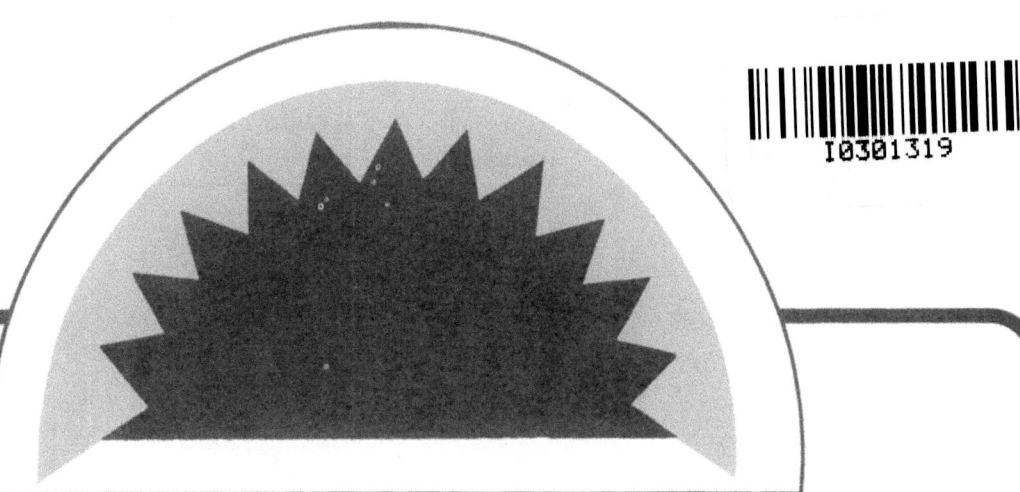

41st Infantry Division

Fighting Jungleers II

TURNER PUBLISHING COMPANY

TURNER PUBLISHING COMPANY

Copyright © 1992 Turner Publishing Company.
All rights reserved.
Publishing Consultant: Douglas W. Sikes

41st Infantry Division Association
Editorial Staff:
Hargis Westerfield, Ph.D.
Nick Russo, Past National President, Secretary
Author: Hargis Westerfield, Ph.D.

This book or any part thereof may not be reproduced without the written consent of the Publisher.

This publication was compiled using available information. The publisher regrets it cannot assume liability for errors or omissions.

Library of Congress Catalog
Card No. 92-80144
ISBN: 978-1-68162-213-2

Limited Edition

Additional copies may be purchased from the publisher.

Co. B, 162 Infantry, 41st Division at Camp Murray, Washington, 1941. (Courtesy Wm. A. Schmidt)

TABLE OF CONTENTS

Publisher's Message 8
Dedication 9
Letter to 41st Veterans 10
Association Information 11
Letter from the Author 12
History Outline 13
Introduction 15

PART I — STORIES FROM VOLUME I

I. PAPUAN CAMPAIGN (Sanananda Operation, Salamaua Operation)

1. 163rd Infantry Regiment at Sanananda
163rd Infantry: Counter-Sniping from Musket Perimeter ... 17
A 163: Forty Minutes to Hell and Sanananda 19
B 163: Battle of Sanananda 21
B 163: Standing Patrol at Sanananda 23
B 163: Sanananda: The Victory Phase 25
C 163: Fisk Perimeter and Afterwards 26
E 163: Seventeen Days at Sanananda 29
F 163: BAR-man at Sanananda 30
F 163: Two Days Infighting at Sanananda 32
G 163: The Killerton Road Block 35
G 163: Infighting at Sanananda 36
I 163: Storming Perimeter U 39
K 163: Combat on Sanananda Road 41
L 163: From Musket Perimeter to the Kumusi River 43

2. (SANANANDA) 186th Infantry Regiment, Medics, Others
G 186: Patrol to the Kumusi 45
41st QM Co: Those Indispensable Quartermasters 46
B 116 Medical Battalion: Medic at Sanananda 49
Chaplain at Sanananda: The Reverend Joseph Castle 51
41st Special Services: Jungle Show Biz 53
D 186: Campaign in Papua 55
Service Co. 186: The Natives—Our Papuan Angels 57
116 Medical Battalion: Medics' Tales 59

II. PAPUAN CAMPAIGN (Salamaua Operation)

1. 162nd Infantry, 205th and 218th Field Artillery, 641st Tank Destroyer Battalion, Medics

2. 218th and 205th Field Artillery Battalions, 641st Tank Destroyer Battalion, Clearing Company, 116th Medical Battalion
1/Battalion 162: Shipwreck Landing 61
1/Battalion 162: Night in Green Hell 63
C 162: Cless-Robson Fight 65
C Battery, 218 FA: Cannoneers Up Bitoi River 67
1/Battalion 162: Assault on Mt. Tambu 70
B 162: Jungle Pursuit at Salamaua 72
162's Information and Reconnaissance Platoon:
Orange, Folsom, Tapioli 74
162nd Infantry Headquarters: Good Soldier Mackechnie's
Salamaua Operation 76
C Battery, 205 FA Bn: Under the Japanese Cannon 77
641st Tank Destroyer Battalion: Volunteer to Salamaua 79

205th Field Artillery: Cannoneers of Salamaua 80
A 162: Battle on George Ridge 82
A 162: Fogel's Survival Patrol on Scout Ridge 84
205th Field Artillery: Cannoneers of Salamaua II 86
I 162: Epic Heroism on Scout Ridge 88
L 162 Perimeter Fighting on Scout Track Ridge 91
116th Medical Clearing Company: Jungle Medics 93
641st Tank Destroyer Battalion: Blue Water Odyssey
to Battle 94

III. NEW GUINEA CAMPAIGN (Aitape, Hollandia, Wakde, Biak Operation

A. AITAPE OPERATION (163rd Infantry Regiment)
G 163: The Marches of Aitape 96
G 163: Patrol to Marok Village 98
M 163: Machine-Gunners at Kamti Village 99
K & L 163: Defense of Kamti Village 103

A. HOLLANDIA OPERATION (186th Infantry Regiment, 146th Field Artillery, Medics)
C 186: Borgonjie River, Hill 1,000 105
D 186: The Show at Hollandia 107
146th FA: Supporting 162nd Infantry at Hollandia 109
A 116 Medical Battalion: Medics at Hollandia 110

A. WAKDE OPERATION (163rd Infantry Regiment, 167th Field Artillery)
A 163: Combat Tour of Wakde 111
C 163: Coconut Hell on Wakde 112
D 163: Weapons Company on Wakde 114
F 163: Our Wakde Hell-Hole 116
H 163: Machine Gun Duel From Insoemanai 118
167th Field Artillery: Fights at Toem 119
M & G Companies: Tementoe Creek and Tor River 121
163rd Infantry Regiment: War of Nerves at Toem 123

A. BIAK OPERATION (162nd, 186th, and 163rd Infantry, 41st Recon Troop, D Company 641st Tank Destroyer. Battalion, 146th Field Artillery Battalion, B and C Companies, 116th Medical Battalion)

(1.) Mostly 162nd Infantry on Biak
2/Battalion and 3/Battalion: Colonel Haney
Forces Parai Defile 125
M 162: Machine Gunners in Parai Defile 127
146th Field Artillery: Battle in Parai Defile
D Co. 641st Tank Destroyer Bn.: Rear Guard
Action at Parai 130
A 116 Medical Battalion: Combat Medic on Biak 132
B and C Companies, 116th Engr. Bn.: Combat Engrs.
on Biak 133
CN 162: Cannon Infantry of 162nd Regiment 135
CN 162: Cannon Infantry of Parai Defile 137
AT 162: Desperate Battles in Ibdi Pocket 139
B 162: In the Slot on Biak 141
C 162: Ibdi Pocket to West Caves 143
E 162: Fighting Around Biak Island 144
12 F 162: Heavy Combat on Biak Island 146
I 162: Parai Defile and Mokmer Ridge 148
L 162: First Against Mokmer Drome 150

TABLE OF CONTENTS

(2.) Mostly 186th Infantry on Biak
B 116th Engineers: Our Great Road for 186th Infantry 152
186th Inf. and I Corps: Gen. Eichelberger's Beachhead on Biak 154
2/Battalion 186th Engineers: Closing the Great Gap on Biak 156
2/Battalion 186th Infantry: Battling Col. Kuzume's Big Banzai 158
B 186: Fighting the Mokmer Ridges 159
C 186: Tank Fighters on Biak 161
D 186 I: Battle for Mokmer Dromes 162
D 186 II: Sluggers with Heavy Weapons 165
E 186: Spearhead Company on Biak 167
G 186: Ridge Fighters on Biak 171
I 186: Our Luck on Biak 173
K 186: The Crossroads 175
L 186: Night fighters and Desert Rats 177
186 Information and Reconnaissance Platoon; Three Tales of I & R 179

(3.) Mostly 163rd Infantry on Biak
41 Reconnaissance Troop: On the Biak Frontier 181
A 163: Slugging at Ibdi Pocket 183
B 163: Battle on Ghost Mountain 185
2/Battalion 163: Irving's Siege of Ibdi Pocket 187
G 163: Ibdi Pocket and G Company 188
G 163: Mopping Up on Biak 190
I/163: Ambush on Biak 192
3/Battalion 163: Last Days of Ibdi Pocket 194
41st Division Headquarters: General Fuller and His Barber 196
41st Division Headquarters: General Fuller's Infantry Navy 198

III. SOUTHERN PHILIPPINE CAMPAIGN (Palawan, Zamboanga, Jolo, Central Mindanao (Riverside-Calinan)

A. Palawan (186th Infantry and 167th Field Artillery)
E 186: First Blood on Palawan 200
186th Infantry and 167th Field Artillery: The Palawan Story 202
G 186th and 167th Field Artillery: The Cockpit on Palawan 204

A. Zamboanga (162nd, 163rd, and 186th Infantry and 146th Field Artillery)
B 162: Good Fighting at Zamboanga 205
E 162: Disaster at Zamboanga 207
F 162: Ridge Battles at Zamboanga 209
G 162: G Company 162nd Infantry Conquers Mt. Capisan 210
L 162: San Roque and Sibago Island 212
1/Battalion 163rd Infantry: Blow-Out Hill and Pasananca 214
G Company 163rd Infantry: G Company's Last Battle 217
146th Field Artillery: Zamboanga—Ring of Fire 219
K 186: Hill Fighting at Zamboanga 220
186th Infantry Regiment: Our Battle of Zamboanga 222

A. Jolo (163rd Infantry and 146th Field Artillery)
163rd Infantry: First Round on Jolo 224
146th Field Artillery: Fighting the Jolo Mountains 227
146th Field Artillery: Blasts Mt. Daho 229
L 163: The Great Ambush on Jolo 231
G 163: Classic Patrol on Jolo 233

A. Central Mindanao (Riverside to Calinan) just one history
3/Battalion 163rd Infantry: Bucking the Abaca Jungle 235
741st Ordnance Company: 741st Ordnance Had to Make Those Guns Work (Just recollections, beginning on Biak in 1944) 236

A. Appendix 239
Our Honored Dead 240
Decorations and Awards 242
Commanders of the Sunset Division 247

PART II — NEW STORIES FROM JUNGLEER 257

Roosevelt Ridge and C Ridge 258
3/BN 163: Mokmer Ridge, Hill 320, the Teardrop 260
641 Tank Destroyer BN/2 PLN: Blasting East Caves, Mokmer Ridges 263
163 Inf. on Jolo II: Winning Mounts Magusing, Datu 265
I Co. 186: Our Two Battles of Zamboanga 268
B Co. 116 Medical Bn: Medic Schooley's Battle of Sanananda 270
E Co. 162: Roosevelt Ridge and Berger Hill 272
B Co. 163: First Wave on Wakde Beach 274
947 FA BN: Our 155mm Howitzers for Biak 276
AT Co.: Our Southern Philippine Campaign 278
L Co.163: Capturing Zamboanga City 280
I Co. 186: Our Hard Luck at Hollandia 282
G Co. 163: Death Valley at Zamboanga 284
2 BN 162 HQ Co.: Bradshaw's War Against Roosevelt Ridge 287
A Co. 163 Figting The Sanananda Road-Bend Perimeters 289
28 FA: Toem, Wakde, and Maffin Bay 291
L Co. 163: War of Nerves at Davao 293
K Co. 162: Cram Hill At Zamboanga 295
41st Div. HQ and 186: General Fuller's Resignation 297
163 I & R: 14 Hard Miles Over Biak 299
54 Inf. Mixed Brigade: Japanese Death March at Zamboanga 301
41st MP Platoon: Soldiers and Policmen 303
A Co. 162: Cutting the Komiatum Track 305
F & G Co.'s 186: The Landing and the Cave 308
L Co. 163: Combat in Abaca Jungle 310
2 BN HQ Co. 163: Ammunition and Pioneer Platoon 312
D Co. 186: Palawan, Zamboanga, and Sibuco Bay 314
116th Engr. Bn.: Combat and Labor in Papuan Campaign 318
K Co. 162: First Two Days in Parai Defile 320
G Co. 162: Breaching Roosevelt Ridge (Aug. 12-13, 1943) 322
G Co. 163: The Kumusi Patrol 324
M Co. 162: Parai Defile Through Death Ridge 326
2 BN 162: Chaplain Smith's Southern Philippine Campaign 328

TABLE OF CONTENTS

M Co. 186: Our Biak Story 330
HQ Co., 1/BN 163: Wire and Water on Wakde
 (Memorial to Service Co.'s 1/Lt. Frank Nugent 332
B Co. 116 Medical BN and G Co. 162 Medic: Medics at
 Toem and Parai Defile 334
C Co. 162: Sgt. Camp's Patrol Against OBA's Raiders 336
HQ Co., 2/BN 186: Into the Slot A West Caves 338
HQ Co. 2/BN 162: From C Ridge Into Salamaua—First! ... 340
HQ Co. 116 Engineers: Priefert's Battle of Biak 342
F Co. 163: Probing IBDI Pocket 344
Cannon Co. 162: Assault Guns at Zamboanga 346
C Co. 163: Bob Burns' Story of Toem/Wakde 348
B Co. 163: Bayonet Charges at Sanananda 350
146 FA and 2/BN 163: Bongao and Sanga Sanga Islands .. 353
162 I&R PLN: Last Days of 1/Lt. Myron Folson 355
1/BN 163: Pasananca and the Reservoir Perimeter 357
186 Inf. and Engr. Boat and Shore Regt.: The Hollandia
 Fire and Lake Sentani 359
205 FA BN on Biak 362
F Co. 163: Fighting the Ibdi Pocket Cliffs 364
HQ Co. 2/BN 186: Thirst on Biak 367
AT Co. 162: Mine Platoon on Biak 369
HQ Co. 2/BN 162: Patrol with Guerillas in Mindanao 372
Navy and Amphibious Engr.: First Wave Fighters
 for Wakde 374
C Co. 163: Battling Perimeters R and S 376
HQ Co. 1/BN 186: Wounded Near Death on Biak 379
205 FA BN (and K Co. 162): Forward Observer
 Schroeder on Roosevelt Ridge 382
I Co. 163: Tommy Gunner Gonzales on Mount
 Mabusing 384
AT Co. 163: Death of Keenan and Sullivan 386
B Co. 162: Our "Soepiori Campaign 387
33rd Naval Guard (Japanese): Saga of the Japanese
 "civilian" Marine 389
B Co. 163: Bernard Marly's Battle of Sanananda 392
218 FA BN: Panek's Career with 218 FA 394
C Co. 162: Battle Before Dawn at Zamboanga 396
1/BN 186: Blunting Col. Kuzume's Last Offensive 398
Japanese Navy: "KON" Operations to Relieve Biak 400
1/BN 163: Conquering Mount Daho on Jolo 402
167 FA: Firing for 186 Infantry and 24th Div. 404
A Co. 116 Engr.: Night Fight at Toem 406
H Co. 162: Parai Defile and Mokmer Ridges 408
E Co. 163: Blowout Hill at Zamboanga 410
162 Inf. and 532 Engr. Boat and Shore Regt.: Miracle
 Landing at Nassau Bay 412
41st Inf. Div.: Biak: Our Biggest Battle 414
K Co. 162: Papuan Campaign 417
167 FA: Concentration 476 to Rescue E Co. 186 Men 419
41st Cav. Recon. Troop (Mech.) at Zamboanga 421
5th Co. 33rd Naval Guard (Japanese Marines):
 Against U.S. Tanks and Mountain Jungles 423
Service Co. 186: Hard Labor, Wounds and Death 425
162 Inf. Regt. in the Salamaua Operation: Results of a
 Divided Command 427
F Co. 163's Most Accurate History of Sanananda 431
146 FA: Wet Landing, Night Combat 433
I Co. 186 Inf. at Zamboanga, II: BAR man Wins DSC
 at Anungan 436
K Co. 162: Balut Island to Calinan 439
E Co. 163: Insoemani, Liki, and Toem Foreshore 442
Our Amphibian Engr. (542 FB and SR, 2 ESB): Beachhead
 Battles for Biak 444
Planning Invasion of Japan (Kyushu Island) 448
G Co.'s Bongao Action (Philippines) 450
Horseshoe Hill and A Company Ridge (Biak) 453
146 FA BN: Escaping the Parai Defile Death Trap 455
E Co. 162: BAR man Floyd West's War 458
148 FA BN: From Darwin to Luzon 461
162 Medical Detachment: From Zamboanga to Namnam ... 464
G Co. 163 (2/PLN): Combat in the Zamboanga Ridges 466
E Co. 163 on Biak: East Caves and Ibdi Pocket 469
148 FA Bn.: From Timor to Luzon 471
Veterans Biographies 474

Sec. group Co A, 116 Eng. ready to go to Nassau Bay. (Courtesy of Rohlffs)

Alongside kips and a slit trench half full with muddy water Sgt. Sam Marinkovich and Sgt. Raymond Pasvogel squat with portable typwriters to record the news for the columns of their unit newspaper. Veterans of the "Fighting Forty-First" Infantry Division, they are battling against the Japs in the Hollandia area of Dutch New Guinea. (Courtesy of Sam Marinkovich)

From back row, L to R: Al Hoffman, Ron Jones, James Jensen, John Demuary, Edward Valles, David Somers, George Destil, Kenneth Cottrell, Meta Sefofonff, Albert Linden, Bill Zemerman, Harlan Rex, George Faira, Bud Lee, Kenny Fore, Ross Spath, Harold Gullikson, Joe Josphson, Jerry Burg, Lup Periz, James Spurgen, William Silver, James J. Oliver, Lee Richardson, Frenchy Rothell, Earl Legge, Tommy Caroll, Aurther White, Edward Misner, Fosteno Pagni, Shorty Qualls, Merle Overton, Joe Czekner, Captain Lee, Little E. Small, George Bestwina, Captain W. Hayden, Bill Hilliker, Louie Bonaveia, Lt. Cameron, Loyd Copertini, Captain Nelson, Florian Laskie. (Courtesy of Mrs. W. R. Rutter)

DEDICATION

Dr. Hargis Westerfield, Historian

This is how Turner Publishing Company's new 41st Division history was written. Although some of us worked on the official history while still in the Army, the book was a failure. Stories of various batteries, companies, or battalions were destroyed or buried in Federal Archives. The editor merely published a haphazard, poorly copied set of documents and called it a history.

About 1957, 11 years after publication of this failure, I was elected historian at the Chicago reunion of my 41st Infantry Division Association. Then I primed the pump by printing two histories of my G Company 163rd Infantry Regiment in our slick paper quarterly *Jungleer*. Other veterans from infantry, field artillery, combat engineers, medics, and other units began sending me histories which I rewrote for *Jungleer*.

Thirty-five years and about 200 histories later, they are still coming in. Even Japanese former enemies have submitted histories!

In contrast to qualifications of the official editor of the failing history, these are my qualifications: (1) In earning my degree of Doctor of Philosophy at Indiana University, I have learned the strict discipline of serious research. (2) As a volunteer from Army Finance Headquarters, I have seen combat as a rifleman, who was wounded in action.

After a few years of publication, the men of the 41st Division realized my deep interest in getting a complete history of our division in World War II. They gave me small grants for office supplies, correspondence, and photo prints of official documents—at first $100 per year and then $200. I collected from Eisenhower Library (Abiline, Kansas) and Washington National Records Center many unit histories that our official editor had refused to print.

In 1981 I made an important discovery. While giving my annual reports at the Division Association Reunion, I lightly said that I had never had enough money to visit a repository of Federal Archives. A $1500 Grant was instantly voted for me at the Board of Governors meeting. When documents were brought to my desk at Eisenhower Library, I made my discovery.

My discovery was that I had not known what questions to ask; although the Archivists had searched for me, they were naturally unable to read my mind at a distance. A new research area was opened to me.

Now I have had a total of 10 such Visitation Research Grants: To Eisenhower Library, Washington Military Archives Division, Washington Naval Yard, Marine Headquarters, and General Eichelberger's Collection at Duke University, among others.

This is how I write these histories. I assemble all the personal narratives I can find (from interviews, letters, diaries, official reports) and U.S., Australian or Japanese histories. Using my background of combat experience and my years of reading military histories, I put this together. I have had to write and rewrite every word.

I have thousands of people to thank for their help—veterans and families and their friends. Especially do I thank these four. Joe Poshka invited my return to the division association and published my first histories. For over years that great San Huntting kept the division association alive and counselled me. (Sam is rightly called "Mister Forty-First") Mike Trapman saw my large softback *Fighting Jungleers* through the press. (Those histories are reprinted as part of this book.) Nick Russo has continued to keep up association membership and fund publication of this book. I salute Poshka, Trapmen, Huntting, and Russo.

Letter to the Veterans of the 41st Infantry Division

Caspar W. Weinberger

The 41st Infantry Division, made up of citizen soldiers, draftees, and volunteer reservists, combined the great strengths of our American military, and this was amply demonstrated by the splendid record the division compiled in some of the most difficult and vital combat of World War II. It has been a source of great pride to me to have been part of the division during that war, and I hope and am sure that this book will bring back memories of both difficult and triumphant times, as well as remind all who participated of the pride they should feel in having been part of the great American military contribution which contributed so much to victory in Europe and in the Pacific in World War II. That victory insured that the freedom of hundreds of millions of people was safeguarded, and that is one of the noblest contributions to history that could have been made.

Caspar W. Weinberger
Secretary of Defense

ASSOCIATION DATA

BOARD OF GOVERNORS AND OFFICERS

Everett Carlsen	President
Bob MacAuslan	1st V.P.
Irwin Soliday	2nd V.P.
Nick Russo	Secretary
Charles Ricks	Treasurer
Dr. Hargis Westerfield	Historian
Nick Russo	Publisher, Editor

PAST NATIONAL PRESIDENTS

Mike A. Trapman	1949-50		Robert E. Mahl	1966-67		Owen A. Peterson	1979-80
Jesse T. Wilkins	1951-53		Dr. Kenneth Binkley*	1967-68		Jack B. Rogers	1980-81
Harold W. Caffee	1953-55		Edward J. Spanier	1968-69		Don Franke	1981-82
Donald M. Cunningham	1955-56		Thomas P. Campbell*	1969-70		William Wewers	1982-83
Joseph Reardon*	1956-57		Albert Repasy	1970-71		James R. Gleason*	1983-84
Joseph C. Poshka	1957-59		Frederick P. Geyer	1971-72		Albert R. Levendusky	1984-85
Lloyd E. Bryant	1959-60		Edward Pernini	1972-73		Milton Fiene	1985-86
Glenn O. Stockdale	1960-61		Allen L. Jones	1973-74		Walter Stelter	1986-87
Robert L. Nelson*	1962-62		Harry Robshaw Jr.*	1974-75		Lynn 'Flash' Gordon	1987-88
Robert C. Keller*	1962-63		Noel R. O'Brien	1975-76		Fred Naegele	1988-89
Charles M. Ricks	1963-64		Nick Russo	1976-77		Louis Reuter	1989-90
Wally Sandberg*	1964-65		Charles E. Lang	1977-78		Francis Willingham	1990-91
Robert F. Dye*	1965-66		John H. Pennington	1978-79		*Deceased	

HONORARY OFFICERS
Maj. Gen. George S. Cook Hon. V.P.

BADGER STATE CHAPTER
President: William Wewers
Sec./Treas. Charles J. Duncan

IOWA CHAPTER
President: Merle Smith
Sec. Marion Criswell

EASTERN OREGON CHAPTER
President: Bob Geiger
Sec. Lee Bowers

GREAT LAKES CHAPTER
President: Chester Clark
Sec. Reuben Shell. Meets first Sunday, January, and each alternate month except July. Annual picnic in June at residence of Francis Willingham, South Lyon, MI.

MIDWEST CHAPTER
President: Ed McNett
Sec. Dave Sacks. Meets first Tuesday.

163 INF. MONTANA CHAPTER
President: Ward Beley
Sec. Fran Roe. Annual reunion.

116 MEDICS CHAPTER
President: Ray Rensink
Sec. Joe Dent. Annual reunions at National Convention.

MIN-DAK CHAPTER
President: Roy Richardson
Sec./Treas. Jack V. Broman. Spring and Fall meetings.

NEW ENGLAND CHAPTER
President: Chester Cheney
Sec. Fred A. Ashman. Annual get-together.

NORTHERN CALIFORNIA CHAPTER
President: Colman "Bill" Weidman
Sec. Frank Bradbury. Annual spring picnic, Valentine dinner dance, meetings as called.

PORTLAND CHAPTER
President: Leland S. Lewis
Sec. Lester: "Don" Culp. Meets at Milwaukee Elks Lodge third Wednesday of each month at 11:30 a.m.

POTOMAC CHAPTER
President: William Murray
Sec. George D. Moore. Regional meetings.

ROCKHAMPTON CHAPTER
President:
Sec. Jack Fleming

SEATTLE CHAPTER
President: Art Mitchell
Sec. Gerald Griffin. Meets first Thursday.

SOUTHERN CALIFORNIA CHAPTER
President: Nelson "Joe" Smith
Sec./Treas.: Ray Warrick

MID-SOUTH CHAPTER
President: Clifford Hughes
Sec./Treas. R. Lee Strickland.

SOUTHWEST CHAPTER
President: Robert Van Campen
Sec. Richard C. Schumann

SOUTHEAST CHAPTER
President: Carn R. Reid
Sec. Francis Willingham

41ST SIGNAL CHAPTER
President: George Startup
Sec. Don Dimoff

WILLAMETTE VALLEY CHAPTER
President: Denton Howard
Sec. Ed Skoubo. Annual picnic third Sunday of August. Midwinter dance.

218TH F.A. CHAPTER
Acting President: Charles Ricks
Acting Sec. Allen Jones

41ST DIV. BANDS CHAPTER
President: Stan Crawford
Sec./Treas. Dean Curtiss

To Correspond with any of the Association officers, their addresses are as follows:

President Everett Carlsen
Box 81
Blooming Prairie, MN 55917

1st V.P. James R. MacAuslan
2120 Robinson Ln. SE #174
Salem, OR 97306

2nd Vice Irwin Soliday
9724 S. Kostner
Oak Lawn, IL 60453

Secretary Nick Russo
4324-175th St. SW
Lynnwood, WA 98037-7433

Treasurer Charles Ricks
6005 NE 121st Ave.
Vancouver, WA 98682

Historian Hargis Westerfield
2914 Ave. B
Kearney, NB 68847

This Great 41st Division History

We 41st Infantry Division veterans can rightly be proud of the great history which we have written over 38 years. In over 200 histories (over 400,000 words) we have compiled the most dramatic and accurate history possible about almost all companies—or battalions where company histories were impossible to obtain.

By combining the first *Fighting Jungleers* collection with a second *Fighting Jungleers* collection, we have a nearly total coverage of our division's three campaigns. We have in the second collection all four histories of ourselves with our Amphibian Engineers attached at our most dangerous landings: Salamaua (at Nassau Bay), Hollandia with the great fire, Wakde and Biak. We have at least one history about every rifle company of 162nd and 163rd Infantry in the Papuan Campaign.

We have total coverage throughout the whole war of D Company, 186th Infantry (Nick Wheeler with other D men), F Company, 162nd Infantry (Chester Young) 146th Field Artillery (Robert Allen), and G Company, 163rd Infantry (Kermit Dulian and Hargis Westerfield). We have masterpieces like Al Schacht's four histories which completely cover L Company, 163rd Infantry in the southern Philippines Campaign, and Joe Bradshaw's in 2nd Battalion, 162nd Infantry from Salamaua to Central Mindanao. We even have four histories of the southern Philippines Campaign as our Japanese opponents saw their combats and retreat.

Although histories of troops other than infantry are harder to get, we have plenty of them. Every 41st Division Field artillery Battalion appears herein. Besides 146th Field Artillery mentioned already, we have histories of 167th Field Artillery, 205th Field Artillery, 218th Field Artillery—and even the 947th Field Artillery attached on Biak. Besides Robert Allen's 146th Field Artillery stories everywhere in battle, we cite William Morse of 167th Field Artillery on Biak and Palawan, and Don Schroeder observing for 205th Field Artillery on Roosevelt Ridge. In the second *Fighting Jungleers* collection, we have another history of 41st Reconnaissance Troop, three more combat engineers,' and three more from the medics' battalion.

We have covered all three campaigns as deeply a veterans' personal histories and public and private archives collections could cover them. The Papuan Campaign (Sanananda and Salamaua) merited some 60 histories—although our two regiments were just part of a larger Australian army—officially. About 100 histories came from our heaviest American campaign (Aitape, Hollandia, Wakde, and Biak), which involved the entire 41st Division. Over 40 division histories deal with the southern Philippine Campaign (Palawan, Zamboanga, Jolo, central Mindanao). Although this southern Philippine Campaign was minor to our first two campaigns, it was a hard-fought, heroic campaign.)

Greatest number of histories (some 140) our three infantry regiments. Fewest of these are about 186th Infantry Regiment, but it was not needed in the Papuan Campaign except for securing the captured ground between the Sanananda and Salamaua operations. Largest portion of all histories comes from 163rd Infantry Regiment, but this majority is due to loss of archives records that were evidently never turned in to public or private repositories. After some veterans mailed me copies of these records from their private files, I had to write new histories of 163rd Infantry, especially at Sanananda. Of a total of some 140th Infantry histories, about 30 are from 186th Infantry, 48 from 162nd and 64 from 163rd Infantry.

To produce these 200-odd histories, I have interviewed and corresponded with 41st Division veterans and researched among archives for over 30 years. It has been hard work, but writing this *Fighting Jungleers* with the help of many other division association veterans has been one of the happiest acts of my life.

Dr. Hargis Westerfield

Our 41st Division in World War II
by Dr. Hargis Westerfield, Division Historian

I. THE PAPUAN CAMPAIGN
Our first 41st Infantry Division Campaign was the Papuan Campaign in the Australian sections of New Guinea called Papua and NW New Guinea. Sanananda Operation of 163rd Infantry was about three weeks of water-logged fighting against hidden Japanese positions. Salamaua Operation of 162nd Infantry was fought over two regions of jungle ridges until we took Salamaua Town. This is a brief history for orientation.

SANANANDA - Our Sanananda assaults of January 2 to 22, 1943 were 163rd Infantry Regiment's final great operation of the Buna-Gona battles. In a Japanese jungle and swamp of log bunkers and machine gun nests, we replaced battered Australian sluggers. With only three Australian cannon in support, we fought heroic Japanese of 15th Engineer and 41st Infantry Regiments.

Our 1st Battalion at first failed to storm two Jap perimeters north of regimental headquarters. Then 2nd Battalion blocked Killerton Trail to cut off the Japs' escape route to the coast. Fighting east to Sanananda Road, G Company had to slay Jap fighters from among corpses in the "Hospital Lot." After F and K companies great fight down the road, all three battalions teamed to destroy Japanese perimeters east of the road.

SALAMAUA - Next 41st operation was against Japs in mountains and jungles of the Salamaua area 150 miles northwest of Sanananda, June 30 to August 14. In the first beachhead of the Southwest Pacific, 162nd Infantry's 1st Battalion landed after midnight June 30 on Nassau Bay. Although cut off among wrecked barges, we won a bitter night combat. Then with C Battery, 218th Field Artillery, we hiked up Bitoi Ridge to help Australians cut Komiatum Track to Mubo Strip. Despite a costly repulse from Mt. Tambu, we harassed the Japs from that stronghold.

Meanwhile, our 3rd Battalion hiked up the coast from Nassau Bay to battle the Japs of 102nd Infantry on Roosevelt Ridge. With their mountain guns, the Japs held Roosevelt Ridge through August 14. Our fresher 2nd Battalion finally breeched the ridge, and 205th and 218th Field Artillery plus Bofors Ack-Ack guns and Australian guns finished the last Japs on the seaward end of the ridge. We still had to fight over five more ridges to seize Salamaua Town. Whole Salamaua Operation took 76 days.

II. NEW GUINEA CAMPAIGN
Our 41st's mission in the New Guinea Campaign of 1944 was to spearhead other divisions' drives to clear Japanese from Netherlands New Guinea—now renamed by Indonesians as Irian Jaya.

AITAPE - Landing from a large battle fleet on April 22, 1944, 163rd Infantry merely marched for three days to win Tadji Dromes near Aitape Village. Only combat was inland at Kamti Village where I Company's 2nd Platoon cut a trail where 200 Japs were withdrawing westward. With slight losses, we killed 90 Japs. Soon the 32nd Division relieved 163rd Infantry.

HOLLANDIA - On April 22—the same day 163rd landed at Aitape—162nd and 186th Infantry landed near Hollandia with 146th, 205th, 218th, and 947th Field Artillery. Opposition was again light from 11,000 poorly organized Japs (mostly service troops). Our Air Force had already destroyed 300 planes. By April 26 we held Hollandia Harbor and Cyclops Drome. Only large fight was against 400 Japs behind Cyclops Drome.

Japs' great victory, however, was from a single air bomb on a beach crowded with supplies. A great fire on this beach destroyed 60 per cent of our supplies and cut us to half rations. But gaining Hollandia Harbor was our greatest strategic victory of the whole war. We had a gigantic harbor to stage for the Philippine invasion.

WAKDE ISLAND-TOEM MAINLAND - After Aitape and Hollandia operations, our 41st had to storm Wakde Island, about 145 miles northwest of Hollandia up the Guinea shore. Wakde would become an air base to help us fight for bloody Biak, about 180 miles farther northwest.

About 3,000 yards long by 1,200 yards wide, Wakde Strip covered half of the island. Other half of Wakde was a brushy, overgrown coconut plantation. Garrison was some 800 Japs from many decimated outfits in about 100 bunkers.

On May 17, 1944, our 163rd Infantry Combat Team landed unopposed on the New Guinea mainland near Toem Village. Next day, we attacked Wakde with covering fire from H Company's heavy machine guns, 167th and 218th Field Artillery and B Company, 641st Tank Destroyers' heavy rifled mortars.

But all of this preparatory fire had little effect on the the Japs in their 100 bunkers. Continuous Jap machine gun fire almost stopped 1st Battalion with attached F Company on the beach. Aided by two medium tanks of 603rd Tank Company, we pushed north towards Wakde Strip. While A and B Companies fought around the ends of the strip, C Company crossed it under fire. The last Japs were pushed into the cliffs on the northeast corner of Wakde. Not until the third day was battle concluded. At the cost of 40 dead and 107 wounded, we wiped out 800 Japs—except one prisoner. Wakde became a forward air base for attacking Biak.

Regrouped on the Toem Mainland across from Wakde, 163rd Infantry fought a chilling war of nerves against the Japs of the 36th Division East of us at Sarmi Village. One night, Matsuyama Force even broke through 163rd's lines and penetrated almost to the shore before they died. For some time 163rd Infantry elements guarded a staging area for other regiments from other divisions to try to capture Sarmi. Not until June 10 were the last 163rds men ordered west to fight on Biak.

BIAK ISLAND - On Biak Island, our 41st had our last great battles to win New Guinea. Biak was about 200 square miles of mountain and jungle and scrub desert, with Mokmer Strip on its flat south shore. Jap garrison was 10,400 troops with some field artillery—including 222nd Infantry Regiment of the 36th Division which was mainly at Sarmi. Here the Japs tried to build up a base to reconquer New Guinea.

After 186th Infantry landed at Bosnek Village on southeast Biak, May 27, 1944, 162nd Infantry marched west into Parai Defile to try to seize Mokmer Strip beyond the Defile. Parai Defile was a narrow corridor between high cliffs and sea, a perfect place for ambush.

But on the second day, heavy mortar and MG fire from East Caves on the heights and infantry attacks forced 3rd Battalion's retreat. On the third day, seven light Jap tanks attacked with infantry. Our General Sherman medium tanks outranged and destroyed all seven tanks, but 162nd had to leave Parai Defile.

As soon as two battalions of 163rd Infantry arrived from Toem on May 31, 186th Infantry with 2nd Battalion, 162nd Infantry started from near Bosnek Village to make an overland march to capture Mokmer Strip from the inland side. After the first night and following day of battle, 186th Infantry with tanks had little fighting on their westward march. B Company, 116th Engineers built a road through the scrublands. It was a dry, desert march with no water—which must be carried many miles from Bosnek.

Six days after the march began, 186th Infantry positioned on the jungle ridge above Mokmer Strip. Although Colonel Oliver Newman lacked time to clear those ridges, he had to seize Mokmer Strip at once. (For Major General Horace Fuller was under pressure to make Mokmer Strip operationally immediately.)

Meanwhile, during June 3-12, the Japanese Navy made three attempts to blast our 41st to death and land forces on Biak. These were frustrated attempts with the loss of one destroyer, but they did help to slip in 1,200 more Japs on Biak.

On June 7, 186th Infantry marched down from the ridge and occupied undefended Mokmer Strip. Then from the ridge which they had just left, and East Caves, 186th was driven to cover by four hours blasting from field artillery, heavy mortars, and automatic weapons. They were cut off from supplies and reinforcements except for amphib craft under fire on Mokmer Beach.

Even while 186th Infantry was bombarded, General Fuller decided to outflank the Japs in Parai Defile and reinforce 186th with 162nd Infantry. On June 8, 162nd Infantry beached at Parai Jetty and cut off the Japs in the defile east of them. By June 11 under heavy fire, 162nd had joined with 186th Infantry.

On June 11, 162nd Infantry began attacking the crucial strongpoint that kept us from victory on Biak. This strongpoint was low Mokmer Ridge from which Japanese fire could keep our planes from using Mokmer Strip.

After two days' battle, 162nd Infantry had still not cleared the Japs from Mokmer Ridge. So General Jens Doe sent 1st Battalion, 162nd Infantry, and 1st Battalion, 186th Infantry around the right flank of Mokmer Ridge against Jap headquarters in West Caves. In this advance, 186th's 2nd Battalion acted as shock troops to clear the Japs from a 500-yard gap between hard fighting 2nd Battalion and 3rd Battalion on Mokmer Ridge. It was one of 186th Infantry's greatest exploits.

By June 15, however, General Fuller had resigned command of the 41st Division, after Lieutenant General Robert Eichelberger had relieved him from command of the Hurricane Task Force. Generals MacArthur and Krueger were impatient about his delays in making Mokmer Strip available for the Air Force.

Eichelberger and Doe had little difficulty to cut off West Caves from supplies and reinforcements and destroy the garrison with flaming gasoline. On June 21-22, 150 Jap sorties from West Caves and lost 115 dead.

Last large body of Jap troops still lurked in the knife edged coral ridges of Ibdi Pocket inland from Ibdi Village on the south shore. About 1,000 Japs of 3rd Battalion, 222nd Infantry still held out. On June 26-28, five rifle companies of 163rd Infantry assailed the pocket and ranged precise artillery fire on the Japs. The rifle companies withdrew to let 200 of the most able bodied Japs escape, but then 3rd Battalion cordoned the pocket and helped the Air Force to plan a final bombing. On July 22, eight B-24 bombers dropped 64 1,000 pound bombs on the last remaining Japs. So ended the final operation on Biak.

III. SOUTHERN PHILIPPINE CAMPAIGN

 - As in New Guinea Campaign, our 41st was again the spearhead division to annihilate the Japs from Palawan, Mindanao, and the Sulu islands. We ranged over 186,000 square miles of ocean and islands.

PALAWAN ISLAND - The long, narrow semi-wilderness of Palawan Island lay on the west flank of the 41st's main attack for Zamboanga on Mindanao Island. General MacArthur needed Palawan air bases to attack the Japs on Borneo. On Feb. 28, 1945, 186th Infantry with 167th Field Artillery Battalion landed unopposed at Puerto Princesa half-way down the island. The 1800-man Jap garrison of 174th Independent Infantry Battalion lacked field artillery. It fortified in the mountains. Hardest fight was G Company 186ths for the hogback of Hill 1445. For the entire operation, total United States losses were just 12 killed and 40 wounded compared to 890 Japanese dead. By March 30, 186th's 1st Battalion and 3rd Battalion were in combat at Zamboanga to help 162nd's and 163rd's battles.

ZAMBOANGA - On March 10, 1945 162nd and 163rd Infantries endured heavy Jap field artillery and mortar fire from 54th Independent Infantry Brigade while beaching at San Mateo. L Company 163rd Infantry easily captured Zamboanga City on the second day. But on the third day, L Company, 162nd Infantry had bitter fighting to seize San Roque Village west of Zamboanga. Not until 14 days after their landing was 162nd Infantry's G Company able to storm Mt. Capisan. (Our 1st Battalion, 186th Infantry also fought up a ridge to help 162nd take Capisan.)

Meanwhile, 163rd Infantry was having hard fighting to advance to Mt. Pulungbata east of Capisan. In the advance through the heavily fortified cockpit of Santa Maria-Pasananca villages, a platoon of E Company 163rd was blown up. Total casualties for E Company and nearby outfits were 83. Ejecting the entrenched Japs with their deadly 20 millimeter machine-cannon from Pasananca Village was one of 163rd's hardest battles. We never took Mt. Pulungbata because we were ordered over the Sulu Islands to fight on Jolo—left the operation to Filipino guerillas with 3rd Battalion, 186th Infantry down from Palawan.

JOLO ISLAND - After 2nd Battalion 163rd cut off the Japs escape route to Borneo by easily capturing Bongao Island, the farthest west of the Sulu Islands, 163rd's other two battalions landed and occupied Jolo City. We easily overran the "mounts" above Jolo City, but Mt. Daho meant harder assaults. Here about 400 "Jap marines," 33rd Naval Guard, held out for five days under air strikes and 146th Field Artillery shellfire. Companies A and B failed in a stubborn assault of April 20, but the April 22 assault was unopposed. Japs held out on Tumatangas, "the Mountain of Tears," until after World War II was over.

CENTRAL MINDANAO - After our 41st's southern Philippine Campaign was won, battalions still had to fight in south-central Mindanao east of Zamboanga City. Our 2nd Battalion, 162nd Infantry helped liberate Bukidnon Province with almost no casualties. We had harder fighting in the south near Davao, where we helped 24th Infantry Division. Main actions were through "abaca" or hemp fields so overgrown from neglect that it was dark even in mid-day. Here 3rd Battalion, 163rd Infantry between 162nd's 1st Battalion and 3rd Battalion flanking, advanced with tanks to capture Calarian Village. Then 162's men patrolled past Calarian to drive the last Japs into the mountain wilderness.

THE PEACEFUL INVASION OF JAPAN - On November 1, 1945, the 41st Division would have been part of Operation Coronet in the first invasion of the Japanese home islands. We were to land on Kyushu (Koo-Shoo) just south of Japan's mainland of Honshu. We were to land on the eastern side on Miyazaki Beaches—against miles of guns emplaced on low hills behind the beach. But on August 6, the Hiroshima Bomb marked the end of the war. In our peaceful invasion, many of us came to esteem the friendly Japanese people. On December 31, 1945, our division was inactivated. Victorious in three campaigns, we claim some 1,000 dead against 19,000 Japanese fighters. today, we mourn and honor all of those dead, friends or enemies.

TO OUR READERS: The histories you want to read may be in one or both parts of the book. So be sure to look for them in both Tables of Contents. For example, there are three histories of F. Company, 162nd Infantry at Sanananda. You will find two in Part I and one in Part II.

PART I: Histories published before 1980.

PART II: Histories published in *Jungleer Magazine* after 1980 and into early 1991.

Introduction

Just like me, you'll naturally run through my Table of Contents to find the history of your company or battalion first. But you have many other division histories to be proud of. Surely you'll want to read Walt McKenzie's story, Bayonet Charges at *Sanananda* with Bernie Marly's back-up history. Surely you'll want to hear again how G Co., 163rd Infantry got our division the nickname of "The Butchers" after they cut off the Japanese escape route up Killerton Track, and overran the "Hospital Lot."

For Weapons Companies histories, you can't read any better than D-186's two Biak histories by Nick Wheeler and other cobbers of his association. In M Company, 162nd Infantry's Biak saga, you have two superfine histories by machine gunner Louis Botta. Al Schacht's four histories of L Company, 163rd Infantry in the southern Philippines are masterpieces about a rifle company in action. For scouting and patrolling, there are no better stories than Joe Bradshaw's on Roosevelt Ridge and on Mindanao Island.

For heroism in field artillery, we have nothing greater than the story of Don Schroeder's Yanks and natives in the Roosevelt Ridge Jungle with Japanese killers hunting them. Best history of the men behind the guns is 167th Field Artillery's Bill Morse's story of rescuing E Company of 186 men on Palawan. Bob Allen has thoroughly studied all of 146th Field Artillery's actions from the Parai Defile death-trap all the way through the assaults on Mt. Daho on Jolo. Extracting 162nd Infantry from destruction in Parai Defile was the master act of Ben Saunders' 641st Tank Destroyer Battalion with their 12 rifled 4.2 mortars.

Medic George Jackson gives us heroic tales of front-line medics at Sanananda and on Biak. Engineers Bill Andel and Tony Rohlffs have honored their 116th Engineer Battalion in combat at Nassau Bay or at Toem—or in building the great road for 186th Infantry on Biak.

I can fill many pages to glorify battles of our 41st Infantry Division. Instead, I'll list below some important groups of the histories that you will certainly like.

1. Amphibian Engineers' hazardous landings: Nassau Bay, Hollandia, Wakde, Biak.
2. Especially the attacks of A, B, C, E, F, and G at Sanananda.
3. Breaching Roosevelt Ridge—Herman Steenstra's and Gaetano Di Mayo's story on G Company 162 and Chester Young's on F Company 162.
4. B and C Company, 162nd Infantries jungle pursuit of Colonel Oba's raiders.
5. Results of a divided command at Salamaua—reports by Colonel MacKechnie, Colonel Sweeny, and Captain Webber.
6. The whole Battle for Wakde Island.
7. Parai Defile on Biak—162nd Infantry, 116th Engineers, 146th Field Artillery, 641st Tank Destroyer.
8. 186th Infantry's overland march on Biak with B Company, 116th Engineers.
9. 186th Infantry's 2nd Battalion's closing the Great Gap on Biak (with F and G Companies 186).
10. 41st Recon Troop—Biak and Zamboanga.
11. 163rd Infantry's war on Ibdi Pocket (Biak).
12. General Fuller's relief on Biak (See B-3, Numbers 12 and 13 on 186th Infantry).
13. Storming Mt. Capisan (Zamboanga) and Mt. Daho (Jolo).
14. BAR men in action: Jess Fallstick at Sanananda (F 163), Floyd West at Salamaua and later (E 162), Charlie Solley at Zamboanga (I 186 at Anungan).
15. Our valorous and persistent Japanese opponents in the southern Philippines.

Papua, New Guinea. Janurary 1943 near Sanananda. Hauling ammunition through the muck. (Courtesy of Arthur W. Merrick)

Hq. Co. 3rd Bn., 163rd Inf. Anti-tank Platoon. Old U.S. Army tank recaptured. Standing, L to R: Vernard McCaulley, Ernest Brodie. Sitting, L to R: unidentified, Vince (KiKi) Granato. (Courtesy of Curtis M. Huck)

163 Infantry:
Counter-Sniping from Musket Perimeter

BY DR. HARGIS WESTERFIELD, DIVISION HISTORIAN

Core of this story is 41 Division Training Note No. 3; it disappeared from Fed Archives about 1957. Luckily, 641 TD's Capt. Bennett Saunders had a copy for me. E 163's Don Wood and F 163's Jess Fallstick supplied human interest stories. I also used 163's Sanananda Journal and History. Are any former Musket snipers now reading this who can tell me more stories?

When 163's 1/Bn. replaced Aussies in Musket Perimeter 2 Jan. 1943, we faced the chilling threat of hidden snipers from green darkness in trees 100 feet overhead. Even in this jungle swamp, snipers could kill anonymously out of nowhere at 200 yards from the greenery. For a Jap rifleman in a tree, Musket Perimeter was open ground. Our 163 perimeter was covered by vines only as high as a man's belt or his shoulders. And our oval perimeter was just 150 yards wide and 225 yards long. Only 20-30 yards north and east of us, Jap Perimeters Q and R were a ready supply of fresh snipers and more Jap ammo.

Thus, from a tree almost anywhere around our oval perimeter, a Jap sharpshooter could choose a Yank target who had to leave his water-soaked hole. The range could be all of 200-400 yards. The keen-eyed sniper could steady his precision killing-tool on a branch and tighten the butt to his shoulder. He could take a clear sight-picture and squeeze his trigger. All 1/Bn. might hear is a Jap 25-caliber cartridge crack, like a Fourth of July cap sparked on a stone. Then a Yank cowered in a hole might hear the prolonged dying groan of a man in the next squad. Or long after a deadly silence, he might find his buddy a pale corpse with a deceptively small hole in his forehead.

Naturally, Jap sniper fire plunged down regularly at chow time, once the stoves were set up and we had to leave the holes for food. Sniper fire crackled in on us at any unexpected time in 24 hours. And at dusk, ground terrorists would probe into spots that snipers' binoculars had observed to be less protected. Lone men or small patrols would work around our flanks or rear, empty a clip or two rapid fire, then escape.

A group of B Co., 163, men pose for a picture, displaying an enemy flag found on the body of a KIA Japanese. One 41ster is holding a Japanese rifle. Sorry we can't identify the men in the pictures. Can somebody help us out?

Beneath the eyes of these killers, life quickly became not worth living unless we could shoot them out of the trees. Grimly the Musket garrison – 1/Bn. Hq. Co. with A, B, and D Cos and AT's 37mm cannon – developed a system of counter-sniping. Our basic tactics consisted of three main steps – and a fourth which AT 162 added with at least three 37's.

First, we began to deal with the most immediate threat from Jap Perimeters Q-R which lurked in holes 20-30 yards before us. We set up two-man counter-sniper teams in slit trenches on the forward edge of Musket Perimeter. While one man quietly scanned the opaque jungle with field glasses – or the naked eye if he had no glasses – the other man cuddled his well-cleaned rifle and waited. When Jap shots rang out, the observer carefully spotted the green area where the shots came from. He pointed out the direction of fire, let the rifleman observe through his glasses. Then the rifleman fired – until the Jap was silent – or Jap fire retaliated close enough to make him lie prone. Thus we secured our forward area.

Second, we sent counter-sniping teams into trees on flank and rear of Musket Perimeter. To lessen the drudgery and danger of climbing among dead branches in jungle sweat, we set up home-made ladders. Usually we made them of telephone wire with stout wooden rungs.

Once the two-man tree teams were aloft, we got to work. We shot at all trees which seemed to harbor Nippo rifles. When Japs fired, we followed our standing order. All teams returned fire. If unsure of the actual target, we engaged probable Jap trees in the general direction of the popping fire. With our M-1's and 1903 Enfield rifles, we shot at 200-400 yards. Many men preferred the 03 rifle; they believed it more accurate than the new-fangled Garand M-1.

The Aussie outfits that 163 had relieved – and the 32 Div. men before them – evidently had never sniped back from up in the trees. In fact, the Aussies had not briefed us on counter-sniping at all. We believe that they were far too decimated after making and holding Huggins Perimeter, which we had renamed Musket, to take positive action to fight snipers – or too malarious to care.

Third, we needed still another measure, because manning forward slit trenches and trees with two-man counter-sniping teams was not enough. As soon as we had posted sniper teams in trees, we could take the offensive. We could use those teams to guide attack patrols on the ground. We sent out small foot patrols of two-three men. Under direction from tree observers, our foot patrols shot down snipers or slashed other targets on flanks of Jap Perimeters Q and R.

And the ground patrols also set booby traps – grenades tied to two separate trees and connected by a trip cord attached to the loosened firing pins. These booby traps caused Jap casualties, and once definitely effected our capture of a Jap Bren gun. Evidently the Japs had dropped the Bren gun when they fled from a grenade blast.

When we counter-sniped in these three steps, we carefully secured ourselves from accidentally shooting our 163 men. We briefed all men on our methods. We located our own sniper trees so that nobody thought we were firing on him. Most important of all, we made it clear that nobody could fire on Jap snipers – except regularly designated counter-snipers.

Fourth, with the arrival of AT 163's 37mm cannon (at least three) we took another step against these hidden Jap killers. When F Co. passed through Musket on 9 Jan., Jess Fallstick noted that the AT-163 gun crews were hard at work, loading "grapeshot" into the 37mm guns.

Japanese soldiers usually carried on their person, in addition to a good-luck flag, photographs of family, girl friends, even of themselves taken in more tranquil days, dressed in their best uniforms. Shown above are a few such pictures found on enemy bodies near the Musket Perimeter: an officer, probably a colonel; a soldier with an automatic weapon; a group of kimono-clad Japanese girls.

Methodically, AT's carefully aimed 37's were topping the jungle trees around Musket Perimeter. For without tree cover, no snipers could operate. In BAR-man Fallstick's opinion, the number of trees made the task hopeless, but he admitted that he saw a tremendous number of mangled trees on the horizons.

Thus did 163 Inf's 1/Bn. counter-snipe the Nip snipers who took sight pictures on us from above Musket Perimeter. We struck back four ways: with counter-teams in forward holes, with our own tree-snipers, with ground teams that prowled forward, and with AT's 37's.

But how deadly was Jap sniping? And how effective was 163's counter-sniping?

Records of how deadly the Jap snipers were are meager but suggestive. Three days after 1/Bn. took over Musket, sniper activity was recorded. On 4 Jan., Lt. Fitzgerald — evidently of A Co. — reported that a sniper on the west side of Musket had wounded a Yank. We could not locate that sniper, but 163's history states that sniping was "continuous" on 4 Jan.

Sniping and countering were also in full swing Jan 5. On Jan. 6, a Jap sniper was reported to be "over and inside" Musket Perimeter. On 7 Jan., a recon patrol at 40 yards from Musket observed a pillbox at azimuth 347 with eight snipers to guard it.

And when E Co. took over B Co's positions to release for an attack, sniping was heavy. At dawn of 8 Jan., long before B's attack, E's Don Wood heard Jap snipers firing "with deadly accuracy." From our own trees, 163's snipers fired back. Wood thought that it was like a July Fourth celebration.

Somewhere Wood had heard that the Jap sniper was a poor shot. But in that sector of Musket which E had taken over from B, the sniping was surely deadly. Already, here, a Jap sniper — or his buddies — had accounted for five men, although Wood did not say whether they were killed or wounded. He asserted that the "plop!" of the bullet was sickening as it struck nearby — or hit flesh. Yet it was too uncomfortable to lie in a hole and be shot at from overhead. Rather than endure the shooting passively, E men often left their holes and carried on necessary chores before that fight of 8 Jan. began.

This fight of 8 Jan. occurred when B Co. made an abortive strike at Jap Perimeter R. Before it began, about 1030, E's Wood noted that the sniping had slowed up a bit, and that B would attack at 1130. When B attacked, E's job was to stand up and fire cover at the brush and drive snipers down out of the trees. After B withdrew, E men looked around to find McDermeit dead from a shot in the stomach. We can be reasonably certain that a sniper killed him.

On the night after B and E fought, Jap sniping was reported as "unabated." And when E left Musket with other 2/Bn. Co's to set up Killerton Road Block, Wood said that they endured a morning of sniping. Under sniper harassement, E men forced themselves to move forward by rushes from cover to cover. Often they hid from bullets behind Jap or Yank bodies.

And next day back in Musket, on 10 Jan., snipers were again reported "active." The fact is that not until 163's offensive of 16 Jan. did our history report that the jungle was clear of the snipers who had killed or wounded us.

But how effective were 1/Bn's four counter-sniping tactics? When, as already mentioned, the Yank was wounded on 4 Jan. on Musket's west side, 163 got to work. By 1745 that very day, Lt. Fitzgerald announced that three Jap snipers were killed in that area. On 5 Jan., AT Pltn. got credit for killing five snipers; B Co. got credit for two dead — a total of seven. On 6 Jan., a Nippo sniper was killed at 0600. These 11 sniper dead were all that 163's Journal reported.

And perhaps Don Wood saw Sniper No. 12 dead when E entered Musket to relieve B on 7 Jan. Passing along the trail, they saw their first rotting dead sniper, slumped over his position in a tree. The vines which had concealed him still held him aloft. Wood said that these vines would no doubt support him until he became a skeleton. Wood wrote that he had "a spectral look seeing nothing but knowing all that we were to know."

We can get an idea of how effective ground-team sniping must have been from the tale of an unknown sergeant who became a fine Jap killer. Although he was not then in Musket but part of a squad in a standing patrol outside Musket near Voya on our supply-trail, his story is surely like one of the many we could tell about counter-sniping teams in the jungle outside Musket.

Almost as soon as this patrol was established, snipers fired on the men. The ingenuous sergeant devised successful tactics which depended on the density of the surrounding jungle. Prowling into thick undergrowth, he carried a Tommy gun with 100 rounds. He also carried a canteen on his ammo belt, a hunting knife, and a head net against mosquitos. Wearing dyed green fatigues, he stained his face and hands with black mud.

When a sniper fired on them, he took an azimuth towards the crack of the rifle, and moved under cover in that direction. When he had closed in on the sound, he lay still until he heard another shot and spotted the exact tree the sniper fired from. In almost all cases, the sergeant then waited until he saw the target Jap with the peaked cap and the long rifle. Then his heavy .45 bullets tore the Jap from the tree. A few times when the Jap was invisible, he slashed bursts into the foliage to kill him.

When scouting for snipers in more open area, the sergeant carried his M-1 for greater accuracy at long range. Although sometimes he took two-three other riflemen with him, he preferred to work alone. He moved from cover to cover towards the firing until he located the Jap target he longed for. This sergeant claimed a kill of five Jap snipers and perhaps deterred a larger number from harassing his squad.

Effectiveness of 163's counter-sniping was great but not 100 per cent effective without another more drastic measure. Some time evidently after 11 Jan., to judge by 163's Journal, the sniping lessened because of our four tactics. Sniping became limited to distant, inaccurate fire limited to meal times.

But despite these assertions of 163's Training Note No. 3, sniper fire down on Musket Perimeter never did halt completely. Only on 16 Jan. did the storming of adjacent Jap covers bring the sniping to an end.

On 16 Jan., K Co. and L Co., with two plns. each, overran Perimeter R on which many snipers were based. And on that same day, L combed the Jap areas leftward of the Motor Truck Road all the way up to Fisk. Only on 16 Jan. 1943, toward the close of the Battle of Sanananda, did 163 finally clear those fearsome snipers from the jungle around Musket Perimeter.

FORTY MINUTES TO HELL AND SANANANDA
By DR. HARGIS WESTERFIELD, Division Historian

On 30 Dec 42, Aussie planes lifted A Co 163 Inf over the Owen Stanleys into Sanananda Battle — 40 minutes to Hell. Hiding from possible Zero attacks, we flew almost touching giant jungle palms. Dropping into green Hell below, we saw an opening wide as a postage stamp, bumped into Dobadura Strip. Jungle heat struck us; explosives blasted nearby. Dizzily, we heaved packs from planes. Natives reloaded our planes with pale Yank, Aussie wounded for Moresby hospitals.

In Guinea sweat, we hiked to bivouac on Soputa Trail. At midnight 31 Dec 42, Aussie cannon barraged the Nips to celebrate New Year's. At 0300 1 Jan 43, we marched into holes guarding the Supply Trail to Huggins (Musket) Perimeter.

A's first 10 days was a dark time, when we patrolled the rain-forest daily and huddled in muddy perimeters at dark. A's main body new helped garrison Huggins, while 1/Pln outposted the Supply Trail a mile back. There Hasselbring killed A's first Nip; Coult quickly killed A's second. Back at Huggins, Huxhold aimed a shot into the jungle. A Nip toppled from a giant tree and fell at our feet. On 6 Jan a Jap MG 50 yards E of Huggins poured bullets on an A patrol for 30 minutes — but with no casualities. McNally was first wounded — a burst of TSMG fire in the legs. When 3/Pln reinforced C Co by Fisk Perimeter. Murphy was shot in the leg. A bullet caromed off Cpl Thomas' skull but only nicked him.

On 10 Jan, A got in deeper. After AT's Cpl Knight found the Japs' Perimeter Q — E of Huggins — deserted, Gen Doe thrust in 1/Pln at once. We wondered why the Nips left. Q contained a .50 HMG, 2 40mm mortars, scores rifles with ammo, grenades. Here we found the first example of Nippo cannibalism.

On 11 Jan after K Co relieved us on the Supply Trail, all A joined 1/Pln in Q — except for 3/Pln at isolated little Moore's Post. Jap tree snipers were bad; but our own countersnipers climbed trees and silenced them. Soon Japs fired only at night. From Perimeter Q, we now probed Jap Perimeter R, east of the road.

On 13 Jan, Lt McKinney's 2/Pln attacked Perimeter R in A's first assualt of the war. Aussie 25-pounders and our 81s did precision firing against the Nip lines a few yards ahead, while we took cover from possible shorts and awaited orders. After much HMG, LMG drumfire, we charged with assault fire and grenades. Their pillbox slots were low; we crouched and hurled grenades at them in the bowler's position. But entrenched Nips were too strong. Hart died in the aid station 35 minutes after they hit him. Jones, Cheney, Sgt Beesley had arm or leg wounds.

Safe at dark in our wet holes with the stench of dead Nips, we knew that we must fight R Perimeter again. After more recon patrols 14 Jan, Lt Boid planned all-out attack 15 Jan.

So when 2/Pln probed ahead for A Co at 0730 15 Jan, the scouts knew the precise location of Jap fire-lanes. McKinney's 2/Pln crossed the road N to Perimeter R, bypassed the fire-lanes, bored into R before the Japs saw us. Despite heavy fire, 2/Pln was so skillful that only Daly took a bad leg-wound.

Then Lt Houston's 1/Pln lunged into R, shot into the labyrinth of interlocked bunkers, firing trenches — a snake-pit 100 by 150 yards. Surely poor Jap shooting saved us. Under heavy fire, Ziegele crept up to a .50 HMG in a bunker, struck dead 4 of 5 Nips with his M1. Killed in R were Curry, Chambers, Tatarski. But by dusk, we silenced the Nips, although they still lurked in R shadows. Then K Co relieved us and with L spent 36 hours to clean up Perimeter R. Many Nips must have escaped that night, for K found just 3 alive in the final kill.

Despite our 4 KIA, 7 WIA, dysentery, malaria, battle fatigue, Gen Doe needed A Co. Finally under our own 1/Bn CO, Col Lindstrom, we joined the great 163-Aussie push of 16 Jan. A Co was to attack Perimeter S on the Jap main line N of Fisk. Specifically, we were to make a diversionary frontal attack on S through open, sunstruck kunai grass, while E took S in the rear. This diversion cost A Co 9 KIA, 17 WIA, and 20 heat evacuations — 46 lost.

Before we cleared the assembly area, a short mortar round caused several KIA and WIA. But as D Co sprayed both flanks of our advance with HMGs, A moved out as skirmishers, through tall kunai under blazing sun. On our right, a strong point enfiladed us; rifles fired from tall trees. Weapons men rushed up LMGs and sprayed down snipers. Our skirmishers crept on steadily — too steadily.

The Jap gunners let us push within 20 yards of S Perimeter. Then MGs opened up; a cross fire from 1 HMG, 1 LMG trapped us. (Some observers counted at least 4 MGs.) Instead of area firing, Nips loosed bursts at roots of any grass that moved. "A" men dropped dead, or shouted for Medics. Under red-hot sun without a breath of air in that kunai flat, we lost 18 men and 2 officers evacuated from heat stroke. And our LMG belts were empty; sniper fire thickened again.

Col Lindstrom sent in a B Pln to lessen pressure; but without success. With BARs, M1s, we blasted our way out again. We killed 2 MG nests, felled many snipers, forced other Nips back to holes. As dusk confused their aim, we escaped. Besides 20 heat cases, 17 WIA, we had 9 dead — Bunker, Wells, Rowland, Hardin, Belchak, Henderson, Strobach, Johnson, Cpl May.

In the same attack, C and B had but light opposition — swept around the Jap right flank, made perimeter 200 yards behind them. Now from mopping up R Perimeter, K joined us, and we dug in with 1/Bn. Although K had come from the ships only on 11 Jan, it had drastic losses. A plus K now made up only 1 company in strength. At dark, we huddled into mud-holes with bully beef and hard tack for supper. At dawn, Nips grenaded and fusilladed our holes, wounded 1, killed Wojtech, Livermore. Our bullets tore those Nips apart.

After our bitter fight of 16 Jan, A was now on the Japs' right flank. Orders came to attack with K on a given azimuth to determine extent of the perimeter we fought yesterday. Until we turned back, we had no resistance — then hit a strong point 250 yards behind Jap lines, and halted. On 18 Jan, A and K struck the perimeter we probed the day before — which some called Perimeter T. We hit it in the middle, advanced to the very edge before Japs halted us. We remained before these Japs overnight, fought again next day. On 19 Jan, we pushed with A's own LMGs well forward and a HMG Pln guarding our right flank — until our advance masked our own automatic fire. Japs rallied to stop us — close to main Nippo Hq.

This fight climaxed 20 Jan. We pulled back 150 yards with K, and FA barraged 15 minutes to 1030. Then massed 81s and MGs impacted for 5 minutes; and we charged, caught most Japs in holes or trying to come out. We slew them in droves, and K Co had excellent shooting against Nips trying to eacape. Then A Co fanned out on the right, and lent fire power to B and C at work on S Perimeter. As Jap shooting lessened, B and C got in to storm the Japs. As the fight closed, 1/Bn counted 525 dead Japs. A had no casualties, found souveniers galore.

Thinking the battle finished, we still had to clear K's area at dawn. K Co had with stood an attack of 70 Japs, and now needed relief. We killed a few.

Then on 25 Jan, Nips played a last sick joke on us. Relieved from those corpse-filthy perimeters and expecting so more combat, we entrucked under Lt Nugent to guard Ambogo Crossing. We chose bivouac at random in the heavy thickets, began unloading our 3 trucks. Then Arisaka rifle fire rattled at us from the base of an immense stump. We shot back. A Jap grenade thudded against a limb, bounced back, and exploded among Japs. We buried 5 deep under ground right where they died. From 15 Jan to 15 Mar, we picketed at Ambogo, then boarded trucks for small river boats that motored us to Oro Bay.

At Oro Bay, we had a New Guinea paradise — on mosquito-free heights 1800 feet up — a 270 degree view of blue mountains and green ocean. For safety from planes our tents were pitched on the side of a gorge. We framed and platformed our tents in bamboo. Lt Nugent left us for B Co; and after hospital rest, 2/Lt McKinney became CO — a position he had well earned. And we rested from battle and remembered our dead — 13 at Sanananda, and 4 Weapons men drowned in Australia at Torbul Point.

There Cpl Leavitt had saved 2, but Kinsel, Tressman, Hernandez. and Cpl Arpell White had drowned. And we proudly remembered the great days when we struck Jap perimeters point-blank — and above all, those fights of 13 and 16 Jan 1943.

TWO ATTACK ROSTERS — A-163 Inf.
2/Pln, 13 Jan 1943
Lt McKinney; Pln Sgt Wolcott; Sgts Carpenter, Davenport, Brody, Beesley; Cpls Dorris, May, Daly, Murray; Pvts Jicha, Hart, Cheney, Miller, Jones, Behuncik, Reynolds, Olson, Hritz, Hudson, Huxhold, Casciato, J. Smith, McMannus, Stroud, Carlson McGrath, Mattice, Turek, Del Sasso, Wilson, Wanninger, Alires, Urnaza, Fleming, Bunker, Medic Baker.

1/Pln, 15 Jan 1943
Lt. Houston; S/Sgt Henry; Sgts Ziegele, Burrison, Weyer; Cpls Walter, Wittlieb, Rutledge; Pvts Chambers, Curry, Pisapia, Veselka, Johnson, Heintz, Madej, Luedke, Aiking, Macy, Marquart, Haarala, Hasselbring, Lanigan, Hughes, Apida, Beckwith, Cordova, M. Gonzales, Archuleta, Martinez, Max, Tatarski, Bashor, Icenhower, Medic Smith. WEAPONS ATT'D: S/Sgt Harris; Cpl Roberts; Pvts Hoppe, Mack, Collier, Fellows, Taylor.

Prime source is unsigned MS merely called "Headquarters Company 'A' 163d Infnatry/Office of the CO. Capt. Howard McKinney added more data during meetings some 5 years ago with other A Co vets at Poplar, Montana. Also useful were Dr. Samuel Milner's VICTORY IN PAPUA, and Federal Archives reports, "The Battle of Sanananda," "New Guinea Chapter/The Battle of Sanananda," 163's Journal untitled, and George Weller's Chicago Daily News stories. (I have lost the name of a man suggested as the author of this first, unsigned MS, so welcome the chance to make up for this omission.)

THE DIVISION HISTORY, NO. 76

B Co. 163 Infantry:
Battle of Sanananda

by **Dr. Hargis Westerfield**, Division Historian
with **Sgt. James J. Eder**

In the dark before dawn, at 0320 on 30 Dec 1943, B Co., 163 Inf. awoke at Port Moresby to enplane for the Sanananda battle. But deathly mists hid the Owen Stanley mountains that our Aussie planes had to dodge through. Zeroes would hover above us if we came out of the mists. It was three days before DC-3s landed B Co. in the jungle swamps to lose 23 KIA, 34 WIA before the battle ended.

By 3 Jan. B garrisoned Musket Perimeter on that lethal north side before Jap perimeters Q and R. After we dug in, Jap fire began. When we fired back, they wounded mortarman Knoepfle. They chattered just yards from our forward holes. Then they tried to hit our rear, but found we had no rear. After heavy casualties, they withdrew, then struck a final blow. During these attacks, B lost wounded (besides Knoepfle): Robjdek, Al Miller, Guider, Castillo. Capt. Hamilton was narrowly missed. All day Jap fire whizzed by B while Aussie Hanson Troop's 25-pounders fired security, and we blasted with grenades and called down 81 fire.

Next day began the heroic phrase of B Co's Battle of Sanananda. With only light supporting fire, heroes of memorable names led grim combat patrols or all-out attacks against almost impregnable Jap bunkers. With other 1/Bn men, B endured an experimental phase of fighting like that which decimated 32 Div. at Buna-Gona. Losses were heavy.

On 3 Jan. B tried an attack from Musket against Jap Perimeter R. One patrol hit a MG nest 40-50 yards north, but the attack failed. Even while supported by 81 mortar shells, a second patrol also failed before that same MG nest.

Sgt. Reddoor led one of these patrols. When the Jap MG fired, his patrol hit the ground, but Sioux Reddoor leaped behind a tree. Although wounded in hip and right foot, he threw two grenades into the nest to kill eight Japs. Then Chippewa Sgt. Belgarde charged across the open with his Tommy firing .45 slugs as fast as he fed in clips. He scooped up Reddoor and bore him to safety. Belgarde was wounded also. All day 4 Jan. rifle fire was continuous against B Co. in Musket Perimeter.

Next day, Hamilton planned to storm that pillbox which had wounded Sgts. Reddoor and Belgarde. After another 25-pounder barrage, 2/Pln. attacked in front while 1/Pln. came in to the left and behind the Japs.

Roy Ramsey thought that B's timing was off—that 2/Pln. attacked too soon from in front. S/Sgt. Sullender was stricken, to die later.

The enveloping 1/Pln. patrol of two officers and 28 men encountered the crossfire of four cleverly hidden MGs. We destroyed one MG, but at a high price. In this attack of 1/Pln., Limbocker was the first man to die. Both McMeel and Potter tried to save Limbocker, but they saw Jap tracers pass too close to his body. Benske would have tried, but we talked him out of risking another death to save our man. Lt. Ellers and Cpl. Pinkenstein were also wounded. Connor's grenade rebounded to kill both him and Koustrop. Mendoza was wounded and had to be left to die under the Jap guns that night.

Both Potter and McMeel were missing in action and already believed dead. Nobody ever found McMeel's body. Later Chaplain Siqueland found a mess kit in the Jap Hq bunker—a mess kit that S/Sgt. Eder had given to him—with Eder's name on it.

Specially tragic was the death of Sgt. Gaskell. Reportedly hit by a sniper, he threw himself on his own grenade to save the men in his squad. From this attack of 5 Jan., eight B men were dead or missing and three wounded.

It was probably shortly after this holocaust of 5 Jan. that S/Sgt. Eder led a four-man patrol including Cpl. Dolan, the company clerk, to reconnoiter the Jap perimeter. We first moved left to our front on Suicide Trail—the name B Co. gave to the crosstrail which 2/Bn. would use on 9 Jan. to cut off the Jap escape route on Killerton Trail.

At this outpost, Eder had a guide lead us through a booby-trapped area. Quietly, the guide took us through and quickly got away from us. Sliding through the swamp, we crept towards the center of the Jap perimeter. We easily passed between two MG posts to reach that Nippo center.

But the Japs evidently became suspicious and dispatched a patrol to kill anyone they could find. We froze to the ground, Eder and Dolan face to face. Eder was down behind a fallen tree parallel to the trail up which the Jap rifles were coming.

The Jap patrol leader halted on the other side of the log Eder was hiding behind. The Jap stood on the other side near Eder's head and hurriedly scanned the jungle. From concealment, Eder feared to look long at the Jap; he dared not take the risk of drawing the enemy gaze. Eder smiled weakly at the scared Dolan and waited.

Perhaps the Jap was just as scared as Eder and Dolan, for he spoke to the patrol and took it out of there. After observing and memorizing awhile, we also got out of that sinister place.

In escaping past those MGs, one member of the patrol panicked and dashed through our own booby traps towards our outposts. After the shooting stopped, Eder found him repentant and had the kindness never to report the man's headlong flight to Hamilton.

On 7 Jan. attrition of B continued. Hamilton lost the soldier whom he considered his "best enlisted man," S/Sgt. Lockman. Hamilton thought that the same sniper who had shot Gaskell had also killed Lockman. Ramsey saw the bullet strike laterally across Lockman's back. Gorischek also was killed 7 Jan. For 8 Jan. Col. Doe had decided on 163's largest operation of the war—up to this point. Aussie Gen. Vasey gave him permission to strike Jap perimeters Q and R which were dug between B at Musket and C north of us at Kano Perimeter. (Vasey gave permission, but he wisely sent his Col. Pollard to hold Doe back from committing 2/Bn., which was to block Killerton Trail next morning.)

While C struck Q Perimeter, B was assigned to storm R,— the larger perimeter on the west side of Sanananda Road. Each B man took two grenades and two days' rations for the push. Although Doe certainly expected success, B's CO. Hamilton doubted whether he would get through 8 Jan. 1943 alive.

About 1145, Aussie Hanson's FA Troop opened up with 25-pounders. All available mortars and MGs fired preparation. But Hanson Troop was out of impact fuzes to explode on contact with the earth. These Aussie guns fired only delayed action fuzes which exploded harmlessly in muck, if they exploded at all. A waist-deep swamp and heavy fire stopped C Co. dead, and C lost Lt. Fisk, among the 10 wounded and 10 missing that Hamilton recorded in his diary.

And, like C, we B men had an impossible mission. Best direction of attack was from west to east against perimeter R, but Hanson Troop was on the east—out of position to cover B's push.

We had to make a suicidal frontal attack from the south. We ran into fire from the perimeter we fought, and on the flank from Q which C was attacking. To Weapons Pln's S/Sgt. Eder, it seemed that the waiting Japs let his men get just 5-10 feet out of their holes before the drum-fires cracked down.

From long bunkers and coconut-tree pillboxes, the Japs shot —with automatic weapons firing on line 10 feet apart. We recoiled shooting back blindly, with what dead and wounded we could get out. Waist-deep in water, we had our new positions. We were happy that raw E Co. garrisoned those lines for the night. Hot food and some sleep helped our morale, but our losses were again severe.

We never could recover Berg's body. Dead also were Russell, Foltz, Irmen, Carroll, Horan, Sgt. Genther. Wounded were McFarland, Rubens, Cawiezell, Haller, Del Costello, Nore, Kjemhus, Laabs, Tyree Martin, Cpl. Petrovitch.

On 9 Jan. E Co. left our lines to join 2/Bn. in the push to Killerton Trail, and we had to return to our swamp before R Perimeter. Soaked in rain and mud, we learned to sleep with FA firing overhead and grenades blasting nearby. Busha was wounded 9 Jan. On 10 Jan. Hamilton hoped for no casualties, but Hanrahan and Thornton were wounded in the same hole. (An unnamed medic was also killed.) On 11 Jan. Fiscus was killed about 1900 hrs.

Indispensable was Capt. (now Col.) Robert M. Hamilton's rain-blurred diary with casualties' names and dates. Also indispensable was Sgt. James J. Eder's 7-page, single-spaced typescript, B Co. and I, with his ltr. 13 Feb 1973. Roy Ramsey gave me data at Gearhart Reunion of 1971; so did George Weller's 1943 Chicago Tribune *articles and Dr. Samuel Milner's* Victory in Papua.

Then came two days' relief from the lines—back in Musket Perimeter. And no rain fell. B Co. lay barefoot on the ground and began to dry out. Diarrhea and malaria were now prevalent.

And about 16 Jan. Eder got orders for a difficult one-man contact patrol. He had to move north through Jap country and find 18 Aussie Brigade, now moving south from the sea in 163's direction. With his youthful bringing up as an Umpqua Sioux, dark-skinned Eder was in many ways the best possible choice for this difficult mission. During field training exercises, he had made other B men shiver when he would come up out of nowhere among them. In this jungle fighting, he was already notable for his silent, deadly stalking of Jap patrols.

He now alerted B men facing that seaward side of our field-of-fire to be careful not to shoot until sure their target was a Jap and not Eder. He faded into the opaque jungle greenery. Then he crawled patiently northward through muck and water —how long, he never could remember.

But suddenly, he heard Jap voices behind him; he knew that he was past the Nippo lines without having known when he passed them. Eder now felt panic; somewhere in the opaque jungle before him were Aussie outguards—bitter blond veterans of deadly Jap battles—men who might shoot instinctively at a black face. For tropic-tanned Eder was shades darker than any Jap; other Yanks had shot at him for a Jap more than once. (He was in fact, a hundred per cent American combination of American Negro, Sioux, and German.)

He knew that he could not long remain in one place. He began crawling again; he prayed.

Suddenly he was staring into the muzzle of an Aussie Owen gun. Why that Aussie never squeezed the trigger is a mystery to this day. After Eder had identified himself, the Aussie Owen gunner could give no reason why he had not shot Eder to pieces.

The Aussies fought their way south to 163, but their CO kept Eder close beside him all the time. Eder shook too much to be of use in combat now.

And so went B Co., 163 Inf's first, or heroic, phase of the Battle of Sanananda. In this heroic phase, too many were killed or wounded in our own perimeters, or in poorly supported attacks—especially those attacks of 4 and 8 Jan. Our sacrifices were heroic yet wasteful, but perhaps 163 needed them to acquaint a raw regiment with its need to adapt to battlefield reality. And perhaps 163 needed these sacrifices to undermine Jap morale, which was still high when we took over Musket and Kano (Fisk) Perimeters.

By about 16 Jan. B entered into our second phase of the Battle of Sanananda. Operating with other companies, we seasoned and bloodied veterans would wipe out Jap perimeters S,T,U—those surviving perimeters astride the great road-bend north of Kano (Fisk) Perimeter. In the previous heroic phase, our losses had been 17 killed out of a total of 23 in the entire battle, and our wounded 23 out of 30 in the entire battle. In the second and last phase, B's losses would be comparatively few, our fighting superb.

Standing Patrol at Sanananda

By Dr. HARGIS WESTERFIELD, Division Historian,
with S/Sgt. MORTON E. RUBENS

On 3 Jan. 1943, S/Sgt. Mort Rubens was point man when B Co. 163 Inf. tensely hunted through mud and brush to relieve the shattered Australian garrison of Huggins (Musket) Perimeter. B slipped up the Sanananda supply trail in battle formation. We had heard that 300 Japs had cracked Aussie lines. News of this strike by 300 Japs was more than rumor, to judge by the slow trek of B up that trail. We were rightly alerted for trouble.

But B had no Jap trouble—only the disheartening sight of pale, drawn-faced, slouch-hatted Diggers shambling down the left side of the trail almost close enough to touch. These Aussies of 2/7 Cavalry Regt. had fought to hold Huggins since 16 Dec. 1942. (The CO for whom the perimeter was named, Capt. Meredith M. Huggins was seriously wounded earlier, 5 Dec. 1943.) The departing Aussies were sick, wounded, despairing. Their uniforms were rotten. Rubens thought that they could not hold out another day. Right then, Rubens decided that B 163 did not have much of a chance to return alive from that swamp.

So we soaked down into Huggins (renamed Musket) Perimeter. We dug L-shaped holes with two men to a hole. The hole was shaped like an "L" so that if a Jap grenade dropped in, a man could heave himself to safety around the bend in the "L".

Once in perimeter, B was always under fire—snipers and MG's daily, grenades at night. In full daylight, we kept heads down. Their snipers were good; they smashed a helmet any time you lifted one on a stick to test their aim. We left our holes only when light was bad—early morn and dusk— and then in fear.

In an L-shaped hole, we stayed down all day and watched all night, seemingly without sleep, in two-man shifts. Nights in that jungle opening were indeed black. There was danger that a grenade thrown from a hole would hit a tree and rebound into the hole of the thrower. Rubens cannily placed pieces of wood on the rim of the hole so that he could touch them in the dark and guide his grenades into a forest opening where they would menace the Jap raider and not himself.

Sgt. Rubens and his 1/Pln. men spent far too many grenades as far as custodians of supplies were concerned. Early one morning after a bad night of Jap alarms, 1/Pln. was low on grenades. Back at the ammo dump centering on Musket Perimeter, Maj. Hawks said, "You guys out there use up too many grenades at night." Rubens naturally replied, "Major, come out with me tonight. You'll see how many you use."

Hawks had no answer. Boiling with anger, Rubens slung his Tommy gun on his shoulder, gripped two boxes by their handles and strode back toward 1/Pln. (Rubens was 6 feet, 3 inches tall, and then weighed some 215 pounds.)

As he walked, Rubens grew angrier. Suddenly it dawned on him that Musket Perimeter was far too quiet. Something was wrong.

He had trudged out past B's holes which he hadn't seen in his blind anger and was close to where Japs would be lurking. Rubens turned tail, and still carrying grenades and gun, he dashed back in panic and threw himself into a hole.

Then the Nips opened fire. Maybe they were as surprised as Rubens himself at his casual stroll towards them. Or maybe they were going to let him walk into them and then kill him.

That same day, he decided to enlarge his cramped "L" hole. He would also dig a new seep for drinking water, one different from the hole that they had used for some days.

In that soft earth, Rubens dug about 12 inches; then he hit a shoe—a Jap shoe with a foot in it! He covered the foot hurriedly, then dug in another direction. After that, when he filled his canteen, he began sterilizing his water with two drops of iodine instead of one. Using a second drop made him feel a little better.

And now he got his first important mission for 163 at Sanananda. He was to set up a hazardous standing patrol on what Sgt. Jimmie Eder of Weapons Pln. called "Suicide Trail." (Suicide Trail was that strategic route which 32 Div. Infantry and Aussies had used to seize and hold Huggins Perimeter from the Japs. It ran west from Musket-Huggins to Killerton Trail. Maj. Rankin's 2/Bn. would need that trail in their great advance of 9 Jan., when they closed the Japs' escape route.)

A standing patrol was a flexible trail block, a defense in depth to retain the use of a trail or road. Taking 13 men, including two BAR teams, Rubens dug in on both sides of Suicide Trail. He placed the BAR's to cover it all the way to the bend in the trail. Besides guards out front, he also kept an alert man at his rear to prevent being surprised and cut off. And he mined the trail ahead and personally attached trip wires to grenades, preferably the Nippo thin green wire that was hard to see.

On this standing patrol, it was a grim touch-and-go—maybe four-five days, hard for a man to remember just how many days when the time passed in danger. We were on our own with our own supplies and only the phone to connect us with 1/Bn. And daily and nightly, Jap patrols tried to find our position to kill us.

Daily we set up forward defenses on the trail, and sometimes exchanged grenades and gunfire. At dusk, we pulled back some 50 feet and let booby traps deal with Jap night-fighters.

It was through our hidden booby traps that S/Sgt. Rubens guided S/Sgt. Eder about 5 Jan. when Eder made a daring four-man patrol with company clerk Bill Dolan into Nippo territory.

CREDIT: When Mort Rubens read S/Sgt. James J. Eder's mention of being guided by Rubens on Suicide Trail, he wrote to me to identify himself and begin his story. Core of this story are these: Rubens' undated ltr. about May 1974, dated ltrs. 14 May and 29 May 1974, undated note about June 1974. Some aid came also from Dudley McCarthy's South-West Pacific Area First Year, and 163's Extract from History (1 Jan-8 Jan. 1943). Mort Rubens has a small restaurant in the Farmers Market at 3rd and Fairfax Sts. in Los Angeles.

On 7 Jan., another B patrol through Rubens' position came upon Nips cutting poles 70 yards northwards. The Nips fired on the patrol, and the patrol withdrew.

Early one morning, Japs pushed on Rubens' patrol from two directions: from our right flank and from our front over the Suicide Trail we guarded. On the right, our trip wires blew up grenades and halted them. But they came on in front. They were trying to flush us out, for they could not find our exact location. We held fire to draw them on. They lost two on the trip wires; still they came on.

The strain was too great for one of Rubens' men; he started to get up and run. If the Japs saw him, all of our lives would have been in danger. Rubens jammed his Tommy against the man's back and gritted, "Try to run, and I'll shoot both your legs off." Rubens pushed the frightened man down, but kept him in sight thereafter.

Now our BAR's opened up on the Japs and dropped some of them. They pulled back and tried again, and we felled a few more. This was the last time the Japs probed our standing patrol in force.

Thus for four-five days, Rubens with 13 men held Suicide Trail and carried out orders not to let the Japs use that trail. In all that time, we were never aware that our keeping that trail clear was of paramount importance for 2/Bn's great march to cut the Japs' escape route to the sea.

Only contact with 1/Bn. was still by phone. With that phone to his ear on 7 Jan., Rubens got a shock. While hearing B's 1/Sgt. Edeline report B Co's losses to Hq., he heard an echo repeat the top kick's name five times.

At once, he told Edeline that a wire was being tapped, somewhere between Rubens' patrol and the main perimeter. Edeline instantly ordered Rubens to pull back to B with all hands, and to keep ready to shoot. Japs might be hurrying down the wire to blast us.

Thus Rubens pulled out his standing patrol but he was lucky to return. At the last minute, new trouble developed.

No Japs followed him, but he came from the jungle unexpectedly upon newly arrived E Co.—men who had not yet fought. E was casually sitting out in the open with their arms disassembled. They were cleaning equipment at the front.

Rubens found an officer and warned him that Japs could be within 25 yards. E Co. got out of sight fast.

E was lucky then; so was Rubens. For if E's men had been more experienced, they would have opened fire on Rubens' patrol the instant Rubens came out of the jungle.

Rubens had begun that standing patrol with 13 men and he returned to B Co. with all 13 men.

And now Rubens got his second and last important mission for 163 at Sanananda. When B with C made the great assault of 8 Jan. on the two Jap perimeters north of Fisk, we heard that some 80 Japs were before us. We were going to clear them out completely. In this action, Rubens was suddenly called from 1/Pln. to lead 2/Pln's push.

With 35-37 men, Rubens' 2/Pln. headed north to fight the Japs. Soon a Jap MG opened up, and B ran low. When the MG lowered its fire, 2/Pln. crawled. It became rough going; in thick jungle under fire, a man couldn't raise his head to see where he was.

Suddenly Rubens' line of men stopped moving, although we had hardly advanced 200-250 yards from Musket Perimeter. Rubens crawled up to try to spring a few individuals' advances. Every man he contacted was dead or wounded. The Japs had shot them all from above.

Moving over to the right, Rubens tried to find out where that deadly fire came from. He spotted snipers above and before the pillbox that was firing the MG on us.

He raised up his Tommy gun with a 50-shot drum which he had taken from a Jap corpse. His heavy slugs killed a sniper in a tree to his left.

But in firing, Rubens took a shot in the right temple. He rolled over, squeezed trigger, and killed the man who had wounded him.

Then all the rifle fire on earth seemed to strike Rubens at once. Bullets tore the Tommy from his grip, wounded him twice in the right hand. With his unwounded left hand, he threw a grenade at that pillbox; its defenders hurled a lot back.

Rubens then kept passing out. He tied the gun sling around his arm to stop the bleeding and dragged his half-dead body back to perimeter. How long it took him to return alive, he never knew.

Thus went Rubens' war against Jap Perimeter R, with inadequate FA preparation, and without the techniques of carefully timed preparatory fire that 163 would use later at Sanananda. Since he had been reassigned to 2/Pln. just before the attack, he hardly got to know the names of the B men killed or wounded. Perhaps the killed were Irmen and Carroll. Perhaps the wounded were McFarland, Cawiezell, Haller, Del Costello, Nore, Kjemhus, and Laabs.

Despite the wound in his temple and two more in the right hand, S/Sgt. Rubens at first seemed to have recovered. He continued soldiering. After some five months in the hospital, he became an intelligence NCO at Base Section 7. From Base Section 7, he was selected for OCS and appointed in Jan. 1944. In recommending him, the CO of Base Section 7, Brig.-Gen. Thomas E. Rilea, wrote, "I would be glad to have him serve under my command in the grade of Second Lieutenant."

But Rubens' old wounds and privations of Sanananda came back on him. He had to return to Base 7 for limited service, then enter hospital and return to the States. Finally came his medical discharge. He had two disc operations. He now has 30 per cent disability pension from the VA: 10 per cent for the bullet wounds, 10 per cent for malaria and 10 per cent for his back. And he can get no indemnity for his liver after its injury from medication against the tropical hookworm disease, no doubt complicated by drinking from a polluted seep in Musket Perimeter.

Such was the saga of S/Sgt. Rubens in his Sanananda Campaign—a dexterously led standing patrol on Suicide Trail and a brave day of battle against Perimeter R.

B Co. 163 Infantry:
Sanananda: The Victory Phase

by DR. HARGIS WESTERFIELD, Division Historian
WITH COL. ROBERT M. HAMILTON
AND SGT. JAMES J. EDER

Indispensable was Sgt. James J. Eder's 7-page, single-spaced typescript, "B" Co. and I," with his Ltr. 13 Feb. 1973. Also indispensable was Capt. (Now Col.) Robert W. Hamilton's rain-blurred diary with casualties' names and dates. Basic narrative is also probably by Hamilton–"An Unsupported Attack" from "41 Div. Training Notes, No. 2, Part IV." I also used Dr. Samuel Milner's Victory in Papua, George Weller's 1943 Chicago Tribune articles, 163 Inf's The Battle of Sanananda, and extracts from 163's History.

On 16 Jan. 1943, B Co. 163 Inf. began the "victory" phase of Sanananda—as opposed to our earlier, "heroic" phase, of 3-12 Jan. In our "heroic" phase, B Co. had almost single-handedly bucked the Japs' "R" Perimeter north of Musket. We had lost heavily–17 dead, 23 wounded. Weapons and FA support had been ineffective. But in our final, "victory" phase B would coordinate action with other 163 outfits and heavy support fire for ultimate victory.

During this final phase of B's action, we became part of Col. Lindstrom's 1/Bn fight against triple Jap Perimeters S, T, and U. Astride the great roadbend east of Musket Perimeter, S-T-U made the hard core of Jap resistance at Sanananda. According to three prisoners questioned three days after our initial fight, S-T-U was heavily defended. Garrison was 400 strong, with 10 HMG's, 10 LMG's, a 75 AT cannon–with a regimental headquarter of an unspecified regiment.

Yet despite the strength of their perimeters, the Jap garrison was starving. Standard daily ration of rice had been 28 ounces per man; it was down to two by 7 Jan–and to nothing four days before we fought S-T-U. Mortar shells and rifle ammo were strictly rationed.

Unlike B and C's earlier assaults on Q-R, the attack of 16 Jan. was no poorly covered attack of a single company. After 15 minutes Aussie FA, Yank 81's and 60's with MG drumfires, A and C moved out.

B was in reserve at first. But four MG's searched the kunai flat around prone A Co, as 20 A men collapsed from heat. Lindstrom ordered a B pln. in to help A. Because of the hurried briefing, Hamilton almost lost his relief pln.

But probably A's Lt. McKinney himself credited B for drawing fire from A and causing Nip shooting to slacken somewhat. A's support pln. reinforced B. While both plns. fired cover, A slowly retreated about 1200 to reform leftwards behind the original line of departure.

Compared to A's total of 9 dead, 17 wounded, this one B pln. had 5 dead. Besides Hopke, Blumenthal and Sgt. Henry Johnson, we lost Sioux Morin dead on the Popondetta evacuation plane. (Edeline said that Morin had killed 25 Japs.) Cpl. Lingle was listed as wounded, but later as dead.

Despite A's severe repulse, Col. Lindstrom maneuvered successfully on 16 Jan. When C on A's left met little opposition, he ordered C and B's two unfought plns. and drove around the Jap right flank. Here he set up Perimeter A-D, reinforced with A and B men as they returned from frontline combat that day.

Perimeter A-D was strategically located north of Sanananda Road in the 45-degree angle of that road–and some 400 yards from either arm of that angle. We could smash any large group that fled towards the Bismarck Sea. Augmented by Maj. Rankin's 2/Bn. from Killerton Trail, we could infight against Perimeters S-T-U. The Battle of Sanananda was almost finished.

But for B 163, four more days of combat hell remained. On the morn of 17 Jan. we waited for ammo and hot meals–such as they were. C rations and bully beef were hard to take! And after a three-man patrol found the Japs in the same position as yesterday, we made a recon in force on that azimuth which the patrol gave us. Thus began our fight on S-T-U.

CO Hamilton thought the recon in force unsuccessful, but no B man was even wounded. That night, our remnant of B quietly dug in 100 yards from the Jap pillboxes. Our strength was low; Hamilton cut the three rifle plns. to two. Sgt. Eder's Weapons pln. was down to two LMG squads and a 60 mm mortar squad.

On 18 Jan. we left our lone mortar squad and a kitchen detail in last night's perimeter and moved out to fight. Carefully, Lt. MacKenzie scouted the brush. About 100 yards north, we saw 5-6 Jap bunkers on the far bank of a stream five yards wide, and water about chest deep.

Here 2/Pln. pushed first. As it began to cross, Japs opened fire. Everyone was down and crawling. Our right squad fired faster and worked up to eight yards from the Japs. The left squad pushed ahead also. Now the Pln/Sgt. and two men crossed the stream and went to work with grenades and tommies.

They silenced the bunker before them. Nearby Japs fled back through a communications trench, into a second line of bunkers. Now all of 2/Pln's right squad and the other men of the left squad crossed, and 2/Pln's two squads crawled ahead in a skirmish line. Ahead was a second line of Jap bunkers–15 yards behind the first, and 30 yards apart.

After 2/Pln. cleared the way, 1/Pln. closed up behind the center of the line, about 15 yards back. All this movement drew ground fire from rifles and MG's, and tree fire from snipers.

Now the supporting 1/Pln. had orders to push to the left of the 2/Pln. It covered the advance with four 3-man patrols to the right, and three patrols on the left.

But the leftward patrols reported back with bad news. After working west 75-175 yards, they could find no flank to the Jap lines. They were continuous; two lines of Jap bunkers stretched as far as they could see. Hamilton thought it high time to dig in for the night.

And B made perimeter here in that first line of Jap pillboxes. This perimeter was shaped somewhat like a baseball diamond–but with an elongated angle pushed out close to the unbroken Jap second line. The two short angles anchored on two vacated Jap bunkers. The shallow fourth angle was back on the safer side of the creek, for closer contact with our kitchen and 60 mm mortar crew to the rear. We posted Eder's two LMG's at opposite angles to enfilade our front–or, if needed, to pivot to defend the rear point of the diamond. In this diamond perimeter, B had no Jap trouble that night.

On that day of frontal attack of 18 Jan., B had two wounded- Land and Plotts. For some days, we thought Gorichs was dead, but later Ramsey found him alive and well at the Medics.

On 19 Jan. Capt. Van Duyn's C Co. came up on B's left at daybreak. Van Duyn and Hamilton then linked up all four rifle plns. and the 60mm mortars in a telephone party line to their dual CP. Now pln. leaders could report on breaks in Jap fire and coordinate advances. With one CO left at the phone, the other could be at the front with his men.

C breached the Jap line first. Despite heavy fire, S/Sgt. Mohl with Cpl. Rummel crossed the creek, killed six bunkers and blasted a hole for all C to reinforce them. Partially relieved of Jap fire, B also attacked.

Soon the three squads of Hamilton's lead pln. were committed. Each squad lay deployed in a semicircle against a pillbox ten yards away. While their squad fired into the slot, two selected men worked forward and arced in grenades. Thus B cleared two bunkers in the Jap second line.

Just as our attack seemed about to pierce the perimeter, the Japs left their broken first and second lines. They formed a new line some 30 yards back and held us as dusk began to fall. B had lost Burnham, Abbott wounded.

On 20 Jan. B stayed put because Col. Doe needed all FA and mortars to help Capt. Dupre's I Co. attack U Perimeter from the south. (U was south of Sanananda Road.) And two B patrols found that on the left more Jap bunkers were evacuated from the line that we broke the day before. The Japs still held a third line, however.

25

Men of 163 mopping up

And on 21 Jan. came B's last great fight at Sanananda. When A plus K on our left followed a heavy barrage into T Perimeter and gutted it, B plus C also struck.

B had orders to attack across a Jap graveyard and take Perimeter U across Sanananda Road. When our FA and mortars fell on B instead of the Japs, some of us were buried by earth. Yet we dug out our B men with no casualties.

After the barrage, Lt. Radow suggested that Sgt. Eder lead the advance. Badly scared but simply saying "Follow me," Eder stepped out ahead of B's few remaining men. At the road, he saw three Japs watching him. He shot down 1 with his carbine; the other two merely looked at the dead comrade. Eder shot the second; the third dropped behind a parapet and escaped.

Over his shoulder, Eder saw his men halfway across the graveyard. Then an M-1 started the firefight. Too close to the Japs and alone, Eder took a grenade blast that knocked him down and wounded him in neck and elbow. But he was down on the ground when Jap MG's fired over him and drove B back into the jungle.

Somehow back in safety with B, Eder heard that his close friend Compa lay wounded in the cemetery. At first well covered by our fire, Eder crawled in safety and called for Compa. Then Jap Mg's shot close. Eder said he must have gone mad in fear; he leaped upright and fled back to B Co. unhurt. Later, he found that Compa had died at once from MG bursts.

With S and T liquidated, Jap Perimeter U was still untaken across Sanananda Road. It was still too strong to be stormed by B, now down to 30 men at the front.

Now C Co's Lt. Shelley crawled over to Eder's command and said that C had orders to withdraw from our flank. But 1/Bn's Hq. told B to stay there—feverish, tired, and hungry. When another barrage fell on the Jap perimeter before us, we prevented any escapes. We saw other units mopping up along the road. And so on 21 Jan. 1/Bn had overrun Perimeters S-T; B claimed 171 dead Japs out of 531 killed on 21 Jan. And B had lost Compa.

Our phone had gone dead, but B grimly sat in our defensive position from 21 Jan. through 25 Jan. After three days without food, there came B's Mess Sgt. Archiquette sloughing through the mud to Eder's command. He carried two pails of rice and hardtack—the first hot food we'd seen for six days—and cigarettes. "It's all over," said Indian Archiquette. "Just eat and relax." Most of us sighed and quietly fell asleep.

Probable total of casualties for B was 25 dead, 28 wounded. Then we had the sick—so many that Hamilton soon gave up listing—like McGuinness, Poynter, Nelson, Miller, Lara, Magdois.

Hamilton's log of his illness epitomizes what many B men suffered. In the midst of combat, malaria and dysentery hit him—on 16 Jan. when we began fighting Perimeter S-T-U. On 19 Jan. the fever seemed over, but it was back again next day, 20 Jan., into those last days of battle. For six nights in a row, but still commanding B, he went without sleep, endured dysentery. He forgot when he was without chills and fevers and headaches. Finally evacuated to Australia, he was hardly convalescent 23 days after the start of the fever 16 Jan.

Then came the day of B's victory parade—as much as a 41st man ever got. As senior NCO, Eder got orders to form B and hike to Soputa. In route step, B marched out—just 18 of us—with cooks, clerks, KP's. Passing Huggins Graveyard, most of us feared to look aside.

Then a jeep pulled to the side of the road. It sported a two-star flag. Eder ordered B to attention as we paraded past Gen. Fuller. Fuller returned Eder's salute. Eder heard a staff member say: "General, there goes what remains of one company—the raggedest, stinkingest, and fightingest outfit in the 163d – B Company."

C Co. 163 Infantry At Sanananda:

Fisk Perimeter and afterwards

By DR. HARGIS WESTERFIELD, Division Historian
with RUSSELL F. STEVENS, DON C. DIXON and others

On 2 Jan. 1943, C Co. 163 Inf. moved into the Battle of Sanananda. After flight from Port Moresby, we had slept the night of 1-2 Jan. by a small, high-banked jungle stream. On 2 Jan. we crossed in single file, on a slippery log. As we hiked north, guides warned that Jap positions were only a few feet away.

Trudging single file under heavy gear, we developed a dangerous gap between start and finish of our line. When the trail forked, with Jap Perimeters "P" close leftwards, the last 40 men lost contact. We turned wrong and almost got killed. We found ourselves in a brushy opening the size of a city block between Musket (Huggins) Perimeter and Jap killers.

From Japs to the south and Aussies in Musket, lead poured over us in a steady roar. All 40 of us hit ground in waist-high brush, dug in frantically. Stevens used an Aussie butcher knife and his hands to dig in like a dog.

Aussie mortars soon silenced Jap fires. We scurried from no man's land—without a casualty.

Passing through Musket Perimeter, we heard more Jap lead pour harmlessly over us. The sound of lead died down as we hiked up a trail circling right of the road to avoid the invisible Jap perimeter on our left. After another half mile, we arrived at the Aussies' James Perimeter which we were to relieve. ("Kano" was another Aussie name for this perimeter until we renamed it "Fisk" for our lieutenant killed 8 Jan.)

James Perimeter was a little ring of slit trenches about 70 by 80 feet. An alarm system surrounded it—a wire three inches off the ground. Bully beef tins hung there with empty cartridges to rattle and warn of Japs. We had to

41st Division troops arrive at a jungle landing field for the Sanananda operation.

extend James 20 yards to hold our larger company and an attached pln. of D Co's HMGs. Holding James Perimeter had been battered B Squadron and 2/7 Aussie Cavalry, which had dug in under fire 19 Dec., 17 days ago.

These were happy Aussies! Their CO himself received hq. runner Stevens and made him a cup of tea on a little alcohol stove. Lt. J.A. James was the CO; the perimeter got its name from him. (He later became a Brigadier General.)

After 2/7 Cav. got out, it was "C's" war, deep in Jap country. Our perimeter was the farthest Yank outpost north up Sanananda Road. Where the road bent east, there stood large Jap Perimeters S, T, and U. A short way south of us, twin Perimeter Q and R held the road to block us from Musket Perimeter. To get supplies at Musket, we had to send convoys SE in a half circle through A Co's Moore's post to avoid the Japs.

"C's" troubles began. On 6 Jan. S/Sgt. Kuhn was wounded, details unknown. Also on 6 Jan., 2/Pln's S/Sgt. Dixon led "C's" first recon patrol—Cpls. Kassing and Hugh Holmes.

After "C" prepared with several mortar shells, Dixon's patrol started: Kassing and Dixon with M-1s, Holmes with a Tommy. After 150-200 jungle yards, Holmes on the left warned Dixon. We were already among Japs—just past a position—and had to escape fast. Dixon told Holmes to move first. After 20 feet, they went prone, still unhurt. A burst of fire hit Holmes' chest when he rose again. Dixon was never able to keep down his heels; a single bullet cut four inches of his leggings, lodged in his big toe. A shot between the eyes killed Holmes.

To the rear, Dixon and Kassing shot at any movements in the brush. Dixon hurled two grenades. Then Yank fire saved the two prone men; Capt. Van Duyne sent a rescue squad. Unwounded, Kassing later was hospitalized for shock.

Next day, Japs seriously wounded Malizzo on supply convoy. On that 7 Jan. also, Richter died from Holmes' Tommy gun, which the Japs had captured. We killed the Jap who had it.

On 8 Jan. C Co. from the north and "B" from the south made disastrous attempts to wipe out twin Jap Perimeters Q-R between them. While "B" hit Perimeter R east of the road, we struck Perimeter Q west of the road.

Attack plans were defective. Aussie Hanson Troop's 25-pounder cannon shelled "C" men. "C's" line of attack was poorly reconnoitered. The first Aussie short probably killed Aubrey Jones, wounded other men. Another short killed McLemore and wounded more "C" men.

Shortly before the attack, Stevens had seen three "sharp-looking" men in our perimeter—knew that they were officers, even without insignia. With sweat beading his face, one man phoned headquarters, pleaded to call off the attack.

But at 1200, "C" had to move out after a creeping barrage. Shells struck so close that Capt. Van Duyne and runner Stevens hit the ground. As Stevens looked up, a shell holed his right thigh so deep that his hand could go through the hole. He saved his own life with a tourniquet.

Hobbling past Stevens on foot and knee, Sgt. Wheat shouted, "I got him!" BAR-man "Joe" gloated that he had put two clips into a pillbox and killed the Japs therein.

But "C's" push failed. The Aussie shells had only delayed fuzes exploding harmlessly in mud. Last night's rains caused us to flounder through waist-deep swamps around the north end of Perimeter Q. When we attacked against the strongest end of oval Perimeter Q, five MG positions 10 yards apart repelled us.

On that 8 Jan. "C" lost six killed and 13 wounded. McLemore, Jones, Meek, Raley, Berryman and 1/Lt. Fisk were dead. Besides Stevens, many others had grievous wounds. Gillaspy lost his left arm from a bullet. Kundert and T/5 Callantine were both hit on the left side of the abdomen. Cornish was shot in right thigh, 1/Sgt. Ferris in right flank. Bullets struck Sgt. Emil Nelson in left arm and Roy Smith in left hand and shoulder. Shell fragments gave Harrison a "lumbar" wound, and Stevens a wound in right thigh. Wounds of McJames, Strand, Sgt. Wheat and Cpl.

Martin were unreported in medical records. With six dead and 13 wounded, "C" suffered more than "B," which attacked Perimeter R at the same time and had two dead, 9 wounded.

After our repulse of 8 Jan., C Co. for the next few days endured the life of most other rifle cos. in that jungle swamp. On 11 Jan. Sherman died of wounds, details unspecified. Like other "C" men, Roesselet never forgot rains, jungle rot and the blind leafage that kept him from seeing more than a few feet from his hole. All night he heard animals or Japs prowling. Day brought nerve-wracking supply convoys to guard or recon patrols into sweaty brush.

Yet "C" found some bright, hot spots in our holes. In this wet jungle, hot food seemed impossible to get. Soaked wood failed to burn; Jap mortars would have crashed into our smoke if it had burned. But while reshaping his hole, Gewicki found small blocks of Jap cordite in heavy waxed paper. A small block flamed out like a blowtorch. It boiled a canteen cup instantly—even made bully beef less repellent.

South of us, our regiment kept pushing on Perimeters Q-R. On 10 Jan., two days after "C's" attack, AT Co's Cpl. Knight found that the Japs had for an unknown reason left Perimeter Q, which had repelled "B" on 8 Jan. Co. A seized "R" at once. On 14 Jan. "A" safely sneaked an entire pln. into "Q" from the north, then hurled in the whole co. to fight for it.

C Co. also sent a pln. to hit "Q" from the east while B Co. joined "A" to fight from the west. Perimeter Q was

---

CREDIT: Russell Stevens' three-page typescript (23 Oct. 1977) is the important "personal" without which I could not have written this story. Other "personals" include Don Dixon's ltr. (17 Aug. 1977), also ltrs. of Howard Roesselet (11 Oct. 1977) and Frank Kundert (autumn 1977), awards of Maurice Levy, Cpl. Wilmer Rummel and S/Sgt. John Mohl. Archives and books include B Co's Capt. Hamilton's study in 41st Division Training Note No. 2, 163's Casualty Lists, 163 Inf's "New Guinea Chapter/The Battle of Sanananda," George Weller's 1943 reports to "Chicago Daily News," Dr. Samuel Milner's "Victory in Papua" and Australian Dudley McCarthy's "Southwest Pacific Area/First Year/Kokoda to Wau." All 163's rifle cos. at Sanananda now have stories for the Jungleer. But where are stories of nonrifle cos. of 163 at Sanananda?

---

about 300 yards north to south, and 150 yards east to west, a roughly oval labyrinth of interconnecting bunkers and fire trenches. There, fierce resistance continued on 14 Jan. Probably "C's" Staub was killed in "Q" while Baskin and Urnikis were seriously wounded—all on 15 Jan.

But "C" never stormed Perimeter Q. Relieved by other cos., we became part of Col. Lindstrom's great push against Perimeter S, most eastern of the last three remaining Jap perimeters in the triangle at the great road bend. (It took L and K Cos. 36 hours to overrun "Q," but the kill was small.)

When "C" pushed in Lindstrom's all-out 1/Bn. attack on Perimeter S, we had no casualties, although A Co. lost nine dead and 17 wounded. When Lindstrom saw that "C's" advance was unopposed on "A's" left, he ordered "C" to swing around the Jap right flank. With B Co. we dug 1/Bn. Perimeter A-D 400 yards north of Sanananda Road. We contacted 2/Bn. coming down from the north to sever the last Jap garrisons from flight to the sea.

Hard fighting remained. Tague was killed 17 Jan., perhaps while scouting south against Perimeter S.

On 19-22 Jan. we fought our final action—a front-line siege of the double wall of bunkers of Perimeter S. A stream five yards wide and chest deep protected "S." On 18 Jan. B Co. had won a perch across the stream. But except for "B's" three captured positions, the first line of untaken pillboxes still menaced both of "B's" flanks. The second line was unbroken.

On 18 Jan. at 0730, "C" took over to fight on "B's" left. When S/Sgt. Mohl's 3/Pln. pushed, Jap fire from unseen flanking pillboxes cut 3/Pln. in two. Mohl's 16-man vanguard saved itself under the stream banks. But Jap rifles wounded four in seconds. We could not retreat over the fire lane that had cut 3/Pln. in two.

Mohl noted that two Jap pillboxes had only narrow frontal fields of fire; he saw the narrow dead space between them. We had a chance to live!

Deploying his survivors behind the creek bank to cover him, Mohl crawled safely up the dead space. He arced a grenade into a pillbox and killed it. Cpl. Rummel crawled up to Mohl with more grenades. The second pillbox still fired.

Rummel stood up twice and hurled grenades and missed. His third grenade hissed into the slot, blasted silence in the pillbox.

We passed up more grenades; Mohl and Rummel fought more emplacements. Among shell holes and pillboxes, they played a deadly war game with grenades, Mohl's Tommy gun and Rummel's rifle. Panicked Nips fusilladed widly in all directions. Mohl and Rummel gutted six pillboxes in all; they ordered up their eight unwounded and held the dead Jap line.

"C's" fight distracted the Nips before B Co; it easily crossed the stream and killed two pillboxes in the Japs' second line. But they withdrew 30 yards before the breach and held most of the second line intact. That night, "C" and "B" understrength plns. dug a triangle perimeter before the Japs' second line.

"C" had 12 seriously wounded that 19 Jan. Mortars penetrated Nowlin's right chest, Tylick's biceps and thigh. Others had shot wounds: S/Sgt. Nixon in right hip, Robles in right cheek and arm, Busse in right chest and arm, Gunter in right leg, Toelaer in hand and right thigh. Praznoswki was hit in the middle of his back. Mall was shot in left index finger, Perry in left shoulder. Don Smith and Cpl. Freitas had unspecified serious wounds.

But killer Levy was not in perimeter that night. Before dark hid him, he was fighting inside the Jap lines. His rifle killed six Japs, but he still lived, despite his muzzle flash locating him for return fire. Sheltered in the crotch between two great trees that night, he had a fine field of fire with daybreak. Then he slew 19 more Japs and crawled to safety, shot in the left knee.

On 20 Jan. we still fought the double line of pillboxes, but lacked heavy support fire because I Co. used it against Perimeter U southwards. More Jap pillboxes were silent, but their second line still held hard. Besides Levy, "C" had two more wounded; Nielsen shot in the head and Slosar in right leg. We had two dead: Sgt. Whitney and Cpl. Nance, wound unspecified, whose actual death was on 30 Jan.

On 21 Jan. "C's" battle ended. When A and K Cos. stormed Perimeters S-T on our left flank under heavy support fire, Jap pressure weakened before us. We crawled up and overran the second bunker line, then drove in with assault fire as Japs rose up to run and die. Hanenkrat was wounded, hit in left leg. Thus fell Perimeter S-T on 21 Jan. Only Perimeter U held out south of Sanananda Road, which I and L Cos. would storm on 22 Jan.

In our 19-day Battle of Sanananda, "C" lost 13 killed and 30 wounded. With D Co. HMGs, we outposted the Yank perimeter deepest into Jap territory, then fought well in the failing attack on Perimeter Q. On 16 Jan. we made the all-important move on 1/Bn's left flank that sealed off the last Jap garrisons from escape to the sea. And on 19-22 Jan. we hammered to death that double line of pillboxes in Perimeter S. "C" was one of the great fighting cos. in the Battle of Sanananda.

Seventeen Days at Sanananda

By S/Sgt Don E. Woods
with
DR. HARGIS WESTERFIELD, Association Historian

On 7 Jan 1943, E Co 163 Inf heard heavy firing as we sweated knee-deep in the swamps to relieve B Co from front lines at Musket Perimeter. Passing low gravemounds — Jap, Aussie, Yank — inches above water, we looked in the eye a rotting Jap sniper slumped from the vines that lashed him in a tree. His spectral stare saw nothing but knew all that we were to know. That first night, we crouched knee-deep in water to hurl grenades into jungle blackness. Wild hogs slithered like crawling Japs. From his hole, Don Wood with 2 cobbers threw 5 wild grenades; Yanks in the next hole threw 13 wilder grenades, kept E awake with M-1 fire.

In gray dawn, Jap snipers shot too accurately. Before E's arrival 5 Yanks had died from snipers at Wood's position. Today, Yank counter-snipers hit back, somewhat lulled Nip fire. About 1130 after Yank 60s and 81s impacted with 25-pounder FA of the Aussie Hanson Troop, B Co was to attack Jap Perimeter Q. From our holes, E Co was to fire cover.

Mortars and Aussie FA exploded 20 yards ahead. Jap sniping increased. Then B's Sgt Poynter and men dashed from Musket Perimeter, hit the mud, fired, and rushed in. E's men stood up in holes, blasted Japs on ground and in trees. Two Yank 50s fired overhead; Jap shrapnel flew all around E Co. B's attack failed. Shot in the stomach, E's little McDermeit died en route to hospital.

That night, E chilled with bodies half submerged while shrapnel-torn shelter halves let in rain. But at dawn 9 Jan, sleepless wet mucky E Co left fetid Fisk Perimeter—all but 2 Yanks in a hole swept by Jap MGs. (They escaped at dark.)

E Co left Fisk to secure 2/Btn's rear while G and F Cos led west 400 yards to block escape route of the main Jap army up Killerton Trail. E Co followed under fire, past maggot-covered corpses. We often hid from bullets behind Yank or Jap bodies. Mud was often waist-deep. Litter cases passed us—Wood's 2/Btn cobbers Ken Herman with a shoulder wound, Greiner with his leg a bloody stump.

That night, 2 Pltns from E took over F Co holes, with Japs 15 yards off pretending to call for help to draw fire. Again the Guinea rain fell. We lay in water but for hands and weapons sticking out—took turns to rub down bodies to keep blood circulating. Japs MGs sprayed mud to keep heads down. This place we named Hell's Corner—something from Dante's Inferno. Next day, F/Pltn replaced 2/Pltn in water-filled holes. For 3 days, 2/Pltn rested on Rankin Heights 400 yards north —nursed soaked wet feet wrinkled like washboards—had holes in dry, sandy loam near E's kitchen.

Other E Pltns fought in turn. On 12 Jan when Col Tsukamoto smashed 3 tanks, halted Aussie 18 Brigade's push north, E Co slew in the "Hospital Lot" beside G and F Cos. Here armed Nips hid among dead or dying; we had to kill or be killed. For E's Soliday, it was just 1 dugout clearing party after another. In the hospital stench, he lost count of his kill; he wanted no souvenirs here. At Jap Hq, he saw 3 Japs at their LMG—shot them at 40 yards—saw 1 fall back—and 2 just sag to earth. Later, 2 Nips with bayonets crept within 10 yards of Soliday, but Sgt Ashure warned in time. Soliday killed both.

But F's Prinz, Lt Ogden, Sgt Roush, Medic Marcus lay dead on G's left flank. Near dark, Rankin sent E to scout that flank. Capt Buckland's patrol saw Japs transferring a LMG from a well-hidden dugout. Einar Lund, Steiner slew all 3 with M-1s. But not until next morning in that thick jungle did Rankin and Aussie Capt Hirschel find the 4 F Yanks where 2 Nip fire-lanes met.

On 14 Jan, on patrol south of Musket, 163 caught a sick Jap who said the Japs were leaving the Sanananda Road and Killerton Trail Junction. Quickly, Aussie Gen Vasey sent 18 Brigade north and 163 south to crush Nip formations out of their deadly perimeters. With G, E Co hit south. F/Pltn led out, secured a small Nip village, slew 6.

Past the village, Don Wood saw many fly-blown Nippo bodies—the work of Aussie cannon. Suddenly he halted; one Jap body had no flies on it. This Jap raised to throw a grenade. Don's tommie put 2 slugs in head and 2 in chest.

Across a small river 500 yards past Aussie Inf and fox-holes heaped level with dead Nips, Wood's squad got orders to contact G Co. Suddenly Wood yelled at a crawling Jap officer who reached too late for his pistol. As Wood killed, he dropped to the ground with Morly and Larson down behind him. Other squad mebmers stood paralyzed with buck fever; an NCO even stood over Wood to ask loudly, "What should we do?"

Answering profanely, Wood deployed his squad to check the trailside. They found a circle of holes full of live Nips. We had only 2 grenades among us. Don ran back to Mjr Rankin, got Carl Wolker's squad to help him. Wood and Walker cadged all available grenades from resting Aussies and lugged the black steel pineapples up front.

In a half-circle, the 2 squads hunted out the Nip holes. Rifles shot down the Nips who rose to fire; grenades wiped out survivors. Just as a Nip bullet missed Wood's shoulder, Larson's rifle jammed from defective armor-piercing ammo. Wood threw a grenade but heard no explosion. Larson cleared his rifle. They rushed the hole at rapid fire. Under a shelter-half, lay officer and orderly both dead. Except for a few minor wounds, Walker's and Wood's men had no casualties; we counted 60 dead Japs.

But seated upright against a tree, they found Potts of Walker's squad, shot in the leg. He had taken sulfa, bandaged himself, and swallowed a message from Rankin to Buckland—not to risk capture by Japs. Potts died in hospital.

Thus on 14 Jan, E and G Cos had wiped out 3 Nip perimeters they first struck on 9 Jan. Meanwhile, other E men battled Nips on days they never dated—in that hell of fatigue and fear and mud. After Rankin set up 2/Btn's roadblock, Japs might recoil from Rankin to overwhelm 163's Musket garrison. For 2 days, spiky-haired, aggressive young Lt Rottman kept fighting Japs. Men in forward holes ran low on supplies. Rottman, Sgt Nay recoiled from daylight carries in heavy Jap fire. But Cpl Ashcraft rushed to the men with food, ammo. He died trying to return.

Another time, Lt Rottman as point lead a patrol 100 yards deeper into the jungle among Jap positions. Suddenly Barman Arevalo, on a flank, raised his arm to warn Rottman—who was almost on top of the blinded front of a pillbox. Flames shot through the overhanging line of foliage which the Japs had replanted. Sgt LaCounte backed up, fell over a vine, seemed dead. But finally safe in jungle, LaCounte and Rottman found grenades which they lacked—3 Nip grenades in a foxhole. Now each leader took a squad to attack—one from each side of the pillbox. From each side, we chucked grenades—rushed the dugout after the blasts. There lay 3 Nips—2 dead, 1 dying.

After liquidating Hell's Corner and the Jap triangle on Killerton Trail, both Aussies and Yanks cut sharply right to strike snakelike Sanananda Road north of Fisk Perimeter. The Aussies fought north to the sea. But southward, the battle was wholly 163's. Both F/Btn and 2/Btn now had a position behind the Nips where we could hold and annihilate them.

On 17 Jan, E Co's mission was to support 2/Btn near the road. Hearing other Cos' grenades and Aussie shell-fire ahead, we hiked through kunai grass towering above. Soaked in sweat, we floundered then into waist-deep swamps. We sniped back at snipers, that night held a trail-junction.

About 1130, a Jap MG whizzed bullets just over the hole of Schultz, Meyer, Larson, Wood. As one man, we rolled into firing positions. After some minutes' combat, heavy rains fell, dashed sand and mud into eyes that had to be open to watch for Nips. Rain filled the holes; the MG again skimmed low over us. But we had to chance bullets and bail with helmets—or drown. At first gray streaks of dawn, we rolled out to kill Nips; but they were gone.

After 17 Jan, E men's memory for dates grew blurred in our mist of rising fever, fatigue, sleeplessness where day and night seemed the same. For Gen Doe sent 163 in for the final kill. On 19 Jan, E Co hiked south of Sanananda Road to relieve Capt Ellers' F Co—short of ammo and badly chopped up after losing 5 Yanks to a pillbox—a rumored 12 dead, 27 wounded.

Thus E begin battling Perimeter V—east of U but not on a map. Coming in, we had MG fire. Our rifles quelled a possible counter-attack. When Lund mistook a crawling Jap for a Yank, a bullet put out his eye. Covering the eye, he located the Jap MG for us, walked unaided to medics. He said, "I'll have a different glass eye every day in the week—a bloodshot one for Sunday mornings."

E Co was wedged between 2 converging shoulder-deep streams in thick underbrush. Three Jap MGs slashed down from high ground front and flank on E's boxed in riflemen. By dusk, 5 were wounded—including Lund, Strong, Stack. But Capt Buckland and NCOs knew that to charge them was suicide. While riflemen held ground, our attack would be with fire from company weapons.

But on 20 Jan, E's weapons were not up. Jap fire was heavy. In a shell-hole, BARman Arevalo got the leg wound he would die from. Sgt Skinny Larson found in his shoulder a Nip bullet he had carried 3 days. Heavy rains put us neck-deep in the holes. Back in brush, Cook Labidy staggered around on his bandaged leg to prepare food.

Just before dawn 21 Jan, Torgeson and detail brought up

> Prime source was Don E. Wood's 330,000 word memoir of his years in the Army in 2 bound MS intended for Oregon Historical Society in Portland—and George Weller's 12 articles in CHICAGO DAILY NEWS on Sanananda in 1943. Don also supplied Weller's articles and identified E Co men in the articles. Other sources were Dr. Samuel Milner's VICTORY IN PAPUA, and Col. Wm. C. Benson's "History of G Co 163 Infantry." E Co Sgts Don Hulin and Ralph Oswald also contributed information in letters.

that MG we had begged for. Set up in dark, it shattered Nips with dawn fire. Norm Cooper slew 20 all day. In turn, Paul Warner at the MG triggered 5 Nips trying to escape—saw rifles fly from hands, pieces tear from uniforms, helmets fly from heads. Good hot Guinea sun dried out E Co, and we zeroed our mortars in on the Jap high ground.

Setting up E's mortars was heroes' work. To get proper range for close fire, Sgt George Jacobsen and Cpl Walkowicz had to stand up in the open to pace off yards down Sanananda Road —not creep, but walk erect and exposed. Yet the 60s were ready to blast any Jap night attack. And we got another reward.

As our second ranging shell impacted, 3 Japs dressed in white strode up the road. Followed 30 Japs deployed to take advantage of our surprise—an old trick worked on the British in Malaya. Jacobsen alerted our mortarmen behind him. As our shells detonated in their tubes, Walkowicz shot down the lead officer with his tommie. A second Jap picked up the officer, turned to run. Then our mortars hit—5 rounds—a great red flash. Next day, we counted 70 dead Japs.

Aided by support fire overhead and pressure from other 163 Cos., E Co soon had the Jap position under control. Next day, we even detached Wood's 2/Pltn over the river to interdict Japs outside their perimeter. And next day, Jan 23, all E mopped up the wrecked Jap area. And against those pillboxes that hurt F Co, we found 3 unknown dead Yanks.

Thus fought E Co in its nightmarish 17 days at Sanananda— in waterlogged swamps and nights of chilled terror. Thus we cleared the Triangle, smashed the Japs at Perimeter V. We had 17 proud days of combat at Sanananda.

BAR-Man At Sanananda

By J. A. FALLSTICK (F Co 163 Infantry)
with Dr. Hargis Westerfield, Division Historian

On 5 Jan 1943, F Co 163 Infantry landed from Aussie Hudsons at Dobodura Air-Strip SE of the Sanananda Battle. Heat and fear closed down on us in the high kunai grass as we hiked west. At every sweating halt, we dropped excess weight. Among trees evidently shelled and burned, we found Aussie artillery. A few nights before, Japs had infiltrated, muzzle-loaded a gun with explosives, and peeled it back like a banana. We saw a native who had refused to guide for the Japs —a starved thing of skin and bones who could hardly stand. Slogging along in the heat, we took 10 minute breaks every half-hour.

South of Soputa, we crossed the Girua River on a log bridge. Here we met up with Aussies from the line—"desert rats of Tobruk." Our pride for our Yank Tommy guns dropped when we inspected their light-weight Owen guns impossible to jam in mud and water. We found a pleasant Salvation Army Post.

* * *

Our first night we bivouacked in the swamp—built up log platforms on the ground and guarded in turns in threes. But a man was shot in another platoon. Next day, we had our most pleasant experience north of Moresby —a swimming break, with sniper guards posted. Here we had orders to discard all tell-tale tracer ammo. We passed native villages and noticed unhappy faces if we took water on their side of the stream. We were warned to be careful: some had scouted for Japs.

Early on 9 Jan., we were finally at the front. Crossing Sanananda Road at Musket Perimeter, we watched wounded being evacuated. A Lieut. died that morning attacking a bunker. Here sniping had been heavy, and 37 AT guns had blasted the tops

Men of 163 aboard plane enroute to New Guinea . . . and Sanananda.

of many trees to rout the Japs. But we had to be careful. It lifted our morale to see Colonel Doe in a Hq dugout.

* * *

From Musket, F patrolled west on a muddy trail—ankle-deep when you didn't hit a hole. Soon we saw a grim warning—on the right of the trail a skeleton in Aussie helmet and uniform, and across the trail a skeleton in Nip helmet and uniform. But we still had nothing to worry about save being thirsty all the time and the sweat and eternal mud.

* * *

Then a big MG opened up on G Co in the lead; we hit the mud. From the waves of fire, a heavy fight went on; but that Nip HMG dominated the situation. We had orders to bypass the trail north to high ground in tall kunai. While we formed perimeter, a tommy-gunner in another Pltn thought we were Japs and fired. His slugs sounded like a hornets' nest in the kunai, and we flattened out and tasted dust until he stopped.

Despite 4 heat prostrations in our squad alone, we dug in on the west side of our perimeter—V shaped 2-man holes. Ground was high here; you dug all of 2 feet before you hit water. Then our squad, under Cpl. Pop Reynolds, must contact the part of G Co cut off in the fight that morning. We hacked 30-40 minutes in the jungle—back in a circle almost to our starting place. With another compass the second time out, we found G Co behind logs dug out of the muck. We were glad to bed down in our higher perimeter.

* * *

Thus began F Co's jungle war at Sanananda — the sweaty patrols, the fearsome night silences. Next we were assigned for a holding action under Sgt. Hundahl—to set up a diversionary fire on the Jap perimeters astride the Killerton Trail, while Aussies pushed north to us. We fired, but only snipers replied with Close misses. We got 2.

* * *

From Rankin Perimeter, F sent patrols mostly to our rear—towards Coconut Gardens south of Killerton Point. It's amazing that maps show no Jap position in this area northwards; each time we heard snipers mark our progress with bird whistles. They didn't fire often; but found new signs every day—sneakers, bayonets, packs by trees they had climbed.

* * *

Each day in perimeter, we missed more buddies; dysentery, malaria took toll. The first night, somebody in another Pltn with dysentery left his hole after dark and was killed. You don't hear much of one hazard—big black rats. One night a big one rattled in our mess-gear, and guns cocked all down the line. I stabbed him with my knife and silenced him, but ruined my mess-kit and ripped both tents.

* * *

Cut off from supplies, the Japs in Killerton Perimeter weakened. We did not attack, but we drew the nauseous burying detail. On the trail from Musket, we found 10-12 Yank bodies recognizable only by dog-tags and uniforms. That day, slouch-hatted Diggers passed through us to fight in the north.

We left Rankin Perimeter forever and headed east through the Coconut Gardens. From here on it was 1-night stands; we never slept in the same hole twice. Eastward our Pltn hacked a trail through a solid mass of vegetation. Why we cut that trail I'll never know; we backtracked then and turned south.

* * *

Then MG fire stopped the head of our column. As Sgt. Bain remembers, there died Lieut. Ogden, Sgt. Rush, PFC's Marcus and Prinz—with 8 wounded. We drew burying detail again; and Marcus and Prinz were personal friends. Thus began F Co's war on the Hospital Lot.

That night was grisly. Before dark, we dug in a whole foot before we touched water. Just after sunset, the Guinea rain began—in 2 hours up 6-8 inches; chin level. On the right flank of our Pltn, my ammo-bearer Compton the Texan and I found rest was out of the question. We were all soaked and super-alert.

Somebody fired down the line to our right. Muffled by the rain, Japs crept in. You couldn't see 3 feet ahead, but the brush moved with bodies. I got off 30-40 rounds—and jammed my BAR. It was long before daylight — with only Compton's M-1 and 4 grenades against the dark. At dawn, he had 2 clips, and I had 1 grenade. Cpl Ray was killed, PFC Herman badly shot in the shoulder, PFC Paul wounded in the leg.

Morning brought orders to attack—and me with my BAR full of sand. With 5 minutes to pack and go, I oiled it heavily and got in on single fire. While the others went in with bayonets, I tagged along. The Japs were gone. But a Jap runner crossed the trail without seeing us. Sgt Dickey finished him. I had time to take apart the BAR and get it back on automatic. We returned to the track and headed north again.

* * *

The first huts in the Hospital Lot must have been for Headquarters; I saw more dead officers than enlisted men. We found large jars of quinine but feared they were poisoned. The Japs had put much work into the Hospital Lot—probably forced native labor. There were drainage ditches and some footbridges with Japanese arches. Huts were platforms on stilts with thatched roofs. For isolation cases, there were smaller 1-patient hunts—but no mosquito nets or screens anywhere. Here and there were small, well-built bunkers with limited fields of fire. In this low terrain, brush was thin and trees giants—a sniper's paradise.

* * *

Patrolling took on a different form here. Instead of first finding enemy resistance, we knew where it was, and we had only to hit at the right time, in fast, hard raids. (Thus we got the name of "Rankin's Raiders," after Mjr. "Barney" Rankin.) Here Sgt Hundahl used automatic weapons very successfully.

From the time of that ambush of 12 January until we quit combat in the Hospital Lot was about 4 days and nights. We never knew how many Japs we opposed, nor when they would concentrate on us. On these small, fast patrols, we were not inclined to lose time checking every move in a darkened bunker or hut. Apparently their more able-bodied patients were issued grenades to throw, or booby-trap their bodies if we arrived before they died. Some of our men saw grenades roll out when we got near the huts. In these dangers all around us, we took no chances; we threw grenades or shot first.

Yet that world of jungle and swamps and corpses was funny. "Digging in" was building up with logs. It always rained. The ground was so soggy that a new rain just piled up on top. One morning Compton awoke to look right into the eyes of a dead Jap who had floated up to his billet. Compton starved before he ate bully beef again. And we got lazy; instead of digging for underground water in drier spots, we got lazy and used a clear stream. The water wasn't bad; but one day Etchingham spotted corpses floating in it.

In these initial raids, my Pltn had no casualties; but now we fought Nip fortifications. We rendezvoused with G Co, headed east and south. There were no huts in this jungle; artillery or bombs had chewed the trees to hell. About 40 yards out the trail to our right, an Aussie helmet on a cross warned me, then a movement in the brush.

I motioned to Compton; he had seen it too: Japs all over the place 30 yards away. Sgt Hundahl caught our signal, but what saved Brown and Mohn our scouts I don't know. But the Japs hadn't seen us; we rushed towards them and into our closest protection—a ditch with 3 feet of water and jammed with trees that cannon had shattered into it. From their perimeter, Japs fired and missed.

Sgt Olson underestimated them; he ordered his squad up and at them. He died just above the ditch. Another Sgt tried to crawl over instead of under a tree in the ditch and was shot in a hip; another was hurt in the arm. The rest of the Pltn wriggled into forest cover ahead and fought.

Now we could look down into a line of holes and bunkers 40 yards off. They were trying to reenforce the line, but they couldn't see us. The shelled area behind us was so open that no snipers could hide to fire on our backs.

Compton, Etchingham, Chyboski, and I teamed up here. While they took turns loading and firing on Japs dodging down the trail across to our left, I covered the holes and bunkers directly before us. Clip after clip I threw in at any movement. But we did not fire on men in white coats; they looked like doctors. We silenced our sector and were withdrawn through a swamp of tall thin bush. The Japs fired too high; the bullets hit the brush and sounded like a rivet-hammer on your helmet.

* * *

Next morning we scouted a short-grass clearing, but only a ditch in the middle saved us from their rifles and MG's. Next morning we went back there and battled with them. With our Pltn on F's left flank, we almost crossed the clearing. Hahn beat me to a hole; I bounced out, rolled into the brush and found a ditch with only a little water in it.

The ditch ran diagonally with our attack and into the Jap perimeter. Some of F to my left in the brush moved up with me, and M-1's fired from the clearing. And when I looked up, a column of 10-15 Japs moved across my field of fire. I cut half-way down the column before my magazine ran out and they hit the dirt and scattered. I

CREDIT

A tall, darkly tanned, well-informed typographer, J. A. (Jess) Fallstick of South Indiana and Chicago did not look like a lean, scarred jungle butcher with a BAR when I met him last summer at the Chi Reunion. He wrote, "What influenced my writing in the first place was the reticence of others to communicate their experiences." "I hope that this will arouse them to help you." Prime sources were his untitled MS and ltr of Jan. 18, 1959. Also useful: Col Wm. G. Benson's "History of G Co 163 Inf," T/Sgt Richard Bain's ltr of Feb. 8, 1958, Dr. Samuel Milner's **Victory in Papua**.

was about to fire low into the bush; but bullets plunked around me.

I ran up the ditch and rounded the curve to another jog in it under a tree. Now I saw 2 bunkers, 25-30 yards ahead to my left. There was movement in 1; I put a magazine into the firing slots of both. Our fire had died down; it was silent in the brush to my right; 2 Yanks had stopped on my left. After alternating fire between the bunkers again, I stepped back down to reload. And my war was ended—suddenly.

The sniper was probably above and behind to my left. The bullet struck the ammo belt strap on my left shoulder, tore the belt completely off, made a large hole in my back. It angled down through the lung, missed my heart ¼ inch, came out between my ribs. It entered the right wrist, stopped behind and on top of the knuckle of my little finger on my right hand.

I fell into the ditch with 8 inches of water, but luckily the bank saved me from falling prone and drowning. Before losing coordination, I got the sulfa pills out of the kit in the water beside me and swallowed them. I wondered how many quarts of blood are in the body and how many reddened the water around me...

Thank God for Cpl Ward Williams. At the risk of his life and in pain from a rupture, he dragged me back through the ditch to the CP and Medics. I lost a lung; but Sgts Billsbough, Dickey, and Cpl Ernest (Pop Reynolds) died in action.

Men of the 2nd Battalion, 163 Infantry, seek graves of buddies who fell in in the Sanananda battle.

F Co. 163 Infantry:
Two Days of Infighting at Sanananda

By DR. HARGIS WESTERFIELD, Division Historian

CREDIT: Dr. Leeon Aller is primarily responsible for this second Sanananda story of F Co. He sent me 41st Division Training Note No. 2, which is no longer available from Federal Archives. F Co's Jess Fallstick helped identify F Co. men's names from Chicago Tribune stories by George Weller (Nos. 9, 10 published in 1943). Fallstick's "BARman at Sanananda" (Jungleer, XII, 2) was important, and E Co's Don Wood's "Seventeen Days at Sanananda" (Jungleer XVIII, 2). (I made the error of placing the Jacobsen-Walkowicz incident in E Co's history because of inaccurate information deduced from Weller's stories.) Dr. Samuel Milner's "Victory in Papua" and 163 Casualty Reports were indispensable. I consulted also 163's "The Battle of Sanananda" and two documents both called "Extract from History." Dates of casualty report seem inaccurate. Comparative reading of other sources has caused me to move dates of casualties from 19 and 20 Jan. to 18 and 19 Jan. Probable author of Training Note 2 is F's CO, then Capt. Conway Ellers, per ltr 5 Nov. 1976.

On 18 Jan. 1943, battered F Co. 163 Inf. got orders to find and fight Japs in the last great strongholds of Sanananda. These strongholds were Perimeters S-T-U-V astride that prominent east-west curve of Sanananda Road north of Fisk Perimeter. F Co. had battled since 9 Jan., when we aided G Co. to block the Japs' northern escape route on Killerton Trail. As "Rankin's Racers," or "Rankin's Raiders," F Co. had then cut back east across the jungle in short, fast raids in the area near the Jap Hospital Lot. In killing some 100 Japs, our ranks had thinned from fevers, wounds and death. We were lean and hardened to fight one of the most heavily defended perimeters of Sanananda battlefield. We did not know locations of Jap positions, but we had to find and fight them.

Although we heard that nearest Japs were full 400 yards southward, we dropped packs and deployed to fight now.

Our scouts had seen Japs much farther north than 400 yards the day before.

At 0900, 2/Pln. and 3/Pln. pushed down the sides of Sanananda Road where water in holes or streams was two-six feet deep. We moved in squad columns: two squads forward, one squad back. Two scouts hunted ahead of each lead squad—just 10 yards ahead, the limit of vision in this jungle-swamp. Our supporting 1/Pln. and Weapons Pln. followed in double columns down the road. We carried full loads of ammo and two grenades per man; rations were delayed two hours behind us.

Sanananda Road was a one-way strip of corduroy for jeeps through a 30-foot wide jungle clearing. Off the road where 2/Pln. and 3/Pln. waded, water in ditches, holes and small streams was two-six feet deep. We splashed in mud knee-deep to hip-deep, with our maximum 10-yard vision. After scouting 200 yards south, we met light Jap rifle fire, and about this time contacted Capt. Reams' K Co. on a mission like ours. To give K room to fight, we shifted our roadside platoons leftwards on the east side of the road. We were still receiving light rifle fire ahead.

We sent 1/Pln. from Sanananda Road to envelop those Jap riflemen on our left. In column of files, 1/Pln. hiked 150 yards to find huts beside a stream six-eight feet deep—a stream which was not shown on the map. Then 1/Pln. deployed and moved obliquely towards the other two plns. deployed as skirmishers in front of the roadside. Some 20 Japs broke and ran like rabbits ahead of 1/Pln.; the other plns. slew all 20.

F Co. reorganized and moved 50 yards farther in the same formation before the shooting began. We then started up more Japs in the same maneuver and hunted them toward their road, killing 25 with Tommy guns and rifles.

Having slogged 250 yards with no casualties, we now advanced on a 150-yard front. The jungle opened up before us, with visibility of some 35 yards. Our two lead plns. moved with two squads forward, and one squad back. Two scouts preceded each squad, with a distance of 15-20 yards ahead. In the next 75 yards, we flushed out and killed nine Japs. Our total bag of dead Japs was now 54.

And then late that afternoon of 18 Jan. 1943, F Co. began its greatest day of battle at Sananada—against Perimeter V, deeply hidden in kunai grass and jungle swamp.

Despite careful patrolling, the squad of BAR-man Fallstick almost lost its scouts in the first shootout. With rifles ready, tense F Co. had now moved south into an area where FA or bombs had slashed the trees to fragments. About 40 yards down the trail to our right, Fallstick was alerted by an Aussie helmet on the cross of a dead man. Cross and helmet led his eyes to a movement in the brush. He saw Japs all over the place, 30 yards away. We were walking blindly into their perimeter.

Fallstick motioned to Compton, his ammo bearer; Sgt. Hundahl caught the signal also. But what saved Brown and Mohn, the scouts, Fallstick never knew.

The Japs had still not seen us. The whole pln. fanned out to our closest protection—a ditch with three feet of water, jammed with shell-torn trees. From their suddenly-discovered perimeter, the Japs opened fire.

When the dripping pln. crawled far enough ahead to get out of the ditch, we were in a position above a line of holes and bunkers. We looked down their throats 40 yards away, but they couldn't see us in the brush. Best of all, our backs were turned on the shelled-over ground, and they could not

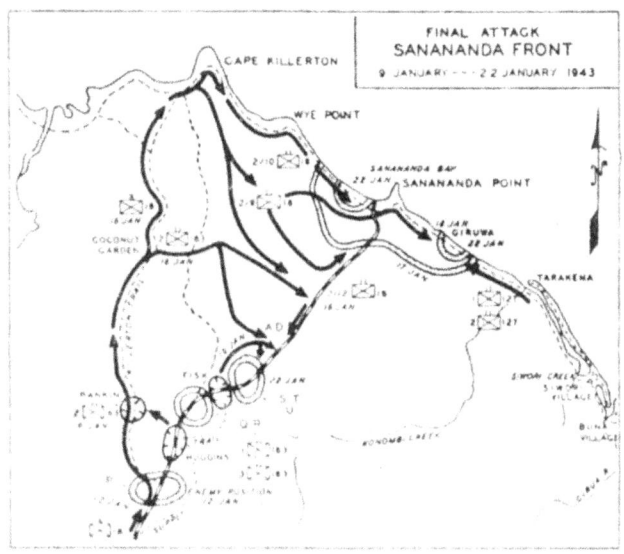

infiltrate and fire from concealment behind us.

Chyboski, Etchingham, Compton, and BAR-man Fallstick teamed up for fighting that Jap line. Down a trail crossing before us to the left, Japs were hurrying into their positions. While the other three men took turns loading and firing at Japs dodging down the trail, Fallstick's BAR kept the men down in bunkers and holes directly ahead. Clip after clip he launched into any movment, of the eight or nine in his belt. These Yanks did not fire on men in white coats because they resembled officers. (They probably were officers.)

When we thought that we had silenced our sector, Sgt. Hundahl withdrew us to reinforce the other F men. To escape from our firing position, we four men had to circle back through a swamp of tall, thin brush. Jap bullets behind us sounded like rivet hammer on our helmets, but they were too high to hurt us.

Despite the good fight of this pln., F now halted dead in our tracks under heavy Jap fire. An LMG and an HMG traversed the kunai, or searched it top to bottom in 50-round bursts. Riflemen also lanced at any movement. A 40mm mortar exploded some 20 shells near us, but these were apparently fired without observation. Any splash in this water surely drew Jap fire—even on runners from F's headquarters. Perhaps Cpl. Pulliam died here, and Horrocks was wounded in the neck.

F Co's front was a bottleneck 200 yards wide, between Sananada Road swept by MG fire on our right and a deep stream on our left. Ahead of us were Jap bunkers behind that ditch jammed with shell-torn trees and three feet of water.

It was now 1630, close to dark in New Guinea's January. Rations meant for us at 1100 had now caught up. We made a drenched perimeter 150 yards wide, with its right on the road. Water was nowhere less than six-eight inches deep. We ate miserably behind logs and brush. All tobacco was wet, but vengeful snipers would have prevented smoking anyway. All night, half of us tried to sleep while the other half took turns on guard. We expected a Jap attack any time.

In this chilly, soaked dark, F men did not understand the position we had to fight tomorrow. This was Jap Perimeter V, which on today's available maps is probably the eastern part of Perimeter U. The Jap line ahead protected a roughly square area containing a truck park and more Jap positions. The day before, F had faced west against the eastern side of that square, across a 200-yard length of water-filled ditch. On our right, the Jap fire lane of Sanananda Road sealed off our advance. To outflank that eastern side of the square, we had to cross another ditch, then fight a double line of bunkers 200 yards long which rested their right flank on a creek six-eight feet deep. The ditch and the creek would channel our frontal attack down a 200-yard lane under fire from riflemen, two LMG's and one HMG. Lacking the heavy FA with unlimited shells, F Co. would find this position impregnable. But on 19 Jan. we fought valiantly.

With daylight on 19 Jan., sodden F faced a battlefield of heavy casualties. Lt. Raber patrolled 150 yards left front to locate the Jap lines. At the deep creek, we turned westward. Just 20 yards ahead, we discovered a group of Japs preparing breakfast.

Raber deployed us as skirmishers and placed one of his two BAR's into the best position to sweep the group. This BAR-man Heisler was to trigger the attack when he fired. But unavoidable sand and water had fouled his action. Slipping the bolt forward and recocking alerted the Japs. We fired too late, hit only a few. They scattered back to their first line of bunkers and returned fire. Our pln. was forced down to earth. Raber was the only casualty; a bullet bored his helmet and stunned him.

A walking casualty, Raber told Sgt. Slyter to ask Capt. Ellers for heavy fire support. Weapons Pln's Sgt. Jacobsen gave Ellers protection while he set up an OP to range in 163's 81's in battery at Musket Perimeter. About 1330, bn. CO Rankin and Aussie FA observer Peter Hirschel joined Ellers at the new OP—only 30 yards from Jap lines. We could see two ranks of bunkers blocking our way.

About 1400, Aussie 25-pounders and our 81's barraged. In 90 minutes, the Aussies fired 156 shells. Our 81's registered with 12 heavy shells on the double line of bunkers, but 10 of them were duds in the soft ground. Shifting to light shells, they impacted 200 rounds on the bunkers. Ellers meanwhile sent small patrols to clear out individual Japs slipping past us towards the road.

At first, this accurate support fire made F's war seem easier. This fire split the double line of softwood bunkers and slew most of the Japs inside. Firing where necessary, we passed both lines of shattered bunkers and counted 50 Jap dead. The battle was going well for F Co.

But after 150 yeards, the Japs halted us again. Our advance was wedged between the deep stream on our left and the deep ditch on our right, with Jap bunkers above that ditch. An LMG fired frontally at us, on the firm ground between the two watercourses. Shooting down the ditch that we had crossed on our right, an HMG enfiladed our front. Starting now, we probably had most of our casualties—all seven of our killed and 12 of our 13 wounded. (Lt. Raber was wounded early, as told elsewhere.)

Against the HMG on our right, we made a daring charge, led by a sgt. name unknown. Maybe he underestimated Jap resistance, or the fervor of combat carried him and his men away. Against that HMG, he led a six-man charge across that ditch. He made it himself just over the top of the ditch; four other men died with him.

We can only conjecture the name of this sgt. and the four dead with him—from a total list of two sgt. and five other men killed in F on 19 Jan. No one has said how Sgt. Dickey died, but Billsborough was killed within a yard of a Jap bunker; so Billsborough must have been the sgt. leading the charge. Beighey was killed also on the lip of a Jap dugout. Cpl. Reynolds also led a charge against an MG before his mortal wound; perhaps he was part of the same attack. Molitor was seen wounded among Jap bunkers; then he disappeared. BAR-man Kramarick was shot behind by a Jap who feigned death in a hole. When Kramarick was found, he still clutched an unexploded grenade in his right hand. (He was probably the same corpse whom relieving Sgt. Don Wood of E Co. saw still erect before a pillbox with a grenade still menacing it even in death.) Surely some of these men were in that charge: Billsborough, Beighey, Reynolds, Molitor and Kramarick.

Attacking on our right, BAR-man Fallstick positioned in a ditch leading into Jap lines and shop up a column of 10-15 Japs with half a BAR clip. Dodging answering bullets, he rounded a bend in the ditch and shot into movement in a bunker. While alternating bursts between this and another bunker, he was wounded by a bullet through lung and right arm. He was drowning face-down in shallow water, but Cpl. Ward endured the agony of hernia to save Fallstick for the Medics.

F lost one more killed and 12 more wounded, totaling seven dead, 14 wounded that 19 Jan. Harry Scott was killed. Alfred Brown was wounded in right arm and leg, Arguello in right forearm, Denton in right albow and Brune in right hand. Helmer was hit in the neck, Lawrence in left shoulder Payne in left leg. Locations of Zimmerle's wounds are unknown. When a Jap rose to hurl a grenade, DeFrisco tried to warn others, himself took wounds in left arm and mouth from it. Shot in right wrist and left arm, Babicz wanted to keep on, but Sgt. Olberg ordered him to the medics.

For protection on Sanananda Road from a night attack, Lt. Libke angled our mortars close to Jap bunkers. To sight accurately, Sgt. Jacobsen and Cpl. Walkowicz had to pace off yards in open road. After we zeroed in three shots, five Jap officers in white marched up to draw fire and spot our weapons for suicide attacks. Then 20-30 Japs charged. Walkowicz Tommy-gunned an officer; then our mortars impacted in a great red flash. Later, we counted not 30 but 70 dead Japs nearby. Mortarmen like Mark, Reese, Bob Myers and Draski had done well.

F's bitter day of battle ended with wondrous news. We were almost out of ammo, chilled and soaked, and Capt. Buckland's E Co. relieved us. The heroic Japs countered during our relief, but only lightly. E Co's fire repelled them.

But E Co. wisely failed to attack that formidable

Smashed Japanese landing barge and dead Japanese litter the beach at Buna.

combination of natural and Jap-made defenses. When, two days later, I and K Co's struck from the south and wiped out Jap Perimeter U and adjacent Perimeter V, E Co. lay in F's old lines and gave only fire support against the penned Japs.

And worn, decimated F Co. was long gone north to relieve Aussie 2/9 Bn. at Sanananda Village. Our two-day battle against Perimeter V was ended. Total cost—14 wounded and eight dead.

G. Co. 163 Infantry:
The Killerton Road Block

by Dr. Hargis Westerfield, Division Historian, with Col. William Benson and George Weller

Basic narrative, although unsigned, is probably from G Co's CO Benson—No. 5 in 41st Div. Training Note No. 2, supplied by Dr. Leeon Aller after disappearance of original from Fed Archives. Correspondent George Weller reported on this fight in Nos. 3, 4 of his 1943 articles in the Chicago Daily News. Details of wounds are from AGO's recently received casualty reports. G Co's Lt. Braman added more details in Sept. 1973. Australian Dudley McCarthy's South-West Pacific Area, First Year, and American Samuel Milner's Victory in Papua afford strategical background. This G Co. story ties in with Jess Fallstick's "F" story (Jungleer, XI, 2), and Don Wood's "E" story (Jungleer, XVIII, 2).

On 9 Jan. 1943, G Co. 163 Inf. led 163's 2/Bn. west from Musket Perimeter into the regiment's first major strategic move of the Battle of Sanananda. This move was to block Killerton Track north to the Bismarck Sea. We would thus cut off the main Jap escape route from their great inner perimeters. Fugitive Japs would have to flounder through almost impassable swamps or trackless jungle.

We would also give the Aussie 18 Brigade a jumping-off place for their drive through to the coast. So important was this move to the Australians that Gen. Vasey sent his Col. Pollard to Col. Doe in Musket, to have Pollard insist that 163's 2/Bn. be kept intact for this operation of 9 Jan.

G Co's specific mission was to lead Maj. Barney Rankin's 2/Bn. 1200 yards west of Musket Perimeter over a long disused native trail and set up a roadblock across Killerton Track. Although patrols from nearby Jap perimeters to the south would surely be prowling for us, we had the impossible order not to fight the Japs until we were dug in.

We sent a small precautionary patrol some 800 yards west along the trail we were to follow, but it had to turn back because we feared to signal this major bn. move to the Japs.

And at 0945, Benson's G Co. led the long, lean files of 2/Bn. into our first combat. We carried full packs with usual arms and ammo and one grenade each. Rations per man included one "C" tin, one of bully beef and three Aussie dehydrates.

B Co. 163's Sgt. Poynter acted as guide. While two scouts led 20–30 yards forward, G's Capt. Benson hiked with his point, consisting of the rest of the squad the scouts belonged to. Maj. Rankin naturally accompanied this squad. After them came the main body of G and then F Co. Probably next in column was H with 4 HMG's, but only three 81 mortars. Last of all was waterlogged E Co. which had already helped B Co's assault of 8 Jan. at Musket, and had lost McDermeit, the first man to die in 2/Bn. Benson's point found the mud just ankle- to knee-deep, but E in the rear had to wade in our tracks waist-deep. The heat of the sun seared our sweat-blackened shoulders.

Now G came to Killerton Track, a silent north-south corridor in the kunai between two walls of jungle swamp. Since an almost impassable swamp bounded this 100-yard-wide corridor, it was actually like a defile for Jap mortar fire.

But as yet we had no Jap battle. When our two lead scouts signalled "Halt," the point squad with Benson and Rankin crept to almost the edge of the trail opening for observation. One scout went 50 yards further to the Track and reported that he saw no Japs in either direction.

Then Benson deployed G's 3/Pln. and 1/Pln. less one squad at the angle between the trail we had come over and Killerton Track. If they had to, they were to fire leftward (or south) in the direction where the Jap perimeters were supposed to be. Across the trail as security to the north, Benson posted 1/Squad of 1/Pln., to watch up Killerton Track in the direction of the sea.

Here at the angle of Track and trail from Musket was a great log which hundreds of 32 Div. men had crawled around to reinforce the Huggins Perimeter roadblock in earlier days. (We had renamed Huggins to Musket Perimeter.) At that time, we did not know that a Jap HMG lay in ambush behind that log, 25 yards southward.

Nothing went wrong at first, but death waited. After deploying 3/Pln. and 1/Pln. as security, Benson started to cross with the rest of G Co. They had to climb up a two-foot bank, which was one foot higher than the Killerton Track itself, and hurry over 100 yards of open ground into cover. Thus 2/Pln. and part of Weapons Pln. crossed the Track. No shots were fired. Other G men were prone in the kunai grass.

This jungle was all too quiet; the silence could not last. The first Jap came down the trail towards outguards Sgt. Tullis and Seipp. Sgt. Tullis told Seipp to hold fire a little longer. A second Jap moved towards them.

Seipp's M-1 blasted. Ejected shells rang out and both Japs fell. Then Jap MG's fired; 40 mm mortars dropped death from the sky. Seipp was knocked down to die before G men could get to him.

Joe Murphy saw Gorlewski fall, never to stand again. Robert L. Murphy fell nearby. Tree snipers began working on our prone men outlined in the kunai. Fatally wounded, Monsted lifted himself once, then fell and lay quiet. Joe Murphy himself lost his pack and squirmed to safety through tufts of kunai grass that a Jap MG searched just after he had crawled away from them. Finally, Joe Murphy heard Aussie 25-pounder shells fall nearby. He took advantage of this distraction to dash for safety and lay in a hole where he chain-smoked to calm his nerves.

Besides our four killed, G Co. had 7 wounded. Lt. Braman said that Chalberg was down in almost the first burst of fire—shot in the right leg. While caring for other wounded men, Mivelaz was struck in the right side of his chest. Sgt. Hopstad was hit on the index finger of the left hand, Cpl. Ewing on the second finger of his right hand. While prone on the far side of the trail, Wertenberger was hit in the left foot. Garborg was wounded in the left knee, and Trevino in the right calf.

And so, using the 100-yard opening around Killerton Track as a fire lane, Jap MG's and riflemen in trees had cut G Co. in two. Already across the track with 2 Pln. and some weapons, Benson had his men dig in. So did Maj. Rankin with G's Lt. Braman and 1 and 3/Plns. on the Musket side of the Track.

Then Braman with Sgt. Tullis made a try to rescue Seipp; they thought they heard him groan out in the kunai no-man's land. But on creeping forward they found Seipp dead. Suddenly Japs in trees opened fire, and Tullis and Braman were in the same trap where Seipp had died. They succeeded in dragging back his body to where Sgt. Molina's squad held ground under Jap fire.

Groans still came from somewhere up front where Jap riflemen had hidden and where they could look down over a wounded man. Another Yank—reportedly Robert Kreiger—volunteered to risk his life with Tullis to recover the wounded G man. Fire flickered over the two Yanks. They dared not touch Monstead; they promised to bring him in after dark.

But that night, they found no one in the place where Monstead had lain. Later in the battle, someone recovered Monstead's dog tags from a Nippo corpse. And G never discovered the bodies of Robert Murphy and Gorlewski.

While Jap and Yank rifles duelled above him, medic Harold Marshall got to work with the seven wounded whom Bay and he had helped back to safety. By the time litter men had come forward, he had neatly sheltered G's wounded in a ditch. He had systematically dusted

35

"We have the enemy spotted..."

wounds with sulfa and bandaged them. He had given morphine shots and tagged men for evacuation.

And although G Co. was contained by hidden Japs, 2/Bn's Barney Rankin carried on. When F tried to cross the trail a short way above G, Jap fire was too heavy for the losses that would be sure to come. (F's BAR-man Fallstick had heard the big Jap HMG that dominated G Co's fight.) And Don Wood and other E men hid from bullets on that muddy crosstrail behind old Jap corpses and saw litter cases of their 2/Bn. cobbers pass them back to 116 Medics at Musket.

Rankin now ordered his 2/Bn., less G, to hike 250 yards north. They filed along the east side of the jungle-swamp corridor and set up a great perimeter which filled the whole space on both sides of Killerton Track. Perimeter Rankin was perhaps derisively called "Rankin Heights," for we could not dig a hole over two feet deep before the water started seeping in. But F Co's Reynolds' patrol with Fallstick made contact with G crouching in muck behind logs they had dug from the swamp. The F men returned to appreciate the healthful, arid "Rankin Heights."

And so, on 9 Jan. 1943, 2/Bn. had precariously dug in—the main body 250 yards north of the first crossing, and with bifurcated G Co. lying soaked in the swamps. And south of G the Jap perimeters were hidden: three small adjacent perimeters, according to one earlier reconnaisance. These Japs were in a curve of Killerton Track on the side next to Musket. A swamp protected their rear towards Musket, and the kunai openings gave them a fine field of fire on the track.

Since the big Jap MG was too deadly for frontal attack and Jap 40 mm shells could search the area from jungle invisible to us, Rankin tried a new American tactic. He called H Co's Cpl. Escobar, a former acrobat, to climb a tree for observation. With a phone strapped to his back, Escobar went hand over hand up a great vine on a jungle giant. Escobar called down that he could see the Jap gun clearly; his voice was so loud that Rankin had to hush him. After an experimental shot or two from Musket where our 81's massed in batteries, a regular saturation blasting began. Company 60's joined in. Jap mortar shelling ceased, and that Jap HMG died on Killerton Track. We heard that it fired on that great log against 32 Div. supply trains for the last five weeks.

Next morning, Rankin and Benson used the safest possible way to reunite G Co. separated by Killerton Track and Nippo fire. From both directions, G Co. men lay prone and began digging a trench across the Track. Tropical heat made the work hard, and we were lucky to have S/Sgt. Bates with a pln. of B Co. 116 Engrs. to help us. We tried to guide them towards a meeting place with shovels of dirt that we occasionally heaved high into the air.

Once the trench was dug, Benson distributed his G Co. properly on both sides of the track and brought up H's HMG's to seal off the passage permanently from Nip attacks.

Five days after G's first fight on Killerton Track, we pushed southwards. We teamed with E and drove south to crush the Japs, whom the Aussies were pressing north against us.

With the Japs' southern perimeters obliterated, the Aussie 18 Brigade passed north on Killerton Track through "Rankin Heights" to mop up Japs on the coast of Sanananda Village. Then G with 2/Bn. was released from the Killerton Road Block and "Rankin Heights" to trek north, and then to cut east through trackless jungle to the main Sanananda Road. There we would join 163's other bns. in the final infighting to wipe out Jap perimeters S, T, and U.

Thus did 163's 2/Bn. complete the regiment's first important strategical mission of the Battle of Sanananda—to set up the Killerton Road Block and cut the Japs' escape corridor to the Bismarck Sea. And that's the story of how G Co. 163 Inf. acted as spearhead company in its first fight.

G Co. 163 Infantry:
Infighting at Sanananda

By Dr. HARGIS WESTERFIELD, Division Historian,
with S/Sgt. JOE MURPHY and other "G" men.

After G Co. 163 Inf's fight to block Killerton Trail on 9 Jan. 1943, we fought again on 14 Jan. Three nameless little Jap perimeters faced G Co. a short distance off. Slanting in echelon NE, the three Jap perimeters outguarded four P Perimeters some distance south which had defeated the Aussie tank attack 12 Jan.

On 14 Jan., when Aussie Gen. Vasey discovered that a Jap retreat had begun, we teamed with E Co. to meet Aussies pushing north to squeeze out remaining Japs.

While G crouched in tall grass, Doherty and Murphy scouted south. Through abandoned Jap bunkers and slit trenches they scouted 300-400 yards southward in eerie silence. They passed Jap corpses. Finally in open ground, they sighted Aussies who waved at them.

But when Doherty-Murphy led Lt. Braman's 3/Pln. in, a Jap ambush blasted in our faces. From an opening in the underbrush, some 20 Japs fired heavily. Doherty-Murphy flattened in short grass in an open, level ground. With Doherty following, Murphy threw himself behind a large log.

Once behind the log, Murphy learned that a Nippo bullet had ripped off a rear pocket but failed to draw blood. More bullets crashed through the spongy log. Lying on their backs, they dug in like moles. Dirt flew from digging heels and sheath knives.

From trees behind the unbrush, snipers fired. Shooting from a deserted Jap hole, Belin fought back. A grenade bounded from underbrush into the hole. Belin did not panic from the hole to death in the open. He threw back the live grenade to explode among the Nips. G Co. slew maybe 20 Nips—and without reported casualties in G Co.

And so G and E Cos. teamed up with Aussies and wiped out the Japs' southern perimeters. Now G participated in 2/Bn's second great strategic move of Sanananda. Hiking north up Killerton Trail, we were to turn east into the jungle, then south against the northern perimeters of the Japs. In this move, we could find and destroy any strongpoints behind Fisk Perimeter, and join 3/Bn. and 1/Bn's fight against the great stronghold on Sanananda Road. These marches and fights made our 2/Bn. known as "Rankin's Racers," or "Rankin's Raiders."

That afternoon of 15 Jan., G patrolled up Killerton Trail and relieved Aussie 18 Brigade men in the Coconut Garden. While the Aussies fought north of us, G marched to help 163 in the final week of battle, 16-22 Jan.

About 0815 16 Jan., G headed east from the Coconut Garden 1,000 yards, then south by compass 1,200 yards into what we called Perimeter T. We surprised some 25 Japs in bunkers and went in to kill. Notable was the fight of Indian Butch Ackerman—a one-man army who lobbed grenade after grenade into rear exits of Jap bunkers. (He died fighting on the Kumusi.)

Then came the famous fight in the "Hospital Lot," in an area near Yank Perimeter AD. About 1200, 2/Bn. contacted 1/Bn. so that 163 now enveloped the last great Jap perimeters.

With F Co. leading, 2/Bn. started to cut Sanananda Road. When F met Jap opposition, Capt. Benson led G north some 100 yards to bypass the Japs and block the road.

G Co. was patrolling up a narrow trail. Our 3/Pln. scouts—one was certainly Baird—slipped through a swamp, then up the trail between two yet unseen pillboxes. An unwary Jap guard was squatting in a lean-to; they killed him.

And 3/Pln. moved forward and found a clearing with thatched native huts on three-foot piles, with fine hiding places for Japs behind thatched walls. The "clearing" was thin jungle 300 yards wide. Benson said that maximum visibility was 100 yards and minimum, 25 feet.

While deployed, waiting for orders to advance, 1/Pln. had two wounded. At least one Jap rifle fired, maybe more. Steblay was hit in right thigh, Cpl. Beverley Johnson in right forearm. We could still see the bullet under the skin in his arm. After medic Marshall treated them, both could walk out.

Sudden intense rifle fire met 3/Pln. A light mortar impacted nearby. As Lt. Braman and another man entered the clearing, a LMG opened up from the rafters of a hut. All that saved them, Braman thought, was that the gunner believed he'd killed both men on the first blast.

We decided that this was a Jap hospital area, but deadly armed men held it, in defiance of international law. "What should we do?" we asked Benson. "Do? Do what you always do," he answered.

G opened up on the shacks with all possible firepower. A hut collapsed under a stream of bullets. We flanked the shacks, picked off the riflemen. Sgt. Doherty sneaked behind the LMG man who had almost killed Braman and knocked him off the rafter. From the nearby cemetery the light mortar fired only three-four times, and we killed it. Meanwhile, grenades began exploding among the huts as able-bodied defenders and hospital invalids blew themselves up—or tried to blow up G Co.

Some Japs fought in the open; some fought from foxholes and trunks of large trees. Others ran and were cut down. And in the huts, our tense riflemen found live Japs under blankets and dead Japs under blankets. And G Co. had no chance to check each corpse with a stethoscope—not when a pale hand might reach out to blast a grenade in your face.

So G fired first and pulled blankets off corpses later. Some Nips were dead or dying of wounds, malaria, dysentery and blackwater fever. Some patients held live grenades under blankets and tried to blast us or blow themselves up. Murphy saw one Nip rifleman with an amputated leg—prone and firing from the floor of a hut. We found newly-dead grenadiers hiding under blankets beside skeletons.

We did not count the bodies in the Hospital Lot. Lt. Braman of 3/Pln. said that he did not hear much shooting. But when Tokyo Rose learned of the Hospital Lot, she named the whole Division "Butchers" and said that we would never leave New Guinea. The Division took the name of "Butchers"; at that time "Jungleers" was a name not yet in use.

That night of 16 June, G blocked Sanananda Road and partly made perimeter north of the road. With Morales, Sgt. Muryphy lay in a slit trench with a gob of mud as parapet. They were exposed on a point with a Jap bunker a few yards on the left rear. Far behind was a two-man Yank hole. Left, a terrific 20 yards off, were BAR-man Mayberry, his assistant, and an ammo bearer.

Murphy and Morales had a bad night. Darkness brought crawling Japs and grenade throwing. By 0300, Morales was so tired that Murphy let him sleep. Half an hour later, Murphy heard scuffles and grunts from Mayberry's hole. Had a Jap knifer got in? Was a Jap LMG set up already to strike from the rear at dawn?

Two grenades blasted the dark near Mayberry's hole. Then came black silence, and the minute hand of Murphy's watch dragged on to daylight, with perhaps snakelike death lurking from behind.

The slight New Guinea night breeze gave way to the dead calm that comes before dawn. Muted sky beyond the fringe of jungle branches hinted at daylight.

Ready to strike the supposed Japs behind him, Murphy

> CREDIT. Murphy's ltrs. (6 Apr., 15 Apr., 6 Aug., 1974) caused complete rewrite of this story. Other ltrs were from Capt. Arthur "Buck" Braman (18 Feb. 1963) and Sgt. Frank Steblay (10 Dec. 1974). Highly important were Col. Wm. C. Benson's "History of G Co.," George Weller's Sanananda articles in Chicago Daily News (1943). I used also Dr. Samuel Milner's Victory in Papua and these 163 documents: "Casualty Lists," "The New Guinea Chapter the Battle of Sanananda" (15 pp.), a 19-pp. "Extract from History" and a 106-pp. journal also called "Extract from History." What I write here will stand as corrections of early data published in Jungleer on E, F, and G 163.

strained eyes into the decreasing darkness. A helmet stirred. Out of the mud came Mayberry's face, and two more G faces. Nobody knew who had thrown the two grenades that missed.

Although most of G now left the road for Perimeter AD, Braman's 3/Pln. held the roadblock for some four nights. After our bitter ambushes several times the first day, the Japs tried to pass mainly at night.

Doherty and Lt. Braman devised fine ambush tactics. By day, we hid in swamp 15-20 feet off the road except for two forward scouts. When the scouts alerted G, the men eased in from the swamp and prepared to kill. We had two MG's. At night, we manned positions on the road shoulder.

Once, 11 Japs hiked up the road. Gunners let them go 10 feet past to where they could see us—then piled up 11 dead. Wrongly, we tired men let the 11 lie there. In 30 minutes came 20 Japs—perhaps to check on their 11-man point. When they saw 11 dead, the 20 ran. G slew 15, but five still ran. Giessler killed four of these five with one sweeping burst of his BAR.

About 0230 on 20 Jan., 15-20 Japs hit 3/Pln. to break our

Dead Japanese soldiers at Sanananda.

ambush. All died. Not until daylight did Fred Bennett report the bullet in his leg. To keep Bringard in the same hole from worrying about him, Bennett had endured the wound in silence all night. Some Japs we killed even carried suitcases containing silk shirts, perhaps for furloughs in Australia after conquering it. (Also on 20 Jan., Treangen was shot in the right foot.)

Such was G Co's dark fight at Sanananda. Besides Japs, mud and fever, we remember minor jungle horrors. Rats scurried from corpses into our holes at night. Snakes squirmed in for warmth. Bats or maybe flying squirrels attacked wallaby rats in the trees at night. Then we heard screams like that of a woman in labor. Our hearts beat in fear like trip hammers. Worst of all for G were the sweet sounds of jungle doves, for often they were Jap signals. We counted the systematic number of coos and tried to figure out meanings that could indicate death for us.

Even after 163 had destroyed the last Nippo perimeter on 22 Jan., G had a last deadly fight. On 24 Jan., two Japs surrendered. They claimed to be Buddhist monks. They promised to lead us to 26 Japs ready to yield but afraid to be shot on sight.

At 1045 on 25 Jan., Lts. Corts and Braman led 32 men to help "monks" bring in the 26. Some 400 yards into jungle, we found four bewildered, unarmed Jap medics. Maybe their surrender made us too relaxed.

We then found a chain of dugouts filled with dead Japs. At one chain of dugouts, Pingatore saw five live Japs. When one ran, Pingatore killed him with a Tommy gun. (The two "monks" evidently escaped about this time.) From behind a pillbox, a Jap rifle wounded Pinatore.

While we covered with fire, Lt. Corts crawled in to aid Pingatore. A rifle bullet punctured Corts' Adam's apple and shoulder. An explosion from a pillbox deafened us. Evidently a Nip tried to throw a grenade through a narrrow slit, but it rebounded.

Medic Woodman crawled up to bandage Pingatore and Corts. Although Pinatore could walk with an arm wound, we made a litter for Corts. A dazed Jap shuffled from the exploded pillbox to be spared and received the first aid he loudly demanded.

Fifteen yards farther on our return, Japs shot up our rear guard: Cpls. Vierra and Kozing, Capt. Braman and Sgt. Jack Anderson. Earl "Bud" Hall of 2/Bn. Hq. died without a sound. With three dead and two wounded, Braman retreated. We had five prisoners: the Jap wounded by a Jap grenade in the pillbox and the four meds. Next day, the captain recovered the bodies. Pingatore and Corts both survived; Corts with a metal whistle in his throat for talking.

Such was G 163's saga of Sanananda—after 9 Jan. 1943, when we blocked Killerton Trail. (Its story is told elsewhere.) We teamed with Aussies to kill P Perimeters, then cut off the last great Jap perimeters on Sanananda Road. We wiped out T Perimeter, cleared the Hospital Lot and held the roadblock. After the main battle, we had a treacherous ambush. Casualties—with those on Killerton Trail—were at least six killed and 14 wounded. Known dead from disease were typhus victims, Cpl. Mercille (28 Mar.) and Sgt. Molina (6 Apr.). Our kill of Japs was surely over 10 times all our casualties.

Strictly speaking, G Co's Sanananda concluded with our ambush of 26 Jan. Yet our fighting record was the cause, we believe, of still more casualties. We got another combat order. With G 186 Inf. attached, we battled Nips at the Kurerda River crossing, then fought their tenacious rear guard all the way to the Kumusi River. In the Kumusi Patrol, we had three killed and 10 wounded. But the Kumusi Patrol is another story of G 163 in the Papuan Campaign.

41sters take time out for an evening meal on the outskirts of Mokmer. Our guess is that the men were dining on Spam and processed American cheese with bits of bacon.

I Co 163 Inf Storms Perimeter U

By DR. HARGIS WESTERFIELD, Research Historian

On 14 Jan 1943, I Co got sudden orders into Sanananda battle – 12 days after 163 took over the Aussie positions. Suddenly freed from work on Sanananda Road. "I" Co hiked a hot muddy mile to Nicholson Dump, 163's supply depot 150 yards south of the first Jap perimeter. Occasionally, Jap rifle bullets sang through nearby trees.

At the dump, "I" men received 3 grenades, extra ammo, then fearfully followed Maj Wing. Knee deep in mud and water, we skirted Jap perimeter "P" for a dirty quarter-mile then came to little Huggins perimeter astride the road.

Huggins – which 163 renamed Musket – was 163's forward CP – sandwiched between the Jap perimeter we bypassed and Jap perimeters Q and R a few yards north. We heard scattered shooting while we set up tents, over slit trenches already dug. Nobody seemed concerned when a Nip rifle bullet or two whistled overhead. We were too low in defilade for danger, but other 163 killer teams hunted the snipers.

On 15 Jan, Nips got mad at us. Sent up the trail from Huggins 200 yards to salvage a blitz buggy, a 1/Pln squad walked into a Jap MG sighted on the buggy. We dived off in all directions. S/Sgt Van de Riet fell into a hole beside an old Jap corpse, but did not mind the company. With 2/Lt John Olson and Sgt Whitehorn, Van de Riet pulled us all back to safety.

Back at Huggins, most of I Co fearfully regarded a tall dead jungle tree with only a few green vines up its trunk. Invisible except from a side view, a Jap sniper still hung by his safety rope. Meanwhile, we worked on Sanananda Road again. And a large "I" detail also helped dig up the few Yank dead at Musket, to rebury them in a more suitable place. The memory of this horror of corpses stayed with us in the next days of combat.

15 Jan was the day Gen Doe committed all 1/Bn to attack north of Fisk. When 3/Bn relieved 1/Bn, I Co that afternoon got orders to down tools, and take over C Co's position in Fisk perimeter. To reach Fisk, we again left the road to bypass Japs at perimeters Q and R. Fisk perimeter was smaller than Huggins – a rude circle of log-walled foxholes, with a kitchen shack in the center. From here, we detached 3/Pln and Weapons Pln across the road to Luna perimeter. We sent Lt Ross and S/Sgt Pomenter's 2/Pln 400 yards east, to hold Moore's Post. All 3 perimeters were mud, with the stink of dead Japs.

On 16 Jan, "I" supported 1/Bn's attack northward. When Aussie 20-pounder FA and C's 81s geysered Jap positions, our weapons men at Luna threw in 60s, sprayed trees with LMGs. After the barrage, "I" men hid in a great blown-down tree and 2 abandoned Yank trucks, and sniped many Japs.

Next day, 17 Jan, Sanananda Road was clear behind us. Perimeter P above Nicholson Dump had fallen, and Cos K and L had cleaned up perimeters Q and R. Large workparties sweated to repair the road. Blitz buggies hauled in food and ammo. I Co was now ready to fight the great circular perimeter U, south of the road.

By 1330, I Co had 12 patrols probing into perimeter U to find the latest Jap strongpoints. Sgt Colby's patrol of Brklacich and Riddel crawled 100 yards directly before our perimeter and lay within a few yards of Jap diggers. Goldbricking Japs and our own patrols barley missed finding us, and we brought back important data. And at dusk, Lt Slade's patrol with Sgt Whitehorn and his squad spent hours close to the Jap holes.

On 18 Jan, I Co started its great action against perimeter U. At 1305, Lt Slade's 1/Pln combat patrol left Fisk on azimuth 1350 to a swamp. Then we turned left to advance against the Jap lines NW and North. We hoped to cut off the right wing of perimeter U.

We slipped up a trail directly into perimeter U – with no outguards. We spotted 2 pillboxes, estimated that 100 Nips held the perimeter. A shack 40 yards behind the pillboxes seemed to be their headquarters.

At Slade's orders, we lobbed grenades into pillboxes and nearby holes. After the last explosion, we went in hard with M-1s, to shoot down Japs we had forced out of their holes. As they fell dead, we held perimeter U – for a short time.

But more Japs manned their guns, got fire superiority, almost wiped us out. Sgt Jerrett took a rifle slug in his shoulder; Lund was hit in head and shoulder. Maniecalce had a bad chest wound. Arneson was struck in the shoulder, Ciazzo serveral places in the upper part of his body. Attending wounded, Medic Holtmeier was hit. Pierced in the jaw, Voloshen. died a few days later.

Covering withdrawal of our wounded, Brklacich slaughtered 5 Japs with a swing of his TSMG. We fell back to man a perimeter close to the Japs, while our mortars barraged perimeter U. Our own mortar put a fragment into the cheek of our cook, T/4 Manda. Although many volunteered, I Co had a hard time to evacuate these 8 wounded, one of whom was to die.

And to 1/Pln's new perimeter, Mess Sgt Burckhard sent a detail with hot food, over the new trail in the dark. Next morning, 2/Pln sent 2 squads to reinforce 1/Pln, headed by Stuckenschenider and Tays.

On 19 Jan, after 40 rounds of 81 shells, 1/Pln, reinforced, attacked again. But the Japs threw us back after we made 10 yards. We killed many, but Clyde Henderson died of head wounds, and Lt Slade was reported dead. Trying to rescue Slade, Whitehorn was shot in the back, and Wyatt in the head. The bullet struck Wyatt's steel helmet, lifted him off his feet, threw him yards. He escaped death narrowly, with a deep graze across the top of his head.

But Slade was not dead — McCall lay inches below the Japs' bullet-stream until he felt sure his Lieutenant would never move again. Hours later, at dusk, Garcia crouching in his hole saw movement — then a crawling man. Garcia took 4 separate sights on the man — yet for some reason did not fire. It was Slade, who crawled back to medical aid and life.

On 20 Jan, all I Co had its greatest hour of battle and sudden death. Reassembled with the hard-fought 1/Pln, which had fallen back from the Jap front, we waited at Moore's Post while shells looped overhead into perimeter U. From 1130 to 1330, our barrage flailed intermittently — 750 81s from the mortar battery at Musket, 250 25-pounder Aussie shells. From Fisk, H's MGs tore the jungle overhead as we moved out.

With 2/Pln and 3/Pln in line, Hq slightly behind, I Co shoved off as the mortars still impacted. After 200 yards a short 81 dropped between the lead plns. Klingbeil took a hit in the leg.

For a whole minute, all "I" flattened in mud. Just as we started again, another 81 blasted 25 feet from Hq Pln. Dead were Capt Du Pree, 1/Sgt Boland. Shell fragments cut Hale's knee. Although just a yard from the CO, Com/Sgt Rogers was not killed — but knocked a few yards off by concussion. The writer of this story was close but unhurt.

While other CP men evacuated the casualties, 1/Lt O'Dell, the exec, led I Co on into perimeter U. But that cruel mortar burst slowed the charge; the Japs heard the lull when our mortars stopped impacting, manned their hole. In that blast of unseen fire, we failed. At close range, a Jap MG killed 3/Pln's 2/Lt John E. Oleson and Pease, his runner. Bullets in both legs felled Bedingfield; he lay 2 hours in a fire-lane before rescue. Carlson was shot in the chest. Barnett of 2/Pln died with a bullet in his brain; Bedingfield and Carlson died later.

Unable to retreat until dusk, we slipped back 100 yards among old Jap huts. Here we formed close perimeter, cowered that miserable night in thick rain where we could never have seen a Jap attack in time. M Co saved our wounded.

On 21 Jan, swamp-tired I Co rested. And 3/Bn's S-2, 1/Lt Jacobucci, volunteered to make I's next attack easier. Despite the price I Co had already paid for finding the Japs, supporting weapons officers needed more accurate data that seemed unobtainable. A 1-man patrol might succeed undetected, and Jacobucci volunteered. Jacobucci did the impossible — this Wyoming Yank, who slithered across firelanes, often watching 10 yards from Jap pillboxes. Out in that swamp 3½ hours, he came back with the final data necessary for victory.

Meanwhile, 21 Jan, we lost 1/Lt Leibach from a light mortar wound at his OP the previous day. Malaria and wound sent him to Australia. After rest 22 Jan, "I" had a black perimeter night. At 2300, some 5 to 20 Japs fled from perimeter U — right through our guards and fire-lanes. As they penetrated, we wisely held fire, not to kill I Co men. But after they passed, Morris' grenade killed 1, wounded 1. The dying Jap kept us awake until dawn.

On 23 Jan while E Co watched for Japs to reveal themselves, "I" formed with L to hit perimeter U again. At 1028, Aussie cannon blasted 260 rounds in 16 minutes. Two minutes before the Aussie cannon stopped, M's 81s shot 150 rounds in 4 minutes. From Luna and Fisk, 4 HMGs fired medium speed at treetops and bushes — 3 periods of 2 minutes each — the last 2 minutes' fire as the lines moved out. Three minutes before the attack, I's 60s fired a rack of 50 each.

Again, "I" hit the line under mortar-barrage, 2/Pln and 3/Pln abreast. Again an 81 played hell with us. Killed in 2/Pln was Sgt Bill Taylor, Dardeyn and Hatfield seriously wounded. Lux and Cerma (or Cerza?) were wounded and evacuated — Tays wounded slightly.

But this time, our rifles made the final breakthrough. MGs had silenced snipers; most Japs were still in their shelters. Just a few riflemen stood up to fire, we shot them dead. We caught mortar crewmen in their holes, riddled them. We moved, firing several hundred yards north back to Sanananda Road, then turned back and probed the holes again.

Leaving L Co to garrison perimeter U, we marched back to Fisk perimeter; it seemed like home to us by now. We rested a whole day; feet were in bad shape, especially in 1/Pln where the men had 2 days longer in the swamps than anybody else.

Then I Co marched 9 miles to Gona Mission — packs too heavy with Jap souvenirs. But not a Yank fell out. We ran mop-up patrols from Gona; at Dinwati 2/Pln alone killed 56 Japs. We even took 10 prisoners. Now the stored up malaria and dysentery of Sanananda come to a head with us; we had 50 hospitalized at once, and were down to 74 company strength. But after losing 10 dead before perimeter U and at least 18 wounded, I Co had it light at Gona. And this is how I Co stormed perimeter U at Sanananda.

Basic story is from unknown writer — maybe in I Co's CP. Additional data are from 163's Sanananda JOURNAL, a Field Report — "New Guinea-Sanananda Phase. 1/Lt John Jacobucci's DSC story. I also used a map from the original Division history. Background is from Dr. Samuel Milner's PAPUAN CAMPAIGN. Third Battalion stories from any regiment are hard to find? Can you help?

K Co. 163 Infantry:
Combat on Sanananda Road

By DR. HARGIS WESTERFIELD, Division Historian
with C.O. ED REAMS

Debarking from Aussie C-47's at Dobodura, K Co. 163 Inf. got lost at once. Too quickly gathered in the landing area by planeloads and dispatched into the kunai, K was not reassembled until 9 Jan. 1943. (By this time, 1/Bn. 163 had already battled from Musket Perimeter, and 2/Bn. had sealed off the Jap escape corridor on Killerton Trail.) On 11 Jan. came K's first memorable assignment.

When Japs deserted Q Perimeter near Musket, A Co. moved from a position on the supply trail to occupy Q. K in turn garrisoned A's position en route to Musket Perimeter. (Voya was the place where supply convoys had to leave closed Sanananda Road and take to the jungle to bypass the Japs and supply Musket Perimeter.)

On 12 Jan., K covered the right flank of Aussie 18 Brigade which tried to storm the southern Jap Perimeters P frontally. The Aussie attack failed, with heavy casualties and loss of three tanks. K Co's action was not reported.

On 15 Jan., we began operations that continued through 22 Jan. to the close of the main Battle of Sanananda. About 1200, we slew our first Jap—perhaps a marine because of his anchor insignia. At 1230 on 15 Jan., we patrolled with three NCO's and five pvts. While on a bridge across a creek, Marr took a bullet in the left foot.

At 1645 that 15 Jan., we teamed with L Co. to relieve A and B against hard-fought Jap Perimeter R, north of Musket. While those companies joined other 1/Bn. elements for their great offensive of 16 Jan., we pressed Perimeter R. About 2000, 12 Jap rifle grenades struck K, but all were evidently duds. Dresen probably died in action before R—from a shot in lower abdomen.

On the morning of 16 Jan., K was holed within 30 yards of the Japs and had taken some MG fire. But by 1410, K and L finished mopping R Perimeter. Capt. Reams slew his first Jap, who died hard under 15 .45 caliber Tommy gun slugs. Our Jap kill was light; many had escaped. In our final day against R Perimeter, we had no casualties.

Now all Jap perimeters south of Fisk were overrun. But concealed in jungles and swamps where Sanananda Road bent east, the Japs held hard in Perimeters S, T, and U. North of these Jap positions after the great fight of 16 Jan., 1/Bn. established Perimeter A-D. This perimeter interdicted Jap retreats seaward and based our attacks on S, T, and U.

At Perimeter A-D 17 Jan., K reinforced battered A Co. While one platoon chopped a supply trail for 2/Bn. which had crossed from Killerton Roadblock, the other platoons scouted south to find Jap positions in Perimeter T. We hit swamp south of A-D and were recalled.

At about 1515, six Japs with fixed bayonets rushed an outpost against Novolli, reputedly the largest man in K Co. Novolli pulled a Jap up by his own bayoneted rifle. He seized the Jap's body and beat him to death on the ground. In this fight, we killed five Japs and wounded one who evidently escaped.

On 18 Jan., K had heavy combat. With A Co. on our right at 0815, we pushed south towards a section of T Perimeter that A had found yesterday. This section consisted of three bunkers across a 75-yard width of kunai jungle. After a short approach march, K took heavy MG fire on our left flank across Sanananda Road in the recon zone of another bn.

To avoid this fire, both co's fell back to the same starting point and moved off more to A's right. In changing directions on this blind jungle, we got lost for about an hour until striking the new supply trail we had cut for 2/Bn. Japs fired again—heavy fire on K from the SE.

While Jap fire halted A also, we pivoted on A's flank and turned down the road back towards Fisk Perimeter. I Co. also deployed a platoon before Fisk to dispose of Japs K might drive towards them. I Co. sprayed the right side of the road with automatic weapons to keep down snipers.

Here by the one-lane corduroy Sanananda Road, we contacted F Co. shooting its way SW to hunt down Japs. F had shot both sides of the road, but now gave way for us to fight on the right (west)side of the road. But a MG fired from a concealed trench on the road behind us on our left flank. We halted. F Co. fought on southward to where a deep stream a Jap MG's halted it with heavy casualties. But K Co. kept contact with A and rested for battle against T Perimeter tomorrow.

On that battle day against T Perimeter 18 Jan., K lost at least three killed, 14 wounded—all wounded marked as "serious." Actual time of casualty is unknown. Once, Japs in T Perimeter called that they were surrendering. Capt. Reams told 2/Lt. Rawstron to try to take them prisoners—but to be careful. When Rawstron stood up—perhaps with Price and Barger, Jap fire killed them and pinned down K Co.

Medics tagged all 13 wounded as "serious," mostly from bullets. Six took high bullet wounds, Burre in upper arm, Rogers in right shoulder, Campion in left hand, Gernentz in left ear, left cheek. Sgt. William B. Miller was hit in left hand, Sgt. Nemec in back. Four had low wounds—Cawood in right leg; Riddle, right knee; Roy Hall, left thigh; Zawko, right thigh. Cambra suffered mortar fragments in chest and left shoulder. Simons had a fragment in right arm, a bullet in left shoulder. Salvaggio's and Shaheen's wounds were in unspecified parts of bodies.

CREDIT: Most important sources are Capt. (now Lt. Col. retired) Ed Reams' 5-page, legal-size handwritten letter, undated, 163 Casualty Lists, "41st Div. Training Note No. 2, Sections II, III." Other sources, all important, are Samuel Milner's Victory in Papua, 163's "Extracts from History," Murray Noble's 15-page handwritten ltr. (after 22 May 1973), 163's detailed journal of Sanananda. (I quote also deceased Don Emil Rohrig's ltr. of about 1947 from memory, for I destroyed it back in the days when I had no plans to write this history.) I now have stories from every 163 line Co. that fought at Sanananda with the exception of C Co.

41sters blasting away at enemy bunkers hidden in the jungle.

Next morning, 19 Jan., K still fought Perimeter T. Advancing again A's left, we had no trouble at first. Enfilading the brush from A's right, a HMG pln. raked the way clear for us. LMG's pushed ahead and shot for us. Then our MG's had to cease as our advance moved ahead of them. The Japs rose from defilade and slew three A men, wounded six. K Co. lost six wounded that day. Both A and K had to dig in below Jap small arms fire.

Repulsed by a strongpoint, K killed a few Japs and seized a Bren gun. Better still, a wounded Jap crawled into K's lines with important information. He warned us that we were fighting toward 10 MG's in a trench system guarding the former Jap hq. for all Sanananda. This news undoubtedly saved us many casualties.

On 19 Jan., most of K's wounds were in the upper parts of our bodies again. Japs shot Sgt. Gore in left radius, Ruskin in right radius of their forearms. Cpl. Floyd Smith was hit in the bone of the upper left arm. Rizzi took a wound in right shoulder, Steele in upper back. Bingham was hit on the right side—upper forearm bone and knee. Martin Johnson was wounded, place unspecified.

On 20 Jan., K and A were back to 1/Bn's Perimeter A-D and out of action while I Co. made an abortive attack on Perimeter U, to the SE. There I Co. used all available FA and 81's of 163 RCT but failed.

On 21 Jan., harassed A Co.—and especially our K Co.—had good hunting. After pulling back 150 yards while Aussie FA fired and our 81's blasted from Musket Perimeter like batteries, we moved out while HMG's fired overhead. This time, we struck to the right of the 10 Jap MG's and drove home our attack with assault fire.

While Lt. Grisson, a little to the rear, phoned directions to platoons, Capt. Reams led K Co. in. We caught most of the Japs still underground or trying to extricate themselves from shattered bunkers. The garrison panicked and ran up Sanananda Road across our line of fire. We had great killing. The attack of A plus K was so demoralizing and firing so heavy that B and C were enabled to storm Perimeter S to the westward. While an A pln. now turned west and mopped up the roadside westward, our K pln. cleared it eastward.

Together, A and K and support weapons killed some 530 Japs that 21 Jan. 1943 in the heaviest slaughter since the Aussie massacre back at Gorari 12 Nov. 1943. K Co. estimated that our share of the kill was 80-100. K had just two wounded—Kausalik with a fragment in left leg and Sgt. Barnes with a shot in left heel.

That night after the destruction of T Perimeter, tired K men relaxed in 3/Bn's nearby perimeter for a good night's sleep. The last organized Jap Perimeter U was strongly besieged, but we took turns on guard against chance collisions with stragglers. The moon was full above the misty jungle.

About 0600 22 Jan., just as the moon was setting and just before sunrise, some 150-200 escaping Japs evidently halted to rest with the head of their column against K's perimeter. When they sensed K Co., they leaped into our foxholes and started shooting.

Some K men with blistered, mud-caked, soggy feet had bivouacked above ground. There was some momentary panic. Rohrig heard Jap bayonet men charging us. Like pigs, they grunted as they charged: "OUGH! OUGH! OUGH!"

But Capt. Reams and his men were now coldly alert and firing back. When one Yank got a bayonet in his breastbone, he grabbed the Jap rifle, kicked the Jap in the teeth, and shot him dead with the Jap rifle. We readily repelled the attack.

In broad daylight, we saw 31-33 Japs lying dead in what seemed to be a hastily formed skirmish line. We found an abandoned HMG on half-load. We took one seriously wounded prisoner—a Jap officer who spoke English.

K's own losses were surprisingly light. Japs shot one mortarman when he left his hole to put his weapon into action. This casualty was either Nash or Snedaker. Nash was hit in the back and the left hand to die 27 Jan. Snedaker was wounded with bullets in chest and right leg. Sgt. Goldsmith was accidentally shot dead. Novolli and Tom Pierce had slight wounds.

From the wounded Jap officer, 163 HQ learned that this body of Japs had landed at Giruwa to reinforce the Sanananda garrison just 10 days before. Originally 500 strong, it had lost some 200 in battle and in sickness, with 150-200 unaccounted for. Although urgently dispatched southward, none of them had ever got into action in the front lines near Musket Perimeter. Unaware of their location, they were trekking west when they collided with K in the dawn. Nobody knows anything certain about the rest of their career, but it is possible that they faced G and L on the Kumusi, the 100-odd still alive.

Such was the war of K Co. 163 Inf. at Sanananda. Committed late to battle, we helped mop up R Perimeter, then forayed down Sanananda Road with A Co. In two days of good combat, we finally destroyed Perimeter T. In a Japanese dawn attack 22 Jan. 1943, we climaxed our war with a smashing repulse. Our losses were comparatively light: with six dead, 17 wounded. We had fought well, with minimal losses.

41sters and Aussies seeking protection behind a Jap structure during a firefight in the Sanananda sector. The Aussies proved to be invaluable combat comrades.

L Co., 163 Infantry:
From Musket Perimeter to the Kumusi

By Dr. HARGIS WESTERFIELD, Division Historian,
and Rifleman RALPH WESTERMAN

At Sanananda, L Co. 163 Inf. was among the last Co's to begin fighting. But 30 days after the battle ended, our malarious outfit can claim the honor of having the last 163 casualties—on the Kumusi Patrol, 21 Feb. 1943.

On 9 Jan. 1943, when 2/Bn. blocked Killerton Trail and 1/Bn. held Musket Perimeter, L Co. boarded Aussie planes at Moresby for the front. Landing on a dirt strip at Dobodura, we shouldered rifles and packs and regretfully saw our plane at once take off for safety from possible Jap raiders from the dark jungle.

Hiking three miles over muddy trails, by 12 Jan. we relieved our battered B Co. cobbers garrisoning that cockpit of Musket Perimeter. We heard our first Jap rifles crack from the trees, and 163's answering M-1's. Our holes were 150 yards from the Japs' backs in that green hell.

Rations were short. We ate rice and GI chocolate and some hard Aussie biscuits. The planes had dropped those biscuits in 5-gallon tins, but they had not broken. We also drank strong, green tea.

Next day, 13 Jan., L had its first casualty—Sgt. Deval Cassidy with a bullet through his brow. Evidently a Jap sniper had fired down from a tree and killed Cassidy.

In the swampy old B perimeter, living was wretched. Many slit trenches had water in them. Our drinking water came from a well only two feet deep. A few steps from the well in one direction was a slit trench—and a Jap grave a few steps the other way.

On 15 Jan., L Co. saw grim action, jungle style, with invisible death. Officially, the report was that A Co. and two L plns. attacked Jap Perimeter R north of Musket Perimeter. For L however, the action was mainly combat patrols in blind jungle, with two dead and three seriously wounded.

L Co's Lt. Wall and his combat patrol thrust into the Jap jungle. They drew fire, hit the ground, and had to stay there under the bullet-strike. Then 3/Pln. sallied to unspring Wall's patrol.

Although Westerman usually ran as second scout, that day Sgt. Camerata moved Westerman one place back in line and replaced him with Bob Weaner. (Actually, we were only three steps apart to keep contact in those Sanananda thickets. But those three steps could make the difference between life and death.)

Supposedly, our 3/Pln. was attacking a pillbox that Lt. Wall had been attacking. Instead, we hit a barrier of Jap bullets. Some 20 yards from unseen Japs, we heard the crash of their MG. Then bloody Weaner crawled out past Westerman. "Westerman, be careful!" he warned. "I heard them talking before they shot me."

For the next three hours, 3/Pln. had to hug the ground. Intermittent Jap MG bursts slashed bark from trees three feet over out heads. With darkness, we changed to safer positions. Lt. Wall told us to form a listening post and stay there.

All night under the moon, sleepless Westerman lay by his Tommy gun with Price nearby. They listened but heard nothing, and dared not doze. It was 24 hours before they were back in safety to eat again. When they returned, rations were four ounces of chocolate, a canteen of water—and nothing else.

On that same 15 Jan., L was actually helping A to fight Jap Perimeter R, which had held up 163's northward advance. Besides Weaner seriously wounded, L lost Cleland and Zurawski killed; Milligan and Horning badly wounded. Medic Churchill was killed also.

Next day, 16 Jan., L Co. became part of the all-out Aussie and Yank offensive that Aussie Gen. Vasey had organized the day before. North of us, the Aussies fought eastward, and 163's 1/Bn. and 2/Bn. thrust at Perimeters S and T north of the great road-bend. (This was the torrid day when 163 enveloped those Jap perimeters. A Co. was saved after losing nine killed, 17 wounded, and 20 evacuated with heat prostration.)

On this great offensive of 16 Jan., L with K replaced A and B in that old siege of Perimeter R. But after a fortnight's attrition by B Co. and supporting shelling, L found Perimeter R an easy fight. Aussie 25-pounders and Yank mortars blasted. Then we pushed.

We met MG and rifle fire, but L reported no casualties. Patrolling through jungle so thick that he could see only a few yards, Westerman found his first visible Japs—several dead men.

By 1410, this Jap Perimeter R was wiped out. L Co. then assembled at the south end of Musket Perimeter and deployed in the jungle 200 yards NW of Sanananda Road. We combed the area on the left side of the road as far as Fish Perimeter. For the first time since 163 had occupied Musket, the jungle was clear of Jap snipers who had killed in Musket Perimeter. But on 18 Jan., snipers again hit Musket, and the garrison killed five of them.

On 17 Jan., L salvaged R Perimeter. We collected Jap equipment, and some B dead nobody could recover before. We found a butchered Yank cadaver—perhaps of Lt. Fisk.

With L were now a few Aussie soldiers and they brightened up the jungle for us. We were scarred with jungle rot, racked by dysentery and malaria. But these rugged Aussies in their khaki shorts and wide, sideswiped sombreros looked debonair as they soldiered with us.

On 21-22 Jan., the main Battle of Sanananda came to a crashing finish. After 1/Bn. with K attached wiped out Jap Perimeters S and T north of the road-bend on 21 Jan., our L with I had to smash Perimeter U south of the road, on 22 Jan. Thus L reinforced I and E to wipe out the last uncaptured Jap perimeter at Sanananda.

By 0855, L had moved east from Musket Perimeter to fall in on I Co's right. But not until midmorning did action begin—after elaborate and carefully planned support fire. For by now, Gen. Doe had developed a science of crushing Nippo perimeters.

Starting 19 minutes before our midmorning attack, Aussie FA fired 260 rounds into Perimeter U and ceased three minutes before H-Hour. Also starting at 19 minutes before H-Hour, four HMG's of 163 fired two minutes' medium rate of fire from Luna and Fisk Perimeters north of U. These four HMG's fired two minutes more at 13 minutes before H-Hour—and fired again for the last two minutes before we jumped off. They concentrated on treetops and the bushy fringes of clearings.

And both calibers of mortars impacted also. From Musket, 15 of 163's 81's began while the Aussie FA kept firing. Our 81's fired from 1040 to 1042, ceased, then impacted again with 13 pieces for the last two minutes before H-Hour. And I Co's 60's took up the fire. For three minutes, up to one minute before H-Hour, I Co's little 60's shot a total of 50 rounds per mortar.

CREDIT: Heartfelt thanks to L's Ralph Westerman for his replies to my Jungleer notice—a six-page legal-size MS of extracts from his diary, and letters of 15 April and 15 May, 1974. Background is from Dr. Samuel Milner's Victory in Papua plus 163's "Extracts from History, 27 Dec. 1942–19 Mar. 1943," and "Journal, 1 Jan. 1943–30 Mar. 1943." Bennett Saunders supplied 41 Div. Tng. Note No. 3, which D C's Fed Archives no longer has available. Ralph lives on a farm beside Interstate Highway 70 near Ellsworth, Kansas. His wife waited 44 month for him to come home; he has two sons and two daughters.

Then at 1047, L plus I attacked, while E Co. quietly awaited targets NE of Perimeter U. I and L then struck for the Jap lines on a 30-degree azimuth from Sanananda Road.

Behind the last mortar salvo, we were on the move, despite some Nippo fire. We caught dazed Japs still in their holes or trying to leave them. Other Japs ran. Four Jap strongpoints were seized and 35 Japs killed. We captured three AA guns, MG's mounted in trees and rifles with unused ammo. Perimeter U was overrun by 1152.

But L Co. continued its war with malaria, jungle and Japs. Some 1,000 able-bodied Japs were finding trails west across the north-south road to Gona and living off the natives until they could regroup to fight again.

On 24 Jan., fevered and hungry L Co. followed two Aussie guides through the mud to camp about a mile from Gona. On 25 Jan. L had neither lunch nor supper, and a breakfast of tea only. We saw two Japs by a tree; the Aussies slew both. Here were the first Japs Westerman had seen die in the whole battle.

In the next few days, L despatched a few stragglers around Gona Mission, where only the cross was left standing. Mader was seriously wounded 28 Jan.

About 29 May, L had a 3/Bn. order for a killer patrol inland to Elwaada vicinity. Lt. Wall chose the most physically fit survivors of L, but to get 20 men, he had to take many with a temperature of 100. In five hours, we slogged NE up the coast, and turned inland and south to Watrasata Village on the near side of Amboga River.

Hearing Jap voices at Watrasata, we slipped up covered by tall kunai grass and shot dead five stragglers. At 1630, we reached Elwaada and saw two Japs 125 yards off at the far end of the village. Fearing ambush, Wall first enveloped flank and rear of the village. Then his point killed the two Japs. But Elwaada's six huts were clear of Japs.

At about 1800 hrs., after we had dug in, natives came to make friends with us. Two more natives arrived to complain that two Japs were in their gardens some 10 minutes' hike north of Elwaada. A five-man L patrol killed them. Next day, natives guided us to slay three more Japs on the trails. Then we had five hours' fevered hiking back to Gona. We had ended lives of 12 stragglers, but had found no menacing concentration SW of Gona.

Then came the final chapter of L's jungle war. On 4 Feb., Maj. Wing picked four 10-man squads to help Capt. Benson's G Co. Advancing towards the Kumusi River, G had halted three days before a strong Jap position on the Kombela River – the Japs' first show of strength since Perimeter U fell on 22 Jan.

We boarded 35-foot motor boats and chugged up the shore some three miles. We landed and joined Lt. Carsner's G 186 pln. and sloshed through jungle where we were often waist-deep in water. At a native village, a scout told us that we were the first white men they had ever seen. They gave every L man a boiled potato which we ate happily with a crumbled salt tablet. It was the first fresh edible we'd tasted in a long time.

The natives ferried us across a river – probably the Bakumbari – in an outrigger canoe. Reaching the coast again, G 186 and L 163 were now behind the Japs holding back G 163, and where we could have destroyed them on a retreat.

But we contacted the Japs just before dark. After a brief fire fight, 186's Lt. Carsner decided that a night attack was unwise. By daybreak, the Japs had escaped along the shore. G 163 with G 186 continued their march to the Kumusi River.

On 14 Feb., all L Co. relieved G 163 at Kumusi Mouth, and on 21 Feb. L's last fight took place.

On 21 Feb., L heard that Japs were swimming in the sea two miles south of the Kumusi River. Lt. Stark took 11 L men, six Aussies, and two native scouts after them. A band of some 30 Japs split into three groups of 10 men each to escape more easily. We made an unsuccessful ambush against these Japs on the north bank of a dry riverbed, then had to cross that arroyo under cover of Aussie FA. We killed four Japs, wounded others. Later we found what must have been their raft and cut it adrift, and destroyed supplies of food and medicine.

But a Jap grenade wounded Civetta, Cpl. Wooten and Lt. Stark (who was either an Aussie or an attached 186 man). Wooten was

41sters cross a creek in the Sanananda area. Even though the famed triad of Gona, Sanananda, and Buna was a strip of beach not more than 8 miles in length, troop mobility under jungle combat conditions was a hazardous and time consuming undertaking.

dead that same 21 Feb; Chaplain Siqueland prepared his funeral service. Hughes was wounded on 21 Feb., to die two days later.

Not until 10 Mar. did 2/Bn. 162 Inf. relieve L at Kumusi Mouth. Meanwhile, Westerman with 11 more L men was evacuated. While aboard the Dutch ship **Bontekoe**, bound for Port Moresby, Westerman saw the burial at sea of L Co's Gill, our last known dead man in the Papuan campaign.

Sewed in a canvas shroud and covered by an American flag, his body lay in state on the starboard after-deck for burial services. His body slid into the deep; the ship made a right turn; a guard of honor fired a rifle salute.

Such was the story of L Co. 163 Inf. in the Papuan campaign. We helped overrun two Jap perimeters, yet had only minimum casualties. We had only six known dead and five known wounded. Although we did not suffer so heavily as the line cos. of 1/Bn. and 2/Bn., we carried out orders. Although late in battle, we came back fever-stricken from the Kumusi, back to hospital or rest camp.

Historian wants more individuals' stories

Association Historian DR. HARGIS WESTERFIELD (G-163), **414 W 25th, Kearney, Nebr. 68847**, in his report to the last annual meeting, listed history stories on hand for a number of units. However, these outfits are on the critically short list as regards stories, and Hargis asks men from these outfits to write him with whatever details of actions they can remember: A-186 & F-186; A-162, G-162, K-162; C-163, E-163; **all** F.A. batteries. Medics and other special troops. Stories of all units at Zamboanga. And, everything anyone can remember about the circumstances surrounding these casualties (in what part of the field was he when he was hit? In what part of his body was he hit? How was he evacuated? What other fighting went on in that position after he left? What else do you remember? Every small detail is important to get your company story into history, recorded for all time. THIS MEANS YOU! Please help. I want to hear from every wounded man, too – all details.

★ ★ ★ ★ ★

Our Historian, Dr. HARGIS WESTERFIELD (G-163), Kearney, Neb., has been commissioned an "Admiral of the State of Nebraska" by Governor Exon. Hargis has retired from the faculty of Kearney State College, and is in the midst of ceremonies marking this milestone in his life. Ship Ahoy, & Brace the Mains'l, Admiral!

G Co. 186 Infantry:
Patrol to the Kumusi

by DR. HARGIS WESTERFIELD, DIVISION HISTORIAN
with LT. HENRY CARSNER

I dedicate this story to the memory of Henry P. Carsner, who looked so healthy when I met him at the Gearhart Reunion in 1971 that I thought he'd live to read it. Prime credit is due to his three-page typescript of 22 Apr. 1971 plus a six-page holograph supplement of 28 Dec. 1971. Also important were George Weller's three articles in the Chicago Daily News, dated 8 Apr. 1943, and Col. Wm. C. Benson's handwritten report, "Company G Activity .... Feb 1 .... through Feb 14, 1943," provided through courtesy of Col. Charles R. Dawley. Excellent overall historical data are from Aussie Dudley McCarthy's South-West Pacific Area, First Year, *and Gen MacArthur's* Japanese Operations in the South-West Pacific Area, Vol. II, Part I.

About 31 Jan. 1943, Col. Murray ordered G Co. 186 Inf's 1/Pln into what became 186's first fight of World War II. Actual mission of Lt. Carsner's pln. was to patrol 22 miles west then north around a great bend of Guinea shore to secure the mouth of the Kumusi River. In this patrol we had to assist Capt. Benson's G Co. 163 Inf.—battle-tested veterans of Sanananda. At Kumusi mouth, we were to slay Jap fugitives from Sanananda, and other Japs rafting down from Aussie victories. At Kumusi mouth they had hoped to block our westward advance, or to escape in Nippo craft.

Gen. Fuller ordered us to avoid battle until we dug in on the Kumusi. But gallant, die-hard Nips would naturally block the narrow coastal corridor between jungle and sea at strategic crossings. Long before we saw the Kumusi, G 186 saw 186's first combat.

Reinforced with two extra BAR teams, G 186 hiked towards Gona where danger would begin. To carry rations and extra ammo, we had 120 natives led by Aussie W/O Bill Brannigan of ANGAU. Despite native carriers, we soldiers had too much on our backs. Surplus equipment weighted us: two extra fatigue suits, a jungle suit, and that back-breaking jungle hammock. We had everything but an iron cot, mattress, and blankets.

At Gona, Carsner left the extra pounds with a 163 Hq. outfit. He never saw this surplus again, and later he had trouble explaining this shortage to Col. Murray, who threatened court-martial. But no court-martial ever materialized.

Next morn, on 1 Feb., G 186 shouldered packs, ported rifles, and sweatily marched west—combat ready. For a report came that a pln. of fresh Jap marines had landed across our march. On the beach, we saw

At Kumusi mouth

signs of Japs: empty food and Sterno cans. So we kept clear of long sweeps of sandy beach, where snipers could kill from far off. We scouted well within the jungle, that awesome, quiet tangle of brush and giant trees where no animals moved and no birds sang.

Then at the mouth of a small river we saw our first Jap. He ran up gladly, as if he thought we were Japs also. Our surprised M-1's shot haphazardly; our scouts had buck-fever, and the Jap got clear away

Crossing the river hot after this fleeing Nip, we hit trouble. A Jap MG lashed out from jungle, killed a native scout at 10 feet. Remembering Fuller's order to avoid battle before Kumusi mouth, Carsner pulled back some 600 yards to Sebari Village. He planned to probe with small patrols and find a way around the Japs to reach the Kumusi.

There at Sebari, Capt. Benson's G 163 veterans met us 186 rookies. This little company of underweight and fevered Sanananda men took over the action, pushed out a fighting patrol. Since this patrol found no Japs, Benson ordered his own G Co. to lead out to the next river, already midway between Gona and Kumusi mouth. (This river was probably the Kurerda, although a reliable account names it the Kombela.)

Seeing no Japs, Benson tried a quick crossing, and G 163 found wounds and death. On the wrong side of the Kurerda, Benson's three-man point was cut off—men who had volunteered. Sgt. Bretzke was killed. Ramsey and W/O Dixon (an Aussie) had to strip and swim out to sea for their lives. Using three observers for mortar fire, Japs wounded G 163's Sahs, Gonzales, Kubista.

And Carsner's 186 men helped 163. With Cunningham and perhaps Rheinfels, Sgt. Bolen manned a captured Jap assault boat to evacuate a wounded G 163 man. Under heavy Jap MG fire from a tree position, the 186 men made the farther shore and rescued him. Carsner himself ran down to the boat and grasped the 163 man's shoulders to help him from the line of fire. This man was hit in the chest, but Carsner later saw him at Fort Lewis, fully recovered.

Benson took five days to force Kurerda Crossing. For it was a naturally strong position. The estuary bent at right angles on two sides of a jungle thicket 75 by 100 yards. Behind this long peninsula, an open sandstrip gave Jap mortars, MG's, and rifles a clear field of fire. To displace the Japs, Benson brought up M 163's four 81's with 47 Yanks, and a pln. of L 163. For two days, M's 81's with G 163 60's hit the Jap jungle, and on 5 Feb. Carsner's G 186 men had action and were blooded.

On 5 Feb. Benson ordered G 186 to move on an inland route around the Jap right flank to Fuffarda and Kumbardo Villages and thence to the coast. We were to hit from the river and drive the Japs into Benson's men who were now over the Kurerda, but checked by Jap fire two whole days.

In that heavy jungle, the march of G 186 was unavoidably delayed. Pressing forward with his scouts, Carsner heard a shouted Jap command 50 yards ahead. A MG opened up on us. BAR-man Collier hit the ground; Carsner stood astride his prone form and directed fire. A bullet shot Collier through the hips.

As we pulled back with Collier, darkness closed in, with 186 squads still coming out of the swamp. It was sensible to withdraw 100 yards and dig in. Willing natives carried out seriously wounded Collier while G 186 rested and waited quietly for dawn. But 1/Sgt. Desler and another Yank were caught in the forward position and lay there under heavy fire for the night.

That night, the Jap defenders of Kurerda Crossing escaped up the coast, and 186 contacted Benson's men without a fight. In that jungle strongpoint, 163 found two Jap bodies—only mementos of five days' resistance.

Next morning, 7 Feb. 43, Carsner's men led out before 163. The Japs waited for us, across what was probably the Bakumbari River, for it was now 186's honor to attack.

This time, Carsner commanded a regular landing craft and drove in from the sea. He had selected a landing site halfway between two Jap MG positions, and both MG's opened up as we charged in. Ordering his men down, Carsner manned a Bren gun mounted on the bow and silenced both MG's. But meanwhile, the Yank coxswain sheered hard about and headed for safety. Jap bullets stitched the gunwales, but no 186 man was hurt.

Benson welcomed Carsner back with good news: 186 was to try this one-barge beachhead tomorrow. By this time, however, an Aussie 25-pounder cannon was up front, and along with M 163's 81's it drove the Japs from the Bakumbari Crossing. G Co. landed without opposition.

We continued the pursuit of the Japs toward the Kumusi. Here and there lay crumpled Nippo corpses—a total of some 25 dead. Surely these were soldiers wounded at Kurerda Crossing who had died in flight.

Natives came in canoes

We came upon a Jap hospital vacated probably the night before. A forgotten wristwatch still ran. Carsner thought that this hospital had been the post of that fresh Jap marine pln. we had heard about in Gona, that they had furnished security for the patients until they were moved.

And so went G 186's fighting mop-up patrol with 163 in the 22 miles of beach and coastal jungle from Gona to the Kumusi River. Besides Japs, we faced the terrors of the primeval jungle coast. Most of the many streams were too deep for direct crossing. Water transportation was too slow and too hard to come by.

Best method to cross a river, we learned, was to avoid it. We avoided a deep tropical river by wading out to sea where the slackening current had piled up a shallow half-moon of a sandbar. Under heavy gear, we floundered calf-deep to neck-deep with shorter Yanks held up by taller Yanks, or with nonswimmers hanging on to legs or parts of old canoes.

In crossing, we shuddered—and still shudder today—at the sight of salt-water crocodiles at inlets—no doubt already corpse-fed. Sharks cruised in inlets as we crossed—sharks that we now definitely know were man-eaters.

Official rations were, of course, poor. We had Aussie C rations. We had peanut butter and jam—and sand—on hardtack that seemed as difficult to chew as concrete. Yet some of us managed to find tasty native foods. Carsner and others ate squash prepared in a waterless cooking pot with banana leaves. ANGAU Brannigan displayed his knowledge of native food. He roasted a grass seedhead—like our manna grass—in hot coals as one roasts an ear of corn. Carsner found it tasty and nutritious. Men also ate great watermelons, bland-tasting but a good source of needed water in that disease-ridden land.

Thus G Co. 186 Inf. had already helped veterans of 163 in two fighting crossings en route to Kumusi mouth. Then on the same day that Carsner made his unfought landing, we came to another unnamed river. This time, we threw down a barrage at dusk, the next day we crossed unopposed. Thence forward, the Japs did not try to block our way to the Kumusi. The main problem now was to get craft to cross the deep water: Higgins boats sometimes, or salvaged Jap assault boats— even a native dugout which G 163 rebuilt for the trips.

And on 10 Feb., after M's 81's silenced Jap fire across a lagoon to our left, we closed in on Kumusi mouth. After six miles of heavy slogging in sand, we neared the most eastern of the Kumusi's two branches to the sea. In the jungle were Jap shacks and dugouts. Offshore, surf foamed around shattered Jap barges which A-20's or Beaufighters had broken. For it was here that on 2 Dec. 1942, despite wild air battles over them, four destroyers had succeeded in landing 500 Japs of 3/Bn. 170 Inf. Here Col. Yazawa had also gathered other fugitives from inland battle against the Aussies. Under Yazawa's command, some 400-500 Japs had reinforced Col. Tsukamoto at the Battle of Sanananda. And as late as 24 Jan., a company from 102 Inf. had moved east from Lae to garrison at Kumusi mouth. But these were gone.

Here at the mouth of the dirty-brown Kumusi, we already found a tiny, straw-haired Aussie CO with a slouch-hatted little war party of Diggers. For three months, they had seen no other allied soliders. They had been picking off Jap refugees, but their kills had dwindled until 163 with G 186 had pressed new Nips towards the Kumusi. This Aussie CO estimated that he had killed 100, although official estimates totaled 600. He exhibited two full chests of officers' swords–along with officers' silver cutlery for banquets, and sctoch and cognac.

But for weary G Co. 186 Inf's 1/Pln. the great news at Kumusi mouth was that Benson had his field ranges up. He invited us to a dinner of the best pancakes we ever had in our lives. During the next few days, G 186 also killed a few Nippo stragglers. And about 14 Feb., we gratefully boarded Higgins craft to motor back to our regiment.

Such was 186's first combat—in its Kumusi Patrol of about 31 Jan. to about 14 Feb. 1943. We had excellent combat discipline, and no problem of tropical illness. With only Collier wounded, we had carried out assignments in three firefights and teamed with experienced 163 men on patrol.

---

41 QM Co.

Those indispensable Quartermasters

By DR. HARGIS WESTERFIELD, Division Historian
and COL. H.B. CARY, QM

To forward rations and ammo into infantry perimeters, we truckers and clerks of 41 QM lived a life of overwork in the deadly jungles. Of course, we were never as often in danger as were riflemen, and living conditions usually were better too. But without our supplies carefully allocated, no rifleman could live for a day at the front. Here is a part of our story—of men who kept our infantry fighting the Japs.

We began the war as a regiment: 116 QM Regt., 3 Bns, 13 company units. On 1 Nov. 1942 at Rockhampton, we became the small 41 QM Co., but with a full colonel commanding—Col. Frederick C. Roecker. We were now six plns:

Hq, Office of Division Quartermaster, Sv Pln, and three truck plns.

By 5 Jan. 1943, our 35-man detachment saw action against Japs at Sanananda, as far as 41 QM could act. From our supply dump 2640 yards west of Soputa, jeeps trucked supplies up Sanananda Track. With 163 Sv Co., we guarded native carriers for Musket Perimeter. We labored with light trucks to clear Dobodura Strip and dropping ground and forward loads into dumps for Sanananda.

From near Musket, our QM ammo trucks returned wounded from the front to Dobodura airlift. Medics brought to us men in stretchers, but could spare no aid men. Often our drivers had to halt in danger en route to give wounded what aid they could.

Rations for 163 were bad indeed: bully beef, Aussie hardtack and tea. These were so nauseous that when C rations first arrived on about 15 Jan., front-line men called even the C's a delicacy.

To fairly allocate supplies was itself a hard task that QM well performed. During 5-25 Jan. 1943 at Dobodura, Sgt. Powell operated like a computer. As chief clerk, he performed hard mental work daily. He had to calculate fairly the rations for 6,000 Aussies and Yanks and 2,000 natives.

Because of shortages, Powell could not use proportions from Army manuals. He had to use percentages based on fluctuating lots of various supplies on hand. He also had to supervise dispatching of our limited number of small trucks to haul supplies and return wounded from the front. Powell had one of the excruciating jobs of 41 QM.

Beginning 27 Jan., we faced a ration shortage. For eight days bad weather halted the airlift of supplies from Moresby. We had only three days' rations and two days' gasoline on hand.

In this crisis, supplies had to come over the rough jungle road from Oro Bay, 16 miles east of Dobodura, even though four bridges were washed out. Other units carried our supplies until the last crossing. We had to get our motley fleet of little trucks and trailers to where they could haul from Warisota Plantation to Sambogo River Crossing. We could not float these trucks across the river; a shallow bar blocked us off in midstream. At the west bank, the river was three feet deep before a bank with a 55-foot slope of black loam. With natives, we got down into the river to manhandle them over: 32 quarter-ton Aussie trailers. These transported supplies back to the ferry, where natives carried them across. This is how we kept the men of Sanananda supplied until the bad weather ended.

Although 41 QM started the great Dobodura dump, we had to move it to a new area, remote from the main center. Too many troops now bivouacked too close to it for us to protect supplies from pilferage. But in the new jungle area, we were too shorthanded to adminsiter it adequately. Sickness had dropped our detachment from 41 to 25. We secured 25 men detached from infantry to truck supplies. We few remaining QM men had to issue supplies and safeguard the new dump. Back at Moresby, some 38 QM soldiers were the nucleus of a Provisional Air Supply Co. We packed parachutes and sacks for air-dropping on Dobodura. Meanwhile, small homesick detachments of 6-16 clerks and drivers labored at obscure jungle villages with exotic names: Hariko, Boreo, Buna. We supplied 162 Inf. and leapfrogged up the coast to Nassau Bay.

Such are 41 QM's highlights of the Papuan Campaign. We dumped supplies, guarded supplies and issued supplies. Like other 41st men, we endured homesickness, monotony, heat, sun and rain, hard work and fevers. But we kept the infantry fighting.

After our return to Australia, we voyaged back north into the great New Guniea Campaign of 1944. Each D-Day, our cargo-carrying LST's landed at about 0900. Besides a capacity load of personnel and vehicles, and LST carried 200 tons in bulk. To secure from twilight plane attacks, all LST's had to be at sea by 1700. The Navy spared us little time to unload.

To help 41 QM, we pressed every soldier not at the front to unload ships—any man who could lift a box or shove it down a conveyor. Since we lacked workers in the beach dumps, when the ships left, all of our supplies were badly stacked in the dump. Using partly untrained personnel, 41 QM had to stack, store and issue at the same time. We were always short of hands until their release at the end of fighting in Europe.

At Hollandia Beach, 20 minutes after 186's first wave landed, 41 QM had four men ashore to find dump sites. In this necessary recon, we were exposed to Jap MG fire. Maj. Reid was an officer thus exposed; another at Hollandia was Capt. Myhr who was early ashore on Biak also. Supervising sailors, amphib engrs, and Cn 186 and 162 Co's, we unloaded seven LST's and the attack transport "Westralia" before dark. But swamps retarded road building to clear White Beach 1. On 23 Apr., our detachment went to Pim Jetty to set up an alternate base for 186 Inf. supplies.

And shortly after dusk 23 Apr., a lone Jap bomber guided himself down on us by smouldering fires from wrecked Nippo dumps. One bomb detonated Jap ammo; the fire spread to aviation gas and other supplies. Fires raged all night of 24 Apr. QM had eight wounded in this bombing. Fragments hit Maj. Frank Moore, who spent 30 days on his stomach in the hospital.

QM men were heroic among explosions in smoke and in flame. Schweitzer dashed into smoke and saved a wounded man before the ground flamed up behind him. Sgt. Mitchell raced through exploding gas and ammo to rescue a second wounded man. Cpl. McGinitie carried another wounded man to safety, placed him on a litter, and ran back for others. Even with incendiary burns on his hands, Shell brought out a man. Although wounded himself, Maj. Gerfen helped in evacuations, dispersed troops from danger zones and helped move FA.

In the entire campaign, QM had probably ten wounded— all but one in that bombing. On 24 Apr., an unknown QM man drowned. He believed that an LST was still on beach and walked off its ramp into deep water.

During two days, over 60 per cent of Division rations and ammo were burned or blown up—the equivalent of 11 LST's of supplies. Frontline infantry went on half-rations. For three-four days, 186 Inf. lived mainly on Jap fish and rice. Continuing explosions kept us from the best landing beaches for more supplies while 11 loaded LST's waited offshore.

While flames died down, we detached 38 men to bypass the destroyed dumps. They set up a new dump across Jautefa Bay, south of Pim Village. From here, we supplied 186 Inf. at Lake Sentani and Cyclops Drome. We used "buffaloes" on Lake Sentani. Capt. Ruedy instituted and operated the emergency dumps near Sentani. His system of coordinated trucks and "buffaloes" supplied 186 Inf.

Other QM men were outstanding in the Division's emergency after the bombing. Charged with unloading rations on the beach, Sgt. Justus had to start rations from five different holds to five different beaches. He named destinations to coxswains and kept accurate records of all supplies, and relieved critical shortages. Sgt. Krejci was efficient in computing shares of rations to various outfits and in trucking rations forward. With 11 trucks to haul supplies daily over bad roads, he prevented a critical bottleneck in transportation. Capt. (later Col.) Cary had notable skill in setting up dumps in the right places.

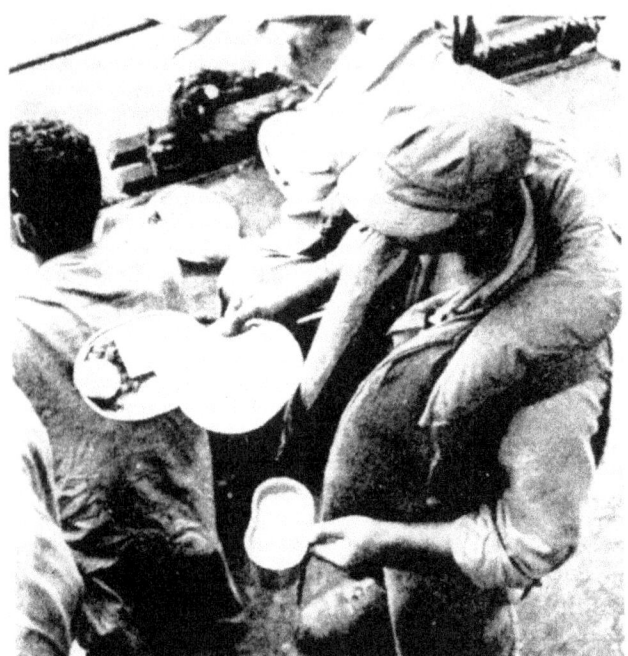
Three times a day each mess kit had to be filled with food by the QM.

We saved lives on 28 Apr. Swann, Cpl. Hogg, and two unnamed men leaped into the sea and rescued two drowning men caught in an undertow dragging them into the depths.

While most 41 QM men beached at Hollandia, a 22-man detachment landed for 163 Inf. at Aitape. Attached to Sv. 163, we distributed rations. Some of us rode an LCM to supply G 163 stationed on the main Hollandia trail at Sserroe.

After Aitape, the same QM detachment landed at Arare on the mainland near Wakde Island. With Sv. 163, we perimeted at Unnamed River west of Arare, some two miles east of Tor River front.

While guarding a captured Jap truck, two QM soldiers scouted the area selected for our night perimeter. They killed two Japs in a Jap perimeter; found on them two pistols, a saber and a stethoscope. One body disappeared that afternoon, the other next morning.

After Wakde was stormed, we moved with Sv. 163 and 741 Ordnance detachments to 163 Hq. at Toem Village. We were actually assigned posts on 163's outer perimeter. On the night of 27-28 May, we were in holes when a Jap charge of Matsuyama Force broke through 163 and charged the beach. Next day, we counted 14 dead Japs at a 163 MG post 50 yards away.

Then nine QM men were attached to Sv. 158 Inf. trying to capture Sarmi Dromes. We crossed Tor River in LCM's to make a small supply dump ¼ mile westward and forwarded supplies from here. When Japs halted 158 Inf. we rejoined our detachment.

For 41 QM, the Biak operation was more heavy labor. We serviced the whole task force and supervised many supply units.

Three hours after 186 seized Bosnek Jetties, with some fighting nearby, four QM men landed and scouted inland to previously selected dump areas. By 1100, cargoes from eight LST's and five APD's (high speed transports) began pouring across the reefs in "ducks" and "buffaloes." They brought 10 days' supplies—rations, clothing, gasoline and other necessities. As at Hollandia, we had to unload 500 five-gallon cans of water because no one knew where and if water would be quickly available on Biak.

This had to be a speedy unloading to save ships that were immobile and thus especially vulnerable to Jap raids. At 1600, four Jap planes bombed harmlessly. By 1700, we finished unloading so that all ships were departing into safer Geelvink Bay.

> *CREDIT: Col. Cary supplied core of this history, a 31-page typescript entitled "Historical Record and Events of the 41st Quartermaster Company Covering Period 16 September 1940 to 31 December 1944." Almost as important was Maj. Frank W. Moore's Article, "Mission Unexpected," from Quartermaster Training Service Journal, 7 Sept. 1945, which Cary also supplied. Other sources included R.R. Smith's Approach to the Philippines, and Medal Award stories. Awards were for Cary, Maj. Herbert E Gerfen, Sgt. Ken Mitchell, Cpl. Tom McGinitie, Maj. Clarence Reid, Sgt. Joseph Krejci, Pfc. Clemen Schweitzer, Capt. Melvin Ruey, Capt. Boyd Myhr, Pfc. Reuben Shell, Cpl. Norman Hogg, Sgt. Robert Justus, S/Sgt. Ward Furness and Sgt. Weldon Powell. Some of these men may not have been 41 QM men, but their stories connected with other known 41 QM men's stories. (Col. Cary left the 41st at Biak to study civil and military government at Leland Stagford U. and the University of Virginia, to rejoin us at Zamboanga. Retiring after 20 years' military service, he earned teacher's credentials and taught for 12 years before retirement in 1974.*

On two of the next three days, 41 QM with attached units unloaded two other large convoys. With infantry guards, our own trucks now supplied 162 and 186 forward areas—a 20-truck team for 186 alone. On the road from Parai to Mokmer, Jap mortars damaged a truck and wounded two QM men. Total QM casualties on Biak were four wounded and one missing in action.

On Biak, however, 41 QM's greatest achievement was administrational. Besides our primary job of supplying our 41st, we acted as a back-of-the-lines SOS (Service of Supply). Having the most know-how, we provided QM services for 52,000 troops, even including 5th Air Force men. Division QM is supposed to service 13,000; we serviced 52,000. Attached to us was a truck co., two regimental Sv. co's, a bakery pln, a 601 Graves Registration Pln, a gasoline supply pln and a depot supply pln.

For 120 days 41 QM handled this job, until Service of Supply finally arrived with the fighting ended on Biak and took over. When we dropped from 52,000 to 13,000 men to service as in earlier days, we did not know what to do with ourselves.

Such is the story of the 41 QM in the Papuan and New Guinea Campaigns. In the Papuan Campaign, before Sanananda and Salamaua, we were mainly homesick little detachments supplying infantry in jungle holes. In the New Guinea Campaign, we underwent a greater variety of experience. We were caught in the holocaust of the bombing at Hollandia. We shared in the nerve-wracking actions of 163 and 158 Inf., either at Toem, or even across the Tor River. Climaxing our action in New Guinea was the unloading of heavy cargoes and administering all the forces on Biak. Casualties were few. In the final reckoning: one dead, one missing and 12 wounded—if we go by offical figures. But we earned our safety by the grueling hard work of keeping 162, 163, and 186 Regimental Combat Teams in action. Without QM, you could not have lasted a day.

MEDIC AT SANANANDA

By T/5 GEORGE L. JACKSON

With Dr. Hargis Westerfield

On 4 Jan 1943, B Co 116 Medics' 2/Pln crammed into an Aussie Hudson at Port Moresby, to sneak through the Owen Stanleys into Sanananda Battle. Unarmed, heavily loaded, the Hudson flew the passes close to steep ranges above us. Often we cowered to the floor. Jap Zeroes haunting the passes could shoot us down into jungle where our bones would be lost forever. But we landed safely north of the blue ranges in dazzling kunai grass, and started the feverish trek north into the "Horsehoe" of Sanananda.

This was beyond the end of civilization. Rushton somehow learned that his wife was in critical condition before childbirth. He was frantic, but he could not return. He lived in the knowledge of her agony, and did not know for a long time that she survived. He did not see his child until she was 2 years old.

B Co hiked in sweat 2 days north to Sanananda. The first night we slept cocooned in shelter halves under downpours, the second night in native huts. No rain fell the second night, and the crawling myriads of insects did not awaken us in our fatigue. By now, drinking water had turned bad — blue with sediment and impurities and bitter with halazone. Bowel complaints began: with malaria, they would invalid all but 4 of 20 medics in 2/Pln.

On 7 Jan, we straggled up the muddy trail, bypassing Jap-guarded Sanananda Road, and into Huggins Perimeter. Huggins was a raised area of white sand above jungle swamp. It contained rings of holes, the 163 Hq, Message Center, poised mortar batteries, and a graveyard. It was actually one great crowded fox-hole. That night, we slept in a trench in the fairly safe SE section.

Then on 9 Jan, B Co 116 Medics went into action. We slogged west in mud with Mjr Rankin's 2/Bn of 163 Inf to block Killerton Trail, the Japs' last escape corridor. During a break, I found my first dead Jap when I sat down on him. I had dropped to rest beside a log. I looked right to see his boots — and to the left, his helmet. Nearby lay a complete skeleton in Aussie battle-gear. Still in helmet and boots, the skeleton reclined on a poncho.

This hike to the new Perimeter Rankin was through swamp often hip-deep in muck and water — over sunken logs and tripping wires. From Perimeter Rankin, we looked across a kunai grass clearing to another depth of jungle hiding Jap snipers in trees. Soon our counter-snipers turned them into corpses, swinging from the high perches they were tied into. Aussie observer, Capt. Peter Hirschel would use them for FA aiming points.

Beginning with G Co's wounded when Perimeter Rankin was established, Medics started litter carries. Dysentery so weakened me the first day that Harnack took my turn to slosh under a litter back to Huggins, then to the Portable Hospital back down Sanananda Road. This carry took the labor of 11 Medics.

First night in Rankin was sickly, and tense under threat of Jap raids. Dysentery was rampant among us. When 2 Yanks left fox-holes in the night, others shot them down. We played safe by digging a latrine in our hole. Next day, Aussie FA and 163's 81s back at Huggins beat the kunai southward to clear the way for the Aussie Brigade pushing toward us. One piece of wild shell fragment ripped out shelter halves over the hole, buzzed past Harnack's ear, landed spent — but still hot — on my right sleeve.

Mike Zaleski took time out from medical duties to become a 1-man army. In kunai grass before us, observers located a Jap MG. Zaleski took a tommie, and without orders, crawled behind that nest and wiped out the gunners with 45 slugs. He returned to settle down and work hard.

On 12 Jan, Aussie tanks and infantry unsuccessfully attacked the Japs' track-junction perimeters. Here I dressed my first wound, a small blue hole in a rifleman's rear. He had got his embarrasing hit when crawling away from an attack. He was not so much hurt as chagrined.

After this aborted Aussie attack of 12 Jan, Rankin's 2/Bn evidently could not break through the Jap lines to the east. Instead, we looped around north of Huggins, closer to the Bismarck Sea. Here we dug in to cut off the Japs' last perimeters. In moving, we Medics were in luck. We hopped a ride with a jeep-and-trailer — 4 Meds, 13 natives, and all equipment. In the new perimeter, we saw maggotty, fly-buzzed Japanese corpses floating in the tidal swamp. We then heard that G and E Cos had wiped out a fortified Jap hospital area. Within hours, Tokyo Rose had named us "Butchers of Sanananda."

First night in the new perimeter north of Huggins was horrible. Our holes were already water-filled to 6 inches of the top. Heavy rains fell. Thunder roared. Lightning illuminated the perimeter for sustained moments. In those protracted flashes, Japs spotted us — killed 1, wounded 2 — kept us shivering awake. Del Duca threw a grenade that hit a stump and exploded among us — harmlessly Derrick risked his life to crawl from his hole to try to save a wounded Yank.

Water ruined all my medical supplies. I had tried to use my pack for a perch in my bath-tub of a fox-hole and soaked it completely. But for some time, I had no first-aid work — just took temperatures, carried out wounded in litters.

We had only a little sleep in this chill water. With a bully beef diet, dysentery, malaria, some of us had high tempers. The second morning in this perimeter, our 3 top NCO's blew; alleged we were loafing. Cpl Haraseth took over 2/Pln. Three Sgts departed 2/Pln with quick malaria, or were reassigned; we never knew. Our CO, that fine Lt Buzzard, was called back in emergency by 7 Portable Hospital. There he did surgery for 17 solid hours.

Dysentery continued in this perimeter, where swollen Jap corpses rose and fell with the nearby Girua River. Out of perimeter with dysentery, Cudney was seen by an armed Jap. But the Jap failed to shoot. Terribly weak myself, I kept going — even did some litter carries. Two T/5's alleged I was getting favors and decided not to carry litters because their feet were infected. These two had gone barefoot — had laid themselves open to ulceration from bugs, leeches, scratches. They squared off against Haraseth. In a tense scene, he invited them to do something more, but we others were ready to ring them and hold them back if they tried to lay a finger on him.

Malaria soon took out Red Day, Dan Sullivan, and finally, Harnack. Day worked himself down to Brisbane. Harnack was done completely; malaria hit him for 2 years. His initial case must have been severe, for it was not easy to evacuate a Yank with malaria; you had to have 104 degree temperature — or stay up front.

One morning came a call to save a casualty where 163 fought those perimeters to the south. We started out 8 in line. Sgt Mohl led us — a fighter from C 163. At perimeter edge, we hit the ground one after another. Mohl wheeled right, fired his M-1 from the hip, killed a Jap rising to get a bead on him. Last in line, I fell as the Jap was groaning in death agony.

Now we met Aussies with casualties. One walking Aussie was hit in 6 places, but he was good for many more miles. We helped them into perimeter and went on to our original mission. While firing went on, we waded up a trail now 3 feet under water from the tide up the Girua River. Firing increased. When I slipped to sit hard in the Girua tide, buddies thought I was hit. Up ahead, the terrain was bare of trees and the firing heavier. We had to fall flat in the water with just our helmets showing. This we endured to save another wounded Yank, as we sloshed back with our sagging litter.

Getting around the Jap perimeter to 163 at Huggins — renamed Fisk — was always a problem. Jap raiders often cut wires and set up ambushes. Nervous young Trascyk got an emergency assignment to guide some walking wounded and fever casualties on that trail — and at 1700 hrs in the afternoon. Going was fearsome because of expected ambushes, but Trascyk came back totally sure of himself thereafter.

One morning, we followed a combat patrol that had to force its passage 10-15,000 yards. Starting down the trail, we took sniper fire. The sniper slew 1, wounded 1, and pinned half our column around a blind turn in the trail. When orders came to move up, Trascyk led off. "Ping!" went a sniper bullet. Headlong he dived through mud in a slide for safety, as 1/Sgt Richard "Pinky" Bennett never got tired of remembering. I hurdled Trascyk and ran on. Around the turn, came another sharp "Ping!" I felt a sharp stab in the ear, but believed it to be a vine. Later, I found a bullet groove across my ear.

As 163 forced the fight, I remember 5 Jap prisoners. The first was vicious — an officer graduated from U.C.L.A. who radiated hatred — ready to kill anyone he could lay hands on. Native carriers would have punched him full of holes, but Yanks bore him back for questioning — heavily guarded.

Near silent Jap AA guns and a 1940 Plymouth Sedan, bullet-riddled but in running order — we got 4 Jap prisoners. One private was weak, fearful; we all pitied him. He was grateful for a scalding can of hot tea we could not bear to touch; he drank it down and shed tears meanwhile. But he was too weak to walk, and outside the perimeter, we heard one shot. His memory remains. Another prisoner we dragged from the swamp — his hand blackened from a bullet wound and maggoty. Capt Harry Smith and another Capt Smith from 163's 2/Bn operated at once — with a well-sharpened key-hole saw-blade — all we had. I tried to talk to him, but all I heard were fearful sounds. Despite the operation, gangrene took him. Another was a Marine paymaster resembling Billy Graham. He was very happy to inform us of all Nippo troop locations. He violated no Jap order in telling us; he wasn't supposed to surrender. Telling him to say nothing if taken prisoner would have contradicted his orders not to surrender.

Resistance was broken, and we trudged a mile away to set up at Sanananda Point—falling out often with dysentery or malaria. Matuscyk now shipped out, and Haraseth with a temperature of 105. We were down from 26 to 4, and were now ordered to bring a litter for a carry from an outpost 5-6 miles up the beach. Wary of Japs, we crossed a rushing river by holding to a single rope, and walking a log under water. On the other side lay Japs killed that morning. We counted 34 Aussie graves in the soft sand at the jungle's edge. Our patient, Hildebrand, was in better condition than we with his malaria, and insisted on walking most of the way.

For 3 weeks, we camped at Sanananda Village. It consisted of some 3 shredded shacks, many coconut palms lopped off midway by shell-fire, and a gigantic bomb crater. It was on clean sand, with jungle behind and the cool Bismarck Sea in front. And the best part of our whole Sanananda Campaign was to laze dry and cool on the beach while the great tropical sun sank in the westward ocean. As our sick began to return, we started our recovery from the black, mucky inferno of Sanananda — the nights cowering in mud, the sun-bitten, staggering litter carries, the dysentery and malaria, the Jap corpses rising with the tides. B Co 116's 2/Pln men had passed a vicious test in battle, which they would proudly remember in years to come.

JAPANESE DEAD ON NEW GUINEA BEACH.   U S Army Photo 157-2

Basic source is thrilling holograph diary of George L. Jackson (A, B, C-116 Med), who now teaches art at Everett (Washington) High School. I also used references from Dr. Samuel Milner's "Victory in Papua", together with my own studies of Sanananda. Jackson re-evaluated his diaries during his 1956 vacation — began by listing names of men in his outfits, and events for which he remembered them. A graduate of the University of Washington, George is presently working on his Master of Arts degree in Education. He organized 116 Med Chapter of the 41st Inf Div Ass'n, and is it's secretary. His colorful diaries also provide a rich source of material for stories of 116 Med at Hollandia and on Biak.

CHAPLAIN AT SANANANDA

By DR. HARGIS WESTERFIELD, Division Historian
with Chaplain Joseph E. Castle

At daybreak 31 Dec. 1942, I crammed with my chaplain's pack into an Aussie Lockheed Hudson, with 13 enlisted Yanks. We were bound from Port Moresby to Sanananda aboard a battered plane, with the doors removed for quick landings and turn arounds.

Unused to air travel, we sat on the floor as the plane was airborne. Suddenly a Yank saw, through the open door, a stream of liquid flowing off the port wing. He alerted the radio operator; the plane landed at once. The gas cap was off; gasoline was flowing freely over the motor exhaust. We refuelled the tank — this time secured the cap — and flew again.

It was a clear day over the dark Owen Stanley Mountains. The plane struggled up 6,500 feet into a pass, successfully made an S-curve inside the pass, and dropped down over Kokoda, to hedge-hop to the kunai strip at Dobodura.

Without signals, the Hudson slipped in at tree-top level, landed, and was turned. Forty minutes after Moresby, we piled out, and the pilot started to the runway for the takeoff. Japs had raided Dobodura a short time ago, and Jap planes were nearby then. But Yank and Aussie wounded were waiting, and a medic Major held the plane until natives carried 2 litters aboard, and 2 walking wounded followed.

Such was this Chaplain's first meeting with the War — a year after I felt the call, while a Methodist pastor in NW Iowa. For the young men of my church and others' churches needed my help at the Front. When conditions permitted I was to set up places of worhip and hold services. But at Sanananda Battle, my work was more complicated. At the risk of my life, I must assist in holy living and holy dying — help the dying to die in Christ, and keep up the faith and morale of the living.

Besides personal equipment, I had a very portable "religious office": a pack with my Bible, a few prayerbooks and Testaments, some sacramental wine and wafers, paper and envelopes — some rosaries for Catholics. I also had with me Pvt. Lyle Brady, Chaplain's Assistant. He cooked, made camp, acted as bodyguard, helped in religious services.

From Dobodura Strip, we hiked 2 days thru kunai and jungle towards Sanananda front. Appalling sights were Yanks coming back sick or wounded — their thinness, the haunted look of their eyes. In single file, we forded Girua River — waded 200 yards hanging to a rope in often shoulder-high water. I was already fevered, with a touch of dysentery.

But I had no right to be sick. On 2 Jan. 1943, I trudged up the swampy supply trail to bypass the Japs, and into Huggins Perimeter.

Huggins was a perimeter of heroism and horror. On 30 Nov. 1942, 126 Inf's Capts Shirley and Keast had shot up this Jap bivouac area, dug in, and held it as a road-block 22 days, until relief from the Aussie 2/7 Cavalry. (Keast and Shirley were then long dead.) The Aussies then hacked out Kano Perimeter farther up the road, but with huge losses. Sanananda was a stalemate until 163 took over Huggins Perimeter — a maze of waterlogged trenches under intermittent Jap fire from jungle giant trees overhead, and a graveyard was begun the day I arrived, with reburials from previous battles.

That first night of my arrival, C's Tony Schmidt was killed. Next day, I had services for him — and four more. Four 32 Div. Yanks and an Aussie had been exhumed from resting places, and brought with C's Schmidt to start 163's first battle graveyard.

On 6 Jan, I buried T.W. Conner and Koustrup, and 7 Jan Jan Gorishek and Richter. Next day, it was Cpl Neuberger. After B and C Cos made 163's first unsuccessful attack — 8 Jan — I buried 5 on 9 January — Ashcraft and McDermeit from E Co in support, and Raley, Aubrey Jones, and McLemore. On 10 Jan, I buried Beard. But not until 11 Jan could I perform services for C's 1/Lt. Fiske, whose body was finally recovered from the attack of 8 Jan.

During these burials, snipers' bullets some times narrowly missed me. Burials were out in the open, although we had outguards. Strangely enough, I was never fired upon when making a burial, but I usually was shot at when returning.

Burials were not all my duties, of course. Giving spiritual aid and keeping up morale were also my duties. When casualties were brought to medics, I talked to everyone to satisfy what request I could, and also give religious or other aid.

I remember Yank wounded brought to the aid station — men with gaping wounds were treated, with never a sound of complaint. I remember wounded who smiled and took cigarettes, and thanked me for a little hot tea, and asked only about a wounded buddy.

I saw another type also — a man in a B Co attack who had frozen under fire a short way from the line of departure. He screamed that he was going to die. Finally another Yank roped him and dragged him to safety. A litter squad brought him to us; a medic held him from rolling off. In agony, he kept throwing out one leg. Medics cut his pants off and found only a little jungle sore. Stripping him, we found only a small scratch on his neck. This real or shammed case of conversion hysteria we bore out — and treated serious wounds of 2 other Yanks who endured their treatment like men.

Gen. Fuller visited the aid station, and sat on the edge of a slit trench with me, to ask about the mens' morale. The usual Nip fire began; Yanks shot back, even if jungle targets were hard to see. Leaves dropped as Jap bullets whined off trunks overhead. Fuller wondered why someone didn't stop those Nips. I assured him we were stopping a few more each day, but that some Japs were persistent.

As Fuller entered the med station, new wounded were brought in. It often happened that too many Yanks gathered then — drew fire. Sgt Pete Johnson howled, "All you men that got no business here — get the hell out!" Fuller was minus insignia, and he got out with the others. Just then, our fire had silenced the Japs, and Fuller left us. I never did find out just how the general reacted to the sgt's "Get out!"

Being sniped at when returning from burials was only one of my experiences. MG bursts missed me by mere inches. A grenade or mortar splashed me thoroughly, and bit skin from my left side. The Japs shot up my shelter.

Existing in a slit trench was an agony of its own, with or without Jap fire. Rations were meager, and drinking water was almost unendurable, although plentiful. On that old battlefield, many men had to keep low in their holes — a latrine in one end, a well in the other. We chlorinated canteens with 4 times the usual amount of tablets; they still often stank of rotting flesh.

Besides sporadic Jap attacks, we could almost set watches with Jap fire each forenoon and afternoon. After intense duels of rifles, MGs, the Japs were quieted by a few mortar rounds or Aussie 25-pounders. That FA certainly did quiet Japs! On nights of battering rain, lack of FA fire would make us nervous. Noises were then frightening — rifles, grenades, or just jungle noises. Then Aussie shells would impact, and I lay back in mud and water, sighed "All is well!" and slept again.

We had just begun to learn trench warfare. After Japs stirred about and talked considerably one night, we set up booby traps — often 2 grenades tied to adjoining trees, the loosened pins connected with a cord.

Incidents of that day made us fear a night charge by the Japs. At midnight they moved toward us, loudly chattering. A booby-trap grenade detonated. Japs ran back, but talked again. Then with less talk, they moved at us from the flank. Another booby-trap burst, and someone was then surely hurt, carried out; the brush rustled. A third time, they came from a new direction, with greater caution. When the third trap blew up, out men saturated them with grenades. At dawn, we found blood and other signs that more dead or wounded Nips were borne off.

On 13 Jan, the inevitable fever knocked me out. I left Huggins in a stretcher carried by natives — 2 alternate teams of 4 and a leader. Although no longer weighing 185, I was still heavy. They took me on logs over streams, and waist-deep through swamps. When a native slipped and nearly fell, the chatter told me that he had committed a major offense. (They were not so careful with a Jap wounded man.) To my surprise, I was flown down to Port Moresby, but after a night between white sheets, I bounced up, restored by good food, sleep, and cleanliness. The white nurse thought I was crazy to go back. Off my plane at Popondetta on 15 Jan — 3 days after leaving, I got as far as the portable hospital, and another burial serivce. That night I slept in Kano Perimeter — renamed Fisk — in a filthy jungle also called "the Pigpen."

After attacks of 16-17 Jan, Jap resistance ended south of Fisk. North of Fisk, 2/Bn and 1/Bn assailed the Jap rear. Besides burying C's Cpl Morin at Soputa No. 2, I buried 5 more: Talbert, Belchak, Rowland, Harden, Nauman — at Fisk. These were on 17 Jan. On 21 Jan, I buried S/Sgt Henry Johnson, Don Smith, C Co's Cpl Freitas, T/4 Clair Rice. On 22 Jan back at Huggins, it was H's Sgt Goldsmith with C's Bunker; and Leo Johnson, Cpl Otto May, Hapke. On 23 Jan back at Huggins, were buried Livermore, Wojteck, Pease, Barnett, 2/Lt John Olson, Merton Henderson, Strobach, Oscar Wells, Staub, Sgt Ellis Olson, Cpl Lingle. Don Hughes was buried Feb 24. All these were identified, but 4 bodies were never found: F Co's McMeel, Cpl Hugh Holmes, M's Cpl Marvin Berg, Frank Rogers. For them, we had memorial services 7 Mar 43.

Each man we buried in rites of his faith; I read full services for a Jewish man. Later a Catholic Chaplain read services for his men. I had buried 43 163 men, 23 32 Div men 2 Aussies — and 2 Aussie missionary women killed by Japs.

On 22 Jan came my narrowest escape from death — the day after the campaign "closed." While 1/Bn's S-2 Lt Fitzgerald went to check on Jap equipment, I went with him and 3 men. I was seeking Yanks for burial. While we searched hq records, 4 Japs slipped up on us — or blundered in — and died. After wading 2 creeks neckdeep to the Jap Motor Pool, we heard firing. Almost too late, we were behind a Jap LMG patrol shooting at our pltn guarding the motor pool. In seconds, our pltn shot down 12 Japs — and fired on us. Finally, a Sgt heard me or saw me and ceased fire. Perhaps this scare helped kill Fitzgerald, who died days later of fevers that seemed mild to the doctors.

Such was the life of an Army Chaplain on Sanananda Front — helping Yank morale, counselling wounded, finding and burying the dead — cowering in muddy holes to survive. As the campaign closed, I had 9 days' malaria — some of which days I do not remember. My weight dropped from 185 to 155. But I was among the Men of Sanananda who had survived. And I had done the Lord's Work among the Men of Sanananda to the best of my ability.

Sources are Chaplain (and First Lieutenant) Joseph Castle's "Chaplain's Activities on the Sanananda Road" (Jan 1 — Feb 28, 1943), an appended roster of burials with dates, and some replies to my queries. Presently Chaplain of the 41st Assn, he recently moved from Gorie, Iowa, to be pastor of Trinity Methodist Church at Ritzville, Washington.

41st Special Services:

Jungle Show Biz

by DR. HARGIS WESTERFIELD, DIVISION HISTORIAN
and SGT. MERLE EDMUNDS

At the 1971 Gearhart Reunion, Merle exhibited his fine scrapbooks, but your historian confesses he was too "thick" to catch on to this fine story for the Jungleer. Sources include program of "Meet the Soldier," and Edmunds' MS, "Rockhampton," "Traveling with Joe E. Brown," "New Guinea Scandals," and "The All in Fun Revue." Edmunds also helped with letters dated Feb. 1, 6, 25; March 4, 14, 19, and 31. Historical background is from Japanese Operations in the Southwest Pacific Area, Vol. II, Part I. After the war, Merle played in a trio in Chicago's Hotel Sherman's Celtic Room, among other places. He formed his own band in Bloomington, Illinois, played in Illinois and in San Antonio. Since 1953 he has been writing insurance for American Family Insurance in Bloomington, Ill.

The "Show Business" of our 41 Special Services was important in making our Division great. Morale before and after combat was important. A rookie before his first fight, and a veteran after action - both had the same problem. We worried too much about battle. Nothing could help us more than hearing a bright concert under lights—or laughing hard at a comic skit. This is the tale of Sgt. Merle Edmunds and cobbers of 41 Special Services—the tale of how they made "Show Biz."

A few days after the brand-new Queen Elizabeth left San Francisco on 19 Mar. 1942, young Pvt. Edmunds of H Co. 163 met Charles Kenney and his buddies. Kenney had his fiddle which Edmunds also played. And guitarists Eddie Biehl and Tom Van Wagoner with accordion man Larry King gathered around them. Biehl and King were vocalists also.

Meeting Maj. Butterworth, Edmunds made the most important decision of his Army career. Having organized shows during his college years at Illinois State U., Edmunds asked for Butterworth's help. And down in those crowded compartments of 10,000 Yanks going to battle, a call went forth for more musicians and other entertainers. More band instruments came up from deep in the hold.

Edmunds' first Army show, "Don't Get Overboard," was memorable. It was in the spacious officers' mess, which probably became Queen Elizabeth's ballroom for first-class passengers after the war. A 163 Inf. chorus vocalized. Other 163 participants included Dick Davis, Pete Jenson, and Phil Reitan. Little Aussie Max Braybrook played his harmonica.

We did well that first night—so well that we repeated the show three times on the afterdeck. We played without lights because of blackout rules, but on that moonlight deck, it was like day. As Queen Elizabeth drove down west over the world's edge, farther from home, men who might never come back forgot the jungle in their future. They laughed and cheered and went back to their holds where they still sang.

And so, after Queen Elizabeth docked at Sydney on 6 April, Edmunds transferred from H 163 to 41 Special Services in Div. Hq. Later he became a Sgt. in charge of Division entertainment. His group comprised some seven men. Cpl. Wegner was assistant, with Cpls. Moeyer and Lynam directing athletics, and Cpl. Filo as electrical technician. Maj. Bishop and Capt. Walker were officers in charge.

At Rockhampton, Edmunds' first show was for the Red Cross, with W/O Bix Huffman's Div. Arty. Band. Players included 1/Sgt. Bill Faulkenstein, George Doris, Boggie Geirhart, Arnold Orman, Kryl Thorlakson. Presented at the Rocky School of Arts theater, the show succeeded all too well—700 had to turn away because of lack of seats.

Then Edmunds had another brilliant idea. Why not produce a great musicale with Yank and Aussie talent—and with Aussie girls? It would enhance both Aussie civilian and Yank morale. Edmunds' CO, Maj.

"Rocky" girls entertain the 41sters in Merle Edmunds' production in Australia. The male is Chester Dorn. A stray dog, front left, is enjoying the "La Conga" number.

Glen Bishop, got Gen. Fuller's approval. So began Edmunds' production of "Meet the Soldier."

Huffman's Div. Arty. Band was ready; so were other fine 41st players and singers. Miss Leishman of Rocky and Cpl. Wegner designed costumes and stage sets. From 162's Special Services, Fred Devenney took over rehearsals for comic skits. (Devenney had played bit parts for our "Our Gang" comedies in Hollywood.) The wife of a Rocky MD, Mrs. Voss brought in some Aussie girls; others came from Miss Mona Kinsman's ballet school.

Most unforgettable girl was vocalist Peggy Yewdale, a languishing, long-lashed brunette: weight 129 pounds, height five feet seven inches. She had one of the finest feminine voices in the show.

Presented at Rocky's Wintergarden Theater, "Meet the Soldier" was a huge success and played three weekends. It was a 2½-hour musical with two acts of 23 scenes. It was rich with deep male Yank voices, light with the songs of Aussie girls. It flashed with naked Aussie thighs and throbbed with the FA Band.

Opening was the band's celebration of "Rockhampton Rock," written by our Sgt. Eddie Hornberger. Then came "Jersey Bounce." Edmunds and Wegner had included all forms of Yank pop music for cheering Aussies. There was a Gay Nineties Revue, clusters of Hawaiian songs, plantation songs, and Western songs. A full-blooded Sioux, Roland Pusich, stopped the show in the Western theme. He sang "Tumbling Tumbleweed," and "Home on the Range." Devenney was great as an uneducated Southern black preacher lecturing his congregation on sex. After the lecture came "Evening Hymn," written by Eddie Dimond himself.

The girls were everywhere in the vocal parts and had their own ballet number. For sweet memories of vets of the Rocky Beachhead, we name them all here. Besides Peggy Yewdale, there were Mona Kinsman, Joan Mith, Kay Olive, Dola O'Hanlon, June Brady, Phyllis Wilson. There also were Marjorie Shaw, Joy Monroe, June Courtis, Seamie Lindon, Delroy Young. And Lorna Belz, Pam Rudder, Beryl Saunders, Daphne Glore, Mary Schmidt, Daphne Ireland, Amelia Belz, Alison Hansen. (Some reader remembers as he reads!)

And "Meet the Solider" was Edmunds' great hit. From MacArthur's Hq. Col. Cowan phoned. He wanted us to take the show on tour all over the Pacific Islands. But after Sanananda was won, the Division needed us in New Guinea to help the morale. We disbanded "Meet the Soldier;" March found us deep in New Guinea's green hell.

At Dobodura, Edmunds learned that comedian Joe E. Brown was coming to tour the forward areas. As ordered, Edmunds hastily got up 186's band and two acts to work with Joe. On 4 April, Edmunds took his convoy with Joe to Oro Bay—a convoy of seven jeeps on a jungle road.

Oro Bay was 18 miles up the Guinea shore over a corduroy road of logs laid side by side in the mud. Because of displaced logs, it was 18 miles of jogging up and down—a long mess of logs and mud and water. Driving the lead jeep, Edmunds worried over a broken spine. Joe said we'd travel better off the road. We drove 3½ hours to make 18 miles.

Entering Oro Bay, we had trouble that would recur later and cause Edmunds lasting harm. A guard halted us; we had forgotten the countersign. Joe dismounted, walked up to the guard, and gave a silly grin. He said, "I'm Joe E. Brown." The guard passed us.

At Oro Bay, Brown gave a marvelous show, of course. And 186's 5-piece band jazzed up Oro Bay: King's accordion, Biehl's guitar, Kendrick's trumpet, Edmunds' jazz fiddle, with Jim Wells as vocalist. Fendall's mouth organ got a bigger hand than Joe Brown himself.

In two days, we did four shows for lonely, homesick Yanks. Once we splashed nine miles deep into the mountains. So steep and slippery was the final hill that a big "cat" had to lift all seven jeeps over it. Returning to Dobodura, we got stuck twice on the road. For four days then, we had three shows daily—hard work to please Joe and the Yanks that needed us.

After Brown, the job was dull with limited equipment, but bands played daily, and we had a few movies. When more instruments arrived, we planned a new show—"The New Guinea Scandals of 1943." For six days Edmunds and Wegner toured camps for volunteers and effected releases from company details.

When the first show opened at Dobodura, homesick Yanks sat with their eyes popped out—the performers wore civilian clothes! (Back in Rocky, Edmunds had the foresight to pack a chest of clothes we all yearned to return to.)

A small section of 163's band played for "New Guinea Scandals." The show had music, gags (jokes) and short "blackouts"—brief little plays. Dick Davis, who had worked under Orson Welles, did the script for the "blackouts". King, Biehl and Edmunds jived with accordion, guitar and fiddle. One highlight was a male ballet—six men, called the "Dobodura Adorables," in native grass skirts and huge coconut bark headdresses. Hayden Bolander had tears in men's eyes when he sang "White Christmas."

Besides "White Christmas," the other big hit of the brave, homesick war days was "You'll Never Know." And we remember "Give Me One Dozen Roses," "Paper Doll," "White Cliffs of Dover," "Miss You," "Praise the Lord and Pass the Ammunition."

After Dobodura, the "Scandals" hit all the GI towns—Popondetta, Hiranda, Simemi, Soputa. We had one audience of 4,000. Then we took that damned road to Oro Bay again.

This second trip of 18 miles was worse than the one with Joe E. Brown. In some spots logs had sunk under mud. In places, we unloaded the jeeps to relieve the drivers of the weight. Sometimes we got stuck and heaved the jeeps out by our own muscles. Mud fouled us, yet in dry places mud caked on our sweat.

But the trip, partly over high mountains, was scenic. Edmunds saw coconut groves hundreds of feet below, and a winding river with the deep, dark jungles on either side. All along the road hundreds of natives hacked down trees to widen the way. This time, the three-jeep convoy took 4½ hours to make 18 miles. On the first night we arrived too tired to play. Yet on return to Dobodura a week later, 31 SS got a Letter of Commendation from Oro Bay's CO, Col. "Snuffy" Smith himself—that picayune disciplinarian who terrorized his casuals and replacements.

Then 41 SS hosted another great show—the veteran Aussie "All in Fun Revue." It was homing from stellar performances in North Africa. Now we had transportation problems—to conduct on jungle tours a cast of 35, plus band, curtains and stage sets.

A third time we followed that same theatrical circuit of Joe E. Brown and our "New Guinea Scandals." Once again, Edmunds led over slushy corduroy 18 miles to Oro Bay. We got stuck in mud two miles out. After unloading and helping pull out the jeeps, the Aussie actors were mud-covered, head to foot.

But these old troupers of 500 performances from Cairo to Tobruk were real soldiers too. At Tobruk when the Germans recaptured it, they

The Division Band poses for a group picture on Biak in 1945.

had to take arms and fight. In the battle, their band lost four members. After the hard corduroy road trip, they forgot it all in a swim in Oro Bay's beautiful lagoon.

On 11 April, we got deep into war; Admiral Yamamoto loosed one of his heaviest raids on Oro Bay. That afternoon, following a morning show at First Evac. Hospital, Edmunds drove the lead jeep high into mountains on a new road to put on a show for 116 Engrs.

Suddenly, a captain leaped out from a jeep to warn us off the road. Obeying, Edmunds halted and warned the convoy to take cover. The sky was still clear.

Five minutes later, the sky was filled with screeching Nippo bombers and Jap and Yank fighters slashing each other with streams of red tracers. A fleet of 72 Jap fighters and 22 carrier bombers swooped down on Oro Bay's shipping. Edmunds saw two P-38's shoot down a Zero and cheered as the Zero flamed and fell.

A Jap formation of 16 bombers and seven fighters laid direct hits on two transports from a convoy that had anchored a half hour before the raid. A Zero flamed down from AA fire; then a P-40 shot down a Zero. When AA fragments thudded close, Edmunds took cover.

Of Yamamoto's 94 planes, only 32 got through defenses in an hour's battle. But the two transports were sinking. Three bombs fell on the transport Chinese Tiger; it sank a foot an hour.

The 116 Engr. show was called off. Returned to Oro Bay, we volunteered to man barges, land supplies and casualties. Before the two ships sank, all troops were saved and most of the supplies.

After four Oro Bay performances, "All in Fun Revue" was back to Dobodura. As with Joe E. Brown, Edmunds supervised three daily shows. Over the jungle circuit he conducted all 35 actors, band, and stage sets. He never forgot those fine soldier-actors. These veterans went where ordered, gladly ate what food we had, slept anywhere. Despire heavy fatigue, they kept the show going on.

Having served two years overseas, the Aussie showmen flew home on furlough, and suddenly Edmunds' days on jungle circuit came to an end. Capt. Walker innocently caused the change. Walker was an enlisted man's officer, well-liked, but he made what to his superiors was a major error.

While conducting a show on tour, Walker forgot a password. Without the password, the guards at one camp could not tell a "cry" of actors from a Nippo raiding party.

Walker was transferred to a line outfit. Edmunds got sick; the next thing he knew, he was sent to G-163. The Band protested, but Chief of Staff Col. Sweany upheld that transfer—blamed also Edmunds about forgetting the password. And 163's battle-thinned line outfits did need replacements.

But Edmunds was not long in G-163. Returning to Dobodura for supplies, Edmunds and some of G's men came to a river crossing. These veterans were too wise to ford without scouting for Nips on the other bank. Edmunds and another man climbed a tree.

When a limb broke, Edmunds fractured his shoulder and collarbone. Flown to Townsville, he had malaria during the operation—and 12 recurrences later. Unfit for New Guinea, he was in Special Services in Australia until rotation in 1944. Edmunds now has a steel plate in his shoulder, and a disability pension for it. Thus ended Edmunds' war.

But, as veterans, you and I will never forget shows like Edmunds' in 41st Special Services. As an unfought recruit, you shuddered in fear as you looked from New Guinea out into the night and the ghostly black rollers of the Bismarck Sea. You were as afraid of the Japs as they were afraid of you. Then was the best time on earth to head for a 41 SS show and laugh and forget New Guinea. Or you were a hospital patient after combat with typhus or malaria or battle wounds—and almost mentally ill from the world of mud and corpses. And here were Aussie or Yank vaudeville performers to lift you up with humor and melody. Such was the wonderful work of Sgt. Edmunds and 41 Special Services, creators of "Show Biz in the Jungle."

Merle Edmunds: then (1943), left, and now (1970's), right.

D Co. 186 Infantry:
Campaign in Papua

by LEROY (NICK) WHEELER
and DR. HARGIS WESTERFIELD, Division Historian

On 14 Jan. 1943, battle-trained D Co., 186 Inf. boarded a Liberty ship at Gladstone, bound for Port Moresby. (The Battle of Sanananda would continue into 21 Jan.) Crowded into Hold 3, D men spread strips of plywood with comforters on the steel deck—used packs for pillows and backrests.

This steel "mattress" was hard to sleep on, but we could still expect fresh rations. For when he learned that 2/Bn. had only C rations for travel, Col. Anderson turned over his account in Rockhampton Bank to Bn. Supply Officer Rohan and sent him ashore. Rohan's detail found a slaughterhouse and bought the entire stock. The Liberty ship had refrigerators ready. Rohan also brought aboard 850 pounds of bread from two private bakeries. At Townsville, the second day out, Anderson radioed for a boat so that Rohan could requisition a day's issue of fresh bread from an Army bakery.

Bn. mess sergeants set up field kitchens above D Co's hold just forward of the bridge, and we had a cool mess area topside, with good food, thanks to Anderson.

Without escort, we left the Inside Passage of the Great Barrier Reef above Townsville and, covered by night, headed into the Coral Sea. On this smooth green "lake," we did not think of Jap planes or subs. At the bow, we watched flying fish, or turned to books or card games.

This voyage to New Guinea was a pleasant, routine trip, with no Jap attacks. At Port Moresby, D Co. landed and bivouacked the first night near the dock, just on the crest of a small coconut-covered hill. In this bucolic grove, we lashed up hammocks for the night.

Before dark, we noticed an Aussie 90mm AA battery nearby, and looked at piles of supplies and ammo stacked for miles. Night came. After observing total blackouts on the voyage, we were amazed at the lights making Moresby bright as day. Ships were unloading day and night, yet Moresby was then the most bombed city in the world.

But soon air alerts sounded and the lights went out; searchlights crossed the sky. At 30,000 feet, Jap Betties in formation struck for the docks. The Aussie 90's cut loose. Nobody had

---

Prime source is Leroy ("Nick") Wheeler's 38-page MS on D 186, "The Papuan Campaign." Nick is at work on a monumental history of D 186. He gives "information credit" to Gerald LaHaie and Arthur Anderson. For background, Westerfield used brief notes from Samuel Milner's Papuan Campaign and Gen. MacArthur's Report of Japanese Opns in SWPA. (While on his supposed deathbed from typhus after his Kumusi patrols, Nick got orders to leave D 186 for OCS.)

to tell D Co. what to do. One group from D crouched for shelter—in a pile of live bombs! Two men dived into a pit of hot coals. Most of us just froze in fright.

After the bomb run, lights went on; ships kept unloading. Next morning D Co. laughed, but Moresby continued getting night raids for months.

On 21 Jan.—final day of 163's Battle of Sanananda—D's NCO's saw remants of 2/Bn., 126 Inf. with perhaps some Cn and AT elements. These 32 Div. men had obeyed the stupid order to hike directly across New Guinea to the Bismarck Sea. A beaten, decimated, malarious outfit, they warned us that we'd soon be like them. But D Co. was lucky enough to rate the air lift over the Owen Stanley Mountains. And after three days' wait at the Moresby staging area, we thought we were used to Jap raids and tremors of explosions.

On 21 Jan. before dawn, D Co. queasily lined up to load on C-47's of the 347 Troop Carrier Wing. This was at 5-Mile Drome, largest of many Moresby strips. As our C-47's warmed up, a flight of B-17's flew down from a bomb mission. The strip was fully lighted, and the B-17's came down with landing lights on.

Suddenly, explosions blasted across our end of the strip. The C-47 intended for D's Hq. Pln. flamed and blew apart. A daring Jap bomber had got into the landing pattern of the B-17 and unloaded his bombs on us. He escaped, too late for AA fire that broke out from the end of the strip.

Although our corner of the strip flamed and exploded, no D man was even scratched. And D's discipline was so fine that we did not panic into the dark.

Then D Co. loaded swiftly into nine C-47's, with shivering Hq. Pln. reassigned to a plane that had not blown up. As the planes taxied for the takeoff, crew chiefs briefed our NCO's. We had no convoying fighter planes. If forced down, we must keep together until somebody found us. For protection, we stationed a D BAR man at each window to fire through a rubber-circled hole in the glass.

Now airborne into the towering Owen Stanleys, we endured the agony of air pressure on throat glands. We thought our ear drums would burst. Many men bunched up on the floor. But some of us admired the smooth mountains covered by a solid mat of jungle.

In 30 minutes we landed on the sheared kunai of Dobadura Strip—with Hq. Pln. first off the plane. As we left, a two-star general boarded and wished us "best of luck." Supply Sgt. Pozzoli called him a dirty name which the general did not hear; we did not know then that this was Gen. Eichelberger.

Fearing Nip snipers who sometimes shot at planes, we cleared the strip. Our C-47's were gone, and 186's Col. Murray gave orders from his jeep. He did not make it clear why we were rushed forward. Then D began ten horrible miles of tropical hiking to the front, after an early rest and a swim near Simemi that day.

Next day, jungle closed in on D. The road vanished. On a muddy track, often knee-deep, we shuffled under heavy weapons, with a unit of fire, packs and jungle hammocks. Despite warning, some of us threw away equipment for which Col. Murray would charge us. In a temperature of 110 degrees, with 80-100 pound packs, D Co. waddled through a final four miles of muck. Although wringing wet, we could not drop our loads into mud at a break. Capt. Arey called off all halts.

Some ten miles NE, D staggered to the beach to relieve the remnants of 128 Inf. after the Buna-Gona operations. This was Maggott Beach by Cape Endaiadare which 128 had helped

"On a muddy track, often knee deep, we shuffled under heavy weapons..."

capture—with Aussie tanks and infantry. In a stench of death, they held the beach in two to four-man positions. We never forgot the tired look of their eyes. Most were sick and running a fever. They gladly left us their heavy weapons to stiffen our defenses, and then departed.

Japs were buried with feet sticking out. Many dead Yanks and Aussies lay where they fell; we could picture the whole story of many a fight. Three Yank corpses rose and fell in the shallow surf near the beach. But we knew why the surviving fighters of 128 Inf. left them for D Co. to bury.

D Co. saw why we were rushed forward three days before our riflemen. Japs still held ground a few miles north of Gona. Jap stragglers roamed the area, and D Co. patrols had to hunt them down until 2/Bn. riflemen took over the hunt. After a while, we could no longer hear M-1 fire where they killed Japs who would not surrender.

During the second week of February, D heavily fortified an area south of the cape under mangroves, between the beach and a coconut grove. We expected a Jap counterattack; the night raids already had scared us from our hammocks.

So we built log bunkers for HMG's—two guns per squad—which we placed to cover every inch of the beach. We stiffened the line with AT 37's from Hq. Co. and placed riflemen to guard the weapons. With fifteen 81 mortars in two batteries, we could arc 76 shells in the air at once. D Co. thought we could beat a division.

Alerted 1 March by an Aussie coastwatcher in New Britain, D expected to fight a heavy landing force. On 2 March, 5th Air Force dispatched every available plane out to sea—some on two-three missions. We saw them straggle home, some aflame, some on one motor. Some also crashed into the jungle.

Then came wondrous news of a "wholly Air Force" victory in the battle of the Bismarck Sea. Four destroyers and all eight transports were sunk. Of 6,900 men of the Nip 51 Div., only 800 reached Lae. (Later we found that the annihilated convoy was not bound against 186 but was destined to defend Lae-Salamaua against 162.)

Despite the Bismarck Sea battle, Jap aces often defeated Yank airmen in the skies over D Co. Based at Lae just 110 miles north, these aces had the new Zero—built to turn easier and climb faster.

Capt. Masahisa Saito flew aces like Mishizawa, "The Devil," who killed 100 allied planes, and Ota and Sakai, who together downed 60 of ours. Handa and Okabe shot down seven Yank planes in one day—a theater record. Sugita, Sueyoshi, and Sasai seemed more like birds than men.

Over Buna, nine Japs caught five B-17's with four P-39's covering. The Japs shot down all nine. Once Sakai with wingman Ota downed four P-39's in five seconds of action. With "Devil" Mishizawa, these two hit four flights of P-40's and killed seven planes before the rest turned tail. These three triple-looped a fighter strip at low level twice in one day. Our gunners could not get off a shot at them.

Against these veterans of China, our green fliers suffered initial defeats. D Co's area was a maze of wrecked planes. We buried nine Yank fliers in the new cemetery. Air Force called for volunteers from 186—experienced .50 HMG gunners. And 186 lost 19 killed on a detail at Dobodura Strip.

But our fliers learned. We had reserves of planes and trained men to replace them. And our Mitchells and Marauders struck Lae Strip and drove Saito's Lae Wing back to Rabaul.

Although D did not fight in Papua, we had casualties or near-casualties, direct and indirect. Bleeding dysentery, malaria, scrub typhus—all took toll. And monotony got men into trouble. When 1/Lt. Jarrett killed a supposedly wild boar, we placed Jarrett under guard from the native owner until ANGAU arranged a settlement. A 20-foot shark chased Sgt. Strebig, who practically flew over water ten feet deep to escape.

Monotony was the basic cause of more serious suffering experienced by D men. When S/Sgt. Wheeler volunteered for L 186's Kumusi patrol, he caught typhus. Although he learned that 11 had died of it already, the first experiment with sulfa was to save him. Experimenting with salvaged aviation gas, McGough was burned so badly that he lay near death for a long time. And Bob Cooper died from the explosion of a Jap knee-mortar shell he was disassembling.

And D lost five good men by transfer to other outfits. Cliff James walked down from Sanananda Point to report deaths of Limbocker and Potter in B 163. Another source reported deaths of three D men sent to 161 Inf. of 25 Div. before we shipped overseas. Thorpe, Fry, Joe Wallace were KIA on Guadalcanal; some of D's older NCO's took the news hard.

Such was the tale of D 186 in the Papuan campaign. After the close call of the flight over the Owen Stanleys, we relieved battered 128 Inf. men on corpse-strewn Maggot Beach. After that, we had six months of jungle garrison under Jap planes and endured the agony and monotony of savage New Guinea. Now D Co. looked forward to getting paid—to a furlough and drinks and women and civilization.

Service Co., 186 Infantry:
Natives-Our Papuan Angels

By Captain Herbert C. Johnson
with Dr. Hargis Westerfield, Division Historian

Major credit is due to Herb Johnson's unpublished MS, 18 pages single-spaced, entitled "Our Papuan Angels." For background, I used a few brief comments on Hariko by Dudley McCarthy in his *South-West Pacific Area/First Year*, and the "Buna East Special" map of the Lt Sconce Survey.

This is the tale of 186 Inf's "Papuan Angels" — natives who fought heavy surfs off Hariko Village to land precious and cumbersome equipment for Dobodura Strip. We first met those wonderful guys in 1943 shortly after Sanananda. Capt Herb Johnson, Sv Co's CO, got orders to hike with 20 men from Oro Bay just 10 miles NW up the Guinea Shore and develop a supply dump at Hariko Village.

"Just 10 miles from Oro Bay to Hariko" turned out to be 18 miles over soft sand and across 5 rivers, usually in a bath of sweat. Inexperienced in jungle hikes, we carried 60 pounds of new stateside "jungle" equipment that we feared to throw away. At one river, an Aussie ferried us in a clumsy skiff, but we waded the other 4 rivers — always in a few feet up to our knees and sometimes shoulder deep.

By the third day as Sv detachment neared Hariko, we were a staggering, disordered mob men kept dropping out from. Thank God that after Sanananda the Japs had been cleared out of the 4-mile area between Hariko and 186 Inf Hq at Simemi. Slanted forward because of the heavy pack and reeling from the heat, Johnson found a Yank officer in charge at Hariko and asked him to send out a few natives to help our stragglers.

At once a dozen natives dashed off down the trail and became our first "Papuan Angels." First, they trotted back 10 miles to rescue one of Sv Co's Sgts who had dropped out with malaria the first night.

The Papuan Angels found our feverish Sgt and in minutes chopped from the jungle a litter of poles and vines and trotted gently back towards Hariko with him. Every time they passed a straggling Sv man on return, a native picked off his pack and shouldered it and trotted along with the litter. Even without packs, our unacclimated Yanks could not keep up with these trotting litter men. Sv's 18 miles to Hariko took 3 days; the Angels' round trip took 5 hours. And they came into Hariko under that litter as if they could trot 10 miles. The feverish Sgt said it was his easiest ride of a lifetime, at a trot over the sand.

Now trail-weary Johnson thought he was the butt of a vicious Army joke. The Yank Col already commanding at Hariko said that he had orders to flee with his 6 officers and 185 men at dawn tomorrow. And here was Johnson with just 18 effectives to replace 191. The Col added that several cargoes of supplies would be offshore for unloading that very night — and no port machinery of any kind to swing them in.

But the Col also said that the Aussie Native Overseer would have the natives unload the crafts. To find that Overseer, the Col said, Johnson needed only to go down to the native village and ask for that Aussie with these magic words in pidgin English, "Master belong you?"

After asking only 5 natives, Johnson found Scotty Dausett, a grey-bearded, grey-eyed Aussie in khaki shorts with his side-swiped Aussie hat over one eye. Scotty gladly began briefing Johnson on this crazy new assignment — unloading clumsy Army gear through heavy surf with natives speaking semi-foreign English. Well-educated, Scotty was a mine of information about the native workers. He started teaching Johnson pidgin English. Amazed Johnson learned that he had 700 natives to command — under a Boss Boy who was once king of a tribe. This tall, twinkling-eyed Aussie was so interesting that Johnson forgot his command worries.

Before Johnson realized it, night had fallen, and they sauntered down to the black ocean to start unloading. A gang of two "boongs" (100 men in white GI shorts) were there already. From the mysterious blackness came a blinker signal. Safe in the dark from Nippo planes, a barge was waiting 400 yards offshore, to be dragged in from the coastal motorized lugger that had towed it north from Oro Bay.

While Scotty and the Yanks watched, natives launched an Aussie skiff — a clumsy, flat-bottomed thing 30 feet long with 3 sets of oarlocks. A native in the stern grasped the end of a 2-inch rope coiled on the beach, and the skiff rowed out into the black.

Half an hour later from far off in the ocean, we heard native calls that ended with what sounded like "Tight im rdrdrope!" This meant that they had secured the tow-rope to the barge.

Silently the natives on the beach lined up face to face on this rope. None of them seemed to pull, but the rope to the heavy barge out on the waves was going through their hands at least 2 miles per hour. As the rope came in, they laughed and talked like kids.

Finally the dark wooden barge loomed from the blackness — 50 x 80 feet, and accurately packed to cram all available space. With one of the weirdest and most beautiful chants Johnson ever heard, they warped the barge inshore. Then one group jumped onto the barge. The other group waded into the sea, and the men above loaded the supplies on their shoulders to carry to the beach. They bore the supplies 100 yards back into the jungle for concealment from Jap planes. Usually they ran with the shoulder loads. Johnson once saw a native win a contest with others when he trotted ashore with 500 pounds on his shoulders.

And when George got what sleep he could late that night, he slept better because of those native workers—those "Papuan Angels." During many nights afterwards, he marvelled at their hard work and high morale.

Sometimes our Aussie luggers came laden with gas drums. The drums were too heavy to manhandle into skiffs, but the contents had such a low specific gravity that the drums would float. Some 400 yards offshore, the lugger crew and the natives rolled them overside. Then the drums bobbed apart until they seemed to cover the ocean.

These were shark waters, but our natives swam out for the drums. Each man got behind a drum and started slowly kicking to shore. Barrels bobbed over the ocean, and behind each of these barrels bobbed a black native head until every drum grounded in the shallows and was pulled in.

One of the natives' toughest jobs was to use skiffs to lighter cargo ashore. The groundswell kept shifting and banging gunwales together and threatening to crush bare native feet. We could not risk dropping in crates of food or ammo; they might knock a hole in the skiff. Natives must pass every case by hand down in the bouncing skiff.

Once loaded, the awkward flat-bottomed skiff was almost impossible to row. The craft nearly always listed and lifted one side of oars partly out of the waves. The skiff became a plaything for offshore breezes. A slight breeze once wafted natives with a cargo 5 miles out to ground on a sand spit. It was hard to recover that cargo.

To unload 2 radar units, we really had trouble. Mounted on 4-wheeled trailers, these were among the heaviest units the Army ever had to move. We had no power unit to pull them, and no ramp to carry them through the sand and mud of the beach. It was like trying to land a 155 mm gun with no prime mover.

But our wonderful Aussie cobber, Scotty Dausett, went to work for us. In pidgin English, he explained to the Boss Boy how to build 2 ramps. Then the natives drew their machetes and scattered into the jungle to find certain poles and vines for the ramp.

Back in the jungle, Johnson saw 1 native gang of 50 working a log towards the beach. The log was 2 feet thick and 30 feet long. When Johnson saw it, they had the log waist-high. They would chant in beautiful native voices, *"Eesaloooo!"* Each time they hit the "loooo!" the log went up 6 inches more until they shouldered it and bore it to the beach.

There they began an astonishing construction job. Without nails or spikes, they lashed together 2 long ramps with raised sides. Those raised sides were to act like rails under the trailer ties.

Natives manned both ends of a trailer, then eased it up on the runners. When the tractor started down the ramp, the natives ran madly — 10 miles an hour at least. Their speed would have frightened a US government inspector. But in 2 hours, both units were safe on firm ground to be dragged to where we needed them. Again, Johnson said, "God bless the natives!"

And Johnson blessed natives another night — there on that lonely dark beach under Jap air-power. The boongs were unloading D-8 Caterpillars and Carryalls. They had warped a loaded barge up to an old sunken barge to use as a ramp! They had finally managed to get off a bulldozer to fill in a causeway and unload the other Cats. With natives sandbagging this causeway, we had 4 D-8s off. Motors deafened Johnson as he stood among them beside a Boss Boy.

Suddenly he saw Boss Boy look up. Answering Johnson's query, Boss Boy said: "Master he go. Thing b'long Jesus b'long Jaapaan come long." Now "thing b'long Jesus" was pidgin for an angel — and for a Jap plane. Jap bombers were coming.

Johnson and Boss Boy raced for a bomb crater. All the natives had disappeared. As Johnson hit the crater, a string of bombs impacted the sand — but harmlessly. Thenceforth, Johnson watched the job with one eye and the nearest native with the other. Natives were the best air-raid watchers we ever had.

And of course, these Papuans carried supplies; at first, we had no roads west of Hariko that were fit for even a jeep. After Sv men broke down rations into units, a Yank guide led out a group of natives. Using vines, each native lashed a ration case on a carrying pole, started off up the trail. Even if the hike was 5 miles long, no native took a break, and our unburdened guide found it hard to keep ahead of their swinging jungle gait. If a can fell from a case, the native carried it in his hands all the way and turned it over to the guide when the trip was finished.

During Sanananda Battle, the natives gently carried wounded to the Air Strip. Eight men were assigned to a litter —4 to carry and 4 alternates. The 4 carriers held the litter above their shoulders and had their hands take up the jar of the walk. When the 4 carriers tired, the relief slid under the litter and traded places without the patient's knowledge.

But the Papuans refused to treat Jap invaders so well. Hq naturally needed Jap prisoners for information. Since able-bodied Japs never surrendered, we had to get wounded unable to commit hari-kari in time.

So twice they sent natives back with Japs, but these Japs never arrived. The natives simply said the Japs died en route. Next time, we sent a Yank guard with the carriers, but for the wounded Jap, the trip was a horror. Their hands above their shoulders travelled against the steps they took and jolted the poor suffering Nippo. Inexplicably, they fell without the slightest cause and sailed the Jap off the trail. He was almost dead on arrival, and he certainly would have been dead without our guards. Our Papuans naturally thought that the Japs had caused the war, and we could not make them understand being humane towards the Japs to get needed information for defeating them.

Such were some of Capt Herb Johnson and Sv 186's first experiences with the indispensable Papuan angels. Without those dark allies, we might never have won that jungle war.

And Johnson and his Sv Co detachment will never forget that first night with those Papuan longshoremen. We hear again the weird and beautiful chant of 200 dark voices in the ocean night, before the black rollers coming forever out of the north. As they lean to the tow-line, the chant starts high and the dark voices drop just slightly as the chant is finished: *"Eeesaaaaa LOO."* And out of the ocean dark, they heave one more great black barge that will forward 186 Inf to victory.

116 Medical Battalion:
MEDICS' TALES

By DR. HARGIS WESTERFIELD, Division Historian
and Medic GEORGE JACKSON

Medics' tales for Jungleer stories are hard to find. A few of their tales have appeared as part of company or battery histories already published or stockpiled for publication. Only other mentions of medics are in Divisional medal stories, which are not publishable because we could not connect them up with narratives of units wherein they served. We are therefore lucky to get enough information about these gallant medics to write them up in the Jungleer. It is only by good luck that we had our 116 Medics' Chapter secretary, George Jackson, to supply three stories already in the Jungleer. (These were stories of B-116 at Sanananda—Vol. XX, No. 2; A-116 at Hollandia—Vol. XXIII, Nos. 1-2; and A-116 on Biak—Vol. XIV, No. 1.) Frank Cray honored Clearing Co. 116 Bn. with his story of Salamaua (Vol. X, No. 4).

Here, however, are a few more medics' tales. George Jackson, again, is responsible for most of them. We have found two more from USAFFE Hq. As DSC stories, they are certainly authentic; they are also detailed enough for short Jungleer writeups. We are grateful to 3/Bn. 162's Dr. Milton Drexler for his personal story. We hope that publication of these medics' tales will prod other men to tell other medics' tales. Those tales will never appear in print unless someone writes them up.

1. On or after 16 Jan. 1943, Kantes of B-116 Medics' 2/Pln. had a wild birthday party. Exact date is not available, but the party occurred after B-116 moved through the jungle north of Perimeter Rankin (founded 9 Jan.) and then east and then south to Sanananda Track. We set up perimeter here, a short distance west of the Track, and behind the corpse-littered hospital lot which G Co. 163 Inf. had cleared on 16 Jan.

Our camp area was somewhat open, with short, scrubby trees around us and mud underfoot. Water table was six inches below the mud. When we dug slit trenches here, to be roofed by two-man pup tents, we created our own personal tubs to sleep in, which overflowed into muddy ponds.

That night with high winds, more rain poured down in waves. Lightning flashed occasionally. A wandering squad of still unbeaten Japs took up positions in a dense thicket to our left. Now and then, among lightning flashes, they shot at us.

When our B-116 men replied, DeLucia's grenade hit a tree before our perimeter. The grenade rebounded and wounded DeLucia himself. Derrick left his wet hole under a shelter-half to patch up DeLucia. For a time, Derrick was the only live man exposed out there by the lightning, in front of the Japs, until he had save DeLucia.

Although the exact date is not available here, it was the date of John Kantes' birthday party, probably the most memorable of his entire life.

2. In the Salamaua Operation, A Co. 116 Meds. endured hard labor. This was long before we had our own dead and wounded in the disastrous attack of A and C Cos. of 162 Inf. on Mt. Tambu. On 1 July 1943, our hard, painful work occurrred two days after 1/Bn. 163's "shipwreck landing" at Nassau Bay. Following the night fight of 30 June-1July— the attack on the beachhead perimeter—we dug probably 21 graves. We buried four officers and 17 enlisted men, from A or C 162 Inf. and A-116 Engrs.

Afterwards, when 162 moved inland up Bitoi River, we too slogged inland, up and over Bitoi Ridge, which some called "Heartbreak Ridge." We cared for their wounded when 162 outfits pushed against the Japs to pinch out the Buigap Creek Salient. Rations were short, of course. We slept in wet clothes every night.

But some of A-116 Meds' finest hours came on 30 July 1943, when A and C Cos' attacks failed agnist the highest peak of Mt. Tambu. Here Col. Taylor lost a third of his four plns. Besides losing nine dead, he had 36 wounded that A-116 had to rescue under Japanese fire. (This was the attack that Col. Taylor believed the Aussie CO—probably Col. Conroy—ought never to have ordered. Taylor said the Aussie col. sold him "a bill of goods" to make this deadly attack.)

During these assaults of 30 July, from 0905 to 1225, we meds labored to save our 36 wounded. (We did have some great help in these rescues. DeRooy remembers an Aussie bull of a man who helped us mightily. Name of this man was probably L.C. Allen, a Cpl. of Capt. L.A. Cameron's

---

CREDIT: George Jackson, Secretary of our 116 Meds Chapter, has credit for three of these six stories—and most of the space. Stories Nos. 1 and 2 appeared in Jackson's "Pill Roller," published in 1970. Story No. 5 came from George's interview in Jan. 1975 with Col. Leeon Aller. I also used medal stories of Aller, Stasiowski, Hudon and Thomas B. Williams, to which George referred me. (Williams got a DSC for his bravery.) Story No. 4 bases on Dr. Milton Drexler's ltr. of 5 Aug. 1976. Stories Nos. 4 and 6 are from DSC citations of Randall Balch and Frank Gehrman.

Coy. of 2/5 Inf. Bn. Aussie historian David Dexter credits him with advancing 12 times under fire to rescue 12 Yank wounded.)

But in that black jungle among razorback ridges, in an area some 200 yards long, our 116 Meds of A Co. saved most of our wounded. They paid a price in their own wounds and death. In many places, the Jap MGs were invisible.

Without covering fire, Medic Hurley tried to save a wounded man. He crept too close to a Jap MG that killed him pointblank. We could not recover his body until days later, when we found his skull.

DeRooy and Ron Jones were more lucky. They crept under a Jap MG nest and pulled out a wounded Yank. Both returned unscathed and saved their casualty.

Another four-man litter squad of meds answered a call to extricate a wounded man. He lay near the left flank of Taylor's attack where A Co. had advanced, and later, near that lone pln. of C Co. that had been our final hope of the assault.

Crossing a clearing on our return, this litter squad with its wounded man came under a sniper's lash. A bullet in the back killed Sather. Another bullet clipped Major in his ankle. Carrying the litter beside Sather, big, wide Lysecki was untouched. We conjecture that the sniper first aimed at Sather because he was the leader of the party.

To get some 36 wounded back to hospitals was a hard job. We were short of GI litters, and GI handles were too short for those steep, tortuous carries. We improvised more effective litters from jungle poles and gunny sacks. It took eight carriers to lug a wounded man down through almost impenetrable mountain jungle. Our carries were slippery, sloppy, steamy. Boat service was usually lacking at Nassau Beach. Native black "angels" then carried our wounded eight more miles to a jeep-head and transportation to a hospital of sorts.

Such is the medics' tale of their valor in the abortive attack on Mt. Tambu and the rescue of the wounded that followed.

3. In the fight for Scout Track Ridge, on the approaches to Salamaua, A Co. 116 Medics' Balch distinguished himself. On this day, Japs lobbed in howitzer shells on our ridge positions and wounded four men. Our aid station was a shell hole that could contain only three of the four men. The medic giving first aid had to work outside, exposed to Jap fragments and bullets.

S/Sgt. Balch ordered the other meds to take cover, but one med delayed and was seriously wounded. Balch continued to work at his station—now with five casualties to care for. Having given aid to the wounded, Balch then toured front-line positions. Although exposed to fire, Balch pried into our holes for men too seriously wounded to call for help. (Date of this citation, 3 Aug. 1943, is probably erroneous, for we can find no report of action on that day. We only know that it occurred while 162 was pinching out that long Scout Track Ridge extending down from Salamaua.)

4. On 29 May 1944, while 162 Inf. retreated from the Japanese trap in Parai Defile, Capt. Drexler of 3/Bn. Medics led a litter party to save a wounded Yank. While 162's men were pulling back we laid our wounded man on the stretcher and started to pick him up. A shell exploded nearby.

It slew the wounded man. All of the party but one was hit. Drexler himself took a fragment in the leg but was able

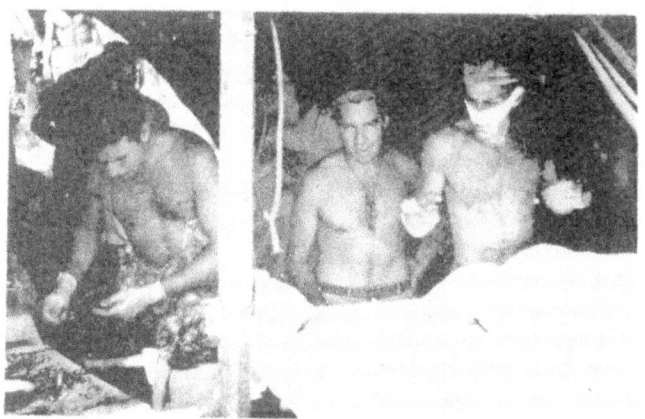

A surgeon and his assistants operate on a soldier for shrapnel wounds at the 26th Portable Hospital on Biak.

to walk. We turned back with the body in the litter.

Somewhere in that brush, we saw a 162 man. He wanted to know what we were doing in that dangerous ground, for 3/Bn. was getting out of there.

Suddenly from thickets around us, a crossfire of our own guns halted us. Four Japs dropped dead nearby.

Safe in our own lines, we heard a 3/Bn. say, "You're lucky we didn't gun you down. We shot some Japs five feet from where you broke out of the brush."

Next thing that Drexler remembers was letting wounded men down over the cliff to LCMs waiting to ferry them to safety. He was far too busy to attend to his own "walking wound." During the evacuation, he remembered jumping over MG nests and being fired at from a rifle company. Not until next day did Capt. Lederman, Drexel's assistant, cut his leg to remove the fragment of Japanese steel.

5. On 5 June 1944 on Biak, C Co. 116 Meds carried out another great action of devotion and bravery for our combat infantrymen—and probably for B Co. 116 Engrs. We meds were then supporting 186 Infantry trying to find a trail up and over Mokmer Ridges so that 186 could take Mokmer Strip from the rear. C's medics were probably in an area of opaque tropical scrub some 10 feet high.

Suddenly Japs attacked. We fell prone on our faces in the midst of explosions and rifles blasting all around us. Grenades and mortars slashed at us.

Fragments slew a casualty that our CO, 2/Lt. Aller, was caring for. Jap fire perforated a water trailer. A probable mortar blast knocked the wheel off our only ambulance, which we needed to haul wounded back down the new 116 Engr. supply road to 12th Portable Hospital. G Co. 186 Inf. was probably the company that returned Jap fire and hunted down the raiders.

Despite danger of continued, long-range mortar fire, 1/Sgt. Stasiowski and S/Sgt. Thomas B. Williams tackled the job of replacing the ambulance wheel.

A mortar blasted us again. Fragments penetrated Williams' abdomen and liver, but Williams was hard to kill. With devoted Stasiowski, Williams stayed on the job and replaced the wheel. We then evacuated Williams with the riflemen he was trying to help. But he refused treatment until other 186 wounded were cared for.

Meanwhile T/5 Hudon, our driver, also helped in treatment of the wounded men. Then he hauled them in the dangerous drive through Jap territory, back to 12th Portable Hospital.

1st Bn 162 Inf's SHIPWRECK LANDING
By DR. HARGIS WESTERFIELD, Association Historian
with Col. A.R. MacKechnie and Fred Devenney

Best tactic for committing 162's 1/Bn against the Nips at Nassau Bay seemed to be a midnight landing. Embarking from Morobe and Mageri Point, we would have a peaceful blacked-out ride safe from Jap coast-watchers, the planes they would bring down on us. Aussie scouts from inland would light the beach. Dug in by daybreak, we would then annihilate demoralized Nips on the shore with 218 FA's 155s. Then we would strike the Nippo rear in the mountains at Mubo while the Aussie 3 Div broke them in frontal attacks.

This night beachhead sounded simple. But we lacked experience with the black night waves of the Guinea Shore.

As dusk thickened at Morobe 29 June 1943, we lines of riflemen filed aboard 3 PT boats — 70 men per boat. Meanwhile at Mageri Point with more infantry, we loaded jeeps, guns, and bulldozers on 24 LCVPs, 1 LCM, 2 Jap barges. Then the craft took assigned places, moved into the dark ocean in 3 waves leaving at 20-minute intervals.

In the black outside the harbor, waves hit us at once. The Guinea rain fell in sheets. Here our first 2 waves of barges contacted the first 2 PT boats from Morobe to serve as guides. Third Wave could find no PT boat to lead it, but wallowed along hopefully with an Amphibian Engineer Officer as pilot, although the high black waves were already bewildering.

Jammed with some 30 others and communications gear on the LCVP with Col A.R. MacKechnie, Devenney huddled under dripping poncho as seas grew rougher and rain heavier. Lt Hoyt had told him to expect at least 6 hours bouncing in open seas. Devenney longed for a cigarette, anything dry and warm. He remembered the remark from a girl friend's letter: stateside, all the bars now had to close at midnight. Devenney almost wept; things were sure tough at home.

By 2030, Devenney's LCVP had trouble holding formation in these high waves. The motor conked out. We flashed the trouble signal. A PT boat slipped alongside at once. Now we got a clear idea of just how high the seas were. One minute, we looked far down into a trough; then a wave towered overhead. Continually, newly seasick men kept crowding to gunwales; some men never got that far but were seasick anyhow and anywhere.

Although the LCVP with Devenney and Col Mack in it was repaired, Col Mack decided that even the low deck on a PT boat would be better OP from which to see the Aussie lights when they appeared on the beach. He needed the best possible vantage point to help him make the final decision to land — or even turn back. In these high waves, a landing would be calamity — wrecked boats, losses of equipment difficult to replace — and drowned Yanks washed ashore.

In the dark, the PT boat with Col Mack ran past the beach. In turning back, it lost several boats, and spent 20-30 minutes recovering them. Other boats were even more astray.

Thus it was that the second wave of barges stood off the beach-front first, while officers peered over the black tossing waves at the Guinea Shore. Why was the beach blacked out? Did Yanks or Japs hold it? Where should they land? Where were the Aussie guides and the lights?

(That morning, the slouch-hatted Digger Pltn from 2/6 Inf had fair going when it left 3/Div on the mountains. Then to cross one river, they built a raft to carry 3 at a time, pulled it back for repeat loads. But they did not well remember the trails from an earlier scout, and travel by azimuth slowed them down. Dark found them splashing into great swamps behind the beach where they feared mangling or death from crocodiles. They became lost in the swamps; they separated in groups of 5 or 6 to discover high ground at the beach. In this dimness, they had to climb a rail fence; it cracked and broke. But it was not booby-trapped. Very late in darkness, they rushed piecemeal onto the beach. Had the Yank flotilla got past them and grounded among the MGs and cannon in Jap-held Salamaua?)

Out at sea, second wave leaders saw 2 small flashlights blink from the beach. A rifle fired; both lights blacked out. The right light now flashed; Devenney read the Morse: "Let's go!"

Midnight disembarkation begain in confusion. Lurching over black combers, barges converged dangerously at that one light. Seasick men cowered to the floor as other barges threatened to crash into them.

A PT man shouted to Devenney's barge to pull over, wait. Only 300 yards off, surfs pounded the shore. Devenney nervously readjusted flotation bladders in his jacket.

At 1240, the LCVP motor revved up; the boat straightened out for the beach. Collapsed seasick men came to life. A wave lurched them sidewise, "Saddled up" with pack, extra gear, Devenney saved a fall by clutching the gunwale; men piled up at his feet. He tried to pull up another man, but a roller topped the side, felled both men into deep water.

"Back up!" men screamed to the helmsman. The motor reversed; the crash was averted while just seconds away. A foot of water sloshed in Devenney's leggins.

Lt Hoyt of Communications ordered the drive to try for the beach 50 yards right. He herded the 30 passengers to the rear; the ramp would need plenty of room if the beach was high.

"Here we go again!" yelled Hoyt. The helmsman put the LCVP prow into the beach again — gunned full throttle. Surf thundered; the boat struck. Waves broached it sidewise. Men leaped into a foot of sandy water. A new wave beat Devenney's helmet, yanked the throatlatch to choke him.

Under heavy rolls of wire, Hoyt's pltn staggered up the beach into pitch black. We kept touching each other to keep contact. No Aussie guides came to show us bivouacs; we milled around in blackness on a Japanese beach.

After 10 minutes' black confusion, the Aussies lit all their lights, while Yanks cursed. Then all along the beach, jungle lights flickered up and down. Yanks regrouped in formations — or rushed to unload heavy equipment. Devenney saw 2 tractors clank ashore.

It was risky with those lights on, despite the necessity. One Jap MG could flank the beach and play hell. So could blasts of rifle fire — or charging bayonet-men.

Luckily, no Japs came. Meanwhile, C Co's Capt Newman landed from his wrecked barge and ordered his boat-teams to assemble 300 yards south. In blackness, he accosted slouch-hatted figures and got answers in Aussie accents. The Aussies seemed confused. He found no guides — and no one who knew about a screening force to protect the Bn. At the center light, no officer was in charge.

But Col Mack soon arrived, after his lost PT boat reassembled the First Wave that ran past the beach. This 47-year old regular army Colonel hurried his PT commander back to the beach. But a direct landing from the PT boat would be disastrous. Boats 11 and 13 — which had carried A Co men ashore — retracted from the beach, dangerously hove alongside the PT boat. Only Col Mack and 6 men could jump from PT boat to LCVP.

Watching at the LCVP ramp driving for the beach, Col Mack discerned a naval graveyard — broached and foundered craft pounded by waves. In black waters, his barge struck an open ramp of another craft. Everyone was knocked flat; but Mack kept his TSMG above water. The ramp fell; they jumped into knee-high seas to struggle up the beach. At once, Mack closed the beach — sent A Co north, C south, his CP and Hq Detachment inland. No guns landed — only Lt/Col Cochran and a small artillery advance party. With no Japs reported, Mack ordered the 2 PTs with 170 B Co Yanks back to harbor.

Getting 162's 1/Bn ashore in a midnight gale and positioning it for battle was only the start of the day for this soldier who had bluffed past a retirement board despite serious osteo-arthritis. Col Mack got no sleep that night — nor the next.

Communications men scouted the jungle past the new CP. Pillette, Stewart set up the radio. Devenney, Forbes, Albright nosed the brush for Japs. But the night was black; rain beat the fronds and smothered all sound.

They tried a zany way to hunt. Albright, Devenney crouched, grenades ready. Forbes flattened behind a log, flashed the light 30 seconds. No Japs stirred. Similar flashlight patrols scouted on their flanks.

Devenney's group found a small trail and blocked it. They found an empty pillbox to shelter the radio. Devenney was among those who slept in the rain and hoped for dawn — 4 hours off. In gray daylight, he saw heavy clouds over jungle, and surf dashing around wrecked barges.

At daylight, lines of riflemen strode up the beach past Devenney. They would fight the Japs to the north. One threw away his empty C ration can. "Put on strikes, chum!" he called. "We'll be back for lunch." Did he ever come back?

That morning while Capt George's A Co probed north to fight 162's first action, the foreshore teemed with wrecked boats, scattered supplies, life-jackets, salvage details. Of 32 craft leaving bases, just 22 had hit the beach. Of the 22, just 4 retracted and got to sea again. Of 10 not landing, 7 returned to Mageri; 3 hid out at Buso, could not land until 2 nights later.

Of some 1,000 assigned to land, about 740 made it — 96 in A Co, 166 in C, 110 in D, a squad of B. Others included 52 Bn Hq men, half of 24 Portable Hosp — and motley groups from A 116 Engr, 542 EB & S, Service Co, other advance groups.

Of the 740 who landed, only 440 were infantry. We lacked 218 FA's 155s, 209 CA's AA. Only 1 radio was serviceable. I & R had got lost — except for Lt Folsom with Svagdis and Tapioli who swam ashore with an important message. And minus FA, Col Mack fought the Nips at dawn.

This beachhead debacle caused far too many Yank deaths and too many Jap survivals. No Yanks drowned; but 21 killed and 27 wounded were too many losses. Route of C's isolated 2/Pltn on the South Lines next day and deaths of many service troops on perimeter that night may have been due to lack of B's rifleman. Lacking FA, we let many Japs escape to fight again.

But why this holocaust of landing barges? Col Mack pointed out that no Yank beach expert had seen the area. Despite excellence as scout and soldier, Aussie Lt Burke who made the report was unfamiliar with landing barges. Barges had to come in at a dangerous angle where wind and high surf could readily capsize them. Deepest reason of all, however, must have been due to the nature of the landing — in black night where boats would eventually lose their way and gales were almost certain.

But Col MacKechnie's 162 landing begain the Division's Salamaua operation. Avoiding Nippo coast-watchers at Dinga Point and a possible concentration of Japs at the moment of landing, he had 740 Yanks ashore who knew that they had to fight. A small Jap force heard landing noises and took to the swamp. According to a Jap sgt, the premature arrival of the bulldozers — which were in the original Second Wave but landed first — had made the Nips fear that tanks were landing. While the Japs were still off balance, Capt George took A Co and hit them hard at dawn June 30.

Basic documents are from Col. A.R. MacKechnie's personal papers and Fred Devenney's unpublished MS, Hell is Green. Both "Col Mack" and Fred supplied magnificient "human interest". "Col Mack" also obliged with detailed replies to my questionnaire.

Night In Green Hell

By FRED J. DEVENNEY and HARGIS WESTERFIELD, Divisional Historian

Credit Lines

1) Prime source is Fred J. Devenney's unpublished MS *Hell is Green*. Additional sources include: 2) C CO Capt. Delmar J. Newman's "Report of Landing"; 3) A CO Capt. John D. George's Ltr 12 July 1944; 4) Col. A. R. MacKechnie's "Notes on Operations, Morobe, Nassau Bay Area, 8 July 1943"; 5) MacKechnie, "The Salamaua Campaign"; 6) MacKechnie, "Military Monograph to Adv Officers Class No. 1, Armored School, Fort Knox, Ky."; 7) 162 Inf Rep of Operations; 8) War Journal, 162 Inf. The story of A Co's fight was especially difficult to write, and I shall appreciate data and critiques of all kinds.

FRED J. DEVENNEY (1 Btn Comm 162) fought on Bitoi Beach, climbed Bitoi Ridge and signalled for fire on Mt. Tambu. A few weeks after he found Aussie pounds on a Nippo corpse, he was spending them in Brisbane, mate! He had been ordered Stateside to become an Air Cadet. At Air Force Shows, he raised sums amounting to six figures. How? He told the Base Commandos about what 162 was doing in New Guinea, and they bought bonds by the hundreds. Fred sells property and insurance and handles loans in Santa Ana, Calif. It's a treat to read his great unpublished MS *Hell is Green*. (And any Butcher knows Hell IS Green, Fred. hw)

THE DEADLY NIGHT combat of 162 Infantry's First Battalion at Nassau Bay 30 June 1943 resulted from a calculated risk that Col. AR MacKechnie could not avoid. If he did not strike first, he could expect 400-500 veteran Japs to butcher his bedraggled castaways in the surf. For with daylight, Nippo scouts would report that 18 U. S. landing-craft were wrecked in the surf. Then Jap officers would assume that we were understrength and demoralized. On that narrow beachhead, without artillery protection, we faced annihilation.

With only two rifle companies and some motley advance elements ashore, MacKechnie did what he could. he secured the flanks of the beach. C Co's 186 Yanks moved south to the Tabali River and dug in, unopposed. He sent A Co north towards the Bitoi River.

But Capt. John D. George's 96 men of A Co with a D Co HMG hit the Nips head-on. After they advanced a short distance into the green jungle hell, an ambush of about 50 Nips blasted A Co with rifles, knee-mortars, machine-guns. Japs let our forward elements pass, then fired on the rear, and shot at the Hq group from hidden positions.

Although A Co was under fire for the first time in the war, the men plied their M-1's like veterans. They held their ground and deployed their squads to block the envelopment which was sure to follow.

But A was short a platoon plus a squad which had not landed. Jap fire thickened. A Co fell back 2-300 yards to reorganize. Then Col Mack sent up that lone platoon of D Company 2/5 Aussies which had daringly lighted the beach for last night's landing.

We had planned to throw the Aussies in on our right and envelop the Japanese flank; but the Aussies met a fire that halted them before they could get in line with A Co. A gap was left, and the Japs threw a command straight at it. Only our D Co HMG crew saved the day; their drumfires stopped the Japs until A Co men came up on the double and shot them to pieces.

After only an hour of this, the Aussie D Co Platoon had to be relieved. They must have gone into action short of ammunition, in fact, since they came out of the hills only to light the landing-barges into the beach. A detachment of 116 Engrs and 532 Boat and Shore Engrs replaced our Aussie allies. We zeroed in on the Jap mortar and MG positions with a D Co 60 mortar and silenced them; but sniping continued. We expected another attack. To secure the beachhead, we had to smash a concentration of Japs that apparently stood before us and push on to the defense line of the Bitoi.

Now Battalion Hq took the calculated risk that caused a deadly night combat. Since C Co's 186 men on the South Lines had not been in action, most of them were ordered to reinforce A Co and drive to the Bitoi.

Only the Second Pltn of C Co with 4 MG's would remain behind on the Tabali as a holding force. Captain Delmar Newman of C did object to leaving 1 Pltn too far south; but he heard that his main body would return to their lines before darkness.

This was a military risk that turned out wrong. Although C's main body with A Co knocked aside the Japs and reached their objective, Lieut. Brown's 2 Pltn of C Co caught hell.

At 1630, Brown reported that Japs were across the Tabali and working to his rear. At 1640 he got orders to withdraw and dig a new line; but by 1645, the Pltn was fighting for its life.

What happened in this rout of C's 2 Pltn may never become entirely clear. Daugherty reported a Banzai charge right into our position that caught us off balance. We killed a number, but they were in on us with bayonets. Kyle died there, and somewhere in close combat three more GI's with Lieut. Brown himself. One man cowered in a fox-hole unobserved by the Japs for three days before he could escape.

Daugherty shouted to his gunners to leave on the double. They seized MG's and fled down a narrow trail to the beach—some 300 yards in tropical heat and slithering sand. About 200 yards south of Btn CP, they dug in for a last fight. Under cover of a ledge of sand scooped up by the shipwrecking surfs of last night, they now had three MG's and a line of riflemen from the beach a short way into the jungle. Part of the line was the great unused bulldozer that had frightened the Japs on the previous night's landing.

Dug in waiting with Chavez, No. 2 gunner Daugherty craved a last cigarette before the death-dark. In the rout, he had lost his haversack and four packs of Luckies to the Japs. Meanwhile, everything had grown quiet as a tomb except for the roar of the breakers—too quiet, in fact. And there were not enough men in depleted 2 Pltn to hold the line against a determined charge.

But reinforcements came through the dusk—mainly from that central core of Hq and service troops that riflemen enviously called "Commandos." Force S-3, Capt. Paul Cawlfield led them. Besides Combat Engineers and Amphibs, Lieut. Clem Day's D Co mortarmen, and the CP Defense Pltn, there were clerks and chauffeurs—even Capt. George Ross, S-4, and Pvt. Iler, chauffeur for Colonel MacKechnie himself.

Under protection of the bulldozer blade, Devenney and Forbes dug in with the telephone. In the dark, a line of Yanks—about 60, he thought—passed Devenney to strengthen the cordon back in the jungle. It was already dark so that Cawlfield whispered to have each man hold on to the ammo belt of the man before him. Brush scraped leggings; branches ripped against rifles, loudly in the scared night.

Like pistols, the first Japanese grenades detonated; shrapnel splattered the foliage. The line of men slammed into the ground. With the silence, they dug in desperately.

Another grenade exploded; a Yank screamed, started to run, crashed to the ground. Behind us at 20 yards, Jap rifles crackled—maybe 10 of them. A Nip MG sprayed us, ricocheting from the bulldozer. Again Nips threw grenades; and the sand stung Devenney's face.

This was the moment for Devenney's buddy Prem to whistle on the phone from the safety of the CP. In an agony of fright, Devenney struggled to shut Prem off; at any moment a Nippo grenade might burst in their faces. At last he whispered, "Shut up, Prem. Every Jap in 20 yards can hear you!" But Devenney lived, in a silence of horror and the sudden reasonless pandemonium of attack. There were attacks at 8:00, at midnight, at 4:00 in the morning, at 4:45, and at 5:30.

All night long we played a deadly, silent game with the Japs. It was a silent game broken only by blasts of grenades, MG's, and the cries of the wounded and dying. Some men died quietly; some moaned; some cursed the Japs. A grenade mortally wounded Baldini about 9:00, but he did not die until morning.

Now Daugherty's MG duelled a Jap gun at 30 yards. A knee mortar burst behind Devenney but merely stung the end of his finger. By the bulldozer, Turk challenged a Jap in Yank helmet, and fell dead from a burst of sub-machinegun fire. We fired back, but the Jap escaped in the dark towards Btn CP. Ray Ford was shot in the foot. A nearby Corporal had lain prone on a medical kit to avoid the prickly jungle growth, and a Jap MG shot it from under his belly. The fire ripped open another man's pack, but the M-1 tool in it stopped the bullet.

Cpl. Linneweh had crawled the length of the line to check the placing of his men, but he mistakenly stood up, tripped on wire, and staggered. In 2-3 seconds, two M-1's, a tommy, and two BAR's stabbed the night. Although badly wounded in the side, he crawled back to the 24 Portable Surgical Hospital and saved his life with plasma.

The Japs tried a new trick; a MG fired to reflect light from our own MG barrels. But the sound was phony; the gunner evidently was back in a hole and firing with a wire attached to the trigger. Nobody fired to give away the position, but our grenades burst nearby and shattered the night with Japanese howls.

Silhouetted against the sea, two dark figures ran through the shallows to take our guns. Devenney did not need to fire; other bullets knocked them dead.

Now the Japs ganged on one MG. Figures stood up and swung rifles at low shapes around them; a butt-plate clanged on a helmet. A .45 barked; two men fell. Then the Yank figures drew apart and dropped suddenly into their holes again.

Through blurred eyes, Devenney watched the end of a night that had lasted forever. Dark forms were taking shape—a detail bringing up more chests of ammo and grenades to the guncrews. And with daylight, Cawlfield ordered everyone to dig in deep; in the frightened dark many Yanks had been forced to risk themselves on top of the ground. Devenney and Forbes found a ready-made foxhole, with one of our Engineers dead in it.

When ordered back to the CP, Devenney had to step over three Yank dead. Near Daugherty's guns he noticed spots of blood where men had crawled. Here lay a dead Jap in khaki and puttees beside his bayoneted rifle. His features were surprisingly light, and he looked young and well fed. The bullet had holed him in the temple.

"Grenades look big as coconuts when they throw 'em at you," quipped Daugherty from beside his gun. He puffed hard on a cigarette. "Look here, Dev," he said. "See this Nip? He found my four packs of Luckies back in the old position and brought them all back here to me—the little darling!"

At gray dawn in many areas, the Nips fired for a quarter-hour and then pulled back except for the inevitable snipers who had to be combed out of the trees. Despite the terror of the night attack, it had failed—failed even though a grenade struck 10 feet from the Force Message Center, and a sniper died only 50 feet from the CP at daybreak. With the daylight, the main body of C Company turned south again and joined with its Second Platoon to fight on the Tabali River, but found only stragglers.

And this is the saga of the Night Fight on the South Lines at Nassau Bay 30 June - 1 July, 1943. It had resulted from a calculated risk that went wrong. The Australian PIB force at Dinga Point apparently pushed an estimated 200 Japs to head northward for their main body over an obstruction of 162 Infantry. They had struck the South Lines of C Co at the opportune moment when only Brown's 2 Pltn had been left in position. After his defeat, quick action was needed to save our whole beachhead from destruction.

The fight on the South Lines cost nine Yanks killed, 12 wounded and four missing, according to the initial report—no small number in the SWPA where a few must do the work of many. We had killed an estimated 50 Nips on both lines and secured both ends of the beachhead, from Tabali River to Bitoi River. Now we could wait for supplies and plan to push inland to climb

Historian's Thanks

The first half of 1959 has been great for collecting historical material," reports Dr. Hargis Westerfield (G Co 163). "Although 162 led in contributions, 163 kept up its contributions. And 186 Infantry, "the lost regiment," has sent its first material, along with 116 Medics.

162 Infantry leads. Vernon Townsend (CO Cannon Co) has sent us the first full-length company history to arrive — along with a magnificent box of reports and records of Salamaua and Biak. Marvin B. Noble (Exec A Co) wrote us a letter about the death of Marshall from a croc, and promises a detailed history on A. Bernie Schimmel (I 162) wrote Alvin Taylor's brother the story of that Oklahoma kid's death, which letter was passed to us. H. M. Kelley (I 162) is now preparing a company history.

163 Infantry continues its high quality of performance with a spirited account of hot MG action at Kamti Village by S/Sgt Vernon Magee (K 163). His other comments on Kamti Village will be printed with those of Arthur Merrick (Lieut. L Co). Curtis Huck (Hq 3 Bn) also promises historical material.

186 Infantry has begun to be heard from. Alan E. Rock (Sgt. I & R) forwards a section of his history on Dictagraph tape, also an article from "Infantry Journal" on "Jap Ambushes" on Biak. Sgt.-Major Fred Larey (Hq 2 Btn) promises a story soon. Also promising is Col. John Nielson, 186. Don Hollnagel also wrote to us.

116 Medics comes through with a history of D Co, Salamaua through Hollandia — the first non-infantry history to arrive. S/Sgt. Frank Cray submitted this material.

Bitoi Ridge, cut the Komiatum Track, and besiege Mt. Tambu.

This was Green Hell

C Co. 162 Infantry:
Cless-Robson Fight for Salamaua

Prime source was in Col MacKechnie's papers. I regret that no names of enlisted men were mentioned. (And neither 162 nor 163 left adequate Morning Report lists of casualties for the Papuan Campaign. Federal Archives are no help here.) I also wonder whether these papers have confused the "Lt Grey of A Co with that fine soldier, B Co's Lt James Gray. If this is so, I apologize to "Jim" Gray.

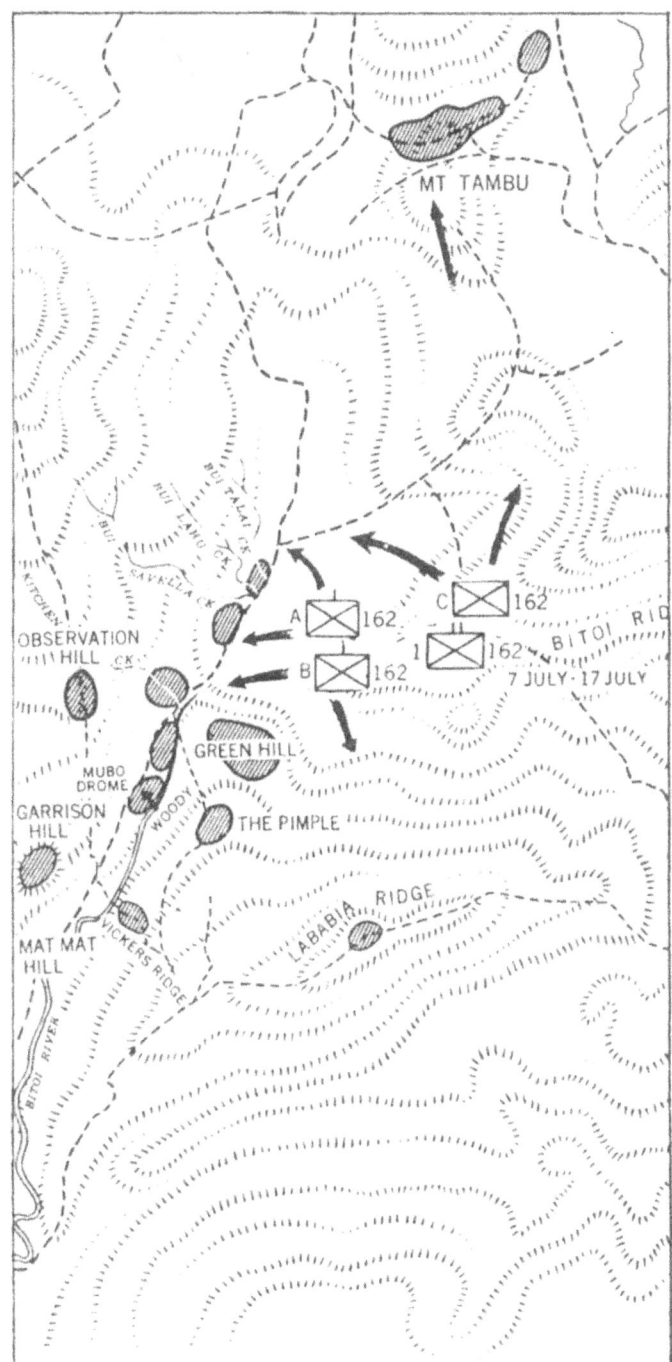

On 12 July 1943, 162's 1st Bn was deep in its 5-day Battle of the Bitoi River on the approaches to Salamaua. On 12 July, Lt Ralph S. Cless had orders to take 25 men from our 1st Pltn plus one LMG with 5 crewmen and 3 natives to lay an ambush on the Komiatum Track against Japs withdrawing to Mount Tambu. Leaving Ralph G. Robson's 3 Pltn outpost, we began to climb Bui Kumbul Ridge. Luckily for us, Robson's Pltn—on a different mission—was scheduled to follow our trail up the same ridge in 15 minutes. For without Robson and 30 men, there may have been no Cless Pltn left alive.

Although he expected to fight no Jap army, Cless took all precautions in the wet, slippery mountain jungle. For 25-30 yards ahead, 3 black Papuan Infantrymen smelled their way. After these scouts, alertly strode two A Co guides, then Cless with Lt Grey of A, then our pltn at 5-yard intervals in single file. Already jungle-wise, we moved quietly in the hot, steep, 45-minute climb. About 75 yards from the summit, the jungle thinned to a steep, rocky slope.

Near the lip of that ridge, our natives signalled—"Japs!" We halted; packs slipped off; we checked M-1's, got off the trail, waited. Cless and Grey hurried up to whisper with the natives.

Just 10-15 yards over the ridge-lip, they had seen a Jap officer and several men at a trail crossing.

Cless deployed his 10-man First Squad left of the trail, and his Second to the right. The Third half-squad remained in reserve with the LMG crew.

Combat-ready, the 1st Pltn crossed the ridge-lip, struck for the crest. Then Japs spotted our riflemen near the trail, at 15 yards.

Our M-1's spoke; 2 Japs fell. From the cross-trails, a Jap LMG rattled; Arisaka rifles stabbed at us.

With Jap fire heaviest on our left flank, we could not push forward there. But on the right in thinner foliage our squad met only scattered fire. Hoping to gain high ground above the trail crossing, we moved ahead. But at 15 yards, a Jap HMG opened up; we took cover.

With both 10-man squads committed frontally, Cless ordered the Second Squad to work up a gully on the right flank to enfilade that Jap HMG. While the half-squad tried to flank the Japs on our right, the Japs also made a flank attack on our left. They sent at least 10 men to our left to come in on our rear.

But the Sgt of our left squad had 3 men out guarding that flank—SOP in Cless Pltn. These 3 spotted the Japs' flank attack, blew them back with rifles. Still guarding our rear, the 5 men of the LMG crew jumped into the fight; one gunner emptied a pistol clip into a Jap who had crawled within 5 yards of us.

Meanwhile, our half-squad was stopped in its flanking movement by heavier fire. Already Cless' entire pltn was deployed, and the Japs had no flanks. We could do nothing but use the half-squad to fight a holding action. At this point, a Jap advance on both flanks could have enveloped us and wiped us out.

But half-way up the ridge behind us, Robson heard the firing. Ordering his pltn sgt to hurry the pltn, he panted up to Cless, got a hurried briefing. Quickly Robson swung his Second Squad in on our right, his Third on our left, and his First to our rear. Thus we had an all-around perimeter defense of riflemen, with our LMG secure until needed.

Jap pressure increased on our left; we counted at least 3 knee mortars and another MG in action there. All along the line, more Jap rifles fired. Japs assaulted frontally; their bodies thudded wounded or dead on the stones. A few snipers climbed into trees and fired down on us; grimly we sighted and knocked them down screaming.

We knocked out several MG gunners with rifle fire; but the MGs' fire did not cease. When a gunner was down, his number 2 man pushed him aside, continued shooting at us. Our only hope was to spot the guns precisely and disable them with grenades.

Our officers exposed themselves to find the MGs. The Japs' fire-control had by now improved. MGs, mortars, rifles would build up a barrage, then remain silent for minutes. But knee-mortars—4 of them—caused no casualties, many of them were duds. Under the barrages, we lay prone until they ceased and they set up targets for us. That's what it was—target shooting.

For Japs would rush then—and fall hard. Or Jap riflemen would actually rise to their knees in the open and look for targets. Before their rifles touched their shoulders, we picked them off; they dropped their rifles and died.

Scouting the jungle on the left, Robson thought he had spotted the MG that had blocked our right flanking movement. As he started back to CP, 11 slugs from that HMG struck him. But he crawled over the slope to safety.

Shortly after Robson was hit, Japs blasted hard into our left flank. With 1 dead and several wonded, Robson's Third Squad fell back, almost shattered. Cless called up Robson's fresh First Squad from the rear into the fire-fight. The Third Squad Cless reorganized to hold our rear.

The fusillades continued on our left. Every movement brought streams of MG and mortar fire on our riflemen. We realized that we were hopelessly out-numbered; we could not capture that high ground and dominate the cross-trails. Japs in the jungle were now within 5-10 yards on our left; we blasted them with grenades.

Cless decided to withdraw to Robson's smaller perimeter of last night. Over the sound-powered phone which Robson had ordered connected during the firing, Cless called A Co's Grey whose orders had been to place his men in Robson's old position. Cless requested Grey to send a squad forward to help extricate our wounded.

Evacuating our men took a long hour. While we lay on the defensive and made every shot count against actual targets, we lost 1 more Yank dead and several wounded.

Now our wounded were safe; orders came to disengage. First, Cless pulled back the MG squad, then Robson's battered Third Squad in the rear. Then the 2 squads on the right filed out. The Second Squad of Cless' 1st Pltn, also on the right, fell back 50 yards, formed a temporary line on both sides of the trail. Finally our left flank fired a few more rounds, and man by man dropped downhill to the protection of the covering squad. Tired but grinning with relief, we left the dark-green Bui Kumbul Ridge.

Breaking contact took 15-20 minutes. We were orderly and quiet; no man left his position until he was told; the NCO's kept full control of their squads all the way. We lost no equipment; each man shouldered his pack where he had left it.

Withdrawal was, in fact, so orderly and quiet that Jap fire on our old positions still echoed on the ridge for 20 minutes afterwards. The Japs seemed to have too great a respect for our small numbers to press again.

Back at the Robson outpost, we dug more and deeper holes and planned for battle. We even sent a reconnoisance patrol back to observe the Japs. We spotted 2 Japs 100 yards down the ridge from the top, but they turned away. But we had returned to Robson's old outpost about 1630 hrs, and the Japs lacked the morale to attack. Except for the agony of the wounded, we had a quiet perimeter night.

Water, mud and slush, not to mention the anopheles mosquitoes, were the 41sters inseparable companions in New Guinea.

Next morning, Lt Griffith, CO, arrived with the rest of our Co. Already, at dawn Cless had sent 3 Yanks and a native to check the ridge. Japs still held it. About 1000, a FA observer arrived and directed the shelling of the ridge. Then all C Co probed the ridge again but found only 22 Nippo graves, bloody bandages, discarded equipment, arms, and ammo.

Evidently Cless and Robson had hit the head of a Nippo column withdrawing from Green Hill, The Pimple, and Woody Island. We estimated that 400-600 Japs must have been in their little army. And with our natives, we had a total of 65!

Despite the odds, C lost only 2 KIA and 4 seriously wounded. (The historian finds no report of Robson's death.) Yet we fought them to a standstill for over 3 hours. Probably we caught them by surprise; they were not dug in and had not planned their action ahead of time. Surprise was the only reason why we did not fight a Custer's Last Stand.

But on our part, the Cless-Robson Fight with C Co's 1st and 3rd Pltns was a classic of scouting, teamwork, and frontline tactics.

C Battery, 218 FA:
Cannoneers up Bitoi River

By DR. HARGIS WESTERFIELD, Division Historian
with CHARLES RICKS, LOUIS REUTER and AL JONES

At 0130 that dark morning of 5 July 1943, the first detachment of C. Btry. 218 FA beached at Nassau Bay and dug in for a few hours' sleep under protection of 162 Inf. and B 218 FA. Our "pack" howitzers were 75's. Although C 218 had missed Col. MacKechnie's "Shipwreck Landing" of 29-30 June, we faced danger immediately. That very dawn at 0715, Sgts. Al Jones and Vernon Bates were wounded by a booby trap grenade which our engineers had not removed. Both men were hospitalized, Bates was the more seriously wounded. And by 1600 next day, 6 July, Col. Cochran ordered C to prepare to strike inland. We were to move up the Bitoi River among jungle swamps and floodlands and on into the wilds of Bitoi Ridge.

Overall mission of 162 Combat Team from Nassau Bay was to help Aussie 17 Brigade to pinch off the Jap salient of the Komiatum Track and capture Mubo Air Field. Fighting from almost impassable inland mountains, the Aussies could not capture Komiatum Track Salient alone and overrun Mubo Air Field at the extreme south end of the Track.

And C 218 FA's first objective was to slog and slosh with our 75's far enough inland to cover 162 and Aussie 17 Brigade against Komiatum Track. After that, we were to climb 2,800 foot Bitoi Ridge and harry the Japs northward until we drove them from Salamaua Town itself.

Already C was moving north from 162's Nassau Beach through sago swamps, and in fear of ambush from Japs fleeing from 162. That second night ashore, we had to sleep in holes—in six inches of water. Reuter never forgot that rain in the holes. He was grateful for the flotation bladders that pillowed his head above the water and kept him from drowning.

And on 7 July, the third day after C Btry. had landed, Capt. Burelbach was responsible for the massive job of heaving four 75's and ammo five hellish miles inland to Napier Village. Besides the four officers and 80 men of C, he had with him as helpers 35 men of Service Battery to penetrate the swamps of the south arm of the Bitoi and possible ambushes.

At first, C moved the howitzers on wheels over a half mile of jeep track, then inland by tractors, and then through the first mud and water. Working along the Bitoi River, we came to what we called "Dry Creek," although we called it "dry" only because the water was lower in this creek than in any other creek along the trail. Now the Caterpillar tractors failed us. We had to use ropes fore and aft to help the howitzers onward.

The Bitoi River was swift and swollen from mountain rains, but we had to cross it. While some men pulled ahead chest-deep, others held the howitzers with ropes to keep them from being thrown back downstream. And we had bamboo poles lashed together in the river to keep us from being pushed down into drowning holes under the current. Tall Reece began carrying replacement Hargan on his back through high water, for Hargan was only five feet tall.

Soon we had to disassemble the 75's and carry them, part by part. They were designed to break down to eight parts: barrel, recoil mechanism, two parts of the tail, the axle and two wheels. Largest part weighed 200 pounds. Some parts we carried on poles—four men to a team for relieving one another.

Records say that C Btry. with Sv's help crossed and recrossed Bitoi River anywhere from two to six times. There were good reasons for these different numbers. In our own mist of fatigue and incipient fever, it was hard to remember how many times the howitzers did cross. And in the swamps and wide curves of the south arm, it was hard to remember which was a crossing of the real river and which was a creek crossing. Away from the river, we climbed slippery rises that foreboded even rougher ascents in the days when we would have to push four guns up a real New Guinea mountain. We carried with us 400 rounds of ammo—another heavy job, for each projectile by itself weighed 14.9 pounds. (Yet in field operations, we could fire 400 rounds accurately in less than 30 minutes.)

That night of 7 July, C dug two separate perimeters on the Bitoi trail. Each perimeter protected two howitzers. We looked back with pride on a great day's march—we men of C and Sv Batteries. Both Cols. Cochran of 218 and MacKechnie of 162 praised us for a marvelous job.

On 8 July, 50 AT 162 men came back from forward infantry positions to help us progress. And by 1600, Maj. Hintz reported that two C 75's were emplaced at a point on a stream a mile down the Bitoi River from Capt. Burelbach's CP near Napier on the north side of the Bitoi.

And meanwhile, 218 FA's Hq. Btry. men were setting up an advance observation post to spot Jap targets for us among those blue jungle mountains and valleys. Here the Japs were dug in to protect the Komiatum Track which had been their main invasion salient from Salamaua.

This Air Forces photo shows the rugged terrain over which 41st Division troops fought their way to Salamaua. After the capture of Mubo and the Japanese positions on Lababia Ridge and Green Hill, the attack moved along Buigap Creek to Komiatum, gateway to Salamaua.

Although the Aussie 2/6 Bn. guarded Brown's OP on the main Lababia Ridge, our Jap targets began only 6,000 yards north on a round, forested peak of that same Lababia Ridge. Aussies called the peak "The Pimple" because it resembled a pimple among taller mountains, but it was all of 1,500 feet high. On it were at least 25 pillboxes and 50 weapons pits. The Japs on "The Pimple" had broken three Aussie attacks and cut off an attacking company for three days. "The Pimple" had been staging point for the Japs' all-out attack on Lababia Ridge on 20-23 June.

And north of "The Pimple" was the 1,000-foot Green Hill, thus named because among all the greenery of Vickers Ridge it appeared greenest. The precipices of Green Hill guarded the Japs from Yank pushes up the twisting, mountain-protected Bitoi

River. "The Pimple" and Green Hill were C Btry's first targets; they had baffled Aussie attacks from inland for over two months.

And so, on 8 July 1943, Capt. Brown reported to C Btry. that Maj. Holmes of the Aussie 17 Brigade had given permission for registration fire on "The Pimple". For 218 FA, it was a great moment of the war—preparing to fire our first round in battle against the enemy. All of us signed our names on the shell. Sgt. Rethlefen's section had the honor of firing 218 FA's first round at "The Pimple." Shortly after 1700, 8 July, C fired the first registration shot.

And at 1010, 9 July, registration fire was continuing on "The Pimple" and Green Hill, despite poor visibility. We registered again at 1200. Two hours later, we had orders from Aussie Maj. Holmes to fire what was a large number of shells from our limited supply. At 1500, C shot Concentration No. 500 on Green Hill—32 shells in nine minutes. Capt. Brown reported, "Excellent effect."

And that night from 2130 through 0430 on 10 July, C harassed Points A, B, and C around Green Hill with 28 rounds. Brown observed Japs evacuating these positions.

On 8 July, C had begun fire with only 400 rounds on hand, and demands on our ammo were heavy. On 10 July, 56 men had to portage 112 rounds in from the coast on those harsh, man-killing trails up the Bitoi. By 2000 that 10 July, we had expended 48 rounds on Concentration 502, which was "The Pimple." (That same day, we alerted for an air raid—nine Jap bombers and five Zeroes, 20,000 feet up. But they bombed near the coast and vanished.)

On 11 July came C's "big shoot-out." At 1115, Lt. Walwyn (B Btry.) requested fire for Capt. George's A Co. A had by now crossed Bitoi Ridge and was bucking Komiatum Track. We fired 37 rounds—but not the "big shoot-out."

But the orders for the "shoot-out" came at 1504 that memorable 11 July, 1943. Aussie Maj. Holmes requested FA fire at Bui Lahu Creek on the Komiatum Track—urgent! Target was an estimated whole company of Japs resting in full field equipment.

Viciously, we manned those guns. With delay fuze, we ranged in all four guns. Gunners like Ricks, Ryan and Burke sighted on the firing stakes, then opened up. As four howitzers recoiled, four Number One men caught four empty shells and clanked them on the refuse pile. Four more shells leaped into four howitzers instantly. Four gunners checked firing stakes and found the range still right; Four Number One men pulled lanyards.

We had four rounds per gun—16 rounds in the air in 36 seconds—fired a total of nine rounds per howitzer! After the concentration reports came back—Japs in trees, or pieces of Japs. Walwyn reported 50 dead Japs and many more wounded. We fired, finally, 50 rounds. C never forgot that "big shoot-out."

On 12 July, after we fired Concentration 502 the last time, unopposed Aussies took "The Pimple." One 13 July at dawn, we fired four concentrations into Woody Island; the Aussies seized it. At 0900, we hammered 100 rounds between Bui Lang and Bui Talal Creek for A Co. A then advanced up Buigap Creek— Komiatum Track itself—past abandoned holes and hundreds of dead Japs and fresh graves. At 1100, Col. Taylor requested 60 rounds for Newman's C against dug-in Japs. The first few rounds panicked them. C's mission in clearing Komiatum Track was finished.

C headed on deep into the diabolical jungle mountains, two howitzers at a time. A pln. of 116 Engrs. helped us carry the disassembled 75's. We went up Lababia Ridge—the first half a climb straight up—to captured Green Hill, and then down to Buigap Creek near Kitchen Creek.

And from about 18 July to about 19 Aug., C fired mainly for Col. Tylor's 1/Bn. against the unstormable Mt. Tambu. On 30 July, when A and C Co's of 162 made the attack, we helped other Yank and Aussie guns fire preparation. From 30 minutes before the assault until five minutes after it began, we blasted the SW slope of Tambu with 208 rounds apiece. Like the Aussies' attacks on "The Pimple," this assault was a costly error, but through no fault of C 218.

On 4 Aug. we had our only battle casualties, but not from Japs. The Aussies had not yet learned that FA was more reliable than mortars. One defective Aussie mortar shell impacted a combined observation party of C and Service Btry.

Although the party was behind a log, C with Sv. had five dead and one wounded. Dead were C's Lt. Osterholtz, Cpls. Newson and Copp. C's Lindenau lingered to die in hospital 15 Sept. Sv's Cpl. Salice (or Solis?) died also. Wounded was C's George Miller.

During this month of heavy fire, the work of C's artificer, Sgt. Totten, was outstanding. Since all our ammo was now air dropped, many shell casings were badly dented and not fireable. Often projectiles jammed in the case, with danger to gunners.

Totten headed the detail which repaired these shells— and Cpl. Demonnis with Reuter and two natives. Under Totten's instructions, they extracted primers and projectiles and refitted them into cases already empty from firing. (After a shell fired, concussion actually improved the case for future use.)

Once a brass crosshead was broken, the crosshead that activated the firing pin on the gun. This break should have made the gun unworkable, but Totten fabricated a new brass crosshead and the gun worked perfectly again.

After Mt. Tambu fell to 162, C rejoined A and B Btrys. on Tambu Bay and began blasting Japs all the way into Salamaua. We registered on Salamaua at 1445 on 22 Aug., and at 2100 we heard a great explosion, as if we had blown up a large Jap ammo dump.

Final report of C 218 FA at Salamaua concerns our Capt. Burelbach. Attached as firing officer to the Aussie 15 Brigade, he became a savior for Capt. Provan's Dawn Co., attacking up D Ridge. Trapped high up the Ridge, Dawn Co. was low in ammunition and in a precarious position before Nips protecting their Scout Track escape route. Twice the morning of 1 Sept., Burelbach called down 218 and 205 FA to smash Jap charges.

At 1800, wounded Capt. Provan himself stopped at 218's "Smith Btry." for personal thanks for our 75's. And later in the day Aussie wounded came by to repeat Dawn Co's gratitude for being saved from annihilation. And on 2 Sept., Burelbach was a hero again in protecting Dawn Co. from another attack of these fresh, aggressive Jap marines. (They were members of Commander Takeuchi's 5th Sasebo Special Landing Force and had orders to wipe out the Aussies in one week.) Next day, Burelbach reported that he had got direct hits on three Jap pillboxes and had totally destroyed several LMG's. And this is the final tale of C Battery, 218 Field Artillery, which helped capture Salamaua and saved many Yank and Aussie lives in doing so.

CREDIT: Indispensable were notes from interview with Charles Ricks, Allen Jones and Louis Reuter at 1972 Chicago convention. Important also was Australian David Dexter's The New Guinea Offensives, with maps and mountain descriptions. Other data came from "Report of 218 FA, 27 June '43 to 30 Oct '43," and "Journal June 26 to Oct 4, 1943." I also used Col. A.R. MacKechnie's "Operations of 162d Inf. in Salamaua Campaign," and "Notes on Operation Morobe, Nassau Bay Area." (I mentioned 218 FA in my article on Mount Tambu (Jungleer, May 1959), where I erroneously said that 218 had 105's instead of 75's.) I need more Artillery stories; only other I have is that of Ted Helmer's C 205 FA at Salamaua. We'd like to have more stories of 218 FA; this is the only one available thus far.

162d Infantry Assails Mount Tambu

by DR. HARGIS WESTERFIELD with COLONEL A. R. MacKECHNIE (162 Inf.)

Wounded being evacuated from SCOUT RIDGE to 162d Inf. beachhead at TAMBU BAY, N. G., August 1943.

Credit Lines

For this article, I used these sources: 1) 162 Inf Rep of Op; 2) Col. A. R. MacKechnie's "The Salamaua Campaign"; 3) Gen. Harold Taylor's "Notes re Mt. Tambu"; 4) Taylor's map; 5) a water-color from Mt. Tambu; 6) Col. John George's ltr dated July 12 1944; 7) George's ltr to author Dec. 1958; 8) Rep of First Lieut. James Clark, 186 Inf. This is the approved way of writing history—assembling data from many sources and interpreting such data creatively. hw

FOR THE FIRST BATTALION 162 Infantry, the fighting for the approaches to Salamaua came to its most deadly climax in the frontal attack on Mount Tambu 30 July 1943. Mount Tambu was one of the toughest battalion strength positions that 162 Infantry ever faced. This position was actually the northern peak of Mount Tambu still held by the Japs after two Australian attacks. Sixty feet above the men in the holes loomed a rising wall of dark, shell-battered jungle. It was a triple tier of pillboxes, and the Japs garrisoned it from an underground network of tunnels often protected by ten feet of earth overhead, and from an unbroken supply-line north over the ridges.

The two previous Aussie assaults had only made it harder for the Yanks' attacks. On 16-19 July, Aussies had overrun the southern hump and held it. On 24 July, Cos. A and C of the 2/5 Btn had tried without artillery against the northern peak and got nowhere. The Japs had abundant time to dig deeper and test their defenses before we attacked.

On 28 July, C Company 162 Inf took over the Aussie perimeter 100 yards down the slope from the Nipponese lines, while the Aussie D Co 2/5 Infantry still held a firm base of fire on our left. Some 75 yards behind C, First Btn Headquarters and our D Co garrisoned the southern hump. And 300 yds from our front line on the same hump, were emplaced our 81 mortars and the Aussies' 3-inchers.

C Company reconnoitered for the safest possible lines of attack, and spotted the lurking pillboxes on the withered jungle terraces.

On 29 July near dark the artillery assault began. The eight 105's of Batteries B and C, 218 FA, and five Aussie 25-pounders struck at Tambu Peak from 1715 to 1725 Hrs. Our 81's and the Aussie 3-inchers also blasted the jungle mountain in the last light of day. But the big show began on 30 July. From 0730 to 0905, the two batteries of 105's with the 25-pounders again played hard on Mount Tambu.

What effect did the final morning's shelling have on the enemy?

With only 208 rounds per gun, the effect must have been light on their dug-in positions, even from remarkably accurate firing. For with a three-minute silence in firing at 0840, enemy machine-guns opened up defiantly. Our mortars apparently silenced them. At 0843, two 75's went to work on the near slope of Tambu, while the 105's and 25's renewed their barrage; and in a final five minutes, the 81's and 3-inch mortars arced their concussions down on the Japanese front

Our last mortars impacted on the crest at 0905. From the far left, two of our heavy 30's fired obliquely against the shoulder of Jap pillboxes to the far right, but the enemy's counter-fire was quick.

With the last mortar shell at 0905 and the opening machine-guns, C Company moved out from its assembly point at the right rear of the CP. These little 30-man platoons of veterans wisely made no direct frontal attack at the first terrace with its embankment of eight pillboxes and an easy slope for grazing automatic fire. With the First Platoon in support, C's Second and Third Platoons kept working their business-like way to the right flank of the towering hill position, against emplacements poorly guarded by flanking fire. Japanese rifles, machine-guns and mortars opened up sporadically. Our riflemen called for counter-fire against mortars, or from cover blasted the machine-guns into comparative silence. Rifle-grenadiers latched on launchers, attached AT grenades, sighted carefully over weighted rifle-muzzles and pressed triggers. Shells blazed into pillboxes.

Yet the Jap was master of Mount Tambu, where his observers could see for miles over dark jungled Charlie Ridge to the Tambu Bay to the SW. Untouched by shell-fire, he could look down on gray blurs of Yanks and correct his sight-pictures and squeeze off shots when it suited him.

But C's attack continued, slowly, desperately. In 43 minutes, the Second and Third Platoons had moved only 150 yards along an oblique line towards the right front of the Japanese line. Then we had advanced a weary 50 yards up to the right shoulder—the first line of pillboxes.

We knocked out six of the eight pillboxes in the Nipponese forward wall; our AT grenades made certain kills of two Nipponese heavy M.G.'s. With virtually the whole first Japanese line over-run or silenced, we felt momentarily successful.

Then, just on the first crest, we met the massed fire of Japanese heavy guns from the second line of pillboxes 10 feet above us where the mountain narrowed to a neck 100 yards wide. Frontally, two of them blazed at us from 50 yards. Grenades rolled down on us. From the far left of the ridge, an enemy gun had 100 yards of terraced enfilade at our right flank. Our riflemen were pinned down, unable to charge or retire. And leftwards, new Japanese forces with automatic weapons infiltrated into the pillboxes we had cleared, and directed new fire on our flank.

With C's Second and Third Platoons both in jeopardy and unable to move under fire, it was time to send in support troops. The First Platoon had been inactive and safe in defilade near the C command post. Now it formed up and moved out in a long climb to the left of the other platoons, and towards the very center of the Japanese lines. We hoped that this advance would take the pressure off the other platoons, but the Japanese held the second line unbroken, and a machine-gun could work on the First Platoon from the far left of the first line.

We made still another bid for victory. An unexpected push on the extreme left shoulder might do it. A sudden onslaught on this

Services were held in small clearing for men not actively engaged in the battle 300 yards ahead. Background shows typical jungle growth.

other anchor of the Japanese forward defenses might divert the fire that played on the left of the C attack. It might draw reserves of manpower and automatic weapons, and the battle might still be won.

From Captain John George's A Co, which now manned the vacated C perimeter, this forlorn hope started out with A's First Platoon of 31 men, including First Lieut. James A. Clarke, observer from 186 Infantry. To protect the A Platoon's left flank, we also moved a Heavy Machine Gun even farther left.

With two squads abreast and one in reserve, "A" moved out. With the Heavy Machine Gun firing into the pillbox on the left shoulder, and the protection of a dip in the ground, the platoon was briefly safe. Then from the Japs' far left, we were in the field of fire from an outposted pillbox hard to reach. Soon we had masked the fire of our own M.G.

At the base of the hill, a Nippo Heavy opened, and knee-mortars impacted among us. Platoon Lieut. Barney Ryan and a corporal were wounded immediately. All told, we had four killed and 21 wounded, and only six unmarked. Here Lieut. Clarke of 186 Inf got his training for combat first-hand, as he lay under the drum-fires and wondered that he still lived.

This last flurry of attack lasted just 25 minutes. At 1200, C's First Platoon was slowly advancing, and A's First was making the last hard attack. At 1225, all units were down flat and taking all that the Japs had to throw. Even Capt. Del Newman of C got worked over by an MG that fired through his sleeve and shot the pockets off his web belt yet left him unscratched.

What was to be done now? An estimated 135 men — half of A and C — lay imprisoned under Jap fire — or wounded or dead. Could we send in another wave? Where could we find them? The Japs' second line was unscathed, and the first was rebuilt over our prone riflemen.

At 1242, Col. Harold Taylor ordered our withdrawal. The Heavies fired 17,000 rounds against the pillboxes and partially stopped the gunners. The Yank 81's and the Aussie's 3's smoked up the C positions, and we pulled off with one one more killed and six more wounded — half of these casualties due to a short from a 3-inch smoke shell. C's First Pltn on the left towards the center escaped first, then the Second to its right, and finally the Third on the far right. By 1330, C had cleared, but extricating A's Pltn was another problem.

A was supposed to leave before C; but because of the terrific fire, not an A man could move. Long after C was gone, Capt. George was hard at work saving his men—the 27 left alive. He called for smoke, and our section of Heavies shot 1800 rounds against the Japs' guns before we withdrew. C Co. returned by 1330; it was not until 150 long minutes later that A's men were home in their holes with four dead and nearly all the others stung by Japanese steel.

Over one-third of the attackers were killed or wounded—a total of nine KIA and 36 WIA (estimated) out of perhaps 135 who started.

What were the names of those who died or suffered severe wounds? Lieut. Barney Ryan and Pltn. Sgt. Ted Richter with two squad leaders were among those wounded in A's First. In C Co, we know only the name of the wounded Juarez, a proud Spanish-American rifle grenadier some 6 feet tall.

Why did the attack fail? Aside from the sure risk of fighting uphill on a narrow front against automatic fire and rolling grenades, the answers are many. The time for reconnaisance was short. The CO of the Aussie 2/5 Btn was optimistic; he had sold his Brigade CO on the frontal attack —by someone else.

As for the assault itself, even the most accurate 105's with delayed action fuses could not penetrate 10 feet of enemy ground. Moreover, all participants agreed that bazookas and flame-throwers would have succeeded in the frontal attack; but New Guinea infantry of those days still had only rifles, hand-grenades, and launchers for close combat.

It was over two weeks later that the First Btn again attempted Mount Tambu in force—after days of artillery fire and harassing patrols. And the Aussie 42 Btn had cut the Japs' supply track. Only after three direct assaults and a month of attrition was Mount Tambu ours.

by Dr. Hargis Westerfield
(Pfc G Co 163 Inf)

Col. A. R. MacKechnie

As CO of 162 Inf at Salamaua, Col. MacKechnie was awarded the British DSO for his exploits by the Australian Third Division. After Salamaua and until retirement in 1946, he served on the Ground Force Rocket Board and wrote a TM of Rocket Tactics, as well as several Infantry Journal articles.

His career is proud and colorful. Born in Carrington, N. Dak. (1895), he graduated from Port Angeles High in Washington. After becoming Sgt (F Co 2nd Wash. Inf., N.G.), he returned to play two years of football at U. of Washington. Although a stateside RA looey in World War I, he rose to chicken colonel by World War II. (One of his two sons is a Major RA now.) He also played and coached Army athletics. In 1926, on the Infantry School football team, he was coached by none other than President Dwight D. Eisenhower.

Retired in Healdsburg, Calif., "Colonel Mack" is chairman of the local Red Cross Chapter and Sec.-Treas. of the Boys' Club.

40 mm Bofors (AA), 50 Cal. MGs. (AA), 81 mm Mortars and 75 mm and 105 mm Howitzers were used to support successful attack on Roosevelt Ridge, TAMBU BAY, N. G. by 162d Inf.

B Co. 162 Infantry:
Jungle Pursuit at Salamaua

**BY F/LT WENDEL C. MESSEC WITH
DR. HARGIS WESTERFIELD**

CREDITS

Basic MS is F/Lt Wendel C. Messec's "Report Pltn Action in Mt. Tambu-Salus Lake Area," 18 Sept 1943. Of major importance also was an unsigned personal narrative. Col. AR MacKechnie's "Operations of 162 Inf in Salamaua Campaign" gives overall picture. All 3 MS are part of the treasure-trove "Col Mack" sent me in 1958 — which gave me basic material for 8 162 stories. We badly need more stories of 162 on Biak and Mindanao. (Hargis Westerfield, 6248 Study Avenue, Cincinnati 30, Ohio).

On 12 Aug 1943, 162 Inf besieging Mt. Tambu got alarming news. A Papuan track worker had seen fresh spoor of Japs crossing Boisi Trail—an estimated band of 40 headed SE. At once, F/Btn's CO, Col. Harold Taylor, knew that the Nips were out to kill Aussie and Yank FA 4 miles off on the coast at Lake Salus. And Taylor's men were observing to help these guns decimate the Japs on Mt. Tambu and save Yank lives. (He had lost 9 killed, 35 wounded in the frontal attack of 30 July.)

At once, Taylor ordered a B Co Pltn in pursuit—Lt. Messec's 3 Pltn. For B Co was in the best condition of all F/Btn's Cos. Orders had held us from the shipwreck landing at Nassau Bay and the 2 days' fight for the beachhead. On the 30 May assault on Mt. Tambu, B Co was in reserve. But B Co had had its share of patrols and minor fights. Promptly that afternoon of 12 June we moved out—32 of B Co plus 4 Btn Communications men with wire. We had just 1 day's rations.

At 0730, 13 Aug we prowled in a long line of riflemen among mountain jungle. We trailed by bits of Nippo equipment, and saw where they had halted to eat. At noon, we oriented ourselves from a hilltop, found that we were 8 miles farther from Lake Salus than when the patrol began. The Japs were lost—or trying to mislead us. At the first Jap bivouac area, we were scared. Instead of 40, our 32-man Pltn was chasing at least 75-80 Nips.

Out of wire now, we left Communications men Perez, Smith, Greenlee, Coker to keep phoning for rations and to forward cargadores to us. We missed supper that night; we saved our last ration for dawn. In that clammy mountain jungle 2,000 feet up, we spent the night huddled close together, dozing fitfully.

Finishing our last ration for breakfast, we moved to Jap Bivouac No. 2, 12 hours old. Signs still indicated some 100 Nips ahead. We starved ahead of time; we were hot, thirsty, sore-footed. Then our Communications Detail caught up with a message. Japs were already before us at the coast; the news was 8 hours old. We left 2 sick Yanks for the expected carrying party. We alerted again to the green jungle wall of death ahead, dragged our weight of steel over confusing ridges.

At 1700 Hours, we saw light on Salūs Lagoon, pushed on fast. An M-1 fired; Lead Scout Ransom shot at a Nip outpost of 4-5, hit 2. The Nips hid and fired back. We crouched low while bullets cut the leaves overhead. We busied the Nips with persistent frontal fire, until Ransom and Sgt Orton climbed a cliff on the flank and hurled grenades and routed them.

Dark was coming. As we dug in, a short burst of firing stabbed the night. We thought that FA guards on the shore were fighting a Jap attack. We waited for what sinister truth dawn would bring us. Ours was a bad perimeter here. We had no food since dawn, and no water since 1400. At noon, however, 12 A&P men broughte us meager rations. The A&P men would not keep any food for themselves. After lunch, we moved out despite blistered, scalded, jungle-rotted feet.

The Japs' trail led down a deep ravine. To avoid ambush, we turned north and inland 500 yards off the trail, then back to the coast. With scouts far ahead, we cleared 2 villages, but Jap sign was old.

In the last melancholy jungle sunlight before dark, we heard the heavy buzz of flies. We found 6 Aussies dead beside overturned billy-can and scattered mess-gear—and 2 dead Nips in full pack. Here had been the firing of last night—the defeat of an Aussie patrol like ours sent to protect FA.

After searching for wounded Aussies, we dug perimeter. Men on guard knelt alone thinking and staring into darkness.

As we doped it out, we had lost the trail of that first Nippo patrol we had started to chase. That patrol must be positioned before our guns a day's hike northward. But the Nips we chased looked formidable. They had much ammo, full packs, a month's rations. If both parties of Nips united, they would number 200—enough to kill our FA. Messec decided to smask one or both parties before they joined forces —our little patrol of 29, counting 2 Meds.

At earliest light, hole guards roused us to hit the trail. Supperless yesterday, we saved our last ration for when we

Jungleers in a fire fight.

might need it more. Fearing ambush, we left the trail for the jungle again. About 1000, we had our last ration, then waded north 4 hours at the edge of the salt marsh.

Down a steep hill, we saw an unalert Jap sentry. Not to alarm other Nips, Cox—with his squad covering him—slipped through the brush to brain the Jap with his BAR. But we still climbed hills 3 hours before we hit the Nippo main body.

Lead Scout Ransom saw 8 Nips 150-200 yards before him taking a break. When they moved off, he signalled his Second Scout and the lead squad to count them before we fought. Ransom slipped away first with TSMG ready.

Suddenly Ransom came face to face with 8 Nips and 2 automatic weapons outposted. As the Nips saw him, he took cover, emptied the whole clip into them in short bursts before they reacted—as in slow motion. Two fell dead. Their return fire was wild. We heard the groans of wounded.

Then 2 Nip MGs blazed out. But it was evidently pre-arranged fire—and nowhere near us. Yet our scouts were pinned down, and most of the covering squad in defilade. But with BARman Edin's heavy fire, we attacked and got out Ransom and the other scout.

Now as planned, our rear squad made hasty perimeter, while the 2 forward squads fell back. In the delaying action, Edin's BAR was again effective.

Many Nips seemed to shout orders, but we had no counterattack. After 20 minutes, we formed a new perimeter 300 yards back, whlie Medics Davis, Bailey dressed Broder's arm wound.

Messec selected a perfect position to fight from 300 yards farther on—a small knoll off the trail and to the Nips' right. It was a nose jutting off a higher hill. It was a pretty ambush.

Half an hour before dark, outguards heard movements from the Japs' direction. With a BAR on each flank, we massed the other 2 BARs with 8 TSMGs against the main Nippo thrust. "Hold that fire until 15-20 yards' range!" ordered Messec.

The Japs pursuit came single-file up that trail. Heavily armed in camouflaged uniforms, they still trudged too close together and chattered.

Already the Nippo point of riflemen climbed on a level with us. Followed the main body—a long line 100 yards down to the bottom of the ravine—which ravine was only 40 yards from our position air-line—and in plain view. Other Nips kept hiking downhill behind them. It was a BAR-fighters dream come true!

At 20 yards, Briggs squeezed BAR trigger, burst after burst. Seconds later, Cox' BAR shot up the rear of the column descending the ravine. Our 8 TSMGs and most M-1s opened up. We wiped out the point; 35 Nips rolled downhill and lay groaning. A few got free to return fire.

Another Nip force across the trail opened up. We shot from standing position with M-1s and somewhat lessened their fire. Now they probed for our flanks and began pushing—hardest on the ridge above to our vulnerable left. Jap bullets hit closer.

Cpl Burrell shot 2 with his sniper's '03. Their barefooted corpses rolled down on us. A TSMG killed 1 Jap; he fell in the open. Our accurate fire kept others from pulling him back behind a tree.

They almost quit shooting, but yells told us that they had found both flanks of our position. Occasionally Nips ran across openings; we picked off a few. Burruel got busy again; he dropped an AT rifle-grenade on the leftward high ground and blasted them and halted the movement past us. As Burruel stood up to trigger his kicking rifle, they fired back; but he grenaded front and right flank with more good results.

The firing died out in the dark. We took stock and decided to pull out—rearward where no Nips seemed to lurk. We had whipped them decisively; but our automatic weapons ammo was about gone.

Followed the fright and confusion of even a planned night retreat. With the first half of 3/Pltn, S/Sgt Meier missed a rendezvous at a stream junction. While trying to find them with the second half, Messac rescued 4 men who were lost in the dark.

Next morning, Messec's half left the rendezvous and arrived at 162's Nassau Bay Base by 1200 2 days later. Despite orders, Meier's group hiked to Tambu Bay—a shorter distance but a rougher track. Once they saw 4 Nips with LMG; but the Nips fled. Their march took a night and day of continuous footslogging. BARman Isely was lost and alone 36 hours before he saved himself.

Meanwhile, what of the Nippo lia or raid to kill our guns? Besides routing the Aussie patrol, they did penetrate an Aussie battery, plant dynamite under a gun. But the charge never exploded. In that night's fighting, Aussies killed 15.

What of the surviving Nips? Only the jungle can answer, and the jungle tells no tales. But 3 days after Messec's great ambush, guards with a litter party saw 12 Nips moving north on Tambu Track. The guards killed 8, scattered the other 4. We believed these to be the last organized remnant falling back to the garrison on Mt. Tambu.

All told, Messec reckoning totalled 6 Yanks evacuated—wounded Bruder, 4 men with bad feet, 1 hernia case. By 21 Aug, however only 15 of the original 32 rejoined B Co; the others remained with the Clearing Co. longer. Messec also conservatively estimated that we had killed 35 Nips. And most important of all, Col. A. R. MacKechnie credited B Co's fine patrol with ending all attempts of Jap raiders to kill our FA.

But perhaps these dates are most important of all to prove the success of Messec's patrol to Lake Salus. Messec rejoined 162 at Nassau Bay 17 Aug. On 18 Aug, another 162 patrol found that the Japs had begun to evacuate hard-held Mt. Tambu. One of the deciding factors in the Japs' retreat may well have been Messec's great patrol.

Orange, Folsom, Tapioli — 162nd's Great I&R Men

By DR. HARGIS WESTERFIELD with FOLSOM, WHALEY, SMITH, RUSSELL, PEEL, LeBARON

Lean, red-headed Rod Orange created 162's I&R in midsummer, 1942. With a core of 6 trained men from S-2, he sharked up (they say) the 18 men considered most troublesome of the CO's. Orange trained us brawlers to hike 30 miles daily, climb every mountain at Rockhampton, relax by judo.

But in New Guinea, Orange volunteered too hard. He raced I&R into Morobe too late to catch the Japs. He set up OP with two natives behind enemy-held Salamaua, gave Gen. Fuller thorough information about the Japs. He planned to scout Finschhafen, but crashed near Lae while observing from a light bomber. Nobody ever saw Rod Orange again.

Then saintly Myron Folsom took command—an All-American wonder boy—tall with snapping black eyes—a Californian, a star tennis player. He had a towering sense of duty, front-line courage, and a high sense of humor. If we respected Orange, we loved Folsom—this religious-minded leader who never pulled rank on us—who preferred to bivouac with us even in garrison.

Yet when 162 shipwrecked itself at midnight 29 June '43 at Nassau Bay, the black night and the gale nullified us. Our third wave with I&R on a cranky Jap barge, got lost. On a second try, Folsom, Svagdis, Tapioli swam ashore an important order for Col. MacKechnie. Folsom said, "We should have joined the Navy."

On July 2-7, we patrolled around Col. Mack's beach perimeter, booby-trapped trails, set up OPs. We learned how green we were.

For LeBaron, Kazor, Merz, Willis, Russell, Sgt. Cooper went mostly unarmed in a carrying party up Lababia River on 6 July. We wise guys knew that the Japs were all north of Bitoi Ridge. When they blasted us from ambush, we cowered behind wooden boxes, desperately broke out "C" ration cans to fight Jap rifles. Although three Yanks died, no I&R man was hurt. But we learned a lesson.

When 162 moved inland, we guarded a first native carrier train to "Mack Forward." When 162 pushed over Bitoi Ridge, we guarded the left flank. Up Bitoi River almost to Nippo Green Hill, we scouted between sheer slate bluffs, sometimes waded chest-deep, spent nights in ambush. Wallace, Kazor, LeBaron became outstanding scouts.

Then Col. Taylor told us to find a carrier route to Mt. Tambu. On our first three-day patrol went Folsom, Whaley, Peel, Wallace, Smith, Meyer, Berrigan, four naives. On 15 July in the brush, an Aussie scout missed a shot at Tapioli. We identified ourselves to the Aussies, took the point for them. At a creek-bend, Tapioli killed a sleeping Nip with his rifle-butt. We located the carrier trail for 162, put the Aussie outfit on it.

CREDITS

I have Folsom's "Diary—I&R Pltn;" his untitled report 8 Sept. 43; "Use of I&R Pltn in Jungle," 17 Sept 43; "I&R Pltn Rept." 20 Oct 43; "Folsom Recon Patrol," "Ambush of Jap Party." Additional data came from John Justin Smith's "Soldier of the Dusk," and Ltrs from Smith (Dec 1960), Raymond R. Russell, Jr. (Jan 10 1961), Milan Peel (Feb 18 1961), Tex Gould Whaley, Jr. (Apr 18 1961), Clyde LeBaron (June 8 1961). Useful also was 162's "Journal of Salamaua Operation." Thanks also to Col MacKechnie, CO of 162 at Salamaua and Col. Towsend (CN 162) from whose papers I took everything above but the ltrs. [McCartney's "history" briefly mentions Orange's missions to Salamaua; but Folsom, Tapioli, I&R go totally uncited.] Folsom's Dairy lacks detail except at the start; I had great difficulty on dates and individual patrols. I wrote all I&R men whose addresses I could find; but I have yet to get accurate data on Folsom's last patrol on Biak.]

HARGIS WESTERFIELD

While Taylor besieged the Nip Btn. at Mt. Tambu, we were attached to help Col. Roosevelt's major operation against the tangle of unknown jungle ridges around Tambu Bay which barred us from Salamaua. It was a nightmare of everlasting patrols for information, always the mountains, the pressing hot jungle, the smell of dead Nips. Some times we went in force, as many as 15 men to a patrol; other times there were three, two, even one. Patrols lasted an hour, a day, or as much as a week. We ranged far inland from Tambu Bay, went into the Nuknuk network of trails long before the Japs were driven out. We scouted the NW coast so far that we looked down on Salamaua weeks before the riflemen.

Closer to the battle, we manned OPs, questioned natives, mapped positions, guided others, cut off Jap supply trails. On 2 Aug., Rumack, Folsom registered H Co. mortars on pillboxes, caused much damage, saw 12 Jap dead. At one OP, Russell spied a Jap CO in full uniform—sword, epaulets—on a ridge at 1500 yards. He called for mortars, 105's, often drove this bantam rooster underground. But he never saw the Jap's bunker blasted out.

Although I&R's job was to see Nips without being seen, we had some sharp exchanges of fire, were sometimes grazed. On 8 Aug., Milan Peel guided an Aussie Capt. to his new outfit, over a well-traveled supply trail inside our lines. Topping a ridge, Peel stood up to face a Jap rifle-butt swinging at him. It knocked him 15-20 feet. He called the Aussie, heard only a groan. A punitive expedition found the Aussie dead with a bayonet in his back, hunted down and slew the two Nips. Evidently they were a recon party who became tempted to kill. Peel survived with 24 stitches in his face.

If Peel was I&R's only serious combat casualty, it was due to the six PIB men who joined Folsom 29 June, just before the first landing—Lance-Cpl. Tapioli, Liokina, Sau, Arnau, Trumuet, Orosol. Tapioli was the greatest. Once he led Folsom, Smith, others down a river 6 miles inland. We expected Nips at every bend. Near the end of a straight ¼-mile reach, Tapioli halted, said "Japanese." Folsom was indignant; the patrol was stopped for no reason. "How do you know?" he queried. Tapioli pointed to his nose. Just around the bend lay many Japs by camp-fires.

Such was Tapioli—5 feet of him, a mop of kinky hair, two phenomenal eyes, a toothy smile, powerful legs. The

Japs drafted him in New Britain; he carried for them at the Buna Beach. He escaped in the Owen Stanleys, joined the Aussies. The Aussies gave him to Folsom.

Once Bob Randall, 162 cartographer, jeered that our reports too often mentioned Jap axmen chopping down trees. Randall said, "You write this because it sounds good on a report." Next patrol, Folsom sent Tapioli to the Nips for evidence. In 15 minutes, he brought back an ax, a twig with Nippo blood on it. We ceremoniously presented these to Randall.

After 162 took Roosevelt Ridge, we hunted Nips on other ridges blocking us from Salamaua. Notably 15 Aug., Whaley, Pedersen, Cornie checked B Hill for an alleged Aussie outfit, reported only vacated Jap trenches to occupy. On 19 Aug., Whaley, Smith, Pedersen checked Charlie Hill, also said to be Aussie. Pussyfooting first, Tapioli, Whaley halted and stared into jungle black. It took some time before realizing they stared into a Jap pillbox. Aussie Hq. called us crazy; later they apologized through a call from Col. Roosevelt. They had stiff opposition to capture Charlie Hill.

By late Aug., hardened I&R's patrols were a fine art. For example, about 23 Aug., Folsom hunted NW of L Co. on Scout Hill Track to find a Nippo supply line, and observe from ridge-spurs. With four others, he left L Co. perimeter at 0700. (Equipment was probably carbine, ammo belt with canteen, "D" chocolate bar, fatigue hat.) Formation was Indian file—Tapioli first, then Folsom, Cornie, Willis, and Liokina last. Near the top of the saddle between Charlie and Egg Hills, Tapioli halted, signaled for quiet.

After 30 yards' slow advance, Tapioli motioned Folsom up. Folsom saw a track of packed earth, Jap wire high in the trees. He beckoned the others. Cornie, Willis, Liokina took positions to protect flanks—or cover a quick withdrawal.

Suddenly we heard noise on the track. A column of 30 Nips in full field equipment, well worn and dirty, passed eastward. As usual in Folsom's experience, they trudged eyes front without scanning the jungle. He decided that they must be doped, to walk a trail without security.

Then we followed the track ourselves. Worried Tapioli led, with Liokina at our rear. Both natives feared our Yank clumsiness would alert Nips; the track was well travelled in both directions.

Just in time, they signalled. We hid in the bush. Another Jap party passed. We left the trail and reconnoitered four ridge spurs more. Everywhere Nips were passing or digging in. We made a fat report for our infantry and FA to work on.

About 27 Aug., Folsom had a field day of combat. First he booby-trapped Scout Camp Trail, probably in the approved way. He had Tapioli scout several reaches of trail to find it all clear.

Then Tapioli took position down the track; his native cobber guarded in the other direction. Quietly we three Yanks got to work. While two set booby-traps with black thread, one cut wires. Now Tapioli pulled off the trail to guide our withdrawal; his cobber covered our rear. Shortly afterwards, the booby-traps exploded. We stopped and laughed silently.

On 27 Aug. also, Folsom's group worked with A Co. and Aussies to cut that supply trail. While forming off the track, they saw six Japs pass—in clean uniforms with full field equipment. Then we sent four Aussies with a Bren gun 50 yards up the track—and four more Aussies down the track, while eight Yanks wanted for frontal fire.

Now came 11 Japs fully equipped, with Arisakas slung on shoulders. Our Bren gun fired first—and then the rifles. The Japs fell dead before they could even unsling arms.

Thus I&R campaigned for Salamaua, found the Nips, and led the heavy armaments against them—something like 200 missions in July-Sept 1943. We were first into Salamaua from Roosevelt Ridge in 10-12 hours' time. With Kazor, itself. It was a hard, careful patrol; we marched 3 or 4 miles from Roosevelt Ridge in 10-12 hours time. With Kazor, Ihme, Peel, and LeBaron, Folsom swam the Francisco River to find only corpses, shell-torn ruins. Shortly after capturing Salamaua, I&R was back to rest and training at Rockhampton—to steak and eggs and beer and booze and Aussie blondes.

How we avoided court martials no one knows; but Folsom must have fronted for us.

Will any I&R man forget that last house-party at Rocky before New Guinea again—when the party got down to Australian Aqua Velva?

For the New Guinea Campaign, I&R could not take Tapioli along, because he would be outside the Aussie Mandate, no doubt. At Finschhafen, I&R pilgrimaged to Tapioli. He wept in greeting Folsom, begged to come along.

At first, we were lucky without Tapioli.

We were first into unoccupied Hollandia.

On 27 May in Biak, we were the point into the Parai Defile. We saw Nips 13 times that day, yet passed them without being hurt. Seriously wounded in the leg 28 May, Smith saw Folsom come out of the jungle to wish him well. As with Orange, Tapioli, Smith never saw Folsom again.

On 31 May, 1944, Myron Folsom died from a MG burst while heading a patrol to the caves N of the Mandom Waterhole. Details of his death are still obscure. We believe that a Javanese (or Korean) in the service of the Nips had led him into ambush. When we brought him out, we identified him by the captain's bars he carried in his pocket for his coming promotion. If Tapioli had been there, Folsom might still be alive.

162 Infantry:
GOOD SOLDIER MacKECHNIE'S SALAMAUA OPERATION

By DR. HARGIS WESTERFIELD, Division Historian
with the late Col. A.R. MacKechnie

When Col A.R. MacKechnie, with 162's 1/Bn, charged in through heavy surf that black midnight at Nassau Bay, he faced the strangest campaign the 41st ever fought. For Col Mack had more than Japs to fight. He fought the problem of divided command. Although under direct Aussie command in roadless jungle mountains, he still must please Gen Fuller 200 miles back at Oro Bay. Then Gen Fuller appointed Brig Gen Coane to command part of Col Mack's own 162 for the next operation after Nassau Bay — The Tambu Bay operation.

But the Aussies had already ordered Col Mack to make the same attack at Tambu Bay that Fuller had ordered Coane to make. Both Mack and Coane were to attack with the same troops; nobody knew who commanded whom. With a background of misty blue jungle mountains, MacKechnie, Fuller, Coane, 2 Aussie generals, even Maj Roosevelt, played one of the wildest farces in U.S. military history. Due greatly to Col Mack's initiative, these men finally solved the problem of divided command and no doubt saved many lives of 162 men.

Actually, first error of the divided command came long before Mack's disastrous landing, the night of June 29-30, 1943. On 9 June, Aussie Capt DB Burke made the error that caused Mack's shipwreck landing. During his patrol into Jap country, Burke chose Mack's landing beach. In full day, Burke saw the 300-400 yard clearing on the Nassau Bay foreshore, and then "got the hell out," as the cobber put it. Thus the hasty opinion of an officer who did not observe the surf on the beach at night, was to trigger Col Mack's stormy black night landing that broached half of his barges. So Col Mack made his "shipwreck landing."

Dawn of 30 June '43 found Col Mack dug in minus 218 FA, B Co, and AA guns. Jap planes with infantry could destroy him. And the high casualties of the next night — 21 dead, 17 wounded — were probably due to lack of guns we could not land. And 218 FA could not smash Jap perimeters at Bassis and Duala until the Japs had fled in little bands to fight again farther north. Of course our combined operation with Aussies in the mountains later pinched off many Japs, but without 218 FA, we failed to cut down hundreds on the foreshore.

And 2 days after the landing, Mack wrote Gen Fuller that he hoped never again to have dual commanders. Despite no FA, AA, combat Engrs, native carriers, Mack had Aussie orders to move inland through 10 miles of jungle swamp to Napier to attack the Jap mountains. With no native carriers, he must use only a few jeeps — or take Yanks from duty to be pack-mules. His 3 rifle Co's he must string out over 10 miles to guard his CP, Napier, the new supply dump at Bitoi Mouth. A Jap counter attack front or rear could still happen. That night, Mack heard much fire from Bassis behind him yet no information from where Capt Hitchcock's Papuan Infantry harried the Japs.

And 2 days later, 4 July, Col Mack balked at hurry-up orders of Aussie Brigadier M.J. Moten. Mack had understood the campaign schedule to be subject to change because of emergency; but Moten tried to hold Mack to a Hq time-table of 13 June. Just 5 days after the wrecked landing. Moten expected Nassau Bay beaches cleared of Japs, a supply base set up, a 10-mile road over swamps to Napier, and all Yank fighters into the high jungle.

On 4 July, then Mack wrote Moten that Aussie Capt Hitchcock still had not reported that he had cleared Dinga Peninsula of Japs in Mack's rear. Yet Mack had forwarded Col Taylor, with almost all 1/Bn, to Napier for the seizure of Bitoi Ridge. Mack had, however, retained C Co for 24 hours to secure the beach until other Yanks arrived. Building a supply-road to Napier by 7 July was also impossible — even if that was the day Moten wanted 162 to strike into the mountains. Above all, Mack insisted that his Yanks' lives must not be sacrificed to meet a prefabricated schedule.

Upshot of Mack's resistance to these hurry-up orders was that Moten found a better way to expedite 162 into combat. Moten ordered an air-drop to Taylor on 5 July at Napier. Then Col Mack obtained L Co to garrison Nassau Bay so that C was released to join Col Taylor, to help Aussies fight Japs. But Mack started a chain reaction that caused Moten's CO, Sir Stanley Savige, to suggest to the Aussie CO of New Guinea Force that Mack should be replaced. Aussie Lt Gen Sir Edmund Herring had the tact to make no protest about Col Mack.

Thus, divided command again caused Mack trouble — yet no doubt saved Yank lives. For Gen Fuller had told Mack not to mount an offensive until he had the base installed and fully protected. Aussie Gen Savige later concluded that Mack's delay was really due to Col Taylor's inability to land that stormy night of June 29-30. For Taylor's task was to fight while Mack set up the base. Since Taylor failed to land, Mack had a dual role: secure the base yet command in the field. Despite Moten's dissatisfaction, however, Mack had served both Aussies and Gen Fuller effectively.

Then Mack really got involved in a wild farce of divided command — with 3 Aussie generals, 2 Yank generals — and even Maj Archie Roosevelt. Finally, good soldier Mack lost his cool — was relieved of command — reinstated through wisdom of Aussie Gen Savige and Gen Douglas Mac Arthur — and won Salamaua.

Farce began when tactful Lt Gen Herring decided to install a coastal base at Tambu Bay to supply Savige's 3/Div, now impossibly far from supplies at Port Moresby. A gunner himself, Herring wanted Yank 105s to blast Japs before Salamaua — itself only 5 miles air-line from Tambu Bay. We were closest, and Herring asked Fuller to command. Herring's deepest reason for having a Yank CO was that he feared to jeopardize morale by having Savige command Yanks from a distance.

And Gen Fuller placed Brig Gen Coane in command of the new operation. On 12 July, Fuller assigned Coane his troops. Important for the farce is that Fuller specified Mack's 162's 3/Bn to Coane.

And now erupted a battle-royal with 5 generals, Col Mack, and Maj Roosevelt in the ring. At his Port Moresby command conference of 3 July, Herring did not make clear who would command the Tambu Bay Operation. Gen Savige got the idea at Moresby that he now headed all 162. Savige told Brigadier Moten to detail Roosevelt's actions at Tambu Bay. Others' messages now flew every way — querulous, puzzled, angry.

But on 12 July, Savige was unsure what units he commanded. He repeated to Herring signals from Mack to Moten that Fuller said Roosevelt's 3/Bn was removed from Mack's rule to direct control of Fuller himself. Savige had not heard Coane Force was formed and asked who commanded whom. Herring replied, ". . . all units Mack Force under operational control of 3 Aust Div."

Savige now thought that he commanded all Mack's 162. But Herring merely meant that Savige had all Mack's present 1/Bn BCT with elements as Nassau Bay.

Trouble really began. For as both Coane and Mack found, CO Moten of 17 Aust Brig still know naught of Coane Force. He was sure that he ruled Roosevelt's 3/Bn. Perhaps because of advice from Capt Hitchcock's overworked Papuans now scouting Boisi, Moten told Roosevelt to send just 1 Co to fight Jap trenches where 200 reinforcements had just landed. (Yet on 29 June Roosevelt's largest — Co L — had only 138 men.)

And Coane informed Roosevelt: "Roosevelt Bn is not repeat NOT part of Mack Force and is not repeat NOT under command of 3 Aust Div or of 17 Aust Bde." And Coane told Roosevelt to continue following Coane's orders.

Now Roosevelt lashed out. After Coane's signal, he refused to comply with an order from Moten. He also gave Moten "friendly advice." He said that Moten's plans showed improper recon and lack of logistical understanding. Roosevelt then told Fuller that Moten's orders might cause disgrace or disaster. If Fuller disagreed, Roosevelt asked relief from command. When Savige in turn informed Roosevelt that Aussies commanded him, Roosevelt refused to recognize Savige's message. He said that he took orders only from Fuller.

But the real CO of 162 took the heaviest blow from this

confusion. Back at Mubo in the mountains, he had orders to plan to take Tambu Bay with 3/Bn. Returned to Nassau Bay, however, he found that Roosevelt was told that Mack did not command him — but Coane Force instead. Yet Mack took the front for Roosevelt and apologized to Moten for the provocative messages — which messages Mack condoned because the confused situation had put Roosevelt in a difficult position.

Although Coane now had Mack's 1/Bn and 2/Bn with attached units, Mack still felt responsible. For he learned that Coane had been assigned his combat mission evidently in a hurry. Coane Force lacked personnel for the mission. Mack turned over to Coane all his available Hq staff and service men and signallers.

Mack himself was detailed to Coane Force as S-3, Operations Officer. Only infantryman among FA officers, he found them unfamiliar with tactical procedures. They held long conferences with 6-8 discussants, divided decisions. But they gladly used his experience for coordinating troop movements.

The confusion of messages and commands now angered Mack. Moten had told Mack to plan for seizing Tambu Bay with 3/Bn. Returning to Nassau Bay to execute these plans, he learned that Coane had the mission Mack through he had, with 3/Bn to do it. Then Coane learned 3/Bn was not his, also. NOBODY had it!

Mack exploded — and well he might. He had borne the brunt of the whole Salamaua Operation far too long. And only he knew what physical agony he suffered despite medical sedatives. An old football injury racked his spine with osteoarthritis. He had successfully bucked a medical board, to fight in New Guinea.

So on 17 July, Mack radioed Fuller harshly. Mack complained he never had a direct reply to any report to Div Hq. He was left with only a few rear elements to command from all 162. Since Fuller lacked confidence in him, he asked relief from command. Or he requested "an additional pair of scissors so that I may continue present accomplishment of cutting up paper dolls at which I am rapidly becoming an expert."

Next day, Fuller relieved Mack, called him to Hq for inquisition. Irate Fuller was unaware that any confusion existed in the chain of command. Yet Fuller finally retracted his charges down to 3. Charges were: failure to keep Fuller informed of operational details, carrying out Savige's instructions to the letter, and sending the "paper doll" sentence. (One finds evidence for and against Fuller on all these charges — except, of course, the "paper doll" message.)

Then Fuller sensibly did not throw Mack away. Rather, Mack took Coane a letter to assign Mack to any job "regardless of organization or present assignment." But with Fertig now CO of 162, Coane would not reassign Mack without Fuller's specific approval. Finally, Coane sent Mack as liaison officer to 3/Div.

But the Yank Tambu Bay Operation was too slow for the Aussies, even if Coane with only. 3/Bn had cleared the foreshore, penned the Nips on Roosevelt Ridge, and rightly placed his guns to support Aussie drives on Salamaua. Roosevelt's men did well despite each company's averaging 100-120 men under strength even before Tambu Bay. And 3/Bn had changed four COs in the last 2 months. Yet Roosevelt Ridge was untaken even when 2/Bn later attacked and got footholds on lower ridges. (Mack had earlier recommended an initial offense with all 3 Bns in action.)

Reporting to 3/Div Hq, exiled Mack found that Aussie Gens Herring and Savige knew a great CO when they saw him. They insisted that we storm the Ridge, and trusted Col Mack. Herring went over Fuller's head to Gen MacArthur, to ask that Mack again command 162. And MacArthur agreed.

After Coane was relieved for illness, Mack returned to the Ridge, which our howitzers had denuded of jungle. That bright morning of 14 Aug, Mack trained all FA on that ridge — even the Bofors AA he had got to Tambu Bay after Fuller relieved him. The guns blew the top off the Ridge, and Mack guided 162 into Salamaua by 12 September. And for Good Soldier MacKechnie, Lieut-Gen Sir Stanley Savige procured a prize medal — the British DSO. Thus grandly ended the farce of divided command which Col A.R. MacKechnie endured to win Salamaua.

Prime sources are Col Mack's Ltrs: to Gen Fuller, 2 July, 14 July, 21 July, 28 July — and to Col Kenneth S. Sweany 29 July, 1 Aug — all 1943. Highly important also is David Dexter's THE NEW GUINEA OFFENSIVES (Canberra: Australian War Memorial, 1959). I used also Col Mack's "Notes on Opns, Nassau Bay Area" dated 8 July 43, 162's Journal beginning 12 July 43, Col Mack's citation from Gen Savige, 26 Aug 43 for DSO, and my two earlier brochures in JUNGLEER — "Night in Green Hell," (July 1959), and "1/Bn 162 Inf's Shipwreck Landing (Dec 1968) from materials submitted by Fred Devenney of 1/Bn Communications and Col Mack. This article is far more exhaustive than either David Dexter's study or earlier comments by Dr. James E. Miller, Jr in OPERATION CARTWHEEL.

C Battery, 205 FA BN:

Under the Japanese Cannon

By DR. HARGIS WESTERFIELD, Division Historian
with CAPT. TED V. HELMER

Ted Helmer sent me the basic dossier for this story, his undated letter in 1973, also "Log of Shellings Received by Battery C", with Chicago Tribune's correspondent Robert Cromie's news story, "Salamaua Susy Kills the Japs for Battery C." Other data are from 205 FA Bn's "Unit History, 16 Feb. 43 to 4 Oct. 43", with "Appendix XI—Casualties," "Unit Journal 218 FA Bn—Lae-Salamaua Campaign," Col. W. D. Jackson's Report 24 Sept. 1943, and David Dexter's The New Guinea Offensives. *Cross-references are to two previous* Jungleer *stories on entire 205 FA Bn at Salamua, March 65 and Oct. 72. I regret that a vague record from another source caused me to scramble A and C Batteries' casualties in the Oct. 72 story.*

In late afternoon, 23 July 1943, C Battery, 205 FA, loaded our four 105's with tractors and men into ten LCV's at Oro Bay and headed north to fight for 162 to capture Salamaua. C 205 was now attached to 218 FA, which was already in action. Under the cover of a moonless night, C Btry chugged some 100 miles up the Guinea shore to beach at Tambu Bay under Roosevelt Ridge. (Only the day before had I and K Cos of 162 failed in the first assault on heavily defended Roosevelt Ridge.)

Arriving on the south side of Tambu Bay about 0300 in pitch-black jungle darkness, our well-trained men unloaded four howitzers, four crawl tractors and gear. Why Japs did not open fire was a mystery. We were in Jap HMG range, and tractors and LCV's made noises that carried far into the night.

At daylight 24 July, C started to set up firing positions. At 0945, our No. 1 gun was laid ready to fire. By 1100, we had registered a few rounds. In return, Jap guns lobbed in seven rounds on us. We continued firing to complete registration, but we were down on the ground when Jap shells came, then up to pull lanyards again. When a shell cut communications with Hq., Sgt. Klaas ran wire in the shelled area to connect up C again.

As we registered the guns, C also made the dirt fly behind them. Slit trenches got deeper and deeper. Under threat of Jap shells, we thought that a spade was worth its weight in gold.

At 1800, when C was firing a mission, ten more Jap shells smashed into the area. Although they hit nothing, we had orders to cease firing.

On C's second day of action, 25 July, Japs blasted us at 1130 – again with ten rounds. Again we ceased fire, but we were back in action for Capt. Walter King's A Battery, 205 FA, which had by now set up near us on Tambu Bay. An annoying Jap gun had repeatedly scored near-misses close to King's Btry—had just placed a shell 50 yards from his No. 4 howitzer. King thought that he had spotted that gun—

The 41st artillerymen in action

had seen what were probably its camouflage net and smoke puff about 1315. He adjusted Helmer's Btry on the suspected position for fire with results that could not be determined.

During evening mess, we had a Jap air raid. A lone Jap bomber dropped three bombs in C's area between our guns and the beach. Only the wire to 205 FA's Col. Poinier was cut, but the bombs each made a hole in the soft earth deep enough to drive a 6x6 truck into. Since C had as yet no AA protection, the plane escaped. Next night, 26 July, we did have AA guns defending us, but they missed the lone Jap plane that again raided. The Jap took warning, and we never had another raid.

By 27 July, all 205 FA was reunited under command of Col. Poinier, whose CP was now set up for action at Tambu Bay. He now registered all 205 howitzers on a common base point. Thus he could construct an observed-fire chart to support 162 Inf. battling Japs on Mt. Tambu and Roosevelt Ridge.

C Btry was now deep into the Battle of Salamaua. We would fire 17,638 shells on the Japs from 24 July through 11 September. We would fire more shells than any other 205 FA Btry.

And the Jap guns replied, although their fire mostly amounted to mere sniping from the mountains with a field piece. Beginning at 1200 27 July, we took four Jap rounds. Our fire director, probably Lt. Sitton, discreetly ceased firing so we could hit our holes. He stopped fire again on 28 July when we took six rounds starting about 0900.

Then on 27 July, from 1030 to 1700, we took all of 100 rounds—more than double the 37 already fired at us from our landing at Tambu Bay onward. Probably the Jap increased the number of rounds drastically because C was shooting at specific Jap guns until 1400. And we had our first wounded—T/5 Ed Anderson with a hand wound.

And on 30 July, C was firing a barrage to help Col. Taylor's 1/Bn. in his impossible assault on Mt. Tambu. The Japs threw in 30 rounds, but C continued shelling. Prendez took fragments in the leg; Lt. Segar had a hand wound.

And so for four successive days, 27-30 July, Jap shells hit in the C Btry area—137 shells, and lightly wounded three men. In contrast to C's own heavy fire, these Jap shells were few and inefficient.

No Jap shells struck C Btry from 30 July through 10 Aug—a lull of 11 days. But on 11 Aug. we fired bn. missions—probably beginning the all-out assault of 162's 2/Bn.—and the Japs replied with their heaviest shelling.

As we started firing at 1500, they also started shelling. In the period from 1500 to 1815, they struck back with 133 shells—their record fire for the whole operation. Fragments punctured a howitzer tire and holed a howitzer trail. Henninger had slight wounds in left shoulder and arm. Lt. Segar was again wounded, this time in the leg and more severely than before.

When Kulczyki was more seriously wounded in the left leg, medic Russ Thomas and Bergstrom dashed to help him, even amidst a hot Jap shelling. Segar hobbled along on his wounded leg behind Kulczyki in a stretcher. *Chicago Tribune* correspondent Robert Cromie heard Segar call, "I'm okay. Look after him."

After taking 133 shells 11 Aug., C had 25 rounds at 1100-1215 on 12 Aug. and again ceased fire. The Japs damaged some personal gear. Next day, while C aided in the great blast-off that finally gave 162 the entire Roosevelt Ridge, the Japs fired eight rounds on us at 1430, and again at 2330.

As any 205 men can tell us, those Japs shells were actually inefficient. For example: the 133 rounds that they fired on us in 3 1/4 hours on Aug. 11 were about the same number that C's four guns could put into the air during 12 minutes' firing.

Just the same, those few Nip shells kept C well dug in and alert. During three weeks, C had to move the btry position three times. (And the guns nearby of Aussie A Troop, 2/6 Field Regiment, had to move twice.)

Then came the day when the desperate Japs tried to use infantry to silence our devilish and persistent allied guns. Under Maj. Oba, they loosed about a company-sized raiding party down from the mountains. Alerted by 12 Aug., C posted extra guards and set up MG's to cover all the dead spaces like the depression Sgt. Dwyer pointed out in front of Prendez's MG. All C men got orders to sleep in holes every night. Despite the threat of raids from those ominous mountain jungles, we continued round-the-clock firing on call against the tenacious Japs, now driven back to heights beyond Roosevelt Ridge.

When Oba's raiders drove home their attacks, C's probable location was on a little peninsula on the outer SE end of Tambu Bay. The first Jap drive swung north in C's general direction, but instead struck B Troop of Aussie 2/6 Field Regt. and was thrown back after a sharp fight. This attack was a mile south of us. And the Japs also thrust at 205 FA guns half a mile south of the Aussie guns, but Aussie infantry repelled them in three clashes.

On 16-17 Aug., Lt. Messec's pursuing patrol from B 162 broke up Oba's raiders into small groups of fugitives whom Aussies and natives then hunted down. Oba had struck and scattered Aussie Lt. Hoffman's careless Aussie patrol sent to intercept him. In attacking Aussie Gamble's B Troop guns, Oba had killed three and wounded six. But he did not succeed in killing a single allied gun. (As if to emphasize the futility of this courageous raid, a Jap 75 did put a gun of this Aussie B Troop out of action on 18 Aug. and wounded three gunners.) Oba had mainly succeeded in destroying his own force of at least 85 men.

But during these days of awaiting the Jap strike, C's discipline was perfect. Despite three-four tense nights, we did not fire a shot nor heave a grenade at those Japs who never fought us. Perhaps to back up Oba that day of Messec's combat, 16 Aug., the Japs threw in 12 rounds at C from 1430 on. We stuck to our guns with counter-battery fire. On 17 Aug. after 2120, we took 30 more Jap rounds.

And with Roosevelt Ridge seized on 14 Aug., C 205 had its first chance, from the site of the former Jap OP's, to get accurate observation of Salamaua itself. And for Lt. Stephen King, 205 FA could clear a Piper Cub strip from which he would fly safely to spot targets at Salamaua.

By now, C had named all four guns. "Salamaua Susy" was the name of the first piece to blast Salamaua town itself. We called the other three guns "Blood and Guts," "Tombstone," and "Scatterbrain."

At all times, fire director Sitton told the cannoneers what targets our guns were laid on and how close we came to hitting them. When we got a direct hit on a bridge or a building or an ammo dump, we leaped high in the air and yelled because the work was well done. And so we continued day and night, feeding 33-lb. projectiles into our four howitzers—to that total of 17,638. Partly because C was the first battery to go into action for 205 FA, we fired more shells than the other two batteries.

And on 18 Aug. C endured a final flurry of Jap shellfire—as if the gunners had hoarded their last meager supply for one last shoot-out. Between 1440 and 1540, accurate Jap fire caused Sitton to order our guns to stop. The Nips' 43 shells ignited powder bags. They damaged our switchboard. They clipped off a huge tree that crashed across a covered trench with men crouching in it. Although no one was hurt in this trench where Sgt. Shenkyer had taken cover, he suffered in his duties as first cook. Fragments had ruined a field range... and a batch of cookies that he was cooling for dinner.

From a serious point of view, worst result was the second wound suffered by Sgt. Klaas. He was evacuated with a fragment in the right chest wall. Banning had a slight leg injury, and Roberson was hospitalized for shock.

And so, from 18 Aug. 1943 through 12 Sept., C 205 continued blasting either Salamaua or the Jap forces now stubbornly retreating. After Salamaua fell on 12 Sept., C's Capt. Helmer was the only battery CO flown by Piper Cub to that demolished town to find new positions to support ground forces. But the Aussie 5th Division's CO announced the terminus of the Salamaua campaign. No longer needed, C 205 gladly returned to wonderful Rockhampton in Queensland for rest and reorganization.

Under the threat of the Jap mountain guns above us at Tambu Bay, C Btry, 205 FA, did all that a Yank FA Btry should do. Despite their commanding position on the heights, Jap gunners never destroyed a single howitzer. Our official 205 Bn. history finally chronicled only four seriously wounded: Henninger, Kulczyki, Sgt. Klaas and Lt. Segar. But 205 FA was lucky in that Jap gunners were short of ammo and that their batteries did not lay heavy concentrations on a howitzer at a time. Yes, at Salamaua, C Btry, 205 FA, was gratefully lucky.

641 Tank Destroyer
VOLUNTEER TO SALAMAUA

By T Sgt. JOHN H. OLSON
with
DR. HARGIS WESTERFIELD

25 Aug 43 While we 641 TD men were at Morobe base on detached duty, Lt. Salmon asked for volunteers for Tambu Bay where things were pretty hot. Col. MacKechnie had taken Roosevelt Ridge, but he was losing 20-50 men a day against the ridges between 162 and Salamaua. He needed every man. Bill Adams, Van Luven, Lenehan, Tiny Nelson, and I volunteered. We arrived 0900 25 Aug. Our front lines are about 800 yards away. We bivouacked close to Roosevelt Ridge. We moved into a "kip" back in the jungle about 300 yards from hte beach. Our FA fired over our heads all night long. The first night it kept us awake but we soon got used to it. One Btry of 75s was only 100 yards to our rear. Being subject to Jap mortar fire, we dug in.

27 Aug 43 Lenny and I took our rifles and climbed to the top of Roosevelt Ridge, then followed it until we could hear our patrols shooting. Then we knew we had gone far enough for the first day. Up to now, we hadn't heard what our job would be.

28 Aug 43 We found out what we were to do—lead and guard native pack trains to the front lines. This is the only way there is for us to get supplies in and the wounded out. These trains are called "bong trains." We left about 7:30 with 150 natives packing water, C rations, ammo. There were 15 guards. We had to go over Roosevelt Ridge and down a valley on the other side. The far side of the ridge was in full view of a Jap observation post on Roosevelt Ridge.

Just as we gained the shelter of the valley, the Nips dropped some 77 mm shells in the trail we had just come over. The natives at once looked at us when the shells started to whistle to see what we were going to do. You don't dare look as if you are scared, or the whole bunch of them will go bush. We put on kind of a forced grin and they thought everything was all right. After we skirted Lokanu which was in Jap hands, we climbed C Ridge to 3 of our 162 companies.

Trails were so muddy and steep that a mule couldn't climb them. We just carried our rifles or tommies, a bandolier of ammo, and a canteen tied to our belt. And believe me, we were pooped when we got back to camp. Those little banty legged natives would carry about 4½ gallons water apiece. We weren't supposed to let them carry more than 45 pounds. I certainly had a lot of respect for those boys. When we got up to the last Co, we were about 45 yards from the Japs. You darn near had to belly all your way for that last few yards.

29 Aug 43 Led pack train to same destination as yesterday. No Jap fire on us, thank goodness. I sent the train down in charge of another NCO and stayed up on the ridge watching a sniper, an Indian boy, pecking away at some Japs on a distant ridge. He didn't get any while I was there but was giving them a darn rough time.

While back at our kip at 2000, we got shelled by the Japs with their 77 gun. They bracketed our tent with about 40 rounds high explosives. One shell hit about 40 feet from our kip. It sure jarred us in our holes. It put 12 shrapnel holes in the top of the kip, tore all our mosquito bars to ribbons, and punctured Moon Mullins' canteen at the head of my slit trench about a foot away from my noggin. After it, I found my heels knocking together. I thought it was because I was cold from lying naked on my stomach in the wet sand. When I tried to stop them from shaking, I found it to be impossible.

What a peculiar feeling you get under fire the first time! Your mouth goes dry and your stomach seems to be touching your backbone. The guys kept making remarks like "That one was pretty close," "I thought the little so-and-sos couldn't shoot," and "Things are getting awfully uncomfortable around here."

Of course the Japs were trying to kill our FA, but the shells were shorts. After they quit, our FA gave them hell for half an hour. But the Nips were really dug in well. One came right back and fired about 4 rounds—as much as to say, "I'm still here, Yank!"

30 Aug 43 We moved our kip to a new location away from our FA and up against the ridge so the Whistling Charlie couldn't reach us. Our FA blasted away all night long. We are getting used to it.

Today we climbed to a freshly captured Nip perimeter at Grandview. I guess that is what our FA was fussing about last night. Grandview gets its name from the swell view of Salamaua from here. Our boys took 60 rifles, 7 MGs, and 1 77 here. Salamaua seems to be about 1800 yards away. This is a long way in the jungle. We can see the Isthmus very plain from up here

1 Sept 43 I took it easy all day. Rinsed a few clothes in a stream and took a bath. Went back up to Grandview and observed our mortar and FA fire on Salamaua. Aussies of 17 Brigade are advancing down Markham Valley and lobbing FA from there. I'd sure hate to be down on the receiving end.

3 Sept 43 We packed equipment to move—over to Dot Inlet on the other side of Roosevelt Ridge. After the painful climb with full pack and a rest, we started over the ridgetop. Immediately Whistling Charlie opened up. We ran back to the Tambu Side and laid doggo half an hour while Mr. Nip shot everything he had.

Target was our FA again, but the first 10 minutes of shooting, the shells all lit short up on the ridge where we were. When he quit shooting, we knew our big stuff would start, so we lit out over the ridge like scared rabbits taking advantage of our shells to keep the Japs from shooting.

Our new job is to unload LCVs at night and haul mortar ammo to the pieces during daylight. Our new camp is at the foot of Lokanu Ridge. Now we know the only thing could trouble us was mortar fire. But we neglected to consider we had 7 Yank mortars right in this area—a natural target for Nips if they find out.

Time is really taken up now by work. During day, we haul mortar ammo in clusters of 3 and 6 for half a mile through a sugar cane patch. Clusters weigh 60-80 pounds. Nights from 9:30-12:00, we unload all kinds of supplies from LCVs. We can't understand why the Nips didn't shell us at nights when we unload. Nips can surely hear boats coming in; they make enough noise to wake the dead.

10 Sept 43 The Nips shelled with mortars at 0700, wounded Dick Bueler through the upper leg. Shelled again 11:30 but there was no damage. I don't like this mortar business. The first shell always catches us standing up. At least, Whistling Charlie gives you a couple of seconds to hit the ground.

11 Sept 43 Shelled us again at 0700 with mortars and 77s. The 77s couldn't get at us, but they lobbed in mortars. First mortar shell caught both Lennie and me standing up. It landed in a ration dump 75 feet away, wounded a Yank in the ankle, and knocked him down. A nail from a box in the dump landed on Lennie's bed. We dived into our slit trenches. The next one lit 20 feet from our kip. It riddled our tent to shreds, cut down my gun and pack rack.

This shell cut 2 fingers off Houston's right hand. He was sitting up in his hole 10 feet from us, and he just reached for his cigarette to take it out of his mouth when it got him. He went wild and ran as hard as he could go—falling over a brush pile and yelling at the top of his voice. It affects some that way. The same shell caught mortarman Coster as he jumped out of his hole—and ripped his stomach wide open. We had 1 KIA, 10 WIA.

Bill Adams dived right out of his bed roll into his trench. About 5 gallons of rain water had gathered in the canvas flap above him. When the close shell lit, a piece of shrapnel ripped a big hole in the flap. All the cold water soaked Bill. I guess he thought they had got him for sure; he really let out a war whoop. A fellow dived into my hole on top of me without warning and scared me almost into a fit.

At 1600, they shelled us again but did no damage. We had moved our kip again down on the beach and dug in and built us a splinter proof shelter about 5 feet deep in the ground. When we had nothing to do but shoot the breeze, we did it with feet hanging down in the hole so we could tumble in double quick time.

Shelled us again 1800. No damage done this time. It looks like our new shelter is a peach. Early this afternoon, a flight of 6 Mitchells came over and bombed Salamaua. After unloading, they circled and strafed the target 6 times. Boy, it surely was a pretty sight. There is a big battle going on out at sea this evening. Looks like Jap planes attacking a convoy. An awful lot of AA being thrown.

> Only source is a section of T/Sgt Olson's fine diary. For the most part, this is a verbatim copy. Diary runs from date of Olson's notice to report for Draft exam 24 Mar 41 at Kelso, Wash., until discharge 18 July 45. It is such an excellent diary that we regret that in May 1944, Olson was assigned to 24 Div and passed out of 41 Div History.

(Father Monahan buried Coster in our small cemetery under the palms on the beach. Father Monahan was certainly wonderful; he didn't know the meaning of fear. Every day he tramped to the front to carry mail and writing paper and gum and candy drops. Sunday he served Mass. One time at Mass when his boys knelt and he was reading the Bible, a sniper clipped leaves from a tree behind him. Father didn't stop services. After he was through, 2 fellows quietly left and took care of the annoyance.)

12 Sept 43 This morning, we climbed Lokanu Ridge just as the Nips had been driven off. Just as we got to the top, Charlie threw over 40 rounds so we stayed on our own side. All 3 Btn. is moving up, and lots of supplies. Col. Fertig is in charge and doing a bang up job.

Nips shelled opposite our kip at two LCVs but had no luck. Moon Mullins was taking a message to Mjr. Morris when the Japs opened up. Shells were landing all around him while he was rooting in the mud. One lit in the mud in front of his face and stuck there. It was a dud, and when we saw Moon he was white as a sheet. He couldn't even talk. He must carry a rabbit's foot.

Our patrols are in Salamaua; guess it has fallen. All the native old men, children, and Marys are released from the Japs and passing through to a new ANGAU camp. We gave all the kids candy until we ran out. They looked pitiful. I ran into my former boss boy who led my carrying parties. He ran up and said, "All Jappen he gone Salamaua?" I told him I thought all Japs were gone. He asked, "Did you chase them out?" He meant, did the Americans chase them? Again I answered "Yes." "Good, he said. I want to give you 2 coins." Upon saying this, he gave me a New Guinea shilling and a penny. He was so sincere about this and it meant so much to give me something I made a fuss over.

We moved by barges to the Francisco River this afternoon; made our landing about 4:30. It was a bad 6-foot surf; we lost a barge in landing. Japs had been there a short time ago; we found a dead Jap shot through the head, and he was still warm. We set up a guard in case a wandering Nip patrol might come close in. Nothing happened during the night.

At 0300, we loaded on an LCT and landed at Salamaua about 0330. The old place was really blown to pieces, but we were in just after the first patrols and had good souvenir hunting. We picked up cancelled checks from the blown Bank of Salamaua. There were tons of clean clothes — good clothes, too. I found a Jap bicycle in good shape, and a newsreel man took my picture on it. On Sept. 14, we unloaded landing barges all day. I was back at the same job I had at Oro Bay, and my Battle of Salamaua was ended.

205 FA
Cannoneers of Salamaua

By DR. HARGIS WESTERFIELD
Association Historian

Long before 205 FA killed Nips on Roosevelt Ridge, we got the hard first taste of war—sunk at Milne Bay 14 Apr 1943. Up from Australia on the Dutch **Van Heemskirk**, 205 FA (less B and C Btries) was scared at first sight of New Guinea—landfall at Milne Bay where jungle hills hid all sight of our troops, with the fee of lurking fevers and Japs everywhere.

> **CREDITS**
> W/O Lloyd Bryant sent a fine personal letter. Other sources include "Detailed Acct Sinking of VAN HEEMSKIRK" (Lt Col NE Poinier), "Unit Hist Hq 205 FA Btn 16 Feb/43 to 4 Oct/43, "Opns Btry B while attchd to 218 FA Bn," "Casualties," "Messages Relating Effect Arty Fire in Salamaua," "Actions of Forward Observers," "Roster of Officers," report of "Hq, Fifth Australian Division Artillery," and "162 Inf Journal of Salamaua Opn"—from Col MacKechnie's papers. "Detailed Account by Btry on Shelling Received from Jap Field Pieces" was limited to Btrys A and C.

At 1715 came air-raid alert, orders to disembark at once. Only F/Lt Lyle Oaks, 47 men stayed aboard—medics, cooks, baggage-guard, MG crewmen. Leaving all bags, footlockers, we got ashore long after dark, spent a restless night with mosquitoes. By dawn, our ship was gone—no one knew where. She was not back for 3 days—until 14 Apr.

Van Heemskirk brought Nippo bombers over her. As we cowered ashore in our first alert, we saw **Van Heemskirk** and other ships in Milne Bay turn for the pass to the Coral Sea. Like minute black mosquitoes, Nip planes dived through AA tracers at docks across from us at Gili Gili—and at our ships.

Through field glasses, CO Lt-Col NE Poinier watched **Van Heemskirk** twist while 205 FA gun-crews fought planes. A Nip dive-bomber smashed the afterdeck. Poinier saw the blast, flames 100 feet above the deck. Killed were Pvts Gail Smith, Sam Dickson, Jim Dole—Doyle and Dickson of burns. Also seriously burned were Pvts Wm Rush, Don Northrup, Ed Mackey, Les Hayman, Sgt Podolak. The raid lasted 10 minutes longer.

Von Heemskirk turned, tried to beach 1 mile east of 205's camp. Poinier rushed rescue details to the beach, 100 yards away. Number 4 Hold was flaming; FA shells, gasoline exploded continually with the MG belts and AA shells on deck. In 15 minutes, the master ordered abandonment; they took to the rescue boats following the doomed ship.

Safely ashore with the survivors of the gun crews, we watched **Van Heemskirk** tortured in 4 hours' fire and smoke and successive blasts. A corvette fired 6 shots to sink her and stop the explosions—but uselessly. Poinier wisely kept volunteers from trying to salvage personal equipment—until 1700. Then, when 15 minutes passed without explosions, he sent 10 men who landed forward and saved a few bags on deck. Then the ship settled; the 10 leaped into water. She sank in 30 seconds. We lost all personal equipment but the lights packs with us, all Btn combat equipment but the 105s on another ship.

When **Van Heemskirk** was deserted and sinking, Capts Sam Huntting, Walter King with Pvt Jim Riddle risked their lives to return for badly needed medical supplies. When the ship took her dive, they had ot swim. They were just 20 yards off when the ship sank.

Loss of impedimenta retarded 205 FA's operation as a unit from 14 Apr to 20 May. While B, C Btrys detached for duty with 218 FA, A Btry with Service Hq Btries unloaded ships at Oro Bay Depot. Resupplied 20 May, we emplaced at Warisota South to support 186 for possible defense of Buna-Tarakena-Samboga. Our stay with 186 was just acclimatization to New Guinea with advanced training—moving D-2 tractors with guns through mud and jungle—digging in for constant Jap air alerts.

Then 205's Salamaua Campaign began—through Capt Ron Martin's B Btry attached to 218 FA. Aboard 20 LCVPs, we coasted up to 162's base at Morobe, hid from planes by day, and at 0230 12 July emplaced at Nassau Bay where 162's Col MacKechnie fought for Bitoi Ridge.

But Martin's Btry did not hit the Nips from Nassau Bay. We dragged our guns by tractor north along beaches and often through high surfs north to Lake Salus Beach. Here we fired 205 FA's first round into Jap territory—a registration shot by Martin's B Btry 0615 20 July 1943. It was the first of 47,602 105 shells fired by 205 FA in the Salamaua Operation.

And that day we smashed at a Nip cannon high up by Roosevelt Ridge, which Roosevelt's 3 Btn now fought. And B Btry was well into battle for Salamaua; we registered to hit the Lokanu area, Boisi Village, were on 24-hour firing duty. When at 0628 22 July, another Nip gun blasted, B Btry struck at it immediately until it silenced.

Next day, 2/Lt Schroeder heartened 162 facing the embattled Japs on Roosevelt Ridge. On 23 July with 2 PIBs and an Aussie Sgt, he worked his way to the top of the "north ridge" at Boisi, spied a Nip OP. He set up radio, checked maps. Shifting from a previous day's registration, he calculated to bring 105s dangerously close to him. Then he called, "One-fifty left. Repeat Range. Request Btn 4 rounds. Am digging in. Love and kisses."

After Fire Directions Control gave him 5 volleys from a Btry, Schroeder increased range, then fired 10-15 more rounds into Nip targets. Downhill, he joined a K Co patrol, but they ran into ambush. Shrapnel gashed his left shoulder, sent him to hospital.

While Martin's B Btry fired from Salus Beach, remaining 205 FA Btrys pushed forward. Jammed in landing craft, we left Sanananda beaches, furtively chugged up the Guinea shore, alert for Nip planes. On the south shore of Tambu Bay, we beached after dark, dug in under Jap guns. At 0615 20 July, Capt Helmer's B Btry fired its first combat shot. On 27 July, with A Btry now landed near him, Col Poinier began firing as a unit all 205 FA guns.

It was a gruelling, perilous assignment for all 205 FA—observers or cannoneers. Officer observer detachments with radio must sweat forward with all 162 line outfits. With vision never over 50 yards—often down to 10—the observer had to "sense by sound" to adjust fire. He had to judge his distance among those tricky jungle mountains by ear only. The shells must fall close to 162 men to protect them. The observer had to call for minute adjustments in deflection or range, gun by gun, then hug the ground praying that he had not brought the shells down on 162—or his own forward party. But observers were accurate—or lucky. Only Schroeder was hit—but by Nips; and Lt Ed Ross on 16 Aug with shrapnel in left hand and chest. F/Lts Ritter, Jendrjewski; 2/Lts Pellegrini, Dick, Shea, Willard, Wilson, Turner, Galbraith, Porter—all smashed Nips and lived.

And 205 cannoneers were worse off on the beach. Only from that narrow strip of sand under continuous observation could get an effective position for our fires. The Japs

Lae today. The clearing is the airfield. Sticking out of the ocean is a wartime wreck of a Japanese ship.

soon mapped our exact locations. And they outgunned us in the Salamaua area; they had at least 43 guns—24 of them the mobile, more readily concentrated 70-75 mm mountain guns. But for 47 days, in chill night rain or burning sun, we fought 105s against the blue jungle mountains. To hit those close-in ridges, we elevated barrels almost like AA guns—would have got the barrels higher if we could keep the shells in long enough to lock the breach. Ammo was water-soaked, with bent shell-cases. Often we cut gun-crews to 3 while all hands labored to smoothen shells to fit the breaches. But down at Dobodura, Lt Brewster had invented a **shell-straightener**, which W/O Lloyd Bryant got for us. And this left us only ourselves and the Jap guns to worry about—and the planes.

For Jap cannon and planes fought back. As C Btry fired first guns at Tambu Bay 24 July, Nips hit back with 7 rounds —crack of thunder, geysers of sand too close to where we hit the ground. We completed registration, but 25 rounds more drove us into holes at dusk. Next day at 1130, 10 rounds pinned us again. At 1800, 3 Zeroes and 3 dive-bombers swooped. Two bombs shook the ground under our faces, missed kitchen 35 yards, guns 75 yards, made craters 15 feet wide, 5 deep.

The same day "C" got bombed, "A" Btry was firing its first shots. When 12 Jap rounds hammered at us, we held fire, flattened while C Btry fired 258 rounds back in 2 missions an hour apart. The Japs quit.

On 26 July, Martin's B Btry took a strafing and 3 bombs from Mitsubishis with Zeroes—a bomb missing at 500 yards. When a lone Nip gun hit 218 FA with 5 guns, Martin saw smoke in a saddle of the jungle mountains. He judged that the gun hid in a cave or under a ledge, slipped out for a few rounds, then hid again. He neutralized it with 10 volleys.

But 205 continued firing, despite 21 Nip shells 28 July. But the sky was full of enemy shells 29 July. Firing counterbattery, C took 100 rounds from 1030. T/5 Edward Anderson was nicked in the hand. But 43 shells on "A" were more effective. Shells fired powder, punctured brass. A direct hit on his shelter killed Cpl Robt Davis. On 30 July, Nips threw 15-18 more at "A" about 0800, lightly wounded Melheim, Prosser. "C" also drew 30 rounds, but did not halt its barrage which was firing for Mjr Taylor's abortive attack on Mt Tambu. Prendez, Lt Segar had light wounds.

Yet Jap guns did little to halt 205's firing. Nearly 2 weeks later in Roosevelt Ridge's last days, Japs struck at "C"—133 rounds, the record. Shrapnel seriously wounded Henninger, Kulczycki. Shells holed a howitzer track. Next day, they fired 25 rounds. And on 13 Aug while we helped the assault on Roosevelt Ridge, C got 15 harmless rounds.

After 162 took Roosevelt Ridge, the Japs tried again—4 days later. On 17 Aug, they laid 26 round on "A," wounded Les White. As shells fell, we had to man our holes against a Jap raid—which turned out to be our own natives on a maneuver. Shells damaged Number 3 Piece, jammed it with sand. And "C" took our last flurry of Nip shells—12 16 Aug, 30 17 Aug, 43 18 Aug. Sgt Klaas had shrapnel through the right chest wall; Banning was hit lightly. Shells destroyed a field range, damaged swithboard, fired power bags.

Despite Jap shells, 205 FA was first Yank Btn to hit Salamaua itself. On 27 Aug, Aussies set up an OP which sighted Salamaua. And we harassed 162's goal 24 hours daily. Results were satisfying. For instance, on 29 July, we fired a supply dump. On 30 July, we hit 50-60 Japs at a bridge. We burned a Nip warehouse. We blasted a supposed camp in jungle. We holed a road on the narrow neck of the isthmus among fleeing troops. Finally, we got 4 direct hits on an AA gun. And on 5 Aug, Fifth Air Force credited 205 FA for neutralizing Salamaua's AA fire. Our grateful bombers reported that the amount of flak under them was cut 45 per cent.

And 205 FA takes its share of credit for 162's peaceful capture of Salamaua 16 Sept 1943. But why did Nips fail to silence 205 FA, fail to keep us from killing them, from blasting Salamaua?

Jap FA men never realized the value of massed fire from a whole btry on the same target in the same second. (We Yanks knew that while 1 well-sighted gun might miss, 4 on the same target were close to absolute accuracy.) And the Japs didn't or couldn't fire enough shells—no matter how heavy their fire seemed to us below their guns. In 6 days' actual shelling, Btry A took only 107 shells from Nips; C in 12 days took only 440. (B left no record.) Over 47 days, however, 205 FA Btn shot 47,602 (1876 smoke shells)—of which A fired 13,102; B, 16,322; and C 17,638. Div Arty's Col Wm A Jackson rightly says that Nip FA had only nuisance value. Nip fire briefly damaged only 4 guns—2 tires punctured, a sight damaged, a gun jammed with sand from a near miss.

Casualties were low also. Besides 3 killed on **Van Heemskirk** and 5 seriously wounded there, we had just 1 killed at Salamaua, 4 seriously wounded, 3 accidentally wounded. But this is not the whole story. We had 3 Yanks out for conversion hysteria where continuous shellfire and heavy duty make them mental casualties. We had others still suffer mentally also. We remember **Van Heemskirk** reeling under dive-bombers. We remember firing our 105s in jungle darkness, crouching under the fire of Japanese cannon. We killed many Japs, saved many 162 Yanks.

A-162 Infantry
BATTLE ON GEORGE RIDGE

By CAPTAIN JOHN D. GEORGE, (A-162)
and
DR. HARGIS WESTERFIELD, Division Historian

After 162 Inf overran Roosevelt Ridge before Salamaua, next objective was to pinch Japs off Scout Track Ridge. On 27 Aug 1943, Col Harold Taylor ordered Capt George to move A Co less mortars 500 yards east across the Ridge to contact Capt Munkres' 2/Bn on C Ridge. Leaving Lt Gray with the 60s and 36 men, George went with 82 men and 2 LMGs against the dark hot ridges. Orders were to avoid dug-in Nips, but fight our way through to Munkres. At 1300, rifles alert at port, we scouted into the jungle.

Quickly M-1s fired, quieted. Just 300 yards from Aussie territory, our scouts killed 2 Nips at a creek — not stragglers, but unarmed. Their perimeter must be close.

At once we took to a narrow ridge, a broken tunnel of greenery slanting upwards NE to Scout Track Ridge. We wanted to be above the Nips, if they saw us. At 1500, Munkres made radio contact, and at our request, Taylor behind us fired 5 smoke shells to orient us. Hoping to meet Munkres that night, we hiked up this ridge to what we would name George Ridge. We found a well-defined trail, with fresh tracks westward.

Probing east on this track, we hoped to be atop George Ridge by dark. But at 1715, our scouts found Japs dug in at the summit. We would have fought then; but the captain ordered us to withdraw unseen.

About 150 yards east of the Japs, we dug our perimeter directly across their trail, with good fire for MGs east and west. While outguards crouched scanning the dusk, we dug quietly, carefully. By 1930, we set out booby-traps, got into holes, broke out and ate K rations, wished we could light a cigarette.

After a quiet night of sleep broken by turns on guard, we saw daylight faint through the leaves. We put out 2 outposts front and rear, smoked again, had a "K" breakfast. Meanwhile George phoned Col Taylor that we had probably cut the main Jap trail. Taylor ordered us to sit tight, but send out a recon patrol north and another south to contact Munkres.

Then we tried to draw the Nips into ambush. Ten Yanks crept 150 yards up the trail in the early morning. Nips were out of their holes. They drew beads on them, squeezed triggers, felled 6. Then they ran, but no Nips pursued.

At 1400, 10 more picked men filed alertly up the trail on the same mission. We heard M-1s crackle; Jap rifles and MGs spoke out. Our men ran back jubilant, muzzles blackened. They killed 2 this time.

Again the Nips did not attack; but since 0900, our line to Taylor was cut. Our southern patrol reported at 1500 that they could not bypass the Nips dug in along the ridge in that direction. But worst of all, the northern patrol of Sgt Fogel with Renusch and Madrazo never did return.

Our second perimeter night on George Ridge closed down on us. The brush moved around our positions. At 2015, 15 Nips rushed us. With 5 grenades, we slew 9, including the officer. Then the long, fearful dark was upon us. But the night passed quietly.

At 0900 next morning, another combat patrol hit the Japs. We killed but 1. And Jap counter-fire was heavy — rifles and blasts from a knee-mortar. Just as the patrol reported to Capt George at CP, a mortar shell burst in a tree just over us. We had 4 litter cases and 2 walking wounded — all 6 requiring evacuation, and 5 lightly wounded. Seriously wounded were Lt Stark, Sgt Richter, T/5 Dennis of A Co, as were 186 Inf ob-

> Basic story is from personal experience of Capt George, published in Infantry Journal by Col A. R. MacKehnie under title "Rifle Company in Jungle Combat," supplemented by JOURNAL OF 162 INF AT SALAMAUA.

servers Capt Thomas, Lt Barkhurst, S/Sgt McDonald. Lightly wounded were Sgt Morrison, Pvt Michalski, Pvt Sickel, Capt George — and 186's S/Sgt Hegele.

Meanwhile, a 3-man patrol had repaired our lines, and we learned that our patrol was guiding a B Co Pltn plus A & P Pltn with rations for us. But an hour later, outguards to the west saw many Japs heading up our trail. They fired, hit a Jap, fell back to perimeter.

To save our B friends from ambush, we sent a 6-man patrol to warn them by fighting the Nips. There was no fight, but the patrol brought in the carrying party. This group carried only rations; but they left us all their personal grenades and extra ammo. We knew that a bad night was coming. They carried out our grateful 4 litter cases and 2 walking wounded.

Col Taylor promised over the phone that C Co would bring us more grenades and ammo; but A Co faced the third night without relief. Occasional mortar shells blew up in perimeter and kept us in holes. At 1600, we had ominous news: Sgt Fogel and his 2 were missing still.

At 1900, Nips surrounded us, volleyed rifles, MGs for 30 minutes. They yelled, moved in. But it was only an unsuccessful attempt to draw fire; they did not charge home.

Came a third morning on George Ridge — the last morning for some of us. The Nips on the west had moved in too close for us to re-post outguards. Eastward, however, our persistent 10-man patrol attacked the Nips — killed at least 8. But their replying rifles forced us back to our holes.

At 0800, 1 Yank from C Co slipped into our perimeter; his patrol had been fired on and split up. We sent him back with S/Sgt Warnock, Sgt Lukes, and our PIB boy. Warnock was to direct mortar fire on the Nips. Lukes was to lead in a phone line, more Yanks, and ammo. Nobody was able to return.

Japs moved closer and dug positions until 1600 — 100 yards to the east, 50 yards to the west below us. We lobbed rifle grenades into the western positions but could not dig the Japs out. Brush moved everywhere; we tensed for the attack that night.

Despite shortage of grenades, ammo, this perimeter of 70 Yanks in 18 holes was strong as we could make it. To fire east along wider terraces, we dug in a MG flanked by 2 BARs. The other LMG and 1 BAR guarded the western trail down the other slope. We need more automatic weapons; the south flank of our perimeter was weakest with only 1 BAR.

At 1815, Japs fired heavily — rifles, mortars, HMGs. About 1830, fire lifted; they began shouting and came in to kill. As we heard them coming, George feared some Yanks would be caught with their heads down; shouted, "Head up! Here they are!"

Cracking like pistols, our first grenades detonated, exploded. At the flash of Jap rifles, we opened up: rifles, BARs, MGs. Bodies thumped on the ground in the dark. Japs screamed, and grenades put out their screams.

Now we breathed awhile, and prayed. Again their MGs, rifles ripped the trees, the earth below. Yelling began again, and their panting rushes; and we threw grenades, fired, heard more screams.

Some men say that the Japs formed and assaulted in 9 separate waves; most of us never thought about counting. We lay low, listened, then spotted movements; threw grenades; it was squeeze off shots and fire by count without sights until the empty clip rang out. It was reload and fire again while the barrel heated — until a lull ahead or a buddy's hand on the shoulder halted us.

We began to feel chill in the stomach. Every rush meant firing a few more clips, throwing a few more grenades. As the dark suddenly quieted, our hands counted blindly the few clips left in our belts, the last grenade or two on the parapet — like a thirsty man in the desert checking his last water. For when ammo ran out, they would overwhelm us — waves of many Japs with long bayonets. Home was a long way off indeed, over dark waters to Oregon.

Covered by automatic fire, the Japs got in sometimes. One MG ricocheted hard chunks of earth into Paul Adams' left eye. But he fired on. In the same hole, Cpl Elliott was hit 3 times, once in the head from a hand-grenade which he picked up and hurled back. A Nip grenadier hid behind a tree until Mendoza rushed the tree. When the Jap grabbed the rifle, Mendoza kicked him in the belly, freed the rifle, shot the Jap.

The Japs took 2 holes on the SE and SW corners of our perimeter. Peterson's BAR hole drew a heavy attack. A Jap grenade thundered before the fox-hole, killed Kidd, mortally wounded Peterson. While Peterson still fired, Likes killed a Nip whose bayonet then pierced his leg through. Peterson told Likes that he was finished and told Likes to save himself in another hole. Peterson fired 1 more clip before he died on the bayonet.

In another hole, a grenade killed Sgt Johnson, Cpl Cate, holed Moore 22 times. But Moore and Dick fought on until a bullet smashed Moore's gas-cylinder and Dick's carbine jammed. They dived into another hole with other Yanks — were asked to stay. Then 3 Japs took over their hole. At dawn, Sgt Morrison crawled over to kill them with tommy-gun slugs. One Jap beat Morrison over the head with a grenade that did not go off. Morrison smashed his head with a pistol. F/Sgt Baker shot the Jap through the head.

Daylight found 37 Jap dead, two of them officers, inside perimeter. Down a gentle slope from 1 foxhole, we saw 37; the nearby dead totalled 150. We had 4 Yanks killed, 10 wounded, total, in the whole mission.

Without grenades, more men, A Co could not hold its lines another night. At 1100, Capt George sent Muhleman, Kramek to inform Col Taylor. We buried Johnson, Cate, Peterson, Kidd. Muhleman and Kramek got through. At 1300, our outposts to the west heard the welcome sounds all were hoping for. An M-1 at 1/Bn Hq fired 2 strings of 4 shots; it was the order to go.

Protecting our wounded — all could walk — we left our battle-field. For 100 yards downhill, we found dead Japs. We saw 3 more on outpost; they ran.

While George's command fell back, Gray's A Co mortars near Btn in a crater by B Co fired to cover withdrawal and guide by sound. Gray fired a 60 shell each 5 minutes. In this action, Gray shot as much as limited ammo and observation allowed. Lt Bert Thompson (186) saw Gray's first shot knock a Jap sniper from a tree where he had made himself a long-time nuisance.

Thus A Co returned alive from 3 brave nights on George Ridge. Even Fogel's lost patrol reached 2/Bn lines across the ridge unhurt — after 4 days, 3 nights without food and shelter, and after bypassing 6 Nippo perimeters. Iron discipline, bravery, leadership had paid off; Capt John George's A Co fought a classic action American soldiers will long remember

A Co., 162 Inf. at Salamaua:
Fogel's survival patrol on Scout Ridge

By Dr. HARGIS WESTERFIELD, Division Historian,
with Sgt. WAYNE FOGEL

On 28 Aug. 1943, Col. Taylor ordered A Co. 162 Inf.'s Capt. George to send two patrols to contact Capt. Munkres 1/Bn. on the seaward side of Scout Track Ridge. Objectives of the two patrols were to find a route for George to extricate A Co. from its dangerous position between two Jap forces at each end of Grassy Spur. (We renamed Grassy Spur as George Ridge.) Originally, Taylor and George were trying to work with Munkres to cut off Japs defending B and C Ridges after 162 had taken Roosevelt Ridge. But new Jap pressure might become far too great for A Co. to survive.

A Co.'s southern patrol returned by 1500 to report that finding a safe passage through the Japs down there was impossible. But Fogel's three-man patrol to the north could never rejoin A Co. in all the time that it defended George Ridge. We three men endured wild, intense, hungry days and nights in Jap country. Almost at once, the Japs cut us off from A Co.; Fogel's patrol quickly turned into a survival patrol.

Morale was high when we three left George Ridge. We were cool and sure of ourselves. Madrazzo's keen eyes could spot Japs at impossible distances. Sgt. Fogel carried a Tommy gun; Renisch and Madrazzo had rifles. Expecting to return to A's perimeter, we traveled light as possible, with only a bandolier apiece for the riflemen, and canteens of water. We had no food and no maps. But from A Co.'s perimeter, we saw the summit of Scout Ridge across which we were trying to find A's escape route. Distance to 2/Bn. was estimated at only some 500 yards.

Dropping down the north side of George Ridge past our wary outguards, we slipped into a jungle valley. Then we worked up a spur ridge that might lead to Scout Ridge. Near the top of the spur, we saw Jap pillboxes. We spread out to observe that line from distance, then fell back to a thicket to talk over our findings.

Here we made the wrong decision that led to three nights and four days when we patrolled only for our own survival. We decided that the pillboxes above us were empty, and started up the spur ridge to be sure that they were clear. We hoped that we had already found that route open, so that we could inform George that A Co. had a clear way to contact Munkres.

But the pillboxes were not empty. Japs were coming down to kill us. Despite heavy Aussie GI shoes, we ran back down the spur. We ran across the valley northward to another spur to escape. We lost those Japs somewhere in jungle behind us, but we had moved northeast into enemy country. We had started to cut ourselves off from A Co. completely.

Still seeking that route across Scout Ridge for A Co., we climbed another spur eastward. We saw troops ahead, but did not know whether they were Yanks or Japs.

Suddenly we entered on a trail where Japs were filling canteens. They ran from us; we ran from them the other way. Then they rallied and followed us, but dark was falling. After we lost sight of them, it was quiet enough to halt for the night.

That first night we were terribly alone and away from A Co. We lay on the side of a spur where we could look down and shoot first at any Japs coming up. With each man taking his turn on guard, we slept as well as we could where we could touch one another in the dark. We missed the rations we had not brought along, and we would miss them a lot more.

With daylight of our second day cut off from our company, we did not see any Japs hunting for us. Climbing farther up the

A Japanese machine-gun pillbox in the Salamaua area. It was extremely well-built and camouflaged so well it could not be seen from a few yards away.

spur, we looked down on Japs working hard at digging a big hole. We thought they were going to bury supplies, perhaps to cache them for a later return.

Now we climbed a round hill for better observation. Japs were plentiful before us. We counted more Japs out in the open than a man might see in an entire jungle campaign. Once, 50 Japs lined up in formation below us. An officer stood out plainly as he gave orders.

Consulting in low voices at the foot of Round Hill, we now deeply realized that we were cut off from A Co. These mountain jungles were alive with Japs between us and our outfit which we yearned to see again. We had not eaten since we left A's perimeter, 24 long hours ago. Despite the dire feeling of isolation, not one of us ever gave up the hope of coming out alive.

It looked as if the safest thing to do now was to resume our original mission. We decided that it would be safest to cross the main Scout Ridge to where 2/Bn. was fighting the Japs.

We perceived that the main Jap supply trail was below us and blocking the route that we had to travel. So we hiked back up Round Hill and spent a second afternoon in patient and hungry waiting. We heard Jap chatter down there and checked our guns over and over for readiness to fight if anyone stumbled upon us.

With darkness falling and the Japs quiet, we got across that supply trail. In the insect-deafening last light, we slept again in touch with one another and took turns on guard. So passed our second night.

On our third hungry, hot day, we almost topped Scout Ridge. We came upon another Jap pillbox, this time unoccupied.

Then we heard a terrific, continuous blast of fire across the ridges. This was probably the three hours' preparatory fire that the Aussie 29 Brigade made against Charlie Hill, keystone of the Japs' final defensive line before Salamaua Town. In those three hours, some 2,000 105 rounds, 450 mortar shells, and 6,000 MG rounds were impacting Charlie Hill in preparation of an assault that would fail.

But all that we of Fogel's patrol thought was that every Jap movement anywhere near us seemed to have halted. Now might be our one and only chance to escape being slaughtered. We ran across the high mountain; we halted winded and starved but safe on the other side of Scout Ridge.

Again, however, we were in danger; it was too late in the day to risk our lives in the dark. The Japs might shoot us or the Yanks might, taking us for Japs. Although we had begun to hope to save ourselves for sure, we slept and guarded one another again on the east side of Scout Ridge.

And as we carefully scouted our route on the fourth day of absence from A Co., we heard the wonderful sounds of American voices. We saw our own kind: red-faced or dark-faced Americans, with the Atabrine tinge on their cheeks under curved, wide helmets.

We had wandered unknowingly from Jap country into the American sector. At first, they took us for their own 2/Bn. men. Nobody even suspected that we were the forlorn wanderers from A Co. across the dark ridge.

We inquired our way to 162's CP. Here in a tent, we saw a shirtless, elderly soldier before a map spotted with matchboxes

CREDIT: Prime credit is due to Wayne Fogel, who gave me most of these details at Gearhart Reunion, 1971. For background, I used "Battle on George Ridge," based on Capt. John D. George's own story in Jungleer (Nov. 1966), and David Dexter's The New Guinea Offensives. Dexter's Australian history has the best overall account of 162 Inf. at Salamaua that I have yet been able to find despite the Australian bias. I also used a page from Col. A.R. MacKeehnie's "Leadership," published in the Fort Leavenworth Command and General Staff School's Military Review, date unavailable.

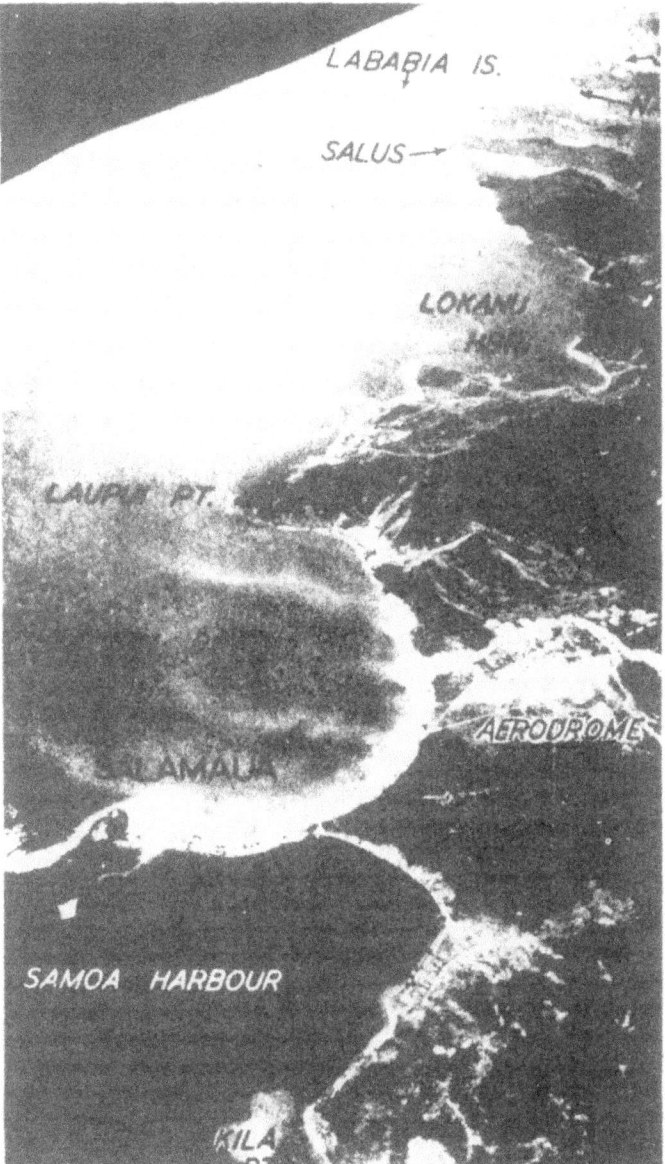

A Fifth Air Force photo of the rough terrain in the Salamaua area, taken just prior to the 41st Division's incursion.

to locate our 162 outfits.

"Who is this old guy?" Fogel wondered. He was Col. Art Fertig, executive of 162. Fertig was then a vigorous young man only 49 years old. (He would not pass away until he was over 80 years old.)

And we gave Col. Fertig our report. No matter what were the details of Fogel's patrol's adventures, we had credit for encountering six organized Jap positions. Fogel had credit for finally leading his patrol across the ridge between two Jap positions. (Plans would soon be made to move a Yank company into the gap between these two positions, but the Japs retreated before 162 could make the move.)

Fertig told us, "Boys, you're better off than A Co. They've been cut off for days." (Actually, George withdrew A Co. from George Ridge that same day, afternoon of 1 Sept. 1943.)

Then we three cobbers—Fogel, Renisch, and Madrazzo—borrowed mess gear and devoured like wolves the delicious food the cooks set before us—hot cakes and canned peaches. We ate without restraint and were sick afterwards.

But in four days and three nights, we three had carried on a classic survival patrol. We had spent those days and nights without food and shelter in a jungle that teemed with Japs. And we had come out alive.

205 Field Artillery

Cannoneers of Salamaua, II

By Dr. HARGIS WESTERFIELD
with Major GEORGE FOULKE

> Prime credit is due to Mjr Foulke's MSS, "History of 205 FA Bn" and "Salamaua Campaign." Col NE Poinier also supplied Foulke's 2 MSS plus his own "Notes" for a briefing to Staff and Faculty at Fort Sill FA School. (Poinier's "Notes" are interesting, scholarly.) Brand-new material comes also from Sam Huntting's Ltr to Russell Merritt 14 Dec 1970; **Japanese Operations in SW Pacific**, Vol. II, Part II; Australian David Dexter's **New Guinea Offensives**. (Dexter's volume is thus far superior to any American work on Salamaua.) To some extent, I used my own "Cannoneers of Salamaua from **Jungleer** (March 1965), especially where conflicts of dates occurred. If other full-length FA stories were available, I would not have published this article at this time; but Foulke, Poinier, Huntting, Dexter have given 205 FA a fitting memorial.

Already under threat of Jap bombers before landing our first gun on a New Guinea beach, 205 FA Bn disembarked hurriedly at night on Milne Bay's shore at 2100 hrs, 10 Apr 1943. For their transport, the old Dutch S.S. *Van Heemskirk* was under menace of heavy Jap air-raids. 205 left aboard the *VH*, to protect her, our security ack-ack MG detachment—Lt Oakes and 47 machine gunners.

And old *VH* tried hard to escape her death. At 0300 that night, she up-anchored for Port Moresby with our gunners, but news of an air-raid at Moresby turned her back to re-enter Milne Bay.

Van Heemskirk's death came at 1230, 14 Apr. Seventy or more planes hit Milne Bay—port and ships. First, Jap bombers struck at medium level. Then Mitsubishi dive-bombers swooped, targeted *VH*.

And Oakes' 205 FA MGs poured out AA fire—damaged 2 Mitsubishis, killed a third. But that third made a direct hit into the No. 4 aft hold. The 100-octane plane gas in this hold flamed 150 feet high. The plane that ended *VH* then crashed in flames 100 yards to port.

Gail Smith was KIA; Doyle and Dickson died of burns. WIA — many with burns — were Hayman, Northrup, Rush, Mackey, Horner, Cpl Dunn, Sgts Howard and Podolak, 1/Lt Oakes. Wounded Horner went into No. 4 hold and saved a man blown down among the flames.

But *VH* was dying. While seared wounded writhed on the hot decks, her Capt had orders from an Aussie corvette to beach her at Waga Waga—where 205 FA had landed 4 days back. The corvette whammed in 6 shells below the water line, aft, which seemed at first to extinguish the fires.

Unluckily, Waga Waga was no sloping beach where *VH* could berth in safety, but a coral reef offshore. Her bow merely hung on the reef, while the corvettes' shell-holes filled the ship with water and began to drag her down. The Dutch crew abandoned ship. Our Medics boarded to give first aid. Under threat of continuous explosions, we got 205's MG Pln ashore.

About 1700, explosions of 155 mm ammo and 100 octane gas eased up. The fires had not yet reached the bow of the ship, and Cpt Sam Huntting got permission to head a group to board again. He wanted to salvage medicine chests and personal equipment in #1 hold forward to raft them ashore. Lt Arnett and several men rowed us in, then backward to avoid possibly exploding ammo.

With Cpt Walt King, Sgt Riddle, 1 more, Huntting tried to loosen a life-raft for launching. Rusty fasteners kept us from freeing the raft. Then *VH*'s stern settled rapidly; Poinier waved from the beach for us to get off. Before we could recall Arnett, *VH* was sliding down the reef. We 4 Yanks went down the rope ladder like greased lightning. Huntting was a couple feet from *VH* as she disappeared. Luckily, she slid down the reef slowly enough that she made no whirlpool to suck us under. Arnett's boat crew picked us up.

The Milne Bay raid was actually the finale of Adm Yamamoto's all-out offensive of 7-14 Apr which had effectively damaged us at Oro Bay, Moresby, and Milne Bay. Japs reported their 149 fighters and 37 medium bombers had sunk or destroyed 10 transports. They claimed a loss of only 10 planes. Our official report was that 61 bombers, 30 fighters had sunk 1 ship, damaged 4, destroyed a fuel dump. And we claimed 15 planes shot down, 9 probably destroyed. Despite heavy damage to ship and shore installations, *VH* was only ship sunk. And in all raids, Japs lost 80 planes, far too many for them.

Many of our 105s were lost in the *VH* sinking, but 205 FA did not leave Milne Bay until 22 Apr aboard *AT Bontikoe*.

At Oro Bay, 250 of us then became part of a Port Bn under Mjr Foulkes and Capt Wright while an advance detail pioneered a camp near Dobodura. And at Oro Bay, the Port Bn endured an air-raid of 45 planes. Men hit their slit trenches immediately. About 12 bombs landed 30-100 yards from us—250 pounders, incendiary, and anti-personnel. Although we found fragments 250 yards from the impact area, no man was hit.

Such were 205 FA's first encounters with Japs, 14 Apr and 14 May 1943. But not until 10 July did any 205 guns get orders for the front. After boarding LCVs for Nassau Bay, Lt Ron Martin's B Btry set up defenses for Col MacKechnie's base, but did not fire. Four days later, B Btry had one of our toughest marches of World War II—some 5 miles' jungle march along the roadless, swampy, forested New Guinea coast to go into action against the Japs.

We tractored the guns through thick forests. We had to ford both north and south arms of Bitoi River. Tractors went so deep into the Bitoi that the water climbed over hoods and engines—finally just below the air intakes. The 105s completely submerged, but the tractors brought them through while water cascaded from barrels. At one point, we drove the guns out into the ocean breakers. We set up about 1 mile north of the north inlet of Lake Salus.

Then, on 18 July 1943 after 3 years' training, 205 FA finally loosed its first shell at a Nip target. At 0800, a lanyard released the first shell at Dot Island at 10,300 yards—1500 yards out in Dot Inlet behind Roosevelt Ridge. Aussie Capt Hitchcock's Papuans had reported a Jap OP there, but we did not find what effect our fire had. By 25 July, A and C Btrys were emplaced on the south beach of Tambu Bay and firing against Nips on bitterly held Mt Tambu.

Especially in early firing, observers had trouble. When 1/Lt Holman observed with an F/162 patrol 22 July, he fell, resulting in a serious back and leg injury. On recon with Col Poinier, Capt Standley fell and left 205 with a knee injury.

With Aussie Sgt F Makin, 3 Papuan scouts, and a K 162 patrol, 2/Lt Schroeder climbed atop probably Roosevelt Ridge. The Papuans spotted a Jap OP. Although it was too close for safety from our own shells, Schroeder blasted the Nip area with a whole Btry—10-15 volleys of 105s.

A punitive patrol of 10 Japs then sought Schroeder to kill him at the ridge base. He took a bullet in the shoulder, but Aussie Makin emptied his sub-machine gun into the Nips, blew them back. Makin then bandaged his shoulder, guided the K 162 patrol back to safety.

Although Jap guns had already shelled B Btry, on 28 July, we took one of our heaviest bombardments. Japs fired some 120 rounds at A and C in their forward positions at Tambu Bay. C's T/5 Ed Anderson was nicked in the hand. Some 43 shells on A Btry fired powder, punctured brass. KIA was Cpl Robt Davis—a direct hit in his shelter.

On 29 July also, 2 dive-bombers struck at Tambu Bay. AA killed 1; the other was forced down disabled on Salamaua Air-Strip. Our 205 observer called down fire on this plane and destroyed it.

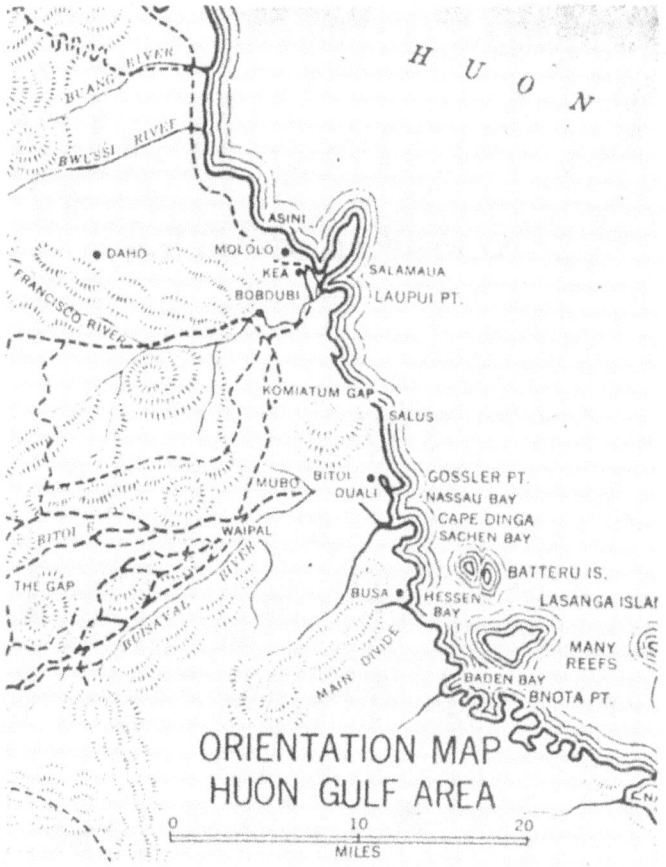

ORIENTATION MAP
HUON GULF AREA

On 30 July, while 45-48 shells hit A and C, we destroyed warehouses at Chinatown — the point on Salamaua Harbor across from the isthmus. When 50-60 Japs unwisely bunched to cross Francisco River on a foot-bridge, we bracketed them and had casualties reported to us. Ordered to hit Jap installations on Salamaua Isthmus, we placed all but 3 rounds on that narrow neck. Jap guns retaliated but inflicted just one light wound on 2/Lt Segar. C's Cpl Melheim had a light wound on the cheek, and Prosser on the left arm.

On 2 Aug while observing at the front, 2/Lt Ross received shell fragments in left hand and chest. But he stayed on duty to deliver fire at close range. On 4 Aug, C's Prendez was hit by Jap fragments.

Then on 12 Aug at 0747, 205 FA's guns announced the master offensive at Roosevelt Ridge, where the Japs had held off attacks of 162 Inf units since 22 July. From 0747 to 0900, our 105s struck at 15-second intervals; shell-bursts rose high on that red ridge. Bofors of an anti-aircraft outfit became field artillery for the occasion. Then 2/Bn men stormed up. With our help, the battle went on until 14 Aug. On 14 Aug, 205 FA's guns were part of the massive shelling that cleared the way for 162's occupation. Besides directing accurate FA fire at close range, B's CO Capt Martin was noted for leading 162 patrols to pinpoint Nippo positions.

On that first day of barrages, 12 Aug, C Btry took the record number of Jap shells for one day—a total of 133. They punctured a howitzer tire, holed a gun-trail. Wounded in left leg was Kulczyki, and Henninger in left shoulder and arm. Lt Seger had a second light wound, this time in the leg. The 133 shells were surprisingly ineffectual.

For, as Col Poinier rightly said, the Japs had guns, but not artillery. To Poinier, using field artillery meant mass firing and surprise firing of as many possible shells in the shortest possible time. Since the Jap guns pecked away one gun at a time, they were ineffective. The 133 rounds fell in 3½ hours. Poinier's FA would have put the whole 133 rounds on the Japs in 12 minutes with 1 Btry in action—or 133 rounds in 5 minutes with the whole Bn in action.

And on 17 Aug, 26 rounds somewhat damaged A's No. 3 gun, simultaneously wounded Les White in the cheek. On 18 Aug, 43 shells managed to destroy a field range, damage a switchboard, flame some powder bags. Klaas took a fragment through the right chest wall—a serious wound. Banning got a light leg wound; Roberson went out for shock. On 20 Aug, B's Sgt Frazier was hit while unloading supplies.

After the fall of Roosevelt Ridge 14 Aug, 205 FA continued round-the-clock firing on call against the tenacious Japs in the blue jungle mountains above Dot Inlet. Like other FA, we shared the dangers of land raids; one missed us by less than a mile. Just 300 yards from A Btry and 500 yards from Bn Hq, some 30-50 Japs of Mjr Oba's great raiding party struck Aussie Lt Gamble's Troop of 2/6 Field Regt of 25-pounders and Lt Grove's 20-man Pln of 47 Aussie Bn. They killed 3 Aussies, wounded 7, left behind 2 of their own dead officers. They left, by the guns, demolition charges that never exploded. In the dawn of 16 Aug, A Btry saw this fight just 300 yards away.

On 31 Aug, 3 Jap guns fired on a small allied ship. The ship put back in to the beach and took Poinier to adjust fire on the guns—and a Jap barge lying inshore. But observation from the water was difficult. Poinier hurried ashore to mount a Piper Cub and fly over the Jap locations. He called for fire from us— and 218 FA. A direct hit destroyed the barge. Jap troops scurried from the area he had called fire upon.

And suddenly Salamaua Opn was ended; 205 FA got the news 11 Sept when Hq refused permission to fire on designated targets on Salamaua Isthmus. Our men were already entering the township.

Thus ended 205 FA's Salamaua Opn. Surviving Van Heemskirk's sinking under dive-bombers, we had fought our guns below those blue Japanese mountains where we had orders to fight. Our total losses—not all mentioned above because we can find no record of the names—were just 1 KIA, 1 seriously wounded, 13 slightly wounded, 3 shock cases, and 2 WIA by their own booby traps. And by 12 Sept, we had expended 47,062 rounds' 105 ammo. C Btry had fired 17,638; B 16,322, and A 13,102. And 205 FA had not lost a gun to the Japs. Most important of all, many 162 Yanks and many Aussies owe their lives to the efficient fire of 205 FA Bn.

I Co. 162 Infantry:
Epic Heroism On Scout Ridge

By 1st/Sgt. M. H. Kelley, with DR. HARGIS WESTERFIELD

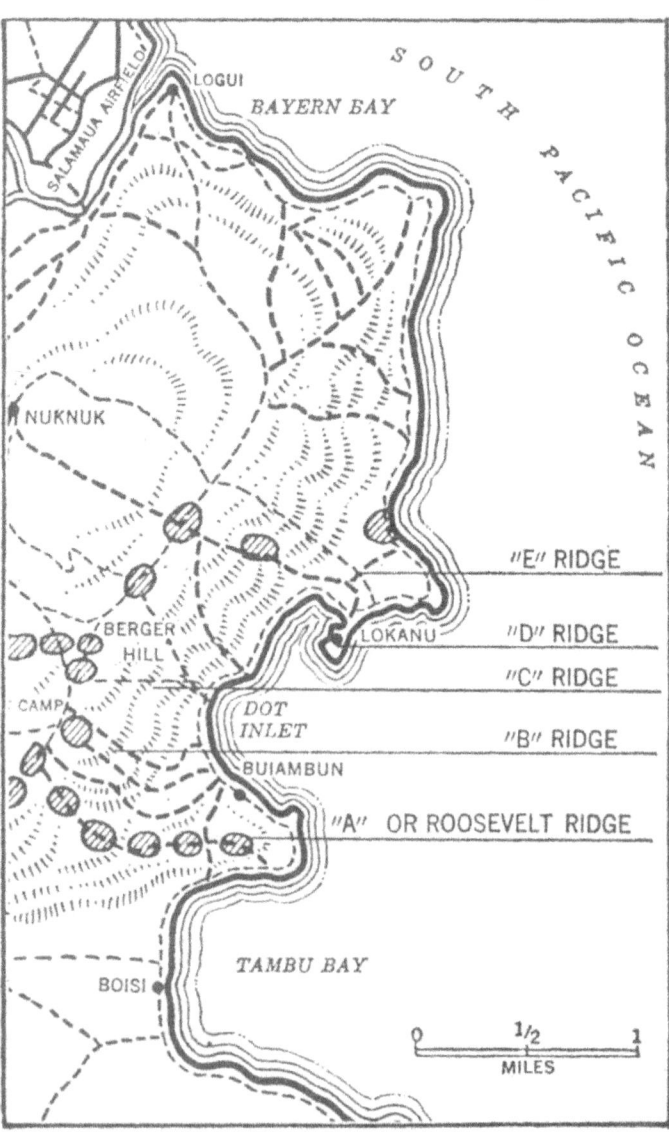

Nuknuk and Vicinity

CONTINUOUS MOUNTAIN trench-fighting was the achievement of I Co. 162 Inf. against Scout Ridge flanking Roosevelt Ridge before Salamaua. For 37 days (with 1 brief rest) our dwindling Co. fought the Japs off 2 ridges.

Four days after K and L's first push on Roosevelt Ridge 26 July, we got orders to follow Scout Ridge to where it seemed to intersect Roosevelt Ridge and the Jap army. Led by black Papuan Infantry, we labored heavily armed up Scout Ridge. A native guide raced down the column shouting, "Smellum Yapan!" An Arisaka cracked. Paul Rober fell dead of a bullet. The Japs volleyed with mortars, rifles, MGs. We blew them back, killed 7. The Japs dragged off other dead.

Next day 2 Pltn. pushed alone up Scout Ridge. We must move until orders or Jap firing stopped us. Where we fought yesterday were only dead Japs with flies buzzing and shallow positions.

More scared now, we hunted the Nips—several hours up a hogback in dense forest. At a round, nearly bald hump, we halted, sent out a recon patrol. It got heavy fire at 150 yards—nobody hurt.

CP phoned our Pltn. to hold Bald Knob overnight. Our thin line did not sleep that night. The rest of I reinforced us, dug in 27 July.

On 28 July, Japs attacked — out of nowhere. They charged uphill, shrieked, called insults in English. An amplifier with an Orient record weirdly heartened their charge. Our MG's, rifles, grenades blasted them back. But we had heavy losses—especially 2 Papuans who panicked from the holes. That night we learned that muzzle flashes made us targets; we began using grenades for night-fighting.

From 27 July-3 Aug., "I" withstood nightly attacks from infantry. But at dark 3 Aug. came new terror—boom of shell, eerie whistle, crash in perimeter, moans. It was their 70 mm "Whistling Charlie." Then infantry howled, drove in. Sgt. Rush, among others, was wounded; but we lobbed in mortars, rolled grenades, beat them.

On 4 Aug. after some days' recon, our 2 Pltn. attacked frontally. (The ridge was too steep for flank attacks.) The 60's registered; then we pushed and tore down a vine fence. Then their MG's, rifles splattered us. Jap fire blew a clip of TSMG ammo from 1 man, snipped chin-strap and ear-lobe off another. Our grenades could not reach them on higher ground; but grenade launcher and overhead fire covered us. A squad crept into close range, grenaded them from their holes. We destroyed 1 LMG, 1 HMG. But live men could not penetrate farther. They countered; our 2 Pltn. fell back with 2 slightly wounded.

During 4-12 Aug., we held Bald Knob, continually probed with trouble. On 6 Aug. of this time, we spotted Japs building 3 pillboxes and had FA smash them. On 8 Aug., we found a strongly fortified line with 2 new bunkers—2 Nips in a tree, 1 on the ground. A salvo from 205 FA wrecked that tree.

At night, Japs crept in, or noisily charged. "Whistling Charlie" struck us. By day, he hid in a cave, this funny World War I cannon on wagon wheels with a short base. By night, he rolled out, fired a few rounds, crawled back into cave while FA wasted shells on him. We never

---

THE AUTHOR

Just after high school graduation in Bend, Oregon, M. H. Kelley was inducted into I Co. 162 Inf.; served 4 years, 11 months, 1 day—except for hospital trips. He became 1st/Sgt. soon after Salamaua, and held this grade until discharge 17 Aug. 1945. He is also a vet of the New Guinea Campaign. Typhus - jaundice-malaria gave him a 30-day furlough stateside. Returned to I Co., he found that he had enough points for discharge. A tobacco and candy salesman, Kelley hunts, fishes, coaches Little League.

knew what became of that gun.

After a brief relief 13 Aug. while other outfits took Roosevelt Ridge, we went back to fight Scout Ridge—but this time from a different side. As we moved inland from the shambles of Roosevelt Ridge, MG's struck our first scouts. Trying to spot gunners, Lt. Gordon took a sniper bullet in the thigh.....

SINCE WE lacked a qualified mortar observer, FA Lt. McKinnon volunteered. With "I" back 100 yards, he slithered forward 20 yards more with Kelley among Japs' final protective lines. He brought our 60 fire close. A tremendous burst clipped leaves overhead. "Let's have a cigarette," he said to Kelley. He meant that

IN MEMORIAM
EDGAR BELL,
I Co., 162 Inf.

Prime credit for this history goes to Edgar Bell, KIA 29 Aug 1943. His brother Alvin so loved Edgar that in 1958, he placed a notice in Jungleer asking how Edgar died. His I, 162, buddies so loved Edgar that they wrote to Alvin, and I got their addresses from the letters he received. F/Sgt. M. H. Kelley then gave me I Co.'s story. Besides Kelley's basic MS, other sources include ltr Bernie Schimmel 10 Sept 1958, Narr F/Lt Watson (from Col MacKechnie Papers), War Journal 162 Inf (from Col Townsend Papers). This is my only story from Roosevelt Ridge.

Without the help of you who read this, the brave deeds of the other Second and Third Btn Companies will be forgotten. God rest the soul of Edgar Bell, and those others whose names I don't know. Hargis Westerfield, Historian.

the next rounds might be down their necks. While they shared their 1 cigarette, the bursts fell just before them on the Japs.

But in this dense forest in clay, our mortars failed; the Japs' mortars dropped a withering rain. By dusk we dug in for another fortnight's battle for Scout Ridge—the last of I Co. From 6 officers, 158 men, we were down to 4 officers, 51 men at the front. Riflemen were reorganized into 1 Pltn.; we still had Hq and Mortars.

On 16 Aug., our riflemen crept in, threw grenades. While we still dug in late afternoon, an attack came—perhaps because of M Co's. mortarmen Sgt. Warren. With Sgts. Dewhurst, Kelley covering him, Warren dropped shells where Japs might be concentrated. Instead of retreating, the Japs pushed.

Dewhurst spotted the first Nip creeping in brush; precisely his M-1 crackled while Kelley's TSMG spat short bursts. Meanwhile Warren droned commands: "Now just elevate a teeny bit—not much now—or you got no Sgt. Now fire 1. Fire 2. Fire 4 for effect."

To Kelley, he said, "I got it. Let's get the hell out of here." He backed off with his phone; Dewhurst still shot. Warren's mortars broke the attack.

Now Pltn. Leader, Lt. Watson foresaw heavy night attacks, spurred tired men to dig deeper—pitched in himself. Later, we wanted holes twice as deep. From dusk to dawn, Japs attacked—snipers from trees, light mortars, MG's. They fixed bayonets, shouted, hit us frontally, enveloped our right. We blew them back with heavy losses.

FORWARD POSITIONS ran low on grenades. When Hq. sent more, Watson and Kelley made several night trips to the front. One man covered the other where possible. Our men would not fire at night; but Watson and Kelley feared knife or machette. But this extra ammo and Warren's M mortars

The most important pieces of equipment in New Guinea were bulldozers and tractors. Here's a tractor pulling a gun to the top of Roosevelt Ridge.

helped back up Jap attacks 4 or 5 a night—dusk, 900, 1300, dawn.

For 2 weeks after 16 Aug., "I" held in grenade range of Japs, broke their attacks nightly. Without men for offense, we gave them no rest. Our alert snipers spotted movements, squeezed triggers. Strong-armed throwers lobbed grenades; mortars hit them, always when unexpected. But among others, we lost Thomas to a direct mortar hit.

How outnumbered we were, we learned in an unusual way. Scout Ridge is red clay. After a few days in holes, we turned red—clothes, face—even hair. But our Japs lived farther below ground than we; they weren't red. For they rotated every 3 days—back to a bath, a full night's sleep.

But we could rotate only from fox-hole to fox-hole—from 4 key positions to other less exposed positions. In each of these 4 positions, we placed 2 comparatively fresh men each night. These smaller 2-man positions were harder to target with blast fire. And these men never slept anyhow.

Soon our narrow front stank with dead Nips; the live ones never retrieved even wounded in their nightly attacks. We volunteered to creep out, throw earth on them. Later Hq. issued quicklime for them.

WE PUSHED on Aug. 20. Covered by HMG's, mortars, we tried to close in; but accurate MGs pinned us down. Then from the Ridge behind, L Co. lobbed mortarshells. FA salvos exploded on them. We charged again; but their HMGs, mortars, grenades, killed 2, wounded 5. FA Lt. McKinnon died.

On 22 Aug., we killed 5 by sniping; but on 23 Aug., they attacked both "I", "K" about 1900. We repulsed them. On 24 Aug., 7 more Japs died from snipers. At 1230, a MG fired for a minute; but our mortar silenced it. Thus our days.

On 29 Aug., we tried again, but failed in tragedy. Two squads sneaked off on flank attack under the ridge-crest; a third squad waited to hit them frontally.

Tense in perimeter, we heard grenades; the flank attack moved ahead. Supply Sgt. Schimmel finished checking the striking squad's ammo, grenades. He smiled at Oklahoma Edgar Bell's kidding, took to his hole.

When Schimmel was just 75 feet off, mortars barraged. Mortally wounded were Bell, First Cook Chitwood, 1 more a litter case. The attack halted. Ironically enough, when reinforced with a few returned casuals, we grenaded Nip holes, crept to the center of their perimeter, stood up unopposed. They had quit a position strong enough for a Btn. We advanced to the next high point on Scout Ridge, again sent out patrols. On 31 Aug., we took a perimeter on "B" Ridge with but 1 casualty. But on 1 Sept. came maybe our wildest fire-fight. Hq. had promised us Heaven itself—relief from the ridges, hot food! (Remember old-type "C" rations—meat and beans, meat and vegetable hash, eaten cold with congealed grease, hard biscuits, no hot coffee?)

All that Hq. wanted us to do for this relief was knock out the Nips with M-1's, break through to "B" Co. In the dense jungle around us, surprisingly accurate rifles replied from everywhere and nowhere. Covering our advance, BARman Reimers took death squarely between his eyes. Smidt jumped on a brush-pile; it was a Jap position; a bullet shot him in the groin. Beserk at his buddy's wound, Prince led the main effort and kicked out the Japs. Higdon was shot through the neck, but a surgeon saved his life with a silver tube through the windpipe. But I Co. won its last fight before entering burned out Salamaua.

And thus I Co. 162 Inf. fought its epic battles for Scout Ridge and "B" Ridge. Credited with 119 Japs killed, we were far ahead of K Co. on the official score.

WHAT HARM DID the Japs inflict on us? By 10 Sept., we were down to an effective fighting strength of 44, with officers —a drop of 120 from the assigned strength of 164. But our casualties were those of a tropical campaign—only 7 dead Yanks not counting others dead later from wounds like Bell's. (We had one more death than K Co.) Tropical illnesses made up over half our casualties.

But to those of us still alive, all that we had been through was as nothing when on 12 Sept., 1943, we loaded at night under threat of air-raids, headed for Australia, long-legged blondes, steak and eggs, Aussie pubs, Melbourne furloughs. We had won our first battle.

Maj. Gen. O. P. Newman

Major-General Oliver P. Newman writes to express his interest in the work of Division Association Historian Hargis Westerfield.

Incidentally we believe that the post-war career of the former CO of 186 Inf who led his regiment to victory on Biak, should b known to the entire Division. After serving as Chief of Staff of the 41st Division in Japan, he was then named Chief of Staff of the Fifth Infantry Division under his old chief, General Doe, at Camp Campbell, Ky. In Sept., 46, he became Chief of Staff at the 3rd Infantry Division with which he served in the Korean War. Readers may remember that it was Newman's Third Division which rescued the Marines after their death-march back from the Yalu River. In Oct., 51, he became Assistant Commander, then in March, 1952 became a Brigadier General and was Assistant Commander of the Ninth Division. In 1954, he was Commanding General, Base Section, Communication Zone, US Army European Command. He now ranked as Major-General. In Sept., 56, he was named Assistant Chief of Staff, G 3, Headquarters US Army Continental Commander Fort Monroe, Virginia. Answered last roll-call on 8 Oct. 76 at Columbia, S.C.

Old Tambu

This is the story of 21 days
When they're gonna turn us loose.
We'll give the Nips a bit of a go,
And live on jungle juice.

We'll rout the Nips from their stronghold
And clean up the mess, ya know,
Because the colonel wanted so badly
To have a First Battalion show.

Now the colonel sez to the general,
"Why don't you give us a chance?
We've come up the coast without seeing his ghost,
And we'd like to make him dance."

Then the general sez to the colonel,
"Okay, it's now your show.
I'll give you the blacks to carry the sacks,
There's the door — now, go!"

So the colonel gathered together his men,
And sez, "Men, this is going to be rough.
There'll be times when you'll be wet and cold,
And the going will be mighty tough.

"But we're going to fight for 21 days,
And death will claim a few.
I know you guys will do your best,
And that you'll get what's coming to you.

"Oh, you'll get what's coming to you, my lads—
You'll get what's coming to you.
After 21 days of heat and hell,
You'll get what's coming to you!"

But the 21 days are over,
And we've fought for twice that long.
As soon as we clean up one damn mess,
They yodel that 21-day song.

We've all come to grief on bully beef,
And most of us are sick;
It's bully beef, it's bully beef,
You can always take your pick.

I can't figure what's coming to us,
Unless it's bully beef.
They're eating cake and coffee at the beach,
And forgotten to give us relief.

So now, I guess, what's coming to us
Is that BEAUTIFUL bully beef;
What did I do to you, Mother,
To come to all this grief?

Poem submitted by
RAY BAUMGARDNER
of Huntley, Montana

L Co. 162 Infantry:
Perimeter fighting on Scout Ridge

By DR. HARGIS WESTERFIELD, Division Historian,
with LTS. ROBERT POPE and JAMES KINDT

On 21 July 1943, L Co. 162 Inf. began some 48 days of ridge fighting against Jap perimeters above Tambu Bay. We bitterly remember red-mud foxholes and slippery, half-blind jungle patrols against Jap-held Roosevelt and Scout Ridges.

On 19 July, Jap cannon on Roosevelt Ridge blasted K Co. with 12 casualties, but L's attacks of 21-22 July found the guns silent after our FA's work. On 21 July with Papuan scouts leading, we almost topped the ridge. Automatic fire repelled us; Bowen was first L man to be wounded.

Next day, 22 July, with K on our right, we pushed two plns.— at first on the tracks of yesterday's patrol. Left of L Co., a Papuan spotted a Jap observation post and LMG. Because of a steep cliff and ridge section held completely, we turned slightly east before attacking.

In single file, we pushed up a slanting trail to the right. A Papuan scout led, then an Aussie NCO. Commanding 2/Pln. supporting, Lt. Pope heard a Jap rifle crack, then a "pop" from the Aussie's Tommy gun, then "popopopop." Then Japs fired rifles, MG's. Pope's men were strung out on a trail paralleling the ridge top some 100 feet below the crest. They hit the ground; a man's helmet fell off and clanked far down the slope. They shot at the crest but saw no Japs.

L Co. dropped down 100 yards, called in .81 mortars. Shelling was erratic; we failed to take the ridge. Later, Pope heard that the fight began when a Jap rifleman shot at the Papuan scout, but missed. The Aussie NCO fired back, but at first with his Tommy gun on single shot before he snapped on "automatic." He missed the Jap. Sgt. Crook died in this attack; wounded were Kirwin and Sgt. Boggs.

Two days later, 24 July, L left Roosevelt Ridge untaken, and hiked to help I Co. already in the long fight of foxholes and patrols on Scout Ridge.

Scout Ridge was maybe 12 miles of tangled, high jungle. From its north end it overlooked nearby Salamaua, then extended south in a wide curve inland to the Jap bastion of Mt. Tambu. Scout Ridge contained the heavily fortified main Jap supply line for all the ridges defending Salamaua. Here and on B Ridge, L fought for 47 days.

On 26 July, we supported I Co. attacking up Scout Ridge. The attack failed; we lost nobody. Next day, we reinforced Aussie Capt. Hitchcock's Papuans against the Jap perimeter south of I.

While a 2/Pln. squad feinted on one side, 1/Pln. and a 2/Pln. squad attacked. When attack failed, we fell back into a perimeter. Then we repelled a counter of 35-40 Japs. Bauman and Cpl. Bird were wounded. We retreated 100 yards to higher ground and perimetered to secure several track junctions.

Our mortars and FA shelled the southern perimeter. After recon patrols of 28-29 July, on 30 July our scouts found the perimeter deserted. Well dug in, some 40 Japs with automatic weapons had held it. Then a recon patrol from our mortar perimeter was ambushed a few hundred yards NW of that perimeter. Wounded were Hayden, Hick and Carter Williams.

During 31 July-9 Aug. we had various patrols and outposts, but no casualties. By 10 Aug. we had fully relieved I Co. in Colvert Perimeter. For the next 19 days, we grimly faced north

CREDIT: Writing this story was impossible without a seven-page, legal-size typescript of Pope, his ltrs. 15 Apr. and 3 May 1976. Kindt supplied Pope's address, his own ltrs. 15 and 24 Apr. 1976. Important also were Award Stories of Morris, Estrada and Colville; 162's Journal 9 July-13 Sept. 1943, and Col. A.R. MacKechnie's Report of Operations. Useful backgrounds were Australian David Dexter's New Guinea Offensives, and Reports of General MacArthur, Vol. II. Important also were maps of Roosevelt-Scout Ridge and a diagram of Jap Perimeter T, both unsigned. (Pope retired two years ago from his career as Research Forester, U.S. Forest Service. Kindt has been a manufacturers' representative for 30 years, selling furniture and related products to retail stores.) We are critically short of 162 stories–notably on Zamboanga where only B, E, F, and G have stories.

against the great Jap T Perimeter which barred our advance up Scout Ridge.

On 10 Aug. a recon patrol 600 yards west of Colville heard Jap voices. A booby trap wounded Lt. Endicott. We mortared an estimated 40-50 Japs in that position; results unknown. Next day two patrols heard chopping, even saw Japs building emplacements. Sgt. Villwock was wounded in the second of these patrol, on the east side of Scout Ridge.

Three days after relieving I, L Co. did not perceive the strength of T Perimeter concealed in jungle above us. On 12 Aug. our eight-man patrol pushed to storm T. Several automatic weapons slashed at us; we fled under our MG's overhead fire.

Then L had moments of stark terror in that blind jungle. With whistle and boom and thuds, four cannon shells hit us—a Jap 70 mountain gun. But we had no casualties—only fear of more shells to come.

On 13-14 Aug. a patrol probed T daily, preceded by 12 rounds of our 60 mm mortars. On 13 Aug. Japs blindly returned rifle and automatic fire at our perimter. All that night we heard chopping and pounding forward, probably because they expected an assault after the loss of Roosevelt Ridge. On 14 Aug. our patrol drew heavy fire, with grenades and mortars too. Thornton was wounded.

On 15 Aug. pressure increased on T Perimeter. Along with daily patrols drawing fire, M Co's 81's and FA shot at observed Jap positions. Their 70 cannon replied with the heaviest shelling we had in the campaign: 20 rounds, but without casualties for us. On 17 Aug. they wounded Colville and Rodriguez on patrol. Our shells cleared the perimeter, but emplacements were still intact.

On 18 Aug. Col. MacKechnie ordered aggressive patrolling to capture T Perimeter. After night FA fire and morning preparatory fire, K led the attack, L supporting. K penetrated a Jap fence by mortar-blasted holes, but MG's halted the push with three unrecovered dead and six wounded. Then the Jap gun fired six shells and wounded two M Co. men in a MG position.

And so went days and nights of perimeter combat on Scout Ridge—full of action but now hard to remember. For days all had the same pattern. We sent out patrols daily. If we got heavy fire, we recoiled, often with casulties, then called for mortar and FA rounds to quiet Japs. Next day, another patrol probed to measure results.

Nights in our holes were almost never quiet. Besides setting booby traps on the outside perimeter, we had thrown out empty ration cans. Nearly every night the cans tinkled. And always somebody shot or grenaded; others caught the fear and blazed away. On 22 Aug., for example, we threw 40 grenades during 1900-2030 hours, results unreported. Pope believed that rats caused most alarms. Dysentery was rife among us, especially a nuisance at night. M Co's shell containers became portable toilets.

Rain fell almost every afternoon. We drained drinking water from shelter halves into our helmet. We could not bathe; many feared to take off their shoes. Red mud was everywhere, coloring us reddish brown all over our scraggly uniforms and getting into our skin pores.

Food bored us: C and J rations, some Aussie bully beef and biscuits. We ate them cold mostly; smoke could draw Jap shells. Pope devised many ways to combine those monotonous rations for variations in taste. Even for antismokers, our limited cigarette rations were better than nothing. Some men even smoked tea from Aussie rations.

Besides a Jap cannon, our own shells also menaced us. Once, Pope watched four mortar shells follow each other overhead in a great arc. Topping the arc, Number 2 shell flip-flopped and was passed by Nos. 3 and 4. Pope yelled, "Short!" We hit our holes. It boomed harmlessly among us—a medium with delayed adjustment to collapse Jap holes underground.

After FA concentrations 19 Aug. a recon patrol saw destroyed emplacements in T. But next day, a 12-man combat patrol failed again to take T. At 2120 the Jap gun placed about 10 rounds on us, wounding Lt. Kruidenier, T/4 Eckstrom and both 3/Bn. medics.

On 22 Aug. Pope told a FA observer that shells from our own guns were coming lower. Observer replied that the fire angle was carefully adjusted to clear L. Next fire would be lower still. Pope wisely hit his hole then; next two of four shells were tree bursts, wounding medics Charnik and Cpl. Gager. FA sightings were to clear a tall ridge which hid L Co. from batteries below, but the trajectory impacted us.

By 25 Aug. we had a good idea of Jap T Perimeter on a wide hump of Scout Ridge some 50 yards before us. This hump was shaped like a short-legged T with the foot of the short leg facing us. Top of the T was a pimple about 125 yards across the ridge and 75 yards deep. Before L, the ridge narrowed to 15 yards with a network of trenches blocking out attacks. On precipices, MG's enfiladed both flanks. Holes were often 15 feet deep; reverse slope had shelters safe from FA and mortars.

At 0810 on 25 Aug. they returned our 500 LMG rounds with heavy, inaccurate fire. Our four-man patrol then fired four rifle grenades and some bullets, but drew no return fire until after 500 more LMG rounds. Then we took light rifle fire, but they received twenty 60mm shells without retaliation.

On 26 Aug. L made a "diversionary attack" to support 2/Bn's attack on our right flank. Our attack was a forlorn hope: a four-man point with 10 backing it, and a full pln. ready to follow on call. Leading the point, Cpl. Morris arced six grenades at an emplacement, but MG fire wounded him. Colville crawled to help Morris. Estrada exposed himself to fire and was hit also. Another man (perhaps Joe Smith of the point) and Colville rescued Morris. With altogether 14 rifle grenades, we thought we destroyed an emplacement.

Then 12 60's on two emplacements brought no return fire. When 117 81's struck T, guided by forward observation, seven Japs fled. We set up a sniper observation post for others.

On 27 Aug. probably one of eight cannon shells wounded Friesen. On 28 Aug. two cannon wounded two M Co. men in an MG position.

At 1000 on 29 Aug. L took T Perimeter. We lobbed in 180 .80mm shells and fired nine shots to signal to B Co. pushing from left flank. Our sniper post advanced unresisted. At 1200 we entered T, then met a B Co. patrol on Bald Hill behind T Perimeter. The Japs had left T several hours before.

Also on 30 Aug., a patrol found a trail from T down a spur ridge and flanked a Jap perimeter retarding I Co. When 4,000 MG rounds got no return, we informed I and pushed. At 1455 we met I in the empty perimeter.

Except for one officer and 25 men attached to I Co, L now spent two happy days of rest in 3/Bn's area. (On 1 Sept. that patrol left with I killed eight pillboxes.) On 3 Sept. we replaced I Co. in a former Jap perimeter at the junction of B and Scout Ridges, which was named Kindt Perimeter after the officer who replaced CO Dicks on 23 Aug.

L still fought grimly the almost impregnable positions at this B-Scout Ridge junction. Scout Ridge was surely the bastion of Jap defenses of Salamaua. So strong was Scout Ridge that a map of our battle lines now formed a "V" with L Co. facing the base of the "V". On both arms of the "V," Yank-Aussie outfits were almost into Salamaua, but on Scout Ridge Jap strongholds kept the "V" arms apart—seven perimeters on the Ridge itself.

Our final battle was on 4-8 Sept. Early on 4 Sept. we fell back some 100 yards while mortars hit our last Jap perimeter. M Co's Sgt. King was wounded. Then FA barraged, and the mortars again, while we reoccupied Kindt Perimeter. Our patrol took three Jap emplacements before our repulse. Wounded were Sgt. Lindahl and Cpl. Inman. Tampke fought notably well.

At 0645 on 5 Sept. 20 Jap 81-mortar rounds barraged, slaying Tampke and wounding Jacobsen and Hubbard. A recon patrol found new Jap construction. Next day at 0630 our weapons flailed the Japs. We killed two Japs but had to retreat. Despite 260 81 shells, our second push of 6 Sept. failed again.

At 0645 on 7 Sept. they missed our perimeter with 8-10 heavy mortar rounds—all duds. With clear forward observation, M fired 200 rounds, causing far greater damage than all our previous fire. On 8 Sept., after more 81's, we seized their silent perimeter. On our last day of combat, ironically enough, a sniper killed Colville, hero of our 26 Aug. attack.

The day before, Lt.-Gen. Hatazo Adachi, CO of the Jap 18th Army, had ordered immediate evacuation of Salamaua. On 10 Sept. L pursued the Jap retreat and on 12 Sept. slept in that destroyed little New Guinea port.

CO Kindt remembered well our staggering into Salamaua on 12 Sept. with about 60 survivors from battle. (We were officially 138 strong on 29 June.) He recalled laughing at, then pitying, E Co. from C Ridge with only 22 survivors. (Official figures specify 94 L men, 39 E men, but those others were probably not at Salamaua.) Officially, L Co. lost only three dead, eight seriously wounded and 12 lightly wounded—figures not jibing with this story, but close enough to seem accurate. Other losses came mostly from disease, although most men recovered.

Thus went L Co's war for Salamaua. It was a war mainly on Scout Ridge—a war of nerves and endurance rather than a war of wounds and death. It was a hard war in a reeking mountain jungle perimeter under Yank and Jap shells with nights of broken sleep and steaming daylight patrols.

Jungle Medics

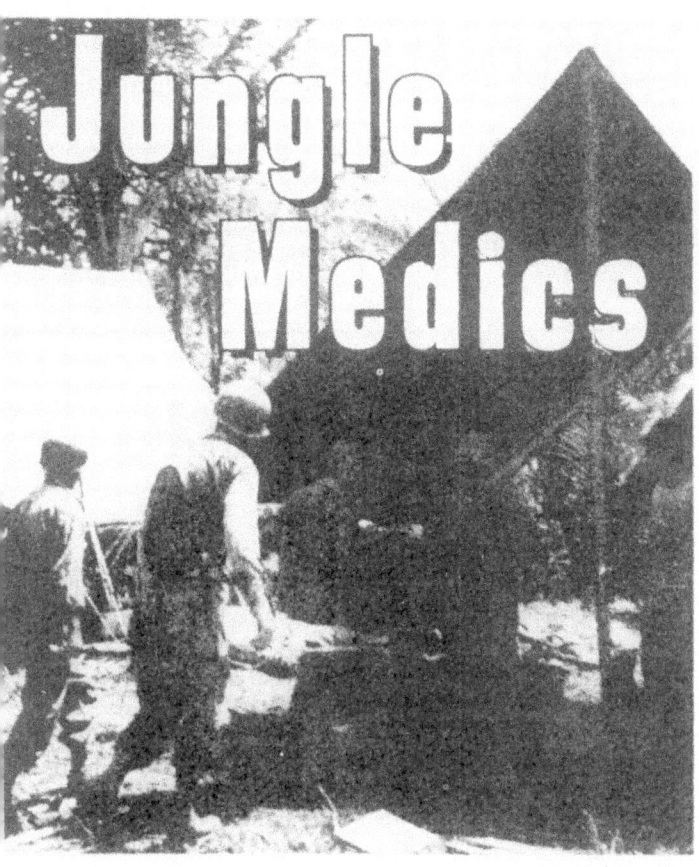

(Clearing Co, 116 Medical Btn)

by S/SGT. FRANKLIN J. CRAY with DR. HARGIS WESTERFIELD

UNDER RED AIR ALERT AT 1500 HRS 12 JUNE 1943, Clearing Co's First Pltn, 116 Medical Btn, boarded a small ship at Killerton Point and hurried overnight up to Morobe in preparation for the Salamaua Operation. We had already endured the New Guinea red alerts, rain, mud, heat, and mosquitoes for 6 months. Landed at Port Moresby 27 Dec 1942, we had flown over the hump to Sanananda, and had done medical mopping up, since 23 July at Popondetta, and then Soputa. Now we had to fight the gruelling medical battle of Morobe while 162 Inf fought on Mount Tambu and Roosevelt Ridge.

Our Clearing Co Pltn consisted of 4 medical officers counting the CO, a dental officer and 54 enlisted men. The Company also had another Pltn and a Headquarters. Technically, we were D Co, but even official reports called us Clearing Co. With a Staff rating, I was Pltn. Sgt; we operated independently of the Co, and I was all-around technician, with all the work and grief of a top-kick.

At Morobe we set up our clearing station about a mile from the dock behind a large hill. The area was brushy with swamps on both sides and a lagoon leading to the sea a half mile below. The Engineers had not yet blasted out a hillside road, so we carried all of our equipment that last half mile. Natives macheted the undergrowth with its mosquito lairs. We dug a well, got new tentage, and set up five wards, some in native-built huts, and a surgery.

By 18 June, the Pltn was ready and receiving patients — mostly recurrent malaria. On 30 June, we buried our first dead—a typhus patient. The next 80 days were sheer hell.

With Col. MacKechnie's landing at Nassau Bay 30 June and the push behind Bitoi Ridge, casualties poured in. On 2 July, Div Chaplain Atterberry held final services for a man dead of gunshot wounds.

With heavy battle casualties and fearing air-raids, we sandbagged and blacked out the Surgery. Surgical teams worked day and night. Enlisted men made the setups for operations, sterilized equipment, prepared patients. We depended on well-trained T/3 Jack Stephen to line up operation equipment. Then our Doctors operated—Capts. Frank Robinson, Armand Gordon, Alan Schofield, or Donald Searing. In the blaze of high noon, in the sweat of a blacked out tent at midnight and rain on the canvas, the doctors calmly operated. While they rested, we did the post-operational sterilizing and policing. Our meager equipment had to be immediately sterilized for a new job. Our technicians did redressings; I handled many chest wounds that made a sucking noise and had to be dressed with heavy compress bandages.

Mostly we had 80 to 100 patients; but when air-alerts drove our ships to hide, we filled up to 200, half of them malaria cases. After 7-10 days' treatment, they returned to duty. Some were soon back—as battle casualties. In most cases, the treatment was simple: a clean dry place to sleep, a place to clean up, the best possible food.

New Guinea's travel conditions and the Nips' planes did not let us function just as a Clearing Co. We couldn't just "receive, treat, and evacuate" casualties. Mainly they used us a week for a Field Hospital and then returned to the lines. We had to evacuate others to Oro Bay, and this was a special problem.

When a ship was available in Morobe Harbor, we had maybe an hour to get 50 or more men the half-mile down to the dock at our shallow little inlet. While able patients walked, we carried others by litter or in our jeep—the only vehicle issued to us. A smaller crew manned the boat to help 532 EB & S men lift litter cases onto the ship. We remember one 162 officer full of MG bullets, in a leg-and-body-cast. He was a big man, and the litter almost cracked. (Historian's Note: will some 162 man please tell me his name.)

August 1943 was even harder. On 5 August the red alerts and actual raids were so many that we could not evacuate patients, and soon filled up to capacity. But on 6 August we shipped out some 100 ambulants. On 11-16 August, with the fall of Roosevelt Ridge, we had a rush of casualties—several Higgins boats a day—60 on 16 August alone. Surgery was almost never empty. For the rest of August, we drew 20-30 patients daily.

In early September, with Morobe Harbor crammed by supply ships, we served naval patients. The Japs bombed 2 LST's, and we worked on burns and shrapnel cases. We buried 12 sailors, and 1 soldier who lived for a while even after the amputation of a leg with 9 bullet wounds.

On 9 September, Jap planes found 262 Hospital fresh from the states—all pretty, with the tents lined up out in the open. There were 3 casualties. In the next 2 days, we had a chance to evacuate most of our litter cases —but still had 150 patients on hand. On 12 June, a formation of Jap bombers could have killed us in chow-line; it blasted the Navy instead. Shortly we had 17, many severely burned, and the odor sickened many of us. We buried 18 more in our cemetery. We sent 17 to a Hospital Ship, and buried 4 more.

Then Lae was taken, the Japs were pinched out of Salamaua, and suddenly Clearing Co's First Pltn's campaign ended. We returned or transferred our last patients and crated up equipment to ship it north for another medical unit. We rode LCT 372 for Oro Bay and new uniforms, and 4 days later boarded the *Sea Snipe* for Australia. Our 2 Pltn from Tambu Bay had already set up camp for us at Rockhampton across from 5 Station Hospital.

From 5 Oct 1943 to 11 March 1944, we got all the furloughs and passes we could. Camp was routine garrison duty. At the Medical Btn parade in the 186 Inf area, we received the Distinguished Unit Badge for our services at Sanananda. Early in 1944, Clearing Co shipped back to New Guinea.

That was when the Army played that grim little rotation joke on me. With 22 months overseas, I was part of the group separated to go home. We remained at Rocky for a fortnight to clean up camp—and then boarded the *Katoomba* for New Guinea again —the land of the long blue jungle coast and the mist from the mountains and heat and fevers.

At Finschafen, S/Sgt. Lyle Donaldson had my place as Pltn Sgt and I filled in where I could. On 22 April, we left LST 466 to land at Hollandia. We camped on Pancake Hill where the Japs had left intact with ammo a magnificent AA gun that could have blown the whole landing apart.

When a sneak plane burned up our supplies, we set up station quickly. Our rescue party picked up casualties on the beach, and Surgery worked all night with 30 serious cases.

On 24 April, we turned over our patients to 92 Evac, and joined 186 for a trip by LCM's south around Cape Pie and across Jautefa Bay to Pim. There we loaded on trucks and moved up

Credit Lines

Assisted by his buddies, Frank J. Cray, 2760 Stolz Hill Road, Lebanon, Oreg., furnished all material for this illuminating tale of our Medics. (CO G and H 116 Meds plan a reunion for 1960 at St. Anthony, Idaho.) Please understand that CO G and H were combined to form Gray's outfit, D 116 Med Btn, which went by the name Clearing Co.

While still in high school, Frank joined Oregon NG in 1938. Inducted in 1940, he became Cpl., then S/Sgt in Australia. Rotated home, he finished the war with 752 MP Btn of Tule Lake, Calif. doctoring Japanese. He married Myrtle Esdaile of Portland, whom he met while in uniform. He has 4 children—a girl 12, a boy 9, and twins 4. He now works for the Cascade Plywood Corp.

Correction

Col. A. R. MacKechnie has asked the Historian to delete his name from the authorship of "162 Inf Assails, Mt. Tambu," in the previous *Jungleer*. He prefers that credit go to Gen. Harold Taylor, Col. John D. George, Lieut. James Clark. Thanks, Col. Mack!

the Lake Sentani shore road right along with the advance.

The second day, we set up station by Lake Sentani just off the new road to the air strip, a spooky place. Japs sneaked around; we heard them yelling and barking and howling all that night. On 27 April, we received our first casualties—and infantry guards to hunt out the Japs. We amputated the foot of a man blown up in a booby trap. On 29 April, gunshot and shrapnel casualties came in, one with a bad sucking chest wound. At dusk, guards flushed 2 Nips on the road 30-40 feet from our receiving tent. They shot one through both hips: we treated him and evacuated both to the stockade the next day.

At dusk on 2 May, we had a tense moment. In a jeep's headlights, 17 Jap prisoners came down the road; at first we thought they were armed enemies. They spent the night with us, then went on to the stockade at Nifaar.

Our Hollandia Operation ended in less than two weeks—hard and bitter and frightening at times, but nothing like the last year's work at Salamaua. We left the Sentani swampland and camped on the open beach. We began receiving routine sick and set up a dental lab.

Then rotation struck on 18 May. Of the original group with me in the old H Co of the Oregon National Guard in 1940, only 10 were left. These were F/Sgt John Schlenk, S/Sgts Harvey Cutts, Stanley Anderlik, Franklin J. Cray himself, Sgts Lynn Blackwell, Leo Crispin, Al Jenner, Gene Sutter, and T/5 Wes Gillenwater. With Hq Co was F/Sgt Joe Dent, and also with the Division were W/O Glenn Kobow, and M/Sgt. William Cook.

We flew from Cyclops Drome to Milne Bay, shipped on the U.S.S. *Fred C. Ainsworth*, and landed in San Francisco 29 May, 1944. Now I wish somebody else would continue the history of Clearing Co 116 Medics the rest of the way to Japan.

641 Tank Destroyer Battalion I
Blue-water odyssey to battle

By DR. HARGIS WESTERFIELD, Division Historian,
with Captain BENNETT SAUNDERS, 641 TD S-3

The blue-water odyssey of 641 Tank Destroyer Battalion is in many ways high Army comedy. Yet underlying this comedy is the deadly seriousness of men striving to battle for their country. We worked hard to get into position to fight!

In Dec. 1941, about Pearl Harbor time, 641 TD Bn. was organized at Fort Lewis. Formerly, we belonged to antitank units of the 41st's 66 FA Brigade, which disappeared when the Division became triangular. The only non-FA part of 641 TD was Recon Co.—originally in 116 Engrs.

Although supposedly an outfit of self-propelled tank destroyers, we never saw combat as a Yellow Tiger unit. At Fort Lewis, no tank destroyers were available. Principal weapons were towed 37mm AT guns.

Two months after Pearl Harbor, 641 TD was 50 per cent below strength. Suddenly on 19 Feb. 1942, our half-manned outfit boarded a gigantic train with all our equipment and rumbled all the way across the USA to Fort Dix, NJ.

It seemed like a great emergency run to save the Union. We halted only at RR division points to change train crews and engines.

We made a fast run to Fort Dix—to a dead stop. For our ship to battle had been "La Normandie." But alleged trouble with electric wiring had caused it to burn at the dock in New York City.

With impact of this news came another impact. To put the bn. on a war footing, we received 500-600 of the N.Y. national guardsmen from Ft. Ethan Allen, Vt. Brooklyners seemed predominant. In the same barracks, we heard the clear, ringing tones of Montana and the softer, quicker music of Brooklyners with the "R2" flattened out.

At first, older TD men and new easterners did not get along well. We were Americans of two different regions and two different American accents. Brooklyners called old-timers "Cowboys," and themselves, "Battling Bastards of Brooklyn." We called them "Dodgers," but disrespectfully. Some of them dodged off at once.

In two hours after arrival, some 40 per cent of them were AWOL in Brooklyn. We placed armed guards to hold them, and some guards made a grapevine to Brooklyn to alert AWOL's on our day of embarkation. Since a mess officer never knew how many would be present for a meal, he usually requested too many rations. We ate like kings.

Then 641 TD entrained from Jersey to embark on the "SS Uruguay". Most AWOL's returned to 641 TD—a few actually on the pier as we loaded that night. All companies had lost men; but Hq. Co. heard 35 "silences" at gangplank roll call.

Instead of the luxury liner "Normandie", now canted and charred at her dock, we boarded the rusty, medium-sized old "Uruguay." She was a 35,000-ton relic of Latin American cruises, but had to serve 5,000 Yanks bound to Australia for 37 days of travail. Carpenters still hammered when we boarded.

First general quarters was called for an emergency. All former plumbers were requested to help get toilets in working order. We needed them badly come Easter!

On 4 Feb. 1942, "Uruguay" left New York Harbor. We saw Liberty's statue sink slowly below the horizon—faced the open Narrows and the gray North Atlantic.

Rumors were that a German sub had torpedoed a destroyer off Jersey last night. We had orders to look out for life rafts or floating corpses.

Before Transportation Corps know-how, our units were badly mixed—641 TD, 162 Inf. and 41 Recon. For two days at sea, reloading gave us something to do.

The antiquated "Uruguay" slowed the whole convoy to a maximum of 10 knots. We were sitting ducks. Yet, along with "SS Santa Paula", we were part of perhaps the most heavily armed convoy of the U.S. Navy. Two cruisers and the old carrier "Hornet" guarded us—with destroyers in large numbers, especially at dawn or dusk. Several times, a Navy dirigible monitored us a few miles. Although depth charges boomed on the horizon, we got safely through the Atlantic.

After sighting the great land mass of Cuba to port, "Uruguay" anchored at Colon on the ninth day, next morning locked through the Panama Canal and into the blue Pacific.

Sailing west in the desiccating heat of the equator, we got dire news. Since the "Uruguay" condensed only 60 tons of water daily and we consumed 90 tons daily, we were rationed on half a canteen every 24 hours.

On 25 Mar., we had landfall at Bora Bora in the Society Islands. U.S. cruisers "Richmond", "New Orleans" and a naval supply ship gave us water, while repairmen labored all night on our defective condensers.

No one could go ashore, but we could trade with natives, even swim. Suddenly the natives headed for shore. Six moss-covered submarines rose from the waves. We almost panicked, but these were Yank submarines.

On 3 Apr., Good Friday, we sighted the long blue foreshore of New Zealand and anchored 24 hours in Auckland's fine harbor. Natives waved bottles from the docks. That night, Brooklyners yearned for home when they heard the bells of

---

CREDIT: Main source is Capt. Ben Saunders' 23-page typescript prepared in 1974 from his huge collection of documents. Supporting details came from T/Sgt. Deane Flett's three-page typescript "The 641 Tank Destroyer Battalion," which I used for an earlier comic story in *Jungleer*. Saunders is a retired "Concrete Consultant" now living in Seattle. Besides data for at least two 641 TD stories, Saunders has given me important documents for 163's history a contribution comparable to that of 162's Col. A.T. MacKechnie. Col. H.B. Cary of Bellingham, Wash., has today sent me papers for a probable story of 41 QM. In non-infantry stories, we need more Medics' narratives. We still have not received data on 41 Sig. and 41 MP.

harbor ferries. But nobody went ashore; this was just a water stop. The crew had given up on the condensers.

A strange-looking New Zealand auxiliary cruiser escorted us west into the Tasman Sea. We longed for firm land in Australia and escape from this prison ship.

But Easter was agony. A roast turkey banquet was tainted. Everyone sickened with diarrhea. Like athlethes trying out for the Olympics, we raced for the toilets, but half of them jammed.

Next day came our first storm in that turbulent Tasman Sea. When the storm peaked, our turbines quit. For two hours, "Uruguay" was dead in the water while our New Zealand escort angrily flashed signal lights and made circles around us.

On resuming our 10-knot speed, we loafed into Melbourne after a voyage of 10,000 miles in 37 days and nights of sweltering blackouts. Diarrhea, dehydration and despairing boredom had so weakened us that we had trouble even carrying barracks bags to the waiting trucks. Our destination was Seymour, 60 miles NW of Melbourne.

At Seymour, we began training. During our first field exercises, the command radio carried Tokyo Rose's welcome to 641 TD. We had our first casualties. S/Sgt. Maurice Johnson died in a Melbourne hospital. On the return trip, Maj. Swift's car ran off the road. Swift was injured seriously; his passenger, Lt. Carl, was killed.

Some three months later, 641 TD accompanied the Division north to Rockhampton and trained again, while other units moved to New Guinea. Then came 641 TD's great jungle "circus" for the general.

T/Sgt. Deane Flett still believes that because we were among the last 41st units to go to New Guinea, we got the chore as guard of honor to 6th Army's new Lt. Gen. Krueger.

At 2359, before midnight, 641 TD rose and entrucked for Rockhampton Schoolyard. For three hours then, we waited for Krueger and marched or marked time in various military formations.

When Krueger finally appeared at 1100, he saw 641 TD in all our glory—850 men, 35 officers, awkwardly marching in outlandish garb. Like men from outer space, we shone in green and brown jungle zoot suits. We wore long-legged green jungle boots—"like tennis boots'" said Flett. Men still laugh at our appearance. As for Krueger, his only comment was, "I guess you haven't done this before."

In Dec. 1942, we were finally alerted for New Guinea; but only Recon Co. flew the hump, Moresby to Dobadura. The other 641 units hung around until March.

Suddenly we were at Gladstone to embark on the Dutch "Bontekoe." We watched it unload battlefield salvage—blood-stained blankets, dented helmets.

But we did not sail because these were the days of Adm. Yamamoto's all-out offensive against our shipping. For five days "Bontekoe" holed up in Townsville Harbor while Jap 100-plane raids hit Darwin, Moresby, Milne Bay, Oro Bay. On the sixth morn, G-2 predicted that the sky would be clear for us to slip into New Guinea.

Besides "Bontekoe", convoy included unlucky "Van Heemskirk" with 205 FA Bn. aboard, a Liberty ship, and an Aussie corvette as guard. Full speed ahead, we left Australia, crossed Torres Strait, and by late afternoon anchored near the head of Milne Bay. Here was the horror of New Guinea—air that was thick with humidity like looking through glass, unbroken seas of jungle.

Just as we anchored, we heard three rounds of ack-ack from probably No. 3 Airstrip. We up-anchored and ran 10 miles across the bay to Waga-Waga Jetty. We docked; orders came to disembark.

While "Bontekoe" scurried for open sea, we marched NE up the coast to bivouack. About 0200, a message waked us: Jap task force heading for Milne Bay! And 641 TD was to defend the coast. In cold gray dawn, we desperately dug in.

Then nothing happened for two days while 641 TD waited by our holes. Suddenly "Bontekoe" came out of the ocean to anchor at Waga-Waga again. We filled in holes, policed area, and waited another night in tropical rain.

In morning sunshine, we boarded "Bontekoe" again. Hanging out bedding and clothes to dry, we settled down for a sleepy afternoon.

Three shots rang out from the warning ack-ack. Col. Fertig ordered all 641 ashore; the real air raid crashed down.

In beautiful formation, high-level bombers marched down the bay, wheeled majestically, then blanketed the airstrip and dock area with bombs. Then came fighters and dive bombers. They worked over all ships—all but "Bontekoe." Five bombs splashed near the Aussie corvette.

Suddenly it ended. Machine guns, bombs and ack-ack blasted wildly. Then came silence. Five ships were flaming and sinking—including 205 FA's "Van Heemskirk" and the Liberty ship in our convoy. But the corvette was safe.

And "Bontekoe" was safe! Moored at the dock, we had been unnoticed and not even shot at.

Boarding again, we soberly watched salvage crews beach five burning ships. "Van Heemskirk's" 205 FA shells and aviation gasoline boomed and banged all night long.

Such was 641 TD's "Battle of Waga-Waga." Before dawn, we ran for Oro Bay and arrived after midnight two days later in a wild tropical storm. Lightning showed a small harbor with wreckage of ships protruding from waves everywhere, and a bombed-out jetty. A small launch towed a barge out; we crammed aboard. At dawn, more rain fell as we lightered ashore guns, trucks, and supplies.

As "Bontekoe" departed with the Aussie attack unit we replaced, 641 settled down to a useless defense of Oro Bay. We set up three Aussie 25-pounders back from Tobruk, along with our 37's.

Morale climbed on 14 May. A heavy Jap bombing attack ceased; our newcomer P-38's dived hot on the tails of those planes. The P-38's cleared those bombers from the sky; at one time, 12 Jap planes were splashed down in Oro Bay or fireballed in the sky.

Suddenly 641 TD moved to Borico, north of Oro Bay, and was delightedly ready for action. We were attached to the First Cavalry Division for the Admiralty Islands Operation. We turned in our obsolescent unfought 37mm cannon. Ordnance dept. rolled in new, self-propelled tank destroyer units. We trained enthusiastically.

But a telegram from War Dept. ordered us to turn back in the noble tank destroyers. Our bright dream of battle for 1/Cav. Div. had faded.

Then ships and planes brought in the 4.2 chemical mortars that became 641 TD's prime weapon in combat on Biak and the Toem Foreshore. These were heavy close-support weapons as powerful as cannon. Although we lacked even one training directive, with the help of Col. Cochran we improvised our own table of organization and training manual. We now had 48 heavy mortars—12 per company, six per platoon. Each section had a ¼ ton tractor pulled by jeep.

Within three weeks, we had qualified all officers and a good many NCO's. By Apr. 1944, we were with 41 Div. at Finschhafen for the great New Guinea Campaign—for Aitape, Toem-Maffin Bay, Hollandia, Biak. We fought to hell-and-back all over New Guinea. But here the tragicomic epic of 641 TD's attempt to get into combat comes to an end. The story of our battles is another great story.

G Co. 163 Infantry:
The Marches of Aitape

Prime source is my own MS, collated with 163 Inf Journal of Aitape Opn. Original MS was given the editor of our first history book but not used and could not be relocated in Federal Archives. But I brought a carbon copy home with me.

Before dawn 22 Apr 1944, G Co 163's riflemen sleepily waited orders overside from a great "Landing Ship Dock" off Aitape. In the black well behind us, G's Weapons Pltn crowded into LCVPs for the sea to rise and float them out.

Suddenly, we saw yellow flashes landward in gray light. Tremendous red shells thumped the beach; planes dived into reddening light below. Smoke of burning oil rose straight into the sky. Point-blank, a destroyer broadsided Tumleo Island— an endless chain of red-ringed shells.

Now came G's orders overside. Crushed with our weight of steel and packs, we sagged down landing-nets. Bruce Baird held my net away from the heaving side of the ship. Jammed with packs against LCVP bulwarks, my 3/Pltn had room only to stand.

Already it was broad daylight, the sky a blue washed clean by the Guinea rain before dawn. Forward, a gunner joked, "Let 'em send a plane now. We're ready!" But no plane struck. Through a crack in our ramp, miles off, I saw a clear stretch of sand with barges nosed into it, a dark-green jungle wall.

But G did not go in then, for 3/Bn in the first wave was securing the beach for us. Our craft slowly turned in a wide circle. Lt Kreiger said we could light cigarettes. My right arm took a pack from my chest pocket, but my left was jammed into the next man away from my matches. Giru lighted my cigarette. After long waiting, Kreiger called, "Lights out! Fix bayonets!"

In that jam, Giru and I had to reach atop the other man's pack and latch on bayonets. We smelled diesel fumes and brine. Our LCVP straightened for the beach. Through my forward slit, I watched the empty beach, our closing into an ominous silent jungle wall. Even with 3/Bn inland, I was afraid.

Barge grated the sand; ramp took too long to fall. I leaped out first—happy and scared. But with no training at Torbul Point, I made a brave leap that was laughable. I sunk deep into wet sand, fell and jammed my rifle muzzle. Lt Kreiger and 3/Pltn sprinted across the beach past me.

Up and running under heavy pack, I crossed open beach, dashed through brush past 2 Jap bunkers thatched and sand-covered. A hole was stove in the top of one. I saw my first Jap dead—crumpled little pale corpse in white—the bare delicate feminine arch of a foot—red star of a bullet. Cortez had killed here.

We riflemen landed unhurt, but down shore, Weapons Pltn dashed in under Jap rifle-fire. Old-timer Gorsline took an arm-wound, never fought again. Other Weapons men panted safe into cover. Cappuccino lost contact, turned up with Amphib Engrs 3 days later. (A Jap sniper would kill him on Biak.)

In a shaggy kunai meadow, I found 3/Pltn making combat packs. Sweatily, I yanked from my pack that foolish heavy jungle hammock, raced through a labyrinth of straps to reassemble my gear, fearfully ramrodded sand from my rifle muzzle.

The surrounding meadow seemed a confused mill of green-clad men and piles of rubber bags. Yet long, orderly lines of rifles were filing into the jungle. Outguards with slanted rifles crouched at jungle's edge. Farther off, M-1s splattered as 163's rifles hunted for stragglers. (And the fresh, clean smell of crushed mint comes back to me from my first beach-head.)

My line of riflemen struck up a faint jungle track. Tough lawyer vines hooked our packs. One green vine ran into my useless stacking swivel, halted me until I yanked it loose. I learned to keep a hand over that swivel. Bent low at a pause, I saw a yellow man moving parallel at a crouch. I slipped off safety. It was a Yank lineman. "Take it easy," warned Tex Fowler behind me. It was good that Sanananda vets had us rookies sandwiched in line between them—Fowler behind, Mayberry ahead.

G came out on a rain-pooled macadam road. We saw into a cavernous Jap kitchen. Clean utensils hung in orderly rows. A steer carcass lay by the road. The Japs were gone.

From the G point, guards brought 2 prisoners. "Who caught him?" asked a correspondent. "Bronis Kiselus of Brooklyn, NY," 3/Pltn's S/Sgt Daugherty replied. This was untrue—just an Irish trick to get Kiselus' name in print. But we never saw that paper.

G Co halted among native huts. Automatic fire from the rear drove us to earth. Surely a Jap MG had ambushed us. Wriggling in grit, I tried to aim my rifle on the unseen target. I thought, "He's searching for me. If I don't shoot on sight, he'll kill me!" But officers' shouts halted fire. A misguided Yank souvenir hunter was taken for a Jap and shot up badly. And me—I hiked on angrily nursing abraded skin where sand in sweat cut my tender stateside flesh.

We marched to Tadji Dromes and found them unguarded. The maneuver of our great invasion fleet had sucked in Gen Adachi's men to garrison Wewak, for an attack we never made. Tadji Dromes were not worth taking. Like most Nippo fields, it's just a bit of coral surface in the kunai with a few wrecked planes.

Orders were to dig in; FA would shell the jungle before us. With my flimsy little shovel, I dug in fear. I dug a fox-hole waist-deep, and kept on. Black with sweat, I saw veteran Kiselus idly grinning at me. We moved on; FA never fired. I still resent what happened to my fox-hole. It hid 3 unarmed Nips later until an E detail—perhaps under Lt Rottman—found and slew them.

Our hike went into wetter ground. Many a Yank threw off his terrible sweaty pack and flopped against a log. For besides M-1, regular combat pack with shovel and poncho, we had 2 days' K rations, 1 day's C rations. (Capt Braman left most of his aboard the night before.) We had gas mask, full ammo belt, extra bandolier. Banging my side was more torture—a big canvas pouch with grenade launcher, a kit of 5 AT bombs. (Never in the whole war did I fire that launcher in action.)

Water was short; we had just 1 canteen. But we heard that trailside water was poisoned from phosphorus. We nursed a few pallid drops from our canteens.

We moved so fast that by 1044, we were at the fighter strip. By 1300, we crossed First Phase line—a low bridge over the muddy canyon of Waitanan Creek. At the creek, I rebelled. That gas-mask weighed as much as my whole pack. Officers had promised we could drop it here. Orders never came. I splashed mine into the swamp. Losing this weight seemed to save me from collapsing.

The trail became a chain of logs over shallow water. Halts were frequent, to make us stand and balance full pack on those logs. Our feet ached. Some of us sat on the logs with water over our uppers.

The afternoon darkened. Crossing another creek past the pale, stained bodies of 2 Nips the FA had tossed dead, we made perimeter in the coconut grove by Pro Mission—a big native hut under a cross. Here we dug a circle of 2-man slit trenches. Louisianan Anderson and I carried empty canteens back to the stream where outguards watched. After the halazone took effect I drained 2 full canteens.

Back at the slit trench with Fowler, I heard "Giant" Harrison, 3/Pltn T/Sgt, call, "You're on your own now!" Outguards fell back to their holes, eyes still on the trails they had guarded.

While Fowler slept, I had first watch, grenade in right hand. I knelt very much alone. Thick brush tangled around me; I could not see even the next hole because of brush. Only in front could see any distance—our field-of-fire—a wide gray void downslope between coconut trees.

My tired eyes played tricks. Tortured eyeballs jerked; I saw Jap grenadiers creeping up. I knew that I had better throw that grenade first. But the grenadiers turned back into bushes. After 2 dazed hours, I roused Fowler to take my grenade, fell dead asleep.

Only a minute later, as it seemed, Fowler awoke me. "I can't hold my eyes open," he whispered. "You gotta stay up awhile." And something must have stirred out front; another Yank had thrown a grenade at it awhile back.

41sters rest on a beach in the Aitape area.

Strangely enough, it made me feel good to take his guard for another 2 hours. Fowler had spent the afternoon on that excruciating job of scouting before G Co. And now for the first time since I joined G Co, I felt good for something. No Jap troubled us, and I finally took my turn to die asleep again.

After troubled sleep, we packed at dawn to march. Sun blazed as we hit the trail. After the first sweat, we settled into the slow, wet plod onward, the jungle over ported rifles. Our shell craters secured the route. We saw no Japs.

That second night, G Co dug in under coconut trees before Raihu River. On inner perimeter with S/Sgt Murphy my squad-leader we could sleep all night without turns on guard. We dug a deep, dry trench. Fowler had let us sleep boxed in our shoes, but Murphy told me we could get rid of ours. Nobody would be fool enough to fight above ground, said Murphy. I never wore shoes in a hole after that.

Murphy hoped for a good night's sleep, but a G grenade sparked like a pistol. "The Battle of Raihu River" began. As giant land-crabs "attacked" over dead coconut fronds, a long series of grenades blasted and knocked sand down on our ponchos. Once Hardesty loosed his great MG Fifty at the jungle. (Conforti had fired on a Jap at sunset, then hit a hole.) But we had too many green men on outer perimeter. It was an almost sleepless night.

Next morning, Capt Reams assembled G and swore hard: "If any Japs were there, we'd be pinned down under knee-mortars right now." But we forgot his just anger when he finished with, "Intelligence says the Japs withdrew 2 days ago."

It seemed that we had a third day of sunstruck hiking to look forward to. And I got another hot jungle lesson. Sitting waiting orders on a dead coconut branch, I felt my back pocked with fire. A chain of great scarlet ants was biting me. Peeling off pack and jacket, I slew them viciously. I swore like Reams.

G Co forded Raihu River in a long winding line around step-offs, while our tall men marked the underwater trail and looked after our shorter men. Water came to my arm-pits, but I kept dry my M-1 and ammo atop my helmet. And now, despite Reams' assurances, I felt danger. We crossed the Aitape River on the beams of a half-wrecked bridge. Our line of rifles curved uphill—past a cumbrous Jap automatic AA gun with a clip of live shells in the breach.

Shots rang out at the head of G's column. Around my right shoulder, Sgt Slaga's M-1 fired uphill at a target I never did see.

In the green Aussie hospital atop Windy Ridge, scout Mese had surprised 2 Nips at breakfast. They reached for their rifles.

41sters aboard an LST on their way to Toem, Dutch New Guinea, a stage in the Wakde operations. The group of soldiers in the foreground, seemingly unconcerned about the impending operation, enjoys a game of cards.

Mese's tommy-gun blew out a Jap brain. The other Jap fled across the ridge-brow while our M-1s chased him and missed.

Such was G Co's "battle" of Windy Ridge. It was one of the few actions in the whole main operation to seize Aitape—although 3/Bn did have a murderous assault from escaping Japs on a back-trail 3 days later. But when we inspected the network of Nippo trenches defending Windy Ridge, G was happy that we never had to attack. Those slopes were perfect for grazing fire.

Thus ended G Co's Beach-Head at Aitape—except, of course for wilderness patrols and the sad landing at Marok Village where Vivorito drowned. At Aitape, we had defeated the Japs by marching. After 32 Div took over, the Japs came boiling back out of Wewak and did the long Battle of the Drinumor, but G Co was long gone for Toem and Biak where we had 11 killed.

G Co had lost only Gorsline—no doubt grateful for the wound that got him out of the lines forever. Like G's other recruits, I had learned about front-line action without undue agony. I had not fired a shot nor thrown a grenade. And our campaign had ended as I wish all campaigns would end—with a long bath in the sweet, cool, rain-sweetened River of Aitape.

G Co., 163 Infantry:

Patrol to Marok Village

By DR. HARGIS WESTERFIELD,
Association Historian

After seizing Aitape 24 Apr 1944, 163 Inf needed jungle patrols. For the day after G Co took Windy Ridge, a Piper Cub over Sissano Lagoon west of us received harmless rifle fire from 3 Japs in 3 canoes. At a Jap Hq upstream across Raihu River, Lt Schille's 5-man patrol was shot up and scattered, and I&R man Benge killed. On the same day, 3/Bn men killed 3 Of 6 armed Japs at Kapoam, where the Kamti Village fight would explode on 27 Apr.

And on 28 June, G Co sent 30 men of Kreiger's 3/Pln for a 4-day patrol to Marok or Malol Village, some 6 miles west on the beach. With us, we had an Aussie officer and an ANGAU Sgt to recruit native labor. (ANGAU—"Australia-New Guinea Administrative Unit"). We had 4 native guides. Just after a good night's deep sleep in my commodious jungle hammock, I didn't want to go. But I found Beavers on the damp ground against a coconut tree and left the back-breaking weight in his charge.

Back under helmet and weighty pack, I faced the garish daylight in our long line of men in green. On the edge of a sago swamp, we turned uphill on a slippery trail with pools of rain water in the rock underfoot. New Guinea sweat fevered us, and we helped BARman Jim Wilson and assistant Mayberry by carrying most of their heavy clips.

But from the ridge top, the slope tumbled sheer, and we stood unhelmeted in the lean, cool breeze from the Bismarck Sea. Descending ledge by ledge, we revived in those chill winds. Through stately avenues of coconut palms, we saw long breakers foam on miles of white beach.

This was Tepier Plantation, where hungry Nips would surely be foraging. The village was a little knot of native huts. In line of skirmishers, we went in and cleared the village, rifles ready at port.

And the big Aussie Sgt with his little Yank carbine took the surrender of a skinny little Jap — the only live one I saw in the whole Aitape invasion. He bowed to the waist and hissed in courtesy. To reassure him, we lighted a cigarette in his mouth. We put a pack on him, and with Sgt Shumaker and 4 volunteers guarded him back up the steeps we had just come down.

Then we fired the village and sat down to lunch. But downwind came waves of angry rifle-fire. We leaped up and grabbed rifles and doubled back without our packs. We thought we'd never see those 5 good friends of ours again. Yet we found our detail again — the guards grinning and the Jap grinning. The gunfire was miles away over the hills — or wind-borne waves of sound from Jap ammo in the village we had burned.

Later, we learned that Shumaker's detail arrived at G Co safely and forwarded our live Jap to Persecution Task Force Hq for questioning. The Jap was a sgt from an air force labor bn at But Village — 100 miles east of Aitape — with orders to report to Hollandia, after our bombers had left only 2 damaged planes at But Field. Starting out with 2 friends, he had a wound 22 Apr and told them to fare to Hollandia without him. The But garrison had been 600 strong.

Returned to our beach after farewelling Shumaker again, we had K rations and great draughts of the effervescent, foaming green coconut. Then we struggled west along the flats through the sleepy afternoon. Feet sank in the sand, and helmets were heavier step by step. Once we passed a wrecked Jap lugger on the beach. The Aussie sgt fired his carbine over it but got no reaction.

And by late afternoon, we arrived at Marok Village — a scattering of shadowy, deserted native huts among weeds and desultory coco palms. It sat on a flat a little above the beach of packed white sand. The Japs had left bags of rice, a manual of field fortifications, and poor little red-scratched post-cards that would never be mailed.

We made a rude perimeter on the clean beach — but above ground since our natives said no Japs were near. About sunset, we had a swimming detail in the tall waves. Our patrol was like a vacation jaunt. And that night at my turn on guard in the moonlight, I sat with rifle across my knees and contemplated the long dark foaming rollers breaking — God's grant of beauty among our rifles.

At dawn, a fine black native spearman in red loincloth stood up before our outguard. The big Aussie sgt went to parley with him. Then Kreiger called all Yanks off duty from our swim in the surf to act as an informal guard of honor. "Don't put your bayonet on the end of your rifle," Sgt Slaga told me. "It will scare them."

With his sgt attending, our Aussie officer sat in a newly built little booth of coconut palms. The natives were coming in to ally with us and work for us.

For Americans reared from childhood on Indian tales, it was a dream of pioneer days come true. A village group came up to be counted — a white-eyed, friendly throng of black families. They seemed not to understand how to line up.

Then a slender, clean-looking chief stepped forward. He had a scarlet loincloth with a curved slender naked blade at his side. He helped the Aussie sgt to set them in ranks for counting.

And that tribe in line we never forgot. In front stood grinning little blacks in their brightest loincloths, with often naked machetes at their belts. Around their legs peered skinny little ebony boys. Little grey-faced kinky-headed mothers waited behind them. These young mothers had long, drooping bare breasts and wore heavy packs. Babies peered over the grey mothers' shoulders. Tump-lines from the packs covered the mothers' foreheads.

After this tribe made treaty with us, it hiked past us towards Aitape. Then other tribes of the long white beaches and the dark rain forest presented themselves in turn before the ANGAUs at their booth. And all that afternoon into sunset, the sands up past the curve in the shore was black with the tribes of natives coming in.

And that night, the huts of Marok Village glowed with cooking fires. A naked little black boy with a machete as long as himself climbed high in a coconut tree and hacked at a frond. The Japs were gone forever.

So Kreiger's 3/Pln had 3 delightful nights on Marok Beach. We slept in a little ring between that dark-faced village and the giant, long rollers from the north and the sea-road towards Tokyo.

Then the third morning, 4 landing-barges cruised in, beaked like Viking long-ships with their turned up ramps. From a foredeck, big black-headed Capt Reams shouted, "Put on your packs and come aboard!"

So we came back again to the Twentieth Century in the fumes of half-burnt diesel oil. We sat by our packs in the slime and

---

Prime source is "Aitape, Marok, Serra," from my unpub MS, "History of G Co.," with background from 163 Inf Operations Journal and Awards Stories of Allison, Bust, Walker. I left a copy of my "History of G Co" with MacCartney at Kure in 1945, but Federal Record Centers have not reported having it on file. Fortunately, I carried a copy home with me.

A combat patrol in the jungles of SWPA, as seen by the late artist Kerr Eby.

sludge and nausea of our Landing Craft Mechanized and fared some 20 miles up the coast for a surprise landing at Serra Village. Besides all G Co, we had a section of 81s and of HMGs from H Co. with 2 more ANGAUs and 3 native police.

G Co was back into the war indeed. Even before I could finish my many home letters, I was up at orders behind the landing-ramp. I faced my second beach-head. I fearfully gripped that M-1 and peered through the slit at another wall of dark-green jungle coming at me.

Long before the shore — as it seemed to me — the landing-ramp dropped into blue water under my eyes. Like others, I walked in through blue water. It got deeper — over my leggins, my belt — over my shoulders. I lifted M-1 over my head. I kept wading. The water was a blue-green wall over my eyes. (I hadn't time to be afraid; I was brought up in Kentucky's Licking River.) When the water shallowed and daylight came, I dashed for scrub at the beach-edge, formed a line of skirmishers against Japs who weren't there.

Only later did I learn that our landing was premature — a tragic mistake that caused G Co's first death in the New Guinea Campaign. A sand-bar 25 yards from the beach had made a cross-current that swept out deep, concealed holes. And our coxswains had decided we were close to the beach and dropped ramps.

Off 1 ramp stepped 11 Yanks and began to drown in deep water, before CO Reams could halt others and curse the Amphibs into lifting ramps and closing in to the beach. Vivorito was dragged under the LCM and drowned; G Co never saw him again. Laurie Walker, S/Sgt Allison, Medic T/5 Bust slipped off equipment and saved others. Half-drowned men littered the beach. Walker saved Kubista and worked with others to bring him back to consciousness. Other men recovered Vivirito's body long afterwards. He was a veteran of Sanananda.

G Co carefully hunted the sweaty trail into Serra (Sserroe) Village. A rifle bullet crackled the brush 10 yards behind 3/Pln's rear guard. Forward, Osen's 2/Pln slew 2 stragglers on platforms of native huts, but 3 escaped. Half-bare in ripped fatigues, Louisiana Kid Anderson envied the green trousers on a Nippo corpse.

By now, sunset was near. Hanson's mortars zeroed in on approaches. G Co dug perimeter in the sand. Serra Village was 2 clusters of huts separated by a shallow fresh-water lagoon which the natives later drained.

And for the next week, Serra Village Outpost meant for G Co, long black nights in perimeter. It meant hitting that hole at sunset with angry, stinging mosquitoes singing their song of malaria. Rain fell almost every night in the blackness, and we had to dry out at dawn. I could have slept dry with my magnificent jungle hammock for a tent, but I had left it with Beaver. He had lost it.

By day, G Co patrolled through wilderness and knee-deep swamps to wide, unknown rivers and saw blue, unexplored uplands in the distance. (I can now name the rivers: Biru, Zar, and Niger.) The day after the landing, a patrol killed 3 Japs. On 3 May, an ambush on the main trail SE of camp slew 2, but 3 escaped. Our trails showed much Jap sign, but the main body was long gone. And G Co was thankful indeed when news came that 126 Inf would relieve us on 7 May, and LCMs would take us to rejoin 163 at Santa Anna Plantation. G Co had bagged just 7 Nips. Intelligence had misled us and deprived us of much needed rest.

But we men of Kreiger's 3/Pln had lived at Marok in a New Guinea wonderland denied to most Americans. Scout Kenneth Clark and I never tired of talking about that morning at Marok Village. Before darkfall in holes on quiet inner perimeters or on rusty ship decks at twilight, we used to remember that wonder out of the wilderness. We saw the natives coming in.

K and L Cos. 163 Infantry:
Machine Gunners at Kamti

By DR. HARGIS WESTERFIELD, Division Historian
with S/Sgt. VERNON MAGEE

This is mainly the battle story of K Co. 163 Inf. in S/Sgt. Bren's death fight against Japs at Kamti Village behind Aitape. But it begins with a brief account of other 3/Bn. cos. in the Aitape Operation before K-163's great fights in defending Kamti Village. At Kamti fought a "K" LMG section and "L" riflemen.

Arriving off Aitape about 0500 on 22 Apr. 1944, 3/Bn. swarmed down landing nets and into barges and circled offshore in half light. After attack bombers strafed, naval gunfire lasted 30 minutes. In full daylight, the sky was a fresh blue, washed clean by the Guinea rain before dawn. Our barges drove hard for the sand and the green jungle wall.

K's riflemen headed directly inland. As Lt. Arnold's M Co. barge grated the sand, the landing ramp stuck. Sgt. Powell's No. 13 boots kicked it down.

K Co. advanced inland on a few Japs by fire and movement. Almost every "K" man seemed to be firing. Past native huts strafed full of holes and shell-topped palms, we killed our first Japs. M Co's Arnold saw eight to ten dead Japs, two prisoners and one with a leg wound. Prisoners were in good condition, well-equipped. K's one casualty was Nye, shot in the leg from a naval plane's ricochet. "M" lost an injured man, Parenboom, his foot smashed between barge and ship as he left the landing nets.

K Co's assignment was to secure the coast straight inshore for other 163 cos. to swing west and push lengthwise down the two Tadji Strips. Some 300 yards inland, we set up at edge of a kunai opening, 750 yards long paralleling the shore and 125 yards at the widest. Our first night ashore was quiet.

Meanwhile that day, "L" advanced east alongshore to secure the rear of 163's beachhead. By 1230, we advanced 750 yards to dig in at Rilia Village. A reinforced "L" pln. passed through Lemieng Villages, some 1750 yards more, to outpost on the point of the Nigia Estuary. We killed two Japs here; several escaped into the swamps. We found an LMG. At 0620 on 23 Apr., we sighted a Jap barge ashore, east of our Rilia Perimeter. We slew five, wounded two and captured the barge.

I Co. did a curving march through the jungle, west of "K's" post on the Kunai strip, and made perimeter on the east end of Tadji Strips. At some time, Sgt. Carl Anderson was shot in the face.

Thus with light action, 3/Bn. cos. secured the rear of other 163's bns. that overran the Aitape area by 26 Apr. Opposition was so light that by 26 Apr. 127 Inf. relieved us to go into garrison at Tadji Plantation.

But events were leading up to 3/Bn's sharp fights at Kamti Village. This village was high in Kapoam Hills, some six miles SE of Tadji Strips. Separated by jungle defiles with narrow trails were three villages: Marnge, closest to the ocean; Matomute, a mile farther south; and Kamti, 500 yards farther into the hills.

First mention of Kapoam Hills occurs in 163's Journal on 23 Apr., when 163 took Tadji. Kapoam was important enough for Aussie ANGAU Capt. O'Donnel, assistant, and five PIBs to go there on a two-day patrol. Meanwhile back on Nigia River, where our "L" was relieved, 127 Inf. found a trail from Chinapelli to Kapoam. On night of 24 Apr., tracks showed that 50 Japs had hiked east, in the direction of Gen. Adachi's great, bypassed Wewak garrison.

This report from 127 Inf. was probably enough to send 3/Bn's Maj. Wallis with a strong detachment on a three-day patrol into Kapoam Hills. On 25 Apr., Wallis led out 42 men of L's 2/Pln., a "K" LMG section of 15 and four men of 3/Bn. Hq. Lt. Candella commanded "K's" LMGs. Wallis took also an Aussie ANGAU capt. and a sgt. with three PBIs. Total number was probably 69. We carried three days' rations, arms, ammo and entrenching tools. Those shovels certainly came in handy!

Ours was a hard trail in thickest New Guinea jungle, some eight miles inland from 3/Bn. Hq. And old Jap trail went to the Kapoam foothills, where a narrow path twisted up and down the jungle hills. The track was steep and slippery; many men fell into that mud. With important "K" LMGs and ammo boxes to carry and the need for scouting, we took from 0912 to 1730 to arrive at bivouac in Matomute Village—eight miles in eight hours.

About 1000 o'clock during our hike, "L's" scouts slipped into a silent, empty village, probably Marnge. They shot at five well-armed Nips, killed two and wounded one, who fled with two others. Heavy rains were now soaking us.

About 1600, after we completed maybe seven miles, a PIB checked a track off our trail. Just 15 feet from our

> CREDIT: Heart of this history is a story by K 163's S/Sgt. Vernon Magee about K's defense of Kamti Village. Also useful were 163's Aitape Journal, Casualty Lists, R.R. Smith's "Approach to the Philippines" and Lt. (later Capt.) Jack Arnold's diary. Remainder of Kamti Village story appeared in Arnold's "Defense of Kamti Village" (Jungleer, Feb., 1959, Vol. X, No. 1). Magee wrote this story in 1945 when asked for information to appear in our former Division History. When no one told him whom to send it to, he took it home with him, then submitted it to me after he read Arnold's story.

A patrol moves along a jungle trail at Wakde. Trucks, jammed with supplies, wait at the side of the trail until it is safe to deliver and distribute their cargoes.

trail, he pointed to a barefoot Nip asleep behind a log, with rifle and bayonet.

Our mission initially had been to seize a prisoner for information on troop movements. The PIBs awoke him, repeatedly signed to him to get up. He tried to explode a grenade and died trying.

In Matomute Village, atop a 500-foot ridge, we had a peaceful perimeter night. It was empty of Japs, or even of natives. We hoped for a second peaceful night and the coastal trail that morning.

About 1030 on 26 Apr., natives started returning to Matomute. Five days earlier, they had seen 300 Japs pass through Kamti, bound for upland Bes Village, on the Wewak Trail. These Japs had few arms, but plenty of food.

And the Japs were still in those hills! About 1500, two natives ran chattering into Matomute. Japs were in Kamti Village, 500 yards air-line across the jungle defiles.

Maj. Wallis' patrol arrived too late at Kamti. We shot at one and missed. Still, we knew that 10-15 Nips passed through daily. We found a Jap rifle and maps.

At once, Wallis cancelled our return to the beach, even though we had only a K-ration dinner left. Leaving Lt. McKenzie's "L" squad at Matomute, the other "L" men and "K's" gunners slogged over the hills to Kamti.

On guard and homesick all night in the perimeter, and hoping for dawn to return us to the sunny ocean waters, we did not know what we had stumbled into. For our ambush was really blocking the main Jap escape trail, from captured Hollandia to Wewak. The Japs had a field order to hold it at all costs. A copy of this order was on a Jap maj. killed at dusk, but nobody among us could read Japanese.

For other reasons, the Japs wanted to garrison Kamti Village. Dated 25 Apr., a captured report outlined a grandiose plan of attack to regain Tadji Strips. Written by the Aitape garrison unit CO, this plan probably went only so far as to effect the coming attempts to storm Kamti Village. A map of the Aitape region demonstrates the strategic importance of Kamti in an Aitape campaign by the Japs. Located on the high ground above the wide Aitape coastal swamps, it was on the only mostly dry trail from Korako to the coast. Out of reach of most naval gunfire, it would be hard for 163 to assault. It could become an assembly point for Aitape refugees and for reinforcements from Wewak.

But on that battle morn of 27 Apr., nobody in 3/Bn. knew that the Japs were massed to storm Kamti. At 0700, when K's Weapons Pln's Parrish saw three Nips probe towards our holes, he thought that they were stragglers. We held up MG fire until they closed in.

Instead, they spotted a BAR hole on our right, shot first. Heavy fire broke out on both sides, some 200 Nips came in on three flanks to destroy 39 entrenched Yanks. With his nearest MG on our right flank, S/Sgt. Bren kept the trail clear, fired bursts into any suspected thicket on that flank.

But the heaviest Jap attack hit our right, where Sullivan, Fredericks and Maggiore with Sgts. Brientback and Kempas battled with "K's" other LMG. Bren got orders to reinforce the right flank.

While Sobrero carried the gun still on tripod, Bren led the way. Second gunner Magee and ammo carriers Osborne and Poole doubled after Bren.

In the hilly country on our right flank, a clear field of fire was hard to get. Bren pushed his crew forward into the danger zone. When his eyes caught the telltale flash of Guinea sun on Nippo bayonets, he ordered his gun crew down. We flattened above ground, too late to dig in. But Bren stood up tall to spot our targets.

Bren saw Nips mass in a clump of trees 15 yards ahead. More bayonets gleamed; they grouped and broke into a charge. "Let 'em have it, Bill!" he called to Sobrero, prone behind the gun.

As Bren's carbine slew one, Sobrero's LMG instantly smashed dead bodies into the ground. The Jap rush died. Again Japs rushed; again Bren's carbine slew one; again Sobrero piled up their dead.

As the third charge began, Bren moaned and fell. But he still told his gunners that he was all right. While Sobrero with Magee at the belts broke up the third attack, Bren lay in agony. After rushing up with more MG belts, Poole tried to save Bren.

Nippo bullets clipped branches down on our heads; Japs were squeezing triggers on us from everywhere. Other Japs tried to flank our MG and riddle us. But "L's" protecting squad picked off every infiltrator.

A third and fourth time the Nips charged. Often we slew by firing bursts low at the sound where they jabbered, or at the thud of their footsteps. And again the sun dazzled from long bayonets, and we fired at the dazzle and killed.

Then we heard a thud where Poole worked to save Bren. When we called to Poole from our gun, there was only silence from Bren and Poole.

After we broke the Japs' last rush, our right flank was under control. Orders came to return our MG to its original hole. Crawling back, Magee noted that both Bren and Poole had died of head wounds.

In leaving the right flank, Sobrero and Magee saw that the crew of Sullivan, Brientback, Kempas and Fredericks still delivered a weight of fire into the Japs' moves. Probably they were not wounded because they had time to dig holes before the charges. Meanwhile, "K" riflemen Parrish and Rogers flanked our gunners and knocked out Nippo infiltrators with M1s and grenades. When two "L" men were hit on our left, Parrish and Rogers piled into their hole and staved off the Nippo rushes.

Thus died "K's" Bren and Poole. L Co. on that 27 Apr. listed three wounded: Reisner shot in right chest, Beauchamp in left leg, Sgt. Ubert in right leg. Medic Blount, probably at Kamti also, had a concussion on the back of his head.

By 1000, MGs were down to just two boxes of ammo. We had no Tommy clips left, and there were critical shortages of grenades and BAR clips. The Japs might be quiet until nightfall. Maj. Wallis ordered withdrawal. Since direct Matomute trail might be ambushed, we slipped back out of the village into the jungle. We carried an "L" wounded in a poncho; the three others evidently walked. Lt. Candella was among last to leave Kamti.

In three hours of floundering in the sweltering hill jungle, we got lost—came out on the Matomute trail just 15 minutes from Kamti battlefield. But on returning to Kamti, we found 65 Yanks dug in there, mostly poorly armed. Here were Lt. McKenzie's squad from Matomute and some 50 "L" men in a ration party commanded by Lt. Arnold with Lt. Ellison. The ration party had only pistols and carbines—no grenades. But no Jap attacks came at that crucial time.

We still had half a day left to ready for those attacks. By wire laid in from Matomute, we asked for help. Supplies and men arrived. At 1500, planes dropped 25-30 cases of ammo and rations. (One case crashed through a hut roof and broke the leg of Arnold's orderly, Jenkins.) About 1930, M Co's HMGs reinforced us, and more of L Co. came.

While we buried our two dead, Maggiore saw a Nip corpse move; a rifle fired. Marion Jones died, perhaps from that Nip already dying. Nobody knows for certain.

Such was the first day's battle at Kamti Village, where "K's" two MG crews secured us. "K" had three dead; "L" had probably three wounded, and one medic. Official count of Jap dead was 42.

At 2100 that night and at 0600 next morning, Japs charged our perimeter again, but Arnold's HMGs helped our security. "K's" guns then held the back trail to Matomute.

But the rest of the story concerning the defense of Kamti Village has already been told in the Jungleer.

41sters at Kamti Village.

More on Kamti Village

Dr. Arthur W. Merrick (L 163) writes that the reinforced 2 Pltn, L Co got the Unit Citation for Kamti. "Led by Lt. Wes Candella, the Pltn was to scout the area but not sever the main Hollandia-Wewak trail. A doubtful native source tipped off our mission. The third night out, an L man knifed a Nippo runner with a message vital to our G-2. Then Candella set up on the ground above and inland from Kamti.

"The first night (27 Apr 1944), the 64 EM and three officers halted attacks by a force estimated at the size of a Yank company. Maj Wallis ordered aid from the rest of L Co. As Exec, I led the party. Rough going forced us to sleep by our trail 28 Apr. At Kamti, my LMG's covered the coast trail, and M's HMG's faced the main track. Then Wallis got a native report that approximately 2,000 Nips headed for our perimeter from the Torricellis. Report was unconfirmed, but we withdrew, despite enough supplies and Candella's excellent defense lines.

"Japs attacked the night of our return (29 Apr); but Candella called their charges less severe. Sgt. John W. Klobofski was our one-man army. He refused to stay with the L's LMG's. He constantly checked ammo, line of fire, support, casualties; thus he died. . . . A grenade landed in the hole of Cpl. Drinkwater together with a man, possibly named Davis. The man leaped out; Drinkwater dropped his helmet on the grenade and stamped on it. The explosion broke a leg, but I think that he recovered.

"Next day my patrol checked the trail to Wewak. We saw dead Nips and signs of other activity. We did not know that three Nips trailed us—must have thought us Nips. As we cleared the trail back at Kamti, M's HMG cut loose. One for certain, and maybe two Nips died. We had no attacks 30 Apr."

Dr. Merrick is now Professor of Physiology and Pharmacology at U. Missouri Medical Center, Columbia. He was in L, then B, then 1 Bn Hq 163, Dec 1941 until 1 May 1945 and rotation. He well remembers Lt. Roger Quackenbush and Runner Neil Rahm, both of L.

Vernon K. Magee (K 163) writes that approximately 40 Yanks stopped the 27 Apr attacks on Kamti. "They were an L Pltn plus K's LMG's—less a squad of L returned to the coast for rations. A message on the corpse of a Jap Major said that with 200 men he was to keep Kamti open at all costs to allow Nips to bypass us and rejoin forces farther north."

Magee helped serve the LMG where two men died—Bill Poole of Reno, Nev., and Frank Bren. Marion Jones died on K's other gun. Co L had two wounded. They carried one on a poncho; the other walked, despite rough trails. Mr. Magee lives at 413 Hungerford St., Lansing, Mich.

Dr. Westerfield, Division Historian, comments: "In some ways, these two accounts differ from Jack Arnold's in the last Jungleer, and from each other. I print these to keep the record straight as I can. Their data go into the definitive history. I ask that more Yanks send me their memories of Kamti—and of any other operations. I need many different stories of the same action to get a true history. But why do my readers leave our great history to just a devoted few—like Mr. Arnold? I'm speaking to you with your eyes on this word, this minute! Write to me, blast it!"

This Was 163's Finest Hour

Whenever a group of 41st division veterans meet, the subject of Buna-Sananda Operation invariably turns up. This was the grandpappy of all 41st division campaigns. It wasn't the longest show, as jungle operations go. It lasted from mid-November, 1942, thru mid-January, 1943. That's only two months. But it was a bloody campaign and the casualties ran all out of proportion.

The Jungleers entered combat zone with 3,820 men. The operation was initially assigned to the 32nd division, with the 163d Infantry of 41st thrown in at the climactic stages. The 32d division, committing its three regiments, with a total strength of 9,825 men, suffered nearly 100% casualties. The 163d sent 3,820 men into the combat zone of which 923 became casualties.

(Casualties include the sick in action as well as those killed or wounded.)

The campaign, the first for most of the men, saw many individuals give a fine account of themselves. Their efforts were appropriately evaluated. The whole division in its later campaigns at Hollandia and Biak didn't collect as many high decorations as did the 163 regiment in the Buna-Sananda show. There were four Distinguished Service Crosses awarded and at least 36 Silver Stars.

Defense of Kamti Village

by JACK ARNOLD (163 Inf.) and HARGIS WESTERFIELD, Divisional Historian

About the Author

A veteran of Aitape, Wakde, Biak, Zamboanga, Jolo, Davao, Jack Arnold of Cuyahoga Falls, Ohio, was CO of M and later L Co 163. I based this narrative on the detailed diary that he sent me, and a few letters to clear up debatable points.

I'd like to have some more diaries from other men of the Division. If you have such information, please write me. I want material from 162, 186, 163, and the artillery outfits and your outfit.

Hargis Westerfield
Divisional Historian
6248 Sturdy Avenue
Cincinnati 30, Ohio

ON 28 April 1944, 50 men of the Third Battalion 163 Infantry, with me in command and seconded by Lieut. Ellison, volunteered to carry rations to Matomute Village, 8 miles back in the Kapoam Hills, behind Aitape. There Major Wallis had set up an outpost with 51 men from K Co.

The call came at 1100, and we left at 1300, light-hearted. It sounded like a "good deal," to get away from "garrison" on the beach. Our landing at Aitape, five days before, was a breeze. No Japs were reported at Kamti; we were just a carrying party.

Except for steel helmets, we hiked like boy scouts — light packs with ponchos and K rations. We thought that the men who wore pistols were lucky; the rest of us had light carbines. We didn't trouble with grenades. Our burden was only 20 cartons of 10-in-1 rations. Two men carried a carton on a pole between them, and more than two men were ready to relieve the bearers—at first.

It was just eight miles, a good distance for a walk in the sunset. We'd picnic for supper on the trail, rest overnight at Matomute, and return to a hot meal on the beach at noon. And the purple Kapoam Hills beckoned ahead.

Then the heavy jungle closed around us, and the sweat soaked our packs through our fatigues, and the mud sucked underfoot. That mud was as sticky as fresh cement, often half-way up the leggings, and slippery with hidden rough spots underneath. Men began falling and we quit laughing!

At 1800 we tiredly halted to lunch off those noble K rations, and it was a job to start the column again. With the dark, the Guinea rain slapped down on us. The men were too exhausted to swear. In black night, they sloshed and slipped and fell. And we found discarded Nippo gas masks and helmets at the trailside. We kept Sgts. Powell and Stallcop up ahead as a point for what security was possible.

At 2000 the trail lifted dimly up for some 500 feet into the Kapoam Hills—a slippery uphill struggle in pitch dark. We had to rest now every 20 yards or so. An hour later, we were out on our feet, on a mucky climb at an angle of 65 degrees. We had muck up to our waists; the jungle was perpendicular to our left, with a dripping void to our right. We couldn't sweat those bloody rations a step farther.

Then I sent Powell to try another way and contact Matomute Village, which must be at the top of this trail. He returned with Lieut. McKenzie who told us to leave the rations until daylight. We climbed an ugly thirty yards of black wet hillside, and on top the men instantly went to sleep in the mud while the rain soaked them. I coaxed them into some kind of perimeter, but I was sure they wouldn't stay awake.

About 0600, we awoke in the painful tropical chill and made hot Nescafe. Heavy firing started off in the hills to our left. We hurried from our bivouac 300 yards into Matomute to join Lieutenant McKenzie and his small outpost. After 30 minutes, the fire died down.

As MacKenzie had already briefed me, Major Wallis had spent the night in Kamti Village just across the hills with a single rifle platoon and LMG section. Then the fire opened up again. I can still hear those LMG's pouring it in. We assembled our two detachments and set off—cautiously now, to avoid surprise by Nips. It was a long and sweaty business— that hike to reinforce Wallis.

Although Kamti was only five hundred yards air-line from Matomute, we took 3½ hours up and down the hills, halting for panting breaks and shuddering whenever our scouts signaled a halt. We sweated out the fear of ambushes, again and again.

Three hundred yards from Kamti, a Jap popped out of the jungle. He brought up his long rifle; but a Yank put three M-1 slugs into his chest. Even more cautiously, we moved up to the village. Nothing fired. We climbed a hellish 400 feet into the village.

Kamti Village was quiet as death — those 15 silent huts.

103

Then we began finding Japs strung out everywhere among abandoned Yank fox-holes. I found an officer's saber. The corpses had not been plundered of souvenirs.

MacKenzie and I logically assumed that Wallis was pursuing the Nips, although the silence was nerve-racking. Hurriedly we set up a defense with our 65 poorly armed men, and waited for Major Wallis, up ahead in those jungles.

To our surprise, his detachment of 48 men and Lieut. Candella returned to the village behind us, by the same trail he had come up. Somewhere along the line, they must have deviated off on a side trail and missed us coming from Matomute. Then they had returned to Kamti for new bearings.

Major Wallis told us about the fights. At 0615, Japs had attacked with 60 men in a fight of half an hour. Then they left their dead and re-formed and fixed bayonets and came in determined to wipe us out. Our guns had cut them to pieces. We had two killed. But our two MG's had just half a belt, the grenades were expended, and the riflemen were down to a clip or so per man. Falling back was the only thing to do.

We redistributed ammo and made a hasty perimeter. Then we sent a wire-party to link up with Matomute. As soon as we telephoned, Col. Mason started up supplies and men.

At 1500 we set up a cross in the middle of the village. Planes dropped 25-30 cases of ammo with more ration cartons. Some .45's detonated as they hit. One case crashed through a hut roof and broke the hip of my orderly, Red Jenkins, who was storing supplies. It was a painful wound eight hill-jungle miles from a hospital, with attacks on our perimeter expected hourly.

Then Wallis pointed out our two dead Yank machine-gunners whom we had overlooked, and burying details started digging in the cruel heat. Before we had finished, one Japanese rifle-shot rang out—no more.

A third Yank lay dead, and nobody knows who killed him. It could have been one of our mortally wounded Nips who fired and perished in that last effort. The buddy of the dead man found one Japanese in a slightly different position, and thought that this corpse was the killer.

So we dug three graves. And while the outguards crouched and waited for help from the beach or the next Nipponese attack and most of us manned our holes, we gave them Christian burial. Lieut. Ludinus read a psalm, and we marked the heads of the graves with crosses.

I had also called for my own Platoon of HMG's, and they arrived about 1930 with some L men—a forced march of 6½ hours.

Major Wallis set up my guns. Two of them he concentrated on the north trail, and two on the SE trail—each pair only a few inches apart. I wired the guns and set up my CP in the center of the perimeter. Night fell.

About 2100 they started moving in around the base of the hill—preparing to come at us from all sides. Until 0300 they kept us keyed up and hurling grenades at rustles in the jungle.

Then they rushed us. Every gun opened up; red tracers criss-crossed; grenade shrapnel and bullets ricocheted off the huts. My men were too busy on the guns to answer my phone, and I just kept low and listened. The attack was over in a pall of black smoke. We had no casualties.

At 0430, they were moving in on us as before. Now and then we broke up a noise by rolling down a grenade or so; but we knew what was coming.

At 0600 came the first streak of light—and the attack. Again we opened up — harder than before. This time the fight lasted over an hour, with slight pauses when they re-formed and built up another advance.

At one lull in the firing, somebody called "Medic!" Pfc Fields crawled out of his hole and dragged one of our best machine-gunners off the line into the aide station. He had been shot through the back and out the stomach. Doc Barrin poured in plasma, but the yellowing of his flesh revealed the inevitable. Thus died Sgt. Kobofsky; those two HMG's firing side by side had drawn a concentration of Japanese bullets.

In the quiet, we held a council of war. The last attack had been cannily conducted and with discipline; it was no blind rush. Surely the attacks had been planned to spot our automatic weapons. The consensus was that we ought to pull out.

Only one officer dissented. He thought that the Japs were only a small group in flight to the Torricelli Mountains; there had been no mortars and no automatic weapons among them. We had just landed in the strategic spot, he asserted. If we left this high ground, we might have a hard time retaking it.

But withdrawal was ordered in thirty minutes. After burying Sgt. Kobofsky with all the ritual we could give him, we pulled back to Matomute—in mud and sun and fear over those treacherous trails—and with Red Jenkins in a litter.

At dusk, we bedded down in Matomute, and over the wire, Major Munkres ordered us back to Kamti Village, although one officer protested that we would be wiped out.

I spent my third successive night without sleep in water up to my knees in a fox-hole. All night artillery and Air Force worked on Kamti. At 0630, we had all that marching and climbing and fear to undergo again. But we scouted back into an unoccupied village and set up again. We buried 30 to 40 Japanese in 3 or 4 common graves. They had no identification tags, but we made crosses and hung helmets on them. And there they lie nameless until this day, and nobody in Japan will ever know what became of them.

At 1700, three Nips sauntered into Gore's section of MG's and disappeared when he blasted them. One was found dead with three slugs in his ribs.

And that was the last time the Japanese came to Kamti Village. From May 2 through May 7, we sent out patrols. On May 2, Lieut. Jenny's patrol killed three—and on May 4, he killed six. On May 5 in a cleared area, Sgt. Powell said, "I'm going to get a Jap." Three minutes later, he put two bullets through a Nip's head at 200 yards.

Meanwhile, the Medics shot crippled Jenkins with morphine, and Angau's natives carried him to the coast. Chaplain Appleton with a detail of natives came to exhume our four dead and rebury them on the beach. And Headquarters began to rotate our garrison—until elements of 126 Inf came straggling in all day May 7 to relieve us. You may not believe me, but some of my men did not want to return to the coast. (Historian's Note: Many of us believe you; that's why we're writing this history.)

ROSTER M Co 163 INFANTRY
(Kamti Village,
Apr. 28- May 7, 1944.)

Platoon HQ

Pltn. Leader—Lt. Jack Arnold
Pltn. Sgt.—S/Sgt. Powell
Instr. Cpl. Gustafson
Transport Cpl. Johnson
Driver Pvt. Pete
Messenger Pvt. Cacas
Messenger Pvt. Podracky
Sniper-Mess. Pfc. Hill
Medic Pfc. Fields

1st Sect. Ldr. S/Sgt Stallcop
First Squad
Leader—Sgt. Moore
1st Gunner Pfc. Parker
2nd Gunner Pfc. Heil
No. 3 Man— Pvt. Mitchell
No. 4 Man—Pvt. Forbes
Driver Pfc. Matusak

Second Squad
Leader S/Sgt Mount
1st Gunner Cpl. Brown
2nd Gunner Pvt. Stockmyer
No. 3 Man Pvt. Reynolds
No. 4 Man Pvt. Wallace
No. 5 Man Pvt. McFarland
Driver Pfc. Helund

2nd Section Ldr. S/Sgt. Reed
Third Squad
Leader—Cpl. Moyer
1st Gunner Pfc Smith
2nd Gunner Pfc Hughes
No. 3 Man Pvt. Seib
No. 4 Man Pvt. Gonra
No. 5 Man Pvt. Larra
Driver Pvt. Russell

Fourth Squad
Sgt. Showman
1st Gunner Pfc. Holmes
2nd Gunner Pfc Williams
No. 3 Man Pvt Kaminski
No. 4 Man Pvt Visconti
No. 5 Man Pvt Parkey
Driver Pvt. Pierce

C Co. 186 Infantry:
Borgonjie River, Hill 1000

By DR. HARGIS WESTERFIELD, Division Historian
with TED COTTER, other C 186 men

This is the story of C Co. 186 Inf's first combat experience—the Hollandia Invasion. On 22 Apr. 1944, before 0645, we were ready to hit the beach. As our LCIs waited for orders, destroyers and LCI rocket craft pulverized the coast in smoke and debris. From Vice Admiral Mitscher's Task Force 58 carriers, hundreds of planes dive-bombed the shore.

With other 1/Bn. 186 men, C Co. followed all 162 Inf. (less A 162) into White Beach 1 and the jungle-swamp. Our first mission was to cut the motor road from Pim north to Hollandia. While 162 fought north to Hollandia, we were to penetrate 1500 yards inland, then turn south to capture Pim Village. At Pim, we would be on the road to Lake Sentani and the three airstrips north of the lake.

Under cloudy morning tropical skies, C rushed off landing ramps at 0750. A newsreel man photographed us piling off the ramps. Unexploded shells and bombs were scattered all over the beach. For what seemed an hour, we waited for orders to push inland. Some 150-200 yards ahead, Navy Hellcats strafed pillboxes, but Levick saw no Japs in them.

Turning north to miss the impassable jungle, we began a mad dash inland. Skirting rising ground, we saw flaming drums of gasoline hissing and surging down toward us.

We crossed a swamp among scattered mangrove trees. Their roots projected above water and tried to trip us. Water was often knee-deep, or even belt-deep. Men like Levick—five feet, five inches tall—were in chest-deep. It was hard to wade and watch for Japs too. Our planes worried us, diving law for Jap targets.

One bazooka ammo man fell into a shellhole with water over his head. Another Yank saved him by pulling on his jungle pack.

Dripping from the hot, wet swamp, then from higher jungle and more heat, C craved water. Dipping his canteen into a small stream, Levick looked up at a dead Jap in the current, 30 feet above him. Levick went without the water.

C now turned south, away from 163 Inf. paralleling our inland march. While 162 Inf. advanced on Hollandia Town, we hiked south towards an even more important objective.

Our objective was the Leimok Hill—Pim Village area. Japs on 730-foot Leimok Hill could have mangled 186 men on White Beach 4, where most of our regiment was to land. Here we found loaded MGs—some of them 20 mm machine cannon—but no Japs to man them. C dug in on Leimok while 3/Bn. landed below us at Pim Village. Support fire from Amphib Engrs' craft had wiped out a small Jap force and fired Pim Village.

Pim Village headed a road leading west some 3000 yards to freshwater Lake Sentani. North of the lake below Cyclops Mtns. were the three Hollandia strips we had to take.

In C's first day of action, we had executed five Nips, of whom two had rushed an unnamed Lieut. They were armed only with bayonets. We do not remember how the other three died.

At 0800 23 Apr., C left Leimok Hill and hiked slowly west on the narrow road towards Lake Sentani and the strips. Passing 3/Bn. securing Pim, we now pushed on supported by 205 FA and 218 FA and Task Force 58 carrier planes. Despite only light Jap opposition, Col. Newman wisely posted C and A to guard our right flank.

Passing a Jap soldier village on the road, C evidently got orders to check out a possible Jap force in Cyclops Mtns. foothills NW of us. With A, we pushed up Borgonjie River, which wound about six miles down from Cyclops into Pim Swamp.

Starting our company patrol, we had a mile of track through jungle along a road into a canyon. But the canyon narrowed; the way got rougher. In the river, boulders loomed as high as a small house. Ominously, the radio was useless here; we lost contact with other outfits.

In late afternoon in the wilderness, we halted at a stream intersection. While Sgt. Simpson's squad worked upstream to find a way out of the canyon, we filled canteens and washed. We were about to open K rations for supper.

Glancing up towards an outpost, S/Sgt. Yarbrough observed men moving down toward u8 in the riverbed. At first, he thought it was Simpson's patrol returning. But they were Japs.

These Japs took no pains to conceal themselves; Yarbrough surmised that they had not seen us. Yarbrough grabbed a pack and attached ammo belt from a rock eight feet off, and jumped behind a large boulder. His signals alerted his two BAR men posted on each side of the stream. Our two outguards were working their way back among the boulders.

About 30 Japs were now in view. Our BARs shot; Yarbrough threw down his rifle on this target.

Suddenly Yarbrough could not breathe. He expelled wind; blood spewed out on his hands. He felt the hole where the bullet entered—felt the back of his neck where the bullet must have gone out. For some reason, he was relieved to find no hole in the back of his neck. And Yarbrough remembered nothing more until next day.

Fighting about 10 feet from Yarbrough, Levick guessed that the deadly bullet had glanced from a rock into the sergeant's throat. Levick saw blood and a bubble from the wound, but a medic could do nothing for Yarbrough.

From trees and brush, invisible Japs fired down on us below them in the canyon. Our LMG men had no time for tripods; they cradled barrels in their arms and sprayed where bullets seemed to come from. Firepower and falling light combined to stop the Japs; darkness came about 1835.

In our first combat, C spent a bitter, frustrated night. Most of Sgt. Cotter's 3/Pln. ran up the left bank of the Borgonjie and hit the ground within 50 yards of the river. Night fell at once.

Cotter guessed that the Japs left the area in 30 minutes, but the scare remained. Every noise brought volleys from our own men. Cotter's hardest job was to keep quiet the two privates next to him. He threatened to bayonet one overgrown child trying to cry for his mother. Trigger-happy rookies kept us awake all night. Cotter believes that most firing came from 2/Pln. on the other side of the Borgonjie.

With the first shots just before dark, C's Hw. Pln. and

another squad took to high ground on the left bank and lay prone. Shortly after dark, we heard a large group of Japs directly ahead, but hidden by dense brush. They spoke loudly and clashed rifle/bolts. We expected a charge; 1/Sgt. Lathrop ordered "Fix bayonets!" With only his bayonetless carbine, Hi Norton was a scared man.

41sters crossing Lake Sentani in LVTs.

Then-MGs from the right of the stream enfiladed the Japs before us, broke up the possible attack and slew a number. Norton was uncertain whether A or C gunners fired. Later, he heard that a Yank Air Force prisoner died when we shot down those Japs.

On that 24 Apr. after sunrise at 0634, daylight was bitter for 2/Pln. Just before light, 2/Lt. Collins and S/Sgt. Ted Norton were killed. (Ted Norton was the brother of Hi in Hw. Plt.) By 0800, Cruce was dead of wounds.

Also seriously wounded were Ernest Davis and Fanning. Wallace was wounded also. Cotter believes that Wallace and a buddy were AWOL Seabees, whom we rated as top scouts. Our Capt. Anklam returned them to Seabees with written commendations. We hoped that their punishment would be light.

In our night fight of 24 Apr., we lost three dead and four wounded, but killed 18 of an estimated 160 Japs.

Miraculously, Yarbrough was still alive, despite that bullet through his windpipe, which lodged in his right lung. C cleared a trail wide enough for us to drag him from the canyon on a makeshift stretcher. We took nine hours to carry him five miles to the medics; had to halt our carry to kill more Japs. Despite horrible thirst, he had to go waterless. (Today, Yarbrough still carries the bullet in his right lung. In good health, he is a barber in his own shop in Cave Junction, Oregon.)

Marching west 24 Apr., we still secured 186's north flank in the westward advance. We killed eight more Japs, probably from the 160 who attacked last night. About 1630, we rejoined 1/Bn. where the Air Strips Road branched off to Koejaboe on Lake Sentani, a 21-mile long freshwater lake meandering west.

Next morning, 25 Apr., C was part of 186's two-pronged move to capture Hollandia Strips. While 2/ and 3/Bns. slogged along the shore, we boarded LVTs for a 10-11 mile ride. After five miles of open water, our barges passed right between Ase Island, with Ajapo Village on the sharp point to port. Air Force planes guarded us. Firing on suspicious native huts, we saw no Japs. Rounding the great swamp peninsula on the north shore, we landed safe at Nefaar Village, near a flaming Nippo dump that 186 had machine-gunned.

We dug in on barren hills south of the strips. From the north, Jap AA fired heavy concentrations of time-fuze shells on us. Although demoralizing, they made only a few light wounds—hospitalized overnight a shell-shock casualty.

On 26 Apr. by 1030, we took Cyclops Strip unopposed. Wreckage of 288 Jap planes littered the strips. Although Jap 6th Air Div's CO thought himself out of range of Arm; planes, our Gen. George Kenney attached extra belly tanks

> CREDIT: Most important sources were personal letters of C-186 men: Ted Cotter—10 Dec. 1974, 7, 10, 14 Dec. 1976, 2 Jan. 1977 and one undated late in 1976. Important also were ltrs. of Granville Levick, 15 Nov., 14 Dec. 1976 and Hi Norton, 20 Jan. 1977. (Yarbrough's undated ltr. in 1976 first alerted me to the fact that I had a story. Cotter contacted John Brazille for me.) Nick Wheeler's D Co. 186 "The Show at Hollandia" (Jungleer XX, 2), was useful, also B-186's Durand Mandoline's map of "B's" attack on Hill 1000. Useful also were 186's Casualty Report, "C's" April Morning Report, R.R. Smith's "Approach to the Philippines," George Kenney's "General Kenney Reports" and "New Guinea Terrain Handbook 25".

to his fighters. In three days, beginning 30 Mar., Kenney's fleet of some 230 planes of 5th Air Force, had wiped out Jap 6th Air Div. This Jap disaster explains why Task Force 58 landed 186 safely at Humboldt Bay.

On 26 Apr. also, a C patrol contacted a 24th Div. patrol near Weversdorp Village. With this contact of 41st and 24th Divs, main objective of Hollandia invasion was accomplished.

But C still had battle ahead. Some 400 Japs—last organized fighters at Hollandia—were entrenched on Hill 1000, 4000 yards NE of Cyclops Strip. In Cyclops Mtns. foothills, they overlooked a long ravine leading up from the Strip.

While B advanced up the lower benchland right of the ravine, C occupied the crest of a kunai grass hill to B's right. Far too exposed for safety, we took heavy Jap fire from the rain forest before us.

Lingerfelt got a deadly chest wound. Medic Shelton tried to save him, while we called down FA on the woods. Our FA's first salvo struck our own 3/Pln. and killed both Lingerfelt and Medic Shelton; also wounded Alex Schneider and Shimek.

We returned some fire. With telescope sights, 3/Pln's sharpshooter Beaty killed a Jap at 500 yeads. Seeing Japs at 300 yeards, Brazille had orders to fire his LMG on them. Before he emptied a full belt, three bullets wounded him in shoulder—put him out until he was able to land on Wardo Beach on Biak in mid-August.

Hq. Pln. had better luck. On rearguard for C, we saw six Japs sneak from the brush on B's right and take position behind a rock. Unsuspecting B had for some reason pulled in their outguards. We killed at least four with carbines or rifles; the others fled. On a patrol of our own that day, 1/Sgt. Lathrop took point-blank pistol fire from a Jap officer. The Jap missed; Lathrop killed him.

D Co's 81s barraged the Japs' position to cover B and C's withdrawal. With two dead and three wounded, C had just twice B's number of four dead and six wounded. In return, we reported six Japs killed at 1030 and 16 killed from later patrols.

On 29 Apr., heavy shellfire broke up the Jap concentration on Hill 1000. Although C Co. was positioned to attack as late as 1600, we took no part in 1/Bn's occupation of the hill where the others slew 72 shell-dazed Japs. Preparatory mortar and FA fire had slain 37. An estimated 100 had retreated into the Cyclops Mtns. wilderness.

Such was B Co. 186 Inf's war at Hollandia—a memorable day of landing, afternoon and night battles on Borgonjie River and daylight battle at Hill 1000. It was all infantry jungle mud and sweat and blood. Although opposition from a planless Nippo defense was light, we still lost five dead and seven wounded. In sweat and blood and mud, C Co. 186 Inf. underwent a strenuous training session that tempered us for our great Battle of Biak.

D CO 186 Inf - THE SHOW AT HOLLANDIA
By DR. HARGIS WESTERFIELD, Division Historian
with Nick Wheeler

On 22 Apr 1944, D Co 186 Inf landed from its LCI at White Beach 2 in Humboldt Bay when 186 followed 162 ashore. D Co's first objective was Leimok Hill – a 2-mile march through mangrove swamps. A Marine tank pln chugged past us – complete with photographers. It was a great movie scenario in action.

At the swamp edge, we queasy, overloaded footsloggers raised a loud yell. The tanks had charged gung-ho into the swamp and drowned. Now only turrets stuck out of the water. Never again did we see Marines at Hollandia.

Scattered Jap MG fire came from Leimok Hill crest. When a fighter plan strafed, Jap fire ceased; the gunners hid behind the crest. When the plane left, more desultory MG fire broke out. After a few passes, the fighter pilot called a brother plane. Now 2 fighters strafed both hill slopes simultaneously. The Jap MG fired no more.

But 186 took most of the morning to labor through swamp and brush, in single file. Tropical sweat was heavy; water was knee-deep and waist-deep again and again. Under heavy weapons and extra ammo, D Co sloshed, cursed, and fell. Pietras, with his heavy tripod, hit a step-off and went totally under. Sgt Marinello yanked out

INFANTRY FILTERING THROUGH THE MARSHES NEAR HOLLANDIA.   U S Army Photo 157-14

Pietras; his squad dived to save the tripod. Meanwhile, D had many scares, from diving Air Force lads hungry for targets. (They shot up I Co badly.)

Now pushing dripping up a ravine in mid-afternoon, we heard M-1s where a rifle company killed a lone Jap. We seized Leimok Hill and were perplexed. For we found Jap trenches, MGs set up, even a 20 MM AA gun – but no Japs. As D's 1/Pln – attached to C Co – dug in, we looked out over the whole Hollandia seafront – landing craft everywhere – and Yank ships crowded up to the horizons.

South of us, we saw 186's other 3/Bn men land from Amphib craft, below a small village built on stilts above the sea. Suddenly the village erupted with rifle and MG fire. Supporting Amphib craft blasted the village with automatic weapons. An uncounted number of Japs were killed or drowned.

Next morning 23 Apr, at 0800 we started out to capture Sentani Dromes, some 18 miles east over a rough tropical road. Supported by 205 and 218 FA and carrier planes, D Co of 1/Bn jammed through 3/Bn, past a Jap motor depot crowded with trucks. At a rest halt just past the Hollikang Road Junction, D men saw a Jap messenger ride a bicycle down the road behind us. Rifle was slung on his shoulder. He did not know we were there. With his carbine, Lee Ward slew our first Jap of the campaign.

At Brinkman's Plantation, 2200 yards from our start, A and C Cos left the main body to patrol NW 2000 yards, up to a fork of the Borgonjie River. With A and C Cos went Sgt Hannegan's 2/Sect of D's 1/Pln.

Seeing no Japs, our D men dug in among A and C riflemen a few hundred yards short of high ground, beside the boulder-jammed Borgonjie. Then from the high ground, an estimated 150 Japs struck. All night they made uncocordinated attacks. Seriously wounded was C's Sgt Moore – hit 4 times. Another C man took a gut wound but walked back to aid station. At dawn 24 Apr, A Co attacked uphill on the left, and flushed the Japs. Later, we counted 119 dead Japs. (Meanwhile, most of D had slept peacefully with 1/Bn back by the road.)

While 186's 3/Bn drove 150 Nips before it, and seized Koejaboe Village 24 Apr, our 1/Bn regrouped at Brinkman's Plantation. D Co's men came down from the hills with A and C Cos. And on 25 Apr, D Co embarked in LVTs (alligators) to seize Nefaar Village, some 8 restful miles west on freshwater Lake Sentani. (Unlucky 3/Bn with B attached slogged parallel to our easy ride, enduring an overland march on a muddy track.)

But a fighter plane zoomed low over us on Lake Sentani, and warned us of trouble ahead. While troops landed at Nefaar, Sgt Herd on his 50 HMG spotted a Nip on the steep hillside, and played a cat-and-mouse game with him. Then D Co, with riflemen and 205 FA observers, dug in on the ridge to protect Nefaar Village. That night, blasts of Jap AA fire stung us-time-fuzed and effective. Spent fragments nicked a few D men. We dug deep that night.

Strangely enough, we found an unused Jap 20 mm gun on the ridge commanding Nefarr. It had not fired a shot.

Then on 26 April, D pushed with 1/Bn against the Jap dromes, which were the real objectives of the whole Hollandia operations While 24 Div's 21 Inf hit eastwards, 186 pushed west. Preceded by 24 Div's heavy FA concentrations, we captured Cyclops Drome, while 186's 2/Bn took Sentani Drome — and no shot fired. The last large Nippo force had retreated under 24 Div's FA fire that morning.

It was frightening to see — air-strips covered with perfect fields of fire from bunkers and pillboxes — MGs and field pieces still positioned. So well placed were guns at the cliff base, that neither long range FA nor air-strikes could hit them. Only assault guns and 81s could touch them. And Jap fighters, bombers, recon planes covered Hollandia Drome. They looked operational, but on raids of 30 Mar through 3 Apr, our Fifth Air Force had killed these planes — over 300 planes. Uncrated engines and parts lay everywhere.

That night, we expected attacks from vengeful Japs, but we had just one alarm. Something tripped a wire in a fire-lane. We killed 3 pigs, 5 dogs. Laughter relieved D Co, but a small force did attack K Co 21 Inf and lose 12 dead.

Then 186 did find combat. On 27 Apr, 1/Bn patrols found some 400 Japs strongly entrenched on Hill 1000 — a foothill of Cyclops Mtns, 4000 yards NE of Cyclops Drome. These Japs had failed to escape west to Genjem Village — the rallying point for all Hollandia Japs — and they now looked down a long ravine to 186 Inf forming to kill them.

On 28 Apr, D's 1/Pln and mortar observers pushed with B and C to take Hill 1000. With Lt Messec back in command position, B attacked up Hill 1000 into trouble. Up the lower plateau of the hill B's 3/Pln advanced, with rain forest on its left flank, and a hill of many boulders and tall kunai grass on its right. From those boulders, Japs blazed down on 3/Pln. Surely the first Jap fire killed or wounded the most Yanks. For the rest of B — men like Dolan, Donahue, Gonzales — dropped down out of sight safe unless they moved and drew fire.

Although twice wounded and his assistant killed, BAR man Tharpe silenced a Jap MG while heavy fire flared back at him. He slew 5 Japs. Although wounded early in the fight, S/Sgt Reidburn fought back with rifle and grenades, and directed aid to wounded Yanks. D's Connally stood up to go forward and fell with a bullet in the ankle. Rushing up to help extricate 3/Pln, 1/Lt Messec took a shot through the dorsals and was out of action. Capt Strecher was also wounded.

Next in command, 1/Lt McCahren ably handled the withdrawal. While 2/Pln — on the safer far right — struck uphill through kunai, and at the top turned left to hit the Japs' flank, 1/Pln pushed directly on the Japs firing down on the ambushed 3/Pln.

When surviving Japs withdrew, 1/Pln came down to help 3/Pln with casualties. Dead were 2/Lt Laws, with Grant, Les Brown. Rhoden would die of a stomach wound tomorrow. Besides Reiburn, Tharpe, and Messec of B, Capt Stretcher would never fight again in B Co. Other wounded were Elmer Sullivan, Sgt Jochens. B Co lost 4 dead, 6 wounded. But 50 Japs died that day. And as B fell back, D Co's observers — Sgts McCartney, Crumb, Imhoff called down D's 81 mortars. Then FA barraged the Japs.

On 29 Apr, after 205 FA fired 5 concentrations and D's 81s barraged, all 1/Bn attacked Hill 1000 again. We found the surviving Nips crazed with shell-fire. A, B, and C slew 72, found 37 dead from shelling. We drove 1000 yards past the hill, smashed all organized resistance. Later estimates said we had fought 115-150 Nips.

To D Co's relief, the Hollandia Invasion was more show than battle, but we had one final show that beat them all. On 6 May, returning to Hollandia Beach for embarkation to invade Biak, D heard the guns again — like a Jap strike on our rear.

Without warning, our ships opened fire before us — AA units going crazy around us, and the whole far-spread flotilla in Hollandia Bay. Our NCOs barked orders; D Co dug in frenziedly. Now a fleet of Yank landing barges broke for our beach. D Co held fire in wonder at the last moment. But who came ashore but Gen Douglas MacArthur himself! Then a wave of camera men dashed in and shot everything. We stopped digging and laughed in relief. MacArthur had returned — to White Beach 4 at Hollandia.

It was a real show and cost Uncle Sam plenty. We were all angry because of the extra labor digging in and the wasted ammo. Later, however, most of us realized that the show was Gen MacArthur's outburst of publicity against Navy and Marines. MacArthur wanted to return to the Philippines to rescue the Army he had left there, and this was his way of tipping President Roosevelt's command decisions in his favor.

Such was D Co 186 Inf's Hollandia show — from watching Marine tanks in a mud-bath to a water tour on Lake Sentani to the movie scenario when Gen MacArthur hit White Beach 4. Of course, we had discomfort and fear and death. Even with no D casualties. Hannegan's MG fight beside C Co on the Borgonjie River had not been easy that night. And we suffered compassionately with B Co's disaster on Hill 1000.

But Hollandia was mostly a big show for D Co. We fortunately seized Hollandia, before Gen Adachi could carry out his plan to bring the hardened 51 Inf Div up from Wewak. And at Hollandia, Gen Kitazono got the assignment to organize the Jap defenses too late to hamper us. D's actual campaign lasted from 23 Apr through 29 Apr. After a week's patrolling by Cyclops Air-strip, the mopping up of a few Nippo stragglers, and some freshwater bathing in the nearby stream, D Co was back on the beach by 6 May. Biak Was next.

Essential for this story was D Co's Nick Wheeler's 25-page MS, composed from tape recording sessions with Wayne Strebig, David Herd, Alvin Mazuti, and Albert Hannegan. Durand Mandoline of B 186 detailed the ambush on Hill 1000 in a letter of 21 Oct 1964. Other sources included RR Smith's Approach to the Philippines, Gen MacArthur's Japanese Operations in the SWPA. More personal data were from award stories of Reidburn, McCahren, and Tharpe — as well as the B 186 Morning Report — which entries were made the month after the fight — in May. Nick Wheeler is preparing the most thorough history of any company or battery of the Forty-First Infantry Division ever written — a real challenge to the rest of us.

146 FA BN Supports 162 INF At Hollandia

From rain-mists hiding the black Hollandia coast, great yellow fires shot up from our first bombing planes. As 146 FA gun crews on LSTs saw daylight on curving beaches, cocoanut palms, jungle mountains, the thousand guns of our Navy opened their bombardment. Scarlet tracers, searing yellow flashes lighted the skies. Our planes dive-bombed the beaches; then 162 Inf assault craft hit the Hollandia beaches.

With 162, two 146 FA observer parties hit the beach, each party containing an officer, a noncom, 2 radio men, 2 linemen. Capt. Murdock, B Btry Co, was with 3d Bn 162's observer party; Lt. Wilkins Jr., C Btry Co, with 2d Bn. While 162 riflemen struck inland, C Btry, with a 218 FA Btry of 155s attached, was set up for firing, on White Beach 1, 20 minutes after landing. Meanwhile, A and B Btrys labored frenziedly with tractors and manpower to get the howitzers north up the slippery wet clay sides of Pancake Hill, and were set to fire at 1030 hrs.

As the artillery stood ready, 146 observers accompanied the 162 Bns over unknown, unmapped hill jungles to cut the Pim-Hollandia Track, then turned north at day's end to halt on a ridge 1000 yds south of Hollandia Town. For the entire D-Day, artillery support was not needed; only a fre Nip MGs and riflemen had opposed 162. But division intelligence reported the Nips strongly held Hollandia Town.

On 23 Apr, from 0945 to 1005 hrs we blasted Hollandia with 105s, plus 600 rounds from 218's 155s--first, roving fire in the town, then heavy concentrations on the hills at the outskirts. the Nip riflemen were silenced. But both 162 and 146 suffered. During cose support firing 8 Yanks were wounded by a tree burst. Those men would have been safe if they had heeded warnings to get in their slit trenches when we were firing. Btry A's Cpl Northrup was 146's first casualty' while laying wire on the main axis he tried to free a wire caught in a box of emplosives; lost most of his hand from the explosion.

That afternoon, 2d Bn 162 took a ridge commanding a narrow valley in the hills west of Hollandia. Then F Co sent a patrol of an officer and 14 men thru the kunai at the ridge base and towards rocky, broken terrain before a village. Altho Lt. Wilkins wanted to shell the village first, his offer was turned down. The officer and 6 men were casualties. F Co then sent in a reinforced pltn that extricated remnants of the patrol; but the Nips held out. That night, Lt. Wilkins, with Lt. Ridenoure, liaison officer, shelled the village, and threw in 200 rounds at dawn. The Nips fled.

Thus for 146 FA against ground troops, Hollandia was mainly a rehearsal for Biak; but the Nip air force taught us a flaming, gory lesson. Since 162 might need support at any time, the howitzers had to use the only firing positions available--bare, brown Pancake Hill, and adjacent White Beach--jammed with AA and FA emplacements, bivouac areas, Yank supplies, and smouldering from half-burned Nippo dumps. We were stitting-duck targets for a Nippo bomb run over Pancake Hill. In the dusk at 1910 hrs that second day, a Nippo sneak bomber buzzed vengefully upon us. He sped south over Hollandia town, too low for radar to spot him. Guiding on the 2-day-old fire from Nippo dumps, he dived low and loosed 4 bombs.

The first 3 missed, but his fourth hit the edge of a Nippo ammo and fuel dump on the beach below Pancake Hill. Fire blazed skyhigh, exploding ammo and bombs and

LSTS UNLOAD ON A BEACH NEAR HOLLANDIA. 30 APRIL 1944.   U S Army Photo 157-1

streams of flaming gasoline spread the fire south down the beach towards 146's gun positions. As the flames neared the gun positions, the fire seemed to slacken, but shell fragments from continuous explosions endangered all of us.

Anticipating that forward observer Lt. Wilkins probably would need concentrations on the pocket west of Hollandia, B Btry's exec pulled the men back until the heat from the fires died down, but left the gun positions set up. But, hours later, the fires flared again, from explosion of another gasoline dump, and spread to an ammo dump 200 yds from the howitzers. Upon the exec's orders, the 146 gunners leaped to save howitzers and tractors. Desperately, in the firelight and shadows, we heaved out three 105s and their tractors, and much other equipment. We had to leave only one 105 and tractor, mired and wedged against a stump, and 2 ammo trailers dug in near a heap of TNT stacked there by a shore party after we had emplaced. Borgford took a wound in a leg from a shell fragment. Hardly had we gotten clear of the position when the TNT exploded. Cited for gallantry in action were, among others: 1/Lt Thomas, Cpl Dominguez, Sgt Hafter, T5 Morrison, S/Sgt McLoughlin, T4 Robt Nelson, 1/Sgt Orr, Cpl Vavra, Pvts Kempel, Lassegard, Schiefelbein, Templeton.

All thru 24 Apr the dumps blazed fiercely. Not until 25 Apr could we get back to C Btrys old position. We found most remaining equipment unhurt, but had to winch the 105 sidewise to unmire it from the swamp. The two trailers with 560 runds of ammo had been dug in so deeply that not a round had exploded.

Recovered and reimplaced 27 Apr, 146 fired its last concentrations to protect 162's 1st Bn in capturing Cape Soeadja. While searching the long peninsula guarding Humboldt Bay rom the sea, we fired 17 concentrations, totaling 768 rounds. In this landing, 162 killed 4 Nips on Hill 640; then 1st Bn wiped out scattered groups of Japs farthur up the peninsula.

On 28 Apr, 146 began to build a new bivouac area on Imb Bay, near Cape Soeadja. A security patrol for our advance party found a Nip rifleman. We tried to capture him, but he was so well dug in we had to kill him.

But just before 146 was given orders to move from Pancake Hill, death found us. On the evning of 2 May, 2 Nip bombers flew in from our radar's blind spot just behind Cyclops Mtns. They dived low on the crowded hill, dropped 4 bombs. two landed in Sv Btry and 1 in A Btry. Killed were Sv Btry's Sgt Landicini, Pederson, and Cpl Boyett of A Btry. Wounded were Bn S4 Capt. Rushing, Sv Btry's Ned Lewis, Lishinski, T4 Revell, T5 Kinter; B Btry's Norman Larson and T5 Paul Ludwig, A Btry's S/Sgt Griffin, Pvt Griffith. Injured were Bn Co Lt. Col. Virgil Anderson, Hq Btry's Beede, Rosin; A's Flaton; B's Serzynski, and Sv Btry's Charles Day and Omer Martin.

The bombs also set off an AA ammo dump on the crest of Pancake Hill. Exploding shells sprayed us. Near Sv Btry, engr trucks blazed and spread streams of flaming gasoline. 146 men rescued wounded, fought fires, gave first aid. Among those cited were Capt Fletcher, Lt Duncommun, Sgt Roseth, and Pvts Flaton, Halvorson.

Up on this exposed, bare hill, 146 Fa was very vulnerable. But on 3 May, just after the Nips' last bomb run, the division commander and staff arrived to notify Col. Anderson that arrangements had been mae with the Navy to provide fiepower for support, so 146 could evacuate this exposed position. Next day we embarked gladly, to encamp at Hollekang, native village at the southern end of Hollandia Bay. Ill-fated Pancake Hill was left behind except for a radio station and our 3 dead in a new graveyard.

Such was the tale of 146 FA Bn at the capture of Hollandia. The operation had been less dangerous than it would have been if even a single reinforced Jap regiment had been left to hold Hollandia. But the Jap strength had been lured elsewhere thru their guessing wrong on where we were going to hit them. We had 3 KIA, 10 WIA, 8 injured in action. Jap planes had done all of this with just 4 bombs. At Hollandia, we had forebodings of what could happen in our next operation. And it did happen on Biak!

Copyright 1968 By Hargis Westerfield for 41st Infantry Division Association. No part of this article may be reproduced in any form without permission.

Credits: Main source is Capt. robert Allen's Opn Rept, 146 FA Bn, Hollandia Campaign, with R.R. Smith's APPROACH TO THE PHILLIPINES, and a few details from the original Division History. However, the latter hardly mentions 146, and says nothing about F-162 or the second holocaust which directly caused evacuation of Pancake Hill.

A Great Soul Goes To His Reward

Association Cahplain Percival Michael Blenkinsop, chaplain of the 186th Infantry rom 1926 to the S.W.P.A., succumbed to a heart attack April 6.

Chappy (Colonel) Blenkinsop was active in Portland Chapter of the 41st Infantry Division Association, in the American Legion, the 40 & 8, and many other organizations. He was 78.

He served almost four years in the Canadian Army in WW1 as a machine gunner, and became army Chief of Chaplains in the S.W.P.A. in WW2.

Pallbearers, and most of the honorary pallbears, were from Portland Chapter of the Association.

Chappy was awarded the bronze star with clusters, as well as many distinguished service awards by veteran and civic organizations.

116 Medics at Hollandia

by DR. HARGIS WESTERFIELD, Division Historian
and GEORGE JACKSON (116 Medics)

Slipping into Humboldt Bay in the dark before dawn 22 April 1944, A Co 116 Medics waited landing orders from the Aussie liner Westralia. Suddenly next to Westralia, Cruiser Boise let go in gigantic red flashes and swirls of smoke. From 7 carriers, Navy Hellcats whacked the beaches. And at 0705, A Co 116 Medics scrambled down boarding nets into LCMs, with Yanks of 162's 3/Bn. One Yank lost footing and fell into the calm waters. We never saw him again.

Instead of landing at supposedly well-defended Hollandia itself, we had hit the west beach of Humboldt Bay—just one small bay south of Hollandia. North of us was Pancake Hill where Yanks found an undamaged AA gun abandoned. It could have butchered many of us deploying on the beach below.

Wading ashore, Jackson tripped on submerged wire and got more ankle sprains from concealed holes on that beach. We then hiked north up a 1,000 foot hill on a slippery clay path. Every time a Medic stood still, he lost footing on that rain-wet clay and fell. Some Japs fired at us from caves, but 162's bazooka teams quickly bounced rockets into holes and shattered them.

That night of 22 April, A Co 116 Meds dug in with 162's 3/Bn on JARREMOH Hill overlooking Hollandia. Some die-hard Nips infiltrated and picked fights with us. Boucher took a slug through both cheeks and upper jaw. One Jap tried to wrest Howard Williams' carbine from him but failed. One large Mongolian type was seen by the water-hole. On the east edge of the perimeter, 2 Japs died.

On 23 Apr, A Co's Medics went to work twice before we moved out. First, one of our own mortar muzzle blasts laid out some Yank casualties for us. Second, as we stood up full pack, the final round of the 105 bombardment of Hollandia struck a branch overhead. It burst with a terrific concusion; Jackson's hearing was addled for weeks. It had struck down the Yank between Devaney and Jackson. When he reached for his medical pack, he found that a shell-fragment had slapped through the pack and scrambled his supplies. With not a Nip in sight, we had 50 killed or wounded that hard morning before Hollandia.

Now A 116 marched with 162 down on Hollandia. It was a town of some 8 blocks of scattered buildings in a shallow valley through which a creek meandered. A jetty stretched over shallow waters into the harbor.

Our riflemen chased a few frustrated Nips on up the cliff projection toward the sea on the opposite side of town. In organizing the position, we had to take extreme care; Hollandia was heavily booby-trapped by us—and countertrapped by Japs.

A Co 116 Medics set up shelters on the beach and helped evacuate 20-30 wounded Yanks. Jackson accompanied the detail with them on an LST back to the west beach of Humboldt Bay where we had first landed. At the beach, we made much effort to give some shade to the supine wounded who could not move. Jackson even held his own helmet for a long time over one Yank to give the sufferer a little shade.

Back at Hollandia, the sailors and we dug into the buildings for souvenirs. The Japs had abandoned even jelly candy and tangerine pop—and beer and whisky. Men found saki, and they lost all inhibitions. One Yank swallowed so much that he loaded up with weapons and went out to kill a man he hated. MPs halted him—and then took charge of all the liquor they could extract from us. Zirk with other medics made a financial killing from gullible sailors. They discovered bales of Nippo cloth and dye. Out of this cloth, they sewed together countless Jap flags, and sailors bought them wildly.

Such was A Co 116 Medics' risky but light 2 days' combat duty at Hollandia—with only Boucher wounded and a near miss from our own 105 and no Medic dead. Came then a month of garrison duty with 162 Inf. (Meanwhile, 163 Inf was painfully working its way up the coast from Aitape to storm Wakde and fight a war of nerves on the Toem foreshore.) But on 25 May, A Co 116 Medics boarded LCIs for that hell-hole that Biak would become.

A Co., 163 Infantry:
Combat Tour of Wakde

By DR. HARGIS WESTERFIELD,
Association Historian

> Prime source is "History of Company A, 163 Infantry," which is complete through Biak. Dale Adams and Col. Howard A. McKinney both submitted copies. Also important are "Awards Lists," although I could have missed some stories because I could not link up every man's name with the company where he got the Award. Also indispensable were "One Step Westward, by a Battalion Commander" (attributed to Mjr Leonard Wing, which appeared in *Infantry Journal* and is used by permission), and RR Smith's *Approach to the Philippines*. Our original history on Wakde is mainly a rehash of "One Step Westward."

Jammed into LCVPs striking for Wakde Island at 0915 18 May 1944, A Co 163 Inf expected no Japs. But at 500 yards, bullets slapped the water like New Guinea rain around us. Bullets pierced gunwales; 2 navy coxswains died in Weapons Pltn and Hq boats. We hit the beach in the third wave at 0930—dashed off barges, dived into sand below bullet level. The first 2 waves of 163 flattened out and blocked us almost completely from attacking. MG slugs hit flesh; Harrera died at once; Sgt Behuncik was shot in the back to linger dying until 5 July. Stevens took bullets in leg and hand. Lt. Rhodes was wounded; Lt Jensen became CO.

Already Sgts Russ, Davenport scouted inland, returned to guide 1 & 3 Pltns on our primary mission. We had to take "Mt Wakde," a knoll 20-25 feet high on the SE spearhead cape which commanded our beach-head. Weapons and E Co men on Insoemanai had been shot from there; Mjr Wing expected heavy resistance.

We cut the neck of the cape, then slowly bombed out pillboxes. From a pillbox, a Jap fired and grazed Hendrix' helmet. As the Jap raised his head again, Sgt Russ killed him. On top of Mt. Wakde, we destroyed a troublesome MG nest. A bunker held us briefly; we bombed it out—killed just 12 Nips on the height.

Leaving 3 Pltn's 3d Squad to garrison Mt. Wakde, A Co went to help F Co clear out the nearly destroyed plantation houses 300 yards NW of the beach. Here Nip MGs had halted F and pinned it down. F Co was in a bowl with Nips firing down their throats from the rim.

While building up a line behind F and waiting for tank assistance, we found several cases of saki, wine, whisky which we stuffed into our packs. While Lt Jensen was briefed by F's Pltn leader, T/Sgt Russ got angered at Nippo riflemen firing at us. He scaled the steep slope and slew all 9. Now the tanks helped us help F Co out of trouble—half an hour of violent infighting. Sgt Krushevsky guided a tank against a pillbox. In the debris, he advanced before the tank, drew fire, and then blasted the pillbox with his BAR until the tank killed the pillbox.

Meanwhile securing our rear, Sgt Mandy's Weapons Pltn killed 3 Nips overlooked in trenches behind us. Hearing suspicious noises in 3 bunkers on our right flank, Humphrey volunteered to secure the bunkers. In a bunker, a Nip was manipulating a MG bolt. Humphrey fired, threw 6 grenades into the bunker to quiet it. When he poked a bayonet at a "dead" Nip, the Nip revived, tried to wrestle Humphrey's rifle from him. Surprised Humphrey finally unlatched the safety, killed the Nip.

Now A Co continued its tour of Wakde. Moving past the rear of F Co, we rounded the north end of Wakde Strip to clear the west end of the island. While 1 & 2 Pltns moved abreast of F on our right, and 3 Pltn's two Squads covered our rear, we pushed ahead. Past the north end of Mokmer Strip, we extended our line leftwards and combed the area thoroughly. Heat was almost unbearable. We had no water, and coconut milk had to quench our thirst.

With F Co, we attacked the NW curve of Wakde Island. Pushing down a dispersal lane SW of the Strip, we found 3 Jap bunkers to our right. At 20 yards, tank 75s smashed them; but from foxholes to our rear, Japs threw grenades and attacked. Our BARmen dispersed them—or dropped them dead.

Parting with F which went to assist B on the south side of Wakde Strip, we probed eastward 500 yards in the narrow space between the north shore and the Strip. We found coral crevices and rocks, caves and thick brush, and a congeries of wrecked planes, trenches, and other equipment.

Here A Co found wounds and death in the confused battle of the revetments at the east end of Wakde Strip. On first contact, CO Jensen formed a temporary perimeter, then sent 1 & 3 Pltns to fight the Japs. We advanced up a narrow coral dispersal strip flanked by revetments—into Jap rifle-fire.

Fletcher took a head-wound; Jap fire pinned 3 Pltn down. When 1 Pltn formed as skirmishers immediately before 3 revetments, Lt Thompson was out of action with a hand wound. T/Sgt Hansen took command; but both Pltns remained flat under rifle fire.

Then S/Sgt Byrum Jones' squad moved in to scout a revetment. As his patrol fanned out into the brush, Jones came in behind 17 Nips with 3 MGs in a large hole in the side of a revetment. With John A. Adams volunteering from a LMG crew to help, Jones attacked them. Nip MG fire from the opposite revetment cut them off, wounded both men slightly. With rifles and grenades, they cleared out the Jap position. But when they tried to rejoin their squad, HMGs killed them. Jurasin assumed command of Jones' squad, pulled it back and redeployed on the flank of the deadly revetment. With BARs, grenades, they silenced that revetment.

Here 1/Pltn's Sgt Gibbs won honor and death. Called to A's CP to bring information, he was told to take 4 men for protection. Gibbs refused to weaken the firing-line, evaded MG

First wave of 41sters on Wakde Island in 1944.

and rifle-fire to go alone. After giving Jensen his data, Gibbs again returned unguarded.

About 200 yards from CP, Gibbs saw 3 Nips mounting an LMG on a wrecked plane. They were about to shoot up A's CP; but Gibbs bombed them out instead. A rifleman killed Gibbs.

Meanwhile A Co's Weapons Pltn fought its own action in the CP's rear. When Nips killed our D Co observer, Sgt Mandy with Tombleson, P. Jones, and other Weapons men scouted rearward. We spotted Nips behind fallen palms. Mandy chose a position where he could observe any movement; he killed 5 Nips. One of them stood up with a rifle in his hand and called "Me no Jap!" Mandy killed him also.

Now Jensen sent runners to call in the tired Pltns to form night perimeter. Jap fire had died down; 1 & 3 Pltns could pull back. Now dangerously exposed north of the Strip with nothing on our left flank and B Co too far to our right across the open ground, A Co dug in for the night. Eight Nips walked into 1/Pltn's field of fire. Gordy, Zirkle, Sgt Charles Jones killed them a few yards from our holes. Our night was pleasantly quiet.

Our second day on Wakde, 19 May, was much easier. All morning, we crouched in perimeter to wait for B and C to contact us. Light sniper fire peppered us all morning; but Sgt Curry was the only casualty—with a leg-wound. In late afternoon, B and C arrived. We had the Nips in a pocket. The tank with B Co knocked out the Nip position. In the ensuing wild shooting, Devine, Whetstone, Sgt Wilson picked off 5 Nips.

And 19 May's fight ended when we pulled back into Bn perimeter. While the last Wakde Nips died of wounds or cowered in holes, we had a surprise hot meal under Mjr Wing's auspices. On 20 June, we returned to the revetment area to flush out more Nips. When our skirmish-line found some out of reach in a cave on the NE beach, Fallinger helped. He climbed into a precarious position and killed the cave with a flame-thrower. Tom Moore teamed with B Co men to rescue B's mortally wounded Sgt Case.

On 20 May 1944—after 3 days—we left Wakde forever; but trouble waited for us on the nearby New Guinea mainland on the Toem Foreshore. On 27 May, a week later, A Co sent 100 men to Hurricane Task Force Hq back up the beach to unload LSTs. At 1930, air-raid warnings caused our party to be sent ashore. About to entruck for camp in the dusk, we learned that Nips were fighting back in our 1/Bn lines. We spent that night protected by a few Engrs at the beach—and wondered what had become of our buddies left back at the camp.

Back in camp next morning, we learned that the main Jap thrusts were on both sides of us—C Co on our left, and A 116 Engrs on our right. In the A Co street, the Japs set up MGs, sprayed our tents. Yet all the A men in camp regrouped in the rear—but for men on outpost—LaRoue, Denny, Hill, Einboden. The Japs missed these men who came back alive at dawn. A Co had no casualties; but we spent the next two days building positions and manning them all night.

On 30 May we boarded LCIs to fight the Nips who were rumored to be defeating the Division on Biak. Leaving flat-wooded Toem Foreshore in our wake, we had shell-withered "American" Wakde on our starboard before we turned west for Biak. We were glad to leave that spooky Toem Foreshore. And our combat tour of Wakde was a tough little action—the machine-gun blast on the beaches—helping F Co out of that frightful little hollow—the battle of the revetments. We had been lucky to lose only 5 Yanks killed in action. Eleven would die in the coral ridges of Biak compared to 5 in the brush of Wakde.

C Co 163's COCONUT HELL ON WAKDE

By LTS. WALTER LARSON and FLOYD STANFIELD
with Dr. Hargis Westerfield, Division Historian

On 18 May 1944, about 0900, C Co 163 Inf's battle-loaded Yanks looked peacefully, like tourists, from LCMs at the quiet sands and shell-torn coconut palms of Wakde Island. Ahead, B's LCMs bobbed along in the first wave. A-20s dived low at the beach and bombed up dust-clouds. LCIs loosed banks of rockets. But Wakde returned no fire; it looked more harmless than AITAPE's Shore, 3 weeks back.

Then a rain of bullets plunked into our LCMs. We huddled below gunwales. TJ Smith of Lt Walt Larson's 2/Pltn was hit. It seemed like hours of battering drumfires before C's LCMs struck the beach, ramps clanged down, and men erupted into a chill horror of sunlight where bullets were slaying. The second-in-command of Pesavento's squad fell badly wounded, under menace of a ditch full of Japs. Pesavento crawled within 4 yards of that ditch, with M-1 kept the Nips down until his squadleader carried off the wounded Yank.

C Co scattered flat in wet sand along the water's edge, in the partial shelter of a low bank. It cost wounds and death to get off that beach and into shell-shattered coconut groves and rubble. While Smith lay dying, George Leonard was wounded about 0920, about the same time fragments hit Rich in his right shoulder, and Tuszynski was shot in the right hand. At 0920 also, S/Sgt Seeger had a nose wound but stayed on duty.

With A Co hitting the high point on our right, and B and F on the left, C probed into shattered rubble and brush 200 yards directly ahead, to meet fire from Jap automatic weapons. We had little time to see where men fell. T/4 Sunderman was killed at 0930 and Gene Lewis wounded, and Cpl Suits killed about 0945. A falling tree killed Harvey Hayes.

About 200 yards inland, C spotted a cluster of mutually supporting pillboxes. We took nearly an hour from 0915 to clear them — with grenades and riflemen's assault fire. Moving 100 yards more north to the Air Strip, we found more Jap bunkers well hidden by undergrowth of the neglected coconut plantations, or long logs splintered across aisles. Now C asked for tank support — at just the right time, for the 2 tanks that had landed safely on Wakde, had left off fighting for B and F Cos at the plantation houses, to reload with more ammo from the beach. Now we used tank 75s to stun pillbox garrisons, then lobbed grenades into fireports, shot dead any Jap who showed himself.

Now Mjr Wing planned a complicated maneuver. A Co had secured Rhodes' Ridge which flanked the beach, and all other companies were also ashore, nearly full strength, and pushing Japs. But the Japs' part of Wakde was still larger than ours and all in one piece. Inside Jap country, their troops were free to reinforce at any point at will. Worst of all, if our 4 rifle Cos continued advancing, they would fan out in 3 directions, and leave gaps for Jap infiltration and Yank disaster.

So Wing utilized his 4 Cos wisely. Using A and C Cos as tactically most important, he planned his maneuver with the open air strip as a base. C Co and tanks were to cross the air strip at its narrowest part — move south to north over the middle of the strip. And A Co was to hike 1,000 yards west to round the Wakde point, then turn east and clear the north side of the strip. Then Japs trying to reinforce those opposing or fleeing A Co would meet blockage where C had crossed the strip.

This crossing manuever C never forgot. For when Larson's 2/Squad under Seeger made it safely and returned, Capt Kent of Wing's staff decided to send C over without tank protection. A mortar barrage would assist.

Lt Moore's 1/Pltn started across the bare ground among the wrecked planes. Distance was an easy 135 yards — although some of us felt strange at being in this open space. Just as 2/Pltn started, Larson heard Capt Peterson bawl, "Run!"

Bullets rowelled the ground all around C's men on the strip. Moore's Pltn was across and into brush — and Larson's first 2 squads. A slight drainage ditch on the far side became filled with prone Yanks — heads to toes. Killed were Kleeman and Yeats; wounded were Hurley, Zerr, Henry Johnson. Each Pltn lost 1 killed.

In retaliation, our BARs flailed trees but with no results. Later, C heard that fire had come from a Jap MG on the side we started from, and that an outfit on our flank — where B was fighting — killed the MG. Then 218 FA and 167 FA crashed in from Toem, to silence other reported MGs.

While Moore and Larson's men waited, the rest of C and a tank rounded the safe west end of the strip, to reunite us. Now A Co pushed from the western corner of Wakde, and on past C Co between the strip and the sea. After crossing the strip, C slew 5 Nips, but A Co met MG and mortar fire after passing us to the NE corner of Wakde.

After seeing A past, we recrossed the secured air strip and moved back south through more coconut groves and across long, overgrown avenues. Although F and B had fought east before us, Jap pockets remained, and firing was abundant. Wounded were Lee Perkins, Lou Schwartz.

At night, C dug in with right flank on the south shore of Wakde — the side of the landing. On left flank was B, then C to form a line to the air strip. (A was dug in alone north of the strip.)

On this first day of Wakde Fight, Jap casualties were at least 200 dead, but 163's 2/Bn with F Co had 19 dead, 86 wounded — including 7 officers and 14 first-three-graders. B Co had 42 casualties. C had 6 dead, 9 wounded and out of action.

Behind our night perimeter, Air Force had prematurely moved in acres of equipment. Near us was a gasoline truck holed by bullets and dripping. Yet that night, no Nips hit C Co.

At dawn, from holes, we watched 5 Nips come down from a ridge to fire several trucks we would not guard. With so many Yanks in our rear at the beach, we held fire. It was not our skirmish.

On 19 May, F, B and C Cos were to advance in line to clear 500 yards of Wakde SE of the strip. Then F, B and C would turn NE and join with A Co to pin the Japs in the restricted NE peninsula.

Thus, on the beach flank that second morning, C became the turning element. Our friends the tanks came up — now 3, since beach crews had rescued and bailed out Tank No. 3, which had landed in 7 feet of water. Capt Peterson sent 2 to Stanfield's 2/Pltn and 1 to Larson's 3/Pltn.

Stanfield's 2 tanks came up on line 50 yards apart, and advanced — with a 2/Pltn squad protecting it. About half a squad followed close behind a tank for all possible shelter — although supposed to be 15 yards away from the steel sides to lessen danger of ricochets. Other men of the squad fanned out some 30-50 yards to the rear, and scanned brush ahead and to the flanks for Japs. Squad 3 echeloned left, to keep contact with pushing F Co.

Up the eastern slope towards the Japs marched C, with 3 clanking, throbbing tanks. A few Jap rifles cracked. Tank MGs began strafing. Left, a lone Jap sniper whined bullets too near, but 3 Yanks converged fire on him and killed him.

Topping the crest of the slope, 1/Lt Stanfield saw the Jap air control tower and more log and earth bunkers among bomb craters, fallen trees, and rubble. As C men spotted strongpoints, Jap fire grew suddenly heavy; bullets hammered tank armor. As shells blew up bunkers, Japs fled, and HMGs shot them down running — as did our rifles.

A Jap charged Larson's tank. At first the Jap seemed bent on putting rifle bullets down the 75 barrel, then mounted the tank as if to jab bayonet down an open hatch. As he topped the tank, Larson and Seeger gunned him down. An unarmed Jap leaped on a Stanfield tank, but Stanfield was unable to determine just what the Jap had in mind; the Jap died too soon.

A Stanfield tank bypassed a slit trench full of Nips. To recall the tank, a rifleman exposed himself, to hammer on the turret with a gunstock. Finally, we turned the tank and brought his guns to bear on the trench, then finished the Japs off with a few grenades and rifle-fire. We slew 13 Japs and then one Yank wounded.

And some time in this tank-inf strike at die-hard Nips, 2 C Co Yanks became memorable. Working on a Jap position, Sgt Siemenkiewicz took a rifle bullet into his shoulder and out his back. Although wounded, he crawled within 10 yards of the Japs and directed the attack, then passed out from loss of blood. (He was an invalid still, a decade later.)

Medic Forest Andrews was called up to give first aid, while most C men lay low under Jap fire. Despite warnings to let the increasing fire die down, he prepared the man for evacuation. (We believe the slain man was Lt Nugent, shot with 2 others when Japs infiltrated between C and F.)

Tank 75s were effective at 25 to 200 yards, and soon C had no return fire, although Japs still holed up fled before F's advance. We could not risk shelling F men. Orders withdrew 2 tanks to fight elsewhere, and C formed a skirmish line with Larson's Pltn and Tank No. 3, to shoot up other Jap hide-outs. Movement was slow; we must dig all Japs from holes, in brush often covered with coconut fronds. But by 1815, all 4 rifle Cos cordoned the Nips in 500 square yards of NE Wakde.

All Cos withdrew to the beach for hot meals and a night's rest. On 21 May, some C men had details counting bodies, while others worked on the Jap pocket with A Co. Crossing the south end of the strip, we met fire. Possich took a gunshot wound in his face. At the coast, we cornered 5-7 Nips in a cave, again had tank help. Working perilously around the coast under a coral shelf, we mopped up more Nips, finally contacted A Co coming south towards us about 1530. And this ended C's battle on Wadke; we were aboard LCMs and out of that coconut hell by 1910 21 May after 3 days action and back to the Toem Foreshore.

On 27 May at Toem, however, C Co had a bad night when Matsuyama Force hit us in our tents. KIA were Buck, Gilkison. Shot in left arm and right foot was Prerost, and Schneekloth in right shoulder. Fragments wounded Schoening — tore Spear's right arm, Schecke's right leg, Limpert's left knee, Neilsen's right eye. T/5 Lindsay was hit in right arm. At 0500, Bystrek took fragments in his ear. Our morning patrol found 5 dead Nips, but we had 2 dead, 10 wounded, including Valero.

Thus fought and died C Co 163 Inf men in 3 days battle on Wakde, and that bad night at Toem. With 6 dead and 12 WIA on Wakde, we totalled 8 KIA, 21 in hospital. The tanks had certainly saved us more casualties. And C was now a veteran beachhead assault Co and tank-infantry Co.

Most useful were Lts Larson's and Stanfield's reports. Larson's MS was written in 1967; Stanfield wrote his 31 July 1944 on "Infantry-Tank Assault Teams." Other documents include Journal 163 Inf beginning 12 May 1944; "One Step Westward," attributed to Col. Leonard Wing; award stories of Andrews and Siemenkiewicz; RR Smith's APPROACH TO THE PHILIPPINES — which also contains abstract of Stanfield's report. (I knew Larson as Weapons Pltn leader in my G Co on Biak, later as 163 Staff Officer on Jolo. Larson is now a business man in Billings, Montana.)

D Co. 163: Weapons Co. on Wakde

BY WILLIAM LAWLER AND JAMES J. EDER
WITH DR. HARGIS WESTERFIELD

> **CREDITS**
> Bill Lawler started this from recollected material originally turned in to MacCartney at Kure and never used. Also useful were medal stories of Eder, Retterath, Marion Reed, Dean Henry, RR Smith's APPROACH TO THE PHILIPPINES, D Co's "Morning Report" for May, 1964. Important also is "One Step Westward," attributed to Col. Leonard Wing, and used by permission of INFANTRY JOURNAL — published March 1945. Of equal value with Lawlar's story is James J. Eder's "Two Feet Between Gun Muzzles," reprinted in an undated ltr summer 1963.

Beside dug-in weapons on Insoemanai Island, D Co 163 Inf lolled in the open with other outfits of the Provisional Groupment. FA shells raised dust-clouds on shaggy Wakde. We were sure Mjr Wing would seize it tomorrow without losses. But Lawler had heard Wing loudly refuse a Naval officer's suggestion to halt fire and take Wakde now.

About 1600, Jap rifles cracked from Wakde — 500 yards off. We hit the holes; but an E Co man died from a bullet in the head. He was drinking from the largest spring on Insoemanai — clearly seen from Wakde. A second Yank raced over the low raise into brush. A third Yank crouched in a catch-basin of coral blocks until nightfall. Despite FA from Toem, Nip MGs fired. The Groupment had 4 wounded.

Our other spring was in defilade — but a mere trickle. We had enough water for MG jackets, but had to line up until dusk for our ration of half a canteen. Worst still, when FA shelled Wakde, shorts fouled us with mud and water, killed 1 more Yank, wounded 6 more.

By 0900 18 May, while F/Bn plus F drove in LCVPs for Wakde, D Co and other outfits barraged an estimated 10 MGs until we burned out all barrels. But F/Btn closed on the beach and masked our fires. Japs shot back at us. With ammo spent, we rushed over Insoemanai's hump to safety— all but D Co's F/Pltn of MGs.

For D's F/Pltn was in the LCVPs storming Wakde. As the steel hail of Jap fire struck, F/Pltn saw 2 flanking LCVPs of riflemen turn back. We got ashore minus rifle protection— but had no casualties. Eder's squad mounted his MG at the mouth of a concrete "trench" — a drainage ditch. We didn't see a deadhead Nippo MG crew watching us until we could fire. We wiped them out.

Ordered to support A Co with MGs, we skirmished into Wakde Town — well laid out streets, wrecked buildings. Eder hoped Wakde was taken; but B Co found the toughest fight — as usual. Dodging Nip bullets, we dug in on B's flank.

Meanwhile an LCVP with a resupply of amo ferried the rest of D Co with Lawler from Insoemanai to Wakde. Laboring ashore under heavy gear into Wakde Town, we dug in under the Nip hospital built on concrete pillars 3 feet above ground. Nearby a water-tower stood tall above a Jap bathhouse.

A stream of walking wounded from the front passed D Co en route to Medics — many men with bandaged wounds or crimsons gashes — everywhere on heads or arms or shoulders.

Lawler thought the Japs were winning. But Wing's positive voice on the radio to Gen Doe was reassuring: "Everything under control, Sir." Lawler's morale rose; this tall blond handsome authoritative man was very sure of himself. Lawler continued digging in. Glancing up at the water-tower, he rejoiced that no bullets pierced it — remembered his thirst last night.

By his MG on B's flank, Eger got orders with Marion Reed, Sgt Garrison to bring back ammo for the other MG. Pushing forward with 3 belts apiece, they caught sniper bullets like a hailstorm in the coral around them. Eder lost Reed, Garrison; he came to crouching behind a mound. Japanese voices sounded through a crack in the mound. Eder peered inside and almost fainted. A Nip officer seemed to be arguing with other Nips. Eder got 2 grenades from his pockets, pulled the pins, thrust them into the mound, ran. The mound bounced once; Eder thought he was safe. (Later he found a handsome sword on the Nip officer, who was a Col.)

Then at a distance, B men yelled at Eder, pointed overhead. He was under the water-tower; a sniper was potting at him. Like a scared cottontail — he said later — he scurried back to B Co's front with his ammo.

Safe with his MG beside B Co, Eder shook so that he could not find his mouth with a cigarette. Finally calmer, he looked toward the beach. He got another shock. The place was crawling with Japs. In a strong flank move, they were firing towards B Co, and at the beach.

Eder's crew reset the MG on the beach road for a better field of fire. An official voice behind Eder growled, "why the hell is this gun pointing at the beach? Your position is on B's flank." It was Col Moroney himself. Eder tried to explain, but Moroney must see for himself. He stepped out on the road; Nip bullets shattered coral around him. Moroney hurried away. With D's MGs blasting, B got F's support and 2 tanks and built up a line that threw back the Nips' attack.

Crouched by his racketing MG, Eder never forgot how 163 saved many lives of B's seriously wounded — even while cut off from the beach. We loaded the wounded into tanks and ran them direct through Nippo fire while MGs covered the tanks. Near the beach, the guns on the LCVPs took over to cover the men until they were out of danger and could be lifted from the tanks for medical attention. Nothing could raise our morale higher than 163's care for the helpless wounded.

The snipers from the water-tank had chased Eder in fear of his life. But they also scared Lawler and the main body of D Co at Wakde Town. While we dug, the spatter of bullets drove us under cover — —several times. We hid keen-eyed watchers and dug to draw fire. Bullets spattered again; we ducked; a private yelled and pointed. Instantly all D Co knew: THE WATER-TOWER. Vengefully 2 D MGs stitched patterns around the tower. We dug to draw fire again, but the sniping had ceased. We found 3 dead Nips inside.

Near Lawler, Japs ran out and fired Yank trucks; but D men in the holes dared not shoot; we might hit Yanks on the other side of the trucks. Out front, a trench came to life with Nips blazing away. A tank rumbled up, blasted them, sat down on their trench. They were alive 1 minute, dead the next.

Although well dug in under the hospital, D Co now had sensible orders: get out of that death-trap where Jap drum-fires could ricochet from roof and concrete pillars into our holes. We dug in protecting Wing's Hq. Infiltrating Nips loosed a LMG on us; tracer fire from it flamed a foot over Lawler's head before we drove them off.

Now a Sgt came to pick a combat detail. Near the shore, a rifle Co — Lawler never knew whether "F" on the beach or "A" across Wakde — needed a HMG with 15 Yanks. Tired and afraid and the oldest man in D, Lawler hoped to save himself. The Sgt looked at Lawler — seemed to forget his name. Lawler glanced down. The Sgt chose another man. Lawler felt guilty in minutes; he had a premonition. Of that 15, 1 Yank died, and 5 were wounded.

D's F/Pltn of MGs with Eder was also dug in beside Lawler and others to protect Btn CP and Medics. At dark, Eder with 2 others lay in the MG position left of the road to Wakde Air-Strip where B and F faced the most aggressive Nip warriors.

While Lawler slept at 2:00, Eder in his own hole crouched on guard. Two gray figures slipped up the road. Eder started to challenge them, but they halted — Japs! These scouts fell back; came an under-strength Jap Btn. Eder surmised that — not knowing that D Co was watching them — they had planned to take B in the rear.

Eder held fire until men farther up the line closer to the Nips could shoot first. He wanted to hear them up in a cross-fire; but he heard nothing. Why Marion Reed held fire from the next hole, no one knows, but Reed did wake Retterath. In another hole, Sgt Dean Henry was also awake beside his MG.

Eder heaved grenades into the road. He fired his MG; but it jammed. He roused the 2 sleeping men beside him; we fired rifles and pistols and grenades. Screams from the road told us we were hitting Nips.

Then a grenade plopped in our hole — invisible in the dark. We leaped out; as it blew up; we hit the hole again. Japs charged; we cut them down. Two more grenades thudded into the hole. We jumped out again — Eder into another hole on the back of an ammo-bearer whose knife-arm he grasped in time to save himself.

Back in the hole, Eder crouched alone; his buddies never came back. Should he pull out the MG breech-block and leave also? But he heard Jap sound nearby — prayed like a good scared Catholic.

Two heads popped up, he blew both brains out with 45 slugs. In the pistol flash, he saw the Nip MG on his parapet. Eder swung MGs towards each other — 2 feet between muzzles! Both fired.

MG bullets ricocheted around Eder; he emptied his MG belt, was still untouched. All was quiet a few seconds. He eased a new belt in. He cocked the MG; a Nip jumped him. Eder caught him by the foot, put 3 45s into him, threw the body out among the others.

Eder felt in the dark in the bottom of the hole for more grenades and ammo. An explosion felled him. A Jap stood above, let go 2 bursts into the trench, then stepped in. Eder put a bullet into the brain, heaved another Nip out. Eder cowered a long time in the silence until dawn.

While Eder and his crew fought, Reed, Retterath, Henry fired also.

Probably they put bullets and grenades into the same Nips that Eder's crew hit. Lawler heard a Yank in a nearby hole — probably Pender — moan and wriggle across the open to find Medics and live. He lost the toes on his right foot. When silence fell, Lawler kept his head down, hoped the fight was over. Then a Yank grenade lobbed from the next hole — Newcomb picking off a crawling Nip. Lawler alerted, fought with grenades and M-1 against dark sounds outside perimeter.

In early light, we eased from our holes with rifles to clear the area — past sprawled Jap corpses. Suddenly Arisakas cracked. We smothered them with M-1's, heard muffled grenade explosions. Besides 2 Nips we killed, we found a third blown in 2 with grenades clutched to his stomach.

With dawn, Eder got deeper into his hole; he knew that a sniper would zero in on the MG exposed on the parapet. He heard firing where his buddies mopped up Nips; but he took no chances. He heard footsteps, readied himself to fire.

But Yanks stood over him: proud Mjr Wing, D Co's Capt Skauge, other officers and guards. As Eder stood up, Col Moroney and staff arrived. Eder saw 2 dead Nip MGs and their crews.

We counted 9 dead Nips in 10 feet of Eder's MG muzzle, found 6 more scattered about — believed 1 escaped. These 15 were probably exclusive of 3 D Co left dead at dawn. Besides Pender, we had 2 more hospital cases — S/Sgt Henry wounded in left shoulder, and Nordmark wounded with fragments and sot in both legs. Eder had light grenade wounds in his hands.

Despite the night-fight, Lawler's conscience still bothered him about missing yesterday's combat detail. Hearing that another Co — perhaps A — was pinned down across the Air-Strip, he joined a carrying party. He felt better, but the trip was hot, eventless

By dark, the Wakde War was almost over; the last Nips were silent in holes in the NE corner. Relaxed over hot full mess-gears, Lawler, Eder, other D men who survived were expecting a deep full night of unbroken sleep. Only a man in each squad would get a 2-hour period of guard duty once all night.

on Wakde, "D" lost 4 dead, 6 wounded to hospital. Smoger was killed on 18 May, Phillip shot in left wrist. On 19 May, bullets in the head killed Nordmark, Pasley. Kuhn died of gun-shot wounds in chest and abdomen. Besides Pender, Henry, and Marshall cited already, Eades was shot in left shoulder, and marshall in left leg. D Co. was lucky to lose so few on bitter Wakde.

F Co., 163 Infantry:
OUR WAKDE HELL-HOLE

> CREDIT: "F" 163's historian, S/Sgt Marlow, provided a 10-page, single-spaced typescript. Cpl Plummer gave me a 13-page handwritten MS, and Lloyd Schulte a 7-page letter of 30 Nov 1978. Useful also were Cpl Frank Feifar's and T/5 Medic Malanca's medal stories, Col (then Maj) Leonard Wing's "One Step Westward," orginally in Infantry Journal; RR Smith's Approach to the Philippines, 163's Journal 17-30 May 1944, and 163's Casualty Reports 17-30 May 1944. I cite Clyde Plummer and his own MS and for contacting others; I could not have written the story without his aid. We now have stories of all units that stormed Wakde: A, B, C, D, F, and H Co on Insoemanai.

Driving for Toem Beach in the fourth wave, F Co 163 Inf saw only one sign of Japs on silent Wakde to port. A small gunboat drew Jap fire, which Navy shells quieted. Smoke from Wakde's flaming dumps obscured Toem, where Naval planes bombed and strafed for us.

"F" landed unopposed and hiked 2 jungle miles behind 1/Bn and dug in near Toem Village. A patrol 300 yards on a trail from 2/Bn CP, found a small Jap bivouac and a .77 cannon with shells and fuzes. Gun had not fired (The harassed Japs had withdrawn another gun with a small 224 Inf detachment.)

On guard that night, Schulte saw a Jap column loom on the trail before his hole, bayonets fixed. With awaking Etchingham and Reeves, he fired and saw them drop to earth. Other Japs ran. One moaning Jap died at daylight. Of an estimated 12 Japs, we found 1 dead officer, 2 dead privates.

About 0900 that great battle morn of 18 May, "F" with "B" abreast on our right, was jammed in assault boats chugging from Toem to Wakde. Smoke and orange flashes of explosions rose from Wakde shaking like being torn apart-- from bombs of 36 A-20s of Fifth Air-Force, 2350 Naval 5 or 6-inch shells, and our 167Fa, 218 FA, and Cn 163. Small craft shot 850 rockets, 20 mm and 40 mm guns, while 641 TD mortars and all 163's heavy weapons fired from Insoemanai.

Then the Japs fought. Bullets at 600 yards sprayed our barges while "F" flattened on the bottoms. S/Sgt Marlow heard the wounded coxswain scream from the barge leftwards. He fell forward. The barge circled unguided until another man steered it inshore.

In 2/Pln's barge, S/Sgt Plummer held dying Dickson in his arms. A bullet knocked out Sgt Al brown's front teeth and burned his lips. Water in the boat reddened with blood from other men's wounds. When the ramp fell, we expected a MG to pile us up dead inside the barge.

Suddenly, 50 yards from the beach, Jap fire lifted, for reasons unknown. Barges grounded; ramps fell; "F" dashed onto the beach and dropped among stumps and logs. Only 2/Pln's ramp jammed. Men swarmed down ramp and sides and raced through shallows and fell prone. We tried to form a skirmish line with "B" on our right.

A "B" Co man screamed that he was hit. Looking over our shoulders from the sand, we saw the second wave of "A" and "C" in a death storm. As ramps dropped, men fell in water or on the beach. Then Jap fire ceased again.

Leaping down the side of 2/Pln's barge, Plummer saw a large concrete blockhouse leftwards, but gunports were silent. Dashing rom shell crater to shell crater up the beach, he found himself alone, under intense Jap fire too high to hit him.

Returned to the beach, Plummer found scared men bunched together like grapes. "Follow me or get killed here!" he warned. As they rose and went with him, Plummer thought that he had sprung all "F" from the beach. By now, CO 1/Lt Liebach lay dead, and 4 more "F" men were wounded. Sellick was shot in right leg, Serby in left shoulder, Edgin in right wrist and elbow, and S/Sgt Charles Larsen in right wrist.

Now "F" moved slowly north from the beach, but for 3/Pln assigned to clear SW Wakde. Nip fire on our left flank grounded our main body.

Plummer saw a tank land from a barge. As its treads hit sand, it pumped 2 shells into that silent blockhouse. With another tank, it drove for 3 Jap pillboxes firing intensely. The 2 tanks blasted all 3 pillboxes into the air. Now with tank protection, we advanced as skirmishers on Wakde Strip. The tanks left us to fight for "C" Co on our right. A sniper wounded Sartibonez in the left shoulder.

Meanwhile, 2/Lt Thomas' detached 3/Pln fought hard on SW Wakde. Trying to clear nearly destroyed remains of old coconut plantation buildings, we battled formidable pillboxes among them. From captured Rhodes Ridge to the SE, "A" Co reinforced us with the 2 tanks recalled from "C" Co. it took a 30 minutes' battle around noon, with rifles, grenades, tank MGs--even bayonets--to clear the plantation houses. Probably here Cpls Von Hoene and Shields died--Shields with a bullet in the head. We had 6 more "F" men wounded by bullets: Lyons in shoulder, side unspecified; Filipone in left shoulder and neck; Galindo in right shoulder; Valles and Sgt Gilley both in left knees.

F's main body now turned west along the south side of Wakde Strip. But we made only a few yards before a MG halted us 150 yards from a revetment (a semi-circular mound of earth to protect Jap planes from bombs). We halted and set up a MG because we had orders to help "C" Co trying to cross the Strip northwards. Maj Wing wanted to cut off Jap attempts to build up a new line on western Wakde. While we waited, a bullet pierced Kraus' head just over the ears. Medic T/5 Malanca saved Kraus to go home for honorable discharge.

"C" started across the Strip. Two Japs dragged a MG from a revetment and fired on "C" men in the open. Machine-gunner Thomas and assistant Rutzatz and BARman Schulte leaped on the strip and drove the Jap MG crew back into hiding.

Jap fire from the east kept half of "C" from crossing the strip, but "F" had orders to fight west again, all 3 Plns in line of skirmishers, our right flank on the Strip.

Jap fire grounded us again from a ravine in high weeds, but the MG shot too high to hit us. Sgt Williams' grenade drew 2 Jap grenades in turn. One exploded between his legs, but the fragments missed him. Williams, S/Sgt Lamb, Reeves, and others charged with grenades and heavy fire and smothered the Japs' wild return volleys.

To the far right, we found the 4 Jap MG crewmen who had shot at "C" crossing the Strip--in a shellhole just a few feet in ront. Miller and Cpt Feifar threw grenades and attacked with M-1s. Hunter dived in with BAR bursts. We slew all 4 Japs.

In that silent ravine, we found 11 mangled bodies on the sides of a long trench 2 feet wide, and 7 bodies in another 2-foot trench. Several rifles were there, MGs, and a pile of unexploded grenades.

Orders came to turn back SE and help "B" Co in heavy fighting. out of water, we had only milk from green coconuts, if we were lucky to find them. A few of us had time to fill canteens from a coral quarry pool--milk-white water almost boiling from the sun. Too soon, we were hurried south to reinforce B Co.

While trying to press the main Wakde garrison into small NE Wakde, "B" was having rrouble. From thick brush, MGs with grenadiers and mortarmen had stopped "B". Japs were slipping around between "B's" right flank and the sea to menace our crowded beach with its supplies and wounded.

Marching 640 yards south, we crouched passing "B" Co's rear and saw men baking in shell-holes under blazing sun. We crawled among pieces of corrugated tin and splitered lumber among smashed buildings.

Orders came to jump up and charge to a new line, 2 at a time. Running across a wrecked, tin-covered remains of a building, Schulte dropped into a small depression. Jap Bullet No. 1 hit 6 feet before him. Bullet No. 2 hit 6 feet before him. Bullet No. 3 hit 3 feet before him. Schulte rose and ran back and saved his life.

"F" had pushed too far ahead of B Co. Cpl Plummer found 6 men alone in a L-shaped Jap trench, and got them back to a shell-hole that was Pln Hq. "F" then withdrew to fill canteens from a water-tank drawn by a jeep. After a cool, liquid moment, "F" deployed farther south. Orders were to dig in for the night; Jap fire was heavy.

Dashing under fire around a rubble pile, Plummer jumped into a shell-hole and took a bullet near the spine that could have killed him. His chest seemed to cave in. he straightened up, shook like a snapped bow-string. He collapsed, head on knees. Blood gushed from his mouth--in seconds a pint or so on that white coral. Able to move on his head, he thought that he called Cowan to bring Medic Malanca. Bent double for safety, 2 stretcher bearers ran in and dragged Plummer out. He lived, but was paralyzed from the waist down.

Meanwhile, our new CO, 1/Lt Ferguson, had convinced 2/Bn Hq that "F" was too far advanced. We crawled back across the north-south road to dig in for the night. Soil was too rocky for holes, but shell-craters were plentiful. That night, our FA kept us awake with 20 harassing rounds hourly. Nips screamed, crept close to fire a few MG bursts. When they sniped from debris piles, we had to stand and empty guns at them.

Next morning, 19 May, without breakfast, we crouched waterless in front-line shell holes under a sun blazing by 0800. South near the beach-head, a fiery smoke-pall arose where Nip raiders had burned 6 Air Force Mack trucks.

About 1100, our 3 tanks clanked up for help. The Nips now put up the last brave fight for their grou. They shot heavily into our perimeter; we shot back. Crawling from piles of tin, rock, and lumber, they fought prone, often just a few feet from us. Tucci rose to his feet and slew a Nip officer creeping on us.

The Japs had perfect cover behind a riddled coconut log felled last night. Rowe stood to fire; a Jap shot him over the temple. While bandaging him, Malanaca was hit in left shoulder, but refused aid until Rowe's life was saved.

In fighting groups around the tanks, "F" fixed bayonets and advanced on a front with "B" on our left up to the Strip, and "C" on our right down to the sea. Nip fire ceased. Our tanks crawled over huge debris piles and blazed down with MGs while we searched out what they had missed.

2/Lt Cammenca suddenly jumped sideways before a dugout mouth and pointed his carbine. But he pressed magazine release and dropped his clip. He tossed in a grenade. The muffled explosion told us that the Nip had hugged it to his stomach. When Sgt Reeves threw a grenade, another Nip died the same way. A third grenade slew 2 more Nips in a connecting tunnel.

Resting on a coconut log, Schulte saw the elbow of a "dead" Jap move under the log, heard a grenade tapping to arm it. Schulte's BAR jammed, but he worked the lever and got off just 1 shot to kill the Nip.

At the beach ahead, all Cos almost stampeded for water welling from a bottomless Jap drum in the sands and drank deep. "F" turned to the heavy timber on cliffs of NE Wakde where Japs still lurked. As we passed a burning Jap dump, a .50 shell exploded and wounded S/Sgt McGowan in his left hand. While mopping up the cliff area, 2/Pln had trouble. From a cave, a bullet hit Sgt Lisieck in the chest; he died in the ambulance. A bullet hit Sgt Cameron's right elbow. Another smashed 2/Lt Houser's .45 in his shoulder holster, and knocked him down. The pistol deflected the bullet and saved his life.

As dark fell, "F" quietly returned to our holes of that morning. Weirdly quiet was the dead Jap line ahead. We had last eaten 24 hours ago. Now our kitchen served hot beans, salmon, coffee. Next morning, 20 May, we awoke in our holes and felt much better. Breakfast was corn-flakes, grape-fruit juice, coffee--with filled canteens and cigarettes.

We returned to NE Biak for the last Japs. When 2/Bn took fire from the caves, we needed special weapons. A bazooka failed. A tank could not approach on that narrow beach, nor depress its .75 from above to shoot into the caves. We poured half a Jap gas barrel over the cliff, dropped the other half to the beach, then lit it with a flame-thrower. After a blaze, we advanced down to the beach, shooting or grenading any suspected dark place on the slope. We saw no more Japs, only huge piles of equipment.

After hot supper again, we had good news. We were leaving Wakde for Toem abroad an LST. S/Sgt Marlow pitied his men with their exhausted, dirty faces under 3-day beards. Fatigues were blackened and torn. Only a few talked, even to buddies nearby. Rationed for just 8 hours on Wakde, we had fought for 3 days.

In 3 days' battle, "F" lost 4 dead, 17 wounded to hospital, of whom 3 died and 15 were wounded the first day. Wakde was costly for "F", despite aid of taks and FA. But on 18 May alone, we slew 87 Nips. Despite thirst and bloodshed, ours was a well-fought battle for Wakde-- on the beach and in frontline shell-holes.

Machine Gun Duel

BY S/SGT HAROLD INGLE, H CO., 163 INF.

On 15 May 1944, H Company 163 Infantry embarked on LCI 340 to fight on Insoemanai in the Wakde - Toem Operation. Already after our beachhead at Aitape, our morale was low.

For we could not forget 13 May at Santa Anna Mission (Aitape). While Mortar Platoon was testfiring, an 81 mm shell just cleared the tube and blew up in the crowd. Dead were Landcaster, Hoelscher, Helland, Dotson, and Anderson. Bostwick and Legleiter were to die in the hospital. What happened to Brooks, Campbell, Houy, and Ingrahm I never knew. (*Historian's note: Division History lists among our dead, "Inghram," two Brooks, and two Campbells, but no Houy.*) But with 7 dead and 4 possibly dead, and 16 others wounded, Mortars were down to half their strength. And just before embarkation on May 15 we saw 2 mentally sick—maybe from F—evacuated for battle-fatigue.

About noon LCI 340 pulled out from Aitape and headed slowly west up the Guinea Shore.

On 16 May, we anchored off Hollandia with the blue cloudy Cyclops Mountains before us. All day we hove to in Humboldt Bay with nothing to do but smoke and think. Barrath left us with a fever of 106. After dark, LCI 340 steamed off for the landing.

On May 17, while the destroyers threw in endless chains of red-ringed shells at the thickets of Wakde on our left flank, and had no answer, we followed the riflemen ashore at Arare Then we hiked to Toem, with the M-1's cracking in the coconut groves southward.

On the foreshore, we joined up with the provisional Groupment to land on Insoemanai Island and fire a protective weapons barrage next morning to protect the assault on Wakde Island. With E Company's riflemen for protection, D and H Companies of 163 with AT Co and the 641 Tank Destroyers' 4.2's would land on this smaller island of Insoemanai to cover the amphibious charge of the First Btn plus F Company on May 18.

On LCV's, we started for the smaller of two wooded islands at 3.500 yards. Our barges grounded 75 yards from Insoemanai. On the nearest beach, Groupment Headquarters set up, with ammo dump and radio station.

First Lieut. Donald Lowe took H up a grade of 6 feet and through scattered forest across Insoemanai. Mid-way we dropped off the 81's and the attached 4.2's. On the far shore, we machine-gunners were posted above the beach on a low coral shelf. To our right around the island's curve were a platoon of E, and then H's First Platoon's MG's. To our left, AT dug in with two heavy 50's.

From the mainland, shells whispered overhead to land on Wakde before us. The coral air-strip ran almost the entire length of the two miles of Wakde. Although its mainland lay dead ahead, a heavily wooded little peninsula of Wakde outflanked us to the right.

Our position was screened by scattered trees, but we could not dig into the coral. We had to fill sand-bags on the beach in full view of Wakde, but we drew no fire—as yet.

With the guns protected by sand-bags and ready, Bruner put on the coffee, Then Japanese rifles struck from that wooded peninsula on our right. One E Company man died with a shot through the head. Another bullet detonated an E man's ammo belt which took fire and burned him severely. Still another was wounded.

We hid by our guns but saw nothing. Regular barrages landed on that wooded point and silenced the snipers. We came out in the open to our coffee-pot. A machine-gun burst plunged among us.

As darkness fell, the shells still tore overhead against Wakde. The inevitable rain machine-gunned down on us. Beside the guns, we wrapped in ponchos and tried to sleep.

I awoke to a tremendous burst of shells. It flung me over the sand-bags.

More shells roared in. Our nearby Artillery Spotter galloped by cursing. The first shell severed his lines, and he raced to Groupment Headquarters to stop the shelling. In the dark, my section scraped at the coral with knives and spoons and bare hands to save themselves from more wild steel. H lost nobody this time, but E had five wounded and one more dead. (*Historian's Note: Was 167 FA or 191 FA guilty? Now 191 FA says that 163 Cannon Co. was responsible because of inexperience in combat firing, according to the U.S. Army History.*)

It was D-day for Wakde. As we gulped our rations at dawn, A-20's started the show with a low-level attack.

Our section's first mission was to cover the beach in the area of the ruined plantation houses—from the pier farthest to the right to a large tree several hundred yards farther. Since daybreak we had waited for orders.

But the Japs beat us to the punch. They opened up and pinned us down.

Then Cumba and Frazer fought them with O'Sullivan and Vados the assistant gunners. They traversed the area with their heavies. Leaves showered down as Japanese gunners' fire lifted too high to hurt us. As the enemy fire slackened, I heard other American sections to right and left as they too fired on Wakde.

Yet the Japanese stuck to their guns. When Roth and I jumped out to break our barrel loose, bullets thudded into the sand-bags around us.

We got in 8,000 rounds of HMG into the plantation area and every other suspected spot on the beach.

At the height of our fusillade, the landing-barges jammed with helmeted green infantry slowly rounded the tip of Insoemanai—A, B, C, and F. Now they were in the slot between us and Wakde.

It was a slow parade of high-ramped landing barges against an ominously silent and threatening island. Wakde still lay quiet under the terrific pounding of our mortars and artillery. The blasts of our machine-guns must have kept the Nips from manning their gun-ports. But as the squadrons of Americans drew abreast of us and masked our guns, we had to cease firing.

Suddenly Japanese Wakde burst into flames. Small arms fire raked the barges. Possibly mortar shells splashed around them.

The leading barge was hit; the coxswain went down before a stream of machine-gun fire. His LCV drifted off course towards us; then some brave man gripped the helm and held it hard on through mortar blasts and bullet-strikes into the beach.

The first wave of barges got in; the landing-ramps crashed on the beach; the riflemen raced through the surf. They made about ten yards on that beach and hit an invisible wall. They fanned out prone, faced inland, fired where they could. It was a hard landing.

Then our attention was diverted to a little donga opposite us. Out of a bunker, a saber-waving Japanese officer led twenty to thirty soldiers up the hill to our landing area. They carried two machine-guns.

I ordered Cumba to fire. But the fire-control officer on our island (from AT, I believe), refused

> The author of this wonderful article on Insoemanai, S/Sgt Harold Ingle, was with the Division from Australia through Sanananda and the New Guinea Campaign all the way to Zamboanga. And this leads me to say that it isn't my fault that we have no feature on 162 or 163 or 205 or 116—or on your outfit. If you have diaries or letters or memories to write up, please let me know.
> —Hargis Westerfield, Div. Historian

us permission. He claimed that we couldn't be sure they were Japs. When was the last time he had seen a Yank officer leading troops into battle with a sword, I asked.

By this time, most of the riflemen had climbed out of sight, but the din of small arms was terrific. For two tanks were ashore: the two surviving tanks of 603 Tank Company had sprung the left side of the beach-head loose. The rifle companies were fighting inland.

Like watching a ball-game, we cheered as the tanks mopped up those evil pill-boxes. At each bunker, a tank slowly thrust the muzzle of its cannon into the slot. The resulting blast killed the pillbox. Riflemen followed closely and fired at every movement in the debris of the explosion.

This tank-and-rifle cooperation continued until the war had worked its way out of sight. Now the beach-head swarmed with movement as service troops unloaded ammo and supplies.

At dusk, H Company with the Provisional Groupment was recalled from Insoemanai. We hiked with our heavy guns across the island again and waited until the barges ferried us back to the mainland.

This was the duel with machineguns on Insoemanai against Wakde. The Provisional Groupment lost 2 dead, 12 wounded. At least 240 dead were counted in the area of our fire, and we know that H got many of them.

Moreover, the Provisional Groupment got credit for keeping the Japs down when they could have banzaied to bayonet the boys pinned on the beach. And we prevented the redeployment of enemy infantry from the other side of the island where the Japs had most expected the landing.

Finally, on 22 May 1944, General Jens A. Doe himself told PFC Louis Frazer, "Your heavy machine guns did a swell job on that little island."

This was you. No worry about the rising cost of living, the dentist bill or higher taxes. Just trying to stay alive.

167th FA Fights At Toem

By SGT STAUB
With DR. HARGIS WESTERFIELD

Assault on Wakde, assault on Lone Tree Hill, perimeter defenses, jungle patrols — wounds and suffering and death and tropical labor — this is the saga of 167 FA at Toem. Besides 163, we killed for 158 Bushmasters and 6 Division.

Ashore with 163's Fourth Wave 17 May 1944, Capt Thomson's Fire Control Party and Recon took over the fire site first observed in air photos. Then we beached our 3 LST's at 0900. At once we set up C Btry on call for the push on Toem. We dragged the other guns into the fire site 2000 yards east of Toem, and took 163's green Cannon Co with us. By 1100, our observers on Insoemanai were directing 105 shells on Wakde. Meanwhile, Capt Helmer's party registered us on the Tementoe flank, and F/Lieut O'Laughlin registered on the Tor flank.

At once Japs retaliated. Our fire on Wakde goaded them to shoot at Insoemanai. When A Btry fired Concentration 100 on the Tor, a Nippo patrol tried to penetrate our perimeter. B Btry endured sniper fire. But by midnight of D Day, we had fired 2766 rounds. At 0100, however, Capt. Connor was killed in Fire Direction Center. Yet at 0830, we began to barrage Wakde, in preparation for assault.

With Forward Observation Parties attached to all four rifle Cos in the barges, Lt Col Beach accompanied Mjr Wing in the second wave. By 1600, Beach was ashore and hammering the Japs with 167 and 218 FA. (Our fire silenced MG's that held up C Co's crossing of the Air-Strip, and protected perimeters all night. That attack day we fired 1586 shells.)

After Wakde fell, 167 FA decimated Japs on the Tor River Line. When 163's 3 Btn's bridgehead was attacked, F/Lt Schumacher secured it with a box barrage. On the Tementoe Front, we smashed a village where Japs were heard.

CREDIT

In Japan, Sgt. Staub wrote this for McCartney's "history." But Mack practically ignored combat at Toem, left a blank space. I bought this with Assn. funds from Fed Records Center, rewrote with RR Smith's RETURN TO THE PHILIPPINES. My only other FA material deals with 146 at Jolo, Zambo'. But it lacks names of men who did things. Can any FA reader help? I am disappointed at lack of FA letters. Remember when you read this, it always gets down to one man — you. Please write.

While 158 Inf was beginning to move against Lone Tree Hill on the way to Sarmi, 167 had to displace forward to the Tor to cover the movement. Quietly taking up position the night of 22 May, we set up the guns. Like Infantry, we posted outguards and sent out security patrols.

Now we fired around the clock for 158 Inf, in its push on Sarmi. When a Nippo Mountain Gun pinned down L 158 from west of Maffin 1 Jetty, our Piper Cub directed 105's on it, and observed for an LCI that was strafing with .50 MG's. Our fire helped 158 edge forward; but at 1600, they again received mortar fire from Maffin 1. We blasted Maffin 1 again.

On 24 May also, we shot at that same Mountain Gun, and placed smoke-shells so that 218 FA could throw heavier metal on it. After 158's lead elements set up a night perimeter east of the Tirfoam River, we barraged the riverbank for a half hour. At 1800, Marvin Larson — with a forward observation party — was wounded by a rifle.

On 25 May, we fired with all Task Force Artillery on an area 400 by 200 yards before "158," 350 yards east of the Tirfoam River. Advancing infantry then found that the heavily garrisoned Jap defenses were destroyed or abandoned. At 0830, Lieblong (Hq Btry) took a Jap rifle bullet in the thigh.

....Near Maffin 1, observers found that we had killed at least 7 Japs and wounded an unknown number. We also found the Mountain Gun position which we had bombarded 23 and 24 May. There were two guns still operational; but 35 Japs lay dead around the guns. They had fought like heroes.

At our batteries east of the Tor, security patrols and MG lanes kept us safe from night attacks; but at 0812 26 May, Springer of B Btry was shot in the thigh and died in 45 minutes.

That night we battered all known howitzers and strong points; and on 27 May, we fired all out with 158's great attack. "A" Btry fired just beyond Lone Tree Hill; "B" and "C" fired near Hill 225. We made direct hits on 2 MG positions holding up the First Btn and got direct hits on both. In 15 minutes, we hit an ammo dump and fired it. And that night — as on most nights — we fired other concentrations on Japs.

But 158 Inf never took Lone Tree Hill. When 163's 1 and 2 Btns were called to Biak, 158's 1 Btn must fall back across the Tor to help 163's 2 Btn secure the Task Force Beach-Head. Then Jap pressure made Col Herndon pull the other 158 Btns back to the Toem Foreshore. Our guns covered the withdrawal, and now our patrols even east of the Tor became dangerous. For greater security, A Btry displaced back to Unnamed River and grouped with CN 163 to protect the beach.

On 30 May, Nips prowled near our perimeter; our patrols killed a few of them. At 1300, they struck our 3 Btn, still west of the Tor. We silenced a HMG and stopped the attack. At 1430, we teamed with mortars and smashed a second attack. But the war closed in again; Wavrick of A Btry died while manning a MG in our perimeter.

Yet when Yoshino Force's 223 Infantry struck in the great attack of 30 May, it must have been the strength of our perimeter that diverted them against the isolated AA Gun Positions on the beach west of Arare and east of our A Btry-CN 163 perimeter. Although the Nips wiped out 2 positions and struck B 158 hand to hand, our night was quiet.

On 31 May we laid down a 30 minute smoke screen to cover 3 Btn's withdrawal across the Tor. By 1 June, we also withdrew to near our A Btry and Cannon Co and made perimeter together.

On 1 June, Japs were too close for howitzer fire. We took small arms and went out and fought them. Givens (Hq Btry) and Galazin (Sv Btry) were wounded — Galazin seriously. We killed 1 officer, 1 private.

Just before dusk, we had a naval war. When 158 men sighted a Jap sub a few hundred yards off Rocky Point, Capt Thomson zeroed in with 3 Btn volleys. Sub crash-dived.

The thunder of our guns, our sweat in the sun, our lurking in perimeter and coming out fighting continued. On 3 June, Hodge (C Btry) died of an abdomenal wound. After midnight 4 June, Japs banzaied on K 158 holding the bridgehead across the Tor. Lt Waters — observing with K — at once put Cannon Co's gunfire on the Japs. He also brought in our 3 batteries to box off the Japs. We threw in 800 rounds and stopped them dead.

119

41st Division artillerymen in action in SWPA in 1944.

On 4 June also, we had fired a concentration on another gun position west of the Tor. On 5 June, a patrol found the gun — about the size of a Yank 75 howitzer. They counted 20 105 holes in 30 feet of the gun. We had demolished the road there, killed 84 Japs. Yet at high noon, Byrd (B Btry) was wounded on outguard.

During the night of 5 June, a Jap plane over Wakde destroyed or damaged all Task Force liaison planes. Quickly, airmen repaired one plane by cannibalizing parts from other planes. Our artillery birdmen had done yeoman service observing overhead. We here honor 2/Lt Robinson for flying 53 missions with 70½ hours in the air, where he was often fired on by AA or even rifles. 1/Lt Van Dyke flew 61 missions with 76 hours.

On 7 June came our last 'infantry" action. With a recon mission to scout 1800 yards south through the Tor River jungle and along the banks, Lt Monroe took 10 men. For security, Monroe put out a scout and 2 men to cover, then followed with his second-in-command and the others in single file. Off the beach road 300 yards, we spotted a Nip scout and slew him. Exploring east along the Tor's banks, we found tracks of a Jap Pltn that had passed that morning. Westward, we found 2 Nips and killed 1 and probably 2.

But our fire alerted a Nip strong point which unmasked and fired with a rifleman and a HMG. Explosive bullets blasted off 3 and 4 inch trees. Our 3-man point was pinned down. Lt Monroe rushed into the fire, shot dead gunner and sniper. By deliberately drawing fire and taking a wound in the foot, he saved us all. Meanwhile back in C Btry's gun pit, Brener was seriously wounded.

Not until 10 June and after 3 tries, did First Infantry (6 Div) wipe out that strongpoint where Monroe's patrol had almost met disaster.

On 10 June also, Yoshino Force began withdrawing from Toem. Already we had our last casualty; but there were 3 days more of forward observation parties, nerve-racking patrols, and gun-fire against Lone Tree Hill.

On 16 June, after twice beginning to load on a Liberty Ship, we embarked in LST's. We left 4 dead behind us, of 11 total casualties; and we were happy to see the last of shaggy Wakde Island and the flatwooded Toem Foreshore. But we went with pride: our perimeters were impenetrable; we had seen the accuracy of our 105's against Japanese artillery. We had worked our guns and saved lives for three regiments: our Division's 163, 158, and the Sixth's First Infantry.

Our Trip To Japan
By S/Sgt Roy Moyer, M Co. 163

When our outfit moved (from Zamboanga), they were embarked northward. A few days out, they were told they were going to Japan, but that was absolutely the only thing they knew. They were supplied rations and ammo and landed early in the morning in the same way any beach landing was made against expected resistance. **(At that time the war was over, and Japan had surrendered.)** After landing in Japan they deployed and sent out two scouts and proceeded donw the beach toward a distant city.

Now some of this outfit was green, but the NCO's and officers had all been in action before. This was the most eerie time Sgt. Roy Reed ever went through. No one had any idea what was going to happen, if they would be attacked at any moment, if there were mines or booby traps around; in short, they didn't know from nothing. They found a road parallel to the beach, scattered, and moved on the town.

Some distance ahead was a burned out factory and the scouts moved through this (scared as only a scout can be), and found nothing. As the rest moved up, two Japanese soldiers came out of a gate. Every man hit the ditches on both sides of the road. When they took time to look, both Japs were standing at attention. They were saluting.

This story was told to Moyer by Sgt. Roy Reed, Steubenville, Ohio. At the war's end Moyer was rotated home, while Reed went on with M 163 to Japan.

M Co., G Co., 163 Infantry:
Tementoe Creek and Tor River

By Dr. HARGIS WESTERFIELD, Division Historian,
with Lt. JACK ARNOLD

This is the double story of how two fighting 163 Co's helped hold the flanks of the Toem-Arara beachhead beginning 17 May 1944. The less bloody story is that of G Co. at rearguard for 163's left flank on Tementoe Creek. But this is mainly the battle story of M 163 in the vanguard for 163's right flank on the Tor River. For M Co. helped make and hold Tor River bridgehead for 158 Inf's advance against the heavy concentration of Gen. Tagami's 36 Division, which successfully defended Sarmi dromes from three different combat teams.

For both G and M, the landing was easy. While PT boats threw red-ringed shells into silent, shaggy Wakde leftwards, G Co. waded often chest-deep from its LSI, passed 163's security guards at Arara Village, and turned east. Our long green line struck east for Tementoe Creek, which is in the direction of already captured Hollandia, 145 miles eastwards.

Soon G deployed to clear Toem Village. S/Sgt. Murphy shot a Jap to pieces. Hoping for my first shot at a Jap, I still held off firing into a diminishing agitation of brush where we knew that another Jap was fleeing. For Kiselus had shouted not to fire; he had a sudden fear that we might hit a G man by mistake.

Advance G patrols crossed Tementoe Creek, here a sluggish tidal lagoon just before the sea. Our patrols surprised 15 sleeping Nips, killed them as they reached for rifles. One rushed Capt. Reams whose carbine jammed; Buckles' Tommy killed the Jap. Although G patrolled 500 yards east of the Tementoe that afternoon, we found no more Japs.

For the whole Toem Foreshore—my name for the triangular jungle flat between Tementoe Creek and Tor River—was almost undefended. Before D-day, perhaps a single Jap company with a two-gun pln. had secured this Toem Foreshore. Our violent naval preparation drove out these Japs, and on D-day F Co. found only an abandoned Jap 75 mountain gun and signs of recent occupation.

Despite occasional shots at stragglers, G Co. peacefully dug perimeter in the sand with Tementoe Creek a shallow barrier to the east. Gen. Doe sent up field kitchens; cooks served coffee. We had a peaceful sunset of soft colors and even mail delivery before T/Sgt. Wm. "Giant"Harrison called in outguards.

After dark, dud knee-mortar shells hit the sand near our holes. A Nip officer and a sgt. waded the Tementoe; Mayberry's BAR felled them. The wounded officer lay shouting in Japanese, but grenades silenced him.

Later in the black quiet on guard, I heard a Jap voice shout, "Don't shoot that bwa." This was the only time in the war that I hated a Jap; he was crying out in foreign sounds my American words. As ordered, I waked Sgt. Slaga to throw a grenade to quiet him. Probably that same Nip pounded a grenade to arm it on a tree 10 yards before Marsh and Bradley. Their BAR and T/Sgt. Frank Hanson's mortars then made a long silence before our holes.

At dawn, our jaded 3/Pln. was rushed to the beach. There we saw radio operators crouched by their walkie-talkies, and a black cloud of smoke north over low-lying Wakde. A long Jap sgt's body lay full length on the beach beside me. And up the beach to my right, BAR-man Barnes was dead before the dark jungle. Last night, Varney and Barnes had slain four Nips against the skyline, but at dawn Barnes did not turn his BAR to automatic and spray the brush with his BAR. When he stood up, a bullet pierced his brain.

Covered by grenades and BAR, a little knot of fighting men—T/Sgt. Sahs and Varney among them—formed up, fired two clips each and rushed the jungle. They tore four dead Nips from the thicket before them.

That fight over Barnes had called 3/Pln. out before our breakfast. Now starved in midmorning, we found a miracle. Since field kitchens had come up, I ate at a table in luxury—hot cakes and coffee. Acting like a waiter in a restaurant, cook T/4 Virnoche stood at my elbow to press helpings on me.

Next day, on 19 May, G Co. found trouble when clearing the area at dawn. In heavy brush near the shore, Cpl. Louis Gordon took a serious wound. That same Nippo bullet gouged both Aronowitz and Lt. Brandon, our exec, in their forearms. Big Brandon yelled, "He got me!" and pumped 16 carbine bullets into the Nip.

Thus on 18-19 May, while 163's main assault overran Wakde Island, G Co. skirmished at rear-guard on the mainland at Tementoe Creek. We lost just one killed, three wounded. Our losses were light, unlike 3/Bn's losses on the Tor River eight miles west. This is the story of 3/Bn's fight as M Co. men saw it.

As with G, M 163's landing was easy. Wading 25 yards to shore waist-deep in surf, Lt. Jack Arnold noticed three large fires east on Wakde. Into dense jungle, M carried mortars and MG's past abandoned Jap medical equipment and three trucks.

Ahead of M, L's rifles shot at both driver and helper in a truck, but both Japs escaped. And by 1550, Maj. Munkres 3/Bn. dug in on the safe side of the Tor River. (But two of I Co's rifle plns. were recalled next day to unload ships, then sent to secure

> CREDIT. Personal sources are M Co's Lt. Arnold's detailed diary, and my own unpub. "History of G Co." Indispensable also were 163's detailed "Journal 12 May 30 May 1944," 3/Bn. 163 Inf's Morning Reports for May, and Dale Falk's Award Story. Background is from R.R. Smith's Approach to the Philippines, and Gen. MacArthur's Japanese Operations in the SW Pacific, Vol. 1. (I contributed a copy of my G Co. history to Division records in Japan, but it's missing from Fed Archives.) I salute Jack Arnold, who has made vital contributions to five 163 stories.

163rd Infantry leaves Toem for a landing on Wakde. A member of C Co. sent this picture home and wrote: "I don't see how there could be any Japs left alive after the pounding our ships and planes gave the island. But if there were survivors they had to have a lot going thru their minds seeing all those American flags and Yanks."

Niroemar Island 15 miles off Sarmi for an Air Force radar warning station. They did not fight on Tor River.)

Not until 1550 18 May, after Gen. Doe was sure that Wakde was taken, did 3/Bn. get orders that would mean combat. While M covered our advance and 218 FA fired, a 12-man I Co. patrol crossed the Tor and dug in with a section of LMG's as protection. The other men of Lt. Charles Roberts' I pln. crossed soon after. Then his I patrol probed a mile up the beach and found signs of Japs.

Although he had lost Wakde Island, Gen. Tagami of the Jap 36 Division now tried to drive 163 from the Toem Foreshore, which 163 had seized as tactical center for the whole Wakde-Sarmi Operation. Tagami sent most of his 224 Inf. four miles inland to hit the center of our beachhead. And he organized 224 Inf's rear elements to push 3/Bn. back across the Tor.

Our 3/Bn. soon found a number of Japs. When an L patrol hunted west up the beach to "Maffin 1" village, they slew one well-armed Jap, then drew fire from 30 Japs with mortars and MG's. We slew three more. Another Yank patrol pushed inland 6,000 yards to "Maffin 2" village in a loop of the Tor, and found 500 Japs. We reinforced Roberts' Tor bridgehead with all L Co., and a K pln. Ominously, our outposts had a firefight with the Japs just before dusk.

And 20 June on the Tor was a day of battle for 3/Bn. Minutes before dawn, some 20 Japs gathered courage and hit our bridgehead with fixed bayonets. Unluckily, these bayonet men charged directly down a LMG lane on Roberts' left flank. The LMG slew all 20—the last just 10 feet before the LMG.

Across the Tor from Roberts' outpost, Arnold's sections of M Co's HMG's had moved forward inside the bend where the Tor met the sea. Although still east of the Tor, his HMG's now enfiladed the Japs on I Co's right flank. And nearby, Lt. Austin's 81 mm mortars exploded among Japs reorganizing to hit Roberts again.

Reported Yank casualties of 20 June were three killed, three wounded. Missing were a squad leader with his LMG and four more Yanks. Perhaps in that same attack, medic Falk died when he ran from CP safety 20 years off to rescue a wounded man (probably Godfrey) in full view of the Japs. While trying to lift this wounded man into a litter, Falk was shot dead.

While Jap rifles kept firing, Arnold's HMG's covered the crossing of a reinforcing K pln. for Roberts. Lacking effective communications on Roberts' side of the Tor, Arnold cleverly found out his cue to open fire. Whenever Japs or Yank M-1's cut loose, he poured in 150-200 rounds per gun of enfilade fire. Since the fire stopped each time, Arnold thought he had credit for breaking at least two attacks. And M's Austin's 81's blew four Japs into fragments up into a tree.

But one sniper infiltrated between Arnold's HMG's and Austin's 81's. When 81's or HMG's fired, the sniper shot at M under cover of the noise. Arnold sent a killer patrol for the sniper and drew fire, but the sniper escaped.

At 1810 that 20 May, shooting still went on. Although the lost LMG was recovered and the five missing men returned, 20 May was a hard day of battle, with five of ours dead and seven wounded. Besides medic Falk, "I" lost these dead: Boyer, Sgt. Strong and Lt. Roberts—a fine soldier with a direct commission from Sanananda. S/Sgt. Else of K was killed. Besides Godfrey in "I," Prenzler, Henry Scott and Cpl. Roy Swanson were wounded. L Co's wounded were Willie Murphy, T/Sgt. Gibney, and McCoy with a bayonet in the forearm.

But next morning the Japs were gone. Munkres relieved "I" and L with all the K, and a section of M Co's HMG's. About mid-morning, Jap heavy mortars or high angle FA fire hit 3/Bn., but no attack came, although Task Force Hq. had alerted us to face an all-out assault.

Then on 22 May, Col. Moroney ordered L Co. to fight on already conquered Wakde. Die-hard Japs still alive there had kept special troops awake all night. They had lost one officer and two men, in return for five dead Japs. Leaving from the Tor in 3 LCM's, L landed at Wakde and set to work. At 1300 next day, L's Capt. Hooker reported that L had killed eight Japs the day before. We had two prisoners, one a Jap pilot scorched from a flamethrower.

Back at Tor bridgehead, however, 3/Bn's action had slipped into the war of nerves already facing other 163 men in that opaque jungle of the Toem Foreshore. We had two days' quiet, but with insecurity enough to make us nervous. Then at 1455 on 23 May, M got orders to cross the Tor into Jap country. We were to protect 158 Inf., newly landed, and about to push on Sarmi drome.

By 1845, Arnold's HMG's were dug in on the Jap side of the Tor—sitting out there all alone without the riflemen's protection. We had dug in where Roberts had died, with Jap graves all around us. K Co. was miles up the coast with other HMG's of M Co. They had moved out without informing Arnold. After a fearful night, however, M got orders to pull out of 158's battle and return to 163 country across the Tor. It had been a quiet night, but all of 3/Bn. felt better upon rejoining 163. On 23 May, 3/Bn's last man to be wounded was Henry Jones of K Co.

But back at Toem from 24 to 30 May, M Co. with its 3/Bn. endured a war of nerves, especially two nights' wild fighting when Japs attacked the center of the beachhead. Even if the Jap night attack of 27-28 May missed 3/Bn. and hit 163 Hq. and 1/Bn., these were bad nights. On the night of 29 May, 163's MG's were startled into wild firing because of a false alarm.

Finally, on 30 May, M with 3/Bn. was more than jubilant to leave what had become a war of nerves on the Toem Foreshore. Like G Co. on rear-guard at the Tementoe eight miles eastward, M Co. had been almost perfectly safe from the night attacks of the Jap Matsuyama Force of two bns. of 224 Inf. plus one bn. of 36 Division's mountain artillery. And unlike G Co., which must remain behind until 10 June, M gladly said good-by to the jungle flatlands at Toem and headed for Biak. We were unaware of the heavy fighting on Biak that would continue deep into July, but our war on the Toem Foreshore was finished.

163 Infantry Regiment:
War of nerves at Toem

By HARGIS WESTERFIELD, Division Historian

On the Toem Foreshore by captured Wakde Island, 163 Inf fought a war of nerves against the blinding Jap jungle. Our war of nerves was on 23 May-9June after we won Wakde and opened Tor River Bridgehead for 158 Infantry to fight for Sarmi.

While 163 Inf grouped near Toem Village after Wakde, patrols found Jap clews everywhere. But we did not know that Col Soemon Matsuyama's 224 Inf and Col Naoyasu Yoshino's 223 Inf were planning to hit us together and destroy us.

Trouble flared first on 163's eastern flank. Here our 2/Bn had spent every night since 17 May in wet slit trenches of sand on the west bank of Tementoe Creek.

On 23 May before 1140, a 32-man E Co patrol sighted 11 Japs after we had crossed the Tementoe en route to coastal Keber Village. Sgt Peters was shot in his left shoulder. Every try to move farther east drew fire from a small position we could hardly see. We were recalled.

Meanwhile, 8 miles westward, a final K Co patrol across Tor River to Maffin Village No. 1 met Jap fire. Henry M. Jones was hit in chest and neck. When relieving us, an L 158 patrol had a man killed. K Co rejoined 163 Inf at Toem.

On 24 May, G Co's Lt Larson led 28 men to kill 11 Japs "E" saw yesterday—with 4 BARs, a native, and an Indonesian guide called a "NICA," (Netherland Indonesian Colonial Administration).

The native led us after a Jap to a log footbridge across the Tementoe. Halfway across the bridge, our point took the crossfire of 2 Jap LMGs. NICA Freddie Marooch died on the bridge; G Co's Vitosky was shot off into the water with a head wound. Native and a 2/Bn I&R man escaped.

Although wounded and under heavy fire, Vitosky directed our bullets on the Jap positions to cover his return to safety. He even demanded a BAR to fight again, but we had to leave Marooch' body on that bridge. An estimated 20 Japs had fought from that blind jungle. We killed only one.

Our Regiment was facing south of Toem against an opaque wilderness. We saw only a few Japs, but traces were everywhere, in 8 miles of swamp and brush and forest, Tementoe Creek to Tor River. On Vitosky's heroic day, Lts Milder and Leslie reported from a plane, a network of trails south of coastal Masi Masi Village 4.5 miles east of Toem. They rightly surmised that these trails headed a main inland route turning west outside 163's front—a staging ground for Japs.

That night at 1820, a Jap rifleman missed CN Co's Lt Steiner directing fire. On M's front westward, Lt Arnold heard shots and grenade blasts against Jap infiltrators.

At 2030, a small Jap patrol penetrated through booby-traps into a 3-man 163 HQ Co outpost. Shovan challenged; a Jap 2/Lt slashed down on him with a saber. Shovan's tommie slew him, but the saber stroke cut deep into Shovan's neck and shoulder. Waking Levitt had a bayonet-thrust in his right arm. When Shovan's grenade and .45 slugs raked the trail, the other Nips fled. Found on the dead officer were a jammed pistol, 2 grenades, and sketches of our positions.

On 26 May, a 5-man "E" patrol and a NICA guide tried to recover Marooch' body, now on the other side of the Tementoe. Two Jap LMGs repelled us, but with no casualties.

Meanwhile, G Co's 2/Lt Larson's 41-man patrol had outposted to draw Jap attacks across the Tementoe on the coast road. Trading shots with 5 Nips just before dark, we had an eerie night in holes while CN Co's gunners were zeroed in to protect us. After a night of silence, we scouted through Masi Masi Village, full of pillboxes but deserted. This nervous patrol ended with no casualties.

On 27 May, E's Capt Zimmerman and 67 men forced a crossing of that log bridge over Tementoe Creek, probably after H Co's .81 mortars' preparation. After vicious skirmishing, the Japs retreated 100 yards and stopped us. They killed E's Moxey with a bullet in the back, wounded H's Holbrook. S/Sgt Newman crawled up under fire, then stood to shoot down Japs. After 2 Nips died, "E" moved forward and drove the Japs farther back, while S/Sgt Muchmore risked himself to draw Moxey's body over a log. We saved bodies of Moxey and NICA Marooch.

E's men found only empty fox-holes, and no LMGs. Despite their minor defeat, these Tementoe Japs had successfully screened us from locating 224 Inf's bivouacs. This Matsuayama Force was coiled a few miles south of us in the jungle—ready to strike that very night of 27 May.

On 27 May after 4 days' patrols, 163 Inf should have readied for Matsuyama's charges in formidable perimeters. We may have been off-guard because vigilant Gen Doe was gone on 25 May to Hollandia to assist in the invasion of Biak. Our temporary commander was 158 RCT's Brig-Gen Edwin D. Patrick. Even on 30 May, 3 days after our attack, Patrick still believed that the Japs were concentrated against 158 Inf far east of Tor River.

Matsuyama's attack in early dusk could have been a 163 disaster. Except for 2/Bn in holes on the Tementoe, tents were up almost everywhere. "D" and "M" had slung hammocks. "A" was short 100 men unloading a ship—sent down unarmed!

About 2000 after a red alert where a Jap plane bombed Wakde, Matsuyama struck. Knee mortars hit 163 Hq and 1/Bn from the dark. Our booby-traps blew; Jap grenades impacted. Suicidal killers charged with 3 grenades wired on their bodies to explode together.

Our fire detonated the suicide grenadiers before they neared us. But by 2005, C's Schneekloth was hit in right shoulder. A fragment took Schoening in the chin.

Perhaps C's line held in the first attack, but by 2030, Buck had died from a bullet in the head, and Gilkinson from a bullet in the abdomen. Jap riflemen had broken C's line.

Screaming Japs burst into 163 Hq. They cut off some staff officers and other CP personnel—unarmed and out of their holds—in a CP tent. Luckily, the Japs missed them in the dark. With fixed bayonets, Japs struck 163's Medics' hospital with disarmed patients, but all patients could walk. Medics saved everyone. (Some time that night, a steel fragment slashed Medic Frye in his right cheek.)

Dug in a Message Center, radioman Norman and phone-central Belenky could not run. When 13-14 Japs charged with bayonets, they shot rapid fire—killed 1, diverted others.

Maybe 200 Japs had breached our lightly held lines. Of these, some 100 attacked 1/Bn's motor pool to blow it up. But from a slit trench, 4 blazing M-1s stopped them. The motor pool chief, S/Sgt Burton, S/Sgt Engbretson, T/4 Switzer, and T/5 Donakowski piled up 13 Jap dead, their last corpses 2-20 feet from the trench. Burton got a bayonet

B-163 men in action at Wakde.

through his shirt. Found on Jap bodies, maps located all staff installations and AA beach positions.

Despite this confusion, 163 Inf riposted professionally. In Hq Co, S/Sgt Cox rallied 20 men for a new defense line, while S/Sgt Knight flanked our line with a .50 HMG. Then they buttressed a weak section of the perimeter.

C Co made an important move. Guided by Schoening, who was cut off in the dark and wounded but still at the phone in his hole, "C" counter-attacked. We reoccupied our frontline holes, linked up with "B" on our right, and "D" on our left.

"C" lost more wounded in the forward holes. About 2100, Limpert caught a fragment in the left knee; Prerost was shot in right arm and left knee. Spear had fragments in right and left legs (time unspecified) and died of wounds 30 May. Although not in a forward hole, T/5 Lindsay was hit by a fragment in his right leg at 2130.

No more Jap attacks came through after midnight, but sporadic rifle fire continued until daybreak. Last wounded was Bystrek at 0500, with a shot in his left ear.

According to available reports, main Jap impact in 163 Inf was against "C," 1/Bn Hq, and 163's Hq Co. But "D" and "B" and "A" had minor parts in the night attacks. (We know very little about A Co 116 Engrs' own bloody fight.)

Without their HMGs posted and being short of ammo, D Co kept pretty quiet on C Co's left. Seriously wounded was T/Sgt Lygren with fragments in cheek, ear, and shoulder. A Jap came through near the hole of Lawler, Pinkley, and probably Sgt Curran. The Sgt dropped the Jap, who later crawled away because they could not spare a grenade to finish him. At dawn, Lawler killed a Jap withdrawing 50 yards away—Lawler's first kill in his career.

In "B," Sedal died, circumstances unreported. In A Co's street, Japs set up a LMG and sprayed the tents, but hit no one. (On Arara Beach, Engrs guarded 100 men of our port detail.) Although cut off on outpost, A's Einboden, Denny, LaRoue, and Hill were safe in the dark.

In M Co, Lt Arnold heard that A Co 116 Engrs killed 17 Japs, half a mile down the road. There 6 Engrs died, with 2 seriously wounded. Gunshots killed 5 men. Renkel and T/5 Zelesniker were hit in the chest, T/5 Mossman in the head. T/5 Russ Larsen was struck in head and chin; T/5 Wilde in the pelvis. T/5 Eichenlaub died from a fragment in left arm. Besides these dead, Robertson was wounded in the jaw, Jim Thomas in the groin—both gunshot wounds. Nothing more is known of A 116 Engrs' fight.

Matsuyama's uncompleted attack could have been 163's major disaster, but he made comparatively few casualties. His total kill was 4 163 Inf men, 6 Engrs of A 116. Wounded were 7 163 men, 2 Engrs, 1 Medic mentioned already. Probably 2 more Medics were casualties that night: T/3 Middleton killed by a shot in the chest, T/Sgt Duff wounded by a shot in right shoulder. Our Regiment counted 18 dead Japs, found 11 new graves outside perimeters, and suspected that other casualties were carried off.

That morning, many bullet-holed tents looked like sieves; looted barracks-bags gaped in the streets. Outside perimeter, an F Co patrol was the only one to fight Japs. Meeting 15, "F" received fire from rifles and an automatic weapon, killed 2 Japs. Patrolling SW 2100 yards on a much-used trail, "K" men found a small bivouac with bloodied clothes. "B" scouted a new-cut trail 1200 yards south of Arare but

> CREDIT: This was a hard story to write because I had to gather story of 163's night fight of 27-28 May in little bits everywhere. Personal sources include D Co's Sgt William Lawler's memoirs, diaries of M's Lt Jack Arnold, H's Sgt Harold Ingle, Westerfield's history of G Co, anonymous history of A Co. Indispensable were 163's 40-page journal of 12-30 May 1944, RR Smith's Approach to the Philippines, 163's May 1944 Morning Report. Important also was Gen Douglas MacArthur's Japanese Operations in SW Pacific. G Co's Capt Arthur Braman gave me G Co's handwritten petition which was basis of Vitosky's medal award. Other medal awards I used were those of Shovan, Newman, Muchmore, Norman, Belenky, Cox, McKnight. Burton himself told me his story about his night fight—interview at Canton, Ohio about 1968.

saw no Japs. Yet Japs were 3 miles south of us in deep jungle.

About 9 June, the last 163 men left for Biak. We still remember Toem Foreshore as a spooky place, despite fairly easy casualties—15 dead, 26 wounded to hospital, 1 missing, later reported as dead. We remember too well, blinded patrols in flat jungle; lurid nights of fire in the coconut aisles; the threat of Jap assasins against laxly fortified lines. Such was Toem Foreshore's War of Nerves for 163 Inf.

And 163's war of nerves intensified. Bulldozers cleared fire-fields; MGs and barbed wire now guarded our front. News came that 158 Inf was defeated across Tor River.

Two nights later, our nervous, unrested front exploded in wild farce. An M1 and a carbine fired in 1/Bn; then almost every MG and some mortars blasted out. One could nearly read by light of our fire, but no Japs attacked. Accidentally killed was M Co's Wall, shot through the head. For reasons unknown, A 116's Sgt McNutt died with a head wound; A 116's John D Brown was missing in action, later reported dead. T/5 Schultz of 2/Bn Hq had fragments in neck and left arm. K Co's Vasquez threw a grenade which hit a tree and rebounded to blow off his left hand.

On 30 May, most 163 men embarked to reinforce our 41st on Biak, but 2/Bn, CN Co, and most of SV Co stayed to secure 158 Inf. Gen Patrick needed us until 6 Div replaced battered 158 Inf.

For us, the war of nerves continued. By 30 May, Gen Patrick had learned nothing from 163's night fight of 28 May. He believed that only roving bands of Japs were south of Toem; actually, 200 organized Japs were within 3 miles of our coast. Patrick's command was scattered in beach detachments that Japs could destroy in detail. For 5.5 miles from Tementoe Creek west to Maffin Village No. 1 across the Tor, were 21 different perimeters. Six were unsupported AA emplacements spread wide to catch low-flying Jap planes.

This time, Yoshino's 224 Inf struck. They hit 4 isolated AA emplacements between Arare and Unnamed River, in the middle of Toem Foreshore.

They overran 2 AA positions, damaged a multiple .50 and two .40 mm guns. They turned a captured .50 HMG on B Co 158 Inf and charged it. They killed 12 of us and wounded 10, and left 52 Japs dead, when they withdrew at 0430. Meanwhile, 163's 2/Bn lay safe in holes where we had slept since 17 May, when 163 landed. And Col Yoshino's was the final attack on Toem Foreshore. On 10-12 June, all battered Jap formations crossed Tor River, to fight again outside 163's sector.

Our 2/Bn's war of nerves continued awhile longer, where we were entrenched near the graveyard where H's Ingle counted 179 graves by 4 June. On 5 June, we had 7 H Co men seriously wounded; a 105 shell from 158's 147 FA hit H's mortar position. Smiley died of the wound in his left leg. Sgt Motheral's left ankle was amputated. S/Sgt Little slashed in right arm and back, LaCoste in right arm, Levandosky in upper left thigh. Stabach was hit in left knee, 1/Lt Flamm in left ankle.

COL. HANEY FORCES PARAI DEFILE

By DR. HARGIS WESTERFIELD, Research Historian-
and General Harold E. Haney

Main cause for 162's near disaster those first 3 days on Biak, was Gen Douglas MacArthur's sudden change in orders. At first, he planned to use the whole 41st to capture Wakde and Sarmi. Then by 10 May, MacArthur realized that Sarmi terrain was unfit for a heavy bomber base. He cancelled the Sarmi attack, but ordered 162 and 186 RCTs to seize Biak, leaving Wakde Island to 163 RCT.

When orders crashed down on 162, Col Haney had no chance to confer with the Navy about support fire. At Hollandia, Haney had an assistant operations officer on the Naval control ship to interpret his firing requests. But for Biak, Haney merely heard that a Naval party would be attached. Without previous understanding after close conferences, 162 was in jeopardy. Any accident could cut communications. Our own Navy could even fire on us.

So even before 162 landed, Haney had trouble built in. And when 162 did land, 27 May 1944, a current the Navy had not charted made more trouble. The current drove 186 to land closer to Mokmer Drones than 162, which Gen Fuller had ordered to make the crucial advance. Time was already running out, and Col Newman suggested 186 move on the Dromes immediately.

But Gen Fuller insisted that 162 and 186 countermarch on the narrow foreshore under the Japs' noses. Disaster threatened then, but Japs, crouched on Ibdi ridges, had no orders to drive our scrambled companies into the sea.

And on 27 May 1944, 162's tense, sleepless column of sweaty, green-clad riflemen pushed westward, under rising morning heat. Tall, jungle-covered ridges closed in on our right, beyond the straggling native huts of Ibdi. The ridges became a weathered wall of limestone cliffs, shouldering us into the reefs, toward our vigilant destroyers offshore.

About 1115, Lt Folsom's crack I&R platoon fired at a Jap squad withdrawing west. After Navy fire, we brought up 5 tanks of 603 Tank Co. With Navy guns and an Army LCI firing rockets, we fought Japs at 1235, at 1400, then at 1450 — at which time our tanks blasted Jap MGs in pillboxes at the cliff base. We had 1 KIA, 5 WIA against 16 Jap dead. The dark jungle cliffs of this narrow Parai Defile had helped Japs of 3/Bn 222 Inf and 14 Division Shipping Unit to fight a successful delaying action.

Meanwhile Col Haney tried to widen 162's narrow dangerous battle front. Earlier, he planned to advance 2/Bn through the ridges to protect 3/Bn's right. But 2/Bn found no Japs up the steep Young Man's Trail at Ibdi. Haney recalled 2/Bn to move down the coast on 3/Bn's left flank, and left only E Co to advance along the cliff-tops above 3/Bn. E Co found no Japs in that blind scrub jungle of upheaved coral, and could not keep up with the march. Haney had E Co rejoin 2/Bn. He was already minus Cn and AT Cos on port details.

Haney tried again to widen 162's front. He gave an early order for 1/Bn to find an embarkation point for buffaloes, to move men around our seaward flank, and cut off Japs opposing 3/Bn. Division refused his request. He could only send B Co to seek a trail on the ridges. B found no trail.

That night, Haney lay sleepless. The Japs held Parai Defile where demolitions and defenses in depth could not make it impregnable. But tomorrow, the Japs had to fight. And how could Haney deploy 162, on a front wide enough to let us fight 162's estimated 4400 Japs (actually 11400)?

Tomorrow, he would hurry 3/Bn down the shore to where flat land widened out. Then he would wheel 2/Bn NW into the flats, and 3/Bn would take Mokmer Strip.

But on 28 May, Haney had no chance to deploy 162. Only the first hour went well. Japs blocked K about 0830, but tanks and the Navy's destroyers drove them back. Jap 81s fell near our LCI rocket ship and LCMs off Mokmer Village. From above Mokmer Drome, a "coast-defense gun" dropped projectiles near our destroyers. (Perhaps the shells were from Mt Hodai's concealed 105s.) Yet K Co led on until Mokmer Dromes were 200 yards away.

Now lurking Nip observers phoned their gunners our precise moves. Beside piled shells, Jap mortarmen stood to. Below, K led I forward. L Co, with M Co HMGs, pushed toward the limestone terrace on the right flank. Some 1200 yards back, G Co led 2/Bn to secure our right flank against those threatening cliffs.

Then Jap MGs sealed off K's front with a live wall of crackling brush. Dashing up to help K Co, I Co angrily recoiled from this deadly wall. Behind us, Jap fire cut the coastal road. On the terrace to the right, Jap 81s, then a wedge of Jap riflemen severed L and M from 3/Bn. Casualties accumulated — with no way of evacuation. Medics shouted for plasma. Then G tried to take 2/Bn up on the right to guard 162 from those deadly cliffs. Tremendous Nip fire stopped G, then cut off G, with many casualties.

Jap mortars kept thundering down on 3/Bn pinned in brush below Parai Cliffs. The shells fell literally like rain-drops, according to I's 1/Sgt Kelley. The Bn now took HMG fire, then grenade-launcher blasts and rifle-fire — and at 1010 a howling Jap attack. We shot that attack into the ground. And L and M found a covered way to rejoin 3/Bn — except for an L Ptn that had to fight back to join 1/Bn at Mokmer Village. G Co fought free to contact 2/Bn again. But 3/Bn still shuddered under mortar blasts. Surrounded on 3 sides, 3/Bn was short of men. Along with an M HMG Ptn, we had to use AT's Mine Ptn to guard our rear.

Coming up with his command party some 800 yards west of Mokmer Village, Col Haney saw his battle going badly. West, he saw his 3 tanks shake with gunfire against unseen Nips. West and NW, Jap guns, mortars, MGs, rifles were crashing. And from NE, he heard automatic fire around 2/Bn, from which no messages came in. Behind, near Mokmer Village, Jap mortars barraged.

Jap fire forced Haney's CP into beachside sumps. We fought futilely to kill Jap support fire on the ridges. 146 FA could not reach positions to hit Jap guns and mortars in caves and defiles facing seaward. But Haney and 162 Hq CO Reed turned binoculars on cliffs where heavy Jap mortars coughed. By 1200 they had data through to 3/Bn Hq to enable the destroyers to blast at what we now know as East Caves.

But destroyers' guns never killed East Caves' mortars. About 1200, Japs slew our naval officer with 3/Bn. Communications fell apart. Requests for naval fire must now go through channels — up to Task Force Hq — down to ships — through 6 different CPs at least. Fire became sporadic. Sloppy planning paid off in death.

Failing naval aid, Haney had to shift CP back from immediate danger and battle noise which hampered messages. Capt Robt Read risked himself to bring Haney a reserve tank for safe transportation.

The tank gave Haney a jarring ride, with Jap MGs stripping the tank clean. (But our mortars pinned down Jap AT men.) Reaching rear CP, Haney pleaded vainly for a new Naval party. He fought East Caves with 81s, 4.2s, 105s, 155s, but uselessly. Jap automatic fire continued.

At best, we could suppress East Caves' mortars, but when we silenced them, mortars from north and west began to fire. Their weapons could cut 3/Bn's supply road at will.

Haney called Gen Fuller for help, and Chief of Staff Col Kenneth Sweany arrived that afternoon. On Sweany's advice, Fuller ordered 3/Bn to leave its forward amphitheater of death. Despite FA and 4 tanks' flank protection, 3/Bn retreated under intermittent fire 2000 yards, to where it dug in under 2/Bn's protection. We had 16 KIA, 87 WIA and evacuated. And without supporting elements' help, 162 claimed 101 Jap dead by our own hands.

On 29 May, third day, Col Kuzume attacked. Beginning 0700, he struck 3 times — first with infantry, then with tanks and infantry. Our tanks killed all 7 Jap tanks and helped 2/Bn shatter the infantry.

Haney perceived that Kuzume had repeated what 162 did yesterday. Kuzume tried to come down the slot between East Caves and the sea on a narrow front. Results were brutal and fatal. Both COs learned lessons. Neither could kill the other's support weapons. But Kuzume could look down on us like fish in a tub and pound us continuously with mortars.

While another Jap attack on our right flank briefly cut off 162, Haney again asked for Fuller's help at Parai, and Col Sweany came. Haney said 162 had 3 choices. First, with adequate naval fire and other regiments guarding communications, he could advance with all 162. Second, 162 could hold ground, but pile up casualties. Third, 162 could retreat to Ibdi Village.

Sweany said that he could not assure naval support. The whole division was already committed — with 163 still at Wakde. He left the decision to Haney.

And Haney had the courage to admit defeat under impossible conditions. Despite his feeling of failure at 162's wasted gallantry, he chose withdrawal.

But how could Haney quickly extricate 162 from Parai Defile? We had to leave before Kuzume's new fire plans would seal off Parai Road. And U.S. military schools had taught but little on getting away.

Then Haney remembered what a World War II Chief of Staff had told him on retreating — and without the clack of a typewriter.

Haney called 4 staff officers — 162's Exec. and a man for each Bn. He told those 3 to stick with their Bns throughout the retreat. While Lt Col Wayne Bailey, Exec, assembled amphib craft, Capt Lawrence Crampton, Adj, helped with evacuating wounded and hospital medics. Probably Lt Col Paul Hollister, Mjr Paul Cawlfield, and Capt David Fowler took retreat orders to the bns. At 1350, Haney gave the command to execute the retreat, and within 10 minutes, all 162 moved east.

While 2/Bn (less G) and L with a Ptn of I left by water, rest of 162 hiked the muddy, war-torn road. Led by 1/Ptn of 603 Tank Co, both 3/Bn and 1/Bn struck east. Although 641 TD's 1/Ptn had to destroy 2 mortars and ammo, 2/Ptn saved its mortars. Along with 2/Ptn, 603 Tanks, 116 Engrs' detachment brought up the rear. Besides FA support, there hovered offshore a naval Rocket LCI, and 542 EB&SR's 2 Amphib tanks and their AA LCM.

To select positions at Ibdi, Haney boarded an LVT, but its engine failed 800 yards off shore. Haney saw Japs wheel a mountain gun atop Parai Ridge. It ranged shots on LCTs and wounded men at Parai Jetty.

Vengefully, Haney manned the LVT's 50. A former Chief of Heavy Weapons 2 years at Benning, he began firing the HMG. But an Amphib Engr boat — perhaps the AA LCM — demolished the Jap cannon. After 15 minutes' delay, the LVT engine was started up, took Haney to Ibdi where he put his bns to digging in as they arrived. Including 2 WIA when planes strafed close to 2/Bn at rear guard, 162 had 16 KIA, 96 WIA, 3 injured 29 May 1944.

Such were 162's first 3 days on Biak. Through no fault of ours, we came near annihilation. MacArthur's sudden change of plans; the failure to organize naval support, started us wrong. Because it could not chart the offshore current, the Navy scrambled our landing on an enemy shore. Then 186 and 162 had to countermarch unnecessarily with armed Japs on top of them. When Haney was shoved into the Defile, his sagacious request to widen his front with a seaborn landing was denied. These 5 errors were major causes of 162's losses in 3 days — 33 dead, 188 WIA, and 3 injured. And 162 came near being wiped out.

Yet Col Haney had done well. He mauled Kuzume's 222 Inf in the Japs' pyrrhic victory. He killed most of the Jap tanks; the last 2 or 3 would not fight again until the last days of battle. And Haney had instilled within every company of 162, a morale which enabled his men to come back, with the offensive that finally broke the Jap army on Biak.

> Prime source is Gen Haney's MS, "First 3 Days at Parai Defile" plus Ltrs 14 Apr, 20 June 1969. RR Smith's, APPROACH TO PHILIPPINES AND REPORT OF GEN MacARTHUR/JAPANESE OPERATIONS IN SWPA, give background; 162 Journal supplies details. Sidelights are from 1/Sgt M.H. Kelley's "I Co 162 Inf: Parai Defile and Mokmer Ridges" (JUNGLEER, Nov 1965). I also used Medal Award stories of Lt Col Wayne Bailey and Lt Col Paul Hollister; Mjr Paul Cawlfield, and Capts Lawrence Crampton, David Fowler, Robert E Read, and Alfred Coffey — the last decorated for his S-2 performance. Gen Haney lives in a seaside mansion at St Augustine, Fla., and decided to write his story after a visit from Mrs. Westerfield and me.

Col. SWEANY, Gens. COANE, FULLER, MacARTHUR.

M Co. 162 Infantry:
Machine-gunners in Parai Defile

by DR. HARGIS WESTERFIELD, Division Historian
and S/SGT. LOUIS BOTTA

About 0900 27 May 1944, M Co. 162 in LCTs crashed over coral reefs through high surfs onto Biak. Some of us jumped off ramps into water over our heads. Almost drowning, First Section's Gunner No. 2 let go his HMG under water and lost it. Section Leader Sgt. Williams stripped and dived 3-4 times but failed to recover it. Yet Botta's MG squad landed safely; Botta even kept his box of 50 White Owl cigars dry. "M" pushed at once for Mokmer Strip, far downshore.

Despite heavy equipment, M Co. moved fast. First Gunner Moore carried the 52-lb. tripod, and Second Gunner Waltemeyer the 44-lb. gun. Shephard, Bauser, Barry, Biancomanno, Muscatello, Reynolds, Botta, Watkins and 2 more men each bore two 40-lb. ammo boxes, with carbines. Along with equipment, gunners had .45s, and Sgt. W.L. Jackson his M-1 and binoculars.

Beached east of Mandom, we passed Ibdi at 1030. As left-flank guard, Botta first saw what then seemed beautiful vertical Parai Cliffs, pink and gray and green. Maybe 2,000 yards long, they fronted a pretty crescent of sand. About 180 feet high, they curved SW around Soanggarai Bay, rising abruptly from coastal rain-forest. Richer, greener forest topped them. A dark gap centered the most prominent line of sheer cliffs. Two tree-lines on their sides marked the 2 lines of galleries that Japs could fire from. M Co. walked unaware into an open-jawed death-trap.

This first day, "M" worked half-way through Parai Defile while Navy and tanks helped 162 clear away light Jap forces. Jap rifles halted us just before the plank bridge over the stream from the cliff half way down the Defile. We withdrew about a mile to perimeter near the beach.

Next morning, 28 May, M's machine-gunners fought in one of the 41st's hardest battles of the war. While some "M" men fought for "K" and "L" far past the Defile near Mokmer Village, Botta and other MG men slogged down the road to the stream. As the road curved to the bridge, we lost our first man—Boothby wounded by plunging fire of a sniper on high cliffs east of the gap. Some "L" men were wounded here also.

From 180 feet above, rifle fire pinned us below the Nips' great stone fortress. Even 250-lb. Maj. Hollister dived and rolled into cover. A few grenades cracked down also.

Nip fire narrowly missed Botta shooting back with his carbine. On that dizzy height in their camouflage, Japs looked like small trees in motion. They were hard to hit.

From his difficult position against the cliffs, Botta's 2 carbine clips missed the snipers. Then 2 riflemen pointed up, aimed a long time, fired together. A sniper fell from the height and hurtled down the cliff with terrifying screams. We hoped that he was the Nip who shot Boothby.

Then a MG in a hidden pillbox fired down on our riflemen and silenced them. Sgt. Moe Jackson's impatient MGs got orders to fire. First gunner Moore slanted his gun for the cliff-edge and traversed slowly in short bursts of 6. His 2 belts (500 rounds) clipped the cliff and impacted the pillbox.

Yet when Moore ceased fire, the Nip MG fired a short

PARAI DEFILE comprised a series of seven sharp coral ridges, the crests of which were 50-75 yards apart and separated by gullies 50-100 feet deep. These separate ridges were honeycombed with small natural caves, potholes, and crevices. There was little soil on most of the coral, yet the area maintained a cover of dense rain forest containing trees 8-20 inches thick and 100-150 feet high.

burst down on us. Moore withdrew to give our .81mm mortars room to fire. Fifty shells lobbed over the high cliffs—and 50 more on the pillbox. Its MG fired again, a challenge to try to pass down the road.

We then cleared the area for our P-38s to batter this cliff fortress. For over an hour, they bombed and strafed. The high cliff flamed like a volcano, but the MG still struck from that pillbox.

Yet the high cliff and hidden pillbox quieted enough for "L" with "M" to bypass them, although we crouched and looked up over our right shoulders and prayed as we passed.

While I and K Cos. pressed up the beach road past Mokmer Village, "L" with M Co. crews had to protect their right flank from the Jap cliffs. We had to advance parallel to them along a cliff terrace about 500 yards wide and 1.5 miles long, with 2/Bn. following us.

This great terrace began with a cliff 15-20 feet before us. Japs lightly held it, and no one knew what was in the rainforest on the cliff-summit above.

Botta helped clear the terrace with his HMG. While an "L" officer observed with binoculars, Botta fired slowly and carefully along the terrace for some 15 minutes. About 250 rounds chopped trees and bushes from the stone terrace.

Then an "L" scout quickly climbed up to the terrace and tied a heavy rope around a tree. Up the rope, "L" men climbed and shot down the Nip opposition with their rifles. (Botta's HMG got credit for a few Nips also.)

Then "M" weapons men scaled the rope also with their heavy killing tools and ammo boxes. Maj. Hollister stood at the rope-end and helped our men up with 40-50 pounds of gear. He braced us to press against the cliff and lever ourselves up.

Once on that terrace, Botta saw 2 dead "L" men as they had knelt to fire and win it. One man still gripped his M-1. There were 10-12 dead Nips also.

Heaving aside the dead Nips, we tried to dig in on the coral—heaped up large loose rocks for protection. While we waited for orders, we did not realize the trap we were in.

Suddenly Jap mortars cracked down, then MGs. L Co. scouts said that they saw Nippo tanks warming up their engines. We had to save ourselves.

With Lattimore beside him, Southard dodged behind a tree. Several more men dropped behind a large pack, but probably Coffman was down in the open. This tall man of 6-3 was the only one hit, however. MG bullets scraped his left foot, almost shot the pack off his back. His steel entrenching shovel deflected bullets and saved his life.

Meanwhile malarious Sgt. W.L. Jackson was wounded and perhaps in shock. He ordered us to leave him because he could not move. But still leader of Botta's MG section, he told Botta not to forget our ammo and water, and waved good-bye. It was 34 years before Botta found that Jackson was not killed.

Our retreat off the terrace was still fairly orderly. We dropped tripod and ammo boxes, but saved the more delicate gun by slinging it down in an old ammo belt. "M" and "L" did wait their turns on the rope we had climbed. M's Hurt, for example, dived off the cliff, caught a branch, swung on it like a trapeze, then dropped to the ground beneath. In his last leap, Botta hit head on into a staggering "L" wounded man and broke his own nose. Cowering under fallen trees from a Jap LMG, and staunching his bleeding, broken nose, Botta saw our wounded run. Two "M" men even dove into the ocean.

About the time when the mortars impacted "M" and "L" men on the terrace, a Jap infantry attack cut us off from 2/Bn. advancing behind us. Probably from a crevice in the cliff on our right flank, a Jap command infiltrated through the brush and charged Sgt. Batcha's HMG crew, which was looking ahead for orders. Batcha was struck to die of wounds later, but the squad fought for its life with .45s and carbines. The Jap officer fell. California Indian Joaquin manhandled the HMG into position and blasted into the Japs and repelled them when only 20 yards away.

Perhaps in this same Jap attack, other M Co. gunners fought hand-to-hand. T/Sgt. Wm. A. Brown, Sgt. White, and Cpl. Loyal fired small arms but had no time to reload. They clubbed their guns and went in fighting and defeated their Japs.

Before dark, we dug our circle of fox-holes in a beautiful coconut grove near the beach. Botta hoped for a quiet night, but Capt. Bland warned that Jap attacks were certain.

Screaming from the night, 2 Japs leaped into a hole near Botta where Salamaua vets Chappy and Harder were crouched. One Nip died from a .45; the other was wounded. He crawled towards Botta on the HMG and pleaded, "Don't shoot, Joe!" Botta kindly did not shoot; he twisted his grenade pin loose and

East Caves Area where 162d Infantry first encountered the Japanese.

heard the "crack" as it armed. He lobbed it gently into the Nip, who screamed once more before he died.

Then suddenly we heard maybe 3 Nippo planes overhead. We hoped that they would ignore us, but suddenly the air was full of screaming and whistling, louder and louder as maybe 6 bombs fell. Flattened in his hole, Botta felt that all the bombs were aimed at him. Finally they exploded close to the perimeter edge. Rocks, dirt, and hot flying shrapnel rained on us while Botta pressed his face under his helmet into the ground. Dingman was killed. Next day, Botta inspected craters 20 feet wide and 15 feet deep.

On that disastrous 28 May, "M" lost only 2 dead but had 15 wounded. Batcha and Dingman were dead. Barkway, Hobbs, Jessap, Cpl. Kendsorn, T/Sgt. Wm. Brown were marked seriously wounded. Besides Boothby, men lightly wounded were Moscatello, Les Davis, Franscisco, George Jackson, Rudd, Lattimore, Periello, Judith, Cpl. Adams, Sgts. W.L. Jackson and King. (It is not absolutely certain that all of these 17 casualties were on 28 May, when records were hard for company clerks to keep. And except for Boothby, and Sgts. Dingman, Batcha, and Jackson, we cannot find out which of the men fought with "I" and "K" near Mokmer Village ahead, or were back with "L" on the terrace.)

HISTORY CREDIT No. 114

CREDIT: Supreme narrator is Louis Botta, whom Mike Trapman of Potomac Chapter brought to me. Answering my queries, he wrote to me 15 June, 2 and 26 July (twice), 9, 30, 31 Aug. (twice), 14 Sept., and 2 Oct.—besides a sketch of the Defile. I used 2 other Jungleer stories—Col. Haney's (March, 1970), and T/Sgt. Bill Brown's of L Co. (March, 1969). Archives include 162's Narrative, Journal, Handbook, and Casualty List with Joaquin's Award Story, and Terrain Handbook No. 27. R.R. Smith's Approach to the Philippines was also useful.

On 29 May, our third day in Parai Defile, the Japs tried to drive 162 into the sea. After 2/Bn. smashed an infantry attack at 0700, they made a tank-infantry attack which became the first tank battle in the SW Pacific.

While "M" marched back through a stately coconut grove, Botta had not seen 2 Nip tanks coming at us 500 yards away, but suddenly he saw one of our 2 waiting tanks revolving its 75mm gun turret. This tank was aptly named "Murder Inc.," and it fired and halted the last Jap tank dead in its tracks to block Parai Road. Already flattened in the sand, M Co. saw "Murder Inc." turn its turret and fire again. The second tank halted and burned; we saw a half-burned Jap corpse hanging half out of the top hatch door. (All told, 6 Jap tanks died that day.) Botta said that the light Jap tanks looked like Vokswagens as contrasted to our medium General Sherman tanks that seemed like monsters.

About 1100 in trying to drive the Japs from their cliff-tops, our Navy shattered us instead. M Co. calmly watched the destroyer firing, but a "short," probably a 6-inch shell, exploded in 3/Bn. Our 162 Hq. reported 5 killed, 31 wounded, "by 1 salvo." As Capt. Bland ordered us to leave that ground, young Drigert called for help. He was hit in the ankle. Botta carried Drigert 500 yards to where Medics bandaged him and Drigert waved goodbye.

Evidently that same shell wounded Southard and T/4 Jack Meyer. From the explosion 200 feet away, a fragment seriously wounded Meyer, prone with malaria at 104 degrees. His temperature dropped to normal! As the shell landed, Southard was reaching high on a native shack to pull off a pole to cover his new fox-hole. A fragment sliced off half his wrist joint and caused amputation of his left hand. The buffalo evacuating him stuck on a reef, but another craft pushed it free to transfer him to a larger craft which took him to the hospital.

On that third day also, Botta's HMG crew again had a close call from another small Jap attack. But we beat them back with carbines. And that night an air-bomb killed Lentz.

"M" had fewer losses than yesterday, on 28 May. Besides Lentz killed, and Southard, Meyer, and Drigert wounded, we had 5 others wounded, 1 injured. Marked "seriously wounded" were Parker and Weldon. Lightly wounded were Hamman, Hardesty, Quill Smith—and Stanfield injured.

By 1200 our third day in Parai Defile, Col. Haney realized that we could not silence the Jap cliffs to enable us to capture Mokmer Strip. As Haney said, "Col. Kuzume could pound us like fish in a tub." By 1400, 162's great retreat was on. Some men of "M" probably left by water with "L" from Parai Jetty; but M's fighters from the terrace slogged up the Defile again. That night, we holed up far east of Parai, on the coast behind Mandom.

As it also happened to 162's other companies of 3/Bn. and 2/Bn., M Co's weapons crews narrowly escaped annihilation. But in June, a few days later, we would return again to fight the Japs in the tall, beautiful, deadly cliffs of Parai Defile.

641 Tank Destroyer Battalion:
Rear guard action at Parai

By Dr. HARGIS WESTERFIELD, Division Historian,
with Captains BENNETT M. SAUNDERS and J. RICHARDS GERTTULA

The giant 4.2 mortars of D Co. 641 Tank Destroyer Bn. were crucial weapons in rescuing 162 Inf. from the Parai Defile disaster on Biak. Fighting rear guard in Parai Defile, we mortarmen battled for 162 to the last 4.2 shell that we could fire. As ordered, we destroyed six of our mortars and retreated.

But before we tell you about combat in Parai Defile, we ought to explain to you the operation of the 4.2 and detail our first action at Hollandia. For even old-timers with the .81 mortar may not know the operation of the 4.2's and their good and bad points.

Best points of the 4.2's were their rifled barrels and their long range. Unlike the smooth bores of other mortars, these rifled barrels spun the big shells into distant targets with great accuracy. Each 25-lb. shell contained some 8.5 pounds of TNT, or as much white phosphorus. Using "instant" fuze, the shell could clear a 30-foot area covered by 6-inch trees. Capt. Saunders said that the shell left the 30-foot area clean as kitchen linoleum.

Of course, the 4.2 had its bad points. Worst of these was the weight. Barrel weighed 90 pounds. Supporting rod ("standard") with its recoil spring in a cylinder weighed 75 lbs. Third and heaviest part was the base plate of 150 lbs. Total weight was 315 lbs. Theoretically, we could hike with it, in a carrying party of six: a man for the barrel, a man for the standard, and two for the base plate, which had handles. Two men could carry two shells each in double pouches on their shoulders. Each shell in its case weighed 40 lbs.

Naturally, the hand-carrying party was impractical for distances, especially in the tropics. And the GI heavy weapons cart was too frail for 315 pounds of mortar — and useless in sand or swamp. And we lacked a jeep motor pool.

Another bad point was the peculiar construction of the traverse mechanism; it did not turn the barrel according to the calibration. We had to learn to change angle of fire by dead reckoning from the forward observer perched on a tree limb or down in a hole.

And still another bad point was that we lacked firing tables or training manuals to assist in understanding nomenclature and fire techniques. But aided by FA Lt. Col. Cochran, while we were at Borio north of Oro Bay, we made our own firing directives. And we qualified all officers and a fair number of NCO's to fire the mortars. We were ready for combat.

Then on 18 Apr. 1944, D Co. was on LSD Gunston Hall to fight at Hollandia. (We had been out of the States since 4 Feb. 1942, and in New Guinea since March 1943). On 22 Apr., from the deck of our LSD we saw planes and naval guns blast the Hollandia foreshore. We saw I Co. 186 Inf's landing craft charge into the beach before us.

And D's 1/Pln. with six mortars piled into LCM's to race for I 186's White Beach 1 at the end of the sandspit outside Jautefa Bay. Our assignment was to fire cover for 186's K and L Co's when they landed at Pim Jetty across Jautefa Bay.

Quickly we set up mortars, fired first round at 0702. We shot 43 rounds white phosphorus shells over Pim Jetty. Conditions were ideal for an excellent smoke screen; 186 Inf. landed without casualties. Gen. Fuller himself praised us by radio — a fine start for 641 TD.

Then 2/Pln. landed at White Beach 4 on the inland side of Jautefa Bay, where 1/Pln. moved to join us. Between our two positions, we discovered a Jap pillbox — and movement inside. With one bazooka round and nine grenades, Lt. Lillie's detail cleared it. Inside lay a dead Jap major and some enlisted men. They had silently watched us for three hours.

Next day, 24 Apr., we registered a defense barrage for 3/Bn. 186 on Suikerbrod Hill south of them — 29 rounds HE. On 26 Apr., D reinforced 3/Bn. 34 Inf, 24 Div., near Lake Sentani. While supporting 34 Inf. pushing up Hoeb River, we drew 20 mm fire. Ordered by 34 Inf.'s Col. Jenni, we shot 29 rounds, but unluckily wounded three Yanks who were not supposed to be there.

Thus ended D 641's Hollandia action — after 101 rounds fired on three missions. We now readied for Biak.

For Biak, D got a splendid reinforcement. Attached were 12 DUKW's — amphibian 6x6 trucks of 1½ tons — and 12 Negro drivers, including S/Sgt. Roy White. These drivers were from 812 Amphibian Truck Co. These 12 blacks were top soldiers — and diplomats — in dealing with white outfits. They liked us enough to procure some fine rations from various QM outfits, such as turkey for our banquet with Gen. Doe near the close of the campaign.

And so D with our black drivers again boarded LSD Gunston Hall — this time for heavy combat on Biak. Landing 27 May at 0815, we finally bivouacked near Ibdi. We had not fired a shot; Biak looked easy.

But on late afternoon of 28 May, we had our grim battle orders. For that morning, 162 recoiled from the great Jap ambush before Mokmer Village and was now almost surrounded at Parai Defile. Col. Haney needed our 12 heavy mortars for all the fire power he could muster against the Nippo cliffs blasting 162.

It might have helped 162 greatly if our mortars could have begun pounding the Jap East Caves that afternoon. But our DUKW's were busy unloading ammo from the LSD at Bosnek. Crowded roads held them from taking us before threat of darkness.

Came 29 May, our finest time of battle. D loaded at Ibdi and turned west for combat. The land road to Parai was too congested; we had to go by water to T-Jetty instead.

But a paralyzing delay occurred before we fought. The Parai vicinity was under such heavy rifle fire that the beachmaster halted water traffic. He held D for some three hours until 1300 that afternoon.

During those three hours, Capt. Gerttula's advance party had moved overland to Parai Jetty. With Sgt. Greenshields, T/5 Goff, his driver and radio man, and Kelly, Gerttula lay behind coconut logs or got up to remind the beachmaster to land our DUKW's with mortars that 162 needed. Back at Ibdi, our pln. CQ's with the DUKW's also strove vainly to strike for Parai.

Yet 162 direly needed direct 4.2 fire on Parai Cliffs. For 146 FA up near Ibdi was so placed that it could fire only laterally on the fissures in the cliff tops. Naval fire was erratic; direct communication with our fleet had broken down. The Navy liaison officer with 162 was killed about 1200, and 162 could no longer contact our naval

---

CREDIT: Saunders' correspondence began this story in 1974, with his "History-1941-1944 641st TD Bn," and many following letters. Starting 20 Oct. 1974, Gerttula detailed D Co's Hollandia and Parai Defile actions. Federal Archives contributed "Operations Report, 98th Cml Bn (Mtzd) 12 Apr-21 July 1944," with "Unit Journal of 8 July 1944," and "Incidents of 5 July 1944." Background on Parai Defile is in R.R. Smith's Approach to the Philippines, although erroneous on 641's retreat. Formerly 641's S-3, Saunders is now a retired concrete consultant in Seattle. Formerly D's C.O. Gerttula with wife, Doris, is farming at Stanfield, Oregon, where he breeds "Doris" Charolais cattle. We have two more 641 TD stories, but I still need help with B-641 TD at Toem and Maffin Bay.

gunners. All requests for fire had to go through some five different CP's – and would arrive too late.

When our DUKW's finally beached at Parai, Gerttula led 1/Pln. into position 400 yards west of T-Jetty, supposedly to fire west towards Mokmer Drome. We were about halfway between Parai and Mokmer Village. Lt. Bell's 2/Pln. took up a position 200 yards east of 12 Portable Hospital which was busy with 162's many wounded.

Meanwhile, AA fragments from the dark Nippo cliffs were screeching through palm tops overhead. Jap rifles fired; knee mortars impacted too close. More fearful still was our own naval gunfire and rocket fragments recoiling from those cliffs almost on top of us.

Now we posted security guards and set up all 12 giant mortars to fight those cliffs. Digging them into the solid coral of Biak was impossible, but the same coral gave our base plates a solid foundation for perfect accuracy against those cliffs – against what were not yet named East Caves.

We sent our observation parties, connected them up by phone to our 12 mortar crews and worked on those cliffs. Our black DUKW drivers built our ammo dump, and shuttled back to T-Jetty with loads of 162 wounded from 12 Portable Hospital.

Against those deadly Jap cliffs, our 12 mortars struck with the weight of a full 105 FA Bn. On all Biak that heroic day of 29 May, D Co. directed the only heavy effective shellfire against the Jap ambush that was Parai Defile.

Our shells crashed down on eight concentration areas and quieted Jap mortar fire. We silenced one MG. We set fire to three dumps. In retaliation, Jap shells could only cut our wire often; but Goorsky and Sgt. Greenshields did notable work in splicing wire and restoring communications with our observers.

Official records say that D 641 had just one glorious hour of full company action that 29 May against Parai Cliffs, from noon to 1300. For awhile, we had indeed silenced Jap plunging fire down on 162 Inf. Then, suddenly, we had to lose in battle six of our 12 fine mortars.

For 162 was quitting Parai Defile; Lt. Col. Bailey informed us that D Co. 641 TD was to fight a rear-guard action to save 162. And since 1/Pln. would have no protection after 162's 2/Bn. had withdrawn, 1/Pln. would have to cease fire and depart with their six mortars in four DUKW's. But 2/Pln. was to hold out longer. We were to fire the last shell possible, destroy our mortars, then save ourselves.

So 1/Pln. escaped by water, but 2/Pln. Lt. Bell's gun crews heroically fought our remaining six mortars against Parai Cliffs. With Capt. Gerttula and our exec, 1/Lt. Sandwick observing, we lashed the cliffs with HE and phosphorus shells. For hours, we shot hundreds of M3 shells containing 25 pounds of TNT.

Scanning fissures in the cliffs with binoculars, Gerttula and Sandwick spotted Jap fires and openings to infiltrate through. They called down repeated fire on crevices whence small-arms fire issued, and on a stubborn 20 mm gun that opened up again and again.

Gerttula skillfully combined white phosphorus shellfire with HE shellfire. He assigned one mortar to mark targets with white phosphorus for the other five mortars to hammer. That same WP mortar also traversed the front as called upon, for the flaming particles crackled into nooks and crannies and flamed what they touched.

But mostly on 29 May 2/Pln. fired by battery on specified targets. On the order, all six pieces impacted on the same crevice on the instant.

Yet D could not shatter that cliff-face shielding the Japs. Any pause in our shelling let that untouched Jap 20 mm shoot again on 162 retreating from the foreshore. Then our shells silenced it again. We are sure that many 162 men owed their lives to 641 TD that 29 May.

Official records say that D got orders from 162 at 1300 to be ready to leave, but 2/Pln. fired until 1640. With no sign of panic, we worked those 4.2 mortars. In 3 hours and 40 minutes, we fired some 400 shells, as Gerttula estimated.

Orders were for 2/Pln. to board last LCT to arrive after 162 departed. (Meanwhile D Co. 442 Amphib. Engrs. guarded the cliff approaches north of T-Jetty with rifles, and LMG's.) Then 2/Pln. shouldered packs and small arms and hiked 400 yards to the jetty. We had no time to carry our heavy mortar parts, even if we had been so ordered. (And 2/Bn. 162's A & P Pln. had already destroyed two precious LCVP loads of our 4.2 ammo.)

But a destructor party remained behind: Gerttula with his wiremen Koskela, Turner and Goorsky. They destroyed probably 180 shells, smashed sights and elevator instruments on mortars. Thermite grenades detonated inside the rifled barrels. (Later D would recover those barrels with no mark of grenade fragments inside, but we never dared to use them again.)

Greatest fear of Gerttula's destructors was to be left behind when Japs swooped from the cliffs. We now scouted east towards safety at Ibdi. Taking a narrow coastal defile route remote from 162's retreat, we saw neither Japs nor Yank wounded, nor even abandoned equipment. Our worst tension was from nervous outguards of 146 FA at Ibdi, but they did not shoot.

When the LCT pulled out from the menacing cliffs, we endured more than did Gerttula's quiet land-party. As our LCT pushed away from the reef, that vengeful Jap 20 mm gun on the cliffs was firing. These murderous little shells followed us out of range, wounding two sailors. They sunk one of our last DUKW's, but a destroyer saved the black driver. A 2/Pln. man went to hospital in shock.

And that night of 29 May at Ibdi, D Co. 641 Tank Destroyer Bn. reassembled tired but proud. We had played a major part in saving a fine regiment from annihilation. We had cannonaded the Jap cliffs with an estimated 400 rounds. We had fallen back in good order, with not even one man wounded. Soon we would replace our last six mortars and help our Division to conquer Mokmer Ridge and East Caves.

The 41st was the first American unit anywhere to meet Japanese tanks in combat. The first engagement took place on Biak, and the enemy lost every tank committed. Photo shows knocked-out Japanese tanks near Bosnek. The 641st Tank Destroyer Battalion won big in its first test.

COMBAT MEDIC ON BIAK

By PFC GEORGE JACKSON
with
DR. HARGIS WESTERFIELD, Association Historian

Standing offshore before the dark Biak ridges 27 May 1944, A Co 116 Medical Bn saw Operation Hurricane starting like one. B-24s raised shock waves as they bombed beaches. Hellcats strafed and bombed. LCI rocketships blasted with incredible volleys. As 162's first LCMs drove for Bosnek Jetty, Jap mortars splashed near misses.

In the second wave—LCIs—A Co arrived on schedule, the second LCI touching the jetty. Next to last off, I held up the ramp's retraction, displaced a naval officer. Grena had to go back for his glasses. As A Co assembled ashore, a dapper Dutch official hoisted the Dutch flag overhead. We said little, but tommies pointed at him. Hastily, he ran up the Stars and Stripes.

In heat, sweat, rain, we hiked under heavy packs with 162's 3/Bn 8 miles down to the edge of Mokmer Drome — with dark jungle cliffs pressing in ominously. But we knew we would end Biak Invasion tomorrow — just another Hollandia pushover.

But next day, 29 June, Col Kuzume's 222 Inf halted 162's 3/Bn with MGs and mortars. MGs fired constantly to keep us down, with mortar shells occasionally to force withdrawal.

Pinned down at first, we Meds made ourselves flat as possible—scrupulously cleared the smallest twig from under us. Called up for a casualty—it was hard to get off my chest—I found a Yank with elbow wound and ruptured artery. I applied compress bandage, put arm in a sling, and wrote his evacuation ticket. He was happy to be safe, despite the shattered elbow. Then 2 buddies were brought in. A dud had hit one in the middle of his back; the other was untouched but just as helpless. This shellshocked Yank had lost all voluntary controls. While he sobbed continually, we could only lead him back by a hand.

We placed the man who was hit on a litter, tried to run with him down a dry creek bed to the aid station—a million to one chance of saving him. Across the road below MG fire we ran, then staggering down a rocky gulch. No Japs shot at us, but he died before we checked in.

As 162's 3/Bn got to the edge of Mokmer Drome, our 2/Pln of Meds went with them. They were cut off 6 hours and used up about all of their medical supplies. Dan Sullivan was in 2/Pln—a grim tired man returning. Official losses 29 June were 16 killed, 96 wounded, 3 injured.

With that first day of combat, dates and events became jumbled in our minds. We worked 12-hour shifts—always in a twilight of deadened fatigue—always under the guns. It became a routine of wishing it was nightfall, then wishing it was daybreak, day after day and week after week. It seemed always probe and withdrawal, leaving behind weapons and capturing theirs to the point when any fire—and we could distinguish each and evrey type—might be the Japs' and not ours. Somewhere on Biak, I lost the whole month of June; it was July before I knew it. For Infantry, it was perhaps easier to remember advances and retreats, probes and withdrawals. For us Meds, it was 12-hour days—and death after death.

A Co 116 Meds pulled back a little to our previous bivouac, dug into coral sand. Here a small white friendly starved dog visited us, like several others we slew later. We welcomed and fed him—then found he was a Nips' aiming point. In the growth below the cliffs, they couldn't pick out individuals, but they could track dogs to a group. The first burst of their MG at long range struck a deep wide hole being dug for Communications Center. First burst killed a Yank, broke another's arm.

> Primary source is George Jackson's 2 handwritten notebooks from 8 Sept 1940 through 31 Aug 1945—his date of discharge. Accurate dating of this story is impossible; George was too busy staying alive and sane to document each day under Jap fire. But better than a dull official record, George's journals bring back the corpses and Jap mortars of Bloody Biak. Now a high school teacher at Everett, Washington, George is also working part-time for his M.A. in School Administration at University of Washington.

A few minutes later, it raised sights and fired again. While others holed up, I crouched behind a big tree while slugs skipped in the roadside dust. As at Hollandia, I was lucky more than once.

That same day before supper, a Zero "zooped" in over the cliff—so close that some tried hitting it with M-1s. Startling so close was that big red meatball. Rumor came that Jap planes had caught a company up at Bosnek fresh from the states and killed 17.

While 162 probed the Japs at Parai Defile, after our forced march in the rain back to Bosnek, A Co dug in close to the cliffs. We helped outfit Whitey Pluid with new equipment. Out with a patrol, he had flattened under MG fire and had to wriggle out of his pack to crawl to safety.

Here A Co was shelled by a Nip Mountain Gun that rolled out of a cave on tracks and slipped back before counter-fire. One evening, he caught 5 of us in a large hole—Devaney and Capt Toussaint among us. Shells dropped behind us, but they whined too close and low over our heads. We could only wait out "Whistling Charlie" until he got tired or the guns smashed him in the open. I fell asleep, and my buddies wondered why I was so quiet. They were badly shaken up.

Next morning at breakfast, we saw 4 Yank planes turn our way—an A-20 with 3 B-25s. We watched them come in, cheerfully confident they were our friends. Our trucks were parked in the open. Our aid station with its Red Cross was nearest their run.

With a fresh cup of Nescafe, I watched the A-20 cross and the first B-25 come in—and open up all 8 50s which made the nose of the plane a bright orange glow. Carefully laying down the cup, I flattened with the others. Two bombs fell. After the planes left, we had 6 dead Yanks—3 by strafing—3 by fragments. A millionaire's son was dead among them, a .50 through his skull. We had 14 casualties by MGs and fragments. A .50 holed Dunkin's helmet, but Dunkin was not inside.

All this may have been about 4 June when we went through the scare that the Jap Navy was coming to Biak. About 7 June, we loaded on Buffaloes, bypassed the Jap roadblock, and landed at Parai Jetty. Only casualty was a rifleman who shot himself through the femoral vein—only time we used a tourniquet. We had to lug him by litter down a 30-foot cliff. We passed the litter from hand to hand with a human chain down the cliff-face.

I stayed with the casualties on a Buffalo trip back to aid station. I had to loosen that femoral tourniquet every 15 minutes. Returning, I found 3/Bn and Japs trading mortar shells. Heading for Devaney's hole, I was glad to hear a Chaplain sing—as he dug in, "What a friend we have in Jesus." We yearned for his reassurance, and never forgot this song.

One hot afternoon as 162 fought, Pluid and I helped exterminate Nips. In that tremendous heat of 120-130 degrees, we deployed off the road—Whitey and me naturally in the ditch on the safe side from Jap fire off the cliffs.

Suddenly, I sensed occasional fire from seaward. Fire could be only from deserted native hut on piling. We leaped over to the other ditch across the road to verify the single shots. On the slight rise from the beach, the 20-foot space above the sea was alive with Yank infantry by a temporary aid station. I told the nearest infantry officer, and he gave orders. Atfer 162's rifles riddled the shack, 2 Nips lay dead inside. Hoping to avoid discovery, they had fired overhead at men closer to the cliffs, until our bullets found them.

Directly ahead was the main fire-fight, a pall of smoke and dust. Closer, a 30 HMG fired steadily. Small patches of grass burned from hot cartridges.

When the call came for a litter, I went along as aid man. The wounded man huddled in the hollow of a solitary pile of rock. His forehead was deeply gashed, deepest over the left eye. We could not help in his cave.

I told the NCO to carry him, and the litter party did—a compact target for a Jap burst. I trotted behind to spread the fire.

We escaped without a shot. Capt Toussaint took a look—angrily ordered him off. It was a mere flesh-wound. Blinded by blood, the scared boy took a step, fell into a hole, and became a casualty from a broken leg.

As Jap resistance lessened, 162 moved up to Mokmer on the beach or in the water. "A" Co halted beside an apparently dead Yank sitting by the trail. We saw no wound, but he was plainly green—our usual sign of death. But I sensed life in his pulse. Rushing to F/Pln's Sgt Cushing, I learned that no one else had checked him for death. As we found the wound in the back of his head, 2 Bn Meds got to work. He responded to treatment, but I heard no more about him, since A Co moved forward again.

Now it was mid-June in combat, and me in fear because I was on the Rotation List. Two other Meds imaged that fear. Willie Shepherd knew that he would die before Rotation. In July while he crouched behind a high bank, a shell hit beside him. And Herb Larsen, who disavowed this belief, also died then.

Devaney and I now decided to play safe but still be useful. Supposedly safe in jungle, I heard a mortar crack and hit a shell-hole. The shell struck 3 feet away, but without tipping. The blast was upward and did not hurt me. I got out while 8 shells more impacted—without one deadly tree-burst.

Shell No. 9 fell as a 162 outfit deployed as skirmishers to relieve another outfit. With 2 other Meds, I waved them down. But a fragment hit a Yank in the chest. From a hole the size of a pea, a small scarlet fountain squirted. He fell on me. But with these 2 Bn Meds, I helped him to a surgeon to save him. I decided that hiding from the Japs would never preserve me for rotation.

Soon 162 broke out of the beach-head and fought on Mokmer Ridges. One day, I took plasma up to a 162 Co badly in need of it. Liaison Man Renna came also to spot Jap pillboxes that unpredictably let large bodies of men through, then targeted single men. Crossing that bare, gravelled area of shell-holes was chilling. We saw the pillboxes—one right at 100 yards, the other above us at 15-20 yards. We saw movement in it. Without being fired on, we climbed a 20-foot cliff to 162's men lining the edge, left the plasma, returned unhurt across the open. Renna reported his data directly to Gen Eichelberger, just arrived at Bn Hq.

For A Co 116 Meds, however, the Battle of Biak died down to routine days in garrison with turns on guard at night in the holes. Expecting Rotation, I was suddenly flown to Hollandia with yellow jaundice, thought it would be my luck to miss the homeward ship. But after 10 days' hospital, I was back on Biak and saying farewell to A Co—along with Capt Toussaint, Pluid, Devaney, Haraseth, Sullivan.

It was a hard parting from soldiers of my own kind. We were off for home, but left behind a camaraderie of like spirits I never found again.

116 Combat Engineers On Biak

By Dr. Kenneth J. Deacon
Office of the Chief of Engineers

ON 27 MAY 1944, 116 Engineer Btn (less A Co with 163 Inf at Toem) followed 186 Inf ashore at Bosnek. As Engr Intelligence had forecast, a fringing reef kept landing craft 100 yards offshore. But Capt. John A. Gallagher, Btn S-2, headed a recon party to find a break in the reef. Directly from our ships, Engrs drove nearly submerged bulldozers ashore, began to repair jetties to expediate unloading assault cargo.

While B Co plus Hq and Sv detachments labored at Bosnek, Capt. Robert A. Strachan's C Co teamed with 163 Inf to push for Mokmer. Up front, we took off mines, duds, other obstacles. A bulldozer helped 603 Tank Co. The rest of "C" worked on the former Nippo supply road.

Despite ominous opposition, 162 broke through to Parai. Almost midway in the defile, we bypassed a ruined bridge which C 116 Engrs never forgot. At dusk, most of C gathered in bivouac at Ibdi; but Nippo mortars zeroed in, wounded 6. We puled back to sleep at Mandom.

On 28 May, we did outstanding combat engineering. Japs cut off and attacked 162's L and M Cos, on the road over the terrace. When 603 tanks moved forward to relieve "L" and "M," T/5 Leslie Winkler supported the push with his dozer. Once he gave mobile cover to 6 stranded riflemen until they reached safety. Fired on by a MG nest, he climbed from the dozer to point out the position so that 603 tanks neutralized the fire. Cos L, M 162 withdrew safely.

Meanwhile the ford east of Parai became badly rutted. An Engr dozer gave continuous assistance to vehicles trying to cross. Despite stalled trucks that created a traffic jam, other Engrs cleared away debris, started to restore the bridge—much of the time under Nippo fire.

On 29 May when 162 fell back from Mokmer Village, 116 Engrs did a masterly job at that critical bridge in the Parai Defile. After 162 broke up 2 Nippo tank-infantry attacks, Gen. Fuller ordered C 116 Engrs to complete rebuilding the Parai Bridge instantly. We had to work under fire to help save 162 from disaster.

While C's 3 Pltn stopped roadwork ahead and came back to guard, our other 2 Pltns toiled feverishly. The 2 Pltn hauled and spread gravel for approaches. First Pltn did carpentry, put together the bridge—a structure of 3 spans, 60 feet long. Our 3 Pltn fought snipers; one man died here.

Three hours after Gen. Fuller's order, the bridge was ready; 30-ton tanks, wheeled vehicles, hiking, sweating infantrymen poured across it. But for the Parai Defile Bridge which C 116 built under fire, 162's defeat might have been a disaster.

While 162 regrouped at Ibdi, B Co 116 Engrs were committed to action inland. For when 186 Inf campaigned through the dry coral scrub behind Bosnek to seize Mokmer Strip from the rear, Capt. Argyle E. Armstrong's B Co made a supply road. We had to build this road partly out of a poor Nippo way and partly out of native tracks inland—roundabout from Opiaref E of Bosnek some 10 miles. We had to build this road just as fast as 186 Inf advanced—almost waterless and stung by Nippo rifles.

It was indeed a hard road to build. Each morning Col. Newman of 186 indicated direction and distance he planned to move; and B 116 had to come up with him by dark. Although we blasted for wells, we found only dry holes in that limestone that drained perpendicular. We labored on 1 canteen of water per day, and the hope of the erratic rains. For protection, we usually had to rely on our own security patrols.

On 2 June, we widened and improved the 5 miles from Opiaref to the West end of the Bosnek Drome area. On 3 and 4 June, we built 3 brand new miles of road, despite heat, drouth, Nippo ambushes. On 5 June, however, a heavy rain about 1200 gave us the chance to spread ponchos and collect water to refill canteens and drink deep,

---

CREDITS

This article is a by-product of research by Dr. J. Kenneth Deacon, Historical Division, Office of Chief of Engineers, Baltimore. He is at work on a book entitled "Engineers in the SW Pacific." Data of this article are from: Engr Sect, 6 Army, Engr History (unpub MS); Hurricane TF Engr Rpt 11 Jul 44; Hq 2 ESB Rpt of Opns, 1-31 Jul 44; Hq 116 Engr Comb Bn, 20 Sept 44 Opns Rpt 10 May–20 Aug 44; 116 Engr Bn Unit Hist 1944; Co B 116 Engr Bn, 10 Jun 44, Opns Rpt from 2-6 June 44, Co C 116 Engr Bn 18 Aug 44, Gen Rpt on Missions Hq 363 Engr Avn Bn, Biak Camp Rpt; Hq 1112 Engr Cons Grp Unit Hist Rpt.

A Sgt. of Engineers in 5 ETO campaigns, Dr. Deacon received training for writing historical research while earning his PhD at New York University. He has written many articles on engineer action for the magazine, "The Military Engineer." The historian will be glad to take orders for Dr. Deacon's book.

disregarding the soapy taste in our helmets.

But on 5 June also, Nippo snipers and infiltrating riflemen were tough. They ambushed one patrol which rallied under and behind a truck and held them off. When one Engr took a severe grenade wound, T/5 Melbourne E. Brooks carried him 50 yards to safety. Brooks was also wounded in carrying his buddy.

Meanwhile Nips waylaid Engrs escourting the dozers. They killed a guard, momentarily cut off others, bracketed the dozers with mortar blasts. One dozer cleared the impacted area, but shells dropped close to a second in the rear. The driver sped into an area protected by 186 Inf.

Japs also stood up out of the brush, hurled an explosive against the windshield of a passing tool truck. The driver stepped on the gas; the charge bounced off the windshield before his face, exploded safely yards behind him.

By nightfall of 5 June, the roadbuilders were still a mile from 186's perimeters. 2500 yards over the ridge away from Mokmer Drome. Despite rough terrain ahead, gathering dark, and possible Nippo raids, the road must get through to supply 186 at dawn.

But with darkness coming, we could not locate 186's perimeters in the sea of 12-foot coral scrub. We radioed 186 to shoot a flare, then took an azimuth. Now First Sgt. Ralph W. Ryan followed the azimuth as far as he could see. Then he flicked a cigarette lighter to guide dozer man T/5 Elmer Brown. We opened a crude but usable track right up to 186, and spent a night of broken sleep in the coral in safety. On 6 June we improved the supply road so that on 7 June, 186 could push over the ridge and begin infighting to secure Mokmer Drome.

While B 116 Engrs built 186's overland desert road, C 116 with 162 Inf was again trying to force the Parai Defile to Mokmer. On 3 June, C 116 reinforced 162's 3 Btn and 7 tanks on the second push between cliffs and sea. In the van, a 162 Pltn probed with 4 Engrs using mine detectors. Followed 3 tanks, a dozer still commanded by our old friend T/5 Winkler, more 162 Pltns, tanks, and Engr Pltn. To the rear came 2 more 162 Cos, the rest of C 116.

Halfway through the defile, we found that demolished bridge which we had built for 162's previous retreat. This time, after the lead rifle Pltn crossed, an Engr Pltn moved up to repair the bridge.

From the cliffs, a torrent of fire struck us. Japs burst out from jungle between road and cliffs, cut off 162's lead Pltn.

T/5 Winkler's dozer helped 2 tanks across the stream to open fire for the besieged Pltn. For 2 hours, the Btn point fought the Nips but could not force the defile.

From nowhere came a Nip in GI uniform. He mounted the lead tank, exploded a gernade down the hatch. With 1 man dead, 2 others wounded inside, an assistant driver seized controls. But logs in the road and rocks blocked the tank's escape.

T/5 Winkler bulldozed aside the obstructions. The tank was saved. Winkler elso gave perfect cover with his dozer to escaping 162 riflemen. Meanwhile C's other Pltns completed the bridge, but futilely. When 162's 3 Btn withdrew with 3 more dead that afternoon, the Nips destroyed the bridge a second time.

From the east, Parai Defile was impenetrable. But on 7 June, 162 bypassed it and landed at Parai Jetty. A Pltn of C 116 repaired the jetty. **We also removed mines and other obstacles so that tanks could move on the beach road. On 9 June, 2 Engrs were working under fire at "Coffin Corners"—a name for Mokmer Village.**

Not until 13 June did 162 mop up Parai Defile which it had earlier bypassed; but at once C 116 got orders to open the supply road from Bosnek to Mokmer in 24 hours. Ruined was the bridge we had twice rebuilt. Bombs and shells ripped the road; coral mounds and fallen timber blocked it. Farther west, shells had smashed sea-wall into road for a long stretch.

Yet Capt. Strachan had foreseen this rush order. He perceived that the bridge was the key to his problem; without it, we could never deploy heavy equipment into the stretch by the sea-wall. Already, he had had his men prepare a prefab, 60-foot bridge to carry 30-ton loads. At once, he dispatched a mine-detector squad to remove naval shells which Japs had used as AT mines. With just 3 hours light left, he trucked the bridge up and installed it. Next morning, we drove heavy equipment over to repair the road at the sea-wall. We did our job on time; now infighting 186 and 162 men had a free flow of supplies from Bosnek.

When 162, 186 made the all-out assault of 19-20 June, Engr and other flame-thrower patrols sprayed many positions guarding West Caves. On 2 June after Jap fire still denied entrance. Engrs perhaps dealt Col. Kuzume the final blow. We poured 5 drums of gasoline through crevices above the cave, fired them with flame-throwers. Although unseen from above, the holocaust was horrible. Col. Kuzume burned his colors, killed himself. His troops Banzaid on 186's lines.

Still on 22 June, remaining cave Japs did not surrender. From A 116, now up from Toem, volunteers F/Lt Elwood C. Call, Cpl LeRoy Hayden, T/5 Everett B. Allison did the final work. They set off several 25-50 pound charges. They filled 3 drums with 850 pounds of gelignite each, lowered them by winch, fired them electrically. Only a few Nips ran out to die.

West Caves were silent; but despite FA and bombs, Nips still fired from East Caves. After E Co 163 took the high ground, C 116's F/Lt Sweetland invaded the caves with volunteers. They shot 3 Nips, killed an unknown number by fire, explosives, destroyed quantities of food, ammo, guns, mortars. East Caves were no longer a trouble spot. At Ibdi Pocket 25-28 August, after 163 destroyed the Japs, Engrs sealed caves, destroyed pillboxes, bunkers.

Such was the saga of the bridge-building, road-building, bulldozing, fighting 116 Engrs of Biak. Able comanders were Col. Herbert G. Lauterbach—over all Engrs operations, and acting Btn CO, Major William L. Morris. Killed in action were Anthony J. Mussari, Allan G. Martin, Michael Bobby. Dead in field operations were Robert J. Hawkins, Lloyd A. Cole, Alexander R. DuMarce. Besides 6 dead, we had 36 wounded, 4 injured in action. We bridged Parai Defile Stream 3 red-hot times, built 2 long roads under fire for 162 and 186 without which they could hardly have taken Mokmer Drome. We fought in the van with 162 Inf; and T/5 Winkler—combat bulldozerman—is a legend among the 41st Division's Butchers.

HISTORIAN'S NOTE:
The Historian sadly announces that he had to write all the way to Office of Chief Engineers before he could get material for this article on one of the leading non-infantry outfits of the Division—116 Engineers. He would like to say that one—just one—member of 116 Engrs had contributed to him. Why have 116 Engrs suppressed this brave story of the bridges in Parai Defile and their road-building feats? (McCartney's "history" says nothing about the Parai Bridges nor 116 Engrs at East Caves—pays little attention to any of the great works of 116 Engrs.)

HARGIS WESTERFIELD
Division Association Historian

Catching Up With History

Cannon Infantry of 162

CREDIT
A blond, broad-shouldered young Lieut.-Col., Vernon Townsend of Tangent, Oregon, was indeed good company at Bozeman Reunion. Still active with Division, he boasts over thirty years' service, all but a few days of it in 162. This history I found in a carton of papers which he lent me, along with 162's Journal at Salamaua, which I used also. Can anyone name the authors of "Cannon Infantry" for publication in JUNGLEER?

Although created a cannon company 7 June 1942 in Australia, we trained as infantry, then as stevedores. After Camp Seymour, Rockhampton, Townsville, Port Moresby, and many air-raids and port details at Oro Bay, Douglas Harbor, and Morobe, we landed at o200 Hrs. at Tambu Bay 22 June 1943. At dawn we saw the jungle tangle of Roosevelt Ridge 1500 yards off, and heard the shelling. Only the day before had the Third Btn's push failed.

Basically, we worked as a dock company, under fear of air-raids, fire from the ridge, and infiltration. In the attack of 28 July while carrying ammo to the forward companies, we first suffered. Schechter, Pajovik got slight mortar wounds. On 29 July, Lieut. Newton had a light MG wound. We were glad to return to stevedoring. One Pltn was sent to guard supplies at Nassau Bay, and Lieut.-Col. Fertig credited it with cutting pilfering by two-thirds.

In the final assault on Roosevelt Ridge 13 August, Cannon Co. with rifles climbed the Ridge also. Following E Co., we suffered from the Nips. Bullets wounded Botiller, and T/4 Crawford, who lost his right arm. Mortars wounded Sgt. Eerkes, with Pvts Brown, Tosh. On 14 August during the great bombardment of Roosevelt Ridge, Cannon Co. with AT and the Band constituted the Provisional Btn that garrisoned the ridge as it was taken. On 15 Aug, Cannon patrols sought out Japs on Lokanu Rridge.

Issued 81 mortars at Dot Inlet, we supported 162's 2 Btn and the Aussie 15 Inf Btn against D and Lokanu Ridges. While guiding Aussies, Kelly was killed and Lewis slightly wounded. On 8 Sept we were shelled by mortars, artillery. Cpl. Culster died there; Lieut. Kness, Sgt. Andreas, and Pvt. Houston were wounded. With 2 killed, 9 wounded, our Salamaua Campaign ended. But our strength was down to 61. We were glad to leave for Australia 28 Sept.

Biak was Cannon Co's toughest infantry battle. Unloading LST's the second day, we hid in the boats from a strafing plane or dived off the jetty. On 28 May, with tanks and 162's 3 Btn in combat for Mokmer, we landed from LCV at Parai's T Jetty. We had it easy at first guarding 162's rear and 26 Portable Hospital.

By 29 May, Cannon Co was the front line. With a few guarding perimeter, we were working on Bosnek road, or burying, or loading wounded on boats. The Japs launched a planned attack; they mortared the hospital where most of us worked. Japs made a main drive for our 50 caliber position above T Jetty. We piled them up dead and repulsed them. Our wounded were S/Sgt Wills, Cpl Lewis, Pfc Biel.

Meanwhile, other Cannon- eers organized and got into position except a few to help evacuate wounded swiftly. Again Japs attacked frontally; we drove them back with our burning crossfire. Under cover of a seawall next the ocean, they ran up a MG and were almost ready to throw down upon us. But a guard spotted the 2 with the gun and shot them down. Finally we moved out as skirmishers and annihilated the last Japs. Besides our 3 on the 50 MG, Danielson and Tominic were wounded.

S/Sgt Rakovich died with a .25 through the head; but we killed 80 Japs for him. According to the U.S. Army History, our fight was part of a movement with B Co that dislodged the Japs from a road-block between 162 and Bosnek.

That night when 162 fell back from the Parai Defile, Cannon stood as rear guard with a landing party of D Co 542 Amphibian Engineers. Then we retreated last. It was 4 miles up a muddy cliffside road; even Shermans sprung their treads on it. Only a drenching rain prevented our collapse.

At dark, we dug in before 205 FA and the next day guarded 162 CP. On 31 May died that boyish wonder Lieut. Myron Folsom of I & R after taking over a patrol started by our Lieut. Mitchell. He penetrated 50 yards farther into Ibdi Pocket and died from a Jap MG in a prepared ambush.

On 1 June, we were setting up defenses around Mandom Water Hole. Before we were ready, Japs assaulted with cover from MG's, knee mortars. But for an isolated 4-man outpost on the hilltop, Cannon would have met disaster. McClure died bayoneted; Gabaldon was wounded; but Howard piled up 9 dead and with Strickland delayed them until we broke the attack.

On the night of 2 June, we were ordered to save an AT Pltn trapped 300 yards north over 3 ridges. At daylight, we set up two MG's and a skirmish line on the third ridge and gave overhead fire to cover AT's run. Lieut. Townsend was wounded in the hand. We evacuated AT's dead and wounded and fell back by stages, half of the men and 1 MG at a time.

Then we landed again at Parai Jetty to aid I and K Cos. On 8 June we pushed west to open up the coast road to Mokmer while L pushed east. About 500 yards off, we battled ferociously for hours against the first Jap pillboxes and caves. Baer

Landing craft carry troops of the 41st Division in for the Biak landing.

died there; Juarez and Bright were wounded.

Although it was late in the afternoon, we had to push again. After 3-400 yards, we hit the worst ambush of our history. Dug in on 3 sides, they blasted us; we expected to be wiped out. They tried to pin us down; then they charged with bayonets. Our heavy fire blew them back.

We had to escape down a corridor of snipers. Several died or were maimed there —especially in our 1 MG squad which pulled out first. We lost our MG tripod; but Lieut. Sullivan and Sgt. Jennings fired the light .30 from the hip. The first men escaped put down a heavy covering fire to bring out the others. Then we fired to protect the volunteers who brought out bodies.

Dead were T/5 Louis Martin, PFC's Hall, Schecter. Wounded were T/Sgt. Glunz, PFC's Allgood, Burns, Chatfield, Webb, Backus. We had that day 4 killed, half of our losses overseas.

We returned 9 June, but slowly, with Clark's squad on the right, Dickerson's on the left—a few yards at a time. Near a 200-foot cliff, we got Regiment's orders to withdraw. L Co had suffered many casualties on the other side. Later we learned that a Btn had to clean up that position. Then we spent a few days unloading supplies, then guarded a trail NW of Mokmer Drome and ran 3-4 patrols a day. We had no more casualties.

After hard training with our 105's on Biak, we landed near Zamboanga and dug in near Wolfe Airfield. About noon the Japs started bombarding. Crabtree was wounded slightly, and Biel while unloading an LST. On 11 March, a barrage fired the petrol dump 50 feet from our positions. That night 8 Japs ignited the surviving gas drums and pinned down one of our positions with a Woodpecker MG and fired on another position at 15 feet.

We forced them out with 1 dead in 5 yards and 3 more 50 yards up the trail.

Meanwhile, Cannon's 2, 3 Pltns were in action finally with cannon. From 16 March to 17 April, we used direct 105 fire to aid riflemen digging Nips out of the mountains. We transported guns over impassable mountain roads, jeeped in or hand-carried shells. Platoons fired independently, often 20 miles apart—for 162, 163, 186.

Relieved from its Basilan Island "vacation," the First Pltn almost got put out of action 20 March. With 1 gun in a palm grove 150 yards from Jap positions, and another 300 yards from them, we suddenly received all the fire-power the Japs had, front and rear. Trucker Sierra took artillery shrapnel in his right shoulder. Dried grass flamed up from mortars and menaced our ammo and guns. Cappola risked his life to beat out the fire and saved us.

Next day we returned to attack this same position, the heights above Masilay. Marine Corsairs attacked first; their shrapnel hit our truck. With F attacking and E guarding our flanks, we ran our guns to 500 yards from the Nips. Jap snipers fired, but we threw a barrage; we saw tree bursts; we dug them out of holes and caves. Our riflemen took the position.

On 28 March, Sgt. Padnuk led 12 men with Graves Registration to recover a rifleman killed days before. Coming back from 400 yards out, they hit the ground in a clearing under fire from a Jap LMG and rifles. But the 3 Pltn commanded this clearing and covered our escape with 50's and 30's. A Jap mortar impacted the area just after we evacuated. Jenkins had a bullet hole through his pants at the knee, and T/4 Howard 3 through his jacket.

On 1 May, we were de-tached to help guard the 31 Division's long supply lines into central Mindanao. Landed at Parang, we trucked to Fort Pikit 40 miles off. We ran motor patrols back to Parang and saw no enemy. Lieut. O'Hara's 3 Pltn went to Pada Palungi, 15 miles away, an idyllic streamside setting in a Moro Village. Then X Corps' CO, Major-General Seibert, desired an escort for inspecting frontline troops. O'Hara took him to Valencia, deep in the heart of Mindanao before the mud made Seibert give up.

The main body turned south over muddy hill-roads and through streams where the bridges had been burned. On 13 June, we guarded a bridge at Mintal near Davao. In the push on Calinan 19 June, we set up a road-block, endured snipers and mortars. On 22 June, a lone Jap blew up in our electrified minefield. On 22 June, Cpl. Watkins got a light grenade wound. By 9 June, we had been shipped back to Zamboanga.

Then Japan surrendered, and we toured in Japan. Peacefully landing at Kure and visiting Hiroshima, we were stationed in the ancient city of Onomichi, although a Pltn accompanied the 1 Btn to Matsue across the island. At Onomichi, Cannon Co kept the peace as MP's. On 17 December 1945 came deactivation. With our 8 dead, Cannon had been more lucky than the straight line companies; but we had done our job — stevedores, riflemen, cannoneers, from Australia to Japan.

162 Infantry:

Cannon Infantry of Parai Defile

By Dr. Hargis Westerfield, Division Historian
With T/Sgt Al Morrow, Cn Co 162 Infantry

Prime credit for this second story of Cn 162 on Biak is due to T/Sgt Al Morrow's letters of 1972: six letters from 8 Aug through 8 Nov, and hitherto unused material from "Cannon Co 162 Inf," an unpublished ms supplied by Maj Vernon Townsend in 1960. Also important were three sketch maps by Morrow, 162 Inf Journal, 162 Morning Report, R R Smith's *Approach to the Philippines*. Necessary cross references are to previous *Jungleer* articles: "Cannon Infantry of 162," Dec 1960; C Co's "Ibdi Pocket to West Caves," June 1968; L Co's "First Against Mokmer Drome," Mar 1969. (When will AT 162 help me on its Biak story?)

About suppertime 28 May 1944, Cannon Co, 162 Inf, boarded LCV's at Bosnek to reinforce 162 on that first day of defeat on Biak. Not yet issued cannon, we were riflemen in two fights for Parai Defile. Landing at Pryor Jetty below ominous gray cliffs, we doubled ashore to dig perimeter on the 20-25 foot cliff above 26 Portable Surgical Hospital.

Cn's first fear was Jap planes which flew safely over Biak in the half hour before sunset, when our fighters had to return to Hollandia to land before dark. But no Jap planes appeared. Our other fear was from the Jap attack on 162 from the west; 162's wounded were filling up 26 Port Hosp—87 WIA that 28 May we landed at Parai. But our trouble began on 29 May.

That morning, CO Townsend assigned Cn to labor on Parai Road, evacuate 26 Port's patients to landing craft 100 yards off, or bury already four dead whom Capt. Waisbrot's surgeons could not save. Townsend naturally left a small security guard at Cn's two 50 HMG's on the cliff above 26 Port.

Suddenly about 1200, when most Cn men ate in the hospital area below the cliff, knee mortars detonated above us. Men like T/Sgt. Morrow hit the earth as shells struck all around us. A Jap command had outflanked 162 and thrust east along the clifftop, an estimated 90 men. Evident purpose was to smash through to the beach and cut off retreating 162. But 26 Port was also menaced.

We swarmed up a ladder to top the 20-foot cliff and to man the perimeter. Already, our guard on one 50 HMG to the east was firing at the Japs trying to seize it. The Japs wounded Biel, Cpl. Lewis, S/Sgt. Wills—probably the HMG's crew. But they stopped the charge and killed many Japs.

Brave men that they were, the Jap force struck again—but hit our fully manned perimeter. Our burning crossfire repelled them. Morrow later saw only dead Japs with gold teeth where the HMG's felled them. From manning his HMG, he saw Cn in action again below the cliff.

The bloodied Jap command then cannily tried to flank Cn and win a position on the beach behind the sea wall. From there they could sweep Pryor Jetty clean of escaping Yanks and hold the coast road to halt 162's land retreat.

But an unnamed Cn Yank spotted the two leading Nips, both carrying MG's to throw down on Pryor Jetty when they came in range. With expert marksmanship, he shot both dead on their MG's. Then Cn piled back down from that cliff and deployed as skirmishers and moved east with M-1's firing. We annihilated that valiant Jap group.

By 1300, 3/Bn Hq had reported to Col. Haney that Cn 162 had opened the road to Bosnek and killed 63 Japs. (Our Cn historian claims that the number of dead Japs totalled over 80 of the estimated 90 who attacked us.) Besides Biel, Lewis, and Willis WIA in the first attack on our HMG, we lost S/Sgt. Rakovich dead of wounds in the final attack. Danielson, Tominic were also WIA.

Later, Cn learned that our fight was only part of a move by 162 companies that saved 162 from being cut off by land from retreating to Mandom. With inadequate Engr. craft to succor 162, the loss in men and materiel could have immobilized the regiment. East of us, B 162 had been the other part of that move to dislodge another Jap force, but with preparatory fire of D Co's mortars, B drove out their Japs without a hard fight, unlike Cn 162.

Such was Cn's victory for 26 Port. Hosp. and 162 Inf. on 29 June. Then defeated 162 Inf. streamed eastward in retreat, and Cn fell in at rear guard. No Japs fought us, but we had to slog four miles over a torn-up road in drenching rain. That road was so rough that even Sherman tanks sprung their treads in boulders and mud, but the rain saved more of us from collapsing of heat exhaustion.

Cn was safe from Parai Defile for nine days, but we still fought. On 31 May, 1962's I & R pln surely saved Cn men's lives. Lt. Folsom took over a patrol from Cn's Lt. Mitchell. Just 50 yards further up that trail north of Mandom, a Jap MG killed Folsom. On 1 June, Cn was assigned to guard the Mandom water hole. A Jap attack expelled us before we could dig in, with one KIA, one WIA. On 2 June, we retook the water hole and smashed a Jap counterattack. On 3 June, we rescued a pln of AT 162 cut off on Ridge 3 of Ibdi Pocket.

But on 7 June, Cn faced Parai Defile again. This was the day 162 began the second try to seize Mokmer Dromes. Col. Haney's strategy was to bypass Parai Defile this time and land at Pryor Jetty near where Cn had defended 26 Port. But a deadly Jap garrison still held 1,000 yards of Parai Defile. And while 162's main body moved west, Cn had to battle east to smash the Jap garrison and reopen the supply road. L's reinforced pln was to drive west to contact us.

Parai Defile was perhaps the Japs' most important tactical advantage on Biak. Beginning 1500 yards west of Ibdi, a 200-foot cliff constricted the jungle foreshore to a width of 100 feet, which widened out to some 500 yards by Pryor Jetty. On D-Day, 28 May, Col. Haney had lost valuable time to break through a small delaying force. After 162's retreat, Jap guns on the cliff and Jap forces below had made Parai Defile almost impenetrable.

We probed east 500 yards to the third low ridge overlooking the jungle flat and here engaged the first Jap outpost about 1020. Here we fronted Japs strongly fortified in pillboxes and caves. During the next few hours, Cn wiped them out. We lost Baer KIA, Juarez and Bright WIA.

Although the day was getting late, we got orders to push again. After 300-400 yards up the trail, we walked into a deafening blast of fire from all sides. Cn had unknowingly hit an ambush of Japs who were well dug in. Schecter was probably killed in that ambush.

We faced annihilation. The Japs tried to pin us down at first, then they charged with bayonets. Although we had only a .30 LMG with us, our heavy fire repulsed them. And now we tried to withdraw, the LMG first. That retreat was a long agony.

Most direct escape route lay down the trail and over a six-foot hump. Hearing the fire from the safe side of the hump, our two getaway men crouched waiting, not daring to cross the hump. Soon Joe Burkett and Morrow heard rustling in the brush and called out to find out whether a Jap or a Yank made the noise. They got no answer.

Just as they decided to shoot blindly, an unnamed Yank officer called out not to fire at anyone crossing the hump. While Morrow and Burkett held fire, the first Cn men ran towards them.

But unseen Japs already had their sights on the hump. Hall's and Martin's bodies thudded dead; the third man made it alive. (The men were all probably from the LMG squad ordered to retreat first).

The remaining Cn men tried another escape route. Scattered groups worked their way inland through brush closer to the

The Parai Defile

cliffs. The first men made it safely, then endured Jap bullets to cover others' retreat. We decided to send two at a time while the others laid down a covering fire. By now we had lost the LMG tripod, but CO Sullivan and Sgt. Jennings sprayed it from the hip to hold down the Japs. Then several men returned under heavy protecting fire to get out every one of our dead and wounded. Although Hall was killed crossing the hump earlier, Martin was still alive, to die of wounds next day.

It was a bad show for Cn Co. 8 June 1944. Besides dead or dying Baer, Hall, Schecter, T/5 Martin, we had eight WIA for the hospital. WIA were T/Sgt. Glunz, Cpl. Juarez, Pvts. Burns, Allgood, Chatfield, Bright, Backus, Webb. Since only 60 Cn men were in action, not many of us remained to fight tomorrow.

Pushing from the east to try to contact Cn on 8 June, L Co. was unhurt. But the day before our attack, L had pushed alone and was stopped with nine WIA.

And then, the day after our bad show, Cn got orders to battle again to clean out the Nips before L Co. Hq reported that Jap territory in Parai was down from 800 to 300 yards.

This time our thin squads patrolled east fearsomely. With Ed Walter Jones at point and Morrow No. 2 man, we started out in three sections. With a squad on the trail, we patrolled with Sgt. Dickerson's squad on the left and Sgt. Clark's on the right.

Slowly and carefully and wary of every sight and sound, Jones and Morrow advanced only a few yards at a time and waited for all three squads to come up with them. Inland, Dickerson's squad saw the 200-foot limestone cliff with a draw below and a small ridge. Firing should start any minute, the tense riflemen thought.

And suddenly, Cn Co. got a reprieve—a life-saving order to retreat. Our battle in Parai Defile was over. Probable reason for this wonderful order was due to what Hq. learned from results of our support fire. A combat buffalo had twice blasted areas in the 300 yards between Cn Co and L, yet could not silence Jap guns. At 1610 came a report that the buffalo had drawn heavy counterfire (8-10 Jap MG's on it) from high ground. Then an LVT of 542 EB&S Regt. directed fire from three Sherman tanks positioned on LCT's. Although the three Shermans shelled only 1000 yards of terrain closest to Pryor Jetty, they could not get results to justify Cn's risk of more casualties.

And thankfully that evening, Cn Co. made perimeter with AT 162, which had also suffered from fighting in the Ibdi Pocket. We were grateful to God for this release from the deathtrap of Parai Defile.

Not until 12 June, four days later, did outfits other than Cn 162 and L 162 liquidate Parai Defile's Japs. While AT replaced L Co. pushing west, C replaced Cn to push from Pryor Jetty. Hardest fight of 12 June was when C's 3/Pln fought on the cliff-top. Here C Co. killed a MG and found 37 dead Nips who had defended it.

By 1335, 12 June, Parai Defile road was open for 162 to expedite supplies for the all-out fight against the ridge which denied our Air Force the use of Mokmer Dromes. But Cn was already long gone from Pryor Jetty to guard supplies and secure trails in 162's main battle.

Such is the saga of Cannon Company, 162 Infantry, in two great battles for Parai Defile. In our first fight, we saved a hospital of wounded Yanks and held 162's escape route open. In the second fight, we braved the Japs in their strongest defenses, yet saved Cn Co from annihilation. The gray cliffs of Parai Defile are now a hard, proud memory of Cannon Company, 162 Infantry.

AT Co. 162 Infantry:
Desperate Battles in Ibdi Pocket

by Dr. Hargis Westerfield, Division Historian,
with S/Sgt Fred Kielsgard and Lt. Ralph Crawford

Indispensable were Kielsgard's two handwritten MSS totalling 23 pp. and Crawford's handwritten MS of five legal-sized pages. (Kielsgard wrote in July and August; Crawford's MS is dated 25 Aug. 1973). Claude Johnson contributed after 24 July 1973; Emil Entzminger on 4 Aug. Cannon Co. 162's paragraph on rescuing AT 162 was previously published in Jungleer, Dec., 1960. Other sources include award stories of Gardner, Hovorka, Helm, Crawford, Kielsgard, Palmer. I also used AT's Morning Report for June, 1944, 162 Inf's Journal and Report of Operations, and R.R. Smith's Approach to the Philippines, but Smith erroneously reports that AT was driven to the beach on June 1944. Westerfield was with G Co. 163 on both its attacks past Shield's body.

On 27 May 1944, about 0800, Anti-Tank Co. 162 Inf. landed from an LST on Biak. While AT's Mine Pln. was detached to join 162 in Parai Defile, other AT men unloaded petrol and ammo from our LST—on the double in fear of Jap planes.

Working like badgers late that afternoon, we heard four Jap light bombers blasting and strafing. MG bullets battered the deck above, like woodpeckers on a shed roof; something thudded overhead. Running out, we heard more planes and took cover back in our LST.

When silence came, a Jap plane lay dead in shallow water to port. The thud was a bomb that hit on deck but failed to explode. The gunners threw it overboard after they had downed the plane.

Up front with 162's 3/Bn. in Parai Defile, AT's Mine Pln. lost Sgt. Miller wounded 28 May, the second day of battle. During 172's retreat that day, Helm and his Pln. Sgt. saved the life of their medic. Because he was too badly wounded to walk, they carried him 75 yards to safety under intermittent rifle and mortar fire from the cliffs.

At dawn, 29 May, Mine Pln. had just got up to admire our fine Navy offshore. But a destroyer fired on us, and Claude Johnson was wounded in the back. Probably later 29 May, a Jap MG hit Fuller. After three wounded, Mine Pln. rejoined AT 162 on 30 May—but only for more vicious battle in a green coral hell.

For the next day AT 162 began our greatest fight of the war against those dark ridges later named Ibdi Pocket. Although we were antitank men, Gen. Fuller was now so short of men that he used us as riflemen.

Between 162 pushing towards Mokmer Drome on the coast and 186 pushing west on the inland plateau, there lay a threatening Jap stronghold—some seven jungle-covered, knife-edged coral ridges. About 1700 yards wide, Ibdi Pocket was one of three main Jap strongholds on Biak. To safeguard 162's and 186's main advances, Gen. Fuller saw that he had to battle Jap garrisons of these ridges.

First, Fuller sent 2/Bn. 162 up from the coast over Young Man's Trail into Ibdi Pocket to wipe out the Japs and contact 186 pushing west. After two days' fighting, 2/Bn. did contact 186. But they left behind them, almost intact, the reinforced 3/Bn. 222 Infantry of Japanese.

And AT 162 got orders to keep 162's supply trail open from the coast. About 1400, 2 June 1944, we entered those dripping green death-ridges—into wounds and suffering and death.

Climbing the last steep slope of Ridge 1, Cpl. Kielsgard carried an extra pack over the slippery, rain-wet trail. He never forgot that his death-marked cobber, S/Sgt. Janosky, reached back to help—gave his hand for the last time.

Gardner led out a recon patrol; Kielsgard heard our first M-1 shot. Gardner returned with a Nip rifle just out of cosmoline. He said that the dead Nippo owner of that rifle was over six feet tall—the tallest Nip Gardner had ever seen.

That night of 2 June, AT set up on Ridges 2 and 3. Lt. Crawford's pln. manned the forward ridges. About dusk, from 300 yards back in that green hell, Kielsgard's squad heard a grenade blast from Crawford's direction, and a scream from Janosky before he died.

Later, we learned that Crawford's pln. had halted on Ridges 2 and 3 at dusk, with no time to try to dig in or heap up coral parapets. Crawford with Janosky and their understrength squad were on Ridge 3, with the other 2 squads under T/Sgt Walen on Ridge 2. Lt. Schottsmans platoon were deployed on Ridge 4.

In the dusk on those brushy ridges, Japs screamed and fired and charged. Although we returned fire, we were outnumbered and began to fall back along the ridge.

Janosky called, "They've cut off my leg!" Crawford pulled him aside and told his men to get out of there. Crawford held Janosky until he died—probably from shock, after what Crawford thought was a Jap saber stroke.

And Crawford realized that he was the last Yank left on the ridge, and that many Japs were somewhere in the dark all around him. All that long night he hid in a coral crevice. Japs covered the ridge, but somehow missed him. Near daylight, he crept down toward the draw and signalled back to Ridge 2. His men came, happy to see him again, and they reoccupied Ridge 3—evidently unopposed.

In the morning, AT pushed two squads forward—probably to Ridge 4—and ran into a Jap ambush. After three Yanks were seriously wounded, Hovorka volunteered to enter ground which Jap MG and rifle fire covered. He saved one badly wounded man, and guided the two squads to safety. When he tried to rescue a second man—probably Ray, Boruch thought that rifle fire killed both men.

On that same night of 2-3 June, Cpl. Kielsgard and his depleted six-man squad endured nerve-racking action, although with no casualties. He had to set up a listening post in a hollow half-way between Crawford's pln. and Ridge 4. Although withour phone or radio, Kielsgard established this strange listening post. He deployed his men on the upper side of the trail—prone among humps of coral.

There we listened to Janosky scream before he died. Kielsgard heard Crawford's battle begin and continue all night and on until noon next day. The whole Jap army on Biak seemed to charge down the hollow between the ridges. It was, indeed, a whole company of Jap commandos. From this hollow, he listened to the Jap leader's orders, then the MG's spraying Crawford's ridge, along with small-arms fire, occasional Jap grenades and mortar blasts.

Soon the Japs worked up the trail by Kielsgard. They stumbled over empty AT water cans and seemed to swear loudly. He trembled—with only six Yanks to help him—and only rifles and a few grenades in the dark against overwhelming numbers.

He tried to lie quiet in the dark, but his own knees rattled against coral like a woodpecker hammering on a log back in his Old Virginia. A rookie breathed so hard as to be heard 25-30 feet away. Another man snored every time he dozed off. But Kielsgard pressed the two noisy men close enough to elbow them to quietness, and jammed his own knocking knees hard into the coral.

Jap commotion down the trail continued until Kielsgard arched a grenade into the Jap noise. After much wild scrambling, they quieted

Landing at Biak

139

down, but we lay tense at our rifles.

But farther down in the hollow and on Ridge 3, action continued all night. After daybreak of 3 June, rifle fire came from all directions hours of it. About noon, many feet clumped down the trail from Ridge 3. Kielsgard's squad alerted to fight, but it was Schollsmans men escaping.

Some men said that a great number of Japs had detrucked below us, and while we shot many of them, they decided to withdraw. Crawford's men bore with them four silent forms in ponchos: Janosky, Hovorka, Ray, and an unidentified man who did not die. Schottsmans was last in the retreat. Kielsgard and squad were assigned as rear guard, but no Japs followed. When we reached Ridge 3, we saw 3 silent forms under poncho's—Janosky, Hovorka and Ray.

Cannon Co. 162 Infantry had extricated Crawford's platoon. Ordered up the night before to help AT, CN set up two MG's and a skirmish line and covered AT's retreat with overhead fire. CN then helped evacuate AT's casualties and fell back in stages, half the men and one MG at a time.

On 3 June, a tree burst of a mortar had wounded three AT men. Crawford thought that one of them was T/Sgt. Walen, wounded by a 4.2 mortar of 641 TD which was zeroing in by sound to try to help us. (No terrain maps were available.) Luckily, Walen was hit not by a phosphorus shell, but a special type of practice shell. Besides our three dead, AT had six wounded on 3 June: Kush, Parrish, Tambakis, Lakis, T/5 Kenney, Walen. The same mortar shell which hurt Walen also wounded two of these six men.

After AT's fight of 2-3 June, Gen. Fuller closed the supply trail across Ibdi Pocket and attached 2/Bn. 162 Inf. to 186 for the overland march to Mokmer Drome. But he decided that he could not force Parai Defile unless he first cleared Ibdi Pocket, which menaced the flank of 162 on the shore. From Old Man's Trail, he planned to send 1/Bn. 162 east to destroy the Nips where Lt. Folsom had died. And he sent A Co. 186 to fight westward on AT's right flank. Although 1/Bn. 162 completed the eastward mission easily, A 186 and AT 162 hit the stone wall.

On 6 June, AT 162 with A 186 advanced westward. With A 186 flanking us inland on Ridges 3 and 4, AT 162 scouted 400 yards but found no Japs at first. In midafternoon, scout Jimmy Shields led us - Jimmy the battler, who on the night of 2-3 June had roamed from end to end of Schottsmans perimeter and claimed 28 Jap dead.

About 1550, 6 June, M-1 fire started up. Shields shot at a Jap who seemed to crumple behind a log. Shields ran up to him and was shot pointblank and killed.

Heavy Jap fire now forced AT to fall back some distance from Shield's body and form perimeter on a ridge. Unable to dig in, we heaped up those little Ibdi Pocket pigpens of coral for protection.

But the key to this position was a little hump of rock at the Jap end at AT's ridge. This hump overlooked the thinly covered coral ridge behind it, where most of AT had perimetered for the night. The hump itself was bare of trees but surrounded by brush to within 15-20 feet of our LMG guarding it. The hump was deadly to hold, but we had to keep it for AT that night, or have the Japs take it and fire down our throats.

Light but persistent fire struck the hump. About 1700, Cpl. McCormick was wounded here behind his MG. A shot supposedly from a Jap pillbox had struck him in the calf.

Under this light fire, Kielsgard replaced McCormick. With him was a forlorn hope of some six Yanks crouched behind coral walls that stood out under the full moon of 6 June–that night of D-Day in Normandy. Kielsgard never forgot the names of these comrades: Sgt. Counts, with Gardner, Helm, Boruch, Thachek, Boston.

A Jap plane strafed harmlessly and did not return. Jap attacks lasted all night with hardly a lull. Once, Kielsgard counted three MG's fighting us, plus two knee mortars and the usual rifles and grenades.

Customary Nip routine was to fire the MG's or, at times, the mortars. Then from one side, bushes shook to get our attention. Then from the other side, a Nip rushed us–and was blown back or slain outright. We formed a grenade brigade. Every hour or so, a man crawled back down the ridge to AT and came back with two helmets full of pineapples for Japs.

Besides Kielsgard, S/Sgt. Gardner took turns on the LMG while the other men did their part with M-1's and grenades, although they were in lower, less favorable spots for action. Gardner and Kielsgard traded positions at the LMG, but Kielsgard was especially happy when Gardner's M-1 was there to fell charging Nips on our right flank.

New Jap tactics were to scare us into a freeze at our MG, then have us empty its belt. While we reloaded, they could rush in with bayonets. So our MG fired only in dire need brief touches of trigger for the

At point blank range

shortest possible bursts. One giant Jap screamed piercingly and leaped at us. Kielsgard shot him on the wing; his body thudded dead before the MG barrel. When Gardner held a chunk of coral against his head for cover, a mortar fragment cut his exposed thumb.

At dawn, the Japs withdrew. Shakily, Kielsgard's seven men rejoined AT Co.—no doubt with an outguard on the hump. Only 19 cartridges remained in the MG belt. When Kielsgard picked up the MG, he found that a bullet had shot off the snap attaching barrel to the tripod.

On 7 June, we pushed again. Sgt. Palmer's squad hit a nest of concealed pillboxes full of blazing MG's. Japs threw grenades, and Palmer, firing rapidly, was lucky to escape with his squad.

Wounded 7 June were Lt. Harbaugh, lightly, also Gunia and Entzminger. A bullet struck the brow of Gunia's helmet and came out the rear. Crawling flat on his stomach on the left flank of a patrol, Entzminger inched past two corpses of men who had died the previous day. He felt a sharp crack in his right shoulder. Despite the shock, he somehow stood up, pinched the bullet hole tight with his left hand, and walked back to our medic. He still held the rifle in his right hand. He never knew why the sniper failed to fire again.

During 7-10 May, AT and A 186 got nowhere at Ibdi Pocket. Lt. Harbaugh brought up a flamethrower team from 162. But deft Jap riflemen kept the flamethrower from a shot into a pillbox. It would have cost most of AT 162's and A 186's lives to win Ibdi Pocket from that reinforced Jap bn.

Relieved from Ibdi Pocket 10 June, by 15 June AT had made perimeter near 162's forward CP before West Caves. On 17 June, Strawser was wounded by a MG while he carried a casualty from another company to an aid station.

On 19 June, Crawford's pln. took two 37 cannons to begin fire into West Caves. Mraz had a light mortar wound but remained on duty. Cpl. Sheppeard was also hit 19 June and hospitalized. But on that day gunner Vogel died at his post when he blasted into West Caves.

Observing the patch of woods where Vogel's killer was hiding, Crawford banged on a nearby tank to ask for help. Under Jap rifle fire, the tank headed for the woods. One Jap rushed the tank with a flaming Molotov cocktail, but our bullets riddled him. And perhaps about 20 June, an AT detail under Lt. Harbaugh was aiding 1/Bn. 162 before West Caves. We dumped a whole truckload of gasoline into the caves and fired it.

Such was AT Co. 162 Inf's war on Biak–unloading an LST under bombing and strafing, enduring the defeat of Parai Defile with our Mine Pln. We battled the death ridges of Ibdi Pocket day and night, then fought the West Caves.

At Ibdi Pocket, we surely blunted Nip 3 Bn. 222 Inf's morale, for after 7 June they were generally on the defensive. And when G Co. 163 Inf. recoiled on 19 and 26 June from that grimly held strongpoint blocking Ridge 1, G's men retreated past the high-water mark of AT's westward advance of 7 June. Some few yards in front of that pillbox under an Aussie blue blanket lay the body of Jimmie Shields, who could not be moved until B-25 bombers had killed Ibdi Pocket. Shield's location best symbolizes the daring of AT 162 at Ibdi Pocket.

In the Slot on Biak

By DR. HARGIS WESTERFIELD, Division Historian

with Major James Gray

Basic personalized narrative is from "Company B 162 Inf Reg; Biak Operation;" supplemented by Mjr James Gray's ltr on Soepori Opn, undated, about Sept. 1962, and ltr of Bob Jacobs 12 Sept 1959. Other sources include June and July Microfilm Morning Reports of B 162, "Hurricane Task Force Narrative of Biak Opn," "Addendum" "162 Inf Journal" on Biak, "Unit Journal/B Co 162 Inf/Soepoeri Campaign, RR Smith's RETURN TO THE PHILIPPINES."

On Biak, B Co 162 Inf battled Nips on D-Day. We made initial assaults on Ibdi Pocket. Infighting Jap tank-infantry teams 14-15 June, we almost got wiped out, but we battled Kuzume to the portals of West Caves.

On D-Day while 162's lead Cos probed Parai Defile, we got orders to cross the dirty-green coral ridge north of Ibdi to flank the Nips. Jap fire halted us before Ridge 1; Mihelic, Palmiotti took serious arm wounds.

On 28-29 May, B secured 162 Hq while Japs drove 2 bns back from Mokmer. On 29 May, Japs hit us with mortars, MGs, rifles. About noon, they cut the road east of Parai Jetty. With CO Townsend's Cannon Co riflemen, we dislodged the Nips behind close mortar support. D Co's Weapons killed 8; Cannon Co took all losses. By 1500, B Co formed rear-guard while 162's battered bns escaped from Parai with 32 dead, 183 wounded.

Back at Ibdi 30 May, B Co dispatched combat patrols to find 1 Bn a flank route through the ridges. Mortars and rifles repulsed 1/Pltn; Sgt Grove hurt an ankle in the cliffs. Then 2/Pltn struck up the same trail — a 1-man trail, slippery with falling rain, up a 25-foot cliff. Mortars scattered us, wounded Godwin. After our own mortar barrage, we failed again. T/Sgt Biedebach took foot and elbow wounds.

On 31 May, a Yank B-25 strafed and bombed 1 Bn. But 3/Pltn had to clear that ridge. Jap fire stopped us. Without orders, Ransom climbed 20 ft up a cliff. A grenade slashed his face, but he shot into Nip positions. After covering Cox, also wounded with a grenade, Ransom pointed out locations to a flame-thrower team. Although flame cleared our way to the crest, Jap fire hit Martin, repelled us.

After 3 days' security perimeter for 205 FA, B headed up Young Man's Trail into Ibdi Pocket, with Bn Hq and 2 HMG 30s. It was again horror for B Co — jagged up-and-down coral trails, dark-green fear, harassing fire from nowhere. We evacuated a "psycho." On 4 June, a B squad with mortar cover helped A 162's push to Ridge 7. Through 7 June, Sgt Alex Schmidt, Nicholls patrolled, slew stray Nips. Schmidt's squad found East Caves.

But B was recalled to help clear Parai Defile. Landed at Parai from buffaloes, we followed 3 Bn and tanks pushing NW to Mokmer Village. In extending 3 Bn's right flank, B's 2/Ptn moved into a Jap mortar barrage that halted the push. Shells from East Caves wounded Galvin, Dunn, Wells, Sgt Hicks. B Co withdrew, dug in, mortared the Japs.

On 9 June, we tried to dig in on high ground above dead Nippo tanks. Jap mortars struck Medic Helland in the head; he died in Sheffey's arms. To save itself B Co dodged back, to drop down a 10-ft cliff to the beach.

Back in yesterday's safe perimeter on 10 June, we sent a security guard with Sherman tanks to Mokmer — 6 men atop each tank. No one was hit. About dark, Lt Cate called for 60mm fire on 2 Nips observing from the ridge. Our own shell knocked observer Pierce. The blast knocked Medic Jacobs flat in his hole. While bandaging Sgt Pierce, Jacobs found that the shell had wounded him also. Souder was also wounded that day.

Disaster struck on 11 June. Following 162's first great assault on Mokmer Ridge, we secured 162 Hq in the dispersal area at 1900. With no time to dig in we clutched the heaving ground under Nippo bombers at 2300. Nosek, Geohlke, S/Sgt Hornbussel died. Seriously wounded were 10 — Leroy Davis, Shea, Duck, Oropesa, Goletz, Sibert, Bonner, Malezynski, Pritchard, S/Sgt Nichols. Also hit were Paul DeWitt, Biggs, Paul Northcutt, John Moran, 2/Lt Cate, S/Sgt Jim Cook.

On 13 June, B Co went "into the slot" for our heaviest combat of the war. As part of 162's 1 Bn, we teamed with 186's 1 Bn to stab the heart of Nippo defenses of Mokmer Dromes. We would cross Mokmer Ridge safely east of 162's fighting 3 Bn, then turn west to capture what natives reported was the last water-hole remaining in Kuzume's hands. (We did not know this was really West Caves.)

But B Co met trouble on Mokmer Ridge. After digging in, we sent 2/Pltn to scout behind 162's E Bn. Finding 30 well-armed Nips who hit the brush and ran, 2/Pltn got back at 1730, had to dig in 50 yards west of B's left flank. At 0600 14 June, 2/Pltn awoke in darkness to battle a determined 15-man Jap attack with bayonets, LMGs, a knee mortar. Diskin, Norman took rifle and grenade wounds. But B's LMGs slew 9 Nips in 10 minutes. Until 1100, Nips held us with small arms, mortars, even AA shells.

Still at 1100, B marched in 500 yards from Mokmer Ridge, turned hard left, deployed all rifle pltns abreast as skirmishers. With Hq, Weapons, 2 HMGs behind the center Pltn, we advanced under FA barrage. Our own FA shorts sporadically halted us, a short wounded Kolowitz, Stricklan. We slew some Nips.

Late that day, we hit the track SW to West Caves. Pushing 250 yards more, we dug in on a slight rise. As Sgt Schmidt returned with a small patrol, Japs attacked. A rifle wounded Schmidt. While Medics tried to save him, Jap fire wounded 2 of Schmidt's outguards — Close, Benedict. Close and Schmidt died that night.

B Co fought on. Leftwards, 1/Pltn prone in a half-circle took heavy fire — front, flank, and rear. We set up 1 LMG that fired fine protection. But when Weapons men tried to position another LMG, Linnville, Roscano, Sgt Kalmbach were hit. The gun could not fire effectively. On their right, 1/Pltn and 3/Pltn had heavy fire, front and flank. At 1800, we brought up B's 60s, but intense fire kept them from positions where we badly needed them.

It was a bad night for B Co. About 1900, Jap tanks with infantry blasted us — tanks with 37mm cannon, HMGs. Jap infantry fired in a continuous sheet of flame. 1 Bn lacked bazookas to fight tanks. Wounded were Weapons Pltn's Varto, Summers, Cpl. Duncan; dead were 2/Pltn's Gafner, Lokofsky.

In 90 minutes came orders to retreat. We left with 7 Yanks missing in action, lost much heavy equipment. But B Co fell back in good order, holed up in 3-man teams behind 186's B Co.

Thus Col Kuzume's sally drove B Co from the field 14 June, but next day, we fought Kuzume again. At dawn, we pushed up to close the gap we had left between 162 and 186. Nips with a tank charged down on us — moving cannon, HMGs, Jap infantry in a withering blast.

We still lacked AT weapons; but we coolly fought for our lives with all our fire-power, while 121 FA threw in shells. We blasted the tank-infantry into carnage, saw the frightened antique little turreted beast veer off into safety. Wounded were Wellbaum, Braun S/Sgt Jim Cook. While taking them to Medics, Imbrone, T/5 Merritt Thomas, S/Sgt Buchanan also were hit. Noble was seriously

141

wounded. Lightly wounded were Swain, Hugh Baker, Glaza, Varto. But at 1100 from "missing in action" returned our 7 Yanks lost in Jap attacks last night.

On 16 June, we stayed in holes. For 186's 2 Bn attack on the left was causing Yank FA and mortar fire across our front. But B's mortars shot all day; Jap fire hit us. A sniper killed T/4 Squires. On 17 June when 1 Bn pushed again, we followed A 186's right rear. Jap mortars wounded Ellis, Sgt Kiepke, T/Sgt Larkins. B's 40-man detachment guarded 186 dumps; Crider, Sgt Comiskey got mortar wounds there. But with Beecroft as observer, our mortar's served 186 well.

Despite — losses we consolidated into just 2 rifle Pltns — B Co became tank-infantry to fight West Caves themselves. On 19 June, we escorted 2 tanks which held down most Nip fire until we got into rifle and grenade range. When Jap fire barred our riflemen, a B LMG section moved to the left end of the Sump Holes and lanced at Jap strongpoints guarding them for 2 hours. For once, B counted no casualties!

On 20 June, in the same tank-infantry assault, B Co found death again. Accurate Nip riflemen waited. 1/Lt Gray, CO, took B men to our left flank, cleaned out a dangerous Jap pocket. Gray was wounded there. On our right, a Jap tried to flame a tank with a Molotov cocktail. Sheltering behind a tank when possible, T/4 Ziebolz killed a Jap pillbox. He then crawled to the other side of the tank and knocked out 3 more positions. We rolled 6 drums of gasoline into the caves and lighted them. But Jap fire continued with almost no decrease in volume. At 1700, we fell back with Ziebolz, Cpl Vinton Williams, Grosshandler dead; Whitaker, Roudian, Quillman, Lts Gray, Cate wounded.

After this fight, B Co consolidated again. We were down to 1 full-strength rifle pltn plus Weapons and Hq. From assigned strength of 189 when Biak Battle started, we were down to 167 — but with only 100 for duty. Luckily, we did not fight West Caves again, we relieved C Co on the high northern ridge for security guard — 4 days' comparative rest and recuperation. On 25 June, most of B relieved A Co to guard West Caves again. But the great infighting and the Jap Banzai (21-22 June) had ended. Remaining few Japs gave no trouble. On 28 June, a few Yanks finally penetrated deep enough into the caves. And B Co participated in a great souveniring party.

But B's war on Biak did not end with capturing West Caves. Men back from hospital rebuilt our pltns; and 2 months later, we found death again in the forgotten "Soepoeri Campaign." On 7 Sept, Weapons and 1/Pltn landed under Soepoeri Island's blue jungle mountains — on the SE coast near Biak. Mission was to interdict Japs wading from Biak to live off native gardens — and to destroy Cmdr Mayeda's Jap Marines trying to rendezvous with subs to take off Adm Senda.

On 10 Sept., 1/Lt Grimm sent a small patrol against Nips in the mangrove swamps by Amirweri. The Nips' ambush was clever. Ellis, Pearce, DeLoof, Lt Cate died. It was weeks before we got out their bodies.

CO Gray blazed with anger. He called B's other pltns from Biak got Bn CO Col Benson's loan of 2 D Co 81s. Gray swore this was one for Irish John Cate, great soldier, God rest his soul! Survivors of Cate's patrol showed how to zero in D's 81s, B's 60s. Eagerly we uncovered gleaming mortar shells, piled them ready. Gray gave orders.

The shells arched down into dark-green mangrove jungle, caught the Nips in tree platforms. Some lay chanting war-songs — a Jap diary recorded this! Mortars mangled many, vengefully our rifles slew 40. We took 12 prisoners.

One morning near Awak, 2 Japs killed an old native who guarded "marys" and children in the yam patches. For the first time in years, the natives became head-hunters. In 4 days, they slew the 2, returned with the head of the actual slayer. That night, the village Kapala or Chief invited B Co to the victory celebration.

Naked black spearmen enacted the killing — crept on the Jap again — leaped high in air with spear-thrusts. We Yanks crouched by our rifles, tried not to watch the fire-light flash on the dead Jap's head. The Kapala asked B Co take part.

Resourceful CO Gray called on our Hawaiian Yank, Sgt Kekipi, to speak for B Co. In the full light of the fire on the beach, Kekipi rendered an old Hawaiian war-chant. And we men of B thought of Kekipi's Hawaiian chant as our own victory song. We

Landing craft carry troops of the 41st Infantry Division for a landing on Biak.

The 186th Infantry's "rabbit squad" smokes Japs out of a pillbox on Biak.

A Sherman tank leads a column of Jungleers through the tangle of Biak.

remembered Parai Defile, Ibdi Pocket, the night the bombers caught us above ground, the night and day we fought the tank-infantry team, the bloody days before West Caves. We remember wounded we'd never see again, our 16 dead. And ours were proud memories of a great battle company.

C Company, 162 Infantry
IBDI POCKET TO WEST CAVES
By DR. HARGIS WESTERFIELD, Association Historian

On Biak, C Co 162 Inf was at first nerve-wracked but fairly safe. When 162's 3d Bn fell back from Parai Defile 29 May, C with three tanks became rear-guard. Then after some patrols and security guards against the Parai Nips, C became part of 1 Bn's operation against Ibdi Pocket. Gen. Fuller decided that Ibdi Pocket on 162's inland flank must be cleared before 162 tried to take Mockmer Strip again.

C Co was again lucky in the push up Young Man's Trail in Ibdi Pocket 4-6 June 1944. On 6 June, C was far up in those knife-edged limestone ridges and facing east. S/Sgt. Fay Murphy was wounded. But since Ibdi Pocket's Nips no longer menaced 162 in the Parai Defile, C was ordered back to the beach for 162's great try to seize Mokmer Strip. This time we embarked on landing craft to bypass Nips still holding Parai roadblock, and put ashore at Parai Jetty where I, K, and C Cos with six tanks of 603 Tank Bn had already landed.

On 8 June, C was part of 162's second march to Mokmer Strip. Clearing out booby traps ahead, C advanced below to the first cliff with the beach on our left flank. To our right, I and K advanced in line with us on the high ground above the first cliff.

At noon break, 162's men were 500 yards east of Mokmer Village—in that coconut grove where the Japs stopped us 11 days before. When we moved at 1300, Jap field guns with 90-mm mortars clumped down. Would Jap tank-inf attacks come, as on 29 May? To secure from such an attack, B hurried to K's right flank to the ridge behind K.

And C echeloned on the beach 2 to 300 yards ahead of I and K. Jap 77s and mortars flailed us. Shell-blasts felled Capt Day five times before he went back to the Medics, and we never saw him again.

Possibly six Jap 77s fired on us from back at Parai, and 3 mortars from the cliffs. Where our mortarmen dug in, T/Sgt Manley begged Vigue to take cover. Manley knew that the Jap fire pattern was such that the next salvo would surely impact here. Manley was already holed up. Just as Vigue turned to walk away, a shell fragment struck him in the head and killed him—a man already assigned for rotation but unable to ship home from Finschhaven.

Later that day, C's mortars and 1/Sgt were almost wiped out. Manley had just pulled his mortars back 100 yards from the Japs' impact zone. Ahead, Yank rifles no longer fired, and he had seen men falling back, but Manley had no orders.

Manley found 1/Sgt Hackos and 2 others forward of his old mortar positions; asked for information. Hackos replied, "I don't know. They don't tell me a damn thing about what's going on."

Between salvos, Manley worked up to the foot of the ridge. He thought we had stormed it and the rifle pltns had moved on. Another Jap salvo was due to land near him. He looked for a hole—and saw none. He threw himself under a broken palm tree—landed feet first in a standing fox-hole. A shell hit so close it filled the hole up to his waist. Nip voices yelled at each other on the ridge.

Manley shot off his carbine clip at the voices and sped for his mortars. He halted only to tell 1/Sgt. Hackos that our riflemen were gone from the front and that Hackos himself was now the company front. Hackos and his men outran Manley in their charge to the rear.

The Yank supposed to tell Manley that C was withdrawing had seen men on the move and had thought we already had the message. His neglect almost killed 4 men. But that night C dug in safely. On that June 8, besides Vigue KIA and Capt Day wounded, we also lost Karnbad and Kuzniers WIA.

On 9 June, a few mortar shells flattened C to earth in perimeter, but hurt no one. With B Co now on our right flank and D backing us, we moved up behind a 205 FA barrage. Sporadic mortar fire hit before us while Nip MGs shot from the cliff and another Nip mortar lobbed shells over the ridge upon us. While D's mortars counterfired, C plugged on. Yank mortars started a fire on Nip cliffs.

At 1300, C patrols contacted 162's 2d Bn, which was attached to 186. (Our 2d Bn had done the waterless inland march with 186 and helped take Mokmer Strip from the rear.) Now C was recalled to the beach to spearhead 1st Bn's attack to clear out Parai Defile, which had long held up 162.

On 12 June, C was back at Parai Jetty pushing east towards Bosnek while AT-162 pushed west. Here, Japs still held a ridge and water-hole and Parai Road. Hardest fighting occurred where 2/Lt Berger took 20 Yanks with 1 LMB to push the Nips off the ridge.

Moving 40 yards along the ridge, we found the Nips on a nearly perpendicular rise of 20-30 feet. They waited until 3/Ptn reached the crest, then fired with automatic weapons. We hit the ground. Throwing a grenade and firing his carbine, Lt Berger took shelter behind a coral outcrop. Berger tried to knock out a gun, and a burst caught him. Sgt Weimer saw Berger get up for a last charge. Berger emptied his carbine, hurled a grenade, was still charging when he died.

The rescued 3/Ptn fell back from this place of death; called for mortars. Nip small-arms fire could not hit us, but grenades rolled down and scarred us. Manley's mortars fired a first round for range with the safety pin still on. It landed among Nips, but the next rounds were tree bursts which hit Yanks. Then 3/Ptn lifted their mortar fire and walked the bursts up the cliff edge and down into the Nips. Next day a patrol found 37 dead Nips on that ridge. Besides Lt Berger killed, C lost Fabio killed also, and Stratton and Charles Kelly wounded.

Thus, on 12 June, C finished off the Jap roadblock in Parai Defile. Now Col Hanley ordered C into the Morkmer Ridges where 162's 1/Bn teamed with 186's 1/Bn to drive for Kuzum'es West Caves. On 15 June, a C Ptn went into the ridges at dawn with plasma and stretchers for men of hard-hit B-162. On 17 June came C's hardest day of battle yet.

While C fought, A and B, while pushing on West Caves, came under Nip fire from high ground that was 186's objective —fire from a Jap 75, 2 HMGs, 3 LMGs, 2 knee mortars. C knocked out several pillboxes, but by 1140 Japs forced us back. Worst fire came from cliffs on our right, but tanks blasted out these Japs. By 1330 C had the last important Jap positions— just as 186's 1/Bn arrived unopposed from the other side of the ridge. But C fought again; Japs shot at A and B from the left flank—from ground which G-186 had taken but had to leave on 16 June. These scattered riflemen and MG crews we cleaned out by dark. On 17 June we had 7 WIA: Hedell, Orosco, Steforsky, Mascarella, Svoboda, Lumpkins, S/Sgt Gardea, 2/Lt Landrum. These men were out of action; Bruning's and T/Sgt Rosenbalm's light wounds let them remain on duty.

That night, Nips hit F hardest, but also cut communications between A and C and the rear. By 0810 next day, C killed 8 to restore contact. Inspecting our captured ridge, we had a Jap 75 cannon, 3 LMGs, 2 HMGs, 2 mortars. We counted 30 more Jap dead. After dark 18 June, we had word of the Japs' main Biak stronghold in the dark below us—the coral sumps called West Caves.

When 1/Bn first attacked West Caves, B hit from east and south while C probed from north and east. In one of C's probes, T/Sgt Rosenbalm died—giant Rosenbalm firing his BAR from the hip like a tommy-gun. He struck everything he shot at. On his last day, he knocked out 2 Jap automatic weapons and was charging a third when Jap crossfires dropped him dead.

C did great work firing from our new ridge. By now, we had spotted down in the flats those Nippo sumps and lined our sights on them. To fight off 162, Nips had to take positions outside. Every night, Nips sallied out and dug in before dawn. As the light cleared, we spotted fresh coral where they had dug in. So every morning, riflemen and gunners sighted down the ridge through the tall, slender trees of Biak and emptied their holes. We named our ridge Turkey-Shoot Ridge.

On 21 June C relieved the single pltn left of B, and attacked the sumps. Flamethrower-rifleman teams cleared Japs from high ground NW, and C with 2 tanks hit West Entrance. We lobbed grenades into all holes and crevices in reach, shot all Japs we saw. Tank 75s fired into the cave mouth, but coral stalactites blocked off penetration of the caves. Engineers poured 5 drums—hundreds of gallons of gasoline—into surface fissures, dropped in phosphorus bombs which flamethrowers ignited. Underground, heated Jap ammo began popping like firecrackers. This night, Col Kuzume burned his colors, and 150 Japs sortied from West Caves to die under 186's HMGs.

On 22 June, C hit West Caves again—staged behind a low knoll with corpse odors heavy in the dawn coolness. We heard a number of explosions from the caves. Most C men neutralized North Sump; 1/Ptn guarded 2 tanks clanking to South Sump. Nip mortars popped; M-1s replied. We caught Jap weapons crews still outside the caves and slew them. From Duck-Shoot Ridge, a C mortar barked.

Seven Japs had gathered in a shell-crater on the North Sump rim. C observed them from Duck-Shoot Ridge. Without base-plate or bipod, Sgt Harwick aimed the tube true; Clifford dropped the shell down the barrel. It got all 7 Japs; the bodies lay dead, radiating like the spokes of a wheel from the center of the hole.

But our tanks' 75s still could not penetrate the mouth of South Sump to cover a C Co attack. Japs still lurked inside. Sixth Army observer's Col Harold Riegelman had an admittely wild idea—to lower 850 lbs of TNT with firing wires attached into the hole for an experimental blast.

Maj Benson assented; Engineers brought the TNT forward in a trailer, lowered it from a winch into the sump. We pulled back C 100 yards, put the tanks in defilade, detonated the TNT. Ensued a roar and a great rockfall. A few Japs— one at least insane from the blast—dashed out to die before our rifles.

With Benson, 3 162 riflemen, and some Sixth Army men, Riegelman checked the cave-mouth for lethal gases. Riegelman saw, dim in the blackness, prostrate Jap forms and smelled foulness. Although uncertain whether or not the odor was from poinson-gas or decomposed flesh, he advised Benson to wait a few minutes, then send C in with the bayonet. (Riegelman had slept well the night before, returned to Hq to write a monograph on fighting Jap caves.)

But Maj Benson saw no need to lose a C man in that Gehenna of corpses and possible poison gases and ambushes. Not until 27 June—with C Co breathing clean air back in the ridges—did other 1/Bn men with 41st CIC men penetrate that place of horrors to find 125 more or less whole bodies of dead Japs.

With the Cave assault of 22 June, C ended our great Battle of Biak. We had fought Ibdi Pocket, run the gauntlet of the Parai ridges, and turned back to liquidate Parai roadblock. We had fought those mouths of hell, the West Caves. Dead were Vigue, Fabio, Berger, and Rosenbalm.

> Human interest is mainly from T/Sgt Wm Manley's letter to the father of slain Lt Arthur Berger, 22 June 1966, and his notes and map done in 1967. Also important was a chapter from Col Harold Riegelman's CAVES OF BIAK (Dial Press). Solid documentary sources include 162 Inf's JOURNAL OF BIAK OPN, Co B 162 Inf's BIAK OPN., R R Smith's APPROACH TO THE PHILIPPINES.

E Co 162 INF: FIGHTING AROUND BIAK ISLAND
By DR. HARGIS WESTERFIELD, Division Historian
with T/Sgt Don Carlson, E Co, 162 Inf.

On 27 May 1944, E Co 162 Inf landed dry at Bosnek Jetty, and labored heavily upward towards the first coral ridge. We slew 4 Nips and took their LMG, then hunted west along the jungle ridge. Mission was to protect Col Haney's right in his Z-Day push for Mokmer Drome. But we had no trail on this jagged ridge — only heat and silence. Although 162 Hq prodded us, E could not keep up with Haney's march along the shore. We found no Nips. Haney was already short Cn and AT Cos, unloading ships. He ordered us to rejoin the main body, to bivouac near Parai.

Next morning, the Mokmer Japs struck 3/Bn, cut it in two, and mauled G on the right. With F Co following, E got orders to reinforce or rescue G Co.

We hurried up to where we saw G's rear guard, but we never got closer. Jap mortars and MGs cracked down. E Co hit the ground but held. We could do little more. Sgt Bill Doescher came up on somebody's request for a LMG, but we had no field of fire for it, and told him to keep it safe in the rear. But Jap mortar fire lulled, and we guided G Co back to the rear, and a battered 3/Bn Pln which had fought its way through.

E Co now retreated 75 yards and dug in. As 3/Bn withdrew in defilade above our new holes, it had new troubles. Being in defilade, 3/Bn men could not tell whether overhead fire was Jap or protecting Yank fire. Thus the men lay low when they should have retreated, or had casualties when they stood up unknowingly under Jap bullets.

Then a squad leader on E's beach flank, Sgt Howard Sullivan, waded into surf where 3/Bn men saw him. Although coming under fire, Sullivan caught 3/Bn's attention and signalled them when to advance and when to take cover. Sullivan stayed out in the open until 3/Bn had cleared E's lines. Later, he led his squad to save wounded, and move dead to where the tide could not carry off the bodies. On this day, E had just 3 reported wounded — with Ken Franzen and Dale Evans to hospital and 2/Lt Engle remaining in action.

E Co's holes were now an important part of 162's front. Backed by HMGs, 1/Pln held a line of 40 yards. from the beach up to a 12-foot cliff. Our lines crossed the road up the terrace where the Japs had stopped our advance yesterday.

At first light 29 May, Japs pulled a banzai charge on E 1/Pln. Our rifles, mortars, MGs knocked them down — like ducks in a shooting gallery. S/Sgt Don Carlson held us back; we wanted to move up and end the war.

An hour later, we heard our first Jap tanks clanking down upon us. 1/Lt Uppinghouse phoned Hq to ask for tank support. Next few minutes were tense; E Co had no bazookas or flamethrowers to hold the line. Just as the Jap tanks crested the ridge and Jap infantry struck, our Sherman tanks came up and sighted on the Jap tanks — 3 heavy Shermans against 4 Nip tanks.

A round of 75 AP shell stopped each Jap tank, while E Co and supporting MGs killed the Jap infantry. But in 30 minutes, a second Jap infantry line with 3 tanks struck us. Again, our tanks killed their tanks; E Co's guns downed the Jap infantry.

But while E Co rejoiced in victory, orders came for the great retreat from Parai Defile. Not knowing that Japs were massing on 162 right and had even cut us off awhile at T-Jetty, E Co saw no reason for retreat. We thought that an advance of a mere 100 yards would capture a point to which we later had to slog all the way around Biak to return to.

As ordered, E Co had to withdraw 600 yards from our present line. An air-strike would impact the line we now held. We managed to retreat 100 yards of the required 600, but supporting troops blocked our trail. Carlson's profanity made even officers jump. But still we fell back too late. When our planes strafed with 50s, Rip Walker died. Killed somewhere on that day also, was Fred Lee. Wounded were 17 — Duffy, Bob Martin, Ford, Drawdy, Malinski, Quinonez, Hart, Fritz, Manzari, Macurik, Hessler, Boren, Fell, Elwood Carlson, S/Sgt Rider, Sgt West.

And with 2 KIA, 19 WIA in 2 days, E left Parai Defile aboard amphibious craft. We rested 2 days in Bosnek Perimeter. Then when 186 started overland to take Mokmer from behind, E Co went with other 2/Bn Yanks to help 186. Mission was to clear Young Man's Trail from Ibdi Village, through the coral hills to contact 186, then trek west over the ridge to Mokmer Drome — an advance that had been E's original assignment on Z-Day.

MOPPING UP ON JAP POSITION IN NEW GUINEA, 22 APRIL 1944.   US Army Photo 157-9

On 1 June, E Co struck north into the Ibdi ridges. At Ridge 2, Carlson saw a Jap striding down the trail — and got him between the eyes. With G Co next in support, E Co labored onto Ridge 3 — then saw Japs on Ridge 4 ahead. By 1550, Japs struck both flanks of E Co's strongpoint on Ridge 3, and soon cut it off from the rear. Gilley was wounded. But we outposted the base of Ridge 4 and safely passed the night, despite our isolation.

On 2 June, we contacted 2/Bn again. Mortars neutralized Japs on our flanks. We advanced up Young Man's Trail to Ridge 5 where a Jap MG stopped us. T/Sgt Bickle's Pln was partially pinned. Newly promoted Pln/Sgt Carlson got orders to flank the Japs on the left, since Bickle and some 6 others were on the ground under Japs' rifles. But the left flank was too open to Jap fire; orders came to pull back in line. Bickle and his men came out on their own. Between MG bursts, they had to jump over a great log across the trail.

Then E Co found it could move safely around the Jap strongpoint to the right. Meanwhile F Co also came up on Ridge 5; our combined fire kept most Japs down. Reinforced by G Co also, we contacted E Co 186 Inf by 1500. Losses included Pritt, Chavez, Huff WIA — and T/Sgt Bill Doescher out with food poisoning.

Now 162 Hq gave up on advancing any large number west, through the almost impassable ridge, while Japs behind us held almost impregnable Ibdi Pocket. And E, F, and G Cos went under 186 command, and hunted west over the waterless jungle flats north of Parai Defile.

And after 4 hot, dry days of miserable hiking in the scrub, E Co followed 186 down to seize Mokmer Drome. When the great barrage of 7 June began, E was caught in the middle of the air-strip. The screech of depressed AA cannon was sickening. E Co faced about to the ridges, and dug at coral for protection. We could not get 3 inches below the surface, but heaped out little piles of loose stone where we found it. We sent out ineffectual patrols. The Jap emplacements finally quit firing, and we set up perimeter. We lost Sam Allen KIA, and 13 WIA: Clayton Adams, Clay, Hawk, Winegardner, Baker, Carroll, Fields, Mason, Hendrickson, O'Brien, Cox, T/4 Brownson, Cpl Herron.

Next day, 8 June, E Co marched and suffered again. Ordered east to rejoin 162's main drive west from Parai, we hiked under Jap barrages. With F on our left, E had to clear Japs from the beach. Deployed on a 15-foot shorecliff, 1/Pln took the brunt of Nip shells from those sullen ridges. And 800 yards east of Mokmer, a rain of shells halted 2/Bn until 186's D Co mortars slowed Jap fire. (And G Co 186 hunted those ridges, seeking to kill those emplacements.)

E moved again, but heavy automatic frontal fire stopped us. From the sea side, streams of small shells cracked across our front into coconut trunks and exploded. We seemed to need a tank or assault gun to smash this formidable menace. Angered at 45 minutes' halt in hot sun, Carlson borrowed a 2/Bn bazooka team. The Jap gun was a 20 mm Killer, in a coral cave 50 yards up the beach. Crouching, peering around a coral bend of cliff, we saw only the gun muzzle in the firing slot. While riflemen and an E LMG fired on the cave-mouth, bazooka men crawled around the bend to sight their tube. First 2 rockets — adjusted for tank armor — were duds, but one crashed through the slot. We fired 6 more rounds which blasted the cave-mouth open, knocked down the stone walls, smashed the gun. But the 2 Japs within had fled already, to be shot down when they ran across F's front. Later, we decided that Jap security measures had unintentionally saved E Co lives because their coral embankment below the gun had kept them from depressing the muzzle for deadly low fire.

That night, 2/Squad of 1/Pln expected a quiet night on inner perimeter. But as we arrived on the upper bench, a Jap mortar killed Ted Brown, wounded Sterner, Harbin. And at midnight, Jap mortars killed Massey, our radio man. Japs tried to infiltrate. Being low on grenades, Vetrovsky would throw a few rocks, then hurl a live grenade, conserving grenades and keeping the Japs out.

On 8 June, 5 died — Able, Pollock, Cpl Horn, Brown Massey. Wounded were 13 — Munoz, Joyce, Tromble, Harbin, Gorman, Capella, Conley, Head, Toton, Holton, Sterner, Lewis, Sgt. Sullivan.

And on 9 June, E contacted 162 again, pushing from Parai Defile. Home with our regiment, we learned that we had credit for killing 600 Japs and 9 tanks — 2 more than actually fought us. But now came orders for E to hightail it back up the beach we sweated over. Jap watchers on the ridges must have been as surprised as we were.

And on 12 June, E was part of the infighting to clear the Jap positions on Mokmer Ridge, which denied our use of the airstrip. A thumb-shaped resistance pocket — with West Caves centering it — pointed towards Mokmer strip. While 3/Bn pressed west on the "thumb", 2/Bn with E Co pressed east.

Perhaps because of earlier suffering on Biak, E Co had these ridge actions comparatively easy. Although F Co garrisoned the ridge at once, E had to send up only a pln. Not until 16 June, after 186 made its great assault, did all E Co take over a ridge-top mission. But our action was still nerve-wracking, as on 12 June when 1/Pln took over an old F perimeter. For 947 FA crashed hunks of 155 mm shell on us, and an air strike had a near miss with a 100-pound bomb. We were unhurt, but no Japs were near us either. Sgt Bemis' relieving pln suffered our own fire also. Finally, E Co took over a ridge position that seemed safer.

On 17 June, Capt Robinson sent Sgt Carlson on a recon patrol. Moving 3-400 yards west on the ridge, Carlson then patrolled north. Exposed on barren land, his 5-man patrol took a classic diamond form and hunted into a Jap supply dump on both sides the road and up the hill north. We heard 2-3 Japs hammering and talking before we pulled back to report distance and azimuth. Gen Doe called Carlson in for details, gave him coffee and a pack of cigarettes and said he'd capture the dump with 2 tanks and 2 rifle Cos.

The night of 17 June, 15-20 desperate Japs hit the ridge between E and F with a MG and knee mortar. Of 12 casualties in 2/Bn, E lost 3 — the only dead — Funk, Gower, Cpl Jack Brown. From 17 June on, E Co did not fight again — but did carry on endless marches, patrols, and mop-ups. We had done well on Biak, had stopped the tough tank-infantry attack of 29 June, fought up Young Man's Trail to help 186, then fought back to 162 at Parai before the final assault to seize Mokmer Ridges, at a high price in killed and wounded.

Prime credit is from T/Sgt Don Carlson's 15-page, legal sized holograph MS in diary form. Especially useful were Gen Harold Haney's letter 20 June 1968 and a paragraph from INFANTRY JOURNAL'S "Bazookas on Biak." Pentagon records include RR Smith's APPROACH TO THE PHILIPPINES, 162 Infantry Journal, E 162 Morning Report, and Sullivan's Award Story. Carlson is today Loan Officer with US Civil Service's Small Business Administration in Hawaii. Graduate of University of Washington, Carlson has a son David aged 18, prep school grad accepted for Stanford University.

F Co., 162 Infantry:

Heavy Combat on Biak

By DR. HARGIS WESTERFIELD, Association Historian with SGTS CHESTER YOUNG and FOWLER SUMMERS

Prime source is T/Sgt Chester Young's typed MS—"F Co 162 Inf Biak Journal," plus his story of night combat identified in 41 Div Training Notes, his Ltrs Oct 31, 1970, and Jan 4 and Mar 16, 1971. Fowler Summers wrote 10 Pp of Ltrs May 24, 1970, July 5, 1971. I also interviewed Maurice Winslow early in 1971. Official materials include RR Smith's *Approach to the Philippines*, F 162's May-June Morning Report (corrected by Young), Extracts from 162's Biak Journal, awards of McKeller, Winslow, Capts Olson, Ratliff. Thanks also to F's Walter Stelter for his roster of members of F Co's present group.

On 27 May 1944, F Co 162 Inf landed on Biak and struck down the coast behind 3/Bn to fight for Mokmer Strip. We passed several gas dumps afire and a deserted village, but no Japs fought us. Bleakly F remembered our second day at Hollandia, where one ambush cost us 7 KIA and 3 WIA. But here on Biak, the only incident came when a Jap plane lighted us with a flare.

But on 28 May, instead of taking Makmer Strip, F found death. When Nip charges stopped 3/Bn on the shore, our 2/Bn tried to mount a terrace north of 3/Bn to outflank the Jap forces below. Jap fire halted us, cut off G Co before us. Chester Young's 3/Pln went to safer high ground on the right, but F men on the road suffered. Incessant Jap mortars wounded Patton, Krieger, Headley, Temple, Bruno. Fox died of wounds.

And 29 May was heavy combat. For 2/Bn repelled tremendous tank-inf charges under East Caves' bombardment as we held 162's main road under cliffs. S/Sgt Summers watched Sgt Goalby's M Co HMGs kill Japs until gun-barrels were useless.

On high ground below cliffs, Young's 3/Pln endured FA, mortars. A mortar shell impacted a MG crew holed next to Young. It killed 2, wounded others—missed Young to wound the rifleman next to him. A coral chunk blacked Young's eye, but great Capt Edwin Olson died from mortars.

Soon F Co got orders for a delaying action while 2/Bn saved itself on landing craft. Orders never got through from our 2/Bn CO to retreat. Summers saw a Yank bomber dive to spew 7-8 streams of red death on what the pilot mistook for Jap pursuers of 162. On 29 May besides Capt Olson, F had 3 more KIA—Meadows, Lahaze, Burgess. WIA were 1/Lt Phillips; T/Sgt Fehrenbacher; S/Sgts Button, Lowe, Woodall; Sgts Burke; Barber; T/5 Wittman. Bates, Gurynski, Gonnelli, George Jones, Hayes, Dixon, Hanning, Petrasko also were WIA. F had 4 KIA, 16 WIA.

Then F boarded Alligators to leave Parai Defile for ridges behind Bosnek. On 1 June, F became part of 2/Bn's battle with Ibdi Pocket. Mission was to clear Young Man's Trail over 7 knife-edged coral ridges above Ibdi Village, then contact 186 trekking to capture Mokmer Strip from the rear.

In that green hell of jagged ridges, rain seemed to fall always. E Co pushed to Ridge 3 on 1 June; Japs cut E off for the night. While G Co moved to Ridge 1 in support, F came up on G's right. We caught MG fire from a cave to our left, Young thought. Blackburn, Kovack, Puckett were wounded; Roehm died of wounds. F could not dig in that night, but lay soaked and cold in little pig-pens of heaped up coral.

On 2 June, E reestablished communications, pushed to Ridge 5. After our Capt Ratliff's fine recon, F was on Ridge 5 by

1150 also. E's and F's fire kept down Japs until G came up. We pushed over Ridge 7—had fought through Ibdi Pocket. In contacting 186 then, Young's patrol took a Jap strafing.

Then 2/Bn 162 flanked 186 on its march, helped search for a trail over ridges down to seize Mokmer Strip. On 5 June, E's Lt Uppinghouse-led Young's 15-man F patrol to hunt that trail. Someone failed to tell Div Hq this patrol was out. FA observers evidently thought we were Japs.

Suddenly 947 FA heaved 155s on Young's patrol. First shell cut our wire; some 18 shells exploded around us—miraculously missed. A Jap patrol hunted us. It passed Young but blundered into 2/Bn and fought. Back scared from 18 explosions, Young thought his Bn CO would send him out again. He slipped off his safety, growled that if anyone wanted him dead, he'd take a man with him. But the CO merely needed more details about that other patrol. On 5 June, another 3/Pln patrol lost Simunovic killed. F lost Alvarez, Massey, Brewer WIA.

On 7 June, F 162 with 186 took Mokmer Strip unopposed, then endured the Japs' FA ambush. Caught crossing the strip, F cringed under FA, AckAck. Projectiles often hit the rock at such a slant that they caromed off with the ear-splitting scream of a buzz-saw. MGs and rifles also pecked at us. Oklahoma Indian Harjo was hit in the foot. That night, Stein was shot in the leg, died from shock during treatment.

Then on 8 June, a 57-man F 162 patrol struck into the Jap ridge to kill an especially vicious battery of 4 20 mm guns. (A G 186 patrol and a K 163 patrol hunted those guns also.) F's men slept on the last ridge inland, at first light patrolled back down towards Mokmer. A fine azimuth reading sent F straight for the Jap guns. Down 400 feet, we found a little ammo dump and just over the ridge, the 4 20s revetted in coral with an unused spare—on a bench 100 feet wide. We had expected tanks' help from the beach, but they feared to hit us.

The Japs lacked outguards to alert them to pick us off as we filed down. Not one Jap gun pointed at us. S/Sgt McKeller ordered volleys that drove off the Japs. Then S/Sgt Summers used his reading in the life of John Paul Jones to help him "spike the guns." Sgt Dean and he planted grenades in breeches, pulled pins, ran. The guns never fired again. F Co had no casualties but for a man who broke a leg and a man wounded. Woods had a bullet through a sleeve.

We spent a few more days with 186 on Mokmer Strip. For East Caves' fire held us from contacting 162's main body now trying to join us. One night Japs bombed the Strip—the planes so low overhead we heard the bombs crash into Jap bomb-racks. One night under Jap mortaring, Prielipp and Young ordered a lad to hole up with them. He did not heed the warning; a fragment evidently cut his jugular to kill him.

By 11 June, 162 had fought its way west to gather up 2/Bn. Now F Co was part of the team with the most important mission of the Biak Operation. We must capture the low ridge above Mokmer Strip. Taking this ridge would end Jap control of Mokmer Strip. Fine was wounded 11 June as we got into position below the Ridge.

On 12 June, F struck straight into brushy Mokmer Ridge. Art Richter met a Jap face to face. The shock was such that both backed away. That night, a Jap crawled into CP. A Medic struck him, then thought the Jap a sick GI, sheltered him all night. When he saw the Jap at dawn, he broke a gunstock to slay him. Senner was wounded 12 June.

Most of the next few days, F Co anchored 162's left flank on the ridge—with 900 yards' scrub between us and 3/Bn eastward. When a patrol spied 3-4 Japs, Woodall exploded a grenade under the first, and we killed them all. Long was wounded 15 June.

And by 16 June, 186's 2/Bn had closed the gap between us and 3/Bn, and cleared out some menacing gun positions in the gap. But when 186 fell back, F Co must spread out to dig a thin line of holes to guard that ridge. Even arrival of all E Co on our left was but little help. The dangerous gap was now between E and F Cos—where Japs surely crawled to spot each F hole. And F's left flank was a mere 9-man outpost —3 holes of 3 men each in a triangle of shell-torn brush 30 yards from F's main body.

And so at 0400 in the dark 19 June, desperate Jap warriors with mortar cover hit F Co's left flank outpost. Hole-guards suddenly had us alert in the dull dark. Brush crackled; Japs 200 yards off were kicking empty MG boxes. Suddenly from Les Brown's Hole No. 1 on the extreme left, Yank grenades exploded. From a little knoll, Jap mortars pounded us; fragments fell around us.

After mortars quit, Japs screamed, fired, attacked in 3 groups. One advanced on Hole No. 1, 20 yards from Young's hole. Another shot on Young's left flank. Worst of all, a third group struck for our left rear; 3 rifle-groups flamed at us from the dark.

And all 3 groups converged on Hole No. 1 where Les Brown and 2 other new men fought. From all 3 holes, we threw grenades, heard Jap screams, halted their attack briefly. But they overran Hole No. 1, killed 2 Yanks—expelled Les Brown. From Hole No. 1, Jap rifles blazed at us.

Brown ran toward Hole No. 2 with Barrett and 2 new men in it. Brown was too quick and quiet; the occupants thought Brown a Jap and killed him.

Now F's MGs fired their final protective line but could not save us. F's holes were in a straight line on the ridge; F's MGs could not traverse far enough left to clear the dead space close to the holes. A Jap voice called in English, "Watch out for the MG! Work to the right." Young snarled at the Jap's clear English; he could almost smell the rice-breath as Japs closed in.

Japs now lanced at Hole No. 2. Although Young's men in No. 3 grenaded around Hole No. 2, only Barrett's tommie shot from there, then silenced. Then Barrett and 2 cobbers rushed for Young's hole—and almost died because they did not identify themselves. Panting Barrett said that both M-1s had jammed; he was down to 1 clip of tommie ammo.

Virginian Young kept cool. We had only 3 M-1s and 4 grenades for the 6 of us. To run up the line to alerted F men in the dark might mean death. But to remain in Hole No. 3 was certain death.

Young told the other 5 to fall back across a draw 30 yards off—to talk slowly to the men in the dark holes—and to wait for him.

After the 5 left Young alone in the dark hole, his wait seemed to last forever. Then 5 Japs rose on the sky-line; his last grenade impacted them. Something blasted Young's rifle from him, split the heel of his hand. But he found his 5 men waiting for him. Since we moved slowly but frantically called our names, F men let us through to form a line on the left rear.

S/Sgt McKeller already jumped from his hole to rally F Co, restive with the wild firing from Young's outpost. Young helped the MG Sgt—probably Robshaw—to line the MGs down that draw between F and the overrun outpost. For the only way to save F Co seemed to be to fire those guns and seal off the Jap front.

But there in our field-of-fire lay our own wounded crying in the dark. Medic Winslow rushed into the blackness and panted back 3 different times with Yanks. Although slightly built, good Medic Winslow carried the 3 50 yards to defilade. He brought back Hale—whom Hopkins had shot accidentally—and 2 more.

Now F's MGs stabbed flame into the dark to seal off the Japs. With his slight wound, and his M-1 shattered, Young could only help bring up more MG ammo. He heard the strike of the bullet that knocked Silvestri's helmet over the ridge and killed him. After Silvestri died, Jap fragments silenced 1 Yank MG. The other was low on ammo. Just in time, our 60s lobbed in; came then D's 81s and closed the night action.

At dawn F counted 28 dead Japs. No accurate list was kept for F's casualties for that night's fight; but for 17 June and 18 June, we had 5 KIA, 6 WIA. Killed on those days or nights were Brown, Hale, Shaw, Bordner, S/Sgt Silvestri. Wounded were Lindstrom, Grigone, Dean, Perone, Sgts Robshaw, Kaercher.

And thus ended F 162's main Battle of Biak. The Japs never tried F Co again. For information only, we sent small patrols over to the cornered Japs in West Caves—but took no chances. The Japs fired every time we tried to look into those caves.

When the Engineers crammed those sink-holes with dynamite, detonated with gasoline, F men had orders to hit the ground. We expected the top of the world to blow off, but we could hardly feel the explosion. Most of the concussion must have spent itself in the great caverns underground.

Last man wounded in F was Wintermeyer on 28 June. Rumor says that he was unloading a truck and somehow pulled the pin on a grenade attached to a pack. On 7 Aug, F was part of 2/Bn 162's contact patrol towards Korim Bay—15 days to meet 163 coming south to meet us. It was good to have no more deadly battle with Japs. For since F's landing 28 May, we had 14 dead and 39 wounded—as far as accurate figures can be had. Such was the price of F's great fights—in the slot at Parai Defile—up and over Young Man's Trail at Ibdi Pocket, and in the night defense of Mokmer Ridge.

Bottle, bottle - who's got the bottle

By Colonel John H. (Herb) Neilson

The date was 15 September 1940. The place was Medford, Oregon. It was the last day of civilian life for the author, Bill Lovell, Howard Schrecengost, Joe Roberts, Joe Dallaire and several thousand other 41ster's. The next day we were all scheduled to enter active duty for "one year of training". For some reason, it never entered our heads to evade this duty by declaring ourselves as conscientious objectors, students or "hardship cases". In fact, we looked forward to it, and celebrated the event exceptionally well—but not very wisely! The only member of our company who didn't celebrate the occasion was Joe Dallaire (Hq3-186), whose girl friend frowned on tasting the grape. It was quite an evening!

The next morning we were greeted by a first-class hangover and a physical examination that included an urinalysis. We feared that we all risked being flunked on the physical because of our previous night's drinking bout. We also logically decided to have "Sober Joe" provide for each of us what is known as a "specimen" in medical circles. However, Joe's puritanical girl friend had fed him copious quantities of chocolate fudge the night before. You guessed it! Doctor Bob Sleeter (Med-186) promptly declared eight of us disqualified for diabetes. After a red-faced explanation, a few hours' wait, Doc Sleeter made a retest which we all passed, and the whole crew made it through to the SWPA except Schrecengost and Joe Roberts. Schreck finally wound up as G-2 of the Alaskan Command after a stint at O.C.S. He later transferred to the Intelligence Corps (Cloak and Dagger), and retired from the Regular Army in the late 1960's.

Joe Roberts made it through the induction physical, but got caught up with at Swamp Murray when Colonel Ralph Cowgill made an inspection while Joe was on latrine detail. Colonel Ralph walked into the latrine and found Roberts bent over a wash basin. In response to the regimental commander's question as to what he was doing, Joe replied, "I'm washing out my glass eye, you dumb b———, whatdya think I'm doing!" Joe's military career with the 41st ended forthwith! Strangely enough, Joe was later killed with the 503rd Parachute Battalion at the Kasserine Pass in North Africa. We do know that Joe was an expert at reading the eye chart with his good eye, and then repeating it when the only vision he had was with his glass eye!

I Co., 162 Inf: Parai Defile and Mokmer Ridges

By S/Sgt. M. H. KELLEY
with
DR. HARGIS WESTERFIELD,
ASSOCIATION HISTORIAN

On 27 May 1944, I Co. 162 Inf began the battle for Parai Defile, crucial for taking Mokmer Dromes. Leading 3/Btn's push, Cpl Rose and squad slew 4 Nips. A bullet wounded Jim Wilson in the abdomen. When supporting tanks broke the Parai Bridge, F/Lt Goggin called the nearest Yanks to protect tankmen saving their monster. Jap fire from the cliffs wounded 1 Yank, drove others to cover. Goggin scaled a 50 foot cliff, surprised the Japs on the flank. He slew 4, routed the others. We saved the wounded Yank.

Now I Co's 2/Pltn scouted ahead with the tanks. A Jap shot S/Sgt Clyde Woods square between the eyes. Le Moine was hit on the left side of his scalp. But naval rocket ships smashed the Japs on the cliffs with tremendous volleys. Under inaccurate harassing fire from Jap rifles, I Co pushed west around the narrow point. In wide brushy flats west of Parai, we dug in with 3/Btn. About 2200 in bright moonlight, 2 unarmed Japs rushed a MG position and died.

On 28 May, those brushy flats with Jap cliffs behind us became 162's death trap. The day began well. K struck down Mokmer Road and shot up light Jap resistance. But at a trail junction 1500 yards west of Mokmer Village, heavy MG and rifle fire struck K Co. Our F/Lt Goggin ordered Camack's and Madeira's Pltns into line with K Co to flank the Japs into withdrawal.

Scared but eager for first shots at Japs, I's Pltns sweated through the 15-foot scrub to fight beside K Co. Then we hit the ground—scared, frustrated, angry— all at the same time. For Jap HMGs hacked a line through the brush across our front. We could not pass it. From sinister Parai Ridges we had bypassed, heavy mortars lobbed into I Co—Jap 81s like rain drops from the sky. Lost in brush, wounded were moaning. At this moment, turreted Jap tanks staggered evilly down the road at us—with Jap infantry columns. Jap 81s kept impacting.

From Camack's Pltn, S/Sgt Jack Perry ran to the rear to tell Btn/Hq of the tanks. AT Co hurried up to take positions. I Co's bazooka-men waited confident and ready, but orders came to fall back. Now our own Shermans clanked forward. With naval aid, 603 Co tankmen drove the Nips to cover—with 3 tanks hit by Jap FA and 3 men wounded. M Co's HMGs and I's LMGs moved down the Jap infantry.

While Jap mortars still fell, Jap warriors hit 3/Btn's inland flank. I Co faced their attack and stopped them. We shot at least 6 Nips.

CREDITS

Absolutely essential to this great saga were M. H. Kelley's Diary 17 Apr-7 May 1944 plus Ltrs 11 Feb., March 22, May 3, 1965. Background data were from "Report Opn 162 Inf 27 May-19 Aug 1944, 603 Tank Co. Report Aug 1944, 41st Division Medal Awards List, and RR Smith's Approach to the Philippines. Also author of earlier story of I Co at Salamaua. Kelley is one of 162's few historians — now a forest ranger in Chemult National Forest in Oregon. We have only one other 162 story of Biak—Jim Gary's on B 162, soon to appear. Help!

But the beating the mortars gave us was terrifying. We could not dig holes in the coral. The hard surface intensified each burst; as much coral flew through the air as shrapnel. Second growth limited our own observation; but the Japs in the cliffs saw almost every move we made and followed us to a new location with a new salvo. In East Caves alone were 5 81 mortars battering us, with an unestimated number of others lobbing shells in on us.

The entire 3/Btn cowered under bombardment in an area 200 yards deep and 500 yards long, squeezed between sea and cliffs. Superior fire-power sealed us off from advancing; we could go only one way from annihilation—back.

Three hours after the tank attack, Lt Goggins got orders to withdraw I Co. F/Sgt Kelley long remembers the cool, clear, concise manner in which he gave instructions to Pltn representatives and Kelley himself. Mortar blasts punctuated many of his words, and several times Kelley felt himself lifted 6 inches off the coral by an explosion.

Kelley's orders were to find Lt Eulon Richardson, assemble F/Pltn and 3/Pltn on the right, and meet with the other units for full retreat. Kelley could not find Richardson at first, but he led out the fighting Pltns. In the low scrub, he sighted Richardson limping towards the Japs. Kelley swore above the blasts and saved Richardson; this dedicated officer would have gone into the Nip lines to help his men.

I Co's retreat must be across a narrow tidal flat several inches deep in water. Half way through, Kelley sheltered behind a log and shouted to the men to hurry—never to stop. From the dark cliffs, Jap MGs and rifles fired. Bullets spouted water all around them. Men stumbled, righted themselves, ran on. Regrouping, Kelley was surprised to find no serious casualties there. Radioman Smith from Virginia had a walkie-talkie radio shattered in his hand. A bullet shot the watch off the lapel of Buro's jacket. A part of the watch pierced his nose where natives wear ornaments.

But I's casualties were heavy — Dunlap killed, 16 wounded. Two mortar shells exploded in the Pltn where Stanek was squad leader. With shrapnel in his back and a leg wound, Stanek first helped other wounded to aide station before Kelley persuaded him to get treatment. Besides Stanek, I's wounded were Larry Thomas, Ulgener, Disney, AC Sellers, Vollman, Key, Webb, Godsey, Stegall, McMillan, Wayment, Frost, Russ Lewis, Miles. Out of 162's 16 killed, 87 wounded, I Co had 1 dead, 16 wounded that day of defeat at Parai Defile.

On 29 May, we had horror indeed. While I Co rested quietly in perimeter, Richardson called Kelley from listing yesterday's casualties in the Morning Report. Kelley walked 20 yards to talk. The next thing he knew, he was picking up his blood-splattered self. It was other's blood. Back where he had worked on the Morning Report, Hq was a shambles—bodies in grotesque positions tumbled over one another, the Medic already working at shattered Alberghina. "Don't bother with me. Help Dick," said Al, referring to Thorne. Both died. Helping Melcher to Btn Aide, Kelley saw Doc Drexler operating on a K man on a table—medics' tents jammed with bloody men. Our heavy naval guns had fired short. Besides Alberghina and Thorne dead, we had 10 more wounded—Sealey, Foshee, LaBonte, Melcher, Yagatich, Simcox, Snyder, Rose, Liguori, and 2/Lt Madeira who lost an arm.

I Co gladly led 3/Btn's rteretat from Parai Defile—except for Huffman's 2/Pltn at rear-guard with L Co. In pelting rain, we hiked 4 miles back to Mandom, dug in around FA and AA. In chilled fatigues, we gladly found Nippo canned heat for boiling coffee, wondered what next. Huffman's Pltn returned by buffalo craft.

From 31 May to 6 June, I Co had only drudgery and attrition in probing Parai Defile. At night 1 June, a Jap cannon fired a Jap gas dump in our perimeter, also wounded T/5 Shovan. At night 3 June, a Jap grenade killed Sgt Norman Smith outposted near Parai. On 6 June, 6 I men joined an L patrol across Parai Stream. Pedersen, Mulkey, Sides each killed a Jap. Richardson now directed fire on the Japs from a destroyer. Morale was low; some I men wasted grenades at night.

Then on 7 June, I with K boarded buffaloes to bypass the Defile and land at the jetty after rocket bombardment, unresisted. On 8 June, we made another useless attack—with K on the terrace, and back to where the Jap tanks struck on 28 May. Again, heavy mortars hit I Co from right rear, on our unprotected flank. We could only withdraw. Wounded were Woodrow Jones, Don Hall, Reeder, Ed Brown, Willie Rice, Gallow, Lagerstrom. Killed were Titting, Sgt. Lincoln "Powerhouse" Williams.

Morale was never lower than after the defeat of 7 June. We had again fought across the impossible terrain of our first defeat. We wondered why no unit helped us on our open right flank. Constant rumors came that Jap reinforcements were landing on northern Biak. If we couldn't crack Nip defenses now, fresh Japs could drive us into the sea. And the death of the diminutive giant "Powerhouse" Williams with his happy grin and ready wisecrack—this death hurt our morale more than anything else.

About 1400 9 June, we again probed to Mokmer, to the second northsouth road. Mortars and MGs halted us again. So next day, we pulled back to the beach and slid westward again. With some protection from a low coral shelf, we hiked Indian file through reefs that were waist deep mostly. Jap mortars opened on the rear squads and splashed us. Each concussion in that water slammed us like a foul kick below the belt. But once out of the water, we turned inland, crossed the east end of Mokmer Strip and dug in on high ground. We faced the Jap ridges at last.

We killed on 11 June. Part of 186's and 162's offensive, our patrol scouted a Jap pillbox 150 yards ahead on a coral ridge deep in rain-forest. A small Nippo patrol hunted toward us. We pulled back, ambushed them, slew 4. At 0930, I Co withdrew to give mortars and 947 FA's 155s room to geyser the coral and timber. At 1230, we pushed on the exposed right flank, with dark 60-foot ridges to our right. At 1300, we drew rifle, MG, mortar fire.

S/Sgt Dewhurst spotted a large, well-concealed bunker which only a direct hit could destroy. He deployed his squad for cover, then crawled up in defilade. When he was 12 yards from the pillbox, Jap automatic fire lanced at the covering squad. By short dashes, he got to 5 yards, and dropped. He then leaped for the corner of the pillbox. He chucked 2 grenades down the slot. He emptied an M-1 clip into the Japs as his men closed in. We found 11 dead Japs—4 from grenades, 7 from M-1 bullets.

In the next push, another pillbox pinned down Dewhurst's squad. Dewhurst's jaw was half shot away. Pedersen and squad volunteered against the Japs' flank, worked up to 10 yards' distance before the pillbox opened up on them. A grenade bounced off Pedersen's helmet, seared him with shrapnel over arm and shoulder. Pedersen ordered his squad to fire and rush. He killed 2 Japs with grenades, and 4 with his rifle; his squad killed 9. Pedersen refused evacuation.

I Co's morale soared. Out of that mortar impact area on the flats, we now had jungle ridges where we could maneuver.

On 12 June, we hit hard. When Jap fire held us, we pulled back to let M Co's 81s smash the Japs. With L Co attacking on a terrace northward, and K on the slope south to Mokmer, we took the hard way up the ridge. L and M had it light, but Sgt Bandy's squad of I Co took heavy fire. Bandy's squad killed 3 Japs but fell back with Murkli, Muldoon, Lipinsky wounded and left under fire. Com/Sgt Whalley left his radio and with Seiber and others dared the Jap fire to save the men. Murkli died later.

With MG and 60 mm mortar cover, we pushed through these positions to the next higher ground. Manford Price was slightly wounded. By 1130, we fought through a second set of positions; but 50 yards west was a third series—and a fourth reported 50 yards farther west. L Co began advancing on the right flank to help us. On 12 June, I Co advanced just 200 yards; but now we felt success in our bones.

For on 13 June, we passed through the deserted Jap positions to higher ground. We bypassed a small pocket of 2 Jap pillboxes on our right to tie in with L Co, called fire on them. A K patrol later found them deserted. I Co was ready to drive west with 3/Btn at dawn.

But we never had to drive west. On 13-15 June, we rested or cleaned weapons, while other 2Btn and 3Btn elements narrowed the Japanese gap on the ridge between them. On 16 June while 186's 2/Btn closed the remaining gap, Jap mortars hit us twice, seriously wounded Janaskis—our last casualty. We did not have to butcher in the abbatoir of West Caves. By 25 June, we were back in the sun on the beach.

On Biak, I Co fought as well as in the old-time trench warfare on Scout Track Ridge above Salamaua. But on Biak, we survived 2 heavy mortar ambushes what would have annihilated us. Yet we survived Parai Defile and led off in the crucial storming of Mokmer Ridge to free Mokmer Strip for raids against Mindanao. We lost 8 dead and 40 wounded—a minimum of casualties for the dangers we endured. The replacements after Salamaua—stateside teenagers and "old men" over 30 had been welded with our Scout Track Ridge veterans into a finally unbeatable I Co 162 Infantry.

L Co 162 Inf - FIRST AGAINST MOKMER DROME
By DR. HARGIS WESTERFIELD, Association Historian
and T/Sgt. Bill Brown, L Co 162 Inf

Standing off Biak in our LCI at dawn 27 May 1944, L Co 162 Inf's men were exuberant. For Biak seemed another easy victory – like Hollandia. Our turreted battle-fleet and convoys moved in from every sea-horizon. Waves of B-24s smote the beach. Two heavy cruisers, 3 light cruisers, 21 destroyers, 5 rocket craft slashed the land. Five fast transports, 21 amphibious craft drove for shore.

Landed by 0900, L Co was sure no Japs lived after this bombardment. Ashore in the second wave, we moved west down the narrow Jap coast road, sweated in the scrub. By 1030 as we hiked, the brush ridge on our right closed us in to the beach. But L Co did not worry.

When 5 tanks rumbled abreast, L men growled. At Salamaua, our lives depended on seeing and hearing Japs; but tanks din and dust made us hike blind. Short of water, we filled our 2 canteens from the slimey coastal swamp. Then after drinking, we found Parai stream 500 yards ahead – underground river of clear, clean water.

Bivouacked about 1600 above Parai Village, we watched 8 Jap planes – bombers and fighters – strike low at the fleet. They skip-bombed, strafed, made a suicide dive, disabled a transport. But our Navy shot all down instantly.

That night, L Co slept on the east side of Parai Village. Despite orders, many never dug in. We slept well. By 0730 28 May, L advanced confidently to take Mokmer Drome – advanced into disaster.

At Parai Defile, tall, mossy cliffs of rain-forest pressed L Co's march almost into surf. It would be a bad place to retreat through. Then, around the curve in the beach, the cliff fell away into a long inclined terrace, slanting towards the sea. And L Co, with a section of M's HMGs, advanced up the roadway like a ramp, to get on the plateau above Mokmer Drome.

We never reached the Drome. Just as Lt Minner's riflemen sighted the airfield, a Jap heavy mortar barrage flailed the top of the ramp we climbed. Accuracy was unbelievable. Bill Brown saw a direct hit on a mortar base-plate. A 30-50 foot cliff penned L Co on the seaward side, while the Japs bombarded us from a 50-foot cliff lined with Jap gun emplacements.

Japs drove a wedge of riflemen behind us down the ramp and cut us off from 3/Bn already being pushed back along the shore.

Heading L's riflemen pushing on the Air-Strip, Lt Minner was hit and died before plasma arrived. T/Sgt Koelfgen lay under mortar fire with a leg almost torn off. T/Sgt Ray Kliever ran in and carried Koelfgen to safety. As casualties grew, S/Sgt Healy took over Minner's men, maneuvered the battered squads from cover to cover, back to the comparative safety of L Co.

Although L was cut off, Capt Kindt acted immediately. With T/Sgt Kliever again volunteering, Kindt took a patrol which found a concealed way to get L back down to the beach. But L's 3/Pltn was initially surrounded, and could not rejoin Kindt. This Pltn fought its way back to the higher ground where 162's 2/Bn – with G Co cut off – also fought for its life. (Meanwhile, news came that a company – probably G – was cut off 500 yards to the rear. We had to get a message through Jap ground to this company by runner. From a squad protecting 3/Bn's right, Lombardozzie volunteered, and successfully carried the message through.)

While casualties mounted as Jap shells continued impacting, not a man of L Co expected to get out alive. Angrily resigned, we decided to sell our lives for as many Nip dead as we could. But by 1600, the Jap barrage lifted. The Jap counter attack died. And one fighting L Pltn moved forward of 3/Bn's main body, then turned to the right flank to reinforce I Co.

Then L had orders to dig in – a real shock to us at the sea's edge like sitting ducks, with coral rock to dig into. But then 3/Bn received new orders to withdraw. With tanks at hundred-foot intervals up the road, L formed for retreat – two lines a few feet apart – just like a parade. From the cliff, Jap gunners and mortarmen threw down all they had.

An unidentified officer - big, red-headed, bemustached – bellowed, "Every man for himself!" Taking cover where possible behind tanks, L Co ducked to a point where we could slip down over the cliff to the beach. Brown leaped over men dead unscratched – from shock or concussion.

Just as Brown threw himself behind the first tank in the column, a mortar shell impacted it. A fragment slashed Brown's left arm. Taking cover, Brown scrambled down a 15-foot cliff, which sheltered L Co until we rejoined 3/Bn near Mokmer Village. On a strip of open land, Virseo died, and some L men were wounded. Besides Minner and Virseo killed, L Co had many wounded. Besides Brown and Koelfgen, these were wounded: Battenhorst, Sgt Bowman, T/5 Brewer, and Williamson, Epstein, Trager, Sam White, Sobolski, Kirwin, Bileyeau, Kevil, Pleasant, Teetor, Hawkins, Mel Williams. We had a total of 2 killed, 15 wounded.

Picketing the upper plateau for 3/Bn, L Co endured the night; but on 29 May, our own destroyer shot a salvo into 3/Bn. Ten were wounded: S/Sgts Healy, Loverich, with Brimley, Nugent, Chas Kelley, Conley, Kramer, Valdez, Ball – and Theriault killed. Jacobsen died of wounds. Thus by 1445, L Co gladly joined the retreat from Parai Defile. Loaded on buffaloes from T-Jetty with an I Co pltn, we landed below Ibdi, where 3/Bn regrouped to fight again.

Now we were part of 3/Bn's new attempts to force Parai Defile – which we called "Bottleneck." Kuropatka was killed 2 June. On 3 June, L Co was with 3/Bn and 7 tanks to force the Parai Defile. By 1355, Jap fire halted 3/Bn. Japs burst from the scrub, cut off 3/Bn's lead pltn. Tanks helped save the pltn, but 3/Bn failed to break through. We found 2 Jap road-blocks. Grenades crashed down the cliffs on us. As we fell back, a Jap leaped on a tank, dropped a grenade inside, killed 1 Yank, wounded 1. A D-8 Caterpillar towed out the tank.

On this day while his LMG fired overhead cover for the retreat, Brown heard a FA major start to order a barrage on Scott's 3/Pltn. Barrage did not fall. A sniper killed Newhouse. Temellosa was killed, T/Sgt Kliever wounded. That night we killed 2 Japs. On 4 June, Steinhibler died of wounds.

From its patrol base at Parai Stream by Sonegarai Bay, L Co sallied on 6 June, advanced safely 250 yards by 1435. But by 1550, after the first road-junction, we took heavy fire. Brunotti died; Cacioppo was wounded. We fell back to Parai Stream again.

When I and K embarked to bypass the Parai Japs and landed again at T-Jetty, L Co remained behind, to continue pressing those bypassed Japs. This time, on 7 June, we made 500 yards before Japs stopped us, at 1445. Five Yanks then volunteered to seek a way to contact I and K Cos at Parai Jetty. But Jap fire stopped the 5 – Sgts Bill Ferguson and Walling among them. Not until dark could they escape. L Co wounded 7 June were Cobb, Powlowski, Stanton, Lapis, Kearns, Scott, with S/Sgt Estrada, Greenwood, Low.

On 8 June again, an L reinforced Pltn tried to clear Parai Defile in a pincers movement with Cannon Co, pushing east. But a dug-in Nip ambush cut Cn in half, repelled them with 4 KIA, 7 WIA. L was unscathed. (Not until 12 June did 162 liquidate the Defile with C and AT Cos.)

But on 10 June L was released from that narrow, corpse-foul jungle shore and its overshadowing deadly cliffs. In amphib craft we rejoined 3/Bn in fighting against Mokmer Ridge which denied us use of the air strip. Mokmer Ridge was jungle on coral terraces with 600-700 Nips – infantry, combat engineers, guarding AA, mountain guns.

On 11 June, L was mainly in reserve while 3/Bn fought west against Mokmer Ridge – against emplacements so difficult that 947 FA's 155s must clear the way. Evidently L detachments assisted. Bill Brown's overhead MG fire silenced a large Jap pillbox until I Co men worked in to kill 5 Japs with grenades, and overrun it.

Then on 12 June, L Co found death again. To relieve pressure on K, we got orders to work along K's right flank north of the ridge – with just 2 Pltns, while the third remained in security guard on the flats. Moving warily west, our two Pltns with weapons men contacted Japs in position, had 1 wounded. At 1225 again, L drew fire from a Jap pillbox on that ridge. Since Japs on Mokmer Ridge thus made us sheer off north, we cut directly south at 1445 to climb Mokmer Ridge safely. L had hoped to contact I Co fighting west. Instead, we located ourselves 500 yards from I Co – all 500 yards thick with Japs.

On this night of 12-13 June, we had wedged a ridge perimeter between those Japs resisting I Co eastward, and Japs in the 900 yards separating us from F Co westward. (These 900 yards made up the Great Gap not fully closed until 186's 2/Bn offensive of 16 June.) And Japs crept in through the dark to kill. A mortar slew Sgt Gardner in his hole, wounded 2 more Yanks with him. Before daybreak, Japs lay 10 yards from our holes. A Jap officer reached for a MG barrel during the daybreak attack; the gunner shot him dead. Besides Gardner and Sgt Dennis Jones KIA, we had Bak, Frank Burns, Rodriguez, Ingle, Trudillo wounded 12-13 June.

Morning of 13 June found L isolated from 162 communications, and low on water, food, ammo. Another attack might force L off the ridge. T/Sgt Little volunteered to apprise 3/Bn Hq of our predicament. He ran a gauntlet of fire, but luck and poor Nip shooting saved him. Then 3/Bn laid wire to put us back in contact with 162. Rations, more ammo came up. Litter cases went out, despite Jap MG fire that drove carriers to earth awhile.

Now, on 13 June, depleted L Co had the impossible task to attack Japs both ways on Mokmer Ridge – west 900 yards to F, or east to I Co. The westward gap L never did close – although Yank shells fired to help us seemed to light almost in our hip pocket. Not until 1314 did L make contact with I Co. Even then, 2 Jap pillboxes held out – one 100 square feet of reinforced concrete, the other a log corral with dirt reinforcement. By 1600, tanks knocked out both pillboxes. L's reserve pltn came up, and we readied for another attack west. On 13 June, Zieglmeir died of wounds; Lombardozzi was wounded.

But L Co made no more attacks. On 14-15 June, L kept low, under menace of Yank FA supporting 1/Bn's strike towards West Caves. On 16 June while 186 closed the gap between 162's F and L, we hit the ground but had more wounded. Sputaro caught fragments in the back but remained on duty. Koram, Everett Gardner, Guy Stewart, Lassier, Keith were wounded. And now, but for mop-ups and security duties, L's war on Biak was ended.

L Co 162 Inf lost 12 KIA, 47 WIA. Cut off in Parai Defile, then shelled by our own Navy, we had rallied to make costly probes into Parai Defile. Being ordered from Parai Defile, L Co had cut itself off again, for a night fight among Japs on Mokmer Ridge. L Co 162 Inf has a proud record of combat on Biak.

> Prime narrative for L CO story is T/Sgt Bill Brown's 6-page memoir. Also essential were RR Smith's APPROACH TO THE PHILIPPINES, L's MORNING REPORTS, 162's REPORT OF OPERATIONS, and JOURNAL, Award Stories of Little, Kliever, Lombardozzi, Healy. JUNGLEER stories of Cannon CO 162 and 116 Engrs on Biak were useful. Bill Brown and beautiful wife operate Bureau of Credit Control (Salem, Oregon). Bill has 2 daughters 15 and 16. Week-ends he retreats to a 3-acre farm where he raises his own produce and plans to breed horses.

The Association Trophy

As all old-timer members know, back about 1949 the Association laid out a good-sized chunk of dough for a beautiful large silvered punch bowl and ladle, as a trophy of the 41st Infantry Division Association to be awarded annually to that unit of the 41st Infantry Division (National Guard) which showed the highest efficiency rating for the year. The Division Headquarters annually appointed a Board to rate the units and determine the trophy winner, and a formal presentation of the trophy, with the winning unit's designation engraved upon it, was made by Associaition officers and members in the area. When the bowl became completely filled on all sides with engraving, a handsome stand was made for it, and the winning unit's name engraved on a silver plate and affixed to the stand.

Now that there is no complete 41st Infantry Division any longer, but the former Division units are several large separate units and a host of individual separate companies, etc. (41st Infantry Brigade, 81st Infantry Brigade, 163rd Armored Regiment, 116th Combat Engineers, and many smaller units), there is no central headquarters to rate these units scattered over four states. Continuing award of the trophy became impossible. At the Gearhart reunion, it was decided to have the secretary pick up the trophy and hold it until the Association could determine what to do with it.

The State of Oregon Military Dept. requested that the trophy be given to them, to be displayed on a handsome stand, with a special glass case, in their headquarters. Since a count of the unit designations engraved on the trophy showed an overwhelming majority of them were Oregon units, since no other state headquarters had expressed an interest in the trophy, and since it would be discriminating against the other units if it was awarded only within any one of the separate brigades or other successor units of the 41st, Association President Ed Spanier directed that a mail poll be made of the Association's Board of Directors on this request. The ballots were almost unanimous in favor of it, so this presentation will be arranged for. It was felt that having our trophy prominently and permanently displayed in a headquarters where The Adjutant General, State of Oregon, Maj. Gen. DONALD N. ANDERSON (186) and many of the staff are veterans of the 41st, and where ex-41st men will be continually passing it, was far better than bundling it up and letting it gather dust with the old records of the Association. It would be impracticable to ship it to each reunion for display because of its bulk and the probability of damage or loss.

B CO. 116 ENGINEERS:
Our Great Road for 186

by DR. HARGIS WESTERFIELD, DIVISION HISTORIAN
and T/5 William A. Andel, B Co. 116 Engineers

On 24 May 1944, B Co. 116 Engineers boarded an LST for the Biak operation. Leaving Hollandia next morning, our convoy started north. Then one night, we turned south to hit Biak. That night of 26 May, many Engineers did not sleep; we had to be up at 0430. Men sang in the holds; guitars twanged.

At 0800 27 May, B-Co. trooped down an LST ramp onto a narrow beach at Bosnek. Too many disembarking outfits jammed too close together; a high ridge menaced us a short way north.

At once we dug a fine shelter trench 100 yards inland from our LST, then got to work unloading. Attached to 542 Engr. Boat & Shore Regt., B Co. also cleared and repaired the two Bosnek jetties. Our bulldozers worked where they needed us.

About 1600 came the Jap planes—four 2-engine bombers and 3-4 fighters. They flew low over that menacing ridge to escape radar detection.

As the planes bombed and strafed the beach, B was already deep in the wonderful trench we had dug. One plane evidently tried to crash into our LST. He missed it by ten feet to land on the other side on the beach. The two Jap crewmen were already dead. The other three bombers were also shot down. Next day, 28 May, a Jap plane flew low over us—seemed to be photographing. Furious gunners on the beach and the LST fired at him, but he escaped untouched. (It was two days later when our AA killed our own B-25 from Hollandia with badly needed maps; it flew in just as Jap planes were expected about 1600 hours.)

On 29 May, B's Sgt. Hubbard was wounded and taken to a hospital; details are unknown. While C Co. 116 Engineers supported 162 against Parai Defile and were repulsed, B worked on Bosnek Beach. Later 186 Inf. made its tortured overland march to seize Mokmer Drome. The movement would have failed without B's new road.

On 1 June, B Co. moved east up the beach away from Mokmer, then inland through the ridge-gap north of Opiaref. We began 186's crucial road overland to capture Mokmer Drome. First, we had to improve the poor Jap track five miles from Opiaref inland. Andel was dynamiting obstacles on the road, and spoiling Jap rice or ammo dumps.

In a perimeter back on the beach that night, we had our second casualty. While guarding heavy equipment in mid-perimeter, Wiese saw a man move in the dark, and shot him. Wiese hit Moratore; he had got cold in the hole, and tried to sleep in a truck. Wounded through arm and shoulder, Moratore did not rejoin B for two months.

On 2 June, we finished putting the five-mile track from Opiaref into condition for heavy traffic. We also built 1½ miles of road west of Col. Newman's 186 CP, now in the area surveyed for the Bosnek Drome.

With K 186 preceding, we followed 41 Signal Co. which had already laid wire. Andel got orders to guide our bulldozer to point out the location of the wires so that they would not be torn up.

B's work party was now on a level stretch where few trees grew, and Andel was some 40 feet ahead of the "cat" as he pointed the way. Then from three trees half a mile off, a sniper shot at Andel; a bullet whistled so close that Andel froze. He thought the Jap was trying to pick off someone acting like an officer.

CO Armstrong ordered Andel to keep moving. Although the sniper fired several times, no bullet came close. The work party got rapidly out of range so that the fire was ineffective. Nobody in B knew what happened to that sniper.

That night, B with K 186 guarded perimeter with our important road machinery in the center. (With 186's 3/Bn, B was in the van of the push to Mokmer Drome) In the dark, Andel headed a MG crew on a trail. Since the other two were rookies, he had trouble to keep them from shooting every shadow or rustle of the grass. But his MG stayed quiet.

On 3 June, with just one "cat," B labored on five miles of new road. We were deep in jungle scrub 12 feet high, with visibility not over ten yards. We believed that our own guards secured us.

While the "cat" growled at coral rubble in the draw below, Andel was in a group blasting the way with dynamite over a small hill. Like others, he leaned his rifle on a log while he worked at the dynamite. Eight guards protected us—four on each side of the road.

In a sudden commotion, Andel looked up into brown faces and eyes like Japs' eyes. Some 25 Koreans of a labor gang had slipped past our guards to surrender. If they had been Japs, B skeletons would still be bleaching in that scrub. We halted the truck to take the Koreans back to MP's.

Also, on 3 June, a B detail jeeped back on the road to locate a badly needed second bulldozer. About 1500, Zeroes swooped to strafe the jeep on a bare, stony knoll. The men flattened on the ground, but Sanchez took a fragment in the leg. Some 300 yards farther, a tank medic bandaged Sanchez. A second swoop of Zeroes drove Andel under a tank among scared tankmen. (The "cat" came to help us the next day.)

On 3 June, B made three miles of road. That night in the perimeter, somebody accidentally exploded a phosphorus bomb. White smoke covered our perimeter; somebody yelled, "Gas!" We panicked to find those misplaced or lost gas masks. Luckily, no Jap bayonets charged into the smoke. That night, Hawkins was ill with malaria and jaundice in his hole, but we dared not aid him in the dark. He probably died that night.

On 4 June, B merely improved the last three miles of road. Gen. Fuller halted all advances until he knew that a Jap naval

Moving the 41st Inf. division out of Finschaffen on a two-pronged attack of Hollandia and Wakde was the greatest challenge the 116 Engineers had to face up to that point in the war. That the operations went off with clocklike precision was due to the excellent organization and performance of the engineers. Picture shows a portion of the beach in Finschaffen in late April, 1944.

task force was turned back.

On 5 June, B advanced the road again, but our water shortage was serious. We had just one canteen issued daily, but a little light rain had helped our supply. Now we were down to a few swallows in our canteens; our last ration had come up at midmorning the day before. The tropical sun beat down out of a cloudless sky.

For the dynamite gang, labor was agony; they had to dig holes for charges, then help the "cat" push the debris aside. Just as we started up a small hill, Mike Bobby—a lad with an altered Polish name—cried, "I can't go no further!" Displaying his rosary, he called Andel and Mikus to pray for rain with him. They did pray until a sergeant called out, "Move on!" Andel doubted; the sky remained clear blue.

Then in 15 minutes, the sky clouded. Down crashed a heavy tropical rain. Gratefully, we spread ponchos to drain water into

> B 116's story was impossible without Andel's 10-page handwritten MS. Important also was Dr. Kenneth Deacon's 126-page unpublished MS from Ch. IV of Combat Engineer Operations, which I condensed by his permission for Jungleer of May 1962. Deacon wrote about all 116 Engr. Bn. on Biak. Mel Brooks' letter on his medal award helped greatly. Other useful sources included S-3 Mjr. Wm. Dorner's "Extract—116 Engineer (C) Bn." R. R. Smith's Approach to the Philippines, and 186's Biak Narrative and Biak Journal. Morning Report of B 116 presents such difficulties that in case of conflicts, I have preferred Andel. Bill Andel owns and operates a 400-acre farm near David City, Nebraska.

canteens and helmets. Although almost immobilized, B worked our road again, and 186 patrols climbed the western ridge to sight Mokmer Drome 2500 yards southwest. To this day, Andel believes the three Yanks' prayers caused 186's great rain.

Back working, we ran into Jap fire but were unhurt behind the halted bulldozers. Somehow, we were ahead of 186's protection. After 186 rescued us, we succeeded in building three miles on 5 June.

Next day came more Jap trouble. After unloading supplies for the medics, an engineer truck convoy halted for lunch. A 186 runner warned of a Nip attack, but guards laughed at him until CO Armstrong spoke sharply. We kept helmets, M-1's handy, but relaxed against truck wheels and read Yank.

Out of nowhere in that opaque scrubland came a Jap attack of 10-15 riflemen with grenades. T/5 Brooks, Sgt. Langager, and Andel rolled under the truck and fired at the Japs. Brooks thought that they killed at least six.

The first Jap grenade detonated thunderously but harmlessly on the empty truck above them. The second grenade was a dud. The third fragmented into Langager's left rib. But the Jap attack was broken.

Langager thought he was killed, but Brooks staunched the blood with his own white T-shirt. Despite Nip fire, Brooks carried the 200-pound Langager 50 yards to the medics, while others patrolled for Japs in the scrub. Brooks and another engineer volunteered to ride ambulance fenders to convoy Langager to the hospital. Langager lived. And Brooks himself had a few days in the hospital with a hand wound from a grenade—a wound received in the same action.

Also killed that day was the miracle-working Bobby who had prayed for rain with Andel and Mikus. Bobby was the only B man to die in action; a sniper shot him from a tree.

Later that same afternoon, several Japs leaped from the brush and hurled a charge at a passing tool truck. The driver accelerated and bounced the charge off his windshield. The charge exploded harmlessly behind the now flying truck.

Although these Jap raiders caused few B casualties, they delayed our work. With hardly an hour's daylight, we were still a mile short of 186's new perimeters. And 186 badly needed supplies for pushing down on Mokmer Drome. Yet in that sea of darkening scrub, we could not locate even the direction of 186's perimeters.

B radioed 186 to shoot a flare, and we took an azimuth on the flare. 1/Sgt. Ryan followed the azimuth as far as he could see the "cat" behind him, then flashed a cigarette lighter to guide T/5 Elmer Brown to drive his bulldozer forward. Laboring for two hours after dark despite the risk of Jap assassins, B made a crude but usable road for three miles to bring up 186's supplies.

After days like these, we were up to the foot of that ridge with Mokmer Drome beyond. And when on 7 June 1944, 186 Inf. swarmed down the ridge onto the airstrip, B 116 was responsible for that attack. Without B 116 Engineers' supply road, 186 could never have completed the great overland march.

But to B, another move was more important. A few days later, B entrucked for the beach—hot food, the first bath in three weeks, and a shave. Then we moved across Biak, built camp, and dug a waterhole for all the troops on Biak. We spent days at this well with our jackhammers battling solid coral.

Then B built a road through the ridges and found death and wounds again. Dynamite caused the agony. A crew relieving Andel's crew brought a new circuit tester that was to make sure that all loads of dynamite would detonate simultaneously. It was raining at the time. This new crew put some five cases of dynamite on the hill and was about to test it.

Instead, the five cases blew up while B men were on top of the hill. DuMarce was killed. Carmichael and Larry Clark were so badly injured that B never saw them again. They went Stateside for plastic surgery.

Such was B Co. 116 Engineers' war on Biak. More lucky than our brother combat engineers of C 116 who saved 162 at Parai Defile, we too dared Jap rifles in the waterless scrub outback of Biak. For 186, we built that important strategic road that supplied 186 for seizing Mokmer Drome.

Finally, for T/5 William Andel, the great day came on Biak. While hospitalized for a week with inexplicable tropical swelling of hands and feet, Andel was visited by B's S/Sgt. Godfrey. Andel's name had been drawn from a hat; he had won first prize. After 35 months overseas and a total of 40 months off his farm at David City, Nebraska, he was going home—on B 116 Engineers' quota for Dec. 1944.

GENERAL EICHELBERGER'S BEACH-HEAD ON BIAK
By DR. HARGIS WESTERFIELD, Association Historian
with Major General O.P. Newman (Retired)

After dark 14 June 1944, Lt Gen Robt L Eichelberger got surprise orders from Sixth Army's Gen Walter Krueger in Hollandia. At dawn, Eichelberger must fly 300 miles to Biak, take command of Hurricane Task Force – our 41st Division – and make Biak's three dromes safe for Yank planes to land. Even though 162 and 186 now battled Japs above Mokmer Drome, Yank planes could not land there. Evidently Krueger, backed by Gen MacArthur, believed at least one drome should have been operational by 10 June, to back up Yank assaults on the Marianas. They blamed Gen Fuller.

At 1200 15 June – while 186 and 162's 1/Bns repulsed Jap tank-inf teams east of West Caves, Ike's 2 Catalinas flopped into squally waters at Biak. Fearing to shatter a leg, Ike crawled astraddle the plane's nose while awaiting LCM's gunwale bounced dangerously close. The young Catalina pilot tried to help Ike, was washed into heavy seas, stroked back to safety minus his braided cap. Ike leaped into the LCM. At 1230 at Bosnek, Ike relieved Gen Fuller from Hurricane Task Force command. Fuller was still 41st CG, and Ike tried to persuade his friends and West Point classmate to remain. But Fuller requested reassignment and left SWPA, became Deputy Chief of Staff with Adm Louis Mountbatten's SE Asia Command.

Late that first night on Biak, after recon trips and many conferences, Ike bedded down at Bosnek, dry in a sandbagged tent on a wooden floor 5 feet deep in coral. Rain drummed the canvas. At 0300 when rains stopped, Nip planes struck. With I Corps Chief of Staff Gen Clovis Byers and 41st Chief of Staff Col Ken Sweany, Ike spent his first and last hour in an air-raid shelter. He never forgot its discomfort.

On 16 June, Ike met Gen Doe where you'd expect Doe to be – at 41st advance CP – dug in on Mokmer Beach. Ike preferred to watch, while Doe – on Col Newman's suggestion – sent 186's 2/Bn shock troops to close the sinister ridge-gap between 162's 2/Bn and 3/Bn. Ike phoned E 186 for news – prone in earth under fire. Angry junior officers held up phone receivers to catch the crackle of Nip Arisakas, said: "Come and see for yourself." Ike was understanding enough to attempt no disciplining of Lts Pronobis, Crawford, Capt Boyd.

Ike's study of 41st situation reports "dissatisfied" him. He had no clear picture of the front. He lacked reliable figures for Nip strength. Nips popped up from caves to fight, relieved each other at will; yet nobody knew exactly locations of main caves.

Yesterday, Ike had jeeped precariously through Parai Defile, still dangerous from East Caves' Nips. But on 17 June, he found an easier way – speed-boat to Owi, then Cub to Mokmer Strip. As they hit Mokmer Strip, Nip fire at 2000 yards missed them. (Ike thought himself first man to land at Mokmer.) With Byers, Doe, he jeeped up to see our attack of 17 June.

Scared Ike never forgot his attack. While 162's 1/Bn and tanks hit SW toward West Caves, 186's 1/Bn backed east, then turned north into dense broken ridges, to assail the Nip rear. In jungle, 186 and 162 collided; a momentary American-American fire-fight blasted off.

For better observation, Ike and a young Lieut climbed a steep hill to a Yank OP. Several hundred yards ahead lay a ridge that the Lieut said Roosevelt's 3/Bn took that morning. Below, where Ike could hit them with coral, our tanks were buttoned up and firing. Suddenly Japs volleyed from the "captured" ridge – rifles, MGs, Jap 90mm mortar fragments thudded near Ike.

The tank-turrets pivoted, blazed away – at Ike's ridge! Actually, Nip caves on the hill under Ike had unmasked and drawn tank fire. Ike called up Doe, Byers, to see. Now grenade-throwing Nips surrounded the tanks, battered them into retreat.

After this fight of 17 June, Ike called off Doe's attack of 18 June. (Doe had planned to attack West Caves with all 162 while 186's 1/Bn secured the Hill 320 plateau.) Ike wanted no more battle-field scrambles. He demanded reports of all companies' moves, day and night. He sent Col Bill Bowen, I Corps operations officer, with Cub observers to fly low over Nippo country repeatedly and spot all cave entrances. Flyers' reports, careful study of Jap documents, personal visits, interviews of the few prisoners – all enabled him to unscramble our lines on Biak.

Rightly, Ike surmised that Nip replacements were getting through to West Caves. He decided to block them. While 163's 3/Bn guarded the plateau below Hill 320 to halt Japs from the NE, Ike planned to seal off the NW corridor from Korim Bay. Using the newly arrived 24 Div's 34 Inf, he could relieve 186 from the coast and place it across the western approach to West Caves.

Doe feared knee-mortars would kill 186, but Ike ordered his major move. On 19 June, 186's offensive-minded Col Newman put Cos E and F on high ground east of the motor road into West Caves' rear, linked with 3/Bn on left, 1/Bn on right. On 20 June, while 186 and 163's 3/Bn protected it, 162 began infighting for West Caves. Now 34 Inf left garrison duties on the former 186 coast, and readily took Borokoe and Sorido Dromes. Despite greenhorn errors, 24 Div smashed 3 Nippo counter attacks – with 167 FA's help.

On 20 June, Ike was close to combat again. When Gen Sverdrup, I Corps Engr, he had jeeped to Sorido Strip to find how much work was needed to make it operational. At noon, his jeep halted by the shore while Sgts Dombrowski, Ventura gave out K rations. Then 34th Inf Yanks found Nips in a cave under Ike. Japs threw unexploded grenades back at 34th men. Although Ike's G-3 Dan Edward – wounded beside Ike at Buna – wanted to clear the cave, Ike checked him. Finally a phosphorus grenade blinded the opening; TNT killed the Japs. Ike's men finished lunch in peace.

On 22 June, the morning after 186's 3/Bn broke the great Jap "Banzai" attack, Ike ordered 186 to delay clearing up the bodies. He drove up to the lines with a cameraman in his jeep.

Piles of dead Nips blocked the road. Ike dismounted and walked up to 186 men still at their guns. "Something explodes within me, and pleasantly, when I meet up with gallant men," said Ike. Assuming that the 12 men on the 50-caliber guns had fought the whole fight, he promised to decorate them that very day. He announced that he would give 2 Silver Stars and 10 Bronze Stars, and he had the men decide among themselves who merited the Silver Stars. (Yanks fighting in France in June 1944, were getting most of the publicity in the States; and Gen Newman believed that Ike staged his little drama partly to bring SWPA men back into prominence.)

What kind of man was this mild-looking blond General of 60 years, who must order men to death to win battles? The answer is not easy.

Courage he had, certainly. At Buna with 32 Div, he wore his 3 gleaming general's stars and walked through "pinned down" companies to lead them. On Biak when he inspected 186's 2/Bn with Col Newman, Japs fired mortars. Two shells impacted close. Ike ignored them, stood up talking to Newman for what seemed to Newman eternity — really a long minute or two. Ike then ordered 186 men to remain in holes, but with Newman, he climbed a ridge to confer with Bn Cos, enlisted men in bad spots.

Ike's manners were gentlemanly. Toward officers and men, Newman observed Ike was polite, considerate, friendly, outgoing. Never did he use profanity — or speak harshly to anyone. But Newman thought Ike was tougher, more ruthless than even gruff, outspoken old Teutonic Gen Krueger. Unlike Krueger, Ike never expressed concern for officers or men. He was arbitrary.

After 3 weeks contact with Nips, 1/Bn's morale would improve if we had a day or two at the beach to rest and clean up. On his inititative, Newman ordered relief of the Bn. But 1/Bn rested on the beach overnight only; Ike ordered it back to West Caves. Again, after the Banzai of 21-22 June, Newman got Ike's orders to storm a hill behind 186. Approach was up a sheer cliff. Newman suggested to Gen Doe that a 162 Bn do the job; the map revealed that this Bn was dug in near a slope offering an easy way up to the Japs. Doe agreed that 162 should storm the hill; but 2 days later, Newman got an order from Doe. Ike had told Newman to take the hill — or be relieved. Newman did as ordered (probably with 3/Bn); he knew Ike would have carried out his threat if he refused the attack.

How do we reconcile Ike's gentle manners and this sharpness? A man can make errors — especially in a lonely command position. Ike had seen high officers of 32 Div act disgracefully at Buna. He evidently had got the habit of being hard whenever he was crossed. During Buna fight, he refused a Dr.'s request to visit badly wounded men in a hospital; he feared to wreck his ability to make merciless combat decisions. Yet this was the Ike who stood weeping among the graves of Buna.

What did Ike do for victory on Biak that Gen Fuller had not done? Fuller's strategy was good, despite Krueger's oversights. For Sixth Army Hq did not reconnoiter accurately, assigned him too few troops, loaded him with dual posts — both CG of the Division and of Hurricane Task Force.

Fuller secured Bosnek for a base, contained Ibdi Pocket. In bypassing Parai Defile with 162 and putting 186 on Mokmer Strip to face Kuzume, Fuller saved many lives. By 186's move overland, he took the pressure off 162, enabling 162 to open Parai Defile more easily. Fuller's men were ready to storm West Caves. He finally got 2 full Regts as reinforcements — to total the 4 which Krueger failed to give him in the first place. At first limited to 2 Regts at the front, Fuller had sadly chewed up Kuzume's Btns. But Fuller's greatest achievement, perphaps, was to develop the Jap offensive on Biak, and demonstrate to Krueger that he must re-evaluate the whole problem of conquering Biak.

Then, besides following Fuller's plans, what did Ike do? Perhaps freeing outspoken Gen Doe to use his front-line wisdom was Ike's salient achievement. Perhaps Ike's achievement was simply that he was willing to pool his ideas with those of our own great general. (Ike called Doe stubborn and opinionated; said by implication that he respected our stubborn and opinionated general enough to confirm his appointment as Division CG.) In battlefield strategy, Ike's main contribution — over Doe's opposition — was to throw 186 athwart the Nips' supply route from West Caves to Korim Bay. Perhaps these were Ike's achievements for the 41st.

With Mokmer Strip secured and Doe commanding the Division, Ike flew back to Hollandia 27 June. His order to Biak had come as a surprise; and he got another surprise on his return. Krueger angrily ignored Ike. Ike learned that — against Krueger's objections — MacArthur had formed the new Eighth Army, which Ike was to command. Krueger liked Ike, but his anger was at first directed against Ike. Later, however, Krueger consulted with Ike to recommend Gen Doe as CG of the 41st. And if we are to judge by the date of Ike's appointment as CG of the Eighth Army, it was his work as expediter of the Battle of Biak that prompted Gen MacArthur's decision to give Ike command of Eighth Army. Such is the tale of Generals Eichelberger, Fuller and Doe in the Battle of Biak.

> Most important original source is Gen Newman's ltr 4 Aug 1962. Other sources are RR Smith's APPROACH TO THE PHILIPPINES, Gen. Robert L. Eichelberger and Milton MacKaye's OUR JUNGLE ROAD TO TOKYO.

186's Second Battalion Closes The Gap On Biak

by Dr. Hargis Westerfield
with Lt. Joe Crawford

On 16 June 1944, 186's 2 Btn grimly attacked to close the 500-yard gap between 162's tired 2 and 3 Btns. From that ridge, Nippo artillery still kept our planes from Mokmer Drome. Backing it lurked a strongpoint later named the West Caves.

By 0820, we relieved 162's 2 Btn. For 15 minutes 641 TD's 4.2 mortars impacted 4 Nippo gun positions. Followed 5 minutes' barrage from E's 60's, D's 81's. We shuddered while bursts smashed the tangle of broken trees and coral where Nips waited to fire.

At 0900, E's 2 and 3 Pltns pushed with the First Pltn in support to left rear. We struck east along the ridge, with the crest separating Block's 2 and Crawford's 3 Pltn. Flanks were unguarded. On Block's right far down to Mokmer Drome was "Nothing," said E's Capt. Foltz. On Crawford's left north of the ridge were only silence and terror.

South of the ridge, Block's 2 Pltn with E and H MG's pushed on a 50-yard front where no man saw over 15 yards ahead. Although somewhat protected from Nippo long-range fire by the ridge, we endured small-arms fire. We passed Gun Position No. 1 which was silent, but met rifle fire from 3 more positions. Our 3 Squad took Position 2, killed a Jap. Position 3's rifles stopped us.

Then 3 Squad's Eddie Morales volunteered. Bitter Morales had lost a brother earlier in the war. While 3 Squad fired cover, he threw grenades, tommy-gunned out Position 3, killed 8. With more ammo, he moved out on Position 4, but died from distant fire.

From Position 3, we covered 2 Squad's attack on Position 4. A bazooka team climbed to the crest. Totally exposed, a Sgt. at 15 yards fired 14 rounds into the log bunker, captured it.

Thus Block's Pltn fought up the ridge, destroyed 1 HMG, 1 120 MM, demolished 3 Jap 6-inch cannon. For full contact with 162 S. of the ridge, Mjr. Horace Bradbury ordered G's First Pltn to push up on a 70-yard front of broken ground. At 1100, they closed the gap which the Japs had kept open for days.

But N. of the ridge, Crawford's 3 Pltn with 2 HMG's had hard going. Moving 50 yards through brushy shell-torn terrain, we took hot fire that Block was protected from. From our front, left front, left rear, heavy fire halted our attack.

We made holes by hurling our bodies into shell-pulverized earth among old dead Nips. A Yank fired behind Crawford, almost blew his head off. A slug knocked down Pltn Sgt Sullivan. It pierced his helmet behind, creased his head, exited in front. He couldn't find the bullet, was scared stiff, thought it still in his head.

In mid-air diving for a hole, Crawford took 5-6 bullets in the fatigue jacket under him. One crumpled his dog-tags, nicked his chest. He darted for a stump. Something holed his thigh. Safe at the stump, he picked knee mortar shrapnel from his back.

Here Crawford found Scout Asla, another red-haired rifleman, the phone. They fired crazily at smoke from a vicious LMG, but uselessly. Crawford directed 6 rounds of 60 mortars on it, stopped it in 30 minutes. He put 18 rounds into the West Caves area, killed 2 knee mortars. Exposed on the ridge, Lt. Kossl directed E's mortars also.

Headquarters sent 2 stretcher-bearers to save a wounded scout. Crawford angrily told them not to go. Just as they stood, a Nip HMG killed both at his feet, wounded Asla, wrecked Crawford's carbine. The scout was dead already. Sgt Rothschild died keeping contact with Block at the crest.

Now Lt. Pronobis' First Pltn of E Co. attacked left of Crawford to relieve pressure so that he could withdraw. But Nippo fire pinned Pronobis. It was futile to send in Lt. Minor's 2 Pltn of G on Pronobis' left. By 1130, Minor was stopped after 50 yards. Our whole attack bogged down. At 1330, Minor broke a Nippo counter-attack on that dangerous left.

Lying at the stump, Crawford enjoyed a cigarette, listened on the phone to the other Pltns. Headquarters asked CO Boyd of G Co., "Is it hot up there?" "Listen!" said Boyd, and held up his phone. Fire crackled like popcorn.

Gen Eichelberger queried, "How many MG's have you taken? What positions have you overrun?"

Crawford retorted to the General. "You can go to hell. Come up here and see for yourself." On his phone, Pronobis shouted, "That goes for me too." Capt. Boyd said,

CREDITS

Prime sources are 41 Div G-3 Joe Crawford's Ltr 29 May 1961, with 186 Inf Report on Biak, RR Smith's APPROACH TO THE PHILIPPINES. Also used were Frank Kraska's Ltr 4 June 1961, and these 186 Inf Co Records of Events: 2 Btn HQ, Cos E, F, G, H. (But Smith ignores the dangerous situation before the retreat, makes the retreat seem like a Sunday School picnic.

Crawford spent all evening with me discussing various points. Credit goes also to Dwight Shonyo (E 186) and Mrs. E. Mary Bolduc whose advice helped me to obtain Training Note 8, without which I would not have contacted Crawford.

Commissioned from Overseas OCS at Brisbane, Joe Crawford was in the New Guinea Campaign. at Palawan, Zambol His Civil Engineering degree is from U. Michigan, and General Electric in Cincinnati is his employer. He is well over 6 feet tall, has 1 wife, 4 girls, 1 boy.

"Count me in on that also. Eichelberger shut up.

Now Mjr Bradbury ordered a new offensive to break the deadlock. He brought up Lt McGovern's 3 Pltn of G with 2 50 MGs from 2 Btn AT Pltn to Minor's left. After 600 rounds from 121 FA's 75 pack artillery had blasted the Nippo mortar and MG emplacements, the 4 Pltns moved out — from left to right, McGovern, Minor of G; then Pronobis and Crawford of E.

This attack was stopped after 200 yards at most; but McGovern's G Pltn stormed high ground at a Nippo bivouac area, halted most of the automatic fire holding back the others.

Minor's G Pltn had it harder. We exchanged fire with the West Caves themselves. From the first cave mouth, the 3 Squad took MG and rifle fire, even grenade blasts. After 50 yards' farther advance, we halted at fire from the second cave mouth, from high ground N. of the cave, from the hill to front.

Now despite Nippo pressure, we thought we could today conquer the West Caves area. We did not know that it held 500 Nips, many automatic weapons. We thought we had only to reduce the easy hilly position north of the caves. Then all Pltns could advance without enduring flanking fire. We could drive through the last few 100 yards to where 186 and 162's 2 first Btns were holding but unable to help us because of our overhead fire. (It took 11 days more.) McGovern's Pltn of G Co. pushed for the hill. Losses had cut us to 2 squads. Between the 2 squad-columns marched a .50 MG section of AT Pltn. When astride a road, we drove off a small Nippo counter-attack. About 100 yards from the hill summit, we took rifle and MG fire from a Jap position. The AT 50's returned fire. Now we deployed as skirmishers, First squad to front, 2 squad on flank. The First made 60 yards; but we faced a cliff—MG's on top, riflemen defending the base. The 2 Squad tried the NW slope of the hill; but sheer sides, rifles, MGs repelled it.

At 1400, G's Capt Boyd tried to re-enforce McGovern with the Weapons Pltn armed with rifles. Crossing the road where McGovern had met attack, they had heavy fire, a number of casualties, took cover just past the road.

Thus ended the advance of 16 June. Casualties mounted up; the slightest movement drew terrific fire. We had found the west side of the West Caves; but night was too close for further action. Could we take what the two First Btns of 162 and 186 had fought for days?

Could we even hold out

HERE'S HOW THE 13th Air Force men saw Biak Island before the 41st division landed there. That's Bosnek going up in smoke while a B-24 is going back to its home base for a refill.

here through the night? Ominous to Gen Doe were the Nippo infantry milling around on the road N; our left flank lay open to attack. Meanwhile F Co's 1 and 2 Pltns were now up from reserve. By 1445, F's First with LMGs was positioned on our left flank, and F's 2 Pltn was evacuating G's wounded. And we planned to extricate the Btn.

At 1515, 81's fired smoke mixed with explosives on all known Jap positions. Although blinded by smoke, G's 2 Pltn withdrew without straying because Minor had warned them to orient their retreat before blackout. The Japs attacked during the retreat; but Pronobis' E Pltn held them.

Now Pronobis' covering Pltn fell back correctly. At each halt, a BAR team protected by riflemen blasted the enemy while the main body retreated a short way. Then an alternate BAR group fired protection to extricate the exposed BAR group and then cover the next step in the Pltn's retreat. During this move, Japs tried to envelope our left flank; the alert BAR group spotted them, dropped them dead.

At 1515 also, G's McGovern Pltn withdrew from its honorable advanced position near the cliffs. While the First Squad and the 50's retreated, 2 Squad fired cover. The Japs pursued us to near the road. But here F's First Pltn, the mortars, AT Pltn's other 2 50's and H's 4 HMGs smashed the attack.

Now with all Pltns safe on the low ridge, 162's 2 Btn relieved us at our original objective where we had closed the gap. Thankfully those of us who could walk returned "home" to our bivouac area a long morning past.

We killed 65 counted Japs plus unknown numbers who came under fire in the smoky retreat. We had lost 15 Yanks killed, 35 wounded — compared to, for example 16 killed, 87 wounded with 162's 3 Btn at the Parai Defile 28 May.

Wounded in Hq Co were Lt Blanton, Pvt Phipps. H had Jankowsky killed, 3 wounded. At 1430, F's First Pltn lost one EM killed, and Lt Dikeman wounded. But E, G Cos had more men engaged, suffered most. E had 6 killed — with Morales, Rothschild, 15 wounded, with Lt Crawford, Asla Sullivan. Although G left no record, a computation leaves it with 7 killed, 14 wounded, among them Capt Boyd, Lt Minor. It is sad to relate that no one can name our 12 other dead, or 27 wounded.

Despite our dead, we men of 186's 2 Btn who survived rejoiced in our holes that night. We had sealed the gap for 162 on the jungle ridge over Mokmer. We had spotted other Jap emplacements, located the western limits of the West Caves. In 5 days, we would be close enough to make Kuzume burn his colors, order his men into "Banzai" attacks. By 21 June, we would win the crucial strongpoint of the Battle of Biak.

2nd Bn 186 Infantry:
BATTLING COL. KUZUME'S BIG BANZAI
By DR. HARGIS WESTERFIELD, Division Historian

On the nights of 20-21 June and 21-22 June 1944, 186 Inf on Biak smashed the biggest "banzai" the 41st Division ever encountered. But by definition, it was really no banzai. A banzai is a fanatical, mindless charge, but those attacks of 20-22 June seemed like coolly planned attacks of disciplined soldiers.

On 19 June, 186 Inf had dug in across the West Caves' garrison's supply route and escape way into the NW Biak wilderness. On 20 June, 162's 1/Bn smote West Caves' outguards and rolled drums of flaming gasoline into many caves and crevices. Thus the two regts held West Caves in a vice. Since the Japs' code of honor prevented surrender, they preferred the 'honor' of death in battle.

That night of 20 June, after 162 had flamed its gasoline drums into West Caves, Nips made small harassing attacks against 162's 1/Bn in the opposite direction of their intended break-through. Others drove north up the main road, to strike 186's south flank. They dragged mortars and light cannon from West Caves and threw a few shells on the beach road and Mokmer Dromes. Before daylight, they were back in West Caves for dazed slumber and preparation for the banzai.

For events of next morning could surely prove to Col Naoyuki Kuzume that a heavy attack was his only hope to extricate the most aggressive warriors from the rivers of flame. On 21 June, 1/Bn 162 with 603 Tank Co's 2 tanks, shot dead or burned to a crisp West Caves' outguards. Five more drums of exploding gasoline seared into the most westerly large mouth of the Caves.

Yet with no thought of surrender, Col Kuzume continued plans to battle to the last. His main cave garrison of at least 375 were probably the best combat Japs left on Biak. They were mostly unblooded — men of 221 Inf Regt smuggled in from Manokwari after the 41st landed.

Before the last night battle, Kuzume assembled his staff and in an impressive ceremony, burned the colors of his own 222 Inf, to save them from the shame of capture. Although reports say that Kuzume killed himself then or later in West Caves Japanese historians state that he did not commit suicide but was killed in action 2 July in the 24 Div area north of Borokoe Dromes. (The ranking naval officer, Rear-Admiral Sadatoshi Senda, did not die until December where he had hidden in the jungle.) It seems reasonable, therefore, to believe that the well-organized Jap attacks of 20-22 June were under command of a live Kuzume.

After the attacks of 20 June, 186 crouched firmly ready for the certain fight of the next night. Astride the road were dug in 186's 2/Bn AT Pln under T/Sgt Bill Hall, with T/Sgt Cornegay's Pioneer Pln. Lt Roll's G Co — one of 186's top combat outfits on Biak — anchored the right flank.

A trip wire stretched across the road to trigger a great heap of empty 5-gallon gas cans and water bidons. On each side of the road, AT Pln had .50 HMGs sighted to hit the trip wire, even in the dark. Another .50 HMG was mounted on a waiting tank. Next to AT's .50 on the right of the road, G Co's holes began on higher ground — a little half-circle of shallow coral pig-pens with G's CP 100 feet behind them in thick foliage. S/Sgt Roger Jensen had the third hole to the right after AT Pln's .50 HMG position. The line of G Co holes curved back behind him so that his was the most exposed position.

And so, about 2100 21 June, in black, tropical night, heavily armed Japs pushed along the road to 186's lines to try to escape. As expected, Jap soldiers tripped the wire across the road. The cans clanked down, and at 50 yards, the HMG 50s ricocheted down on the Japs. While wounded screamed, live Japs impacted knee mortars, set up LMGs, blazed away at our lines. Sheets of flame made the night into broad day. Within 40 yards, the screaming charge collapsed into moans and silence. But the living began to work forward through the brush in small groups.

In his hole with Francis Davis and a new man, Jensen at first held fire. Then the new man's rifle blasted in Jensen's ear. A Jap fell dead 3 feet from the edge of their hole. Since the Japs were totally silent, Jensen phoned for G Co's mortars. To kill what Japs he could or drive them into G's fire, he walked our 60 shells in as close as 50 feet, despite objections of Lt Minor, T/Sgt Jordan Davis, and an officer from 2/Bn Hq.

To men like G's Jensen, and I & R men Allen Rock and Nick Kalember, the "big banzai" was one continuous probing Jap attack all night long. But farther back, other 186 NCOs and officers strained eyes and ears into the dark and noted various lulls and changes in the volume of Jap fire. They outguessed the Japs.

For the attacks seemed to come in 2 stages. First stage was for the Japs to gather at a small clearing around a great tree 100 yards from our roadblock. Once assembled and organized, they deployed to rush.

The Nips did not know that by daylight, M Co had carefully calibrated that great tree for an aiming point in the dark. When 3/Bn's Col Maison sensed that the Nips' first stage was to clump around his mortars' aiming point, he ordered all M Co's 81s to crash down on that tree. These mortars broke the back of the 2100 fight. Remaining Nips fell beneath the 60s and .50 HMGs.

Attack No. 2 came at midnight — this time with only light mortars to help the Nips. This time, G's light mortars, with .30 LMGs and AT's 50s held the line. The attack died.

Thus, it seems plain that the Nips didn't stage a wild banzai on 21-22 June, but that the attacks were orderly and planned. About 0200, small commands of Japs hit 162's 1/Bn — notably the holes of A 162. Small groups moved along 162's front — suddenly fired rifles, or hurled grenades — yet never drove home a charge. Although 162 men had no casualties, they killed 17. The Japs saved their final strength to rush 186's 2/Bn roadblock at 0400.

In this third and final attack at 0400 on the road-block, the Nips' best weapons were stealth against tired Yankee defenders — then grenades and bayonets. This time, their attack drove home — even from men wounded by our .50s; they landed in Yank fox-holes. All along the line, we fought hand-to-hand. One jumped for Capt Pendexter, Bn Medic, in his fox-hole. Although a mild gentleman, Dr. Pendexter operated without anesthetic — cut out the Nip's life with a machete.

Prime targets of this last desperate rush were AT Pln's two .50 HMGs. Most of all, the Japs wanted to kill these .50s that barred the motor road escape corridor. At one .50, First Gunner Klovas with LaBebe were efficient and lucky enough to keep the Japs off. But where Ted Howe, Charles (Pinky) Lang, and Tom Morrisey manned the other HMG, death struck back.

A wounded Nip crashed the brush, fell over the barrel of the .50. Ted Howe leaped from the hole to pull him free. The Jap clutched Howe, blew up his suicide grenade between them. Both Howe and the Nip died. In the confusing dark lit by flashes of explosives, Lang wrested a bayoneted rifle from a Jap, and reportedly killed 4.

Desperately 186 Inf riposted with every weapon it could bring to bear to save its threatened road-block. M Co still dropped 81s around the great tree in the clearing where Nips probably still assembled to follow their initial plan that usually did not change. Since G Co next to the .50s was facing the same Jap thrust, and Sgt Jensen had to pull G's 60s in perilously close to G's riflemen, we used another stratagem. We called for I Co's mortars to angle in from our extreme left flank; and nearby F also helped with its .60s. our mortars still often impacted just 25 yards before us. Thus while rifleman slew Nips who got past our MGs' final protective lines, M and F and G's mortars cut down the dwindling Nip reserves.

Before dawn, the "big banzai" was over. We mopped up their bloodstained wounded, often still holding suicide grenades. We found and slew the few lingering Nippos playing possum in the brush at the road-edge.

In the silence by 0830 with corpse-flies already thick on the Nips, graying Gen Eichelberger arrived, dismounted from his jeep, and inquired about the night's disturbance. Rumors were that he objected to stray bullets from 186 which that night had shot up his I Corps Hq. (Another rumor was that the Air Force near Mokmer Dromes had complained, they had leave their beds and cower in holes while our .50s caromed off the coral. An Air Force bed was set afire and a quart of scotch was shot out of a Col's hand.)

Whatever the rumors, Ike behaved like a general when he dismounted and reviewed the jubilant, loud-talking Yanks and the silent heaps of Nips with the stain on their faces. The dead Nip still bestrode the .50 where he had died with T/Sgt Howe. We had counted 115 dead Japs, including 6 dead that morning. Howe was killed, and 5 wounded.

G Co 186's CO, Lt Rolls, told Ike the story of the night's combat. Standing clean and tall in his shining helmet while cameramen worked on our pictures, Ike listened with pleasure. Someone pointed out to him PFC Lang, who had killed Japs with their own rifle. "You're almost as ugly a man as I am," Ike told Lang. Exultantly, Ike said, "Wait until 163 hears about this!"

And there among the silent Jap dead with our blackened gun muzzles looking on and 162 mopping up for us around West Caves, Ike awarded medals. He let the assembled Yanks decide by vote who had earned the medals he was to give out. "Something pleasant always explodes inside me when I hear of brave men," Ike said later of his impulse to award those medals.

Thus ended 186 Inf's and our Division's biggest Jap banzai of the whole war. On first thought, an American reader might say that the Japs had foolishly thrown away 115 good men. But if we examine the Jap military mind of that war, we can see what they gained from this night battle.

Since surrender was not bushido code, the Jap banzai was fitting and proper and got good results. West Caves still held out — would not fall until 27 June. By leaving to fight, the Japs had relieved the crowding in West Caves, and given the remaining garrison room to fight on. And if Col Kuzume escaped through our tight lines, presumably other Japs escaped to fight again. For the Japs, it was not wholly defeat.

But for 186 Inf, it was wholly a triumph. Never fully used in battle until Biak — if we were fully used even then — we had again shown that greatness on Biak which would make 186 a superb fighting regiment on Palawan and at Zamboanga.

Original sources were Ltrs of Tom Morrisey 27 Mar 1960; Fred Larey 16 Nov 1962; Roger J. Jensen 10 July 1969; Joe Poshka's "And So It Goes," (Jungleer, Oct. 1962), backed by Medal Stories of Ted Howe, Chester Klovas, Howard Lang, and Jensen. Background includes R.R. Smith's APPROACH TO THE PHILIPPINES, Gen Eichelberger's OUR JUNGLE ROAD TO TOKYO, Alan Rock's "Three Tales of I & R" (Jungleer, Mar. 1960), and REPORTS OF GEN MacARTHUR, VOL II, JAPANESE OPNS IN SWPA.

FIGHTING THE MOKMER RIDGES

By SGT DURAND MANDOLINE (B-186)
and
DR. HARGIS WESTERFIELD, Division Historian

At 0724 27 May 1944, B Co, 186 Inf, sloshed 300 yards into surfs of Green Beach 3 at Bosnek. With 2 AT 37s attached, we hurried east 1200 yards — on special Task Force duty to guard Bosnek Beachead's right flank. AA men followed with .50 MGs, Bofors guns; and F Co guarded our rear. Some B men found saki, like Winters.

As we perfected perimeter in late afternoon, 4 Zeroes slipped past, single file over treetops. Despite surprise, AA men got tracers into No. 4 diving at beach. At 1200, after the throb of Jap landing craft from east, Japs volleyed B with mortars, MGs, grenades. We thought their MGs fired from barges. B drove them off; they wounded Gil Howerton, Al Henderson, Sgt Gustafson.

On 28 June with F backing us, B's 3/Pltn scouted east up coast to Opairef, past bristling jungle ridges. As a Yank spotted the dark, narrow slot of a pillbox concealed on a knoll, Mandoline, Sgt Maurer, others flattened under a bullet-blast. What saved us was the height of the narrow slot; the gunner couldn't depress the muzzle low enough to kill. He did nick S/Sgt Sowers on the hand. After a flame-thrower came up, we crawled close under the pillbox to get safe from its fire-lanes. We lanced the slot with flame; impacted grenades to be sure all Japs were dead. Wounds there were negligible; but next day, a 2/Bn patrol accidentally killed Lavene.

Now Col Newman recalled B to 1/Bn at Mandom. Japs had repelled 162 at Parai Defile, and 186's 1/Bn (less A Co to fight Ibdi Pocket) became part of the overland move to take Mokmer Dromes from the rear. On 2 June with other 1/Bn men, we hiked north from Mandom 500 yards over coral ridges and down into sweaty scrublands of inland Biak. 1/Bn turned hard west here and patrolled in line with 186's 3/Bn. While C flanked the southern ridges, we hiked on their right, in contact with 3/Bn north of the road. Our squad columns hunted Nips on the lines where 116 Engr built the supply road.

Coming up a rise before B's 3/Pltn, Scout Larry Wade saw a Jap. The Jap saw him. The Jap grenade hit within a few feet of Wade; Wade fell, and the fragments missed him. Wade cut the Jap down with his M-1.

Maybe other Nips mistook 116 Engr's bulldozer for a tank; they let us alone. But our trek in the glaring dry stony scrub with no breeze was agony. All day, Mandoline, other old-hands nursed that canteen we had on leaving Mandom.

Next 2 days, B men had only a canteen-cup daily. When the great rain fell 1200 5 June, machine-gunning the dry scrub, Col Fields halted us. We spread ponchos to drain water into helmets. Dehydrated men dropped their water-discipline; drained full helmets of that nectar-like rain.

After B and other 186 outfits swarmed over the ridge and seized Mokmer unopposed, many men took a first break in a great Yank bomb crater. As F/Lt McCahren told us to dig perimeter, we saw Navy LCTs with tanks and supplies coming to the beach. Then Japs on the sand shot at them. They thought B Co was Nippo also, and struck at us with MGs. Flattened in a small depression, "using my nose for a pick," Mandoline heard bullets snap just over his back. "Let that guy drop his MG a notch, and I'm gone," he moaned.

A Lieut identified B Co and stopped the fire; then began the great Nip bombardment of 7 June — about 0945 — MGs, mor-

---

Prime credit is due Bernard Mandoline's 6-page, single spaced MS in ltr 25 Aug 1964. He also supplied notes from interviews with Sgt. Bernard Maurer. Ray Gonzales supplied ltr from Mike Landi. Indispensable background were 186 INF REPORT OPERATIONS ON BIAK, RR Smith's APPROACH TO THE PHILIPPINES. Federal Records used include B 186 MORNING REPORT (JUNE, 1944), and Award Stories of Capt Richard Shrow, S/Sgts Palmer Ehrlich, Carlton Greigg, Guy More.

---

tars, FA. Every few minutes what sounded like a freight train ripped air overhead — a Jap naval gun shell. We saw one explode on an LCT as the Navy headed for Geelvink Bay.

And B dug deep among explosions — but still thirsted. We hope to fill canteens at a well 10 yards off. Jap gunners held fire until several Yanks lined up for water. Then their shells narrowly missed the well. We lay low and thirsted. All this time, B men got hit — Lt McCahren, McCloud, Regner. Cook Kuzma took a shell fragment in his back — and get a ticket Stateside.

That night, Japs prodded our lines along the east edge of Mokmer Strip to the beach. They sent dogs first to blast off our booby-traps. Then B shot every dog we saw. But the main Jap night attack hit farther inland, to our left.

That night besides landing precious water, Amphib Engineers took off wounded, brought supplies — and 3 Sherman tanks. On 8 June, the 3 Shermans went to fight the Jap ridges — with 2 squads of 3/Pltn to protect from Nip infantry. The Shermans rolled out 200 yards while scared men ran forward and hit the dirt. The tanks then shot with HMGs, 75s, while scared B men tried to spot Nippo counter-fire. Results of tank fire were not known, but B's men were greatly relieved at orders to return to perimeter.

On 9 June, B Co was first company in the Division to strike the main Jap force on Mokmer Ridge — those blind low coral jungles of ambushes and pillboxes and caves with cannon. Here fought some 1200 Jap Inf, countless AAF Construction troops acting as Inf, backed by FA and the unstormable West Caves. In the lead patrol of the attack, BARman Mandoline probed towards the ridge west of the Strip. As we came to a jungle opening 25 yards across, the Japs fired. We dashed across unhurt.

Then we formed a skirmish line below a rise facing the ridge. At 250 yards, we saw a large cave, and Japs moving 100 yards to our right, and a Jap OP in a tree. We shot at OP and moving Japs, but Jap MGs drove us to cover. And, unknown to our forward elements, Japs flanked us and got behind us.

Withdrawal orders came. Prone with his BAR, Mandoline heard the squad-leader's call to pull back. He turned his head but hesitated. A Jap bullet hit near his foot. If he had obeyed the squad-leader instantly, he would have got the bullet in his brain.

With Japs menacing B's rear, we had to withdraw — although we killed 10 Japs. Back at the 25-yard jungle opening, we minimized the danger — took off one by one — full field equipment and all. Nobody was hit.

On 9 June also, Sgt Maurer had the detail to bring back 162's dead from Parai Defile. Jap fire from the ridges wounded Cal Kramer. We reburied 162's men at Sboeria Beach.

On 10 June, B Co moved on the same Jap positions — but now reinforced. After B's observers called in FA on the ridge, C waited in reserve while Col Fields supervised. After the shelling, B moved east along the ridge, while C kept even in movement down on the flats.

But 25 minutes later, B and C both found combat. Jap HMGs, mortars, rifles were firing. In B, First Scout "Deacon" Forrest Rice fell mortally wounded from HMG fire. Scout Greigg shot back at the Nips until his squad escaped. Despite his jammed Tommy-gun, Greigg crept up to help Rice. Rice was already dead, a rotation man who should never have fought that day. And Capt Shroy risked Jap fire to bring B's 60s on the Japs. He silenced mortars and rifles and relieved Jap pressure; but HMGs in pillboxes still ruled the ridges. Tanks, 75s, bazookas did little against coral and log emplacements — except where Greigg led bazooka fire to kill 1 pillbox.

And at noon, Japs drove around C's north, right flank. C slew 22, but the others got into C's rear. Col Fields then got Newman to send F Co to guard Bn CP. After 2 hours' fire with 75s and bazookas, Fields pulled all 3 Cos 400 yards south of the Jap ridge. He planned to call 947 FA's 155s on the Japs, but Gen Doe now ordered 162 Inf to take over the attack.

Besides Forrest, B Co lost Sgt Kledzik killed by a mortar — and Potts and Sgt Curry wounded.

For 2 days while other 186 Bns pushed with 162 on the right flank ridge 1/Bn with B Co fortified the beach perimeter at Sboeria. Then Gen Doe teamed 186's 1/Bn with B Co included to 162. We were to team with 162's 1/Bn to drive west to a reported Nip waterhole halfway between Hill 320 and 162's 3/Bn which was stopped dead in its tracks by Nips. (No Yank yet knew of Kuzume 'West Caves.')

On 14 June, 186's 1/Bn drove west. B secured the rear. That night, we dug perimeter carefully across an important road below a jungle ridge. Small Jap groups pressed both B and C near the ridge. Just before dawn, Japs blew a booby trap before 3/Pltn. A Jap officer shouted in English, "You Yanks are going to die!" We traded grenades with the Japs. In a crater, S/Sgt Hrubes giggled like a girl every time he threw a grenade. At dawn, the Jap officer lay dead before Hrubes, sword still clutched to slay.

At dawn 15 June, B got orders to dig in left of the trail we guarded the night before, where D's heavy weapons and 1/Bn Hq were in position Then Jap rifle bullets hit our position.

We surmised that Jap snipers shot from tall trees some 200 yards left front. Our M-1s and BARs lashed back. Right, we saw a cave opening in the forest, and 4 Japs moving at us. We killed them or stopped them — had no more sniper fire. D Co shot into that cave entrance; now and then a few Japs ran out and fell.

And B Co heard Jap tanks rumbling forward, while B 162's men ran back to take shelter in our holes. Col Fields had rounded up all 1/Bn's bazooka shells — only 4 or 5 We heard him shout back over the phone to 186 Hq for more. A phosphorus shell from our own FA fell short in a nearby hole. We never forgot those screams. Back in CP, Supply Sgt Ehrlich was seriously wounded when heavy Jap fire swept over. With jaw almost severed and in shock, Ehrlich refused a litter crew's help; we did not want to deplete B's front in the coming attack. Unaided, he crawled 20 yards under MG fire to cover.

Up the road, big Olecik saw a Jap tank careen over the ridge. He raised his great brass bazooka for the shot of his life. But BARman Bill Cook fired first. The tank turned back. Olecik almost mortared Cook out of his hole with profanity. But probably 186's C Co and 1/Bn Hq did most to halt the last Jap tank offensive on Biak. Besides B's S/Sgt Palmer, other wounded were Englund, Grassmeyer, S/Sgts Greigg, Guy More, Dick Price. But Japs still fought; on 16 June, 2/Lt Redding died from a sniper bullet.

After 186 and 162 penned the Nips in West Caves, B tied in with 186's AT and D Cos to guard the Japs' northern escape route. In pitchblack hours before dawn 22 June, we heard our mortars and MGs explode, while 37s and flares made daylight before us. B Co lobbed in grenades, and on 22 June had to count the dead Japs and line up bodies and parts of bodies for the bulldozer to shove into the common grave.

But for more tedious patrols and outposts, thus ended B Co 186's Battle of Biak. We had guarded the Division's right flank on Bosnek, then fared west on the waterless march to take Mokmer in the rear. We fought well at Mokmer Ridge until 162 replaced us; we drove home the last great attack with 1/Bn buddies against West Caves. We got off light on casualties; but what hurts most is that 3 of our 4 dead went unnamed until now. Besides Lt Redding, we honor here these 3: Lavene, Sgt Kledzik, "Deacon" Rice.

GENERAL FULLER PASSES

Maj. Gen. HORACE H. FULLER, retired, who commanded the 41st Infantry Division from Ft. Lewis to Biak, died Sept. 18, after a brief illness, on the Isle of Man. He had lived in Calvert County, Maryland, since his retirement in 1946. Gen. Fuller was born in 1886, the son of an army officer, and was graduated from West Point and commissioned in the artillery in 1909. During WW1 he served in staff and artillery command capacities. Prior to taking over command of the 41st Infantry Division, Gen. Fuller was commandant of the Command and General Staff College of the Army. After leaving the division at Biak, he served on the staff of Lord Louis Mountbatten in India. His awards include the Distinguished Service Medal, the Silver Star, and the Legion of Merit, and he has been honored by France, Belgium, and the United Kingdom. News of his passing was sent us by Col. MIKE A. TRAPMAN (218, DHQ).

C Co 186 Inf- TANK FIGHTERS ON BIAK

By DR. HARGIS WESTERFIELD, Research Historian

with T/4 Arnold Feldman and T/Sgt Francis Snell

At dawn 7 June 1944, C Co 186 Inf filed from the waterless jungle scrub on Mokmer Ridge behind a barrage, to help seize Mokmer Drome — unopposed. But the air suddenly screamed with high velocity AA shells, from the dirty green ridge we had just left. For 4 hours on Mokmer Strip, we crouched in fear, while 186's mortars flailed back at each discernible Nippo muzzle-blast.

S/Sgt Scheena's BAR man was struck down in the open. Scheena dashed 10 yards, carried him to a shallow hole. Scheena then gave first aid, dug him in deeper while shells burst within 10 yards, then dashed for an abandoned litter to speed evacuation. Of 14 killed, 68 wounded this day, C had only this one known casualty.

On 8 June, 1/Bn less A Co, (still fighting at Ibdi Pocket) went back to fight the whole Jap army on Mokmer Ridge. B Co topped the ridge into heavy fire; C on the right flank sent out patrols — saw 6 Japs, killed 2. S/Sgt Biedelschies was killed; Pointer, Boyce, and Zant were wounded.

Next day, after 95 minutes' FA fire, B again secured C's right flank, to attack the Jap positions. This time, Scheena's mission was to secure our flank with his squad. B sent a LMG past us, without adequate protection. When 30 Japs attacked the gun, B's MG Sgt called for Scheena's help. C beat off the attack; Scheena slew 2 himself. Afterwards, dead Nips lay 15 yards away from the MG. Scheena also found time to help a wounded B man to Medics.

Both B and C were under HMG, knee mortar, and rifle fire. Hearing Jap officers shouting commands was unnerving; but C's Lt Gilmore countered by shouting his own orders. The Japs quieted down, and our 60's drove them off. But HMG fire continued from Jap pillboxes.

At 1200, numbers of Japs rounded C's north flank. We slew 22, but the rest were loose where they could cut us in two. Although Col Fields had Col Newman advance F Co for security, we had to regroup 400 yards back. Newman planned to demolish the Jap pillboxes with 155s, but 162 now relieved us for its turn at the dirty-green coral ridges.

Then, on 13 June, C got orders that sent us in fighting for West Caves, against Kuzume's secret tank reserve. Nobody then knew that West Caves existed, but mission for 162's and 186's two First Bns was to envelop left flank of Kuzume's 222 Inf, which still denied our use of Mokmer Strip. On this low jungle ridge, the die-hard Nips had fought 162's 2/Bn and 3/Bn to a standstill. So Gen Doe ordered 1/Bn 186, with 1/Bn 162, to strike the Nips on their left and rear, to relieve pressure on the tired 162 Bns on the ridge.

On 14 June, C led 1/Bn across the low ridge which stopped our pushes of 9-10 June. But we crossed at another point, 500 yards behind 162's 1/Bn, which also bypassed Nip positions. Our long line of riflemen filed into the dense ridge jungle, turned west on the trail, scouted 600 yards.

The first squad of acting 2/Lt Ackley (a T/Sgt) surprised the Nips in hasty positions astride the trail. Severson killed 4 surprised Nips in a long BAR burst. Scouting parallel to the right of the trail, Sgt Wilkenson found a Jap ambush before it was sprung. His squad wiped out a whole Nip squad. We had Schlabach wounded — but 15 known Nip dead.

While Ackley's Pltn fought, other C men guarded our flanks. Horn, Cpl Viscioni, Sgt Snell fired to the right on 2 Japs. The Japs hit the ground among giant ferns and shot back. Their rifle-fire increased; 15 more had reinforced them. Horn got a leg wound; Edwards was shot high in the head. We heard the Japs fan out, readied our grenades. They howled and rushed; but our BARs and grenades felled them. Lt Peterson's A Co pltn meanwhile fought down trail on the other flank, slew 6 Japs — including 2 officers, 1 NCO.

Now Ackley's 2/Pltn advanced as skirmishers, along with Sgt Snell's command. After 300 yards, 2/Pltns took fire from a Jap LMG on a knoll. Heavy jungle hampered us, masked our fire. Then Lt Strong's 60s dropped 5 rounds on the gun. We killed a Jap, took the Mg.

C Co now advanced into steep, jungle-matted terrain. Pace was slow but deadly. Heat exhaustion knocked out Dayle Hall, Bowell, S/Sgts Rupp, Von Tobel. Scout Boggs got a grenade fragment wound while he cleared an opening on the crest. Between roots of a great tree, S/Sgt Cottingham found a dying Jap doubled around his own grenade. A fragment of the suicide grenade had wounded Boggs.

At 1400, we contacted 1/Bn 162 fighting forward in our rear. To protect 162's right flank, we dug in on a low ridge slightly behind 162's low ridge, where a road led from Jap country into our lines. Nips were strong ahead — on a third ridge west, on the embattled low ridge S.W. to Mokmer Strip, and in the sinkholes southwards. And 162 patrols brought ominous news before dark. We confronted the new-found West Caves — Kuzume's most powerful center of battle on all Biak. Down that low road between 2 hills, Jap attacks would surely come tonight, and at dawn.

And all night, small Nippo groups deployed near that road and shot at B and C, stiffened with a D HMG section. D's HMGs slew many. At dawn, 50 Nips howled and hit C's left flank — rapid fire and bayonets. Again, D fought well, and C fired its 60s with deadly effect. From perimeter edge, we counted 30 Japs dead.

Dim daylight of overcast 15 June was a bad dream to us jungle-soaked, chilled, sleepless Yanks. Jap MG fire sparked from high brush upon us, and heavy Nippo rifle-fire. Down the road, Nip tanks rushed upon us, with infantry. Brutal, dark bulks lurched down at us — 2 squat, wide-fronted gray monsters; they bristled guns. At 250-300 yards, they blasted us — each with a 37 mm cannon and 2 flashing MGs. Yanks were hit.

The 2 HMGs from 2/Bn AT Pltn were at first too deep in defilade to fire. But while riflemen and mortars drove back or scattered the tank-infantry, the AT gunners ran uphill, reset the gun, blazed away — just as the unprotected tanks turned to flee. Our right AT gunner thought his bullets harmless against the steel broadside of the last tank. But he emptied his whole bag of 50s into it. The tank smoked, sheered left of the road, halted out of sight. A tall column of smoke rose from it for a long time. The other tanks escaped.

For 6 hours now, C's riflemen lay low from a Jap MG we could not kill, and picked off stray Nips. Our patrols slipped out to find Japs. Scheena's master recon patrol drew MG fire, was followed by Nip patrols going and coming. But he got valuable fire control data against the Nip garrison on the hill. He brought his patrol back unharmed.

But at 1310, Jap tanks struck again. Ominous was the clank of treads, 400 yards off, behind the hills. C's 121 FA observer called in his batteries, and 600 rounds of 75s shattered Nippo tank-inf formations, neutralized MG fire.

The tanks struck us alone, drab steel monsters spitting flame, while riflemen and three C bazooka teams knelt in the holes to fight them. No brush grew here; C had a clear field of fire. At 300 yards while AT's 50s flailed the tanks, George Schultz fired his bazooka. Round 1 was a dud. Round 2 was short; Round 3 rain-soaked and useless. Jewell ran to CP for more rockets.

Cottingham and Wilkinson's 2 bazookas held fire until the first tank was 200 yards away. Jap fire hit the parapet close enough to Cottingham to slash his face with flying coral. Cottingham stood and fired into the turret of Tank No. 1 just above its track. A dazed Nip tanker opened the turret, foolishly looked around. Every rifleman on C's line slapped the turret with M-1 bullets, but the turret closed again. Another rocket hit the tank, but bounced off and exploded harmlessly. As the tank turned, Sgt Wilkinson and Hyde, his loader, got a rocket into its rear. And Les DeWitt, at the same time arced the AT shell from his grenade launcher into the tank. The tank disappeared 300 yards away, into the brush, halted and burned.

Yet Tank No. 2 moved up the right side of C's line in a blaze of automatic fire, and struck at our emplacements with its 37 cannon. But Jewell was back from CP with bazooka rockets. Running 20 yards up a hill for better vision, Schultz and Jewell sighted the tank again. This time, Schultz' rocket smashed its tread and stopped it. The spot was too exposed for us to close with the crew, who fled. About 1500, a small C patrol smashed its guns with thermite bombs.

By 1656, we had our tanks up — 5 tanks of 615 Tank Bn for security and the expected advance tomorrow. On 16 June, C killed 4 Nips at 0815; but no one in 1/Bn 186 attacked, for they were immobilized. This was the day when 186's 2/Bn closed the Mokmer Ridge gap, between 162's 2/Bn and 3/Bn on our left flank. The rain of Nippo and Yank shell bursts on our front, would make our attack too closely. That night, C killed 7 more Nips.

On 17 June, C's advance was easy, for we were in the middle of the column of companies which reached Hill 120. Meanwhile, C's Bernheisel died of wounds.

Thus fought C Co 186 Inf on Biak — in 186's first push of 9-10 June, against the Japs' ridge above Mokmer Dromes, and then in the advance to the portals of West Caves themselves — a day of combat against Jap infantry alone, and a second day against Kuzume's last 3 tanks. Our casualties had been light — 2 dead, some wounded. But we had leached away more Nip man-power, relieved the pressure against 162, and killed 3 Jap tanks.

> Basic human interest stories come from set of unsigned notes collected in U.S. Federal Archives originally made by T/4 Arnold Feldman of 163's 3/Bn after my suggestion that he visit Lester DeWitt — whom I had known in 741 Ordnance, and from "Two days Above Mokmer Strip," by T/Sgt Francis Snell, obtained for me by Capt Edward Anklam, CO C Co. I used also Annex 23, "History of First Bn 186 Inf (While Detached from Regimental Control . . . 13-18 June)." "Narrative of Hurricane Task Force," 186 Inf's and 162 Inf's Reports of Operations, RR Smith's Approach to the Phillipines. Lt Glenn Gilmore's "Notes" were also useful, and Medal Awards stories. Smith's official history is notably lacking in its account of tank-infantry combats.

D Co 186 Infantry:
BATTLE FOR MOKMER DROMES

By LEROY "NICK" WHEELER, D Co. 186
with Dr. HARGIS WESTERFIELD, Division Historian

On 25 May 1944, D Co. 186 Inf. embarked at Hollandia for Biak. Morale was high. Old-timers from Sanananda and rookies had integrated well in our march to take Hollandia. Despite lack of briefing and maps, D was confident—confident despite a rising apprehension of the unknown.

En route to Biak we had two alerts the night of 26 May. One was radar contact with a Jap plane, but it turned away without troubling us. Early on 27 May, we had sonar contact with a sub. We were alerted and called to stations, but sonar lost contact quickly. Perhaps it was a Yank sub.

Beginning 0650 on 27 May, D enjoyed the devastating Air-Navy attack that pounded the beaches and often hid landmarks. But as our fleet neared the shore, we old-timers from amphibian training sensed something wrong. A strong, unexpected current was moving us west. After training at Toorbul Point, many noncoms were excellent water readers and understood the flow of currents better than the Naval sea-control party. We landed with bns. far off assigned beaches.

Attached to B Co. to defend 186's extreme right flank, Lt. Gerber's D Co. Pln. of HMG's and Sgt. Crumb's squad of 81's landed at 0742, 2,250 yards west of their objective. But these D men with B had no opposition, and moved east to Green Beach 1, their objective.

The rest of D came ashore by 0742 at Mandom, 2,000 yards off target, then hiked east to Bosnek. Part of Col. Fields' reserve bn., we set up a temporary 1/Bn. defense line 100 yards inland.

Then we got orders to unload LST's, along with all other men available at the beach. Filing through coconut trees to the ships, we took cover from a sudden Zero strafing—with no casualties. After rolling gasoline drums ashore, we set up perimeter defense for Div. Hq.

Jap planes were over that afternoon—four bombers protected by six fighters. We thought that 9 of 10 planes were shot from the sky in minutes, that the last plane fled over Geelvink Bay. One falling plane crashed SC 999, the naval beach control ship about destroyer size. For some time we saw smoke and fire; the wreckage was dumped overboard.

Our concern about Jap raids made a tragic background for killing a Yank B-24, from our own AA fire. MacArthur so badly desired Biak's airfields that he sent us into action without accurate maps. FA and mortars were firing blind on Biak. Then on one of the days when D was still dug in near the beach, Sixth Army Hq. told Div. Hq. that a B-24 was flying in accurate maps from Hollandia.

All units had orders to hold fire; the air drop was to be near the Bosnek coconut groves. When Sv's Lt. Baldwin at 186's CP mentioned his premonition that somebody would shoot the plane down, Col. Newman told Baldwin to knock it off. Newman seemed highly irritated with Baldwin.

D's 1/Sgt. LaHaie used every phone connection in D to warn us to hold fire on the B-24. He sent D runners to nearby units to warn them. He nagged D noncoms and recontacted every pln. by phone.

Minutes later, the B-24 flew in from the west. In a wide S pattern, it passed over harbor shipping. Approaching 41st Hq., it lowered bomb-bay doors. At least one sack fell out. S/Sgt. Pozzoli screamed, "Somebody will shoot him down!"

Somebody did fire—by rumor a gunner on a multiple .50 HMG. Some other gunners then fired too. Tracers streamed through the ship; it jerked skyward. Then it came down at a steep angle, not 100 feet above Div. Arty. CP. Men saw bodies slumped at the windows. It landed in flames some 200 yards from Div. Arty. CP. Of a rumored five-man complement in the plane, Capt. Huntting of Div. Arty. counted two charred corpses afterward.

Meanwhile, about midnight, 27-28 May, D Co's detachment with B Co. on the east, was in our first action against the Japs. Gerber's gunners and Crumb's mortarmen heard engines of Jap barges coming from the east. A Jap recon group landed to probe location of 186's right flank. Attack lasted about an hour, but the Japs withdrew before daylight.

Although 162 was badly mauled at Parai Defile, 186's 1/Bn. remained in reserve but for D's detachment which returned to us from B. On 30 May, when 163's 2/Bn. and 3/Bn. reinforced the Division, D was free to start west on 186's waterless trek to seize Mokmer Dromes from the rear.

On 2 June, D Co. left its defense of Div. Hq. and crossed the ridges above Mandom to turn west towards Mokmer with 186. We moved on the left flank inside the coastal ridges. Although maps showed a trail with easy access to Mokmer, we found a hard march ahead. Soon we climbed in single file across ridges and broken terraces. The land was far rougher than the mountains D had trained on in Queensland. With our heavy equipment, we floundered sweating up and down jagged coral ridges and into draws and up again. We mostly travelled by azimuth, not by trail.

By 3 June, we had advanced 4½ miles into that scrub-coral hell. Japs skirmished with 186's riflemen, but D had no fights. Dysentery, however, was D's agony; we thought that our bodies were rejecting the water.

Sgt. Criswell cites 3/Pln's Howard Nelson for martyrdom to his illness. Nelson was in agony and often dropped out of the line. Yet despite the weight of his 40-pound base plate and other equipment, Nelson kept staggering back to his place in the column.

Mortarman Fersch had to leave perimeter at first light because of dysentery. He walked down a small cliff to a terrace below. He suffered terribly from cramps. When he climbed back up, the pln. was gone; his squad leader had not missed him. Trying to follow our trail, he became lost in the maze of twisted terraces. Cowering in a cave that night, he realized that either Japs or 186

A foxhole at Mokmer. It wasn't as deep as the 41ster would have liked it to be. It was tough digging in Biak coral.

might shoot him on sight. Finally, he stumbled onto 116 Engr. unit and served there until rejoining us.

Water was a crucial problem. To fill canteens, we used night rains caught in ponchos. (Water was so short that when L men shot a Jap, they raced for his canteen. About 1/3 of L Co. soon wore Jap canteens.)

On 4 June, we had hourly reports that the Jap navy was coming. Probable hour of attack was 1630. We were to dig in deep and hide in all the caves nearby to shelter from naval gunnery. Actual number of battleships, cruisers, and destroyers in the task force varied from hour to hour in the reports.

A frightening rumor was that Japs had landed north of us. Rumored number of Japs grew from a Division to a Corps. (Actually, some barges with a co. of 221 Inf. and two light FA pieces did beach at Korim Bay the night of 3-4 June. And by 25 June, some 1,200 had arrived.)

With the end of this threat of Jap naval intervention, on 5 June, 186 neared Mokmer Ridge, which curved in such a way that we were headed due west instead of south towards the sea. While 3/Bn. occupied the ridge top, our 1/Bn. bivouacked near the base. And D drew blood. In the night, a Jap officer with six men blundered over a tripwire into a HMG fire lane. We slew all seven—well-equiped, clean-shaven, young-looking and seeming full of fight.

After getting water on 6 June, on 7 June, behind heavy supporting fire, 186 seized Mokmer Dromes. D backed B and C when they occupied the main drome area.

Occupation was peaceful, but 186 had walked into another regiment-sized ambush like 162's at Parai Defile. For four hours, Jap FA, AA, mortars and automatic weapons crashed down on us. E Co. 162, which had followed us in the approach, was caught in the middle of the Strip, with no cover. An AA gun shelled D; one died, 13 were wounded.

A big field gun, which D called Whistling Charlie, was firing shells fuzed to explode over our heads; it showered the Strip with fragments. Col. Newman called D's Capt. Klink to his CP and gave us the mission of killing that big gun.

Our adversaries at Mokmer. Photo, found on body of a KIA Japanese soldier, was taken in Japan before departure for Biak.

CREDIT: Main source is Wheeler's 69-page MS "Escapades on the Island of Biak," with information credits from Geral LaHaie, Rueben Klink, David Herd, Thornton Crumb, Wayne Strebig, Marion Criswell, George Imhoff, Alvin Mazuti, Ernie Gerber, Willmar Stender, William Baldwin. For Nick, I compiled a full dossier: 186 casualty list, personnel roster and operational reports. Nick used my stories already in Jungleer, and MacArthur's Reminiscences. We both used Eichelberger's Jungle Road to Tokyo, Riegelman's Combat ("Caves of Biak" chapter) and R.R. Smith's Approach to the Philippines. Herd reviewed the story in Wheeler's MS. (Help! Nick says he can't get D's story of Palawan or Zambo.)

When Klink returned to D Co., a Jap mortar chased him with shells. Klink ran madly; shells dropped just behind him. Finally, he fell safe into the hole made by a 500-pound shell.

D Co's mortars fired "battery right." Two Jap AA units immediately saturated the area with shelling. Our 1/Sgt. Strebig had his back plastered with fragments. With bloody hands, we tore at the coral ground like madmen, trying to dig in. D was soon out of mortar shells; but Navy and five Air Force bombs blasted the hills while 121 FA adjusted fire for itself and 205 and 947 FA. The fire decreased before dark. The Jap guns that were still in action began moving to new positions.

Despite this heavy shelling of 7 June, 186 still held Mokmer Dromes. The Japs made no daylight ground attacks, and only ineffective night attacks on 3/Bn. on 8 June.

But during daylight hours 8 June, D's mortars had good shooting to help 2/Bn. 162. (This was the bn. that had joined 186 on the overland trek to Mokmer Dromes.) When 2/Bn. 162 moved east to contact the other bns. of 162 fighting west from Parai, East Caves' mortars and automatic weapons halted 2/Bn. (The Japs' East Caves had been silent for nine days after they broke up 162's offensive of 29 May.)

And D 186 was primed to help 162 in distress. First, Lt. Hudnall and S/Sgt. Imhoff registered our mortars. They fired a ladder of smoke shells to put our 81's on target. Set up in a parallel line, our six mortars detonated and impacted at the same instant. Often a gun crew had six shells in the air before the first one blasted the Japs. We poured in hundreds of shells on that Jap high ground. D stopped enough Jap fire to let 162 continue pushing; we got high praise for this day of good shooting.

On 9 June, D came out of our holes at Mokmer Dromes and fought to help B and C clear that tactical low ridge that was the anchor of Jap resistance on Biak. Nobody then knew that we were battling 1,200 infantry plus a naval guards unit plus FA and other supporting units.

Again, D's 81's adjusted mortar fire to get a base point close to the ridge line, and went into "battery right" again. For 20 minutes, our 81's saturated the ridge. Then D's HMG's went forward behind the deploying rifle squads. The ground was fairly open, cover was limited. Moving up that ridge, we faced the Jap threat. We were a scared bunch of young men.

B with D's 1/Pln. of HMG's almost reached the crest of the low ridge, but Jap MG fire drove us to earth. Jap infantry almost surrounded us. Our Lt. Cox's MG crews were down on that ground "half digging and half firing" to take pressure off B's forward riflemen. We delivered overhead MG fire while even D's ammo carriers fired their M-1's.

When the Japs counterattacked with two rifle plns. on our left flank, D had a great little victory. After B smashed one Jap pln's attack with heavy fire, B got orders to withdraw 400 yards. D's right flank HMG's fired cover for that pullback.

But no order to retreat got to gunner Helphrey on the left flank. He was bitterly complaining that his HMG had not fired enough belts in B's advance. A high terrace had masked his fire.

Suddenly Helphrey saw a Nip officer blindly leading 29 men into his field of fire. Unaware of the Yank HMG 20 yards downhill, they halted and grimly fixed bayonets to smash B's unguarded and retreating flank. They could have caused panic in B.

Helphrey hardly believed what he saw—a gunner's dream come true, at 20 yards a 30-man target. Half-sick with tension, he squeezed the trigger of his HMG. His bolt shot back; he

Colonel Oliver P. Newman (center), CO of 186th Infantry, and Lt. Gen. Robert L. Eichelberger, CG of I Corps, get the latest details on the fight for Mokmer Airdrome from a 186th soldier. The grim-faced soldier in camouflage uniform in back of Col. Newman is Lt. Col. David Dillard, CO of 3rd Bn. 186. Less than fifty yards to right of the group there lay a heap of several hundred dead Japs who unsuccessfully tried to break through the 3rd Bn perimeter.

emptied the whole belt into the Japs. All 30 crumpled and fell. Surely Helphrey saved a pln. or more of B from disaster.

On 10 June, B plus C again attacked this same Jap ridge. This time, heavy FA fire preceded that attack; then D's 3/Pln. 81's took up fire before B and C. This time the companies gained some ground, but a line of pillboxes held them. Again, a Jap counterattack hit 186's flank and forced withdrawal. F Co. had to come up to rescue C. From 1300 to 1500, D and other outfits battered Jap position, but they were impregnable.

Col. Newman would have mounted a third attack, but Gen. Fuller changed plans. He called off our attacks and brought up 162 to help us against the ridge. He replaced two companies with two regiments, which would take over a week's fighting to clear that sinister, low, dark-green ridge.

Thus ended the first phase of D Co. 186 Inf's Battle of Biak. We had come through the dry overland maneuver, the great ambush at Mokmer Dromes and the hard two days' battle for the main Jap ridge on Biak. Allthough still holed up under Jap guns at Mokmer, we had high morale. We were ready for the next phase of infighting the Japs on Biak.

D Co 186 Infantry, II:
Sluggers with Heavy Weapons

By NICK WHEELER, D Co. 186
with DR. HARGIS WESTERFIELD, Division Historian

After fighting in 1/Bn. 186 Inf's unsuccessful ridge attacks of 9-10 June 1944, D was back on the beach at Sboeria. Although 1/Bn. was again in reserve, we worked and slept under threat of shells from Horseshoe Hill, that U-shaped ridge position that was a series of jungle terraces above Mokmer Dromes. Jap binoculars on Horseshoe Hill observed every move we made below. Any large movement of men or trucks or tanks drew instant, accurate shell fire that drove us cringing into hard coral.

D's 81's had helped silence some Jap positions, but the cave guns seemed untouchable. We had seen that many guns were mounted on railroad tracks. They rolled out, were quickly manned, then shot accurately. Some of them we identified by usual number of rounds they fired—or by their span of time in action. Many of us gave names to those guns. D's mortar observers became more familiar with those Jap guns than anyone else.

Thus expert mortarmen—Lt. Hudnall, S/Sgts. Crumb and Imhoff—got orders to accompany a tank to kill Jap guns. Our three men originated a firing plan with the tank unit CO. We would put the tank in firing position, then wait for a gun to come from its cave. Our three D men would stand on top of the tank with field glasses. When the Jap gun fired, it threw up a short burst of white smoke. When that smoke flew up, our observers would spot it and give the range data to the young Lt. behind the tank. He would phone the tank crew to set their guns to fire for effect.

Thus went D's observers into action with a tank and a protecting rifle squad from a line Co. In 20 minutes, a Jap gun stuck its muzzle out. Shells crashed on Mokmer Strip. Reading the mil scales on the glasses were Crumb sitting above the right track and Imhoff above the left track. Hudnall observed over the turret top to the rear. He soon ordered the tank to fire.

The tank fired and rocked violently. Following the tracer shells, Crumb and Imhoff corrected fire with changes in elevation and deflection. The gun was now precisely on target; Imhoff was about to call, "Fire for Effect!"

Suddenly the three D men felt a dull explosion and a rocking sensation. Using our tracer pattern, the Jap gunner had scored a direct hit. Right track below Crumb was blown off, a rifleman was killed, two more wounded.

Yet the tank gun was still operable; we were on target and could kill the Jap cannon and complete our mission. But we hadn't noted the nervousness of the tank crew. The tank Lt. ordered, "Abandon tank!" Instead, our Sgts. ordered the crew to fire for effect.

Yet, the tank Lt. kept shouting, "Abandon tank!" Cowering in a great shell hole, we found a field observer team with a young shavetail commanding. He was so frightened that he would not register FA on that gun. After a few minutes, the Jap gun destroyed the tank. (We have no record of whether that Jap gun was ever punished.)

A staff officer saw D's action. Since the shell had burst directly under Crumb, he wanted to put Crumb in for a medal. Crumb then asked for medals for Hudnall and Imhoff also; they had shared the risk. When the staff officer said that three awards were impossible, Crumb refused. Although easy-going and well-liked, Crumb let his temper flare at what he considered an unequal offer. No award was presented.

During 10-13 June, D had nerve-wracking fire from the ridges. Jap FA, AA and heavy mortars sprayed us with fragments daily. Often we moved to alternate positions to confuse gunners. Worst of all were Jap AA; they screamed after us constantly. We feared those gunners more than anything else in the world. They fired time-fuzes close to ground, and we dug like moles to save ourselves.

Although we realized that we had it easier than riflemen under fire of accurate Jap Arisakas, we labored to give line outfits their needed support. D's observers and wire crews surely worked overtime. We got support fire where it was needed and when it was needed. D probably knew more about locations of Jap guns and caves than anyone else on Biak. Time and again, Col. Newman singled out our observers and wire teams for tough missions of rifle plns.

On 13 June, we had our first dead; a Jap gun crew tried to wipe out our 81's. The blast caught 3/Pln's mortarmen in shade under ponchos where they were playing cards with 1/Pln. men.

In seconds, the gun pulverized the area. It ruined most ponchos, but the men under them were deep in holes. Griffin of MG's was killed; seriously wounded were Scott, S/Sgt. Budach and Cpl. Newport. An FA observer at once engaged the positon; the fire stopped almost as fast as it began. D's mortarmen manned the untouched tubes and kept on firing.

Now Lt. Col. Fields got orders to team his 1/Bn. with 162 1/Bn. for a flank attack on Horseshoe Hill. For the Japs so strongly held the forward side of the hill that 162's 3/Bn. could not dominate that ridge even with 2/Bn's help. Friendly natives reported that the Japs were guarding the last waterhole midway between Hill 320 and Horseshoe Hill. Although Gen. Doe did not know that this waterhole was actually West Caves, he believed that here was the strongpoint—the key to Horseshoe Hill.

At 0800 14 June, D with 1/Bn. 186 left the beach and hiked 100 feet high to the Japs' left flank. D led 1/Bn, then came A, Fields' CP, 116 Collecting Co., D and finally B. C had D's 2/Pln. of HMG's, while 1/Pln. HMG's was in bn. reserve. (Our 81's stayed on the beach in regimental battery.)

In the jungle climb, 1/Bn. bypassed three known Jap positions. At a wide space between contours 80 and 100, we turned hard left to a westward trail. C killed two patrols of 36 Japs. Advance continued through a hot, matted jungle—D's 2/Pln. of HMG's with C's 60 mm mortars.

About 1400, signs were ominous from 162 leftwards. C passed word not to fire on a B 162 squad that was forced back. When annother B 162 squad came through C's lines, its leader told Sgt. Herd that two HMG's were lost.

C 162 pushed through a third ridgeline before dusk, and dug in with our two HMG sections to defend them. Throughout the night, small groups of Japs attacked from

Heavy weapons company men advance cautiously through the jungle.

near a road that entered our position from the west. D men thought a full company attacked; we had good shooting. The Japs struck between two of D's HMG's; we worked on them with help from C's rifles. Early in the morning, we had a great kill. Shouting war cries, some 50 Japs hit C's left flank on the road. From the shelter of our perimeter at daybreak, we counted 30 dead Japs.

And D was angry after a sleepless night. We were miserable in the heat; our uniforms were shredded. Morale was down because Gen. Fuller was relieved from command. We only knew that Eichelberger of Buna was now CO, and we feared being thrown away, as we thought 32 Div. men had been thrown away.

Now Lt. Gerber with S/Sgt. Herd went forward to high ground in our perimeter to search with field glasses for Japs. Japs were moving in small groups to a suspected defense position behind the road. At the base of a large clump of bushes to the right of this position, Gerber looked right into binoculars of a Jap inspecting us. When a Yank observer called for a few rounds of FA on the Japs, a short gave Gerber a light wrist wound. He ordered our HMG's to search the Jap area now and then.

And by 0730 15 June, D was in close combat with Jap tanks. Their overhead support fire slashed at B and C—from the high ground before us and Hill 320 on our right. We heard Jap tanks clanking from behind the hill before us; it made hair curl on the back of our necks.

At 300 yards, tank No. 1 opened fire with a 37 mm cannon—a grim, smoking little machine with high turret. Officers and NCO's got everyone into firing position, but we really needed no help against this tank. The 1/Bn. AT Pln. HMG emptied a full .50 belt against the tank; rifle clips emptied into it too. Suddenly the tank turned off the road and disappeared, trailing smoke. We saw another tank coming; riflemen guarded it, but it abruptly withdrew.

For the next five hours, B, C and D kept low beneath Jap MG fire. From behind us, C Btry. 121 FA dropped 600 rounds on the ridge and halted some of the Jap fire upon us.

At 1310, we had a second Jap attack headed for us. At 300 yards, the tanks fired and rolled in fast. A C bazooka team fired but had only near misses.

Dug in on a small nose on ground above the road, D's 2/Pln. had an excellent field of fire. Our MG's shot fiercely at tank No. 1. Gunner Click almost had his head blown off, the slug tore his helmet from his head.

But as tank No. 1 closed in, Click kept firing; he helped C's morale greatly. The C bazooka team scored a direct hit and stopped the tank. It had closed to 100 yards; all of us fired crazily into it.

Absurdly, the turret popped open; a Jap soldier stuck out his head. Our steel striking the turret sounded like popcorn on a hot skillet. The turret closed; two more bazooka shells hit the tank. It turned back into brush and burned.

With its .37 belching fire, tank No. 2 now charged us. Our hot guns blasted back. As it closed to 60 yards, the .50 HMG damaged its turrets and hampered the .37 from firing into us. C's bazooka men launched three rockets uselessly. One bounced off the turret; one bounced off the track. The third merely destroyed the tool rack.

A 4.2 mortar now fired on the tank; one short hit a foxhole and killed a C man. In trying to bring the damaged .37 into position to fire, the tank turned left and caught on a coral ledge and stripped its tracks. The tank crew left and rushed for cover under a hail of rifle fire.

Gerber, Herd and two C men volunteered to check the tank for more Nips. In hurrying, they triggered a 186 booby trap but were unhurt. A Hq. Co. flamethrower and three Jap mortar shells caused the tank to flame and explode. In this fight, D lost one man wounded and evacuated—Lee Ward.

At 0815 16 June, 1/Bn. killed four more Japs. It amazed us that the Japs were fresh and attacked vigorously—probably new arrivals on Biak. Meanwhile on 16 June, 186's 2/Bn. shock troops stormed Horseshoe Hill and closed the Great Gap between 162's 2/Bn. and 2/Bn. Although D's men in 1/Bn. had to keep low during 2/Bn's attack, our mortarmen down on the beach lobbed in many of the 1,000 shells that tore up the Jap ground before the push. Back with 1/Bn., D's Boyce was wounded.

That night, 2/Pln's HMG's were protecting five tanks. Knee mortars impacted; we also detected a Jap suicide team crawling before our MG's. In the dark, Gerber felt frenziedly for his carbine to signal his guns to fire. When he found it and pulled the trigger, we killed seven. The Japs carried stachel charges and grenades—no doubt to kill the tanks.

And on 19 June, when 186 in a great tactical move enveloped West Caves in the rear, 1/Bn. moved out to contact 186's 2/Bn. and seal the Japs' escape routes. On 21-22 June, the night of the Big Banzai, D's HMG's placed heavy fire on Jap attacks. Crawling forward to a MG hole, Capt. Klink took an ugly wound in his knee from a mortar

---

CREDIT: Main source is Wheeler's 69-page MS "Escapades on the Island of Biak," with information credits from Gerald LaHaie, Rueben Klink, David Herd, Thornton Crumb, Wayne Strebig, Marion Criswell, George Imhoff, Alvin Mazuti, Ernie Gerber, Willmar Stender and William Baldwin. For Nick, I compiled a full dossier—186 casualty list, personnel roster, operation reports. Nick used my stories already in Jungleer, and Mac-Arthur's "Reminiscences." We both used Eichelberger's "Jungle Road to Tokyo," Riegelman's "Combat" ("Caves of Biak" Chapter) and R.R. Smith's "Approach to the Philippines." Herd reviewed the story from Wheeler's MS. First part of this story was No. 94 (Jungleer, XXVII, No. 1—March, 1976).

---

blast. Next morning, a litter jeep evacuated Klink. Twice en route to the coast, his three-jeep convoy had to take cover from Jap fire on the terraces. Luckily, there were no casualties.

For D, the main action on Biak was over with just one man killed. We had three good men who were still to die.

When the Japs tried to reorganize at Wardo Bay in SE Biak, D was ashore with 1/Bn. on 17 Aug. Although Jap opposition was light, we were worn down from combat. One dark night, Rue at his HMG challenged a man relieving him. Another man went berserk; his rifle wounded Rue in the arm and killed Ward when he awoke and raised his head from a foxhole. (Ward was wounded earlier, on 15 June.) To save the berserk man's life from Ward's friends, we hurried him off on a barge next morning.

On 29 Aug. died beloved Joe Palmerio—master of mortar gunnery and indirect fire. When Lt. Harper's A Co. patrol filled two of 10 Japs in native gardens, Palmerio helped S/Sgt. Crumb with mortar adjustments. The second time Palmerio raised his head above a log, he took a bullet between the eyes. Another unseen Jap group joined the fight. When the Japs broke for high ground, D avenged his death; our mortar slew 14 of 25.

Returned from Wardo, D had a tragic accident. While setting up a motor generator to light the camp, Lawrence caught fire from high octane gas fumes that lay low in the heavy jungle. The fumes exploded from contact with fires that had smouldered from the previous day. Although McGough amd Moore extinguished the flames, Lawrence died in the hospital days later. We thought that a letter from Lawrence's stateside wife had finished him. She was getting a divorce; his doctor said that Lawrence had given up wanting to live.

And thus ended the second phase of D 186's Battle of Biak. Repelled after 9-10 June to emplacements under Jap fire at Mokmer Dromes, we joined Col. Fields' 1/Bn. to fight the tanks before West Caves. Although D's losses were fortunately light, our expert gunnery and mortaring had saved lives and served 186 wherever Col. Newman needed us.

Biak. The caves were located beyond the ridge.

Spearhead Company on Biak

By DR. HARGIS WESTERFIELD, Research Historian

At 0657 27 May 1944, E Co 186 Inf piled into amphtracks and charged for Biak, with a Navy LCI rocketship guarding our flank. At 1100 yards, the Navy LCI volleyed all its rocket-launchers ashore. Then E's Lt Crawford saw Jap shells splashing dead ahead. From above Mokmer Dromes, a Jap 120 mm fired while E's first wave drove directly into the shellfire.

Then Crawford saw that our helmsmen had locked on his wheel. Since he sat above him, Crawford kicked his helmet and made hand signals. The driver curved the amphtrack around the shell-bursts, which continued steadily at the same range and deflection. It was like driving a car around a corner. Evidently the 120 mm gunner could see only a small part of the sea because of a steep headland projecting between him and E Co in the amphtracks. (Or perhaps the dim morning light and TNT made correcting range difficult.)

Safe behind the Biak shoulder, E landed embattled — to flounder in the only swamp on South Biak — 1500 yards west of our assigned beach. Sloshing through mangrove muck, Crawford set up a road-block on Bosnek Road to secure 186 from a Jap push from Mokmer.

E Co was unaware that Japs of the Ibdi Pocket ridges could have mortared us off the road — or even dropped rocks. When Joe queried prisoners later, they replied, "We had no orders."

E Co now hiked east past Bosnek Village to fill a gap between G and F Cos, and secure the coastal ridge. About 1200, we found a track through a draw north — and its Jap guards. As his squad climbed the steep draw, Sgt Jesser pushed aside vines and saw a narrow-mouth cave. Jesser took bullets in right arm and back, kept firing into the cave mouth.

From above, S/Sgt Granger tried to save Jesser; he shot down the narrow slot uselessly. Crawling behind pinned Jesser, Granger passed grenades for Jesser to throw. But Granger died with a bullet in his head. Other Yanks lobbed grenades from above, and covered men who dragged Jesser to safety.

167

Maybe the Japs inside heard our orders for satchel charges, for 5 bayonet men charged us and died. After more grenade throws, we brought up S/Sgt Morehead and flame-thrower. S/Sgt Wells assisting, Morehead flamed cave-mouth and nearby crevices. To be sure of target, Morehead stood up with flame-thrower, flamed into black depths where jagged stalactites and 2 boulders shielded the Japs. Two Japs rushed Morehead. A bullet hit Wells in the leg; another pierced Morehead's flame-tank. But we slew both Japs; Smith killed another who stuck out his head. E threw more satchel charges and thought the cave was clear.

Detached with 5 Yanks and BAR to guard another cave, Sgt Santilli got no briefing from the vague F squad he relieved. Cave mouth was a pit 25 feet deep with a ramp up the left side for exit. The night darkened so fast that we could not scout the area. Hearing noises in the cave, we again and again threw grenades or fired the BAR. Some parachute flares blazed overhead; the cave perhaps had other exits.

At dusk, Cacamo had fired at a sound. Moans followed. Just before day, a Jap Marine walked out. Santilli called, "Put up your hands." The Jap came on with rifle. At 15 feet, Santilli ordered us to fire. Cacamo's bullet last night had smashed the Jap's rifle-bolt. We threw the Jap back down the pit.

Next 2 days, E guarded this cave area, on 186's main route to the Japs' projected air-strip above Biak. Each day we killed another Jap crawling from the cave where Granger died — a total of 10. On 29 May, Mitchell was burned by our own smoke-bomb thrown into the cave, and Mueller wounded — probably on patrol.

Then after 3 easier days near the beach, E moved to the Surveyed Drome, became a point company for 186's overland march to capture Mokmer Drome from the rear. During the night attack of 1-2 June at the projected strip before 186 started, the Japs hardly bothered E Co. A Jap officer died under our LMG at dawn.

And on 2 June, when 186 thrust out on the great thirsty march to take Mokmer, E Co with 2/Bn secured the north flank. Returning from an all-morning recon of the projected strip, our patrol fought Japs at a supply dump. Action was sharp and vicious. A Jap threw a grenade at Miazza, it was a dud. Miller and Montore slew a Jap apiece; both Yanks had close calls and were badly shaken. Wounded were Neil, Swanson, and Siliski — 2 back wounds, a leg wound. We killed 6 Japs and fired a warehouse of rifles and engineers' supplies. Our AA flak wounded Morgan.

The 186 overland March of June 2-7 was days of suffering and confusion for E's thirsty men, burdened with rifles, ammo, mortar and MG parts, and ammo boxes. No man remembered well those days of fatigued marching and dark nights of heavy sleep. By day, we hobbled through waterless 12-foot brush, or gratefully dropped to earth for rest when we could. We were down to a canteen of water per day. Even in daylight, the jungle was dark where no men saw over 10 yards ahead. Jap opposition was lighter. The night of 4 June, Japs threw 3 light mortar rounds that fell short of E's perimeter. About 1400 5 June, Japs attacked supply trucks which E guarded. Jap rifle fire was heavy, but we beat them off. Morehead was wounded, part of Weapons pltn was momentarily cut off, but safely rejoined E.

Perhaps at the end of this road, E found water — an abandoned tank truck holed by Jap bullets and spouting the precious fluid. Men like Montore and Santilli dropped all caution — as they thought — and rushed to catch helmets of water and drink enough for once in what seemed a lifetime.

But the march overland concluded, after 186 seized the crest behind Mokmer Dromes. And on 7 June when 186 swooped for the Air Strip, E was last up and over the crest. With Cn and Sv and 162 Hq Cos, we carried supplies. When the Japs Great Bombardment struck 186 men already on Mokmer Strip, E was still descending from the ridge. We arrived at noon to dig in north of the Strip. Although Nips blasted 186 some 4 hours until 1345, E Co was unscathed. Sporadic fire came from small arms, MGs, mountain guns, and AA. One 120 mm was notably obnoxious. At dawn 9 June, Riddle died from long-range fire. Santilli's squad killed a Jap with dog coming up the dispersal bay.

Then on 11 June, now that 162 had cleared Parai Defile and joined 186 by Mokmer Strip, E Co became part of the last great offensive on Biak. While 162 moved west against the ridges, E Co paralleled 162 — but on the levels near the shore. No Japs faced us. But from that untaken ridge 500 yards right, Jap MGs and rifles fired. S/Sgt Santilli saw probable MG bullets kick up dust before him. He saw A. Smith wounded, and probably saw Maurer hit. Our 60s laid fire on observed Jap positions; then we fired LMGs and rifles on them. After 400 yards, E held up until 1400 before we moved again. After 1/Pln cleared the open dispersal bays, the rest of E Co was shot up. Wounded were Morgan, Refice, Kelley, Rachor. Since 162 could not capture the Jap strongpoints, E Co occupied security perimeters on the shore and waited orders. While in perimeter 14 June, Newland was shot in a foot.

On 16 June came 186's greatest battle of the war, when E Co spearheaded the Division to close the Great Gap and fight the Japs point blank at West Caves. Although 162 in 5 days' offensive had topped Mokmer Ridge, 162 had left a 500-yard gap between 2/Bn and 3/Bn. The gap contained 4 Jap coastal defense guns which denied our planes the use of Mokmer Dromes. And when Gen Doe told Col Newman that 162 needed relief from its sustained battle, Col Newman asked for and got the assignment to close the gap.

Col Newman then designated 186's 2/Bn to close the gap; we were closest to it and had done no heavy combat. And Maj Bradley chose Capt Foltz' E Co for the prime effort. Foltz was steady, loyal, and dependable, according to Col Newman, who was in 2/Bn CP but left the job of commanding to Maj Bradbury.

Beginning 0840 16 June 1944, 641 TD's 4.2 mortars blasted the Jap guns for 15 minutes; followed 5 minutes' mortaring of all 186's 81s and E's 60s. Then E attacked.

E's mission was to storm east 500 yards along a low ridge to L 162's perimeter. Days of FA barrages had upheaved the ridge forest into a tangle of logs and branches. Lt Craword's 3/Pln would push up the gentle inland northern ridge-slope, while Lt Block's 2/Pln pushed on the steep southern side where the Jap guns were.

"What's on our right?" asked Lts Block and Crawford. Answer was "Nothing." "And our left?" they asked. "We don't know," replied Bradbury.

With the chopped up terrain and narrow "front," Crawford deployed his lead squad as skirmishers. Other 2 squads deployed in column but echeloned on left flank of lead squad. Crawford used this formation because he did not know what hid in the ridges to the left. (Only the Caves of Biak, heavily garisioned!) Now 2/Pltn grouped in light cover on the gap's west side. Crawford placed his section of H's HMGs to enfilade his left flank, then moved out with his riflemen.

Scouts out ahead, we kept close to the ground and made some 50 yards quietly. New Guinea heat blazed down on terrain stripped bare by shells. We smelled fresh earth and Jap corpses. Jap fire began. We sweated 60 yards more.

Then Jap fire enveloped us; from front, left front, flank, and rear. Bitter and close, fire screamed from a Jap LMG 75 yards left front. A scout fell; we threw oursleves into depressions and writhed into the churned up earth which was so pulverized with shelling that we did not need to shovel.

Caught stringing wire, Crawford flattened, then made short dashes to a great stump. Here he made his forward CP with Yanks crouched beside him — Asla, a scout, a red-haired riflemen, and Sgt Sullivan crimson-capped by the Carlisle bandage tied like a bib under his chin. Jap fire had nailed 3/Pln tight.

But Crawford's 3/Pln fought. We shot to earth uncounted Japs crossing our left flank. Furious fire at the Jap LMG hacking on our left front failed; so Crawford phoned E's 60s on the flat south of the ridge. After 6 rounds, Lt Kossl's men silenced the LMG for 30 minutes. E's mortars also whammed 18 rounds on 2 Jap knee mortars near West Caves, and silenced them.

Crawford ruefully lay by the stump, and fingered the grooves which Nip bullets had put in a dog-tag and carbine stock. Bullets had holed the fatigue jacket under him as he hit the ground. Something unknown had pierced a thigh. Picking mortar fragments from other minor cuts in the seat of his fatigues, he found his cigarettes were still good, and tasted delightful smoke. His pinned Pln kept firing.

A scout lay wounded and exposed. Someone sent 2 stretcher bearers to follow Crawford's wire to the stump and save the scout. Just as they reached him, a long slow burst of HMG killed both bearers and the wounded man. It also wrecked Crawford's carbine and wounded Asla.

Sgt Singer took a detail of 2 Yanks to save wounded. They braved heavy fire to bring a badly wounded Yank to cover where they could give first aid. Sgt Rothschild died crossing the low southern ridge to contact Lt Block's Pln pushing parallel with us.

Thus formidable Jap fire halted Crawford's Pln from closing the gap north of the ridge. But perhaps Crawford's push helped force out Japs because it threatened to cut them off. And Crawford surely absorbed much of the fire that could have smothered Block's Pln.

But Block's 2/Pln had heavy going anyhow — against 500 yards of steep terrain barred by shell-torn jungle and against 4 naval gun emplacements — even if FA made the guns useless.

With Crawford securing his left flank across the ridge, Black advanced an a wider front of 50 yards. He advanced 1/Squad and 3/Squad in 2 squad columns on a 50-yard front while 2/Squad moved in support 10 yards behind 1/Squad. The low ridge somewhat defiladed us from long-range Nippo fire, but small arms fire struck from NE and N.

Safely past the first silent coastal gun position, we suddenly faced close-range infantry fire from 3 other positions. On the left, 3/Squad penetrated Position No. 2 and killed 1 Jap. More intense rifle fire struck from Positions 3 and 4. While the forward squads took cover, 2/Squad maneuvered to the right of Pillbox No. 4.

Then 3/Squad's Morales became a hero — Eddie Morales, who had already lost a brother. Morales hurled grenades into the log-coral emplacement, then shot with his TSMG. He slammed a final grenade into the entrance. He ran to the side of the emplacement. crouched, and sprayed the pit with all his fire. Dead were 8 Japs, and the gun-pit silenced.

Coolly angry still, Morales returned to his pack for more ammo. He doubled up to strike Position No. 4, but he exposed himself on the low ridge-crest. A Jap sniper killed him. Now 3/Squad occupied the emplacement Morales had won and fired cover against Position No. 4 so that 2/Squad could protect a bazooka attack. When his squad leader was seriously wounded, Sawyer took command. With grenades, his squad neutralized No. 4 for our bazooka team to hack at it.

At 15 yards, the bazooka sgt stood exposed on the crest to blast 14 rounds into the gun position. (Watching north of the ridge, Crawford wondered why the sgt lived.) Now 2/Squad rushed and silenced No. 4.

Block's Pln now had visual contact with 162's 3/Pln, but a 70-yard gap remained. G Co's 1/Pln now pushed directly to the low ridge and finished 186's 2/Bn mission. The Great Gap was filled; the Division held the low Mokmer Ridge. Mokmer Dromes were now safe from Jap fire. and the Engineer Aviation Bns could repair the shell-pitted fields in safety. E Co had done the crucial task that won Biak for the Division.

But we had to save Crawford's Pln north of the low ridge where the men lay pinned. Pronobis' 1/Pln attacked across the west end of the depression, to relieve pressure on Crawford. As skirmishers, we moved out – 2/Squad and 3/Squad in line, and 3/Squad supporting. Desperately we infiltrated across the depression, under Jap rifle, MG, and mortar blasts. Just before a Jap truck raod, Pronobis committed 3/Squad in line to the left towards that position of greatest Jap strength on Biak – West Caves. The Division was still hardly aware that West Caves existed!

To lessen fire on Pronobis, Maj Bradbury ordered Minor's G Pltn forward on E's left – where it fought with a forested ridge on its left, exposed flank. Pronobis was now 75 yards forward of Crawford, and Jap fire crackled on our front and flanks. After G's Lt Minor crawled to consult Pronobis, and Pronobis let Minor pass through E's safer ground, both E and G advanced side by side. But a bullet holed Minor's helmet, dazed him. Pronobis knocked Minor down to save his life.

And E could advance no more. Even though Lt Kossl repeatedly exposed himself on the low ridge to call Weapons' fire, E's 60s were useless. In Pronobis' Pln, S/Sgt Vanalstine, the veteran of many Biak patrols, who never risked his men unless he first scouted the way, was killed.

There died Medic Dietsch. When wounded Yank lay in cross fire 75 yards ahead of him, T/5 Dietsch left the extreme right of Pronobis' Pln where he was safe, and went extreme left of Block's Pln. Capt Foltz' CP warned Dietsch against the mission – and Block's CP. As he crawled through heavy fire, even the wounded Yank begged him to return. But Dietsch started plasma transfer, and a Jap rifle killed him.

In 1/Pln's advance, Scout Joe Montore crouched in a small rocky ravine, and sighted a heavily defended pillbox with its MG – a key to the whole Jap defense. Soon Japs spotted Montore with Pronobis behind him. Bullets rattled off the rocks and angered killer Joe Montore, with his TSMG and grenades. What berserk Joe did then he does not remember. But he evidently charged the pillbox slot, and shattered the Japs' bodies with heavy 45 slugs – clip after clip. Then he grenaded the pillbox and killed the MG.

Then Joe and 2 Nips in a small trench saw each other simultaneously. They traded grenades. After warning Pronobis back to safety, Joe heard a grenade boom in his ear. Fragments seared him – under right eye – in right arm and right leg. Brought to 1/Pln aid station, Joe did not leave until Pronobis' Pln saved itself. (After operation at 12 Portable Field Hospital on Owi, Joe would go on to 92 Field Hospital at Hollandia for x-ray and special traatment. Yet he was back with E after 30 days.)

And thus ended E Co's push against terrific odds 16 June 1944 – 186's greatest day overseas. Beginning at 1330, G Co, on Pronobis' left flank next to West Caves, threw in all 4 Plns – all as riflemen – slew many Japs but could not overrun the ridge above West Caves.

Both E and G Cos fought back under Jap fire. Although Col Newman ordered 2/Bn to form night perimeter, Gen Doe had seen to many Nippo infantry grouping on our left rear. (And we realize now that Col Kuzume would surely have attacked desperately by dark – fresh troops against a tired 186 Bn.)

So E Co retreated gallantly. After smoke and explosives covered the Japs, Pronobis' 1/Pln covered withdrawal of Minor's G Pln, carrying 3 wounded. As G left, Pronobis faced 2/Squad NE and 1/Squad N to cover G. With E's 60s aiding, we killed the expected Nippo counter attack.

Now E fell back behind BAR cover. At each 1/Pln halt, a BAR with rifle protection smashed Japs while the main body retreated a short way. Then an alternate BAR group fired protection to save the exposed BAR group, then covered 1/Pln's next retreat. Japs tried to envelop our left flank- the alert BAR group spotted them, dropped them dead. Capt Foltz did not leave until his last E man was safe. Secure on the low ridge. E happly turned over to 2/Bn 162 500 yards' hard won jungle from which the Japs had denied us the use of Mokmer Dromes.

Of 15 killed, 35 wounded in all 2/Bn, E counted 6 dead, 16 wounded. But no one has told how many of them were hit. Besides S/Sgt Vanalstine, Sgt Rothschild, T/5 Dietsch, Morales, Wyman and Heglund. were killed. Besides T/Sgt Sullivan, wounded were S/Sgts Robinson, Summers, Sumpter, St Marys. Besides Montore, Asla, and Lt. Crawford, McGinnis, Morse, F. Adams, Little, Robuck, Roberts, and Windham were wounded.

Having closed the Great Gap 16 June, E Co now regrouped for our second great maneuver on Biak. Despite Gen Doe's assertion that the Japs would mortar us to death, Gen Eichelberger sent 186 to interdict West Caves from the rear – to cut off Jap supplies and reinforcements from overseas.

On 19 June after four FA Bns' preparation, E Co moved out 5 minutes behind F Co. We caught up with F at the Jap motor road 1400 yards behind West Caves. Objective was a long, narrow, sharp rise – the first slope of Mokmer Ridge. Santilli's squad deployed as skirmishers and fired, then moved to the crest. Suddenly Santilli and his scout jumped behind a fallen tree; a grenade arched over their heads. At 10 yards, Japs hurled 5 grenades; not one hit a Yank.

To break the line, Santilli decided to throw a grenade, then have Musch fire his BAR from the right and pin the Japs. Then Santilli and scout would bore in and kill them. But a grenade wounded Musch in the arm. Assistant BAR-man Musto was hit also. Santilli thought his own grenade nicked Musch. The Japs escaped.

Next few days from high perimeters, E probed deep into the coral ridges, met Jap fire, killed a few. We were above the motor road so that the Big Banzai of 21 June from West Caves did not strike us. And beginning at 1200 24 June, E Co went up against the Teardrop.

The Teardrop was a long, narrow valley off the NW shoulder of Hill 320 – over 300 yards long north to south and 100 yards wide. Over 200 Japs with MGs held the western slope. Through hill jungle, Santilli's squad saw a skinned branch hung from a tree – a Jap trick for attention. Lais halted to look at it, and a Jap shot him in the back. But Lais was able to walk back to Medics. Wounded across the ridge from Crawford's Pln was McBride. Seever was killed.

On 25 June, E tensely entered the Teardrop among Jap defenses on NW and west side, but merely contacted A Co. We found 1 HMG, 1 20 mm AA gun, and 20 dead Japs. All told, 186 counted 38 Jap corpses. Yet because Col Newman could not locate 163's 3/Bn to come and close the northern escape corridor at an earlier date, a well-armed company of 200 Japs had escaped annihilation. E Co was lucky indeed to have but 2 wounded, 1 dead, that day we penetrated the Teardrop, rifles ported and ready.

On 26 June, E gladly rejoined 2/Bn in the flats. (E's real war was over this day that 163 made its first all-out attack at Ibdi Pocket.) For the next 3 days we sent 25-man parties to the beach for well-earned bathing and laundry picnics. We set up tents, but laborious patrols continued. And on 27 Aug, E replaced B in 1/Bn for the Wardo Bay landing in SW Biak. There we easily shattered the Japs' last hope to reorganize. Santilli had the scare of his life A Formosan soldier slipped up behind Santilli and pulled his pants leg. Santilli pulled his Webley pistol from its holster, but the grateful Formosan yearned only to surrender. Santilli was even more grateful when he found the grenade and sword-blade the man was armed with.

Thus campaigned E Co 186 Inf — spearhead company of 186 and the 41st Div on Biak. Landing in the first wave under fire, we gallantly fought the cave in the Bosnek pass where Granger died. On 16 June in our finest hour, we closed the Great Gap in Mokmer Ridge. On 19 June, we cut the Jap rear at West Caves, later penetrated the Teardrop. E Co won 3 DSCs — Morales, Dietsch, and Montore. Only Montore survived. E Co had at least 38 wounded, and 10 dead. E Co's is surely one of the Forty-First Division's great company histories.

Sources include Capt Charles Foltz' Diary, sent by his widow Winifred; Lt Joe Crawford's ltrs 29 May, 1961, 4 Apr 1969, interview 1961; ltr Joe Montore 10 Jan 1965; ltr Maj Gen Newman 17 Feb 1967. I also used RR Smith's APPROACH TO THE PHILIPPINES, Ross Santilli's 14-page MS, medal stories of Foltz, Sawyer, Singer, Vanalstine, Granger, Jesser, Morehead, Morales, Dietsch, Montore, 41 Div Trng Note 8, 186's Biak Journal, and Crawford's and my story of 2/Bn (Jungleer, July, 1961). Thanks especially to Mrs. Winifred Foltz, whose husband's Diary was essential. Montore also sent a Diary.

G Co 186 Inf-RIDGE FIGHTERS OF BIAK

By DR. HARGIS WESTERFIELD, Association Historian
with 1/Lt Albert Minor and S/Sgt Jordan Davis

On 27 June 1944 G Co 186 Inf piled into buffaloes and struck for the Biak Beach. An LCI ran in with us and blasted the jungle with rockets. Jap cannon and small arms splashed near misses. G slogged knee-deep into the only coastal swamp in Biak. Maj Bradbury hurried us back east to find the Nips in cliffs 150 yards behind Bosnek.

We scouted among sheer cliffs, unopposed; but T/Sgt Don Meyer probed a large cave and died from Jap bullets. Our flamethrower, rifles, grenades overwhelmed the cave, killed 2 Nips. Then Jap rifle-fire and strafing Zeros harassed us. 1/Lt Minor was out of action with a ricochet into his nose, closing one eye, almost closing the other. Minor went to hospital in Hollandia.

On 28-30 June, G slew Japs behind Bosnek — took a prisoner also. On 30 June, Acosta, Arnall, Lloyd Bailey were wounded. On 1 June when 2/Bn joined the march behind Bosnek to take Mokmer Dromes from the rear, G was in support. Uselessly we searched the waterless scrub for a rumored Jap Hq. On 3 June while guarding a bulldozer building the road, we fired on 2 Nips — and missed. Near the base of Mokmer Ridge 5 June, 15 Nips volleyed, mortared, and grenaded 2/Bn's rear. G's patrol cleared the area. For 2 Yanks dead, 17 wounded, we killed 13 Nips.

After leading bns of 186 crossed Mokmer Ridge and took the air-strip, G was still hiking down the ridge when the surprise bombardment started. We lost no men then, nor during days of shelling. Ordered to clear Nips from the beach caves, we found that our tanks were there first, let them burn the Nips out with napalm.

Now G Co took over important 186 missions. On 8 June we got orders to strike back into Mokmer Ridges and take out Jap AA guns that had smashed supply parties and litter squads. That morning, in fact, Jap fire from those ridges had stopped dead 162's 2/Bn trying to rejoin its regiment.

So on 9 June — Minor's birthday — we panted up jagged coral outcrops into rain-forest. No Nips fired, but we found well-travelled trails and discarded Nippo phone wire. In the dark ridges ahead, Japs were shooting.

Minor's pltn led out, searched the distances of 2 rolls of wire from G's CP. We found nothing. On 10 June Minor led out again up the same ridge. Brush thrashed, but we held fire, contacted K-162 on the same mission. Below us, AA fire broke out; we were near the end of the ridge and the Japs hidden below in the scrub. Then K Co from 163 met us. The 163 CO told Minor that his men had hunted Nips for days with no success, except that 2 K-163 men were dead, shot between the eyes.

Then S/Sgt Davis reported that the ridge ended in cliffs: the best way to get those guns was to climb down those perpendicular cliffs, where Jap mortars, MGS couldn't miss. Davis volunteered to lead with his own squad — mostly Papuan vets. Thirsting on those waterless ridges, David told Minor: "I'll be where I can get a drink of water by dark — or never have one again."

Now Davis' men tackled the worst mountain climb in their lives — 70 feet and higher sheer Biak cliff. With rifles slung to free hands, they grasped trees and coral outcrop to keep from falling — hoping to jar no rocks loose to cause Jap fire. The brush cut our view to 5 yards; we could not see or free hands to fire back.

Yet no Japs saw us. Davis' squad deployed at the cliff base to guard the others — Minor and a Spanish-American lad with the phone — then the whole pltn with Sgt Granito's squad securing the rear.

Davis' squad led out to battle. In 20 yards, our taut squads found spider holes — a Jap bivouac — but no Japs. In 50 more yards, we found a monstrous Jap 90 mm mortar — and enough ammo to level a mountain — or chop our pltn into dead meat on the ridge we had descended.

On the second low ridge, we saw Jap AA HMGs, and helmeted Japs in holes ready to strike 186 below us.

Exultantly Davis quickly formed his squad in line, assigned targets. We blasted out a cliff; Japs toppled and fell. Among their corpses, we formed a half-moon circle for security. We began smashing breeches of the vicious little shrieking guns that fired 25 mm shells.

The Japs counterattacked. On the right, their MG cut brush inches over our prone backs. From the left, Jap rifles fired; grenades exploded.

Our M-1s stopped the right flank attack; but the MG still flailed us crouching into the coral. One scared Yank shrank backwards unknowingly — to where Davis could see MG bullets hitting the ground. Coolly, Davis got up to tie the man's suspenders to a tree-root. Later, Davis found 3 holes in his own fatigue pants leg — front and rear.

Davis crawled to kill the MG, but heard Jap chatter from a cave on the flank. He must take the cave first. He threw in several grenades; a Jap rushed out to die. The MG withdrew. G destroyed 1 LMG, 1 90 mortar, and 2 AA 25's. We counted 12 Japs dead — Davis took credit for 7.

Then Tennesseean Faris stood up on the sky-line. A Jap sniper knocked him down the cliff. Although Granito and others fought to save Faris, the Jap fired again, roared "HOI! HOI!" in triumph. Minor seized a bazooka and fired at the Jap yell. At that close range, the rocket fins recoiled and almost chopped off Minor's head. But the Jap fled, and we saved Faris. Gleefully, we hiked back to the air-strip, to 186's welcome — and the water that Davis earned for us all.

On 16 June G Co fought its greatest fight of the war — when 186's 2/Bn had to close the gap — to storm 500 yards of jungle ridge between 162's 2/Bn and 3/Bn. From this ridge, Japs great guns still smashed any planes that tried to use Mokmer Drome — still held the Division from conquering Biak.

E struck the ridge first, stormed the cannon bunkers, almost closed the gap. For full contact with 162 south of the ridge, Maj Bradbury sent in G Pltns — McGovern's and S/Sgt Bob Murphy's. The Nips let Murphy's pltn reach the objective, then cracked down with rifles and automatic weapons. A Yank was hit in the head and lay in the open where Nips covered him from high ground; Murphy crawled 10 yards to save him. But McGovern's and Murphy's pltns closed the gap.

North of the ridge, E Co's 2/Ptn push met Jap fire that pinned it down. Maj Bradbury ordered Minor's G pltn to strike on the left flank and free E. To Minor, the order sounded murderous. Although Pronobis' E pltn protected his right, he must attack with his left flank open to a thrust from a silent jungle ridge where cliffs indicated hidden caves.

But Minor's pltn pushed with left flank exposed to that silent jungle ridge. Dark caves gaped in the ridge. Minor detached Sgt Garner with 2 men for security. Japs struck our rear from those caves; but Garner blasted them off. As we contacted E Co, Jap frontal fire increased with each attempt to push. Some G men were dead or wounded. A bullet creased Minor's chin.

Yet Col Newman insisted that Minor attack. Minor sent Sgt Cummings' squad to advance by fire and movement. Someone garbled the order; Cummings' men charged with assault fire. Japs blasted us back, struck down several Yanks. Here medic Jette died trying to save wounded; an E medic was hit also.

Minor decided that G's pltn would do better if we left Pronobis' flank and pushed through his E Co pltn. The push succeeded at first; but Minor raised his head too soon. A bullet pierced Minor's helmet; the afternoon went black.

Pronobis ran out to knock dazed Minor down, drag him to a hole. Minor remembered little of the next hours of combat. His pltn made only 50 yards by 1130, then had to fight off a Nippo counterattack from that flank ridge.

Maj Bradley tried a new push with G Co. He called down 600 rounds from 121 FA's 75s, then struck with E's Crawford and Pronobis' pltns, and Minor's and McGovern's pltns in line. This 4-pltn attack halted at 200 yards, but McGovern's pltn accomplished what Minor had wanted earlier — cleared high ground in a Jap bivouac area — smothered automatic fire retarding other advances. Minor's pltn had it hard again — fought West Caves themselves. Despite the rifle and MG fire and grenades, we made 50 yards more before being stopped by heavy fire from a cave-mouth on our flank and frontal fire northward.

Now Maj Bradbury sent McGovern to drive through this Jap area and contact 162 and 186. (We did not realize that we had sent him against Kuzume's most formidable position — West Caves with 500 Nips and heavy weapons.) McGovern hit with just 2 squads remaining, and a 50 MG section of AT Pltn. Astride the road, we repelled a small Jap counterattack. About 100 yards from the ridge summit, Japs shot at us with MGs, rifles. Our 50s silenced this fire.

As skirmishers, McGovern's men attacked cliffs or sheer slopes defended by rifles and MGs. CO Boyd now sent in Weapons Pltn men with rifles. But heavy fire from the road where Boyd had crossed was too much. After some casualties, Weapons riflemen took cover just past the road.

Although G 186 had closed the gap in 162's ridge-line, our new mission had failed. With casualties mounting, we had to retreat before dark. F Co guarded our flanks, bore out our wounded. After 81s fired smoke, Minor's pltn fell back. McGovern's 2/Squad fired cover while other elements pulled back. Japs pursued to the road where a concentration of Bn weapons stopped them.

G Co had the most casualties on 16 June. Killed were T/5 Bossany, Skogrand, Villanueva, LaPlaca, Shayne, Cave, Woulfe, Korsmo, medic Jette. We had 14 wounded. Boyd got a bullet through the elbow, Sgt Marcos a bullet through his knee and the heel of the other leg. Minor had recovered enough to work with Boyd extricating G Co; but both were evacuated. Names of other wounded went unrecorded.

And G still fought. On 19 June, after 186 blocked the Jap road behind West Caves, we got hit again. Patrolling with 2 tanks that shot up Jap MGs, we took fire from a Jap cannon which killed 1 (Granito, perhaps), wounded 8. Only recorded wounded were Chester Davis, S/Sgt Bevernitz. On 21 June, we took the main thrust from the Nips' great Banzai charge to escape West Caves. In the final attack at 0400, Nips were so close that our 60s were useless. An unnamed G Sgt directed I Co mortars on our flank to nip Japs off within a few yards. Besides 1/Lt McGovern, 2/Lt Roll, men like Cheass, Mericle, Willie Jackson, William May, Andrew Johnson, Shope — who was slightly wounded — held the line. Next morning, we saw truck-loads of Nip dead, heard Gen Eichelberger praise us.

Such were outstanding actions of G Co 186 Inf on Biak. We raided Mokmer Ridges and killed Nippo guns; we closed 162's gap on 16 June, with 9 dead, 14 wounded. With a total of 11 known dead, over 20 known wounded, we were rated among 186 Inf's most reliable fighting companies.

Most important story sources are 1/Lt Albert Minor's 38 page handwritten MS and Ltr dated 17 Dec 1964 — and S/Sgt Jordan Davis' Ltr 3 Mar 1964. Jordan also sent me official story of his DSC, difficult for me to get in Federal Awards. Also highly important for 16 June 44 battle was Lt Joe Crawford's E-186 story in my "186's Second Bn Closes the Gap on Biak," (JUNGLEER, July 1961.) Other sources are R R Smith's APPROACH TO THE PHILIPPINES, "Company G, 186 Inf/Record of Events," G-186 Payroll Roster, "Annex 71/Operations of Co G 8-11 June 1944," and several medal stories. Unfortunately, Minor was twice out of action from wounds — before the overland march, and during part of the fight of 16 June. Now that Jordan and Minor have broken G-186's silence, maybe other G Co men can fill out more about this great company.

I Company, 186

Our Luck On Biak

by DR. HARGIS WESTERFIELD

About 0720 27 May 1944, I Co 186 Inf was dumped from buffaloes into sea a mile west of Bosnek. Unprotected, we waded 400 yards to the beach without Jap fire—139 men, 6 officers, crews for 2 M Co HMGs, one .50 HMG.

Remembering our Hollandia deaths, we were grim on Biak. At White Beach 3, we had destroyed a Jap pillbox—killed 11, took 2 prisoners; but disaster followed. South of Cape Tjewri, 4 Navy Hellcats made each a strafing run, killed 6, wounded 15. Massengill, Does, George Mitchell died at once. Sponsler and Koprada died of wounds—Koprada 2 days later, April 24. He was buried at sea. Also wounded were 1/Lt Haedicke, 2/Lt Burl Cox, S/Sgts Harden, James Johnson, McComber, Kropp, Christopherson. Other wounded were Swain, Spino, Al Watkins, Carl Anderson, Stan Williams, George Hess, Wolfley, Lenbeck. Hollandia was useless death.

But on Biak, I Co's luck was good at first. Although 6 Jap planes raided in 2 waves, AA fire killed 4, with 1 possible. For 4 days, we helped Fields' 1/Bn guard already secure Task Force Hq. Umphlett was injured in action May 31.

Released from this useless guard late 31 May, we entrucked into the scrub to rejoin 3/Bn near the projected Jap Air Strip. But release from 41st Hq came too late to close the southern gap between K and L Cos. In the night fight beginning 0100 1 June, we killed 1 Jap of a few trying to infiltrate, then silenced noisy Japs 300 yards off with 6 mortar rounds.

In 186's thirsty march through the upland coral scrub to seize Mokmer Drome from the rear, I's luck continued. On 2 June, we killed 6 Japs. On 4 June Pittman was accidentally wounded. Cook Oehler broke his collar-bone on 5 June.

On 6 June, we crossed the highest ridge above Mokmer Drome, dropped down to a lower ridge, killed 1 of 2 Japs we saw cross our trail. S/Sgt Ulshoeffer was wounded. On 7 June when 186 took Mokmer Dromes, "I" was left assault company. Safe across the Strips, we pushed west some 600 yards on the beach, slew 2 Japs in a dugout. After positioning to guard 186 from the west, we cleaned out Jap caves in the ledge at the beach. "Killer" McRoberts bayoneted 5 Japs here. Besides killing some Japs, we captured many automatic weapons.

When the Great Bombardment of 7 June began from the Jap ridges we bypassed, I Co had 4 wounded in 4 hours. Swain, Janke were seriously wounded. At 2200 that night, knee mortars blasted us. In 30 minutes, jabbering Nips hit 3/Pln from the beach—at 25 yards showered grenades. Their MG fired wildly overhead. We fired back with a concentration of 30 60mm mortar shells, our .50 HMG on the beach road, and a captured Jap MG.

Then M's 81s fired for effect 100 yards before perimeter. Then L's 60s barraged—some shells as close to our holes as 20 yards. These blasts turned the Japs upon L's 3/Pln; but concerted fires of I and L stopped the assaults. About 0500, the last Nips pulled out. Our captured Jap MG had killed most of the 15 we found dead.

On 8 June at 0900, we had our first dead on Biak—Medic Ringglein from a shell that seriously wounded Oehler also, and S/Sgt Emerson Koenig, who lost a kneecap. The barrage from the ridges wounded 4 more. At 0900 also, 1/Pln sortied to protect 2 tanks that duelled guns across Mokmer Strip. But a shell smashed off a tank-track, killed S/Sgt Simmons, wounded 2. Back in perimeter, we were shelled continuously, with 4 wounded at 1500. Another Pln prowled the beach again, slew 12 Japs in caves. Besides Ringglein, Simmons, Japs also slew S/Sgt Rear. Known wounded besides Oehler, Koenig, were Sgt Villa, T/5 Canby, Jordon, Lenbeck, Arnold, Tom Adams, Epps. Seriously wounded were Calvert, Voss, Gianakis, Glynn. Wounded but still on duty were Lane, Wheat. Dead totalled 3, wounded 16.

In the 186-162 offensive of 11 June when 162 went into the Jap ridges, "I" was 186's flank assault Co on the beach west towards Sorido. When a tank hit a land-mine, Voorhees was seriously wounded. On 12 June, early morn, Nips lobbed in knee mortar shells which hit no one. While registering, our FA killed Luby, seriously wounded Ussaitis, Mayo; and Lane was hit but still on duty. On 14 June, our patrol 1200 yards west spotted an ammo dump with automatic weapons. FA destroyed the dump. Daniely had a light wound 17 June.

On 19 June, we went inland to be part of 186's great offensive to cut the supply road to West Caves. Without casualties, we set up defenses on the supply road, meanwhile killed 4 Japs. On 20 June, 1/Pln probed 500 yards inland, met heavy automatic fire front and right front. Then we protected 2 tanks that came to protect us. Tanks drew fire; 2/Lt George Swenson was badly wounded, and 1 man not named in reports.

Basic documents are I 186's "History of Biak Campaign by 1/Lt William B. Foster, "186 Inf's Report of Biak Campaign," "First Two Days at Mokmer Drome." For night combats and the Waters Patrol, I used detailed reports left by unnamed 3/Bn CO. Useful also were I&R man Alan Rock's "Three Tales of I&R" (Jungleer, Mar 1960); Sgt Robt Hedger's "Historical Records—Med Detachment 3 Bn, supplied by Don Wiseman; Maynard L. Clark's ltr 8 Aug 1961; RR Smith's Approach to the Philippines. Medal Awards stories were Trgina's, Wheeler's, Wholey's, Charles E. Smith's, and McRoberts'. To Kenneth Wheeler I owe special thanks: his 2 long-distance calls first let me know that McRoberts' story was an I Co story, since his DSC story was filed in a different file from other medal stories of the 41st.

DR. HARGIS WESTERFIELD

41st Infantry Jungleers pass by shell craters and burning fuel dump on Biak. The date was May 27, 1944, remember?

On 21 June, I Co found the start of heavy fighting for 22 June. Skirting a strong Jap ridge position, 3 Pln spotted pillboxes, killed a Nip. On return, we took MG fire where the road crosses the ridge, had Strand and Stern seriously wounded.

That night, I Co sideswiped the Big Banzai of Col Kuzume's men from West Caves. Although I's western perimeter did not face the Jap thrust, we helped break it. East of us, Japs closed in on G Co. Since G could not elevate 60s high enough to blast infiltrators, I Co's mortars took over. When G's S/Sgt Jensen called for help, Lt Wholey reversed his mortar positions and flanked G's front with a barrage—250 rounds—many within an estimated 50 feet of G's holes. We interdicted Jap reserves, helped kill 109 Japs.

Sleepless after last night, "I" struck the position 3/Pln found yesterday. Our losses had caused us to consolidate to 2 plns. With 3/Pln leading, we set up a base for LMG cover with 1/Pln as security. In 3/Pln, S/Sgt McRoberts advanced his squad within 25 yards of 2 heavily built Jap pillboxes. Alone, "Killer" McRoberts charged a Jap pillbox—rapid fire, slew 2 Japs, wounded another. Seriously wounded, he ordered in his squad leading 3/Pln to overrun a line of pillboxes. We pushed 50 yards more into heavy fire—and an AA gun cracking in our faces. A direct AA hit killed 2 Yanks; a MG wounded another. 3/Pln took cover behind 1/Pln which had moved up 150 yards. FA and mortars barraged the Japs; but we withdrew before dark to let other 186 men finish off those Nips tomorrow. Trgina died from MG fire when he dragged to safety a wounded man—probably McRoberts. Dead also were Usher, Vorse.

On 24 June, "I" was mobile reserve—either for K fighting north or L pushing 400 yards out towards Sorido. We went to help L Co in the third day of a fight against a strongpoint with 2 or 3 75s or AA guns. After 600 yards, 3/Pln's left squad deployed to fight a Jap position. Terrain was flat and blinded with brush. After a few yards, MG fire struck from front, right flank. Then Simmons' squad of 1/Pln attacked the MG. At 15 yards, a scout fired 3 rifle-grenades on the MG. All were duds. A Jap grenade killed Simmons; MG fire wounded 4 more Yanks. Men of 3/Pln now skirmished against a MG which stopped them.

Now our attached HMG opened on the Japs from our right flank while our LMGs shot from the left. But with only 15 yards' visibility, they could shoot only at Jap sounds and were ineffective. Jap return fire was heavy. Now 2/Bn sent 2 tanks in with us. With 2 squads of 1/Pln, tanks overran a Jap MG, killed a Jap. But having to veer left, tanks took both HMG and AA fire. In thick brush, drivers must stick heads out of turrets to observe. Shell fragments wounded Lt Cross, lead tank CO. Cross was hit in the head. The tank-inf team fell back.

Meanwhile, attached radio man—T/4 Ken Wheeler—helped us find the Jap guns. Climbing a tree, he called fire directions for our 60s and M's 81s. When 947 FA's observer arrived, Wheeler pointed out 5 Jap FA or AA positions. After Wheeler's help, only one of the probable 2 or 3 positions was left undestroyed by the 155s, as L Co found in its clean-up attack 25 June.

In this attack of 24 June, besides Simmons, we lost Mason, Gemell, Manning killed—and perhaps 5 wounded whose names were unreported. Next day, L Co liquidated this Jap strongpoint. I's Boyd was seriously wounded 25 June.

Long after Biak was won, I Co patrolled in the native gardens, where I&R reported 500 Nips. On 6 Aug, we shot up 5 Nips cooking, took 4 rifles, 2 knee mortars. On 7 Aug, we had 1 badly wounded in an ambush from 10 Nips riflemen, 2 LMG crews, 2 mortar crews. Same group wounded 1 Yank 8 Aug.

So on 9 Aug, we tried to outfox those Japs. Since they had fought us 600 yards north, we would leave the trail 400 yards below them, circle to take their rear. (They were not supposed to change positions!) With Lt Waters commanding—a hawk-nosed man in first action—we took a large patrol. We had I&R men Rock, Sullivan, 3 Sgts, 12 riflemen, 4 weapons men, 1 medic, even 2 observer officers.

The Japs outguessed us. Ambush came with our patrol in column over 3 low coral hills about 50 feet high. From Hill No. 1, the Japs looked south down a straight trail 4 feet wide—then over Hill No. 2 to crest of Hill No. 3. Our cover and concealment were sparse; the Japs' Hill No. 1 was horseshoe-shaped. Its arms outflanked the trail.

But we probed blindly up that trail past Hill No. 2 across a small clearing, on up the steep slope of Hill 1. Although the first scout reported smoke odors to Lt Waters, we moved a few yards more.

From the left of the trail, a rifle shot hit the scout. A Nip Woodpecker put 4 slugs into Waters. A second MG opened up, and riflemen on the crest—MGs about 20 yards off trail—riflemen 50-75 yards off. S/Sgt Charles Smith heard them pounding their sticky bolts.

After 10 minutes forward, Lt Hawkins worked his way across the clearing under Hill 1, despite heavy rifle and MG fire. Safe behind Hill 3, he gathered the 7 men there, tried to crawl to the Nips' right, SE of Hill 1. But MG fire and a knee mortar prevented this. Trying from farther left, they were halted again. The Japs shifted 1 MG to an alternate position to strike Hawkins, even shifted field of fire 180 degrees, as Pln/Sgt Boone noticed. With a final mortar blast, came hot silence in that tropical heat.

Second Scout Konen called for help for Lt Waters; the Japs were gone. Hawkins and his 7 took the Japs' area, found 3 LMG positions, a knee mortar hole, 3 riflemen's fox holes. The Nips had fled by a trail cut 15 yards from the main trail to where their escape route was hidden from Hill 1. Dead was hawk-nosed Waters in his first action. Seriously wounded—his second wound on Biak—was Lt. Lattanzi, 1 enlisted man. We never caught that clever Jap fighting patrol.

So fought I Co 186 Inf on Biak. Because of 6 unfairly slain by our own planes at Hollandia, death seemed to hold back for us. (L Co lost 19 dead.) But even after the Big Banzai, we had 7 dead in those sharp tank-infantry actions NW of Mokmer, to total 10 dead for all Biak. Despite the holocaust of Hollandia's White Beach 3, I Co became a great battle company.

K Co., 186
THE CROSSROADS

**By DR. HARGIS WESTERFIELD
with BILL AGUE (K Co 186 Inf)**

On 27 May 1944, K Co 186 Inf's warriors hit the Biak surfs, floundered in 250 yards to cut Bosnek Road at Mandom. Second and Third Pltns hiked 1500 yards east, dug in on a sharp coral ridge behind Bosnek. With Japs everywhere, we shot up 15-20 patrolling the north road, slew 1. Arriving at 1530, F/Pltn and Weapons killed 1 more. At 1730, K hit another small patrol, with 2 dead Japs. At 0645 28 May, Jap planes dropped 3 bombs, wounded Isaac Baker. Planes struck again at 1730, but K's luck had started. We had no losses.

After 162 failed at Parai Defile, K led 186's overland march to hit the Japs' rear. On 1 June, our patrol seized the crossroads 1600 yards north of Biak. We saw 6 Nips, killed 1, dug in fast beside AT Co's 2 37s.

At 1330, 15-25 Nips attacked while rifles, MGs, a light mortar drove us to earth. Mess Sgt Brewster flattened under the lister bag, but the MG fired high, wild. At 75 yards, our mortars silenced their weapon. Three Nip riflemen charged from brush. Rifles killed 2; 1 escaped. Fight lasted 30 minutes; 5 hours later, we had to send a flank Pltn to root out other Nips.

L Co dug in east of us but could not tie in to make an unbroken north front. For L must guard a second north road 800 yards east of K. We left a dangerous gap; but Lt-Col Maison could not get I Co back from guarding Gen Fuller's Hq until too late to fill our gap after dark. Expecting I's arrival, Ague, Kleupfel, McDonald waited to arrange for cutting fire-lanes. But the Nips never saw them in the brush that night.

At 0300 2 June, a booby trap exploded on the road to our right. Brush rustled; shoes thudded the road; Jap voices spoke 35 yards from 2/Pltn CP. 2/Lt Giessler estimated 35-40 Nips in a draw 40 yards SE, called down mortar fire. Expertly even in dark, mortars corrected left from the road, fired 6 for effect. Japs jabbered; we shot 6 more rounds. But Japs crawled around mortar holes, blasted grenades at every shell-flash. CO Don Anderson stopped mortar fire; instead, Giessler's men tried rifle grenades. Runner Voos placed the rifle-grenadiers, directed fire.

Nips blasted down the road between its F/Squad and 2 Pltn's CP. Grenades, BARs stopped them. Another attack made for Giessler's hole. Knowing Nips would cut his wire, Giessler phoned for mortar concentrations at dawn. The wire went dead; grenades hit close. We threw Yank grenades that sparked and located us. They replied with more sparkless grenades. We stopped throwing, grasped rifles; but the Japs did not close in.

Now Japs fought all 3/Btn. From the south, 1½ Nip Cos attacked; other Nips struck between K and L Cos. Thirty minutes after exploded booby traps by Giessler's 2/Pltn, K's 3/Pltn fought infiltrators. Two impacted grenades at the hole of Acting Lt Cram. He killed 2; a third died in the dark by 2/Squad.

We fought in the dark. With phones silenced, we didn't know that the Nip southern horde was trapped inside 3/Btn, trying to fight their way out. In F/Pltn, attacks hit near dawn. Small fighting teams tore in from the road; 2/Squad met a drive from Nips evidently sheering off from 3/Pltn. In 30 yards' range, we barraged them with grenades—and in 10 yards killed the last Nip with M-1s.

In F/Squad, Sgt Horace Young heard Nips calling Pltn Sgt Ward by name from his hole. A Nip charged Young, but 3 45 slugs from his tommie killed the Nip. The gun then jammed. With Mauch, McCartney in the same hole, Young fought with grenades to dawn. All night, Ague, McDonald, Kleupfel heard Nippo feet thud past their flank on a brushy track, lay tense by their rifles. They could see no Nips; a thrown grenade would foul in the scrub and spray them, or bounce back on them. They lay quiet.

Main action lasted 30 minutes, piling up 16 dead Nips. But Sgt Parsons, rooky Cibulski, a third Yank were all wounded. They got credit for smashing a possible breakthrough; 11 dead sprawled within a few feet of their hole. It was worse in another hole; there Pometta and Pagno were wounded, sent back to CP. Starret had a direct hit on his helmet. The bullet penetrated the steel at mid-forehead, made a horrible racket screeching on the steel. Starrett spent months in hospital for brain surgery. Sgt Hegle was wounded in the eye. At dawn, 3 Btn counted 3 Yank dead, 8 wounded. K lost just 4 wounded evacuated. Of 128 Jap dead, K had 16.

Despite the sleepless night, at 0900 2 June K Co led out beside L in 186's "desert march" through the scrublands of central Biak to take Mokmer Drome from the rear. Dead-eyed without sleep, we sweated under packs, doled out the last water in canteens, drop by drop. Japs could be anywhere in that 12foot scrub; but only "I" found any—wiped out a 5-man patrol.

By 1330, we made 4100 yards, dug waterless perimeter for the night. By dawn, Ague and others were licking Biak dew off the leaves of scrub foliage.

Waterless and loaded with equipment, we expected a walking nightmare. But stray showers filled helmets, canteens. We made 3,000 yards. On 4 June, we halted to 1000 hours for supplies and a little water from Bosnek. Then Gen Fuller delayed 186 until he learned that the Jap Navy had aborted its chances to relieve Biak. We hunted west 1500 yards into scrub, but got no Japs. K Co got by on ½ canteen's water per man on 4 June.

On 5 June, Newman's officers advised him to wait for water, but he moved us 2400 yards to the base of the first steep ridge rising out of the scrub north of Mokmer. Newman sent K to find the trail over the ridge. Miraculous heavy rain fell; silvery water pooled on ponchos, tinkled into empty canteens. And at 2400, Giessler's Pltn first topped the ridge. K Co with other 3 Btn elements followed Giessler, to bivouac on top. On 6 June, we made 1600 yards, dug in where we could view the sea far off. In the tangled ridges, we saw no Nips. They were surely between us and Mokner Strip; but K Co scouted downward to make perimeter in ominous evening silence.

On 7 June after 30 minutes FA, K Co with other 2/Btn and 3/Btn captured Mokmer Air Strip, in total silence. Then at 1030, the low ridges opened up with Jap fire—75s, AA, 90mm mortars, MGs. The whole 186 perimeter was in a Jap ambush. Fire went on all day while we flattened under near misses or leaped up to give first aid—or dig in for the expected attack of Jap infantry.

CREDITS

Prime credits belong to Bill Ague, K 186's Company Clerk who initiated all contacts and spent much of his own money calling his buddies long distance. Bill's letters brought the dead records to life. Through Bill, Horace Young, Joe Roscoe, Sgt Ward—all gave Bill information. Bill also led me to Mjr. Gen. Don Anderson of Oregon National Guard (then K's CO), who got Teardrop Story from Major (then 2/Lt) Vernon Barkhurst. Official records include K Co's "History of Biak Campaign," untitled story K's fight June 2, untitled Journal of Third Btn 186 Inf Operations Report," R. R. Smith's "Approach to the Philippines." But Smith omitted the Teardrop Fight from his history.

Lt. Barkhurst in a picture taken by one of his 186 cobbers in 1945, just a few days before he returned stateside.

Laboring to direct fire of his 2 mortar sections at Jap gun flashes, T/Sgt McGill had to dash around without cover. Orders came to send his ammo carriers to fill in a gap in the line. He leaped from a crater to lead them. A shell gave him his death wound. Another shell wounded Hoyt, shocked Ague for several days. But by later afternoon, Jap fire slackened 40 per cent. K had countered with mortars, like all 186; and 121 FA fired 2000 rounds, adjusted for heavier 205 FA and 947 FA. K had 9 WIA, McGill dead. Among wounded besides Hoyt were Julius Jones, Ogden Erickson, Louis Reynolds.

On 8 June, we had another hell of shells. A tank's shellfire could not damage a pillbox on our right. At 2145, Japs fired mortars and LMGs at us. Our 60s with M's 81s diverted their attack into L Co. Michener was lightly wounded that day. On 9 and 10 June, Jap AA and FA fire continued with less intensity. But K's luck continued; we had no more losses.

On 11 June, K was part of Gen Fuller's offensive with 186 and 162 to wipe out the Japs. K's luck held up. Although 162 operated inland and got entangled in that hedgehog of resistance around West Caves, we found no Japs where we expected them. And for the next 7 days, while all other Btns slugged at Nip strongpoints, K's Btn mainly held rear guard perimeter but for security patrols often 1000 yards out. K's luck was bad only on 13 June; Yoacham died accidentally.

Then on 19 June, K became part of K's great offensive which enveloped West Caves, cut the Jap supply lines, and forced Kuzume to come out fighting. At 0645, we followed 2/Btn NE to the road NW of West Caves, while Jap mortars flailed us, hit 19. We deployed left of 2/Btn, crossed the road, seized a razor-back ridge 250 yards north. Jap rifles fired on us afternoon and night.

And on 20 June, K Co battled for the Teardrop. Since 186 must protect 162 fighting West Caves from heavy Jap forces northward, K and F went to fight Japs under Hill 320, which dominated the whole ridge-line above West Caves. K and F were to fight to contact each other, and L Co 163 Inf already atop Hill 320. But the Japs halted F Co; and L Co 163 had temporarily left Hill 320's summit.

For K Co, 2/Lt Barkhurst's Pltn led out from our razor-back ridge to clear the slopes under Hill 320. Hardly had we cleared perimeter when Nips fired. As Barkhurst squatted Montana fashion to consult with scouts "Beaver" Morales and Saunders, a Nip rifle bullet exploded coral, banged Barkhurst, knocked down Morales but merely bruised him.

Some 40 yards right stood a 50-foot promontory shaped like a teardrop lying on its side—or maybe the Rock of Gibraltar—a chunk of Hill 320 that had broken free of it ages ago. Barkhurst told Sgt Glen Hall to seize it now, and we luckily found no Japs to oppose us.

We made perimeter on this Teardrop. Some 75 feet wide, it was sheer on the face we climbed, but it sloped toward Hill 320. In coral holes hidden by brush and trees, Barkhurst's 35-man Pltn at first felt snug and safe.

On the slope of the Teardrop near Hill 320, a Nip HMG in a log pillbox fired on F Co's patrol. The gunners did not know that we held the crest of the Teardrop. Scheill crawled around the side of it, tip-toed to the front, dropped a grenade into the slot. He crawled back grinning; the grenade killed the gun.

But Japs moved in fighting. We kept killing them, but in a sense, we were the ones pinned down. From high on Hill 320, grazing fire shattered our coral—even richocheted into 186 Regt and 3/Btn Hq on the flats below.

We were happy that Jap MGs informed Hq of our predicament, but about 1300, Barkhurst got orders to storm Hill 320 overhead. With Baldy Larson's squad leading with the 2 other squads covering, we pushed up the more gradual leftflank slops. BAR men Hassler, Schiell took Jap fire but were the decisive men in neutralizing a pillbox. As 3 Japs fled it, our rifles slew them. But 2-3 Jap MGs raked us; we had to withdraw.

Larson's squad was too deeply involved; it seemed doomed. But Hassler's and Schiell's BARs opened up in rearguard action. Hassler died then. Schiell's BAR pinned the Nips down until the others escaped; but Schiell was killed also. We could not bring out their bodies.

Back on the Teardrop, we crawled under Nip drumfires, beat off attacks. It was 2 hours before we got orders to leave. Then Barkhurst had to ask for Giessler's Pltn to help us. With this extra fire power and more mortar cover, Barkhurst's men got out—just as the Nips repelled the F Co men and might have concentrated on us. Sgt Larson died then. With Larson, Hassler, Schiell killed, we also had Short, Pillola, Mellinaskas wounded. But we brought back the Nip HMG Schiell had silenced, and killed 25-30 Japs. (Not until 25 June, could Gen Doe team 186 and 163 against the Teardrop and the strongpoint in the box canyon nearby. Most of the Nips escaped.)

But after the battle of 20 June, K Co 186 Inf's luck was almost all good. For even with many combat patrols through 3 July with other 186 men clearing the ridge pockets north of Mokmer, we had no casualties but 3 wounded 3 July. We had battled at the Cross Roads, spearheaded the "desert march," taken the shelling on Mokmer Strip, battled on 19-20 June. But K Co had only 5 dead.

L Co. 186 Infantry: Night Fighters and Desert Rats

BY DR. HARGIS WESTERFIELD

On Z-Day 27 May 1944, L Co 186 Inf landed on Biak, took over K Co's mission on the ridge behind Bosnek. S/Sgt Foote died in our first fight with a Nip patrol. At 0615, daybreak, 28 May, Japs attacked our perimeter. We killed 14 Japs (1 officer); but Mecello, Tiberio, Oppegard took grenade wounds. At 3 Btn Medics, Capt Tontar, Cpl Wiseman, T/4 Skaggs gave plasma. At 0400 29 May, Jap planes lit flares around us bombed the beach. Such was Biak for us before the overland march to Mokmer, the final infighting.

On 1 June, after 1962's retreat from Parai, we moved to our jump-off place for the "desert march" overland to Mokmer. We killed a Jap, set up 3 Pltn perimeters on the E-W Road N of the Bosnek Drome area.

At 1500, a rifle pltn with I&R patrolled by trucks—6 trucks bumping along without mufflers 5-10 miles an hour into scrub jungle with visibility down to 10 yards. Our lead BARman fired from a truck at surprised Nips 200 yards down the road, missed. After 1500 yards, we dismounted to hike 350 yards, killed a Nip, called for FA fire where we heard 50-80 Nips' voices. But the noisy patrol scared us. Sgt Verges said that a foot-patrol would have walked as far in the same time, been safer. I&R man Love averred he had never been with a worse patrol.

At 2030 in those scrublands, night fights began. Japs chattered in brush 50 yards N of 3 Pltn. Sgt Hazelton got CO's approval, had his attached 60 drop 3 rounds on them. The 60 blasted the Japs' attack, dispersed them. But at 0300 came a heavy Jap attack, 40 yards E up the road. While we telephoned CP, 8 Japs threw grenades among us, rushed the mortar. They killed 1 mortarman, wounded 1. With grenades, we killed the 8 Japs.

At 0300 also, F/Pltn took an attack. From within 20 yards of Pltn CP, 2 threw grenades. The Pltn Guide also threw grenades, heard Japs groan and weep through the night. A soldier in a 3-man hole turned to see a Nip rise, thrust with bayonet. The soldier dodged, slew the Nip with a bullet through the head. Then 7 Nips charged with fixed bayonets. The 3 Yanks in the hole killed all 7 with short-range M-1 bursts. Meanwhile L's 2 Pltn took grenade fire, killed 3 Japs.

Just before daylight, 3 Nips, 1 with LMG, rushed 2 Pltn's mortars. Our rifles killed 2; the third died only at the edge of the perimeter where a mortarman emptied a pistol clip into him, finished him with trench-knife.

At dawn before the F/Pltn, 1 Jap officer walked nochalantly down the road, died from M-1 fire; and 7 riflemen walking into a HMG firelane, were cut down there. At daybreak also, 2 Pltn men saw 5 Japs leap from the track into brush. A 37 AT-cannon fired canister at the place; later we found no bodies, only blood.

All told, L Co killed 28 Nips that night; but Lloyd, Freiman died of grenade wounds, while Jernagan, Tilenis, Skora were wounded in action.

At 0900 2 June, L Co plunged into the scrub desert of inland Biak on 186's 4-day march to take Mokmer Drome. Water was already short; we learned to race for a brown little Jap canteen even while the Nip was still dying. In that dry hot sea of scrub where even the coastal ridge arcs far southward, we lost sight of all landmarks. Between hot green walls of 12-foot scrub that caught the breeze, our little patrols moved carefully SW up and down slippery coral slopes, over tricky heaps of coral debris, now in sunshine, now in hot wet twilight. Japanese warriors we did not meet; but we scouted many small bivouac areas, well-worn new-travelled trails.

Thirst was our problem: we had only a canteen full issue on on 2 June, again on 4 June. On any halt when it rained, we took every opportunity to spread ponchos, catch water for canteens, or to drink from often soapy helmets. On 5 June, no water was issued; but a rain about noon and Col Newman's order let us stop to irrigate ourselves for that climb to Mokmer Ridge behind K Co.

Late on the day of that great rain, we followed K Co up a rough trail to Mokmer Ridge, glimpsed Mokmer Drome through brush 2500 yards SW. After a day on the plateau above Mokmer, we moved on the Drome—squad-columns in a hot march through 12-foot scrub and among coral openings—expecting Japs.

In dispersal bays at Mokmer Drome, we found only a few empty pillboxes. We hiked on ready for Nips to fire. At the beach, we saw a 12-foot coral cliff ideal for Nippo caves. I Co got into a little fight which our 2 Pltn supported. Phosphorus grenades brought Nips out on the jump. They slapped their clothes like wild men until we mercifully shot them. Our F/Pltn had 2 casualties in knocking out one little hornets' nest.

The beach was still too quiet. After we turned W 375 yards on the beach, it happened. Heavy Jap automatic fire crashed down from a ridge 1000 yards N. As we formed perimeter, field guns, depressed AA fire whistled around us, drove us to earth. We wormed into coral, dug with anything handy. But we organized quickly. While 2 men per squad outposted 20 yards ahead, half of the rest dug; the other half crouched to clear fields of fire. When the cannonade creased, we expected a screaming attack with bayonets and grenades. We did take rifle fire, but it was too high. But their FA and AA saw us accurately, scored us again and again. As we furiously dug for our lives, there came an order (rumored from Division) to stop disturbing brush and drawing fire!

After twice digging in, we pulled back at 1400 to a road-junction, organized tight perimeter—2 squads forward, 1 back in each Pltn. Shrapnel still caused wounds; but M Co's 81's shot off heavy battery fire. Jap shells became intermittent.

CREDITS

U.S. Archives Collection was unusually rich, thanks to foresight of 3 Btn CP on Biak: "Record of Events Co L, from May 25, 1944;" untitled story of L's motorized patrol; untitled story L's fight June 1-2; untitled story L's fight June 8-9; "First Two Days on Mokmer Drome" (by unamed Squad Ldr 2 Pltn); untitled report 26-29 June 1944 from Hq. 3 Btn., 186 Inf. Also highly important was 186 Inf. Opn Report on Biak, with Col. Oliver I. Newman's "Notes". Also useful were RR Smith's **Approach to the Philippines**, Sgt Robert Hedger's **Hist Record Med Det 3 Btn.**

Don Wiseman of 186 3 Btn Medics sent me Sgt Hedger's report, and visited my home.

HARGIS WESTERFIELD, DIVISION HISTORIAN
6248 Sturdy Avenue, Cincinnati 30, Ohio

LCI's, carrying part of 186 regiment to Biak, push along the coast of New Guinea on a misty day in May, 1944.

We had 5 dead—T/4 Vaughn, S/Sge Kepford, Bohuslav, Oplatka—all from shapnel. Sgt Harrison died from rifle fire. Wounded were S/Sgt Larson, T/4 Soderburg, Davenport, Guerrero, Robey, Lt Fallon. Heavy fire greeted 3 Yank tanks that landed at 1400. M's mortars cracked late into dusk; but no Japs attacked.

On the next night, the moon rose bright by 1900. Before F Pltn, a dog howled; then dogs howled from the trail outside Btn, and on the ridge N of Mokmer. Their coordinated barks made us interpret them as Japs' signals.

At 2130, a Jap MG opened on 2 Pltn; other MG's with knee mortars fired heavily. Observing a MG, a knee mortar 75 yards direct front, 1 squad leader reported them to L's mortar Lt. But our 60's were over, and Jap MG's silenced the mortars in their shallow emplacements. Then M Co's 81's tried to hit the MG and knee-mortar; but they landed so dangerously close to our front that we had to halt the fire.

Now their main attack turned from 2/Pltn to 3/Pltn which held the N side of the beach road next to I Co. Our 2 Pltn's BARS and Weapons Pltn's light 30s enfiladed the attack. Our fire crossed M's HMG fire about 40 yards out. In turn, Japs fired MG's against our MGs—6 minutes at a time, then made long pauses. Again our HMGs traversed the brush; then Jap grenades, rifles opened up until we fired final protective lines again, broke up incipient attacks.

At 2400, 5 Nips crouched in a bomb crater 35 yards before 2 Pltn, threw grenades. Our grenadiers had already gauged the range earlier. At 35 yards, we blanketed them with grenades, evicted them, found 2 bodies at dawn.

Beginning at, 2130, 3 Pltn began to suffer grievously, situated as it was where an inland road turned off from the beach road. Despite M's HMGs and 3 Btn's 50, men of 3 Pltn died.

At 2130, a dark group of Nips moved down the inland road. One part of them hit "I" Co on the beach; the other hit 3 Pltn of L Co. They fired mortars, grenades, some rifles. A trio of Nips sheltered in a coral crevice 5 yards in front where they saw silhouettes when we raised to fire. Covered by rifles, all 3 charged with bayonets. We killed 2; the third killed Sgt Bingham, Adam Walker, but died from a trench knife. Nearby died another Yank from rifle-fire. We had to reenforce 3 Pltn from other holes.

At daylight, each rifle Pltn sent 1 squad on recon 150 yards front. We found 41 dead Japs; blood showed that others had crawled off, or had been carried away. Besides Bingham, Walker, 5 more died—Sgt Spicer, T/5 Sneeringer, Weber, Cutting, Schreiber. Wounded included Sgt Corland, Wilbur Olson, Helgesen.

But after 8 June, Japs made no more night attacks. L Co luckily did not spearhead any major offence; but men still died. While 162 Inf and 186's F/Btn assaulted the ridge on 11-12 June, we pushed west towards Borokoe on the coastal road. On 15 June at 0300, Boyd Hall died accidentally.

On 19 June we followed 2 Btn against the ridge NE of the West Caves, took mortar fire. Going into position atop the ridge, we had 6 wounded: McGinnis, Westlund, Lloyd Taylor, Leibowitz, Charles Collins.

On 20 June while patrolling towards Hill 320, we found more death. Salvon's Pltn met heavy resistance, had trouble withdrawing. Hazelton's Pltn rescued a K Co patrol that was pinned down, escaped before a counter-attack. A MG killed Sgt Salvon; rifles killed Gorski, Jerry Walker, wounded Sgt Christie.

On 24 June, L Co moved with "K" and 2 tanks against a Jap FA position. Trying to contact "I," Hazelton's patrol ran into an AA point, took MG fire, which wounded Greer. On 25 June, 947 FA impacted 155s here. Following Hope's patrol, L Co overran the area, found 4 shattered AA guns.

While other 186 Btns stood guard N of West Caves, 3 Btn had its last large action of 26-28 June. With 2 tanks Hazelton probed a sheer, brushy ridge. The point squad was driven back; S/Sgt Palmberg died from a rifle, while James Williams was wounded. On 27 June, Lt Badger, Sgt Hope with a 60 mortar squad in support, tested the Japs thoroughly. Covered by 28 mortar rounds, we pushed up the cliff, fell back from snipers. We then contacted other Yank outposts to block off the Nips, threw in 22 more mortar shells, called for FA, 4.2's, 81's. Reenforced on 28 June by a "K" Pltn plus "I" Co 60's, we had orders to attack. Atop the ridge were only 20 dead Nips, some stuffed in holes in the coral.

And L Co's war on Biak was done except for patrolling. During 2-5 July we cut brush, set up kitchen. During 14-18 July, we had only routine patrols, lined up tents for garrison duty. Luckily, we missed some tough assaults; but we had in our history 2 vicious night battles, the gruelling march over the scrub desert of Biak, the bombardment at Mokmer. We had fought and won like a Line Company—with at least 21 wounded. And we had 19 dead.

186 I & R
Three Tales of I. & R.

By Sgt. Alan R. Rock with Dr. Hargis Westerfield

When I smelled salt water and Diesel fumes and rode the landing barges into the Guinea Shore, I was 19 years old and an I and R man in 186th Infantry. We were a cocky bunch of patrol experts working close to Col. Newman and we had it easy — until the two nights of 21 and 22 June, when the Nippos came boiling out of the West Caves to die. This is my first tale of I and R.

The first night they merely probed against 106 Hq. and Service Co. and two AT 50's straddling the trail. Next morning, blood spotted the perimeter front. We expected an all-out attack during the coming night of 22 June, especially on the trail that led into the Native Gardens.

Then came the moonless night of 22 June. We felt them close in. But I wasn't worried. I had a good buddy and plenty of ammo. In the next hole was Nick Kalember—a muscular guy who could dig a foxhole in coral faster than you could dig one in sand. We had a half-case—24 grenades each—and little compartments in the sides of our holes to keep them handy.

All night the Japs seemed to probe rather than attack. Along with the chatter of AT's, two 50's, some small arms, and the rain's beat, we heard them close in. They talked, rustled the brush, struck grenades on helmets to arm them for firing.

I pulled pins, threw and ducked, while fragments of things rained down on me. Somehow or other, this fight for life seemed comical to me—heaving rocks at rats on a dump. Maybe I was more afraid than I thought—maybe I threw too often. I ran out of my 24 bombs. But hard-digging Nick Kalembar whispered over from his hole, and passed me his grenades. My throwing arm was better. I chucked bombs while Nick waited with his M-1 for any Nip who might get through.

Some Japs detonated themselves with mines around the waist, others attacked. By 0400 Hrs. they mounted an actual battle. I saw Nips in groups of three or four charge those 50's. They drove one charge home. I saw two Nips astride the barrel of a 50. One Jap had killed himself and the First Gunner with a grenade. That was our one death and we had five wounded. But one of ours was blinded.

The Japs had set up mortars under a big tree fifty yards out—a tree which was also the base for our mortar fire. Japs died there before they could even stack the ammo and set up to fire. We counted 109 dead—including the officer Lieut. Francis McGovern found playing possum under a Nippo truck.

At the break of dawn General Eichelberger and Col. Newman came to investigate. Some unhappy P-38 pilots over on Mokmer Air-Strip had complained. Our 50's had ricocheted and disturbed their rest. The poor guys must leave their cots and sleep underground like us rifle-jerks. Eichelberger forgot about the Air-Force complaint and singled out a number of us for Silver Stars and Bronze Stars.

Now for my second I & R Tale—of our 6-day patrol into the Native Gardens. After the Air-Strip was won, Col. Newman assigned I & R the mission of ascertaining how many Japs still held out north of us. The night before I wrote in my Diary. "Tomorrow will be one of the most exciting days in my whole life."

On Sunday 23 July 1944, we started out, eight of us—Lieut. Dick Highland, Bill Huskey, Wayne Holman, Big Murphy, Nick Kalember and me. On those patrols, we wanted fire-power but only a light load otherwise. In addition to a couple of Tommies and the Lieut.'s carbine, we had M-1's, full belts, two extra bandoliers, a minimum of two grenades and bayonets and hunting knives on our belts. We wore soft caps and shoes with leggins. Besides two canteens apiece, medical kits and K rations, we had only a light pack with toothbrush and poncho.

As the sweaty green jungle closed in, we moved in the only possible formation—single file, five yards between each man. We moved forward silently with hand-signals. Nick Kalembar with his Tommie and I alternated at First Scout and followed compass traverses.

At the rear, Lieut Highland or Wayne Holman wrote down azimuths and checked the map-case which served as a sort of rudder in that sea of jungle. For these Native Gardens on Biak were surrounded by dense rainforest. There were tremendous trees —some six feet in diameter, often lying across native trails in the actual Garden areas.

That first day of shadows and silence, we had nil contacts. But on the second morning we found evidences of bivouacs. Then we saw Japanese soldiers, but they didn't see us in those thickets. One would have had a hard time seeing his hand before his face in that. They may have thought that we wouldn't follow them in from the coast this soon with fighting going on in the Ibdi Pocket. They were talking loudly; they sounded relaxed, happy.

We wanted to stay invisible, but later in the day, our dense brush popped a Jap, luck ran out. Out from the three feet before us. We tried to capture him; he saw us motioning him to come to us. He walked away talking aloud to some Japs who were out of sight.

There was no order to fire; but our blast from M-1's, Tommies, even the Lieut.'s carbine drove him fifteen feet. In the next moment's silence we got out of there.

As far away as we could get, double-quick in the darkness, we made two-man positions on top of the ground and tried to sleep. It was a moonless night. Phosphorus from dead wood glowed eerily in the dark and birds or animals made noises that kept us awake.

It was early morning, June, 1944, when Gen. Eichelberger (right), then CG of I Corps showed up at the 186th Infantry perimeter on Biak to "chew the hell out of the blokes who did all that promiscious shooting" all night long. After Co. O. P. Newman (center), CO 186th Inf., told him the facts of life, Gen. Eichelberger passed out a mess of decorations to the 186th boys for successfully stopping a Japanese do-or-die attempt to break out of the West Caves.

At daybreak we found that even K rations tasted good because we were alive. We took a long roundabout course and spied on the Gardens from another direction. Again we heard many Japanese.

To make an exact check of the Nips, we remained on jungle patrol three days more in the green, the heat, the wet. At night we lay close to a large tree during the dark or on a coral knoll to give us a dawn view in the distance. Before dark, we paired off in two's and took turns with grenades or rifles on guard. It worked better for us not to use a watch; it was too hard for a worn-out patrol to stay awake an exact time. It might be only minutes a man could watch, but nobody ever slept before he punched another man awake—all those black nights until the beautiful light came.

With the light, we all awoke listening and guarding the green. Then with the jungle secure, somebody outguarded while the others splashed a little water on their faces and brushed their teeth. We never shaved. Breakfast was cold "K's", we dared not build a fire of wood and canned heat was too heavy to carry. Then we went back on patrol the livelong day, watching the compass and the green hell before us, checking the map. Even in the hourly breaks, we smoked less than any soldiers I ever saw—maybe a couple of us in pretty safe spots. As for the water, we found almost no streams; it rained continually and we filled our canteens from dripping ponchos. It was a tough life, yet a good one that reads today like a green dream—the green dream of New Guinea.

On the sixth day we patrolled back to Hq. We reported we had spotted some five hundred Nips, but Col. Newman didn't believe us. This time, Chuck Johnson, Wayne Holman and I accompanied a dog with his master. Everywhere the dog went, Nips popped up like rabbits. Now Newman believed us and we were glad they invented dogs.

And now for my third tale of I and R—of the disastrous ambush. Once we had spotted the five hundred Nips, Col. Newman acted against them. Long after the real Battle of Biak ended, he rotated 186, company by company, to raid the Gardens and keep the surviving Nips disorganized.

But 186 I and R did not rotate back to rest camp, instead, we took our turns in pairs on little fifteen and sixteen man patrols. Since death and wounds and illnesses had dropped our original strength from sixteen to ten or eleven, there were usually only seven or eight of us fit for duty as guides. We guided repeatedly. If the Nips' morale had been a little better, the I and R men would have rotated to their graves.

On 11 Aug 1944 we came nearest to disaster—so near disaster that a version got into **Infantry Journal**. It happened in a peculiar way. The day before, a patrol of a company whose letter I can't remember, had been ambushed on a trail about six hundred yards from its Hq. So our commanders told us to outfox the Jap. Instead of going six hundred yards this time, we'd stop about four hundred yards from the Jap's ambush, leave the trail, circle the area, and take them in the rear. (The Japs weren't supposed to move their ambush.)

Off we went then, a file of hunters sixteen strong. First, two company scouts, then the officer in command, then Sullivan and me of I and R, then two BARmen, then riflemen. Last came two officers, one a mortarman, the other a short, blonde crew-cut Joe I didn't recognize.

The patrol CO had just come from Stateside—a conscientious sort, capable, tall and slender, with a hawk's nose. We started laying sound-power from the CP. Just out of sound of the company, he told us to check the sound-power. Then we moved over a low ridge, down a gentle slope, then up between the arms of a horseshoe-shaped hill. About fifty yards up a slight incline, we halted so I could take an azimuth of the trail. Then it happened.

The lead scout signalled back that he smelled smoke. A few steps later, a rifle bullet struck him from the left of the trail. Simultaneously, a Woodpecker slapped four slugs in the hawk-beaked Lieut. Our whole patrol hit the dirt; the Japs lobbed in knee mortars also. Our BARmen raised up and answered the fire, and leaves dropped. I don't think he saw any target. Sullivan and I began to fear the Nips would clip us from the rear.

Then the crew-cut officer took seven men and tried to crawl around the Japs' right flank. In that cover, Sullivan and I thought they were Japs and almost pulled trigger on them. That officer made two attacks with his men; but the Japs had an alternate MG position—and used it, too. One MG shifted 180 degrees to fight us again. With the Japs on the left arm of the horseshoe ridge, the officer withdrew his men to the right. The Japs fell back under cover of knee-mortars.

Our First Scout swore at us from where he lay out of sight. "Come and help us! They've pulled out. The Lieutenant's bad hit."

Sullivan and I and two others ran to the high ground and found three men down. One scout was wounded seriously; a bullet had cracked a scout's helmet but missed him. The mortar officer had his nose shot off. But the fate of the hawk-nosed Lieut was one of the ironies of war. He had just come from the States; he had never seen the enemy; and he lay dead. I cannot remember his name or his outfit. As for the Nips, they escaped completely; a relief patrol found only their firing positions.

In I and R I saw plenty of war after Biak—mountain patrols of exploration on Palaguerellas on Zamboanga Peninsula, the clean-up in Japan. But these are three of my best tales—the perimeter on Biak, the six-day hunt in the Native Gardens, the disastrous patrol. Even in that hell-hole of Biak, I loved that crazy jungle. But these are three of my best tales.

Now, I'd like to read some of yours.

CREDIT

Prime credit for this pioneer record of 186 Infantry's history goes to Sgt. Alan E. Rock, I & R, now with Western Adjustment & Inspection Co., Wilmington, Ohio He "talked" me three long letters on Dictabelts, and patiently answered my many questions. The rest is the best study yet published of the life we actually lived on the Guinea Shore. Alan also sent me "Jap Ambushes" from May, 1945, *Infantry Journal*, and Arthur Veysey's item in the *Chicago Tribune* for June 22, 1944. These I used also.

Can other 186 men dictate or write to me about their regiment? Can anyone tell me the name of that fine officer who died or the others' names and the name of the Company involved? Sadly I must admit that 186's contribution is inferior to that of other infantry outfits.

Alan cautions you that he speaks from memories 15 years back and is open to correction. Both he and I will be delighted to receive any letters of amendation or correction. And we still want help on the history from Engineers, QM, Medics, Finance, Chaplains, ARTILLERY, 163, 162.

HARGIS WESTERFIELD,
Division Historian.

41 Recon Troop: On The Biak Frontier

By LT COL GEORGE S. ANDREW, JR.
with DR. HARGIS WESTERFIELD, RESEARCH HISTORIAN

Originally Wyoming National Guards, 41 Recon Troop hit Bosnek Beach after 186's assault Cos—D-Day, 27 May 1944. Specially trained in Marine Scouts' & Raiders' Course at 7 Fleet Hq, we used our skills to help take Ibdi Pocket by fighting on 163's north frontier against Nips that might hit the Montana Regt in the flank. Then we became a private army to knock out Jap warriors in forgotten combats of SE and NE Biak.

While Biak was still quiet after the landing, 41 Recon met death. A misguided staff officer sent F/Lt Cain to check a cave near Bosnek. A Jap rifle killed him. We blasted that cave—slew a Nip officer, 2 men—claimed first blood on Biak—Yank and Jap.

But early Biak days were inactive; we guarded Gen Fuller's Hq while Jap raids became nuisances. On 28 May, Cedric Fields got a serious chest wound. We had several strafings. On 7 June, 2 light anti-personnel bombs hit kitchen areas, wounded Ralph Gaston, 2/Lt Jack Casey. Earlier, Wm J. Jones had a knee-wound from a grenade accident. Thus we lost 4 Yanks.

Meanwhile, G-2 wanted Recon volunteers to land at night by Korim Bay to check on Jap reinforcements in barges. We were to land in rubber boat from a PT craft—be picked up by that PT within 3 nights—or be given up as lost. Or we could trek back across Biak through the Jap Army. G-2 plainly said we had 50 of 100 chances to come back.

F/Lt Andrew swore privately he'd take no chances, but S/Sgt Don Miller, 6 more volunteered. The night before, however, they were scared—begged Andrew to come. And he went!

On 13 June, we 8 landed in pitch dark—1.5 miles away from tranquil Korim Bay. Surf on the reef almost drowned us. One Yank kicked an empty drifting gasoline drum; it rang like a gong. We thought we had surf-ridden into the Jap barge refuelling station.

Shakily, we flattened in a little arc on the blacked out beach. We heard at least a Jap Btn creeping through bush at us—the land-crabs, of course. Just as nerves got taut, Andrew heard Miller's stage whisper from the other flank of the smallest beachhead the 41st ever held. "Jeez! I wish my poor old grandmother was here an' I was there. The old lady never gets to go interestin' places an' do interestin' things." Everybody chuckled, relaxed; Andrew even slept an hour before moonrise let us see to patrol for Nips.

Near Akraak Village, we contacted natives, and got details of Jap barges into Korim Bay. Three nights later, a PT boat took us back to Bosnek. (Later we tried a similar patrol to Wardo on SW Biak, but cliffs stopped us.)

On 19 June, 41 Recon finally entered into the Battle of Biak. Div Hq was now safe; our Regts were infighting for West Caves and probing Ibdi Pocket. But 163 needed us for securing their right flank. So we went to battle in our strength and pride—dismounted cavalry who added an elite touch to a great infantry division.

We were indeed an elite outfit. Half of us were vets of the Papuan Campaign—Wyoming men of a recon Regt—many former cowpunchers. Since we were an intelligence gathering section, G-2 gave us the pick of replacements before the new campaign. CO Capt Lyle Hammond and F/Lt Andrew handpicked our new troopers—all under 21—high school grads, with high Army Test scores. Wyoming vets and bright young statesiders blended into a perfect recon team. Basic unit was the 4-man scout team—3 teams a section, then 3 sections a Pltn. Each man selected his own weapon—M-1, carbine, TSMG, BAR. We knew all about staying alive in the jungle.

Our mission beginning 19 June was to protect 163 on the unmapped north frontier past Ibdi Pocket. Based on 163's water-point where we kept guard, we must stop Japs from hitting our line men. We also sought for the reported Nippo supply trail, made maps as we patrolled.

In 12-man sections or 28-man recon patrols, we hunted Japs. We shot up any group not too large to handle. If they were too many, we drew back—and marked their perimeters for FA strikes. All told, we made 20 patrols, destroyed supplies—even recaptured Yank gear—and a 20 mm AA gun.

One patrol surprised some 50 Nips, drove them from perimeter by sudden attack, killed 5 before they reformed. We escaped from their gathering counter-attack. Another patrol found and entered a cave area — apparently Hq of 222 Inf. In the extensive office and living quarters of 1 cave, we discovered quantities of maps, code books, records. And we hit on and mapped the E-W Supply Trail. Breeding was seriously wounded, lost a toe, our only recorded casualty while we helped 163.

Then was our finest assignment on Biak. We became a small army on our own, under Div. Hq's direct orders. Released from 163 9 July, we based at Opiaref on the beach 3 miles east of Bosnek. We were to liquidate the Japs in SE Biak from Cape Lomboe on the north shore to Cape Wararisbari. Here their F/Bn 222 Inf had resided before invasion—among native gardens — in great native-type barracks—even with a brewery and "comfort girls."

CREDITS

With this article, a salute to Lt-Col George S. Andrew, Jr. (V Corps G-3, Frankfurt, Germany). Andrew left his "Narrative Hist Biak Opn 41 Recon Troop" for Fed Archives Repository. When I contacted him in Nov., Col Andrew generously wrote a long letter 8 Nov 1963, put me on trail of his masterly "Patrol to Saoeri" (Sept-Oct 1946) **Armored Cav Jour.**). I also used "146 FA Report Biak Open," "Addendum to Biak Opn'" "Provisional Map Schouten Islands First Revision," RR Smith's **Approach to the Philippines.** Jim Gibson, a North Carolina Cherokee of 41 Recon, had next cot to me in Clearing Co on Biak, before his death in Base Section Hospital.

Col Andrew's name is forever honored by us for his article, "The 41st Didn't Take Prisoners!" in **Sat. Eve Post** (1946)—the best article ever published on the Division as a whole.

And 41 Recon's little campaign was more important than plundering or shooting stragglers. For G-2 believed that F/Btn's Nips had not been committed to defend Mokmer—still intact and dangerous. Prisoners said F/Btn had pulled back north, stockpiled supplies in the Saoeri ridge 17 miles SE of Korim. Our G-2 captured documents, gathered that Japs would watch us go into garrison, then rendezvous to drive us into Geelvink Bay. Actually, raids could play havoc with Mokmer bases — supply dumps, hospitals, shiny bombers, flammable mountains of gasolene drums. Keeping a tight perimeter was impossible, and the Division was tired, under strength. So G-3 planned this strategy: we would pinpoint Nip positions, then call for FA and planes to blast them.

On 10 July, a 3 Pltn patrol probed high ground 3000 yards east of Opiaref at Warwe—killed a Jap, but lost Dick Whittaker wounded in right forearm. On 11 July, 36 3/Pltn and F/Pltn Yanks found a supply dump at Wadiboe, 1000 yards farther east. On 12 July, at Anggadoeber, we found another Jap dump. Another patrol probed 8000 yards north to Arfak-Saba. Usually we operated like a small army—at least 1 Pltn, plenty of automatic weapons—40 Yanks for the core. Also we took native scouts, cargadores, radio. Often 146 FA's Piper Cub flew overhead to call down 105s on targets Wonded with our command was 146 FA's radioman Collier. Now came our 2 memorable patrols on Biak.

Word came that Nips had a 20-man OP with radio on the east tip of Biak—20 miles off at Cape Wararisbari. On 14 July, 61 Yanks went to get that radio. On the second day, we left the beach, hacked most of our way through jungle. At dark, we found the OP, but the Japs were gone. At dawn we trailed the slower Nips east towards Sawadori. We surprised them at 1200—12 Nips of 19 Naval Guards—in 60 seconds slew 8, wounded 4, seized radio, OP telescopes, documents.

These patrols of 10-16 July secured our forays to spot the great Nippo base at Saoeri. On 20 July, 2/Lt Lewin took 46 Yanks, 3 natives, a dog, from Wadiboe north 6 miles across Biak. On the second day, we left the trail before Saoeri, cut a path to coral cliffs, then down the coastal side to find the Jap left flank.

Freauff, our scout with a native, spotted a Jap bent over drawing water from a well. A Jap MG fired from a tree. Nips right over us in the trees dropped grenades. The first Jap stood up; Freauff shot him down the well. A grenade thudded at Cpl Rundle's foot; he dived sideways but in mid-air caught multiple shapnel wounds in abdomen. A clever Yank in the rear latched on grenade-launcher, lobbed fragmentation bombs into tree-tops. One Jap squawked, fell dead from the trees. Japs wounded a native, gashed Lewin in the hand, Freauff in right cheek and ankle, and Wm Moody and Kuestner in the legs. But Rundle was slashed deep enough to need a surgeon. We built a litter, fled for camp in black dark with 2 Yanks limping on wounded legs, even a mile through swamp mud. A native ran ahead, roused out Miller and others to bring us in with flash-lights by 1200. Kuestner's leg sent him to hospital; worst casualty was Rundle with shrapnel in his intestines—Rundle about to be made F/Sgt next morning.

Yet Lewin had marked the Nips' left flank. And on 24 July, Andrew took 3 Pltn—36 Yanks, 3 BARs, MG, radio, 2 Meds. At seaside Wadiboe, we got native carriers, scouts; we got 16-year-old Diminoes, the chief's son. He had killed 1 Nip with his long spear.

North 3 miles past Jap barracks, we saw where a Nip had spied us—his prints still filling with water in the swamp mud. At Arfak-Saba, our trail ran 100 yards in a ravine. Observing from a bank, "Bunny" Barber spotted three unwary Jap riflemen. Andrew or Putnam killed 1. Then an ambush of 8 more Nips fled from a depression behind a shack. Next morn, at a break in a Jap barracks area, our rear guard saw 3 following us. But our TSMG opened too soon at 75 yards; we got 1 only.

Despite 2 fights in Nip territory, Andrew pushed on to Saoeri Ridge—great bulk of cliffed, knife-edged coral ridge smothered in jungle—a mass of roots, boulders, pinnacles, crevasses. With the date late, he took long chances. His radio was out; rations were low. MG crew, radio men, natives, 6 riflemen made perimeter in the village. He sent 2 sections into the ridge to find the Nips, waited below with a half-section. While Andred waited, Nips passed on the trail. He was sure that the Nip CO had discovered him, would wipe out his 4 little groups.

Sgt Tippetts brought his section down first, with nil contacts. But Mann's section delayed. High on the ridge above him, Andrew heard a TSMG, 3 quick shots from an M-1; then in 15 minutes, Nip rapid-fire—at least 20 rounds. Since night was falling, Andrew took his remaining men back into perimeter. He felt as if he had murdered his brother, visioned Mann's section in the dark among the Nips.

But after a sleepless night in perimeter, Andrew fround Mann's section back over the ridge, intact—except that Mann had a bullet through his biceps, a crease across his chest. They had stayed out too long, blundered into the midle of Nippo country. A Nip with a towel came down the trail to go swimming; they had to kill him. In falling back, they drew fire from behind the Jap flank. Yet Medic Rabinowitz patched up "Abner" Mann, and they spent the night tracing their wire down the ridge to safety. After the patrol's return, we sent 12 fighter-bombers to smash Saoeri. Patrol No. 3 found only 1 Nip; a native killed him.

Thus fought 41 Recon on Biak — protected 163's north flank, cleared SE Biak. After brief rest at Opiaref, we forayed in wild NW Biak until 15 Sept., killed over 45. We fought well on Biak. Intense training, careful personnel selection paid off. We had just 1 killed (Lt. Cain), Jim Gibson who died in hospital, 13 known wounded. We killed at least 82—we frontiersmen of Biak.

CO. A, 163 Infantry: Slugging at IBDI Pocket

By Dr. Hargis Westerfield, Association Historian
with Capt. Richard J. Satran, others.

A 163 scout ducking enemy fire at Ibdi Pocket, Biak, in June of 1944.

AFTER OUR COMBAT TOUR of Wakde (and the war of nerves at Toem,) A Co 163 Inf headed for Biak—its toughest battle since Sanananda. Leaving LCIs at Bosnek 31 May, we panted up a 700 foot ridge to relieve K 186. Our first night was lurid with Nippo raids on the beach. But on 2 June, we were on LCIs south of Biak to take some islets for the Navy.

We beached at Owi unopposed, left F/Pltn there, then seized Mios Woendi, which became a PT base. Woendi's palms and sands made it a South Sea paradise—only without girls. We did 2 more landings. For a week, CO Satran had 3 Padaido Islands named for him—Satran 1, Satran 2, Satran 3. Next morn, Nip Zeroes and bombers attacked our support LCI.; but P38s and 47s sent them flaming into the sea. (As F/Pltn left Owi, we took a harmless strafing also.)

BACK ON BIAK 3 JUNE, we had security guards while AA fought off Jap planes. On 6 June, though, we hiked to 163's perimeter, smashed a Nippo patrol en route—killed 2. On 7 June we found death again when Lt. Teeters' 3 Pltn scouted 3,000 yards around Nippo country. About 1430, our scouts topped a low ridge next to a native garden. Hinkley died shot through the chest. Hodge took a bad wound in the left forearm. Fellows was lightly hit in the leg. Guarding a hospital on 10 June, Zirkle was accidentally killed.

On 13 June, we marched deep into brushy native gardens to cover a water point while 116 Engrs brought up pumps and purification equipment. From there, Lt./Col. Rankin led 2 Pltn under CO Satran to probe the lurking Nips, after 2 sick Javanese had warned us.

RANKIN ORDERED our 60s to fire a light barrage first, then moved out the patrol. About 450 yards off where Hinkley died, we split up. Rankin took 3 Squad with Sgts. Davenport and Wilson right along an overgrown swampy trail. Crossing a stream, we saw Jap tracks everywhere. We started up a short, steep rise.

Just before the top, the Jap ambush blasted into us. Davenport fell then. Wilson behind him took a bullet in the left arm as he dived for safety. Rankin was grazed on the hand; he flattened into a stream-bed until the shooting ceased.

SATRAN'S PATROL RETURNED to help. Armed only with trench knife, Krushevsky went in alone to see whether Davenport lived. Finding him dead, Krush spotted 12 Nippo positions on which he later vengefully directed support fire overnight. Our reenforced patrol next morning found the Japs gone.

After 2 weeks' water-point guard, then as carrying parties for 3 Btn above Moker Strip, A Co entrucked back to F/Btn on 25 June. We were alerted for next morning's all-out assault on Idbi Pocket.

But after B and C stormed Ridge 4 and stopped dead before tougher Nippo positions, A's 2 and 3 Pltns secured the right flank on the ridge 100 yards west of Wing's F/Btn CP. On this half-moon ridge, Vest was shot in the head and lost an eye. Gritter had a neck wound.

IN THAT THICK BRUSH among jagged cliffs, Japs and we traded rifle-bullets and called down mortars on each other. They held the ridge 35 yards from our ridge.

Next morning from security guard at F/Btn CP, Sgt. Russ led his reinforced F Pltn to work around the Nippo left flank opposite A's other riflemen on the far right of the battle-line. Over the brushy flats and up to low gray ridges guarded by columns of white-trunked jungle giants, we hunted with rifles. Nippo rifle-fire blasted us back. Sgt. Ingram was cut off, but escaped with a light hand wound.

F/LT. JENSON, Exec., assumed command. He ordered a mortar barrage on the brush where the fire seemed to come from. F Pltn then advanced safely for some time. But as we fell back, a Jap MG spoke out. Borjorquez, Sgt. Ingram died; Kisiel was wounded; Rivera was missing. Jenson died trying to locate the MG. Rivera flattened in the coral for hours until our mortars again flailed the Jap position. He crawled off and returned to CP just before dark.

At 1330, Lt. Satran reinforced 2 Pltn Ridge on the right flank with our MGs. Nippo pressure became heavier. But the blow fell on Lt. Teeters' 3 Pltn at the extreme end of the Btn firing line.

TEETERS HAD WORKED his way high on a coral pinnacle to see Nippo positions clearly. From here he directed accurate mortar fire and picked off a number of Japs.

But at 1700, Japs poured in automatic fire, arced over grenades, stormed up the blind side of the pinnacle. We had to withdraw; but BARman Virgil Gordon with Archuleta fought a delaying action.

Shrapnel killed both Gordon, Archuleta. By 1710, Nip infantry poured over the ridge. Unless we smashed them, the Btn line would be out-flanked, and F/Btn Hq 100 yards below would be overrun.

THE ADJOINING 2 Pltn struck back. Pltn Sgt. Luedke ran down a slope to a good field of fire. M-1 to shoulder, Luedke broke that Nip offensive, killed 3. Before he could climb back to safety, he had to fight again. He emptied M-1, threw all of his grneades, disorganized the attack. Then a Jap rifle wounded him to die the next day.

With M-1s, BARs, MGs, we shaved the ridge-top, blew the Nips back off. Then 60s, 81s, 105s pulverized our front—only 50-100 yards before us. But we lived, held the line under Lt. Teeters.

Before dusk, Teeters, Sgt. "Krush," a few other 3 Pltn men counter-atacked for the coral pinnacle which we had lost with Gordon's death. Weigl, Sgts. McManus, Batson were wounded slightly. Lt. Teeters fell from a ridge into enemy fire, mortally wounded in the head.

T/Sgt. Hansen slipped over the crest, dragged Teeters back to Medics. Perhaps it was in this assault that Jasinik took bullets through his pack when he crawled into a pillbox firelane to save another Yank.

NEXT MORNING, 28 June, the tired, dirty 3 Pltn fought again. Jap grenades or automatic fire wounded Howell, Sgts. Fleming, Mattice, Jasinik, Hansen. About mid-morning, F/Pltn (once Jenson's) took over the positions. As we changed guard, a Nippo hit among F/Pltn. Flowers and Crompton were wounded.

Nor did 2 Pltn fare better on 28 June. Automatic fire killed Erdley. After a day of ineffectual sniping, the Nips drew blood again. A grenade wounded Coult in arm and shoulder; we got him out an hour before dark.

THUS BY 29 JUNE, the fight for Idbi Pocket was strictly a trench warfare of attrition. When his squad ran low on ammo, August Leonard, acting squad leader, dodged to the rear through snipers to load himself with bandoliers, grenades.

Although shot in the back, he returned with ammo before he died. On another ridge, his brother in B Co heard August's death-scream and had to be evacuated.

So passed 3 of A Co's toughest days since 16 Jan., 1943, at Sanananda. Although last rifle Co in F/Btn to fight in Ibdi Pocket, we were first to be relieved. For on that rugged coral in the teeth of the Japs on a ridge 35 yards across the coral crevices, men went 48 hours without rest of any kind.

WHEN L CO TOOK OVER in mid-afternoon of 30 June, the understrength A Co gladly entrucked 5 miles back to 163 Hq perimeter—to rest until 5 July—to sleep on canvas cots, stand out in the open in a chow-line and eat hot food from a scalded mess-gear again.

FINALLY ON 6 JULY, A Co did a final great patrol against Lbdi Pocket. With 88 men, we went to find out what was left of the Nips in those dirty shell-withered ridges. While our main body kept covered near the base of the cliffs we had fought on before, Sgt. Russ led a Pltn west of the old F/Btn CP. At 1000, a Nip rifleman fired. We killed 2 other Nips, heard others yelling to our front. Russ' Pltn probed south.

At 1215, 3 Nips moved towards A Co. We killed 1, wounded the other. Meanwhile, Russ' Pltn had moved on to high ground overlooking the old B and C positions 50 yards east. They saw 3 Nips cutting logs evidently for a new bunker. A knee mortar shell exploded 75 yards from them. It was time for Russ to get out alive with his Pltn and rejoin the main body of A Co.

MEANWHILE HANSEN'S Pltn moved close into the old F/Btn's ridges and encountered automatic weapon and mortar fire. Now that A Co had the desired information, we were washed up with Ibdi Pocket. We left that sweltering coral waste-land for the die-hard Nips and the 3 Btn, the 146 FA, the 641 TD 4.2's, the 947 FA, and the B-24 planes to play out the game.

Both Hansen and Russ were to get direct commissions as Lts.; and A Co called it our greatest patrol. For we had no casualties, claimed 6 Nippo dead.

And A Co settled down to life on Biak. Besides a few light patrols, we cleared camp of the typhus brush and set up garrison camp with straight, tent-lined streets of glaring white coral. Beginning 27 Aug, we labored 6-8 hours daily unloading supplies at Live Rock Jetty. We never forgot our first beer ration 30 Aug.—6 bottles per man.

LET A CO'S HISTORY on Biak end with the beer—6 bottles per man around each of our cots in our tents. Once there had been 12 more of us—12 good men now dead in the coral scrub. With them, we had sweated out patrols and held the coral ridges. We had broken the only great Nippo counter-attack from Ibdi Pocket. And we had paid for it in the lives of 12 great men, hard men we cannot forget.

B Co., 163 Infantry:

BATTLE ON GHOST MOUNTAIN

By SGT. WILLIAM C. DAVIDSON, CPL. RAY WILCOPOLSKI
With DR. HARGIS WESTERFIELD

In black dark at 0315 26 June 1944, B Co 163 Inf padded to assault Ghost Mtn—B's name for Ibdi Pocket. As D's 81s cracked behind us, B led C and A Cos south across native gardens. Ahead, 105 blasts lighted up jungle ridges where men of 3 Rgts had died already.

With S/Sgts Larsen, Hawkey, Erickson, Coop, Sgt Bilboa as point, we filed up low Ridge 1. Cutting booby-trap wires, we headed for Ridge 2, outlined by 105s' flashes. In the dark, riflemen fell into crevices and over trees our shells had crashed on the road. Topping Ridge 2, we spotted Ridge 3 in smoke and gray dawn.

Coop warned us to step over Jap wire too heavy to cut, but Sgt Fetterman tripped and fell with grenade fragments in him. From the dark, a Jap lunged on Coop with bayoneted rifle. Coop felled him with TSMG. Another jumped BARman Avila. Too shocked to get the BAR off safety, Avila smote him down with his gun-butt.

Day broke fast now among jagged coral ridges with shell-torn brush. On Ridge 3 in column, S/Sgt Cawiezell, Sgt Pinkenstein, Cpl Talley saw a Nip in a cave with field-glasses. Another Nip looked over a pillbox at Lt Houston. But everybody held fire.

Now 4 Sgts and 4 squad-columns abreast halted on Ridge 4. CO Merrick sharply ordered the 4 squads down Ridge 4 left to deploy on the crest. Scouts saw Jap pillboxes and caves below us—except for a HMG above us in a cave to the right. Like wildcats screaming, 3 bazooka shells zoomed into the cave. The third rocket boomed inside, and that HMG was dead.

Down-slope, our 4 squads fusilladed. We slew 26 Nips in a cave, 9 in other positions. Behind our attack line, a Jap leaped screaming at Hq runner Ceja and died full of holes. Reporting back to Merrick, Hawkey dropped another Nip.

B Co had won what we call the first pre-dawn infiltration assault in the Pacific. But now our combat patrols found defeat and death ahead in this brushy plateau of Ibdi Pocket with its low, hidden ridges and masked pillboxes.

Gagnier and Kees' patrol started south around Ridge 5 before us, but a solid wall of Jap fire hit our flank. We had 2 grim choices—run and be wiped out—or fight and lose several. We fought. Gagnier died at once; the LMG tore out his chest. Kees killed some Nips, but died from a bullet in his right temple. The others escaped.

Of Gagnier's patrol, mortarmen Fabe, Greer, Drake were happy to be back alive on Ridge 4. Cpl Fabe crept to the crest to guard other fleeing Yanks, but saw 3 Nips. Before he could fire, a bullet creased his skull, sent him to the rear.

And 2 forlorn Yanks with carbines were left to hold a trail before a Nippo push. Then A Co moved a BAR team in on their right flank behind a fallen tree. Drake tried to point out Jap targets to them. The BARman shot, but a Jap MG tore chunks from the log before them, wounded all 3. (A's Gritter and Vest were 2 of these.)

Greer's carbine crackled into the brush against the moving Nips. Drake crawled down to get A's BAR and ammo belt and returned to Greer. Drake knew that his BAR fire would bring Jap MG fire on him, but the Japs were coming. But he shot several clips into the dark-green jungle. Jap noises ceased in front. The Jap MG rapped out, but it still hacked the log where it had silenced A's BARmen. Now Greer was throwing grenades, and it looked as if Drake and he had better run back to Ridge 3.

Just then, a second "A" BAR team opened up on our right; we could see it below us. Already, Greer had almost spotted the now silent Jap MG at the base of a giant tree, but a sniper bullet exploded a coral block beside Greer and showered him with fragments.

Again the MG fired—but at A's BAR. And Drake now saw the Jap MG's muzzle blast. Viciously, Drake slammed 3 BAR clips into the Jap and quieted him forever. And by now, a B Co squad was rushing up to help Drake and Greer and tie in tight with A Co's line.

Meanwhile, Pinkenstein's and Bilbao's patrol prodded left of B's new CP—across a ridge—down a ravine among Nippo pillboxes. We caught MG fire from a cave above the ravine. Jarvis fell with a light rifle wound in the side. Cantagello told Jarvis to roll into a hole, but a bullet in the temple slew Jarvis. Smith tried to fire Jarvis' bazooka, but had to leave it. Bilbao loosed over 200 rounds into the pillbox, saw Nips fall. We killed 10 Nips, claimed 10 probables; but Smith and Coppage were wounded, and Jarvis dead.

All B now took heavy fire from the Jap hornets' nest we had poked. North of the CP, Japs pinned down a squad, wounded Hughes and Goddard. We got them out by stretcher at 1130. Every 5 minutes, Jap HMGs opened up, kept B down at least an hour. When C Co tied in with 3 Pltn on the left, Jap mortars flailed us. Bassett, Brostead, Hoots, Bertoldi took serious wounds; Coppage, Campbell, Clifton were slightly injured and stayed—on this 150 yards of ridge we held with C Co. A mortar blew up CO Merrick, but he stayed with us.

CREDITS

We salute Sgt William C. Davidson and Cpl Raymond H. Wilcopolski for their MS "Biak," which is a history of B 163 begun by Sgt James J. Eder. Highly useful also were Capt Arthur Merrick's Ltr 9 Oct 1961, and mortarman Ted Drake's MS. Background is from R. R. Smith's "Approach to the Philippines."

Other histories of Ibdi Pocket available are those by Westerfield on G Co and 3 Btn. We lack stories of C and F Cos.

Hargis Westerfield

Jungleers on road near Ibdi Pocket on Biak in June, 1944.

All afternoon, D's 81s and 146 FA's 105s searched the Pocket. As hot dusk fell, we crouched sleepless in shallow holes in coral pigpens. Just after nightfall, Jap voices jabbered below us within 20 yards. We wanted to light the Japs with phosphorus bombs and riddle them with BARS; but a C officer ordered us to let them by. D Co men and 163 Hq men slew 2 as they crossed the road 1000 yards away. In front of us, mortars fired flares, but we saw no Nips.

When the Japs counterattacked A Co next morning, they opened up on us heavily to contain us. Their riflemen hit us in front; they traversed us from 3 positions on our right. Mortars nicked Cumely, Curtiss. We countered with grenade launchers, TSMs, MGs, bazookas, BARS. We shot up all pillboxes we could spot—blew 1 up with bazooka, otherwise slew 2 Nips, 7 probables. Guillen killed a Nip down a trail 50 yards ahead, but the next Jap smashed his elbow with a .25. And 4 Yanks went to hospital with dysentery, or other fevers—Cardozo, Flood, Kassebaum, Bermudez.

By 28 June, the third day, B's attack on Ghost Mtn was a siege. No Nips could dislodge us; Gen Doe did not throw men away in an all-out attack. While 81s and 105s pounded the pocket, Gen Doe sent us unbelievable morale-building food—fresh pork sandwiches, doughnuts, a bottle of Osaka beer for each 2 men. We caught rain to shave and wash.

Attrition continued on both sides. S/Sgt Belgarde with Gulley and Waters found a pillbox built by Nips last night. They threw in 3 BAR clips, 1 bazooka shell, destroyed their MG before it ever fired. At 1200, Lt Merrick accepted relief for his wound of 26 June. Lt Houston became C. Nip mortars wounded Scopelito, Waskiemicz, Drake.

June 29 was hard. While we sat talking after breakfast, Japs retaliated on us for D's 81s. Their second round killed Sgt Bilboa with a splinter in the brain—Bilboa whom Lt Merrick had personally tried to keep in rear echelon because Bilboa was due for Rotation. That same shell also lost us 7 wounded—Andrews, Harvey, King, Lawdowsky, Lundberg, Sgt Smith, Waskiewicz. Coward, Foss, Clausen had light wounds. When August Leonard of A died, his brother in B Co heard his screams and had to be hospitalized. But we scored 7 dead Nips, 5 probables.

That night we threw grenades at Japs heard digging. On 30 June, Belgarde with Waters knocked out their new pillbox. Kummer, Sgt Wojnarowski were evacuated; Sgts Erickson, Coop were slightly wounded. We killed 2 Nips. Rumors came that we would be relieved; that afternoon, we saw rainbows.

On 1 July early, Nips fired 3 knee mortar rounds but missed. Sgt Erickson's wound was infected, and Guzy and he were evacuated. All day, F/Pltn's tall Southern Moore sat by a tree near his hole and sniped at Nips. On 2 July, 4 Nip mortar shells had near misses on our carrying party returning to the lowlands. With Cardenas' TSMG, Campbell's BAR, Gulley's bazooka, we blasted a pillbox on our right flank. Japs squealed like swine, but none ever came out.

Back at CP, T/Sgt Tessmer saw a wild boar but ordered Ceja not to kill it and foul up the area. They forgot it. The boar climbed a trail toward the Nips, rushed Mijal on guard with his BAR. His safety jammed. Mijal ran. A tusk slashed him, knocked him 12 feet down the cliff until he frantically clutched some vines to save himself. Mijal went to hospital. Later, a carrying party killed the boar.

About 1430, Nip MGs tried to shear us off the ridge. After the fire-fight, wounded Kjemhus, Daniels, Irwin went to hospital. Fever sent Kenney, Sgt Talley. B Co had gone from 192 at Aitape to well under 100 men.

On 3 July, B Co's morale went up. Crouching in the dark before dawn, Waters heard bushes move, waited grimly. With the light, he saw 2 Nips spying on our positions. He killed both, said, "I can eat a good breakfast now." Late that afternoon, Gulley slew a Nip lying in the bushes watching us. And Lt Houston brought great news: B Co would be relieved tomorrow.

On 4 July, day of deliverance, F/Pltn hit hard. Cardenas, Sgt Laab saw a new Nip pillbox just over a little ridge south of the perimeter. From K Co—which had relieved A 3 days ago—we borrowed a flamethrower and operator. While Cardenas covered with TSMG and Laabs and Gulley and Sgt Nowacki watched with M-1s, the operator glided in. At 15 yards from the Nips, the operator rose from a squat, sighted the slot, touched trigger. Japs screamed, crawled out, ran afire. One fell then; we mercifully killed 4 as they ran; 1 died inside.

And starting at 1200 with the mortarmen, B Co left Ghost Mtn forever in little 5-man squads. Just back from hospital with his wound on Wakde, Lt Anderson with F/Pltn made the screening force and traded a few shot with Nips. Last off the ridge with him were Cardenas, Campbell, Schroeder, Rickenberger, Medic Halverson, Sgt Laabs, S/Sgts Jokela, Sidwell, Nowacki. We left behind us the pigpens of coral we had crouched in all night, the maggoty open latrines, the unburyable Nippo dead. And somehow or other, we left behind great days of our lives that we can never forget.

For B Co had spearheaded the great night attack on Ghost Mountain 26 June 1944 and won the outworks to Ibdi Pocket. We had taken our losses and held on those jagged rocks in green jungle hell. It had been 9 days of silence and monotony broken mostly by low-voiced commands from non-coms or by whispers when a buddy woke you to go on guard in the dark and passed a grenade to you. It had been 9 days of monotony—and the sudden deadly splatter of automatic fire and the boom of mortar-shells.

Yet after the heavy losses of Wakde, B Co had become either battle-wise or very lucky. In comparison to the 9 dead in 3 days' assault on Wakde, or the 19 dead in 18 days at Sanananda, B Co had just 4 dead in 9 days at Ibdi Pocket. If the ghosts return to where B Co fought, they are mostly Japanese ghosts on Ghost Mountain.

2 Bn 163 Infantry:
IRVING'S SIEGE OF IBDI POCKET

By Dr. HARGIS WESTERFIELD, Division Historian
with (then) Major Robert L. Irving

On 12 June 44, Mjr Robert Irving's 2/Bn 163 Inf landed at Bosnek to help the overworked Division. We got a Jap welcome; 3 Zeroes dove from Bosnek Ridge at us, but fell in AA fire. On the beach, Gen Fuller said, "Irving, I'm sure glad to see you." For on D-16, Col Kuzume still fought well.

Irving sent E Co to fight East Caves downshore at Parai. F Co faced Ibdi Pocket cliffs — above where 116 Engrs again built a bridge across a little stream. G Co made base perimeter in a flat above Ibdi Village. G patrolled for outposts high in those wet, green, jagged coral ridges. Some 500 yards east of G, 2/Bn Hq Co set up near a water-point. We guarded the end of Old Man's Trail which crossed ridges 180 feet at the highest point, and down to an east-west supply trail we had to interdict. The departing Exec of 162 warned Irving to expect shelling from those silent ridges.

Although Gen Doe had Kuzume almost surrounded at West Caves, Kuzume got little help from 3/Bn 222 Inf at Ibdi Pocket. With 1000 men, mountain guns, 90 mm mortars, they could cut our main supply road, but they took no offensive.

On 15 June, a bullet cracked close to Irving's jeep back from F Co. His scared driver eased up on the gas. "Get the hell out!" yelled Irving. The jeep skidded up a rain-slick road between lines of supply trucks parked for orders, and holed up in 2/Bn Hq's perimeter. Some trucks were gasoline tankers, but hidden Jap cannon did not fire.

Not until 1700, with most of the trucks gone, did the Jap 75s fire. Then rounds struck an engr bivouac, wrecked a truck, a G Co mortar and slew 2 engrs, wounded 6.

But a Yank spotted the Jap gun-flash. We sighted three 37-mm guns on the spot of that flash, loaded them with armor-piercing shells for tracer fire. We alerted a gunner to be always on duty.

At 1900 next evening, Irving's peaceful talk with Sgt Nelson of D 162, ended with a deafening blast. Jap 75s holed his tent. Under his bunk, Irving phoned his 37s to fire. Some twelve 75 shell-blasts had deafened Irving, but Raybon already had off 6 rounds.

Trees masked fire of two 37s, but Raybon swiftly corrected No. 3 to the Jap gun-flash, viciously zapped in 6 rounds AP fire, then changed to High Explosive fired again. In the silence, Raybon chilled. Would the Jap gun depress to shoot back down his tracer pattern? But the gun never fired again.

After Ibdi Pocket fell, Irving learned the gun had hidden in an "L" shaped cave. It would fire 12 rounds, then roll back into the cave and around the "L"-angle for safety. But Irving's plan with Raybon's split-second gunnery killed the Jap cannon in the open before the cave mouth. There it rusted in late July. On that day of Raybon's cannonade, 2/Bn Hq had Eino Johnson wounded and evacuated, with Parrish, Beaver; Moran wounded but still on duty.

Meanwhile 2/Bn fought Ibdi Pocket. Seeking Jap batteries, G patrols climbed Old Man's Trail over the shadowy labyrinth of ridges, then set up an Observation Post near the east-west supply-trail. The guns we could not spot, but we did find Jap strongpoints westward — across Young Man's Trail. Irving set up G's 60s and H's three 81s to enfilade G's new front.

Deadly combat patrols began. On 18 June, F prodded from the SW. F's 14-man patrol topped a cliff just before a Jap patrol arrived. We killed 14, then fell back to throw in 36 60 mm shells. Wounded were F's Campbell, Schott, Taspean. On 19 June, G's 3/Pln did not top a cliff before the Japs. Pushing down a ridge in view of Ibdi Flats, we came under a blasting from a cross-cliff. We saved Arnold Johnson, to die of wounds. T/Sgt Giant Harrison and S/Sgt Murphy took multiple grenade wounds head to foot and never fought again. From farther inland, 1/Lt Brandon's Pln probed into ambush, lost Belin killed, but rescued Dulian with a bad arm-wound.

Nobody yet realized how strong was Ibdi Pocket. On 21 June, only F actually attacked — from a point NW of the ridges. Scouts evidently missed Jap outposts, for fire suddenly struck from 3 directions. We left Walter dead, had Sgt Crilley seriously wounded in right hip. Lucky to escape Jap MGs, mortars, rifles, we retreated 200 yards, called down support fire on the Japs. We saw no Japs.

Our overhead MG fire alarmed the whole Jap garrison. Jap guns blazed away all along the ridges, outlined a Jap front of 600 yards — Ibdi to Parai. We now estimated that Ibdi Pocket held 200-300 men — about a third the actual number.

To save lives, Irving got Col Moroney's permission to halt attacks and soften up Ibdi Pocket. He had H's Lt Radow fire his 81s day and night — a round a minute to disrupt Japs' normal duties and defoliate the ridges. (When one 81 shell exploded near Radow's mortars, Irving had the whole lot of shells sunk in Geelvink Bay. For we remembered too well how another bad 81 shell had wrecked a whole H gun-crew at Aitape.) At night also, our 60s fired FA star-shells to alert Japs to attacks that never came. On 23 June, 146 FA threw in 2,600 rounds HE; while Cn 163's 6 howitzers fired at 1,000 yards, with 641 TD's 4.2s and our mortars.

But 146 FA's trajectory was so flat that half a sheaf of fire passed over Ibdi Pocket. So at nightfall 24 June, Irving suddenly ordered G off Ibdi Ridges. In pitch dark, a cursing, tripping, floundering line of men worked its way up knife-edged ridges to descend Old Man's trail to safety. At dawn from the flat, Irving watched 146's 105's fireworks 500-700 yards into the Japs' hell-hole. Under ponchos in a heavy rain, G Co had hotcakes and scalding coffee, then morosely reoccupied positions before the stunned Japs could seize them.

After 4 days' FA and mortars, 163 massed its greatest attack. While 1/Bn struck from NW at dawn, 2/Bn attacked from east and south. Despite notable gains by 1/Bn, no attack truly succeeded. Our 2/Bn suffered most of 163's dead. F Co. lost Chyboski, Sgt Edmund Williams killed, and Krull wounded. Cowan died of wounds. G Co lost Holmes, Tholund, Cappuccino, Martinez, Cpl Porras—all killed— and Zuzky and S/Sgt Huckabee wounded. Wilhelmi was injured. All told, 2/Bn had 8 dead, 3 wounded, 1 injured.

Despite 38 Japs dead from both bns 26 June, Ibdi Pocket was hardly touched. And 163 could ill afford 11 dead, 26 wounded — some of whom died. And 2/Bn did little on 27 June. On 28 June, 2/Bn thrust again. A G Co bazooka slew 2 Japs in a pillbox. Pushing 150 yards, F fought a pill box guarded by riflemen on coral pinnacles overhead. Grenades arced down, wounded Compton, Tucci, Lt Torrman. For Gen Doe, further advances were unnecessary; shells were cheaper than men.

And in this Ibdi Pocket fight of 15-28 June, Irving was everywhere that a good Bn Co could be. (Already have we told how a Jap sniper and a Jap 75 had singled him out personally to try to kill him.) Irving inspected G Co's forward OP back in those deadly ridges. There a G Sgt warned him not to touch a sapling the size of Irving's arm. The slightest move of that sapling drew Jap fire.

That same night at the phone, Irving heard G's fine Capt Braman relaying firing orders from this front-line OP down to his 60 mm mortars. Starting to register 75 yards before the OP, Braman moved the impact area in 25 yards towards the OP — then 15 yards in — then 10 yards closer. Irving interrupted on the phone to warn Braman that 25 yards menaced G's perimeter. Braman replied, "That''s where the Japs are." Braman assured Irving that G's men were safe behind coral, then brought the lethal blasts down to just 15 yards from G's perimeter.

And Irving flew over Ibdi Pocket to call down fire on the Japs. One evening in a Piper Cub, FA observer Capt Rainwater and Irving saw smoke columns out of 2 deep ravines in Ibdi Pocket's jagged coral and rain forest. That night with 641 TD's CO, he figured out a fire order to kill the Japs under the smoke — despite the maps' uncertainties.

Flying with Rainwater next morning, Irving radioed to the 4.2s to execute last night's fire order. Suddenly Irving had a hunch, called a correction of 500 yards right before a 4.2 shell could fire.

G Co. 163 Infantry:
IBDI POCKET AND "G" COMPANY

By Dr. Hargis Westerfield
Division Historian

> CREDIT: Prime personal sources were interviews with other "G" Co men in barracks in Kure, Japan, and my own 3/Pln experiences. Important sources also were 163's Casualty List, "G's" June and July Morning reports, and detailed Journal on Biak. (Narravtive of 163 was meager.) Col (then Maj) Robert L. Irving supplied his "Recollections" of 2/Bn on Biak--written about 1970. Useful also were Award storeis of Karkoski, Higgins, heidt, Miller, Osen. 146 FA's Capt Robert Allen's "Reduction of Ibdi Pocket," RR Smith's Approach to the Philippies. This is my third complete writing of "G" Co's story.

On 12 June 1944, badly needed "G" Co 163 Inf landed at Bosnek on Biak with "CN", "SV" Co., and the other 2/Bn men. Red alerts warned us into coral pits. Three Jap planes dived over low green ridges north of Bosnek, fell in AA fire. Jammed in trucks, "G" rolled west alongshore past a raveyard and AA guns stencilled red with many Jap flags for destroyed planes. Unloaded near Ibdi, we had 2/Lt Brandon's warning, "Keep scattered. You may be under Jap mortar fire!"

We waited orders in a bare little limestone valley pointed at the ridges. Coral walls protected our new CP against a Jap pillbox, a hump on the ridge. "AT" 162 men returned from battle. M-1 muzzles were black from destroying that last Nippo roadblock at Parai Defile. An "AT" Yank had died. We wateched our own T/5 Geral Shields walk to CP to learn what we knew already: his brother Jimmie from "AT" 162 dead on that ridge, body unrecoverable.

Like other 2/Bn Cos, "G" now guarded the coast supply road pat Parai. Our 1/Pln and 2/Pln outposted high on the coral ridges--on bare rock crests tunneled under dripping jungle. We could not dig holes; we huddled in coral "pigpens." We found debris where "AT" 162 fought. Where the coast ridge dropped slightly west, we secured our left flank with an abandoned "AT" 162 LMG. Our 3/Pln was more lucky at first. On the flats near the kitchen, we held a line of pigpens. The sun dried our washing from rainwater collected in drums. Such were "G" Co's first days before the silent Japs and guns of 222 Inf Bn entrenched in Ibdi Pocket.

In the late sunset hours of 15 June, 7 Nippo 75s flailed 2/Bn from Ibdi Pocket--2 of them striking near "G" and 116 Engrs. Close to our CP. shells drove cooks and weapons men into holes. Jester and Walker fired back with a .60 mortar, the gun expelled them from the mortar pit to hide behind steel pipes left by the Japs. A shell destroyed the mortar. Northcutt was hit in the groin. Two men of 116 Engrs were killed, 5 wounded. Yet the Jap guns failed to mass enough guns on "G" to wipe us out. And no Jap infantry attack anywhere justified with 7-gun preparation.

On 16 June, "G" patrols failed to find the guns to kill them. They were easy to hide in that green wilderness of jagged ridges like foaming waves. But by 17 June at 1105, we had patrolled a dim trail north to arrive at 186's old supply road to Mokmer Strip. We laid "130" wire to that point.

Important were "G's" patrols' discoveries of the Japs' new positions. The Japs were now 3000 yards west of their emplcements above Mandom where they had fought 162 Inf probes and killed that great scout, 1/Lt Myron Folsom. Now entrenched NW of Ibdi, they no longer guarded the north-south supply trail where we could deploy to attack the east flank of Ibdi Pocket. On the coast, 2/Bn's Maj Irving set up a fire-base for our attacks--3 "G" Co .60 mortars and 3 "H" Co .81s. Without excess dispersion, they could enfilade the Japs' east flank while "G" pushed west.

But on 18 June, an "F" patrol first attacked Ibdi Pocket. "F" slew 14 Nips but was blasted back with 3 wounded. On 19 June, "G" battled the Nips with 2 bloody patrols. "F's" men topped the ridge ahead of the Japs, but we found them there above us, and lost good men.

Early on 19 June, 2/Lt Kreiger's 3/Pln patrol filed down "G's" southern position on the ridge, west into Jap country. We crossed a stone wall and our MG guarding it. We passed a small Nip corpse hanging in vines on the cliff, and Gerald Shield's brother under an Aussie blue blanket. We gripped tree-trunks and climbed around a cliff. We were in a shallow grassy vale with a clif across the ridge, and a tall, silent pillbox on the cliff. Scout Clark saw a Jap helmet jerk back from the slot.

Men in front fired at half-seen movements, but we heard Jap grenades arming like pistol shots. "Knee mortars! somebody yelled. After a second of silence, we flattened under a rain of grenades that jangled our ears. Hot steel seared us; Arnold Johnson cried out; his rifle thudded to the ground. Most of us cleared that ridge in seconds.

There were still 3 men left in the vale, and wounded Arnold Johnson onthe ground. Clark and Westerfield guarded with grenades while Karkoski bandaged Johnson, then carried him to safety. Karkoski took the direct way over the almost impassable summit of tumbled coral. Clark and Westerfield slung M-1s, gripped tree-roots to clim around the cliffs. Two Jap grenades exploded above them.

A grenade gouge in his left temple caused Johnson to die 17 days later, 6 July. T/Sgt Harrison, S/Sgt Murphy had multiple grenade wounds, head to foot, never fought again.

Farther north in the ridges, 1/Lt Brandon's 28-man "G" patrol also met wounds and death. S/Sgt Belin, Sgt Higgins, and Dulian led on an open trail up a ridge. Belin died from a bullet in the abdomen; Dulian was wounded in his left arm.

To save prone Higgins and Dulian, 2/Lt Brandon and Pln battled hidden Japs 1 hour and 45 minutes. To fight the Nips. Brandon converged 2 lines of BAR fire on the ridge overhead. Sweat-black Dulian and Higgins with Belin's corpse would squirm a foot or two. The Nips would fire and our BARs would silence them while our men crawled a few feet more. Than a log blocked them--with a Jap MG nicking the top. Still dragging Belin, Higgins and wounded Dulian writhed under the log in knife-pointed coral and saved their lives.

Pressure on the Pocket mounted up to 163's all-out assualt of 26 June. On 21 June, "F" failed its one-company attack. By 22 June, all G's Plns manned the ridges. From other "G" men, 3/Pln took over our part of the seaward ridge east of where the Japs had ambushed us on 19 June.

On 22 June, 146 FA's 105s began blasting the Pocket. They fired smoke to hide CN Co's guns positioning 1000 yards from the Japs. Col Moroney requested 3000 rounds to expel the Japs. FA fired nightlong, but the Japs held their log-and-coral pillboxes. Infantry must grapple with them.

On 23 June, a tree-burst killed Barbour with a fragment in his right chest--in 2/Lt Brandon's outpost on ridges east of 3/Pln. Same tree-burst wounded Sgt Schumacher in his back, and Zobel in left leg. "G" believed that our own gun killed Barbour, but a nearby "F" Pln leader had heard no short. Col Moroney's report was that the shell was from a Jap .90 mm.

On 24 June, "Lucky" Frank Miller led a 5-man patrol east from 3/Pln's ridge. He penetrated silent jungle ridges past 2 Nip positions that corssfired on him, cut him from contact with Scout Bradley. He killed the Nip firing automatic from a cave, rolled safe from Nip No. 2's grenade. Miller's answering grenade damaged the Nippo rifle. Hearing the Jap trying to fix it, Miller rose and ran, his forehead bloody from a bullet in his helmet. "Lucky" got months in a hospital to recover--was even lucky to have a love-affair there.

At darkfall 24 June, "G" had to leave the ridges while 146 FA shelled them. No Japs pursued as we staggered blindly through black, stoney jungle. Back on the flats, we heard no shells and and awoke in heavy rain to reoccupy our same positions. FA did shell Ibdi Pocket at dawn, but we still had to attack.

At first light in the leaves on 26 June, phones aroused "G" Co for our great attack. While "A" and "B" Cos pushed east and "F" Co pushed NE, "G" Co was to drive west until Japs halted us, and then block and hold.

Filing down the coast ridge past the dead jap and dead Jimmie Shields, 3/Pln attacked where we had suffered on 19 June. Martinez led with his grenade launcher to fight the tall pillbox from the left side of the ridge. He died from Jap automatic fire inthe midriff. Wilhelmi dislocated his knee in the coral and could not fire his rifle-grenade. Lt Kreiger recalled Clark from attacking with his launcher.

On the right of that ridge, Vilicich fired his BAR into the slot of a short pillbox to silence automatic fire menacing Beane and Westerfield. Prone in the field-of-fire, Beane passed grenades to Westerfield who exploded the last one on the pillbox sill. But with Martinez' body lost, 3/Pln wisely withdrew. Our 3/Pln push ended early in the morning.

Farther north, "G's" main attack lasted longer and cost more me. Moving off 450 yards west of the north-south trail about 0710, by 9030, "G" found many log and coral positions empty. By 0950, we saw our first Japs, in HMG pillboxes.

When scout Holmes rose to his knees to signal, he died from a MG burst in head and chest. As fast as a LMG, Wascovich shot 7 BAR clips into the slot of the main pillbox. Berserk S/Sgt Bob Wilson charged the box but saw no Japs in it. Japs fled over the ridge while our rifles blazed away. At 1021, 3 Jap 90s exploded harmlessly nearby.

By 1345, "G's" lines of rifles had advanced 50 yards more on our ridge, and faced a higher ridge ahead. In the ravine under that ridge, we saw a good trail with a railing.

About 1530, we tried to envelop those ridge positions, and took heavy fire. S/Sgt Huckabee fell with MG bullets in both legs and abdomen. T/Sgt Osen dragged Huckabee to temporary shelter and exposed himself among Jap fire-lanes to direct 1/Pln's fight against the ridge above us. Two men on the ground by helpless Huckabee saw no way to escape from the plunging Jap fire. But nearby Heidt saw a safe route. He crawled under Jap bullets with another man--perhaps Cappuccino--rescued Huckabee, and guided the others to safety.

About 1530, heavy fire and knee-mortars again hit 1/Pln. Tholund, Cpl Porras died, each with a bullet in the brain. Perhaps at that time, a fragment wounded Zusky in the chest.

Without heavy losses, "G" could go no farther. Cappuccino died on outguard just as he lighted a cigarette. Bullets pierced his head and right leg.

"G's" casualties of 26 June were comparable to our losses in our first day's fight at Sanananda. We had the most deaths i all 163 Inf--5 men--while "B" had 3 and "F" had 2. At 1300, we killed just 1 Jap--by 3/Pln at 1300.

About 0830 27 June, we zoomed 5 bazooka rounds into a cave which the Japs had reoccupied before 1/Pln and 2/Pln, and saw no more Japs there. "F" Co moved from their position of 26 June SW of us to our right flank and fought the Japs. We overed their bried attack by fire and had no losses. But on the coast ridge, 3/Pln's Cpl Hardesty was knocked down the cliffs with a sniper bullet. With BAR help, we rescued him, but despite Medics' care, he died at 0300.

On 28 June, "G" made minor advances beside "F's" advances until a strongpoint halted "F" after 150 yards--a strongpoint protected by riflemen on pinnacles of rock above it. "G" slew 2 Nips when our bazooka killed a pillbox.

And 28 June was the final day of 163's offensive. Shellfire was cheaper than men against Ibdi Pocket. In 2/Bn, "G" Co was down to 65 effectives; "F" Co down to 42. From 28 June to 4 July, "G" held the lines with other 163 Cos. We huddled miserably in little coral pigpens on bare rock ridges under dripping leaves of tall, slender trees holding back our sun.

Men on guard at night dared not risk cover under ponchos because they would foul a grenade throw. Or if we slithered off our ponshoc, the sound would reveal our positons to a crawling Jap. At night, a man's turn on guard always seemed to cause a heavy night rain. He would be awakened from comparative warmth in dark fatigues under a damp poncho to crouch with his grenade in the dark. At once like MG fire, heavy rains rattled the trees over the ridges towards him. instantly drenched in twill fatigues, he spent 2 chill hours listening darkness--but happy that no Japs attacked.

"G" Co had our 2 last casualties on Biak. On 29 June, a fragment wounded Cleveland in right wrist. About 1400, 1 July, the last of 5 sniper rounds killed Schmitt, who was snt up from the kitchen crew. he was last man of "G" Co's 10 dead on Biak.

On the right morn of 4 July, "G" Co left our dark ridges forever. Gen Doe evacuated all 1/Bn and 2/Bn Cos to enable 146 FA to smash the Pocket without endangering us. Doe also expected many of the Jap garrison to leave the Pocket and die in our ambushes north of the supply road. "G" Co left behind Martinez' stil unrecoverable body. Dirty and sleepless and released from confinement, the thin ranks of "G" Co left behind a greatness of herosim only soldiers can understand.

Stumbling off the ridges, "G" Co staggered like drunkards over the flatlands. With soft Jap soap, we bathed in the spring flowing into the sea at Ibdi. We washed our only suit of blackened fatigues and wore them damp to dry on us. Messgear tinkled as we lined up for hot garrison rations again.

At dusk, "G" watched the most memorable Jul 4 fireworks of our lives. For 15 minutes, the ridges shook with 81 mortar blasts. It was a fitting salute to our 10 dead, and the Japs still holding hard in Ibdi Pocket.

First shell — a white phosphorus smoke shell — hit the cliff-base — some distance off target. If Irving had not changed orders the 4.2s would have endangered a Yank Engr unit. He never knew whether the map directions were wrong, or the mortarmen failed to correct for compass variation He continued correcting ranges until he fired for effect into Ravine No. 1.

Each time as Irving gave fire orders, Rainwater flew directly at the target. When Irving finished ordering, Rainwater turned sharp to head out to sea. Then Rainwater turned and flew at the target for Irving to osberve the burst. Tight turns made Irving almost seasick, but they killed Target No. 1 at 1800 yards.

Now Irving shot at Target No 2 — at 1000 yards, the second ravine where they saw smoke at evening. From the first target, Irving had his direction, but this was a target harder to hit. It was a deep ravine at the cliff-edge, with a narrow ridge fore and aft. Ravine was also narrow, and at right angles to the fire.

To use 4.2 mortar shells was impossible; they would go over the cliff — or fall below it. Irving called for 146 to fire salvos. First salvo had 2 over, 1 short. Second had 2 short, 1 over. After several tries, Irving placed 2 in the ravine, 1 at the cliff base — a terrific concentration and ricochett of fragments in that narrow ravine. Now 146 fired for effect; the shells blew apart the ravine.

Thus fought the Division at Ibdi Pocket. But to save lives, Gen Doe decided to pull back 163, yet continue blasting the sullen, unbroken Jap garrison. On 4 July, F and G Cos left those stinking ridges forever — unburiable dead, maggoty latrines. Back on the flats, we found it hard to walk after those rough coral ridges — at first reeled like new-landed sailors.

But that day, Irving had a last fight against Ibdi Pocket. With a Jap telescope from Aitape, we found a sniper in a tree platform NW our perimeter — and a pillbox at the tree-base. Irving climbed to a bank outside perimeter and guided a little 37 mm to knock out platform and pill box.

So battled 2/Bn 163 Inf against Ibdi Pocket from landing on 12 June to a stalemate 4 July. Against a heavily armed reinforced Bn among coral ridges impregnable to any reasonable land assault, we carried out orders and had minimum losses. We overran Ibdi Pocket's edges, found strongpoints for FA and mortars to batter. Only after 2/Bn took Ibdi Pocket 22 July when B-25s pulverized the Japs, did we learn what 2/Bn had battled. We had fought not just 1000 Japs — but those Japs in unbelievable positions — 4 large caves, 17 small caves, 75 log or coral pillboxes. Minimum heavy arms had been 3 75 mm cannon, 8 90 mm mortars, 2 37s, 2 20 mm guns, 3 HMGs — not to speak of other weapons probably blown into nothing. Under Mjr Robert Irving, 2/Bn 163 Inf had incurred comparatively minor casualties but had performed a mission of the highest type of military craftsmanship.

Basic MS is Col Irving's 19-Page MS dated 22 Mar 70, compiled 25 years after the battle. Irving used 163's JOURNAL, NARRATIVE REPORT, RR Smith's APPROACH TO THE PHILIPPINES. I researched all these items, 146 FA's Capt Allen's "Reduction of Ibdi Pocket," and my own unpublished MS, "History of G Co. (I fought in Kreiger's 3/Pln.) I regret that no F Co man has given me his story. Except for Irving's story, I have only these stories of 163 on Biak: A Co, B Co, and G Co. Where E's, F's, C's, the whole 3/Bn and other 163 outfits?

G Co. 163 Infantry:
Mopping up on Biak

by **Dr. Hargis Westerfield**, Division Historian

Prime source is my own MS from first-hand experience, although I wrote it from memory in November, 1946, to submit to McCartney's Jungleer. I also used 163 Infantry's Biak Journal, but found it hard to collate the two.

On 4 July 1944, G Co., 163 Inf. lifted our siege of Ibdi Pocket. We left forever our narrow, dark jungle ridges—left forever those pigpens of coral we lived in, and our unburiable dead for Graves Registration. Hiking on level ground from 2/Bn. Hq. back towards Ibdi, we staggered like drunks to adjust our walk to flat ground.

Waist-deep in limestone springs in the living rock below our CP, we luxuriated in soft Jap soap. We laundered the set of black fatigues we'd lived in for two weeks. Clean again, we lolled in the cool moving water to look south towards Jappen Island, that purple mountain wall of wonderland.

It felt good to stand in a chow line with a scalded mess gear and get hot stew again. The sun dried that pale set of fatigues on our backs. And at nightfall came our own July 4 fireworks. Mortars of 641 TD bombed the Ibdi Pocket. Dim Jap ridges trembled for 15 minutes under mortar blasts— back where G's dead lay under Jap pillboxes.

Then on 8 July, G entrucked to set up tents at 163's permanent base camp on Biak. The camp lay in a coral scrubland on the semidesert plateau behind the coastal ridges.

After our "hitch on the rock" above Ibdi, life was good in G Co. We still had no reveille. We woke only for chow call, in broad daylight. We awoke a little chilled. A pale red sun over coral barrens made us remember autumn in Ohio or Montana. We hacked our campsite clean with our machetes. While the sun dried our jungle sores, we hoped that our war on Biak was ended.

But shells still tore the air above to strike Ibdi Pocket, where 163's decimated 3/Bn. still fought the Jap 3/Bn., 222 Inf. And Gen. Doe needed exhausted G Co. to link with 186 and cut down escaping Japs before they could flee north to regroup at Korim Bay. (At Ibdi Pocket after our assaults through 26 June, G Co. was down to 65 effectives; we now totalled 137 men, 3 officers.)

So on 18 July, G's lean, yellow-faced columns in faded green left a

At the mouth of the Big Cave on Biak.

truckhead at the end of the road-under-construction to Mokmer Drome. Bulldozers still dug with armed guards. "You're out only a few days," said an officer as we shouldered our packs. But we knew better. Besides hunting Japs, we must contact victorious 186 Inf. in from the west after winning Mokmer Drome.

Slogging 4,500 yards down the east-west trail to Mokmer Drome, we found no Japs that day. We made a perimeter on a little plateau above some native gardens. Journal reports that our recon patrol killed a Jap with rifle, rice, paybooks and pictures.

That dark, rainy dawn of 19 July, S/Sgt. Slaga woke me out of a hole. He said, "Westerfield, you run first scout today." I said, "Why pick on me? My eyes aren't good enough."

"It's easy this time," said Slaga. "We got you a dog. He does the work."

My breakfast was a canteen cup of black Nescafe which I had time to make lukewarm by burning the paraffin paper of a K ration under it. Sgt. Jim Wilson was already yelling, "Let's go!"

Heading the Indian file of G's rusty-helmeted riflemen was a giant of a strange GI. He was leashed to a giant of a shepherd dog.

"It's easy," the giant said in a Texas drawl. "Just let the dog tell you what to do."

"What does he say? What do I watch?"

"Just watch him. He'll pull steady down the trail. When he jerks, there's a Nip around."

"Then what?"

"Then we pull back to save the dog."

"Hell, that makes me the dog!"

"Yeah, you make a good hound with a rifle. Them dogs cost money to train."

So G Co. took off down the yellow, twisting trail into scrub jungle. We followed Honorable Dog, a member of 262 QM Dog Plan, with his Texas butt boy.

Then a blinding rain hit me like a waterfall, instantly soaking my coarse fatigue jacket and leggings. I ran on, squishing and shivering. Then my GI toe hit a concealed rock under a muddy pool. I fell and fouled my M-1 muzzle.

By the time my folding Jap ramrod had cleaned it, Piotrowski, the regular first scout, had replaced me. The rain halted; the sun blazed down on a red afternoon. We filed into a native garden, a brush-choked depression with shallow soil.

Honorable Dog lunged hard. We left the trail into the garden, rifles ready. The giant Texan heaved his dog to the rear.

Then Piotrowski became the dog. Backed by Slaga and Scout Ken Clark, they padded up the curve of a narrow track. We others of 2/Squad, 3/Pln. followed bent over double where the brush made a waist-high palisade.

Sudden fire broke out ahead. Our column turned and doubled back. I also turned. Then Sgt. Jim Wilson swore at us, and I was down with my rifle to face the silence at the trail's turn, where I thought we'd lost two men. Looking back over my shoulder, I saw a grin of approval from good soldier Kiselus. He was down behind me.

As 2/Squad rallied, we learned that Peter had almost collided with a fat-faced little Jap in netted helmet, ten feet ahead. The Nip drew a bead on Peter, who then lowered his M-1 to waist level and shot the Nip through the heart. By a confusion in orders, our whole squad had turned to run from a dying Nip. Only Slaga remained to guard Pete. But Pete now ignored our panic, grandly divided the souvenirs—even gave away the little Jap's squad flag.

And so during 18-22 July, G patrolled the Jap east-west trail that Kuzume had used to reinforce his battle for Parai Defile. G executed a few stray Nips, but not until 21 July did we meet 186. Prowling over 5,400 yards west, Osen's 33 men finally contacted 186. Now all-tired G yearned for the little heaven of cool tents in our clearing in the coral scrub.

But my own 3/Pln. sadly learned that we must remain behind to set up a trail block where a northward trail crossed the east-west trail. But as we hiked, Sgt. Doherty's Donegal laugh broke out. Through openings in the brush we saw Ibdi Ridges battered by B-25's. Dive bombers like black mosquitoes aimed on the Japs. When blockbusters struck, limestone dust and fragments flew high. White jungle giants toppled; great gaps opened in the summit forest. This was the last day for the brave Jap defenders of Ibdi Pocket.

Our 3/Pln. ambush was an opaque green world where dim trails crossed—the main one being Kuzume's supply trail from the east. We secured that cross trail with two H Co. HMG's, posted outguards. We stretched our ponchos for the rain. Stony soil kept us from digging in, so we sheltered behind logs. The ration party left us 10-in-1 rations and an apple pie each from baker "Ma" Perkins.

But G's luck was bad. About 1000, Conforti shot too soon at a Jap. At outguard, he masked our HMG; it fired too late. Just at dusk, I heard a Tommy gun and an M-1 fire. Piotrowski came in with his muzzle blackened, Doherty shrilled at Pete, "What's the matter? You slipping?"

Pete said that three Nips hiked up the trail at right-shoulder-arms. Kroll and Pete held fire until they closed in. Then Kroll let go with the new "Buck Rogers" Tommy which he'd never fired before. Kroll missed; the smoke was too thick for Pete to aim his M-1.

Good soldier Doherty left with the threat to court-martial any man who smoked while on guard. (Pete did not smoke.) Ken Clark, Piotrowski and I bedded down behind our log. On first guard, I saw the last green light die in the cathedral light among tall trees. Insects sang a soothing chorus. Calling Clark for his turn, I slept well until my next guard four hours later.

On 23 July next morn, Max Scott and I took outguard to the west. We sat on cardboard ration boxes to keep the water out. Because of Pete's mishap last night, we made a new plan against possible Japs. My M-1 would fire first—and at the hindmost Jap, if we saw more than one. Scott's "Buck Rogers" would then open on the others.

But we expected no Japs; I was sure Conforti and Kroll had scared them off already. I waited for the morning ration party—maybe "Ma" Perkins' doughnuts and mail would arrive. It now sounded like the ration party clumping up the trail. My eyes watched for the first scout.

This was no ration party! It was a Jap in a long, pointed cap like a horn, his archaic long rifle at port. For me, it was my heart's desire—a clean Jap target about 40 yards off down a long, clear vista of trail.

From his place, Scott couldn't see him. The M-1 went to my shoulder—in the classic sitting position of the rifle range. My safety was off. I thought he looked down my sight blade. I remembered the words of my coach in training: "Take up the slack in your trigger. Just close your hand."

My M-1 No. 232719 leaped in my hands; gas flew from the breach; a body thudded hard instantly—all on the flick of a finger. Max fired; Doherty rushed out from Pln. CP. To be sure that no suicide grenades waited under the Jap's armpit, we executed at once. Then a detail of us hunted the trail to be sure that no other Japs were with our man. For me at the head of the detail, it seemed like an Indian scalp dance after the kill.

While I was on outguard that afternoon, Clark saved Piotrowski's life—and his own also, back at our bivouac. Battle-tired from Ibdi Pocket and in thick jungle off the trail, we had seen no need to watch for Nips. Jap-yellow from Atabrine, crop-headed Pete snored out in the open.

Lazily lying by Pete, Clark thought he saw two Yanks 30 yards off in a green shadow. "Mayberry!" he started to shout at one who looked like our Texan. "Get out of there; you'll get your head shot off!"

Then Clark realized that they were Japs. He snatched Pete's rifle. Looking down the barrel without using the sights, he cracked off a clip. One Jap fell; a Jap officer and three more ran to the left—right into an enfilade from Beckner's BAR position!

West Virginian Beckner's BAR flailed them. Texan orderly Fowler and Irish Doherty ran from CP and shot in the field-day that followed. After they thought all the Japs lay dead, BAR-man Jim Wilson saw one pretending death under the brush, and threw down on him with two M-1 slugs—for his first sure kill of the whole campaign. Fowler got a saber from this kill; Beckner got a fine Longines wristwatch in perfect running order for which he at once refused 50 Aussie pounds.

Next few days on the outpost were a green dream for me—that green dream of New Guinea. I never got another shot. Most Japs straggled across the outguards' post behind us, where I heard that Baer led in the number of kills.

But for me, tired from the sleepless ridges of Ibdi, it was like a green dream. With Scott, I took my turn on outguard. With rifle scoured and oiled daily, I waited for Japs that never did come. My faded green fatigues were clammy below the knees, the cuffs caked with stiffened mud that never dried. Off duty at our log while Pete slept, I made coffee with Jap Sterno, and had little menus with Spam and sweet condensed cereals—and "Ma" Perkins' bread or doughnuts. I also had mail; I could even read from a small paperback for a while—mailed to me first-class. At twilight, when the green jungle closed in and insects chorused, I pillowed on a flotation bladder, yearned for home, and slept warm in my poncho. No Japs troubled me after Clark woke me for my turn on guard.

On 28 June 1944, G Co.'s reinforced 3/Pln. forever left that green dream of an ambush, now odorous with some unburyable Jap dead. (Back at silent Ibdi Pocket, Father Lynn with six G & F men found our dead for burial.) Gratefully, 3/Pln. boarded a waiting truck and sprawled over benches among our packs. We sat unhelmeted and laughing as a light rain wet us; we did not care. Poles and Mexicans and Slavs and Swedes and Assiniboins and Southerners, we were one ethnic group, one nation, blood brothers, Americans all.

Mayberry had a bawdy song. We laughed hard at it, yet with tears in our eyes. I remembered upturned faces of Jap corpses under that cold rain; I asked for forgiveness. But we laughed hard; we were still alive after Ibdi Pocket and those ambushes...

I Co. 163 Infantry:

Ambush on Biak

By DR. HARGIS WESTERFIELD, Division Historian
with I Co's TIMM, STANCHFIELD, PRANDI, HOLMGREN and SULLIVAN

On 19 June 1944, I Co. 163 Inf. dispatched an unlucky little, partly-armed convoy for K Co. behind Mokmer Ridges directly north of West Caves. We I Co. men knew that K needed our supplies badly. But we did not know why the detail totaled only 25-30 men, and why we were mostly unarmed.

We had heard nothing of the importance of 3/Bn. in Gen. Eichelberger's masterly maneuver of 19 June against the Japs' West Caves. Only the day before, I and K and other 3/Bn. elements supposedly had received Gen. Doe's order to assist Eichelberger's great move of 19 June. While 186 Inf. got behind West Caves and blocked the Japs' supply road, 3/Bn. had this assignment to help 186's other companies.

We were to assemble along the northern slopes of Mokmer Ridge near Hill 320. From there we were to prevent Jap reinforcements from attacking 186 Inf. on its move. Yet survivors of this I Co. carrying party had no knowledge of I Co's place in this grand strategic design.

Nor can survivors of this carrying party explain why we went unarmed and not over 30 strong. It is true that—if we go by a map of 20 June—only 1,000 yards of scrubland separated us from K Co. And of course, our own arms and ammo would add extra weight for us. But on days before this carrying party, 3/Bn. had some bloody little skirmishes with Japs in this area. So we went mostly unarmed!

We know that K badly needed food and ammo, but we believed that I was in a sort of rest camp. Scout Sullivan said that we were supposedly in a safe area. And for the first time, he did not wear his steel helmet.

Survivors remember something of our order of march, and a fair number of the names of the men. T/Sgt. Ed Wilson led the way with his M-1; followed John Sullivan and his Tommy gun. Next came unarmed carriers, Mihoover and Labencki, then Bender with a .45 pistol which could be valuable at pointblank jungle ranges. Stanchfield was sixth in line with another .45, then Petersburg, unarmed.

This line-up is the memory of Stanchfield, 30 years after the fight, but changes in the order could have occurred by the time that the Nippos hit us. At the time that the attack began, Timm says that he himself was about fourth or fifth in the column. He was certainly close to Petersburg, as his story of the action will make clear.

In this column also were Holmgren, Prandi, Beznick and Sgt. DeVries. Prandi says that he was near the end of the column, with DeVries.

And so I Co's convoy sweated forth in midafternoon, on a trail following wire towards K Co. Suddenly the ambush crashed down on us.

Under packs already heavier, I's men were laboring from an area of huge rocks, trees and heavy brush when it happened. We were still in what seemed to be safe territory, only 200 to 450 yards from our home perimeter. As the first six men started into a kind of clearing about 30 feet wide, the Japs hit us.

Sullivan says that he was then first in line. Timm heard a grenade or knee-mortar shell explode among us; men fell. Along with the blast and the thud of bodies, it seemed to Timm as if a whole side of the jungle trail was moving in on us. Japs in camouflaged uniforms charged in on us with rifles and bayonets and even the barrel of a knee mortar. Light was on their bayonets as they leaped at us from 5-6 feet off the trail out of the kunai grass.

The fight was all over in 10 seconds. It seemed to Timm that a wave of 15 Nips bore down on us, although statements from others cut the number down to eight.

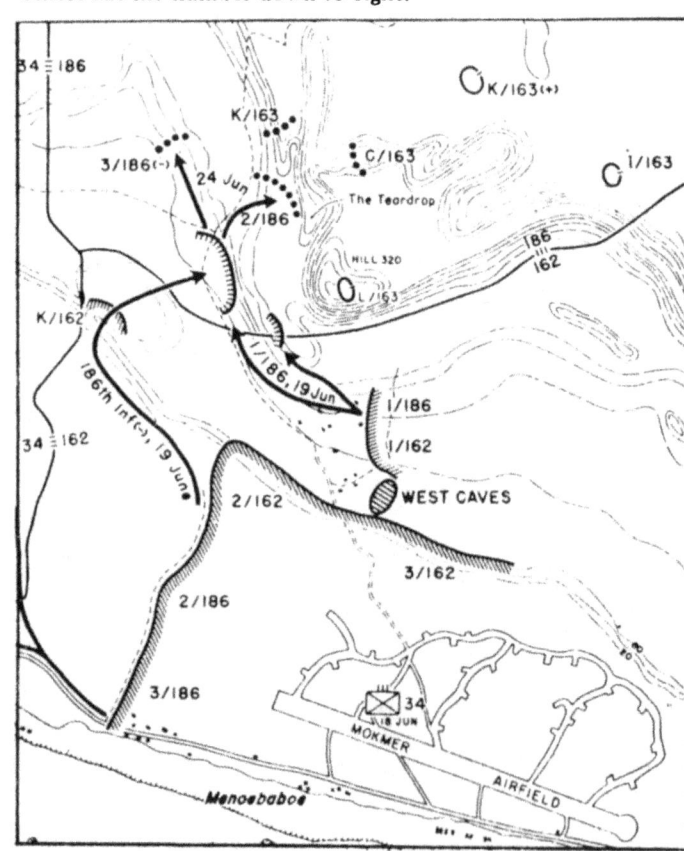

The grenade or shell detonated between Miller and Milhoover. Clarence Miller died instantly; Mihoover was fatally wounded, John Sullivan wounded also.

Timm was sure that T/Sgt. Wilson killed one Nip with his M-1; then a shot in the head killed Wilson.

Timm fought briefly with a Nip armed only with a bayonet. The Nip was on Timm's back briefly; then Timm threw him off. Somebody else slew that Nip.

About this time, a grenade impacted close to Timm. He hit the dirt just in time to save himself, except for a few steel fragments. Timm thought that this grenade fatally wounded Mihoover, although Stanchfield thought that the first explosion had done it. In this melee, it was hard to be certain on the cause of any casualty.

Having hit ground with the first explosion, Stanchfield saw a Jap trying to bayonet Labencki. Bender got that bayonet man with his .45; but as the Nip fell he pierced Labencki in the thigh.

Bender then wrestled another Nip to the ground. Labencki and he beat the Nip to death with their helmets.

Petersburg and Stanchfield leaped to their feet. Stanchfield killed one Nip; Petersburg snatched a rifle from the ground and killed another. Both shot at a Nip far to the right, but they never knew whether they wounded or finished him.

But this is the way Sullivan saw the mix-up—Sullivan who was then in first scout's position, unhelmeted but carrying his Tommy gun. For him, the ambush broke out on the narrow trail, just after he had passed the small clearing. The Japs let Sullivan and two others pass. Then he heard grenades explode on the trail; fragments pierced the back of his neck and shoulders. Turning, he saw maybe eight Japs charging. His Tommy gun emptied a clip into them, but he did not know how many he hit. The others rushed in to kill too fast for thought.

A Jap jumped Sullivan with a bayonet and broke his cheekbone. And worse still, what he thought to be a knee-mortar barrel crashed on his head.

At the moment he did not even realize that a bayonet had slashed him. Desperately he grappled with the bayonet man and fell to the ground with him. He had the Jap on his back and on his own right side on the ground. His right hand passed around the Jap's neck and strangled him to death.

Believing to this day that the other four armed men with him at the head of the column were wiped out, Sullivan ran back down the trail to the unarmed men. While on the run, he saw another Yank down, trying to evade a Jap bayonet over him. Sullivan saw the bayonet lunge all the way through the man's thigh. Then another Yank—he thought it was an Indian—gripped the Jap and killed him with a .45. (Was this the same Labencki whom Stranchfield saw receive the bayonet, and was Bender the Indian who slew the bayonet man?)

By the time he reached the ration train, Sullivan was dazed and half-blinded from blood in his eyes which were swelling shut. He would be blind for several weeks.

Prandi was a lucky man in this ambush. By chance, he was not up forward in the action. He had delayed a little to help an unarmed replacement replace his pack properly, and so was near the rear of the carrying party. During the wild struggle he crouched behind a great rock at the trail bend. To Stanchfield up front, the action seemed to last 10 seconds; to Prandi, it seemed long and drawn-out until all unarmed men got orders back to I Co's perimeter.

It looked as if the rescurers had only to tend the wounded, but a "dead" Jap detonated a grenade. T/Sgt. Morris took a large fragment in his shoulder, and we had to kill the Nip all over again.

Thus ended I's ambush of 19 June 1944. K failed to get the supplies needed that day. For I had hands full to doctor and carry our the wounded before the dark fell. I Co's dead had to lie where they had fallen until an armed detail went for them next morning.

Miller and Wilson were dead already; Medina lived until the rescue party was about ready to carry him back to I Co. Fourth dead was Mihoover, who died from shock, according to Stanchfield.

Besides losing four killed, I had three wounded: Labencki, T/Sgt. Morris and Sullivan.

The badly-wounded Sullivan remembers that men lifted him up and carried him for what seemed a long time. Then they jeeped him to a field hospital. No medics worked on him for some time; he heard that others were dying. He remembers that one boy died on the operating table—the newest man who joined I Co. just three weeks ago, tall and very young. Sullivan forgot his name, but perhaps this was Mihoover whom Stanchfield remembers.

All told, Sullivan had received four separate wounds. He had a shower of fragments in neck and shoulders from that first explosion, then the bayonet wound that broke his right cheekbone. He had a deep gash from the knee-mortar barrel. He found a fourth minor wound under his chin from another grenade. But for him, the most painful part in the field hospital was to have the hair shaved off his head for treatment. This blade must have been several years too old for its job.

Medics transferred him to the local evacuation hospital, then to general Hospital at Hollandia. They tried to return him to I Co., but he kept on passing out. After three months, Sullivan went to reclassification center so that he ended up in AFWESPAC G-4 Hq. in Manila.

Back in I Co., we surmised that the Jap ambush had been a matter of sheer bad luck for our supply convoy. Judging by the knee mortar, we supposed that a reinforced mortar crew had started out to drop a few shells into I's perimeter.

But then the "mortar snipers" chanced to observe our supply patrol. Without risking I Co's probably vigilant outguards and hidden MG's, they could kill a large number of Yanks right there before their eyes. They could also halt supplies needed for another outfit. We were lucky that they did not hold fire until the leading armed men were farther up the trail so that they could have erupted among the defenseless "cargadores." And in this ambush all of the eight Japs may have been killed, but they had indeed made of I Co's supply train a successful target of opportunity.

CREDIT: Prime credit is due to letters from I 163's Walt Timm, Ballard Stanchfield, Dante Prandi, C.A. "Bud" Holgren and John Sullivan. Background is from R.R. Smith's Approach to the Philippines. I Co's men wrote these letters in 1974 after I queried in Jungleer about 163's Casualty List of 19 June, when I supposed I 163 was out of action. After 30 years' elapse, some data in the letters were contradictory, naturally. (Neither 163's Narrative nor Journal on Biak mentions 3/Bn. for 19 June. And Journal entries have disappeared.)

Timm now raises wheat in eastern Colorado. Stanchfield is a retired printer in Minneapolis. Prandi owned a bakery in California. Holmgren is in painting and decorating in Portland, Oregon. Sullivan owns and operates Pioneer Wear with 400 employees in Albuquerque, which manufactures exclusive Western styles.

(Except for I Co's story of Sanananda, this is all the history available on I Co. 163. Can you help?)

East Caves area on Biak

163 Inf's Third Battalion:
Last Days of Ibdi Pocket

by DR. HARGIS WESTERFIELD, DIVISION HISTORIAN

This story would be better if even one man had sent me one unit history of any 3/Bn Co. Main source is 163's often indefinite journal, collated with 163's July 1944 morning report, Harris' and Almos' Medal Stories. Jack Arnold's diary was indispensable for the bombing of 22 July. Dean W. "Bill" Poole's letter 13 June 1971 throws light on K Co 17 July. Background comprises 146 FA's Capt Allen's "Defense of Ibdi Pocket," 41 Div Training Note No. 4, and R R Smith's *Approach to the Philippines*. I regret that my own story is about as nearly adequate as any that I have hitherto discovered. Won't *you* please help me?

By 7 July 1944, Gen. Doe realized that 163 Inf. still must conquer Ibdi Pocket with 2/Bn 222 Inf. dug in. Our two-bn attack of 26-28 June had failed. When we raised the siege of Ibdi Pocket and increased bombardment, we had failed to coerce the Japs out. After withdrawing our rifles 4 July, we blasted the Pocket with D and H's 2400 rounds 81 mortars while 146 FA shot 5500 105 rounds. But 7 July A's recon in strength under Sgt. Russ had found Nips building new emplacements.

Now Col. Moroney sent in 3/Bn to clean up. Although worn down after a month of Hill 320 north of Mokmer Dromes, we still had made no attacks like the other bns. on Wakde or Ibdi Pocket.

Tactics were now more clever than 163's earlier tactics. Rather than encircle Ibdi Pocket and attack, we would use mainly one rifle Co. at a time. Pushing west, we would leave the rear exits unguarded. But north of Ibdi, we set up ambushes to kill fugitives or reinforcements.

On 10 July 1946, FA laid down concentration of 1134 105 shells. Then L entered the low ridges of shell-withered forest. Slaying a Nip at the ridge base, we deployed on Ridge 1 and cowered under three mortar bursts from a pillbox. A bazooka killed the pillbox, but new automatic fire held L's 1/Pln. from taking Ridge 2. In that coral hell, our 2/Pln could not flank that Jap automatic fire. The pillbox we had killed came alive twice; twice we slew its garrison—two Japs in two successive garrisons.

About 1220, two Jap mortar shells exploded close; rifle bullets chipped coral close. We chased Nips from one pillbox with a flamethrower. Another pillbox held until we drew back and threw in 60 rounds of mortar shells. We then reoccupied the ridge unopposed. Meanwhile, a K Co. Pln. secured L's right flank against Japs moving east.

But at 1700, an L 60 mm mortar shell was short. Dead was Pospyhala and seven WIA from that same shell. Wounded were Sena, Perlin, Torres; S/Sgts. Pangle, McClaran; Cpls. Dixon, Viramonte.

L pushed again with flamethrowers and bazookas on 11 July. We cleared five pillboxes; three held a man each, evidently blown up by our bazookas. Lively was WIA in the top of his head at 1025. By 1110, L had won 200 yards, ahead of G 163's old position of 4 July. Sgt. Rollie Harris had expertly placed bazookas and flamethrowers to win with minor casualties.

Resistance stiffened. Six mortar rounds hit L's right flank. At 1100 on our left, paratrooper Gundermann died from a head wound from a pillbox. He was a volunteer from G 503

Pcht. Bn. who had gone AWOL to fight for 163. Avenging Gundermann's death, L Co. knocked out the pillbox, KIA two Japs behind it. By 1410, L had three more WIA: T/Sgt. Gilfeather, S/Sgt. Doug Olson, both by MGs, and Sgt. Nunnelley also WIA. We dug in that night with six more Jap pillboxes menacing us on the next ridge.

And K's combat patrol guarding L's right flank had trouble. From a ridge north of a strong pillbox, MG fire killed AWOL paratrooper Hudson, WIA Cpl. Smick seriously. When Sgt. Almos' litter squad tried to save them, a MG bullet pierced medic Chambers' lungs, hit another unnamed man. Almos exposed himself to give first aid; but Chambers died. K's patrol retreated to 3/Bn CP.

The third day, L got nowhere. The six pillboxes ahead were in stronger locations and reinforced overnight. Even from higher ground we could not knock out a MG. By 1020 Coffee was dead—a third AWOL paratrooper of G 503 Bn. to give Col. Moroney trouble in arranging death-benefits. At 1145, Poli died from a head wound. From front and left rear, 40 Japs shot at us. Sgt. Harris controlled his fire so well that L escaped almost unhurt. About 1705, two tanks of 603 Tank Co's 1/Pln. shelled the cliffs, killed four pillboxes, had four possibles. But L was stopped.

On 13 July, K relieved L from the ridges, while I moved up to take over K's assignment at L's right flank on the ridge top. About 1300, K lost Capt. Charles Peterson near death with two slugs in him. Magee and Perkins were injured; Perkins from a falling tree. In front of K Co. right and on our left flank, Japs kept up heavy fire. Meanwhile, Division began working on the Pocket with 947 FA's 155s.

We had good news 13 July. In the dark of dawn at 0435, at AT outpost on the north saw Japs leaving Ibdi Pocket—three groups of some 60 men, all of them armed. And at 0530, an H Co. outpost for a mortar Pln. saw 15 more Japs leaving the Pocket. The five whom H saw clearly were unarmed and without packs.

Besides good news of Jap withdrawals, I's careful patrols learned that the leftward ridges towards the sea were free of Japs. Our Bn Hq surmised that only a rear guard now held Ibdi Pocket. Yet on 14 July, I Co. lost Sgt. Brklacich wounded with a bullet in left forearm.

On 15 July, we expected easier fighting. After 744 rounds' FA in 75 minutes, K and I pushed at 0815. A tank pln also fired on targets. But Jap fire stopped K and an I pln. dead. From lower ground on the landward side, another I pln. tried to move south against the cliffs. Japs killed Russell M. Smith with a bullet in the head; they wounded Larry Larson, S/Sgt. Trjoski.

Next day, 3/Bn. Hq's main effort was to find flanks of Japs' new positions after their great withdrawal of 13 July. The day was deadly again. Still fighting frontally, K's Walter Scott threw in 80 rounds of bazooka fire to reduce a troublesome pillbox to rubble. When Sgt. Henry M. Jones crawled up to inspect damage, he died from a Jap bullet in the brain. The same bullet penetrated Shepard's stomach to kill him. Early, Sgt. William E. Johnson was wounded. K Co. was stymied by two Jap MG's with 12 accurate riflemen to protect them.

And on that 16 July, I Co. fared worse than K in front. Patrolling the old cliff area west of Ibdi Pocket, we took a heavy mortar burst that killed four, wounded one. Dead were Bender, Branch, Godfrey, Jim R. Scott, with Chavez wounded. On digging up the nose cone, we identified it as one of our own 81s. By now 3/Bn's fight for Ibdi Pocket had entered its final phase. When I replaced K Co. 17 July on the eastern ridge front, we just held ground—or harassed Nips at a distance—along with 81's and FA, around the clock.

In our final phase, accurate maps were all-important. Other bns. helped us patrol. Some patrols prowled below the cliffs; others infiltrated the quiet western approaches where 1/Bn. had fought 26 June-4 July. For example, a 28-man AT patrol penetrated 1000 yards up Ridge 4. AT men here slew four Nip sentinels, found Japs felling trees and sawing logs for new pillboxes. Location of these new Nip lines showed that Ibdi Pocket had contracted. AT men were only 400 yards west of I Co's ridge position. AT's attached FA observer called down 146 FA and 947 FA to smash the new Japs' lines. Yet more important than calling down shellfire were the maps AT and other patrols brought to Hq.

After no reported 3/Bn. casualties 17-20 July, we began the final attack. On 21 July, we started with sham assaults. At 0710, along with 81's and FA, we dropped 34 smoke shells, with small-arms fire from I and L Co. took this turn to replace the weaker I Co. again on the ridges. At 1030, 603 Tanks' 1/Pln. blew up seven pillboxes on the landward side of the cliffs, to make Nips mass for a push from that direction. At 1830:30, we faked another attack—FA, smoke, automatic fire, M-1's.

Their last night alive, Japs prowled near our holes, grenaded ineffectively. Then at dawn 22 July, 105's and 155's barraged Ibdi Pocket, with 100 smoke shells to blind the Nips and scare them. Under smoke cover, L fell back to the road; our planes came.

About 0850 with the lifted smoke, the planes (B-24 Liberators), soared down blockbuster bombs. Eight B-24's, like vicious buzzing black mosquitoes, dived to 4000 feet; bombardiers sighted precisely on assigned targets and launched the first bombs of their 64,000 pound load. To M's 1/Lt. Jack Arnold 700 yards off, the bombs seemed to just float down.

But when they hit, the crash surprised Arnold more than anything in his whole life. The ground exploded and trembled like an earthquake. The horizon danced before his eyes. Black smoke shrouded Ibdi Pocket. While Arnold hit dirt 700 yards off and fragments clinked near him, the planes made two more passes—64 blockbusters in a space 400 by 600 yards.

Panting back uphill under FA and smoke cover, L retook the old position, then jumped off west among rubble and shattered trees of the Jap lines. And 1000 yards west, mortars on call, K moved into rear trails to Ibdi Pocket. FA and mortars stopped. Both small green files moved silently, carefully, fingers on triggers: bearded, atabrin-yellowed, burning-eyed Yanks with clean, quick rifles ready.

At 115, L shot our first Nip, moved in past others dead from concussion against a bunker on a high coral pinnacle. By 1255, we reached Paratrooper Knob where Hudson died 11 days ago. By 1315, we were 300 yards unscathed into Ibdi Pocket. We found two giant 90 mm mortars, perhaps those that hit G Co. 26 June. Among many pillboxes, we halted at signs of life, knocked out a pillbox, found one dead Jap inside. At 1650, we killed another pillbox with three Japs, captured a 400 mm cannon. At bivouac, we killed six Nips in a cave. Meanwhile patrolling towards L, K Co. at 1635 knocked out a pillbox, slew three Nips. At 1650, we killed another pillbox and one Jap, seized a 40 mm gun. Once Japs fired and threw grenades. We smashed that pillbox with two Japs killed, captured a 20 mm AA gun, much ammo. At dusk, K dug in 300 yards from L.

And at 1030 23 July, L and K contacted without casualty in the shallow rubble among the ominous, dark, silent cave mouths and pillbox slits. Higher rose the stench of dead, buzzing of corpse flies unheard only as 116 Engr. teams blasted caves shut. An automatic 37 mm cannon under a roof thickened with nine layers of logs was guard to one great cave with supporting pillboxes. The cave was four stories deep; a rope ladder led down into its darkness. This was Pocket Hq., with its records of 3/Bn 222 Inf. and 2 Gun Co. We slew two more Nips, blew the cave shut.

In an area 400 by 600 yards, Ibdi Pocket held 75 pillboxes, 17 caves, four of them extremely large caves. Armament still evident included eight 90 mortars and these guns: three 75s, two 37s, three HMG's—also LMG's, knee mortars, rifles. We found 228 recognizable bodies.

Such were the last days of Ibdi Pocket. Through 10 June 1944, it menaced all attacks on Mokmer Dromes; it took toll of 162, 186, 163. But why did Col. Kuzume fail to vacate Ibdi Pocket in those final days when he needed every man and gun to hold Mokmer Dromes and West Caves? Ibdi Pocket had only nuisance value after 10 June, and Gen. Doe liquidated it with almost minimum losses. Yet in difficulty of terrain and gallantry of Japs' defense, Ibdi Pocket is comparable only to the 81 Inf. Div. and 1st Marine Div's coral hell of Peleliu, far off in the Mariana Islands.

41st Division Headquarters:

General Fuller and his barber

By DR. HARGIS WESTERFIELD, Division Historian,
with Barber CHARLES RUOCCO, Orderly ART PIERCE
and Cook TED SENFF

CREDIT: Barber Ruocco first suggested this story at the 1975 San Francisco Reunion; he backed it with a 15-page handwritten MS that fall. Senff's ltr. is dated 25 July 1975; my neighbor Pierce gave oral and written data up through March, 1976. Lt. Gen. Robert L. Eichelberger's Dear Miss Em contains a few items that I used. (How about some stories about other important leaders of our Division?)

About 15 Jan. 1942, Pvt. Charles Ruocco was cutting hair of another K-186 man outside Division PX at Copalis, Wash. (The 41st then guarded Pacific beaches against a Jap invasion.) Two more K men waited their turn. Aged 21, Ruocco was a barber college grad with three years in San Francisco's fine Hotel Empire. He had no plans to cut Army hair until K men bought him clippers and scissors and got a box for a chair.

Suddenly Gen. Fuller's staff car braked by Ruocco; Lt. Cain jumped out. "Are you a real barber, soldier?" Aide Cain asked. Ruocco saluted, "Yes sir!" Then Cain said, "The General would like a haircut now."

The K men vanished. Ruocco grabbed his equipment and rode to Fuller's quarters. Ruocco saluted the first general he'd ever seen. "Hello, son!" said Fuller. "How about giving me a haircut?"

The surprised Ruocco cut so well that after the staff car returned him to K, he was transferred to 41st Div. Hq. When "Queen Elizabeth" left for Sydney in March 1942, Ruocco had his own civilian barber tools aboard. Fuller had sent a courier to Ruocco's home for the instruments. Later he had a chair again—a half-ton truck seat mounted on a giant tire rim.

In many months overseas, Ruocco was Fuller's barber; he both liked and respected the General. Usually every 3-4 weeks, Div. Hq's Special pln. had orders to release Ruocco from other details to barber Fuller. At Fuller's Rockhampton mansion, Ruocco found the General in suntans and boots often just having returned from riding his own Australian horses, riding crop under arm.

Usually they talked casually about everyday Army life. Fuller always asked about his men's welfare but almost never commented on military operations. At times, he was a little moody. When he was notably happy, Ruocco knew at once.

Fuller had light-brown hair graying at the temples, and behind—fine hair thinning over the forehead. He did not insist on a careful cut. For a social function, he wanted a light trim. But a request for a short short cut told Ruocco that the Division's moving out.

Like Charles Merritt, the other Hq. barber, Ruocco cut hair for many 41st "big brass." He cut for MacKechnie, Trapman,

Private Charles Ruocco gives a trim to General Fuller outside the Division Commander's tent during a lull in the fighting.

Doe, Sweeny and Maison, among other. For Fuller insisted that they all get haircuts when visiting him.

Such was Ruocco's first experience with Gen. Fuller on the 41st's initial stay at Rocky. Orderly Art Pierce and Cook Ted Senff also joined Fuller at Rocky.

A B-186 private, Pierce met Fuller uniquely. When Fuller readied an Aussie mansion for his quarters in Rocky, Pierce had a weeding detail in the former occupant's garden. Pierce remembers himself from those days as a green, uprooted Nebraska farm boy.

Kneeling to weed, the farm boy saw rows of vegetables planted by the former owner. Pierce had no heart to uproot them, and carefully weeded around them.

Seeing the neat ranked rows of weeded vegetables, Fuller asked who had spared them. Stepping forward, Pierce did not know whether to expect praise or reprimand. Three days later, Fuller made him an Hq. gardener.

Sometimes Fuller gardened himself, and Pierce had a variety of duties. Pierce was a groundskeeper, readied the tennis court, did some guard duty, and once was a barkeeper.

When the 41st moved to Dobodura, Pierce grew a large garden to augment meager rations. Fuller loved radishes, but in that climate they were mostly tops. Some misguided men erected a fence that marked Hq. for Jap raids. Pierce planted cucumbers whose vines quickly climbed to hide the fence.

To get hard work from his men, Fuller never actually bullied nor pulled rank. In building the great Oro Bay Road, he might promise enlisted men a can of peaches to push the work, yet he would award the peaches anyway if the men worked hard enough. He might promise an officer a bottle of Scotch for completing a mile of road.

Once he ordered Pierce to take a bottle of Scotch to a visiting Aussie brigadier for a nightcap. Arriving at the Aussie's quarters, Pierce was to pour a drink for him, but to keep his grip always on the bottle. Then he was to slip the bottle under his coat and return it to Fuller.

Pierce was now Fuller's orderly. He cleaned Fuller's carbine—then one of the few in the Division. He sent out uniforms daily to a Papuan laundryman, but shined the shoes himself.

To Pierce, Fuller was no harsh officer—martinet; nor was he "superwarm" in personality. But Pierce respected him.

Unlike Pierce, Cook Ted Senff did not encounter Fuller dramatically. A former civilian chef, he was preparing Rocky hotels for officers and took a chance to cook for Fuller. Except when hosting other officers, Fuller liked simple foods: stews clear or brown. He enjoyed corned beef and cabbage with plain boiled potatoes. When the cooks had heated C rations in New Guinea, Fuller ate from mess gear and even washed it himself.

He hated unfair rationing. Once in New Guinea, a QM officer flew to Fuller's mess with a case of fresh eggs. Surprised, Fuller lunched on devilled eggs served by Poggetti, the other cook. After lunch, he called Senff and asked about the eggs. Learning that no other mess had fresh eggs, he ordered Senff never to serve them again. The remaining eggs in the case went to a nearby field hospital.

He disliked complaints and pretence. Once a new Yank officer from Australia complained about service at the officers' mess. Fuller called him aside, braced him to attention, berated him and flew him back to Australia on the next plane.

In Papua, Red Cross men presented Gen. Fuller with a radio and took pictures of his acceptance. Then they asked for their radio back. Fuller refused downright and donated the radio to a Div. Hq. mess hall.

Senff also drove for Fuller in New Guinea, with orders "Get there fast as you can, but safely." Once Senff unintentionally erred and delayed Fuller. When a gas-dump guard told Senff to help himself to petrol, Senff poured in a 5-gallon can of supposed gas. After lunch, Fuller drove the jeep off with another officer. Then a runner summoned Senff to bring the other jeep to Fuller. He was marooned in a big puddle in a dead jeep. Senff learned that he had filled Fuller's jeep with five gallons of water. With no comment, Fuller drove away in the other jeep. He never held the accidental error against Senff. He often complimented the cooking, and Senff rose from corporal to T/Sgt. while under Fuller.

Like Cook Senff, Barber Ruocco remembers how Fuller cared for his men so much that he hated unfair food service. Once when cutting hair in Papua, Ruocco voiced the complaints of Div. Hq. about certain mess sgts.

On that day, Fuller was talkative under Ruocco's clippers. Ruocco said, " The men are complaining about the food. They told me to tell you, sir."

Fuller queried, "What's that you say, son? What's that you said?" When Ruocco repeated the complaint, Fuller was visibly shaken up. He replied, "Why, you men are eating the same food as we are!" Ruocco, said, "Maybe so, sir. But it doesn't taste like yours."

"Son, tell the boys I'll do what I can about it," Fuller replied. At once, Fuller sent his personal chef of the day to the Div. Hq. mess sergeants with orders to cook all rations as the General liked them. Next time in the barber's chair, Fuller first asked, "How's the food now, soldier?" Ruocco answered, "Just delicious." Fuller proudly smiled at him. The era of good food lasted until our next beachhead at Hollandia.

Came 1944, the great year of invasions up the Guinea shore. Soldiering in Defense Pln., Ruocco had less contact with Fuller. While patrolling near Lake Sentani, Ruocco and two other Yanks found three moaning half-dead Japs, too helpless to lift their rifles beside them. Ruocco insisted on their carrying the two thin bodies back to Hq. perimeter. Much information came from them.

On Biak at Parai Defile, Ruocco was a runner for 41st Medic Hq. He had to contact front-line medics and return information on the daily toll of casualties. Once at Parai Water Hole, Jap crossfire pinned him down.

Ruocco remembers Fuller in full battle gear giving orders right and left from his jeep. After Lt. Cain looked inside a supposedly cleared bunker and died from a lurking Jap, Fuller profanely ordered clearance of all bunkers. This was the only time Ruocco saw him truly angry.

Before Biak's West Caves were taken, Ruocco has a final great memory of Fuller. Suddenly Ruocco got orders to bring his barber tools; somebody wanted a haircut. About dusk, he came to Hq. through heavy security—MP's armed to the teeth.

Inside the tent, he saw most of our "big brass" from Division and the SWPA. He saw MacArthur, Eichelberger, Fuller, Doe, Sweeny, Coane, Maison and aide after aide after aide. Booze was abundant. Lights shone on a wall of maps.

Ruocco set up his chair at the end of the tent opposite the maps. Fuller asked, "Who wants a haircut? I got my barber here." After MacArthur said that he had just received one, Ruocco cut Eichelberger's, then Fuller's, then Chief-of-Staff Col. Sweeny's, then another general's. They all called one another by first names. They called Ruocco "soldier" and offered him whiskey also.

Ruocco knows that after he left them, the generals' meeting continued far into the night. This was the night he gave Fuller his last haircut, because Fuller left the 41st shortly afterwards. Ruocco remembers this generals' meeting as a good-by to Fuller.

After Fuller left the 41st, Ruocco still cut hair for Div. Hq. On our D-Day landing at Zamboanga, however, he was a battle casualty in an unusual way and had a complicated journey back to his outfit.

When his LCI lurched under near-misses from Jap shell fire on D-Day, Ruocco was climbing down a ladder into a barge. On the ladder above him, a Yank dropped a rifle on Ruocco's head. Knocked off balance, he fell 40 feet and hit the rail of the barge underneath. He passed out and came to on the deck of the LCI which he had just left. He was en route to a hospital ship, and back to New Guinea.

At 10th Evac Hospital in Hollandia, Ruocco suffered horrible pain at the base of his neck. He was temporarily paralyzed. It did not matter to him that New Guinea was not the same now, with war nurses and WAC's everywhere. After six weeks on a stiff board bed with plenty of drugs, he was released, although still wobbly. And he could not get transportation back to Division in the Philippines. He was told to find his own way.

To get started, he hopped an Army transport plane to Biak, but malaria halted him there. He was sent to 1st Evac Hospital. A Jap air raid hit the next ward and killed two patients. Released from the hospital, he emplaned on another air transport to Leyte, then to Clark Field outside Manila. No planes were leaving Clark, so he went to Manila, which MacArthur had just captured. There at Intramuros, with thousands of troops around, he was hard put to get a meal. But when mess personnel learned that he was a 41st man, he ate like a king, or as near like a king as Army cooks could serve him.

Back at Clark Field, where he slept on the ground, Ruocco learned that one plane was leaving. It was a Navy bomber heading for Australia to buy liquor. It would fuel en route at Zamboanga.

Introducing Ruocco to the gunner's blister, the Naval pilot said, "All guns are synchronized. If you see any Zeros, squeeze all triggers when ready. I'll notify when to put on the oxygen mask." He assured Ruocco that this was no joke and ordered him into the gunner's seat. (No doubt the pilot knew that no Jap planes were alive in the Philippines, but Ruocco never knew this until 1976).

Forty-five minutes later, Ruocco made his delayed arrival on Zambo soil and came home to his barber chair and Army details until the end of the war.

But neither Ruocco, Pierce, nor Senff ever saw Fuller again after he left Biak. He had been promoted. He was now Deputy Chief of Staff for Admiral Louis Mountbatten's SE Asia Command. Lt. Gen. Robert L. Eichelberger himself had wanted Fuller as a corps commander.

And these are Barber Ruocco's, Orderly Pierce's and Cook Senff's memories of the late Maj. Gen. Horace Fuller, 31 years later. They remember him as an emotionally restrained and respected general who respected and understood the men under his command.

41st Division Headquarters

General Fuller's Infantry Navy

By Dr. HARGIS WESTERFIELD, Division Historian,
with S/Sgt. JOHN MYERS, B Co. 116 Medical Bn.

The "Infantry Navy" of the 41st began after July 1942, when Gen. Fuller started our combat training at Rockhampton. He needed small, seaworthy craft to aid in amphibious training. And he also wanted these craft for antisubmarine patrols along the Great Barrier Reef. Jap two-man subs were playing havoc with shipping to Brisbane, to the extent that as late as Jan. 1944 the Dutch liner New Netherlands would dock no closer than Sydney.

Down in Sydney, the Aussie government commandeered boats for our navy. They requisitioned three private cabin cruisers—all over 40 feet long—and manned them with a special crew of civilians and soldiers, and brought them in short hops to Rockhampton.

Then we put the three cuisers on war footing at a small shipyard in the Fitzroy River. On the foredeck, we mounted a .50 HMG, and on the afterdeck, a .30 LMG. We installed auxiliary private gas tanks to afford the cuisers 10 days' cruising time at sea before they would have to return for refueling. We had to replace some planks in the hulls. And we sheathed their wooden hulls in copper against the teredo, a dangerous wood-boring shipworm.

For combat with submarines, we considering arming the little boats with depth charges, but we gave up the idea because of the danger. Their speed was some 20 knots, and the discharged ashcans would detonate too fast for safety. We needed a speed of 25-30 knots, or else risk serious danger to hulls and men.

But these were great little cruisers. No. 74 was longest—52 feet; Nos. 42 and 76 were 42 feet each. They were 10½ feet in beam, with a draft of four feet. All had twin propellers.

Inside they were luxurious, these former cabin cruisers of rich Aussies. Interiors were sheathed with teak and mahogany. Even dishes were monogrammed.

All three were compartmented like small floating hotels or luxurious old private cars on the American railroads. They contained cabin, salon, galley, wheelhouse, and bunks for 5-6 men. Exterior appearance of all three was dashing. Our CO, Capt. Skielvig, from 41st Div. Hq. called No. 76 "a long sleek gray job."

Meanwhile, the request for crews for our "Infantry Navy" had gone out. Personnel clerks culled their "rare bird" files for 41st men with nautical skills. First sergeants no doubt announced Gen. Fuller's need for experienced sailors. For our three crews we needed navigators, machinists (called "engineers"), gunners, cooks and medics. We needed two crews of four men, and one of five men—probably for that longer No. 76.

Senior NCO was S/Sgt. Myers from A Co. 116 Medical Bn., qualified both as medic and as navigator because of previous sea experience. (Myers was a graduate of a school for chiropractors.) Cook Adam Sax had been on the Matson liner Lurline. Besides Sax and Myers, these were among the first to report: Budge, Munneke, Guy, Kalen, Holmes and Andy Johnson.

Australia contributed a superpilot who knew the labyrinthine depths, shallows, shoals and islands of the Great Barrier Reef. The man was George Richmond, a fisherman who had owned his own boat. Over 45 years old, Richmond was 6 feet tall, weighed 200 pounds, and was an expert swimmer. He would dive from No. 76 down on a sea turtle and wrestle it into submission. In personality, he was always pleasant, kind, generous and pious. Above all, he knew the Great Barrier Reef—its shoals, its tricky currents and dangerous winds.

And now that "Fuller's Navy" was copper-sheathed, armed and manned, our duties began on the waters around Rockhampton. One of these duties was just a little off the record. Nos. 76, 74, and 42 were sometimes private cabin cruisers for the big brass. There generals, colonels and other top officers could relax from the tensions of command.

At one time, Myers' No. 74—on which Munneke was machinist—became a floating motel for some of the top CO's of the SW Pacific. Eichelberger himself, Gen. Fuller, Col. Doe and others boarded No. 74 for an "overnighter" down the Fitzroy River. We motored down the Fitzroy and anchored out in the stream far enough not to be spotted form the shore. Myers said that the guests consumed "much Johnny Walker medical supplies." After duty was ended, Myers said that "each crew" got a bottle for its uses.

When Johnson of the Judge Advocate General's Dept. and an unnamed finance officer got promoted, they also had a week's Cruise on Myers' No. 74. (And surely other high-ranking officers made use of the three cruisers. And did women—Aussie or Yank—

CREDIT: Total credit for this story is due to John Myers. Ltrs. were all in 1974—20 Aug., 10 Sept., 27 Aug., 4 Oct., and 8 Oct., plus undated MS probably in 1974. Myers supplied Col. Walter Skielvig's ltr. of 21 July 1955. Thanks also to George Jackson, secretary of 116 Medics' Chapter, for contacting Myers. (Myers was not with the "Navy" in New Guinea, and I had only Skielvig's letter to rely on. Can any reader help me with the story of Fuller's Navy in New Guinea?)

ever enjoy these parties aboard: civilian girls, nurses, Red Cross women? Not even a rumor of that sort came to Myers' ears.)

But "Fullers's Navy" had serious duties to perform on the Fitzroy River and out on the Great Barrier Reef.

Raw amphibian infantry of the 41st had to be trained for disembarking down rope ladders from merchant ships. In full pack on the way to battle, they must learn to disembark from sagging rope ladders into collapsible boats. We did not want panicked rookies to freeze on the ropes and block other descending men. Nor did we want them to step on hands beneath them and cripple those hands with GI shoes.

So 116 Engrs. built a simulated side of a merchant troop carrier down the river from Rockhampton. For conditioning in unloading, Division men under arms and in full packs made descents down rope ladders. They learned to grip the vertical ropes for safety from the descending feet of men above them. They learned to voyage in collapsible boats—20 to 22 men per boat.

"Fuller's Navy" had the duty of towing fully loaded boats to the far shore of the Fitzroy River.

One of those little trips was tragic indeed. On 11 Sept. 1942, an overloaded boat collapsed, and 7 men—probably of 163 Inf.—were drowned.

More would have drowned but for the bravery of men like Holloway and Sgt. Hughey of Hq. Co. 3/Bn. 186 and LaSalle of I-186, who dived in among the struggling Yanks. LaSalle dragged a man to the lifeline; others helped this survivor ashore. Hughey rescued another man, and Holloway saved a third.

The "Navy's" most fascinating duty, of course, was blue-water duty—scouting for two-man Nippo submarines in the labyrinthine Great Barrier Reef. Besides danger from Jap submarines, there was continuous danger from the Barrier Reef itself, skerries and shallows and currents and reefs. Its waters were vicious with unexpected high waves and hurricanes.

In those elusive islanded labyrinths, however, the "Navy" never saw a Jap submarine. And it may be by God's grace that no sub ever surfaced and fired on us. Our high octane gas made us deathtraps. One small tracer could have ended a cruiser's life—and the life of every man aboard.

Dangers of navigation were indeed great. In those days no accurate map of the reef was in existence. We sailed with information based on Richmond's fisherman's knowledge of the waters—and by dead reckoning. The small craft bounced too much and often forced us to grab for railings.

Myers never forgot one storm of hurricane force which caught them among the coral shallows in the Great Barrier Reef. Fortunately, each boat had extra anchors, and Myers' No. 74 had three. In that blast of wind, Myers thought it safest to down all anchors, and try to ride out the rough weather. For the wind had No. 74 caught in a pocket of deep water from which they could be blown into coral shoals that would rip out even the copper bottom.

Grim at the wheel, Myers felt two anchors and chains clink past the boat. Luckily, he had the foresight to attach a third anchor to a "cable-laid" line to ease the strain.

This last anchor and the cable held hard against the storm. But for 12 solid hours Myers gripped the wheel and kept the motor on half-speed to save the last anchor that kept him and his crew from drowning.

General Fuller with General MacArthur at Hollandia.

But in many ways, a 41st sailor in "Fuller's Navy" had the finest career a man could have in wartime. Despite the bounce of the light craft, waters inside the reef were too calm for seasickness. Fishing was wonderful. Choicest of catches were the bluefish, and the emperor fish that looked like a great goldfish. We even caught two giant sea turtles for headquarters' mess. Myers thought that the best fun of all was simply to bask in shorts out on the deck in the sun and dream of home. And the night when the big brass of the SE Pacific had their gathering, he was proud to guard for them.

But this wartime paradise had to come to an end for "Fuller's Navy" and S/Sgt. Myers. He was recalled to duties with A 116 Medical Bn. And the Division moved out for New Guinea.

Aussie George Richmond piloted little 76, 74, and 42 into the battle zone. Although other reef pilots said that he would lose at least one craft, Richmond brought all three cruisers to New Guinea without touching a reef.

In the Papuan Campaign, we used them strictly as survey craft and in carrying mail for troops in forward areas. And we had two deaths in line of duty shortly after Gen. Doe sailed in No. 74 to inspect defense positions. Names of these men are not certain, probably Sgt. Johnston and Clemmer.

Temporarily acting as cook on No. 74, Johnston was baking biscuits when a stove exploded. He had put the biscuits on a Coleman stove and placed it inside the craft's oven, which at that time was not working. The biscuits were getting the benefit of the heat reflected from the oven's sides.

Unluckily, he had closed the oven door—against which Act. Capt. Skielvig and Richmond had warned the previous cook. Nobody today knows whether or not Johnston knew of the warning, but closing that door meant death to two men. The Coleman stove melted in intense heat, and when the door opened, the gasoline tank exploded.

Flames seared the bare flesh of Johnston and Clemmer, both of whom had been in shorts in that tropical heat. They ran up the steps from the galley and collapsed.

Skielvig and his crew pulled the men free of the flaming galley. Foamite killed the blaze before it engulfed the main fuel tank.

No. 74 raced for help to the nearest installation, 10 minutes away. Skielvig grabbed a jeep and drove for help over a corduroy track to the nearest field hospital. He did not carry the men, for the jolting on their seared bodies would be murderous.

He returned with a doctor and medics who gave them morphine and plasma. But both Johnson and Clemmer died four days later in an Oro Bay hospital.

Off the Guinea Shore, the "Navy" had our one and only encounter with Japs. Returning with mail, Richmond on No. 76 was caught by a Washing Machine Charlie. Several bombs hit the waves just behind us.

Richmond drove over a reef and inshore and stopped, to be

less of a target in the phosphorescent waters. Being out of bombs or believing he scored a kill, Charlie departed. No. 76 survived. The timing was knocked off the motors, glassware was broken, but no man was hurt other than sustaining slight bruises.

About Aug. 1943, when the Division returned to Rockhampton, we had to leave Nos. 76, 74 and 42 for others to use. One, perhaps No. 76, "a long sleek gray job," went to a PT squadron. This naval outfit had been our comrades, and we were happy to give them our collection of tools. We had gathered more equipment than these PT boys had seen in ages.

We left a second cruiser at Oro Bay for the port commander. The third, probably No. 74, went to Oro Bay for the use of Gen. Eichelberger himself.

Such was the saga of Nos. 76, 74 and 42, sleek cabin cruisers of Gen. Fuller's bluewater "Infantry Navy." Nevermore have we heard of them since New Guinea, but we trust that they are still alive and that they still cruise off the coast of down under.

186 Infantry on Palawan in March, 1945

E Co 186th Infantry's First Blood On Palawan

By Dwight Shonyo with Franklin Sawyer and Dr. Hargis Westerfield

On MAR 1945, 3 days after 186 landed on Palawan, E Co's 2 Pltn entrucked for a routine patrol N of Irahuan on the Tagburos Trail. No 186 outfit had met trouble on Palawan; but CIC had found Nippo maps with circles on them. We probed into 'Circle X."

From the jungle hills, our trucks rumbled back, and left silence. Our scouts moved out. We slipped after them, rifles alert to fire. We sweated over a well-beaten path through bamboo. To the right stood a deserted cannon, to the left 2 camouflaged trucks, surely booby-trapped. The scouts nosed into an empty fox-hole on the hill above us, led us over the crest.

A booby-trap exploded too soon. From a gulley, a Jap screamed, charged with bayonet. Sgt Holston emptied an M-1 clip into him. A second Jap charged. Holston drew a six-shooter and killed him.

We had spotted the first Jap resistance on Palawan. Lt Reeves told us to circle the Jap area, return to Hq to report. We moved down a river-bed. The sound of Nippo chopping died away to the right. Tired and hot and short of water, we forgot the crossed cleavers on our helmets that promised death to the Japs who had burned alive 150 Yank prisoners on Palawan.

On high ground, we took a 90-degree azimuth to turn through a clearing with a hill for the coast. We filed slowly ahead. The point squad moved around the hill. Shonyo ached to recall them, but it was too late.

A thousand bull-whips cracked overhead; a Jap MG with Arisakas felled or pinned down the lead squad. We had 2 killed or dying, 3 wounded, F/Lt Reeves one of them. The whole Pltn hit the ground under fire. Shonyo rolled into an arroyo; he felt safer when Watkins, next squad's scout, moved into the same ditch with his TSMG. Sgt Holston slipped back unhurt, then Filipino Riviera, a lifer paroled from Iwahig Penal Colony to fight Japs. Riviera had fired up all of his carbine ammo.

Some 50 Nips with a MG were dug in to shoot down our throats at a move. Their main body lay close behind. An attack from our left rear would wipe out the Pltn.

Gamely, Lt Reeves lay in pain behind a log and called back to his message-center. Frantically, our radio cried for help from 167 FA on the coast. But their fire-control answered terrifyingly. They couldn't even find us on their inaccurate maps. And we cowered deep in Palawan's jungle hills with a heavy Jap charge coming.

Then a Piper Cub buzzed overhead. Some bright GI pulled out a mirror, caught the plane's attention by reflecting the sun at the pilot. The pilot radioed, "This is the Cub. I will guide your first round."

The first shell screeched low over treetops. Would it fall short among us? With a faint thud, a cone of smoke rose 100 yards right of target. From among the wounded, Reeves' voice was calling back to us. After Sgt O'Malley's correction on the radio, the second shell was left, but closer. Japs yelled. If shell No. 3 went wrong, they might charge.

The third shell blasted on target. "Fire for effect!" we screamed. The wind of each 105 pushed us prone men down, then pulled us up; it fluttered the tails of our fatigue jackets.

We planned to save our wounded. While Singer's picked riflemen blasted the Nippo right, 167 FA would fire smoke. Covered by frontal fire, an unarmed party would rush for the wounded. Many of us had trouble leaving comfortable holes; but Watkins, and a Sgt coaxed them to the take-off line. Matey, Sgt Musch, Watkins, Shonyo, another man prepared to rush for the wounded.

Finally smoke-shells exploded; our M-1's, BAR's struck the Japs' right. Over the crest dashed the 5 men, hoping the smoke would hide them.

But Shonyo nearly cried like a child as he ran. No smoke covered Reeves, and Shonyo knew that he must save him. Luckily the Japs thought we were attacking under the smoke and threw all their steel into it.

Shonyo still tried to save Reeves. Running at top speed, Shonyo could not feel his legs move. Yet one foot kept planting itself before the other; he ran on air down to Reeves behind his log.

"Are you hurt bad?" Shonyo called, hitting the ground by Reeves. "Can you move at all?"

One leg was grazed, but the knee-cap of the other leg was two-thirds shot away.

Shonyo thought of heaving Reeves on his shoulder. The blast of the Jap MG hurried him. In a split second, Shonyo decided that the easy fireman's carry was impossible; he wanted to save Reeves' leg. He turned Reeves over on the less injured leg, began dragging him by the shoulders.

Reeves had been hours on the ground. His body throbbed horribly with pain. He did not cry out; but his face turned whiter and whiter. Shonyo prayed that Reeves would pass out; but Reeves urged him on.

Now they were up and over the crest alive, with bullets barely clearing their heads. Shonyo fell exhausted by Reeves, calling for help. Some 3-4 men ran up to aid Shonyo carry Reeves to a safer place, assist the Medic to splint his leg.

Shonyo ran for his rifle. The shelling increased. But he found 2 rifles. "Which is my rifle?" he asked excitedly. "Get down!" we tried to warn him. A shell bowled him over; he thought he was hit in the spine; his finger touched the hole to feel the splintered bone. After he took sulfa, they carried him to a low place in the line of riflemen where he could lie safe as possible with the other wounded.

After withdrawing 2 hills off from the Japs, we lay in perimeter above ground and waited for help while still directing 167's shells wherever they could do most good. We were without entrenching tools; we were short of ammo.

The radio said, "Easy, this is Able Co. We are on our way to relieve you. Over." In 30 minutes came a request to lift FA fires, shoot an M-1 for direction. Our shot was answered, but at a distance; we wondered if it was Jap or Yank. A third call said that A was close, and to watch out for shooting a Yank, and to fire again. This time, we truly heard an M-1; 5 minutes later, A was there to take over.

Then came the relief of the wounded, by now 4. Shonyo never forgot the long carry by litter with 5 rifle-armed Medics or helpers. Once they bypassed 2 Nips whom they heard chattering. By 2000, Shonyo was last in line for surgery at 168 Evac Hospital. There he lost a piece of his back the size of a pork-chop. The shrapnel had severed his waist-belt, was found in his clothing.

Thus ended 186's first day of combat on Palawan, with Reeves' 2 Pltn of E Co in the catcher's position. Killed were Maurer, Sansbury. Wounded were Reeves, Shonyo, Huber, and finally, Scout Watkins who had first helped organize the rescue party and had shared in getting out the men already down. All 4 wounded lived. After 2 years' hospital, Reeves could walk despite his stiff knee. He was discharged as Capt. His wound still handicaps Shonyo.

Some of us veterans of Bald Hill on Biak said that Hill 1125 on Palawan was tougher. For it took all of 2 days more for 186's First Btn plus 167 FA plus Cannon Co to overrun Hill 1125.

On 2 Mar 1945, we were in contact with the Japs from 1255 to 1715, while 600 105's impacted them. That night while emplacing, the First Btn drew fire from 2 MG's and many rifles. On 3 Mar after more FA softening, the 1/Btn tried to storm Hill 1125 3 times. Heavy MG fire drove us back, but with minimum casualties. Our shells lighted off an ammo dump.

On 4 Mar, we began with FA; then Cannon Co brought up 105's and fired them "rumdum" pointblank into gunports until Jap riflemen seemed to run around in circles. Then mortars and MG's covered flame-thrower teams which reduced the first pillbox with its MG. After clearing the hill, we found several dead Japs, 2 MG's, a 20 MM dual purpose gun. Thus ended the first fight on Palawan, which E Co 186 Inf began.

CREDITS

Sources were 186 Inf's Report of Palawan Opn, ltrs from Franklin Sawyer, Dwight Shonyo (E 186). Although McCartney's history mentions E Co's first contact with Japs on Palawan, it mentions no casualties, asserts that the Japs got away in the dark, the same day. He omits all mention of Hill 1125 and the First Btn's 3-day fight with it. This reminds me that we still need more stories from 186 men—especially the First Btn.

HARGIS WESTERFIELD

186 Infantry and 167 FA:
THE PALAWAN STORY
By Dr. Hargis Westerfield, Division Historian

> *CREDIT: Main sources for this new Palawan story are untitled 186 Inf Journal (21 Feb-8 Mar 1945), "History of 167 FA During Palawan (V-3) Operation", "Report of Commanding General, Eighth Army on Palawan and Zamboanga Operations," Samuel Eliot Morison's The Liberation of the Philippines, RR Smith's Triumph in the Philippies, 186's "Battle Casualties 27 Feb to 27 Mar 1945," and 186's March Morning Report. Extremely useful were Probationary Medical Officer Tosimichi Urata's "Action of 3 Co (Tominaga Co) of 175 Bn," letter of Chaplain (now Lt-Col) Frank Trayler (12 Oct 1978), and "Guerilla Organization and Radio Communications," (27 Nov 1944). Dwight Shonyo wrote of E 186's first fight on Palawan (Jungleer, Feb 1962); Roy Bennett wrote of "G" 186 on Hill 1445 (Jungleer, June 1962). Shonyo's was first of 186's stories, now totalling 26, from Sanananda through Zamboanga.*

At 0650 28 Feb 1945, 186 Inf's 80-ship convoy of 8,000 men deployed at the throat of Puerto princesa Bay, mid-way on the east coast of Palawan Island. Missions were to seize an air-base 150 miles closer to the Jap life-line in the South China Sea, and to free the fifth largest Filipino island.

Bay shores were reported undefended, but Rear-Admiral Fechteler took no chances. After 2 days' XIII Air Force sorties, Rear-Adiral Riggs' light cruisers *Denver, Cleveland Montpelier*, and 4 destroyers salvoed for 15 minutes. (Jap sources reported that we had 2 battleships and an escort carrier!) By 0845, 186 Inf was landing at the end of the peninsula east of Puerto Princesa Bay. Gen Eichelberger watched from a B-17 overhead.

Although LVTs of 532 Amphib Engrs had trouble hitting assigned beaches, we fought no Japs. Beaching farthest east on the peninsula, 1/Bn rapidly advanced 8 miled north across the Air Strips and dug in on Irahuan Road on the NW side of the bay. Detached "C" Co hiked east to Canigaran Beach and took 3 deserted 20 mm guns before "I" Co from 3/Bn floating reserve relieved us. other 3/Bn Cos blocked roads to the north.

Since battered Puerto Princesa city was clear of Japs, 2/Bn (Less "G" Co and some "H" Weapons men in reserve) boarded LCMs at 1600 and crossed the bay. We hiked 2 miles through rice paddies to Iwahig. Next day at 1200, we contacted 1/Bn at Irahuan School.

There was still no fight; the Puerto Princesa plain was secure. But where were the Japs, and hw many were there?

Of the estimated 2735 Japs in the Palawan area, 1800 had garrisoned Puerto Princesa. The others outposted on little islands to guard the small ships en route to Luzon. Except for occasional patrols and raids to harvest rice, they left the interior to guerillas to govern themselves.

Hard core of Puerto Princesa garrison was CO Obayashi's 4 Co 174 Independent Infantry Bn less a Pln. Other outfits were 131 Airfield Bn, 1st Independent Maintenance Unit. CO Tominaga's 3 Co, 174 Bn was divided into Plns on outlying islands and never fought at Puerto Princesa at all.

Yet without air cover and FA, the 3 Puerto princesa units fought well--slew 10 186 men and a 167 FA man, and wounded some 35. (We also lost a "K" 186 man by drowning.)

On 2 Mar 1945, 1/Lt Reeves' "E" co patrol fought our first Japs--on Hill 1125 north of Irahuan. A booby-trap exploded too soon to slash Sgt Holston on the point of a patrol. When 2 Japs charged from a gulley with bayonets, Holston killed the first with an M-1, the second with a 6-gun.

To find liits of the Jap position, Reeves tried to circle the hill back to the coast. Suddenly a Jap MG and rifles shot down the lead squad, killed 2, wounded 4, Reeves included. While our wounded lay exposed, 50-75 Japs fired down into us. We expected a charge.

S/Sgt Tyrell of 167 FA radioed for gunfire, but gunners could not find our position on the poor maps available. Then Lt-Col Beach'es Piper Cub flew near enough to catch the sun on a mirror which some clever "E" man flashed up at him.

The Beach ranged in 105s on the Japs. "E" fought to save our wounded. While Sgt Siner's picked riflemen hit the Japs' right flank, Matey, Watkins, Sgt Musch, Shonyo, and another saved the wounded. Shonyo dragged out Reeves, but later took a back gouge from a 167 FA fragment.

Reeves lost 2/3 of a knee-cap, but later could walk with only a little stiffness. Shonyo had a "pork chop" sliced from his back. A bullet holed Huber through his left side. A fragment hit Vezane on the wrist. Watkin's type of wound is unknown. A neck wound killed Sansbury. After his first wound, Maurer moved and drew more fire that surely killed him.

The "E" Pln withdrew 2 hills off from the Japs while 167 shelled them. At 1715, "A" Co relieved "E's" Pln. "A's" Moulton was probably killed then. "D" Co's Fersch took a sug in left bicep, and McKenzie another in right knee.

On 3 Mar, "B" tried to take Hill 1125 where "E" fought yesterday. On our first attack at 0800, MGs drove us to the earth. After 167 FA's 1/Lt Ehrlich adjusted fire from "C" Btry, "B" Co attacked again. But MG fire from a pillbox halted us. A third time, after "C" Btry neutralized that pillbox, "B" tried and failed again. "B" lost Kimberly killed, and 4 wounded: Kilgore, Rauktis, S/Sgt Sorensen, and T/Sgt Moskila.

Only on the third day, 4 Mar, did "B" Co overrun Hill 1125 after FA, mortar, and MG fire. Using a flame-thrower, "B" took the pillbox by 1440. Our "C" 167 Btry had made a hit on it, and other shells had exploded nearby. "B's" Hiller was wounded. By 1600, Hill 1125 was ours. To help 1/Bn, "C" fired 341 runds in 3 concentrations on those die-hard Nips.

While "B" fought bloodily on 2-5 Mar, "E" Co began another action against the Nips on 3 Mar, and fought until 5 Mar. Near Iratag at 1430, "E's" advanced Pln occupied a position which Nips had just left. Food was still warm in a shack; cigarette butts smouldered. When the other "E" men reinforced us after 1600, Jap fire hit several men. Perhaps Harrington was killed then, and 4 others wounded: Nemyo in the calf, Sgt Mueller in the thigh, Creed in the chest, and Sliski in an unknown place. Creed survived his chest wound, after an operation. That night, Jap fire was intermittent on "E."

But next day, 4 Mar, "E" seized the Jap position without fighting, found a MG, a truck, and 13 dead Japs. On 0945, however, when we tried to occupy Firm Hill on our right front, Japs resisted strongly. After "CN" Co shells, we tried again, but a MG and other automatic weapons halted us. "CN" fired again; we attacked at once but failed again. T/Sgt Hopkins died there--a man said to have been comissioned Lt the day he died.

Patrolling 3 miles behind Hill 1125, "L" Co had 3 unfortunate casualties. At 0400 5 Mar, 2 men were wounded accidentally, and that mornig 1/Bn unintentionally shot another man. Landry and S/Sgts Lager and Letendre were wounded, but exact time and place of each man's wound are unknown.

"E" found Japs' resistance still so hard that on 5 Mar, 167's "B" and "C" Btrys plus "CN" Co and mortarmen planned a barrage together. Adjusted on target at 0715, we crashed down surprise fire at 0830. By 1145, "E" secured Firm Hill, without losses. Firm Hill had been Jap Hq for a large group, with motor park, food dump, and hospital.

On that 5 mar also, "G" Co replaced "E" and began battle for Hill 1145, the last stronghold on Palawan. Only 8 miles north of Puerto Princesa, Hill 1445 was a tall, blind jungle hogback under giant trees where Jap pillboxes were invisible. At once, a "G" patrol scouted up a pur of Hill 1445 through dense rain-forest. From a steep slope, MG hail drove us to cover--perhaps some 20 mm shells also. Our BARs and rifles sprayed the jungle but could not silence the guns. Our 167 FA silenced the Jap fire.

Probing on 6 Mar, we met that fire again. Rifles were useless against those 2 unseen MGs. Wounded were Schultz, Hubbard, 2/Lt Melton. Unable to pinpoint the guns, 167 FA blasted the trees overhead with delayed fuze.

With no regular forward observer close, Capt O'Laughlin, 167 liaison officer, volunteered to help "G" Co. Creepting to 30 yards of the strongpoint, O'Laughlin died in 43 minutes, a rifle bullet in his chest. "G" Co's S/Sgt Davis thought that the same bullet wounded his own foot. Radioman Gower observed for 167 FA until M/Sgt Weinberg replaed him, and then 2/Lt Bain. But FA could not find the pillboxes.

At 1850, 167 ceased shellfire, but "G" faled in another attack. Garoutte was killed and unrecovered. Hubbard had a bullet in his shoulder; Schultz was wounded, McCurly injured in action.

Withdrawing 150 yards into hasty perimeter, we guarded the narrow downhill trail with a LMG flanked by 2 foxholes for riflemen. Japs fired down on us that night, and charged with daylight at 0415. Our LMG slew 4 Nips and broke their charge. Two other Japs kiled themselves behind a large tree.

On 7 Mar, despite FA smoke markins, P-38s with 1,000-lb bombs totally missed Hill 1145. After FA and mortar shells, 1/Lt Kossl's 1/Pln attacked. MG fire killed Kossl; his dying body rolled behind a tree and took a final burst after death. A bullet pierced Engburg's lung. Ed James, Wallace, Drinkard, Mansfield, Rod Murphy were all wounded from "G"; "H's" Daily was probably wounded here also.

Despite our bloody repulse, 2/Lt Harbig's Pln brought good news. Harbig found a trail on "G's" left flank which Sgt Bennet's squad with Scout McQuaid leading, had traced to the crest of Hill 1145. Setting up a trail-block for the night, Harbig got a LMG section for secrity--and Capt Fulmer's order to fight up that trail on 8 Mar.

On 8 Mar, 167's "C" Btry precisely adjusted each gun. After removing a fre trees with quick fuze, the guns covered the forest with delayed fuze. At 1,000 yards, 2 guns of 186's "CN" Co fired directly into the hogback.

As Harbig lifted FA fire, his killer Pln stormed the hogback. Sgts Smith's and Atchinson's squad charged over the crest into the Nip foxholes. Scout Kirby's tommie slew Jap on the trail. The squad fired into Nip foxholes, heaped dead around at Jap MG that never got off a burst. Horn was "G's" only wounded that day. We found just 8 Jap dead, but "E" and "F" patrols saw clues of Jap wounded, walking or carried.

The small Battle of palawan ended, but hunting down the other 1900 Japs on the mainland and offshore islands never ended. This fith largest Filipino island (4550 square miles) is still frontier country--in 1945 with ony 10 people per square mile on the mainland. Although only 25 miles wide, it has a mountain core averaging 15 miles across. These mountains are a labyrinth of rainforest where Japs were elusive.

But we cann account for most other Jap infantry on offshore islands. Their duties had been as guard and port details for small Jap ships that came no longer. On 8 Apr, "F" Co with 2 "CN" Co guns and "H" weapons landed to clear Busuanga Island just north of Palawan. Here were grasslands for cattle and manganese mines. Near San Jose, an "F" patrol fought some 30 Japs, probably 4 Co 174 Bn with some navy men and killed 7 and routed them. Other Japs panicked into the hills. On 7 Apr, we left Busuanga to Filipino Capt Amores of Palawan Special Defense force, to hunt down over 1000 remaining Japs.

Our PT boats discovered a Pln of 3 Co 174 Bn on Pandanan Island just south of Palawan and smothered its return fire. After securing nearby Balabac Island on 16 Apr, a "G" rifle Pln and Weapons men landed safely on Pandanan 22 Apr, and found nobody. Japs sources say that the Pln was wiped out before "G" landed.

When orders had come for Jap HQ Pln and 2/Pln to gather with other outfits for battle at Puerto Princesa, they were far north on Palawan. Embarking in a sailboat and native canoes towed by a motor-boat, they could travel ony by night, and hid by daylight. Seeing our Navy blasting Puerto Princesa, they landed safely up the coast, and tried to reach battle by slogging through the mountains. Rations ran out. They stopped to forage, then heard of their defeats from refugees of 4 Co. From time to time, they fought Filipinos--often had to disperse and regroup in the mountains. Many died in action--or from malaria or starvation. Fighting became impossible; ony 22 men of 3 Co, for example, were known to have survived.

Our 186 Inf lost just 3 more. On 15 Mar, Herman James of 1/Bn was shot. "I" Co's Gilbert was wounded 18 mar, probably somewhere on SW Palawan where mountains come close to the sea. On 19 Mar, "K's" Campbell was trapped by a wave when he tried to walk between 2 seaside boulders. Dragged into the sea, he was hurled by other waves against cliffs and killed. Chaplain Trayler emplaned to the beach to conduct his funeral.

All important Palawan action ended by 8 Mar, however; most 186 men were not needed. Maj Pablo Myce's Filipino Special Bn, 1,000 strong, was fighting the Japs. By 18 Mar, all 186 men but 2/Bn and "CN" Co were reinforcing the Division at Zamboanga.

Of 2735 Palawan Japs, there were 502 known dead by 30 Apr, and 8 prisoners. Of 186's total of 11 dead and 35 wounded, "E" and "G" lost the most. "E" had 4 killed, 9 wounded; "G" had 3 killed, 12 wounded. "B" was third with 2 killed, 4 wounded. Thus, 3 Cos had 34 of our 45 Palawan casualties.

From Puerto Princesa Strips, our Air Force now slashed at Jap lines of communication from the East Indies, and sup-supported Army landings on Borneo. Our 186 Inf had completed assigned missions.

G. Co. 186 and 167 FA BN:

Hill 1445 – the Cockpit on Palawan

by DR. HARGIS WESTERFIELD, Division Historian
and SGT ROY D. BENNETT

On 5 Mar 1945, G Co 186 Inf with 167 FA's help began 4 days' fight to storm Hill 1445. Some 8 miles north of Palawan's key harbor of Puerta Princesa, Hill 1445 was the Japs' final stronghold—in wilderness behind Thumb Peak, altitude 3645 feet. Hill 1445 was a tall, blind jungle hogback where death lurked invisible.

Pressing up from 186 reserve at Puerta Princesa, G Co on 5 Mar relieved E Co which had captured Firm Hill in 2 days' fight. After advancing up a streambed to replace E Co, G Co set up CP at the intersection of another stream. At once, a G patrol struck up a trail on the left side of the stream's right fork. The trail left the stream and climbed a spur of Hill 1445.

Our file of rifles scouted through dense rain forest with some great trees. Slowly our scouts led around a giant tree and up a steep slope. A hail of MG fire drove us to cover—some of it perhaps 20 mm shells. Our rifles and BARs sprayed the jungle near those guns, but we could not silence them. We called in 167 FA shells to help extricate us.

G Co had found the final Nippo stronghold; and on 6 Mar our F Co cobbers sent a pln NW up Irahuan River to block the trails NW of Hill 2060. F's objective was to interdict the expected Jap flight from Hill 1445 to the west coast.

Simultaneously with F's move, G Co probed up that right fork trail again. With rifles useless against this jungle hogback, we fell to the earth when 2 HMGs struck down at us from the nose of that hogback. Since 167 FA could not pinpoint either HMG emplacement, our 105s hammered with delayed fuze. Jap fire wounded Lt. Melton; we evacuated him.

Safe under cover 75 yards from the Nips, G Co waited while 2/Bn Hq requested a FA observer to help our lead pln against Hill 1445. With no regular forward observer available, the 167 FA liaison officer volunteered to "sense" 105 howitzer fire to prepare for the attack. About 1330, O'Laughlin started his mission to help G Co. Accompanied by his detachment, he crept within 30 yards of the strongpoint on the dark hogback. But about 1410, a rifle bullet pierced O'Laughlin's chest and killed him. Probably the same bullet wounded G's Sgt Davis in the leg. Radioman Gower of 167 FA then took charge until M/Sgt Weinberg replaced him—and later, Lt. Bane. Unluckily, 167 could not find the pillboxes to kill them.

At 1850 that same 6 Mar, 167 lifted the barrage, and G attacked again. We failed again. Garoutte was killed; we could not bring out his body. Hubbard took a bullet in his shoulder; Schultz and McCurly were injured in action. As dark fell, we withdrew 150 yards, made a hasty perimeter with all G Co. The Nips would surely counter-attack before dawn.

We secured the narrow downhill trail from the Japs' hogback with only 1 LMG and a foxhole on each side of the LMG to protect it. But our perimeter was deep and strong.

That night of 6 Mar was wild; Nips fired down into us but hit no one. At 0415 when day broke, they crashed a charge down on us.

We broke that charge; we dropped 4 dead before our LMG. Then 2 Japs committed hari-kari behind a great tree. When T/Sgt Atchison, Sgt Smith, Scout McQuaid went up to check the Nip dead, more live Nips crouched watching us from the trail. They did not shoot, and we were ordered back to G's CP at the creek fork.

Then 2/Bn Hq called for an air strike. At 1300, P-38s of 13 AF ran over Hill 1445 with 1000-lb bombs. Although 167 FA had marked targets with smoke and had the Piper Cub up 5000 feet to spot the target, the air-strike was useless. The P-38s missed Hill 1445 completely. Two 1,000 lb. bombs straddled G's CP, far to the rear.

Prime credit for this full story is due Roy D. Bennett of Cutler, Ohio, with Ltrs 7 Feb, 4 May 1971, and his MS "Co G Fights for Palawan Hill 1445." To get his data, Roy called Scout McQuaid long-distance in Pontiac, Mich., then visited him and Ed Barosky in Detroit. Roy also drew a fine map of Hill 1445. Also useful was an earlier ltr from G's Jordan Davis, G's Morning Report, "Hist of 167 FA Bn During Palawan Opn," untitled Journal of 186 21 Feb-8 May 1945, and "Report of Com Gen Eighth Army on Palawan and Zambo Opns." Now who can tell me full stories of other 2/Bn 186 elements on Palawan? Roy is inspector for Ohio Dept of Highways and also handles weather reports for Ohio Highway Dept in winter.

Now Kossl's 1/Pln attacked from a distance of 1200 yards up that trail where we had been stopped before. Kossl called for and got mortar preparation, then pushed with 1/Pln. But deadly MG fire struck Kossl. He fell behind a tree, seemed to know that he was dying. He gave his field glasses and map to Pln/Sgt Atchison, told him to take command. As he rolled over, another MG burst struck his dead body.

Engburg took a bullet through the lung; James was seriously wounded. Wallace, Dinkel, Mansfield, Maybury were also wounded. A bullet hit the rim of Rod Murphy's helmet and cut his face. We saved all wounded, but Kossl's body was unrecovered.

Yet promise of success had come to Lt Harbig's 3/Pln. Harbig's men had scouted a trail they had found up the left fork of the creek. Their original purpose had been to intercept Japs fleeing from Kossl's attack that had aborted. After making a trail-block where the trail up the left fork cut another trail to Hill 1445, Harbig sent Sgt Roy Bennett's squad to reconnoiter that trail. When Scout McQuaid spotted 3 huts on the nose of the hogback which ended Hill 1445, we checked the huts but found no Japs.

It was near dark when Bennett reported his find to Harbig, and Capt Fulmer ordered Harbig's 3/Pln to fight up that trail tomorrow. A section of G's LMGs reinforced us at dusk. During the night, those 2 LMGs blazed out—killed a wild pig. Krauser almost shot a monkey.

Before 3/Pln's attack of 8 March, 2 105s of Cannon Co emplaced 1000 yards from Hill 1445 and blasted this hogback of hidden pillboxes. C Btry of 167 fired a precision adjustment with its 4 guns. Great limbs crashed from giant trees. Then 167 shifted to delayed fuze over the hidden Nips who must have been half-crazed by the amount of shell-fire.

While these 6 guns of Cn 186 and C 167 were thundering on the Japs, Lt Harbig's killer pln had stormed to the ridge-top, rifles ready. Harbig ordered FA fire lifted. Then Sgts Smith, Atchison charged over the crest with their squad into the surprised Nips.

A burst from Scout Kirk's tommie slew a Jap on the trail. Another Jap hit a hole to delay his death awhile. Into a perimeter of Jap foxholes charged Smith's squad. They fired into fox-holes—shot anything moving above-ground. Horn was wounded; but we found Jap dead around a MG that had never got off even one burst. In the perimeter, we counted 8 Jap bodies. The others must have surely escaped on a trail that G Co could not interdict—a trail from the hogback of Hill 1445 down the reverse slope. It would lead fleeing Japs to the west coast of Palawan and possible escape to Borneo.

And so these Jap survivors got clear away into the hills, safe from all pursuers. G Co men saw Japs dodge into the dense growth between Hills 1445 and 1460. E Co followed the valley NW; orders were to block all trails, but E found only where

Nippo wounded had fled. And F Co saw signs along the Irahuan Valley where Nips had carried off their casualties.

Thus ended the Japs' tight gallant little defense of Hill 1445 on Palawan—a defense presumably by 4 Co 174 Independent Inf Bn—since they were the only combat troops in the nearby area. (Other Japs outfits in the Puerta Princesa Sector consisted of only the 131 Airfield Bn, First Independent Maintenance Unit, with mixed personnel from Navy, Army, and Army Air force.) Against overwhelming FA superiority and G 186's men with high morale, these Japs had held 4 days in this well-chosen position, had killed FA Capt O'Laughlin, G's 1/Lt Kossl, and Garouette. They had wounded 9 of us, with 2 injured in action.

And why had G Co 186 Inf fought on wild Palawan, home of the Tagbanaua Moros, and far off on the periphery of Filipino civilization? Aside from keeping Gen MacArthur's promise to free the Philippines, and aside from cleaning up Nips who might have been nuisances, we had other good reasons. As the map shows, the 300 miles of narrow Palawan makes an almost continuous land-bridge north from Borneo. Jap planes and small boats had used Palawan as a stepping-stone to supply and reinforce Luzon and Leyte. The long coast-line had provided a sheltered passage and innumerable safe anchorages for small supply ships for the Philippines. Hub of this important communications link had been Puerta Princesa with 2 air-strips, a seaplane base, and a good harbor. And when 186 drove the Japs out of Puerta Princesa, G Co had followed them in and rooted them out. Such was G Co 186 Inf's last important fight overseas, with the help of Cn 186—and, above all, 167 FA.

Elements of G Co. 186, after landing at Puerto Princesa, Palawan, advance toward the mountain. Hill 1445 is in the background.

B Co. 162 Infantry:
Good Fighting at Zamboanga

BY DR. HARGIS WESTERFIELD, DIVISION HISTORIAN
WITH T/SGTS. DON BIEDEBACH AND ALLEN COOK

Prime inspiration is due to two letters: from Don Biedebach – Jan. 2, 1969; and Allen Cook – Jan 28, 1970. I used also the fine, detailed Opn Report of 1/Bn 162, and Overall Report of 162 with casualty lists. (We have no more full-length stories of the 41st in Southern Philippines campaign. Published were these E, G 186 on Palawan; B, E, F, G 162 with K 186, G 163, 146 FA at Zambo; G 163, 146 FA on Jolo; 3/Bn 163 at Riverside-Calinan. Only 12 of 108 stories are on Palawan, Jolo, Zambo, Riverside.)

On 10 Mar. 1945, about 0800, B Co. 162 Inf. unloaded on buffaloes for the dusty, battered foreshore of Zamboanga at San Mateo. Churning the surf to that palm-fringed beach, 2/Pln. Sgt. Biedebach and his men rejoiced that we could reach our first beach cover with protection from our Navy. But as we waded in, 1/Pln. Sgt. Allen Cook and his men looked apprehensively into the black slots of Jap concrete pillboxes.

Cook's whole pln. froze or flattened into sand, and T/Sgt. Cook's first scout turned to him for orders. (Our shortage of officers was such that a T/Sgt. commanded 1/Pln.) "Let's go!" yelled Cook, and we were up and at those pillboxes. To our surprise, they were empty!

With A Co. on our left, and 2/Bn. 162 on our right, B's little squad-columns pushed inland. Behind B, C 162 went left and set up a roadblock against flank attacks from Caldera Point (until F 162 could push through us and break up that Jap concentration).

And B with A abreast pushed easily inland for 1,000 yards to seize the abandoned Wolfe Airfield. Ground opposition was negligible; B killed just one out of four Japs killed by all 1/Bn. that first day. B Co. lost S/Sgt. Vandiver killed, and Stinger and S/Sgt. Jim Cook wounded.

As we watched his pln. front for Nips, Cook had a hair-raising scare. He felt a hard prod in his back. A stateside recruit had an M-1 muzzle pressed into Cook. Carefully drawing aside, Cook saw that the recruit had his safety off, ready to kill. We evacuated this strange character back to Medics.

After finding an abandoned Jap hq. and taking some documents, B contacted Japs about 1600. By now, our 1/Bn. had crossed Wolfe Airfield, and before us was a great impenetrable swamp – a disused rice-paddy 200–300 yards north of the strip. And at 1600, 1/Bn. began digging in for the night.

But Biedebach's 2/Pln. could not dig in safely. Instead, we got a fine bit of combat conditioning under Jap fire on the first slopes of a ridge behind Zambo. During the final daylight, we had orders to set up a strongpoint on B's right flank – isolated from all other units. Probably 2/Pln's mission was to interdict any possible Jap attack around the end of the swamp protecting 1/Bn. frontally.

The tropical night was falling, and we lacked time to dig deep into the hard ground. Some of us managed shallow holes, but with the night and the unknown closing in, Biedebach ordered a stop to digging and all other noises.

Some 20 per cent of 2/Pln. were green, and Biedebach doubted whether he had adequate perimeter discipline. He doubted whether we would obey his direct warning not to fire except at a real Jap assault.

About 2000, Jap MG fire opened up in the blackness. Beginning some 100 yards left of our men who often lay unsheltered above ground, the MG raked our position, then traversed to the right 100 yards past us. The gunner seemed unsure of our location. Their tracer bullets revealed that they were firing 50 yards behind us on another ridge. When shooting ceased, Japs shouted obscenities, dared us to fire back. Their shots were sporadic all night, and Biedebach was proud of his canny 2/Pln. that held fire and did not needlessly locate us for Jap infiltration.

But what strange type of an MG were the Japs using? To our T/Sgt. it sounded like a BAR; it certainly was no Jap weapon he knew anything about. Next morning, he ordered Sgt. Taffe to take a recon patrol and find out what type of secret weapon had fired on us last night. Although he encountered no Japs on this patrol, Taffe did turn up the drum of an obsolescent Lewis MG from the conquest of the Philippines in 1942.

On 14 Mar, B Co. with 1/Bn. started to push on Mt. Capisan – the Japs' main stronghold NW of Zambo. While 2/Bn. moved on the eastern of two roughly parallel ridges heading for Capisan, B Co's 1/Bn. scouted to take up a position on what 162 was to name West Ridge.

On this 14 Mar. B Co. was point for 1/Bn.; and Biedebach's 2/Pln. was point for B Co. When we reached the first high ground with no opposition, Biedebach was suspicious of the Japs' evident permission to move into the rough country. B seemed to have full freedom to maneuver. Then we saw the Japs' reasons for letting us into the mountains: Our new position was on a pimple half-circled by high points 400–500 yards away.

Then Jap fire broke out, drove 2/Pln. to cover. But 3/Pln. on our right was more exposed. It now seemed folly to try to advance farther downslope in the face of plunging Jap fire – and folly to try to hold this exposed ridge. Biedebach sent a runner to advise B's CO Jim Gray of 2/Pln's predicament.

Orders came back from Col. Benson not to give ground. So Biedebach contacted 3/Pln's Sgt. Larkins, whose men had now come forward upon this exposed ridge, and helped them to get cover. (Larkins would die near Davao.) As yet, B had no casualties.

Guarding B Co's rear with his 1/Pln. in comparative safety, T/Sgt. Cook saw Col. Benson go forward on our left flank. Then Cook heard Benson's heavy body thud to the ground. A rifle bullet had struck him an inch below the heart. We carried Benson out, but this great veteran of G Co. 163 Inf. at Sananada and of 1/Bn. 162 on Biak would live to lead again.

But 2/Pln. and 3/Pln. were still in jeopardy from Nips who were

A convoy, carrying two regiments of the 41st Infantry Division (162 and 163), approaches the beaches in the vicinity of Zamboanga. It was a clear, sunny morning.

firing down our throats. The new Bn. CO, Benson's former executive, now came up to examine our position. Medics evacuated the aggressive Benson. The new Bn. CO realized at once that it was not worth even one man's life to maintain that target range we had set up for the Japs on their mountains. He ordered a withdrawal.

While Biedebach set up all BAR's to fire periodic bursts on Jap sources of trouble, 2/Pln. and 3/Pln. crawled to safety. By 1900, all men were out except good leader Biedebach, whose duty was to be the last man to leave.

Then a Jap bullet struck him in the shoulder. Sgt. Hodgins helped him out of that trap of an exposed pimple. The pln. runner then conducted him to B Co's rear where 116 medics did a tremendous job of lifting him up the next ridge. All that night, he lay on a stretcher in the medics' perimeter and listened to the firing where nearby C Co. stood off a dire attack. Biedebach would get as far as Mindoro for his hospitalization before he would rejoin B some months later.

Also wounded 14 Mar. were Aaron Cook, Sheridan Hall and Cliff Lyon. On 15 Mar. Simon White was wounded.

On 16 Mar. in the black night between 0200 and 0400, some 50 Japs struck hard in two assaults on both B and C. Long before attacking, they sprung our booby traps. Then they hit B Co's front. With a heavy concentration of B's 60's, and D's 81's, and FA also, we blasted them off and killed an estimated 20.

Evidently this frontal attack on B was a decoy for a more desperate strike against C. Before they attacked C, these Japs took off their shoes and bound their feet in rags. They fixed bayonets and went in for bayonet-work with no thought of surviving after they charged in.

Thus C met a well-planned attack of nearly 50 Japs also. This well-organized detachment was divided into three commando groups with three different missions. No. 1 was to kill C's MG's. No. 2 was to wipe out C's Headquarters Pln. No. 3 was to destroy 116 Engrs' two bulldozers with high explosives. Charging up the brand-new supply road that 116 Engrs had conveniently finished for them yesterday, they broke into C's perimeter, drove for the CP, and caused many deaths. Capt. Krist took a bayonet wound from which he never fully recovered. That night, C Co. lost five killed: Sullivan, Layne, Colucci, S/Sgt. Larry Myers, Sgt. Bowman. Sumpter died of wounds. Besides Capt. Krist, C had five more wounded: Glen Hansen, Brownhill, Lt. Peters, S/Sgts. Azevedo and Falgout. But C beat off attacks on weapons pln. and bulldozers and next morning counted all of 25 Nippo dead.

And on 16 Mar., B lost three killed and three wounded when an 81 mortar shell burst among 1/Pln. men. Killed were Shumate, Berry and S/Sgt. Seibert. Wounded were Borrell, Arsaga, Woodson. Later, the hardest job T/Sgt. Cook ever had in his life was to collect the three dead Yanks' personal effects and label them and turn them over to Graves Registration for mailing to the three dead men's homes.

But now B joyfully heard that E Co. was relieving 1/Bn. from this deadly position below the Nippo ridges. Since we were most exposed, B Co. was the last of 1/Bn. to leave. As the other rifle companies moved out, B halted a small Jap attack at 1115 – no doubt a probe to find out what 1/Bn. was up to.

Before leaving our front, B Co. had prudently sent back a security detail to post an HMG in the old A position, perhaps to forestall Jap infiltration into 1/Bn's rear. After beating off that small attack at 1115, we left our forward perimeter at 1300 to wait for E Co. take over from us at 1330. B was happy to escape this cockpit of battle for 162 at Zambo. We'd have been even more happy to escape if we knew what 2/Bn. had to undergo before it stormed Mt. Capisan eight days later.

Some time afterwards, B learned that 1/Bn. left West Ridge because Division wanted to capture Basilan Island. Division had to redeploy units to get a spare outfit for Basilan. After changing fronts, 1/Bn. teamed with AT 162 and thanks to flight up San Roque Valley and drive the battered Japs NW into an encirclement which other units would complete.

Despite the power of our Victor IV Task Force, the San Roque Japs, some of them Naval Guards, battled courageously. They still had land mines, and at least one FA piece and one 20 mm gun that were hard to range. On 18 Mar., for example, they disabled a tank, killed one C man and hospitalized four more C men.

And B had more casualties. On 17 Mar. Eaches was killed – last death in B Co. at the Zambo fight. Wolfe was wounded. On 18 Mar., Sgt. Abrahamson and Collier were wounded and Torres injured. On 19 Mar., Braun, Will Williams and Maddox were wounded. And on 20 Mar., it was T/Sgt. Allen's turn to be wounded, along with Dickey and Alvardo.

This 20 Mar. was so quiet that a man might write letters home – if he had anything to write with. Just as a "Spanish lad," who was

Helpless service troops watch a fuel dump go up in smoke on the southern edge of Wolfe Airfield. The dump was hit by a Japanese artillery shell.

surely Alvardo, came over to talk to Cook, Jap mortars fired from close in.

One shell exploded near their feet on Alvardo's side of the trench. Knocked out for a split second, Cook heard Alvardo's cry of anguish. Alvardo started crawling away. Thinking himself untouched, Cook and his buddy dragged the badly injured Alvardo back to their hole and called for medics. Dickey was wounded also.

Then Cook saw blood on his own combat boot. A fragment was lodged near the tendon in his calf. Although helped out by two medics, Cook thought the wound was light. Down at the schoolhouse hospital, the doctors took out that fragment but missed another fragment. After Cook believed that he was healed and began to hobble on crutches, infection and fever of 104° set in. Although the leg healed well, Cook found himself ticketed for the USA and permanently out of World War II.

On 22 Mar., T/Sgt. Larkins was wounded but still on duty. On 25 Mar., Sgt. Barrett was wounded – the last to be hit in B at Zamboanga. And by 28 Mar. San Roque Valley was so quiet that 1/Bn. left to patrol in the Pitogo River Valley, with the exception of B Co!

B got the idyllic mission to garrison Basilan Island – that paradise of plantations and pretty Filipinas, which stretches like a great purple pavilion over the waters to the south of Zamboanga City. Then B's battle for Zamboanga was ended.

B 162's tour of duty at Zambo was not too hard. Our well-timed withdrawal from the pimple on West Ridge, after Col. Benson was wounded, no doubt saved many lives. And our drive up San Roque Valley was against Japs already much less aggressive than in the days when their marines pushed L out of San Roque Village. But even at San Roque, we believe that B had comparatively few losses because of our seasoning in New Guinea and our fine discipline. Still to win the battle for Zamboanga, B Co. 162 Infantry lost five killed in action, and 21 wounded and hospitalized.

Zamboanga, D-Day' + 1: LST's unloading the 41st Division's equipment and supplies.

DISASTER at ZAMBOANGA

By T Sgt. WILLIAM DOESCHER
with
DR. HARGIS WESTERFIELD, Association Historian

Five days after Zamboanga Beach-Head, E Co 162 Inf and 6 tanks attacked Nippo hills at San Roque Village west of Zambo City. Tank 75s smashed 2 Jap bunkers on a low northern hill. T/Sgt Wm Doescher's 3/Pltn raced up to seize the Jap trenches.

But a ditch stopped 2 accompanying tanks. Heavy small arms and MG fire kept 3/Pltn low in brush. A Jap Pltn attacked up the low saddle ahead, almost got to us. Pltn Guide S/Sgt Gartman pushed Franzen's and Zebelian's squads to the edge of the brush. Our M-1s blew the Japs back. Each time he felled a Jap, Conley gleefully signaled his kill back to Doescher. Below the hill to 3/Pltn's right, intense fire sprang up between 2/Pltn and more Japs.

Doescher saw E's chance to wipe out these fully committed Nips — despatched runner Roy Mason for all E Co plus 4 more tanks to envelope them. But F/Pltn and 4 tanks were wasted against an unheld ridge. And loaded on these tanks were all E's LMGs and 60 mm mortars.

A Jap squad struck 3/Pltn again. Layton took a bullet in his throat — to die on an LST on the ocean days later. Franzen's and Zebelian's squads killed the attack. Franzen's tommie slugs blew up the satchel charge on a Nip's belt. The blast stunned both Yanks and Japs.

Below to Doescher's right, 2/Pltn chased Japs in 2 hours' running fight until intense fire from high ground stopped us. We fronted pillboxes. With fine cover fire, Langham hurled grenades to soften Jap defenses. He charged a pillbox of mangled Japs, bayoneted a gunner. When 2 Japs in the next pillbox shot at us, he turned his Jap MG on them, slew both. Thus 2/Pltn smashed their line, but resulting over-confidence may have caused disaster 21 Mar. But remaining Japs withdrew next day.

Thus E on 14 Mar drove a deep wedge into Jap lines, and on 15 Mar, AT took high ground on our right to widen the wedge. Japs still held hard, however, on East and West Ridges protecting Mt Capisan. Meanwhile, E Co had idyllic days pulled back to quiet West Ridge. Then, the night of 17-18 Mar, a stray bullet killed Juhl sleeping alone in his hole.

And E's idyl on West Ridge was over; we had attack orders for East Ridge — against a position which G Co had probed for a week.

On 21 Mar, E Co dismounted from trucks by G's perimeter on East Ridge and scanned a higher wooded pimple 700 yards NE. Heavy, concealed fire had met G patrols every time. Now E Co must storm it alone — although G's Capt Feddersen had had repeatedly warned Hq that Jap concentrations there were formidable.

Despite pleas from Lts Belikove and Archie Smith for permission to run just one quick recon patrol, we fought that pimple blind. Btn CO Caulfield remarked, "I'm going to side-slip an E Co Pltn onto that hill." E Co's attack began.

After a Marine air-strike and FA, E Co moved out NW of G's perimeter to intersect the ridge in dead ground away from the Japs. MacKay's 2/Pltn led; followed 2/Lt Dikeman's F/Pltn, then Bill Doescher's 3/Pltn. LMGs were back with CP; mortars stayed with G. Two Jap .80 mortar shells totally missed us.

E safely climbed that ridge curving SW from the Japs. On the ridge, we were covered by a knoll 150 yards from them. Now Lt. MacKay's 2/Pltn pushed on the Nips as ordered — without recon — or further advice from CP. Disaster ensued. Some Japs fired, but expert scouts like Langham silenced them or got 2/Pltn unhurt past fire-lanes. Then 2/Pltn halted before a hedge of tall trees. It was an impassable barrier of willows planted by a farmer long ago and grown tall and thick in tropical luxuriance.

Absolutely essential were T/Sgt Bill Doescher's 16 pp MMS plus 3 maps and several letters — all written in 1966. Next in importance was Lt. Archie Smith's ltr 20 Apr 1965, Col Richard Feddersen's "G Co 162 Inf Conquers Mt. Capisan," and background material including Langham's DSC Award Story, and 162 Inf Report of Operations (1945). Bill is a Commercial Reporter for Hooper-Holmes Bureau, which serves the Insurance Industry as Dunn & Bradstreet serves the credit world.

MacKay ordered 2 Yanks to chop a hole through the willow barrier with machetes. They made a small opening, and 2/Pltn filed through man after man — all the time under perfect observation from the ridge itself and a second Jap pimple 200 yards east across a draw. When 2/Pltn was all through but still not fully deployed, a stream of fire from a Jap MG closed the gate. Japs shot us down like caged animals inside that willow

207

fence — raked us with MGs, the new Jap .30 rifle — aimed fire such as E Co had never met before. Most casualties were shot in head, shoulder, chest. Lt MacKay died first; Sgts fell early; casualties piled up.

A runner got through for help — not for reinforcements but for evacuation of casualties. Instead, F/Lt Belikove ordered in 2/Lt Dikeman's F/Pltn to win the fight. Intense fire had made the willow barrier easier to penetrate. But Dikeman's Pltn met a bullet-hail, was halted and decimated. A storm of bullets enfiladed us from the pimple across the draw on our exposed right flank. The Japs made full use of our costly failure to reconnoiter.

Past Doescher's unfought Pltn on the knoll came a stream of hobbling wounded and Yanks carrying bodies. T/Sgt Robinson came crying with corpses of Keith, Vallier, once young princes of Sergeants. Bieber was carried piggyback — shot through chest and right shoulder — finger-size bone fragments protruding from a great hole in his shoulder-blade. Busby and Sgt Whitley had scalp-wounds; Whitley walked unaided, but Busby was led along in shock. T/Sgt Jim Anderson was wounded. Now Dikeman's men were coming out. Unaware of a bullet in the abdomen, Dikeman rushed down for an M-1, ran back to kill a Jap, returned with another bullet in the same hole before he let himself lie on a stretcher. Migliore tried to stagger on a leg that Medics would amputate.

E's surviving 3/Pltn got orders to extricate the shattered remnants of 2/Pltn and F/Pltn. Doescher questioned surviving NCOs about locations of casualties, ordered Franzen's squad to bring out all bodies, dead or alive. He formed his last 2 squads ahead of our knoll to meet the expected Jap counter — his brother Dick's LMGs set for overhead fire above him.

S/Sgt Franzen was shot in the throat while he led the rescue party. He could never talk above a whisper after that day. When the casualties were drawn out, Exec Archie Smith sent in men to retrieve or smash our abondoned rifles. While Rowe's squad covered withdrawal, E withdrew under .81 smoke shells. A heavy rain chilled survivors.

On this disastrous 21 Mar, E Co had 6 dead, 13 wounded. Besides MacKay, Keeth, Vallier, died Keeling, Hampton, Arvon Johnson. Besides Anderson, Whitley, Bieber, Migliore, Franzen, and Dikeman, also wounded were Tomas, Hulse, Moyer, Harbin, John Owens, S/Sgt Robertson. Next day, shock and other causes would chop Dikeman's Pltn to 12 effectives — and dead MacKay's to 6.

As the dark came, 105s fired concentrations on the Japs, and then 155s crashed in. Firing each heavy 155 alone, the observer sniped down every large tree. After 105s' harassment all night, E's hill was nude at dawn and F's badly scarred. Now Cn 162 shot at 800 yards, while 14-16 Marine Corsairs laid 500-lb bombs on our hill. Daltry saw Japs' bodies fly up. One pilot fouled his bomb on the front shackle of his plane. He turned over the plane, secured the bomb, flew back and dropped it. But another pilot bore his wobbling bomb back on E Co — drove us to earth with an impact 200 yards off.

Now Doescher's unbroken 3/Pltn marched first. This time, he got Weapons Pltn next behind him with Sgt Corbell beside him. Trailed behind them shattered Pltns — Dikeman's down to 12, and dead MacKays down to 6. Wounded or shocked men had dropped out.

As E started, a veteran runner collapsed against a tree, cried, "It's a trap! They'll kill us all!" E hardly moved before others in Doescher's intact Pltn dropped rifles and ran in hysterics. Doescher tackled each man, held him to see he was incoherent, let him run. They were old-timers shot over too often.

E again sideslipped to the same unguarded part of the Japs' ridge, again filed unhurt to the knoll we had fought from yesterday. Here we emplaced weapons, formed Doescher's Pltn with a squad across the ridge, the others in squad column on each flank.

"Fire a clip and let's go!" he told the front squad. They fired but didn't go. He called Gartman to urge on the left while he urged on the right. The squad would not move. He slung rifle, cut a switch, went alone. He looked back at unmoving men. Finally, he lashed the rears of 2 chicken pvts. We started.

At the shattered line of willows, we executed unresisting shell-shocked Nips in their holes. A little Jap threw back Durante's grenades until Durante held his live grenade long enough to detonate on impact and kill the Jap.

Despite Belikove's agitated orders, we snooped each hole carefully. Dick Doescher's LMGs fired overhead. Then, some 20 feet below the crest of the knoll, Belikove yelled "Charge!" F/Pltn's Heath or Miller — both died that day — was first on the crest. An unseen Jap shot him dead into a foxhole.

Portland chapter trophy for efficiency among present units of the 41st Division is present to Hq Btry, 41st Div Arty, by chapter commander CHARLES PAUL (218). At his right are Association past president LLOYD BRYANT (218,205) and Col. ROLAND JENSEN (218), present commander of 41st Div. Arty. The trophy is being presented to the battery commander, Capt. CHARLES D. YOST, Jr. Other chapter members attending the ceremony included RON URICH (Hq-218), BOB STITES (218), and ALMA HUNTER (186).

The military crest was a long, boulder-strewn outcrop. Men tried to fire over or lobbed grenades but dared not cross. Too far left, Lambiotte got a bullet which rolled up sheet metal on his helmet, yet merely cut his scalp. Doescher ordered mortarfire. Observer Jarvis terrorized us; he miraculously cleared the crest with 3 rounds on the Japs. We feared trying more.

With 3 KIA, 9 WIA, F now had the hill on our right, and demanded that we take the reverse slope. Our Japs still shot into F's backs.

Doescher told 3/Pltn to crawl in line for the crest. With Zebelian on the extreme right flank, Doescher rounded the shoulder. Zebelian turned on his side to speak. A Jap fired. At 8 feet, Doescher looked into Zebelian's eyes in death: saw intense surprise, then almost joy, then a rapid gentle glazing of the eyes. It was the easy, sweet death of a devout Catholic.

To get Zebelian out, we covered with smoke grenades, and Sgt Wm Reid dragged him back. But E could not cross that crest. Jap fire was light and inaccurate, but we must expose ourselves individually yet could not return fire. Dick Doescher grew so angry at F's and Hq's demands that he set up Sanderson's squad with gunner Crandall to fire a belt from the exposed crest. They shot a Nip who ran in the open, but E Co could not clear that reverse slope. We lost Lowe, Flyzik, Holmwood, others from battle fatigue; Al Miller, Heath, Zebelian KIA; and Hahaj, Earl Peterson, S/Sgt Vantta WIA. Compared to yesterday's loss of 6 KIA, 13 WIA, on 23 Mar we had 3 KIA, 6 WIA. Sgt Conaway had the top shot from his helmet but grinned unhurt.

That night, E bedded down on that bare slope in little stone forts, but we did not hear the Japs steal away. We probed at dawn to get no Jap fire. When the KP's brought hot coffee, we drank like nectar what we had thought we would never taste again.

So ended E Co's Battle of Zamboanga — surely the heaviest combat of any 162 formation there. Fighter Langham would die 18 Apr when Japs slipped between 2 patrols on the same trail and provoked a fire-fight. In all Zambo Fight, E lost 12 KIA, 19 WIA, far more than any other 162 formation. Yet with three great attacks including the disaster of 22 Mar, E Co was still a lucky outfit.

F Co. 162 Infantry:
RIDGE BATTLES AT ZAMBOANGA
By Dr. HARGIS WESTERFIELD, Division Historian
with T/Sgt Chester Young

At 0932, 10 Mar 45, battle-loaded F Co 162 Inf splashed from LCI 774 into deep seas, and floundered for Yellow Beach 2 at Zamboanga. We dragged out several dripping F Co men. While 162's other bns drove for Wolfe Field and other 2 Bn outfits secured the beach, F had a special mission. Now named "Ratliff Force" along with 2 Bn's AT Pln, F Co was to secure the 41st's rear. We were to seize Sinong River Bridge 1500 yards west of San Mateo and hold there.

At our landing beach, Jap mortars impacted close, but did no harm. Regrouped at the road junction, F hiked west on the beach 1200 yards. Mines were everywhere. At 300 yards from Sinong River Bridge, Jap fire signaled that we were outnumbered. After taking up defense positions for an attack that never came, we probed across the Sinong with S/Sgt Shea and two squads.

From commanding ground with a 500-yard view, Japs waited grimly. When Scout Misiewicz checked some locked outbuildings of a farm, Jap fire cracked down, wounded Shea in the leg as the 2 squads took cover across the road. Misiewicz made a tourniquet for Shea, then raced back along the beach for help.

Returning with Allison, Mach, and an Alligator, we tried to save Shea. As we tried to get him into the Alligator, more Jap bullets hit Shea. A head wound was mortal. Joe Mach was killed; Allison was wounded, to die later. In getting out Shea's and Mach's corpses, Marufo and Lindsay were wounded. This fight lasted 3 hours.

Next day, an Alligator ferried Lt White to our Navy offshore, to direct support fire on the Japs. (The Division had learned much from its mistakes at Parai Defile on Biak.) Sgt Chester Young now led Shea's former Pln behind the sea-wall on the beach, to where we could jump off behind naval gunfire and rockets, to storm the Jap ridge.

But the Japs had fled. Leaving 2/Pln to guard Kawit Village, F Co dug in on Caldera Point at 1108 13 Mar. Maidwell was wounded. Previous air strikes had left nothing on Caldera Point but steps and fragments of a cement building. By 1445, F Co was relieved. K 163 took over, to furnish security for Seabees making a base.

By 15 Mar, Ratliff Force disbanded. F Co rejoined 2/Bn, which had to face vicious Jap opposition in the push up from Masilay Village, over East Ridge, to ultimate capture of Mt. Capisan, the final Nippo strongpoint.

But while E and G Cos of 2 Bn battled East Ridge before Mt. Capisan, F Co had another special mission, which was more pleasant than seizing Caldera Point. We headed the assault against great Basilan Island — which spreads out like a luxurious purple pavillion 10 miles south of Zambo City. At 0805, 16 Mar, F Co embarked for Basilan — with 1 section H Co's HMGs, 1 section H's 81s, 1 pln Cannon Co, 41 Recon, and a detachment of JASCO for liaison with Navy and Air Force.

At 1130, Lt White's and Sgt Young's 1/Pln landed unopposed on a "sort of a dock" — the only safe place on the rough beach. While Lt Hansen's and T/Sgt Hansen's 2/Pln took Lamitan village, a little way inland, White's 1/Pln patrolled the beach. The men enjoyed the taste of real "shell eggs" which grateful native families gave them.

Since 2/Pln was unopposed at Lamitan, 1/Pln took a HMG and an 81 mortar for another beach landing — around the north hump of Basilan Island at Fort Isabella on 18 Mar. Despite 1/Pln's apprehension at being isolated from the main body, our dock landing was unopposed. We landed just 150 yards left of a fine old Spanish fort of stone, with a moat around it, but no Japs held the fort.

From 17 Mar through 20 Mar, F Co helped guerillas rehabilitate civilians. Collaborators were punished. Guerillas tied the puppet governor "Chee Chee" to a pole in the center of the square and tortured him. Chee Chee took 3 days to die. But guerillas claimed he had ravaged loyal Filipinos far worse. The guerilla Lt said that Japs had killed his sister just 2 days before the landing — to punish the Lt for helping the Americans.

F Co could have fought the "Battle of Basilan" indefinitely, but on 20 Mar, we left only 3/Pln for security and mopping up. Just before departure, Lt Hansen investigated smoke on the beach and took bad burns from explosion of a phosphorus grenade.

And F Co was back into the front-line hell of 162's push on East Ridge. When E Co ran into its disastrous ambush of 21 Mar, F Co began a fight more desperate than at Caldera Point. F's Capt Gerlach detached Young's 1/Pln to help Capt Belikove's E Co, after a deadly morning that cost E Co 6 KIA, 13 WIA. By the time Young arrived, F could only help get out wounded and salvage equipment. We saw an E man come back who had been left for dead — stunned or unconscious or shamming death under the eyes of Jap killers.

When 2/Pln arrived at E's perimeter also, Sgt Chester Young greeted his brother Lester who carried a litter. That night, 1/Pln and 2/Pln doubled up in the same holes. This was the first time the two brothers had guarded at night in the same hole. It was to be Lester's last night alive. E's Pruitt was killed — probably that night.

On 22 Mar, F made its toughest attack of Zambo Fight — against the ridge to the right of that ridge where E Co took its defeat. Both 105's and 155s smashed E's and F's ridges all night. This morning, Marine Corsairs dropped 500-pound bombs. E's ridge was bare, F's badly scarred.

At the appointed hour of 1030, F Co attacked its ridge, but E Co on the right failed to come up. While Chester Young's 1/Pln struck right around a small pimple on the ridge, Roy's 2/Pln moved around on the left. About 1132, F drew MG fire and returned that fire.

But by 12:15, F had reached its objective; Sgt Young's and Sgt Johnson's plns had started around the hill in opposite directions and were in contact. F had no casualties. Chester Young had just talked to his brother Lester who was Sgt of Johnson's lead squad, and had learned that the two plns' scouts were in contact. All was going well.

Meanwhile, we could not learn what E Co was doing. Then suddenly E moved and took Jap fire. Then Roy's squad and Lester Young's of Johnson's pln delivered support fire to help E advance. They tried to find and kill a Jap MG that held up E Co.

Then Jap fire crashed down on Johnson's pln. Lester Young's squad had gone too far ahead into an exposed position, and it was slaughter for that squad. Sgt Roy started in to help them, but an F Lt ordered him to hold back. (T/Sgt Johnson must have been killed about that time). Roy ordered up 2 LMGs and 2 BARs and thought that his men cut down every remaining bush on the E ridge to root out the snipers.

Christodolov set up his BAR between 2 rocks and called out: "Lettum come! I gottum covered!" As he turned, a Jap rifle bullet drilled both helmet and head but did not kill. A Jap sniper singled out Roy. The first bullet hit a tree before Roy's face; the next cut off a shoe-string. Roy threw himself safe into a bomb crater.

When Jap fire struck Roy's 2/Pln, Chester Young thought a Jap MG was atop F's ridge. But he bravely crossed that ridge top to get back to his own pln and found no MG. Word came to Young that 2/Pln had lost 5-6 men, including medic Hatton. Young's own pln medic, Robert Dunlap, went where F Co needed him.

Dunlap brought out several men. Suddenly the call came that Lester Young was hurt, and Dunlap ran in to help. Sgt Young also started for his beloved brother, but Lt White and Sgt Prielipp held Chester back. They told Chester Young to return to CP and see his brother there.

When Dunlap got to Lester, he bandaged the boy's head. The sniper struck again, and Dunlap fell dead over the dead body of

Sgt Lester Young. Surviving Chester's world seemed to end right there; his twin brother and he had been inseparable throughout their lives. He fell to the ground.

From encouraging F Co, able 1/Lt Gerlach lifted Chester and took him to a safe place where the medic tagged him and sent him to hospital for sedative shots. And 2 days later, Chester assumed the hard duty of writing to Mother, to get the news in ahead of the cold, formal telegram from the War Department. Mrs. Young was already ill. A month after Lester came home for re-interment in Sept 1948, Mrs. Young died.

Lester Young had been one of the fine NCOs of F Co — a fair man who assigned details strictly in turn. Lester was the kind of soldier whom CO Gerlach would place in a Pln — along with his brother Chester — to help break up a personal clique of its leaders. Although several F men owed Lester $200-300 at his death, he had asked that their debts be forgiven. F Co will never forget this gentle and brave soldier.

On 22 Mar when Lester Young died, F had 4 KIA, 10 WIA — in contrast to 3 KIA and 2 WIA at Sinong Bridge. Besides Young, Johnson, Dunlap, we lost Rivera. Besides Christodolov, wounded were McCaffery, Baker, Jensen, Zulave, Hanson, Jackson, London, Madison. And Chester Young was out with battle fatigue. 1 Lt Barnes WIA.

But these were F's last Zambo casualties. Although Japs still held the reverse slope on E's ridge which enfiladed F Co, they quietly retreated by daylight 23 Mar. Unimpeded, F now advanced to the junction of the ridges and contacted E moving up the other ridge. About 1000 yards north, an F patrol lashed out at 30 Japs, slew 1 before we made perimeter. And on 24 Mar when G overran Bald Ridge and charged up palm-topped Mt Capisan, F seized a spur on the left of Bald Ridge, then reinforced G for night defenses, where Japs killed 2 H Co men in a final attack.

Such was F 162's main Battle of Zamboanga. After a bad first day, we were lucky to get assigned to capture Basilan Island. Came then the hard fight of 22 Mar where Lester Young and other good men died. For F Co, Zambo was not so protracted and bloody as Salamaua or Biak. But — as we did at Hollandia, on that one disastrous patrol of 23 April 44, when Lt Polimac and 8 men died — we met agony and wounds and death at Zambo — with 13 wounded and 8 men killed.

First honors are to T/Sgt Chester Young's Ltrs 4 Mar 1970, 25 Sept 1970, and 5-page single-spaced MS. Casimir Misiewicz helped with an undated ltr in 1970. Chester and I both used 162's REPORT OF OPN 10 MAR — 2 MAY 1945, 2/Bn 162's JOURNAL beginning 10 Mar 45, CASUALTY LIST, medal stories of Allison, Gerlach, Misiewicz, T/Sgt Jack Roy's Ltr 10 Mar 1970 details action of 2/Pln 22 Mar 1945 when Lester Young died. Thanks also to Mjr John Jacobucci for 3 fine Zambo maps. Also useful were previous JUNGLEER articles: Col Dick Feddersen's on G 162 (Vol XVI, No 4) and Bill Doescher's on E 162 (Vol XVIII, No. 2) I still need H 162's and Hq 2/Bn 162 stories.

G Co. INF Conquers Mount Capisan

BY COLONEL RICHARD FEDDERSEN (ARC)
WITH DR. HARGIS WESTERFIELD, HISTORIAN

At 0932 10 Mar 45, G. Co 162 Inf's Higgins boats broke for shore at San Mateo Beach west of Zamboanga. Capt. Feddersen's barge grounded on a bar. We waded in hip deep. Peering through rocket smoke from craters, the CO with his lead squad struck inland past wrecked Zambo' Country Club.

Unknowing, we crossed the First Phase Line; Jap mines had obliterated the road marking it. A MG felled S/Sgt DiLaura with a shot through the leg. In a crater with our CO, he ignored the medic at his leg, pointed out the MG. A squad flanked and killed the MG and a Nip. By the road, Feddersen nearly tripped on dead Gerold Gordon — a MG bullet through the head. Bob Carr was also wounded.

Next day, tanks and mortars helped us clear the coast ridge. Then FA asked G's help: 2 mtn guns 300-400 yards ahead had blasted the 41st supply dump. In 15 minutes, binoculars found the Jap observer tied to a tree with his phone. At 200 yards with M-1, our CO nailed his corpse to the tree.

On 12 Mar, our CO stared through binoculars at an unarmed Jap camouflaged in a cornfield — who also stared back through binoculars. Btn Hq wanted prisoners. Lt Muzall tried to take him from behind with a patrol, but we kept a LMG on him. The Nip turned to run when he heard the patrol. Our gunner fired the LMG; the Nip blew up in all directions. He had lashed a mine to himself for a suicide rush. G voted to take no prisoners.

On 14 Mar, G relieved C Co at Masilay Trail Junction. We had to begin the push to East Ridge. A "C" Co corpse huddled on the dark trail forward. At once, our CO sent F/Lt Osen to take his Pltn and a Hutson squad against the ridge — a move C called deadly.

After careful recon, shrill blond dynamic Osen pushed down a draw, past a left ridge, seized a knoll below East Ridge above the Trail Junction. Osen lost no men, killed 4 Nips at a MG on the knoll, dug in beside the dead gunners still at the MG. That night while the CO felt helpless at CP, Nips hit Osen's 4 squads. But F/Lt Wingo with G's 60s and Lt John Smith with H's 81s shattered Nippo rushes. At dawn they fled, left 3 dead 20 feet from the holes.

Our CO took all G except Wingo's 60s with security, to save Osen. From the left ridge, a MG hit a Yank. Two wounded ran down to report Osen heavily attacked, cut off. Our CO checked the panic, led G to dash across the trail opening. But the MG wounded Weapons' T/Sgt Shaffer. Feddersen spotted the pillbox on the ridge at 150 yards. A rooky bazooke man put his first rocket into the slot, silenced it forever.

Feddersen found Osen at home with his depleted 4 squads, with 21 dead Nips. G rolled the Nips downhill, enlarged perimeter. On 15 Mar, we had lost 9 wounded: T/Sgt Shaffer, Sgt Rutka, Siarkoski, Lander, Flowers, Harold Thompson, Coffman, Diniwiddie, Goraczniak.

During 15-20 Mar, G held Osen's Knoll. From East Ridge, snipers drew beads on exposed spots in our perimeter. Day and night we skirmished. At night 15 Mar, they attacked, cut wires. Next day, we found and destroyed their former Yank 75. Marine bombers hit the ridge; our flank patrols slew 17 Nips. Stafford was wounded. On 17 Mar, B-17s impacted 7200 pounds of bombs 250 yards off. Our patrols sallied to kill 3. But at 1320, snipers wounded Dudley and Wirth — shoulder and face wounds.

Next attack started 18 Mar; 2 Nips leaped into a hole 75 yards above us — a G Co mortar concentration area! We blew them out. At dark, Jap MGs marked our flanks with tracers. Japs massed and chanted on the ridge above. Sgt Lehmann guided FA upon them. H's Smith impacted 81s. Japs still broke in. One fired 2 pistol shots at Feddersen, holed his mess-gear. The Jap leaped into the next Yank hole, died from TSMG slugs pointblank. Firing over us at the

---

CREDITS

Brother Florian Donatelli so loved his brother Tony that he inquired of Oregon National Guard Bureau how Tony died in battle. The Bureau contacted JUNGLEER. Prime sources are Col Feddersen's unpublished MS, and ltr dated 2 June 1964. Feddersen and I both used also (untitled) Journal of 2 Btn 162 Inf at Zambo, "162 Report of Casualties 10 Mar — 2 May 1945, S 162 Report of Operation" (same dates). Feddersen drew the map. Feddersen joined 162 at Roosevelt Ridge with rank of Captain, took over G 162 on Biak. He is now President of Nall Motor Co., Iowa City, Iowa. So far, only Zamboanga stories available for JUNGLEER are Feddersen's story, the G 162 story, the 146 FA story. Help, please!

ridge, Filipino soldiers (121 Inf) also fired into us. But the Nips fell back with moaning wounded. We had 1 wounded that night, 1 on patrol next morning — Klebonis, Barton.

So for 5 long days, we held Osen's Knoll under sniper fire from East ridge. Once Osen crossed perimeter under fire to save 3 wounded. On 19 June, after another air-strike, 2/Lt Kalled V. Kalled (AT 2 Btn) observed for his 37 mm cannon to lash those deadly snipers. As he lay in a slit trench, a Nip probably saw the sun flash on his binoculars. The bullet pierced his forehead — this tall dark hanndsome Yank who was perhaps Arabian and Moslem. Kalled's avenging 37s smashed a pill box fronted with 4 16 inch logs, silenced ridge snipers with canister. But next day, a Jap mortar wounded Lowe and Flowers in the same hole.

By now, 162 Hq saw that G fought the anchor of the Nip defense of Mt. Capisan — fully a Btn of Japs. Terrain was impossible for tanks. So 162 gathered all 2 Btn — E from West Ride, F from Basilan Island. On 21 Mar, E grouped behind G's perimeter to take East Ridge. G started it; we blasted a 5-man Nip patrol, killed 1, picked off 3 snipers.

E did get to the top of East Ridge — with air-strike, FA, G's fire support. E made 800 yards — into heavy frontal fire, MG enfilade from the right. Major Caulfield withdraw E— with 6 KIA, 13 WIA. That night, Nips hit G's holes, wounded Robertson, Lockridge.

On 22 Mar, E plus F and a G Pltn attacked again. Besides Marine planes, FA, Cannon Co's assault gun did direct fire at 700 yards. We took East Ridge. E had 3 KIA, 3 WIA; F, KIA, 9 WIA. G lost Nieto wounded, shared a kill of 20 with F. But at 1530 next day, a Jap MG hit Farmer at our CP.

On 24 Mar, G attacked Bald Mtn — the last strongpoint guarding Division's Task Force objective — Mt Capisan. At 0845 from F's position on East Ridge, we scanned Bald Mtn. Its pillboxes on the crest shook from FA, 81s. HMG fires criss-crossed the forward slopes.

Without adequate recon, Feddersen has orders: attack at once to get full benefit of 162's heavy preparation. Muzzall's Pltn led; followed Hutson with out CO, then Osen. We climbed at first under jungle concealment, overhead fire.

Jungle cover ended 600 feet from Bald Mtn's summit. Muzzall deployed his Pltn as skirmishers to drive for the top. Hutson's Pltn came up on the right. A Nip MG raked us, wounded 2 Yanks — 1 through the head.

Sgt Lehmann fired 2 MGs from our flank against the suspected MG next — a thatched hut on the ridge-nose. Tracers marked hundreds of rounds shot into the hut. It blew up in a cloud of thatch — a hut full of land-mines. But bullets still whined; Cannon Co blasted into ridge pillboxes that still shot at us.

Although briefly checked when 3 wounded men panicked, Muzzall's Pltn attacked. As FA fire lifted, Japs bolted from holes — up and over Bald Mtn. But Muzzall's shouts and hand-signals to rally the Pltn had marked him. A die-hard Nip in a hole killed Muzzall — a bullet in his chest. Another Yank killed the Jap. A second Yank was now dead — Donatelli struck through the forehead — and 3 wounded.

Heavy fire-fight began. Many Nips died, but Muzzall's Pltn was badly shaken up. Hutson got orders to move to the right; but Nip — or perhaps Yank — light mortars halted his Pltn. Just then, a runner reported success on the far right. Previously ordered by Muzzall, Dillard took a reinforced squad behind Bald Mtn and routed the Nips there. Feddersen instanly ordered Osen's Pltn to strike left around Bald Mtn to contact Dillard. G Co had won Bald Mtn.

Our CO found Dillard with TSMG staring at dead Japs far down Bald Mtn's reverse slope. They heard Japs running away downhill, or dragging moaning wounded up a little stream bed NE. We hurried up to MGs to blast any noise or movement.

And standing on Bald Mtn above a carpet of dead Japs, Feddersen and Dillard beheld a massive unknown tropical peak — still palm-topped, but brown and shell-torn. Log bunkers and trenches guarded its summit. From a lower two-thirds of rain-forest, the next attack — we hoped it wouldn't be from G Co — must climb past caves over open cogon grass under the pillboxes' crest. Not yet did G realize that this was Mt Capisan — Division Task Force Objective!

Mjr Caulfield congratulated G Co — and asked G Co a favor. Could we scale Capisan now — before the whole Nip Army poured in to make it Roosevelt Ridge all over again? If we did not take it today, we might have to fight Capisan many days. G forgot thirst, fatigue, fear.

An hour after winning Bald Mtn, G moved out below air-strike, FA shells, HMGs raking the draw NE of Capisan. Morale was high. When Japs fired near a hut under Capisan, Hutson's men slew 12-13 Japs, yet had no losses. Our CO said, "Take Capisan!"

Now G almost run—past Jap voices and caves probably mined. But the Japs were only wounded and aid parties. By 1530, G was two-thirds up Capisan; the pillboxes on the crest lowered over us.

Suddenly a runner brought bad news to Feddersen, 3 squads behind Hutson. A heavily armed Nippo column was pushing around Capisan on a collision course. But the Nips were noisy, unalert. Our CO had kept G silent and ready.

Instantly Feddersen thought and struck. He ordered Hutson, Osen, Dillard (with Muzzal's Pltn) to hurry our rifles to the top of Capisan. But he pulled back all BARS and MGs to tear apart the Nippo column. As our automatic crews

Zamboanga beaches on fire Mar. 10, 1945

ran before him on their mission, he radioed for all available help — even called for medics and litter-bearers. Caulfield saw from Bald Mtn; he called down FA shells at once.

G's automatic fire crumpled dead the point of the Nippo column; FA turned the others into corpses or scared fugitives. And above on Capisan, Hutson's rifles were killing Nip outguards, while Osen and Dillard shot stray Nips on right and left slopes and climbed with Hutson. In the bright mountain skies with the sparkling ocean in view, we grenaded pillboxes, left shrapnel-pocked scarlet dead. Most of the Jap garrison had hidden from our shells on the reverse slope. Now they looked up at tall Yanks firing down their throats— and fled if they lived. G had but 1 wounded on Capisan— just 4 wounded, 2 killed all day. Wounded were Kammerling, Bryce Dixon, Skow, M/Sgt Cunningham; but dead were Donatelli, F/Lt Muzzall. In a bitter night fight, the Nips would come back; they would score 3 casualties on 3 H men at their HMGs — wounded Aragon, killed Haggard, Henry Smith. But the Jap night attack failed.)

But that moment in the light on the summit of Mt. Capisan was one of the greatest in the life of G Co — Go Co 162 Inf which had stormed Roosevelt Ridge and infought for Mokmer Dromes on Biak. Before Capisan, in 2 weeks' combat, with but 3 KIA, 29 WIA, G had by actual count killed 119 Japs, plus a share of the 216 killed while we fought beside E and F Cos. On Capisan, we captured 3 20 mm guns, 1 HMG, 2 LMGs — and put 1 LMG back to fighting Japs. Of 14 KIA plus 42 WIA in the whole 2 Btn in the push on Capisan since 20 Mar, G had but 2 KIA, 8 WIA. In the 2 hard preparatory days, E and F had 5 times our losses and had seriously hurt the Japs. But G Co had begun the fight for Capisan — and finished the fight for Capisan. G Co had had good luck in fighting the Japs; but luck was not enough. Battle wisdom and heroism had won Mount Capisan.

L Co. 162 Infantry at Zamboanga:

San Roque and Sibago Island

By DR. HARGIS WESTERFIELD, Division Historian
and L Co's 1/Lt. DAVID CAMACK

On 10 Mar. 1945, L Co. 162 landed after heavy bombardments at San Mateo Beach, about 3.5 miles west of Zambo City. We pushed inland unopposed through silent Jap trenches with pillboxes, many intact from gunnery and bombs. At 1220 with 3/Bn. we advanced from temporary positions around NE end of Wolfe Strip. Orders were to skirt east end of swamp near Wolfe Strip and occupy San Roque Barrio, about three miles away.

Thus "L" began our Southern Philippine Campaign—against Japs supposedly less tough than the hardened veterans of Salamaua and Biak. Organized in the Philippines in 1943, Lt. Gen. Tokichi Hojo's 54 Independent Mixed Brigade was a miscellany of garrison units, fragments of other commands and replacements. Mostly lacking combat experience, they still had Jap courage. And like the Japs of Cebu City, 54 IMB held some of the best defences in the southern Philippines. On a front five miles wide, often three miles deep, they had barbed wire, extensive minefields and plenty of automatic weapons, mortars and FA. They had 56 20mm guns and 23 75cm cannon.

Yet on this first day, opposition was slight. Out of 11 3/Bn. casualties, "L" had three marked lightly wounded: Hopple, S/Sgt. Peiffer and Capt. Goggin. After fighting a few rearguard Japs, 3/Bn. bivouacked south of San Roque Village and that night endured only slight harassment from night fighters.

Goggin was replaced as CO by 1/Lt. Camack, exec. officer of I Co., on 11 Mar. L Co. moved through low, wooded foothills until about 600 yards south of San Roque. Patrols reported Jap defenses ample for a regiment, but we made just slight contacts. "L's" Sgt. Campione was lightly wounded—out of only four in 3 Bn.; of whom one died. That night, Japs against harassed.

On 12 Mar., our 3/Bn. began its real action against the great San Roque strongpoint. First, I Co. moved 2500 yards north and seized a trail junction at a village which we renamed Harlowton. Here I Co. blocked a NW-SE trail joining a southward trail. We interdicted the main Jap front. Eastward, one main Jap body faced 163 at Pasananca. The other Jap group faced us men of 162, extending from San Roque north and west to the Sinonog River and the final stronghold of Mt. Capisan.

L Co. readied to attack San Roque. This village area was bowl-shaped, about 1,000 yards in diameter, and surrounded by rising ground. Here the Japs had almost completed a naval forces headquarters—numerous offices and barracks, even with running water. It was an area of trenches, bunkers, and pillboxes, notably on the south road. North and NW, two adjoining valleys held a large hospital, a plane-parts dump and several shops. Both valleys were strongly fortified. Our air strikes had levelled most buildings.

Thus, San Roque bowl was an excellent position for Japs to conceal a large body of troops. It was also excellent for a stubborn defence, or a massed counterattack.

On 12 Mar., "L" went up against that concealed threat. Specifically, we had orders to seize one of the ridges overlooking the bowl. If we held the ridge, we could cover other 3/Bn. men's entrance into the bowl.

So CO 1/Lt. Camack sent a recon patrol to find the best avenue of approach. The patrol was also to report whether one ridge would be a safe position for "L".

The patrol found the approach from the south safe enough. Even though brush was heavy and entrenchments ample for a whole Jap regiment, the patrol saw only a few stragglers. But it erred greatly—selected a ridge too small for L Co. to occupy. Only a few men could see from it to cover 3/Bn's advance into San Roque.

When he moved "L" up to the ridge, the alarmed Camack wondered why Japs had let L Co. get even a foothold. The knifelike ridge was too narrow and too short to hold. Only a few men could actually look down on the town. A pln. could hardly find space on it to dig in, let alone all of L Co.

CREDIT: Most important sources were ltrs. of Dave Camack (12, 23, 27 July 1972) and his notes to my ltr. of 18 July 1977. Important were Award Stories of Bentley, Camack, Geske, Rummell, Stokes and Waynick. Rest of this I pieced together from 162's "Report of Casualties", 162's "Report of Operations, Zamboanga Area, Mindanao," and "Headquarters 41st Division Artillery, Narrative Report of Zamboanga Operation." Thanks also for Major John R. Jacobucci's "Special Report No. 68" on Zamboanga (14 Feb. 1945) from Allied Geographical Section SWPA. Credit is due also to U.S. Eighth Army's "Operational Monograph on the Zamboanga Sulu Operation."

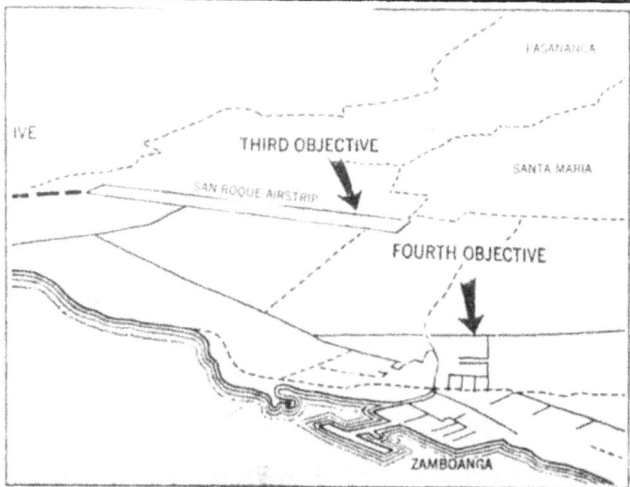

Camack had to spread "L" out over 100 yards of second growth.

At once, Camack phoned 3/Bn's CO that this terrain was useless to protect an advance. And this ridge was impossible to hold. L Co's right flank on the ridge was open to fire from higher ground. And that high ground was now coming alive with Japs. Directly in front of us, Japs were occupying a ridge 200 yards away.

But 3/Bn's CO seemed unimpressed by Camack's report of danger to L Co. Camack had orders to do everything possible to hold his ground.

Already, Jap fire had begun from the right flank of "L's" short and narrow ridge—against an exposed squad probably in Lt. Geske's pln., dug in 10-15 feet from Camack. From the forward ridge at 200 yards, sporadic fire also struck at us. L Co. was already in a bad spot.

We could not clearly see those moving Japs in the brush and behind ridge crests. We could only fire in their general direction with our small arms, "L's" LMGs and two of "M's" HMGs. We had set up one "M" HMG to fire from the left front of our ridge, with five protecting riflemen on the top close by. Despite our failure to discern individual Japs, Camack would later find that we had hit some, however.

First death in all 162 Inf. at Zambo was of 1/Lt. Bentley, bn. communications officer. He had volunteered with "L" for liaison and observation. Twice he traced a broken phone line 30-50 yards while fully exposed to Jap fire. This time, he moved into the open for 100 yards to mend the break. An allegedly stray bullet killed Bentley. Others were wounded.

Camack finally persuaded 3/Bn's CO that L Co. was uselessly exposed and got permission to retreat. With 1/Lt. Geske, Camack ably organized the withdrawal, despite mounting Jap rifle fire against our ridge. We were lucky that the Japs were firing only small arms. With MGs or mortars, they could have maimed or killed many more.

Camack's first duty was to save M Co's two attached HMGs. To protect them, he set up our two L Co. LMGs in final protective lines, with covering riflemen. And 1/Lt. Geske with 1/Lt. Rummel—hardened old vet of C 163 at Sanananda—risked Jap fire while they tried to extricate other men unaware of our retreat order. FA now fired smoke shells over our retreat to conceal us from Jap plunging fire.

But one group of six Yanks was still isolated in firing positions and unaware that Jap killers were moving in. Stokes and Waynick dodged back from tree clump to tree clump to spot the six men and recall them to "L's" covering force.

Among last to leave, of course, was CO Camack. All wounded got out. Camack became one of a party of eight— he remembered youthful Calvin Young among them—who gathered rifles some men had dropped. Besides the walking wounded, men helping the wounded had dropped rifles— no doubt on orders. As many as eight may have been wounded; two more fell from heat exhaustion.

When Camack reported in person to bn. CP, a visiting brigadier general complimented him for setting up his fine delaying action to protect our retreat. More important to Camack, however, were the profuse thanks of M Co's Lt. Walt Kelly for saving his two HMGs and their crews.

On that 12 Mar., "L" had nine hospital casualties. Bauder was seriously injured. The other eight hospitalized were marked lightly wounded: Griego, Jamison, Epstein, Horner, Amaral, Waldecker, T/5 Gagliardo and Sgt. Weaver. Two more were heat exhaustion casualties. (On that 12 Mar., only other 3/Bn. men to suffer were from K Co. with five casualties—but three of them killed.) We were unsure, however, if all of "L's" casualties came from that San Roque ridge. For that night, "L" repelled an hour-long attack, which could have caused some of these losses.

Yet 41 DivArty's "Narrative" differently records L Co's San Roque fight of 12 Mar. DivArty said that at 1400, we repelled 800-1000 Jap Marines, in a situation so fluid that FA was useless to assist L Co. It added that at 1645, Japs expelled us from San Roque, which we retook within hours.

But 162's "Narrative" numbers the Japs not as 800 but 300. And Camack did not even have FA observers with L Co., for 162 had not planned to use FA in attacking. For another, 162 Co. was to seize another ridge in front of L Co. to work with "L" to mortar down the Japs in San Roque bowl. Moreover, "L" and other 3/Bn. units never did take San Roque. Orders came next day for us to bypass San Roque, while E Co. with tanks and AT Co. choked out resistance.

With other 3/Bn. men, "L" reinforced I Co. at Harlowton NW of San Roque. We became part of a 162 encircling movement against the main Jap body opposing our regiment on the western front above Zambo. We were to drive the Harlowton Japs NW to their strongold of Mt. Capisan.

On 13-15 Mar., all 3/Bn. had few losses—and all of them in "L". Weis, Stewart and S/Sgt. Kliever were lightly injured in action; one of these men with a sprained ankle. On 14-15 Mar., we lost none—with only an "I" man injured in all 3/Bn.

On 16 Mar., "L" occupied I Co's perimeter while "I" and "K" abreast attacked the first hilltop NW of Harlowton. Here two Jap co's resisted until 1125 next morning. Counted were 40 dead Japs; certainly many more were killed and sealed inside caves that we blasted shut. Inactive that 16 Mar., "L" lost none; "I" and "K" together had five dead, 15 wounded. On 17 Mar., our Sgt. Losinski was wounded from a stray U.S. plane bullet; other 3/Bn. outfits had only two wounded, one injured.

On 18-19 Mar., we captured two steep hills and had almost all of 3/Bn's casualties. On 18 Mar., "L" advanced about 700 yards NW against some Jap opposition, including mortar shells, and secured the next hill. We contacted 163 Infantry from the east. Although "I" and "K" together lost just one killed and one wounded, we lost Costello (killed) and nine wounded. Lew Wilson was recorded seriously wounded. Lightly wounded were Kramer, Trager, Foreman, Grazer, Archie Kelley, T/5 Hattabuch, Sgt. Beck, S/Sgt. Blumenfeld and Ed Wilson. On 19 Mar., we took another hill to the NW, with fewer losses. Lightly wounded were Karam, Conley, Weldon, T/Sgts. LaVelve Davis and Blanchard. Rest of 3/Bn. had an injured officer.

On 20-24 Mar., "L" was part of 3/Bn's continued advance along with 162's other two bns. and 186's 1/Bn. against Mt. Capisan. On 22 Mar., our bn. stayed in place for FA and planes to pound Capisan. But we lost O'Neal Wood seriously wounded and Goedecke dead of wounds.

When a three-pronged drive stormed Capisan late 24 Mar., our part was to overrun the hill mass east of this supremely important mountain. We lost no one. All of 3/Bn. had one killed and one wounded. We then went to work with all of 162 to clean up Jap remnants in the Zambo Mountains.

A month later, L Co. was the main outfit in 162's last Zambo shootout. This was the four-day fight for Sibago Island. Lying 28 miles SE of Zambo City at the eastern entrance to Basilan Strait, Sibago is just 1.5 miles long by 3/4 miles wide and shaped like a kidney bean. Highest of its two hills was 630 feet, with a lighthouse topping one hill. A large detachment of diehard Nips held its wooded cliffs.

Local Filipinos told us only that some Japs were on Sibago. After air-dropping 500 specially prepared leaflets uselessly on their positions, we took direct action. Following a light air strike, 162's I & R landed on Sibago at 0900 on 26 Apr., with two PT boats supporting. Advancing up a ridge, I & R halted under intense rifle and MG fire. Unable to maneuver in that small area, I & R found its position untenable. T/Sgt. Schramm was wounded.

Withdrawing to Lanhill Island, 1,000 yards north, I & R got reinforcements from an "L" pln., and two 81mm mortars, probably from M Co. A CN 162 pln. also emplaced on Lanhil to fire on order. We had another air strike with 105 bombardment and landed again at 1005 next day, 27 Apr. No MGs fired this time, but lively rifle fire impacted near us. Cpl. Inman was killed, Forte and Sgt. Darrell Brown wounded.

The 41st Division received important air support from the MAG groups (12, 24, 32) operating out of the San Roque airstrip secured by 163 Inf. The strip was enlarged and was renamed Moret Field, in honor of a Marine flyer, Lt. Col. Paul Moret, who was killed in a plane crash at New Caledonia in 1943. After the Zambo compaign was over, the 41st Inf. Division honored Magzam (Marine Aircraft Groups Zamboanga) with presentation of a plaque. Picture shows Col. Thomas (G-1) reading citation, while Gen. Doe, Gen. Sweeny, Gen. Haney and Gen. Zundel stand at attention.

Trying to top the Japs' pointed ridge, L's CO Camack saw no sense wasting men to storm it. We had scouted the heights from all directions, but most approaches were almost perpendicular. We needed mountain-climbing equipment. Camack withdrew us to the beach and called for more bombing before advancing again. Not until two days later, 30 Apr., did we leave Sibago Island. Instead of 26 Nips originally suspected there, we had slain 58.

Already on 27 Apr., 162 was alerted to embark from Zambo Peninsula to the Mindanao mainland for our final battle of World War II. In the Zambo Operation, "L" had suffered only minor casualties, with three dead, 30 wounded and four injured in action. After our repulse at San Roque—through no fault of ours—we had done well in the advance on Mt. Capisan and in clearing Sibago Island.

Headquarters Co., 1/Bn 163 Inf.:

Blow-up Hill and Pasananca

by DR. HARGIS WESTERFIELD, Division Historian and CLIFTON JAMES, SR. (Hq. Co. 1/Bn. 163 Inf.)

When Hq. Co. of 1/Bn. 163 Inf. charged into San Mateo Beach on 10 Mar. 1945, Jap fire struck our LCI. Runner Cliff James thought that all the Jap 20mm guns of Zamboanga fired at us. We beached under a bank 8 feet above us, impossible to scale with our heavy gear.

A tankman of A Co. 716 Tank Bn. saw our trouble and drove into shallow water nearby. We jumped on his tank, ran to the rear, and climbed onto the beach. Jap fire hit nobody, and passed on. Hq. Co. pushed inland a mile to hole up in deserted Jap trenches, near Wolfe Strip.

(Only years later do we realize how near disaster 163 came from our own planes. While Gen. Thomas White—C.O. of XIII Air Force—Gen. Doe, and Gen. Eichelberger watched from the deck of their Navy command ship, 3 flights of Liberators almost bombed us. Arriving late from Halmahera, they ignored Air Control, and bombed while we were already ashore. After the first 2 strikes, Gen. Doe asked Air Force Gen. White to stop the bombing. Pacing the deck nervously, Gen. White blanched and said that he had no radio contact. But even Flight No. 3 hurt no 163 man; a swamp had retarded our advance. But Gen. Doe did credit XIII Air Force for hitting Caldera Point, which could enfilade our landing beach.)

On 11 Mar. about 1050, we had our first casualties. When getting out of a jeep, James heard the Jap shell coming, threw himself into a hole just in time. Reichenberger was killed; 2/Lt. Seiler died later. The same shell wounded Maj. Alfred, S/Sgt. Duvall, T4s Barnes and Barnard, T/5 Kisser, and Pvt. Leach.

Although briefly in reserve, 1/Bn. moved into combat the afternoon of our second day at Zambo, 11 Mar. When E and F Cos. pushed into palm groves below Santa Maria Village, 1.9 miles north of Zambo City, Jap MGs, a 20mm cannon, and small arms fire lashed F Co. Withdrawing 200-300 yards south, "F" needed reinforcements.

But when 1/Bn. forwarded under cover of combined fires of "F" and 146 FA, opposition was light. Our Bn's greater fire power drove back the Japs' first line. They retreated 200 yards, and held. Hq. Co's 1/Lt. Foster's team knocked out a Jap 20mm gun too close to us. At 1655, 1/Bn. had 3 litter cases and 2 walking wounded still to evacuate that night. Our 1/Bn. casualties totalled 5 dead, 10 wounded. James saw many dead that day—including, of course, Jap corpses.

Runner James got little sleep that night of 11 Mar. All night, men shot and threw grenades at the dark. Two men panicked from holes somewhere in 1/Bn. and were killed, but the Japs did not attack.

On 12 Mar., 163's 1/Bn. and 2/Bn. tried to advance north against the entrenched Japs. While our 2/Bn. pushed left of the Zambo City-Pasananca Road, 1/Bn. pushed on the right of that road, with Tumaga River on our right flank. We fought a suicidal defense in depth of 2,000 well-armed men of 33 Naval Guards—the crack "Jap Marines." Their holes and pillboxes were nearly invisible in coconut plantations overgrown with brush. Besides deadly little 20mm guns, they had several 75s not detected yet.

On that 12 Mar., 1/Bn. took fire from probably AA guns of 20mm at 0940, but attacked at 1005 and by 1158 was through heavily mined and booby-trapped Santa Maria Barrio. But by 1345, we were stopped in an area of pillboxes guarded by barbed wire, and called for tanks. In 2 hours of intense battle, the tanks destroyed six 20mm guns and several MGs with maybe 100 dead Japs. We fought side by side with 2/Bn.

But with C Co. leading, 1/Bn. made just 400 yards that day, despite probable tank help and 146 FA's 2 direct hits on 2 Jap guns. When digging in that night, James saw his hole of last night; Hq. Co. had not moved far. Our 1/Bn. counted 5 dead, 10 wounded. Of these, Bn. Hq. Co. lost 2 wounded—T/Sgt. Cliff Davis and T/5 Stern.

Japs cut our communication lines that night. Reports came that 2 plns. were to hit us in the dark. Maj. Kent hoped for a suicidal "Banzai" charge so that we could mop up the survivors. But no attack came.

On 13 Mar., 1/Bn. pushed again into the deadly coconut groves before Pasananca, with 2/Bn. again on our left flank. This third hard day of battle led up to Blow-Out Hill that afternoon.

C Co. was on the point a second day, but "B" moved in front of "C" and took fire from "C" men who thought that they were Japs. Casualties, if any, were unrecorded; but C's T/Sgt. Yates halted us and ran to inform "C" men. As Yates rejoined "C", a sniper killed him. Maybe because Yates carried Capt. Houston's binoculars and so seemed to be an officer.

Then a 20mm and a .75 opened up and stopped 1/Bn. When we called for a tank of 3/Pln. 716 Tank Bn., and C's Gould volunteered to guide the tank. Shortly after, the tank returned to report that Gould was killed.

Then Sgt. Stuart went out on the trail before the tank, but 3 Japs jumped in front of him. Stuart slew all three. But before he could shelter behind the tank, a 30 mm gun ricocheted off the steel sides and killed Stuart. The tank now spotted the .75 and smashed it, and maybe 100 Japs.

Again 1/Bn. pushed on Pasananca—"A" on the left, and "C" on the right. A bunker on the other side of a creek halted C Co; 2/Lts. Moore and Worthly wiped out its 5-man crew. But another MG at the base of a hill stopped C's 1/Lt. Irish's Pln. and killed one and wounded one. A bullet in the groin seriously wounded Irish himself.

In this area where "C" halted, barbed wire was pegged 6 inches above the ground; we wondered why. To our left, Runner James saw a hill about 100 feet high which was covered with coconut palms, surely the same hill near which Irish was wounded. James did not then know that he was looking at Blow-Out Hill. He did not know that an E Co. Pln. had finally fought its way to the summit while other "E" Plns. waited below for tank-cannon to blast concealed Japs holding both flanks. James was, in fact, cutting a souvenir belt-buckle from a Jap killed by Moore and Worthley.

Suddenly the whole hill lifted up. James dove into a trench as deadly debris fell—shattered trees and chunks of earth. Abbott fell on top of James in the trench. He leaned an arm on James' helmet, and a falling rock broke his wrist.

Now we saw why the Jap wire was only 6 inches above ground. As men ran for cover, they tripped on wire while hill fragments crashed down on them. C's Tegeler ran down the road toward a bridge that was mined. At Maj. Kent's warning, James grabbed him and took him to where Capt. Baron and other medics worked on men lying everywhere around.

Flames, chunks of earth, rocks, and even whole palm trees erupted from Blow-Out Hill. At 1500 feet over the blast, 146 FA's observer saw debris fly far above in this explosion that tore a 200-yard crater in Blow-Out Hill.

In C Co. where coconut logs fell, Burns sensibly embraced a tree. He still took a dent in his helmet. But "Uhler the jeweler" died of a broken neck, and 14 other "C" men were first listed as lightly injured in action, which must mean that they were struck.

41st's supply dump at Pasananca

HISTORY CREDIT No. 115

CREDIT: Indispensable core story is Cliff James' ltr, 8 Nov. 1978, backed by 163's Journal 17 Feb.—29 May 1945, 1/Bn. 163's S-1 Journal 10-29 Mar. 1945, 146 FA's Capt. Robert Allen's "Zamboanga Recaptured," and 716 Tank Bn's "A Co. on Zamboanga—Jolo." Important also were Morning Reports of all 1/Bn. Cos., and "Special Report No. 68/Zamobanga," donated by Maj. John Jacobucci. These men supplied important letters: Maj.-Gen. Jens Doe, 27 Jan. 1961; Col. (now Brig.-Gen.) Kenneth Sweany; A 163's Sgt. Clifton James and Robert "Ace" Heleman, and C's Bob Burns and 1/Lt. George Irish. Dr. Arthur Merrick (then the newly transferred captain of B 163) phoned from Washington, D.C. on 28 Mar. Only other 163 story of Zambo ever printed in Jungleer was about my own G 163. Won't other 163 men help me with their companies?

Far left of Coconut Hill, A Co. also suffered. As palm trees flew through the air, Sgt. James was thrown up 5 feet, sprained his ankle coming down, and could not hear for an hour. Sgt. Hyde was killed; A Co. reported a total of 4 casualties. D Co. had 4 "lightly injured in action," probably blow-up casualties.

In Runner James' 1/Bn. Hq. Co., Branden was killed, and S/Sgt. Harrison lightly injured—both Blow-Out Hill casualties.

Our recovery from that deadly blast was rapid, however. Unhurt men dreaded a Jap assault at once. Perhaps no attack came on E's front because the hill blew out on the wrong side, against the Japs. On C's front, the Japs seemed leaderless. C's Burns heard them loudly talking. Without orders, he and other "C" men set up MGs and mortars and fired at close range. Jap talk turned into screaming; they did not attack.

In all 1/Bn., probable final figures for the blast were 2 dead, 20 wounded. In 2/Bn., E Co. alone lost 3 dead, 18 wounded. Total in 163 was perhaps 5 dead, 38 wounded. The hill had blown prematurely, or losses would have been far greater.

Yet both Bns. quickly moved out against the Japs again. While 2/Bn. leftwards got a foothold on the west ridge of Pasananca and fought there, 1/Bn. had our own hard fight. We advanced step by step against small arms and mortars to the groves' edge just south of Pasananca. In open ground, fire from 3 sides hit us, forced back into the groves to dig in. From Santa Maria to Pasananca, 1/Bn. had made 1.5 miles on 11-13 Mar.

On 14 Mar., all arms blasted the powerful Jap lines holding Pasananca—FA, Air Force, and infantry—including CN Co. At 0800-0830, 146 FA fired 8 concentrations, and marked with smoke the air-bomb lines. At 0920, 2 squadrons of B-24s hit the Japs, then 3 minutes' FA. Four more B-24 squadrons then struck between 0936 and 0945. After mortar preparation, "B" and "C" advanced.

Even after heavy preparation, 1/Bn. had hard going. Tropical growth had hidden many Jap bunkers. After a few hundred yards, Jap 20mm guns, FA, and some small arms slowed us. We reached the cross-roads below Pasananca by 1225; but 2/Bn. on our left had not come up on line. We were exposed to Jap flanking fire. At 1300, Japs began circling our right flank. Six 1/Bn. Hq. men had to provide security until an "A" Pln. came to take over.

About 1200, 5 tanks forwarded and claimed destruction of 16 pillboxes and one 20mm gun. B Co. gained 700 yards; but by 1615, 1/Bn. had to dig in for the night. Brightest spot of 14 Mar. was that we heard Jap demolitions going on in Pasananca. In Bn. Hq. Co., Sgt. Myers was wounded; total 1/Bn. losses were 3 dead, 9 wounded, and 1 injured.

Next day, 15 Mar., we progressed, however. Some Japs were still in Pasananca, but our objective now was to capture Zambo City Reservoir, 1.7 miles north of Pasananca. An "A" patrol on our right flank reached the reservoir, and passed it to meet a "C" patrol which had come directly up the main road from Pasananca. Following these men, 1/Bn. by 1625 held the 2-mile

The Blow-up Hill in Pasananca, north of Zamboanga, where 163 suffered heavy casualties.

circumference of the reservoir. (It could hold about 1,500,000 gallons; but Jap neglect and guerilla sabotage had made it useless. C Co. 116 Engrs. would soon make it operational again.) On 15 Mar., 1/Bn. Hq. had just 1 injured—Delrial. Two men were wounded in 1/Bn.

From high ground above the reservoir, the Japs still menaced us on 16 June. At 0710, their 20mm gun drove 1/Bn. to ground, forced Maj. Kent to dive for his hole with the gun shooting at his heels. Two "D" gunners fought it with their .30 LMG; but even FA and mortars failed to kill it. AT Co's .57 recoilless cannon broke it with 3 rounds.

When Maj. Kent had a council of Bn. officers that afternoon, a knee mortar shell impacted his CP about 1425 and caused havoc. When the shell hit, Kent was out of his hole while Hurley bathed his eye inflamed from a centipede bite of last night. Capt. Merrick, new Bn. S-3, sat on the edge of a hole with his helmet off. On the side of Runner James' hole, C's Capt. Houston sat. The CO of A Co., 116 Engr, 1/Lt. Call, stood at one end. Call said that he did not know how to disarm a new type of Jap mine. Capt. Merrick heard the shell coming.

The Jap mortar shell killed Call by a fragment in the chest. Another fragment mortally wounded Houston in the side. Kent was wounded in both knees, Hurley torn up badly. James, Merrick were struck in the head—James 3 times. Capt. Skauge, Bn. Exec., was also wounded, and Merrick's orderly in shock.

Already badly holed on the way, an ambulance arrived with 2 volunteer drivers. As they helped lift us from under a big tree, more Jap mortar shells fell nearby. The drivers evacuated at 80 miles per hour to save us—right through the Japs. Wounded Merrick and James lay on either side of Houston in the hospital when he died. On 16 Mar., 1/Bn. Hq. lost 1 dead, 5 wounded, from a total of 2 dead, 18 wounded, and 1 injured.

In the next few days, the other 163 Bns. helped drive the Japs from the overhanging ridges. On 17 Mar., 1/Bn. lost just 2 wounded. When "C" with 2 tanks won a hill north of the reservoir, on 18 Mar., "C" had 1 dead; 1/Bn. Hq. had Marsee wounded. By 23 Mar., all 1/Bn. was relieved and safe in a rear area. Of 19 killed and 70 wounded in all 1/Bn., Hq. 1/Bn. had lost 5 dead, 17 wounded against Jap Marines without planes, tanks, heavy FA. But we had killed many more Japs and driven them from their Pasananca stronghold into starvation jungle ridges.

Zamboanga: G Co., 163 Inf's Last Battle

By DR. HARGIS WESTERFIELD (G Co., 163 Inf)

At dawn 10 Mar 1945, up from New Guinea, G Co 163 Inf tensely waited to hit Zamboanga beach. While cruisers, destroyers, Liberators made fireworks, we skeptically scanned a lordly terrain. Coconut groves spread back miles to lordly blue mountains straight up. Far right towards Zambo City, the mountain wall broke into a blue gap at deadly Pasananca.

Mortar shells fell too close to our LCI. A landing-ramp failed to drop. Half of us must detour through holds, bulkheads to climb off the other ramp, but shells still missed us.

Now our great battle company slogged up the beach—long green files of helmeted Yanks bristling with clean rifles, heavy BARs, mortars, MG barrels. Vets of 2 hard New Guinea campaigns, our green columns made a proud sight despite our fears. We were sunbitten yellowed vets of Sanananda with an Aussie drawl—scarred vets of Biak yellowed as the Sanananda men who had schooled us—light-skinned lads just from Stateside Basic scared and trying to do right. (And hard to see in the bright Filipino sun, ghosts of 24 New Guinea dead.)

We saw no Japs at first; but signs were bad. We sweated past Nippo cannon in concrete pillboxes, empty bunkers. Down straight roads through coconut groves, we saw marks of a thriving civilization. We looked for women!

Yet not until the second day did G Co kill 2 Nips. Past San Roque Drome, we were in reserve when F 163 met shell fire and fell back with casualties before taking Santa Maria. Here fought our Japs—2000 Marines of 33rd Naval Group—in pillboxes on mined roads, with mortars and FA masked under coconut fronds.

On 12 Mar 45 at 1000 outside Santa Maria, G Co walked into the greatest concentration of shellfire in our history. Always we blamed 1 Recon's 2 Pltn; it drew fire from a low jungled rise behind the coconut groves, hightailed for the beach.

But a line Co cannot run from a barrage. We echeloned leftwards from the heavier fire, dug in. Glass, Hardy felt safe in a hole between native huts. But a fragment hit Glass in the thigh; Hardy was shell shocked. We mortared some MG positions, called for tanks to kill other MGs, enabled B Co to advance also.

Again G Co attacked through everlasting coconuts, shell bursts. On the far left of our skirmish line, Bradley drew fire in an open spot, fell dead. Across a clearing, Nip cannon and riflemen in bunkers fought us. A 20mm shell struck Marsh in the side, killed him.

In holes or behind coconut logs, we writhed flat. Shrapnel tore down fronds overhead, thudded into ground—or soft flesh. Mortar concussion blasted ears. Because of heat, battle-fatigue, we evacuated 4 men. Besides 2 killed, we lost 9 wounded—Jackson, Brodeur, Heidt, Glass, Sgts Detzel, Carter, Skelton, Musgrave, 2Lt Tower—who had several bullet wounds.

But now that G had drawn fire, 146 FA's Piper Cubs spotted Nip emplacements under coconut fronds. FA shells made 2 direct hits on guns in Pasananca. Compact and close, G and H mortars hit Jap trenches. We advanced to Santa Maria 400 yards, killed 18 Japs. By dark, we had dug perimeter in a palm grove south of Santa Maria.

On 13 Mar, G Co awoke from snatches of sleep between night watches into this world of foxholes, coconut groves, shell-blasts. We moved 1000 yards north of Santa Maria, met a Nip heavy mortar barrage at 1545. BARman McCorkle died from a direct knee-mortar strike. Flat behind a tree, Rider watched the right tree break from a shell, then the left. The third shell hit his tree, broke it down, wounded him. But Kickel dodged from the right tree, hid by Rider unhurt. Wounded also were Peterson, Cpl Mechlinski. And on 14 Mar, G Co advanced 400 yards north until pillboxes and rifle-fire halted us. Gilbert Smith was wounded, and Sgt Zawora; Abbruzzesse was injured.

On the fourth day of battle whole F/Btn and 2/Btn elements captured Pasananca Road Junction, G Co held the same perimeter. Yet Austin was wounded; and Lt Messenger killed at dark by a defective Bouncing Betty, 14 Mar.

On 16 Mar while repairing wire which Jap mortars had damaged, Bombardier himself died of mortar shrapnel. F/Pltn flushed a sputtering Jap MG, but had no casualties, let the supporting weapons deal with it.

But 2 Btn's main effort was against the bunkers where a Nip mountain gun and 20 mm cannon held up 163, on the road up the Tumaga Valley. And 20 Yanks from G's 3 Pltn joined other 163 men to become tank infantry and clean out those bunkers.

Passing black-mouthed pillboxes which tanks fired into, we could not hear Nippo drumfires for the clank of tanks. But Parks, Huddleston saw HMG tracers gouge earth before their feet—saw men drop rifles, lurch back wounded.

The lead tank also carried a bulldozer blade; it charged a pillbox, sat down on it. The dying crew inside moaned awhile. The tanks shot to death 4 smaller emplacements; the 75 in the largest was silenced. All 4 tanks blasted into that strongpoint; 50-75 Nips in dirty khaki charged wildly with bayonet; the tank HMGs toppled them dead. We drew back triumphant—with somehow or other not a G man hurt, while 146 FA battered the area clear of the last Nips. On 17 Mar, we pushed after more FA, plane preparation, had only the silence of corpses, the buzz of flies.

The Nips struck back after midnight against G Co astride the roadblock 1000 yards west of Pasananca. At 0030, Gordon heard footfalls before his hole; an H gunner across the road coughed harshly. A 4-man MG crew dropped behind the coconut log before Gordon, and set up for the H gunner. In the dark, the Nips never saw Gordon and his 2 alerted buddies.

Pointblank, Jewell shot 1 Nip through the head; Smith killed 1. Gordon wounded a Lieutenant. All 3 Yanks riddled the fourth. The Lt cracked a grenade, blew himself apart.

That noble H gunner fired a stream of flame before our holes. Bodies thudded; Nips screamed for aid in a twisting mass. From the right, a Jap MG dueled the H gunner. But from the next hole, Beckner's BAR flailed out, silenced the Jap MG.

But isolated guarding a riverside path, Pltn Sgt Utigard's position took a fatal attack. Two Nips stalked him; 1 yelled in English. Utigard fired at the bush the Nip shouted from.

CREDITS

Prime source is my "History of G Co 163 Inf." Highly useful were 146 FA's Capt Robert M. Allen's "Attrition in Pasananca," "Battle for the Ridges." "Historical Narrative—V-4 Opn," signed by Gen Doe, afforded excellent overall background, and 163's "Journal of Events" contained scattered data. But 163's "Report of Operations" was worthless. McCartney's chapter on Zamboanga is desultory, unsatisfying, mixed with irrelevancy, wasted space on Basilan, a cursory treatment of Jolo. In actual space about the battle, he spends about the same amount of pages as he did on the far less significant action on Wakde.

My G Co MS, I based on the Morning Report, plus interviews in barracks in Japan with LaMar Gordon, Wascovich, Boberg, Parks, others. I prepared this material while in McCartney's office at Kure, left a copy with him. Fortunately, I brought two other copies home with me. I find no evidence that McCartney used a detail of it, and have queried 3 Federal Archives curators without relocating the copy that I literally placed in his hands when I went home from Japan. Except for the trip to get Hoffman, I did not participate in Zambo's Fight.

Copyright 1963 by Hargis Westerfield for Forty-First Infantry Division Association. No part of this article can be reproduced in any form without permission.

The Nip hid behind another bush, lobbed a grenade on the M-1 flash. Shrapnel tore into Utigard's neck; he fired 15 rounds before he died. T/Sgt Rudningen took deep slashes on the shoulder blades. Barrett awoke deafened; his rifle probably slew the Nip. His hearing did not recover for years. Past dying Utigard, the second Nip charged G's Hq Pltn. Boberg shot from his hole at 10 feet. The Nip fell on Boberg's poncho; Frederickson clubbed him. G Co claimed 10 Japs killed, including 3 by a Pltn on the ridge to the north.

Daylight brought death again. Heading a patrol into a bamboo thicket, Scout Fiorello dropped with 5 30s in his legs from a Jap with a Yank BAR. Sgt Fields heard Fiorello cry that he was too weak to move. With BAR cover, Holtz and Fields rushed the thicket. The Jap riddled Fields, and fled. But Field's death saved Fiorello's life. Wounded also on 19 Mar, were Black, Sgt Bruce.

About 20 Mar, G Co pushed with 2 Btn towards Hill 1000—Coconut Hill. We patrolled in hill country—black earth slopes, bamboo thickets, stray coconut palms. Best paths followed crests notched in Nippo rifle-sights.

Climbing unopposed the shoulder towards Coconut Hill, we looked down the next slope to see E Co men digging furiously. George's keen eyes spotted Nips firing on E Co, and moving in to the kill. Berzac's BAR, and our riflemen piled up 6-7 Nips; others crawled back wounded. A Yank scout from E Co fell; his buddy shouldered him, ran downhill. A Jap officer's saber flashed in the sunlight as he ran for a death-blow; then our BARs found the officer, made his medieval bravery a mockery.

Taking Coconut Hill was not easy. G's F/Pltn probed; but mortars hit us on the open bench just before the top. Pltn Sgt Kozing saved us without casualty. On 21 Mar, however G Co met death in battle for the last time in our history.

G's 2 Pltn climbed to the horseshoe bench around Coconut Hill, sought a trail to the top. Pressing left, we recoiled from a sheer slope and Nippo riflefire. From across the hill we heard a Yank BAR; we thought that E Co was attacking simultaneously. But that BAR was Jap.

So G's patrol tried the bench to the right. The day was dark, misty. A light rain began. Below a steep bank, we found ourselves in fire fight with a dark blur of Nips, 40 yards in front. With only a few feet interval on the path, we knelt behind logs and fired.

Tall, quiet Iowan Wayne Hoffman, a Mindoro replacement, was firing when it happened. The bullet made a small hole in his forehead. We believe that one of our men shot Hoffman's slayer in the temple as he ran. When the firing stopped, Hoffman still knelt as if alive.

Carrying Hoffman's body, we floundered over the black hills in the Filipino rain. Misled Vanderwelt of the MGs left our bogged line on the difficult slope and profiled himself on a crest. A sniper toppled him on the exposed side of the ridge. Yet we saved him: he lay paralyzed for days with a bullet near his spine, but he lived.

Not until the next day could Father Lynn come with a ration-party to bring back Hoffman—first carried in our arms, then in the kitchen-truck, where grades were easier. Tired in that truck, Westerfield envied Hoffman; his worries were ended, and the war seemed useless. Then the truck halted; it took on a frightened Filipino family of refugees—mother and father and children—a bundle of clothing, captive chickens, a crucifix. When Westerfield pointed to Hoffman under a shelter-half, a Filipino lad took off his hat. Westerfield had his answer.

Just before Hoffman's body came down from G Co, McInerney slew a Jap on the next ridge at 500 yards. A Marine plane in an air-strike lost directions, dropped a bomb that missed the sheer crest by 10 feet, bowled over the whole outfit in a blast from below. Mjr Munkres shouted over the wires to the Marine Col to call the planes down. It was probably the next day that G Co advanced with 2 Btn at dawn, took Coconut Hill, to find the Nips gone—except for 5 corpses.

Thus G Co 163 Infantry fought its last battle. After undergoing heavy shelling, a Banzai, sweaty hill patrols we added 8 more to our ghostly platoon of 32 dead overseas. After an almost bloodless raid into the Sulus, our 3 Pltn had a last great combat patrol on Jolo, but our roster of dead stopped with 32 at Zambo. A tough little scrape against Jap Marines was Zambo Fight; we were lucky to lose only 8—although, God knows, one Yank was one too many.

Men of the 41st Division enlarge beachhead near Zamboanga in March, 1945.

146 FA - ZAMBOANGA RING OF FIRE

By DR. HARGIS WESTERFIELD, Division Historian
with Capt. Robert M. Allen

On 10 Mar 45, 146 FA's Lt-Col Alfred Hintz and Advance Party drove ashore at San Mateo Beach, behind 162 Inf's assault waves. While Jap shells blasted the beach, we hiked 600 yards W to our area, arriving just as A 162's point ptn. cleared it. During our recon, a Nip MG raked the area; "A" silenced it. Hintz designated btry positions, and our 105s ran the gauntlet of Nippo FA, from ship to position. Shells splattered close; T/5 Guest had a shattered arm.

Quickly we placed all btrys; B registered by 1215 to assist 163's 3/Bn, pushing to take Zambo' City. When Nippo defenses east of Baliwasan River halted 3-bn at nightfall, Eighth Army's Capt John Green requested our 105 neutralizing fire.

We had no Cubs up yet for spotting, but Capt Emanuel Levenson adjusted fire from a floating OP, which ranged up and down the waterfront from San Mateo to Zambo', dodging Nippo FA, mortars, small arms. But Green's radio broke down. He risked his life on the exposed beach, to confer with Levenson. On 11 Mar, his OP barred from shore by low-tide reefs, Levenson swam in for conference with Green. Thus we found the ranges; Green with 1/Lt Simpson cleared the way for 3 Bn to take Zambo' City.

At once 146 FA btrys encountered Nippo FA fire. At 1600, 2 Nip 75s impacted us. One 75 fell between, and less than 20 feet from CP and Fire-Direction Center. Lightly wounded were T/5 Hamann, S/Sgt Barstow, Cpl Hautamaki. (A shell also hit 205's CP, killed 5, wounded 13 key personnel.) But 146 FA harassed for 3 bn all night, and at dawn, our concentrations cleared the way for 3/bn's seizure of Zambo'.

While Zambo' fell, 146 FA helped 163's 2/bn begin the 7-day fight for Pasananca. While Nip MGs, 81s, 20 mm cannon fire drove "F" out of Santa Maria, 146's 2/Lt John Jacobson used our 105s to protect F from counter-attacks, and further the relieving 1/bn's successful push. But the Nips fell back from 1/bn just 200 yards, to prepared positions. That night 146 FA guarded against a "Banzai" and harassed Nippo lines. Meanwhile Col Hintz and staff pored over Cub observers' photo maps, and studied intelligence reports for 12 Mar.

For 163 now faced Jap marines – 2000 well-trained, well-equipped Nips of 33rd Naval Group. Concealed under palms' thick foliage, these marines guarded every ridge and road around Pasananca, with mazes of pillboxes and trenches. Their observers watched every 163 move from the hills. Mines underlay the roads; gunners stood to FA pieces not even yet detected by our troops.

Better to aid 163, 146 FA moved to the mouth of Baliwasan River in echelon. While rear btrys continued fire, A Btry moved up, registered in 30 minutes, began firing, while other btrys in turn moved in to start their fire for effect.

While 163 advanced 400 yards 12 Mar, we harassed the Nips' rear, threw shells on Pasananca emplacements. Fired on in their low-flying Cub continuously, 1/Lt Ralph Evans, the pilot, Capt Duff, Eighth Army Observer, ranged close above palm fronds hiding the Nips. Several bullets holed the Cub; one hole gaped between seat brackets. Duff scored 2 hits on FA pieces, blasted weapons, pillboxes. By dawn, after all-night fire from 146, Nippo FA fire lessened noticeably.

On 13 Mar, ground observers working with Lt Allen in his Cub, pounded hills guarding approaches to Pasananca. Allen neutralized a 75, flamed an ammo dump near San Roque. About 1400, as 163's E Co topped a hill defending Pasananca, flame, earth, debris—even whole palm trees— erupted from that hill. Allen's plane shook with the blast. At 1500 feet altitude, Allen saw the column of smoke and debris soar high above his plane.

1/bn and 2/bn continued advancing. When 2/bn occupied the W ridge commanding Pasananca, Nips lashed the ridge with everything—even a 20 mm and a 75. It was the same 75 position near San Roque, which 146 had neutralized 12 Mar. 218 FA this time, destroyed that 75, and Allen from the Club located the 20 mm. We smashed 20 volleys into the Nip defenses; Allen's precision adjustment of our 105s then wrecked the 20 mm.

On 14-16 Mar, 163's advance bogged down, while FA and planes duelled the dogged Nip emplacements. For on 15 Mar, 163's first two bns pushed against concealed FA and mortar positions in Pasananca and on the ridges above. The Japs had prepared these positions months before, and tropical growth now hid them. Allen located a high velocity 75 commanding the road into town; but before 146 could fire for effect, 163's CO asked us to let the tanks deal with the 75. The tanks never killed that gun; it fired for another hour, was found abondoned later.

In 1/bn's attack 14 Mar, 146 observer Capt Clifton Thomas' party dashed across the clearing with the 163 point. Thomas tried to bring fire on that 75 commanding Pasananca Road, took a rifle-bullet in the chest, lay 15 minutes before aid men reached him. T/5 Hayslip volunteered to continued directing fire; 2/Lt Rietheimer replaced him. By next morning, the Nips had left that 75 behind.

Although 1/Bn got a patrol into the Reservoir Area on 14 Mar, and seized the Reservoir on 15 Mar, Japs still held the ridges, observed and fired almost at will. Lt Allen with Lt Evans the pilot, flew dawn-to-dusk, observing and adjusting fire on Nip OPs or telltale puffs of smoke. Both 218 and 146 observers saw the mortar position on the ridge W of Pasananca, and 146 FA's 2 rounds killed it. But on 16 Mar, key 163 1/Bn personnel were lost – C's Capt Houston KIA; and WIA: bn CO Mjr James Kent, exec Capt Skaugie, S-3 Capt Merrick.

Then a 163 recon patrol located strong Jap defenses, astride the road NW of Pasananca. Nips shot up that patrol, then repulsed a strong tank-inf team. We wanted to catch the Nips with surprise fire. We used an auxiliary target for adjustment, then placed the bn's 105s on target. It was a perfect execution of surprise fire. Our first volleys blew up the strong point—the heaviest single concentration of the Zambo' fight. The Cub observer saw fires, Nips fleeing north.

Thus on 16 Mar, we located Jap position after position and silenced them; but new ones kept opening up. Only by late afternoon, after over 1000 rounds, did Nippo fire dwindle. Several Jap groups retreated N into the hills. And on 17 Mar, after Marine Group 32's air strike and 146 FA's barrages, 2/Bn advanced at Pasananca to find that the Japs had abandoned the positions. Casualties for 163 were 45 KIA, 266 WIA — in return for 700 Jap corpses. And 146 FA had supported with 7000 rounds at Pasananca.

But 1/Bn at Pasananca Reservoir still endured Nip marines' fire, from close-in OPs and ridges rising 1000 feet on 3 sides. When 1/Bn secured high ground also, 146's Lt Rietheimer got a clear view and hammered back around the clock. Once when a dual 25 mm halted the whole 1/Bn Reitheimer crept up to within 35 yards of the gun, and adjusted fire to kill it. Then after 2/Bn cleared the ridge on 1/Bn's front by a flank movement, the Nippo pressure slackened. And by 20 Mar, 163 had won the Pasananca ridges by the reservoir.

Before 2/Bn moved against Hill 1000 on the west, 163's 3/Bn pushed on the eastern ridges. East of Pasananca across the Tumaga, 3/Bn struck bunkers near the Tumaga a coconut covered knoll 300 yards east — once Nippo Hq of Zambo', by Filipino report. On 18 Mar, 146's 105s marked targets with smoke, and marine bombers swooped in with 1000-pound bombs, with our 105s shelling in turn. This ended 3/Bn's troubles opposite Pasananca.

Now on 21 Mar, 3/Bn faced strong Nip fortifications on the E hill mass — on forested Sugarloaf Mtn, the ridge, and the saddle between. Here, despite a few misunderstandings on fire coordination between 163 and 146, our cannon and Marine Aviation enabled 163 to seize control of all high ground, without undue casualties.

One more great stroke remained for 146 FA at Zambo. While 162 and 163's 2/Bn pressed on the Nips in west — especially about Mt. Capisan, Filipino guerillas contained them at the rear. But on 22 Mar, a Nippo concentration broke through the guerillas, then separated into 2 forces. The eastern force moved towards Moroc. With 218 FA, 146 acted on guerilla reports, which precisely located a large force and Nippo General Hq. At dawn, we zeroed in on a cooking fire — which went out fast — with several volleys of surprise fire, then marked Hq with smoke for an air strike. Our inf did not need to mop up this area.

Then 146 FA's battle for Zamboanga ended. On 30 Mar, 167 FA down from Palawan relieved 146 FA for the Jolo Operation less than 10 days off.

We had done well at Zambo'. Our casualties were comparatively light — T/5 Dale Fredericks dead of illness, 4 WIA, 4 Injured in Action. We had given round-the-clock shelling when called on, despite having to displace forward 3 times. At Pasananca, We had helped minimize 163's losses to 45 KIA, 266 WIA. In 20 days' battle, we fired 20,000 rounds for 163 Inf. Zamboanga was one of 146 FA's most important battles.

K Co 186 Inf-HILL FIGHTING AT ZAMBOANGA
By DR. HARGIS WESTERFIELD, Association Historian

On 30 Mar 1945, K Co 186 Inf entrucked from Red Beach 1 to relieve men 163's 3/Bn in the eastern Zamboanga Mountains. Jeering at Marine Air Force sentries, we passed the air-field. Our trucks climbed the brand-new 116 Engr road to the foot of the last American hill. Panting under heavy armament, we scaled on foot this hill to relieve our 163 cobbers. They were happy to give us their hill — after 20 days' action at Zambo.

From the former 163 hole, Phil Kechele and Sgt Keenan of Glen Hall's squad looked regretfully down at Moret Air Field and clean ocean. A brushy hill shaped like a haystack loomed to their right. But deadly Jap country lay forward. Fronting us a little off center to the right was a higher ridge. We knew that our Nips were dug in on the reverse slope of that ridge. In this open country under threat of accurate Jap rifle-fire, we saw that the safest route was up a saddle (a sharp connecting ridge with sheer slopes on both sides) — up a disused trail ankle-deep in grass.

Despite 20 days' combat at Zambo against 162 and 163 RCTs (and 186's 1/Bn for 10 days), Jap units were still intact. They were entrenched and fairly well supplied. They were determined to die rather than to retreat inland, for their rear was the dark mountain core of Zambo Peninsula — unexplored mountain jungle with disease, starvation, and venomous guerilla trackers.

In the hole with Phil Kechele, Sgt Keenan rubbed his hands gleefully. A regular army man over 50 years old, Keenan was a veteran of World War I. He considered jungle war a poor type of combat. Looking forward at bare ridge beyond ridge, he exulted: "Now we'll fight that war the way it ought to be fought — in the open. This is just like World War I!"

At once, Lt. Geissler's 1/Pltn moved to assail that ridge. Rumors were that 163 had failed to take it even after 2 Marine air-strikes; but K Co had a different tactic. Without preparatory weapons fire, even, we tried a sneak attack — while Kechele and Keenan sat as if on the 50-yard line to watch the big play before them.

The attack worked. Two of Geissler's scouts — probably Jones and Tucker — charged over the ridge and blasted into the Nips with TSMGs. Geissler's following pltn poured over the crest to strike the dug-in Nips on the reverse slope.

What outfit do you suppose Nick Wheeler and Ken Brant belonged to?

Now Lt. Cloud's 2/Pltn advanced in squad column up the path on the saddle. There S/Sgt Hall got orders to leave the saddle and hunt out a small banana grove on a knob 200 yards downhill to the right. If Japs held the knob, it could cut off K Co's advance and threaten Lt. Geissler's pltn from the right.

There was no cover for this advance — just ankle-deep grass over a bare slope. Hall advanced 20 yards downhill with Kechele and Maurice Kelly, his scouts at 5-yard intervals - Stovall with his BAR and the rest of the lead squad and 2/Pltn still strung out in the open on the saddle. Now Hall signalled to Kechele and Kelley to move out as scouts.

From the banana grove, a HMG fired on the pltn point. The first burst hit Hall. He screemed and fell. Scouts Kechele and Kelly dropped to the ground, heads downhill in that ankle deep grass which confused the aim of the Jap HMG.

Other 2/Pltn riflemen fired blindly over that wide-fronded grove to try to neutralize that vicious MG and save the 3 yanks. But Hall was already quiet. Living Kelly and Kechele frantically worked their way up the slope side-ways, chins grooving the dust. Kechele dared not even raise his head enough to sight his M-1. The Jap gun fired in bursts at them — head and then feet and again head and feet. Lumps of Filipino dirt rattled Kechele's helmet; but he still lived and crawled when he could.

After a few bursts, the 2 Yanks lay tensely quiet — their sweat wetting the Filipino earth. The gun gave part of its attention to the pltns on the ridges. Perhaps the Nips believed that they had seriously wounded all 3 — except when a movement made them stab in a burst to be sure of a kill. Those last bursts hit no one — perhaps because the men were harder to hit because they lay in narrow straight lines in the direction of the MG's fire.

Still unhurt, Kechele and Kelly rolled on top of the saddle and safe into the indentation of the trail. Elbows were raw and bleeding; they gasped after the uphill struggle that seemed to have lasted a long 30 minutes. And the assault on the Nip positions was still going on.

That Jap HMG still raked the saddle. Part of the 2/Pltn struggled to extricate Hall. Most of 2/Pltn, however, was supporting Giessler's 1/Pltn attack. By dropping down to the left of the saddle safe from the MG that killed Hall, and clinging to the steep slope, they had worked their way up to where they reinforced Giessler and began to build up that line against the Japs on the reverse slope.

On that narrow ridge, we were terribly crowded. We emptied BARs or M-1s and threw or rolled grenades among the Nip holes. Despite the height above them, some Japs hurled grenades in retaliation. From up and down their line, they fired a few knee-mortar bursts, but the ridge-crest was hard to hit.

By 1130 after a barrage of Weapons Pltn's 60s, Giessler closed in for the victory. We worked 1/Pltn with part of 2/Pltn down among the Nips' dugouts. We hurled white phosphorus grenades into dugouts, shot dead the khaki Nips rushing out. Kechele saw a cross-eyed bazooka man in 1/Pltn fire against a Nip position — the first a dud, the second a direct hit.

Among these numerous pillboxes and caves, K Co captured 1 HMG, 2 LMGs, and found 16 Jap dead from the attack. Leaving supporting I Co to scavenge for snipers holding out, K Co moved out for more Japs. Late in the afternoon, we were on a ridge line above a mass of people moving along a river. Orders came to fire — then orders to hold fire. Never did we know whether these below us were Yanks, Japs, or Filipinos.

As we bivouacked on a ridge, Nips were still out front, 1/Pltn probed 400 yards north and stirred up Jap small arms fire. We pulled back with data for our artillery to work on them. At dusk, a Jap walked towards us and shouted something in his language. When a Yank missed him at 300 yards, he saved himself. And that night I Co — in the position we took at noon — endured 5 minutes! MG fire and five mortar rounds, but had no losses.

On 31 Mar, K Co's 2/Pltn led out north with Sgt Isaac Baker's squad at the point. With his scouts, Baker knocked out a 2-man outpost. He led an advance that caught Japs off-balance in hasty positions perhaps made since yesterday's defeat. Baker slew 6 out of 9 Japs killed. Panting up hill to reinforce Baker at the edge of the rain-forest, Kechele saw a dying Jap. He heard Baker and squad already deep in rain-forest. Baker was shouting for more grenades and positioning his men while he tongue-lashed Nips between M-1 bursts.

About 1230, K Co moved NW for 3 hours to reach Masilay. From the new perimeter, a patrol westward killed 5 Nips. Moving SW, this patrol found a food dump and destroyed it and killed 6 more Nips. But on return trip, we battled Nips — 5 riflemen and 1 LMG. We drove them off, with no casualties — Jap or Yank. Next day, another pltn destroyed another ration dump but was stopped by a LMG commanding the draw. Another pltn hit Jap position in the rear, found only blood. Our cost was 2 Yanks wounded.

From the first day's fixed position combat, K Co's war evolved into patrols from our ridge perimeter of March 31 in all directions. But main object was to reach Masilay River and cut the Nip's retreat.

Initially, we seemed to butt our heads into stone walls. Every trail seemed an ambush. And K's ridge perimeter was overlooked and unsafe; we crawled from holes at dawn to expect bursts from a LMG on the wooded hill behind us. (It never happened.) Our only spring was down a sheer slope in a little open vale with cover for Japs in the nearby rain forest. One morning, snipers lashed our water party of 5 Filipinos. No Filipino ever visited that spring again. And this was where we found Seneca Mann dead. One day when 2/Pltn returned with a litter carrying another outfit's wounded Yank, we almost stepped on Vaught dead in the dusk by the spring. So K Co never had enough water!

K Co pushed laboriously through mountain forests to cross Masilay River and contact L Co. Then orders came to return to rest camp on 7 May. Unbelieving, we filed down the rain-forest trail, through Masilay River, up the ridge on the other side, broke from the rain forest at Brea to hold a beautiful 116 Engr road and a squadron of trucks. We rode singing back to the beach and the sun. Amen!

But by 14 Apr. K fought again 9,000 yards north of Wariwari. There 41 Recon saw a completely equipped Nippo Co building camp. From guarding radar on the coast at Manicahan, Lt Cloud's 2/Pltn moved in.

It was bad business. The patrol advanced through a clearing to see 2 Nips on a knoll above. Maurice Kelly with two 41 Recon men slipped up to kill them. Instead, rifle and MG fire struck down the Recon men. To save them, Kelly pushed ahead and drew Nip fire to let the Recon men crawl out of the fire-lane.

Raging like a whole arm, Kelly accurately blasted the Nip position. A handful of Nips struck at him; but he broke up their attack. After medics treated and evacuated the Yanks, Lt Cloud pulled us back while Otto Schultz and Kechele covered withdrawal. After an unpleasant night with half his Pltn carrying back the Yanks and the other half hiding beside the trail, Cloud sent 4 scouts to draw Nip fire. But the Nips vanished into the bush, and Cloud returned to guard radar.

A month later, Cloud's Pltn battled again — this time in the pagan Sibuko country on the opposite side of Zambo Peninsula. Landing 17 May at Panganuran, Cloud's Pltn led K's advance. When heavy Nippo fire struck in a clearing, Cloud pushed to storm the bare hill commanding the area. When Japs halted lead elements at the hill base, Cloud shot 4 Nips dead, pushed forward until a bullet felled him.

S/Sgt Davis took charge, and stormed the hill with 2/Pltn. Hastily placing us, under Jap rifle-fire, we got set for the instant counter-attack. As 2/Pltn fought the Nips frontally a Jap MG and knee-mortar set up and fired before Davis could warn us. Davis charged in with a grenade and knocked out MG and mortar. This counter-attack ended with 12 Japs dead, of a total 30 killed in that action. But K Co lost Lt Cloud, who did not fight again.

Thus K Co fought at Zambo — drove the Japs from their last fixed positions on the Peninsula. We lost 5 dead (of 11 in all

186), and 12 wounded (of 43 in all 186). Dead were Hall, Vaught, Mann, Maddox, Fred Miller. Wounded were Frank Travis, S/Sgts Davis, Baker; Sgts Foreptak, Stovall; Ken Miller, Clint Watson, Solomon, McGhee, Mounce, Timmons, 1/Lt Cloud. Injured were Steensma, Bob Tucker. Casualties were minimal; but as Gen Newman emphasizes, we ought to measure 186's work at Zambo by results. Never was 186 more efficient than at the Battle of Zamboanga.

Basic narrative MSS are ltrs of 18 Jan and 1 Aug 65 by anonymous writer contacted by Bill Ague, K Co 186 Clerk. (Bill has done much work to keep alive the memory of K Co.) Important were excerpts from Gen. O.P. Newman's Ltr 10 Feb 63. Other data are from Zamboanga Opn 186 Inf, Casualty List 186 Inf from 30 Mar 45, and Medal Awards. This is only 186 Inf Zambo story available.

186 Infantry Regiment:
186 Infantry's Battle of Zamboanga

by DR. HARGIS WESTERFIELD, Division Historian

This is the basic history of 186 Inf. at Zamboanga—history that has had almost no space in print. After we easily defeated the Palawan Japs, Col. Newman sent 1/Bn. and 3/Bn. to fight in the Zambo hills. We reinforced 162 Inf. and released 163 Inf. for the Sulu Sea invasions. Ten days after the 41st's D-Day at Zambo, 1/Bn. saw action beginning on 21 Mar., and 3/Bn. fought on 30 Mar.

As 186's Col. Newman later saw the Zambo situation, the Jap units were still intact in hill entrenchments and fairly well supplied. They were determined to hold out; they had nowhere to go but the unexplored mountain rain forest. Newman thought the other 41st units were making no real effort to conclude the operation. (He made these statements without considering the earlier heavy fights of 162 and 163 Inf., nor the difficulties arising when front-line troops had to pull out for invasions on Basilan and Jolo.)

Orders were for our 1/Bn. to relieve E-162 on the Division's left flank on West Ridge, east of the Sinonog River. Mission was to protect 162's left flank for the assault against the ultimate goal of Mt. Capisan.

At 0630 21 Mar., C Co. and a D Pln. of HMGs relieved E Co. on West Ridge. At 0800, "A" positioned west of "C" on that same ridge. B Co. protected Bn. CP and D's 81 mortars. AT Pln. brought up a 37mm AT gun and two .50 HMGs.

On 22 Mar. "C" had orders to attack "Ridge X" about 300-400 yards north. Moving out at 0935, "C's" lead pln. took heavy rifle and MG fire at 300 yards. Killed was lead scout Linton at 1100. At 1115 through 1500, our MG, mortar and 37mm fire impacted the Japs. By 1445, "C" held the Jap position. We slew two Japs, found seven dead and captured two LMGs.

On 23 Mar "C" struck again. After fire from CN Co's two 105s, "D's" 81s and our 60s, we overran the Jap perimeter. At 1000, rifle fire killed a "C" man. We slew seven Japs and captured an LMG.

At 1330, "C" sighted a large body of Japs west of us on another ridge. We ordered a .50 HMG and mortar to fire on those Japs. Covered by the sound of our weapons, concealed Japs killed one more "C" man and wounded two others. By 1530, we had slain 15 more Japs, seized two more LMGs and a 90mm gun. At 1900, 10 Japs walked in on us to die. We lost McCone and newly promoted S/Sgt. Sachs dead, Gerecke and Slomka wounded.

As early as 0810 that 23 Mar., B Co. and a section of "D's" HMGs pushed on "C's" right flank, to contact "C" on a ridge junction to our left. Although we seized two Jap pillboxes, we failed to contact "C". While A Co. fired five mortar missions supporting "C," 2/Lt. Maschko was lightly wounded by Jap mortars.

On 24 Mar., while G Co. 162 overran Bald Hill on our right and captured the ultimate objective of Mt. Capisan, 186's 1/Bn. also fought to secure the ridge on 162's left flank.

Moving out simultaneously at 0940, C and B Cos. tried to make contact. At 1225, fire from a Jap pillbox wounded three D Co. HMG men (Kreager, Earl Jones, McCoy), probably attached to C Co. At 1300, "B" and "C" contacted—and found the Japs leaving. By 1420, "C" had killed 15 Japs and captured a deserted 20mm gun. At 1845, 1/Bn's AT Pln. saw a few Japs bathing in a river (probably the Sinonog) and slew four with a .50 HMG.

On 25 Mar. A Co. moved 1400 yards north and east to the already captured Mt. Capisan, found another Jap 20mm and contacted 162 Inf. At 1030, a mortar short wounded Bondurant, Huff and Sellers. A "B" patrol on the ridge killed a Jap, found seven dead, seized three 20mm guns and 4 MGs.

Thus 186's 1/Bn. supported 162 Inf. against Mt. Capisan. Fighting on West Ridge with only light losses, we cleared the ground east of the Sinonog River. We now denied the Japs further observation of the coastal plain. We had driven them across deep gorges into the mountain rain forest.

On 26 Mar. 1/Bn. 186 Inf. moved eight miles NE to relieve 163's 1/Bn. and fight Hill 2000. (The "163" men left to fight on Jolo).

On 27 Mar. B Co. advanced 1800 yards up the ridge and met heavy fire from Japs on the reverse slope. We slew eight Japs, began blasting out caves and trenches with bangalore torpedoes. Shortage of bangalores and rough terrain held us

CREDIT: This story was hard to write. Only usable personal story was K-186's (Jungleer, Sept. 1968). Most of this history I pieced together from "History of 1/Bn. 186 Inf. (17-30 Mar. 1945)," 186 Inf's "Zamboanga Operation," and 41st Division Artillery's "Narrative Report of Zamboanga Operation." Important also were Col. O.P. Newman's ltr. to me (10 Feb. 1963), 186's Casualty List and Morning Reports, and Maurice Kelley's and Isaac Baker's Award Stories. R.R. Smith's "Triumph in the Philippines" contains a too brief overall story of Zambo battle. This history was still impossible to write without discovery of a map buried in "8th U.S. Army's Operational Monograph on Zamboanga-Sulu."

An air view of Zamboanga City after it was cleared of Japs and occupied by 41st Division troops.

from completing the job. Next day, 28 Mar., "B" advanced again, killed six Japs at 1000 and established a new position. S/Sgt. Heal was wounded.

At 0720 29 Mar., with heavy support from MGs, mortars and FA, A Co. stormed Hill 2000. Finding 11 Japs already dead, we took a knee mortar and dug in. Small groups of Japs harassed us all afternoon, wounded Hudson and Bucy. We had a 30-minute air strike from 1230 to 1300. At 1800, "B" killed 15 Japs, captured an LMG and destroyed a large ammo dump in caves. Again we had to use bangalore torpedoes. At 2120 that night, Japs mortared A-186 and K-163. Newly arrived from Palawan, 167 FA Bn. barraged these mortars and silenced them.

On 30 Mar. Col. Newman with 3/Bn. 186 was down from Palawan to fight at Zambo. At once, his 1/Bn. reverted to him from attachment to 162. With 163 gone to Jolo, we took over the 41st's right flank—all ground east of San Mateo and Harlowton. Instead of the already captured Mt. Capisan, objective was now 163's objective of Mt. Pulungbata. We were also to drive NE to pin the Japs against the Filipinos' 121 Inf. pushing southward.

On 30 Mar. 1/Bn. fought from Hill 2000. At 1500, "A" endured Jap MG, mortar and small arms fire. Kopecky and T/5 Howard Kelly were wounded. At 1820, "C" fought off three desperate banzai charges from 30-40 Japs wielding at least one LMG. Next day, 12 Japs lay dead before our lines.

Also, on 30 Mar. K-186 poised for heavy action in that NE corner of our front towards Moroc. Left of a never-forgotten hill shaped like a haystack (or sugar loaf), we looked up at grassy, open ridges. A higher ridge leftward was our objective; we heard that 163 Inf. could not take it even after Marine dive bombing. "K's" Lt. Geisler made a sneak attack without FA or air strikes. He slipped his pln. up a saddle to that higher ridge and fired down on Japs on the reverse slope. The Japs resisted stubbornly.

On Geisler's right, "K's" 2/Pln. had trouble when it probed a banana grove atop a small knob. From that grove, a Jap HMG killed S/Sgt. Glen Hall, pinned down scouts Kelley and Kechele. Kechele thought the grove held only three-four Nips at the gun. Not until "K's" 1130 barrage of 60mm mortars did we overrun the Japs on the reverse slope and in the banana grove. We found 16 dead Nips, one LMG and one HMG. Pushing north of our captured position, "K" took rifle fire again.

At 0900 31 Mar., "K" pushed north once more. At 1131 we had rifle fire from hastily prepared positions. Leading 2/Pln's point squad under rifle fire, S/Sgt. Baker killed the Japs' two-man outpost. When 2/Pln. won their position, Baker had slain six of the nine Jap dead. On that 31 Mar. "K" advanced 1500 yards north and occupied Masilay Village.

Late that 31 Mar., Lt.-Gen. Tokichi Hojo ordered remnants of his 54 Independent Mixed Brigade to withdraw northward. He knew that effective resistance was now impossible. Because Filipino 121 Inf. Regt. held his easier escape route NE up the coast past Bolong, Hojo's army had to retreat inland among the starvation mountains of Zambo Peninsula. Of the original 8900 Japs, 3900 still lived. Only 1385 would survive to the war's end.

On 1 Apr. both 186 bns. continued combat patrols deep into the dark mountain rain forest. K Co's Kechele said that the rain forest was like a stone wall that they butted their heads against. Every trail was an ambush.

On that 1 Apr. Jap mortar fire wounded a "K" man, perhaps Ken Miller. One "K" pln. destroyed a ration dump in a stream valley, then halted 300 yards farther upstream, under LMG fire from a commanding position. Another "K" pln. pressed the Jap position from the north but found only deserted equipment and signs of wounded Japs. Perhaps Mann was wounded here, to die later. Perhaps on 1 Apr. Vaught was found dead near dark on a trail to the spring near "K's" perimeter. That spring underwent occasional Jap sniper fire.

At 0500 2 Apr. "C's" Pedine took mortar fragments in the thigh and middle right finger. At 0930, B Co. fought 30 Japs, killed seven, seized or destroyed two LMGs, two knee mortars and a 20mm gun. At 1700, "C" captured one HMG, also 15 saddle horses and a blacksmith's shop!

Also on 2 Apr., an "I" patrol up Misuloy River met hard resistance and had men wounded. In relieving pressure on that patrol, an "L" patrol won a fire fight. In another "I" pln., S/Sgt. Wheat was wounded lightly, and Sgt. Cook died in a carrying party. M Co. had two losses, probably from men attached to I Co. Saware was lightly wounded; Langel was missing and recovered dead on 7 April.

Highly important on 2 Apr. was the contact of 186 patrols with 121 Filipino Inf. Regt. in a river valley two miles north of Mt. Pulungbata. Now the Jap escape route up the south coast had fully closed, but Jap resistance continued.

On 3 Apr. at 0645, "K" withdrew 500 yards south from our perimeter while Marine dive bombers struck the rain forest before us. Then 167 FA fired 148 rounds into the forest. Our patrols found 10 Japs, but no resistance.

Crossing a ridge, "K's" 2/Pln. drew fire. Retaliating first with a LMG, we attacked. The Japs charged us downhill. We slew 20 Japs, had at least two wounded: McGhee and S/Sgt. Baker with a stomach wound. A FA barrage at 1815 let us take the position without more shooting.

A six-man "L" patrol with a Filipino co. struck 1700 yards down Misuloy River into Jap country and slew five Japs out of a group of 14. Four hundred yards farther, we saw 100 Japs bathing. From carefully chosen positions, we killed 47 of the 100. Still drawing fire from a bluff north of the river, we called for 167 FA shells at 1730. Next day, with an "L" pln. reinforcement, we dispersed or slew all Japs in this area.

At this late hour at Zamboanga, Jap tactics seemed clear. With no hope to inflict even token losses on us, they were surviving in tactically isolated pockets and withdrawing slowly. They would show fight only when our patrols found their bivouacs and routes of escape. With abundant ammo, they would show fight when confronted. But our patrols were rushing their slow withdrawals; we had a knack of catching them unawares.

After 31 Mar. most of the actual fighting and most of 186's few casualties were with 3/Bn. to the east. Yet 1/Bn. continued the risky hard work of searching out Jap concentrations. C Co's Sgt. Runge died of wounds 3 Apr. On 4 Apr., when "A" moved to cut off Jap retreat north of Brea Village, 1/Lt. Vick died on a recon patrol.

In 3 Bn. on 5 Apr., "L's" Brough was seriously wounded. On 6 Apr., while pursuing Japs on a bloody trail from Misuloy River, L Co. met ambush from 100-200 Japs on a horseshoe ridge. They shot at us between the horseshoe heels. Despite our mortars' preparation, the Japs repelled attempts of our two patrols to take the heels. Japs attacked our mortars. Slaying 15 Japs, we withdrew, while 218 and 167 FA impacted 120 shells on the ridge. With more FA, we cleared the ridge on 7 Apr. (Lagro of M Co. was wounded on 7 Apr., perhaps in this action.)

Motor patrols began. After a 41 Div. Hq. motor patrol, "K" men followed through with a foot attack. On 14 Apr. 1/Lt. Cloud's patrol fought those Japs on the east coast NW of Wariwari. "K's" Kelley and two 41 Recon men pressed through a clearing at two Nips on a little knoll. Heavy rifle and MG fire wounded both recon men. Kelley rushed the Japs, drew fire; the two wounded crawled to safety. His heavy, accurate fire stopped a small Jap attack. The Japs withdrew silently.

Such were 186's outstanding actions in the fortnight after Gen. Hojo ordered the Jap retreat. (And, of course, we made many other nerve-wracking patrols with meager results.) The Zambo City vicinity was cleared of Japs. By 26 Apr. 186 Inf. began landing on the west side of Zambo Peninsula to shatter new concentrations of Hojo's 3900 fugitives. The real Battle of Zamboanga had ended.

As of 20 June 1945, we claimed killing 2331 Japs, with 103 Jap prisoners and 114 non-Jap prisoners. In return, 186 had 15 dead, 39 wounded and 13 injured in action. (Of course, these figures include Jap casualties and ours for 55 days after the real battle had ended.)

As Col. (later Major General) Newman once wrote, our few casualties emphasizes the masterly achievement of 186 Inf. in the Battle of Zamboanga. By 1945, 186 Infantry was a skillful battle team capable of great fighting in the Japanese home islands.

163 Infantry Regiment:
First Round at Jolo

By DR. HARGIS WESTERFIELD, Division Historian

On the night of 2-3 Apr. 1945, 163 Inf's small bloody battle of Jolo began with overseas recon patrol of I & R's 1/Lt. Pfirrman. For accurate data on the Jap garrison, Pfirrman went by PT boat from Zamboanga, with the Navy's Lt. Sinclair, 41 Recon's Lt. Downs, and CIC's Garcia.

Slipping into Bunbun around the coast curve ten miles east of Jolo City, we met Lt. Sindayan, CO of a guerilla battalion, and Governor Vulawic with other guerilla leaders at Taglibi Barrio.

On 8 Apr. at 1600, 163 Inf. (less 2/Bn.) boarded some 30 LCIs, LCMs and probably four LSTs for the 100-mile overnight Zambo—Jolo run. At least one LCI was with a complement of casuals, also had clothing for Jolo civilians. Submarines, two destroyers and a destroyer escort were our guards.

Landing was easy. Guerilla Col. Suarez had marked our beach with great fires; naval shellfire was heavy. Without opposition, A and C Co's landed from Alligators at 0825 on a 1,000-yard beach of coral sand before Taglibi, eight miles west of Jolo City. By 0942, we contacted Col. Suarez with guerillas. From positions 800 yards inland, A and C Co's found no Japs. Both 146 FA (less B Btry) and 163's Cannon Co. were ashore through the surf to support us. Planes and Navy were busy on Jap targets behind Jolo City.

To capture Jolo City, we had to overrun forbidding forested 823-foot Mt. Patikul blocking Route 5. At 1015, Air Corps B-24s dropped 12 500-pound bombs on Patikul. At 1200, nine Marine SBDs (Douglas dive bombers) planted nine 1,000-pound bombs on Mt. Bangkal, two miles SW of Mt. Patikul to retard possible reinforcements.

Starting north into thick forest around the lowest slope of Patikul, I Co. reported no Jap contact at 1225. We slew two on the west side of the main summit and pushed eastward where we expected trouble. At 1403, we had automatic fire from some five Japs. To knock them out, we sent a platoon around the south side. At 1525, a few rifle shots wounded one "I" man. At 1044, we fired 60mm mortars on Japs to the south. By 1615, we had taken Mt. Patikul with nine Jap dead. Grate was slightly wounded and Bernard seriously wounded. Presumably Bernard was the man who hooked a grenade pin on a vine, to explode the grenade on his hip.

Meanwhile, I & R spearheaded 1/Bn's move on Route 5 to seize Jolo City. Minefields were heavy: box-type mines and .75 shells buried nose upwards. By 1530 I & R had one wounded in a firefight below Mt. Patikul among foxholes and dugouts. We killed two Japs. On 9 Apr., 163 HQ Co. lost Golden, Sexton, T/5 Belenky wounded and Tom Harris killed—probably all I & R men.

A Co. relieved I & R and at first knocked out some opposition along Route 5 in the advance on Jolo City. But by 1730, a roadblock had halted us. We encountered several Jap riflemen, killed one. When we fired, Jap return rifle fire was heavy—from an estimated 15 Japs. The day was so late that "A" ceased movement. S/Sgt. Jurasin was killed. On 9 Apr. also Eckert was killed and Barnard wounded, from units unidentified.

After mines and Jap fire checked 163 west of Jolo City, we tried another approach. Guerillas said that Japs defended roads outside Jolo but held the city only lightly.

To secure the vital dock area before Jap demolition, we planned a daring attack. While clearing deepwater approaches to Jolo, naval minesweepers incidentally swept the sea close to the dock. Destroyers hovered to fire on call.

Then Capt. MacClennan (outfit unidentified) with two officers, 30 men of C Co. and a "D" HMG section boarded two LCMs and charged for the dock. No Japs fired; the dock was undamaged. We quickly captured the street junctions near the docks.

Next day, 10 Apr. at 0857, C Co. reported holding all Jolo City. Sporadic .75 shellfire struck at us from the low mountains south of the City, but we had no counterattack.

Held back outside Jolo overnight, at 0740 A Co. pushed on Route 5 again. We recovered Jurasin's body. Opposition had vanished, but heavy minefields hindered our arrival in Jolo City until 1143. Back in the city, beginning about 1122, other 163 men already were unloading two LCTs at the dock. By 1400, Taglibi Beach personnel were following A Co. into the city to make it our main base for battling the Jap army entrenched among mountains 4.5 miles inland.

With beach personnel came also a large contingent of replacements for 163 after Zamboanga Battle—and a smaller number of Zambo' casuals. Just before dusk, some men unofficially visited the ruined, half-burned city. It was touching to offer a cigarette to a Filipino and see an old crone

> CREDIT: Core of this narrative consists of 10-page 163 Inf. Journal, 6-10 Apr. 1945, 146 FA's "Return to Jolo," Operational Monograph No. 10, Maj. Tokichi Tenmyo's "55th Independant Mixed Brigade/Outline of the Jolo Operation" and "Terrain Handbook 57". (Actual author of "Return to Jolo" was Capt. Robert M. Allen.) Also useful were A Co. 716 Tank Bn's "A Company on Zamboanga-Jolo," M Co's 1/Lt. Jack Arnold's diary, my "146 FA Battalion: Fighting the Jolo Mountains", casualty lists, and 163's Morning Reports for Apr. 1945. (Morning Reports were incomplete, and fire at St. Louis Personnel Bureau destroyed all hope of identifying companies to which many casualties belonged.)

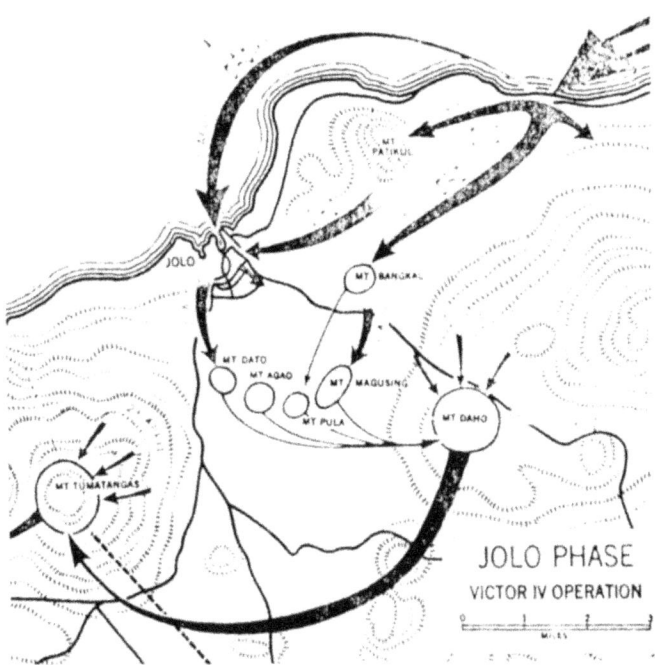

JOLO PHASE
VICTOR IV OPERATION

hold up a stick from a fire to light that cigarette. Matches did not exist. We took friendly Filipinos to our 116 Medics to arrange for treatment of malarious families. The Japs lacked medicines for them.

At twilight, a few mortars still impacted the Jap southern mountains. Casuals and replacements bedded down on canvas cots in a large empty warehouse near the dock. About 2020, veterans recognized the whistle and thud of a Jap cannon—"Whistling Charlie"—at it again. Perhaps the shells aimed at our dockside LSTs. But inside the warehouse, casuals thought that the last shell drove directly at their cots. From trying to reassure G Co's rooky Czuleger on the cot next to him, Westerfield suddenly flattened to the concrete floor under the cot. The shell splintered a nearby building and wounded an unidentified man.

E Co's rooky Lt. Ruben cleared the warehouse and ordered a protective line of three-man prone outposts around the casuals. G's Westerfield and Czuleger with an attached dark-haired guerila lad spent the night in the grass-grown, mosquito-loud gutter before the Jolo post office. But no Japs attacked.

From 1/Bn. positions south of Jolo City, observers counted five rounds of Jap fire, from about halfway up the north slope of Mount Datu. Fifteen minutes later, 146 FA silenced the gun for the night.

Next morn, 11 Apr., 2/Bn. rejoined 163 Inf. which we had left at Zambo on 2 Apr. Sunrise gleamed on our helmets as we formed up at dockside. We had forayed 200 miles west from Zambo and 100 miles west from Jolo to capture Sanga Sanga Island near Borneo from elements of Jap 33rd Naval Guards. Against small opposition, we had secured the Jap barge escape route from Mindanao. Leaving F Co. garrisoning Sanga Sanga, we now held Jolo's rear areas for our other two bns. to fight in the mountains. On 11 Apr. arrived also 146 FA's B Btry from Sanga Sanga to add much needed preparatory fire for 163's battle.

For despite our easy seizure of Jolo Island's capital, the real battle was only beginning on 11 Apr. Two of the three battalions constituting a Jap infantry brigade were entrenched behind Jolo City, with FA and a fine Naval Marine unit. Some 2,200-2,400 Japs manned a mountain defense line half-circling Jolo City. Within two miles of the city, they held a knot of peaks some 800 feet high—and Mts. Bankal and Awak 1.5 miles north of that knot of peaks.

They dug in on Mt. Tumatangas west of those peaks. And 3,000 yards SE was 2247 Mt. Daho with its 33 Naval Guards garrison (Jap Marines).

On first study, however, our Jap enemy seemed weak. They lacked planes, tanks and a navy. No supply ship had got through since they took over Jolo on 5 Oct. 1944—six months ago.

This Jap 55 Infantry Mixed Brigade less one bn. was no frontline outfit of seasoned veterans. Formed in Luzon in 1943, it was a conglomeration of garrison units, replacements and other miscellaneous groups without combat experience. Morale was low. Knowing that we had bypassed entire Jap army units in New Guinea, they had expected to be safe while we fought in Japan or Indonesia. They could repulse guerillas indefinitely.

Over half of 55 IMB had malaria and jungle ulcers. Of the sick, only half were strong enough to fight—or 1/4 of the whole. Beginning in March 1945, they underwent daily air raids. Our planes had reduced approximately half of the positions on Mts. Bangkal, Magusing and Dato. On Bangkal, fire had destroyed all ammo, medical and ration dumps.

But these 2,000-odd men were Japanese—men of a proud nation willing to die for their homeland that they knew they would never see again. We could not use tanks in the mountains. The caves and ravines around the great Mount Daho crater were all but impregnable to ground troops and FA. On Mount Daho were 350-500 "Jap Marines" detached from that 33 Naval Guard unit that had held Pasananca from 163 as long as men could hold it. Their morale was high. Proudly had Major General Tetsuzo Suzuki written to all of his command on the day we landed: "Jolo will be our grave. It should be of great satisfaction to every Japanese warrior that he fights on his grave." To men of their tradition, it was a noble message.

With two months' food on hand, they had enough ammo for one major engagement. They had 400 rounds per rifle, 700 mortar rounds, 700 FA shells for their 12 guns. For each of 16 air-cooled MGs, they had 12,000 rounds. On Mt. Daho the Naval Guards had at least 12 20mm automatic cannon—deadly antipersonnel weapons, as we had learned at Zamboanga.

For 163 Inf., the Battle of Jolo would be small but bloody. Japs would kill 35 and send 125 to the hospital, with 14 injured in action. (Five dead and five hospitalized wounded would be officers.) Despite the overwhelming force against them, these mainly untried Japs fought well.

Even on 10 Apr. while we cleared Jolo City, approaches began on those nearby peaks. Against only light small-arms fire, C Co. moved to within 1,000 yards of Mt. Datu abutting Route 1 from Jolo City across the island.

But direst action of 10 Apr. was K Co's push on C's left flank against forested 768-foot Mt. Bangkal and 572-foot Mt. Awak on a ridge leading SW from Bangkal. Bangkal was apparently the right anchor of the Japs' first line. When we landed on 10 Apr., our Marine bombers neutralized it to protect our attack on Mt. Patikul. The pilots saw excellent cover on its summit and gun positions on northern and western slopes. When eight SBDs dropped eight 1,000-pound bombs, two MGs fired at them from the west slope and were strafed in turn.

Capturing Bangkal would afford our first clear observation of Jap positions southward. It also commanded Route 10 SE into Jolo's interior.

At 0710, "K" with "M's" HMGs marched to storm Mts. Bangkal and Awak while A Co. 716 Tank Bn's 2/Pln convoyed us. Destroyers hit Bangkal. Beginning at 0745 before us, two Marine SBDs blasted Bangkal for 35 minutes. Guarded by an "L" platoon, four tanks went up with "K." A tank-bulldozer made a 5,000-yard road on past "K" so that L Co. could approach Mt. Agao (836-850 feet) which was farther south.

Patrolling through alternate clearings and banana groves, "K" was well on the way up the north slope of Bangkal at 1121. By 1145, we were safely on top. "K" men scouted down the saddle to Awak, secured it by 1250.

At 1356, L Co. with tanks moved south past "K" on Mts. Bangkal-Awak to take Mt. Agao. From the heights, "K" seemed to guard our left flank. But suddenly, the surviving Japs fought back.

At 1425, two Jap rifles fired on "K" from Awak. From the south slope of Bangkal, where they had survived shellfire and bombs, four-five Japs charged from a tunnel and trench system. They tried to run 20 yards to the Bangkal summit and slash "K" with a mortar.

A watching M Co. machine gunner slew three of them. The fourth dropped the mortar and ran into the brush. The "M" gunner kept the mortar covered and hoped that another Jap would try for it.

In this brief fight, K Co. had seven wounded and two more by 1549. By 1605, "K" slew seven more Japs, then two at 1623. We claimed a total of 22, captured an abandoned HMG and two officer's sabres. That night, eight more Japs died in a counterattack.

Because of the menace to our left flank from Mt. Bangkal and the late hour, L Co. held back when it faced Jap pillboxes 1,000 yards from Mt. Agao. Lt. Walters of M Co. spotted a Jap ammo dump some 300 yards from a 3/Bn. perimeter. Moving to seize the ammo with 20 men, he encountered 30 Japs, killed three, with no Yank losses.

Total recorded casualties of 163 on 10 Apr. were nine wounded and three injured in action. "K" had all nine wounded: Hillary, Glen Langley, George Moore, Neely, O'Bar and S/Sgts. Kausalik and Brad McDonald. Injured in action were two "A" men (Cirino, Kafer) and Myron DeWitt of an unidentified outfit.

Thus went 163 Inf's preliminary two days before the main Battle of Jolo. With only three killed, 14 wounded into hospital and three injured in action, we had done well. Jolo City was ours, and the attack on the mounts had begun. But out 2/Bn. was containing bypassed Japs between

Halftracks and armored vehicles of the 41 Recon Troop gave a big helping hand to 163 on Jolo.

Jolo City and the sea near Daingapic Point. And unbroken battalions faced us in an almost continuous defense line of mountains stretching east from Tumatangas through Datu, Agad, Pula and Magusing. And 3,000 yards east of Magusing loomed the nearly impregnable Mt. Daho, with its Jap marine garrison.

163 Inf's Battle of Jolo would be small but bloody, with 174 casualties in all.

146 FA Battalion:
Fighting the Jolo mountains

*by DR. HARGIS WESTERFIELD, Division Historian
with CAPT. ROBERT M. ALLEN, 146 FA*

Only 15 minutes after 163 Inf. (less 2/Bn.) made the initial landing on NE Jolo Island at Tagibi Barrio, 146 FA prepared to fight. At 0845, 9 Apr. 1945, CO Col. Hintz landed with his recon party. In 30 minutes we had selected battery positions and started our terrain survey for accurate fire. A wet landing delayed A and C Btrys., but by 1045, we were positioned with ranging surveys complete. (Cannon Co. 163 Inf. was with 146 FA Bn., but our B Btry. was on Victor IV invasion, farther west in the Sulu Archipelago.).

Although battle-ready soon after landing, 146 FA had no fire missions for 9 Apr. Aided by naval guns and airstrikes, I 163 Inf. took Mt. Patikul 823 feet over the beach, and seized Jolo City and Zettel Field. Jap opposition was from only 3 Infantry Bns. and a Naval Guards Unit—under strength, some 2,000 survivors of originally 4,400 men. They had no air force, and just 12 75-caliber cannons, most of which probably never fired.

Our opposition were typical Jap soldiers, courageous and tenacious, and with no idea of surrender. They were entrenched in formidable mountain defenses over Jolo City. They would kill 35 men of 163 and send 125 wounded to the hospital. And 146 FA Bn. would have one killed and 8 wounded. After our wet landing and the capture of Jolo City, the real Battle of Jolo remained to be fought.

And so we began the real Battle of Jolo the morning of 10 Apr. against the twin peaks of Mts. Bangkal and Awak, some 3 miles east of Jolo City. We believed that Bangkal (766 ft.) was the right anchor of the Jap defenses in the hills SE of Jolo. From it, we could get our first good observation of the Jap mountains southward. Across the saddle east of Bangkal stood Mt. Awak (572 ft.) which the Japs defended also.

Using our Piper Cub, we placed 146 fire on the closest positions, and marked for an air-strike and destroyer gunfire both Bangkal and Awak. With the help of Marine dive-bombers and destroyers, we also shot up Bangkal and Awak. By 1330, K Co. had taken both hills without opposition.

Our Shore Fire Control party under Capt. Levenson, set up an OP on Bangkal, and 1/Lt. Jacobson got orders to join L Co. to attack Mt. Magusing to the south.

Just as Jacobson started to lead his party down the south slope of Bangkal, a command of Japs charged from a tunnel and covered trench system. They tried to reach a mortar commanding the hill crest; 5 were killed in the attempt. Simultaneously, a surprise attack struck the K squad sent out to make perimeter on Awak. There "K" killed 22 Japs but had 9 wounded from grenades, mortars and small arms. That night, "K" with 146's OP had another attack—and slew 4 more Japs.

And that night, 146 briefly fought a Jap 75. From Mt. Awak, some two miles south of Jolo City, shells fell briefly and harmlessly on the town area. After our forward observer called 105 shells down on it, no further action was necessary.

Thus by dawn of 11 Apr., that third day of the Jolo Battle, we had captured Mts. Patikal, Bangkal and Awak. But guerillas reported that Japs still manned a solid defense line of the mountains across our southern front. The line extended from Mt. Tumatangas on the west, eastward across the Jolo City road, then along a close rank of peaks—Datu, Agad, Pula, Magusting—all steep peaks 800-927 feet high. Garrison of this Jap "Left Defense Zone" was mainly 365 Inf. Mixed Bn. less 1 Co. (And 3,000 yards east of Magusing was formidable Mt. Daho with a 33 Naval Guards garrison, but that assault is another story.)

The American attack had two prongs. On 163's left, "L" was to storm Magusing on an advance over open grassland. On 163's right, "C" must advance down the axis of the Jolo City cross-island road and overcome Mt. Datu. Both "L" and "C" had some tough fights, and 146 FA men took prominent parts.

Without FA or AF preparation, "L" and 146 observers accompanied tanks up 874-foot Mt. Magusing. Lead Pln. of "L" with Lt. Jacobson's 146 FA observer party almost reached their objective with no opposition. Suddenly, heavy enfilade fire from covered trenches and concealed pillboxes lashed us from a spur ridge south of the summit. Fierce knee mortar fire also fell from hidden positions on that south ridge.

CREDIT: Basic narrative is from 3 unpublished MSSS attributed to Allen. These are "Return to Jolo," "Reduction of Mt Daho," "Battle fro Tumatangas." Most useful also were Terrain Handbook No. 57, and award stories of Harp, Lee, Ludeke, Morgan, Marquis, Poston, Calldneer, Simpson, and letter of John E. Johnson (aided by Peter Tortorello of 7 Aug 1978. Mjr Tokichi Tenmyo's "Staff Study of Japanese Activities in Jolo..." was also helpful. After Gen Suzuki died, Tenmyo was CO of Jap forces. (My 146 FA Mt Daho story appeared in June 1963 Jungleer.)

41sters in the Jolo mountains.

Tank fires extricated this Pln., but 146's Lt. Jacobson could not aid the men with 105 shells. For we were directly on 146's gun target line, and on ground higher than the Jap spur. Jacobson, Sgt. Nims, and other men of the party were under virtually point-blank fire, but they saved all equipment. Jacobson dared Jap fire to bring out L Co's wounded.

Although "L" had 14 wounded, we could locate Jap strongpoints only approximately. While "L" established covered positions south of Magusing for mortars and MGs to support our tomorrow's attack, Jacobson's party went into action. Working with 2/Lt. Evans, our liaison pilot overhead, Jacobson directed shell-fire on the south slopes of Magusing.

While 146 FA men fought for "L" on our left flank, other 146 men fought for 163 against Mt. Datu on our right.

About 1200, "C" and 146 FA's observers were advancing up a cobblestone road towards the crest of 800-foot Mt. Datu. This road reached the crest through a deep ravine which slashed the rim, halfway around the western slope.

C Co's lead Pln. had passed up through this ravine while the CO and 146's Lt. Ludeke's party and two squads remained below at the bend of the road where it turned to run up the south slope of the ravine. A 146 man spotted Jap cave defenses 40 yards across the ravine and called them to the attention of "C." Perhaps because "C" had earlier found almost abandoned pillboxes on the approach to Mt. Datu, we felt fairly safe. But the patrol to clear the caves hit a hornets' nest.

A blast of Jap fire from the ravine, hit this patrol. Jap fire also pinned down C's men and 146 men on the road.

For 2 hours, we cowered prone on the stone road in blazing sun to save our lives. Although in defilade on the road, we could not leave it. The hidden Japs shot anyone who so much as moved.

After we endured 2 tortured hours, a HMG—probably D Co's—was manhandled into the unique position where it could plunge fire into the caves. Covered by this fire, we made a run for our lives.

About this time, T/5 Lloyd Lee silenced a Jap MG. But when he tried to escape, fire from a cave trapped him again. Lee threw a grenade into that cave and silenced it long enough to save himself.

Down on the cobblestone road, T/5 Harp took a grenade wound in trying to save his radio. On his second try, Harp got a head wound. He kept on firing at the Jap positions.

Pinned down on that sunstruck, heated road, 2/Lt. Ludeke passed out from heat and shock. Regaining consciousness and finally saved, Ludeke refused to leave for the rear that day.

Because the Jap pocket was in dead space behind the hill, FA shells could not hit it. With 163's Major Armstong, Ludeke adjusted mortar fire on the dead space. We tried to destroy our abandoned radio and 2 infantry radios. Despite earlier heat prostration, Ludeke stayed with "C" to adjust night FA fire. (That day, C Co. had three killed—two officers—and 9 wounded. It took 4 days to clear Japs from those 15 caves and pillboxes.)

On 11 Apr. also, 146 FA blasted partly captured Mt. Magusing again. Coordinating with mortars and air-strikes, we helped I Co. to conquer Magusing. "I" had two dead, 8 wounded—and 45 dead Japs.

On 163's right flank, the Jolo Road, we battered Mt. Kagangan (1095 feet), south of Mt. Datu. From their plane, Lts. Evans, Allen adjusted 2 shells before a cave evidently occupied, made direct hits on a pillbox commanding all 1/Bn's sector. We shelled for 3 days until "B" took Kagangan 15 Apr.

Rejoined by B Btry returned from Sanga Sanga Island, all 146 FA batteries lined up on the beach near Jolo City. We were now 3 miles closer to the Japs—but in danger of raids.

From tall cogon (kunai) grass before our guns, they mapped us. About midnight 15-16 Apr, some 16 Japs attacked with bangalore torpedoes, rifle, grenades. We repelled them, with MGs, even grenades and sub-MGs.

About 0200, 4-5 unseen Japs got within 30 feet of S/Sgt. Morgan's MG guarding C Btry on extreme east of 146's firebase. We swung our gun and felled the Japs. Attack ended, except for low moans that we feared to investigate in darkness. But at 0600, a Jap grenade exploded on Morgan's men. Cpl. Souza died of wounds. It hit all 4 others: Callender, S/Sgt. Morgan, T/5s Poston, Marquis. They fought on; Callender risked Jap fire to bring in more MG belts.

Three days before this night attack, 146 FA already fought Mt. Tumatangas, last great Jap stronghold on Jolo. Garrisoned by 365 Independent Inf Bn and most of 55 Ind Mixed Brigade's 12 mountain guns, it held other fragments of broken commands.

Tallest of all Jolo mountains (1264 ft), this massif with Mabusing and Batu Puti comprised some 30 square miles of forested sheer slopes. Overhanging Jolo City, Tumatangas with its combination of cannon and infantry was the last great challenge to 163's combat team.

On 12 Apr, 146's Lt Rainville spotted extensive trenches and gun positions half-way up its eastern slope. They were dug into sides and rim of a huge crater shaped like a "Figure 8." And NW of the crater was a stream bed with much-used water-holes. Rainville surprised many Jap troops in the open to blast them with 105s. That afternoon airborne, he saw more trenches and activity. Over 100 rounds crashed among them. Making a precision adjustment, he got target hits on a gun position commanding Jolo City.

That night of 12 Apr, a Jap 75 shot on Jolo City which B 163 had seized that afternoon. One shell smashed warehouse timbers and narrowly missed killing some 50 casuals from Zamboanga who had bivouacked there a few minutes before. So on Apr. 13, 14, and 16, Marine bombers smashed Figure 8 Crater, water-holes, and gun positions. No gun fired again until 17 Apr.

Attacking towards the crater 17 Apr, guerillas encountered another hidden Jap strongpoint. They took a Jap 75 pointed at Jolo City, but MGs and mortars repelled them.

That night, the gun shelled Jolo for the last time. A direct hit on the hospital killed 3 civilians, wounded 7 more, killed 163's Medic Jiminez.

On 18 Apr, we zeroed in. With delayed fuzes, we heavily concentrated fire on this position by centering sheaf. Our pilots saw 4 target hits. Later, 163 found the gun knocked out. An "L" Pln burned it up with a magnesium grenade. Thus ended the last fire of 55 Independent Mixed Brigade's 12 guns.

Reports now pinpointed the Crater area as the strongest Jap concentration on Jolo—with 500-1000 Japs. When 163's CO Col Moroney flew over it with Lt Rainville, a HMG and several lighter "woodpeckers" shot at them.

On 24 Apr, "K" with 146 support began the action to liquidate the Crater garrison. Although Jap fire at first repelled "K" from the intricate net of Jap trenches, 146's Lt Simpson performed miracles of close FA support on 26-27 Apr. Simpson crawled through the brush within 50 yards of the Jap positions to call down fire. Once, shells fell 35 yards before him. On 27 Apr, 163 Inf used direct fire— brought up a Cannon Co 105, 2 57mm AT guns, and HMGS. After this fire, "K" easily occupied the eastern rim of the Crater.

This memorable action of 27 Apr against Figure 8 Crater still did not conclude fighting on Tumatangas. Again and again, 146 fired on Tumatangas—but only to break up diehard Jap concentrations. For 163 made no wasteful all-out effort to kill the last Jap in that vast wilderness. Guerilla action was of limited effectiveness except over a long period. After the last 146 men left Jolo—2 guns of A Btry about 27 May—small-scale fighting continued until Black 93 Div men forced the Japs off Tumatangas in early July. But the last 87 Japs did not surrender until 26 Aug 1945, 12 days after Tokyo admitted defeat on 14 Aug.

Such was 146 FA's great 7-week operation to conquer Jolo. Our shells broke the major resistance on the Magusing-Datu range, ended the siege of Mt Daho, made Mt. Tumatangas harmless. We did this with 4393 shells,—with 77 "missions," 85 "concentrations," and 43 "massed fires." (At Zambo, we fired only 11813 total rounds.) We had done well.

146 FA Blasts Mount Daho

**By Capt. Robert M. Allen
and
Dr. Hargis Westerfield**

On 12 Apr 1945, 146 FA began fighting Mt. Daho on Jolo. Supporting a guerilla force that evening, we threw shells on a Jap Marine position blocking the highway at Kilometer 7½. Flying low next morning to observe results, Lt. Evans felt his plane rock; 2 twin-mount 25 mm Nippo guns bracketed him. He dived to tree-top level, circled to the guns' blind-spot, happily called for another concentration of our 105's.

We exploded an ammo dump; but the 25's stopped the guerilla attack. That afternoon, Evans with Lt. Allen flew again to fight the 25's. He thought he now knew where the battery's blind spot was and that he had a safe place there to direct fire. Again he was nearly blown from the sky from 3 twin-mount 25's. Again he threw in 105 shells on the 3 guns; but results were nil.

That night, Evans arranged a plane-artillery attack with Capt. Leuktmeyer, liaison with Marine Air Group 32. At dawn, Evans drew fire from three 25's. First he threw in 105's, then market targets with smoke shells. Now 18 Marine bombers dived vertically; bomb after bomb fell in the area of 2 guns west of the road, and into a patch of rain forest hiding a third. Then our 105's barraged with time fire.

Only 2 guns fired when the guerillas probed again; but Jap MG's and rifles protected those 25's too well.

Now from the ground, Lt. Martin Van Buren of 146 FA crept with a guerilla patrol within 75 yards of the closer gun to pinpoint targets for Apr 15. On this day, the 12 guns of our FA Btn plus the 4 of Cannon Co 163 were trained on that stubborn strongpoint.

To achieve maximum kill for surprise fire, the 16 guns blasted together before our plane was sighted by Nippo observers. Volleys of 105's burst in black puffs at tree level; dust rose in clouds.

After air bursts, mixed quick and delay fuse shells hammered their network of trenches and gun positions—over 300 shells in under 30 minutes. Then we marked with phosphorus, and the Marine planes bombed again. The strongpoint was silenced.

Thus ended defense of the strongpoint at Kilometer 7½. Although the Japs' 33d Naval Guard Unit began pulling out 2 days before Apr 15 attack, Lts. Inouye and Sato had held out stubbornly with their 2 pltns. We found two 25's damaged but still usable. Nearly half the estimated 100 Japs were dead and the survivors loaded with wounded as they fell back to the main line on Mount Daho. Other Jap formations had to help carry wounded. In the afternoon 100 men with 40 guards carried 15,054 rounds of AA ammo to the Jap's new position. This retreat went on in the shade of deep ravines; but our planes found them and bombed and strafed.

That night Japs raided our 105's at the airstrip. At midnight, some 16 creps across the airstrip; but grenades and small arms beat them off. In a final attack just before dawn, they hit Btry C. One grenade landed in a MG hole. Cpl Souza died there; and Morgan, Poston, Marquis, and Callender were wounded. After daylight, we found that C had killed 3 Nips, and B and A killed 1 each—and blood on their escape trail.

Now we prepared for the main battle against 2300 foot Mt. Daho, whose wooded flat-topped crater loomed against the horizon. The Japs held the crests of 2 partly bare ridges runing south to the base of Mt. Daho, with numerous commanding outposts facing us. On the flanks of these ridges and between them were deep forested ravines which concealed communication lines and supply dumps.

After heavy bombing early 17 Apr, all the First Btns' riflemen probed the Nips' lines. In the center of the push, B Co was stopped in its tracks; a 25 mm and plunging MG fire pinned it down. Our 146 FA observer neutralized the 25 with battery salvos. That pillbox caught 2 direct hits. But just as B found the 25 silent, Jap mortars and MG's took up the defense, despite our FA preparation. Japs counterattacked downhill. They lost 15; and B had 1 dead, 3 wounded, 4 missing.

After B repulsed the Japs, three 25's opened up from new positions. Lt. Swanson of 146 Btry A was forward observer with B Co. He placed smoke and shells before B, and they withdrew safely. Meanwhile, Lt. Allen—grounded because of the muddy airfield—caught the flash of all three Nippo 25's in an aiming circle at the Btn's survey base. Observing 7000 yards through a BC scope, he shelled the guns and silenced them, although A Co had 3 wounded during the fire.

On 18 Apr we stepped up shelling and bombing. Lt. Allen placed 1 salvo where he had observed the 25 mm fire last night. The salvo tore away foliage; they saw a half-closed cave, and prepared for the kill.

Covered by bombardment, Cn 163 men pushed a 105 and a 37 mm cannon up for direct fire on the Nippo guns, with 146 FA Capt. DuCommun and Lt. Hornefius as guides. But we drew a concentration of MG's and 25's and were silenced. Bracketed, we cowered in a bomb crater. During lulls, the gun crew fired again; but the Japs hit back, wounded 1. We had to withdraw the gun under smoke.

The ridges hid the last Nippo 25 from us. But Lt. Evans flew over with Capt. Bedke, Asst S-3, and spotted the cave it fired from. Then we dropped 2 rounds into the cave-mouth, and the last Nippo dual-purpose 25 was dead on Mt. Daho.

On this day, we had fired 500 rounds. A Nippo diary reported that the Japs remained in their air-raid shelters all night. Cannon had wounded Lt. Io.

On Apr 19, we prepared for the assault of Apr 20. Morning brought after the cannonade a heavy air-strike—36 planes in 2 hours. The bombers tore apart supply dumps in the ravines, stripped away what jungle the guns had left, discovered Nippo caves on reserve slopes. Meanwhile 163's AT 1 Btn from a hill 200 yards NE had sited two 57 mm AT guns, a 105, and some HMG's on the Japs' positions. Cos A, B, C moved into perimeter on the road near Kilometer 8 ready to jump off at dawn. The same Nippo diary wrote that our air-raids had blown apart huts and collapsed shelters.

Of the 2 Jap ridges guarding Daho, East Ridge had the less well fortified cave defenses. Maj. Armstrong therefore planned to attack East Ridge with Cos A and B. After taking East Ridge, both Cos would fire on West Ridge—hub of the Japs' defenses—while C would overrun that final Nippo stronghold.

CREDITS

Only source is "Reduction of Mt. Daho." from *Hist 146 FA*, purchased by Division Assn Funds from Washington's Fed Archives. Peter Tortorello, 146 FA Co Clerk, says author is Capt. Robt. M. Allen.
Can anyone send me more information on Zambo, Jolo, Davao?

HARGIS WESTERFIELD
Association Historian
6248 Sturdy Avenue

On Apr 20, 146 FA had planes over Daho to direct fire —with Col. Hintz and Lt. Evans in the first plane, and Lt. Allen with Lt. Rainville in the second. With 163 as observers were Maj. McDougall and Capt. DuCommun.

At 0800, 146 FA marked East Ridge, and 45 Marine bombers dropped 1000 pounders for an hour, then strafed with 50's. Then cannon shelled with time-fire; smoke palled the air after the orange flashes of explosions; infantry mortars pounded.

In the sudden silence at 0900, A and B Cos moved on the enemy—but slowly through unexpectedly heavy undergrowth and up steep ridges. At 1015 B Co on the right was under fire from a pillbox. Lt. Hornefius placed a direct hit from a delay fuse and blew up the pillbox.

Meanwhile A Co broke out into the open at the center of East Ridge, about ⅔ up the slope to the Japs' lines. A Co was stopped dead; but our observers scored direct 105 hits on the 2 pillboxes firing against A. The delay fuse artillery shell demolished 1 pillbox.

A Co would have pushed again; but B was not firing support on A's left. Only then did we find that in those torturous mountain paths, B was on the wrong ridge—on the stronger held West Ridge 200 yards short of the Nippo's fortifications.

It was too late to revert to the original plan; but B's CO ordered a Pltn to hurry back up the right side of East Ridge for fire support to A. Then he threw the main body of B directly at West Ridge.

With 146 FA and weapons protection, A and B Cos hit East and West Ridges. But when we had to life the fire to avoid killing our own infantry, the Japs rallied. They volleyed the leading pltns of both A and B. Although our Yank pltns won footholds, they lacked adequate reserves or flank protection, and fell back.

Now the Nips counterattacked, and 146 FA and direct fire weapons caught them in the open and rolled many dead. B Co fought back until 1600, then withdrew under smoke shells laid down by Maj. McDougall.

Reorganizing an hour later, B found that 2 men left for dead were only wounded. With Lts. Evans and Allen to place a smoke screen, a B patrol found the enlisted man and rescued him, but the officer was dead. Meanwhile our observers saw many Japs scrambling down the rear slope, and had them shelled. Just before sunset, the same plane helped a patrol locate 2 more wounded men, but threat of darkness prevented it from standing by until the men were saved.

In this battle of 20 Apr, we lost 3 KIA, 3 MIA, 32 WIA against an estimated 100 Japs we had slain. An example of our vicious fire-power comes from the Jap diarist, who reported that of the Naval Meteorological Unit, 8 out of 10 were wounded.

But the abortive attack on Daho was our final attack. On 22 Apr, we wasted shells and bombs in pushing against defenses loaded with 235 dead including the stragglers we could count. Perhaps 150 naval troops escaped, and an unknown number of the Army. Originally, Daho was manned with 500 naval troops plus 100-150 refugees from Brigade Hq on Mt. DaTu, with General Suzuki commanding.

Thus went the stiffest battle against the Nips on Jolo. Outranged by our artillery and without planes, these Japanese soldiers had fought like equals. They held tenaciously at Kilometer 7½, riposted by night at 146 FA, repulsed us on 20 Apr. As General Suzuki prophesied, it was of great pride to each Japanese warrior that in Jolo he fought on his grave. As for us of 146 FA, we did a workmanlike job with the Air Marines and the 163 Infantry to overrun Mt. Daho.

L Co. 163 Infantry:
The Great Ambush on Jolo

**By DR. HARGIS WESTERFIELD, Division Historian
and CAPT. WILLIAM F. SCHACHT**

On 27 Apr. 1945, L Co. 163 Inf. moved on Japs defending Mr. Tumatangas, the great semiwilderness overhanging Jolo City southwards. This was the last phase of the Battle of Jolo. Here entrenched were the Japs' unbroken 363 Inf. Bn, and fragments of 365 Bn which had held the first line of Mounts Magusing and Datu.

Prominent core of Jap resistance was a great brush-filled crater supposedly shaped like a figure 8, halfway up on the NE Tumatangas slope. Japs were dug in on the rim of the Great Crater, with mortars and MG's. And after 3/Bn stormed the crater rim, the Japs were still strong and clever enough to ambush Lt. Schacht's 1/Pln in a memorable disaster.

Trucked up a rugged road into a palm grove 27 Apr., L Co. had our first panorama of the Tumatangas wilderness. It was high, steep ridges covered with cogon grass—like the tall coarse kunai of Sanananda. It was also deep ravines of bamboo thickets and banana groves. Grassy ridges, thicketed ravines—they stretched over many miles to the final steep peak of Tumatangas (2664 feet), sheer above heavy rain forest. As L learned after fighting the Great Crater, the Tumatangas wilderness was a labyrinth perfect for a deadly Jap ambush.

L's first assignment was to relieve K Co. now battling Great Crater point-blank. The crater lay some 1500 yards NE of Tumatangas Peak, between the rocky lower pimple of Batu Puti on the west, and Hill 1020 on the east. Although reportedly shaped like a figure 8, the map shapes it like a whale with the wider forepart swimming west. Great Crater was 600-700 yards long, 300 yards at its widest, and 200-300 feet deep with a brushy floor. Japs held its rim.

When L came to the Great Crater, K still blasted it, and Cn Co's 105 gun, two AT Co's 57mm cannon, MG's and HMG's with 146 FA's howitzers. Dust and fragments hurtled high overhead. Twice already, Jap fire forced back a K Pln attacking the North Rim. Toward late afternoon, K won the rim and killed eight Japs surviving the shellfire.

Relieving K by dusk, most of L entrenched on Hill 1020 east of the crater. Schacht's 1/Pln holed up on the North Rim among Jap fragments and fired all night and grenaded dislodged, living Japs. At dawn, we counted nine more dead Japs.

CREDIT: L Co's Otto Matjeka first told me about the Great Ambush before 1964. Recently, Lt. (later Capt.) Bill Schacht sent me his 32-page diary of action on Jolo. Important also are Gene Stafford's brief story to Matjeka, letters of Carl Phillips (5 Feb. 1976), R.J. Benson (2 June, 19 July 1976). Other sources are Capt. Robert Allen's "Battle for Tumatangas," 163 Inf's Casualty List and Journal. (Schacht manages a 180-acre farm at Huntingdon, Ind.—soy and corn and Black Angus cattle. Look for the trademark "Daisy" on his rubber or plastic products which his company manufactures for Sears, Woolworth.).

After the Great Crater was silent, heavy concentrations of Japs still waited to kill, in the maze of ridges and ravines NE toward Tumatangas Road. Tactical objective was for L to contact I Co's perimeter, some three miles north. Between L and I lurked vengeful Japs who would set up our Great Ambush of 29 Apr.

On 28 Apr. Schacht's pln left the North Rim to contact I Co. Mortars barraged ahead; 3/Pln flanked us on the right. We maneuvered safely 600-700 yards across cogon grass against a dark, dense thicket. Unexpectedly, we faced the outside curve of a concrete or stone half-circle, 50 yards from end to end. Guerillas called it an old Spanish OP against Moros. Its crannies and peepholes menaced us; we found some pillboxes and dumps. We blew up dumps and hideaways in the wall; Cap. Evans of 3/Bn Hq. brought a demolition squad to destroy a bunker and part of that wall. Our check at the obstacle of the "Stone Fort" was a factor in the Great Ambush of 29 Apr.

Suddenly late that 28 Apr. Maj. Milford gave an order that led to Schacht's pln's disastrous ambush. At 1700, T/Sgt. Brownhill was to take a 15-man patrol to contact I's perimeter before dark. Orders were to move fast. In that stinking terrain, we found seven Japs newly dead from FA. But after an hour, the tense Schacht heard that we made contact.

Back on the North Rim among putrid Japs, we slept and guarded that night with fearful knowledge. All 1/Pln was to patrol three miles to I Co. through that same Jap maze of ridges and brush. And Brownhill's 15 men reported Jap signs everywhere.

Orders were unchanged at dawn 29 Apr.; we grimly rolled combat packs. Ahead of us, guerillas shot up their ammo at the "Stone Fort." The slight mortar barrage before us could well have shown our route to the Japs.

Also before us, Lt. Steege's I Co. pln crossed cogon grass to the west near the palm grove where L detrucked two days ago. Midway in the cogon, Jap automatic fire hit an I Medic—either Evar Peterson or Kurkoski—who died later that day. The Jap fire halted; I took up security for our left flank.

Leaving the North Rim of the Great Crater, Schacht's pln crossed unharmed the same cogon field where Steege's medic was struck. We began the march that led directly to ambush in the Small Crater.

Start of the best route to I's perimeter was down from high ground north of the Great Crater, then across lower end of the Small Crater northwards. Small Crater was just below the ridge, where the "Stone Fort" stood. In fact, the high ground where the "Stone Fort" stood was a U-shaped ridge that surrounded the small, oval crater, except at the north end.

Schacht's pln did not try to descend to the Small Crater from the right or east arm of the U-shaped ridge. The

"Stone Fort" blocked the right arm of the summit of the U-ridge, and slopes down to the Small Crater were so thick with forest that they seemed impenetrable. (Later, two Jap LMG's would shoot down on us from there.)

About three-fourths of the way on the ridge, we turned right to hike across the level floor of the crater. We did not know that a Jap HMG waited on the ridge just before we turned off.

Descending the steep ridge into the crater about 1100, Schacht halted the lead squad to take a breather for the other men to catch up, near the low north exit of the crater. Schacht forever remembers the tall, wooded conical peak on his left.

Then from all sides, Jap fire blasted out. Wounded men shouted in pain; American bodies thudded to the ground quietly or crawling for cover. A steady stream of bullets kicked up dust everywhere. Prone in agony, we crawled for even an inch of defilade, but on that flat surface we had none. There were few big trees to crawl behind, where bullets plunked also.

The prone Benson heard men return fire. BAR-man Shilliday excitedly called, "Fire! Shoot back!" But Sgt. Benson already was wounded in the head with a bullet through his helmet and could not fight. In a few moments, he did not hear Shilliday again; the BAR-man was dead.

Three Jap MG's arced down on us from the U-Ridge; a dozen riflemen fired from all sides. The HMG shot from the end of the left arm of the ridge where we had turned down, and two Jap LMG's shot from thickets just below the "Stone Fort." All Japs were invisible and sighting on us down on the floor of the crater. There we crawled like worms searching for any kind of a hole.

In seconds, Schacht lost control of squad leaders and the radio man, who in turn could do nothing. He crawled some feet towards the radio, but about six bullets impacted on all sides. One hit between his legs; another ticked his helmet.

Schacht tried to relay messages back down the column. While he squirmed under fire and awaited a reply, two men yelled, "I'm hit!" A MG burst hissed over his back and impacted between him and Phillips, lying close together. A round clipped a grenade from Phillips' shoulder strap. An MG bullet grazed the skin high on Phillips' chest. The nearest squad leader to Schacht, Sgt. Dixon, was wounded. And so it kept on—several more minutes' of pure hell.

When no word relayed back from the radio operator, Schacht saw that he could get no message through for help. As bullets whipped above or thudded close, he wondered, "Which one's got my name on it?" Men under fire felt hopeless, but Schacht, who could do nothing for some 30 men, suffered far worse.

He had long ago given up hope for an organized withdrawal. He passed orders to survivors to leave in groups as best they could. He'd take two men, try to dash out of sure death to get help. With a lump in his throat, he ordered Romanenghi, Phillips and McBath heading the prone column, to hold the ground and try to round up others to lead to I's perimeter.

Hearing more cries of the wounded, we crawled, ran and ducked; bullets followed our every move. Crossing the low crater-mouth ridge, we had a little cover. Inaccurate bullets indicated that we had to run the long way to I.

Far off the route that Brownhill took last night, we fled through fields and bamboo thickets. Suddenly McCullough shouted, "They're Yanks!" We were safe within the I pln perimeter. Leaving Bronwnhill and McCullough to fire three shots in strings and smoke grenades to guide any survivors, Schacht jeeped back towards the crater. At AT Co's roadblock, seven men had come out alive. Dave Johnson had a chest wound. Next to arrive was Tramel, lucky to have four mere nicks. Sgt. Dixon had two wounds—1 in the leg. Roger had lost lower jaw, teeth and tongue.

Back at the ambush crater, Schacht found confused and silent men who had escaped. Jap fire had stopped. It had lasted 15 intense minutes, and now we had to rescue the last men.

T/Sgt. Dostal's 2/Pln rescue party and Lt. Steege's I pln entered the crater and reassembled survivors with a string of three rifle shots. Several men were still unaccounted for: Blakemore, Benson, Dahlstrom and Shilliday.

Returning with three seriously wounded in litters, Dostal's men saw a pillbox blocking the only feasible exit

41sters in action on Jolo.

from the crater. With I men's help, they angrily cleared it without more losses. Steege shot three Japs running out of it.

Late that evening, Schacht accounted for all of his men. Of some 30 on patrol 16 of them were casualties. Besides Tramel and Phillips mentioned already, two more escaped with light wounds—Beach and McCullough. Besides Johnson, Dixon and Rogers with wounds specified already, we had seven more seriously wounded. Wounded in the shoulder, Cronin (like Rogers) had lost tongue, teeth and lower jaw. Hickman also had a shoulder wound. With his head wound, Benson lay some three hours quiet with red ants crawling over him. Finally, he heard our voices and worked his way to Dostal's rescue patrol. S/Sgt. Stafford was hit in the leg. Brazzanovich and Delmonico also had serious wounds.

We lost two killed. Last body we found, and by accident, was S/Sgt. Dahlstrom's—a bright reliable veteran with some two months before rotation. Shilladay lay dead beside his BAR, with only five rounds left in the breach.

But how, when the Japs had surprise, invisibility and overwhelming firepower, did 1/Pln escape with only two dead, 10 seriously wounded? The Japs lacked grenades and mortars. But why did they fail to follow their surprise volleys with a bayonet charge? We like to believe that they feared close combat because men like Shilladay would not be killed until his last five rounds were expended. (We had no evidence of any Jap casualties.)

Japs attacked L that night, both on Hill 1025 west of 3/Bn's garrison camp and back at the crater. After 3/Pln's Lt. McGee killed a Jap that night, his comrades lurked nearby to barrage our holes with grenades at dawn. A grenade in Young's hole cost him a foot.

While Schacht's decimated pln lay safe in camp on 30 May, we awoke at 0600 to a burst of fireworks up at the Great Crater and steady streams of tracers from our own MG's. In attacking Hill 1025 over open terrain, the Japs made good moonlight hunting. L slew there 28 Japs, took two LMG's, one knee mortar and 23 rifles. We hoped that among those Jap dead were the men who mounted that clever ambush in the Small Crater.

Such was L 163's heaviest combat on Mt. Tumatangas. After the ambush, Schacht's understrength pln was soon back on patrol. Although the Great Crater fight of 3/Bn had broken serious Jap resistance, some 90 fighters held out on Jolo until surrender after V-J Day. For Schacht's I/Pln of L Co., the Great Crater and the Great Ambush are a memory of self-sacrifice and heroism.

G Co 163 Inf-CLASSIC PATROL ON JOLO
By DR. HARGIS WESTERFIELD, Association Historian

On 10 May 45, G Co 163 Inf entrucked to relieve K Co against Japs holding Tumantangas, Malayan name for the "Mountain of Tears" on Jolo. Jammed standing in our roaring trucks rising blast, we peered between others helmets for a last look at homes we had visited, dark pretty girls we knew. They waved from porches.

Off Scott Blvd, our trucks on the Baunu-Timbangan-Maimbung Road southward drove for the long north slope of Tumatangas, upslanting massif of jungle. Dismounting, we climbed a low ridge to take over slit trenches in brush, quizzed a Yank waiting for us.

"Our patrols never got past that spring across the road," he said, cheerfully. "You can't see where the shots come from in the shadows. It's fine for mortars too. You'll see! You'll see!" Somebody shouted, and he ran under humped pack to entruck for Jolo and our girls.

For young 2/Lt Sprague, CO of 3/Pln, orders came fast. Sprague took Baer's 1/Squad downslope behind us and across the road, where the departing K man had cautioned us. While we other 3/Pln men remained to guard the lines, Baer's M-1s and BAR blasted once, muffled by the hills. Silence fell suddenly; it seemed over.

Tall Sgt Vilicich burst in among us, shouted, "Second and third squads! Leave your packs! Let's go!" As we riflemen doubled across the road, Sprague shouted, "Where's that stretcher?"

Across the road, we hit a trail. Jungle closed over us. Sprague ordered 4 men, "Leave your files and come with me."

Slipping past other sweating riflemen, we were happy to see Baer's first scout, Piotrowski, jacket dark with sweat, muzzle blackened. Westerfield and he exchanged slaps. Around that curve clustered another knot of wet green backs with a casualty, and down the next trail-reach, riflemen were prone on guard.

Here lay Holley, our only seriously wounded, red blood on his pale bared chest. Having no stretcher, we slipped a poncho under him, with difficulty hefted him a rough 100 yards back to the road. Here stood BARman Acree grinning. A Medic swabbed the great gouge in his right back just above the belt.

What happened? With Piotrowski and Holley as scouts, Baer's squad hit the trail-block at the spring. Piotrowski spotted a squatting Nippo outguard, rolled him dead. Crossing the stream below the spring, he took the squad up a mountain trail. The Nip LMG was well camouflaged in shadows by banana fronds left of the trail.

The trail was a perfect fire-lane for the LMG, but its 4 men reclined beside it with cigarettes. Pete threw down on them – eight clips from his M-1 fired fast as a BAR; and they died.

Japs up the hill lobbed in knee-mortars, rolled grenades. Scout Holley leaped into a hole with 3 Nips. He slew 2, pressing his M-1 into them. The third shot him across the chest, nipple to nipple. Acree fought with his BAR until a mortar gouged his back. We ran ... Holley lived and got home early to the States; Acree had a few days' hospital. This was Baer's third light wound; it gave him points enough to be home far ahead of other replacements who had joined G Co with him at Rocky.

So effective was Baer's thrust that when Sprague's full pltn pushed, we found only a few dead Nips in cloven jungle boots asprawl by the tracks. Baer's squad claimed 11 Nips killed.

Now we cleared the area by the spring. Just across the stream, Bittner spotted a Nip on the brushy right slope, pointed him out to Ryder. Ryder fired over his M-1 barrel without using sights. The Jap disappeared.

A squad burned out that slope with a BAR. Two men carried out Shoopman; he thought his own BAR had shot him in the hand. But the bullet was Japanese.

On the ridge-edge above the trail-block, we dug in. Suddenly outguard Berzac up the ridge passed work for silence, called S/Sgt Rudningan, runner Nading. In a chattering stream, his BAR with other guns lashed out at 6 Nips trying to escape. At dawn, we found 2 dead.

A carrying party brought our packs and 10-in-1 rations. Digging in on the downslope between Williams and Ryder, Westerfield ate corned beef and crackers ravenously. A can of peas was a prize because of its moisture. We ate peas directly from the can, each taking a turn with his spoon. Nobody minded an old Nip body 10 yards downhill.

Westerfield finished supper with an "O Henry" bar from his pack no tropical chocolate but a fresh American candy-bar.

233

How far they were from the beach of Aitape a year back, he thought as he knelt with rifle ready on first guard, here where brush grew too thick to throw a grenade. Chocolate bars, Filipino girls waving at you en route to war — it was good for a change. But G Co must fight in Japan, he thought, and he would have to live through tomorrow.

At 1000, he woke Ryder, passed the watch to him. The night was dark and peaceful. He stretched full length on poncho, pillowed on flotation bladder, and slept. He had a second turn of only 90 minutes in blacker night. After the chill and damp, he breathed warm under poncho, slept again.

At daylight we had K-rations, hot coffee made instantly with paraffined K-ration covers. But no water-party came up. Westerfield stole time to refill his 1 empty canteen at the spring; it was the wisest act of his life, he learned.

For Filipino mountain-fighting was hard as jungle-fighting only tilted. The cover was thicker but shorter, the sunlight more intense; and there was the water problem. And many men had just 1 canteen.

In a first burst of sweat, we probed down a slope of slippery green, to the edge of a deep ravine. Back up the slope we labored, then up the shoulder past the dead Japs we had shot from our holes. Then we dropped back down a 75-degree slope.

Ahead, our TSMG and M-1 fusilladed. Back uphill we doubled; a Nip MG might hit us in the backs. Texan Fowler, Californian Cortez had killed 2 Nips in the draw; but it was no place to fight. Four gulleys coverged there masked by banana fronds, undergrowth. Chattering Nips were forming to attack; a knee-mortar shell would have killed a squad. A dismounted MG lay on the ground.

Safe again, we flattened on the reverse slope of the ridge. Williams spoke on the phone. Now a low, tearing sound — 146 FA's 105s — curved close to us, blasted in that draw. The ridge shook; great waves of concussion blew up from the doomed pocket. We never bothered to go back there.

We growled as we descended into that ravine a third time. Hard labor was our climb up the next shoulder. Our scouts moved by inches. A man in column would pull rifle, pack grenades, assorted steel up 6 feet, cling by brittle weeds as he tried not to stamp on the next man climbing too close below him. And we feared that a sniper would fire from behind us.

On the second ridge, the climb was easier, but the scouts more scared. Finally we halted before signs of new Jap digging, posted outguards. While most of us lay on our backs and nursed the first water from our second canteen, we learned the mission of this patrol. First, we were not on Tumatangas as we had thought, but on Mabusng, an independent massif 1,900 feet high. Japs were in a valley between us and a rocky pimple called Batu Puti, and we were to contact E Co working toward us through the Japs from Batu Puti.

From Outguard uphill, Ogle's BAR chattered. As Vilicich and Westerfield rushed up beside Ogle and Bennett, a Jap grenade detonated. Flattened behind a tree, we heard it blast harmlessly, 10 feet away. Ogle and Vilichich sprayed the bush.

"A big Nip rifleman!" South Carolina replacement Ogle exulted at his first kill. "Right in that open spot." On Vilicich's order, Westerfield threw 2 grenades. Nothing happened.

Followed an annoying delay while these men of Bill Smith's unfought squad chafed for an attack. At last with BAR cover, Westerfield moved up and ended the wounded Nippo rifleman with a grenade into the foxhole where he lay.

Vilicich pulled ahead to scout the track along a sheer slope, turned right. Suddenly he turned, swung his M-1 back left, lanced the bushes with it at close range like killing a snake.

"Shoot him! He's still alive!" cried Vilicich to Westerfield running up. The wounded officer's body stiffened to the bullet-strike — a young handsome lad whom his men must have liked. His right hand relaxed. On his chest lay a little red grenade. He died smiling.

Sprague massed our 3 BARs to thin the brush, but they hit no Japs among the fox-holes. A squad pushed to the summit of Mabusing, but found only some Nippo fires still burning. Only later did we realize that man, 1 officer, had fought a brave little delaying action to save the others to kill more Yanks.

But already G Co's 3 Pltn faced an ordeal worse than combat. After the hot, tilted mountain fighting, we had no supply party with water. We dug perimeter and sweated out the little moisture we had left. That night we treasured the last drops from our canteens on our tongues. At dawn, he had only a swallow from what E Co spared, and hoped for a relief party.

But at dawn of 12 May, what sounded like an automatic cannonade rolled from our left. Japs hit E Co; there died Sgt Nylaan trying to save another Yank; E Co had 2 killed, 3 wounded. Our water party was diverted to carry out wounded. Long hours we lay on outguard in a fever of thirst while we saw in fantasy tumblers of cold water waiting us at a never-never soda fountain somewhere stateside. Even the rifle-barrel felt cool to the fevered cheek. Not until 1300 that afternoon did the bidons come.

Next morning, guerillas relieved us, and we forgot that bad day of thirst when the trucks drove us back past the pretty dark Joloanos on their porches. Sprague's patrol on Mount Mabusing was a classic patrol: we had killed 17 Nips, in return for 3 wounded, of whom Holley alone came near death. Slender blue-eyed little Sprague led us well, with fighters to back him like Piotrowski, Holley, Cortez, Fowler, Ogle, Villicich, and many others. We came back to our Filipino and Moro girls in Jolo City, glad of the war. It is only as the years pass and Jolo is far away overseas that the sadness comes down upon us. For this was great G Co 163 Inf's last fight.

Prime sources are my "Mountain Patrol" and "Jolo Patrol," part of "History of G Co 163 Inf." Useful also was Capt Robt M Allen's "History of 146 FA" in the chapter "Battle for Tumatangas." My friend Irv Sprague carefully checked my story and offered some recommendations.

BUCKING THE ABACA JUNGLE

by DR. HARGIS WESTERFIELD, Division Historian
with Lt. Col. Jack Arnold

On 4 June 1945, 163 Inf's battle-tired 3/Bn got a third major attack mission in 40 days — after combat at Zambo', Jolo. In southern Mindanao, 15 miles NW of Davao, we relieved 34 Inf's 3/Bn in the dark abaca jungle of the Talomo Valley. Jap MGs, rifles, knee mortars welcomed us, seriously wounded K Co's Pace, L's Wayne Johnson.

Our mission was to buck center against Gen Jiro Harada's Second Defense Line — Ula to Riverside to Calinan, through thickets of abaca run wild. (Abaca — or hemp for making rope — is a tall blue-green plant taller than a man. After 5 years' growing wild with cogon grass and small trees, it made an impenetrable jungle dusk even at noon where 3/Bn must dig out Japs.) Originally detached from Jolo to guard 24 Div Communications, 3/Bn woke up in battle northward with 21 Inf on left and 162 on right. For Ger Eichelberger had only 2 Divs plus 7 extra Bns and a Filipino Army to conquer Mindanao. He couldn't do without 163's 3/Bn.

First fight was to force a crossing at 100-Foot Bridge west of Ula where Talomo River wound SE across our front. L Co sought a tank route to the bridge, but 500 yards west of CP, our patrol drew fire from a Nip patrol, fought back. The late hour caused us to break off and return to perimeter. Meanwhile, K Co had prodded for crossing the Talomo near 100 Foot Bridge. From the north bank, 3 pillboxes shot at K. Continuous automatic fire penned the Nips until our bazookas killed the pillboxes. But Nip rifle-fire still spoiled our recon. Back in perimeter at 1835, Orzenowski was wounded by Nips. FA barrages drove off Nips lurking in twilight.

On 5 June, L and K Cos tried to cross the Talomo. After L's patrol at 0800 was halted by HMG fire, L made a push. With 2 tanks, LMGs, M's HMGs, we grimly attacked. At 1015, L's men killed a MG and 5 Nips. Since Japs were well dug in among abaca thickets, we called for tanks.

Despite raking automatic fire, Jap rifles and MGs rattled bullets off tanks. A Jap leaped out, blasted a mine under Tank No. 1. Concussion ripped the turret open, hurled Sgt Danciu through the turret into the road. Danciu yanked out other crew members — except a corpse. Tank No. 2 thought our men were Japs killing tank, and fired on us. But Danciu jumped before the tank's guns, saved us. L Co lost McBeth killed and 3 Yanks wounded — Brain, T/Sgt Fenley, Sgt Pahmahmie. K Co also pushed, lost Garrison, Ray McDaniel dead; Paysano, Sutton, Mackiewicz wounded. That afternoon, K Co traded fire with Japs across the Talomo, killed 4. That night, Jap 75 FA hit L Co. Orders were to attack at dawn.

On 6 June at 0950 after FA fire, L Co flanked 100-Foot Bridge with tanks. But this time, patrols riskily kept 25 years ahead in the abaca to find Nips and give tanks room to maneuver. We spotted a pillbox, guided tank 75s to kill it, grinned when smoke rose inside. Nip resistance lessened; only L Co's Gloyna, Sgt George were wounded.

Past a rotted body with carbine in Yank uniform beside a shell-torn jeep, L Co cut Highway 1-D north of the bridge, halted at road mines. We sent a Pltn back to secure K's crossing on the piers of the collapsed bridge. We could easily repair it for jeeps.

Now it was I's turn on 7 June to pass through L and attack frontally up Highway 1-D — 2 Pltns abreast with the road between. K Co secured our right flank. By 0830, I Co met heavy small arms fire, halted for M's 81s to smash Nips. Still held back, 85 minutes later, we sent a 7-man patrol 75 yards to our left flank, then north 75 yards. Patrol found a pillbox and spider holes, killed 1 Jap, fell back to let 81s work the ground over. We pushed at 1155, killed 1 Nip, but had Sgt Prewitt wounded. At 1545 after mortars and FA, we shoved a Pltn up reinforced with MGs. We slew 2 Nips, still fought as night fell. Wounded were Direen, John Rhodes, Poinsett; but Sgt Clayton Ford died. But K Co had it far worse on flank security — at 1245 took MG fire that killed Munoz, wounded 6 unknown Yanks.

By 8 June, 3 Bn had 5 killed, 15 wounded and had driven half way to Riverside — 5,000 yards by direct frontal attack. Today, we changed tactics. While K Co and I Co kept slugging ahead, L Co was to flank the Nips, then get behind them to make a retreat.

Thus on 8 June, I Co's patrol hit the Nips, killed 2, had 2 Yanks wounded, then impacted Jap positions with FA and 81s. We lost 4 — Bragg, Petersburg, Sgt Novle wounded, Prociw injured. K tried to protect 2 SPMs (self propelled mounted 75s) to open a new road to the next road-junction. By 0940, we hit Nips ambushes — had Harrington, Harmer, Sefcik wounded; Mosher seriously injured. We could not recover dead Padilla, Herrera until next day. SPMs got a new mission; but K dug in there with MGs to build up a base of fire.

Meanwhile on the flanking operation, L moved west to the Talomo, turned north. At 1540, we slew 2 Nips, bypassed a trench system. We dug in behind the Japs. Co Arnold found our position creepy; but he knew the Japs facing L and K were worse off with L in their rear.

On 9 June, I Co tried to clear Japs from a proposed road up the east bank of the Talomo to reach L Co. But even FA shells and tanks failed I Co. Japs mortared or shot Larry Larson, Weatherley, Gilson, Sgt Leon Weaver. We killed 7 pillboxes.

Now by 10 June, results of L's left end run on Riverside were plain. Jap resistance slackened. Moving out 30 minutes before dawn and without breakfast, Hamilton got K and Hq Cos up to L without casualties. Only "I" had trouble trying to open the supply road. During the fire-fight, tanks help flush Nips. Sgt Don Daugherty was wounded.

Again L Co flanked the Japs, entered Riverside triumphant — a clump of broken-down huts along a Talomo branch. Tiredly entrenched at Riverside, L men did not realize that with 34 Inf and 162, we had spearheaded the destruction of Gen Harada's Second Defense Line. And after midnight, 0445, Jap mortars struck, with an attack of 40 Japs. We slew 12, had 1 Yank wounded by grenade.

In Bn CP, tough Mjr Hamilton epistomized 163's Mindanao war. After 7 days, we had a cigarette issue of 2 packs. Riverside was wet, dirty, fly-ridden as a Filipino latrine. Mosquitoes had 7-inch prongs! Our 4 81 mortars were all salvage — impossible for close support. And 34 Inf wanted back the 2 borrowed ones. Rifle Pltns were down to 20 men. It could be worse.

At 1022, 11 June, Marine Douglas bombers winged south over our crossroads perimeter. Hamilton saw a bomber flipping like a fish overhead with a "hung" bomb — saw it loosen and impact — a 250 pound bomb directly into L's perimeter. Killed were Mayfield, T/Sgt Howard Wood; 16 were wounded — 9 litter cases to be borne 1400 yards over mud-slippery trails. M Co's Stallcop lost a leg. Among wounded were Pollen, Shields, Deason, Breitze, Don Bailey.

But Japs still surrounded Riverside. On 11 June, K and "I" backtracked 800 yards below Riverside to wipe out a roadblock. F/Lt Steege crawled under MG fire to remove mines. Despite a wound, he directed tanks shells to route the Japs. Next day, Jap 90s impacted K's perimeter, killed Ken Martin, wounded Weeks, Horn, Gillock, Cleon Arnold, S/Sgt Milton. Our 81s failed to silence the 90s. After heavy rain, 3/Bn slept in holes often 6 inches in water. CO Arnold's L Co was down to 86 — half-strength from before Zambo.

On 14 June, we struck for Calinan, center of Harada's lines west of Davao River. Here Harada placed his best remaining troops to hold until Japs from the east could hole up in mountains. Winning Calinan took aid of 21 Inf plus 162's 2 Bns.

L Co 163 pushed 1000 yards on flank, hit Nip trenches, killed 2 Japs, had a Yank wounded. After FA help, we drove again — into nerve-wracking quiet by 1400. K Co advanced 1000 yards behind L Co, endured mortar-snipers who fired, moved weapons after each shell. Hiatt was wounded.

On 15 June, L had 2 scares among abaca thickets. We started with first light. A Nip MG at 25 yards drove us to earth, was routed out with 60's. We hiked again, but rested to let I Co through at 1200. Ordered to follow at 1600, we lazily filled our holes to deter Jap reoccupation. Suddenly L Co ploughed a wild blast of HMGs into L. Feeling 12 feet high, Arnold grabbed phone, halted the MGs. A poor map had caused M's gunners to decide High 1-D was straight; they believed they were clearing

Credit: Personal interest comes mainly from Lt. Col. Jack Arnold's World War II Diaries plus Ltr of 26 Feb 1965. Stimulating are Col. (then Mjr) Robert Hamilton's 3 Ltrs dated 12 June, and 20 June 1945 — supplied from Col Moroney's files. Other sources include Morning Reports of all 3/Btn companies, Report of 3/Btn V-5 Operation, Gen Robert Eichelberger's Jungle Road to Tokyo, Col Arnold supplied maps: Tugbok and Baguio Sketch Maps (Mindanao), and 3 aerial maps. I also used Steege's medal story. The V-5 Operation of 162 and 163 is almost a forgotten story.

the road shoulders instead of flushing L Co. L Co's morale lowered — we were down to 72 haggard, sleepless, limping jungle-rotted Yanks.

K and "I" led for Calinan. Wounded 15 June was I's Howard E. Brown — K's Pace 16 June. Averaging but 60 effectives, we had to use tanks for any base of fire. To bypass Nips, we squirmed through often hip-deep mud. Tanks and SPMs seemed always out of ammo, stuck, or broken down. Yet on 17 June, K found the Talomo bridge mine-free, by 1250 got 2 tanks across. K held the bridge; I co and 4 tanks shot up Calinan. Tanks and rifle grenadiers shelled Jap pillboxes. Calinan was larger than Riverside — 800 yards of Filipino huts on both sides of 1-D, scattered huts, 2 road junctions. Expelled Japs still fought. At dawn, K slew 4 grenadiers. SE of Calinan, Jap FA dropped 5 shells on L — wounded Serpas, Pitchford, Buck Wilson, Sgt Ray Miller.

To cover 34 Inf's right flank, L Co led out to seize the road-junction midway to Malagos. We had just 600 yards to go up Highway 1-D — and a promise of immediate relief and rest. Wild battle ensued.

With 2 Pltns, Exec Lt McGee reached the road junction safely, but he took to the woods on the left of the road to bypass Japs on the right. McGee radioed to Arnold to come ahead, but omitted other information. Blithely, Arnold assumed the road clear — hiked all 17 members of 3/Pltn directly up 1-D. Luckily, we had Sgt Ratto's mortar.

From woods on our right, 10-15 feet above, Jap fire poured in. Left was open ground; Jap fired also from above and behind us. L Co cringed in roadside ditches 1-2 feet deep. McGee radioed back that he did not know our exact position and dared not risk his mortars. He had to fight back carefully.

Calmly Sgt Ratto set up his mortar without base-plate out on the bare road, at 25 yards lobbed shells in on the Nips. Arnold's little Pltn arced grenades up the bank. The Japs were gone. Two Yanks were scratched.

Back in Calinan, K Co had wry luck. Assigned to a rest area, we found a Jap MG, had to kill it and 5 Nips with a tank. Bland was seriously wounded — and L's Pavao, that night.

Thus, except for 2 weeks' nuisance patrols, ended 3/Bn 163 Inf's Mindanao War. The Japs and the abaca jungle fought well. Despite our planes, tanks, assault cannon, FA supremacy, Harada's old-style tank-less, plane-less ground army killed 14, wounded and hospitalized 72. K Co had 7 killed; L lost 3, "I" lost 2, and M lost 1. Lichon was 3/Bn Hq's only dead. Medics had 3 wounded to hospital — Greenwood, Charles Cooper, T/5 Baranowski. Of the other 69, I Co led with 29; K had 19, L 17, and M had 5.

For these few casualties, in just 14 days, Ula to Riverside to Calinan, Col. Hamilton's 3/Bn 163 Inf had done well. We had bucked the line 7 miles, effected 2 important river crossings, taken 2 important objectives, and racked up 250 Japs a day. Yet it had been dirty abaca jungle fighting.

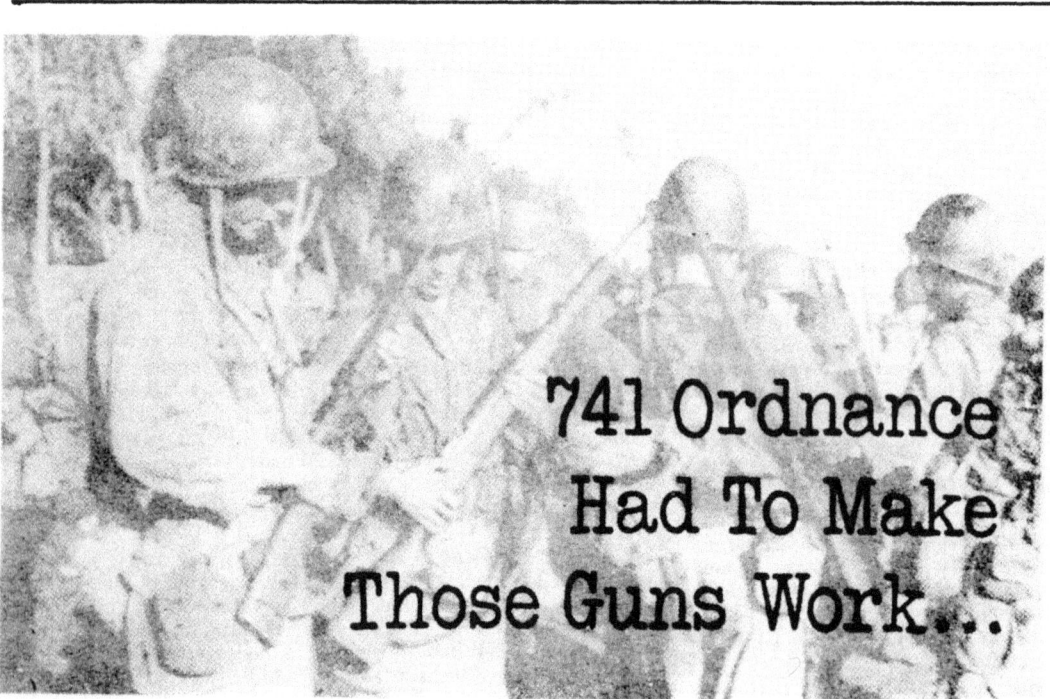

741 Ordnance Had To Make Those Guns Work...

Memories of 741 Ordnance

(Note from the Historian: If any member of 741 Ordnance will send me additional memories, I shall be glad to print them. I'd like to have your personal memories — and better still, stories of your most important labors, or of your casualties by disease, combat, or accident. With your information, I could have written an account better than this one from my limited experience.—HARGIS WESTERFIELD)

These are recollections from my three months with the Division's 741 Ordnance Company—good guys, expert technicians, hard workers. Remember the camp in the beach east of Bosnek under the live-oaks, with the bushy Padeadori Islands on Geelvink Bay to the southward?

On Biak after the battle, most Ordnance men seemed to be still old-timers from the original complement who made up the Ordnance Maintenance Platoon on September 28, 1942. They were tanned and atabrin-yellowed homesick men. They never let us forget their adventures in jungle pioneering at Dobodura, like "Jake" Kirkcalde, a tough broad-shouldered Sioux Indian truck-driver. Others had served a turn with a rifle at the front—like black-jawed DeWitt of 186 Infantry. Up in the coral by Mokmer Air-Strip, DeWitt spied a Nippo tank driving hard at his position. He made a direct hit on it with a grenade-launcher, and it scuttled away and disappeared.

741 Ordnance actually stood GI military formations in the Battle of Biak until one memorable morning. Perhaps on the dawn when the Second Battalion of 163 arrived for reenforcements, the company stood stiffly at attention. From the low jungle ridge but a mile north, two Japanese Zeroes came helling it down at just the level of tall Captain Burns' cowpoke campaign sombrero. Individual privates took charge of themselves without orders and leaped for their foxholes. The Japanese pilots had no time for Ordnance, and they died over the crowded shipping of Bosnek Landing. But never again did 741 Ordnance hold a reveille for a Nipponese inspection.

But a man remembers the little things about warfare best. I remember blonde First Sergeant Elmer Ahola and his effectively managed orderly room. Then there was "Chuck"—whose name I never used—that fine Sergeant and leader of men in "parts" with his ability in handling a combative drunk one night. There was the wrestling match between DeVaca and Slim that started in the showers and concluded under our cots. Wichita Indian Edmonds was a wrestler too; he had a bout one night with "Chappie Old Boy" (George Chapman). There was dark, heavy-set Grimm the Company Clerk who has a fine history of the Company somewhere if we could locate him. He had a knack for getting his tent-mates to run his personal errands for him. There was big Sgt. Prosak with his "roar," and that joker of a Szezwyzk. He loved to hear us pronounce his name literally with all the "z" in it, but he said it to rhyme with "Prosak"—which is "Susak." A man remembers the little things like Bill Caldwell's little blonde Aussie Mrs. and the plate-glass over her picture on his desk, which he

741 Ordnance Veterans Today

● LOU POHLMEIER (Supplies) now is in the cabinet and millwork business at Helena, Mont. GEORGE HUBBARD (Shop) now farms outside Kalispell, Mont. FRITZ MILLER (Shop) is a wheat farmer near Wilbur, Wash. GORDON FAGAN (Shop) has a new butcher shop in Seattle. JACK MAGEE (Supply) is a big wheel in local politics in Klickitat, Wash., and a trucker.

BOB WARD (Welder) owns a restaurant in Portland, Ore. FRED KANE (W/O Supply) is in the butcher supply business in Seattle. SHORTY DIAZ (Shop) owns a garage at Pescadero, Calif.

CHRIS HIRSCHI (Dog Robber) owns a chicken ranch in Petaluma, Calif. GEORGE CHAPMAN (Shop) has a floor business in Seattle. After spending quite a time in the hospital after the war, F/Sgt. ELMER AHOLA is in the sheet-metal business in Seattle with a small firm that enjoys a good national business. (When the historian builds his house—if ever—he wants it furnished with Elmer's Firehood, the Modern Functional Fireplace.)

dusted daily . . . and also Sgt. Posner, who had a gift for repartee during police-calls. Who can forget Chris Hirschi the dog-robber with his prayer to the rising sun when we got him up for reveille?

To the men of 741 Ordnance, the man most deserving of a medal was Dick Crosswell, whose right name I forget. In Australia, a curvaceous Mrs. Croswell languished for his return at Christmas, and here he was alone with a bunch of men on Biak.

At Christmas, Crosswell got a pass to the yon side of Biak to visit a pilot pal of his. With his overnight bag beside him, he sat down in the cockpit of his friend's plane. The plane took off for Australia while he sat in it, and he was too valuable for the Division to risk his life by jumping. Arriving in Brisbane, he boarded a train for his Australian beauty and spent Christmas in her arms. After two days' passionate bliss, he emplaned for Biak again. He was a couple of days AWOL, but Captain Burns knew nothing of his adventure—or was at least officially unaware. Well, Dick Crosswell got a week's confinement to quarters for company punishment, and he should have gotten a medal, in the opinion of many an Ordnance man.

Then we loaded ship and said good-bye to New Guinea — the battered caves on the cliffs by the air-port and the coral ridges and our graves. On the Navy transport *Storm King*, we had good American food as we sailed north to the Philippines. And Captain Burns kept us happy with calisthenics every morning. After a day of waiting for orders by the coco-flats south of Leyte, the *Storm King* drove NW in convoy into the center of the Philippine Islands.

The men of 741 Ordnance will never forget that day of travel into the Visayan Philippines. After dizzy mountain gorges alongside, we cut the water among purple islands with gigantic volcanoes lost in the mists overhead. Then we sailed out of sight of land among great inland oceans. And always the sailors stood to their guns above us to watch for Japanese planes. Again and 'again the cry came, "Flash Red!" as Radar probed every "blip" on the screen. But we had no air-raids.

On the great empty island of Mindoro, we staged with the Division for the Southern Philippines Campaign. Mindoro was anyhow better than Biak; we were out of the jungle and among people again. It was almost cold on that dry, dusty plain below the dim mountains where the pagans still lived. But San Jose village was small and crowded; soldiers were many and girls hard to get. Why was Mindoro a big empty island, and that close to Manila and the heaviest population in the entire Philippines? Historians tell us that the Moros had used Mindoro for a staging area also for raids on Luzon, and that it has never recovered from that systematic destruction, centuries ago.

Now Zamboanga was invaded, and our First Echelon men came back with dire stories. Jap shells struck the foredeck of a nearby LST and killed a half-dozen men. And then WF Rear Echelon of 741 Ordnance embarked with carbines on an LST and spread our blankets on cots on the crowded decks. It looked like war when we pushed into Zambo! In the mountains above the city, planes were still machine-gunning a pocket of Nips.

But except for our truckmen and front-line details, 741 Ordnance got nothing at Zamboanga but hard work in Ordnance fashion—seven days a week and details at night until the grumbling was loud and there was a complaint to the Inspector-General. And we were indeed a chicken outfit! We couldn't even guard our tents without first shining up and enduring a formal guardmount. Those of us with no "T" under our stripes even had to live segregated on a little knoll at Zamboanga away from the technicians of higher grade than we were. Exasperating indeed was the episode of the sliding mosquito bar. Deft with hands, one carpenter devised a holder for his net that folded into the side of the tent. No officer could rest after that until we all fabricated sliding mosquito bars. . . . Perhaps some 741 men remember also the beautiful two-story native bungalow our carpenters erected so that natives could sell refreshments to us. Prices rose, and those same carpenters (I have heard) poured gasoline on it and burned it to the ground.

Such are my memories of 741 Ordnance; I left the company in its big camp on the flats to the west of Zamboanga City. While on Jolo, I visited the detachment which lived there in a local skyscraper. They had refurbished the Power Plant of Jolo City—three stories up in the sky. And at Kure near Division Headquarters, I found 741 Ordnance back in barracks again, and most of the old Dobodura men gone, and the later men up for rotation. . . . Such are my memories of 741 Ordnance, and I forgot now the monotonous grind of labor — seven days a week, and the chicken when a non-com was not even allowed to work with the detail he was in charge of. I remember instead the camp under the live-oaks on Biak, Geelvink Bay lazily rolling down among the Padeadori Islands—and lying on my cot listening to the talk of good guys in the tent with me.

—HARGIS WESTERFIELD

Formation of 741 Ordnance (LM)

● 741 Ordnance was a brand-new outfit formed on September 1, 1942 from other outfits to which its members had been attached. From Lieutenant-Colonel M. C. Ruedy (now Exec of the 121 AAA, Nevada N.G.), I received the details in a most interesting letter. He writes:

"On September 1, 1942, the Maintenance Platoon of Hq and Hq Co 116 QM Bn. was transferred to Ordnance, but we remained attached for rations and quarters. At this time the QM Bn. was converted from Bn. to the 41 QM Co.

I procured F/Sgt Cilk, Cpl Brown and a supply Sgt from their excess plus the ten men from the Ord. Det. at Division Headquarters and the Maint. Platoon which I already had, and formed the 741 Ord (LM) Co. At that time I was a First Lieutenant, and assisting me was Second Lieutenant William E. Backus (died from a heart attack about three years ago). Also Second Lieut. Shirley Swann, W/O Charles C. Carver joined us shortly afterwards.

On October 14, 1942, Lieut. Backus was promoted to First Lieutenant, and I was promoted to Captain. I commanded the Company until November 13, 1943, when I asked to be returned to QM and Transportation, for which I was better qualified." It is to be hoped that Col. Ruedy will write some of his memories for the *Jungleer*, whether in 741 Ordnance or in 116 QM.

The Medics of 162 Inf. celebrate Christmas at Biak, 1944. (Courtesy of Clark)

U.S. Armed Forces Cemetery, Zamboanga, P.I., 1945. (Courtesy of Herman)

APPENDIX

OUR HONORED DEAD

Donald Abbott
Edward F. Abel
Raymond A. Ackerman
Clayton L. Adams
John A. Adams
Glenn H. Ainsworth
John F. Alberghina
Madison J. Aldige
Floyd E. Alison
Loren R. Allen
Sam Allen
Clyde E. Altemus
Robert L. Amans
Willie Ames
Arthur C. Anderson
Virgil Anderson
Lawrence J. Andrews
Robert Angelo
Lawrence M. Ankrum
Benjamin C. Archuleta
Saturnino Arevalo
James F. Armany
John W. Ash
Charles D. Ashcraft
Murray Axel
Gaylord G. Badberg
Nelson K. Baer
John J. Bagis
James Bahuslar
Claud S. Bailey
Issac J. Baker
Anthony Baldini
Joseph M. Balisteri
John Banaszek
Claude L. Barbour
Walter L. Barger
Francis S. Barnes
William G. Barnes
Howard L. Barnett
Emil J. Baron
Felix Barrera
Frank W. Batcha
John Beard, Jr.
William J. Beaudoin
Harry W. Beausoleil
Cyril E. Beck
Gerald F. Beck
James L. Beck
Heinz Behrendt
John J. Behuncik
Bruce N. Beighey
Frank Belchak
Otis B. Berlin
Edgar L. Bell
Virgil A. Bell
Meyer Belofsky
John Bender
Edgar W. Benge
Robert K. Bentley
Carl C. Berg
Marvin A. Berg
Arthur L. Berger
William D. Berry
Raymond A. Berryman
Julian P. Bilbao
Harry L. Billsborough
Maxwell Bilton
Donald Binkley
Albert J. Bitterman
J. B. Blackburn
Lloyd J. Blakemore
George R. Blanich
George O. Bloomquist, Jr.
LeRoy G. Blumenthal
Michael Bobby
Laurel I. Bodding-Field
Miguel P. Bojorquez
James W. Boland
Richard H. Boliek
Eugene H. Bombardier
Leland O. Bone
Ernest D. Bordner
Steve Bossony
Herbert C. Bostwick
Glen J. Bowen
John J. Bowman
George Boyer, Jr.
Duke R. Boyett
Hugh Boyle
Paul J. Braden
Thomas L. Bradley
William H. Bragg
Elbert E. Branch
Otto J. Brandel
William J. Brandes
Elton L. Brann
Ralph B. Breitwiser
Frank Bren
Ronald M. Bretzke

Harold Brill
Fred J. Brittingham
William B. Brooks
William D. Brooks
Doyle L. Brown
Jack Brown
John D. Brown
Lester E. Brown
Robert C. Brown
Theodore J. Brown
Albert B. Brunetti
Rosario A. Bruno
Francis M. Buck
Floyd A. Bunker
Quinton R. Burcham
Fred A. Burgen
Gerald A. Burgess
Neal L. Burgess
Oda Burgess
Paul M. Burgos
Chester A. Burnette
James R. Cain
Elwood C. Call
Richard L. Calvert, Jr.
Frank Campa
Russell E. Campbell
Samuel A. Campbell
Samuel G. Cappuccino
John G. Carey
Alfred Carlson
Denton B. Carroll
Deval A. Cassidy
Angelo Castelli
Daryl L. Cate
John M. Cate
Carlton S. Chambers
William Chambers
Earnest Chappell
Eugene R. Christie
Victor E. Church
Frank L. Churchill
John L. Chute
Norbert R. Chybowski
Anthony P. Ciarle
Ernest Cisneros
Frank M. Cleland
James C. Close
Robert B. Coers
J. T. Coffee
Lloyd A. Cole
Robert A. Cole
Gerald M. Collins
Anthony Collucci
Marion H. Colster
Ottis C. Colville
Estel C. Conner
Philip G. Conner
Thomas W. Conner
Hugh Connor
Eldon F. Cook
Lawrence R. Cook
Robert E. Coons
Robert E. Coors
Harry L. Copp
William H. Coppedge
Edward F. Correia
Joseph T. Costello
David T. Cottle
Jack M. Courney
Melvin H. Cove
William B. Cowan
James L. Cram
Anthony S. Crispino
Harold V. Crook
William A. Crow
Buner G. Cruce
Donald J. Crunican
Clifford N. Curry
Bernice Drwin
Kenneth M. Dahlstrom
Richard C. Dandwrand
James A. Daniels
James F. Davenport
Charles P. Davis
Mike Davis
Robert J. Davis
Clifton A. Deason
Howard Dehart
Louis S. Delgado
Aldred DeLoof, Jr.
Ralph DeDominia
Carl DeRyke
Aaron K. Dickey
Other E. Dickson
Sam H. Dickson
Roy L. Dietsch
Joseph A. DiGiacomo, Jr.
Wilford J. Dingman
Edward I. Dittrich

Anthony Dombroski
Edward A. Dominski
Anthony L. Donatelli
Edward P. Dotson
James W. Doyle
Theobald Dreher
Jacob P. Dresen
Arthur J. Drigert
Carl F. Duell
Charles I. Duke
Eli Dullont
Alexander R. DuMarce
Ella Dumont
Humbird Dunlap, Jr.
Robert W. Dunlap
Duncan V. DuPree
Fred L. Dutton, Jr.
Howard F. Eaches
William C. Eaker
John J. Edgerton
Paul S. Edwards
George E. Eichenlaub
John J. Ekert
Alexander Elliott
Harold W. Elliott
Donald E. Ellis
Oren E. Else
Robert E. Ely
Richard G. Erdley
Joseph S. Escalona
Stanley Evanoff
Earl E. Ewing
Nicholas J. Fabio
Clarence E. Fair
Charles E. Farr
Kenneth E. Felix
Richard W. Fennemore
Sebastian Ferreira
Lloyd K. Ferren
Stanley W. Fields
Shirley H. Fiscus
Eathel I. Fish
Hal C. Fisher
Harold R. Fisk
Erwin H. Flemming
William B. Flesch
Myron W. Folsom
Lester B. Foltz
Thomas J. Fowey, Jr.
Emery C. Fox
Carl L. Frazier
Wilbert H. Fredericks
Dale A. Fredricks
Geron R. Fredrickson, Jr.
Gerald R. Frees
Albert L. Freitas
Lloyd E. Frost
William L. Funk
Norman R. Gafner
Raymond C. Gagnier
Joseph E. Gaither
Joseph E. Galus
Elmer W. Gardner
Robert Garoutte
Glen Garrison
Edward J. Garski
Owen D. Gaskell
Joaquin N. Gayaldo
Angelo F. Gemelli
Adam Genther
Adolph L. Gibbs
Everett W. Gilkison
Clement W. Gill
James W. Gillespie
Virgil A. Girard
Jimmy R. Girardo
Joseph G. Glessner
Junnie Godfrey
Fritz H. Goedeke
Raymond W. Goerke
Robert D. Goiner
Zalmen Goldberger
Arthur T. Goldsmith
Ralph Golhke
Gerald E. Gordon
Virgil H. Gordon
Frank J. Gorishek
Stanley J. Gorlewski
Perry Gould
Major H. Gower
Samuel Graff
Roderick N. Granger
George W. Grant
Nick J. Grant
Roscoe Graves
Leland G. Greenlee
Charles G. Griffin
Robert R. Griffith
Frank L. Griggs

Arthur M. Gritzmacher
Ollie Grizzle
Bennie T. Gronito
William R. Groschen
Jerome L. Grosshandler
John T. Gruhala
Pascual Guerrero
James E. Guier
Salvadore J. Gullotta
Franklin W. Gunderman
Glen B. Gunter
William C. Haffner, Jr.
Beauford H. Haggard
George W. Haines
Jack D. Hale
Boyd Hall
Earl E. Hall
Fred L. Hall
Lloyd Hall
Robert V. Hall
Odell V. Haltzel
Charles T. Hampton
Alfred H. Hanenkrat
Clarence L. Hanna
Clarence R. Hanns
Thomas P. Hanrahan
Richard A. Hansen
Ruessell S. Hapke
Ted Hardan
Dallas Harder
Clark B. Hardesty
Pete Harrera
David W. Harrington
Thomas L. Harris
William Harris
Frank K. Harrison
John R. Hart
Harold O. Hartman
Wayne A. Harwood
Paul S. Hassler
Frederick V. Hatton
Eugene Hausman
Robert J. Hawkins
Harvey C. Hayes
Walter G. Hayes
Raymond F. Healson
Morris C. Heath
Herbert C. Helland
Clyde F. Henderson
Merton E. Henderson
Henry H. Hermsen
Modesto Hernandez
Michael C. Herrara
Darold J. Hess
Harold T. Higgenbotham
Wilbur L. Hill
Henry O. Hinkley
Ira W. Hodge
Frank A. Hoelscher
Kenneth H. Hoffman
J. C. Holder, Jr.
Hugh M. Holmes
Robert C. Holmes
Frank Hopkins, Jr.
James W. Hopkins, Jr.
Thomas P. Horan
William W. Horn
George F. Hornbussell
Harold B. Houston
Francis J. Hovorka
Theodore P. Howe
Raymond W. Howerton
Irving H. Hoyt
George T. Hudson
Wayne W. Huffman
Arthur W. Hughes
Byron D. Hurley
William A. Huse
William G. Hutton
Neil W. Hyde
Lester Hysche
Joseph Immerman
Robert W. Inghram
Ralph Inman
Bernard Irmen
Merne A. Jacobsen
Frank S. Jankowsky
Fred L. Janosik
Albert F. Janosky
William L. Jarvis
Herbert L. Jenkins
George R. Jennings
Howard B. Jensen
Norman F. Jepson
Francis Jette
Albert N. Jimenez
Yee N. Jin
Bill A. Joaquin
Arnold G. Johnson

Arthur C. Johnson
Arven E. Johnson
Clayton D. Johnson
Hannes W. Johnson
Henry L. Johnson
John S. Johnson
Lawrence N. Johnson
Leo R. Johnson
Aubrey C. Jones
Byrum D. Jones
Dennis D. Jones
Henry M. Jones
Ivan E. Jones
Lester Jones
Marion Jones
Marion W. Jones
Gilbert H. Jordan
Ralph W. Juhl
Felix Jurasin
Fred R. Kabkee
James R. Kain
Andrew Kaisel
Kalled V. Kalled
Seymour R. Katz
Edward T. Kearney
Richard A. Keefer
Carl J. Keeling
Robert P. Keenan
Bernard G. Kees
Darrell D. Keeth
Randall A. Keiler
Norman Kelly
Harvey L. Kennedy
Chester E. Kepner
Richard A. Kessler
Bryce H. Kiberd
Howard H. Kidd
Leon L. Kimberly
Anton F. Klepec
Louis J. Kline
John V. Klobofski
Walter J. Kloeckner
Walter Kmicinski
Dale C. Knauss
Joseph M. Kondili
Thomas C. Korsmo
Andrew A Kossl
Lester Koustrup
John J. Kranerik
Albert R. Kroll
Earl E. Kueker
Howard J. Kuhn
Louis W. Kuhn
William R. Kuisel
Edmund H. Kurkowski
Walter P. Kuropatva
Richard J. LaHaze
Richard J. Lahrig
Lee B. Lampe
Charles R. Lamphers
Troy C. Landcaster
John A. Landicina
John P. Landman
Laurence H. Lane
George F. Langel
Albert J. Langham
Wilbur J. Langston
Charles M. LaPloca
Earl W. Larkin
Howard J. Larkins
Russell C. Larsen
Herbert Larson
Joe E. Lashapell
Jack B. Laws
Homer L. Layne
Brown R. Leavell
Marvin S. Leckman
Lavern M. Ledbetter
Fred O. Lee
John B. Lee
George A. Leet
Alois H. Legleiter
Kenneth J. Leibach
Paul Leisnig
Chester A. Lekberg
Robert E. LeMieux
Cecil T. Lentz
August Leonard
Jesse W. Lester
Arthur E. Leudke
Constantine Levasseur
Russell E. Lewis
Robert S. Libera
Judson E. Lillie, Jr.
Leo J. Limbocker
Howard L. Lindenau
B. F. Lingerfelt
Harvey C. Lingle
Herbert L. Lisiecki
Ernest T. Livermore

David A. Lockefsky
Stanley S. Logadon
Rogelio T. Lucero
Earl W. Lukes
Albert G. Luley
Joe G. Mach
Eldred W. Madden
Clyde A. Major
William W. Maloney, Jr.
Louis J. Mangold
Robert M. Mann
John E. Manning
Juan V. Marcelles
Jack Marcus
Joseph C. Markland
John J. Marlowe
Frank Marrello
Kenneth D. Marsh
Raymond A. Marshall
Allan G. Martin
Arthur F. Martin
Harry W. Martin, Jr.
Kenneth E. Martin
Louis R. Martin
Verle Martin
Adelaido Martinez
Douglas H. Mason
John H. Massey
Charles R. Maurer
Otto L. May
Carl R. Mayfield
Harry W. McClean
William D. McClure
David F. McCorkle
Raymond McDaniel
Gay L. McDermeit
William McGhee
Robert L. McGill
John R. McHugh
Carrol I. McIlvanie
William J. McKay
William McKenzie
William P. McKenzie
Garland McLemore
John McMeel
William M. McNulty
Earl F. McShane
Woodrow Meadows
Raymond P. Medina
Lloyd B. Meek
Gordon B. Melody
Julius B. Mendoza
Hugh Mercille
Frank L. Messinger, Jr.
Alley D. Messingill
Donald D. Meyers
Edwin D. Michael
William C. Michaels
William M. Middleton
Harlan Milder
Ralph B. Miles
Jesse K. Miley
Godfrey W. Mihoover
Albert E. Miller
Clarence J. Miller
Frederick C. Miller
Robert W. Minner
Onecimbo M. Mirabel
Ernest P. Miraldi
George H. Mitchell
Max M. Mitchell
Edward C. Molina
Fritz Moliter, Jr.
Owen T. Monagham
Richard M. Monger
Thomas O. Monsted
Howard D. Moore
James P. Moore
Carl P. Morales
Edward Morales
Barney Morgan, Jr.
Willie D. Morin
Bernard F. Morrell
Norman A. Mosher
William J. Mossman
William B. Moulton, Jr.
Otto P. Mounce
Richard E. Muldoon
Richard L. Mullis
Julian J. Munoz
Robert H. Munson
Julius Murkli
Robert L. Murphy
Anthony J. Mussari

Murray E. Muzzal
Earl W. Nance
Sam Nash
Gusta Nauman
Edward Nedza
Alonzo R. Neisler
LaVerne O. Nelson
Russell C. Newhouse
Mandell Newmark
Erby Newson
Joseph C. Nichetti
Roger L. Nicholas
James L. Nixon
William H. Noel
William A. Nordstrom
Perdin O. Nore
Claude Norman
Theodore H. Norton
Victor J. Nosek
Frank M. Nowicki
Eugene M. Nuberger
Frank T. Nugent
Edward Nylaan
Walter J. Oakes
Clarence J. Ogborn
Ralph H. Ogden
Frank M. J. O'Laughlin
John E. Oleson
Edwin S. Olson
Ellis W. Olson
Selmer I. Olson
Dick M. O'Malley
John T. O'Malley
William P. O'Meara
Rodney W. Orange
Abraham R. Orosco
Harold S. Ortoleva
Larry D. Ortwein
Frederick G. Osterholtz
James W. Ostrowski
Erwin W. Overbow
Norman G. Packard
Jerry J. Padilla
Robert L. Palmberg
Joe T. Palmiero
Silvio Pametta
Joseph A. Paradiso
William L. Parsons
Earl V. Paslay
Turner R. Paulsen
Wilburn W. Pearce
Ervin G. Pease
Victor P. Pedersen
Lewis G. Peeler
Rudolph B. Peralta
Matthew F. Perpich
Lloyd Perren
Evar Peterson
Paul E. Peterson
Robert L. Phillips
Douglas A. Phipps
Arthur P. Pineo
William T. Pinkley
Robert Place
Arnold E. Pohle
Harold A. Pohlmann
Paul J. Poli
Michael Polimac
Dale O. Polk
Frank Pollock
Walter G. Pomplun
Eugene B. Pool
Billy S. Poole
Jack Popp
Lorenzo J. Pormigiano
Cayetano R. Porras
Tony N. Portel
Leonard A. Pospyhala
Otis H. Potter
John J. Potts
Donald R. Prenzier
John T. Price
Emil F. Prinz
Paul E. Pruitt
John Ptasynik
Harold E. Pulliam
William J. Pulver
Everett Pyle
Howard L. Pyle
Frank H. Quam
Lloyd Quon
John Qurco
Jack C. Rakovich
John F. Raley
John E. Ramstad

Kent A. Randolph
William J. Rankin, Jr.
Teddy L. Rasberry
John G. Rasmussen
Joseph Rauktis
Douglas H. Rawstron
Cecil I. Ray
James F. Ray
Fred D. Rea
Lester D. Rector
Edmond T. Redding
John H. Redmon
Harry L. Reed
Edward J. Reichenberger
Frederick W. Reichert
William L. Reiling
Charles H. Reimers
Richard E. Renkel
Ernest W. Renz
John W. Reyes
Ernest C. Reynolds
John T. Reynolds
Eduardo Reys
Robert C. Rheinfels
Donald E. Rhoades
Donald E. Rhodes
Clair F. Rice
Silas C. Richards
Arthur H. Richter
Floyd M. Richter
Theodore Richter
Rex Riddel
Dale F. Rider
Fred Riley, Jr.
Milo E. Rinholt
Trindad D. Rios
David Rivera, Jr.
Hoyt Roberson
Charles W. Roberts
Roy R. Robinson
James V. Rochford
Arthur C. Rodrigues
Ramon M. Rodriguez
Charles H. Rogers
Frank A. Rogers
Charles G. Rosenbaum
Harold Rothchild
Harold W. Roush
C. T. Rowland
Leon Roy
Henry Roza
Ray Runnels
Hobert F. Russell
George C. Sabo
Joe P. Salazar
Ralph E. Sallender
Arville L. Salomon
Everett J. Salvon
George M. Sanders
Refugio Sandoval
Edward J. Sanocki
Roy R. Sansbury
Joseph A. Saratowicz
Samuel A. Sather
Herman Schecter
Wenzel H. Schiell
William J. Schirmer
Frederick G. Schlereth
Alex M. Schmidt
Anthony F. Schmidt
Earl Schmidt
Eddie C. Schmidt
Fredder J. Schmitt
Jacob Schoenblum
David J. Schortgen
Glenn L. Schreider
Victor Schumacher
Harry Scott
James R. Scott
Milton D. Scriber
William D. Sedall
Ernest J. Seevers
Joseph A. Seibert
John L. Seiglmeier
Joseph C. Seilar
Gerald H. Seipp
Ralph R. Shane
Frank Shaw
Milton Shaw
Emmet V. Shea
William J. Shea
John H. Shelton
William H. Shelton
Cloral C. Shepard

William J. Shepherd
Bert V. Sherman
Everett R. Shields
James F. Shields
John C. Shields
Stanley H. Shilliday
Dorsey Shuler
Arthur Shults
Raleigh C. Sieber
Harry E. Silvestri
William O. Silvey
Orville M. Simmons
Raymond M. Simmons
Lawrence Simonian
John Simunevic
John Simunovic
Stanley Siscavage
Milton E. Skogrand
Charles C. Smiley
Alfred L. Smith
Don A. Smith
Edward Smith
Floyd L. Smith
Gail D. Smith
Norman N. Smith
Robert J. Smith
Russell M. Smith
Thomas J. Smith
William H. Smith
Willis Smith
Walter M. Smoger
Stanley Smolinski
Herman H. Sneeringer
Clifford R. Snodderly
Alfred O. Solis
Victor H. Soroken
Alfred M. Soukup
William A. Souza
Joseph P. Spano
Sidney D. Spear
Harold E. Springer
William B. Squires
James Stafford
Harold Stambaugh
Herman L. Staub
Nicholas J. Steensma
William Stein, Jr.
Howe L. Steinhibler
Arvid Sternquist
Albert E. Stevens
Nelson Stevenson
Nelson H. Stevenson
Donald Stewart
Irving Stockfleth
Richard Stoinski
William W. Stonecypher
Melvin O. Stoops
John W. Storay
Clarence E. Stout
William W. Stout, Jr.
Denton H. Stovall
William J. Strawser
Gilbert W. Strobach
Raymond E. Strong
Edward Strougal
Harvey B. Stuart
Lester L. Suits
Joseph P. Sullivan
Fred F. Sundermann
Fred F. Supino, Jr.
Godfrey O. Suttle
Theron B. Sweat
Edward J. Swies
Francis A. Tague
Ezra M. Tanner
Jan R. Tatarski
Rolland C. Taubert
Verl A. Taylor
William B. Taylor
Shelby W. Teeters
Dionisio Z. Temellosa
James L. Thacker
Peter J. Theriault
Floyd O. Tholund
Benjamin K. Thomas, Jr.
Virgil Thomas
James W. Thompson
Kenneth A. Thompson
Richard W. Thorne
Robert Thornley
Walter R. Thurlow
Jesse L. Timmons
Frank A. Titting
Dee Tomlinson

Rudolph L. Tommei
Rafael Torres
William Toth
Thomas J. Towey
Anthony L. Trashloleros
August Trautner
Andrew J. Trgina
Ernest S. Tucker, Jr.
Wayne E. Turk
Harvey H. Turner
Deluin E. Vaden
James M. Vainter
Thomas J. Valador
Julius W. Vallier
William L. Vanalstine
Glenn O. Vanderburg
Fred L. Vanderpool
Clifford L. Vandiver
Marvin E. Van Dyke
Jack P. Van Hoane
Clifford Van Orden
Robert Van Scherpenzell
Lloyd F. Vich
Donald T. Vigue
Mario J. Vilanuva
Peter J. Virseo
Frank J. Vivirito
Herman N. Vogal
Frank Voloshen
Ralph E. Vorce
James J. Voss
Harley E. Walker
Jack R. Walker
Jerry M. Walker
Lee W. Walker, Jr.
Robert Waller
Charles H. Walter
Douglas E. Walwyn
Roman E. Wantock
Lee Ward
Lloyd L. Ward
William Little Warrior
Edwin R. Waters
Reed P. Waters
Merle O. Watkins
Clinton Watson
Ray H. Watson
Robert C. Watson
Wyatt B. Watts
Arthur W. Wavrick
Keith M. Weeks
David Welch
Oscar G. Wells
Bernard Whelan
Everett V. White
Keith D. White
Lyle Whitney
Raymond L. Wieder
Clyde P. Wilds
Clifford C. Wilkening
Leonard Wilkins, Sr.
George G. Willard
Thomas N. William
Edhred M. Williams
Edmund K. Williams
Fein D. Williams
Lincoln J. Williams
Vinton A. Williams
Ed Wilson
Truman Winkler
Michael Wirnshafer
James A. Wojtech
Donald L. Wolff
Howard D. Wood
Clyde Woods
John E. Wooldridge
Royce D. Wooten
James E. Worthley
John F. Woulfe
James P. Wright
Troy N. Yacham
Glenn W. Yates
Walter D. Yates
Andy M. Yoka
Lester Young
Boleslaus Zdanczewicz
Edward Zebelian
John L. Zeiglmeier
Joseph Zelasnikar
Isidore A. Ziebolz
Junior H. Zirkle
Carliss Zook
Thomas L. Zoto
Victor Zucco
Bruno F. Zurewski

Decorations and Awards

Distinguished Service Cross

Randal K. Balch
Leonard C. DeWitt
Roy L. Dietsch ★
Jordon W. Davis
Jens A. Doe

Frank R. Gehrman
Glen J. Hansen
Nicholas W. Hatfield
John R. Jacobucci
Byrum D. Jones ★

Albert J. Langhan
Harold M. Lindstrom
John H. McRoberst
John L. Mohl
Melvin C. Monroe

Joseph F. Montore
Everett L. Moore
Edward Morales ★
Paul E. Peterson
Walter R. Rankin

Wilmer K. Rummel
George F. Singletary, Jr.
Charles M. Solley, Jr.
Thomas B. Williams
Paul Ziegele

Distinguished Service Medal

Jens A. Doe ★★   Horace H. Fuller

Silver Star

Leon F. Alder, Jr.
Frank W. Aldrich
Lee L. Alfred
Robert M. Allen
Arthur C. Anderson
Donald N. Anderson
Virgil L. Anderson
Forest M. Andrews
Richard Andrews
Carlyle W. Arey
Argyle E. Armstrong
Byron A. Armstrong
Kenneth E. Arthur
Charles D. Ashcraft ★
Merton E. Austin
William C. Baden
Wayne C. Bailey ★★
Isaac J. Baker
Lloyd J. Baker
Wilfred D. Baker
Mark E. Barnard
William J. Barnett
William C. Barson ★★
James H. Bay
Dwight E. Beach
Arthur Belgarde
Benjamin C. Bell
William C. Benson ★★
Otis Berlin
Louis J. Bilek
Stewart H. Boelsen
James W. Boland ★
Lawrence N. Bourlier
George W. Boyd
Frank A. Bradbury
Horace C. Bradbury
Arthur J. Braman
Byron A. Brim
Matt C. C. Bristol, Jr.
Mike Brklacich
Melbourne E. Brooks
Douglas F. Brown
Elmer Brown
William B. Brown ★★
James M. Buckland
Charles R. Buxton ★★
Harold G. Cahill
Claude R. Carr
Guy W. Carroll
Glenn E. Case
Angelo Castelli ★
Sanders M. Castor
George S. Caswell
Paul A. Caulfield
Bill K. Chapman
Charles B. Claypool
Billie J. Click
Robert L. Cloud
Alfred E. Coffey
Ralph E. Cole
Robert A. Cole ★
Rhea A. Cooley
William H. Cooley
Burl L. Cox
Vincent S. Cunningham
Hubert C. Curry
Richard E. Curry, Jr.
Robert F. Dalton
Herman E. Daniels
Foy A. Davis
Stanley C. Davison
Charles R. Dawley
Don D. DeFord
Raymond E. Derrick
Tom Dewhurst
Neal A. Dikeman ★★
David S. Dillard
Jens A. Doe ★★★
Harold H. Doersam

Benito R. Dominguez
Leo B. Doubek
Kenneth C. Downing
Milton Drexler
Albert R. Driggers
John J. Drum
Wilson E. DuBois
Henry J. Dubsky
Edmund G. Ducommun
Karl F. Duell
Duncan V. DuPree ★
James J. Eder
Samuel E. Eley
Conway L. Ellers ★★
Robert S. Elliot
Edward E. Enders
T. C. Epps
Pius Erck
Bernardo C. Escobar
Ralph M. Evans
Russel R. Field
Charles S. Fields
Harold R. Fisk
Lloyd M. Flaten
Maurice M. Fletcher
Ralph D. Floberg
William B. Foster
David E. Fowler
Dan B. Free
Horace H. Fuller
Alcide Gallant
Steven J. Gardner
Owen D. Gaskell ★
Frederick R. Gehring
Ernest Gerber
Herbert E. Gerfen
Ray J. Gibney
Dale E. Gibson
Raymond W. Goerke ★
Samuel P. Gordon
John H. Graham
James M. Gray
Kenesaw Greathouse
Grant S. Green
James H. Griffin
Leslie E. Griffiths
Herman H. Haedicke
Howard H. Hafer
Harold C. Halverson
Ralph E. Hamel
Andrew C. Hamilton
Robert M. Hamilton
Harold Haney ★★
Clifford L. Hanson
Lester E. Hanson
Charles W. Hash
Paul G. Hassler ★
Nicholas W. Hatfield
Harold M. Hawkins
Byron W. Hazelton
Robert L. Heath
Lawrence J. Hebert
Pat M. Heist
Carl T. Hellis
Dean D. Henry
Emory L. Heyn
Russell L. Hodges
Alvin M. Hoffman
John L. Hoffman
William Holder
James Holgnchak
Paul G. Hollister ★★
Charles L. Hornbeck
Francis J. Hoverka
Theodore P. Howe ★
Donald F. Hulin
Paul Hultman, Jr.
Maurice E. Hundahl
Paul E. Hunter

Frank W. Hurliman
Oscar J. Irwin
William D. Jackson
Clifton G. James
John G. Jeffers
Walter J. Jendrzejewski
Howard B. Jensen
Francis Jette ★
Jessie D. Jewell
Raymond V. Jones
Bernard Kaplan
Seymour R. Katz ★
James R. Kent
Walter W. King
Charles G. Kitchens
Louis J. Kline ★
Chester F. Klovas
Louis M. Krist
Earl E. Kueker
Frank W. Kuempel
Sam F. Lambert
Howard M. Lang
Howard H. Lassegard
Herbert G. Lauterbach
Jerome Lazarus
Kenneth C. Leach
David G. LeBaron
Edward L. Lederman
Clarence E. Lee
John B. Lee ★
Charles Leon
Maurice L. Levy
Charles A. Lindsey
Harold M. Lindstrom
Joseph W. Lirzkowicz
Donald F. Locke
Archie H. Lofts
Phillip W. Long
James A. Lufkin
Alois W. Luhr
Einar A. Lund
Robert E. Lundstrom
Thomas C. Lynch
Carl E. Maffeo
Harold G. Maison
Carl D. Makart
Joseph J. Mannerillo
William M. Mantz
Harold L. Marshall
Harry W. Martin Jr. ★
Ronald G. Martin
Jean Martinez
William Matlin ★★
Ray J. Mattice
Frank E. Maxam
Weston A. McCormac
Willard F. McDonald
Jack E. McEachen
Robert L. McGill ★
Thomas A. McGinitie
Frank F. McGuinness
Melvin C. McHenry
Joseph R. McInerney
Carl M. McIntyre
Howard A. McKinney
Jack C. McLoughlin
Keith D. McMilan
Reed D. McMilan
Donald R. McNeil
Lawrence W. McNight
Phillip E. Mead
Arthur Merrick
Wendell C. Messec ★★
Albert L. Meuller
Robert A. Mikkelson ★★
Harold E. Miller
Harry W. Miller
Walter L. Miller, Jr.
Robert W. Minner ★

Robert W. Mipper
Salvatore F. Mirenda
John A. Mitchell ★★
Joseph D. Mitchell ★★
Kenneth Mitchell
Owen T. Monaghan
Walter E. Moore
Earl R. Moorehead
Ralph S. Morris
William J. Moroney
Gerald W. Morrison
Ralph W. Nay
James F. Neely
Emil L. Nelson
Robert A. Nelson
John O. Newman
Oliver P. Newman ★★
Ralph A. Nicholas
Wendall Noall
Frant T. Nugent ★
Loren E. O'Dell
Thomas F. O'Donnell
Kenneth V. Olberg
John E. Oleson ★
Edwin S. Olson
John D. Orr
Ralph W. Oswald
Erwin W. Overbo ★
Ralph W. Palmer
John S. Panek
Elmo R. Parish
Peder P. Pederson
Milan W. Peel ★★
Sidney E. Pendexter, Jr.
Charles E. Peterson
Rudolph B. Peralta ★
Robert B. Pharr
Charles P. Phelps
John W. Phoebus
James A. Poinsett
Michael Polimac ★
Marion J. Porterfield
Arthur Possoni
John J. Potts ★
William J. Powers
Harold E. Poynter
Reed G. Probst
Oscar J. Rainville, Jr.
Walter R. Rankin
Edward L. Reams
Robert E. Read
Joseph Reddoor
Marion F. Reed
Robert L. Reeves
Clarence E. Reid
Albert A. Rendler
John B. Retterath
Robert C. Rheinfels ★
Cecil C. Rhodes
Eulon Richardson
Robert W. Richardson
John J. Rigler
Edward G. Ripani
Harry N. Rising, Jr. ★★
Herve G. Robert
Douglas C. Robinson
Oliver K. Robinson
Fritz F. Roll, Jr.
William L. Rollman
Archibald B. Roosevelt ★★
Victor Rosanio
Raymond Q. Roseth
Edward L. Ross, Jr.
Richardson D. Roys
Charles H. Rue
Alexander G. Rutka
Marcus P. Sanchez
Richard J. Satran
Harry M. Sayka

William F. Schacht
Oscar A. Scheller
Harold E. Schiefelbein
Wenzel H. Schiell ★
Lloyd B. Schiffman
George C. Schultz
Ralph W. Sconce
James V. Schully, Jr.
William J. Shaw ★★
John H. Shelton ★
William T. Sherwood
Archie L. Shovan
Raymond M. Simmons
Robert E. Simpson
Albin C. Sipe, Jr.
Walter D. Skauge
Walter H. Skielvig
Richard S. Slade
Harry C. Smith
Harry R. Smith
Nathan J. Sonnenfeld
John Sponenburgh
Joseph Stasiowski
Eldo E. Sutton
Kenneth S. Sweany
R. A. Sweetland
Stephen A. Swisher III
William B. Taylor ★
Robert D. Teela
Dionisio Z. Temellosa ★
Robert Templeton
Richard N. Ten Eyck
Richard B. Thierolf
Clifton B. Thomas
Haskell S. Thompson
Edwin S. Tipple
Silvior Tontar
Vernon F. Townsend
John J. Tracy, Jr.
Rob D. Trimble
Harry C. Trodick
Henry L. Tullock
Harry J. Van De Riet
Jack H. Van Duyn
Marvin E. VanDyke
Oliver R. Vannucci
Robert Van Scherpenzell ★
William Vavra
Robert W. Vogt
Norman Voorhees
Edward L. Waisbrot
Francis C. Wallace
Phillip Warner
George E. Waterman
Robert C. Watson
Wyatte B. Watts ★
William R. Weaver
Robert E. Wells
Paul V. Wendell
Jack C. White
John B. White
Jerome B. Wilczewski
Edgar F. Wildfong ★★
Charles W. Wilkenson
Hurshal A. Wilson
Robert O. Wilson
Leland S. Winetraub
Leonard A. Wing
Leslie O. Winkler ★★
Maurice D. Winslow
Raymond S. Winther
Henry T. Wise
Hubert E. Wright, Jr.
Horace L. Young
Emil A. Zall
Albert J. Zaleski
Isidore A. Ziebolz
Paul Ziegele
Junior H. Zirkle ★
Edwin H. Zundel

Legion of Merit

Wayne C. Bailey
George M. Baldwin
Elmer Brown
Chalmers D. Corle
Milton Drexler

Myron W. Folsom
Alvin F. Graverholz
John F. Haley
Harold Haney ★★
John A. Harris

Irving H. Hoyt
Edward E. Kramer
Weston A. McCormac
Michael G. Mehilos

Arthur Molyneux
William L. Morris
Charles W. Mueller
Rodney W. Orange
Oscar Rumack

Walter H. Skielvig
Harry Steward
Herbert T. Warren
Gould Whaley
Edwin A. Zundel ★★

Distinguished Flying Cross

Samuel P. Gordon   John A. Robinson

★ Denotes posthumous award.   ★★ Denotes Oak Leaf Cluster.   ★★★ Denotes second Oak Leaf Cluster.

Battle Honors

WAR DEPARTMENT
WASHINGTON, MAY 6, 1943

GENERAL ORDERS
No. 21

IV. Citation of units in the United States Forces in Southwest Pacific Area. As authorized by Executive Order No. 9075 (sec. III, Bull. 11, W.D., 1942), citation in the name of the President of the United States, as public evidence of deserved honor and distinction, was awarded to the following named forces. The citation is as follows:

The Papuan Forces, United States Army, Southwest Pacific Area,[1] are cited for outstanding performance of duty in action during the period July 23, 1942, to January 23, 1943. When a bold and aggressive enemy invaded Papua in strength, the combined action of ground and air units of these forces, in association with Allied units, checked the hostile advance, drove the enemy back to the seacoast and in a series of actions against a highly organized defensive zone, utterly destroyed him. Ground combat forces, operating over roadless jungle-covered mountains and swamps, demonstrated their courage and resourcefulness in closing with an enemy who took every advantage of the nearly impassable terrain. Air forces, by repeatedly attacking the enemy ground forces and installations, by destroying his convoys attempting reinforcement and supply, and by transporting ground forces and supplies to areas for which land routes were nonexistent and sea routes slow and hazardous, made possible the success of the ground operations. Service units, operating far forward of their normal positions and at times in advance of ground combat elements, built landing fields in the jungle, established and operated supply points, and provided for the hospitalization and evacuation of the wounded and sick. The courage, spirit, and devotion to duty of all elements of the command made possible the complete victory attained.

WAR DEPARTMENT
WASHINGTON 25, D.C., 16 JULY 1945

GENERAL ORDERS
No. 57

BATTLE HONORS. As authorized by Executive Order 9396 (sec. I, WD Bull. 22, 1943), superseding Executive Order 9075 (sec. III, WD Bull. 11, 1942), citations of the following units in the general orders indicated are confirmed under the provisions of section IV, WD Circular 333, 1943, in the name of the President of the United States as public evidence of deserved honor and distinction:

1. The *1st Battalion, 162d Infantry Regiment,* is cited for outstanding performance of duty against the enemy near Salamaua, New Guinea, from 29 June to 12 September 1943. On 29 and 30 June 1943, this battalion landed at Nassau Bay, New Guinea, in one of the first amphibious operations by American forces in the Southwest Pacific Area, on a beach held by the enemy, and during a severe storm which destroyed 90 percent of the landing craft able to reach the beach. Moving inland through deep swamps, crossing swift rivers, cutting its way through dense jungle, over steep ridges, carrying by hand all weapons, ammunition, and food, assisted by only a limited number of natives, this battalion was in contact with the enemy for 76 consecutive days without rest or relief. All operations after the initial landing were far inland. Living conditions were most severe because of constant rain, mud, absence of any shelter, tenacious enemy, and mountainous terrain. The supply of rations, ammunition, and equipment was meager. For 5 weeks all personnel lived on rations dropped by airplane, for days at a time on half rations. Individual cooking was necessary throughout the period. Malaria and battle casualties greatly depleted their ranks, but at no time was there a let-up in morale or in determination to destroy the enemy. Each officer and enlisted man was called upon to give his utmost of courage and stamina. The battalion killed 584 Japanese during this period, while suffering casualties of 11 officers and 176 enlisted men. Cutting the Japanese supply line near Mubo, exerting constant pressure on his flank, the valiant and sustained efforts of this battalion were in large part instrumental in breaking enemy resistance and forcing his withdrawal from Salamaua on 12 September 1943. The *1st Battalion, 162 Infantry Regiment,* has established a worthy combat record, in keeping with the high traditions of the United States Army. [General Orders 91, Headquarters 41st Infantry Division, 18 December 1944, as approved by Commanding General, United States Army Forces in Far East.]

WAR DEPARTMENT
WASHINGTON 25, D.C., 22 SEPTEMBER 1944

GENERAL ORDERS
No 76

BATTLE HONORS. As authorized by Executive Order No. 9396 (sec. I, Bull. 22, WD, 1943, 1943), superseding Executive Order No. 9075 (sec. III, Bull. 11, WD, 1942), citation of the following unit in General Orders No. 95, Headquarters Sixth Army, 18 June 1944, as approved by the Commanding General, United States Army Forces in the Far East, is confirmed under the provision of section IV, Circular No. 333, War Department, 1943, in the name of the President of the United States as public evidence of deserved honor and distinction. The citation reads as follows:

The *2d Platoon, Company L, 163d Infantry,* is cited for outstanding performance of duty and for heroism near Aitape, New Guinea. On 27 April 1944 this unit, with personnel attached to make a strength of 3 officers and 64 enlisted men, established a trail block at Kamti, part of Kapoam village in the Terricelli mountain foothills, to cover enemy escape routes. At 280700 an enemy force of approximately 200 attacked with fixed bayonets from three sides, but was thrown back after fierce fighting. Forty-two enemy were killed, while the platoon losses were 2 men killed and 1 wounded. Though communications were cut, the platoon maintained its position for 36 hours, receiving supplies by air. After withdrawing 29 April to receive reinforcements, the platoon again formed and maintained the trail block where, that night, another enemy attack was repulsed with losses of 1 man killed and 2 wounded. The exemplary endurance, determination, and bravery of the members of this platoon reflect the highest credit on the United States Army.

---

[1] Includes the 163d Infantry.

Commendations

HEADQUARTERS 41st INFANTRY DIVISION

26 August 1944

GENERAL ORDERS
No. 65

Recent landings at Wardo and Korim Bay have broken all active organized resistance of the Japanese. The 41st Infantry Division may well be proud of its action against the enemy in the Biak operation. The victory was difficult. We take pride in the fact that the Division came through with a shining record. Information obtained after the landing showed the Japanese strength to be approximately 11,000. The counted enemy dead to date is over 4,700. In addition to that, there are thousands of uncounted dead and over 330 prisoners. The survivors are dying of starvation and disease. We have liberated some 600 Javanese citizens of the Netherlands Indies and 25,000 natives. While our losses cause a note of sadness to each and every one of us, they were only a very small fraction of the casualties inflicted upon the enemy.

Our arduous days of training in learning the use of our superior weapons enable us to keep our losses down. We intend to take advantage of every one of the stratagems of modern war to exploit our material advantages to save the lives of our men.

This is the first time the Division has operated as a unit. Sanananda, Salamaua, Aitape, Hollandia, Toem, Wakde, saw operations of portions of the Division. The Biak operation finally allowed the Division to operate as a whole and to evaluate its worth as a unit. How well it did operate is reflected in the victory obtained at Biak.

The enemy was a cunning, aggressive foe. He was from a veteran division of the China and Burma campaigns. His record was superb and during this action he maintained it. Defeating this enemy was an accomplishment which reflects great credit on the Task Force.

The artillery has well demonstrated its capabilities. The excellent tactical and technical employment of the artillery has made the task of the infantry much easier. The artillery in its support cracked enemy strongpoints; it was accurate, enabling the infantry to close with minimum losses. The artillery forward observers, liaison pilots and their enlisted assistants, have shared the hazards of the infantry. The gunners and the ammunition details performed well in keeping the guns operating.

Our medical corps performed in its usual outstanding manner. Their devotion to duty in caring for our wounded is worth every bit of praise we can bestow. The medical personnel of the Division have received more decorations in proportion to their numbers than any other branch.

Our supply services, the ordnance, quartermaster, medical, signal and engineers were not found wanting. Their contribution to the common effort was notable.

The Division engineers made possible the forward movement of the infantry by construction of roads, by demolition crews often sharing the intense fire of the infantry in order to accomplish their mission.

In communications, one of the most important factors in controlling troops, our signal corps functioned as a fine integrated team. Not only the Division signal company, but the signal communication teams of the artillery, infantry and other units, carried out their duties under trying and hazardous conditions.

No other task in the Division is comparable to the load carried by the infantry soldier. He is our only reason for existence. He is the man who captures and holds the ground. He carries the fight to the enemy. The infantry soldier was the one who met in hand-to-hand combat the crack troops of the Japanese, threw him from his positions, destroyed him, and gave us our victory. To these men we are eternally grateful and a pride rises in our hearts that is going to carry us on from victory to victory in the future.

We had with us attached personnel—antiaircraft units, additional artillery, service troops. Each and every one did his part to assist in securing the victory we have gained. The whole was an integrated team which has carried on to complete successfully the mission assigned.

To every member of the division and attached units I extend my congratulations on the record you have made. You have fulfilled the highest traditions of the military service of the United States Armed Forces.

JENS A. DOE
Major General, U. S. Army
Commanding

HEADQUARTERS
ARMY GROUND FORCES
OFFICE OF THE COMMANDING GENERAL
WASHINGTON 25, D.C.

10 January 1946

SUBJECT: Letter of Appreciation
TO   : Commanding General, 41st Infantry Division

The 41st Infantry Division which contributed splendidly to our glorious victory over Japanese tyranny and aggression, will forever be honored and cherished by a grateful nation.

Your division was committed to action in January 1943, when the 163d Infantry Regiment plunged into combat at Sanananda, Papua. Lacking naval support, and relying on supplies flown in over the Owen Stanley Mountains, the regiment emerged bearing the marks of jungle fighting at its worst. This action, which helped stem the Jap tide threatening Port Moresby, won for the Regiment the Distinguished Unit Citation.

Storming ashore at Salamaua in June 1943, the 162d Infantry Regiment began 76 days of unrelieved fighting, a record in jungle warfare. Your division's 1000 mile campaign through the New Guinea jungles, which included assault landings at Aitape, action at Hollandia, Toem-Wakde, and Biak Island in the Schoutens, will forever be a bright chapter in the history of your organization.

Now, upon the inactivation of the 41st Infantry Division, it is a privilege for me to commend you, your officers, and your men for your outstanding accomplishments on the field of battle.

JACOB L. DEVERS
General, USA
Commanding

COMMENDATIONS

WAR DEPARTMENT
THE CHIEF OF STAFF
WASHINGTON

18 January 1946

Dear General Doe:

I appreciate your thoughtfulness and that of the officers and men of the 41st Division in sending me the Japanese sword taken by your Division in the Kure-Hiroshima area of Japan.

I am aware of the splendid performance of the 41st Division and, having served as Chief of Staff of the IX Corps when the 41st was undergoing its training under that headquarters, I am proud of its accomplishments.

Sincerely,

IKE EISENHOWER

Major General Jens A. Doe, 03743
Hq 41st Inf. Div., APO 41
c/o P.M., San Francisco, California

ORDER OF THE DAY
On Completion of
RECAPTURE OF BUNA–GONA AREA

Headquarters, New Guinea Force,
22 January 1943

The campaign we have been engaged in for the recapture of the Buna–Gona area is now virtually at a close. I desire to express to all Australians and Americans alike who have taken part in this long and tedious campaign my heartfelt congratulations and my appreciation of all you have done.

First to the Infantry I would like to pay a special tribute. Seldom have Infantry been called on to endure greater hardships or discomfort than those provided by the mountains, swamps, the floods, of tropical New Guinea. All this you have endured with cheerfulness and meantime have outfought a dour and determined enemy on ground of his own choosing in well prepared defenses. Your achievements have been such as to earn the admiration and appreciation of all your countrymen.

Secondly, I would thank the Air Forces for their magnificent work, for the shattering blows they have delivered to the air forces of the enemy and his ships, which have tried so often and so vainly to reinforce and supply him. To the air transport service which made this campaign a feasible operation, for your untiring efforts in all weathers, I thank you.

Thirdly, there are all those who have supported so splendidly the Infantry in their fighting, the Armored Regiment, the Artillery, the Engineers and the Army Co-operation Squadron, and the Medical Services who have cared for sick and wounded in most difficult circumstances. You have done magnificently.

Fourthly, I want to thank all those in the Services who have kept supplies of all kinds going to the forward troops, and also COSC and all its personnel and particularly its small boat section that has braved hazardous waters and enemy action in getting supplies up the coast.

And finally my thanks to the Navy for its assistance in protecting sea routes and clearing the waters round the battle area and farther north.

We have won a striking victory but a long and hard road lies ahead. All I ask is that all of you maintain the standard you have set. I know you will.

E. F. HERRING
Lieutenant-General
GOC New Guinea Force

HEADQUARTERS 41ST INFANTRY DIVISION
26 April 1943

GENERAL ORDERS
No.   7

1. I wish to congratulate the officers and men of this Division for the outstanding manner in which they have conducted operations since arrival in New Guinea and also for the praise and compliments which their efforts have brought to this Division in the recent inspection by Lieutenant General Walter Krueger, commander of the Sixth Army.

2. General Krueger stated that General Douglas MacArthur, Commander-in-Chief, Southwest Pacific, wished the 41st Division to know how highly pleased he had been with its performance and the results of its operations in New Guinea. General Krueger added that he felt exactly the same and was proud to have the 41st Division as part of his Sixth Army.

3. General Krueger was high in his praise of the soldierly manner of the officers and men of this Division. He paid special compliment to the military courtesies observed, especially saluting, correct manner of reporting and general discipline of the entire command. One occasion, General Krueger said, "You can always tell when an officer or a man is from the 41st because he salutes."

4. General Krueger, in addition, indicated he was extremely well pleased with the way the Division had improved its living conditions and prepared defensive works despite the tropic conditions encountered in this area.

5. Again, I wish to congratulate the Division for its soldierly manner and excellent conduct of operations which have brought these commendations. It is my desire that every officer and man of this Division be informed of the high opinion held by General MacArthur, General Krueger and myself.

H. H. FULLER
Major General, U. S. Army
Commanding

COMMENDATIONS

HEADQUARTERS 163D INFANTRY
OFFICE OF THE REGIMENTAL COMMANDER

April 29, 1943

MEMORANDUM:

1. A certified copy of Senate Joint Resolution No. 1 has been sent to this headquarters by the Montana Legislature, and is reproduced for the information of all personnel of this Regiment:

SENATE JOINT RESOLUTION NO. 1

A joint resolution recognizing the victories of Montana's 163d Infantry Regiment, USA, expressing the gratitude of the people of Montana to the Regiment and providing for a cable message from the Legislature to the Regiment in the combat zone of the South Pacific Theater of War.

Whereas, the official military reports emanating from General Douglas MacArthur's Headquarters in the south Pacific as released by the War Department, and the news dispatches cabled by observers, make manifest that the 163d Infantry—Montana's own—has won imperishable fame in the jungles and on the heights of New Guinea in most arduous combat against an implacable foe; and has from the very outbreak of hostilities demonstrated the finest attributes of the American soldier, in devotion to training, in fraternization and cooperation with the free peoples of the great Pacific world to the south, and in the deep resolve to establish the rule of law among the nations of the earth; and

The Sixth Legislative Assembly of the State of Montana, by Senate Joint Resolution No. 3, approved February 22, 1899, recognized the same valiant manhood displayed by the military predecessors of the present Regiment, the First Montana Volunteer Infantry, which at that time had distinguished itself near the city of Manila in the Philippine Islands, and such Legislative Assembly, more than forty-three years ago, cabled to that Regiment an expression of the pride and gratitude of Montana's people; in the years between, the Second Montana Infantry Regiment, immediate predecessor, furnished to the American Expeditionary Force in France, officers and men, who with our allies repulsed the savage hordes of the Prussian General Staff, then and now intent on enslavement of those who oppose the substitution of might for right, and brought back their Colors covered with the streamers and ribands of the great victories in France and Flanders; and

Their successor, the present 163d Infantry Regiment, has emblazoned anew the heroic traditions of the Regiment by annihilating a great Japanese army on the Papuan Peninsula of New Guinea to win the first great land battle of the Japanese-American war; and has thereby again demonstrated the unconquerable resolution of Montana's free mountaineers; and

The hearts of all of the people of Montana, while vibrant with affection for the Regiment, are burdened with the pain of its losses, and determined to repay the holy obligation resulting from these sacrifices, by solemnly assuming the responsibilities of free men in support of the reign of law throughout the earth:

Now, therefore, be it resolved, by the Senate of the Twenty-eighth Legislative Assembly of the State of Montana, the House of Representatives concurring, that the Legislative Assembly tenders to every officer and to every man of the 163d Infantry Regiment the deep gratitude of the whole body of our citizens for the great victory which our men have won, purchased with the blood of many of their bravest, hopeful that the Regiment will accept this expression as an evidence of the love and the devotion which we have for it, and which sustains us on the home front and inspires us to dedicate each day to aid our men overseas;

That we asked the Commanding Officer of the Regiment, when this Resolution is placed in his hands, to communicate the continuing homage of Montana people to General Douglas MacArthur, whose father, General Arthur MacArthur, led the Montana Regiment of 1899 to a victory that brought freedom to the Filipinos who have proved their brotherhood with us and with whose help General Douglas MacArthur as his father's successor, and with the aid of our Regiment, will restore those peoples of the isles of the Pacific to the dignity of men.

Be it further resolved, that duly authenticated copies of this Resolution be transmitted by the Secretary of State of the State of Montana, through secure military channels, to the Commanding Officer of the 163d Infantry Regiment, and to each Company Commander in said Regiment and to General Douglas MacArthur; and in order that this long pent-up expression of our whole people, who are represented at large only by this Legislative Assembly, may be made known to the Regiment as soon as possible,

Be it further resolved, that the following message be cabled at once, through military or other appropriate channels, to the Commander of the 163d Infantry Regiment to the combat zone:

"With vibrant admiration for your magnificent victory over the Japanese on the Papuan Peninsula of New Guinea and elsewhere, with prayers for the wounded and with undying resolve to carry on the high purpose of our noble dead, the hearts of the people of Montana are with you, beating as one every hour of every day. The Twenty-Eighth Legislative Assembly of Montana in session at Helena."

Approved March 5, 1943

    SAM C. FORD
    Governor

                ERNEST T. EATON
                President of the Senate

                GEO. W. O'CONNOR
                Speaker of the House

2. The above will be read to all troops at the first formation following receipt.

    By order of Lt. Colonel MASON:

                JAMES R. KENT
                Capt., 163d Inf.
                Adjutant

OFFICIAL:

    JAMES R. KENT
    Capt., 163d Inf.
    Adjutant

General of the Army Douglas MacArthur, Commander in Chief in the Pacific.

Maj. Gen. Kenyon A. Joyce, Commanding General, IX Corps.

Maj. Gen. Innis P. Swift, Commanding General, I Corps.

Maj. Gen. Franklin C. Sibert, Commanding General, X Corps.

Maj. Gen. P. W. Clarkson, Commanding General, X Corps.

Lt. Gen. Robert L. Eichelberger, Commanding General, Eighth Army.

Lt. Gen. Walter Krueger, Commanding General, Sixth Army.

Commanders of the Sunset Division

Major General Jens A. Doe.

Jens A. Doe was born in Chicago, Illinois, on 20 June 1891. He graduated from the Military Academy and was appointed a second lieutenant on 12 June 1914.

He served with the 11th Infantry at Texas City, Texas, until December 1914 and then moved to Naco, Arizona, and a few weeks later to Douglas, Arizona, where he remained until May 1917 with his regiment. Meanwhile he was promoted to first lieutenant on 1 July 1916 and to captain on 15 May 1917. Between May and August 1917 he served at Fort Oglethorpe, Georgia, with the 11th Infantry and then enrolled in the Machine-Gun Course of the Infantry and Artillery School at Fort Sill, Oklahoma, from which he graduated in October 1917. He became an instructor at a division school at Fort Oglethorpe and in December 1917 assumed command of the 15th Machine-Gun Battalion at that post. He sailed for France in April 1918.

He was made a major (temporary) on 7 June 1918 and was 5th Division Machine-Gun Officer in France from June to July 1918, then was assigned as commanding officer of the 14th Machine-Gun Battalion. He participated in the St. Mihiel and the Meuse–Argonne offensives.

He organized and became instructor in the Army Machine Gun School at Langres, France, in November 1918, and one month later was assigned as an instructor at the II Corps Schools. He enrolled in the Artillery Center, Chattillon, France, in May 1919, was graduated one month later and assigned to the 61st Infantry. He returned to the United States with this unit in June, 1919, and went to Camp Benning, Georgia, where in September 1919 he became an instructor at the Infantry School. His majority was made permanent on 1 July 1920. He enrolled in the Field Officers' Course of the Infantry School in September 1921, and was graduated in May 1922. He then was assigned to the 2d Infantry at Fort Sheridan, Illinois. He was Machine-Gun Officer at Camp Custer, Michigan, from May to July 1923, then was assigned to duty at the U.S. Military Academy at West Point.

He enrolled in the Command and General Staff School, Fort Leavenworth, Kansas, in August 1925, and following his graduation in June 1926, he went to China for duty with the 15th Infantry at Tientsin until January 1930. He then returned to the United States and joined the 16th Infantry at Fort Jay, New York. He commanded the Machine-Gun School of the 1st Brigade at Camp Dix, New Jersey, from April to August 1932, after which he enrolled in the Army War College at Washington, D. C., from which he graduated the following June. He was promoted to lieutenant colonel on 1 January 1936 and served as instructor at the Command and General Staff School at Fort Leavenworth until June 1937. His next assignment was as professor of military science and tactics at the University of California at Berkeley. In September 1940, he joined the 7th Division at Fort Ord, California, and assumed command of the 17th Infantry at that post in February 1941. He was promoted to colonel (temporary) on 26 June 1941 and in April 1942 he was transferred with the 17th Infantry to San Luis Obispo, California, where he remained until June 1942, when he was given an assignment in the South Pacific Theater of Operations.

In World War II, Colonel Doe first saw action in the Buna campaign when the 163d Infantry of the 41st Division, under his command, destroyed the Japanese positions in the center, on the Sanananda Track. This action resulted in his promotion to brigadier general (temporary) 2 February 1943 when he became Assistant Division Commander of the 41st Division.

In connection with the Hollandia landing, General Doe commanded the task force landing at Aitape and prior to the Biak operation he landed in the Toem–Wakde area with his force. Upon completion of this mission he relinquished command of the task force and rejoined his division in time for the Biak landing. In August 1944 he became Commanding General of the 41st Division and was promoted to major general (temporary) on 1 August 1944. During February and March 1945, he directed landings of the Jungleers at Palawan, Zamboanga, Tawi-Tawi and Jolo in the Southern Philippines, and in October of that year led his troops into the Hiro–Kure–Hiroshima area of conquered Japan.

When the 41st Division was inactivated in Japan in January 1946, General Doe returned to the United States for a tour of duty in the War Department. He assumed command of the 5th Division at Camp Campbell, Kentucky, on 9 August 1946 and on 29 September, the same year, became Commanding General of the 3d Infantry Division.

General Doe was one of the most highly decorated division commanders in the Pacific Theater. His decorations included the Silver Star with two oak leaf clusters, Distinguished Service Cross, the Distinguished Service Medal with Oak Leaf Cluster, the Air Medal, and the Purple Heart.

His citation for the Distiguished Service Cross awarded in 1943, reads in part as follows:

For extraordinary heroism in action near Sanananda, New Guinea, on January 21 and 22, 1943. As commander of an infantry regiment which was engaged in wiping out the remaining points of enemy resistance, Brigadier General Doe distinguished himself by his coolness and gallantry under fire. In the reduction of these strongly fortified areas his outstanding leadership and courageous conduct were a continuous inspiration to his troops. Brigadier General Doe's presence in the most forward areas and his disregard of personal danger were largely responsible for the high morale of his troops and the successful outcome of these operations.

COMMANDERS OF THE SUNSET DIVISION

An Oak Leaf Cluster to the Silver Star earned in World War I was presented to him in 1943 with this citation:

In the Southwest Pacific in June 1944, he displayed outstanding leadership and devotion to duty under Japanese machine-gun, rifle and mortar fire, and in personally moving among forward assault troops. By his calm manner and courageous actions, he greatly assisted the advance.

A second Oak Leaf Cluster to the Silver Star was presented in 1945 and the citation read:

For gallantry in action at Zamboanga, Mindanao, P. I. from 10 March 45 to 23 April 45. During this time in the capacity of Division Commander, General Doe directed the initial assault and the consequent capture of Zamboanga. His outstanding leadership, indomitable courage and skillful tactical knowledge resulted in his division securing a firm foothold on Mindanao Island. On many occasions without regard to his personal safety, he went forward to units engaged in heavy fighting in order to gain first-hand information about the tactical situation.

He received the Air Medal in 1945 for numerous flights over Japanese positions and his Distinguished Service Medal, awarded in 1945, was for the Aitape and Wakde campaigns. The Oak Leaf Cluster to the Distinguished Service Medal was awarded for service on Biak.

General Doe was appointed permanent major general in 1948 with rank from 6 September 1944.

MAJ. GEN. HORACE H. FULLER

Horace H. Fuller was born on 10 August 1886 at Fort Meade, South Dakota. He was graduated from the Military Academy and appointed a second lieutenant in the Cavalry on 11 June 1909.

He served with the 11th Cavalry at Fort Oglethorpe, Georgia, until April 1914. He was transferred to the 7th Cavalry and served at Fort William McKinley, Philippine Islands, from May to September 1914, and at Camp Stotsenburg, Philippine Islands, to May 1916. In the meantime, he was assigned to the 8th Cavalry. He was promoted to first lieutenant on 12 June 1916 and transferred to the Field Artillery, to rank from 1 July 1916. Returning to the United States, he served at Fort Bliss, Texas, with the 17th Cavalry to May 1917. He was promoted to captain on 15 May 1917. In July, of that year, he was transferred to the 11th Field Artillery, serving at Douglas, Arizona.

In November 1917 he was ordered to Fort Sill, Oklahoma, as a student at the School of Fire for Field Artillery, remaining there until January 1918. He rejoined the 11th Field Artillery at Douglas and accompanied the unit to Fort Sill where he served until July 1918. His temporary promotion to major came on 8 January 1918.

Sailing to France in October, 1918, he joined the 108th Field Artillery at Veronnes in the Argonne. He participated in the Meuse–Argonne Offensive and in the Ypres–Lys Offensive, in command of the 108th. He earned his lieutenant colonelcy (temporary) on 11 September 1918. He commanded the 109th Field Artillery to March 1919 and then served with the Motor Transport Corps until January 1920, when he was assigned to duty with the Graves Registration Service. He reverted to his permanent rank of captain on 15 April 1920, and was promoted to major on 1 July 1920.

He returned to the United States and served at Fort Benning, Georgia, with the 83d Field Artillery from January 1921 to September 1922. He became a student at the Command and General Staff School, Fort Leavenworth, Kansas, and completed the course in June 1923 as a distinguished graduate. He remained at the school as an instructor until August 1927 and then attended the Army War College, Washington, D. C., where he graduated in June 1928.

His next station was at the Presidio of Monterey, California, with the 76th Field Artillery, where he served until November 1929, when he returned to Washington for a tour with the General Staff Corps. He served as Chief of the Publications and Extension Course Section, Operations and Training Branch, War Department General Staff, until September 1933, when he was ordered to duty with the 6th Field Artillery at Fort Hoyle, Maryland.

A promotion to lieutenant colonel came on 1 May 1934 and he was graduated from the Field Officers' Course at the Chemical Warfare School, Edgewood Arsenal, Maryland, in August 1935, and was assigned to duty as Military Attaché at Paris, France. He served in Paris until August 1940, in the meantime getting his eagles on 1 July 1938.

He returned to the United States in August 1940, and following temporary duty in Washington, he was assigned to take a refresher course at the Field Artillery School at Fort Sill in October 1940, preliminary to duty with the 3d Infantry Division with headquarters at Fort Lewis, Washington. He was also promoted to brigadier general (temporary) on 1 October 1940.

In June 1941 he was transferred to Fort Leavenworth as Commandant of the Command and General Staff School. He was assigned to command the 41st Division at Fort Lewis in December 1941 and on 15 December that year won his temporary promotion to major general. He accompanied the Division to the Southwest Pacific Area and in August 1944 became President of the U. S. Army Forces, in the Far East Board. The following November he was made Deputy Chief of Staff, Southeast Asia Command.

He was awarded the Distinguished Service Medal in 1944, with the accompanying citation:

For service in the Southwest Pacific Area from April 6, 1942, to June 17, 1944. Commanding one of the first Infantry divisions to

Major General Horace H. Fuller.

COMMANDERS OF THE SUNSET DIVISION

arrive in the theater, he demonstrated exceptional ability and sound judgment in bringing his division to a high state of efficiency in preparation for jungle combat. He successfully commanded his division in the defense of the Oro Bay–Gona Area and in operations against the enemy from Gona to Morobe, while elements of his division participated in the landing at Nassau Bay and the subsequent drive on Salamaua. Later he led his division in the amphibious assaults against Hollandia and Biak Island. Elements of his division made the successful initial landings at Aitape and in the Wake Island-Sarmi Area. In all attacks he inflicted decisive defeat on an experienced enemy. His personal courage and inspiring leadership made possible the able execution of assigned missions, and contributed materially to our success in dislodging the enemy and forcing him to relinquish his conquests.

MAJ. GEN. GEORGE A. WHITE

George A. White was born in Illinois on 18 July 1880. His first military experience was as a private in the Infantry in the Utah National Guard on 1 August 1895. He entered the Federal service for duty in the Spanish-American War as a musician in the Artillery, serving until 21 December 1898. He reentered the Utah State service on 15 July 1899 and served as private and first sergeant in the Infantry until 3 May 1903. He moved to Oregon where he enlisted as a private in the Oregon National Guard on 4 August 1907, and the following day, 5 August 1907, he was appointed a first lieutenant of Infantry in the Oregon National Guard.

His promotion to captain came on 21 March 1911; to major, AGD, on 14 May 1915, and to brigadier general on 14 May 1915, serving in this rank until 26 June 1916. He was mustered into Federal service for the Border crisis as a captain in the Cavalry on 27 June 1916. He served until 22 February 1917 when he was demobilized and again became brigadier general, AGD.

During World War I he was mustered into Federal service on 10 September 1917 as a major, AGD, and was promoted to lieutenant colonel on 13 November 1918. Following de-

Brigadier General Harold Haney.

mobilization on 23 July 1919, he was appointed colonel, AGD, National Guard of Oregon, on 23 June 1920, and was promoted to brigadier general on 8 June 1922 and to brigadier general of the line on 23 July 1923.

General White was graduated from the National Guard Officers' Course, Command and General Staff School, Fort Leavenworth, Kansas, in 1926; and from the Military Intelligence Course of the Army War College, Washington, D. C., in 1928. He was promoted to major general on 3 January 1930.

During World War II, General White was mustered into the Federal service on 16 September 1940. He became commanding general of the 41st Division which was in training at Fort Lewis, Washington. He died on 23 November 1941.

BRIG. GEN. HAROLD HANEY

Harold Haney was born at Brazil, Indiana, on 2 January 1894. After serving as an enlisted man for three years, he was commissioned a second lieutenant of Infantry in the Regular Army on 9 August 1917, and was promoted to first lieutenant the same day.

Between August 1917 and August 1919 he served with the 57th Infantry at San Benito, Beaumont, and Camp Logan, Texas, later moving with that regiment to Camp Pike, Arkansas. In September 1919 he joined the American forces in Germany, where he first served with the 5th Infantry and later commanded a quartermaster detachment.

He served with the Quartermaster Corps for two years, being promoted to captain on 1 July 1920. He served for a time as salvage officer with the American forces then returned to the United States in May 1922 and was assigned to Camp Dix, New Jersey. There he served as camp salvage officer and as company commander with the 16th Infantry, in September 1923 moving with that regiment to Fort Jay, N.Y.

Major General George A. White.

COMMANDERS OF THE SUNSET DIVISION

He was assigned to the Infantry School at Fort Benning, Georgia, in October 1924, where he completed the Company Officers' Course in June 1925. He then went to Ohio State University, Columbus, Ohio, as assistant professor of military science and tactics. After serving five years in that capacity, he was assigned to the 6th Infantry at Jefferson Barracks, Missouri, where he became a company commander and plans and training officer of the 2d Battalion. In March 1933 he joined the 15th Infantry at Tientsin, China, and remained there until September 1935, meanwhile having been promoted to major on 1 August 1935.

He returned to Fort Jay and was given command of the 3d Battalion, 16th Infantry. In July 1937 he became assistant professor of military science and tactics at the University of Alabama at University, Alabama, and the following September was enrolled as a student at the Command and General Staff School, Fort Leavenworth, Kansas. Upon completion of his studies in June 1939 he became chairman and chief of the Heavy Weapons Section, and later, assistant executive officer at the Infantry School.

His promotion to lieutenant colonel became effective 9 August 1940 and on 24 December 1941 he was promoted to colonel (temporary). In October 1942 he was assigned to the Southwest Pacific Area and served there until November 1943 as commandant of the Officer Candidate School. He later was assigned to the 41st Division and became Assistant Division Commander, receiving his promotion to brigadier general on 7 January 1945.

On 6 March 1946 he reverted to his permanent rank of lieutenant colonel and was promoted to colonel (temporary).

BRIG. GEN. THOMAS E. RILEA

Thomas E. Rilea was born in Chicago, Illinois, on 5 May 1895. He first entered military service by enlisting in the National Guard of Oregon as a private in the Infantry on 8 December 1914, while attending Oregon Institute of Technology, from which he was graduated in 1916 with the degree of Electrical Engineer. In that same year he served on Federal duty with the National Guard as bugler and corporal on the Mexican border. He was again mustered into Federal service on 25 March 1917, just prior to the outbreak of World War I, serving as a sergeant and regimental sergeant-major of Infantry from 25 March 1917 to 16 June 1918, when he was commissioned second lieutenant in the Adjutant General's Department.

His first commissioned service was on Federal duty with the National Guard in the United States and with the American Expeditionary Forces in France. He was awarded the Purple Heart and was cited by the Oregon Legislature for outstanding service.

He was promoted to first lieutenant on 24 February 1919, and to captain on 31 May 1919. He was mustered out of Federal service on 25 September 1919 and was appointed captain on 8 June 1921, major on 17 November 1924, lieutenant colonel on 16 March 1927, and brigadier general on 9 January 1931.

Following his demobilization after World War I he became Executive Officer of the Oregon National Guard. From 1934 to 1935 he was Vice President of the National Guard Association, and from 1935 to 1936 he was its President. In February 1942 he was relieved of assignment as commanding general of the 82d Infantry Brigade and made assistant commander of the 41st Division. In February 1943 he was assigned to Headquarters, Services of Supply, in the Southwest Pacific Area, and a month later was given command of Base Section 17, at Sydney, Australia. In February 1945 he was hospitalized at Barnes General Hospital, Vancouver Barracks, Washington and in July 1945 was assigned to the Infantry Replacement Training Center at Fort McClellan, Alabama.

BRIG. GEN. EDWIN A. ZUNDEL

Edwin Albert Zundel was born at Greensburg, Pennsylvania, on 29 March 1893. He was graduated from the United States Military Academy with a Bachelor of Science degree and commissioned second lieutenant of Field Artillery on 12 June 1915.

He served on border duty at Fort Sam Houston, Fort Bliss and Laredo, Texas, and then at Nogales, Arizona, with various Field Artillery regiments from June 1915 to June 1917. He was promoted to first lieutenant on 1 July 1916 and to captain on 15 May 1917. He then joined the 11th Field Artillery at Douglas, Arizona, and from September to December 1917 was detailed to Leon Springs, Texas, for duty at the 2d Officers' Training Camp, after which he returned to Douglas to rejoin the 11th Field Artillery. From February to May 1918, he was a student at the School of Fire, Fort Sill, Oklahoma, and then rejoined the 11th Field Artillery.

He was promoted to major (temporary) on 3 July 1918 and that month sailed to France with his regiment. The following month he became a battalion commander of the 78th Field Artillery, at Valdahon, France. From November 1918 to April 1919, he served as a battalion commander of the 305th Field Artillery, and then returned to the United States. While stationed in France he participated in engagements in the Meuse-Argonne and Defensive Sector.

His next assignment was at Camp Meade, Maryland, where he served as assistant camp judge advocate until November 1919, when he moved to San Antonio, Texas, as assistant to the zone supply officer. From January to May 1920, he was assistant to the depot quartermaster, San Antonio General

Brigadier General Thomas E. Rilea.

COMMANDERS OF THE SUNSET DIVISION

Brigadier General Edwin A. Zundel.

Supply Depot, and then sailed to Hawaii, where he was named assistant to the department quartermaster at Headquarters, Hawaiian Department, in Honolulu. Meanwhile, he had reverted to captain on 6 May 1920 but was promoted to major on 1 July that same year. He joined the 13th Field Artillery at Schofield Barracks, Hawaii, in October 1920, as a battalion commander, and served in this capacity until he returned to the United States in July 1923.

He served as instructor at the United States Military Academy until September 1927, when he was assigned as a student at the Field Artillery School at Fort Sill. He was graduated in June 1928, and then was detailed to the Command and General Staff School at Fort Leavenworth, Kansas. He completed the two-year course in June 1930, after which he proceeded to Providence, Rhode Island, as an instructor of the 68th Field Artillery Brigade and 103d Field Artillery, Rhode Island National Guard.

He was ordered to Washington, D. C., for duty with the Regulations Division, National Guard Bureau, in September 1934, and in March 1935 was made assistant to the chief of Operations and Organization Division. He was promoted to lieutenant colonel on 1 May 1936. In October 1938 he took a refresher course at the Field Artillery School and then went to Fort Bragg, North Carolina, as commander of the 2d Battalion, 83d Field Artillery. He moved to Fort Benning, Georgia, in command of the 83d Field Artillery in July 1940, and also served concurrently as artillery officer of the 4th Infantry Division.

He became commanding officer of the 42d Field Artillery Battalion at Fort Benning in October 1940 and one year later assumed command of the 1st Antitank Group at Camp Claiborne, Louisiana, and was promoted to colonel (temporary) on 14 October 1941. The following December he was made artillery officer of II Corps at Wilmington, Delaware, later moving to Jacksonville, Florida, in the same capacity.

In June 1942 he was designated artillery officer of XI Corps at Chicago, Illinois, and in February 1943 was assigned to Sixth Army as artillery officer in the Southwest Pacific. He was made a permanent colonel on 14 October 1943. As artillery officer of Sixth Army he participated in landings on Woodlark and Kiriwina Islands and in the landings at Arawe and Cape Gloucester on New Britain, and at Saidor, Aitape and Hollandia on New Guinea, and the Admiralty Islands.

On 24 May 1944 he was promoted to brigadier general (temporary) and assumed command of the 41st Division Artillery at Hollandia. In this capacity he participated in operations on Wakde and Biak, and in the Philippines.

He accompanied the 41st Division into Japan and returned to the United States in February 1946, being assigned as artillery officer of Fourth Army.

He was awarded the Legion of Merit as Sixth Army Artillery Officer, "for exceptionally meritorious conduct in the performance of outstanding services in the Southwest Pacific area from 6 Februay 1943 to 4 May 1944."

An oak leaf cluster to the Legion of Merit was awarded to him as 41st Division Artillery commander for the Biak campaign and for his part in planning and preparing the Palawan and Zamboanga campaigns.

He received the Silver Star for gallantry in action at Ibdi, Biak Island, on 29 May 1944, and the Bronze Star Medal for meritorious achievement in military operations against the enemy on Mindanao from 10 March 1945 to 25 April 1945.

In July 1945 he was awarded the Air Medal for numerous operational flights in Cub planes over enemy-held territory during the operations on Biak and Mindanao.

General Zundel was appointed permanent brigadier general in 1948 with rank from 7 July 1944.

BRIG. GEN. RALPH WALDO COANE

Ralph W. Coane was born in Oakland, California, on 17

Brigadier General Ralph W. Coane.

COMMANDERS OF THE SUNSET DIVISION

October 1891. He enlisted on 5 January 1918 for duty at the Officers' Training School at Camp Kearny, California. He served as a sergeant with the 143d Field Artillery at Camp Kearny and was commissioned a second lieutenant on 28 May 1918.

He was honorably discharged on 18 January 1919, and was appointed a second lieutenant of Field Artillery of the California National Guard on that same date. He was commissioned first lieutenant of Field Artillery, Officers' Reserve Corps, on 13 January 1925; promoted to captain, Officers' Reserve Corps, on 21 July 1930, to major on 8 June 1936, to colonel on 15 January 1941, and to brigadier general (temporary) on 17 March 1942.

General Coane's first assignment after being commissioned was with the 115th Ammunition Troop with which he went overseas in August 1918. He served with that unit until October 1918, when he was transferred to the 143d Field Artillery, then stationed at Camp de Souge, France. He attended the Artillery School of Fire there.

As a Reserve officer he was called to active duty for short periods of training. He was ordered to extended active duty at Santa Barbara, California, on 3 February 1941, and was assigned to duty with the 144th Field Artillery at Fort Lewis, Washington. He was assigned as artillery commander, 41st Infantry Division, Fort Lewis, in March 1942, and the following month accompanied the Division overseas. As a result of wounds received in action, he was returned to the United States in July 1944 and, following hospitalization at Hoff General Hospital at Santa Barbara, California, he was assigned in November 1944 to command the 14th Headquarters and Headquarters Detachment, Special Troops, Fourth Army, at Camp Polk, Louisiana.

BRIG. GEN. ALBERT H. BEEBE

Albert H. Beebe, Washington National Guard, entered the military service of the State of Washington as an enlisted man on 17 July 1907 in Company L, 2d Washington Infantry, where he remained until 28 October 1909. He was then transferred to the Coast Artillery Corps, where he served as a sergeant and sergeant-major until 25 May 1910. On 30 July 1917 he enlisted in Company B, 3d Infantry, Washington State Guard, and on 13 August 1917 he was commissioned a captain in the Infantry, Washington State Guard, and assigned to the 3d Infantry Regiment. On 3 January 1919 he was promoted to major. On 10 January 1921 he was promoted to lieutenant colonel in the Field Artillery and was assigned as executive officer of the 146th Field Artillery. On 30 March 1929 he took command of that regiment and on 3 May 1929 he was promoted to colonel. He continued in command of the 146th until he was promoted to brigadier general and assigned to command the 66th Field Artillery Brigade on 10 October 1934.

General Beebe entered Federal service on 16 September 1940 in command of the 66th Field Artillery Brigade but was released from Federal service on 25 September because of physical disability. On 28 August 1942, he was appointed major general on the retired list of the Washington National Guard.

He was born at Versailles, New York, on 24 February 1878, and graduated from Cornell University in 1901 with the degree of Bachelor of Law.

MAJ. GEN. CARLOS A. PENINGTON

Carlos A. Penington was born in Wilmington, Illinois, on 3 May 1878. He enlisted in Company D, 1st Washington Volunteers at Seattle, Washington, on 30 March 1898 and served with that unit in the Philippine Islands during the Spanish-American War until he was mustered out on 1 November 1899. He reenlisted in Company A, 2d Washington Infantry, on 27 April 1909, and remained as an enlisted man with that unit until commissioned a first lieutenant in the same company on 9 June 1909. On 28 October 1909 he

Brigadier General Albert H. Beebe.

Major General Carlos A. Pennington.

was transferred to the Coast Artillery Corps, and assigned to the regimental staff of the CAC, Washington National Guard. In September 1914 he was promoted to captain and was made a major on 9 May 1916 when he was assigned as Coast Artillery Battalion commander and as State Inspector. From 15 June 1916 to 16 November 1916, he was on active duty at Tacoma, Washington, in charge of recruiting. On 17 November 1916 he was transferred to the Inspector General's Department, and assigned as State Inspector and on 9 June 1917 he was transferred to the Quartermaster Corps and assigned as State Quartermaster.

On 2 August 1917 he entered Federal service as Assistant Division Quartermaster, 41st Division, going overseas with the Division in December 1917. In France he served as Quartermaster of the 77th Division. He was promoted to lieutenant colonel on 10 November 1918 and was relieved from active Federal service on 6 August 1919.

On 23 February 1920 he was commissioned a lieutenant colonel, QMC, in the Organized Reserves, and was assigned as Quartermaster, 62d Cavalry Division. On 17 May 1929 he transferred to the Washington National Guard and was assigned as Quartermaster of the 41st Division. He was promoted to colonel in the Field Artillery of the WNG on 10 April 1930 and assumed command of the 148th Field Artillery with headquarters in Tacoma. His promotion to brigadier general was effective 24 July 1934 and he was assigned as commander of the 81st Infantry Brigade of the 41st Division. He entered Federal service in this capacity on 16 September 1940 but because of physical disability incurred in line of duty he retired on 16 December 1941. On 28 August 1942 he was made major general on the retired list of the Washington National Guard.

After World War I, General Penington took an active part in the organization of the U. S. Veterans Bureau in Washington, D. C., and as an assistant director organized and operated the Insurance Division of the Bureau for a number of years. Later he was business manager of the Veterans' Hospital at Fort Bayard, New Mexico, and at American Lake, Washington.

He died at Madigan General Hospital on 26 August 1947.

Editor's Note:

The stories on the following pages are reprinted as they appeared in JUNGLEER, the 41st Infantry Division Association Newsletter, since the publishing of the first 41st Infantry Division History in 1980. The editor regrets any errors or omissions.

Sunlight for Guys in the Dark

The guy in the dark at the other end of the phone:
Nierman who called in a voice thick with throat cancer
Lamenting how Lieutenant Folsom died when he led his patrol
Too deep under the Jap machine-guns. Nierman went back
To the cobalt treatment and died, a guy in the dark.
Like Vilicich calling to lighten his dark, in the sun
Of that morning on Biak, when mortars thundered, and
His automatic fire pinned down the pillbox where my own
Grenade fell true. And that night in the dark in the hole
Among our own dead when his hand on my shoulder heartened
Me for my long turn on guard, the wait for the morning
Light. Guy in the dark, Virginian Chester, his brother
Dead on the far side of the hill, and the sergeants
Afraid to tell him, that long day when we battled Jap
Gunners raking the ridge-crests. And my own darkness
At my end of the phone: When these men lighten my mind
With their great memories, I find the dark of my coming
Death easy to watch for, waiting my marching orders into
The great sunlight where guys come from the dark to
Welcome me, no longer just another guy in the dark
Alone at the end of the phone.

HARGIS WESTERFIELD

Jungleers hurry up and wait on maneuvers. (Courtesy of William A. Cline)

F Co. 162 Inf:

Roosevelt Ridge and C Ridge

By DR. HARGIS WESTERFIELD, Division Historian
and SGT. CHESTER YOUNG

CREDIT: Personal sources are letters of Sgt Chester Young 28 Feb, 14 Mar, 23 Oct; Sgt Jack Roy 10 Mar; Fowler Summers 24 May; and Walt Stelter 10 Feb—all in 1970. Company Clerk Stelter gave me a list of all known "F" men to contact. When statements conflict and I am unable to reconcile them, I have preferred Young's data to others'. F Co left no Morning Report to be found for July 1943; August Report is meager, unreliable. Other important sources include 162's Report of Opns and Journal, and Australian David Dexter's New Guinea Offensives—which is best for the overall picture—and maps of Roosevelt Ridge from the later Col AR MacKechnie's papers. (I shall welcome more F Co comments to use for later publication of "short incidents.")

On 27 July 1943, F Co. 162 Inf. first struck the Jap 3/Bn 66 Inf Rgt on Roosevelt Ridge, against which 162's 3/Bn had fought since 20 July. Burdened with ammo, F's sweaty platoons moved towards the opaque jungle of Roosevelt Ridge. We were to support E Co in the van. We pulled ourselves and battle loads up by vines and trees—over a craggy shoulder towards a great round jungle knoll later named Fisher Hill because G 162's fine Lt. Fisher would die there.

Above us on the ridge-shoulder, "E" began firing. Too soon then, "F" got orders to leapfrog "E" and storm the Ridge. We passed several E Co walking wounded going down to Medics. Before we reached E's front line, our first "F" man got hit—probably from Japs in the right—either Scales or Churney from Weapons Pln.

Before our attack, Lt Hanson called down a barrage of 81s and 105s. They fell dangerously close in that tangle of ridges and draws. After Hanson adjusted fire, "F" tries a hot uphill push—into Jap defenses among giant ferns and brush.

High on our right flank, Charles Dean knocked out a pillbox. Sgt. Bickel, Louis Shaffer, Chester Young, and Wade infiltrated across a Jap fire trail until they attacked a bunker 10 feet away. As they fired their weapons and grenaded uselessly, Young felt a hot object hit his forehead. He had heard that all a victim felt was the bullet's heat. He fell and decided he was dying. Then Shaffer asked where Young was hit, and Young decided that a man who could hear must still be alive. The hot object was only a spent shell from Shaffer's tommie. But Wade was killed running back for more grenades.

Since "F" had failed to take the ridge that 27 July, orders came to withdraw. Shaffer and Young shrank from crossing the Jap fire-lane. But an explosion behind them—either Jap or Yank—blew them back across the fire-lane. These "F" men had actually topped the main Roosevelt Ridge—but had tried to take the knoll which no riflemen could seize unaided—where G Co's Lt Fisher would die.

Myron Leach of 3/Pln was actually F's first man to die that 27 July. Ely died also; Sgt Jack Roy saw Ely's last moments. A happy, clean-cut fellow who seemed without worries, Ely had gone back for more grenades. Finding a Jap emplacement holding up F's right flank advance, Ely stood erect before a pillbox to lob grenades at its slot until a Jap killed him.

Pushing in a squad on the left, Fowler Summers heard a mortar or FA shell-burst that wounded Purdue's leg, and gave lighter wounds to Cpl Winston. But like all others, this squad gladly obeyed orders to retreat to a lower crest below what would be named Fisher Hill. That night, "F" flattened miserably in new red-clay fox-holes while Jap tracers stabbed close to their helmets.

Next day, 28 July, Guinea rains muddied F's holes. To avoid a frontal attack, we sent out new patrols to find an easier way to take the knoll, but unsuccessfully. One of the Button boys was wounded: we had trouble bringing him down in mud and driving rain.

On the third day, 29 July, hard-faced, sleepless "F" climbed again towards "Fisher" until Jap fire held us in ferns and brush. Mortar shelling was heavy from the far right of Fisher Perimeter, and maybe from a log-roofed pit in its center. It was hard to direct accurate covering fire into that heavy growth. Sgt Sawyer's patrol lost Kendricks, Ortiz dead, and Sawyer Severely wounded. Among those rain-mists and defilades, men were uncertain whether Yank or Jap shells hit them. Steinski was wounded, died on the way to Medics.

Nobody remembers much of F's next few days on that ridge-shoulder below untaken Roosevelt Ridge. We managed to bury some dead just where they fell. An old map bears these crosses: Ely's, Snodderly's, Allen's graves—up and down the twisting contour lines of that shoulder. Nights were an aching half-sleep under fear of attacks. Days were numb with boredom, sleeplessness, fatigue, guard duty, patrols—and gastly fear.

On 5 Aug, Col Fertig replaced "F" to clean up a little, get new fatigues, even a hot meal. Two Jap planes bombed "F"

Co-author of the Roosevelt Ridge story, reminiscing about the old days with cobbers at the Williamsburg reunion. From left: Al Levendusky (H-163), E. Conaway (E-162), Chester Young (E-162), Anthony Parisi (A-116 Engrs.), Harvey Graver (A-116 Engrs.), Lynn Gordon (G-162) and Ken Phillips (E,F,Hq2,K-162;DHQ).

resting. Slagle jumped into the hole dug for Chester Young and George Lowe. Slagle knocked off Young's helmet. Young's hands were jammed under him so that he could not replace that helmet. A big rock hit the helmet, dented it deeply, almost amputated Lowe's finger. But Young was unhurt.

Next day—despite what 162's Journal says—Young was back up the ridge with other "F" men. On 9 Aug, and "F" patrol guarded some fine black Papuan scouts into the Ridge ambushes. They ferreted out 3 Jap pillboxes for our 81s and 105s to hammer. One bold PIB lad crept up to lob 3 grenades into a pillbox. MG volleys from other pillboxes drove us back, with a PIB man wounded in the foot.

On 11 Aug, all able "F" men were back on that ridge-shoulder under the Japs. We relieved 72 G Co men, but a third "G" Pln had to remain to help us. For "F" now mustered only 72, with 5 officers. From a deep, comfortable hole on Roosevelt Ridge, a Jap diarist noted that Yank opposition was weak. He waited orders for an attack to wipe out 162 Inf.

But 162 struck first. On 12 Aug, Capt Munkres' "G" patrol seized part of the Ridge near a bamboo thicket west of Jap Fisher Perimeter. (Narrative of 162 says that Fisher died, that day.) Now all G Co reinforced Munkres' pln that night and fought off many attacks. And that night, "F" had attack orders.

On 0700 13 Aug, FA blasted the Ridge east of "G" while Ratliff's F Co and Couglin's "G" waited orders. At 0900 after 2 hour's blasting, FA shifted to E's right flank and F's left flank to prevent Japs' lateral attacks. From the heights, our "G" friends helped clear the way. Under Lts Steenstra and Herbert, 17 G Co Yanks exploded 4 emplacements, killed 41 Japs, with only 6 "G" men wounded. And F Co climbed the Ridge.

F Co called it a well planned attack of 2/Bn. Only known casualty was an "H" man—Batts, whom Nips shot in the legs when he was talking to Young. Young's brother Lester was hit but unhurt when a Jap Mortar shot so close that the shell failed to nose over and explode. (Lester would die at Zamboánga.)

At dawn 14 Aug, scouts saw that Japs between E and F Cos had withdrawn. But Japs still held the seaward end of Roosevelt Ridge. And this 14 Aug was the great day when Col MacKechnie blew the top off that seaward end of Roosevelt Ridge with all the FA, AA, and Air Force he could get. E Co then safely occupied the Ridge all the way to the sea.

About 1720 that day, Jap knee mortars impacted F's perimeter, killed a Lt. from Mississippi next to Jack Roy. But main Jap attack bypassed the hard front-line riflemen to hit F's rear—truck-drivers, cooks, and Hq men. All night, riflemen handed back ammo to save F's rear—against a persistent attack that never stopped. There died Snodderly, Smoky Allen, and another Yank—and 6 Japs we could find to count later.

By 1042, "F" had a position on Roosevelt Ridge. With an "H" HMG Pln, a 37 AT gun, a .50 HMG, we held 100 yards of ridge, with Japs still facing us on the inland ridge. East were 500 yards' Jap ground, but "E" had also attacked and topped the seaward end of the Ridge next to those Japs. In this 500-yard gap which was too close to "F" and "E" for support fire, Japs held hard after dusk 13 Aug 1943.

As for our F Co, we drove inland up Roosevelt Ridge through hurriedly deserted Jap perimeters. After gaining 400 yards, 3/Pln's patrol leader, Lt Uppinghouse, sensed danger and dug in. When our security guard found Japs again at 200 yards, I Co reinforced us and dug in. Except for some days' guard on short rations, F Co was now done with Roosevelt Ridge forever.

And "F" fought on to take Salamaua town. After losing Roosevelt Ridge, the unbroken Jap army held a barrier of positions on high ground which kept Aussies and Yanks from Salamaua. To judge by the Aussie map, the strongest part of this barrier was the seaward flank in 162 territory. Here, one main Jap supply line to Salamaua led along the crest of Scout Ridge,

205th Artillery boys use tractors to pull a Bofors AA gun up a new road leading to the top of Roosevelt Ridge.

1500-3000 yards in from Dot Inlet. Four strong Jap perimeters held Scout Ridge supply-line.

Now 162 planned to base 2/Bn on Dot Inlet—just the other side of captured Roosevelt Ridge—and overrun the Japs on Scout Ridge. While 3/Bn pushed north from Roosevelt, our own 2/Bn would climb up from Dot Inlet against Scout Ridge. (The whole 2/Bn was now down to 300 men.) Meanwhile, 1/Bn 162 would press the Japs from inland.

And F Co let 2/Bn up from the sea at Dot Inlet in a heart-breaking jungle night march 25-26 Aug. Sgt. Roy never forgot that all-night slogging in the rain and black uphill jungle. While a rope guided the leader, following men held hands for safety. Next day, some of us had skinned noses because men ahead had stopped without warning in the blackness and we bumped our noses into their packs. F Co halted unhappily at our new outpost halfway to the crest of "C" Ridge, which was supposed to intersect our objective, the Japs' trail on Scout Track Ridge. With daylight, FA and mortars blasted the Japs, and "F" occupied the highest part of C Ridge.

But "F" did not cut Scout Track Ridge. Leftwards was a green hill at 75 yards. Right across a deep draw was what we named Berger Hill (after Maj. Armin Berger) 100 yards off. And 50-75 yards ahead was a Jap water-hole, with Scout Track Ridge above it.

Evidently F Co at first had orders to keep quiet. But we were short of water and went for it at the water-hole and saw a Jap there. One rifleman—some say Wally Stone—shot a Jap through his helmet dead into the water-hole. Another story is that the bullet merely caromed the helmet into the air and merited Stone a good Nippo cursing.

Came then F's day of battle, jungle-style. At 0845, Patrol No. 1 scouted for Berger Hill. Just past the water-hole, we heard movements to our left rear, turned, and slew 2 Japs, maybe wounded another. Fearing reprisal from the rear, we hurried up Berger Hill far enough to see Jap defenses, then got safely back to our perimeter.

Patrol No. 2 moved straight forward to try to climb Scout Track Ridge. When a Jap came towards the water-hole, we fired at him, then other Japs, and claimed 11 killed. But grenades from the Ridge forced us back. Patrol No. 3 climbed the hill to the left and fought Japs there.

From 26 Aug through 8 Sept, "F" fought Japs on Scout Track Ridge. On 8 Sept, however, E Co. rather than "F" occupied Berger Hill. But heavy MG fire struck E from at least 2 pillboxes. With their CO the first man wounded, E retreated. This was 162's last action of the Salamaua Campaign. Our own F Co secured Berger Hill on 9 Sept unopposed. And then F Co followed jungle trails past the vacated Jap positions, and followed other trails that put us into battered Salamaua on 12 Sept to close the operation. Last man to die from F Co was Griggs.

Such was F Co's Salamaua Campaign—2 successful missions against Roosevelt Ridge and Scout Track Ridge up from C Ridge, then occupaton of bombarded Salamaua. From an official strength of 133 men on 29 June, F Co shrank to 33 worn-out veterans, by Sgt Young's count at Salamaua. Official 162 report is that "F" lost 8 killed—compared to 17 for "A", 11 for "C", and 7 each for "E" and "K". (These 5 Cos had 50 dead of the 98 total for all 162 Inf, FA, and attached elements.) And some of the additional 14 "Died of Wounds" may have been "F" men. "F" had 11 seriously wounded, and 19 slightly wounded. But for our 8 dead and 11 seriously wounded, we reported 90 dead Japs. F Co had endured gruelling tropical mountain jungle fighting against entrenched Japs, but with minimum losses. F Co 162 Inf's Battle of Salamaua was a brave, dogged fight of expert American infantry.

3/Bn 163 Inf:

Mokmer Ridges, Hill 320, The Teardrop

By DR. HARGIS WESTERFIELD, Division Historian

Crammed into a destroyer for emergency transport, most of 3/Bn 163 first saw Biak 31 May 1944. To reinforce Gen Fuller, we sped up from battle at Toem. Entering Bosnek Jetty, we watched Jap planes above our AA fire. With 1/Bn, we relieved 186 and 162 Inf for a second offensive for Mokmer Strip. Camped on a low ridge north of Bosnek that night, we heard Jap planes dive for the beach. A quadruple .50 HMG hit a Jap plane to explode near us.

At 0930 1 June, K Co moved 3 miles east to Opiaref to secure the 41st's east flank. Two AT Co 37s backed us, and by 2 June, most of 3/Bn.

On 1 June, a prisoner told L's 1/Lt Candella that 500 Japs menaced us 2000 yards NE of 3/Bn Hq. Four tanks joined us. But on 3 June, 163's I & R and 10 I Co men found only supply dumps and a wire to follow tomorrow. Next day, 10 "I" men traced the wire to its end, then slipped up a coral path lined with empty caves. Two Japs made tea down in the last cave. They would not surrender; we grenaded them out a rear entrance.

Later on 4 June, S-3 Capt Reams' 15-man volunteer patrol climbed a flat-topped ridge to check a wide clearing spotted from the air. Here brush was chopped 12 feet wide into far distance. Destroying 6 small Jap mortars trailside, we scouted across. Back to the trail at 1700, we saw bayonets gleam. Fifty-six well-fed, healthy Jap riflemen passed within 15 feet of prone Reams and men like I Co's John Sullivan. Reams still wonders whether his 15 men with 2 BARs should have fired.

But SE Biak was clear of its Jap garrison, gone west to hold Mokmer Strip. Already 186 Inf marched down their new road to Mokmer Ridges. On 3 June, 3/Bn followed 186 down the new road to secure 186's supply dumps. On 4 June, we had orders to assemble 1000 yards west of the land surveyed by the Japs for Bosnek Strip. We were to hunt Japs north and west of the new road.

First casualties were on 5 June. Scouting towards a Jap perimeter, K Co's Ozbolt was hit in right shoulder. Two outposted Japs escaped. We seized an empty perimeter with many abandoned supplies. On 5 June also, L's Sgt Art Brown took a fragment in right chest, circumstances unknown.

On 6 June, "I" and "L" had tense patrols. "L" men endured rifle fire in a village clearing, but killed 6 of 7 Japs we sighted. Scouting outside the village, one "L" squad took fire from some 20 Japs. S/Sgt Deaven was wounded in his right hand, perhaps on this patrol.

On 7 June when 186 swooped from the east curve of Mokmer Ridges to take Mokmer Strip, 3/Bn guarded the ridge pass to secure carrying parties. Our 3/Bn expected to convoy 186's supplies down the land road, but the water route was preferred.

Now began 3/Bn's little known war in the blind Mokmer Ridges jungle above the Division's major war for Horseshoe Ridge below. Mokmer Ridges wind along Biak's south shore like a python. From above Ibdi Village, they curve SW to the sea at Parai Defile and Mokmer Village. Then they bend NW across

CREDIT: This was one of the hardest stories of all to write—based on a too-brief 163 Inf "Narrative Report of the Biak Operation," and the elusive 163 Inf Biak Journal. Important also were 163's detailed "Casualty Report," letters of K Co's Dean "Bill" Poole (13 June 1971; 27 June 1978), I Co's Dante Prandi (14 May 1974), and John Sullivan (4 Nov 1974). Also important were my conversation with Lt-Col (then Capt) Ed Reams in 1971 at Gearhart Reunion and his phone-call 30 June 1978, and Mjr Garlyn Munkres' Award Story. Useful also were RR Smith's Approach to the Philippines, 163 Inf Morning Report (June, 1944), 186 Inf's "Narrative" and "Journal" with "I Corps' History of the Biak Operation, 15-27 June 1944."

Entrances to the West Caves. Photos were taken after the hostilities on Biak ceased and the caves became a big attraction to the 41sters.

186's pass, and dip south to tall Hill 320. Above Mokmer Village were East Caves, and behind Hill 320, Teardrop Strongpoint. Below Hill 320 westward ran the Japs supply line to West Caves.

First 3/Bn mission was to find and kill 4 Jap 90mm guns blasting 186 on Mokmer Strip. With 3 other 41st Cos, "K" searched the ridges. Below us, G 186 and F 162 destroyed the 90s, but K 163 had losses. We lost 6 men on 9-10 June when "K" made perimeter on 186's old trail and 1/Pln sought the guns on the ridges southward.

About 2030 in early dark, some 25 Japs, including 2 officers, charged K's main perimeter. Sabers wounded 3 men. S/Sgt Holman was chopped in right knee, right arm, right eye. Warren was slashed in right thigh, and St. Onge in the back. We slew 8 Japs, the 2 sabering officers among them.

Meanwhile T/Sgt Poole's detached 1/Pln patrolled SE on Mokmer Ridges. We saw several Japs and felt spooked before perimetering for the night. Poole reported 2 wounded that night of 9 June—one perhaps Rabon, a fragment in right hand.

Evidently, crawling Japs spotted us that night and lay in wait for daybreak. Jap rifle fire began. Poole saw Little Warrior shot in the head to die before him. Others killed were Philips, hit in the back, and Maloney, hit in the head. We saw no Japs, but returned fire in their direction. Rifle fire increased and forced us to leave that afternoon. While each squad took turns covering retreat, we withdrew to K Co. Jap fire ceased after we left our 1/Pln's night perimeter.

On 11 June, "I" relieved "K" and probed for the defenses of East Caves above Mokmer Village. Fighting on the north flank of the Caves, by 1040, we knocked out 2 pillboxes, slew 6 Japs. Perhaps here, Leonard Brooks was shot in left arm. On 12-13 June, "I" continued pressure, with intervals of bombardment by FA and Navy. By 13 June, the coast road was finally open for 162 and 186 Inf to get supplies safely.

On 11 June also, L Co began an important strategical move—safely occupied Hill 320. This was a tall, heart-shaped Jungle nubbin about 600 yards north of West Caves. Some 700 yards west below Hill 320 ran the Japs' main supply track. Protected by cliffs westward, Hill 320 was a fine observation post, and the future hook on a tentacle to help surround West Caves.

On this 11 June, 1/Lt Ludviksen's "L" Pln first climbed Hill 320. A good trail led all the way, the last part on a ledge only 3 feet wide. Next day, L's 1/Lt Quackenbush and 31 men replaced Ludvicksen's. We carried brush-cutting tools to clear the view, and a range-finder. Capt Reams and 2/Lt Silbert of S-3 came with a DivArty observer, and a giant 50-pound Jap binocular.

Almost under Hill 320 on 12 June, 162 Inf fought to take Horseshoe Ridge, the bastion for West Caves. Capt Reams observed for Col Miller's 2 tanks supporting 162's attack.

Below him on a ridge 150 by 100 yards, Reams saw 4 large coastal defense guns emplaced to fire towards the sea. Camouflaged with green spots, they resembled Army 155s. Many shirtless Japs were carrying billy-cans up a trail—perhaps carrying laundry. Col Miller's tankmen and attacking 162 Inf could not see those threatening guns.

Reams halted the tanks; L 162 hit the ground; our FA fired. After our FA ceased, late in the day, the 162 men dug in. Reams said later that the FA totally missed the guns, but the shells must have been hard on the laundrymen.

On 13 June at 0915, a Hill 320 observer saw Jap AA fire on our planes, and phoned FA men the coordinates of those guns. At 1025, alarmed Reams heard maybe 100 Japs on the steep western slope of Hill 320. A lone Jap wandered up toward our outpost; Reams had to kill him. We fled Hill 320 to return later, but had no more Jap trouble. Jungle precipices protected us from the Japs below and Teardrop Strongpoint.

And "I" and "K" still probed the concealed East Caves defense lines in the ridges above Mokmer Village. On 13 June, "I" tried to find a trail crossing the ridges to the sea, and to seize a Jap laundry water-hole. By 1215, 2/Lt Amans' patrol had killed 2 Japs on the ridges, and flamed out 2 caves. We slew 7 Japs by 1545, but lost McAtee with a bullet in left arm. "I" then withdrew from the cliffs to let FA and Navy blast them next morning.

Trying to cross the ridges on East Caves' west flank to the horse-shoe-shaped road in Mokmer Village on 15 June, I Co fought Japs at 1600. At 1745, we slew a Jap while MG fire missed us. Just after dark, an LMG ripped into our perimeter. S/Sgt Pfeifle was wounded in right shoulder, and Maki in left leg.

Next morning, 16 June, S/Sgt Holder died with a bullet in his heart while he led I's forward Pln. By 1245, "I" had 2 more casualties—Sgt Novshek with a bullet in his back, and Brann hit in abdomen to die 8 days later. By 1810, we had seized a Jap

HMG, killed 2 Japs, now held their waterhole.

On 16 June also, "K" had 2 dead. T/4 Vaden was shot in head and chest; Floyd Smith in chest and stomach.

Hill 320 was important in the Division's great maneuver of 19 June. On this day, 186 Inf advanced from Horseshoe Ridge NE, cut the Japs' supply road north from West Caves, and lined up with L 163 holding Hill 320. Action was light for 186, while "L" high in the cliffs had no trouble at all.

On 19 June Gen Doe detached 3/Bn's Mjr Munkres himself for an important patrol into the coral hell north of Hill 320. After a recon flight on 18 June, Munkres took 6 men with him. After 3 hours' trek up and down hot jungle ridges and down into narrow, brush-jammed valleys, the patrol found a faint track into a supply route behind Jap lines. Japs working around a supply dump did not see us, but we had to kill one walking towards us, and alarm them.

Our flight was cut off. Munkres wisely hid us near the Jap lines. After a night among the Japs, we started back at dawn. Not until 1125, 20 June did we return with information—hungry, thirsty, and slashed with coral cuts on hands and legs. From this patrol, Munkres found data to cause over 100 Japs to be driven from sheltered positions and cut down.

On 19 June while 3/Bn awaited Munkres' return, an I Co supply train suffered 3/Bn's highest casualty toll before Ibdi Pocket. Supposedly resting in a safe area, I Co sent out a 30-man carrying party, of whom just 10 were armed—and at least 2 with only .45 caliber pistols.

Near I's perimeter, 8 Japs with a knee mortar saw us. Probably they intended to snipe on the "I" perimeter, but we were easier to kill. They impacted a grenade or mortar shell, and charged in. We lost 5 dead, 4 wounded. Dead were T/Sgt Ed Wilson, shot in the head; Gould, shot in head and chest; Mihoover and Medina both shot in chest; and Clarence Miller shot in a thigh. Sullivan had fragments in neck and shoulder from 2 grenades, a bayonet breaking his cheekbone, and a gash from the mortar barrel clubbing his head. Labencki was bayoneted in right leg, Bezenek shot in left hip. In I's rescue, T/Sgt Morris was hit in right shoulder by a Nip shamming dead, who had to be killed twice. "I" slew 5 of the 8; "L" killed the other 3.

Next day, 30 June, 186's Col Newman needed help of our 3/Bn against a company-sized Nip detachment with heavy weapons which was posted north of Hill 320 in the Teardrop. This Teardrop was a narrow limestone rift—a blind alley with a bend in it, and the only entry from the north. On the west ridge above this rift—which was 100 yards wide and 300 yards long—the Japs waited among their MG nests.

While 186 patrolled northwards, Newman on 20 June wanted our 3/Bn to strike south and close Teardrop's mouth against escaping Japs. But 3/Bn was searching thick jungle 3-4 miles north of Teardrop and took several days to contact 186 patrols. On 22 June, after a night's FA fire on Japs, I Co evidently closed in on the Teardrop. Late that afternoon, Jap fire drove us to earth in a hard rock terrain to make a shallow perimeter. About 2015 that night, Japs whooped like Indians and charged. At perhaps 30 feet, our rifles and MGs finally broke them. A

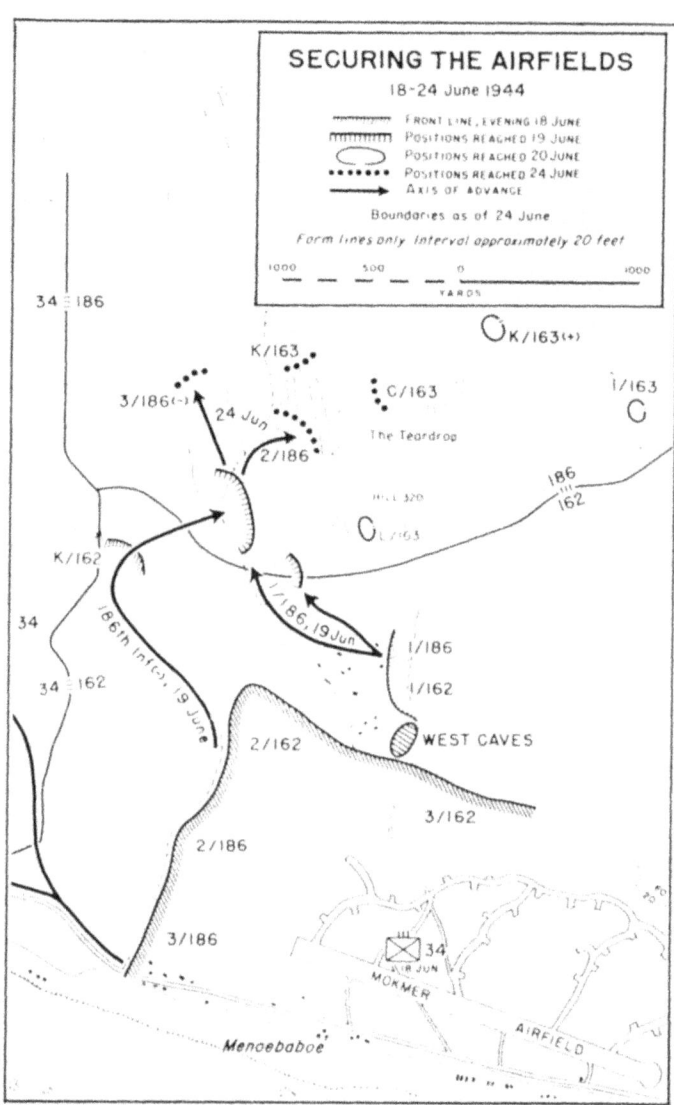

Among the personal effects found on the body of a Japanese soldier killed on Biak was this photo showing him proudly posing with his light machine gun.

bullet hit Prandi in the left leg just below the knee, but his tourniquet stopped most of the blood. At his low cry for help, the nearby MG Sgt phoned the Medic at CP, who came to help him with I's CO (whom Prandi thought to be Capt Sherry). Hours later, the Medic found a second and lighter wound in Prandi's right leg. A heavily armed 5-man litter party carried Prandi through Jap country back to safety. At daybreak, the Japs were gone, but for 2 corpses.

Not until 24 June did K 163 seal Teardrop's north entrance while our C 163 flanked it on the NE and 186's 2/Bn fought towards us. "K" slew 19 Japs that day. On 25 June, 186 overran the Teardrop, captured 5 MGs and 3 light mortars, found 38 dead Japs. But because of 3/Bn 163's necessary delay moving southward, some 200 Japs had escaped.

Our 3/Bn did not enter the Teardrop. By night of 24 June, 3/Bn was finally leaving Mokmer Ridges. Gen Doe badly needed us in the rear areas for 163's all-out attack on Ibdi Pocket of 26-28 June. (On 9 July, 3/Bn would take over the fight for Ibdi Pocket, and fight there until our triumph on 22 July.)

Such were 3/Bn 163's early Biak days, 31 May-24 June. Battle losses were fairly light—12 killed, 18 wounded to hospital. "I" was loss-leader, with 7 dead, 10 wounded. "K" lost 3 killed, 5 wounded; and "L" 2 killed, 3 wounded. Jap dead were far more than have been cited herein. Ours had been only light actions. But they had been indispensable actions—as on Hill 320 and against East Caves. And by 24 June, 3/Bn was well tempered to fight for Ibdi Pocket, in that final struggle.

641 TANK DESTROYER BN/2 PLN:

Blasting East Caves, Mokmer Ridges

by DR. HARGIS WESTERFIELD, Division Historian,
with CAPTAINS H. RICHARD GERTTULA and BENNETT SAUNDERS

CREDIT: Prime credit is due to Gerttula's letters in 1974; but Saunders' 1974 letters started correspondence, supplied invaluable background, found Gerttula for me. But Gerttula alerted me to procure 2/Pln 641 TD's Journal which Federal Archives' employees overlooked. Other records are "Operations Journal 98th Chemical Bn (Mtzd) 12 April-31 July 1944," RR Smith's **Approach to the Phillippines.** *(Late in Biak action, 641 TD was renamed 98 Chemical Bn. Stockman Gerttula now breeds Charolais cattle at Stanfield, Oregon. Former Concrete Consultant Saunders is retired in Seattle.)*

On 2 June 1944, 2/Pln 641 Tank Destroyer Battalion began our second Battle of Biak. We received 6 new 4.2 mortars to replace the 6 which we had lost in rear-guard action to extricate 162 Inf from Parai Defile. (We had to destruct our first 6 mortars because 162 ordered us to leave them.) We spent all 2 June readying our new 6 mortars for action.

The very next day, we fought again. To cover K 162's right flank and C Btry 205 FA which took harassing fire from Parai Cliffs, Lt Sandwick had us occupy positions 300 yards west of Ibdi. Beginning 1930, we shot 8 rounds white phosphorus (WP) and 14 rounds high explosive (HE). When the close fire made "K" nervous, we ceased at 1330. (For these HE shells—M-3—contained 25 pounds TNT.)

And starting 7 June, 2/Pln fought almost daily, nearly 6 weeks through 14 July. We fought Parai Defile again. Embarking on our 4 DUKWs with our fine Black QM drivers, we followed 162's I, K, CN Cos and 6 tanks to Parai Jetty. By 1900, we began registering to protect 162 and tanks—with 4 WP shells, then 6 HE. Our position was 600 yards east of our great rear-guard location of 29 May when we protected 162's retreat but lost our first mortars.

Next day, 8 June, we supported 162's push west to Mokmer Village to try to contact 186 at Mokmer Dromes. Our observation party got badly mauled. This was after the morning when 162 advanced into the coconut plantation where the Japs had struck with tanks on 29 May. At first, 162 found no Jap opposition.

But at 1330, heavy mortar fire from East Caves halted 162. At 1340, D's Lt Russell phoned to request that we adjust fire to spring 162's men from their prone positions under fire. We fired 1 WP, 3 HE shells. Then at 1400, Jap shells cut the wire. We never heard Russell's voice again.

Lineman Kelly rushed back with the sad news Russell was dead, Pendergast and Daly wounded. Gerttula organized a new observer party under S/Sgt Roy White. (White was that kind of NCO always on the spot when "D" needed him.)

Kelly guided the new OP back into the forward area, and by 1700, we fought again—interdictory fire—9 WP, 60 HE.

Temporarily, White silenced those mortars high in the dark-green coral terraces. He got a direct hit on a Nip MG. (White's fine work here and elsewhere would earn him a battlefield commission as 2/Lt.)

Next day, 9 June, Jap fire from East Caves increased steadily while 162's 1/Bn and 3/Bn pushed doggedly west. At 1400, "D" adjusted fire at 50 yards greater range against East Caves. With 2 WP, 22 HE, we momentarily silenced the Jap mortars. At 1730, we shot 16 HE on that same ridge area, but at 1900, the Japs hit 162's Hq. Despite 70 more HE shells, Jap mortars continued fire. (And tanks in LCTs offshore had pounded East Caves all day, but without success.)

On 10 June, Jap mortar fire was again heavy. Their shells hit 162's supply road to the new forward positions at Mokmer Dromes. To safeguard passage of 7 tanks with 15 supply trucks, "D" started battle at 0800. Rate of fire was at a minimum of 1 round per minute, 0800 to 1515. Meanwhile, tanks fired on East Caves from LCTs offshore; and 205 FA and 947 FA arced in projectiles.

But most effective shelling was surely from 641 TD. For when we paused at 1000 to shift base plates, 6 Jap mortar rounds hit Mokmer Road and killed 1 man, wounded 5. Soon fighting again, "D" apparently killed the Jap mortars. On 10 June all day through 1515, we had fired 890 rounds or 18 tons. Apparently the Jap mortars were destroyed.

But on 11 June at orders from 1/Bn 162's Mjr Benson, we fired the same concentrations—beginning 0645. Jap shells were still hitting Mokmer Road. After 145 rounds HE, we quit firing at 0858. From 0858 to 1930, our troops and vehicles travelled the road freely. When the Nips opened up again at 1930, we blasted them silent with 60 rounds HE in 15 minutes.

On 12 June, these die-hard Nips smashed Mokmer Road once again. Beginning 0700, we hit them this time with a third of our shells white phosphorus—38 WP and 77 HE, precisely. The WP was devilishly effective; observers reported that Japs leaped from their holes and screamed with pain. Again, "D" had reopened the road for supplying 162 which now fought to capture the ridge guarding West Caves.

But we still lacked adequate observation of Jap cliff-top installations. Observation planes were unavailable. So on 13 June, G-3 sent Gerttula out on an LCT with 3 tanks to shoot from the sea and help re-register our 4.2s. At 1740, we crashed the ridge with 15 WP and 290 HE. Again we freed the road for Yank vehicles.

On 14 June, "D" got Gen Doe's orders to move into the fight to close the Great Gap between 162's 2/Bn and 3/Bn on Mokmer Ridge before West Caves. Despite 162's dogged advances under heavy FA shelling, the Great Gap was still 500 yards wide. From this gap, Jap warriors denied the use of

Mokmer Dromes to our bombers. And on 15 June at 1645, we registered on 4 Jap naval guns in the Great Gap—with 38 HE shells.

Our fire was surely decisive in helping 2/Bn 186 close that Great Gap. For while 186 waited orders to move out on 16 June, our 4.2's fought for 186 with all that we had. Working with the infantry mortars, we poured in steel on the Japs. We searched and traversed a Great Gap area of 200x500 yards. From 0800 to 0850, we expended 379 HE. Although 162 had been stopped the day before, 186's "shock troops" of 2/Bn had comparatively minor resistance to close the Great Gap— except for E 186's 2/Pln. An estimated 40-50 dead were found in our impact area.

Next day, 17 June, "D" harassed the "main road to West Caves." Covering 300 yards of road, we shot 9 WP, 115 HE. Because of a defective tube, No. 3 mortar shot erratically. We quit using it until we replaced the tube on 21 June. At 1310, the 81s, FA, and we fought a Jap fieldpiece. After 1 WP, 110 HE from us, it ceased fire.

Thus during 15-17 June, we were in battery to help 186 and 162 seal off West Caves for the final kill. After 5 days' inaction, 2/Pln D 641 fired again on East Caves.

Except for sporadic fire at trucks on the coast road, East Caves was inactive. But by 23 June, Jap mortar and small arms fire picked at Engr work parties on piers and roads. We registered on East Caves from the ground; then Lt/Col Cochran adjusted us more precisely from the air. Even then, of 315 rounds WP and HE, only some ¼ of them hit that narrow target of ridge-side caves. Our fire did silence them, but on 24 June, we had to drop 49 WP and 120 HE to quiet them again.

On that same 24 June, we broke down mortars to entruck again. While 162 mopped up West Caves, 186 needed D's 4.2s on Jap positions NW of West Caves—some 600 yards NE of Borokoe Dromes.

By 1830 that 24 June, D's 2/Pln registered—probably on the strongpoint where some 3 Jap 75 harassed 186. Since D's observers with 162 had not returned, CO Gerttula himself and Kelly climbed the steep ridge to attempt observation in an opaque terrain of tall jungle and defiles.

With direct observation impossible, they started registration at long range, then shortened range by sound-sensing— with 8 rounds WP. Then they computed a normal barrage of sweeping fire on an area 400x400 yards. This barrage impacted about 1900, with an unrecorded number of shells. To penetrate the dense cover, they employed delayed fuze. When 186 took the ground, they found that D's fire was accurate indeed. Even our registration rounds had landed accurately on target. Jap positions and weapons were recently deserted. Gerttula believes that this was the shootout after which several dazed prisoners asked whether we fired "automatic artillery."

On 27 June, we fought another Nip strongpoint for 186's 3/Bn. In opaque terrain again, we accurately placed 120 WP, 83 HE. When "L" hit the area, they found 32 Jap dead. Our observer was James White, newly made Lt that 27 June 1944.

But Japs still held East Caves, and shot up Mokmer Road. Gen Doe recalled Gerttula for consultation with G-3 to kill those caves. On 28 June, we displaced a 4.2 to where it could mark the Caves for an air-strike. Gerttula adjusted fires with an Air Force 0C3 and 12 WP shells. Then 405 Bomb Squadron struck, but the Caves still harassed E Co 542 Engr Boat & Shore Regt working in a gravel pit NW of Mokmer Village.

Now 2/Pln had our last Biak mission. On 29 June, we had our old position 300 yards east of Mokmer Dromes. On this exact date in May, we had shelled those caves in desperate rear-guard action to save 162 from annihilation.

Orders were to fire on East Caves until further notice—15 rounds hourly, at irregular intervals. From a DivArty plane, our newly commissioned Lt White adjusted fire. We set up a firing schedule to give each mortar a 1-hour turn to impact its irregularly timed 15 shells and keep 2/Pln in action 24 hours a day.

Division G-3 organized the reduction of East Caves like the siege of a great city. Besides 641 TD's 6-mortar pounding, a gun of C Btry 205 FA smashed 800 rounds of smoke and HE into the caves. North of them, I 163 guarded possible Nips' escape routes or counter-attacks while E 542 Engrs patrolled or hit some caves with bazookas.

Near daylight 0430 30 June, our crews saw a great fire in the cave mouth area. It burned 30 minutes. From his plane at 0800, White decided that we had flamed 2 Jap bunkers. Probably the WP shells had caused these flames.

We continued blasting East Caves every day at 0800 and 1800, from 30 June through morning of 3 July. Gerttula and White flew above to keep our mortars precisely adjusted. Some two-thirds of our rounds landed in the large cave.

At 1025 3 July, orders came to cease fire. During a 4-day span, we had fired 348 rounds WP, 873 HE, all of 1221 rounds. The 348 WP rounds had been mainly for night action, at which time we found aiming lights were necessary.

In those 4 days, not one Jap round had hit road or docks. Actually, the Japs' last heavy rounds fell about 2000 3 July, but Gen Doe knew better than to let up firing until days later. For that sheer cliff wall of Parai Defile was a network of caves and sumps, with AA guns, heavy mortars, HMGs, as 162's 2/Bn and 3/Bn well remember. Although the Japs, for reasons unknown, had failed to make maximum use of East Caves after 10 June, over 3 weeks ago, this was readily the strongest position on Biak.

But after 641 TD ended the menace of Jap heavy weapons, light harassing fire continued. On 3 July, our last firing day, E 542 EB & SR and E 163 penetrated some caves. On 5 July, they dared invade the larger sump holes. In one cave along, were 4 20 mm guns, 500 rounds Jap 81 mortar shells. In another were 2 20 mm guns, a .50 caliber HMG and a .30 LMG. Yet Japs lurked there still—killed 6 Aussie Air Force souvenir hunters 15 July. On 17 July, tanks and infantry killed 2 MG nests. Final resistance ended only on 20 July.

D Co, however, was long gone from Biak by 20 July. For S-3 of entire 641 TD Bn, Capt Saunders, came from Hollandia to liberate us. Saunders wanted to prevent demoralization by post-action labor assignments. Even if all "D" had lost just 1 KIA, 5 WIA, we were close to breakdown. After 2 New Guinea years, almost everyone had malaria, dysentery —Saunders himself with tropical ulcers up to his armpits.

Gen Doe wanted us an organic element of the 41st, but 6th Army Hq had us attached, and Krueger ordered us back to rest-camp at Tahnamerah Bay near Hollandia.

Waiting to embark at Bosnek 14 July, "D" celebrated. Unhappy at returning to their QM outfit, our 12 fine black DUKW drivers scoured Biak for a farewell feast—including canned turkey and fresh fruit. Gen Doe and all of his available staff attended, and Doe presented us a letter of commendation.

D Co 641 TD's 2/Pln waged a great Battle of Biak. After losing our first mortars to save 162 on 29 June, we got new mortars and battled East Caves again. We kept Mokmer Road to West Caves, enabled 186 to close the Great Gap on Mokmer Ridge. And our final 5 days' battered made East Caves an almost harmless shambles. D's 2/Pln played a great part in winning Biak for the 41st Division.

163 INF ON JOLO II:

Winning Mounts Magusing, Datu

by DR. HARGIS WESTERFIELD, Division Historian

CREDIT: Basic to this narrative are 9 pp of 163 Inf Journal on Jolo, and 146 FA's "Return to Jolo," by Capt Robert M. Allen. Ward Beley's Ltr 16 July 1975 and George Groshan's undated report tell about D Co's 2 dead. Other important sources are RR Smith's **Triumph in the Philippines,** 716 Tank Bn's **A Company on Zamboanga-Jolo,** Operational Monograph No. 10 containing "Return to Jolo," with Japanese Maj Tokichi Tenmyo's "55th Independent Mixed Brigade/Outline of the Jolo Operation," Terrain Handbook No. 57 on Jolo, 163 Morning Reports for May, and some payroll rosters. (But Morning Reports seem incomplete, and fire disorganization or destruction of payroll rosters at St. Louis Personnel Bureau, has made identification impossible of many men's outfits.)

On 11 Apr 1945, 2 days after 163 landed, the real Battle of Jolo began. We had won Jolo City, but hard fighting remained. Some 2-3 miles north of Jolo City on Daingapic Point, we contained bypassed Japs in their defense system. But main battle would occur on the low mounts 4-5 miles south of the City. On 10 Apr, K Co had easily climbed Mts Bangkal and Awak, but lurking Japs of 365 Inf Bn exploded a sharp little fight on those mounts supposedly won. This skirmish and the presence of other bands of Japs nearby so menaced L Co that we deferred attacking Mt. Magusing until next morning.

On this morning of 11 Apr, Japs still manned a nearly solid defense line—from giant Mt Tumatangas on our right, east through Mts Datu, Agad, Pula, and Magusing, with other mounts behind them. And 3,000 miles east of Magusing, formidable Mt Daho blocked the horizon. South and east of these mounts and others, our guerilla units with some American advisers kept close guard and later helped fight "Jap Marines" at Mt Daho.

On 11 Apr, strategy of 163 was for a 2-pronged attack. On our left, 3/Bn with L Co leading would strike south over Magusing and Pula to isolate Mt Daho. On our right, 1/Bn with C Co leading down Route 1 would drive a wedge between Mts Datu and Tumatangas. We would then turn left to take Datu in the rear. Thus 163 planned to crush the core of Jap defense and separate widely Japs on Daho from Japs on Tumatangas. But on this first thrust of 11 Apr, both attacks met heavy opposition and failed.

Before L Co pushed, other 3/Bn men must fight off Jap attacks on our rear. Perhaps these Japs tried to rejoin their main body after "K" forced them off Mts Bangkal-Awak yesterday. About dawn, 25-30 Japs attacked down our new tank-bulldozed supply road from the direction of Jolo City. At 0830, they still fought; M's 1/Lt Arnold heard their fire and shouts outside perimeter. Arriving from bivouac near the City, A Co 716 Tank Bn's 2/Pln patrolled 200 yards north and 200 yards south from 3/Bn's CP. By 0900, they had killed 12 Japs. A tank CO even shot one with his automatic pistol.

Before "C" marched against Mt Datu on the west, "L" moved on Mt Magusing (874 feet) to the east. At 0830, we left 3/Bn's perimeter with 5 tanks supporting. At 0920, we went south 200 yards on the new road to the base of Magusing. Fourteen minutes later, L's 2/Pln with 2 Weapons Pln MGs began climbing. Eleven minutes later, we were half-way up Magusing and drawing fire. At 0950, we spotted pillboxes; Japs threw grenades down on us. Tanks worked on the pillboxes, evidently killed them. We slew 10 Japs, had 2 men wounded.

By 1000, 2/Pln was on the summit of round-topped Magusing, with probably a squad in advance and scouting down the south side where a saddle in the ridge led to a lower summit. (Exact action and location of lead squad is obscure.)

Then heavy enfilade fire burst from the brushy lower ridge behind Magusing. It came from well-concealed trenches and pillboxes on that lower spur ridge running off the summit SE to the lower summit. An estimated 40 Japs with at least 3 HMGs and 2 mortars blasted us. Later, we observed fire from some 6 automatic weapons, 1 perhaps a captured Yank HMG.

Jap position was adroitly chosen. If we tried to rise up or even creep forward, grazing fire would strike on crest of Magusing among us. We cowered under the storm of mortars and HMGs.

And 146 FA observer Lt Jacobson, Sgt Nims, and helpers could not call for shellfire to aid 2/Pln. For summit of Magusing was on our 105 howitzers' target line. If Jacobson depressed the 105s' muzzles, they would wipe out "L" men. If he lifted muzzles, they would overshoot the Japs.

Jap fire put our 2 LMGs out of action, and 2/Pln left the Mount at 1122. Six men were wounded retreating; a squad was still cut off.

At 1213, we still tried to save our squad. Since the lower ridge curved a little to the side of Magusing, we had room to lob in mortars and tank 75s on the Japs.

At 1243, L's 1/Pln climbed Magusing to rescue the squad. In climbing, we did not draw Jap fire. But 65 minutes later, we still could not contact the lost squad—feared them all casualties. At 1407, we recovered those 2 LMGs that were put out of action. And 7 minutes later, the squad doubled back to rejoin us. "L" abandoned the hill, with 6 Japs known as dead.

L Co lost 12 wounded to hospital in this fight—1 officer, 11 men. 2/Lt Rumph took a bullet in his thigh; the types of wounds of the 11 men are unknown, although Alvino's, Landman's, and S/Sgt Simicek's were called "serious." Lightly wounded but also in hospital were Beall, Hardaker, Peter Martinez, Ernest Miller, Peugh, Torres, Dan White.

While "L" was repulsed from Magusing on 11 Apr, "C" to the west also had a deadly fight against Mt Datu (800 feet). At first, our attack seemed easy. Six planes bombed and strafed the western slope, and C Co advanced ½ mile down Route 1 to Datu—past empty pillboxes. At base of Datu, we decided to follow a trail leading partly up it. Half an hour later, we still climbed. We executed some 14 Japs on the way.

We had rounded the south slope of Datu and were now working around the east side towards the crest. Starting upwards, we found a Jap .75 cannon and 300 cases of ammo. (Perhaps this was the gun that 146 FA silenced during the night of 10 Apr when Jolo Dock was shelled.)

By 1210, we were half-way up Datu on the east side across from Route 1. Here were deserted positions, 15 packs loaded with .25 caliber ammo, 2 cases of mortar ammo, and clothing. In 15 minutes, we were two-thirds of the way up our 800 feet.

Here we found a road consisting of a rock shelf curving around Datu, and an old truck. Suddenly we killed 2 Japs, 1 setting up a knee mortar. From higher up, a knee mortar shot a few rounds—was evidently silenced.

Our road led up towards the crest through a deep ravine slashing the rim half way around that eastern slope. Despite earlier shells from a knee-mortar, we pressed on up the road, perhaps because of the light opposition and the signs of demoralization from debris of the retreat everywhere.

Our lead platoon reached a point where the stone shelf turned sharply towards the crest while the other "C" men followed a short distance behind. Our CO—probably 1/Lt O'Donovan with two squads and a FA observer team remained below on the road before the sharp turn.

One 146 FA man noted several cave defenses 40 yards across the ravine, called it to "C" men's attention. We sent a patrol to check out those caves.

Pointblank automatic fire flailed this patrol. Fire slashed the road into the main body of C Co, killed Farr, Lts Worthly and James Moore, wounded some 9 men. With dead and wounded, the forward platoon was pinned down on the rock between cliffs. Kleine, for example, fell into a safe space, but no one could rise up to pull him to the rear. CO O'Donovan and FA observer Ludeke were also down among their men.

For about 2 hours, we flattened on that stone shelf beneath blazing sun. Trying to get up or even to move drew a bullet from Japs we could not rise up to shoot back at. FA's Lt Ludeke passed out from heat and shock. At 1500, "C" still took intense fire.

Mjr Armstrong, 1/Bn's CO, led in organizing the rescue. He reconnoitered around the road-bend to observe our platoon pinned down in that sun on the narrow shelf between cliffs. He steeled the morale of C Co.

Climbing up Mt Datu above the ravine, Armstrong and others found the one position on the crest from which we could fire into the caves. We lofted a D Co HMG up where D Co's Pinkley could get the cave-mouths into his ringed sights.

Pinkley began plunging fire to save what had been a doomed C Co. He exhausted all of C Co's ammo, all of his "D" Co ammo, then 6,000 rounds from 1/Bn Hq Co. And "C" with their wounded made a run for it and escaped. (We had to abandon 2 FA Radios and 1 infantry radio.)

Besides Farr and Lts Moore and Worthley killed and Kleine wounded, "C" had 4 more known wounded—Gould, Mahl, T/Sgt Rogney, Sgt Tony Martinez. Wounded also 12 Apr was Ernest Miller, company formation unknown.

That moonlight night of 11 Apr, C Co dug perimeter on the SW crest of Datu. Since FA could not strike the dead space behind Datu where Japs held the ravine, Mjr Armstrong and FA's Lt Ludeke impacted mortars on the area—tried to destroy the 3 abandoned radios.

It was a clear moonlight night over the grasslands and brush of the Jolo mounts. About midnight, "C" fought off a Jap attack. There in a 3-man hole died D Co's Pinkley whose HMG had saved "C" in the ravine ambush. He was shot in the chest with an American 1906 model rifle. Beley pushed Pinkley's body from the hole, helped stop the Jap attack, kill 13.

Other Japs attacked 1/Bn Hq dug in near the base of Datu. Three times, they struck 1/Bn CP with rifle-fire, bayonets, grenades, and a LMG. We repelled them, counted 21 Jap corpses at dawn, saw signs that other Japs were wounded.

Besides Pinkley on Mt Datu, D Co lost S/Sgt Markland down on the flats in our moonlit perimeter straddling Route 1 behind Datu. Seeming in a panicky attempt to escape, Japs got behind our HMG positions. They crossed to the far edge of the perimeter where the HMGs were, yet did not attempt to slip out between those positions or attack them. They recoiled back towards black-topped Route 1. For some unknown reason contrary to 163 practice, Markland slept alone in a hole in the road. Next morning, "D" men found him dead, looking intently towards the outside of the perimeter, as if he had seen Japs. His unfired M-1 lay beside him. A bullet had holed him between the eyes. In return, "D" claimed 8 dead Japs that night.

On 12 Apr, I Co attacked Mt Magusing, where "L" had suffered from cleverly hidden Japs on the reverse slope. Marine planes hit Magusing, but we called the strike "lousy." And 146 FA fired, with tanks of 716 Tank Bn's 3/Pln, and 163's mortars and 81s. "L" fired cover for I Co—had Metonen or Metoxen wounded.

At 1055, "I" prepared to climb the north slope of Magusing while M's 81s pounded the tangled reverse slope. ("L" now saw dead Japs on Magusing.) When about 1200, I's lead platoon took rifle and grenade fire, another platoon moved up to assist. By 1245, an "I" platoon topped Magusing—but under HMG fire. On that reverse slope, we dug Japs from formidable positions, often a Jap at a time. By 1300, we held all Magusing but for the ridge SW to Mt Pula. We took 1 HMG, 2 mortars, counted 45 dead Japs. Supporting tank Pln claimed a kill of 200.

By day's end, "I" reported 2 dead, 8 wounded. Probably killed early was 2/Lt Thompson. By 1542, 1/Lt Amans died, shot by a pretended corpse. I Co's Marek, Newton were wounded. Other wounded of 12 Apr were probably "I" men, Ralph Cooper, Essepian, Joppe, Koza, Sgt Tanner, S/Sgt Alfred Nelson, and Medic T/5 Sheid. T/5 Mandell died of injuries.

While 163 seized the mounts, meagerly reported actions happened near Daingapic Point, 2-3 miles north of Jolo City. On 10 Apr, "I" slew 7 more Japs on Mt Patikul, drove others NW to be contained by I & R with tanks. E Co then fought these Japs 200 yards north of the beach village of Gandasuli. Ambushed by small arms and grenades, we killed 5 Japs, lost Badberg killed. On 12 Apr, we recovered Badberg's body; Cullen was killed. Presumably, "E" annihilated the Japs of Daingapic Point. (I Co meanwhile went south to storm Mt Magusing.)

Such were the first 2 days of 163's real Battle of Jolo, Apr 11-12. I Co had Mt Magusing the second day. Although checked on Mt Datu on 12 Apr, next day "C" readily overran the nearly deserted Jap positions on 13 Apr, found 15 cave defenses. Bosik was wounded.

Actually, remnants of the Jap 365 Inf Bn left the mounts at dawn 13 Apr to reinforce unbroken 363 Bn on Mt Tumatangas. After "I" took Mt Magusing, our tanks threatened to penetrate past Magusing and kill reinforcements from Tumatangas to the great Mt Daho strongpoint on 163's far left.

In return for 500 dead Japs, we had only 11 dead, 29 wounded to hospital. But we admire those brave Japs. They lacked Navy, planes, tanks, heavy guns, yet gallantly fought on reverse slopes of Magusing and Datu. Fighting late in a losing war, they were members of a composite brigade of garrison units, replacements, and miscellanies from everywhere. They should have been demoralized. They should have surrendered in masses. But they were Japanese soldiers, and sold their lives hard.

Sing Song - Dubadura. (Courtesy of Torosik)

L to R: Siefert and Tomaso with 60mm mortar, Zamboanga, P.I., September 1945. (Courtesy of Herman)

I CO 186 INFANTRY:

Our Two Battles of Zamboanga

by DR. HARGIS WESTERFIELD, Division Historian,
with CAPTAIN HERMAN H. HAEDICKE

> CREDIT: Main source is two single-spaced typescript reports of Capt. Haedicke, found in Federal Archives. These are the 2-page "History of Zamboanga, Mindanao Campaign," and the 6-page "History of the Panganaran, Anungan, and Sibuko Bay Campaigns." Indispensable also were 186's Casualty Lists and April and May 1945 Morning Reports. Background data were from 10th Information and Historical Monograph appendix, "The Sibuko-Malayal Operation," and R. R. Smith's **Triumph in the Philippines.** I have no more company histories of 186 Inf in the Battle of Zamboanga.

I Co 186 Inf actually had 2 distinct Battles of Zamboanga. The first was north of Zambo City; the second was in the Zambo Mtn foothills on the other side of Zambo Peninsula.

On 30 Mar 1945, we had our first action, having arrived from quiet Palawan 2 days before. On that 30 Mar, we followed K Co who attacked a ridge near Sugar Loaf Mtn, about 15 miles due north of Zambo City. K Co stormed the ridge and advanced, but we found 10 live Japs still fortified in it.

Those Japs still held out on the reverse slope, in cave-like pillboxes. We persuaded 2 surrenders, but the other 8 men waited for death. We dynamited all 8 in their 3 caves, then dug perimeter. That night, Jap MG fire and knee mortar shells hit near us. Our own mortars silenced their fire. At daylight, we found a dead Jap in the gulley before our perimeter.

On 1 Apr, while part of I Co safely reinforced L Co at Brea Barrio, 2/Pln and 3 squads of 3/Pln took different routes into danger. Moving along a ridge, 2/Pln dug night perimeter to wait for 3/Pln, who had to fight.

While on a different route on the ridge, 3/Pln's 2 squads contacted Japs. Attacking at 1600, we secured a portion of a hill. We killed 7 Japs, but lost Pyle killed. Being too few for the hill, we retreated to protection of F Co 121 Filipino Inf.

We same 3/Pln men had orders to capture a hill 500 yards NE. Long-range MG fire wounded Danieleu (or Danielev) in both legs. Our squad hunted that MG but could not find it. We bypassed these Japs and joined 2/Pln in night perimeter.

On 2 Apr, our detached Plns rejoined I Co, who had moved up to battle the Japs in strongly defended Moroc Pocket. At 1000, 2 squads tried to kill a MG with Japs 700 SW of our perimeter. There we lost S/Sgt Wheat wounded, but knocked out the gun with mortars. While evacuating Wheat, Cook in the carrying party was killed.

On 3 Apr, we fought Moroc Pocket, actually a hill 2,000 yards NW of Moroc Village. Mortars and MGs strongly held it. At 0700, "I" withdrew from forward positions while an air-strike and 148 shells of 168 FA impacted the Japs. But when we pushed, heavy MG fire repelled us. After killing 20 Japs, we withdrew. At 1700, Lt Pierce took a light wound. Back in perimeter, we heard shells slice overhead to strike the Japs. Next morning, we occupied the deserted Pocket and patrolled after the Japs. Searching along Missaloy River, one squad drew fire from a Jap Pln, killed 2, but had to retreat. The Japs departed; Moroc Pocket was clear.

And so, with 2 dead and 2 wounded, "I" ended our main Zambo Battle. By 17 Apr, "I" was in garrison on the beach.

A month later, "I" had our second Zambo Battle. This was a fighting pursuit of the Japs driven from near Zambo City. Of 8900 men from their original army, 5,000 had fled through unexplored mountains of Zambo Peninsula to Sibuko Bay on the west coast, 30 miles north of Zambo City. From Sibuko Bay, they began to move north 30 miles along the coast to Siocon Bay. Here was a rice-growing area where they could base to regroup and fight again, although they were without 75 mm and 20 mm guns.

So "I" battled again. With most of 186 Inf (and 3/Bn 163 back from Jolo, 121 Filipino Inf, and most of 167 FA), we made amphib landings to break up the regrouping Jap units. On 17 May, we rounded Zambo Peninsula on LCTs and landed at Panganaran on the west coast about 30 miles north of Zambo City. Hiking 3,000 yards up Panganaran River, we dug in with K Co at 1800. We slept in native gardens 400 yards NE of the river.

Unlike the fertile plain of Zamba City, the west coast of Zambo Peninsula was like the Guinea Shore which "I" knew only too well. Behind a few small, sandy beaches with a few little streams, the land rose abruptly to jungle mountains becoming 2,000 feet high 5 miles inland. South of Panganran River, there was plain about a mile square rising to peaks 800 feet high. It was New Guinea all over again.

Our Japs were from the same formations we had battled at Zamboanga. These were the 54 IMB (Infantry Mixed Brigade), and the 33 Naval Guards ("Jap Marines"). Before Zambo Fight, 54 IMB was lately organized from a composite of garrison units and rookies. Many were not Japs—but Koreans or Formosans who might want to surrender. The Naval Guards were, of course, a tougher gang who preferred death in battle. Both Infantry and Guards had lost their 75 mm and 20 mm guns. But they still had rifles and MGs and mortars. And it was hard to find out who wanted to surrender and who wanted to kill us.

We found Japs almost at once; 2/Pln killed the first man at 1900—and another trying to enter our perimeter after 2400. At 0800 next morning, a 2/Pln water party surprised a third on a trail and slew him.

On that 18 May, all rifle Plns sent out squad patrols to find any trails that the Japs used for escape routes toward Siocon Bay. Searching 1,000 yards NE up a creek, 2/Pln found no trails—but did kill 2 more Japs. Our 3/Pln probed a ridge-line to our rear for 1,000 yards NW, with no results.

But 1/Pln scouted 800 yards east to a well-used north-south trail. We sent a squad north 800 yards and another 800 yards south. The north squad saw no one, but the south squad saw 3 Japs, killed 1. The other 2 crawled off to safety in the brush.

Now we were sure that we were close to a Jap pocket. At 1130, L Co joined us, and I Co reinforced 1/Pln. Both Cos scouted down the trail to Panganaran River. Here 1/Pln drew fire from a Jap rifle squad in a cave on the bank of the river. After a short fire-fight, they fled—all but 3 corpses, and 1 man who surrendered.

A steep ridge across the river barred I Co's way. At 400 yards up the ridge, our lead Pln took heavy fire from a strong position. Two MGs and a half-Pln of riflemen shot down from the top of a steep cliff. We could not flank the cliff, but 1/Pln attacked frontally and silenced the Japs whose cliff we could not scale.

At dark, I Co minus 2/Pln and 3/Pln perimetered in a safe spot on the trail near the Japs. Meanwhile, Capt. Haedicke had detached 2/Pln and 3/Pln to circle west and post on the top of the main ridge 500 yards SW of the main company perimeter. At 2000 Hrs, the Jap MGs plunged several fire-bursts at us from the cliff, but their fire was high.

On 20 May, 2/Pln and 3/Pln scouted east and killed 6 Jap Marines in a small bivouac about 300 yards from the main I Co Perimeter. All I Co units now reassembled on the ridge-top and prepared for hard fighting.

At 1200, we followed the trail east 400 yards. Here the trail left the ridge, then turned sharp north and dropped back down to Panganaran River.

Halfway down the ridge, the trail turned and led to the cliff-top, where "I" drew fire yesterday. Our 1/Pln slew 11 Japs here, but failed to find the 2 MGs that had shot down on us. At 1500, we dug in for the night. Our 2/Pln then back-tracked to last night's bivouac and killed 2 more Japs. Of the 20 slain that 20 May, 6 were Marines, and 14 Infantry.

On 21 May, I Co left Panganaran by buffalos and landed at Anungan Barrio and bivouacked inland by 1000. Shortly after lunch, a 2/Pln outpost fired on 4 Japs in a cane field 200 yards east. Then 1/Pln pursued the 4 up a draw and killed them—and 8 more—all Marines.

On 22 May, 1/Pln and 2/Pln had hard fighting. Probing directly west up what must have been Montibo River, between 2 high ridges for 2500 yards, we attacked 100 Japs in a large bivouac area. First, their outposts fired to alert their comrades. Then MGs, mortars, rifles blasted at us.

Ensued our careful 4-hour battle in 3 distinct actions. After trying to hold their ground against our heavy fire, they fell back a few hundred yards up the draw and shot again at our advancing Plns. We drove them out a second time. A third time, they made a stand, but we broke them. They scattered in all directions. In the 3 actions, we slew 41, took a prisoner.

We lost 3 wounded, 2 of them BARmen. Sulley was lightly wounded; Wieczarek seriously wounded. One of these men was hit in the side, the other in the back, with names unreported. Wounded also was an unnamed Medic, shot through the arm when he ran to save Sully and Wieczarek.

On an overnight trail-block on a ridge, 3/Pln also fought. A squad patrol killed 6 in the morning, but after noon, 30 Japs tried to crash through our block.

After we repelled them, a Jap called back from the other side of the ridge that they wanted to surrender. When an assistant squad-leader, probably Ortoleva, stood up and signed to them to drop their weapons, he was dead in seconds. An LMG fired a burst into his chest. The Japs attacked again, but Weapons Pln's mortars stopped them. That day, I's total kill was 40 Japs, with 2 prisoners.

On 25 May, I Co lost our second and last man killed in our second Zambo Battle. We climbed to top the south ridge walling the Montibo River. During our march, lead-scout Evanoff died from the bullet of a lone sniper, who escaped our revenge.

Thus went I Co's second Battle of Zamboanga. Despite some memorable fire-fights up the Panganaran River and up the Montibo River past Anungan, our war was mainly a mop-up, against stubborn Japs who held out until they died. After 25 May, we patrolled from amphibian landings as far north as 7,000 yards up the coast, and as far south as our previous post at Panganaran. Then we moved down to Sibuko Bay and mounted more patrols. But we killed only a few more Japs. They escaped 30 miles up the coast to Siocon Bay. At the close of World War II, they had moved perhaps 50 miles more, to concentrate with other Jap units on the north-central coast of Zambo Peninsula. Here 105 Filipino Regt held them.

Of the nearly 5,000 Japs surviving the first Battle of Zamboanga, official figures were that 1,345 had been killed and 377 taken prisoners, of whom 103 were actually Japanese. Of this group of killed or prisoners, I Co claimed 211 killed, and 23 prisoners—from 17 May to 20 June 1945.

With a loss of only 4 killed and 4 wounded (and 1 unnamed Medic wounded), I Co had fought carefully and well; in our two Battles of Zamboanga.

A bottle of Asahi Beer found after the Japanese were repulsed at Milne Bay. (Courtesy of Rohlffs)

B CO 116 MEDICAL BATTALION:

Medic Schooley's Battle of Sanananda

by S/Sgt K. B. SCHOOLEY, B 116 Medics
with DR. HARGIS WESTERFIELD, Division Historian

---

*CREDIT: Core of this story is 3 unpublished typescripts by S/Sgt Schooley. These are 21 pages from single-spaced articles: "Here and There in the SW Pacific," "Action against the Japanese in the SW Pacific," and Chapt. V of "History 2/Bn. Sect. Med. 163rd Inf." "I used also my own G Co 163's "The Kumusi Campaign," (unpublished as of 5 Dec. 1979), George Weller's **Chicago Daily News** Reports of 1943, and Dr. Samuel Milner's **Victory in Papua**. George Jackson, Secretary of our 116 Medics' Chapter, knew Schooley at Sanananda. He writes, "Sorry he is gone—was a good man—made the other men seem human." I am grateful to his mother, Mrs. Josephine L. Schooley and to his son, Mr. K. B. Schooley, for providing these manuscripts, without charge, to the Division Association. (Does any reader know how to contact T/4s Clayton Erickson and Ralph Taylor for their 163 Bn's medical histories?)*

At 0930 on 3 Jan 1943, 2/Bn 163 Inf's Medics emplaned from Port Moresby for the Battle of Sanananda. NCO in charge of 2/Bn's Medics was S/Sgt Schooley, a well-liked leader of men. To Schooley, the half-hour flight was eventless, except for some rough weather above the Owen Stanley Mountains.

But when the plane door opened at Dobodura, we stepped into an oven of humid heat. With nearly 100 pounds' equipment and rations, we floundered along a muddy jeep track. Heat was terrific, especially in those sunstruck kunai openings. In 30 sunstruck, sweaty minutes, 2/Bn learned that the Army routine of 50 minutes' hiking and 10 minutes' rest was impossible. We slogged 20 minutes, rested 30—took 6 hours to make 4 miles. Some of us had more medical supplies in 60 mm mortar bags. A jeep loaded those bags for us. We never saw them again.

That night, our war began. About 2200 while miserably awake under buckets of rain, we heard shots and a scream. A trigger-happy guard saw a small tree fall and shot at it for a Nip. The bullets broke one man's leg, mutilated another leg of a man lying in the line of fire.

Capt Harry Smith and 1/Lt Burleson gave first aid. A litter squad with 12 riflemen to help, slopped into the dark to Dobodura Hospital. They returned sleepless, had to march all day with us.

At daybreak, we hiked 5 miles more to Soputa, ankle-deep in mud on a slippery trail. There we built beds above ground, and swam. To replace the supplies that the jeep carried off, we hiked to Buna for more.

About 2230 the night of 7 Jan, 3 shots alerted us for Jap raids. But another Yank was shot. A guard had panicked when his relief guard crept up in the dark. The 3 shots pierced the stomach of the relief guard. Despite 3 hours' labor with poor facilities, Capt Smith could not save him. Early next morning, he died of shock and loss of blood.

Earlier on that 7 Jan, we detached a litter squad to E Co, which reinforced 1/Bn in Musket Perimeter. PFC Verne Morgan guided Hibbard, Birkestol, and Donahue. A California Klamath Indian, Donahue was so dark that Papuans had chattered when they saw him.

On 8 Jan, when "B" and "C" disastrously attacked Perimeters Q and R, S/Sgt Pete Johnson merely ordered, "Go out and get a casualty." Without direction or distance specified, Morgan's men just hunted towards the firing.

They heard a call for help 200 yards out but could not see the man. Cutting away brush, Hibbard found a Yank with right arm almost shot off. Hibbard dressed the wound, helped lift him into the litter.

Carrying him across fairly open ground, we took fire from Jap rifles and a MG. We ran, but Donahue fell. The casualty rolled off our grounded litter. We hit holes.

Donahue said, "They got me." He held up his holed forearm. Morgan crawled to find 7 wounds on Donahue—the other 6 on legs and hips, probably from the MG.

Hurrying the casualty to the aid station, the other 3 rushed back to Donahue. Pvt Donahue was dead, a Klamath Indian whose name never appeared on 163's casualty list. We pause to honor him here.

On 9 Jan, Morgan's men rejoined Schooley to participate with 2/Bn 163's most important strategy of Sanananda Battle. This was cutting the supply line to Jap Perimeters P—those formidable strong points that were crucial to victory. This was 2/Bn's move past Musket west over Suicide Trail to cut Killerton Track.

Schooley's men long remembered that hike under heavy packs in mud and water waist-deep. Heat was stifling. At 1100, firing began ahead. Prone by the trail, we got orders to rescue G Co's casualties.

While still in the fire-lanes from a dominating Jap MG, Capt Smith and G Co Medics patched up casualties. Ten minutes after the fight began, G Co's Medic Mivelaz took a bullet in right chest while trying to save a wounded rifleman. Passing our Capt, he said, "I sure as hell hate to let you down like this, Smitty."

Meanwhile, Schooley's Medics improvised new litters from jungle saplings and ponchos. Exposed to the Jap MG, we rolled the wounded into litters to carry back to Musket Aid Station, then down to 17 Portable Hospital at Soputa. Even 4 carriers found it backbreaking to carry 170 pounds of wounded man through that mud waist-deep.

While we saved wounded, H Co's Escobar climbed a tree to adjust fire on that HMG from H Co's 81 mm mortars. Over the phone, he shouted out ranges so loudly that we could hear him at 500 yards. Our mortars killed that Jap HMG.

Bedded down in new Perimeter Rankin (named after 2/Bn's CO) 300 yards east of Killerton Track, we had a whole night without rain. On 10 Jan, rifle patrols and Aussie cannon struck the Japs. That night, heavy rains made our slit trenches into bathtubs with water up to our ears.

We heard swearing as men bailed out water with their helmets. By dawn, our aid station was a foot under water. Medic

Scanlon stayed in his hole because the water was warmer than the air. Pillowed on his pack, he smoked his pipe and seemed thoroughly satisfied with life.

On 11-16 Jan, Jap rifle fire was scattered while 2/Bn and Aussies farther south of us overcame Jap Perimeters P. We heard a few Aussie shells hit stubborn Jap positions.

Casualty lists were low for 163, but malaria and dysentery threatened an epidemic. We had too little medicine for dysentery, and doubted that all men—unsupervised—took quinine for malaria. Mosquito nets became so heavy with rain that many were discarded the first day. Mosquitoes were as bad by night as by day; nets made little difference.

Our first action of 9 Jan was fearful, but caring for wounded eased our fears. Casualties shocked us, but it became routine to patch one man and go on to the next. Usually we worked just a few hours, then had only scattered cases until the next large group—maybe in a few minues, maybe in a day or two. Always we had the comfort of Aussie shells over us, with astonishing accuracy.

So lived Schooley's Medics on 9-16 Jan in Perimeter Rankin, sometimes called "Rankin Heights." By 16 Jan, the formidable Jap southern perimeters had fallen, and 2/Bn was free to fight elsewhere.

On 16 Jan, 2/Bn and Schooley's Medics made their second great tactical move of Sanananda Battle. Leaving Perimeter Rankin forever, we hiked 1500 yards north up Killerton Track to the Coconut Gardens, then turned east to seal off the surviving Japs in the Road-Bend Perimeters from escape to the sea.

While the Aussie 2/Bn 12 Inf moved east on our left flank, we also turned east through swamp and jungle to Sanananda Road. Losing all traces of a trail, we had to hack many yards with machetes. Yet our move was so fast that we defied all jungle logistics and reached the Road 6 hours before 163's staff had calculated that we could possibly arrive. Our 2/Bn's march gave us the well-earned name of "Rankin's Racers," although later we were also called "Rankin's Raiders."

Last 300 yards to Sananda Road was combat for our lead Plns. We had some casualties, but few compared to the kill of Japs. By dark of 16 Jan, Schooley's Medics were on the Road among wrecked huts of a Jap hospital area. This hospital had held a Jap garrison with armed patients mixed with dying patients. Attacking G Co had to shoot every man who seemed to be alive.

That night, we Medics made pole beds again. Schooley and Arnold Harrison had 5 dead Japs around them within 10 feet—"all-around defense," as Harrison called it. We slept poorly, hands on rifles. For breakfast, we had one Aussie emergency ration for 9 men, but it sufficed in that place of corpses. Yet we were happy to find medical supplies for our depleted packs, and several complete sets of surgical instruments.

After the fall of the final Jap perimeters, Schooley's Medics moved to Sanananda Point for a brief "rest." This rest meant that we had no more wounded—only men with jungle rot, dysentery, typhus, and malaria—up to 40 malaria cases evacuated daily. Off-duty, we bathed in fresh river water or salt water and sunned on wrecked Jap barges.

But on 1 Feb, a small Schooley detachment joined G 163 for the Kumusi Patrol. This was a trek of understrength "G" for 22 miles up the Guinea Shore to Kumusi River Mouth. We were to disperse Jap survivors trying to regroup for another battle.

Besides Schooley and Lt Burleson, 4 more Medics marched: Brownlee, Collesano, Germak, T/5 Bust, Cpl Katarzy. G Co's assigned Medics were "Red" Evans and Cincio.

On 2 Feb, we slogged over bare beach under blazing sun. Several men fell out with high fevers. Schooley and Burleson halted with them just long enough to write out evacuation tags for them—then catch up with G Co starting from a break to march again. We persuaded CO Benson to slow G's pace—if he wanted most of "G" to reach Kumusi Mouth.

Later that day, we had to slosh 2 miles in water sometimes shoulder-deep to avoid jungle covering our beach trail. Slogging across Killerton Bay, we had heavy marching with soaked uniforms and equipment.

And at 1400, we were back into battle at Kombela River Crossing. Believing that the farther bank was clear of Japs, Benson sent a 3-man point across on a native raft, while others loaded in a small Jap assault boat to follow.

A hidden Jap MG drove 2 of the first 3 men to swim for their lives, killed Sgt Bretzke. Ramsay and Aussie W/O Dixon swam far down the Kombela to escape. Jap fire scattered the men from the boat, wounded Gonzales there. Hiding behind a tree, Schooley watched G's Sgt Frank Hanson run for a hole and take a bullet through his helmet. Rushing to give aid, Schooley found that Hanson was only badly grooved in the head.

Next day, 3 Feb, with Sgt Rennie's M Co 81s to help, "G" crossed farther upstream to strike the Japs in deep jungle. They repulsed "G" with 2 dead, 3 wounded. In this fight, Medics Bust, Brownlee, Collesano, and Germak bravely carried out G's wounded under threat of Jap automatic fires.

Not until 6 Feb with G 186's help did G 163 force Kombela Crossing. Farther west near Buk Village, we had 2 days' fight at an unnamed river crossing, but now 2 Aussie cannon helped us over with no casualties. On 10 Feb, 10 days after starting, we finished the 22 miles to Kumusi Mouth. While "G" and Aussies with Papuan Inf mopped up the area, we had no more battle casualties—just tropical illnesses to doctor.

On 15 Feb, we were relieved from the Kumusi. It took us 10 days' campaigning to trek 22 miles; now we returned by LCV in about 3 hours. Back at Soputa, we hungered for Australia.

Now Schooley was assigned to write the history of his 2/Bn 163's Medics. (T/4 Clayton Erickson was to write 1/Bn's Medics' story, and T/4 Ralph Taylor to write 3/Bn's story.) He named those who were most remembered.

We had 1 wounded, 2 killed. Indian Donahue died on 8 Jan while carrying out an unnamed casualty of 1/Bn. G Co's Mivelaz was wounded on 9 Jan while aiding G's wounded. F's Marcus died as he opened his medical kit to try to save one or more of F Co's dead: Lt Ogden, Sgt Rausch, and Prinz.

Outstanding also was G Co's Marshall serving G Co under fire when Mivelaz was hit. Often under MG fire for 3 days, F's Bay saved 4 men from certain death because he stayed with them to help. H's Colvin was the first Medic to kill a Jap. E Co's Valentic killed 7 Japs, but had to be told to stick to his Medic's duties.

Schooley cited also Capt Smith and 1/Lt Burleson who worked tirelessly with battle casualties and sick men. Schooley cited others' names without comment: T/4 Arnold Hanson, and T/5s Fuller, Becker, Scanlon, Clinton, with G Co's T/5's Bust and Presley "Red" Evans. These were the names of 15 Medics whom Schooley cited especially.

On 30 May 1943, 2/Bn 163's men honored our dead ranked under white crosses wreathed with wild flowers. The Division Band played "Taps," and "The Star-Spangled Banner." Maj Sequiland and Capt Freeman conducted prayers and hymns. After Gen Doe's and Col Mason's speeches, a soldier recited Lincoln's "Gettysburg Address." It seemed to be written just for Sanananda. Then a choir of the Band and 3/Bn 163 sang. Commanded by 1/Lt Rottman, 10 other E Co men fired a rifle salute. While soft music played, Lt-Col Rankin read our roll of our dead—names that could make a man tremble. After dismissal, we read on crosses, the names of dead Medics Donahue and Marcus.

E CO 162 INFANTRY:

Roosevelt Ridge and Berger Hill

by DR. HARGIS WESTERFIELD, Division Historian,
with SGTS. DON E. CARLSON and LES DUNKIN

CREDIT: Prime credits are due to Don E. Carlson's undated 8-page legal sized handwritten MS and Les Dunkin's story to Carlson 14 Nov. 1971. They used my dossier based on Ch. VIII entitled "2/Bn Operations" in 162 Inf's **Narrative of Salamaua**. I used also 162 Inf's **Journal of Salamaua,** and Morning Reports for Aug., Sept. 1943. Helpful also was Chester Young's F 162 story, "Roosevelt Ridge and C Ridge," (**Jungleer,** Dec., 1979). Clearest overall picture of fighting on C Ridge is in Australian David Dexter's **The New Guinea Offensives.** (NOW HEAR THIS: I can print no more full-length Salamaua stories without your help. I need letters on cutting the Komiatum Track, on K Co at Boisi, and B Co everywhere.)

On 27 July 1943, E Co 162 Inf's understrength, jungle-tired men attacked Roosevelt Ridge where 3/Bn had fought since 20 july. "E" was down already form 196 men to 103 men, 4 officers. FA fired preparations; F Co moved in support.

E's dogged, sweaty riflemen led out—up a trail behind the landward end of Roosevelt Ridge. We climbed beside a clear, cool mountain creek. At a break, we filled canteens to drink deep, and refill. No water tastes better than before the first action.

Dark Roosevelt Ridge's jungle towered above us to our right. Now Capt. Bob Hill sent Sgt Red Hill and his 6-man squad to scout uphill. After long, tense, silence, we heard muffled shots. Shortly Hill's squad fell back to grin with relief. A Jap bullet had nicked hill's ear—E's first wound.

"E" now hiked some distance farther up the trail, then turned right towards the ridge. We were trying to get a foothold atop the Ridge—where the Japs were not, if possible. With Sgt. Carlson's squad leading, E Co climbed in single file.

Under our weight of steel, it was a hot, panting climb. Often we had to hand-pull ourselves up by trees, helpless if we saw a Jap. Near the top, Carlson halted his squad behind him—Cole, Tuck, and others.

Quietly we followed a small side ridge near the summit and a brushy knoll or "pimple.". Since the trial was straight, Carlson feared a hidden fire-lane. He passed word for Capt Hill to come up.

Seconds after Hill's arrival, a Jap gun blazed automatic fire at us. Carlson shot two clips at the sound of the fire. The Jap fire ceased.

Here among brush where the ridge was not too steep, E Co made our first tangible foothold on Roosevelt Ridge. A Jap-help pimple was just ahead. F Co came up on our left through heavy opposition and dug in our right. Regimental report said that "E" had advanced 400 yards east along Roosevelt Ridge towards the coast. But E Co had 17 days' delay before we took the Ridge.

On 28 July while both 2/Bn and 3/Bn fought, "E" with FA help attacked the Pimple from the south. Among the foremost fighters, T/5 Bellinger our cook drove in BAR blazing. But his BAR failed him; Bellinger took a wound in the back of his hand. Sgt Lee Dunkin's mortars were too close to us to be effective; Bill Doescher's LMG never got a chance for fire. Bellinger always believed that only BAR failure had kept him from clearing the Pimple that 28 July.

After these first 2 days' assault, "E" settled down in combat perimeter—with fairly heavy patrols and nights of sleepless guard duty. A few days after 28 July, Capt Hill again tried to take the Pimple. While 2 squads hit the Pimple's flanks, Carlson's squad waited in close support. Even though 1 attack squad was heavily reinforced, we failed again.

Counting men withdrawing, Carlson missed Capt Hill, and decided that we must find him. Just then, Hill ran stumbling down the slope. He gripped his chest with both hands, in excruciating pain. A grenade had blasted him, but he walked unaided to Medics and out of action. New CO was 1/Lt Couglin.

After 28 Aug, "E" failed to take the Pimple in various probes, even if we brought up a 37 mm cannon to fight it. On 1 Aug, G Co—newly come from other patrols like that on Lababia Island—passed through E Co to make its attack, but could not clear the ridge. Jap rifle fire and mortaring continued. On 2 Aug at 0730, Beck was killed.

On 2 Aug, "E" was relieved from the Ridge, but we still fought the Japs by patrols from our bivouac on lower ground. Our patrol of 9 Aug drew MG fire which wounded a Papuan scout. On 11 Aug, Lt Genung's patrol with 2 Papuans searched the same area but drew no fire. The Papuans spotted 2 pillboxes which our FA or mortars must have surely destroyed.

Then on 13 Aug. "E" hit Roosevelt Ridge. With "F" attacking on our west flank, 'E' supported by CN Co and an H section of HMGs went to the ridge after accurate FA and mortar preparation. Although 162 Hq called E's a "diversionary action," fighting was deadly. Killed by 1030 were EB Pool and Mike Davis. By 1042, a Pln of CN Co acting as infantry were on a high knoll commanding Jap positions below. But Japs still held pillboxes along the landward Ridge crest west of E Co where F Co faced them and overlooked them on higher ground.

"E" then tried to close that gap towards "F" to the west. Leaving a holding force to secure against the Japs dug in on the Ridge east of us, we pushed west but failed. At 1115, Cpl

Cain was wounded. By 1130, heavy Jap MG and mortar fire had driven "E" to earth. We called for FA help. But neither mortar men nor FA observers could shell the narrow gap between "E" and "F" without endangering our own men. By 1345, Medic Williams was dead, and 218 FA's Sgt Crunican, an observer.

And so, that night of 13 Aug, "E" with CN Co held 100 yards of Roosevelt Ridge's crest. East towards the sea, our rifles faced 800 yards of Jap country. West, again, we faced Jap pillboxes ruling the 70-yard gap to where "F" and "G" men were dug in.

But by dawn 14 Aug, the Japs had fled from this gap. Now while Col MacKechnie concentrated all Task Force FA within range, E Co nerved itself to storm the Japs' last 800 yards of Roosevelt Ridge.

Some 20 B-24s and B-26s dropped tons of bombs on the Ridge. At 1315, 75 mm howitzers, Aussie 25-pounders, 105s, screaming Bofers AA guns, little 37 mm cannon, HMGs, LMGs struck Roosevelt Ridge. Inland mountains thundered with echoes. The top fold of the Ridge lifted into the air, fell into the sea.

In 20 minutes, "E" men had dashed across the denuded, red-scarred Ridge to execute remaining Japs. We advanced through debris and parts of Nip bodies. Stench from remaining holes was terrific. Without casualties, "E" mastered Roosevelt Ridge.

But our Roosevelt Ridge victory merely preluded our second harder and longer operation against the Japs. Their unbroken army still barred us from Salamaua. From Scout Ridge 1,000 yards west of Dot Inlet to Francisco River 3,000 yards farther west, a line of Jap perimeters held off Aussies and 162 Inf. And on 162's front on the sea, the Japs had anchored this line with 5 adjacent perimeters at right angles to their main line of resistance—which was on high Scout Ridge.

Thus, "E" with other 2/Bn outfits got orders to work with other 162 men to crush this seaward right angle of Jap strong-points. While we climbed up from the sea and pushed west, 1/Bn and 3/Bn pushed on them from inland. By now, the whole 2/Bn was down to 245 men.

And so, in the dawn hours of 26 Aug when F Co spearheaded the night advance up the mountains from Dog Inlet, "E" followed and dug in to guard F's supply line down C Ridge. Then we fought to liquidate the Jap perimeters on Scout Ridge, while FA pounded positions that we located but could not seize at first.

From 29 Aug through 1 Sept, "E" patrolled against these Japs, and suffered. On 29 Aug, Guzik was wounded at 1130, and Cpl Blake at 1630. On 29 Aug, fragments wounded Bell, Blake, Vorhies.

On 30 Aug at 1100, E's 6-man recon patrol seized a high knoll directly before FCo. Jap rifles, MGs, some grenades expelled us. But we retook the knoll at 1245. Later that day, E's 2-man patrol probably teamed with an "F" patrol and struck up C Ridge—probably from that knoll which our recon party had gained at 1245.

As we advanced, Jap resistance began within 20 yards after our start. During our push with F Co—all of 200 yards, some 6 Japs died. By 1925, we had pulled back slightly from our farthest point of advance and dug in for the night. We had 2 casualties—Conley wounded, and Heltzel missing in action. Conley saw Heltzel killed, but found that he weighed to much to move.

On patrol 31 Aug, Cpl Sudderth had wounds from fragments. On 1 Sept 43 when recon patrols contacted Japs, Cp Wilson went to hospital from a hand wound. But Cpl Brittingham was killed. Bone died in hospital—in shock from having both legs amputated.

Thus in 4 days' patrols, "E" lost 3 dead and 6 wounded, although only Wilson was marked "hospital" in records. Then came orders for a 5-day "rest"—at least to pull back halfway down C Ridge to "Goalby Outpost," where life was fairly easy until 6 Sept. (Carlson was lightly wounded and evacuated on 4 Sept.)

Then "E" returned to the front at 0900 7 Sept—to fight on Berger Hill—162's final combat of the Salamaua Operation. On 8 Sept, E's 60 mm mortars began the attack with a barrage by experts. After 2 ineffective mortar attacks back on Roosevelt Ridge, our mortarmen had learned how to handle our 60 mm shells which had too much power at those short hillside ranges. Dunkin, Corbell, Jarvis, Ken Baker, and their 3 squads had agreed to pull all charges off the shells, and "fire the tubes by hand by rule of thumb," as Dunkin said it. Our mortar fire was now accurate.

At 1145, "E" struck Berger Hill with our "first wave"—a 10-man combat patrol. Heavy MG and rifle fire pinned down Cpl Virgil Bell's squad and gave Bell his abdomenal death wound. Although even in a Jap fire-lane, Sgt Robinson tried to give Bell first aid, heroic Bell ordered his squad to get out and leave him to die. Probably wounded then was Ospenkowski—in neck and groin and both legs. By now, "E" had sent 4 more Yanks to secure the attack squad's rear.

Now "E" reinforced went up to take Berger Hill. With 8 "F" men attached and an H Co HMG, we reached the summit. But we could not hold Berger Hill; we reeled back from the last spasmodic resistance that 162 ever had to face in the whole Salamaua Campaign.

Jap mortars zeroed in; MG fire swept the hill. Lt Couglin took a fragment in right shoulder; Sgt Wignall had fragments in his face, Hark's left eye was blackened. A bullet wounded Walker over the left eye; fragments hit Miller on his left elbow. None of these 5 was wounded seriously, but it was common sense to fall back and let weapons and FA impact Berger Hill. (Meanwhile, back at Dot Inlet, T/4 Brownson and RH Miller got fragment wounds also.)

That night, "E" rested and licked our wounds back at Goalby's Post, and a day later, on 9 Sept, "F" occupied Berger Hill unopposed. And "F" happily contacted Aussies pushing from inland. This "Jap corner" of Scout Ridge was evacuated; it remained only for decimated E Co to join other 162 outfits in pressing the Jap retreat through Salamaua and towards Lae.

Thus fought E Co 162 Inf to win Salamaua—during 76 days' action of our Regiment. Only 17 E Co men were left to ford Francisco River into Salamaua. Only one of them was a rifleman.

Although most of E Co's casualties were from sickness like malaria or dysentery, we had on our record 7 dead enlisted men. We had 1 officer, 12 enlisted men seriously wounded—and 1 officer and 32 enlisted men slightly wounded. (The Morning Report and our narratives do not agree on these numbers. And we claimed 71 Japs killed in action. Such was E Co 162 Inf's history of Salamaua—a record of hard, professional work in combat.)

B CO 163 INFANTRY:

First Wave on Wakde Beach

by DR. HARGIS WESTERFIELD, Division Historian,
with SGT. WILLIAM C. DAVIDSON AND CPL. RAYMOND H. WILCOPOLSKI

CREDIT: Indispensable personal narrative for this story was 8-pg., single-spaced typescript of Davidson & Wilcopolski from Fed-Archives. Capt. Arthur W. Merrick's "Invasion of Wakde Island" described B Co's tank-inf attack. Other original sources include 163's Wakde-Toem Journal (12-30 May 1944), and Col. Leonard Wing's "One Step Westward," which appeared in **Infantry Journal**. *RR Smith's* **Approach to the Philippines** *is a valuable commentary on these sources. B's microfilm Morning Report was unreadable for Wakde, but I used 163's Casualty Lists, and Award Stories of Korpi, Kroll, Castor, and Bilbao.*

When B Co 163 Inf's high-ramped landing-barges charged for Wakde Island about 0900, 18 May 1944, we expected no battle—even if B Co was the first wave. We were unaware that a Jap LMG had fired periodically from left of Wakde Jetty—a gun that FA from Toem had failed to kill. At 300 yards' range, destroyers and LCIs fired a last covering barrage into the shell-broken coconut groves before us.

As if by remote control, all firing stopped but for our motors' drone. We stared over narrowing waters at the quiet sands of Wakde closing in. A cameraman stood quietly taking pictures.

Then a hail of bullets pounded our gunwales, holed the upper half of our barges. We cowered as low as we could in that jam of men and rifles. Overhead, our barges' MGs fired back, but Amphib Engrs screamed as bullets hit them. On Boat No. 12 coxswain and 2 crewmen were knocked down. Our Sgt Gorichs and Medic Stabek were both shot in their right legs. Sgt Bilbao seized the helm he knew nothing about, jammed our 2/Pln over to Insoemanai Island. A trained driver brought us to Wakde 45 minutes later.

Ramps thudded on sand. We leaped out, fell prone just below a stream of Nippo bullets 18 inches overhead. The shelf of the beach saved us from many deaths. For reasons unknown, the Japs seemed to use no 20mm shells or .50 HMGs on us, but other MGs and rifles kept "B" down and crawling ahead. (Later, we learned that 2 U.S. HMGs had fired on us from left of the Jetty. A 20 mm shell did pierce the side of one LCVP.)

Two tanks of 603 Tank Co landed behind us and silenced the heaviest fire, and sprung us from the beach, but we had to crawl on our bellies like snakes inland. Tying in with F Co on our left, our 3/Pln and 1/Pln made 200 yards by 0950. (Our diverted 2/Pln and S/Sgt Lorenzo's .50 HMGs sent over the night before, still waited for a barge back from Insoemanai Island.) Despite our intense shooting, we saw no dead Japs anywhere. Except for a few squads in delaying action, they retreated to hide and fight. But we had a few wounded.

By 1015, "B" had reached the south edge of Wakde Strip at its narrowest, almost midway between its east and west ends. We saw Jap huts on the strip, a large warehouse, a machine-shop, and some deserted planes. With little trouble, we worked our way about 400 yards east along the south side of the Strip. Heavy resistance delayed C Co on our right, and we halted for orders.

With this halt came more casualties. Nip mortars barraged; a light mortar shell exploded in our CP. Fragments wounded Capt Maxam in chest, ankle, and leg. T/5 Calkins was hit in left forearm, and T/5 Harvey in his back. CO Maxam was replaced by 1/Lt Houston.

Sgt Kees' patrol contacted Japs in the blind jungle eastward and drew fire. There a rifle bullet hit Cargal in left chest; T/5 Rogers gave first aid and sent him to the rear.

B Co now turned at right angles to fight eastward, with the Strip flanking us. C Co needed our 2 tanks, and the heavy jungle ahead would have retarded them. With 2/Pln back from Insoemanai on our left, 3/Pln on our right and 1/Pln reserved to guard Weapons Pln, we moved out. We grenaded some empty bunkers for security—and got credit for thus clearing C Co's front for their push to the Strip.

When 3/Pln's T/Sgt Gardea heard a Jap shouting orders, he seized a BAR and shot rapid fire to smash the expected attack. As he reloaded, a Jap grenade wounded his eyelid and face. A furious attack forced us back to a clearing where we could better form to contain this Jap pressure.

During this attack, our mortars got emergency orders to fire on the frenzied Jap attack. Without time to dig in, Kroll fired his mortar bracketed by Jap motar explosions. Although surely knowing that his death was certain, Kroll shot round after round to defend our hard-pressed riflemen up front. When he corrected adjustment of the barrel, a Jap mortar shell blasted before him and killed him. That shell also wounded Junior Brown in arm and leg, Branch in right arm, and Cpl Talley in the head.

Japs were charging, screaming. Twice, 15-man squads rushed us; twice, we mowed them down in groups of 15. Then they fell back into jungle to reorganize. Third tank was hit so hard that we had to recall the tanks. About 1430, we lost 1/Sgt Shamley, wounded from a bullet in the hip. Intense Jap fire struck down at us from the trees.

Our 2 tanks arrived with an "F" Pln to reinforce hard-fought B Co. Tank automatic fire cut Japs out of trees like hot sun melting butter. Jap bullets ricocheted from the tanks. A frenzied charge mounted one tank, but the other tank's fire sliced them off. The survivors left their dead and wounded and dived back into jungle. Some time during this fighting near the Strip, T/Sgt Korpi had crawled under fire to bandage and save a wounded comrade.

As dusk came, "B" dug in, with a whole bidon of water sent up for the canteens of each depleted Pln. With the Strip on our left flank, we tied in with F Co now moved to our right, with "C" flanking "F" to make a continuous line to the beach. D Co sent 2 HMGs to enfilade our front. We had time for a quick cigarette to soothe our nerves.

On this 18 May, "B" lost more men than any other Co on Wakde. Besides McHugh and Kroll named already, we had 5 more dead—Fish with a brain wound, Correia and Oakes shot in the chest, Witolaski shot in the right thigh, and T/5 Rogers in abdomen.

We had many wounded. Besides Shamley, Gardea, Gorichs, Maxam, Brown, Calkins, Cargal, Harvey, Talley, Branch, Cranford, and Medic Stabek, we had 11 more wounded to hospital. Dean was hit in wrist and head, Curtis in shoulder, S/Sgt Benski in shoulder and right hand. Calderon, S/Sgt Dalsky were both wounded in right arms; Brostad in left arm. Potts and T/5 Hendrickson were hit in left elbows, T/Sgt Charles Larson in right wrist, Chaney in left palm. Location of Greenberg's serious wound went unreported on casualty lists. Except for Scopelite with a fragment in right shoulder, we are uncertain whether any of these wounds were from bullets or mortar fragments.

On this 18 May, B's losses totalled 7 dead, 23 wounded to hospital. Of 21 killed on Wakde on 18 May, 7 were "B" men. Of 53 seriously wounded, 23 were "B" men.

That night, the Japs seemed to fire every 5 minutes, and often with tracers, which we had never known them to use before. About midnight, they attacked in 15-man squads, but B with D's HMGs cut them down. We had no "B" casualties.

At daylight, a Jap voice howled orders before another charge. The empty bunkers which we had grenaded yesterday came alive with drunken Nips. As voices grew louder, the first Jap charged alone and died writhing from 2 "B" rifle shots. Then they hit our perimeter from all sides, but died before they reached us. In broad dawn, a voice ordered their withdrawal. Our casualties were few.

After this fight, we could not advance again, unless we wanted to waste men. Ordered to await tank help, we endured agonizing thirst under danger of Jap rifles. We shot down coconuts and crawled under Jap menace to get coconut milk for our thirsty wounded.

By 1130, a tank forwarded to help us, and we felt safe to straighten up out of our holes. F Co reinforced us on our right flank, and halved our front so that we could concentrate more effectively against the dark jungle ahead. Mission was to contact A Co advancing from their night perimeter north of the Strip to round the east end of the Strip. Water came up for our dry throats and empty canteens.

Then 2Lt White's right Pln moved out with the tank. At 10-20 yards behind the tank, a squad followed it, while the other 2 squads guarded each side, far away enough to avoid Jap ricochets. Ahead were 2 bunkers with 2 or more walls of coral logs and several feet of crushed coral backing the logs. Bunker slots were only 6 inches high, and 2 feet long.

White's left squad fired frontally to seal the slot of the left bunker, and the tank attacked the right bunker. At 50 yards, three 75 mm shells tore the bunker apart. Then the tank MGs covered the charge of our right squad to finish the Japs with grenades and bayonets. Ten Japs lay dead beside their rifles and 2 LMGs.

Now the tank fought Bunker No. 2 about 50 yards on the left front while the right squad protected the right side of the tank and the left squad shot at the slot. At 20 yards, a 75mm shell slugged the bunker. The dazed Japs ran into the open, but our right squad slew all 8, captured their LMG.

With the Japs under control, orders came to push forward and clear the remainder of the south edge of Wakde Strip. We were to contact A Co on the SE end-corner of the Strip.

As our alert rifles advanced again, 4 Nips fired from the nose-guns of a wrecked bomber. At S/Sgt Belgarde's request, the tank charged with MGs blazing, and at 20 feet slashed the plane into a thousand pieces with a single 75 shell. Clanking on, the tank blasted paths for us through impassable brush, but we had to comb every square foot for Jap riflemen in their holes. About 1640, "B" finally contacted A Co at the end of the Strip near the NE corner of Wakde.

With A Co on our left and "F" and "C" to our right, we now formed a rough half-circle around the last Japs. On the NE cape of Wakde, they holed up in coral caves near the sea—in a triangle with its inland leg about 500 yards long.

Terrain was too rocky for tanks in these caves opening towards the sea. Our 20-man patrol perhaps from all 4 Cos fired into the cave-mouths and grenaded them, but we got no return fire. Our 3/Pln's Sgt Case stood and started to enter a cave. A Jap shot mortally wounded Case in the head. Attempting to save his life, B's Sgt Hawkey and an unknown "A" man charged in firing. Under this cover, B's Castor and A's More crawled to drag Case to a waiting ambulance. But Case died shortly afterwards.

Thus ended B Co's second day on Wakde. Our men were among the lucky ones to pull back into the conquered part of Wakde for a hot meal and plenty of water. Sgt Davidson and Cpl Wilcopolski never forgot that hot soup. Most of us slept hard, except for turns on guard.

On that 19 May, we had lighter losses—2 dead, 3 wounded. Besides Case, Dandurand perished from a bullet in the head also. Our 3 wounded were slashed by fragments—1/Lt Houston in left hand and shoulder, Canell in arms and hips, Rumisek in arm and left side of abdomen. (Casualties in other Cos totalled 3 dead, and 19 hospital wounded.)

Next morning, 20 May, "B" briefly mopped up. While "A" and "C" circled the Strip, Sgt Davidson of T/Sgt Tessmer's patrol killed the last of 2 Japs in the open on the south side of the strip near a work-shop. And at 1400, B Co departed forever from that rubble of coral and splintered coconut logs with some 800 corpses that we had to make of Wakde. (Before the war, it had been a quiet, bucolic coconut grove with a leisurely German proprietor.)

Core of the 800-man garrison had been 280 men of 9 Co 3/Bn 224 Inf. including a Pln of 75mm guns, and a few mortar and LMG and HMG squads, from other Cos of 224 Inf. They fought beside 150 men of probably 91 Naval Garrison Unit—"Jap Marines." A Hawaii-born AA observer taken prisoner, said that his own outfit had been 93 strong—perhaps from 53 Field AA Bn. Remaining estimated number of 227 men were from miscellaneous units and fragments of units. Mjr Wing reported that 91 different formations had manned Wakde.

Because of B's heavy fighting, our losses were out of proportion to the losses of the other 3 rifle Cos. We had lost 9 dead compared with the other 3 Cos' total loss of 15. We had 25 wounded compared with the other 3 Cos' total loss of 42 (that is, seriously wounded and into hospital). D Co had 4 killed and 5 seriously wounded, but lighter losses could be expected of a weapons Co.

After running into a beachhead ambush in the first wave—the most serious ambush in the history of 163 Inf—B Co landed fighting. As tank-infantry, we pushed to Wakde Strip, then turned east to battle through the fortified jungle south of the Strip. In carrying on the tradition of valiant combat at Sanananda, B Co had played a major role in winning Wakde Island from the die-hard Japanese.

947 FA BN:

Our 155 MM Howitzers For Biak

by COLONEL HUGH KENNEDY (CO 947 FA),
and DR. HARGIS WESTERFIELD, DIVISION HISTORIAN

> CREDIT: Prime source is due to Col. Hugh Kennedy's 15-page, single-spaced typescript of 947 FA's history at Hollandia and Biak. This typescript is an expansion of a portion of Col. Kennedy's **History of the 947 Field Artillery Battalion/From December, 1943 to September, 1945,** which is now out of print. Kennedy backed his documents with letters of 23 July, 20 Oct., 30 Oct., and 4 Nov., 1980. I used also award stories of Merton Austin, Foy Davis, and Edward Doughty, with 162's Lt-Col. Hollister's "Certificate" of 3 July 1944. Some brief notes came from 41st DivArty's "Narrative Report of the Biak Operation," and RR Smith's **Approach to the Philippines**—neither of which even suggests adequate credit to the heroic work of 947 FA on Biak.

This is the little-known story of how the hammer-blows of 947 FA's powerful 155mm howitzers helped rescue 162 Inf from Parai Defile, then overwhelm the Japs on Horseshoe Ridge. Attached to our 41st Div on 15 Mar 1944, we had battled the Hollandia mud without casualties, and fired just one concentration of shells. But on Biak, our war for the 41st meant wounds and suffering and death for 947 FA men.

On 27 May 1944, Btry C with Lt-Col Kennedy himself, made an easy landing on Bosnek Jetty. We fired only 20 rounds all day, and on 28 May advanced 2.5 miles down the road to near Ibdi Village. Here "C" was to support 162 Inf now entering Mokmer Village past Parai Defile. By 1245, the other 947 FA Btrys had joined us.

Our position was dangerous. Unseen Japs watched from low dark-green ridges above us. About 1400, Japs mortared our constricted clearing of 200 by 300 yards where we tried to dig in through solid coral.

One of their first 81 mm mortar shells blasted Hq Btry's radio section. Four men were killed outright: Putman, McCue, S/Sgt Peay, T/4 James Smith. Cpl Rice, T/5 Hertel died of wounds. Seriously wounded were Neesen, T/4 Savoy; lightly wounded were Fuqua, Zeig, and Cpls Frank Smith and Turman. A fragment hit Col Kennedy in the back but did not wound.

Another shell burst near Btry B's No. 1 Gun and wounded 4 men: probably Reeves, Eichman, Sanders, and Wade.

Sv Btry's men secured our inland flank. After a patrol that found no Japs, they tried to dig in. A lucky Jap round on the coral lip of our MG position wounded Bryna, Sgt Cook, Capt Jackson, killed gunner T/5 Mathes. No Japs attacked. Later we learned that the shells were unobserved that day, on targets set up previously. A charge of Japs could have played havoc with our battalion.

While Btry C began our Bn's retreat to a position half a mile east of Bosnek, Btrys A and B stood to their guns. Down at Parai Defile that disastrous 28 May, 162 Inf needed our shellfire to cover their withdrawal from positions advanced too close to Mokmer Strip.

Our 1/Lt Doughty volunteered to lead an observation party to help 162 Inf, along with Cpl Davis (the only other man named in the party). Embarking from Bosnek on a beach-craft, we bypassed Japs that had cut off 162, and landed at Parai Jetty. Here about 1530, Lt-Col Hollister asked for Doughty's help to smash Jap counter-attacks.

Within 15 minutes after we arrived, Doughty had shells striking those Jap advances with deadly accuracy. Joining the 4 tanks with 162's men on rear-guard, Doughty climbed on top of the lead tank which was drawing mortar and MG fire. Then Doughty left the tank and moved back several more yards towards the Japs for better observation.

Back under Ibdi Ridge, our Btrys A and B fought heroically. While SV Btry's "infantry" crouched in shallow holes to scan the dark Jap ridge northward, our highly-trained 7-man gun-crews continued firing.

Barrage after barrage on call, our great 155mm howitzers hurled 95-lb. shells. As soon as tubes were cleared of left-over smouldering powder that might explode the next shell among us, our gunners pulled lanyards and arced new shells down the shore.

Up front, 162's Col Hollister was amazed at the speed when our shells began falling as soon as he had specified our targets. Doughty's shells accurately impacted 100-200 yards behind 3/Bn. Retreating at 162's rear, he directed those saving barrages—rolling barrages in reverse. He helped 3/Bn back to dig better positions in Parai Defile, by dusk.

That night, Jap planes dropped flares on Btrys A and B. They seemed to try to pinpoint our guns for ground or air attacks. When our MG opened fire with AA outfits, we claimed the death of a Zero that crashed into cliffs about 100 yards NW of Btry A.

Back at Parai Defile in 162's final evacuation on 29 May, Lt Doughty's OP guarded retreating 162 Inf with barrages in reverse until they were saved from destruction. During 24 hours' fire 947 FA had expended 1100 rounds for 162 Inf.

When 162 had cleared Parai Defile and holed up at Mandom, 947 FA had become the front line. So by 1730, we displaced back to Btry C east of Bosnek. The Bn fired throughout the night.

On 1-4 June, we fired often, day and night. In return, Japs harassed us. In the dark of 1 June, a Yank patrol from an unnamed outfit slew 2 men of a Jap patrol on our inland flank. The Japs carried explosive charges surely intended to kill our guns. Next day, however, Btry B's Capt Avery's patrol could not contact any Japs on that flank.

On 3 June, about 1700, Jap planes strafed Btry A just east of Bosnek and fired a powder dump. Btry A's Capt Wiggans led a party to defuze shells already heated, remove nearby powder, and put out the fire.

On 4 June, we heard that a Jap fleet with battleships bore reinforcements for Biak. (That fleet did have 1 battleship.) We dug in our guns facing the sea. HQ and Fire Control covered behind a low ridge. But Jap scout planes wrongly reported that our protecting fleet was stronger. The strike was called off. That night, our own fleet of 14 ships passed by the south coast of Biak and made us feel safer.

Some day on or after 1 June, Lt Runkle headed an observation party for fire for 186 Inf on their overland march from Bosnek to seize Mokmer Strip from the rear. With Lt Runkle, Patterson, Sgt Oldham, and Cpl Lenzner contacted Col. Newman's party about to hole up for the night. As we tried to dig in, Japs sprayed the area with MGs, mortars. Newman urged us to disperse while we crawled.

Crawling on hands and knees to evade a supposed line of fire, Oldham and Lenzner drew a blast of MG fire that passed close between Lenzner's head and Oldham's rear. Each man believed that the other was dead. Meanwhile, 186's men found the Japs and killed perhaps 11. Our position was impossible; Newman radioed the main 186 perimeters and informed them that we were joining them in the darkness. Hiking through mud, water, and darkness, we entered 186's perimeter in safety. We still had to dig shallow holes to sleep in.

Back at our Btrys at 0600 on 7 June, we took 3 bombs near C Btry's No. 1 Gun. Six men were wounded: probably Gulley, Le Blanc, Lannon, T/5 Gibson, and Cpls Davis and Little.

Despite those Japs' bombs at 0600, 947 FA were ready on call at 0700 to help Runkle's OP to help 186 Inf capture Mokmer Strip. At 0700, from Mokmer Ridge, Runkle's OP was directing shells in 30 minutes' preparation for 186 Inf to swoop on the Strip. (Just as Runkle's men started down with 186, a P-38 of ours made 2 passes on us, but missed and turned off. We might have fired back on the third pass.)

Now 186 on the Strip took a heavy bombardment from that same ridge where we had missed the Japs and bypassed them. Their MG fire ricocheted from the Strip before the foot-high revetment of coral stones that we lay behind. Between their MG bursts, we observed smoke rising from the ridge jungle and called our 155 shells down on that smoke. Japs wheeled mountain guns from caves, fired down on us, and hid the guns again. Once the shells bracketed our party, but no more shells came down to split the bracket and destroy us. By late afternoon, Jap fire had noticeably lessened, and at least 6 gun positions were silenced. Later we heard that Runkle's men, unawares, were directing fire for all Bns of DivArty.

Also on 7 June, 947 FA prepared for 162's landing at Parai Jetty which bypassed Japs holding Parai Defile to the east and put 162 in position to join up with 186 on the Strip. Observing from a buffalo offshore, our Capt Austin called 155s down on suspected targets before we landed. Lt-Col Hollister lauded us for our immediate and thorough coverage of every target that he pointed out.

Back at Mokmer Strip that 7 June, our 2/Lt Holmquist's OP lost a man killed, perhaps another wounded. Some time while observing after 1400 while 3 newly landed tanks were destroying Nippo guns, Holmquist lost T/5 Jorgenson killed by MG fire.

Altogether, 947 FA had as many as 6 OPs active at one time on Biak, either for 162 Inf or 186 or 163. Two of our officers were detached as liaison for 121 FA's 75s for the whole campaign. One of our most effective OPs was a floating post offshore on an LCV. Although under Jap fire for several times, it claimed destruction of an ammo dump, naval and AA guns.

On 8-20 June, a number of our guns returned to our old position below Ibdi Pocket ridges, to fire for 186 and 162 against the Japs holding Horseshoe Ridge, that supreme tactical position which denied our heavy bombers the use of Mokmer Strip.

From Ibdi Pocket above us, the Japs shelled around us every night between 1700 and 1800 with mortars and a 75 mm mountain gun or guns. Fire seemed to be directed principally at the cub strip near Btrys C and B. Some times, wild shots impacted our Bn area. This nightly shelling went on until our guns left the area on 20 June. The shells caused no damage. We believe that the Japs sighted those guns on 10 June, but did not again observe the results of their fire—just hoped for the best.

On 11 June while still below Ibdi Pocket, 947 FA began heavy firing to help 162 Inf to capture Horseshoe Ridge guarding Mokmer Strip. Even with our 155s assistance, 3/Bn 162 could not get under way until mid afternoon against the rugged, dense rain-forest of the ridge with its Jap defenders. We had to pound Horseshoe Ridge for over a week to help 162's advances.

On 19 June, 947 FA teamed with 121, 167, and 205 FA to help 186 Inf in Gen Eichelberger's plan to place 186 Inf in the rear of West Caves, which were Jap Hqs on Biak. Concluding at 1040, this overwhelming bombardment helped 186 to advance with but few losses. After this advance, 186 had cut off Jap reinforcements and supplies from the north coast of Biak. Even the escape of any large number of Japs from West Caves became impossible. On the night of 21-22 June, 160 of these trapped Nips tried to break out of West Caves. Here 186 Inf killed 115 of them while 162 Inf killed 17. Not until 27 June, however, could 1/Bn 162 finally enter safely those silent, corpse-redolent Jap Hq.

Our Battle of Biak was almost ended. Taking up a new position 700 yards west of Parai Defile, we helped 186's L and K Cos against the main surviving Jap strongpoint NW of 186's perimeter behind West Caves. On 24 June, we helped to neutralize or destroy 2-3 Jap mountain guns so that "L" and "K" could overrun that strongpoint.

Firing missions became few and scattered until Btry C fought for Ibdi Pocket. On 23-25 June, 947 FA did move to the coast below Borokoe Strip, probably to help 24 Div's 34 Inf to advance. We had good luck on 28 June. Btry A had lent a tractor to "B" of 168 FA, that other 155 mm outfit which came to Biak after the Parai Defile ambush. Probably an overheated motor fired the tractor and exploded 3 155 mm shells on it. No casualties occurred to 168 FA, but we wonder whether 947 would have been so lucky if the tractor had been in our hands.

On 12 July, Btry C saw 947's last heavy combat—ironically some revenge for our casualties in the early days on Biak. For we fired from our early position under Ibdi Pocket on Ibdi Pocket itself. On 12-23 July—but for 3 days—we pounded those coral ridges to help 3/Bn 163's difficult attacks. Some 20,000 shells of 146 FA had already reduced that opaque jungle to mere stumps. After our Btry C's precision blasting of shell-bare terrain, some 200 Japs—most of the remaining garrison—escaped into northern Biak. All told, Btry C expended 2,145 rounds of our 95-lb shells, probably the record number for 947 FA in the whole Biak Operation.

It was, however, necessary for B-24s to drop 64 1,000-lb bombs on the Pocket to destroy the remaining Japs. And even after the B-24s, 146 FA threw in 1,000 rounds of 105 mm shells, while we of 947 FA fired 275 rounds of 155 mm shells. Then 3/Bn 153's assault was almost unopposed.

The death of Ibdi Pocket concluded 947 FA's war for the 41st Div. Firing day or night, our 155 mm shells helped rescue 162 Inf at Parai Defile, and win Horseshoe Ridge and Ibdi Pocket. The 41st DivArty reported that we had fired 9,746 shells in 362 missions. We fought literally in the front lines at times—lost 8 killed and 14 wounded. After leaving the 41st, we would again fight well in the Philippines.

AT CO, 162 INFANTRY:

Our Southern Philippine Campaign

by DR. HARGIS WESTERFIELD, Division Historian,
with STEPHEN COUNTS and GRED KIELSGARD

CREDIT: Fred Kielsgard's letter in **Jungleer** of May 1979 started this story, backed by Fred's second letter of 20 June 1979, and Steve Counts' letters of 21 Nov and 26 Dec 1979, and 27 Jan and 12 Feb 1980. Documents consulted were 162's casualty lists and March, 1945, Morning Report—with 162's Narrative and Journal of the Southern Philippine Campaign in Zamboanga and Central Mindanao. I used also "'A' Company on Zamboango-Jolo" of 716 Tank Bn, "205 FA Bn Historical Record V-4 Zamboanga," and RR Smith's **Triumph in the Philippines**."

At 1615 6 Mar 1945, Anti-Tank Co 162 Inf left Mindoro Island for battle at Zamboanga. In the choppy, land-locked Sulu Sea, our LCI No. 616 bobbed like a cork. At 0939 10 Mar, we beached at San Mateo, weak-kneed and queasy.

Landing was quiet at first but for occasional Jap shells. We hoped for another easy invasion like at Hollandia. With Hoffman borrowed from another squad as first scout, Kielsgard's men were first "AT" men ashore. We had to work our way through barbed wire tangles, but no expected Jap MG fire stabbed at us.

AT Co had orders to hold near the beach until assignment for the attack inland. Then Jap shell-fire increased—rumored from our own 75s captured back in 1941-42. Sgt Counts' squad of our Mine Pln was luckily 4 feet deep in a Jap trench. But forward, Kielsgard wished that his men had carried portable fox-holes. Tanks parked near his prone squad; Jap cannon fire intensified.

Since his squad lacked a phone to AT Co's CP, Kielsgard dashed through shell-file for withdrawal orders. The shells seemed to chase him. Every time he made a short dash and dropped, a shell kicked up dirt behind him.

AT Co had perimetered near the end of a bamboo grove 500 yards north of the beach. Kielsgard brought back his squad, and returned borrowed Hoffman to Sgt Riley's squad. While Riley's squad dug in yet probably stood up while digging, a Jap shell blasted a few feet away. It killed Hoffman. Riley was closer to the exploding shell, but its impact merely stunned him.

As later waves of landing craft unloaded troops and supplies, the bombardment increased. The ground rose slightly from the beach to Wolfe Strip inland, and Jap shells had to whistle low just overhead to impact the beach targets behind us.

Emplaced near AT Co, our 205 FA Bn at first felt safe from Jap guns. Their fire-control trench was only 75-100 feet from "AT." About 1700, a Jap shell burst in a tree about 5 yards behind the fire-control trench. It slew 5 FA men, including Maj Ramstead, and wounded 8 others, including Lt Peterson, Survey Officer.

Concussion wave of this shell knocked down almost all of "AT" nearby. T/4 Marley took a steel chunk in his shoulder. Marked lightly wounded were Simpson, 1/Lt Crawford, T/Sgt Palmer. T/Sgt Counts was partly deaf in his right ear for several months.

Around Zambo, Anti-Tank Co's main duties were like our duties in other operations. We served as riflemen; the Japs had no tanks to fight. (Nearest we ever came to Jap tanks was when they charged down Parai Defile on Biak. But that tank-battle went on above us on our right flank.) At Zambo, we secured 162's flanks or rear, and ran recon patrols. But, as on Biak when needed at Ibdi Pocket, we were needed for battle at San Roque.

After L Co was forced from the strongly held San Roque area on 12 Mar, "AT" had a fighting assignment in that by-passed Pocket. While "L" and other 3/Bn Cos moved to storm the Japs on the ridge above San Roque Pocket, "AT" teamed with E Co to clear the Pocket.

By 0820 14 Mar, AT Co had orders to assist E Co's fight through San Roque. Leaving 1/Pln near Wolfe Strip, we reinforced E Co While "E" pushed into the pocket with 716 Tank Bn's 1/Pln of A Co, we secured the base of our little task force.

At 1310 that 14 Mar, E 162 met small arms fire. Losing Layton to die of wounds, "E" repelled a Jap flank strike, and captured 2 small knobs on the north ridge. Tanks claimed destroying 6 pillboxes, several small arms emplacements. E Co drove a deep wedge into shell-blasted San Roque Pocket.

On 15 Mar, "AT" attacked San Roque Pocket with our 2/Pln and Counts' 4/Pln—better known as Mine Pln because we were originally equipped with mine-detectors. We now acted as tank infantry protectors for 716 Tank Bn's 2 tanks. Forming column on the road a short way south of San Roque Village, we marched northwards, with 2/Pln left of the tanks, and Mine Pln on the right.

Discovery of 2 Jap mines slowed us down on the road. Both were 500-lb Jap bombs buried upright with only their detonators just above the surface for our tanks to hit. Although easy to detect because the hard-packed soil of the road was disturbed in digging them in, we moved slowly. Here was a time when Mine Pln needed our mine-detectors, but we had to lose them 8 months ago at Parai Defile and never received more of them.

About a half-mile north of San Roque Village, we entered a wide valley with a ridge slanting NW about 2-300 feet west of us. In the valley, we deployed to protect the tanks. While 2/Pln advanced 100 yards west of them, we advanced 100 yards east of the tanks.

Both "AT" and the tanks penetrated ground crowded with Jap pillboxes and slit trenches. FA and Air Force had chewed up the earth. We saw many bomb craters. The terrain before Mine Pln was clear of all Japs.

Then about 1010, Jap fire plunged from the ridge at us. Most of the fire fell from that part of the ridge directly north of the column. It caused casualties to 2/Pln men closest to the fire.

Mine Pln took cover in shell-holes and bomb-craters and joined 2/Pln and the 2 tanks in firing back at the ridge. We had no real targets—just quick puffs of haze to aim rifles at. Some of the haze was from MGs. Counts doubted that any Mine Pln man expended over a clip or two.

But 2/Pln on our left suddenly began a harder fight at an ambush of Jap infantry. In firing on that ridge and in keeping up with the tanks, they must have failed to secure their left flank against a slope of supposedly empty fox-holes.

Now these positions came alive with Japs firing on 2/Pln or thrusting with bayonets close to us. As one "AT" man set himself to leap over a slit trench, a live Jap rose and lunged at him with a bayonet. He jumped back and shot the Jap. For a few minutes, 2/Pln had hand-to-hand combat. Probably here, Slack was seriously wounded and big Texan Mueller killed.

The whole advance was stalled. The tanks machine-gunned the ridge, but seemed to have little effect on reducing the Jap machine-gun fire. Tankmen later claimed credit for overhead fire that allowed 2/Pln to crawl back to safety, but they could not silence the ridge.

We could not bring out Mueller's body. In return for Slack's wound and Mueller's death, we claimed 15 dead Nips. Surviving Japs evidently cleared the ridge area before next day, for 162's Journal credits our fight for driving the Japs from San Roque Pocket. We had begun a general evacuation of the Japs that would take them from their Mt Capisan stronghold farther north and into the rain-forest west of Sinonog River.

After AT's big fight at San Roque Pocket, Mine Pln got an easier assignment to secure 162's 81 mm mortar positions at San Roque Village. Some days later, Kielsgard and 4-5 more volunteers went back to recover Mueller's body. Kielsgard still remembers heavy rain forest nearby and steep high ground close to it—a perfect spot for an ambush. Yet we recovered Mueller without firing a shot.

At 0722 17 Mar, Nips mortared "AT" at San Roque with 15 rounds. We had no casualties. Now "AT" was reassigned to outguard 162's Hq. The battle-front was not air-tight; many maverick bands of Japs were still reported at large. But we had no fights with them.

"AT" continued setting up security perimeters. One night we dug in on both sides of a much-used trail. About midnight, a booby-trap exploded up the trail. We heard the "pit-pat" of a barefoot Nip running downward among us. He ran all the way through our perimeter and out the other side and blew another booby-trap. Then he trotted back through the whole Co again—really flying low and fast this time. He escaped back up-trail with his life. We didn't fire a shot, for we feared to hit our cobbers on the other side of the perimeter.

On the night of 26 Mar late in the Zambo operation, "AT" and Counts and Gunia especially, had a frightening experience with booby-traps. By this time, our booby-traps were far more sophisticated than in the earlier New Guinea campaigns. Earlier, we had simply tied a grenade to a tree and attached a trip-wire to the loosened pin. But the grenade took all of 3 seconds after the Jap tripped the wire. It was often just a warning device for us crouched in our holes. Hearing the detonation, the Jap could leap away, hurl himself prone, and be unhurt.

At Zambo, however, we had instant detonators to replace slow detonators in a grenade, or screw into other types of anti-personnel mines.

That night of 26 June, "AT" guarded a well-worn trail on a ridge through dark, heavy rain forest. Counts with Gunia was setting traps with the new, instant detonators about 50 feet outside perimeter. We had one truly deadly anti-personnel mine—a block of cast iron, 6 by 10 inches full of TNT. This was "Big Bertha," to place in the most threatened spot—the only sure killer we had.

Counts placed her on a bench 5-6 feet from the trail, waist-high with the trip-wire crossing the trail. Gunia and he agreed that whoever hit the wire would be "evaporated."

Suddenly at dusk, Counts had orders over the phone. Because a combat patrol was out and might come down our trail, we had to go out in the open in the failing light and disarm our trail traps. While he neutralized the downhill traps, Counts sent Gunia to silence Big Bertha. Just as Counts had secured his traps, he heard a thunderous burst from exploding Big Bertha. It rocked the rige, echoed up and down the valley.

"Damn! Joe's dead!" Counts said in his grief and anguish. He blamed himself for sending Gunia where he himself ought to have gone. Head down, Counts turned slowly back up the trail. He was in no hurry; he had to face what was left of "AT" cobber Joe Gunia.

But Gunia lived! On the other side of the perimeter, Counts saw all of Gunia, with 2 Mine Pln men escorting him to a hole. Although at first stunned from concussion, Gunia soon recovered. Sole wound was a small fragment in a little finger. Gunia had survived by a million to one chance.

On 3 May, "AT" with our regiment and 3/Bn 163 attached, left Zamboango Peninsula to fight on the Mindanao mainland. To conquer great Mindanao Island's mainland, Gen Eichelberger already had his Eighth Army's 24 and 31 Divs, 108 Regt and a 164 Regt Bn. But he needed every handy Bn to destroy the unexpected 50,000 to 58,000 Japs on the island. Landing at Parang 4 May, "AT" helped to mop up the SW corner of Mindanao after 24 Div had spearheaded the landing.

On 13 May, "AT" had 162's first fight against 40-50 Japs near Dilap, 20 miles inland near Mindanao River. When Jap fire grounded our scouts, Counts called for help to save them. We withdrew under heavy mortar fire but had no losses, although our arms were only carbines and rifles. Returning better armed next day, we could not find the Japs.

On 30 May, "AT" was in a truck convoy for Maramag on Sayre Highway, main north-south route on Mindanao. Monsoon rains and other troop moves had turned this neglected road into a quagmire. The mud halted our trucks, and by 5 June, Gen Sibert of X Corps had cancelled this move.

About 24 June, "AT" left Sayre Highway to rejoin 162 Inf, already in heavy combat near Davao City since 10 June. Although 162 Inf and 3/Bn 163 Inf had broken main resistance before Calinan on 18 June, "AT" helped pursue the Nips.

Patrolling a dirt road near Lorenzo, 2.5 miles NE of Calinan on 26 June, we found our last heavy resistance of World War II. At least 4 automatic weapons fired on us. Hagner was lightly wounded. The Nips were well dug in, among many pillboxes. Two days later L Co was repulsed with 5 dead, 12 wounded. Not until 30 June after 205 FA barrages and 2 tanks' help would 3/Bn destroy the 22 pillboxes holding us up and push through to Davao River—this time without losses.

AT 162's Southern Philippine Campaign was for us one of a few comparatively light actions, with just 2 dead and 6 wounded at Zambo, and 1 at Lorenzo. It was hard work and plenty of it, of course. Looking back on the campaign today, however, we believe that the whole Southern Philippine Campaign was mainly to keep us fit for the Division's invasion of Kyushu scheduled for 1 Nov 1945. We are happy that World War II ended.

L COMPANY 163 INFANTRY:

Capturing Zamboanga City

by DR. HARGIS WESTERFIELD, Division Historian,
with FIRST LIEUTENANT WILLIAM F. SCHACHT

> CREDIT: Core of this story is Schacht's retyped Diary of 66 pages, with Award Stories of Schacht, Lemons, Rumph, Neumark, Quackenbush. Backing is from 163's Zamboanga Journal and 146 FA's Capt. Robert Allen's "Zamboanga Recaptured," and "Battle for the Ridges." Morning Report of L 163 for March 1945 names only 7 of the 13 wounded mentioned by Schacht, but Schacht's figure is probably more accurate.

On 10 Mar 1945, 2/Lt Schacht with other L Co 163 Inf men numbly watched the Zamboanga plain appear misty and gray with sunrise over high mountains. From the deck of LCI 1,000, we saw cruisers, destroyers, and rocket-ships hide the land in a smoke-pall shot with flames. At 0840, 48 B-25s' bombs lofted debris high above the water. At 0915, 162 Inf's first waves hit the beach and dashed inland.

Next, in the seventh wave, L 163's men felt LCI 1,000 slide up the sand. Out we jumped and ran across open beach and panted inland 300 yards. It was hard, sweaty going—thick brush among shell-holes and shattered barbed wire.

In 10 minutes, we had dropped excess equipment and were on the line of departure east for Zambo City. Inland on the left, 2/Lt Rumph's 2/Pln moved off, and on the coast on the right, Schacht's 1/Pln. Attached to his Pln were 2 L Co LMGs and 2 "M" HMGs. Dostal's squad protected the 4 MGs. Tanks were on call, and an LCI accompanying us alongshore.

Hampered by more thick brush and barbed wire, we finally halted at an open field about 1313 at Gavilan Point. As we moved again, rifle fire and a Jap MG drove Stafford's squad to earth. Advancing with the other squads closer to the beach, Schacht heard Rumph's Pln return fire. Jap fire came from a hillside and farm buildings across the open field.

L Co's 60 mm mortars were up on call, but Schacht's other 2 squads also lay prone under Jap fire. He wondered how to regroup his Pln and strike back. Our Co, 1/Lt Quackenbush, ordered L's 3/Pln onto the hill to silence the Japs, but Schacht saw unsuspecting Yanks walk right over the pillbox. It ceased fire when our riflemen crossed it, then opened up again. Our Exec Officer, 1/Lt Anderson, took part of Schacht's Pln around to meet the tanks and advance with them.

Schacht led his other men to flank the Japs. About this time, 2/Lt Rumph of 2/Pln also drew Jap fire when he neutralized the Jap pillbox with grenades. Then his squad cleared it.

Now with assault fire, 3/Pln closed in on the Japs and drove them away. Stafford's squad of 1/Pln was now saved; only Hurlburt was briefly missing in action. Meanwhile, L's 2/Pln had killed 2 Japs. Back at the beach-head, I Co had 2 prisoners, but reportedly lost 2 men from Jap bayonets.

Regroupoing again at the buildings ahead, "L" was ready to push again with the tanks about 1500. Pressing on through thick jungle, we fired on every building and pillbox in sight with rifles, MGs, mortars, and tank 75s. At 1410, we took blasts from knee mortars, replied with 81s to silence them.

By 1800, Schacht's Pln was hot, thirsty, and exhausted and took a break lying down while other units came up. Hurriedly we perimetered some 400 yards inshore. We had hardly time before dark to get water, unroll wire, and find a log to lie behind while outguards watched and booby-traps were set up. That night, Schacht slept but little, although nobody in 1/Pln had to fire.

On that 10 Mar, we had not gone far. Baliwasan River was 500 yards ahead, and beyond it was Zambo City 2 miles farther ahead, probably held by Japs for house-to-house fighting.

At 0730 11 Mar, Schacht's 1/Pln again led out, with 3 tanks and 4 MGs. We patrolled 500 yards to the bridge by 0815. Japs seemed to dig in, across Baliwasan River; the road was mined.

To support the tanks' crossing, we fired all we had on the pillboxes and buildings on the other side. By 0940, 4 tanks and 2 "L" Plns had crossed. Four Japs died when a pillbox was knocked out.

Again 1/Pln led out; Schacht had to march first. The tanks and "L" moved steadily up the beach. We advanced faster because Scout Lemons fearlessly checked out pillboxes and buildings.

Schacht still wonders about one silent pillbox with a .50 HMG. Although several 1/Pln men grenaded it and shot into it, rear elements still found 4 live Japs inside.

Three minutes after 1/Pln was nearly 100 yards up the beach past where we had rested, Japs guns salvoed on other men in the same spot. L's Sutton was killed, Balke and Reitz lightly wounded. M Co's Dittrich was killed. Two men of C Battery 218 FA were hit also: T/5 Ripari seriously wounded and Royalty lightly wounded, probably men in an observer party.

Schacht's 1/Pln also expected shelling, cowered behind the concrete sea-wall. Shells did burst within 50-100 yards. Medic Neumark rushed back to aid the wounded—moved them under a bridge for protection, then exposed himself to call for transpoation.

Schacht's men pressed on hurriedly to get clear of this Jap FA fire. While replenishing ammo and scouting the outskirts of Zambo City, we got orders to take it with tanks' help.

At 1430, with I Co on our left, we entered a city of ruined stone buildings 2-3 storys high. It was silent, but we took no chances with Japs. Tanks shelled every building in sight. A network of concrete emplacements covered the waterfront, but no Japs fought us. By 1740, Zambo City was officially captured.

L Co had a blissful day and a half to enjoy Zambo City, bright with the smiling faces of Filipino families returning from the hills in clean clothing. Generals Eichelberger and Doe made a special call to congratulate us for capturing Zamboanga. But other 163 men needed 3/Bn for a reserve while battling Jap Marines in the slot of Santa-Maria-Pasananca. By 1300 13 Mar—the day E Co was blown up—we had left Zambo City to become a reserve for 1/Bn and 2/Bn in heavy combat north of us. We saw our wounded arriving from the front.

On 14 Mar as we entrucked from perimeter near Wolfe Field, Jap shells fell around us. We escaped unhurt up the road to make next perimeter in a grassy coconut grove near Santa Maria. On 15 Mar, our patrol helped rescue AT Co 500 yards ahead. "AT" lost 2 men here; we had no losses.

Pasananca fell without our help, but "L" fought on 17 Mar against Japs holding a village across the Tumaga River. Even with help of 81s and 105s, I Co had failed the day before.

Shortly after crossing the Tumaga, we entered that quiet Jap village deep in a coconut valley some 3,000 yds. NE of Santa Maria. Jap rifles, mortars, MGs stopped us—killed Shea and Freese. On the right flank, Strulowitz of Schacht's Pln was wounded in the leg. "L" returned to our same holes that night. On 18 Mar, FA and an air-strike of 1000-pound bombs drove the Japs from that area into the high ridges.

Just before dark on 18 Mar, Schacht's 1/Pln got a nerve-wracking job. Isolated from even I Co in advance, we were fearful in that thick brush among the Japs. While setting booby-traps, S/Sgt Stafford looked up to face a big Nip Marine. Stafford fired once, and ran. Sgt Dostal and others saw 2 Japs in camouflage uniform. We hit the holes. At dusk, maybe 60 knee-mortar shells lighted just east of us. Nobody was hurt, but nobody slept all night.

On 19 Mar, "L" teamed with I Co to push to the hills 3-4 miles north up Tumaga River. Passing through the deserted village, we seized a ridge ahead under covering fire, and in turn covered I Co's advance 800 yards north to begin a new 3/Bn perimeter.

At night, japs lobbed 4-5 rounds of mortar shells each hour into 3/Bn's perimeters. Schacht thought that they wounded 2 men each time. Caught once in the open while out for water, Schacht heard the first of 5 hit within 15 yards. Throwing himself into a handy vacant hole, he gritted his teeth, heard the other whistle and fall and burst. Yet that night, only "L" man reported wounded was a Weapons Pln man—probably Tedeschi.

About 2200, grenades and booby-traps blasted before 1/Pln at something moving. Dahlstrom phoned that Japs were infiltrating and throwing grenades everywhere. Near the Tumaga 100 yards from Schacht, Dahlstrom had to stop talking to keep the Japs from finding our holes. Finally, Schacht to call for our MGs to fire a final protective line. Yet we have no report of Yank or Jap casualties. A Jap Pln with a MG had successfully crawled through us from the rear and rejoined their outfits to continue battle in the ridges. On 20 Mar, "L" had another day of diving into holes when mortar shells dropped.

On 21 Mar, "L" climbed into an even more dangerous position—a long, narrow ridge that we named "Knee-Mortar Hill." Gasping under our heavy gear, we climbed straight up 300-400 feet on a path of stone and sliding sand.

Here we were on a ridge 200 yards long by 20-25 yards wide with another perpendicular drop on the opposite edge. Across a deep valley of gardens and coconut groves were the Jap ridges. left and north near Tumaga River was dominating Sugar Loaf Mtn, rocks and brush and the steepest of all. Right and NE of Sugarloaf was a horseshoe of 3 high hills, the Japs' main line of resistance, just 1000 yards east of us.

Topping this ridge about 1200 that 21 Mar, we soon took sniper fire and many knee-mortar blasts from the 3 high hills rightward. We scattered to holes carved in the rock on the reverse slope. Our M Co gunners had a number of casualties. L Co's Black Dog was missing.

Morale was down at nightfall. We were dirty, tired, thirsty. Our only water must come up the steep path 300-400 feet. Just below us a few miles away, the lights of Zambo City twinkled at dusk, then gleamed steadily into the night. L Co had only a few hours to enjoy our captured city, but base section commandoes were now happy in it.

On 22 Mar, "L" with MG's HMGs still secured Knee-Mortar Hill, while observers called fire on the horseshoe curve of the 3 hills 1000 yards away. Observers from M Co's 81, Cannon Cos 105s, 146 FA's 105s, and Marine Air's bombers—all targeted heavier fire than the Japs returned. In "L," Shedd was our only wounded, but "M" had several losses.

L Co on 23 Mar still held Knee-Mortar Hill while I Co attacked Hill No. 3, which was closest to us on our right flank. After a Marine air-strike and barrages, I Co's 60-man force with 2 litter squads advanced up the gap to the left of Knee-Mortar Hill, then turned right down the valley before us toward Hill No. 3. At 1013, FA shelled the base of No. 3 Hill.

Schacht watched I Co near the top of Hill No. 3 and face Japs' hidden pillboxes that opened up with MGs, mortars, and rifles. He saw "I" men crawl to the top and form a firing line. After an exchange of grenades against the Japs, "I" cleared the crest in a heavy fire-fight. The fire died down about 1142 with "I" victorious. L Co's 2/Pln then reinforced I Co.

Losses of I Co were 1 killed, 10 wounded. Capt Villwock was hit in the shoulder. But "I" had won a new observation point for directing fire at the main Jap position on the ridge crest 250 yards NW and 100 feet higher, and on a saddle running west to Sugarloaf Mtn. These were the final Jap strong points on those ridges. For reasons unknown, however, 3/Bn never expelled the Japs from those positions, but our relieving 186 Inf stormed them on 30 Mar.

But near nightfall, Schacht's 1/Pln left Knee-Mortar Hill forever. Recrossing the Tumaga, we replaced B Co on nearby Hill No. 8. B Co departed happy and gay from Jap saki and whiskey looted from the Jap Marine village downstream. Next day, Schacht's "recon" patrol to the village returned with 8 cases of liquor and 35 chickens for L's Sunday dinner.

L Co's Zambo war was almost over. On Hill No 8, we had a fine rest except for a patrol up the Tumaga on 26 Mar. Scouting up the west bank, Schacht's men narrowly escaped death on a trail constricted to a hillside ledge. From a hidden pillbox, a Jap HMG and 5-6 rifles opened up on us. We slew 5-6 Japs caught outside the pillbox, and luckily escaped untouched. "L" then called down M Co's mortars on them and cleared them out. On 30 Mar, AT Co 186 Inf relieved us to go into rest camp back down in the Tumaga valley where we had endured the infiltration of that Jap Pln 11 long days ago.

So went L Co's Battle of Zamboanga. Despite the danger and sheer hard work L Co had endured in 19 days from San Mateo Beach to Knee Mortar Hill, Schacht reported just 3 killed, 13 wounded. In our march to capture Zambo City and our fight to help I Co below Sugarloaf Mtn, "L" did an efficient job with minimum losses.

I COMPANY 186 INFANTRY:

Our Hard Luck At Hollandia

by DR. HARGIS WESTERFIELD, Division Historian,
with SGT. EMERSON KOENIG (I 186)

> CREDIT: Important original sources are Koenig's 9-page typescript (14 May 1980), and his letter of 30 May 1980. Somewhat useful was an anonymous handwritten 19-page manuscript from Dwight Eisenhower Library's Federal Archives. It seems to have been prepared after interviews by an unnamed writer at Kure, Japan, on our Division's History Team in 1945. Useful was RR Smith's **Approaches to the Philippines.** This is first time that our Association history mentions death of Sam J. Deese, as verified by I 186's enlisted men's payroll for May, 1944, and overall 186 Inf list for whole war.

Leaving Gladstone Harbor on an Aussie ship, 9 Mar 1944, I Co 186 Inf returned to New Guinea—this time actually for combat. In the 1943 Papuan Campaign, we had endured jungle camp discomfort and bush patrols but had lost no men in battle. In the coming New Guinea Campaign, however, we would fight and lose men killed or wounded.

Ironcially, our greatest losses would be our first losses. It was ironic to suffer many casualties in a holocaust from our own Navy's planes on D-Day at Hollandia.

But at first, I Co's arrival at Finschafen gave us as pleasant a surprise as we could expect in New Guinea after our 1943 experience. The "Finsch" jungle had become a great armed camp. Muddy trails and corderoy roads had become wide streets or thoroughfares. Kunai grass landing strips were now huge coral runways. Our bivouac area was clean, straight tent street. We saw piles of replacement motors for planes.

We soon learned that I Co had an important part in the coming Hollandia Operation. Communications Sgt Koenig found this out when he was the only enlisted man to attend a special briefing with our Exec, Lt Foster.

For Hollandia, I Co had one of our most important tactical missions of World War II. Our mission would be on the Humboldt Bay foreshore, about 4 miles south of Hollandia Town. About the middle of the crescent-shaped Humboldt Bay foreshore, a narrow inlet led into smaller Jautefa Bay. On the western side of this inner bay was our 3/Bn's first main objective. This was Pim Village from which they were to seize flat-topped Pancake Hill, wrongly suspected of being fortified with concealed Jap heavy artillery.

I Co's mission concerned taking the inlet from Humboldt Bay into Jautefa Bay. This inlet was a narrow pass maybe 600 yards wide. Our mission would be on the south side of that pass which Cape Tjeweri nearly closed—and on the narrow sandspit south of the Cape. Here was a Jap dual purpose gun to smash any try of 3/Bn to penetrate from Humboldt Bay into Jautefa Bay and take Pim Village.

"I" was to land on that Humboldt Bay foreshore south of Jautefa Bay—called White Beach 3. After we killed the Jap gun and secured Cape Tjeweri, we were to patrol SE alongshore to fight any Japs sent from the SE to close the Jautefa pass. If possible, we were to get prisoners for questioning.

We laugh at one minor order. A field range, pots, pans, and carving knife were to land and give us a hot meal as soon as possible. Sgt Koenig cannot recall eating anything for the next 36 hours.

I Co's hard luck began at once. A week before leaving, we boarded a little Dutch tramp with a Java crew. Luckily, we loaded days before sailing, or a sick outfit would have beached below Cape Tjeweri.

For ours was a ship foul with dysentery germs. After eating our stew on deck, we had only cold, sloppy water for our mess-gear. The stinking heads had wet floors and leaking troughs. In a day aboard, 80 per cent of "I" was doubled up with cramps and hurriedly dashing for the foul heads. (Koenig thought that dysentery spared him because he never ate much until some time after a change of station.)

"I" hurriedly entrucked back to camp. With knees drawn up, we were hard to carry in litters. Medics made tent-to-tent calls for us. Several days later, "I" again boarded that Dutch ship, now scrubbed and shining—some parts even repainted.

About 0715 22 Apr 1944, we swarmed down landing nets into LCMs and headed for White Beach 3. For miles up the beaches off Humboldt Bay, 3 light cruisers and 6 destroyers fired.

As I's LCMs chugged near a destroyer firing broadsides over our heads, we watched it roll sidewise from the recoil of the guns, then forward again. Its guns dipped into the sea. When it righted, another salvo tore overhead into the Jap coast.

We didn't object to the heavy shelling, at first. Dust rings on the beach, smoke, and fire—all assured us that Jap opposition would be less for our landing. But as we closed on the beach, we feared we would hit it among our own shells.

Shellfire ceased. In smooth water, our LCMs beached on almost dry land, about ¾ miles south of the Cape Tjeweri tip.

As we rushed down the dropped ramp, bayonets fixed, we had hard luck again. Somehow, a Yank stumbled and bayoneted 1/Lt Headicke, our CO. The point penetrated his right biceps. Despite loss of blood, Headicke remained CO for some 4 hours after the wound. He did not leave until Cape Tjeweri was all clear of Japs—left only when too weakened to resist others' pleas to save himself.

Fanning out rapidly ashore, "I" saw our first Jap and shot him down, unarmed and dazed from shellfire. We were angry at his Aussie belt-buckle and uniform. We now hunted to avenge Aussies.

After that bombardment, the sandspit of White Beach 3 was a perfect obstacle course—all shell-craters and mounds and felled coconut trunks and shattered branches. But it was not over ⅓ wide and backed by mangrove swamps. We cleared it easily while our rifles talked.

While slaying 5-6 straggling Japs, we located that battered AA gun emplacement. Naval gunfire had already smashed it into a scrap-heap. But later, we got official credit for destroying that gun.

For some protection, our radio unit set up close to a mound of debris. While sending, the radio picked up faint Jap voices close by. We realized that we had positioned just 6 feet from the slot of a pillbox that had guarded the AA gun. We opened the top and exploded 2 grenades inside. Talk ceased. We detonated another grenade to be sure that all men were dead.

About 350-400 yards south, a Jap wandered onto the open beach. Koenig lost an unpaid bet to Rifleman Wheat beside him. Elevating his rifle-barrel about 15 degrees, Wheat killed the Jap with one shot. For Missourian Wheat, it was like picking off a squirrel from a branch across a ravine.

Ready to move out again, we found another Nip whom we had bypassed. He saw that we did not want more kills, and cannily asked in English for a cigarette. He said that he thought he was on the California coast. He was sent off to Bn Hq, alive.

With this prisoner's guard on a landing craft, Koenig sent an important message: "I Co down beach ¾ miles. Later, he sent another: "I Co over 1 mile down beach—no activity—main body marked with red flag on beach." Those 2 messages could have averted the holocaust from our Navy Hellcats.

Overhead, we heard the steady drone of planes. They were certainly our planes, and some of us approvingly squinted into the sun at 4 Navy Hellcats pointed from the sea at us. On the open beach, Voorhees stood with 1/Lt Haedicke beside him. Voorhees kept our red identification flag stretched tight. Haedicke would try to wave the planes off with his unwounded left hand. Neither Haedicke nor Voorhees would be hit.

Down from the sky, the planes grew larger. They plummeted at us with a roar and a scream. We stared unbelievingly, then hurled ourselves into the sand or swamp mud.

Slugs patterned the sand, splashed into the mangrove swamp, cracked the fallen coconut palm trunks. The planes skimmed the jungle trees and banked out of sight. Relievedly men rose with grit and mud on their faces and saw bullet dents on the sand. The sound of the planes faded away.

A second time, Hellcat motors thundered as the planes hurtled from the morning sun. One by one, they peeled off and struck at us flat on the beach. Bullets thudded into soft flesh. We cried for Medics while Haedicke and Voorhees tried to signal off the planes.

Despite Communications Sgt Koenig at the radio, Haedicke could not contact 41st Hq, nor the 2 destroyers hovering offshore to fire for us on call. Men were dying from our own planes; we could do nothing to stop the fire.

Perhaps the Hellcats made 4 strafing runs; all men are not agreed on the number. But on the last (perhaps fourth) pass, the 50-caliber slugs found a small Jap supply dump on the beach. There they hit Deese in both legs. Deese was caught in the dump fire. Sgt Allen dashed in among the flames and dragged out the helpless man. After evacuation, Deese died of his wounds. The Hellcats were suddenly gone, as fast as they had come.

There is some doubt about whether or not the planes made fully 4 strafes at us. Leopold and Sgt Sharpe said that they had 3 passes; Sgt Clark and Lt Wholey said that they had 4 passes. Koenig, however, thought that the planes lacked enough ammo for 4 blasts of fire. He also thought that the number of casualties would have been higher for 4 alleged strafes—and that all casualties seemed to happen on the same run. Koenig concluded that there were perhaps 2 observation runs, a partial strafing, and a devastating strafing. But our dead and wounded were everywhere on the beach.

Besides Deese who would die, Mitchell, Van Orden, and Messengill were dead already. Koprada and Sponsler died during the evacuation. "I" had 6 dead, 18 reported wounded. Wounded included 2/Lt Cox, S/Sgts Johnson, Rae, Kroppe, Harden, Mc Cumber, and T/5 Leach. Other wounded were Spino, Christopherson, Thompson, Wilfley, Anderson, Watkins, Musgrove, Williams, Miller, Ashby, and Stotler. (Koenig adds names of Swain and Lenbeck, although not on the official list.) CO Haedicke now let himself be relieved, weak from loss of blood after the bayonet.

Other men were narrowly missed. One man lost a heel. Canteens were holed, helmets and shovels dented. Caliber .50 holes were so thick on the beach that a man could hardly lie down without covering a bullet hole.

What caused Naval Air this tactical error? Koenig thought that because the planes lacked enough targets, the primed pilots had to shoot something. Since I Co's landing was isolated from others, the Hellcat leader must have thought that we were a Nip outfit in retreat. I Co may never know the cause.

The rest of our Hollandia Campaign was mostly just hard work. Next morning, we boarded amphibs to cross Jautefa Bay and land at Pim Village. Climbing a steep, muddy road, we rejoined our Regt about 1600. Next day, 24 Apr, "I" and M's HMGs started west towards Lake Sentani and Hollandia Strips. After the muffled sound of a shot, Brown came to Medics with a joint shot off his left index finger. We saw no fleeing Japs, but hiked peacefully west to the east end of Lake Sentani.

I Co had to hike the north shore road to the Strips, but we found a supply of Jap signal corps bikes to ease our hike. On 25 Apr, our march halted because a Jap AA Btry fired predetermined bursts somewhere on 3/Bn. Our answering fire—probably from 205 FA Bn—was about 50-100 yards short of range. Our guns were not close enough; the Nip gunners escaped.

On 26 Apr, "I" captured, the SE corner of Cyclops Strip. We saw 6-8 old dead Nips, many burned out fighter planes, underground supply rooms with intact equipment—but no live Japs.

On 29 Apr, we secured a flank while I/Bn's B and C Cos attacked some 400 Japs on Hill 1,000. From a flank ridge, we watched 205 FA impact a jungle triangle where the Japs were holding. When the Btry fired for effect, a gun shorted into C Co—killed 2, wounded 2. Shelling halted until range was corrected. Next day, "B" with FA routed the heaviest concentration of Nips in the 41st's Hollandia Operation. I Co was now needed only for patrols.

But why was Hollandia so weakly held—the finest air-sea base in western New Guinea? Of 14,000 Jap effectives at Hollandia, 80-90 per cent were only Service Co men. The Japs' 3 generals arrived in Hollandia late in Mar or early Apr—too late for defense planning. Strong defensive positions were lacking. On 30 Mar-3 Apr, Gen Kenney's 5 Air Force had wrecked 275 of Hollandia's 300 Jap planes, mostly parked wing to wing on the Strips.

And where were Hollandia's infantry defenders? Lt-Gen Hatazo Adachi's 18 Army was too far off—325 miles east on the roadless Guinea Short. Our planes and PT boats controlled the sea. When Jap Hq on 25 Mar ordered Adachi to move one division 215 miles from Wewak to Hollandia, he wisely delayed the move until 18 Apr, too late to fight our landings of 22 Apr. For Adachi wrongly believed that we would strike at Wewak or Hansa Bay, and wanted his men there to fight us. He was thus able to fight the Battle of the

G CO 163 INF (2/Pln):

Death Valley at Zamboanga

by DR. HARGIS WESTERFIELD, Division Historian,
(with another G COMPANY MAN)

*CREDIT: Core of this history is 42 pages of typescript by an author who wants his name withheld. Other sources are 163 Inf's "Zamboanga Journal," "163 Inf Officers' Roster/10 Mar 1945," "V-4 Zamboanga Operation" (Casualty Lists), "Narrative Report" (of 41st DivArty at Zambo), and my own "G Co 163 Inf's Last Battle," from **Jungleer,** Oct. 1963). My sources leave me uncertain about some names. I cannot find last name of BARman "Tony." I preferred to spell name of BIEck with an "e," rather than an "i." This history is more accurate than my 1963 G Co Zambo story—which lacks any mention of "Death Valley."*

*As far as I can find, only detailed and reasonably accurate history of all 163 Inf at Zamboanga is in my own stories. My overall history of Zambo appeared in **Montana in the Wars,** a book placed by Montana American Legion in all public or school libraries in that state. My unit histories have appeared or will appear in **Jungleer.***

After 3 days' seasick voyage down the Sulu Sea on an LCI, G Co 163 Inf's 2/Pln saw Zamboanga Beach-Head under heavy naval-air bomabardment. At daybreak 10 Mar 1945, G's veterans grimly scanned 3 miles of rice-paddies and coconut groves to the Japs' jungle ridges. After 162 beached, we waded through water armpit deep and safely landed at San Mateo, 8 miles west of Zambo City. We crossed the beach before Jap mortars and cannon began blasting the beach and the shipping.

While G Co waited for orders, S/Sgt Detzel's squad of 2/Pln detached to secure battered Jap gun emplacements on a hill until 2/Bn could bring demolition charges for silenced naval guns and AA pieces. From here, Arlie Jackson and Sgt Dulian fired at 4 Japs crossing a clearing. Dulian felled the front man, and Jackson the rear man. With 2 more men's help, we slew the other 2 lying prone. At 200 yards, Dulian's and Jackson's first shots missed a 2-man MG crew on the road. Dulian's second shot killed the man with the tripod; Jackson dropped the man with the barrel, who crawled into the brush.

On 11 Mar at 1400—after F Co captured Santa Maria under fire—G Co turned south through light rifle fire to help 3/Bn seize Zambo City. Under heavy fire from a 3-storey stone building in the business section, we summoned tanks with 75s. When the guns failed to cause a surrender, tanks' and G's fire held the Nip garrison from accurate grenading from windows. Bleck and Jackson of 2/Pln lobbed concussion grenades into the lower floor. Sgt Dulian led a 3-man team in through a window, with S/Sgt Waskovich'es men following. With tommie-gun ready, Dulian and Ford behind him climbed half-way up the stairs to smash the door. The Japs then waved a white flag from the window. Fifty-five Jap men and 3 officers surrendered, of which 55, 15 were wounded, maybe 2 of them seriously wounded.

On 12 Mar, "G" left Zambo City for real combat. Past wrecked Santa Maria Village with 1/Bn on our right across Route 8-A, we headed for the hills—over open ground with Jap FA and heavy mortars exploding shells around us. We advanced through a coconut grove where FA snapped trees off like matches. Mortar shells were mostly tree-bursts. A 20 mm gun pounded terrifically on our left front; MGs lashed out.

A clump of 75 mm shells hit among Detzel's squad and wounded S/Sgt Detzel in arm, shoulder, and leg. Hurrying up to take command, Sgt Dulian passed 2/Lt Tower of another Pln bleeding heavily, his shoulder slashed wide open.

Dulian's squad moved 200 yards farther to a road, crossed it in 2 leaps, and dug holes in the protection of a shallow gully. Waskovich'es squad dug in left of Dulian's. We lay at the edge of a coconut grove with 400 yards of rice paddy ahead, then another coconut grove. Jap shells now slithered over us for the easier target of E Co in support.

Jap FA fire ceased. After lunch, G Co pushed again, beside F Co on the right on Highway 8-A. Crossing the rice paddy into the coconut grove, we gained about 12 feet before pillboxes too close fired suddenly and drove us to earth. They cut off Dulian's scouts Ford and Muirfield. Behind a coconut trunk where 2 pillboxes' fire crossed, Dulian had an MG shear off bark within inches of his face. Jackson took MG bursts in both feet; G Co never saw him again. All G Co was stopped in our tracks, but A Co 716 Tank Bn killed the Jap pillboxes.

On 13 Mar, "G" in reserve moved out behind "E" and "F" after 146 FA shellfire. Probably by now, our tanks had destroyed 6 20 mm guns and an ammo dump, but bullets still whistled close. A steady stream of wounded passed us.

We saw a low hill ahead with an E Co Pln on top, and tanks about 200 yards back from it. As we reached the tanks, a terrific blast lifted the whole hill into the sky. The ground shook; flames shot up 100 feet. Men like sacks of old rags and chunks of rock and equipment flew through the air. Through choking smoke and dust, we heard the call for Medics.

Despite falling debris, and the rock chunk that missed "G" by 20 feet, we rapidly deployed astride Highway 8-A while 2/Bn's Medics all hurried to aid E's casualties. Now Waskovich got orders to take a 5-man recon patrol up 8-A and around Blow-Up Hill. We never expected to see those 5 men again.

While we grimly hoped for their return, a Jap dual 40 mm gun and heavy mortars knocked tree-tops down on us. Peterson in Fields' squad took a wound from a fragment in his shoulder. Another fragment slashed MG-man Heidt in the leg.

The fire ahead almost ceased. We saw 4 of Wasko's 5 re-

284

turning. Mortars had impacted all around them; BARman McCorkle's body was left behind after a direct hit. Although Bates was untouched, Cpl Mechlinski had a bullet in his hand, and Bernie Jones had fragments in his back. Wasko was scratched and bleeding.

Capt Braman then sent Dulian with 3 men and 2 medics with a litter to bring out McCorkle's body. Wasko warned that MG and 40 mm and mortar fire covered the road, with 2 snipers. With Ronny leading and Lamb in the rear, Dulian with Bleck worked up the roadside ditch and around the curve to McCorkle's corpse. Dark hills ringed us, where the pillboxes were. McCorkle sprawled by a tree, badly mutilated, his BAR belt blown up, but his face untouched. We retrieved him without a shot, from Jap or Yank.

On 14 Mar, Sgt Dulian got orders to outpost that deadly curve of Highway 8-A around Blow-Up Hill where McCorkle died. He was to locate Jap positions in what we now called "Death Valley." After preparation from FA, mortars, and Marine Corsairs, Dulian, Ford, Bleck, Lamb, and BARman "Tony" started up the road. From Pln Hq, Griffiths and another unnamed man unrolled wire to set up a phone.

Moving about 400 yards with the cover from roadside brush, we positioned in a thicker clump of brush in that open amphitheater which we had named "Death Valley." Our place was almost perfect for safely hidden observation. An open coconut grove gave a field of fire on our left. We could see 100 yards up the ditch—and all Death Valley to our right.

Suddenly through glasses, Dulian saw a Jap enter a pillbox to the right. Pillboxes lined the opposite side of the valley. BARman "Tony" moved and drew rifle fire. From our left, a rifle cracked a near miss. MGs from pillboxes sprayed; a few mortar shells fell. But no Jap patrol sallied out.

Dulian counted 11 pillboxes and some MGs. Mines were on the road. Several Japs were leaning on the edge of a hillside trench. Although he cupped hands over his glasses, they must have caught the sun. A sniper bullet passed through his sleeve.

Two Gen Sherman tanks clanked up the road. Dulian showed the pillboxes to the tank CO in his open hatch. The tanks charged the Jap lines 200 yards ahead. A "waterfall" of bullets glanced off the tanks; they took direct hits from 40 mm shells. After MG fire, they shot with 75s. The Jap fire suddenly halted. The tanks returned with the CO's report that all pillboxes were dead, and the 40 mm gun on the road also. (That gun or another gun were soon back into action, however.) AT Co men with a truck and a 37 mm gun relieved Dulian's men, but Jap fire drove them from this position.

Dulian's men then joined 3/Pln in reserve and followed F Co with the tanks on the other side of the hill. (Other 2/Pln men were already there.) Two air-strikes and tanks failed to pierce Nippo lines. A Jap rifleman fired most of a clip at Dulian, but missed. A 20 mm shell shot 2 fingers off Sgt Zowara's hand. Gilbert Smith of Dulian's squad took fragments in knee and back.

On 16 Mar, we heard that Japs were retreating on our right—before 1/Bn across Highway 8-A. Roads were jammed with hundreds withdrawing. But on our own right, 20 mm guns opened up again. So at 1000, "G" tried a 2-pronged attack on Death Valley. While T/Sgt Kosing's 1/Pln pushed on our right around Blow-Up Hill, Reese's 2/Pln would fight up Highway 8-A.

Our 2/Pln's 2/Lt Beall ordered us to advance down the road until fired on, then call the waiting tanks. When Waskovich'es and Dulian's squads led out abreast on either side of 8-A, Beall then ordered the 2 scouts out from each squad.

Already 2/Pln was in the open before hundreds of Japs in those hills ringing Death Valley, our scouts moved out 200 feet until 100 yards from Jap lines. Then a Jap rifleman shot at 2/Pln from the rear, and missed by only a few feet. Our scouts hit the ditch. Because the Jap fired too soon and grounded us, their 20 mms and some mortars opened a few seconds too late to wound anybody.

Waskovich and Dulian must crawl up to recall their scouts. Muirfield and Lamb of Dulian's squad were caught on the wrong side of the road grazed by Jap fire. Muirfield leaped across and drew only a few rifle shots. Told to wait a minute, Lamb then jumped to safety, but bullets ripped open his pack. Waskovich'es men also escaped.

Beall called for the tanks. Some mortar shells were impacting the road. Beall sent runner Bombardier to clear the phone wire off the road so that the tanks could not cut it.

As the tanks marched up, Dulian's squad flattened into the best of the meager cover they could get against the searing fire that the tanks would draw. Bates, Varney, Sgts Dulian and Beckman, T/Sgt Reece, 2/Lt Beall—all huddled in a little circle 12 feet wide.

About 30 feet from us, our tanks opened fire. Jap bullets skipped over us. A 20 mm shell glanced from a tank and heated the seat of Dulian's pants and hit the bank a few feet away. Another 20 mm shell plunked a tree 3 feet above ground nearby and broke it in half. One Jap mortar dud thudded into the mud near Beckman and Dulian and stood upright. Beckman turned white when he saw it unexploded over his shoulder.

All fires halted after 20 minutes, but we could not advance. On our right, Kosing's 1/Pln could not kill that 20 mm blocking the road. And our 2/Pln's Bombardier was dead following the tanks. A mortar fragment the size of a bullet had pierced his helmet into his brain. Under heavy rifle fire, 2/Pln returned sadly to last night's perimeter.

Suddenly on 17 Mar, 2/Pln advanced through Death Valley unopposed, past pillboxes 10 feet apart, a silent 20 mm gun on the road, bodies of dead Japs in hundreds. On 18 Mar, with E Co on our left, we entered jungle ridges. Lamb and Dulian found a 4-man Jap outpost unhelmeted on a ridge while eating coconuts, and with their backs turned. Lamb and Dulian killed all 4.

While scouting towards a Jap reported in the brush under a cliff, Dulian reached for a grenade. Suddenly he realized that he was out in the open where the Jap might be drawing a bead on him. Dulian whirled to run, but the Jap bullet left a painful flesh wound in his forearm. While checking the wound with Capt Braman and radioman Armstrong, he saw Armstrong felled by a sniper wound in the shoulder.

After other "G" men repelled a night attack, 2/Pln had more Jap trouble next morning. Bleck of Dulian's squad crashed to earth with a rifle wound while Waskovich and he took up booby traps in early morning. While lighting a cigarette, Dulian's outguard Ford saw a Jap rifle aiming at him from the brush. Ford shot 5 unaimed rounds at him and ran; nobody hit anybody.

But S/Sgt Field died with 2 bullets in his brain while he tried to save wounded scout Fiorello. Dulian now tried to rescue him. BARmen Bates and "Tony" sprayed the brush low, then waited for the Japs to leave. Then Dulian, Lamb, Whip, and "Tony" found Fiorello with a shattered right arm, a bullet in left leg, and 3 more in his chest. But Fiorello survived.

Now down to 17 men of 39 who had landed on 10 Mar, 2/Pln still agonized in mountain patrols on 19-22 Mar. Just before dark 22 Mar, we escaped from a hill position too far advanced where Japs could roll grenades down on us.

On 22 Mar, 2/Pln endured with all G Co on a hill what was our lifetime scare. A Marine pilot with 2 500-lb bombs decided that G Co was Jap—even out on the open hill. Bomb

Drinumor River, that last great battle for New Guinea, fought even after Biak.

As for I Co 186 Inf, our Hollandia Operation gave us 3 episodes of hard luck. After having 80 percent of us down with dysentery on embarking at Finsch, we lost our CO accidentally wounded by his own man. Then our own Navy Hellcats wounded or slew us in a little holocaust on White Beach 3. Such was the dire history of our Hollandia Beachhead. After "easy" Hollandia, I Co was hardened indeed for the fight well on Biak.

Smashed Japanese landing barge and dead Japanese litter the beach at Buna. (Courtesy of Rohlffs)

2/BATALLION, 162 INF HQ CO:

Bradshaw's War Against Roosevelt Ridge

by JOE BRADSHAW
with DR. HARGIS WESTERFIELD, Division Historian

CREDIT: Core of this story is Bradshaw's 13-page typescript, mailed to me from Heidelberg, Victoria, Australia, in Sept. 1980. Other help came from E 162's "Roosevelt Ridge and Berger Hill," written with Don Carlson and Les Dunkin, scheduled for **Jungleer** *in October, 1980. Supporting documents include 162's Journal (9 July-10 Sept. 1943), Col. AR MacKechnie's "Report of Operations of 162 Inf... in Papua, New Guinea," untitled Report of Headquarters, 41st Division Artillery for 1943, Australian David Dexter's* **The New Guinea Offensives**, *and an item from the log of Btry A 218 FA for 14 Aug. 1943. Another source is First Sergeant Ken Dillery's letter of March 1981.*

When black tropical night pounced on 2/Bn 162 Inf's LCMs en route for battle at Tambu Bay on 26 July 1943, a mini-typhoon pounced also. Oppressive black clouds hid the stars. Jammed into a crowded LCM, Cook Joe Bradshaw watched our dark crafts ahead with blue tail-lights as they fought the waves, veered from the course, and twisted back into line again. Men were sea-sick. We feared colliding with a fortified Jap island—to be shot down in our boats.

About 0300 27 July, motors coughed, wheezed to a stop. Our lone Amphib pilot said, "This is Tambu Bay—some doggies and Aussies here already. Make for shore real quiet like. The Nips got the high ground."

About a mile west against the night, Joe noted the dark silhouette of a mountain in a half-circle like a horseshoe. The north arm extended to our right into the sea. This arm was the death-ridge—Roosevelt Ridge.

About 0330, our LCM tried to land. The ramp smashed down into churning surf. As the first heavily armed men leaped into foam, the swirl and the big packs pulled them under. Joe slipped off his pack and held it with his tommie-gun in his right hand. A body washed into Joe; he grappled it and sputtered with that body to shore. Nobody was drowned.

While 2/Bn wrung out clothes and ate hot rations, we heard fire from the NW area of Roosevelt Ridge. With FA help, E and F Cos had made 400 yards up the ridge, but a torrent of shot and shell forced them back. They perimetered on a bench 50 yards below the summit just in time to repel a Nipo counter. Jubilant walking casualties now came back for coffee and soup. One man was hit between the eyes, but the helmet had deflected it to graze the side of his head.

After early supper, Hq called for 20 volunteers for the Ridge. Volunteer Joe drew a telephone set. The other 19 each carried 2 empty water-cans. They cached the cans under underbrush by a little mountain stream and returned to Hq, but Joe carried the phone set up the slippery cliff path to "E."

While he climbed, bits of lead spattered exhausted Joe. He hid behind a tree until the high whine of the long Nip rifle had stopped. Laboring on up, he heard more shooting. He flailed back at the sound with his tommie, then squirmed unhurt into jungle and climbed onward.

As night fell, a dark figure guided Joe into E Co's perimeter, but first asked for water. Other men crawled over feverishly to beg for a mouthful from his canteen, but Joe had drained it in the hot climb. Since he dared not return below in the dark, Joe lay on open ground and chewed a leaf for his thirst. About midnight, Nips fired rifles and automatic weapons at "E," then mortared and threw grenades. We fired back at the flashes; their attack ended with only 2 of "E" wounded.

Wide awake with E Co at sunrise, Joe noticed a steep bluff on the ridge-crest to his right. It loomed like a medieval castle—this stronghold where G 162's Lt Fisher would die a few days later. Speaking hoarsely with dry, swollen tongue, Capt Hill advised Joe to return to safety. E Co would attack that stronghold at 0930

Despite some clumsy Jap shooting, Joe easily glided back downhill to the stream. He guzzled cool, rushing water. Then the rising sun reflected olive paint of a water-can left by the carrying party last night.

Now Joe knew what he had to do—whether or not he wanted to—whether or not anyone ordered him to. He sank the 5-gallon can into the stream until it filled, and heaved it with his tommie gun and pack back uphill to E Co.

As Joe sweated back into E's perimeter. Capt Hill was deploying Plns for the attack while FA fired preparation.

Hill gratefully delayed the push until E's fevered, thirsty men could drain the 5-gallon can. Our FA worked on that bluff on the crest later to be renamed Fisher's Perimeter.

Grinning Hill told Joe, "Seems like them snipers don't cotton to you. If you guard our west flank, you might get even."

E's attack failed. Joe thought that many men were wounded, but they made it back alive without help from others. One slim, bemustached Nordic showed where a bullet had gone through his side. Cheerfully he thanked Joe for the water, sauntered downhill to hospital. Joe never saw him again.

Two hours later, the Nips counter-attacked. They concentrated on our MG emplacement, then feinted before Joe's hidden position on the right flank. They disappeared at the first burst of his tommie. Our MG flamed out the frontal attack. We relaxed with parched throats the rest of the day.

At gray dawn, Joe left his slit trench and again slipped downhill—at such speed that Nippo riflemen above him were banging away without aiming.

Gulping great canteen cups of water over that stream, Joe suddenly had a new idea. If he left pack and tommie at an outpost, he could carry 2 cans of water a trip up to "E." He saw his work and did it. In 8 days of serving E Co, Joe estimated that he carried up 80-100 gallons (15-20 cans) before a regular water detail was formed for E Co.

On 31 July while with "E," Joe cleaned his tommie and joked with men in nearby holes, as he leaned on a tree. When Capt Hill yelled for him, Joe propped his gun against the same tree, and ran towards CP. A terrific explosion knocked him down but did not cut him. Forgetting what he had called Joe for, Hill hurried to where Medics gave aid to the wounded. Joe's tommie was hurled to the ground, its magazine neatly sheared in two.

On 31 July, Joe still carried water. Once as he passed a steep open space, a Jap MG burst missed by a hair-breadth.

Near the stream below, he informed G Co men led by Lt Fisher. At once, a "G" patrol went up to hunt that Jap MG. They found signs of an ambush, but the Japs had left after their fire revealed their positions.

Next morning, G Co passed through "E" to attack the bluff. Later, a wounded "G" man told Joe that Fisher was dead, with many more casualties. All the wounded thought that their attack was suicidal. It was foolish to hit well-prepared positions frontally—better to encircle them.

Now renamed Fisher Perimeter, this Nippo bluff was a rounded hill on Roosevelt Ridge with a mask of heavy jungle where we could see no fox-holes. The hill rose to a level top somewhat triangular. But we did not then have a fair chance to reconnoiter to pinpoint the Japs' holes.

On 2 Aug, Joe became part of a forlorn hope to attack with a new "secret weapon." E Co's Capt Hill ordered 2/Bn Hq Co's First-Sgt Dillery, Hughes, Bradshaw, and Sgt Wright to strike on the right side while Capt Hill's group would strike on the left. Joe and Sgt Wright would take the secret weapon on the right side under Lt Couglin's command.

Jap rifles worried Joe's group on the right until they dropped behind a bank. An officer pointed out their general direction of attack, but they saw only jungle—then realized that no recon had been made.

Sheer love of battle prompted Joe to charge up to hurl the "secret weapon"—a grenade wrapped in gelignite. Luckily, someone tackled him low from behind and dropped him while heavy Jap automatic fire slit the air over his prone body.

We withdrew firing. On the other side of Fisher's Perimeter, Capt Hill took a grenade fragment in the chest and was evacuated. On Joe's side "Pappy Hughes," aged about 40, fell with a grenade sliver hitting over his right eye. First-Sgt Dillery dragged him into a gun-pit, but Hughes was dead at the aid station.

On 4 Aug, a native told 2/Bn Hq's Maj Lowe that the Japs had deserted that section of Roosevelt Ridge which K and L Cos had failed to storm back on 22 July. Joe Ramey, and the Missouri squirrel hunter Sgt Daniel formed a party to investigate. (Ramey was a 2/Bn Hq cook like Joe.)

On that 4 Aug, Joe, Ramey, and Daniel scouted up through jungle to where 2 trails forked before a great open space. From the jungle edge, we looked up a gently climbing draw to a crest shaped like a wide-armed "U." Here were shattered trees and red earth heaved by bombardment. We heard no sound.

Padding up the left trail at over 10-yard intervals, we climbed part way up the Ridge. In the lead, Joe noticed an empty slit trench, hoped that the native was right that the Japs had left. In 5 paces more, Joe saw a stream of sparks fly down through dark brush—a rolling grenade that missed us and exploded.

Jap rifle bullets whizzed by. Joe's tommie hung fire; Ramey's M-1 shot once and jammed. Only Daniel's bolt-action Springfield kept firing—under an avalanche to rifle,

MG, and mortar fire. More grenades sparked down to explode. All this fire came from left of the "U" rim, but heavier fire began from the right.

Despite the fire, Joe on the ground had field-stripped his tommie and now fired from left to right at the Japs above. Dropping to earth on the brow of the slope, he hit a soft mound. It was a Yank body; he jerked off the exposed dog-tags and pocketed them with another set from another body 4 feet away. Meanwhile, he kept firing at a circle of Jap shadows firing at him.

Joe rolled farther back down the draw to shelter behind the log, again sprayed the bushes with his tommie in a half-circle. After he had rolled another 10 yards, Ramey's M-1 no longer jammed and Daniel's Springfield still shot to quiet the ridge-crest. Finally safe at the trail fork, Joe fired his last bullets. After we left, the Japs still wasted intermittent fire on that ground.

After a day's rest, we 3 reconnoitered that part of Roosevelt Ridge projecting 1/4 mile into Tambu Bay. We also nosed part way up that shallow saddle 100 yards from where the Ridge started projecting into the sea. As we drew Jap fire from 3 sides, heavy mortar fire slapped the beach behind us, but we could not locate the mortars. Days later, we found that they were not behind the Ridge, but behind the next ridge (B Ridge) 600 yards NNW.

With Bn Hq kitchen short of help, Ramey had to quit the partols, but Joe and Daniel were ordered to examine the Ridge end to end. We were to avoid combat, but to pinpoint Jap positions.

Hearing heavy fire from Fisher Perimeter on 12 Aug, we learned that G 162 had taken it in the way it should have been taken long ago. G's Capt Munkres had spent several days observing it from concealment near Scout Ridge. After sustained frontal FA cannonade, Munkre's men attacked the Japs' rear. Our big guns drove the Japs from their pits. When they ran back towards them after the shelling, their own holes flamed sudden death from our men who had seized them and were firing from them. They helped "F" and "G" to storm the nearby crest. The Japs still held 500 yards of the Ridge eastward to the end of the peninsula.

Early on 14 Aug, before the Great Bombardment began before 162 stormed the Ridge-peninsula, Daniel and Joe guided 50-100 men into their assault position 30 yards below the crest. Hidden on the edge of the ridge-top jungle, we watched Japs in the open below us, talking, laughing, grunting.

Came then the Great Bombardment of the eastern end of Roosevelt Ridge. About 20 B-24s and B-26s bombed it. At 1315, 218 FA's 75s, 205 FA's 105s (and perhaps an attached 155 mm gun), Aussie 25-pounders and Bofors AA guns of 209 FA and 162 FA—all pounded the Ridge. Our DivArty claimed that 20 guns fired 2,228 rounds. (Btry A 218 FA alone fired 236 rounds that day.)

But we men on the Ridge clutched the ground in fear. Some shells fell short near us; fragments ricocheted and screamed around us. Concussion lifted us off the ground, or belted us like boxers' fists. We fought nausea, the urge to break and run.

Suddenly the guns stopped their thunder. A green wall of us stormed into the Jap ground. Jumping over mangled bodies, we tossed grenades into bunkers and heard screams and crazy laughter. We mowed down Japs who tried to fight.

Our 2/Bn 162 Inf had triumphed on Roosevelt Ridge. The Japs would soon evacuate even what they still held of the western crest. But ahead of 2/Bn and all other 162 outfits lay harder combat. We still had to overrun "B" and "D" Ridges to capture Salamaua Town. Joe Bradshaw would scout or fight for his life on B, C, and D Ridges for many more days.

A COMPANY, 163 INFANTRY:

Fighting The Sanananda Road-Bend Perimeters

by DR. HARGIS WESTERFIELD, Division Historian,
with help of DR. LEEON ALLER

*CREDIT: Basis of this second story of A 163 at Sanananda is 41st Div Training Note No. 2 (19 May 1943) with sketches probably by A's CO, Lt Howard McKinney. Dr. Leeon Aller supplied this Training Note from his papers after Federal Archives could not locate it. Also useful were Dr. Samuel Milner's **Victory in Papua** and my earlier Sanananda history of A Co, No. 55 in **Jungleer**. Where my earlier story disagreed clearly with this training Note, I have taken data from this Training Note as being more reliable. I also used official casualty lists which were unavailable to me when I wrote the earlier story. (I have published stories of A Co on Wakde and Biak also. But I still need somebody to help me with A 163 in the Battle of Zamboanga.)*

On 16 Jan 1943, A Co 163 Inf began our final 5 days' heavy combat at Sanananda. On this 16 Jan, we spearheaded 1/Bn's push to liquidate Jap Perimeters S-T-U guarding the road-bend NE of Fisk Perimeter. These 3 perimeters were the surviving hard core of Jap resistance at Sanananda.

In this 1/Bn attack, Capt Van Duyn's C Co was to work its way through lightly held Jap jungle and envelope "S" in the rear. But our A Co had to blast its way straight into Perimeter S. Aussie FA harassed "S" the night before.

A Co bivouacked as comfortably as well as we could 100 yards inside heavy jungle that night. Next morning after hot breakfast, we stacked packs, loaded ourselves with ammo and 2 grenades, then formed for action.

Initially, our preparatory fire seemed fine. Aussie FA barraged, beginning at 0945. D's HMGs sprayed jungle brush on both flanks of 1/Bn's front. From east of Fisk, M's HMGs searched Jap areas on our right to SE and south. At 0957, all 15 81s of D, H, and M Cos blasted from Musket. At 0959, 3/Bn's 60s—in battery south of Fisk—arced their shells down on the Japs.

But to A Co's CO, Lt McKinney, it seemed that FA and mortars impacted too far behind the Nippo front. But when he phoned to place fire closer to the Japs, an 81 short had cut the wires to Col Lindstrom. He could not change the fire.

All told, 163 Inf fired 894 shells of caliber 81, and 789 of caliber 60. MGs shot 6,000 rounds of 50s, and 21,350 rounds of 30s. But only 100 FA shells hit Jap territory. So bunkers were not flattened; McKinney thought that most of our steel had missed the targets. Then before we cleared the assembly area, a mortar short killed or wounded several "A" men.

With C Co abreast, "A" moved out on an 800-yard front. From the jungle edge, many of us saw our battle-field for the first time—100 yards' flat kunai opening, with Jap jungle on 3 sides. Since FA had plowed the ground for days, it was covered with fallen trees, occasional stumps 10-25 feet high, and sparse, 2-foot kunai. Shell-holes and depressions among stumps were hiding prone Jap skirmishers.

With 3/Pln flanking the road to our right, and 2/Pln on the left, we moved out for combat. Each Pln deployed 2 squads forward as skirmishers, and kept a third in squad column.

We crawled across our line of departure; Jap fire was already heavy. Snipers shot down from behind tall trees behind the strongpoint on 3/Pln's right. We brought our LMGs up to our right front and expelled those snipers.

When a LMG and a HMG crossfired on "A," we thought we killed both guns. Our riflemen fired on possible targets now and then, and kept crawling up. (Our tommies did not shoot; they smoked and drew Nippo fire.) In position behind trees on our right rear, A's 60s lobbed in shells to help a little, but Jap bunker roofs were too thick for them.

Jap fire stopped our crawling advance within 20 yards of the Jap bunkers. The combination of bullets in the flat kunai and an estimated 4 Jap MGs was too much for us. Sun blazed; air in the kunai flat was dead and still. Experienced in this kind of fighting, Jap gunners did not rake the grass. They fired at the base of any kunai grass that moved, and struck "A" men.

Under this hidden fire, many "A" men collapsed from heat or nerves. Two officers, 18 men collapsed from heat exhaustion. When our LMGs emptied, snipers re-manned the trees and shot down again on us.

Although trapped under this fire, "A" showed high morale. Occasionally, McKinney heard a man say, "I'm hit," saw him crawl to the rear. Water was just 6 inches below kunai, and unhurt men dug seeps to bathe faces and quench thirst of wounded cobbers.

Wounded were McKinney's runners and 2 unnamed Medics. A third unnamed Medic crawled under fire with sulfa and drugs for those shot down, and stayed untouched.

By now, Lindstrom had the severed phone wire spliced, but "A" was too close to the Japs now to call for 81s on the bunkers. Lindstrom ordered a "B" Pln to attack on the right to relieve pressure, but Jap fire grounded B's Pln. "B" did slacken Jap fire, to some extent.

About 1200, Lindstrom ordered withdrawal from this hopeless attack. To rescue 2/Pln and 3/Pln, he despatched 1/Pln from reserve. Covered by our "A" Pln and B's men, the trapped "A" men started to worm out through the kunai. From under guns of the Jap strongpoint on the far right, 3/Pln began retreat. They crawled to left rear behind covering Plns still in line, then back into jungle. They helped their wounded; not 1 man was left to die.

Then the covering Plns blasted their way out again. As dusk confused Jap aim, our last man escaped. We had 12 dead: Cpl May, Belchak, Bunker, Harder, Wells, Strobach, Leo Johnson, Henderson, Taubert, Rowland, Chambers, Tatarski—who died at 12 Portable Hospital. We had 1 wounded, all but 1 marked "seriously," and all gunshot wounds. Rundelli and Allen were shot in the back, Jicha in right ankle, Bashor and Casciato in right leg, Howell in right hip. Rash was wounded in left foot, Ed Olson in left thigh, T/Sgt Skedsvold in lower thigh and leg, with side of body unspecified. Hit in right shoulder were Del Sasso, Cpl Wittlieb, Sgts Lawson and Webber; and Hillebrand in right wrist. S/Sgt Wolcott took a bullet in left hand, Taylor in left arm, Cpl Dorris in left elbow, with a complete fracture of his right arm. Hinrichs was marked "slightly wounded," part of body unspecified.

Despite A's 12 deaths, 18 wounded, our fight of 16 Jan was a success. For with opposition light on the left of 1/Bn's 800-yard front, Lindstrom made a fine tactical move. He sent "C" with most of "B" in reserve to sweep around the right flank of the Jap lines. There we dug Perimeter AD—200 north of the Jap perimeters extending 800 yards south to Sanananda Road. Then all remaining "A" men and the last "B" Pln reinforced them. Meanwhile, Col Doe had sent Rankin's 2/Bn across the jungle from Killerton Track to team with Lindstrom. Now the Japs were cut off from the sea; "A" could probe for a soft spot—and go in to kill.

After our sunstruck repulse of 16 Jan, A Co huddled into shallow mud-holes. At dawn 17 Jan, Nips fusilladed and grenaded our holes, but with no reported casualties.

On 17 Jan, we were out of combat all day to bring up food and ammo, and regroup. Our decimated riflemen reorganized from 3 down to 2 Plns. Capt Reams' K Co joined us, but "K" was also low in manpower; together, "A" plus "K" was almost 1 company of normal size before battle.

To fight on 17 Jan, we patrolled SE and S to find main Jap positions. Late on 17 Jan, a Pln patrol spotted 3 Jap bunkers of logs and earth on the far side of a kunai patch 75 yards wide. On 17 Jan, Hagedorn was shot in the right leg.

On 18 Jan, "A" and "K" teamed to fight those Japs—but with the fewest losses possible. After a short advance beside us, "K" took MG fire on the left—but across the road in the recon zone of 2/Bn. Both Cos fell back to our assembly area, then started off to the right to avoid Jap bullets.

On this second try, we got lost in jungle for an hour, but found ourselves on the new supply trail "K" had cut for 2/Bn. Soon Jap fire crackled ahead, but we advanced until heavier fire halted us, but without casualties. Dark was coming; we ate and dug our bedrooms for safety.

After breakfast 19 Jan, we made a well-supported frontal attack. While HMGs—perhaps M's—covered our right, we pushed our own LMGs well out in front to protect our rifles. With "K" on left flank, "A" gained ground at first. Then our riflemen advanced so far that they masked our MGs. The Japs rose up and stopped us. "K" captured a Jap Bren gun, and killed a few Nips. "A" lost 2 killed, 7 wounded. Livermore and Vojtech were killed. Murray was wounded in right arm and left shoulder, Rivera in right hip, Cox in right leg. S/Sgt Christian Hanson was shot in left center of his back, Veselka in left shoulder, Hayes in left foot. Area of Mack's wound was unreported in casualty lists.

As "A" settled down for the night, Jap 40 mm mortar shells fell around us. Our light mortars arced in the direction of the Jap detonations and stopped the fire. These Jap mortars reopened during the night, but our 60s were still on target and silenced their fire.

At dusk that night, a wounded Jap had crawled into K's lines. He probably saved many Yank lives. He said that we were ramming straight into Jap Headquarters—into the fire of a trench system with 10 MGs. We planned to miss them.

On 20 Jan, "A" mainly stayed quiet while I Co pushed north towards us—against the Jap perimeter between us which we later found to be 800 yards wide. Next day, we attacked to finish off the Jap road-bend perimeters.

At 1015 21 Jan, after "A" and "K" pulled back 150 yards, FA blasted the last Jap bunker line. As FA quieted at 1030, the Musket battery of 15 81 mortars pounded the Japs, and a Pln of HMGs combed brush and trees around the kunai opening. It was good to see our preparatory fire rip up the jungle edge.

As mortars took up the fire, A's 2 remaining rifle Plns advanced. Our attack formation was in column of Plns. With a squad in reserve, our lead Pln moved in. Left squad went as skirmishers across the deep kunai; right squad filed through hampering jungle in squad column. A combat patrol from D's HMG men secured our right flank beyond our right squad; K Co kept up on our left.

Already, our assault fire started. From FA shells to mortar fire to MG traverses to A's rifle-reports—there was no lull in Yank fire.

This time, "A" struck right to avoid the 10 Jap MGS reported on the left by our Jap prisoner. Crossing the Nip main line, we counted 88 dead already from FA, mortars, HMGs. Then Japs were breaking from their lines and fleeing down our front; without orders, our lead Pln's supporting squad closed to help the killing.

But "A" killed only 20-25; main Jap flight was down Sananada Road towards the Bismarck Sea which they would never reach. And these half-starved, feverish men ran in front of blood thirsty "A" Co. After pushing to the road, "A" sent a Pln to the right to mop up the edges, and "K" sent a Pln to the left for the same job. Securing the road with a Pln, "A" then went back the way we had come to slay those Nips who would not surrender—who hid out or shammed death.

While striking for the road, "A" had fanned out and helped "B" and "C" who were still held up. When Jap eased up, "B" and "C" surged ahead and liquidated the fronts that had hitherto blocked them off.

All told, 163 with FA slew 530 Nips; yet 163 altogether lost just 1 killed, 6 wounded. A Co reported no casualties. It was the largest single days kill since the Aussie victory at Gorari, in the jap retreat from their attempt to capture Port Moresby over the Kokoda Trail. On that great day of 21 Jan 1943, CO McKinney credited FA, mortars, MGs for perfect fire support. The main Battle of Sanananda was now all but ended. Remained only the great attack of 22 Jan by I and L Cos, which attack "A" did not share. But "A" had well avenged the loss of 12 dead and 18 wounded which we had taken in the sunstruck kunai on 16 Jan 1943.

218 FIELD ARTILLERY:

Toem, Wakde, and Maffin Bay

by DR. HARGIS WESTERFIELD, Division Historian

> CREDIT: Most important sources are untitled 24-page typescript history of Btry A 218 FA in World War II, and 36-page legal-size typescript, "218 Field Artillery Battalion/Annual Historical Report, with RR Smith's **Approach to the Philippines**. Other sources include "Sarmi Campaign Unit Journal/Sept. 1-14 Dec. '44," handwritten diary of Service Battery 218 FA untitled, Col Grant Green's letter 8 July 1944, and Allied Geographical Section's Terrain Handbook 26, on Sarmi. I would have never written this story but for T/4 Lloyd Willis who sent me his Btry A history. But without a living narrator, I still had hard work to pull out enough facts for this story. Can any reader help me with another 218 story over the same area, or other battery histories? (In 218 FA, Willis' achievement was in making use of worn gas-check pads and taking the play out of gun cradles.)

On 15 May 1944, 218 FA Bn left bivouac forever on red-dusty Pancake Hill near Hollandia Town to load for battle for Wakde Island and Maffin Bay. By dark, we had boarded 3 LSTs for the Wakde action. After Wakde fell, we would help formations not in the 41st Div to fight Maffin Bay Japs, while 947 FA was on Biak in our place. For over 6 months, we fired for these outfits in succession: 158 Inf, then elements of 6, Div, 31 Div, and 33 Div. In that spooky Toem jungle, we had to guard our perimeters, and train guns to fight in all directions. Btry A even fought off Jap grenadiers blasting our gun-pits.

At 0740 17 May after watching the Navy blast Wakde Island, our advance parties landed on the Toem Foreshore. Deep seas offshore forced us to build a sand bag ramp to land our guns; we could not leave our LSTs until 0940. Positioned 3 miles east of our landing, Btry B was ready to fire by 1020. Btry A registered 17 rounds on Wakde, from 1226 to 1258; by 1300, we had all guns aimed on Wakde. From 1449 to 2220, Btry A fired 274 rounds—and that night 94 more harrassing rounds.

On that same 17 May, Capt Lorraine Smith and his Btry A observers landed from a transport and marched with G 163 from Arare Village to Tementoe Creek, east boundary of the beachhead. Smith tried to set up his OP near the coast, where G Co's perimeter endured Jap harassment. At 0815 18 May, mortar, MG, and rifle fire broke out. Cpl Pulver tried to set up his radio under threat of Jap fire, was hit in the head to die later. Blanchard and Capt Smith on either side of him were not hit, however.

While observing on the beach, Smith's men saw G Co attacked at 0830, and G's Barnes killed. Smith's men tried to register Btry A again at 0900, but Jap fire made observation impossible on this morning.

On 18 May, before 163 Inf assaulted Wakde, our turn to fire came after naval and air bombardment, 0700 to 0825. At 0830, we blasted Wakde for 23 minutes, along with other outfits of 191 FA group. Btry A fired 123 rounds from 0848 to 0901. (Between 1157 and 1315, Btry A helped prepare for the later mainland offensive west from Tor River toward the Jap 36 Div Regts holding Sarmi. After registering 21 rounds westward, we turned all guns but No. 4 back east.)

Our 218 FA's 155 mm howitzers failed to penetrate the Japs' deep coral emplacements on Wakde, but we got credit for one firing mission. When C 163 tried to cross Wakde Strip to the north shore, intense Jap MG fire cut off the advance squads from C's main body. With 167 FA's help, 218 FA temporarily silenced the Jap MGs and got all of "C" across on their second try.

As mentioned already, even as early as Wakde assault day, 218 FA began firing from near Toem across the wide Tor River. Across the Tor—and moving to attack us from the jungle south of Toem also—were about 11,000 Japs of 223 and 224 Inf, with some Jap Marines and 8 75mm cannon. We had to fire on Japs closing in from the dark southern jungle. We also had to fire west across Tor River to help regiments that would push against the Japs holding Maffin Bay and Sawar and Sarmi Strips.

On 19 May, 2/Lt Mead and T/4 Marshall with Tracy and Walker (ranks unspecified) became Btry A's observer party for 3/Bn 163 Inf on board Tor River west of Toem. Jap pressure was strong. On that 19 May, Btry A fought the Japs with 232 rounds, almost our top score of heavy 155 shells fired in one day in the whole operation.

About 1800 that 19 May, Bn Hq reported 500 Japs between us and 163's perimeters, but we never saw them. That swampy jungle close to the narrow beach was a spooky place of many dark rumors. B Co 641 TD sent 20 men to us that night for more security. One man nervously fired at our aiming stakes lights.

On 20-21 May, Btry A fired just 86 shells. On 22 May, Lt-Gen Walter Krueger gave our Hurricane Task Force orders that kept 218 FA detached from our 41st Div for some 7 months. Krueger feared that Wakde Strip was still unsafe until he saw what the Japs' main army could do. While 163 Inf still secured Toem Foreshore, he ordered newly come 158 Inf to smash Jap concentrations westward and put them on defensive. Then followed bitter fighting long afterwards, that kept 218 FA in action months after 163 left to fight on Biak.

Moved to a new position west of Arare, we had to fire westward along 3 miles of beach and jungle. We had to help 158 Inf and later the 6 Div across Tor and Tirfoam Rivers, and to capture Lone Tree Hill, a maze of jungle, cliffs, and caves.

On 23 May, Btry A registered and fired 61 rounds, and on 24 May, 141 rounds. On 24 May also, 218 FA with 147 FA Bn (of 158 Inf's combat team) with M 158's mortars fired to help K and L 158's advance west of the Tor. Later that day also, 167 FA marked with smoke the position of a Jap mountain gun that still held out after pinning down an L 158 advance the day before. We then threw in heavier shells into the smoke over that gun. A few days later, scouts found that there had been two guns instead of one. Both were still operational, but silent, with 23 dead Japs around them.

On 25 May, Btry A fired 220 shells to help 158 Inf cross Tirfoam River 1.5 miles west of the Tor, and secure Maffin No. 1 Village on the coast. Then 158 with our observers went forward to strike the eastern slope of Lone Tree Hill, a coast position tenaciously defended. Of 22 rounds, "A" fired 62, 0817 to 0843. At 1410-1543, we fired 125 shells around a truck and evidently nearby Japs and a supply dump.

On that 25 May, we used an observation party in a buffalo to call fire on japs near Maffin No. 1. A Jap shell holed the buffalo and drove the party to cover. Radio and other equipment were endangered. Cpl Hale, the machine-gunner, rushed back to start the engine and withdraw the buffalo.

For our gunners, Piper Cub observers were invaluable. Flying in danger at 500-800 feet, they saw gun emplacements and bivouac areas hidden from ground observers. They called fire on a strategic Jap bridge over Woske River, maybe 2 miles past Lone Tree Hill. With 33 rounds from 1533 to 1610, Btry A got 2 direct hits and destroyed the bridge. Piper Cubs helped 218 FA to impact several AA guns and bivouac areas.

While battling for 158 Inf, we knew nothing of Jap plans to overrun our beach-head by attacks from the southern jungle. Matsuyama Force and Yoshino Force—each about 2 Bns strong—planned to hit Toem Foreshore together. Luckily, blind jungle kept them from coordinating. They struck 3 days apart.

On the night of 27-28 May, Col Matsuyama's men broke through 163's lines to the beach, yet were repelled. But Col Yoshino did better the night of 31 May-1 June.

Despite small raids close by during 26-31 May, 218 FA was firing as ordered. Btry A shot 62 rounds 26 May, 47 on 27 May. While "A" loosed 155 shells on 29 May, Capt Platts flew 5 miles inland over Jap mountains in his unarmed Piper Cub. After marking a known target with smoke, he still flew low returning. Drawing fire from a hidden AckAck position, Platts hovered above it and called down fire that destroyed the gun.

On 30 May, Btry A's Sigler spotted 2 Japs just 30 yards from No. 4 gun. But over 600 rounds of .30 HMG bullets missed them. Our instant patrol found no Japs in the brush. "A" fired 225 shells that 30 May.

On the night of 31 May-1 June, Yoshino Force hit 4 Ack-Ack gun positions unwisely isolated along the beach east of Arare Village. After damaging 2 40 mm guns, they were repelled. Luckily, our Btrys B and C had that day moved 4,000 yards east of their old positions; but Btry A had a wild night fight. The 2 escaped Japs of 30 May had surely pinpointed our guns.

At 2005, 2 hours before the quarter-moon rose, 8 Japs tried to blow up Btry A's guns. Sgt Smith first saw the Jap rush and fired. But 3 grenadiers leaped between Guns No. 3 and 4 and lobbed 5 grenades into 9 men trying to rest in No. 3's gun pit. Three of the 5 grenades exploded.

Just before the grenades hit, Uzarewicz heard a yell, "Don't let the bastards get away!" Luckily, Uzarewicz turned on his face so fast that he left his hand still behind his back against his belt. His wounded hand may have saved him from paralysis with a fragment in his spine. Uzarewicz, Wertanen, and Cpl Fontana took serious wounds in their buttocks and the small of their backs. Hospitalized also were Golley and S/Sgt Joe Smith—location of wounds not mentioned. Some time in the attack, Cpl Klocko and T/5 Halm were gunshot in their left shoulders.

At No. 4 gun, 3 Japs died trying to grenade us. Rittenhouse and Preston each slew one with his LMG. Vandehey scatthed the third Jap with a .50 HMG. One Jap was an officer with a sketch of our positions and written orders to kill our guns.

At 0530, 4 Japs tried again to blow up Btry A's guns. One crossed the road opposite us and charged Gun No. 3 with a mine bound to 2 charges of TNT. Johnston and Killion both shot him. He fell on his explosives; they blew his shattered body 10 feet high. (Johnston and Killion both fought in pain from grenade slashes in the earlier attack.)

Two other Japs rushed behind Gun No. 3 but were slain. One dying Jap fell into our hole, but Fox threw the Jap's mine safely from the hole away from himself. We found an unexploded mine 10 yards before No. 3 gun. Apparently 2 Japs had lurked in the brush but could not get near enough to the gun to hurl their mine.

About 0730, another Jap hovered near the brush, but our MGs missed him. At the east end of Btry A's perimeter, Estepp and Williams killed 2 more Japs across the road. That night of 31 May-1 June, Btry A killed 8 Japs. We lost no men killed but had 6 wounded and evacuated.

After 1 June, we had no more attacks. While 163 left Toem to reinforce Biak, 218 FA (with 167 FA and B 641 TD) remained behind for 158's offensive across the Tor. On the night of 3 June, a few Japs broke through infantry positions, but 218 FA's fire helped stop them. On 4-5 June, Btry A shot 351 rounds.

On 6-7 June, 158's 1/Bn and 2/Bn recrossed Tor River. (They had withdrawn east to guard Toem after 163 left, until 6 Div relieved them.) On 6-7-8 June, Btry A fired 671 rounds to guard 158's Tor Bridgehead and help 158 to the east bank of Tirfoam River, about 2 miles. On 10 June, a Jap 75 on the beach between Snaky River and Lone Tree Hill harassed 1/Bn 158 for awhile. A 155 howitzer of ours got a direct hit and killed that gun.

On that same 10 June, 218 FA observers saved the lives of perhaps two 158 men. Ripani went forward under intense MG and rifle fire to evacuate a wounded man. Phone operator Walt Miller also advanced in direct line with heavy Jap fire to save a wounded infantryman.

We then helped newly arrived 6 Div to conquer Lone Tree Hill in a 10-day fight, through 30 June. On 3 July, our 155s prepared for that 6 Div to seize Hill 225 and Maffin Strip. The main Maffin Bay fight was now ended. By 9 July, 6 Div needed to advance no more against the decimated Jap Regts. Wakde Strip and Maffin Bay staging area were secured.

But even after 6 Div left for other operations by 26 Aug, 218 FA stayed near Toem as security for 31 Div and then 33 Div's 123 Inf. These rooky outfits held the area, and got their first combat training from the surviving Japs, who fought well when prodded.

On 18 July-31 Aug, 218 hardly fired at all—just 207 shells. "B" fired none! We had fatigue details, training, and sports. Some men got furloughs. We averaged rotation home of 15 men monthly, had 3 sets of replacements. Begining 11 Aug, we supplied 200 men for ship details.

By 1 Sept, 218's fire tripled to 687 rounds by 14 Dec. Beginning 18 Sept, each Btry took a fortnight turn in an advanced position across Tor River on Maffin Bay. Here we ranged the Sawar area to quell Jap activity. On 29 Sept, Btry A performed 218's final notable action of the operation. With 21 rounds, Gun No. 2 destroyed a Jap cannon.

Now 218 FA's time was up at Toem-Maffin Bay. On 14 Dec, orders came to turn in our 155s to Ordnance for replacement. After firing 12,119 rounds since 16 May, they needed repairs. When we arrived "home" to the 41st on Biak, after leaving Toem on 14 Dec, Gen Doe had new M-1 guns waiting for us.

And 218 FA had completed an important combat mission. From Wakde Strip, our bombers had smashed Japs in New Guinea and the Central Pacific. We had helped shatter forever 2 Jap regimental combat teams. We had supported elements of 3 Divs in their first battle experience. Toem and Maffin Bay were now an important staging area for noncombat transports to load troops into amphib craft or transports for new beach-heads. With few casualties, 218 FA had fought well.

L COMPANY 163 INFANTRY:

War Of Nerves At Davao

**by DR. HARGIS WESTERFIELD, Division Historian,
with CAPTAIN WILLIAM F. SCHACHT**

> CREDIT: This story is first half of 66-page typescript extracted from Schacht's original Diary, including his fine maps. Other sources include L 163's Capt. Jack Arnold's Diary, RR Smith's **Approach to the Philippines**, "3rd Bn. Journal/V-5 Operation Davao, Mindanao/From May 10 to July 10, 1945," and "24 Div. Rpt. Mindanao." (Last half of Schacht's typescript supplies main source of forthcoming story about L 163's front-line combat from Ula to Riverside to Calinan.)

On 10 May 1945, L Co 163 Inf with other 3/Bn men got orders to leave delightful Jolo Island and reinforce 24 Inf Div's Davao Operation in southern Mindanao Island. Breaking camp at 0400 12 May, 3/Bn was on LCIs and LSTs by 1717. Topside, we watched rich green Jolo drop behind us into the Sulu Sea. Only Mounts Bahu and Tumatangas stood up longer until the sea swallowed them.

Ahead of us were weeks of often bewildered detachment from our own 41st Div into our rival 24 Div. First came days of nerve-wracking guard duties and sudden moves among Davao Japs. We often exchanged fire with them. Then came our sweat-soaked battle in black abaca jungle to take Riverside-Calinan. Fighting was often as hard as at Sanananda.

At dawn 14 May, the second day from Jolo, our little 12-ship convoy passed captured Zamboanga City and turned NE to round southern Mindano and turn into Davao Gulf. Rumors were that the Japs were harassing the shore with big guns.

Landing at Talomo at sunrise 15 May, we heard FA blasting a few miles inland. Although 24 Div held 80 miles of coast, Japs held the ridges only 1-2 miles inland.

Past the usual coastal flats of coconut palms, we saw a thickly populated country of numerous isolated houses and small villages. Surprising and scaring were rugged and rocky mountains, with beautiful snow-caps. We feared that we would soon have to fight among them.

By 1400, 3/Bn had scattered among trucks to guard approaches to Davao City, on the eastern side of Davao River. K Co fragmented into 8 detachments to guard 3 bridges and 5 road-junctions. I Co occupied Flattop Hill. Bn Hqs with AT Pln was on Hill 120 above Davao River.

Our L Co went to Dry Gulch Hill. Trucked to Davao River, we had to ferry over. Just 2 days ago, the Japs had blown the bridge. We drove through the shattered ruins of Davao City. After 9 miles, we left the main road north of Davao for Dry Gulch Hill.

Morale hit bottom. Dry Gulch Hill was 300 feet high, and full of shell holes and studded with barren tree snags. Sun blazed down viciously hot; corpses of 40 dead Japs reeked from shallow holes. We did not have to dig in, for A Co 19 Inf left us their holes full of red mud. Japs were on 3 sides of us, we heard, and nearest neighbors were I 163, 1800 yards west, on Flattop Hill.

Worst of all, we were totally disarmed for night combat. We even lacked grenades! Weapons Pln had no mortar shells and MG belts. Hq had no communications equipment. Grenades and Weapons ammo and wire had been shipped in boxes. Evidently 163 Hq on Jolo thought that 24 Div Hq would let us equip ourselves on the beach. We now dreaded what else 24 Div would do to us orphans.

Luckily, no Japs attacked that night of 14-15 May. If they had known that we had no grenades or FA on call, it could have been a bad night of close combat with rifles and bayonets.

On 15 May, 3/Pln patrolled but found nothing in a 500-yard radius. Then weapons ammo and wire arrived. We quickly equipped ourselves. About 1400, a Jap MG opened up. Our mortar barrage quieted the MG. A knee mortar shelled us. We called for a heavy FA barrage that silenced the mortar. Meanwhile at 1600, 3 Jap FA rounds hit nearby. About sunset, I Co 1800 yards westward took MG and FA fire that wounded 2 men. Japs were just 200 yards north, on Highway 12. Yet our night was quiet. (We had heard that our only duties for 24 Div would be to act as security guards in rear areas!)

On 17 May, "L" continued our strange security guard. When 1/Pln patrolled 1,000 yards from our hill, they were inside 50 yards of chattering Japs at Road Junction 5 on Highway 13, north of us. Returning, 1/Pln suddenly saw dead Nips 500 yards north of "L." While we patrolled, I Co on Flattop Hill took mortar blasts and countered with 60s and M Co's 81s. The Japs began a little "banzai," which failed.

Things improved for 3/Bn. With the Davao Bridge rebuilt, all Bn equipment arrived. Bn Hq now had a fine building in Davao; company kitchens were set up there. A few from each Co could go on leave into Davao.

On his visit, Schacht examined the fine buildings that were shell-gutted. New markets, stores, and barber shops were flourishing. He saw many Filipino men in white with straw hats, and women in flowery dresses with lipstick and rouge on their faces. But they did not seem friendly, as in Zambo and Jolo. After all, Davao was known as "Little Tokyo" because of Jap colonization. At 3/Bn Hq, Schacht was happy to shave and shower and put on clean clothes before returning to the Dry Gulch hell.

Fear came to L Co that evening: our first Jap rocket. From behind a ridge some 1800 yards NW, the first rocket slowly glided at us—clearly seen with its stream of red flame and black smoke.

When that first rocket soared, we were unsure whether to hit a hole, or see whether it was coming close, and then run. Most of us holed up. It shook L Co and fired brush 200 yards behind us. Nip mortar rounds hit also, but we thought of them as mere pebbles, contrasted to the new rockets. This rocket was like a piece of dynamite 3 feet long by 1.5 feet in diameter, with fins that dropped off in flight. We feared that other rockets would be more accurate, but they were not.

Schacht bedded down in his hole again—a former Jap bombshelter, safe under palm logs. Rats kept waking him, scuttling and rustling nearby. The night before, he awoke with one sitting on his knee appraising him.

On 18 May, L's 2/Pln scouted in a 1,000-yard radius—to Road Junction 5 north, and Davao Race Track east. They found only Jap debris—boots and rice bowls. (M Co at 700 yards distance detected and disarmed 6 mines—all 500-lb. bombs.)

On 20 May, "L" got orders to leave corpsed-up Dry Gulch Hill for Davao City. (We left 24 Div's 19 Inf to fight north on the east bank of Davao River, then turn west to defeat Rear Admiral Doi's infantry and Marines at Mandog. Our own 3/Bn would later get a harder battle assignment with 34 Inf.)

Relieved into Davao City, "L" found a day of heaven. "Heaven" was a concrete floor of a shell-torn old garage with part of the tin roof remaining to deflect that night rain. At church services that night, L Co men sang hymns on the old garage driveway while the sun sat in a heavy cloud-bank. All the strangeness and beauty of religion was once again with Schacht as he stretched out his tired body and relaxed in dreams.

On 21 May, "L" made another repulsive perimeter on low ground about 800 miles west of Libby Village, back west across Davao and Talomo Rivers. Perimeter was in a briary, swampy coconut grove of Jap trenches overgrown by a thicket. That night, guerillas fired heavily 800 yards from us and kept our guards' heads down. They killed no Japs! Next day, we remained in the same perimeter—morale low, with no cigarette issue and no mail in a time that seemed forever.

Suddenly at 1600 23 May, we entrucked to the fighting front north at Mintal Village, to guard 21 Regt Hq that night. While we dug in, Jap mortar and FA barrages fell all around us, but hurt nobody.

About 0030, a night fight began. We barraged grenades at Nips trying to knock out our mortars. Until daybreak, Jap fire and our grenades kept us tense.

But that night of 23-24 May, a 5-Jap suicide squad infiltrated through L Co and hugged the piers of Mintal bridge with armfuls of explosives and blew it up. Next morning, all around the broken span, we saw arms and legs and bodies of the 5 dead Japs. That bridge was only supply line for 2 Bns of 21 Inf fighting east of the Talomo on the drive to Riverside Village. (It was not usable again until late afternoon.)

That morning, L Co had to ford the Talomo in water waist-deep. By 1200, we were on top of Hill 280, a battered, barren knob of broken pillboxes and shell-torn corpses. Our 21 Inf's 1/Bn had won and lost the hill and retaken it in a battle on 8-10 May. In daylight, only stray rifle bullets and MG bursts bothered us.

But far into the night, our FA and some Jap guns were whistling shells overhead. Jap shells kept us on edge and frequently flat in our holes. Just as off-duty men stretched out to sleep, the japs barraged us.

We would hear the gun-report miles away. Came then moments of listening for the steel to whistle down while we squirmed and hoped. Then the shell would hit—all of 75 yards away. Came other reports over and over again until our nerves were uncontrollable and we sickened in our stomachs. The barrage lasted only 10 minutes, and no shell hit closer than 75-100 yards off, but we were mostly awake all night.

So accurate seemed the Jap fire that we guessed that they were using a fine 200-foot tree on our hill for a firing sight. We took 7 charges of dynamite to shatter it. On 25 May, an A 21 Inf patrol south on Highway 12 fought the Nips 600 yards away, and kept us down in our holes awhile.

On 26-29 May, L Co first secured Hill 280, except for 1/Pln's move on 28 May to take over E 21 Inf's position on Hill 220. We replaced guerillas at the bridge with a 12-man guard. While both "A" and "E" of 21 Inf helped their Regt against Japs farther north on Highway 6, 34 Inf was fighting towards 21 Inf from south of us, and trying to make contact.

On 26 May, our partol on Highway failed to contact 34 Inf because the Japs halted us there. When our Co outposts changed guard, a Jap MG opened up from across the river, but fired too high to hurt anybody. Our mortars opened up on those Nips, and we watched them squirming away.

That evening, 5 stray Japs walked upstream towards us. Outposts' fire pinned them to the bank, killed 1. A grenade explosion in the grass made us think that second Jap had committed suicide. The other 3 may have escaped.

That night after our 3/4-ton Bn ammo truck supplied us, a Jap bangalore torpedo exploded under it, half-way between Mintal and Libby. Although damaged badly, the truck returned to 3/Bn area. But a man was killed, another wounded. On 28 May, near the place of this ambush, 3/Bn's wire truck narrowly escaped another bangalore torpedo. K Co then had to patrol the whole Mintal-Libby Highway.

On 29 Mar came glorious news that we were relieved for rest camp. By that date, 34 Inf had squeezed out Jap opposition and contacted 21 Inf. Now 34 Inf relieved us on Hill 280 with AT 34. We cheerfully entrucked back to our rest area near Libby Strip 7 miles from Davao City.

Unloading in a coconut grove atop a steep little knob, we soon had a cool cleared camp, with the help of bulldozers. We set up tents and unfolded cots again. Three miles from our hillstop, we viewed the Pacific, bright blue past the green of the coconut palms. Of course, we still had to secure perimeter holes and share bridge guards with K Co. That night of 31 May, men were writing letters again, or playing cards, or hearing music over 3/Bn radio.

Schacht and other officers helped build their private dining room from fragments of a destroyed house. They built it to house a dish-rack of abandoned Nip china. Even bully beef and dehydrated potatoes tasted better in china than on mess-gear. Fourteen letters arrived! Although still wobbly from recent dysentery, Schacht was happy. He could keep clean, read and write, and sleep above ground in a cot. Then came a second batch of mail!

But on 3 June, L Co's morale dropped—after only 4 days' rest-camp. Tired already from Jolo and Zambo battles for our 41st, we thought that we had also seen enough action around Davao with 24 Div. On 14-29 May for 24 Div, we had spent most of our time in holes or on patrols. We had exchanged fire with Japs—endured Jap FA, MGs, mortars—even Jap rockets and some rifle-fire. Lucky to have no casualties, we thought that we had served this "foreign" 24 Div more than enough.

Now, however, we heard that our 3/Bn would team with 34 Inf to fight north from Ula and then Riverside to meet 31 Div, which was pushing south from 35 miles away. On 4 June, L's 114 men and 3 officers—Capt Arnold, 1/Lts McGee and Schacht—entrucked to reinforce L 34 in the black abaca jungle north of Mintal.

In our understrength L Co of 117, many men were ready to break down from fevers or just convalescent from them. One of these convalescent was our new CO Capt Arnold, an old Guinea vet newly in command. As we passed Zambo on 15 May en route to Davao, his fever of 104 had caused him to be removed to Dr. Katner's ship on a stretcher. After a unit of plasma and glucose—then morphine and codeine—he fell sick again after rejoining L Co on 16 May. Again he had glucose intravenously—but on 26 May was back to "L" for battle. Men like Arnold went north to fight again.

K COMPANY 162 INFANTRY:

Cram Hill At Zamboanga

by K 162's CHARLES BROCKMAN AND ROBERT IRICK,
with DR. HARGIS WESTERFIELD, Division Historian

> CREDIT: Brockman sent me a 4-page single-spaced typescript undated, and letters of 17 June and 10 July 1981. Irick sent me letters of 12 May, an undated letter of about 1 June, dated letters of 23 June, 20 July, and 4 September — all 1981. Each man started writing without knowing of the other's existence; they have now reestablished their "comradeship formed in combat." Important also were 162's Zambo "Report of Operations," detailed Journal, Casualty List, and RR Smith's Triumph in the Philippines. I used a zerox of K Co's Feb-June 1945 payroll to check on ranks and spelling of name, but it was hard to read.

About 0845, 10 Mar 1945, K Co 162 Inf's T/5 Brockman watched from our LST deck while B-24s and Naval guns prepared our landing. About 0915, our Buffalos lined up and drove for San Mateo Beach, west of Zamboanga City. Ahead was a narrow beach, coconut palms, and high blue mountains.

As K Co ran over the beach, we saw a wide plain instead of New Guinea jungle that we remembered too well. Our green, helmeted columns with alert rifles moved inland some hundred yards, but found no Japs. Brockman heard what he thought to be heavy Jap FA firing from the high country ahead — and evidently firing by batteries, not like in New Guinea.

Attached to S/Sgt Chainey's LMG squad with Thompson, Forehand, Dye, and T/4 Peacock, T/5 Cook Brockman got orders to dig in while waiting for orders. The Japs still fired over our heads at the landing. With holes half dug, we had to "saddle up" and move, to attack a small village. We thought that we heard our tanks ashore behind us and opening fire.

The village which we were to attack was probably San Roque, but L Co in the lead found only deserted positions — and no sign of the Japs' great attack tomorrow. "K" had no casualties this 10 Mar, but 3/Bn already had 10 wounded.

We sheltered that night in Jap trenches from small Jap raids. A Jap talked before our holes, but failed to draw fire. He rapped grenades on his helmet to arm them, and threw and missed. We threw back. Next morning, a Jap head hung in the trench about 15 feet from Chainey's squad's LMG.

On 11 Mar, 3/Bn patrolled into the empty but heavily fortified San Roque area. About 1325, B-25 bombed Jap FA ridge positions. Then Jap salvos started again.

That afternoon, Sgt Warehime with Martin and another man strung wire along a road and up a slight bank. While Brockman worked with a wire-coil, Warehime and Martin suddenly fired, hit the ground. Searching Jap bodies afterwards, Brockman found a map which Capt Watson, our CO, hurried to Intelligence. On that 11 Mar, first man to die in "K" was Nava, cause unknown.

On 12 Mar, "K" saw some bitter combat, with 3 killed, 2 wounded. Perhaps some casualties occurred when volunteers went to help L Co, who were expelled from San Roque Bowl by a surprise attack of 300 Jap Marines. But we know only for certain that one death happened during K's disastrous Masilay patrol.

On that 12 Mar about 1430, K Co sent a 20 man patrol NW from San Roque Village towards Masilay Village to try to contact a 1/Bn patrol. Sgt Warehime might have led, but only surely identified man in that patrol was Irick, a replacement who knew nobody's name.

Shortly after the patrol left us, a wild burst of fire came from their direction. Brockman saw 3 men return; others arrived in scattered little groups.

About 1515, some 100 entrenched Japs had hit the patrol from both sides of the trail. The surprise fire broke up the patrol. Fourteen men leaped into the brush and left the leader with only 5 men. These 6 withdrew down a streambed. One man was mortally wounded, and the leader stayed with him until he died at 1745. Three hours after the reported time of the ambush, the leader returned with 2 men, and reported 2 of his small group still missing.

The other 14 returned before dark. After Jap fire struck, Irick hid under a fallen tree behind a rock, and never heard his leader say that it was safe to move. After 2 hours, he returned unhurt to K Co.

Killed that 12 Mar were Morgan, T/5 Schumacher, Sgt Reynolds. Reported lightly wounded were Miller, Kelley. Time and place of all casualties are unknown.

At first dark, Japs machine-gunned K's holes. Three M Co 81 mm shells silenced the MGs, but other Jap attacks marred our sleep that night.

On 13 Mar, "K" watched B-25s hit Jap gun positions, and after several passes, the guns were silenced forever. By 1400, we had advanced unopposed to join I Co at an important trail crossing renamed "Harlowton" after a Montana town.

Regimental strategy now was to envelope Jap Hq high on 1500-foot Mt Capisan. While 1/Bn pushed up West Ridge to Capisan, 2/Bn pushed up East Ridge. Having bypassed San Roque Pocket for others to clear, 3/Bn with "K" was to drive the Japs from near Harlowton NW up knobs and ridges to Mt. Capisan.

That night, Brockman and others in his hole threw nearly a case of grenades at Japs who sang "Dinah" and "Ohmonah" ("Ramona") to men wanting to sleep Brockman thought that his grenade shut up the serenade. All 3/Bn reported 3 Japs killed.

In the next 2 days, 3/Bn consolidated positions and faced Japs in numerous caves northwards. On one day, a Sherman tank halted among our holes and drew so much fire that K covered low. Still under Jap fire, we left perimeter to reinforce "I" on a ridge ahead.

On 16 Mar, K Co fought for Cram Hill, named after 2/Lt Cram who would die there. We teamed with "I" to seize the first hill NW of Harlowton against an estimated 2 Cos of Japs. I Co had 1 killed, 9 wounded, but held their new ground after rifle and MG fire. I Co faced only a single Nip Pln, but we faced a whole Co. And "K" failed.

One cause for K's failure may have been a garbled order. After our riflemen hit the Japs, an order passed down to set up our mortars for badly needed fire. But Weapons Pln got the order to send up the mortars. Mortar crews came up too close to fire on the Japs without hitting our own men.

As the mortars came up, 2 rifle squads were fighting up the trail ahead of Chainey's LMG squad for whom Cook Brockman carried ammo. This trail smelled strong of Japs. Brockman had passed several unexploded black Nippo grenades beside the trail. On both sides of the guns, brush made a thick cover.

Seconds later, we heard Jap fire at our riflemen up the hill above us. "Set up the gun," Chainey ordered. Thompson positioned the LMG. Brockman helped insert the belt.

Brockman moved 10 feet off the trail to the right. Ahead, we heard the firing halt and start over a number of times.

With only a .45 in his belt, Thompson slipped over to Brockman and said, "Hand me your M-1 a minute." Thompson casually put the butt to his shoulder and took aim. He fired 2 shots and returned the rifle to Brockman. "That takes care of one of them," Thompson said. Brockman could not see the body in the brush.

But Thompson did not know that another Jap was near in the brush with the corpse. As tall Thompson knelt by his gun to await firing order, the Jap shot him. A bullet passed through his pistol belt, the gun handles, a .45 clip, and came out near Brockman. Our Medics were forward with the riflemen, but they could not have saved him.

Chainey crept up the trail and pulled the gun back, but had to leave the tripod. Capt Watson called, "We're leaving here in 10 minutes!"

Japs shot at Chainey and Brockman. Crawling backwards on his stomach, Brockman found himself down among more "K" men. He sheltered on one side of a tree, and Turner on the other. Another Jap shot rang out. Brockman felt a hot sting on the left side of his neck. Turner's helmet flew straight up in the air, and landed on Brockman's leg below the knee.

Just then, a man whom Brockman thought to be Lt Doyle Brown crawled back dragging a bazooka. They worked their way downhill in a sitting position. Brockman believed that the Lt and he were the last men off the hill.

"Duck!" called Brown, and Brockman ducked. Brown's M-1 fired twice on their right. Brockman saw 2 Nippos fall.

Now out of danger, they caught up with T/5 Veach helping S/Sgt Shaylor. He had 2 holes in his back, close to his spine. "Don't worry about me!" Shaylor gasped. "There's no need for us all to be killed," They helped him anyhow.

At the foot of the hill, Beaty and more "K" men had halted. They covered Shaylor, Brockman, and Veach with BAR fire.

K Co called this place of death Cram Hill. Brockman heard that 2/Lt Cram died when he stood up firing into a Nippo position. Besides Thompson, Turner, and Cram, we also lost Miraldi killed. Besides S/Sgt Shaylor, machine-gunner Sgt Forehand was seriously wounded. Marked "Lightly wounded" but hospitalized were Leake, Walker, and Kettner. We had 4 dead, 5 wounded.

Next morning when "K" formed to try to take Cram Hill again, Capt Watson mercifully relieved those of us who had fought there yesterday from this attack. Brockman remained below.

Using delayed fuze, our FA blasted Cram Hill for 2 hours. "K" easily took it by 1125. Martin was marked lightly wounded. We killed 6 Japs, found 20 who died yesterday. All told, 3/Bn counted 40 jap bodies. Many more were surely sealed in caves.

That night, "K" took MG, rifle, and mortar fire from the west. T/5 Brockman, T/4 Peacock, and S/Sgt Rush endured close mortar fire. Clear in the night, they heard S/Sgt Jensen's orders to his mortarmen. The Jap mortars ceased, and Brockman threw only 3 grenades all night.

But in another hole while sitting on guard, Stonecypher died with a rifle slug in his neck.

On 18-22 Mar, "K" was in 3/Bn's careful advance over the hills towards 162 Inf's major objective — Mt. Capisan. On 18 Mar, L Co easily took a hill 700 yards north. Our 3/Bn contacted 163 Inf eastwards. No Japs remained on our left flank. That night, "K" killed 3 Japs from a small patrol around us. Through 22 Mar, we made much use of FA and Marine Air Force and advanced short distances.

On 24 Mar, all 3 162 Bns with 1/Bn 186 Inf attacked Mt Capisan itself. While 2/Bn struck frontally, our 3/Bn must secure 2/Bn's right flank. This meant that we had to capture the hill mass east of Capisan. At 1230, after FA preparation, K Co led 3/Bn in this attack.

Leading some 210 "K" men, scouts Testerman and Irick went slowly and carefully with alert rifles while BARman Murphy backed them. From an eye-corner, Irick saw Testerman's M-1 rise to his shoulder. Testerman fired twice; Irick fired once; they hit the ground. Close under a Jap MG, we threw 10-12 grenades and slew the entire 5-man crew. But BARman Murphy took a bullet in his hand half-way between little finger and wrist. K Co overran all Jap opposition, and by 1415, we held that eastern hill-mass so that G 162 could seize Mt Capisan by 1700.

In pitch-darkness that night under heavy rain, we soaked in our holes. Holed with Poston and Sgt Torre, Irick heard Jap grenades thud beside him. In split seconds, his hands found and threw out 3 grenades. Thankfully, he heard 2 of them explode safe outside the hole. Next morning, a Jap Marine 6 feet, 6 inches tall lay dead on the earth above us. He was armed only with a spear.

On 25 Mar, 3/Bn had to push west and south towards 2/Bn now holding Mt Capisan — probably to overrun troublesome Japs who had killed 2 H 162 men in their holes last night and wounded another. Bn objectives were to secure 3 prominent hills — the first 300 yards away, the second 800 yards off, and the third hill 400 yards distance.

The Cos of 3/Bn took Hill No. 1 at 1000, and Hill No. 2 at 1040. There were no casualties all day in I and L Cos but for a man lightly wounded who remained on duty.

But the hour of capture of Hill No. 3 went unreported in 162's Journal. We presume, therefore, that K Co had a harder time to take Hill No. 3, for we lost 2 killed by rifle-fire in mid-afternoon. Dead were Middleton and 2/Lt Doyle Brown. One of these men was reported killed by sniper fire at 1520, but his name is unknown.

And now the main Battle of Zamboanga was over for K Co 162 Inf after a hard fortnight of hiking, taking casualties, and digging in to face Jap harassment after dark. We were in truth lucky that our ambushed Masilay Patrol did not end in heavy losses — and lucky also that our fight on Cram Hill of 16 Mar cost only 4 dead. Our losses totalled only 11 dead — in comparison, for example, with G 163's loss on Biak of 10 dead, in another hard battle.

K Co had been a reliable front-line company. On 27 Mar, we went into a brief reserve with other 3/Bn Cos — and then marched inland to help mop up surviving Japanese.

41st DIVISION HEADQUARTERS (and 186 INF):

General Fuller's Resignation

by DR. HARGIS WESTERFIELD, Division Historian,
with COL (later BRIGADIER GENERAL KENNETH SWEANY)
and COL (later MAJOR GENERAL OLIVER NEWMAN)

*CREDIT: I believe that this study supersedes much of that of RR Smith's on Fuller's command problems in **Approach to the Philippines**. Crucial to the final draft was Sweaney's 7-page letter of 9 Oct 1978. Equally important were Newman's letters of 18 July and 18 Sept 1961, 10 Feb 1963, 7 Feb 1972, with "Newman's Notes," copied for me by Office of the Chief of Military History. Highly important also was **Dear Miss Em/General Eichelberger's War in the Pacific** (Editor Jay Luvaas). Background is from RR Smith's **Approach to the Philippines**, and Reports of General MacArthur/Japanese Operations in the Southwest Pacific Area.*

What are the true reasons why Maj-Gen Horace Fuller requested relief from commanding our 41st Division on Biak? For Lt-Gen Walter Krueger never ordered Fuller's relief as CO of the 41st; he removed Fuller as CO of Hurricane Task Force commanding the 41st. Was relief ordered because of Fuller's own errors? Or was relief ordered because of Sixth Army Gen Krueger's errors? We believe that Krueger was wrong.

Fuller's first alleged error occurred on Z-Day, when our Navy misjudged the current velocity off Bosnek, and dropped 186 closer to Mokmer Strip than 162 Inf. Although 162 was to spearhead the push, 186 landed far closer.

To 186's Col Newman (and to historian RR Smith in 1953), it therefore seemed logical that 186 take over 162's mission. Pushing at once, 186 might gain valuable time. Newman radioed Gen Fuller for permission to march. During beachhead training in Australia, we had readily changed missions when landings went wrong.

But Fuller ordered 186 to move east to Bosnek past 162, while 162 struck for Mokmer. Despite danger of Jap attack from dark Biak ridges, both Regts countermarched on that narrow Biak foreshore, with Japs observing above them. Lt Joe Crawford (E 186) later heard that a Jap outfit looked down on the flank of countermarching E Co. Luckily, the Japs had no order to attack.

Fuller surely lost time here — 110 minutes. Although Newman had his 2/Bn and most of 3/Bn under direct control at 0740, not until 0930 did 162's Bn pass where Newman had beached at 0715. Only a light screening force of Parai Defile Nips resisted 162's push 110 minutes later. It's easy to conclude that Fuller erred in ordering 162 to continue original mission.

But let's stop to think! Our Navy's rockets and big guns were ready offshore to blow a Jap attack apart almost point-blank. The Jap menace was not so great as it appeared.

As for losing time, would 186 Inf have done better in Parai Defile by arriving 110 minutes earlier? It took 4 hours for 162 to neutralize the light Jap holding force in the Defile. Could 186 have done better? And even if 186 had been quicker, the Jap ambush from East Caves would have probably mauled 186 just as 162 was mauled next morning.

And switching missions with 162 might have been disastrous to Newman. In Australia on practice landings, Newman had never switched regiments when a landing miscarried. Newman had changed only Bns of his own regiment. Altering regimental missions in Jap country could lose more men than 162 lost in Parai Defile.

For FA and Navy observers had embarked with 162 units. Location of FA positions, travel routes, command posts, fire direction centers were on 162's maps. Naval gunfire coordinates were on those maps. All units were specifically briefed. To change regimental missions would have meant so many changes of unit assignments that some of them might be missed and fail to get the orders. And reassigning messages must go on the radio in English. Alert Jap listeners would learn unit locations and plans for battle. If Fuller changed assignments from 162 to 186, chaos would result.

Fuller's second alleged error came later, when 186 Inf and 116 Engrs built the new road behind Bosnek to Mokmer Ridge behind the Strip. During most of 186's overland march, only one bulldozer and some few B 116 Engrs labored on that necessary supply road. Col Newman said that abundant equipment was back on Bosnek Beach. We lost time here indeed.

But was Fuller's failure to provide more road-building gear an error? Or was it wise strategy? Since Mokmer Strip was still Jap-held, Fuller on his own initiative built an airfield on Owi Island. He saved many pilots' lives in emergency landings. On 17 June, for example, 15 planes had exhausted their gas in fighting a storm back to their base. They safely landed on Owi Strip. Important also, Owi-based planes guarded Bosnek Beach from bombs like the one that crippled us at Hollandia. (Fuller also lined the Bosnek coast with AA guns so that a Jap raider would meet a solid wall of flak.) And from Owi would fly the B-24s that killed Ibdi Pocket and saved many 163 men's lives.

Fuller's third alleged error came after Newman had hiked 186 Inf to the end of the new road and poised 186 on the ridge above Mokmer Strip. Fuller insisted that Newman seize the Strip without delay.

Newman believed that Fuller crucially erred here. Reasoning that the hidden Jap positions were sighted south towards the sea, Newman wanted to find the Japs and hit them in the rear. He planned to send a 186 Bn down the right side of the high ridge above Mokmer Strip, and another down the left side. Thus he would strike Horseshoe Ridge from the rear. But he failed to get Fuller's order to clear the ridges before capturing the Strip.

While still on the heights, Newman took some precautions. He interrupted 186's push to halt both lead Bns to scout the ridges right and left. But in tangled cliffs and blind jungle, neither Bn found any Japs.

He thought that his right (west) patrol would have made a gigantic difference on Biak, but we have never found the complete story on that patrol. It totally missed the Jap emplacements. Nobody knows why it missed; we can only surmise. Maps suggest that Jap guns were about 1,000 yards off, but hidden in jungle ridges. Perhaps the patrol simply failed to see the Japs — like other patrols with more time. Perhaps quiet Jap outposts saw them pass and miss the positions. Perhaps there was no real patrol — just a few scared flankers fearing to lose contact with 3/Bn.

Newman, however, gallantly rebuked himself for not finding the Japs. He told historian RR Smith that his worst mistake was in not personally supervising the patrol.

At first appraisal, Newman seems right to advocate hunting down the Japs while 186 still held the ridges. At first, Fuller seems wrong in ordering Newman to take the Strip.

For on 7 June after we seized the Strip, the bypassed Japs had us trapped. When we revealed our lines on Mokmer, Jap shells and bullets impacted from 4 different azimuths. They fired from the low ridge NW which our patrol had missed, northwards, NE, and from East Caves. FA, AA, mortars, automatic weapons battered us — 75s, 20 mm guns, heavy mortars like our 81s. It lasted 4 hours, despite counterfire from 121, 205, and 947 FA — our 75s, 105s even 155s. Not until late afternoon, did our FA silence 6 gun positions — and cut Nip fire 40 per cent. We had 14 dead, 68 wounded. We were positioned for a deadly night attack from the Japs. We would have to storm ridges from which we had just descended.

But did Fuller really make a third error in ordering 186 off the ridges? Up there, 186 was at the end of a difficult supply line, and alone among the whole Jap army. Three great Jap fortresses swarming with fighters were on both flanks. Eastward was East Caves and Parai Defile holding back 162, and the Japs 3/Bn 222 Inf free to attack from Ibdi Pocket. West were batteries and infantry of Horseshoe Ridge above the Strip, and the West Caves garrison. Below the Strip, Jap pillboxes held the beach. Col Sweeny, Fuller's Chief of Staff, believes that 186 would have bogged down in the impossible task of extricating the Japs from West Caves.

Fuller seemingly made no third error when he placed 186 Inf on Mokmer Strip. Our FA, plans, and 186 patrols found the Jap FA and smashed it. On the night of 8-9 June, 186's perimeter was so strong that it readily repelled the night attacks on the Strip. (We thought that we had halted a mere night harassment; but Lt-Gen Takazo Numata said that with this "huge" failure, Jap morale began to fail.)

Fuller's fourth alleged error is that he never personally inspected our battle-front. Eichelberger himself made this charge; and Gen Doe himself said as much to G 163's Westerfield at Bozeman Reunion. We can readily attribute this fault (if it was a fault) to a direct order from Gen Krueger himself. On Hollandia Beach when our Task Force loaded for Biak, Krueger told Fuller: "General, I want you to know that I do not give DSCs to division commanders for being in the front lines. Your place is in a command post." It would have been foolish to risk our 41st's CO to a stray Jap bullet, and Fuller obeyed Krueger's order.

(Eichelberger was unaware of Krueger's order to Fuller. Like Doe, he said that part of the slow action on Biak was due to Fuller's failure to inspect his battle-front. But Eichelberger complained about Doe for the same reason! He said that althought Doe was well forward, he lived on the shore and did not keep close contact with battle a mile away.)

We therefore deny that Fuller made these 4 alleged errors. (1) He rightly refused to endanger the Z-Day advance to Mokmer by shifting 162's mission with 186. (2) He rightly assigned most Task Force equipment to building Owi Strip to secure us from bombs like the one that fell at Hollandia. (3) He rightly had 186 Inf seize Mokmer Strip without delay. (4) He rightly followed Krueger's order to command from Task Force CP, rather than to expose his important life at the front.

None of these arguments reflects in any way on 186's Col Newman, who Eichelberger lauded as "aggressive." Newman's was the viewpoint of a fighting regiment which wanted combat on Biak, and which was a prime cause of victory on Biak. But Newman was unaware of Gen Krueger's pressure on Fuller.

Lt-Gen Krueger and his 6 Army Staff made 3 errors that caused Fuller's request to be relieved from command.

Krueger's first error was a glaring underestimate of Jap strength on Biak. His Alamo Force said that the Japs totalled some 4,000, of whom 2,500 were infantry. Actually, Jap sources make the number into 12,000, with 4,000 Army and Navy "combat effectives." (remaining 8,000 were, of course, fighting men also.) During the Jap Navy's KON Operation, about 1,200 slipped in. Grand total of Japs on Biak was perhaps 13,200. Fuller landed with just 2 regimental combat teams, reduced by attrition at Hollandia.

Krueger's second error was his piecemeal assignment of regiments to Biak. Two landed on 27 May; we needed at least 3. First regiment was necessary for a frontal attack. Second regiment was necessary to secure the base on the beach. Third was necessary as a maneuvering force overland. But this third regiment, 163 Inf, did not arrive until 31 May, 4 days after Z-Day, with 2/Bn delayed behind it at Toem until 12 days later. six days later, a fourth regiment, 34 Inf, had to reinforce us against the Japs west of Mokmer Strip.

Krueger's third error was to send insulting messages and letters to Fuller. His directives pressed Fuller and hampered his efficiency in planning and commanding. As his Chief of Staff, Col Sweany says, "Loyalty down the chain of command is as important as loyalty up." Shortly after Fuller's first request for a third regiment of infantry, Krueger's abrasive messages began. They complained of how the daily situation reports were submitted and of our lack of progress. They urged increased action. Fuller's staff would change format of the next report to follow Krueger's wishes, but next day another querulous request would change the desired type of report, and again urge ation.

So angry were these messages that Gen Eichelberger himself had to stop them. The morning after becoming CO on Biak, he got such an angry message. He fired back that he would do nothing on Biak until he fully knew the situation. Krueger sent no more such messages, for Eichelberger had the same rank as Krueger, and presitge as a front-line general. Eichelberger had the clout to do what Fuller could not do.

In summing up, we must conclude that Fuller evidently did not err on Biak. But Krueger (with his staff) made three: 1) He grossly underestimated the numbers of Japs on Biak. 2) He sent 2 regiments to fight where we needed 4. 3) His irate messages damaged Fuller's morale to the point of resignation.

Despite his tactlessness, Krueger still failed to remove Fuller from commanding our 41st. Using the excuse that assigning 34 Inf to Biak had made it a corps operation, Krueger placed Eichelberger in command. Despite pleas of Eichelberger and other high-ranking officers, Fuller resigned, because he thought that Krueger no longer trusted him.

Such is the case for Gen Fuller as CO of the 41st on Biak — and against Fuller's CO, Gen Krueger, in the Battle of Biak.

163 INFANTRY I & R:

Fourteen Hard Miles Over Biak

by PETE GIANOPULOS (I&R),
with DR. HARGIS WESTERFIELD, Division Historian

CREDIT: Main source is Peter Gianopulos' 19-page handwritten MS. "Fourteen Long Miles." In 1946, he wrote it as a high-grade Freshman theme in Taft Community College of California. Pete added further details in a 7-page handwritten letter of 18 July 1981. RR Smith's **Approach to the Philippines** *was somewhat helpful, with 163's Biak Casualty List and Journal. (Where Journal differs with Pete's story, I prefer to rely on Pete because he was closest to what actually happened on that patrol.)*

On Aug 1944, 163 Inf's information and Reconnoisance Pln began an important and memorable 3-day patrol all the way across Biak towards Sawabas Village on the NE shore. Headed by 2/Lt Pfirrman, 24 green-clad scouts with 8 natives and a Netherlands Indies interpreter, hiked north to plot a 14-mile trail and report on Jap activity in that Biak Wilderness. For 3,000 Japs had still not surrendered, even after the shattering of Ibdi Pocket on 22 July. They could regroup for suicide attacks, if we did not keep them off balance.

Although we were strong for a recon patrol, we would not fight except where we would have to. Except for Pete Gianopulos with his M-1 which he would not part with, we carried only light carbines. Our NICA (the interpreter) had a carbine and a long sword — which he would soon use in a grisly manner. Acting as scouts and carriers, 8 natives went unarmed. Besides Pfirrman and Gianopulos, we are sure only of the names of Levitt and Sgt Capirci who were on this patrol. Probable members also were T/Sgt Wedge, Sgts Bunk and Hawes, and Cpls Allen and Crossen, with Cox, Grubich, Haley, and Murray (the assistant to Capt Budge.) Probably on this patrol also were Calkins, McNair, Rhodes, Person, Shosted, Rutherford, and maybe Shovan. (Shovan could not lift one arm to a horizontal position after the saber cut he got at Toem.)

Even deep in the Biak wilderness, we would keep close contact with 163 Hq. Where our radio would be useless, we would have other help. A FA recon plane with 163 Hq's Capt Budge would fly over us 3 times daily to check up. For dire emergency, we had a basket of 4 carrier pigeons.

At 0730, 7 Aug, I&R hit the trail north — the very day that our 163 Inf tried to contact 162 Inf to break up Japs gathered on Korim Track. Our first morning, we made good time. We had covered the first part of the trail before. But for security, we always kept 2 natives ahead who could see Japs before we could. At first, we hoped to complete our mission in 2 days, and return to the luxuries of a garrison camp.

We had to cross a swamp, but it did not hold us back much. Taking our break after crossing, we watched our natives peel the bark off rotting windfallen trees. They found broad worms about 1.5 by 1 inch which they ate — or tucked away dead in their loin-clothes for later eating. One Yank bravely bit a worm, but he said that he preferred even K rations to it.

We hiked onwards in a long single file, with 2 native scouts leading off. Gianopulos' assignment was to plot the trail, and so he was usually third or fourth from the patrol head.

By 1630, we had found our probable first day's objective — a 300 by 400 yard clearing which we believed to be about halfway across Biak. There were a few huts in the clearing.

A 2-man scouting party checked out the clearing. They reported that 6 Japs were sitting beside a hut in the center of the clearing.

Lt Pfirrman tried to encircle and capture the 6 Japs. One group of us would enter the clearing from the right, and another from the left. Pfirrman's group would advance direct up the trail to the huts. We wanted prisoners — not dead men.

But our 3 groups had not gone 10 yards before fire broke out from the center party. One Jap had walked down the trail towards Pfirrman's group. Pfirrman had to shoot him, and the other Japs scattered into the jungle.

While the Lt and others searched the huts, we guarded the clearing edge. Then Gianopulos was scared. He felt hundreds of Jap eyes peering from the jungle at him in the open clearing. For the shots had alerted the jungle to our presence.

After flaming the huts, I&R slept on a small hill under trees at the NE side of the village. After digging 3-man holes, we ate our K rations, then slept — with always a man awake in each hole.

It was hard to sleep between turns on guard in this enemy land, but our night was peaceful.

Next morning, we had our K ration breakfast — the hot Nescafe did taste good — shouldered packs and moved out with carbines ready. We looked forward to an early end of our trip. As Capt Budge in his Piper Cub had reported to Hq at 1500, we expected to reach Sawabas and our waiting landing craft early that morning. We had only 7 miles of our 14 to go. But in less than 200 yards, we found a trail position where an estimated 25-30 Japs had camped last night. Now we were trailing them at a short distance behind. We wondered whether all of us would ever reach the north side of Biak.

About 1130, our 2 lead natives sighted 3 Japs coming down the trail towards us. We hit the ground. Across the trail from Gianopulos up front, another Yank fired. He killed 1; the other 2 escaped.

We moved more carefully now. About 1500, we saw 3 more Japs on the trail ahead. Lt Pfirrman decided that it was time to catch some prisoners. We crept up on them and captured them without firing a shot.

One Jap had a leg injury. Gangrene had set in. He lay smiling up at us from a crudely made stretcher. It was a queer sort of smile, one that is not so graciously acknowledged. A

299

second Jap was thin from hunger and jungle diseases — could hardly stand on his feet.

The third Jap, however, was in good condition, and their leader. Up the trail, he said, was a large group of Japs who wanted to surrender.

Now Lt Pfirrman became eager to catch a large number of prisoners. It would be great publicity for all of us, we thought. For we did not know that any large number of Japs had ever surrendered before.

We ordered 4 reluctant natives to shoulder the litter with the gangrened Jap. We hurried with him and the skinny Jap as fast as we could.

Gianopulos suspected something phony in this promised surrender. He decided that the 3 Nippos were left behind the Jap detachment as bait for a trap. Yet he sensed that it was futile of him to speak up.

The natives had trouble carrying the sick Jap. Through the interpreter, Pfirrman told them to leave the Jap by the trail. They literally dropped him from their shoulders and began stripping him. It would be better to kill this incurable man than handicap the patrol in their attempt to capture Japs who might menace other Yanks if they were left without surrendering. The Javanese lifted his sword overhead and brought it down hard on the Jap's neck. (No doubt he had seen Japs behead his own people.)

As we hiked faster, the skinny Jap could not keep up. Pfirrman dropped 3 men behind to follow more slowly with him. They could catch up later on.

As we neared the coast, the land grew rougher. We climbed through a coral ridge. We scouted through a row of unoccupied pillboxes. Gianopulos was even more fearful of a Nippo trap ahead.

About 1630, when we were 100 yards past those empty pillboxes, Capt Budge flew over us in his Piper Cub. We halted to talk with him, but the dense jungle hid us from the plane. The only way that he could fix our position was to have us tell him the exact moment when he was over us.

While talking by Radio to Budge, Lt Pfirrman sent our Javanese and 2 outguards to take position on the next little coral ridge.

Suddenly heavy Jap rifle fire blazed out at all of us just as we topped the ridge. We hit the dirt, then looked up to find the source of the fire and return it.

All that Gianopulos could see were bullets richocheting off the trees and rocks around us. A bullet took off one of Sgt Capirci's left fingers. An unnamed radio man was shot in his arm. Levitt had a leg gash, probably in his left knee.

As we blasted back, the Jap fire ceased. Gianopulos himself did not fire at all. He saw nothing to shoot at, and did not want to waste bullets and have to clean his M-1 without need to.

Pfirrman detached some men, including Gianopulos, to climb the ridge leftwards to secure us against any Jap attack in that direction. The rear men in our column had instinctively turned to guard us from an attack behind us. Our right flank seemed to be safe because a tall coral ridge protected it.

The 3 men who had dropped behind with the skinny Jap now rejoined us. On hearing the sounds of battle up ahead, they feared that losing contact would mean their deaths. After what was really a mercy killing of the unfortunate Jap, they hurriedly caught up.

What should our patrol do now? If we backtracked, that row of empty pillboxes in our rear might be reoccupied with Japs loaded to kill us. We loosed a pigeon, but the fire had so scared it that it refused to fly away. Luckily, Budge's Piper Cub was still overhead. Capt Budge said that we were within 400 yards of the beach, where we had expected a rescue from landing craft.

When Lt Pfirrman recalled those of us sent to guard our left-flank ridge, we drew fire from our men watching for Japs. We hit the dirt unharmed before their fire halted.

Pfirrman decided that our best possible escape was to climb the high coral ridge on our right where we had seen no Japs, move 400 yards parallel to the beach, then climb down to catch the landing craft that we hoped to be there for us.

With our casualties, we hurried as fast as we could. We had no trail. After the first high ridge, we had to climb up one razor-back ridge and down another. At least, we were escaping the Japs. Most of us were out of water. The natives showed us some vines to gash for water. It did moisten our throats.

As the sunlight disappeared towards night, Pfirrman took 4 men, Gianopulos included, to hurry ahead of the main body with the wounded, to try to make contact with the barges down at the beach. Leaving our packs for the others, we started ahead down the coral ridge in the falling dark. Our feet tripped into coral holes hidden by leaves and broken branches.

Somewhere a short way below, we heard our landing craft circle as they awaited us. But the coral fragments were so rought that we had to stop and lie down in the smoothest little hollow that we could find as the dark fell. To feel safer, we lay as close as possible for the reassurance that touching gave us. We knew that nobody could walk over the coral without awaking us, but we slept with one eye closed and the other open.

With the bleak but welcome daylight, we started down the rough, coral ridge and straggled over level ground onto the sandy beach. The barges were out there — 2 LCMs and a crash boat — 300 yards off and leaving us. Gianopulos threw a phosphorus grenade, and they slowly turned back to us.

We waded out on the open ramps and climbed aboard. The crew gave us water and opened up some cans of tomatoes for us. It was a feast!

While all guns on the craft pointed shoreward against possible Jap riflemen, 4 of us without Lt Pfirrman went with full canteens to bring back to our buddies.

After going inland some distance, we had to climb that first coral ridge before we began calling out the names of our buddies. At first, they were quiet because they feared that we were Nips. Finally came our reunion with them — and their gratefulness as they shared our canteens.

They still had with them our third prisoner, the able-bodied Nip. Carrying 4-5 packs, he followed us, grinning. He, too, was happy to be alive. Later, we learned that he had lived in the States, had gone to school there, and could speak English. He had shared our food and cigarettes and was almost one of us. (When we disembarked on south Biak with this prisoner, an officer chewed us out for not guarding him in the way that the officer thought that he should be guarded.)

Tired, dirty, and sleepy, but happy, we quickly rounded Capes Lombee and Wararisbari on NE Biak and landed near 163 Hq on the south shore. How homelike had our company street become — the sagging, weathered tents, the hot food in our mess-gear, and the springy canvas cots to lie back on! We were glad to leave the Japs who had fought us for other outfits to deal with.

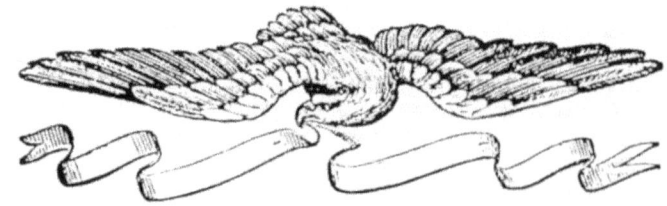

54 INFANTRY MIXED BRIDAGE:

Japanese Death March At Zamboanga

**by 2/Lt RINNOSUKE MAYA,
DR. HARGIS WESTERFIELD, Division Historian**

> CREDIT: Main source is 13-page, single spaced typescript of 2/Lt Rinnosuke Maya, 7 Feb-5 June 1945. Translated by 191 Language Detachment at 41st Division Hq, it was captured at Mialim, 3 miles NE of Vitali on the Zamboanga Peninsula east coast. For orientation, I used 186 Infantry's Journal, "Zamboanga Operation," and RR Smith's *Triumph in the Philippines*. Maya impresses me as a sensitive, cultured officer who kept his emotions well under control, despite his predicament as a member of a starving defeated army. Probably Maya perished, but we hope that he is alive and well in Japan today.

This is a Japanese officer's story of the Battle of Zamboanga, and his part in the death-march among the hungry Zambo Mountains. Actually belonging to 9 Air Brig stationed on Okinawa, 2/Lt Rinnosuke Maya was flown down from Negros Island 7 Mar 1945, 3 days before our 41st landed. Presumably, he went as Air Liaison for air power to reinforce the Zambo garrison — or at least to raise Jap morale for expected reinforcements. With a 3-man detachment, he joined Hq of Lt-Gen Tokichi Hojo's 54 Indept Inf Brig.

On 8 Mar, Maya wrote that US planes were striking Zambo. Bombs fell on Recodo Seaplane Base 7 miles west of Zambo. On 9 Mar, 50 B-24s bombed. At 1000 came a Naval barrage. At 1400, Maya heard that Japs had repulsed our landing craft at Recodo Beach — news totally untrue. At 1400 also, Maya's 3 men and he took up prepared positions behind Gen Hojo's Hq — near Zambo Reservoir.

On 11 Mar, the day after our landing, Maya heard that we had 120 tanks. Since we actually had just a Pln of A 716 Tank Bn, perhaps the Japs confused our tanks with vehicles of 658 Amphib Tractor Bn. By 12 Mar, large US planes had stopped bombing, but B-25s and P-38s observed overhead.

On 12-13 May after our Regts had landed, Maya had great hopes of victory; he said that Jap assault groups were making frequent night raids — as on 12 Mar when Jap Engrs made a "determined assault." (But our Regts' Journals record no Jap attacks at all.) On 13 Mar, he learned that 40 of our alleged 120 US tanks were already made ineffective, at a price of 250 Jap casualties. (Actually, on 12-13 Mar, our Regts had only begun pounding Hojo's main lines.)

On 14-15 Mar, Maya's little group had orders to observe our moves from Hill 385, probably near the Reservoir. With a clear view of our lines, they watched our Air Engrs extend runways on San Roque Strip, working brazenly all night under elecric lights. "Tears of chagrin welled up in our eyes," wrote Maya, who would never fly another plane.

Relieved from observing on 15 Mar, Maya's small command with other service units dug trenches or moved supplies. During 16-29 Mar, the Jap situation worsened, Maya thought that our FA and mortars mainly caused Jap defeat; he marvelled at our great supply of shells blasting down. On 22 Mar, Filipino guerillas began firing at short ranges on the Japs.

Observers flew overhead constantly to direct our FA. On 26 Mar, small "Grumman" planes — probably our Marine Air — struck downstream below Hojo's Hq. Beginning 0600 28 Mar, other planes flew special missions, circled low and sometimes killed engines in trying to hear movements below them. That afternoon, 15 Grummans savaged the area again down Tumago River from Hojo's HQ. Maya still hoped for Jap planes — of which almost none remained in the Philippines.

Maya never really understood our battle tactics. He said that we tried to avoid bloodshed as much as possible. Before advancing, we used thorough air-strikes, then moved under FA cover. Likely, we would penetrate an area where no Japs had deployed. When our barrage ceased, we appeared in the most unexpected places.

But with a Jap counter-attack, we would "involuntarily" withdraw. Then we penetrated from a different direction. "All in all," Maya concluded, our methods were "unorthodox and lacking in sincerity," — "leisurely and totally lacking in offensive spirit." Maya believed in Jap traditions of reckless and costly gallantry.

And now began the travail of a defeated army that refused to surrender. Late 3 Mar, Gen Hojo ordered its retreat. Of his original 8900 men, Hojo still had nearly 5,000 left — but a crippled land army minus planes and tanks and FA. His easiest escape route would have been up the east cost of Zambo Peninsula to the Mindanao mainland, but the Filipino 121 Inf barred this route. He tried to withdraw to the west coast, through the starved and half-explored mountain jungles.

For Lt Maya, those first retreating days were days of heavy labor. He now commanded large carrying parties. On 31 Mar, his men left for a new bivouac area at 0200, 8 hours' trek on hill trails into dawn, where guerillas fired on them many times.

His tired men got a rest all of 1 Apr, while other troops took guerilla fire at a nearby road-fork. A large guerilla force seemed to have many US soldiers with them. On 2 Apr, our FA shells dropped nearer and nearer to Maya. That night, all men took turns guarding against guerillas.

Maya's men continued carrying rations. He equalized each man's load over those rough, wet trails — still over 130 pounds per man. On 4 Apr, his men could carry only 1.25 miles with this load, and we don't know when these loads were lightened.

For a time on this retreat, some formations speeded up until close behind the Marine and Army advance units. Yet each unit had a large following of walking casualties impeding the trails.

A Jap CIC man gave Maya hope for survival. In about 20 days' march, the CIC man said, they would reach country to live off. Only in the first 3-4 days of this 20-day march would they have to guard against guerillas; afterwards, no enemy could hamper them. At the coast, Filipino boats would carry them over seas to the Mindanao mainland. (We now believe that Gen Hojo's true objective was to seize the rich ricelands of Siocon, 40 miles north of Sibuko Bay on the east coast. They would never come to the Siocon rice paddies.)

On 8 Apr, Maya's men left Tumaga River Valley, perhaps 18 miles north of Zambo Beach, and entered Mercedes Valley, near the Zambo Peninsula west coast. Maya had joined his men with 12 Naval personnel who had emplaned from Negros to Zambo with him. Most of the 13 days from 9 Apr through 22 Apr, they spent hiking, or sometimes foraging in native gardens. But they lost about 6 days waiting while the Army decided on its route. Dissension sprang up between Hojo's 54 Inf Brig and 33 Naval Guards (Marines). The Marines often reserved native gardens for themselves, and barred the Army from them. The Marines recklessly built shelters in exposed places, and brought our bombers down on everybody. Where possible, the two arms of the Service decided on separate routes.

By 22 Apr, Maya's men were near Malayal Village, some 2 miles from the Peninsula's west coast. Since their retreat order 22 days ago, they had slogged and carried over 40 tortured miles through the mountain heart of the southern Zambo Peninsula. Now they heard heavy rifle fire ahead. Evidently they had a momentary victory against coastal guerilla where no US troops would land for another month. And they had food: great amounts of newly dug potatoes, and some vegetables.

While digging potatoes on 23 Apr, Maya's men saw a Piper Cub swoop down on them. Only 150 feet overhead, the pilot fired his pistol. Expecting bombing on that garden tomorrow, they fled at once. On 24 Apr while carrying many loads of potatoes, they saw 12 Grummans follow a Piper Cub's smoke bomb down to strafe and blast where they had dug before. Fear of the spying Cub made them cower for hours under trees. On 25 Apr, 12 more Grummans bombed that garden area. For safety from planes, they decided to march at night.

Leaving at 2000 in bright moonlight on fairly easy trails, they marched slowly because the Army column was too long. En route, some Japs endured frequent guerilla sniping. Passing probably Malayal Village and fording a stream 8 times, they finally hid in jungle after 0630 and slept all morning. Hearing that some 10 landing barges were hitting Malayal Beach, they moved again. (On that 26 Apr, C Co 186 Inf landed at Malayal, while 186's other 1/Bn Cos beached on Sibuko Bay, 10 miles northward.) Maya wrote that recurrent malaria and starvation for rice added misery to his overtired body.

On 27 Apr-2 May, this deathly Jap march continued a few miles north each day, with rations fitfully gathered from the fields. For all of 28 Apr, they heard the unbroken roar of US planes. Yet Jap foragers had a great haul that day: bananas, potatoes — even pigs! On 3 May, foragers were not so lucky. Men of Hojo's adjutant section narrowly escaped from either guerillas or soldiers with mortars. At 1400, 1/Lt Kawauchi and 16 men found quantities of rough rice and sweet potatoes, but several men died to get them.

Despite US-guerilla harassment on 4-22 May, the Japs' half-starved death-march continued on the seaside jungle trails of the Zambo west coast. On 15 May, Jap Marines barred the Army from digging sweet potatoes in Filipino gardens.

After 3/Bn 186 Inf landed farther up the coast on 19 May, the Japs had to follow harder inland trails. There was despair on 19 May. US troops fired on the column from front and rear, and slew a large number of the sick and wounded stragglers. That night, Maya pitied the men standing in the rain, wet to the skin and hungry. At dawn, 0630, they marched beneath rain that had begun at midnight. Noontime chills almost made Maya fall out, but he braced himself to trudge on soddenly.

There were deserters already, of course — even 9 men from the elite CIC unit, and Capt Gyomi with 10 men from 67 Air Regt. Chances to get food and even survival might improve away from the slow, harried main columns. Rumors of new US landings were surely convincing men to desert. Looking down from mountains north of Sibuko Bay, the Jap Chief of Staff saw a great tent city erecting, trucks unloading munitions, and Piper Cubs rising from a new strip to hunt the Japs. On 21 May, our 1/Bn 163 Inf from Jolo was landing near Piakan, farther up the coast, to break up the Japs' organized march to the Siocon area.

Meeting 23 May, the Jap COs decided to let their units disperse to try to save themselves. Maya decided to lead his small group all the way to the other side of Zambo Peninsula — through 20 miles more of rainy jungle mountains to Vitali on the east coast. Attaching himself to Makamura Bn (named probably for its CO), Maya organized his little unit into teams of an officer with 2 men. Maya's own group was down to 10-12 men.

It is not clear why Maya decided thus to turn east and labor half-starved and malarious across the middle of the Zamboanga Peninsula. Some units of 54 Inf Mixed Brig were already on the east coast, he knew. Besides the obvious reason of escaping our forces now on the west coast, Maya gave only two other reasons. CIC's Sgt Nishimura said that he knew a trail eastward. And, like Maya, Nakamura Bn was determined to reach the west coast.

On 24 May, our men halted the Nakamura advance guard — killed 1, and wounded 1. The Bn had to take a trail around us. On 25 May, US troops fired at close range. Nakamura's men threw away all excess equipment to help save themselves.

On 26 May, Nakamura Bn with Maya's men marched about 3 miles east, but they were already lost among mountains. On 27, 28, and 29 May, they made only 11-13 miles. Mountain after mountain blocked their way. On 30 May, they rejoiced at a river flowing east, but it twisted west again on them. All day, P-38s flew above them.

On 31 May, with 50 men of the Bn and 8 of his own, Maya was in the advance guard. Frantically, they hacked their way over mountains and forded many rivers. When 4 P-38s seemed to be on a recon run over them, Maya guessed that they were scouting for Jap planes. These Japanese planes were his last hope, that he would never realize.

Time was surely running out for Maya; the last entries of his diary were meager indeed. On "3-4 June," food was exhausted. On 5 June, they thought that they saw the east coast far away. They were extremely tired. The final words in Maya's Diary were: "Cpl Shomojo was unable to catch up with us. Felt lonely because of this."

On 12 June 1945, 61 Filipino Inf men captured this Diary at Mialim, 3 miles NE of Vitali on the east coast. We hope that Maya survived, but he must have died already. Long before his last entry, he had written that his saber was nicked from cutting trees for shelter; both his sword and pistol were rusty. He had never fired a shot at us.

On 3 Mar 1945, from the 8,900-man Zambo garrison, some 5,000 began retreating with Gen Hojo. By 15 Aug, about 1,100 were captured, although many of these were probably Koreans or Formosans. About 1,385 never surrendered until the war's end: Although 3,900 died in battle, their losses in the death-march must have been 2,525 men. We pity and honor the dead of 54 Ind Mixed Brig and 33 Naval Guard, like 2/Lt Rinnosuke Maya.

41ST MILITARY POLICE PLATOON:

Soldiers and Policemen

by DR. HARGIS WESTERFIELD, Division Historian,
with COL. PAUL WENDELL, SGT. LEWIS H. CLARK, and other MPs.

> CREDIT: Personal reports are from Col Paul Wendell's 7-page handwritten MS of late 1982, with Lewis F. Clark's letter of 6 Nov 1976, undated letter early 1981, and letter of 24 Apr 1981. Other letters were from Don Hedburg on 12 Jan 1978, and Paul Robinson on 29 Apr 1981. I used also Award Stories of Col (then Maj) Paul Wendell, Cpls Joseph Sheible and Matthew Trummer, and Jack Welch. Basic archival document is "Historical Report for the Year 1944" of 41 MP Pln. This document I discovered on my Div Assn Grant to Dwight Eisenhower Library at Abilene, Kansas. (With this 41 MP story now in print, **Jungleer** has published at least one story of every non-infantry outfit in the 41st Div — except for 41 Signal Co.)

Outsiders normally expect Military Police to have routine police duties — like directing traffic, arresting drunks, and guarding prisoners; but 41 MPs had plenty of front-line action. For example, during the Salamaua Operation, when Aussie soldiers pilfered our supplies, the Provost Marshall and 12 MP volunteers halted most of this thievery. When supply LCMs unloaded, we endured numerous air-raids — luckily with no casualties.

But at Hollandia, the bomb and the great fire put us MPs into deadly action. The fire and the explosions of 23-24 Apr split up our MP unit. After the Jap seaplane's bomb hit at about 2000 Hrs, most of us MPs with other troops ran towards White Beaches 1 and 2, usually barefoot and unclothed from our bivouac. After regrouping, we MPs returned to the fire for relief duties, despite danger of explosions with fragments and flaming gasoline. Maj Wendell set up an organization for evacuating the wounded. (A total of 24 men were killed, and about 100 wounded.) Removed to Cape Tjeweri across from Cape Pie, we had to use a Jap supply base for rations and re-clothing until LCTs resupplied us from Finsch.

Fire and explosions cut off some 5 MPs from the outfit. Schmidt and Cpl Clark, among others, had to creep 1500 yards up the beach and inland through fire, burning oil, exploding gas and ammo.

Finally topping Pancake Hill, we cowered under tanks until morning. After daylight, we discovered that an unfired Nippo gas dump was at the base of Pancake Hill. If this gas had ignited, all Pancake Hill would have disappeared with us on it.

Clark himself had light wounds from fragments on top of his left arm, left shoulder, and left thigh. When he tried to remove his fatigue jacket, most of it fell off in burnt pieces. His back was a mass of blisters, blood, and sweat.

Near Hollandia on 6 May, MPs' Welch saved an Amphib Engr's life. A beach craft's motor failed, and the driver swam for help, half a mile offshore. He dislocated his shoulder, and was in danger of drowning. MP Welch leaped overboard and saved this Engr's life.

Just like at Hollandia, our Biak landing endangered many MPs. Like 186 Inf to whom we were attached, MPs of 2 groups beached on the wrong shore, miles west of our assigned landing. An unexpected western current and the smoke of the bombardment which hid the beach — these caused the Coast Guard pilot to squish into mangrove swamps 5 miles west of Bosnek.

The Senior NCO of one of those misplaced groups, Cpl Clark was in command. Ashore only 10 minutes after H-Hour, Clark led 48 MPs with 186 Inf east towards Bosnek, out of Jap country.

Just as Clark had posted flank scouts as security for the long hike east, an MP remembered only as "Fred" collapsed with a burst appendix. We made a litter of poles and jackets and carried him with us.

Bosnek road was menaced by our own bomb runs. In rising tropical heat, we hiked grimly through swamp water and brush eastward. Clark insisted on total radio silence for safety.

After some 4 miles, we gladly met 1/Lt Colvert with L 162 pushing west towards Mokmer Strip. Like the other misplaced MP detachment, Clark's men arrived safe at Bosnek.

Maj Wendell's MP Hq had already landed at Bosnek from an LCI at H+45 Hrs. Seeing no other Yanks there ahead of us, Wendell despatched a security patrol west towards Mokmer Strip. This patrol did MPs' duty; they marked Jap supply dumps and warehouses OFF LIMITS. Wendell said that the GIs arriving awhile later made many "caustic remarks" about our signs.

Now based at Bosnek, all MPs worked hard. Some of us had beached in the LSTs and begun directing traffic even while holds emptied of their trucks. Besides taking control of all traffic as it came ashore, we picketed several large Nippo dumps nearby, and improvised a Jap prisoners' stockade.

Finding several 1,000-lb craters near our bivouac behind the jetty, we surrounded one crater with barbed wire. Only 1 Nip was taken the night of D-Day, but he tried to escape tomorrow, and died trying. On D+3, we had another prisoner — then 2 on D+5. By 20 Aug, we had impounded a total of 220, but we never had more than 12 at a time. We continually forwarded them to greater safety, at Base Section in Hollandia.

Although MPs guarded the Jap liquor dumps, some bottles got out — as you would expect. In the first week or so, especially, we had to deal with a number of drunken GIs. Later, we consolidated the dumps to make them easier to secure. Wisely, we destroyed some 500 cases of saki. Later,

41 QM took charge of the beer and rationed it out — about a bottle a day per man.

Such is the official story of how 41 MP Pln safeguarded Nippo liquor. But Clark admits his theft of 4 cases of Nippo red wine that he buried in the chilling sand. Every night, he took a bottle of saki to a nearby QM bakery and traded it for a loaf of fresh bread. Then his buddy and he feasted on red wine with new bread. Robinson unofficially issued beer to front-line troops. An officer could take out beer if he signed a chit, but enlisted men rated no chit. But Robinson let infantry come down from the ridges and hike back with cases. Robinson said that there were so many back-packers that they looked like a safari returning to the ridges.

But MPs' main action on Biak was to perform humdrum police work to make victory possible while other men fought in the front lines. More and more supply and convoy trucks crowded the narrow Biak roads. The Division needed us for traffic cops, especially where the roads were one-way lanes. Three MPs were wounded on road-duty. Ivill was wounded when a Jap mortar made a near miss on a truck. A muzzle-burst of one of our own 155 mm howitzers wounded Witbeck. Martinsen suffered the worst wound of all. When his jeep hit a mine, it turned over on top of him. He still drew a total pension when he died in 1980.

When Division Hq moved to Mokmer Drome after Parai Defile was cleared, an MP detachment went along. Often MPs went to the front to escort back prisoners. Back at Bosnek, our stockade held several officers — one even a Lt-Col.

We built a larger stockade for our US prisoners. Besides 41st men who had gone wrong, we imprisoned Merchant Marines and Air Force men. We had caught them riskily souveniring in restricted areas. Fed on "C" rations and worked at digging graves, they lived unhappily.

On 22 July — the day that Ibdi Pocket was bombed out — MPs' Cpl Sheible performed bravely back of the lines on a US Army transport. An ammonia bottle exploded in an engine store-room. Sheible ran below to drag men on deck whom the fumes had overcome. Sheible himself needed medical aid.

On 5 Oct, Robinson and Sgt Weske fought for a man's life. When MP Ostrowski was draining gasoline from a 55-gallon tank, his 5-gallon pail exploded, and wrapped him in flames. Although only in shorts, Robinson wrapped Ostrowski on a blanket and with Sgt Weske rolled him away from the burning sand around the drum. Luckily, the drum did not explode and kill all 3. Ostrowski died later, however.

While stationed on Mindoro for the Southern Philippine Campaign, guerillas brought us a Nip officer to hold until Chief of Staff Sweeny could interrogate him. We warned Sweeny to question the officer that night, but Sweeny held over the interview until next monring. That night, the officer went berserk — stormed up the sides of our shellhole prison. He reached through barbed wire to try to wrench the LMG from the MP on duty. Other Jap prisoners would not use their Jap language to calm him down. LaFabre had to kill him. After this necessary execution, however, Division Hq thought that we were trigger-happy.

At Zamboanga Beachead, we MPs saw combat again. Landing under heavy shellfire, our LST was bracketed, but the Jap gunners never closed the bracket. Once ashore, we helped organize that shell-geysered foreshore and get the men and supplies safely inland. Then we were first to seize Zambo City Hall ahead of 163 Inf's invasion.

Leading a 15-man MP detachment, Sgts Clark and Tjader landed west of Zambo City on 10 Mar 1945. For the next 13 hours, we endured the heaviest FA and mortar bombardment that the 41st Div ever suffered. The nearby Naval Beach Party took a direct hit. We believe that the whole Naval Command Staff perished.

For 13 hours, we MPs labored to untangle that beachhead confusion of men and vehicles and supplies below the shells arcing down from the hills. We dragged wounded from trucks or the ground and gave them what first aid we could. If blood or parts of bodies were left in trucks that drivers had leaped from under fire, those drivers refused to get back at their wheels. They deserted trucks with engines running and blocked exit tracks. Under threat of Jap mountain guns blasting whirlpools of sand, we MPs extricated 11 ammo-filled trucks from the open beach. Luckily, the Jap FA fired for a few minutes, then let up for a few minutes. We made good use of those lulls in fire.

We monitored a radio team trying to place fire on a Jap gun emplacement high on a cliff. Clark was wounded in the Jap bombardment. He was slashed across left shoulder, right thigh, right ankle, and left calf. Gun-blasts gave him a temporary hearing loss, but he kept on laboring for the Division.

Next day, 11 Mar, Maj Wendell sent Sgt Clark and 4 men with a LMG to jeep into Zambo City to find a new MP Hq. In that advance party were Cpls Well, Berg, and Flint, and one more unnamed MP. (Evidently Maj Wendell was sure that Zambo City was clear of Japs. Probably the jeep patrol started late in the day.)

Entering Zambo City, we found a shack that was booby-trapped and turned back to report the trap to CP. Entering again, we hit a small mine and lost a wheel. Trying once more, we finally reached the silent, deserted city center.

City Hall and Police Station were not badly blasted. With some repairing and cleaning, we would have a fine station for sleeping and cooking and prisoners.

Twilight was beginning. It might be unsafe to drive back to CP. We had seen no Japs, and we decided that we could sleep here securely. Hiding our jeep, we carried our LMG onto the roof of the City Hall. We slept well between our turns on guard.

With daylight of 12 Mar, we heard gunfire and clanking tanks. Looking down one way, we saw 3 Jap patrols scurrying off. We saw a Yank combat Pln arriving. We waved our American flag to welcome the surprised infantry into Zambo that we had occupied before them.

After we settled down to routine MP assignments at Zambo, we had one more memorable assignment for the honor of the 41st MP Pln. Filipinos informed us that they had been hiding an Americna woman back in the mountains for the last 3 years. She was Mrs. Lund, a 78-year-old missionary. Gen Doe's staff now feared that as the baffled, defeated Japs retreated, they might finally capture her and carry her off into suffering. They might hold her as hostage. They might kill her. Even worse, perhaps, they might torture her, or march her to her death in the Zamboanga Mountain wilderness.

Partly because, like most MPs, they had training for combat and patrolling, Sgts Churchill and Clark were assigned to recover her. With a Filipino guide, they passed through our lines and brought her in — a safe trip but one that was full of scares.

Once she was down from the mountains and safe at Div Hqs, Mrs. Lund said, "Thank God! Now may I send a wire to my daughter in California?" A day or so later, she was flown to Leyte and on home to California.

(Earlier in the Southern Philippine Campaign, Capt Murray's Palawan MP detachment had been the first to raise the flag over undefended Puerto Princesa, just as we had raised the flag in Zamboanga City.)

These are some of the highlights of 41 MP Pln overseas. We were fortunate to have only 3 wounded, and 1 non-battle death. We had been efficient policemen — and combat men when our Division needed us.

A COMPANY, 162 INFANTRY:

Cutting the Komiatum Track

by DR. HARGIS WESTERFIELD, Division Historian,
with LT. MARVIN NOBLE

CREDIT: Indispensable source is Lt Marvin Noble's cassette given to me at San Jose Reunion (1981), backed by Bill Davis' and Sgt Glenn Benedict's cassette answering my letter of 20 Aug 1981. (Noble talked his cassette after my letter of 29 May 1981.) Other sources are Sgt Ambrose Burkhartsmeyer's letter 20 Sept 1981, Sgt Robert Little's typescript about 14 June 1969, and Capt George's letter to Col AR MacKechnie of 12 July 1944. Col MacKechnie's official report of the Noble fight is erroneous, but Wm McCartney in **The Jungleers** copied it unknowingly, as did Australian David Dexter (with some modifications) in **The New Guinea Offensives**. Lt Gray did not catch 10 Japs asleep and slay them all at once, and a half of Noble's men did not become casualties. Noble and his men have corrected these misstatements.

After darkfall 9 July 1943, Lt Noble's 3/Pln and Lt Gray's Weapons men of A Co 162 Inf got fighting orders from CO Capt George. We were to cut the Japs' Komiatum Track in the high jungle mountains behind 162's new Nassau Bay Beachhead.

Komiatum Track was the Japs' supply trail to Mubo Strip which our Aussie allies were trying to envelop from the SE. Mubo Strip was the Japs' farthest advance from Salamaua Town. North from Mubo, an estimated 1500 Japs held 8 different positions. While George's other 2 Plns were to press on Japs nearest to Mubo, Noble's assignment was to hit the Japs farthest north and drive down to join George's other men. With Lt Gray's Weapons Pln (less a mortar and a MG crew) Noble's Pln was to descend from 1/Bn 162 Hq on 1800-foot Bitoi Ridge. He was to turn south down Komiatum Track beside Buigap Creek, and strike the Japs.

With a day's rations, we carried all the clips that we could, some grenades, and perhaps 9 rounds for our 60 mm mortar. Lacking a map, we did have a fine guide, Aussie Cpl GL Smith, who had helped light up 1/Bn 162's landing at Nassau Bay. (Smith would die in action 20 Mar 1945.)

About 1800 10 July, we left 1/Bn Hq and hiked NW across Bui Kumbul Creek through heavy jungle that extended north towards Mt Tambu. We made good time early, in fairly light underbrush with 30-40 yards visibility. By 1200, we crossed Bui Kumbul Creek and turned west at about a 90-degree angle. We kept much interval between men, and moved carefully by hand signals in total silence. Without a trail, we climbed 1500 feet over a ridge, then dropped down to Komiatum Track about 1630.

Fresh Jap footprints marked the Track. Crossing it, we dug holes, set up our LMG, and bedded down in a hard rainstorm that lasted all night. Four of us would not spend another night alive.

Capt George later said that Noble's Pln was wrongly led into a position 1500 yards farther north than it should have been. Perhaps Noble's epic fight of 11 July 1943 would have been more successful if they had attacked farther south; but they would fight gallantly and well.

At daybreak 11 July, Noble despatched 2 recon patrols to find the Japs in that mountain jungle labyrinth. Patrolling north up Buigap Creek, Lt Gray was to follow the Track 700-800 yards north to secure our rear. Pln/Sgt Fogel was to take 6 men including BARman Perpick to locate the Japs ahead. Fogel was to avoid combat and report back in an hour.

About 30 minutes after Gray's men went to our rear, we heard heavy rifle and automatic fire from that direction. In 15 minutes, Gray returned, but without all of his men.

Gray had followed fresh footprints to check out a side trail off Komiatum Track. The patrol saw bamboo huts about 100 yards ahead. As they got within 50 yards, a Jap rose up from the huts and exchanged fire. We sprayed the huts, but 9-10 Japs — who may have been caught asleep — poured out and shot back. Gray's men killed them or drove them off, but we were unsure how many Japs were loose to fight again. Rumor had it that some Yank's gun jammed, or we would have killed them all.

Now Noble's men were in a sticky position. Fogel's patrol had not reported back about the unkown number of Japs ahead. Live Japs from the huts could pick up from the rear.

In the next 10-15 minutes, we heard several shots behind us — and a final Jap shot. We hoped that some of Gray's patrol were still alive and fighting back there.

Noble and Sgt McClendon (who had been with Gray) then tried to get into the rear of the Jap huts. Crossing Buigap Creek, they climbed a steep 400-foot hill. From the crest, they looked down 20-30 yards towards the Jap huts.

McClendon pointed out movement in the brush; Noble shifted position for a clearer sighting. This man was surely a Nip. Noble's tommie cut him down at 35-40 yards.

Changing position on the crest, they peered down into the brush again. They saw movement; a Jap rifle cracked and wounded McClendon in the thigh, but came out the other side. With no bones broken, McClendon rolled back to Buigap Creek while Noble covered him.

They hid across the creek 10-15 minutes. The Jap who had evidently hit McClendon looked down from the crest. He crossed over to the open hillside above Noble and McClendon.

They fired together and cut him down. His body rolled behind a big tree on the steep slope with only the legs exposed. Noble's grenade dislodged him to roll all the way down into the creek. They found maps and papers on his body for Bn Intelligence, and rejoined Noble's command.

Perhaps an hour and a half had passed since both recon patrols had gone out. Fogel was still missing. We still did not know how many Japs still menaced our rear where Gray had fought. Yet Capt George's orders were to attack south at 1200 to meet A Co's other 2 Plns battling the Japs.

Noble still had to ascertain that no Japs could strike our rear. He took 2 men back up the trail to where Gray had fought. The place was quiet in death. They saw a Jap corpse in a deep hole where Pln/Sgt Al Miller had probably blown off his head.

Dead with his face to the foe lay Weapons Pln's Miller, and Noble read the story of his death-fight. Miller's rifle lay under his prone body, magazine empty. One hand was under his chest where he had reached for another clip to reload. He was pierced through the chest from the front — Al Miller — the man who remained behind to finish the job. Miller died the ideal death of a soldier — face to the front against the enemy of his nation.

Medics Thacker and Aldige bandaged McClendon's thigh and devised a stretcher for him. It was now 1100, late to get into position for the scheduled 1200 attack with A's other 2 Plns to the south. We moved out quick as possible — at wide intervals — our scouts well ahead.

After an hour, the trail began to widen. Noble now presumed that we padded somewhere near the entrance of Buigap Creek with Bitoi River. Here was a footbridge some 30 yards long with its walkway of poles. Buigap here was 40-50 feet wide — a raging stream at least 5 feet deep. We marched down the Track towards combat.

Now we met Sgt Fogel's patrol which had forayed south hours ago, to find the Japs, avoid battle, and return in an hour. Fogel had escaped the Nips with 5 of his 6 men still alive. But BARman Perpich was left dead on the trail.

The twisting trail had probably led Fogel too deep among the Japs. Probably they crossed Buigap Creek and climbed a little grade around a trail-curve. They had rounded a shoulder of brush sticking up above a bank. Then they had scouted down-trail through a large jungle opening. Perpich's BAR must have drawn a fire concentration that killed him, but Fogel's other 5 men had escaped but left Perpich behind.

Now Scouts Mendoza and Paul Adam led Sgt Benedict's squad and 3/Pln across Buigap Creek and around the hill-shoulder into danger. Among underbrush, with 20-30 yards visibility, we took scattered rifle-fire on our right flank awhile. To halt that fire, Noble detached BARman Elliot, Paul Peterson, and another unknown rifleman. Jungle and Japs caused this BAR group to disappear for days.

Now 3/Pln scouted gradually down-trail to the crest of the next rise. Over the crest, we looked another 50 yards to Purpich's body on the trail.

About half-way up to his body, Scout Adams saw a Jap cross the trail and kneel behind a bamboo clump. This Jap knew that we saw him.

Adams called Lt Noble forward with the Aussie guide. Cpl Smith walked down the hill 10-15 yards ahead of them. "Come on!" he called. "Let's go get 'em! They don't want to argue with us." As he moved out, Benedict's squad and part of another squad deployed as skirmishers to cross the clearing.

Then Benedict thought that the whole Jap army opened up on us — heavy Jap rifle and MG fire. We dropped to earth and blasted back into the brush at them. Instantly we had 3 men wounded. Keast was hit in the foot, Aussie Smith in left wrist, but neither man had a broken bone. Throwing grenades, Noble took a wound in his left shoulder. Just a little behind him, Benedict saw a little spot of blood on that shoulder.

Our rifles and 2 of Noble's grenades and maybe 2 more he got from another rifleman could not quell Nippo fire. With Aussie Smith, Noble ran back to get help from our LMG and mortar with Weapons Pln. He bled somewhat still from the left shoulder wound.

Halfway back, a bullet hit Noble's right elbow, broke both arms, knocked the tommie from his right hand. He dived into a pit where Sgt Stone gave first aid.

Despite his broken arm, Noble dropped 20-30 feet to the creek-bank and moved safely back to where Weapons men waited with LMG and 60 mm mortar. But he failed to have these weapons brought up to crack the Japs' position. Someone misunderstood him.

For by now, it was too late in the day for an attack to succeed. And Noble believed that A Co's other Plns had not attacked on our left flank to the south of us. (They had attacked, but Noble did not find out what they did until years later.)

We lost nobody recrossing Buigap Creek on the bridge, but BARman Elliot and his 2 men failed to answer our calls or our 2 strings of 3 rifle shots. The Japs following our retreat were now in the clearing where we had fought them. Elliot's men dared not answer us — would not return for some days.

We started up a steep hill on the trail just north of Buigap Creek. About 200 yards up it, Jap mortars fired at us. First volley was too long to hit; the second was too short. The third closed the bracket and caused some casualties. Just as he finished bandaging Noble again, Medic Thacker was killed.

We could hear mortar shells leaving the tube. Every time they fired, we hit the dirt. We were now among some Jap holes. When one round fired, Adams fell into a hole, head down. One of the Meds screamed when hit in the stomach just outside Adams' hole. Because of the stomach wound, we could only leave him to die. (We are unsure whether he was Medic Thacker or Medic Aldige; both were killed.) Gunner Wilson got a fragment in his leg; Rifleman Red Nelson was wounded, portion of body unknown. Nielsen was hit — but only on his pack.

In this threat to Noble's whole detachment, we could not carry McClendon up the steep slope on his stretcher. Despite thigh wound and in dazed condition from shock, he had to climb on foot. But we helped him all we could while gripping trees and vines to help us climb. The Jap mortar shells continued walking up the track for some time, then no longer fell. Having seen stakes earlier, we wondered whether the gunners fired unobserving from predetermined sightings.

Next morning, a patrol including Adams, Bury, and Dick and some unnamed men slipped back around a hobgack and shot up Japs just picking themselves up from bivouac to pursue us.

With Lt Gray now CO instead of wounded Noble, 3/Pln and attached Weapons men limped painfully up the ridge north of Buigap Creek and back to 1/Bn Hq and Medics. Battle fatigue struck 2 men; 1 went berserk, and another was shot in the hand. After an operation, Noble was borne back down through jungle mountains to Nassau Bay — a painful trip of maybe 5 days, with 8 Papuan carriers taking turns.

Nearly 40 years later, Noble would learn what Capt George's other 2 Plns of A 162 did on the day that 3/Pln fought. That morning, another "A" Pln killed 4 Nip outguards and pinpointed out their position near Bui Savella Creek, south of where the Japs halted us. Forty Japs died from A's mortars and C 218 FA's 75s. Next day, after 30 minutes' FA preparation, George found the Japs' position deserted. His men then moved north and buried Purpich, Miller, Thacker, and Aldige. More fighting with FA help, remained for A 162 through 13 July before we drove the Japs out of their last positions.

In Cutting Komiatum Track, George's other Plns with C 162 and the Aussies fought well, but Noble's men were among those deepest into combat among all the Americans. Without FA help, we had played an important part in pressing their withdrawal from their long salient down from

Salamaua past Roosevelt Ridge and Mt Tambu into Mubo Strip. Noble had led a heroic fight against the grim, stubborn Japanese. Capt George later gave Noble credit for triggering the whole Jap withdrawal from the Komiatum Salient.

CORRECTION! Hargis asks his readers to scratch out the name of Aldige as one of the Medics who were killed in cutting the Komiatum Track. (It must have been another Medic who died there.) Aldige was killed during A Co's first fight down on Nassau Beach much earlier, on 30 June 1943. Chaplain's Assistant Sid Stafford distinctly remembers taking part in the burial services, on 30 June, at the same time that A Co's Michael was buried. Chester Clark has an entry in his Diary which agrees with Sid Stafford's statement, and Chester witnessed his burial with Sid Stafford. Hargis says that this information reached him at too late a date to make a statement in A 162's story.

Biak Island, Netherlands East Indies, January 1945. Standing, L to R: Jerome Tomkowiak, Paul E. Long, Glen Tobin. Sitting, L to R: Karl Heiman and Joe Culp. (Courtesy of Heiman)

New Guinea: Komiatum Ridge. Entrance to the hut of the Jap Commander at Komiatum Ridge from which he and his troops were driven by the Australians during the advance on Salamaua. The entrance was by slit trench, the door being covered with eight feet of earth. Inside was a shaft thirty feet deep which led to an elaborate underground shelter. In the entrance to the shelter are Pte. George Robinson of Spotswood, Victoria, and Pte. Bill Watson, of Yarram, Victoria. (Courtesy of Rohlffs)

F AND G COS. 186 INFANTRY:

The Landing and The Cave

by DR. HARGIS WESTERFIELD, Division Historian,
with SGT. CHARLES PEARSON OF YANK and G CO 186's ROY D. BENNETT

CREDIT: Core of F 186's story is Sgt. Charles Pearson's "Buffalos on Biak," (**Yank Down Under Magazine,** June, 1944). Core of G 186's story is Roy D. Bennett's "A Cave on Biak Island," 1.5 pages of detailed, single-spaced typescript in small print. Background for both is 186 Inf's "Casualty Roster/Biak Campaign," and **RR Smith's Approach to the Philippines.** (Bennett also gave me G 186's Palawan story. Never, however, have I found one F Co man to help me with the story of his outfit anywhere overseas. I need help!)

I. DAWN LANDING ON BIAK. In the dark before daylight on 27 May 1944, men of F Co 186 Inf crowded into buffalos lined up on the tank deck of an LST standing off Japanese Biak. In the dim glow of the night light, men 5 feet away were only silhouettes of helmets, packs, and rifles. Destroyers were shelling the foreshore; their explosions had a dull ring through the walls of the LST.

"The ramp's going down," said buffalo driver Fennell of Brooklyn. "When we get off, be in back of this job because we dive straight down. A lot of water'll come in, but it'll go right out again."

At about 0630 with buffalo motors roaring, F Co headed for the ramp. When the first half of a buffalo cleared the ramp, it tipped sharply down, and splashed heavily as it plunged into the sea. Day was breaking now. Liberator motors sang overhead as the planes lunged in. Destroyer fire hit the ear-drums harder. An LCI blasted the beach with rockets and automatic fire.

The noise and dust of the preparatory bombardment hid the foreshore until we saw it come closing in on us from 400 yards away. Nervously, we checked over rifles and BARs with our hands, touched inside trigger-guards with our safeties still locked. With its HMG slanting skyward for aerial defence, our buffalo raced for the foreshore.

As the rockets quit thumping, we saw no beach ahead — only black stumps and roots of a mangrove swamp. Our buffalo driver managed to nudge through mangroves and muddy shallows and slide into somewhat firm ground.

F Co jumped out and formed for battle, but no Japs' rifles cracked at us. The unexpected offshore current had pushed us far west of our beach. We were 3,000 yards west of Green Beach 4 where 2/Bn was supposed to land.

But by 0745, all 2/Bn with "F" was ashore and ready. Although 186's Col Newman had asked General Fuller's permission to change missions with 162 Inf and move against Mokmer Drome, he got orders to march eastward to Bosnek Jetties to his assigned landing position. We were trained to swop missions on a scrambled beachhead like this one, but changing FA observer parties to 186 units would have been too complex a task under battle-field conditions.

So "F" pushed east on the little Nippo road to Bosnek. Burning dumps flamed against the background of a cliff. Directly ahead, a column of smoke climbed hundreds of feet overhead.

I and K Cos had also landed in the wrong place 700 yards west of G Co. They marched east to the original assigned position 1,000 yards east of Bosnek's west jetty. We had to pass through I and K Cos, and then 186 Hq's men now crossing our path to probe inland. Then at 0915 just as we cleared the eastern jetty, tank force reserves and FA units hampered our march. But luckily, the Japs at their old Bosnek base had not organized any attack on us.

Behind Bosnek Road, we saw a rise of heavy forest that covered a steep coral terrace. Like I and K Cos before us, "F" men were to occupy this ridge-top as security for Bosnek supply dumps and 162's westward march.

"F" still had met no Jap resistance. T/Sgt Wm Sullivan said to S/Sgt George Grant, "This looks like another Hollandia. But that's too much to hope for."

Just then, *Yank Magazine's* Correspondent Pearson heard that 2 of our men were dead. On the eastern flank of our beach-head, 2 men from an unidentified formation had walked into a pillbox and died. A heavily armed DUKW then blasted out the pillbox so that we could extend our flank. Pearson also heard that some 10 Japs were killed there.

By now, 186's patrols had discovered that there were many caves in the coral terraces — and Japs in those caves. T/Sgt Dikeman crawled up to a cave mouth. Carefully peering in, he saw 3 Japs — and opened fire before they could shoot at him.

And we developed a standard operation procedure to silence those annoying caves that could kill us. We would burn out an entrance with a flamethrower, then explode a 12-pound chunk of TNT inside the cave. Thus F 186 with other outfits went about saving our own lives and neutralizing Jap caves in the Bosnek ridges. After the caves were safe, we garrisoned the ridge-tops and secured our new beach-head. F Co 186 Inf's dawn landing had been successful.

II. A CAVE ON BIAK. In the last blackness before daylight 27 June 1944, we men of G Co 186 Inf already crowded topside of our LST to watch for the light. At 0630 with daybreak, our cruisers and destroyers broke the silence with the roar of 6-inch and 8-inch shells. T/Sgt Atchison ordered the Pln that Bennett belonged to, down into the tracked amphibian crafts.

The LST's doors opened. We waddled out into the sea, circled until all amphibs of our wave could form into line. While another wave formed behind us, we headed for the beach. The Navy still fired shells that ripped the air overhead; small craft (CLIs) smashed the foreshore with rocket clusters.

Large splashes marked the sea on our port side. We decided that the splashes showed that our own Navy was firing short. But later, we learned that big Jap guns above Mokmer Dromes were aiming at us. They missed us completely.

A formation of 12-15 B-24s dumped a pattern of bombs across the nearing Biak foreshore — from right to left. Smoke and dust obliterated the beach. Bennett gripped the .50 HMG mounted on the cab of the Amphib and flamed in a few short bursts against the murk of the shore.

Suddenly the Amphib tracks dug into the sand. G Co swarmed overside and dashed across the narrow beach, then across a disused road to halt panting before a high cliff. By the time we had our squads checked on and together again, somebody had found a rough trail up the cliff. We slung our rifles and climbed hand over hand. Often we slid back on smooth GI soles and badly scratched our knees and hands on jagged coral. (The cuts would make fine open jungle ulcers for the long, hard days coming on Biak.)

With 1/Pln at point, G Co turned left some 2 miles along the cliff top and other ridges almost impassable. For we sweated under heavy gear. Then we turned right with our backs to the coastline and started inland over rough country.

Down came a Jap plane to scout our landing. The ships' guns drove him back. When he passed over us, a few men fired rifles up at him, but without effect.

A Naval gun fragment glanced from a tree-top to strike Lt Minor in the nose and cause his evacuation to Hollandia for a number of days.

Late that morning, G Co had probed inland for what we thought to be 3 miles. (Most of G Co did not know that we were searching for a trail supposed to cross the ridges into the plateau north of Bosnek Village. It was E Co that found the poorly marked track and silenced the pillbox that guarded it.) But nowhere did G Co find any organized body of Japs to put up a fight. Finally, Capt Boyd ordered G Co dig our night perimeter.

Although we had climbed with 2 full canteens, we had depleted our water with hours of sweaty climbing in full pack. From starting to dig a 3-man fox-hole, Bennett was chosen to clink off with a canteen party to find water. He took with him the canteens of Rog, Acting-Sgt Cimbrek — and, of course, his rifle. Bennett joined others looking for water — T/Sgt Don Meyers, Duvall, and Counts.

Our little water-party came upon a little hollow in the coral ridges where we hoped to find a spring. It was a small U-shaped hollow with walls some 15 feet high curving around it. There was an easy walkway all around the "U."

When the whole detail was down on this level, we saw a cave in the wall to our left. Duvall turned left towards the cave to search for a spring. Bennett had the good luck to turn right along the wall.

Duvall probed into the cave-mouth. A Jap rifle cracked. Duvall was shot in the neck, to die in 3 minutes. A second shot rang out; Meyers was down — and crawling desperately to pull himself behind a large rock in the middle of the hollow.

A Jap sprang from the cave, fired more bullets into Meyers. Trying to take position to kill the Jap, Bennett himself was narrowly missed by a Jap bullet. Coral slivers showered Bennett. Bevernitz emptied his M-1 into the Jap, who thumped dead on the coral.

Now the cave was silent under cover from our M-1s. Other "G" men came to help — among them Medic McFarland who had heard the firing from our perimeter. McFarland did what he could to save Meyers, but the four Jap bullets had made his death almost instant.

As we carried out the bodies of Duvall and Meyers, Bennett saw a move before the cave-mouth. A large rock, 4 feet high, lay at the cave entrance. At the edge of the rock, Bennett saw a rifle and a Jap face as he started to aim. Bennett snapped a shot at him; dust flew where the face had been. Bennett wanted to check the cave-mouth for his kill, but orders came to return to G's perimeter. We were all happy to escape from that cave-hollow.

And so as dusk fell that first day of our beach-head on Biak, G Co had buried our first dead and dug in for the night, in heat and sadness. With canteens dry or nearly dry — depending on the type of man who carried one, we bedded down to endure thirst all night. (A man could press his cooler canteen or rifle-barrel to his face, or hold a pebble in his mouth Apache-fashion, for what help that could be.) We had cut our hands and legs in climbing the cliff from the coast. They smarted now despite the disinfectant, and would later become ugly ulcers.

With first light, we were out of our holes as soon as we were safe, and licking dew from the leaves to dampen our dry lips.

Then Bennett with other men made up a 30-man carrying party to go to the beach and return with water in 5-gallon cans. Gratefully drinking and refilling our own 2 canteens apiece at the beach, we returned with 15 cans — 75 gallons for all of waterless G Co on the heights. We took turns as carriers; while one man lugged the heavy can, the next man guarded our trail with his M-1.

Back at G's perimeter about 1200, Bennett found that he was assigned to help a man from 186 Regtl Hq — probably from S-2. This man of an unremembered name — a man from Philadelphia — insisted that Bennett go with him into the cave where Duvall and Meyers had been killed the night before. For 186 Hq wanted to ascertain whether or not this cave was an outpost of the Japs' main defense line above Bosnek.

After they had placed a rifle-squad around the 15-foot cliff to cover them, Bennett and the S-2 men scouted to the cave-mouth. The Jap whom Bevernitz had slain still lay where the M-1 had dropped him.

Inside the cave-mouth another Jap sprawled on his back with his clothes open and a bloody bandage on his stomach. Bennett believed that the sprawled Jap was same man whom he had snap-shot yesterday.

As they started into the cave, the S-2 saw a toe of a Nipponese shoe behind the 4-foot rock before the entrance. The S-2 man motioned to Bennett to climb on top of the rock.

From above, Bennett saw that the shoe was full of a Jap crouched and ready to leap out on them as they went past. Bennett turned the M-1 point-blank about 6 inches from the Nip's head and pulled the trigger. It was quick death.

About that time, the dead Jap with the blood-stained bandage came to life and leaped to his feet with a rifle. The S-2 man turned and put 2 quick M-1 shots into the Jap. This time, he was dead for sure. The blood on his stomach bandage had been red ink.

While Bennett kept his rifle ready, the S-2 man checked the corpses. One was a Sgt with a leather pouch on his shoulder-straps. The pouch contained some maps. The S-2 took these maps, and Bennett covered him until he left the cave.

Then Bennett tossed a live grenade inside the cave and heard it boom deep and loud as he ran to the cliff-top. No matter what was ahead for him and G 186 on Biak, Bennett was happy to leave that nightmarish cavern.

Thus did 186's F and G Cos land on Biak. Despite grounding on the wrong shore, we were luckily unopposed. F Co had no losses, but "G" had lost 1/Lt Minor wounded and Duvall and T/Sgt Meyers killed. Both Cos' hard battle of Biak was still ahead.

L CO 163 INF:

Combat In Abaca Jungle

by 1/LT WILLIAM SCHACHT, and
DR. HARGIS WESTERFIELD, DIVISION HISTORIAN (G 163)

> CREDIT: Indispensable for this story was L Co 163 Inf's Wm Schacht's photoprint from his vivid diary — 14 May to 11 June 1945 — a 55-page typescript with 3 Maps. (Schacht's Diary ends at Riverside, where 3 types of illness evacuated him.) Important especially after Riverside was Lt Col Jack Arnold's "Bucking the Abaca Jungle" (**Jungleer**, June, 1966, and also in my **Fighting Jungleers**). Other sources include 3/Bn 163 Inf's "Daily Journal, 10 May-10 July 1945), Eichelberger's **Jungle Road to Tokyo**, RR Smith's **Triumph in the Philippines**, and 24 Division's **The Fall of Davao**, which is meager and inaccurate about 3/Bn 163 Inf. (L Co 163 Inf men should be grateful to Bill Schacht, who has thoroughly covered their Southern Philippine Campaign. Already published in **Jungleer** are his 3 other stories: one on Zamboanga, one on Jolo, and another about L Co's previous action near Davao.)

On 4 June 1945, L Co 163 Inf's remaining 117 men detrucked near Ula Village to relieve L Co 34 Inf (24 Div) perimetered east of the Talomo River north of Davao City. We hiked down a murky little trail through abaca jungle — an overgrown hemp-field 20 feet high. Abaca leaves wide as banana leaves darkened our path.

While we occupied the main perimeter, 1/Lt Schacht took T/Sgt Howard Wood's 3/Pln to the Talomo River and relieved an outpost of L 34. Jap MGs and rifles greeted us 50-75 yards away. Our BARs and tommies silenced them, but we lifted Wayne Johnson back over the bank with a knee-mortar wound in his leg. Another "L" patrol sought a route for tanks to seize Highway L, main road north to Riverside Village. It drew fire from Japs 500 yards from our CP. Some mortar-blasts harassed us that afternoon, wounded Orezenowski at 1835.

Ahead of L Co fighting from Ula to Riverside to Calinan was perhaps the roughest combat in the whole Southern Philippines. Neglected fields of thick-trunked abaca hemp were now 20 foot-high thickets where nobody could see 20 feet ahead. We had to fight through 4 miles' abaca jungle where Lt-Gen Jiro Harada had deployed his finest battalions.

The Japs held a major strong-point in abaca around Hundred-Foot Bridge in a Talomo River curve NW of us. With K Co across the Talomo, "L" must win that bridge.

On 5 June "L" made 3 tries for that bridge. In early morning, T/Sgt Fenley's 2/Pln was driven to earth by several Jap HMGs at the junction of 2 secondary roads near the bridge. Fenley's Pln escaped without casualties.

Then Lt Schacht headed a 3-tank force with Fenley's Pln and Wood's 3/Pln, with an "L" section of our LMGs and an "M" section of HMGs. We tried to push through to Highway 1 on our side of the Talomo.

After a brief FA-mortar barrage, we marched totally exposed through open ground, next on a secondary road. Jap rifles, MGs, and mortars drove us into the ditches. Every time fire slackened, we moved up, often crawled.

The road ran into an abaca thicket. A Jap leaped out and blasted a mine under the lead tank. Explosion was so thunderous that it drowned out Nip automatic fire pinning us in the ditches.

Tankman Sgt Danciu yanked his crew through the ripped open turret. "L" posted a guard in the ditches beside the tank. Our T/Sgt Fenley was badly burned — his uniform totally blasted off his seared body. Wounded also were Brain, Sgt Pahmahmie, 5 other unnamed "L" men. Concussion shook up several tankmen, and killed a man still inside the lead tank.

To save the lead tank and its immobilized "L" guard, the other 2 tanks and our 2 Plns fired cover for them. A bulldozer hauled the tank with its corpse back to safety.

"L" continued fighting. At 1400, Schacht took all 3 rifle Plns and 3 tanks on a vast flank movement. This time, we crossed the road and dived into abaca 600-700 yards past where the tank was mined. Deep in abaca darkness, we hacked and sweated and hunted for paths. To assist our helpless and blind maneuver, a know-it-all tank major directed us from the lead tank. He swore that he knew what he was doing. After some 2 hours' labor, we filed down a dark, swampy little path where brush hid the sky.

The inevitable happened. Nips lay in ambush where the path joined an unexpected road. Firing on the lead tank, they drove 5 of Schacht's old reliable scouts to cover — McBath, Wilson, and White among them. Leaping for cover, McBath was shot down and hit some more times on the path before the tank. He died on the tank trying to evacuate him.

Since it was after 1700, Schacht insisted to the major that "L" had to retreat and dig our new perimeter, for I Co had moved up into last night's perimeter. The tanks finally turned in that cramped road-space while Japs poked in shots when they could target us. The tank-major smiled and said, "Good luck tomorrow!" but McBath was dead.

Sadly "L" dug into mud while rain fell hard. Word came that we would attack again tomorrow. Thinking of leading men again into that abaca Jap hell, Schacht prayed hard in his water-filled hole. Some Jap fire hit our perimeter that night.

On 6 June, we crawled from muddy holes to attack. Now Wood's 3/Pln and 3 tanks led out — patrolled some 25 yards before the tanks to give them room to maneuver. We blasted and fired all we had, and soon passed where the Jap mine had killed our tank yesterday.

Our FA had shot well before us. We scouted past smoking pillboxes and rotting old Japs with burned uniforms in roadside ditches. By 1010, we spotted a live pill-box. Our tank 75s blasted it; smoke rose from it. For security, tanks fired into one of our own shell-torn jeeps — evidently caught in Jap country. A rotted body lay nearby in US uniform with a US carbine.

Following FA shelling closely, we reached Hwy 1, the Riverside-Calinan road, past deserted Jap fox-holes. North was only sinister abaca for miles, but K Co was moving towards us. We sent a Pln 250 yards south to secure K's river crossing. The shattered Hundred-Foot Bridge was easily reparable for jeeps. Even if we bailed water from our holes during heavy rain that night, we slept better. I Co had taken over our advance.

On 7 June, life looked a bit better for "I." — even I Co was stopped a few hundred yards up Hwy 1. On I's flank, K's 2/Lt Vukovich had his Pln badly cut up. Although the abaca trails were spooky, L Co's Brown's 1/Pln contacted G 34 coming up on the Ula Road. Despite some rain in our mess-gear, real hot chow tasted good, that night.

On 8 June, our new 3/Bn CO, fiery, red-headed Maj Hamilton, tried a new offensive plan against the stubborn Jap lines. While "I" and "K" fought frontally against a Jap stone wall, "L" would flank it. We were to hike up the east Talomo bank 1,000 yards, turn west then to Hwy 1, and cut the Nips' rear. Our danger was that the Nips might slash our wire to 3/Bn, then gather and wipe us out.

Moving out around 1410, we hacked a trail through abaca groves almost night-dark down to the river, and turned upstream.

Silently over vines and up and down steep banksides, we slogged in a 200-yard column. We even feared to breathe here and there among plenty of Jap sign — rice, rags, uniforms, and discarded equipment. About 1540, we broke silence to kill 2 Japs near a deserted trench system that we bypassed.

That day, we made 500 of our 1,000 yards and dug a tight perimeter for that night high on the bank in thick brush. Roar of the Talomo waters made it hard for us to hear, but they muffled much of our necessary noise. It was strange to hear battle behind us; we were even ahead of our FA impact.

Next day, 9 June, in Jap country, we were up by first light and fearfully moving out before 0700. Swishing Talomo waters again covered our sounds, but we have slow going through swamps and over rocks. We had to slash vines. And I and K Co's FA (some of it probably on self-propelled mounts) sent shrapnel knee-high among us. We dived for nearest cover, then moved after each barrage, while MG and rifle bullets often whistled over us.

That morning, we found 6 Jap children under 8 years old, huddled on a camouflaged platform at the water's edge. We passed more platforms with blood and discarded clothing. By 1300, we had our objective — a small road bridging the Talomo. "L" hurriedly dug in to hold the bridge — with Wood's Pln at the Hwy 1 junction. Lying among the Japs, we were down to 1 K-ration and 1 fire-unit against the Jap army. Our phone would be easily cut; our radio batteries were half-spent.

By dusk, Wood's Pln was firing heavily against surrounding Japs. A 40-man Jap Pln dug in frantically while our mortars pounded them. We had to fire nightlong.

Creeping from water-filled holes on 10 June, we happily heard that the other 3/Bn Cos were following our route to reinforce us. By 1100, they all assembled — but for I Co, fighting to open a supply road through the bypassed Jap pocket.

We felt good briefly, but in 30 minutes, puffing "Red Dog" Hamilton was ordering us to make the same forward flank move as yesterday. We were to advance 1,400 yards and take Riverside. Yet I Co was fighting 1200 yards behind us, and we were 1,000 yards ahead of 21 Inf Regt on our left and 34 Inf on our right.

At 1200, Brown's Pln began an advance patrol. By 1400, they had made 500 yards creeping up the Talomo bank, and the rest of "L" joined him. Heading 3/Pln, Schacht labored forward for some 4 hours around natural barriers where Nips could make us a helpless target.

About 1600, we broke from the river-bank thicket into the first great cornfield plain that Schacht had ever seen in the Philippines. We saw Riverside's battered huts and a tall Nip observation tower — saw several miles ahead over open ground to gradually sloping hills.

Feeling terribly exposed after the abaca, we crossed the great field squad by squad — again sheltered by the river-bank until 300 yards from Riverside. We encountered new-dug spider-holes and trench systems maybe circling the town.

S/Sgt Fox'es squad used the river thicket to approach the first houses. On Fox'es signal, S/Sgt Hawko's squad searched more buildings but found no Japs. Then S/Sgt Lemons' squad seized the road junction unopposed. "L" dug in furiously, expecting vicious Jap attacks.

At darkfall, 5 Nips walked towards us from west of the Talomo. We slew 2, but 3 fled to inform their officer. Mortars and rifles harassed us. At 0445 that night, 40 Japs attacked from the east road. Our fire and FA repelled them. At dawn, 10 Japs lay dead 6 feet from our perimeter.

By 0705, all 3/Bn but I Co held Riverside with us. At 1025 that 11 June, a US Marine Douglas bomber flipped a 250-lb bomb on us. From a fouled up bomb bay, it impacted the east side of 3/Bn's perimeter among us. Mayfield, T/Sgt Wood were killed, 13-16 wounded. Known "L" wounded were Shields, Denson, Breitzke, Sgt Bailey. Meanwhile Schacht was out of action with malaria, dysentery, and jaundice for 3½ weeks. By now, "L" was down from 117 men at Ula on 4 June to 86 men, a loss of nearly ⅓ in 7 days.

On 11-13 June, all 3/Bn holed up in the Riverside mud, except for patrols. Japs were everywhere outside. On 13 June, L's patrol contacted 25 Japs, killed 3, but lost nobody.

On 14 June, 3/Bn drove for Calinan 2½ miles north of Riverside, last village before Mt Monoy's wilderness. We were unaware that we were now collapsing Gen Harada's second line of defense, in cooperation with 24 Div. Advancing carefully 14 June, "L" had an unnamed man wounded, but with FA help made over 1,000 yards. Advancing on 15 June, we hit the dirt under a Jap MG 25 yards ahead of us in the abaca, then routed it with our 60 mm mortars.

On that 15 June, other 3/Bn units with tanks led out and captured Calinan by 17 June. Yet at 0700 18 June, L Co endured 5 rounds' Jap FA in perimeter, lost Serpas, Pitchford, Buckey Wilson, and Sgt Ray Miller into hospital.

On 19 June, "L" had our last hard fight to seize a road-junction NW of Calinan towards Malagos. After 1/Lt McGee's leading Plns held the road-junction, a bypassed pocket of Japs fired on Capt Arnold's 17-man 3/Pln bringing up the rear. Sgt Ratto planted his 60 mm mortar without base-plate on the open road and broke the Nips at 25 yards while we grenaded them. Tanks helped us mop up; 9 Japs were killed. Pavao was wounded that night, circumstances unknown.

Now "L" was down to 52 men — haggard, sleepless, dirty, jungle-rotted, a number with minor wounds. Still, we had more nuisance patrols on 19-30 June, while the main body of the Japs' 100 Div men escaped into the mountains. On 1 July, finally, we grouped with our little 3/Bn and built a camp where we rested through 8 July. Then we loaded for Zambo, "home" to our own 41st Inf Div.

SECOND BATTALION HQ CO 163 INF:

Ammunition & Pioneer Platoon

by TECH/SGT NORMAN MATHEWS
and DR. HARGIS WESTERFIELD, Division Historian

*CREDIT: Prime credit is due to Tech/Sgt Norman Mathew's 15-page single-spaced typescript on Toem-Wakde, Biak, and Zamboanga, sent in 3 installments beginning 28 June and ending 13 Aug 1982. Mathews also helped me in letters of 19 June, 16 July, 27 July, 4 Aug, and 13 Aug — all in 1982. G Co 163 Inf's Gerald Varney also helped in a letter of 1 Aug 1982. Although 163's Journals omit mention of A&P, I organized Mathew's story of Zamboanga by reference to 163's Zambo Casualty List. This is the first A&P story that I have ever had for **Jungleer**.*

These are memorable actions of 2/Bn 163 Inf's Ammunition & Pioneer Pln near Toem across from Wakde Island, on Biak, and at Zamboanga. "A&P" was a select specialist group of 25 men, and an officer, 2/Lt Milder (killed at Zambo). Besides supplying ammo for 2/Bn 163 Cos, A&P was a miniature Combat Engr Bn, with the hard labor and danger that Combat Engrs endure. We built bridges and booby-trapped 2/Bn perimeters. (In the British Army, "pioneer" is the name for a combat Engr Co.) We handled tricky explosives. Like combat Engrs, we were combat men.

Wakde-Toem Operation. Just after dawn 18 May 1944, while 163's 1/Bn with F Co hit Wakde Island, A&P got orders to fight on the Toem Foreshore across from Wakde. A Nippo patrol had slipped across Tementoe Creek into the seaside jungle below dug-in 2/Bn 163 Inf. A&P's Lt Milder's patrol hunted them.

Beside our M-1s, we had unlucky Barnes borrowed from G Co for extra fire-power. Barnes was on the point of our patrol, with Lt Milder and T/Sgt Scourbrough. When we entered more open ground near the beach, Jap automatic and rifle fire split the air. A bullet in the head killed Barnes instantly; we others hit the sand under Jap fire.

Shooting from a partly ruined bunker, the Japs had opened fire on our first 4-5 men. If they had waited to see our whole patrol, more A&P men would have died.

Lt Milder ordered return fire, but we failed to see Japs to shoot at. Behind a coconut palm, Mathews watched Jap bullets splash up the sand. Milder led the dash with his first 3 men to a shell-hole about 25 yards away. Leaping over Barnes' body, Mathews followed with McDowell, T/Sgt Scourbrough. In the shell-hole, we found 2 dead Japs.

A large drift-log was stranded from the surf before the Japs' positions. Barnes' body was close by under a dark thicket. Milder jumped up and ran for the log — Mathews, McDowell, Scourbrough still with him. The big log was precisely long enough to protect all 4 men from the deadly Jap fire.

As Milder carefully raised his head, a Jap bullet clunked through the top of his helmet. Head below the log, Milder ordered intense fire from our M-1s. (He had only a carbine.)

A G Co squad-patrol had reinforced A&P and also opened fire on the Japs. All this time, expert riflemen Scourbrough and Mathews were firing behind each end of our log. Jap fire slackened.

From each end of the log, Mathews and Scourbrough threw a grenade; they landed together on the target. Milder sprang up with his carbine firing and charged; Scourbrough and McDowell and Mathews followed, M-1s blazing. "G" men charged also.

Four Japs broke and ran; we gunned down 2 of them instantly. One was a tall dead Jap on his back, in a neat and clean uniform. Two more were dead in the bunker. Besides these 4 now dead, we leaped after 2 more in flight. We killed them in a bamboo thicket.

From this fight Milder got a fine officer's saber. Scourbrough had a wrist-watch off the last Nip whom we killed. As pay for G Co's dead Barnes, A&P claimed a total of 6 dead.

Some days later, perhaps after the air recon of 2/Lt Milder and 1/Lt Leslie, a probable Jap Hq was located 4-5 miles from A&P's holes. Leaving perimeter one morning early, Milder and Leslie led a fast A&P patrol to shoot up and destroy that Hq.

We travelled faster and lighter because we had been persuaded to replace our M-1s with those nuisances of little carbines. We checked out a network of trails pounded by Jap feet. After several miles without trouble, we scouted a large clearing across the trail. Advancing at wide intervals, we saw huts and buildings scattered throughout the clearing.

Not permitting souveniring, Milder ordered all buildings torched, and as much equipment destroyed as possible. When smoke ballooned up, we left. We were afraid that Jap patrols might see the smoke and hunt us down.

As we descended a series of switchbacks on our trail, a scout signalled, "Japs ahead." Our patrol looked down on a sizeable Jap carrying party enjoying lunch, happily chatting. This supply detachment had no security guards.

Slowly we eased into postion above. We looked forward to using our light 16-shot carbines. On signal, we fired as one man.

A few Japs fell; the others leaped into jungle and disappeared. But at rapid fire, some of our bolt-handles flew off our carbines. Despite all of our carbine fire, only 2 Japs lay dead. Some Japs had left blood on the ground. After destroying their rice and other food, we returned to Battalion with their medical supplies. (Surely, those Japs had been carrying to a Hq that they had not known to be deserted.) Back in perimeter, most of us exchanged our tricky carbines for our reliable M-1s.

Biak. On 12 June 1944, A&P Pln landed with our 2/Bn 163 Inf to reinforce the hard-fought 41st on Biak. After watching 3 Zeroes blasted from the sky over our LSTs, A&P perimetered on the coast road west towards Parai Defile and set up 2/Bn's ammo dump. For some 6 weeks until the Japs' 3/Bn 222 Inf died in Ibdi Pocket, supplying our men was our main duty.

We could truck some supplies to Plns close to the Bosnek-Parai Road, but we had to backpack for outfits high on the coral ridges. We lifted loads up almost perpendicular cliffs and along dim jungle tracks. Both japs and Yanks some times fired on us. Often, we volunteered to carry the wounded back to Medics. We must make many perilous return trips through our own perimeters at night, when guards might kill us for Japs. Backpacking was our most heroic work on Biak.

After Ibdi Pocket died, A&P landed in 2/Bn at Korim Bay to mop up north Biak. There we bridged a stream. We felled and floated logs from great jungle trees down to the crossing. Our bridge was strong enough for jeeps.

One cold, wet morning, A&P followed a rifle Co several miles inland. Riflemen spotted a Jap position topping a long slope with a clear field of fire hundreds of yards down before it. A rifle squad probed from both flanks, and found 4 Japs huddled under a canvas square from the rain, and a .50 HMG still cased in waterproof canvas. Jap hands reached skywards when our M-1s menaced them.

Not wanting to scout farther with prisoners, the patrol left A&P's Miller and Mathews to guard them beside the HMG. They spent 2 nervous hours in fear of a Jap attack.

When the patrol returned and relieved us, a Jap Sgt volunteered to tote the HMG back to 2/Bn. The gun somehow became A&P's and part of our perimeter defense.

Later near Korim Bay, A&P manned a trail-block where we had bridged the stream. The air was redolent with Jap corpses. We tried to bury them. Our booby-traps halted some starved Nippo stragglers, but on Milder's advice after a week, the trail-block ended. A&P's Biak war was over.

Zamboanga. In Zambo Fight, 2/Bn 163's A&P operated with greater efficiency than in New Guinea. In place of slow, laborious backpacking like on Biak, we had jeeps to carry ammo. Every morning before the day's fighting, we jeeped in close behind the firing line to restock riflemen, and MG and mortar crews. Each morning, men were anxious to rebuild their supplies of grenades depleted from throwing at prowling Japs last night.

At Zambo, we had our first casualties — some 20 per cent of our small command of 26. First to die was gallant 2/Lt Milder. On 11 May 1945, our second day in battle, Milder with other 2/Bn officers went to inspect our front, or to study the destruction of some Jap positions which we had overrun.

Milder should have been safe, but last night, Jap patrols had probed 2/Bn's lines. Some riflemen were still edgy with fear that Jap snipers had remained behind in ambush. When the officers moved through heavy jungle, a Yank BARman opened up on them. The first burst mortally wounded Milder, but no one else was known to be hit. After some difficulty in making it clear that our officers were not Japs, Milder was rushed to the aid station. Milder died on the way.

As always in 2/Bn 163, A&P was responsible for handling all explosives where possible. Men often asked that we booby-trap their positions at night and remove those tricky explosives at dawn before patrols could secure the area before the front. We had to handle the new trip-flares, 4-pound anti personnel mines, and "bouncing betties."

We cannot forget the large officer who jeeped in one afternoon and requested some "betties." When probably T/Sgt Riggs hesitated to issue them, the officer was wrathful. Riggs finally let go of them. Some days later, we learned that a mine had prematurely exploded and killed him — a "bouncing betty," in fact.

When 2/Bn fought its way up Tumaga Valley against Jap Marines, A&P was called for demolition charges and flame-throwers. (Maintenance and use of flame-throwers was another A&P function.) A rifle Pln needed help to dislodge Japs from bunkers holding a Y-shaped crossroads.

Three Jap positions guarded the jungle where 2 roads merged into another road. The roads made a pattern like the letter "Y." Two smaller bunkers held right and left arms of the "Y," and a larger bunker blocked the road junction where the 2 arms of the "Y" came together. Some fire still came from the bunkers.

While 2 A&P teams flamed out the slots in the 2 smaller bunkers, T/Sgt Riggs and Matthews prepared TNT charges. Their first thrown charges somewhat damaged the 2 smaller bunkers. Their second charges demolished both bunkers; they also unroofed 2 trenches leading to the third much larger bunker at the road junction.

Heavy rifle Pln fire or the flame-throwers had apparently driven the Nips from the smaller bunkers into the large bunker — most likely A&P's flame-throwers.

Riflemen and flame-throwers now concentrated on the last bunker. No return fire came. The Pln leader ordered AP to destroy the bunker so that no Nips could slip back into it.

For a thorough job, Riggs and Mathews had to crawl up the 2 narrow trenches from the destoryed bunkers. They had to place charges under all 4 corners of the supports of the roof of the large bunker — then light fuses and snake out fast.

But the crawl-trenches were shoulder-deep in crumbling earth. The Lt placed 2 men, a man above each trench to help Riggs and Mathews to escape.

Inside the bunker with 2 dead Japs, they placed 4 charges. They counted "Three," saw their fuses light, and scurried on their knees into the light of the trenches.

But no man waited above Mathews to pull him out. And behind him, the fuses were short! Desperately, he grabbed a sapling on top of the ground, but it broke loose and let him drop.

The next second, the blasts blew Mathews up and out of the trench. Dazed, he heard chunks of bamboo logs, earth, and rocks thudding around him. But he was not hit. Never did he find the man who could have helped him up to safety.

At Zambo, A&P men had casualties in our deadlist fight. a Jap reinforced Pln slipped behind 163's advance. Finding an unguarded bridge on a heavily trafficked road, they dug in above the bridge. They covered all approaches with a mortar and a 20 mm machine-cannon. They laid bangalore torpedoes on the bridge.

Finding the bridge-block, 2/Bn ordered an A&P squad to clear the bridge of torpedoes, while 2 squads of 2/Bn's AT Pln covered us. Nobody was aware of the Jap ambush.

On that 16 Mar when A&P began to remove the torpedoes, hot Jap steel struck among us. Paradiso instantly died with a mortar fragment in his back. More mortar fragments seriously wounded Hull in his legs. As we scrambled for cover, a 20 mm fragment smashed Lentz' arm and elbow. Another 20 mm fragment slashed Conners' face.

The unhurt A&P and AT Pln men saved their lives around a sharp curve in the road. When other 2/Bn men reinforced us, Roman Catholic Father Lynn was among the first to arrive. Father Lynn at once ran to carry out a wounded man. A&P men never knew how the fight ended when the bridge-block was finally liquidated.

These are the great memories of 2/Bn 163 Inf in the New Guinea and southern Philippine Campaigns — Toem, Biak, and Zamboanga. A little team of specialists — a miniature Combat Engr outfit — we labored for 2/Bn and handled tricky explosives. For 2/Bn 163 also, we were expert trouble-shooters where needed.

Norm Mathew's story of Barnes' death and A&P's shootout is a correction of my own statements in my story "Tementoe Creek and Tor River" (Jungleer, Sept-Dec 1975). On rear guard at the beach when G Co 163 Inf's 3/Pln reinforced A&P, I never knew until Mathews told me in 1982, that A&P had any part in the Barnes shootout. From a long distance while at the same time turning to watch for more Japs crossing the Tementoe, I thought that I saw G Co's Varney and Sahs make the killing. I apologize to the A&P men who did the killing: Milder, McDowell, Scourbrough, and Mathews of A&P.

D CO 186 INF:

Palawan, Zamboanga, and Sibuco Bay

by NICK (LEROY) WHEELER and OTHER D 186 MEN,
with DR. HARGIS WESTERFIELD, Division Historian

CREDIT: Overwhelming credit is due to a 34-page single-spaced typescript researched and composed by Nick Wheeler and reviewed by 1/Sgt Wayne Strebig, both of D 186. D's contributing authors were CO Capt George Gage, Ross Kreager, Marion Criswell, Lloyd Sabby, and Albert Hannegan — with all 3 Plns and Hq represented. I checked also 186's 2 Casualty Lists from the Southern Philippine Campaign — one from 28 Feb to 27 Mar 1945 (on Palawan) and another from 30 May through 20 Mar 1945 (at Zamboanga — less 2/Bn and CN Co). This last list seems to me inaccurately kept. Where Wheeler and this last list disagree, I have relied on Wheeler. (I may have made unavoidable errors, for the typescript has been nearly unreadable — in some places.) This is the fifth and last of Wheeler's stories — the only full history of any weapons Co ever to appear in **Jungleer***. First four were reprinted in my* **Fighting Jungleers***. Originally, they were published in* **Jungleer** *in Dec 1973 (Campaign in Papua), June 1970 (Hollandia), Mar 76 (Biak), and Jan 1977 (Biak also).*

On 9-25 Feb 1945, D Co 186 Inf staged on barren Mindoro Island across the narrow channel from Luzon to fight for Palawan and Zamboanga. South Mindoro near Progreso Village was a flat, dry plain with a few trees. Despite wind, dust, and water shortage, our tents and cots seemed homelike. Native hucksters sold our kitchen corn on the cob, although our Iowa farmers thought it poor and we joshed them about it.

For Palawan Beach, D's 2 HMG Plns were to load on different LCIs — 1 Pln with AT Co, and 1 with B Co. These MGs would be in the first wave. Our .81 mortars would beach in the second wave. On 24 Feb, we pre-loaded mortars into alligators which went on LCTs, attached to C Co in reserve. Mortarmen carried 2 firing units, and Bn A&P had a reserve unit for us.

Like all 186's Cos, "D" was far understrength — just 133 enlisted men. We had few replacements during and after Biak action. To save their lives for rotation home, we transferred 11 "D" men to SV Co to unload cargo after the beachhead. While we waited for trucks to the beach, replacements arrived and filed off our little squads. These rookies were very scared men.

Just before dark 26 Feb, 186 departed Mindoro to seize Palawan, that long, narrow island southward in the Sulu Sea. At dawn, we got an idea of the size of our V-3 Task Force — 80 ships, 3 protecting light cruisers, 4 destroyers. Our convoy's Ground Force Engrs were to build 3 air-strips.

PALAWAN At daylight 28 Feb, we waited to land while Air Force, Naval guns, and LCI rocketships battered the beach. A and B Cos then hit White Beach 1 at the end of the peninsula east of Puerto Princesa Bay.

When our second-wave LSTs unloaded vehicles, they stuck in the soft sand. Transport Cpl Marv Johnson called the alligator drivers to tow all of our jeeps off the beach.

Landing was simple but for the LST with our rotation men aboard. The tide changed. The sea vanished below us and left us on wet sand. Our LST was a sitting duck for Jap shells. A destroyer threw a line but could not tug the LST into water.

From northward, a valiant Jap 20 mm gun fired on the LST and sprayed the forward gun-mount with vicious little exploding shells. But we know of no casualties. Our cruisers wiped out that gun-crew. Later, "C" found 3 abandoned 20 mm guns.

Although some 1800 Japs had held the Puerto Princesa area, 1/Bn did not fight until the third day ashore. On 2 Mar, when E Co had a few casualties on flat-topped, sheer-sided Hill 1125, "B" and a "D" MG Pln relieved E Co.

While B Co had a fire-fight, 1/Bn's Lt-Col Anderson, Capt Nelson (Bn S-3), Sgt. Maj Pharr, and D's CO Capt Gates scouted on B's left to find a way to advance A Co. Sudden Jap HMGs grounded them for 15 minutes. While B Co tried to save them, D Co's mortar observation party arrived with Lt Rodgers.

Rodgers ordered our base mortar to fire a round to help adjustment on the Japs. By pure luck, this first .81 round impacted a Jap ammo dump. The area just over hill-crest seemed to erupt — a wild fireworks fountain for some 10 minutes. Then D's 1/Pln's 2 HMGs targeted and silenced the Jap MGs. The 1/Bn scouting party of officers escaped unharmed.

Three times after preparatory shelling, B Co pushed but did not drive home with their M-1s because they would lose too many men. Amazingly accurate Jap fire countered D's HMGs. At 1730, a MG slug wounded Fersch in left biceps while a second MG slug hit McKenzie in right knee. ("B" lost 1 killed, 4 wounded.)

By 4 Mar, CN Co had up 105 mm guns on self-propelled mounts to help the attacks on Hill 1125. While 167 FA fired 100 rounds of 105s in 3 concentrations, "D" spent a whole fire unit. They destoryed 2 20 mm gun positions; riflemen captured 2 HMGs. The dazed Japs withdrew from Hill 1125.

Lt Saucier's rank was painted on his helmet. Last night, a sniper had laired in a cave behind our front. Next day at close range, the sniper's bullet cracked Saucier's helmet and knocked him down, but did not kill him. Although "D" men tried to take the sniper prisoner, he prefered death and died from a flame-thrower. Another sniper grazed MG-gunner Franke, but only lightly.

Amusing was 2/Pln's gunners' discovery of 4 full barrels of alcohol in the tall grass. They carried off half a barrel.

On Palawan, D Co endured no more near misses. On 5 Mar, our 81s with CN 186 and Btry C 167 FA barraged the Japs from their Firm Hill Hq. On 6-8 Mar, our mortars teamed again with 167 FA and CN 186 to enable G Co to storm the Japs' strongest position — the Hill 1445 hogback. The stubborn resistance of the outgunned and outnumbered Palawan Japs was ended. Core of their resistance was 174 Inf's 4 Co, with 131 Airfield Bn, and 1st Independent Maintenance Unit.

ZAMBOANGA On 10 Mar, we were placed on a 12-hour alert as reserves for 162 and 163 Inf's landing at Zambo. On 16 Mar, 1/Bn heard that tomorrow we would embark at night for Zambo to reinforce the 2 Regts. They had suffered many casualties, said the rumors.

On 18 Mar, LCIs landed 1/Bn near San Mateo Beach. We followed a stream to junction with another stream and dug in as night fell. On 19 Mar, we moved to a main road and waited for orders. On 20 Mar, we entrucked behind Engrs' bulldozers making a road. Finally, we detrucked and topped a flat-topped hill, and the Japs were dug in before us at the edge of the rain-forest.

While we tensely waited for briefing from 162 Inf to whom we were attached, Lt Hundahl called key NCOs to his hole. Expecting battle orders, they found him dealing out 4 hands for a quick penochle game. Some men tried to improve supper by cutting up tomatoes and peppers from a looted garden into cans of C-ration hash, then heating it in a helmet. The peppers made the hash inedible. Luckily, a mess-truck had arrived by this time with a hot supper.

On 21 Mar, 186's 1/Bn relieved 162's men to fight Japs holding Ridge X before us. Ridge X was on the left flank of 162's drive up West Ridge to capture Mt Capisan, that towering center of Jap resistance at Zambo. D's 1/Pln of HMGs positioned with "C" to fight Ridge X; our .81s would fire from behind a ridge.

At dawn 22 Mar, "C" attacked while D's 4 HMGs fired overhead, along with 1/Bn Hq's .37s and .50 HMGs. D's 4 gunners claimed destruction of many MG nests. Sabby's HMG fired 5 belts with fine results — but ruptured ear-drums of loader Peters. Peters left D Co with his head a bloody mess. Despite death of Scout Linton, "C" took the ridge and 2 MGs — found 7 dead Japs. From C's newly stormed ridge, terrain ahead seemed like an endless series of ridges with short saddles and deep valleys.

Next day, 23 Mar, our .81s and CN 186's 105s helped "C" drive the Japs from Hill 620, the next ridge. Then a MG section of D's 2/Pln supported "B" on the right. B Co tried to fight up Hill 620 and contact "C" on their left. Intense fire wounded D's Bell, Anderson, Sgt Scott, but they came back a few days later. A sniper bullet glanced from a log for a near miss on S/Sgt Kreager. Japs held "B" from Contacting "C" that day.

On 24 Mar while G 162 overran Bald Hill to our right and went on to storm Mt Capisan, our 1/Bn 186 kept fighting for Hill 620. D's 1/Pln's HMGs relieved 2/Pln. Lt Schroeder's 1/Pln split up for B and C Cos still trying to make contact. When "B" assaulted, Sgt Bamber's MGs would try to destroy whatever automatic gun positions they could locate.

At 0940 with our support, B's 2 rifle Plns attacked Hill 620. Terrain was steep, Jap fire heavy. When B's Capt Messec observed with "D" men, a 167 FA shell impacted behind them, slammed rocks and earth onto them, and dazed them with concussion. Rocks in the face cut B's Messec and D's Lt Schroeder, who also suffered minor burns. The shell ruptured Sgt Hannegan's ear drum, also gave concussion to Sgt Stender.

A Jap MG grounded some of B's forward squads. It was firing from 350 yards away across a saddle in the ridges. Gunner McCoy and loader Jones of Kreager's squad finally found a ridge position from which to fire on this long-range MG. Just as Kreager gave firing orders and McCoy and Jones put their second round into the MG receiver, a 20 mm shell hit their gun.

The shell smashed the receiver and damaged cradle and tripod. When the shell exploded, the red-hot largest fragment slashed Gunner McCoy in the shoulder. It turned and buried itself in his chest — luckily failed to penetrate his rib-cage. Loader Jones and S/Sgt Kreager were also down with fragments.

Gillespie, Virginia, Hulm, and Sgt Stender ran up and dropped to the ground to crawl back with McCoy, Kreager, and Jones. The red-hot tracers of shells from the Jap 20 mm gun barely cleared the helmets of our men inching along on their faces. We saved all 3 of D's wounded men.

Meanwhile, Sgt Olsofska's squad silenced that Jap MG 350 yards away across the saddle. Then Sgt Halter's .37 gun from A Co's Pln directed accurate fire on that 20 mm gun. Our Capt Gage saw Jap legs and arms fly through the air.

That battle of 24 Mar ended in victory for both 186's and 162's men. About 1330, 186's B and C Cos contacted on Hill 620, with D's help. And G 162 had taken Mt Capisan. After a skirmish next day, 1/Bn contacted G 162 holding Capisan.

A harrowing D Co accident occurred on that 25 Mar. An .81 mortar shell dropped on a rifle squad and almost buried it. Our "medium" with a delayed fuze wounded 3 men. The yoke locking nut on a mortar had not locked properly. The barrel jerked off its base plate, raised the trajectory, and shortened the range. Some NCOs were chewed out.

The Japs fled from where they had guarded the western approach to Mt Capisan — fled north into the mountain rain forest. After relief by 162 on 26 Mar, "D" blissfully stayed overnight on the beach to eat hot food, bathe, and clean weapons.

Our 1/Bn 186 Inf replaced 163 men who were ordered to capture Jolo Island far west in the Sulu Sea. On 27-30 Mar, we pushed west against Jap pockets on Hill 2,000 — actually a whole series of ridges above San Mateo. Although Japs still stoutly held reverse slopes, they had no chance against aggressive riflemen, D's heavy weapons, FA, and Air Force. On 29 Mar, Leyba and Sharpe took light wounds from Jap mortars, but remained on duty — D's only casualties. By 30 Mar, the Japs were on their great retreat north into the hungry Zambo Mountains. Gen Hojo's objective was probably to seize the rich ricelands of Siocon over 70 miles north of Zamboanga City, but his men would never arrive there.

Last memorable action of D 186 was on T/Sgt Milkovich's patrol inland from Sibuko Bay, on the NW side of Zambo Peninsula, about 30 miles north of Zambo City. At Sibuko Bay, 1/Bn had landed unopposed from LSTs to intercept the retreat of less than 3500 defeated but persistent despairing Japs. Although "D" retained our 81s for security, our 2 HMG Plns now patrolled as riflemen — but now armed also with some .30 light MGS.

In early May, D's 2/Pln of machine-gunner-riflemen were attached to C Co on an outpost 6 miles inland on a river with a name unknown to us. Airmen and guerilla reports made us expect contact with the head of the Japs' main body.

D's T/Sgt Milkovich led 20 men with a BAR and a LMG 4 miles south of C's outpost, and across a river. He talked with C's Sgt Jerecki back from a patrol on the main trail up into the hills. All Jerecki's men felt that somebody unseen had watched every move. Our "D" patrol pushed on along.

Late that afternoon, we had a fire-fight. Milkovich set up LMG and BAR against the Japs. Suddenly their numbers increased; their mortar shell smashed our LMG tripod. Letourneau took splinters in his hips. Our patrol retreated across the river — but for Scott, Crittenden, and Clarke covering their rear.

But the Japs crossed downstream to cut us off. Clarke was missing. There was a second fire-fight; Milkovich's nose was almost shot off. He despatched Ruether and Garrison back to "C" to say that he would fight a delaying action — and to warn C's men in their holes not to fire if we returned in the dark.

Our patrol pretended to dig in, but slipped away at night. Letourneau painfully hobbled along with helpers. We finally reached safety with "C" at 0300.

Clarke came back next morning. He said that at least half a Co of Japs had recrossed the river to a hill. Two "C" rifle Plns found the main body of Japs in a lush wide ravine, and checked their advance while their third Pln and Weapons Pln reinforced "C." There were several fire-fights.

Col Anderson sent D's Capt Gage by PT boat to Zambo to guide a Marine Corsair pilot to bomb the Japs. After the first run failed to find the Japs, our .81s marked target with smoke. Corsair bombs and mortar shells killed or wounded many Japs and forced survivors to leave weapons and supplies. D Co then had mop-up patrols where Thilmony and Garrison were wounded and hospitalized for a few days.

D186's Southern Philippine Campaign soon ended. With no dead and only 14 wounds, we fought well on Palawan and at Zambo.

Robert J. Burns, Henry Johnson, Robert Bouchard and Karl L. Heiman. Zamboanga, July 1945. (Courtesy of Heiman)

Zamboanga and vicinity. Looking NE. 14 September 1944.

An Australian infantry section pass Japanese tanks knocked out at Milne Bay, New Guinea. (Courtesy of Rohlffs)

MID-PACIFIC DREAM

Day by day the engines drone;
The ship drives South: swish of a wave,
Hum of the motors, monotonous
Blue waves, always the same:
Dull blue waters, a few white caps
All the way into the sky. Sleepily
Men lie on the deck: little card-games,
Books, day-dreams of love, drowsy
Smoking—future strikers of beach-heads
Who loll on the dirty decks.

Nothing is real here: no war,
Only western waters forever,
Droning engines, ocean into the sky.
Nothing is real here, not the chance
Terror of twilight, darting torpedo,
Nor what the guards at the guns
Topside wait for, watching the sky.

HARGIS WESTERFIELD

(Aboard Dutch *New Netherlands*, San Francisco to Sydney, 1943)

Wreckage of Japanese aircraft, Hollandis. (Courtesy of Turosik)

116 ENGINEER BATTALION:

Combat and Labor in Papuan Campaign

by DR. HARGIS WESTERFIELD, Division Historian, with ENGRS WILLIAM ANDEL and GENE ROHLFFS

> CREDIT: Main incentive for this history was discovery of "Unit History" dated 26 Oct 1943 of 116 Engr Bn's Papuan Campaign. (I found this at Dwight Eisenhower Library on our Division Association's special visitation grant.) For Sanananda, I used also 163 Inf's Casualty List, S/Sgt John A. Harris' award story, and William Andel's 14-page letter written in 1973. For Salamaua, I used also Historian D. Kenneth Deacon's 10-page typescript "116 Engineers in the Salamaua Campaign," Fred Devenney's "Night in Green Hell" (**Jungleer,** July 1959), Australian David Dexter's **The New Guinea Offensives**, 162 Inf's Journal (9 July-13 Sept 1943), and unpublished manuscript by Col AR MacKechnie, "Operations of 162 Infantry in the Salamaua Campaign." We lack casualty lists for Salamaua Operation.

We Combat Engineers of B Co 116 Engr Bn claim to be the first 41st Div men to contact the Japs at Sanananda.

Docking at Port Moresby from the old Dutch *Bonteko* about 1000 27 Dec 1942, we heard our first air alert, but it was soon called off. After we unloaded supplies, an Engr boarded each truck to accompany the drive to our Sanananda staging area. Climbing the big hill by 10 Evac Hospital, Andel heard the air raid siren again. His Black Omaha driver hit the ditch and yelled for Andel to flatten also. Andel still had never seen a Nippo plane.

While B 116 waited to emplane across the Owen Stanley Mountains, Andel and others volunteered to help man MGs on B-17s to raid Rabaul. Later, we found that we were not needed. Next morning, that plane to which Andel was assigned, was the only one that failed to return from the flak over Rabaul.

On 31 Dec, B's 1/Pln flew across the Owen Stanleys 96 miles and landed on the lumpy, grassy runway of Dobodura Strip. In a stream of sweat, we hiked from Ango Corner to Soputa. Moving quietly up the muddy track to Voya Village, we bypassed the Japs' Perimeters "P," those deadly strongholds. Besides pack and rifle, each Engr carried machete, coil of rope or wire, and pick or shovel. Far up-trail, we heard MG and FA fire, Jap or Aussie.

Probably on 2 Jan 1943, B 116 Engrs' 1/Pln was the first 41st unit to contact the Japs when we entrenched in Huggins (Musket) Perimeter. In the brush menaced by tall jungle trees, we dug shallow holes while fearing snipers from that silent green jungle curtain. A few days later, our 2/Pln joined us to reinforce 163 Inf at the front.

But we Combat Engrs were still labor troops who fought only from necessity. Threatened by Jap MGs, mortars, and snipers, we labored with our hand tools. We dug communication trenches, built weapons bunkers, sandbagged Medics' stations. We some times guarded Aussie FA. We carried supplies, laid corduroy roads — dug graves. We saw some combat.

While building a corduroy road in an advanced area by night, our 1/Pln lost 2 wounded. On 10-11 Jan, Bomall was shot in the right leg, and Sgt Howard in the neck. On an unknown date, 2/Pln killed 7 Japs and took 1 prisoner.

Hard-working S/Sgt Harris was a notable combat Mess-Sgt. Improvising a kitchen in an enlarged trench under threat of Jap fire, Harris provided many hot meals for B 116. When fevers hospitalized his whole kitchen crew, Harris worked on without helpers, finally collapsed with malaria. Despite a maximum temperature of 106, Harris did recover.

While 2 Engr Plns were in combat, Hq and 3/Pln were in reserve — at hard work on labor details. Andel volunteered as mess-Sgt for 3/Pln's 3/Squad which maintained a Piper Cub Strip. He heated rations over open fire — pork and beans from restaurant-sized cans — some canned hash — and dear old Sanananda bully beef. We hated bully beef, but our native laborers hungered for this delicious "bullamacow." Andel traded it for coconuts, papayas, and bananas. Mixed papayas and bananas appetized his hungry work-gang.

After the battle, B 116 regrouped in a coconut grove by Sanananda Track among mosquitos and corpse-flies. Rain fell daily. After work on roads or trails, we slept under pup-tents with mosquito bars — of course in holes for security from remaining Japs. Quinine to prevent malaria made us so deaf that we could hardly hear.

Once Andel and 2 cobbers hunted souvenirs on Sanananda Track. It was spooky among dark, empty pillboxes among shell-shattered coconut trees. We felt that snipers had us in their sights. As we turned back, 3 Aussie soldiers passed us — also out souveniring. That night, a Sgt told us that Japs had slain all 3 Aussies where we had sensed that snipers were watching us.

After we helped 163 win Sanananda Battle, 116 Engs performed our top military achievement of World War II. This achievement was building a network of supply roads through the raw wilderness of the Dobodura-Buna-Oro Bay country. The Army needed supplies for this forward base. Air Force needed supplies to build up Dobodura Field to a base to counter the Japs' New Guinea Air Force.

We built the great road from Oro Bay to Dobodura — 23.7 miles, with 11.7 miles of it in mountains, and 12 in swampy flat terrain. We built 7.5 miles of the Dobodura-Buna Road (The Aussies built the middle miles of that road). We built Buna Dock, with a landing area 30 by 90 feet and a ramp to the shore 75 feet long. We built the 875-foot Soputa Bridge. We laid an aviation gas pipe-line, Buna to Dobodura. We supervised native labor for a hand-made road, 18 miles, Dobodura to Soputa to Killerton. We erected 10th Evac Hospital and Kapala Ordnance Depot, and operated Kota Creek Saw Mill.

SALAMAUA OPERATION. A Co 116 Engrs both fought and labored in our Salamaua Operation. On 29 June 1943, 2 Plns of A 116 boarded landing barges just before dark at Mageri Point to hit the beach at Nassau Bay with Col McKechnie's

1/Bn 162 Inf. It was a black, stormy voyage some 35 miles along the shore — high waves, rain in black, icy sheets.

Under dripping ponchos, 30 men in each bouncing barge were crammed together. We stood in shallow water, or squatted, cowboy fashion. The 15-foot waves tossed barges high; they slapped down hard. Seasick pains racked some men's stomachs. They fought to the gunwales — to get there on time, if they could make it. Some boats got lost; the faster PTs had to regather them. With a speed below 6 miles per hour, the black voyage seemed to last forever.

Although the PT Navy knew the coast well, the PT boat leading our first wave got lost and had to backtrack for its convoy. Several times, our Amphib Engrs thought that they saw a landing signal from the shore, but each time, something did not quite look right. Finally, a white light was blinking from where the beach-side Aussie guides signalled to us.

To 116 Engrs' Rohlffs, the sea outside Nassau Bay now seemed like glass until we turned shoreward. Even in the black Guinea night, Rohlffs made out the 3 dim shorelines of Nassau Bay. As the barges neared the shore, the swells grew higher. Then the long swells became breakers 10-15 feet high which knocked the barges right and left.

Meanwhile 116's Driver Gray had started his D-4 bulldozer to warm it for an instant landing. We shuddered to think that the D-4 made our boat a prime target for MGs.

Finally, we grounded on the beach. The ramp clanked down. First men off Rohlffs' boat were knocked flat and rolled in surf before they clawed in over the sand. But nobody drowned. Next men landing from the boat carried metal network sections for surfacing air-strips — metal networks that we always carried with us. We could walk ashore on these firm sections. They made a surface for the cat run ashore without bogging down in the sand.

When cat-man Gray opened the throttle of this idling D-4, a cloud of sparks geysered up the clouds — as it seemed to Rohlffs. Its clanking tracks and the sparks frightened off a lurking party of Nip soldiers who could have played havoc with our infantry. Little teams of Jap bayonet-men could have slain many of our confused, seasick men in the half-dark of our little jungle flashlights — or donned our helmets and tricked us to shoot into one another. But the Japs feared that our tanks were attacking, and took to the brush.

Only 45 men and 2 officers of A 116 Engrs had beached on this dark Guinea Shore, for high seas had turned back the other Engr Pln. Most of us spent the last 4 hours of the night trying to keep warm in our wrung out fatigues under clammy ponchos — and feeling sorry for ourselves.

The wreck of our barges had marooned us on a Japanese coast. Half a mile NE towards Salamaua Town were 75 Japs of 3/Bn 102 Inf's MG Co, and 2 miles south, 300 more Japs of that Co. A total of 400 Inf and 340 other elements were ashore — but minus 218 FA's guns, which the high seas had turned back. Lack of FA fire cover would increase our losses in the fights next morning and tomorrow night.

With early light, we Engrs got to work. Gray's bulldozer made a track to haul supplies up from the beach. We sheltered a supply dump from Jap planes under trees about 200 yards north up the coast. With a sled built from native wood, we hauled supply loads from the beach to our new dump.

That day and the next night of 30-31 June were a time for labor and combat. When 162's A Co and Lt Burke's attached Pln of the 6 Aussie Inf met heavy fire from Japs north of our beachhead, we Engrs went into action. With Amphib Engrs of 532 Boat & Shore Regt, we replaced the Aussies when their ammo ran low. Rohlffs with 4-5 others volunteered as litter bearers to help "A" men; but that outfit cared for their few wounded. Jap resistance was that day broken all the way north to the south arm of the Bitoi River.

But this A Co victory led into our bloody night fight of 30 June-1 July. Col MacKechnie had sent most of C 162 north to reinforce A Co.

Back at the beach with night falling, Rohlffs found other Engrs excited at the crack of Jap rifles to the SE. Hurriedly, he dug a deep hole into the sand. When water flowed in, he dug a more shallow hole and braced it from caving in with a metal air-strip mat. After Rohlffs returned from helping cat-man Gray with a jam on his .50 HMG down on the beach, another Engr jumped into his too-shallow hole for the night. Rohlfs never even knew this man's name.

A little after dark, a small force of Japs hit A 116's line of fox-holes. Just then, the men of 532 Amphib Engrs ran up from the beach to join us. They had worked late in trying to right their broached landing craft — 21 of them.

To come up beside us in the dark was the worst possible move that the Amphibs could have made. We combat Engrs were lying scared in the dark. We feared that anything moving was Japanese, and fired and grenaded at will.

Rohlffs remembers just 2 Jap rushes at 116 Engrs. In one such charge, catman Gray with a mechanic helper wiped out a whole Jap squad trying to slip past our flank on the beach.

Suddenly the Jap attacks ended. The night was now silent but for moans and death-shrieks until daylight. Too many of the men cried in English, but we dared not move to help them.

Dawn came finally. Up in a tree, a lone Jap sniper drew a fusillade from us. After awhile, somebody broke our tension with, "Looks like we got shredded meat for breakfast."

Now out of his hole, Rohlffs counted 9 dead Yanks, 7 dead Japs. In A 116 Engrs, Rector was our only dead, and Coccia the only name Rohlffs remembers of our 2 seriously wounded. (The Amphibs lost 7 killed and 12 wounded, but claimed 32 dead Japs.) Col MacKechnie, however, claimed a total of 50 Japs killed by his entire force, which number includes all that all Engrs killed. Most Japs bypassed us to rejoin the main Jap army northwards.

Helping Col MacKechnie, we 2 Plns of A 116 built a jeep road up Bitoi River towards Lababia Ridge. We helped C Btry 218 FA carry their disassembled 75 mm cannon over 2,700-foot Lababia Ridge and position them on 1,000-foot Green Hill to help wipe out Komiatum Track Salient.

From Nassau Bay, we boarded barges again and landed at Tambu Bay for the siege of Roosevelt Ridge. We dug in 2 hospitals, operated 2 water-points, built roads and trails to help 162 capture Mt Tambu, and flank Roosevelt Ridge for attacks against it.

On 12 Aug, 10 Engrs volunteered to help 2/Bn 162's fight for Roosevelt Ridge. Against pillboxes, each man carried a charge of 8 pounds' TNT in his hands and a second charge in his pack. Each 8-pounder of TNT was laced with primacord, to fire by an attached cap and grenade. When we pulled the grenade pin, only 5 seconds remained for us to run and hit the ground. Despite menace of Nippo fire, we blew up 7 pillboxes, with perhaps 6 Japs per pillbox.

After the ridge was stormed, we built 900 yards' jeep track with a maximum grade of 33 per cent across the Ridge to supply 162 men fighting on Lokanu Bay. Two of us were wounded there — names unknown. We built a Strip for Piper Cubs. After Salamaua Town was won, we still built roads and bridges for 162 — then rejoined our Bn to work at Base B on Oro Bay.

Such are some highlights of 116 Engr Bn (Combat) in the Papuan Campaign. B Co labored and fought in the Sanananda hell. A Co had a nightmarish fight on the wrecked Nassau Beachhead, and helped heave C Btry 218 FA's guns over Lababia Ridge. Major achivement of 116 Engr Bn, however, was not in battle but in construction of roads and bridges and bases.

K CO 162 INF:

First Two Days in Parai Defile

**by K 162's CHARLES F. BROCKMAN
with DR. HARGIS WESTERFIELD, Division Historian**

CREDIT: Indispensable source is T/5 Brockman's 8-page typescript, single-spaced, of which I have used just the first 4 pages. Other help comes from 162's Biak Casualty List, narrative, and Journal, with RR Smith's **Approach to the Philippines.** I used also Award Stories of Capt Frederick Gehring, 2/Lt Howard Small, and T/Sgt Rex Smith. I could not work in award stories of S/Sgt Darrell Clements and PFC Charles Shaylor, because exact dates of their achievements were not specified in Award Stories. (Clements once volunteered to lead his squad on the extreme flank of any attack, where he overran many Jap positions. In absence of his CO Shaylor risked his life under heavy mortar and MG fire to orient K's platoons, and also rescue a wounded "K" man. But Award Story spreads their citations over several dates, so that I do not know which to use.) Today, I have one story in at least one operation of every 41st Div rifle Co, except 186's A and F Cos.

About 0900 on Biak D-Day, K Co 162 Inf's T/5 Brockman watched from an LCI while 186 Inf landed first. Diving low, B-24 heavy bombers shook Biak Island as they impacted. While DUKWs of 641 TD and 121 FA followed 186 Inf ashore, 3 rocketships cleared the way with a swish of death.

As K 162's LCI landed at one of the two Bosnek jetties, some LSTs were already beached with doors open and unloading. While "K" landed, a 1936 US Chevrolet was aflame on the beach. Our Navy still fired overhead at targets we could not see.

Passing several rocket duds on the beach, K Co with Brockman quickly hit the road west towards Mokmer Strip with I Co marching ahead. (T/5 Brockman was a cook who carried mortar ammo while he was in combat.) At first, Biak seemed like another easy Hollandia type of conquest. But after 1115, fire burst from Parai cliffs ahead. We took cover. Down the road leftward, we saw a captured Jap truck with a few of our wounded lifted aboard.

Now 5-6 tanks of 603 Tank Bn rumbled and clanked past K Co. Brockman never forgot two tanks' names — "Hi-Ball" and "Murder Inc." After tankmen helped drive the Japs from the first Parai cliffs, we caught up with the crews at a halt — saw them taking a break over coffee with canned heat on the tank-fronts. While "K" filled canteens and rested at a spring, we looked up at the pink and gray and green of 180-foot Parai Cliffs. These retarded our March to Mokmer Strip.

Four times on this Biak D-Day, 162's attacking column was briefly checked by Nip fighters 4 times up to 1540. We lost at least 2 killed, 6 wounded. In K Co., Brockman helped dress the knee of seriously wounded Martin. Martin said that an I Co man had thought that he was a Jap, and shot a clean hole through his knee. Brockman believes that K's Sgt Hanna was killed that 27 May. (Report has him "died of wounds" next day.)

Thus by 1500, with tank help, 3/Bn had pushed through the narrowest part of Parai Defile and occupied Parai Village. That night, "K" perimetered on the low bench above Mokmer Road. Cook Brockman and Mess-Sgt Boyes had a shallow hole above coral bedrock inside K's perimeter.

That night, Jap planes dropped flares — but no bombs — to daylight the beach. Jap infantry probed our lines. "K" took several rounds from knee mortars; 3/Bn MGs killed 3 Japs down Mokmer Road.

Brockman was concerned for Cook Newman. Newman was marked for rotation home, but the order was not yet cut. Newman was to spend the last 2 nights of his life in K's perimeteres.

On that disastrous morning of 28 May 1944, K Co came down from their benchland perimeter to the narrow beach area where tanks and men were already forming up. Brockman heard short, slender, energetic Col Haney tell 3/Bn's Lt-Col Roosevelt, "It's time to go." Roosevelt said, "My watch shows we have about 10 minutes." Haney dropped down in the shade with his back against a palm.

One lone Zero fled seaward, evidently out of ammo. Navy and Army AA seemed to hit him, but nowhere vitally. Shortly afterwards, the Zero hit the water just on the horizon edge. A cheer went up from our ranks.

K Co moved out at the point with I Co following to turn inland and come up in line on our right flank. Because of the narrow coast road, T/5 Winkler of C Co 116 Engrs had to widen and level the tanks' road with his bulldozer. He uncovered some cans of food. Brockman and another cook leisurely shared a can of pineapple. Biak still seemed a picnic.

About 0845, "K" hit our first resistance of that evil day on Biak. Tanks easily cleared out those Japs. Perhaps this first little opposition was just to draw us deep into the jaws of the trap. Behind us, back above Mokmer Village, big Jap 90 mm mortars opened up on an LCI, a rocket ship, and LCMs. North of Mokmer Drome, a coast-defence gun fired on our destroyer out at sea. Destroyer returned fire.

Biak still seemed easy. Main body of K Co now pushed on mostly level ground with thick secondary growth inland while "I" pushed on our flank. Here, a ledge was 25-30 feet above the shore. Forward elements of "K" were now 200 yards from Mokmer Strip — as far as 3/Bn would reach for a week.

Then Jap MGs suddenly cracked a path before K and I Cos; Jap 90 mm mortars hurtled down from Parai Ridge to our right and rear. As the shells first exploded, Brockman and Veach were on the roadside next to the water. Ahead, all the tanks' turrets shelled the high ridge to our right.

Veach and Brockman ran for cover across the road, hit a shallow ditch where 1/Sgt Joe Briskey and S/Sgt Charles his brother had huddled already. Looking up in a lull from the shelling, we saw 3 mortar duds back on the road.

About this time, K's CO, Capt Gehring, told the Briskeys that 2/Lt Barnes was dead already, with other casualties. K's mortarmen got orders to fire into the menacing brush to our right — went into position at a dead run.

Good soldier Col Haney was up to "K" Hq for first-hand information. He also spotted a Nippo mortar position on the ridge and sent back to call down mortar shells on it. (Jap fire had cut all 3/Bn phone wires; the only radio left working belonged to I&R).

In still heavier Jap mortar fire, Brockman and other "K" men found a bomb-crater deep enough for us to stand in and watch across the road. The first Jap counter-attack came, but it failed to break through to us.

With a swish, a Jap mortar shell impacted close before the crater. The smoke blackened Brockman's face. A sliver holed Veach'es helmet but did not hurt him. We tumbled from that hole; a Jap observer had almost pinpointed in on us.

After Jap HMGs and heavy mortars halted "K" with "I" on our left near Mokmer Strip, all 3/Bn retreated 600 yards. We were under heavy attack by the Japs' 2/Bn 222 Inf. At 0930, L Co and some of M's HMGs were cut off from 3/Bn by intense fire. Contact was not made again until an hour later when "L" and "M" found a covered route back.

By 1100, however, all 3/Bn (less an "L" Pln still cut off that had to fight their way back to 2/Bn) was down under the slash of heavy mortars. We were in an area stretching 200 yards inland from the coast and 500 yards long on Mokmer Road. We were down in an area of tall brush where Jap observers pounded us from the cliffs. But that brush masked their weapons from our observers. At 1135, 2/Bn was trying to come through from the rear and reinforce us. Beginning about 1201, 3/Bn had to use tanks, FA, and Navy with our firepower to repel a second Jap infantry attack.

About 1200, Brockman watched B-25 and A-20 bombers smash the Jap ridge in several flights. Lying on his back, Brockman saw the bomb-racks in the planes. A crewman later told him how much the airmen feared their own bombs. Fuzes were cut so short that concussion might strike back at them through the open bomb-bays. But their air-strike failed to silence the Japs on the ridge.

Brockman and Beach helped some of K's many wounded down the road to Dr. Drexler's aid station. Among them was S/Sgt Hillman, shot through the foot. Brockman never forgot how intensely in that tropical heat, Capt Drexler and his Medics worked to save our wounded.

Our long, deadly 28 May wore on into mid-afternoon. Once a young man of another outfit asked Brockman to go forward with him to help with some shooting that he had in mind. Brockman said that he had enough trouble already, but to this day wonders how the young man made out in battle.

About 1400, a "K" runner ran back shouting, "Jap tanks are coming!" Our tank-radio ordered, "Deploy!" K's weapons Lt positioned our bazookamen for close-range shots into tanks. Up front when some men began to leave their positions, Capt Gehring exposed himself to send them back into line. He assured them that we could hold where we were.

At 1200 yards, our tanks impacted the 5 Nip tanks with their 75s while our Navy struck at them also. These outranged Jap tanks with their little 37 mm cannon had only a small chance against our longer ranges, but they fought desperately. Our Navy and tanks drove them into low ground while "I," "K," and "M" men slew their accompanying infantry. In this fight, K's 2/Lt Small had done well with his Pln in breaking the Jap attack.

Jap tank fire did succeed in damaging 3 tanks and wounding 3 crewmen. One crippled tank had to withdraw. Its .75 cannon had sustained a direct hit and was unfireable.

Perhaps about this time, K's T/Sgt Rex Smith daringly led a 6-man patrol some 200 yards back into ground that "K" had given up during the infantry attack. His men recovered weapons and other important equipment that had been left — also bore back the corpse of 2/Lt Barnes.

By late afternoon, 3/Bn's position was untenable. Jap mortar and FA fire increased; patrols even briefly cut the road in our rear, until expelled. Gen Fuller ordered 162 back to last night's positions in Parai Defile, 2,000 yards east. K's Capt Gehring told us to destroy any abandoned weapons that the Japs could use. Dr Drexler was not to give aid to any wounded whom we might find while retreating. We were to lay on 2 so-far empty litters to carry with us.

As the next-to-last tank fell back, Brockman sheltered on its coastal side. In almost no time, Jap fire crashed on it from inland. The tank halted killed that fire. In this retreat, Brockman saw just 1 Yank corpse — a young man down by the roadside with his glasses on the side of his nose — his body cold already.

Again, Brockman's tank moved, but stopped almost instantly while Jap bullets clunked from its steel sides. Now the tank fired both its .30 HMG and its .75 cannon.

After the tank silenced the Jap fire and marched again, it forced Brockman off the road because it moved to his side. He fell over the largest unexploded bomb that he had ever seen in his life. Looking up from the ground, he watched pink Jap tracers pass the tank, front and rear.

When tracers stopped, Brockman moved on with his beloved tank. Ahead, M Co's Capt Bland waved him on across an open area. The tank came no farther with Brockman. He raced to a 20-foot drop to the beach and took his turn to climb down a worn tropical vine with his rifle.

Capt Bland now helped other M Co men carry a HMG — even shouldered the barrel to carry it himself. As the men hurried, Brockman saw a piece fall from a gun, and carried it for them. He remembers how courteously Bland thanked him when they reached a safe place.

"K" and other 3/Bn Cos retreated along the shore through 2/Bn's protecting lines and about dark perimetered in the new 3/Bn area along the beach. We had no water and no holes dug yet to sleep in. Brockman doubts that any man ever thought of eating.

Newman was still living — the man who was marked for rotation home. While Veach with Newman holed up, Brockman and a new man dug in closer to the beach. When FA walked protective fire around K's perimeter, a 4-inch fragment struck between Veach and Newman but missed them. "K" men tried to sleep between guard-turns with the deep thankfulness which a combat man feels after a day of battle.

On that 28 May, K 162 probably had our longest casualty list of World War II. We lost 7 killed or dead of wounds, 21 wounded to hospital, 1 injured in action. Dead were Kiberd, Richards, Binkley, Tanner, Walker, Jordan, and 2/Lt Barnes. Reported "lightly wounded" were Maley, Norton, White, Toolan, Gebhard, and S/Sgt Hillman. Fifteen were marked "seriously wounded," 3 of them NCOs — S/Sgt Leach, Sgt Chappelow, and Cpl Mathis. Also "seriously wounded" were Almond, Dyson, Eberhard, Flower, Foley, Gill, Gunter, John Johnson, Kodelke, Magness Martinez, and Welch. Leake was "lightly injured" and hospitalized. Written under dire combat conditions, this list may not be perfectly accurate.

But K 162 was still almost helpless in the closing jaws of the Japanese trap in Parai Defile. On Parai Ridge over us, Jap mortarmen and machine-gunners slept by their pieces with piled ammo behind them. All Bns of 222 Inf were concentrated against us, with 7 tanks of 36 Div Tank Unit — all ready to strike tomorrow. On 29 May was coming the first tank battle of the SWPA.

Tomorrow also would come a murderous shell from our own Navy. Newman was doomed to death; he would never rotate home to America.

G COMPANY 162 INFANTRY:

Breaching Roosevelt Ridge (12-13 Aug 1943)

by DR. HARGIS WESTERFIELD, Division Historian,
with GAETANO DE MAYO, COL. HERMAN STEENSTRA

CREDIT: G Co 162's Cook Grant Ramey triggered this history with his personal list of G's dead in this action, and an official list of Commendations (41 Div G.O. No. 9, 23 Feb 1944). No roster of 162's Salamaua Operation casualties can be found in Federal Archives. Much was missing from 2/Lt John Foley's report on the 2 Aug fight for Fisher's Perimeter, and Capt Garlyn Munkres' report on breaching the ridge, 12-13 Aug 1943. Core of this history consists of Gaetano de Mayo's letters of 7 May and 5 Dec 1982, and 22 Feb 1983; and Col Herman Steenstra's letters of 7 Sept and 5 Dec 1982. Useful also was Ramey's undated letter of about Dec 1982 — with Medic Lewis Weis' letter 1 Feb 1983, and Samuel Beitler's letters both in 1983 — one undated, one of 29 Jan. Ramey reinforced these letters with cassettes of Sgts Chuck Cunningham and Harvey Hutton made in late July 1982. Data from 162 Inf's Narrative and Journal of Salamaua Operation were limited, however. Ramey's love for his brother George is primarily responsible for this history — with the fine help of De Mayo and Steenstra.

On 12 Aug 1983, G Co 162 Inf began our second dogged thrust to breach stubbornly held Jap Roosevelt Ridge, which had repulsed 162 Inf since 22 July. Ten days ago, G's first assault had failed with deaths of 1/Lt Fisher, Cpl Miley, Galus, and Rifleman Rondo. Some time during 3-11 Aug, Jap mortars had killed 2/Lt Silvey and wounded Sgt Ayers. 2/Lts Herbst and Steenstra had replaced dead Fisher and Silvey.

On 12 Aug, F Co relieved us from our side ridge above "F," but we knew that our "G" would soon make our second thrust. But this time we did not expect to make the main attack. Our mission was to support F Co's assault on our left while "E" pushed on the right. Yet G Co finally fought the main battle to breach Roosevelt Ridge.

G's first move was to send 2/Lt Herbst with 4 men to climb to find the best position to support F's attack tomorrow. Sgts George Ramey and Hutton were 2 of the 4 men known to accompany Herbst up the deadly ridge.

Climbing back to G's forward position, we bore left uphill into the jungle ridge. Unaware at the time, we crossed unhurt a Jap MG fire-lane cleverly hidden in brush. On the flatter summit of the ridge itself, we checked out what "Intelligence" had said was a ravine. We were in luck!

The "ravine" was a small ridge — a narrow curving-edged hogback usually about 15 feet wide, but in places dwindling to 3 feet. About 100 yards long, this narrow hogback stretched from near the rear of Jap Fisher Perimeter to the north edge of Roosevelt Ridge. We saw Japs supplying Fisher Perimeter — almost level with us. From the north side of the hogback, we looked straight down into Jap Dot Inlet. Japs peacefully walked the beach or climbed trees or dug holes. We were between 2 Nippo outposts on the Ridge — one 50 yards off, the other 150 yards away.

Capt Munkres at once ordered Herbst to hold that hogback with all of his men. 2/Lt Steenstra joined Herbst with his whole Pln — now shrunk to about the size of a reinforced squad. Munkres counted us as 41 men, 4 officers. De Mayo remembers that we had 3 FA observers — an officer and 2 men.

Prone on the hogback behind Fisher's perimeter, we saw dark fall. Beside our rifles to fight at dawn, we thought of our orders for the long night of fear and silence.

Munkres had told us not to dig in. We must not eat, smoke, or talk. If Japs crawled in, we were to club or choke them.

But like any man of common sense, De Mayo disobeyed the order. De Mayo dug in — and Mundy on his left. Mundy had soft ground for his hole. De Mayo had to grub among rocks and roots.

But G's narrow little hogback turned out to be on the main Jap supply line from C Ridge. Suddenly in semi-dark, Sgt Hutton discerned Jap carriers walking the hogback towards us. Despite orders for silence, a BAR shot down the carriers.

About 10 minutes after lying on his back in this unauthorized hole 2 inches below the surface, De Mayo heard that BAR fire. A crossfire of 4 Jap MGs opened up over G's men mostly on the surface on that hogback.

Watching MG tracers fly harmlessly above him, De Mayo thanked God for his hole. Came then the pistol-crack of a mortar shell detonated from the barrel. He began counting to 60 — the approximate time for one of ours to hit a Jap position. At his count of 25, he heard "Boom" above him. The shell impacted into the 3 feet of space between his hole and Mundy's. It knocked out De Mayo for awhile. At dawn, he would find rifle, ammo, grenades, and pack in a shattered mess — only his photos untouched. Mundy was unhurt.

That same shell that knocked out De Mayo caught nearby Lt Steenstra on the surface. Desperately he pulled web equipment over his head when he knew that the shell would hit close. Fragments riddled his canteen but missed him.

The shell that nearly killed De Mayo was really ours, probably H Co's, although De Mayo never knew it until 39 years later. A second shell from that salvo also struck among us on top of the ground. Concussion blew several men 20-30 feet down the slope. Either Medic Weis or Knopp clambered down into pitch darkness where Japs might lurk, to aid these men

Now everybody dug in desperately. Cunningham said that he dug in deep enough to be called a deserter. When about halfway under, Hutton felt a sickening crash from a fragment breaking his shoulder. He lay helpless in that half-dug hole all night. One shell killed gunner Morales in a burst of fragments. About that time, Capt Munkres was wounded — circumstances unknown. Immobilized, he could only direct our fight.

After that first erratic mortar salvo, our mortars and FA were extremely accurate. We believe that their fire finally killed the Japs' automatic weapons that had defeated the assault of 2 Aug of G Co's Lts Fisher, Swetka, and Foley with E's Powers.

Now Sgt Cunningham sensed Japs coming down from Fisher Perimeter towards our hogback. Our mortar barrage stopped them.

The Japs then attacked with small arms, grenades, MGs. One MG seemd to position itself 30 feet from us until it was knocked out, perhaps by our mortars.

Grenades rained down on our hogback. As they fell, Japs yelled, "Hey, Americans!" maybe 4 times. Or instead of grenades, they threw rocks. For Steenstra, rocks were harder to endure than grenades. When a rock or grenade thudded to earth, we flattened and waited tensely for the explosion. After an actual grenade blew up, we were briefly relieved when the fragments missed us. But nothing was more nerve-wracking than to wait for the explosion that never came.

Battle fatigue made 4 men unfit for duty where Japs seemed to batter us from all directions. One man panicked from his forward hole closest to Fisher's Perimeter and ran sobbing back to Lt Steenstra. The Lt calmed him to return. During the panic, Burcham was killed by a shot in the brain. Steenstra spent all night on guard in the hole beside dead Burcham.

Steenstra estimated that the Jap attacks lasted less than an hour — although Cunningham thought it was 3 hours before Nippo carriers quit pushing up from C Ridge the other end of the hogback. But finally we had silence among our dead and wounded. Men craved sleep but feared to sleep.

Gray daylight found us still surviving in our holes. We were to stay low because our FA were about to barrage the Japs, until F Co would make the attack from the other side. At first, we thought we would only have to pick off stragglers after "F" overran Fisher's Perimeter.

At 0745, our FA and mortars roared down. Like last night's mortars, first FA hit close, within 50-75 yards of us. For 9 minutes, we writhed below this menace while the ground shook. The guns deafened our telephone men trying to lift the range. Better adjusted salvos at irregular intervals blasted again — from 0745 to 0920.

At 0920, Steenstra reported that shellfire had stripped brush from concealing positions on the Japs' strongpoint. Then when support fires lifted, the Japs tried to set up their guns again. Running back to wounded Munkres by his phone, Lt Steenstra suggested that F Co be called up to assail the Japs. Munkres first told Steenstra to pin down the Japs by fire.

Then Steenstra offered to take 5 men and wipe out the Japs. Instead of 5 men, Munkres gave 8 more men to Steenstra, and added Lt Herbst with 7 men. Two officers, 15 men would attack.

Despite intense shelling and our superior morale as assailants, the Japs were still strong. Four emplacements cored Fisher's Perimeter, with 3 LMGs, 1 HMG, and 2 Jap-type BARs. (We did not yet know that FA had disabled their automatic weapons.) "Intelligence" said that only 30-40 Japs faced us, with 2 pillboxes; but T/Sgt Barksdale said later that there were over 100 Japs with 4 pillboxes.

While Cunningham, Sessions, and Ferguson secured the far end of the hogback with a LMG, Steenstra's and Herbst's men rushed single file up the narrow ridge. Japs popped up everywhere screaming and firing.

Steenstra had time for just one order, "Spread out!" Then every man struck for himself. We threw grenades, but Japs hurled them back to explode among us. We then released the pins and held them alive and counted to three before we blasted into the Jap holes. With Japs all around us, we drove into Fisher Perimeter.

De Mayo of Steenstra's men grenaded 2 Jap holes. We saw 2 Japs crawl out to die. Without more grenades, De Mayo fired 3 clips into 2 more holes and heard moaning.

Steenstra's 8 men blew up Emplacements 1 and 2. Short of grenades, however, Herbst's men sealed up Nos 3 and 4 with rifle fire until 2 bags of grenades arrived. Then they gouged out the last two emplacements. Sgt Grant Ramey shot a Jap out of a tree. He took 2 bunkers single-handed but dropped with a Jap bullet in his left ribs. Yet he lived.

All this time, "G" fought unaided. But we had struck at the right time; most Japs fought back only from cover. Once, 3 Japs charged with bayonets; our bullets riddled them.

Below us, F Co was looking up but not climbing to help us. Our fire-fight had made them hold back. By Steenstra's order, De Mayo went over the ridge-crest and signalled to F Co, who moved up to reinforce us. Then De Mayo returned into battle.

Japs still hid in dense jungle around Fisher's Perimeter. One at a time, they tried to dash across open space into a cave on the north side of the Ridge. Borrowing rifles, Herbst and Steenstra hit Japs, just as they squatted two jumped into the cave. Others dived in without halting to squat; we do not know how many more of them we shot on the wing.

Back into the fight, De Mayo saw 2 wounded men: Sgt Scar with a bullet in his left side into the ribs, and Robertson shot square in the forehead. Both men lived — even Robertson with full mental power, although the Medics dared not remove the bullet in his brain.

From a kneeling position, De Mayo fired on Steenstra's order at the heavy leafage of a tree 30 yards away — from which we thought that Scar and Robertson were wounded. Unable to see the results of his fire, De Mayo turned to ask Steenstra whether he had seen results.

As he turned his head, De Mayo took a Jap bullet in the back of his neck. Narrowly missing his brain, the slug knocked out 2 teeth and passed through his open mouth. On the way through, it missed his windpipe but partly paralyzed his esophagus. It would take De Mayo 3 weeks' intravenous feeding and continual efforts to swallow before he could work off the paralysis.

Despite some Jap mortar fire, Medic Weis knelt in the open to give plasma to De Mayo. Two men bore De Mayo back down the Ridge, Summers and a man nicknamed "Pluto" from Hamtramck, Mich.

We had seen Pln/Sgt Ramey unconscious and thought that he was dead, but he walked back down the Ridge. Medics removed 3 splintered ribs, although they could not extricate bits of lead in him forever. One piece remained in his heart muscle, another close to his spine. But Ramey lived many years after.

Besides Capt Munkres and Hutton wounded last night, and Robertson, Scar, Ramey, and De Mayo wounded that morning, we know only a little about the other wounded. A Jap rifle knocked out Meidell when he charged a hole. Persinger lost an ear-lobe. T/4 Virgil Johnson had a Jap MG bullet up his right arm. (We are unsure of the dates when Johnson and Persinger were wounded.) Capt Munkres said that G's total casualties were 2 dead, 4 made unfit for duty, and 7 wounded. (The number of wounded which Munkres reported, does not jibe with the number of names above; but no Casualty List of 162 Inf in the Salamaua Operation has ever been found.)

G COMPANY 163 INFANTRY:

The Kumusi Patrol

by DR. HARGIS WESTERFIELD, Division Historian,

*CREDIT: Bill Ramsey's story at Gearhart Reunion (1971) sparked this article. Captain Arthur (Buck Braman) sent me George Weller's 3 articles from **Chicago Daily News**, all dated 8 Apr 1943: (Although I have Weller's articles on Sanananda itself, I had not known that these Kumusi articles exist.) By courtesy of Col Charles Dawley, I received a Zerox of Col Wm Benson's handwritten report, "Company G Activity from Feb 1 1943 through Feb 14, 1943." Other sources include Braman's undated letter (1972), Benson's "History of G Co 163 Inf," "163 Journals Jan 1-31 Mar 1943," and "Patrol to the Kumusi," my story of G 186 from Lt Carsner's account in **Jungleer** (Sept/Dec 1974).*

On 1 Feb 1943, G Co 163 Inf campaigned again after the alleged termination of the Battle of Sanananda on 22 Jan 1943. Although fatigued and feverish from Sanananda, G Co had to slog and slosh 22 miles from Gona up jungle beaches to seize the mouth of the Kumusi River. Earlier, Kumusi Mouth was a rallying point for Japs retreating down Kokoda Trail from their Aussie battles — and a base for reinforcing their Sanananda garrisons. Trekking from Gona, G Co must cross at least 9 rivers or streams before Kumusi Mouth.

And G Co expected battle. For on 31 Jan, 163's patrol under Lt. Nugent had alerted "G" for trouble. At Sangara Village, inland behind Popondetta, Nugent learned that 200 Japs had raided villages nearby, and that these Japs would surely escape by rafts down the Kumusi and regroup with other Jap commands at Kumusi Mouth and fight again. (One of the major Papuan rivers, the Kumusi flows north from behind Sanananda, then makes a great bend eastward to the sea.)

On 1345 1 Feb, "G" left Killerton Point — a small army in a fortnight's campaign. We had 88 "G" men, 250 natives carrying 6 days' rations, 13 AT men of 2/Bn Hq, radio man Perkins of 1/Bn and Foster of 2/Bn. We had 2 "G" Medics and Capt Harry Smith's 6-man Medical Det.

Because of roadless coastal jungle, CO Benson took the easiest way from Killerton Point to Gona 2 — right into Killerton Bay. We marched over a mile knee-deep to waist-deep for super-6-footers like Benson — and neck-deep for shorter men. Tall men held up shorter men's heads above the water. In Cpl Sahs' memory, most of the march was in waist-high, saltwater marshes. Luckily, the bottom was mostly coral, but some riflemen stuck in mud, and other men had to extract them. Because we naturally straggled, Benson twice looked back to see our 359-man convoy strung out over half a mile of water. Coming out on the beach again, G's point under Sgt Clowes found Jap tracks and discarded Sterno and meat cans.

And on 2 Feb, "G" was back into action. Arriving at Sebari Village after 3 hours' hiking that day, we met 1/Lt Carsner's rookie Pln of G Co 186 Inf. Some 600 yards north of Sebari, they had lost a native scout to a Jap MG. Benson attached Carsner's 45 men including 2 extra BAR teams, and prepared for Japs. Ahead of us was the Kombela River, which was so deep and fast that we could not wade through it as we had waded all other streams after we left Gona.

While most "G" men lunched and rested or bathed, Sgt Clowes led a patrol to locate the Japs precisely. By 1330, Clowes reported that he had sighted no Japs in the 800 yards between "G" and the Kombela River — nor for 400 yards up the south bank.

Arriving at the river, "G" observed a possible Jap village. It seemed to be Jap because the huts were tangled in jungle across the river, unlike the peaceful native villages, which would be in open groves.

If Japs were there, they had a fine position. Where the Kombela bent back parallel to the sea was jungle — 200 yards wide between river and beach. Inland from the jungle all the way to the river was an open sand-flat — a field of fire 60 yards wide. But "G" saw no Japs — only sand or opaque brush down to the Kombela before us.

Benson planned to send 3 volunteers across on a raft to secure the foreshore. Meanwhile, Cpl Sahs' detail would bring up a small Nippo assault boat abandoned in the lagoon behind us and ferry more "G" men over to reinforce the 3 volunteers.

These 3 were G's Bill Ramsey, Sgt Bretzke, and an Aus-volunteer — Warrant Officer Dixon, liaison man with our natives. Natives built a raft for these men, then waded the raft across the Kombela while other "G" men covered the foreshores with their rifles. After the landing, the natives returned with the raft. Still, there was no Jap fire.

Suddenly, G's patrol found 5 Japs repairing equipment, back in the brush. Bretzke and Ramsay each shot a Jap. They then raced for the beach, threw themselves prone, and hoped to be saved by G Co's covering fire across the Kombela.

But Jap MG fire forced the 3 men into the sand. Bretzke lifted his head to return fire and was killed. Ramsay, Dixon kept heads down and feverishly stripped off shoes and clothing and rolled over sand into the water.

Jap fire struck at G 163 and G 186 across the river, but Benson had a BAR team run back up the beach and enfilade the Jap brush in the river-bend below them. Our 2 surviving volunteers crawled through rivulets at the Kombela's edge to where Jap MGs could not touch them without exposure to our BAR team. Then Ramsay swam a hundred yards out to sea and came back to "G" still alive.

From across the river, Jap fire caught Sahs' detail loading the assault boat. When the shooting began, everybody made it safely into the jungle — except Sahs and Gonzales — whose actions made them special Jap targets. Gonzales was in the bow of the boat and holding it inshore by the stringer while Sahs was ashore and holding the stern in by the same rope.

While Gonzales leaped from the boat, Sahs fled wildly for cover. A slug hit Sahs in the elbow; his arm went limp, but he was safe in the jungle. But he saw Gonzales crumpled on the beach where a bullet had caught him as he jumped from the boat. The hollow-nosed bullet had struck him in the back to fragment into 3-4 pieces.

Sahs risked Jap fire to pull Gonzales back into the jungle. Prone behind a log, they heard Jap MG bullets chop it in two. Small mortar shells impacted close, but Sahs crawled rearward and dragged Gonzales feet first into safety. And 300 yards south of the Kombela front, another mortar shell wounded Kubista.

From the south bank of the Kombela, where Benson had earlier posted us, a G 163 Pln returned Jap fire and silenced it. Front-line surgery saved Sahs, Kubista — and even Gonzales, despite the evil fragments in his back.

Next day, 3 Feb, G 163 made an all-out attack. This time, "G" had more than a 3-man forlorn hope to raft across the river. Reinforcements had come up; Sgt Rennel zeroed in 2 M Co 81 mortars with 17 Yanks manning them.

While Sgt Rennel blasted the Jap jungle, some 20 Yanks of G's 1/Pln under Sgt Gammas boated across the estuary and made the beach-head for the rest of "G" to follow. So effective were Rennel's M Co 81s that "G" made 5 trips before ragged Jap fire began. Jap mortar fire splashed near 2/Pln during the crossing.

Rifles ready to kill, Gammas' 1/Pln dashed across the open sand-strip some 60 yards into jungle. Suddenly we found Jap dugouts under our noses — so concealed that we saw them only 3 feet away. Yet we encountered no Japs — not even a corpse.

With G's other Plns supporting, Gammas' men now pushed north 400 yards unscathed. In thick brush, they found a Jap village, and had to search each hut separately. Then 2 Jap MGs tore into Gammas' advance. Indian Ackerman our bugler got his death-wound. Seibert was probably wounded there; he died 6 Feb, 3 days later.

Gammas' Pln crawled back and brought down more mortar fire on the Japs. But Jap bullets still halted Gammas. Next in support, 3/Pln with Benson and Hq were stopped also. At sundown, Jap fire was as heavy as before. About 50 yards from the Japs, "G" dug a hasty, insecure night perimeter, but the Japs did not counter-attack in the dark.

Besides Seibert and Ackerman who were dying, "G" had 4 more men with wounds reported as serious. Besides Meline and Cpl Baird with unspecified serious wounds, Cpl Anderson was shot in the right arm. A bullet holed Cpl Frank Hanson's helmet dead center in the front. But the bullet deflected from his skull bone, then followed that bone up and over his helmet to drop out the back. His hair had a permanent part!

On 4 Feb, "G" pushed again under a mortar barrage and got nowhere. By now, Col Doe with Col Dawley, 163's executive, had come forward to consult with Benson back at Sebari Village. Doe ordered in an L Co Pln for reinforcements.

And by 5 Feb, "G" had taken a Jap key position. It was a high tree platform 500 yards deep in jungle. From here, they had watched our movements and deployed their troops in the jungle to counter our attacks.

On 5 Feb, while G 163 advanced frontally, Benson used Carsner's G 186 and L 163 for a flank movement. These 2 units moved inland to Kumbata and Fuffuda Villages north of the Japs' right rear. From there, they were to hike to the coast, then strike south to trap the Japs fleeing from G 163.

But heavy jungle and poor guidance restrained Carsner until twilight. About darkfall, Carsner's men probed into Jap fire, had 1 WIA, and dug in to wait for daybreak.

On that same 5 Feb, "G" had advanced 500 yards under a rolling mortar barrage and overhead MG fire. Seriously wounded were Ludlow, Rients, and Schultz. Perhaps G 163 actually had pushed the Japs northward to block off Carsner and secure their own escape route. For by the end of the night of 5 Feb, the Japs' Kombela garrison had evaded the trap made by the 2 "G" Cos.

At 1000 6 Feb, G 163 heard 186 fire 800 yards north. By 1315, we had covered the 800 yards to join Carsner at Bakumbari River Mouth. After 5 days' action, "G" found just 2 Jap dead. But against that stoutly held Kombela position, "G" had 3 dead, 10 seriously wounded.

On 7 Feb, Carsner's 186 men led out to pursue the Japs. About 1600, they contacted Japs again, this time dug in on the far side of an unnamed river somewhere past Buk Village. This time, Carsner tried to outflank the Japs by an attack from the sea in our new "Navy" — a single Higgins boat. Two Jap MGS concentrated on the boat charging in. Carsner silenced both MGs, but the coxswain turned back to sea before 186 hit the beach. (This was surely 186 Inf's first beach-head action of World War II.)

Next morning, M's 81s blasted the Japs across the river. And by this time also, an Aussie 25-pounder — probably of Hall's Troop — was in action. With this help, G 186's second sea-borne attack was unopposed, and G 163 crossed and killed 3 Japs. And G 186 led us to the next unnamed river up the coast.

Preparing our crossing, the Aussie cannon began firing, but the Higgins boat was not available. By the time we had salvaged 2 Jap assault boats, it was dark. On that day, 8 Feb, we had advanced 2 miles by 1905. We bivouacked near a Jap hospital ground where we counted 10 unburied Japs who had died less than 2 days before.

Next morning, 9 Feb, we crossed this second nameless river safely. We hiked on to an inlet evidently extending so far inland that it seemed to Benson like a river. With no boats at hand, the natives made a dugout. We ferried clothes and equipment over while the men swam alongside to complete the crossing in the night at 2200.

Beginning 10 Feb, "G" had no further trouble en route to the Kumusi — only some 6 miles' sweaty trekking through heavy sand. We saw 25 more dead Japs, and our Aussie 25-pounder harassed Kumusi Mouth ahead of us.

And by 1050, 10 Feb, G 163 with G 186's Pln were digging into wet sand on the south (or eastern) bank of the Kumusi's nearer of 2 outlets to the sea. We contacted a little warparty of vengeful Aussies; they thanked us for driving 100 more fleeing Japs into their fire. G 163's field ranges came up, and Benson's men welcomed Carsner's 186 command into their chow-line.

After the inevitable mop-up patrols — which killed but few Japs — G 163 with G 186 gladly turned over their mission to L 163 men and on 14 Feb boarded landing-craft back to Killerton.

Even if the Battle of Sanananda had ended a fortnight before G 163's Kumusi Patrol began, these Japs were still in fair condition to put up a fight against Benson's own fatigued men. To judge by their corpses, they were in good condition. Benson thought that they seemed well-fed. They had cooked rice and canned food — mostly Aussie canned food. Benson surmised that these were die-hard Marines of the same outfit that had fought 163 at Huggins Perimeter in January. In losing only 3 dead and 10 wounded for G 163, Benson had cannily used his riflemen G Co fashion and his supporting elements against a difficult Jap position.

Yet G 163 paid heavily in losses from disease rather than from killed or wounded. Before Sanananda, we had flown from Port Moresby with 170 men, 6 officers. But we arrived with only 40 men, 2 officers. We had started out with men already infected with tropical diseases. Men like Lt Braman, G's future CO, had hiked in a daze of malaria until evacuation about 5 Feb. The recuperating G Co 163 had well earned its coming respite — 4-5 months' comparative inaction as security for Popondetta Strip — and that wondrous return to Australia.

M COMPANY 162 INFANTRY II:

Parai Defile Through Death Ridge

by SGT LOUIS BOTTA, M 162,
and DR. HARGIS WESTERFIELD, Division Historian

*CREDIT: Core of story are Botta's ltrs: 31 Aug, 15 Sept, both in 1978; and ltrs of 12 Jan, 19 Mar, 17 Apr, 2 May, and 5 May. Important was Dr. Kenneth Deacon's "116 Combat Engineers on Biak" (**Jungleer**, May, 1962), award stories of Moore, Joaquin, and RR Smith's **Approach to the Philippines**. I used also 162's "Regimental Journal, Biak Island Operation," "Report of Operation," and "Casualty List." Unaided by other M 162 men, Botta did a great job of remembering battles of 34-35 years ago. (Shortly after beginning M Co's story of their Southern Philippine Campaign, Louis suddenly passed away. He left me only the story of M Co when it backed L 162 in the San Roque defeat. Can any readers help me by taking up where Louis left off?)*

After 162 Inf on 29 May retreated under the Japs' cliffs holding Parai Defile, M Co's weapons helped L Co turn back to fight again. With L Co, "M" faced west again. Halfway through Parai Defile at the mouth of the underground stream, 3/Bn set up an ambush against Jap infiltration, with M's weapons as security. From the stream crossing, patrols probed westward.

From 30 May through early June, Botta and other "M" gunners made at least 10 advances and withdrawals, while each gunner toted some 50 pounds of gear. Always Jap fire from the cliffs menaced us. At night, we perimetered in a beachside coconut grove. Always, we seemed to fight Japs around us in the dark.

On 3 June, "M" was part of 3/Bn's formidable thrust with tanks to force the Defile. This thrust was timed well for 162 to press on Mokmer Strip while 186 struck from the right rear.

At 0730 3 June, we advanced. By 0915, our riflemen fanned out to the cliffs at the Defile entrance, had no Jap contacts yet. About 0930, air strikes supported our point squads, who had neared Parai Jetty. At 1044, FA and mortars — M's mortars surely — barraged the cliffs ahead. At 1055, our destroyers shelled around Parai Jetty.

Most of this time, reinforced 3/Bn kept its excellent formation for battle. In the van, "L" riflemen guarded 4 Engineers of C 116 with mine detectors. Followed 3 tanks, and a bulldozer driven by that heroic Engr, T/5 Winkler. After this group, came more 162 Plns, 4 tanks, more C 116 Engrs, and "K" and "L" Cos.

At 1320 at the first road junction, the first Japs fired on us. L's lead Pln got a torrent of fire from overhead cliffs. From jungle between road and cliffs, Japs burst out and cut off the "L" Pln. While C 116 tried to repair the bridge across the underground stream, Engr Winkler helped to drag tanks over to fire for the besieged Pln. For 2 hours, tanks and L Co battled, but could not force Parai Defile.

At 1430, 3/Bn's CO reported us halted at the first road junction, with 3 dead. After 1520, we located 2 Jap roadblocks. Japs dropped grenades down on us from the sheer cliffs. We followed orders to retreat to a position 80 yards east of the river.

And so gunner Botta found himself making another M Co withdrawal from Parai Defile. Plodding 75 yards behind a Sherman tank that almost crawled, Botta slogged on with a slung carbine and an ammo case in each hand.

Suddenly Botta saw his first live Jap of the war. The Nip crouched behind the tank, which had stopped for a second. Botta shouted, dropped ammo cases, unslung carbine. But he was too late.

The Jap mounted the tank and blasted a grenade down the tank, then leaped back into the jungle. Riflemen chased him but never killed him. In the tank, 1 man died; 2 were wounded. An assistant driver seized tank controls, but logs and rock in the road prevented the tank's escape until T/5 Winkler's "cat" dozed them aside.

Orders came to withdraw our HMG crew which was left far down in Jap country so that mortar shells could impact the area. Over 75 yards of fire-swept ground lay between that forward crew and 3/Bn. The Bn CO wanted a tank to deliver the retreat order, but the Japs had again destroyed the bridge.

M's volunteer Moore dashed through Jap fire with the order, showed the MG crew the safest way to retreat. On 3 June, no M Co man was hit, but "L" lost 2 dead, 3 wounded.

In the next few days, we continued pressure on Parai Defile. On 5 June, 3/Bn sent an officer onto a destroyer to show targets to Naval guns, while another 162 man on the beach, marked our advance with a red flag. The destroyer, a rocket LCI, flak boats of Support Btry, 2/Engr Special Brigade — all fired. Then "L" and "I" patrols heard Japs shouting and digging on the cliffs and in the coastal swamp. Just as "I" men saw the bridge, heavy fire repelled them. Except for outposts near the river, 3/Bn again withdrew into perimeter.

On 6 June, we reconnoitered in force. "I" covered "L" with "M" weapons probably attached. Patrols pressed through the gap unopposed, even 250 yards west of the stream and the bridge which our Naval guns had destroyed. The Japs had used many 1-man caves to fight from. At 1550, heavy fire halted us — with 1 dead, 1 wounded in the rifle Cos. We outposted the stream, fell back again.

That night of 6 June, Japs screamed and rushed at our holes. Muscular little California Indian Joaquin crept out into the dark and killed 2. Down in his hole, Botta heard 4-5 carbine shots, then low words passed down the holes to say that Joaquin was dead.

But 3/Bn 162 never finished off the Parai Defile Japs. Leaving L Co and probably most of "M," for a short time there, Gen Fuller detached "I" and "K" to land at Parai Jetty behind the Japs. They were to join with 186 against the Japs above

Mokmer Strip. To help L Co pushing west, Fuller sent Cannon Co (actually a rifle Co then) to take the Defile Japs in the rear.

On 7-9 June, "L," "M," and "CN" tried to break the Defile Japs. But on 8 June, the Japs cut CN in two and forced it back. On 9 June, 3 Sherman tanks fired on them from LVTs, but Japs still held the defile. Then on 9 June, "M," "L," and 3/Bn Hq Co embarked to reinforce the other Cos of 3/Bn at Parai Jetty. (AT 162 replaced us, and pushed against "C," but the Defile was not clear until 12 June.)

During the 12 days after 162's repulse from the Defile 29 May, Botta's crew never fired their HMG in action. During probes into the Defile, we set it up to secure patrols. At night, our guns sealed off 3/Bn's rifle Cos with final protective lines.

But now after M Co left Parai Defile, we used our weapons on "Death Ridge," as M Co named it. Holding Death Ridge made the Japs still winners on Biak, for it guarded all the Biak strips from landing our planes — Mokmer, Borokoe, and Sorido Strips. A low, brushy ridge rising gradually up to 140 feet, it held a garrison of 120 men of 1/Bn 222 Inf, maybe 2 Cos of 2/Bn 222 Inf, combat Engrs, and some FA and AA guns and crews — 600-700 fighters. Core of this defence was shaped roughly like a horseshoe, with the curve towards Mokmer Strip — about 1,000 long by 1,000 yards wide. While Col Kuzume kept Death Ridge, his 600-700 man garrison controlled all Biak.

On 10-11 June, 162 could not reach the Jap core on Death Ridge. Along with intermittent rifle-fire from the ridge-base, some 7-10 LMGs and HMGs opened up every time we tried to cross open spaces. Several batteries of 3-4 mortars fired in spasms, then silenced under our counter-battery blasts.

For 2 days until 12 June, 3/Bn could not even attain the assigned line of departure alongside the advance of the unopposed 186 Inf on the beach below us. At 0940 12 June, all M Co's .81 mortars barraged the Japs. Then with "L" on the right flank, "I" overran 3 lines of Jap defenses. On that 12 June, 3/Bn lost 4 dead, 7 wounded. "M" had no losses.

Starting about 13 June, our Death Ridge offensive was a slower war of attrition while FA, mortars, and rifle patrols pressed the Japs. In return, a Jap mountain gun shelled us. They whistled fearfully and made us flatten in our holes, but they burst in the tree-tops. Despite daily shells, "M" reported no casualty. Our Piper Cub circled above to find that gun, but M Co never knew what caused it to cease fire.

The Japs fronting 3/Bn did not merely wait for FA and mortars to thin them down. Skilled infantry, these 36 Div "Tigers" attacked expertly to conserve as many Japs as possible. By day, small groups infiltrated through brush and shell-holes against us. By night, they screeched and made short rushes where our MGs would be grenade kills if we fired and exposed our positions for them.

Botta never forgot a daylight Jap attack during his last days on Death Ridge. His HMG had the prime field-of-fire to protect a line of L Co riflemen — a shelled out lane in the brush some 40 yards wide by 200 long with a few shell-holes.

Suddenly an "L" outguard leaped from the brush to warn us of a Nippo charge. Close behind Botta, a .60 mortar gunner told us to lower our heads while his 3 practice rounds swished overhead.

Botta hardly believed his eyes when he saw the attack coming that he had long awaited. An officer's blade gleamed in the sun.

Japs dodged in the brush on both sides of our fire-lane. Some hid in the first of a line of 3 shell-holes 150 yards out, then dashed 25 yards more into Shell-Hole No. 2, then 25 yards into No. 3 — just 100 yards away from our lines.

They were too close now; rifles and mortar and HMG fired together. Botta knelt on his firing-step, sighted Jap targets, and touched the little trigger. In battle-joy, he shot bursts of 3-6 rounds at dashing target after target. Expertly, he retracted the bolt now and then to eject a shell to present a stoppage from a possible defective round. He hoped that the Japs would keep on coming, in that great moment when a man's own life seems not to matter.

But our heavy fire broke the Jap charge long before they drove it home. We counted just 3 corpses; other casualties were no doubt carried off. Their dead had fine carbines, and grenades for lobbing into our holes.

Once at sundown, an alert "L" rifleman saw 2 Nips watching us preparing perimeter for the night. The "L" man shot and killed a Nip; another fled while the M-1 blasted behind. We were then sure that Jap scouts spotted us every evening.

On the night of 16 June — after 186 closed the Great Gap between our Bns — Japs slashed our perimeter with rifles, MGs. We fought them with grenades; riflemen slew 7 Nips. At dawn, some 10 knee-mortar shells hit our perimeter, but missed us.

M Co had 8 HMGs fighting on Death Ridge, but we have no report of what rifle Cos they fired for. Once, Botta's gun gave overhead fire for "I" men attacking a ridge. Other "M" guns felled escaping Nips when 3/Bn Cos smashed Jap pillboxes. Unrecorded are the fights of M's 7 other HMGs and .81 mortars.

"M" lost few men on Death Ridge, since we mostly holed up in a stationary line. Only recorded casualties were on 16 June, when the Great Gap was closed. Wounded were M's Underwood, 1/Lt Pound, T/Sgt Hugh Morrison. Botta believes that Morrison was wounded while observing for the .81s.

On 18 June, some "M" gunners got a remembered piece of the action again. With K Co, we had to secure the left flank of 186's great maneuver of 19 June, when Gen Eichelberger ordered 186 to cut off the Japs escape route from West Caves.

With K Co at 1200, Botta's gunners hiked through "E" left of us on the ridge. By 1630, we had occupied an egg-shaped knoll, unopposed. We seized 3 Nip LMGs, "woodpeckers," with neat folding handles. "K" scouts ran to warn us — 9 Nips coming through rocks and brush. While "K" men fired beside us gunner Moore squeezed off a belt. We routed them, killed 4, and scattered the other 5. Our only wounded was K's Jim Sullivan, from a long-range mortar shell.

With our fight of 18 June, M's Battle of Biak was nearly done. For after 186 Inf cut off West Caves, hard-fighting 3/Bn was relieved but for local patrols, while 162's other Bns wiped out West Caves Japs. By 10 July, Botta was scaredly helping unloaded 250 and 500 lb. air-bombs from a Victory Ship at the U-shaped floating dock that he had watched Engrs build while he was still on Death Ridge. Unloading detail ended with a steak dinner, and cigars for Botta.

M's Battle of Biak was over but for the memories even decades later. Botta still remembers the beautiful red-beaked bird with the 5-foot wing-spread who flew over our position on Death Ridge. At first light, the great red-beaked bird with gray and white plumes woke our gunners with 3 screams echoing across the ridges. (He too became a casualty.) Botta remembers his snug fox-hole under the camouflaged poncho with his carefully tuned HMG. There he waited for Japs many an hour with a sweet, bitter White Owl cigar. The cigar aroma covered the odor from a Jap cave that had been burned out. It was a hard life on Death Ridge, but Botta still remembers his cigars, the clean HMG in his hole, and the great beautiful red-beaked bird.

After 162's repulse from Parai Defile on 29 June, M Co was more than lucky in bucking the Japs' stone-wall defense of the Defile, and in guarding our lines on Death Ridge while infighting for Mokmer Strip. It is hard indeed to remember our sole death after 29 June — the death of the heroic Indian Joaquin.

2/BN 162 INFANTRY:

Chaplain Smith's Southern Philippine Campaign

by DR. HARGIS WESTERFIELD, Division Historian, with CHAPLAIN (CAPTAIN) ROBERT C. SMITH

> CREDIT: Prime source is Father Robert C. Smith's 6-page, single-spaced typescript, provided by his Assistant, T/5 Sydney Stafford. Smith also contributed letters of 8 April and 18 April 1982. Important also were 162 Inf's Casualty Reports and Narratives of Zamboanga and Central Mindano — with background from RR Smith's *Triumph in the Philippines*, and *Reports of General MacArthur: Japanese Operations in the Southwest Pacific Area*. For the Maramag-Iglosad background, I have only a half-page from Wm McCartney's *The Jungleers*, which reads like a word-for-word transcript of a report which is not available to me. (Please, won't my readers tell me about their chaplains in battle and out of battle?)

These are the highlights of 2/Bn 162 Inf's Chaplain Robert Smith's career during his Southern Philippine Campaign — from Zamboanga Beachhead into the Pulangi River highlands of Central Mindanao. At 0932, 10 Mar 1945 Cap Smith landed from LCI 700 with G Co 162 Inf in the second wave at Zamboanga. Like G 162's men, he went ashore through hip-deep water. A slight but energetic sunburnt man, Smith was still queasy from 2 days' voyage down from Mindoro.

Chaplain Smith's duties soon began. At 1055 when advancing G Co lost 2 wounded and 1 killed from Jap MG fire, Smith was with Medics at the aid station. As ever, he offered a prayer for every wounded man, if the man consented. (During all of Smith's service, only one man ever refused that prayer.) He prayed for G Co's Carr and S/Sgt Di Laura, who was shot in the leg. (Di Laura was reported lightly wounded, and Carr seriously wounded.)

And with Chaplain's Assistant T/5 Stafford, Smith prepared his first combat burial service at Zambo. At the grave of G Co's Gordon, he carried out the necessarily short rite of burial under combat conditions. Reading some portions of his Episcopal *Book of Common Prayer*, he performed a short ritual for Gordon, temporarily buried in an isolated grave near the beach. And that night, Chaplain Smith also slept below ground in a hole laboriously dug with Assistant Stafford.

On the second day of his beachhead, Sunday, 11 Mar, Smith's life was comparatively peaceful. Except for detached F Co fighting for Caldera Point west of Zambo City, his 2/Bn patrolled for inland Jap positions, and awaited orders. Smith and Stafford bivouacked in the yard of a Moro family — even set up their pup-tent.

That Sunday night, Smith held a General Protestant Service for men at 2/Bn 162 CP. Then he celebrated Holy Communion of his own Episcopal Church. He used a litter as an altar for his Episcopalians to kneel before.

By Army Regulations, Smith had to have a General Protestant Service, and was permitted to have another for his own sect, if men desired it. (Army Regulations classified Smith as Protestant. In much of its ritual and theology, however, the Episcopal Church is much like the Roman Catholic Church. Smith himself is a member of an Episcopal monastic order, the Society of St. John the Evangelist. By permission of his monastic superior, Smith had volunteered for military service.)

Next Monday, 12 Mar, Smith conducted services for men of E and G Cos in the forward areas whom he could not see on Sunday. "E" and "G" were on patrol inland to locate the Japs' positions.

By 15 Mar, 2/Bn 162 less "F" at Caldera Point was also committed for front-line action. While E Co with attached AT Co fought in the hills above the Japs' San Roque Village, G Co began pushing up East Ridge to capture Mt. Capisan.

With Assistant Stafford, Smith also moved forward to the action. While Smith set up their pup-tent, Stafford dug a hole which they named "Stafford's Cemetery." Smith had another difficult chaplain's duty. A sister of a 2/Bn Hq officer had died back in the States, and Smith had to break the news to the officer.

Next Sunday 18 Mar, Smith jeeped alone to E Co, well forward on a mountain. Stafford was ill. (In E Co, Juhl had been killed near his hole the night before.) Smith's E Co congregation met safely below a rise in the ground. For greater security, the men took intervals so that no group would tempt Jap automatic fire. Relievedly, Smith then jeeped down to G Co for his second service. The prayers and praise of his congregation were punctuated by firing at G Co's forward CP.

Against Jap pressure from the north, AT Co had reinforced "G" with 2 37 mm guns. So when Smith went to G's forward CP, he found "too much confusion" for another service. (That night, Japs would make an abortive attack on G Co.) That Sunday, Smith had 4 services — 2 General Protestant services, and one Episcopalian. He had once more endangered his life.

On 21 Mar, Smith expected to relocate in a new 2/Bn forward area, but E Co's attack through a hedge of overgrown poplars was repelled with 6 dead, 13 wounded. Next day, 22 Mar, when E Co overran that position and 2/Bn closed in on Mt Capisan, Smith was on his usual duty at the aid station. He ministered both physically and spiritually to 2/Bn men. (In E's successful attack that 22 Mar, "E" had 7 wounded, and "F" had 10 wounded. "H" had 3 wounded, and "G" 1 wounded.)

Smith gave the last rites before death to a Greek Orthodox soldier with a frightful head wound. (This man was probably F

Co's Christodolov, shot through his helmet into his head. But his name does not appear on 162's death-list; we hope that he survived with total recovery.)

In the next 2 days, 2/Bn 162 stormed Capisan. On 25 Mar, Palm Sunday, the day that Christ entered Jerusalem, Smith and Assistant Stafford early began their 2-hour climb afoot to Capisan summit. After much needed rest, they gathered a congregation of some 100 men. But as services were to commence, a Jap sniper decided to consecrate us with his bullets.

After moving "Church" to a safer spot, he continued his rites. He blessed and distributed palm crosses that were made yesterday. He read the names of 2/Bn's casualties during last week — 20 killed and 6 wounded in that push which took Mt Capisan. After a lunch of "C" rations donated by E Co, Smith held services for that outfit. At Bn CP, he conducted a third General Protestant service, and Holy Communion.

On 26 Mar, he visited 2nd Field Hosp to counsel the wounded not yet evacuated from Zambo. On 28 Mar, he moved with Bn CP to Mt Capisan, with a breath-taking view of Zambo Foreshore. Next day, he celebrated communion to observe Maundy Thursday, when Christ instituted the Holy Sacrament. But bad weather kept him from celebrating Good Friday.

Easter Day, 1 Apr 1945, was one of Chaplain Smith's greatest and hardest days of work in the Army. After sunrise services on Capisan, he celebrated Holy Communion. Third service was on another hill near Capisan, at E Co CP. Fourth and fifth services were in G Co's area. G Co gave Smith and Stafford an Easter banquet far different from "B" or "C" rations: fresh roast pig, corn, sweet potatoes. Sixth and seventh services were for F Co with attached "H" men. Finally, at 1600, he celebrated Episcopal Eucharist with a sizable congregation of his own Church assembled from many outfits.

On 5 Apr, Chaplain Smith crossed to large, mountainous Basilan Island 12 miles south of Zambo mainland. At Isabella, he conducted a late Protestant Easter service for B Co. At Lamitan, he baptized 3 children of an Episcopalian Filipina mother, and served Communion which was for them the first time in 4 years since the Jap invasion. To give communion for another Episcopalian, he had to cross by native boat over a crocodile infested stream.

He had indeed worked hard and risked himself to serve Christ. On 19-24, he suffered even more for his hard work — spent 5 days in 2 Field Hosp with dysentery.

But on 1 Mar, recovered Smith took the field again when 162 Inf was attached to campaign with 24 Div and 31 Div in the great half-wild land of central Mindanao across the Moro Gulf from Zambo Peninsula. Landing unopposed from LST 531 on the west coast of the Mindanao mainland east of Zambo Peninsula, he left Parang on 4 May to jeep south and bivouac outside battered Cotabato Town.

Especially did Smith remember services at nearby Tamontaka SE of Cotabato in the Roman Catholic church. Japs and Moros had desecreated it, but Smith rejoiced that Sunday of 6 May. It was a long time since he had heard God's praises in hymns in a real church building. Three days later, he jeeped some 10-12 miles to give E Co a service at Libungan on the edge of the great Libungan swamp. Because Stafford was ill, Smith travelled alone but for his organ. Moving from conducting ritual to his organ and back would make him smile later; he said that he felt like a jumping-jack.

The mop-up of 2/Bn in the Cotabato area was finished. On 19 May, 2/Bn was attached to 31 Div and ordered to move inland to Sayre Highway, then turn north on it to guard Valencia Strip and nearby supply dumps. On 19 May in a motor convoy, he penetrated 44 miles inland to Kabakan, where 24 Div had seized a road junction, and separated the Jap 30 Div on the north from 100 Div in the Davao area to the SE.

Turning almost at right angles northwards when they hit Sayre Highway, Smith's 2/Bn drove over almost impassable roads, but after 3 days, arrived at Valencia.

Mistakenly, Smith believed that he was settled for awhile near Valencia Strip. He even tried to teach a Bible class, but attendance was poor. By 26 May, he was erecting an attractive chapel — a squad tent decorated with a blue parachute brought from Biak. Assistant Stafford built an attractive altar, altar rail, pulpit, and credence table for the bread and wine. All were made of graceful, fresh green bamboo.

So well settled had they become at Valencia that they had to move some miles south to Maramgag Strip 1 and rebuild "church" again.

On 30 May, of course official Memorial Day, Smith had a sizable congregation despite torrential rain. Names of 2/Bn's dead since departure from Finschafen long ago in April, 1944, were read, and prayers said for them. By the time services were over, the rains had made the chapel floor into a pond. (At some time during the evening also, he had taught a Bible class of a fairly large number.)

A few days later while returning from Protestant services from an E Co Pln several miles north, Smith and Stafford were briefly again in 2/Bn's front lines. A sniper made a near miss against them on the road, and they raced out of danger.

While Smith with Stafford carried on their ministry at Maramag, all 162 Inf except 3 Bn and 205 FA got orders to move north from Kabakan. They were to drive north from Kabakan up Sayre Highway and assemble at Maramag to reinforce 31 Div's 108 Inf against the Japs. But heavy rains deepened muddy, war-torn Sayre Highway and bogged down wheeled traffic. After 5 days' labor, 30 May to 5 June, order was rescinded. All 162 Inf but Smith's 2/Bn went SE to battle for 24 Div in the Davao area. But 31 Div needed our 2/Bn 162 Inf.

Smith became part of one of our 41st's final combat operations of World War II. Ly-Gen Gyosaku Morozumi's 30 Div had withdrawn east across Pulangi River into the mountain foothills. So 2/Bn 162 and 108 Inf had to fight Morozumi there.

On 13 June, Smith without sick Stafford accompanied 2/Bn eastward towards the high mountains of central Mindanao — a chain that runs north and south all the way across the island. Bivouacking that night by the Pulangi River ferry, Smith conducted a sunset Vesper service which the approaching storm caused him to cut to 10 minutes. In the next 2 days, he carried out burial services for 2 guerillas who had been with them.

During 13-30 June, Smith went with 2/Bn to penetrate 20 miles NE from Maramag into the Iglosad-Namnam area. And 2/Bn fought the Jap delaying groups, but with only 2 casualties reported — Morris and Maj Ratliff — both marked wounded lightly on 23 June. These casualties probably occurred when 2/Bn fought 200 Japs in a strong perimeter near Luminatao. Here mortars and planes helped E and G Cos to overrun this perimeter.

By 30 June, Smith was in 2/Bn's return from the Glodsad area, taken over by Guerilla 112 Inf to drive the Japs into a starvation mountain wilderness. He required only a day to cover a distance that had taken 5 days for the 20-odd miles across the Pulangi from Maramag. By 3 July, he was in a motor convoy north from Valencia to Bugo on the Mindanao coast. Here he boarded LCI 611 with E Co, happy to get back from the wilds into the Filipino-Army civilization of Zamboanga.

Such was Chaplain Smith's Southern Philippine Campaign. He had inspired the troops by devotion to duty, steady courage, and coolness under fire. Often he had gone afoot over hazardous ground and climbed to crests of various hills to hold services and administer to the wounded. This Episcopalian member of a monastic order had been one of our many dedicated Army chaplains.

M CO 186 INFANTRY:

Our Biak Story

by DR. HARGIS WESTERFIELD, Division Historian, with M 186's JOHN LAPHAM

> CREDIT: Personal stories are from letters of John Lapham, 26 Nov 1982, 12 Jan 1983 — and Clarence Malcolm 27 May 1983. I used also award stories of Lapham and Richard Ten Eyck. "Record of Events" of M 186 on Biak was almost useless, but some fine help came from "Record of Events of Company L, from 25 May 1944." Other important data came from 186's Biak Casualty List, 186's Inf's "Journal" and "Narrative" from 2 May 1944 to 20 Aug 1944, RR Smith's **Approach to the Philippines,** and **Reports of General MacArthur: Japanese Operations in the Southwest Pacific Area.** l 186's Biak story appeared in **Jungleer** of Oct 1972; K's was in the June 1965 issue, and L's in Feb. 1964. All 3 were reprinted in my **Fighting Jungleers.**

About 0735 27 May 1944, most of M Co 186 Inf landed unfought with our 3/Bn at Bosnek on Biak. Two HMG sections attached to I and K Cos landed 2300 yards west because of an unknown inshore current and had to hike back to Bosnek.

One HMG section with L Co climbed a trail to secure Bosnek Ridge. About 1345 an "L" patrol scouted to our right, halfway up the trail. After gunfire, we saw L's S/Sgt Foote borne back dead from a bullet in his chest. Japs of 1/Bn 222 Inf were putting up scattered resistance in jungle north of us.

Now with L 186, that same "M" HMG section guarded over 100 yards of a ridge behind Bosnek. About 0630 28 May, Japs howled "Banzai!" and attacked. "L" had 3 wounded, but we killed 14 Jap men, an officer. Probably lightly wounded that day was M's Lawrence.

In our early days on Biak, Nippo plane raids seemed continuous. So trigger-happy were our AA gunners that they even killed a plane of ours which was flying in maps. At 2020 the night of 30 May, bombs from Nippo planes killed T/4 Sternquist, seriously wounded Reed and Gant. Gant lost an arm. All 3 men were mess personnel.

When 162 Inf failed to force Parai Defile, Gen Fuller needed our 186 Inf to march overland to bypass Parai Defile and seize Mokmer Strip. So on 31 May as soon as 163 Inf's 1/Bn and 3/Bn arrived from Toem, we turned over Bosnek Beach to them and crossed Bosnek Ridge into the dry jungle scrub.

On 1 June, 3/Bn with M Co moved north across the ridge and by 1100 was entrenching at the west end of the area which the Japs had surveyed for an air-strip. At 1330, K Co repelled a Jap force of some 25 men. In dead night after 0300 1-2 June, a company and a half of Japs struck 3/Bn from the south while other Japs hit from the NW.

Main attack, of course, came from the company and a half to the south, with support of mortar and MG fire. Four hours' hand-to-hand fighting began, when 3/Bn rapidly adjusted our lines and trapped most of them.

In this wild combat, 2 L Co men were killed within 10 feet of the hole where Pate and Lapham crouched. In a nearby hole, probably L's Lloyd was killed at once. Freiman would die of wounds on 4 June, 2 days later.

When some L Co riflemen called over to M's gunners for more grenades, ammo-bearer Lapham responded. He left his safe slit trench near the HMG and collected M men's grenades in his helmet. He slipped behind the first line of holes and dropped grenades into the hands of grateful riflemen who asked for them. Although naturally in great danger from being shot in the dark by our men, and with Japs yards away firing automatic weapons, heroic Lapham was unhurt. He may have averted a Japanese breach of our lines.

That night, 186 Inf slew 86 Japs. Entire Regt lost 5 killed, 10 wounded — including Bunnell of AT Co. Most of our 186 Inf losses were in 3/Bn — 3 killed, 8 wounded. In M Co, Ellmore was reported lightly wounded (probably in this action), other circumstances unknown.

Despite the sleeplessness and confusion from this night action, 186 Inf marched forth at 0900 2 June. While 3/Bn plus 1/Bn slogged west, 2/Bn with AT Co secured our north flank against the Japs. The road died out. In that rocky coral scrubland, our 5 attached tanks became useless. Without their protection, we had to advance against the Japs. In this progress of 2 June, 186 Inf lost 6 killed, 10 wounded — but killed 96 Japs who battled with MGs and rifles in little patrols. M Co had no losses. The Regt made 400 yards west from their tentative plan of going 500 yards. It was not easy going.

After the first day of our westward advance, Jap fighters almost disappeared. But in the heat and humidity in the breezeless 12-foot scrub that walled us in, our march became a thirsty trek.

In that dry scrubland, water was our greatest problem. Well-drillers dug only dry holes. Once we found a well that held water for a single company, but it was dry 10 minutes later, on 4 June. We had a shortage of water-trailers and 5-gallon bidons. Water had to come slowly by truck up 10 miles of rough road. Water had to come by a circuitous road that backtracked east to Opiaref, then bent north and turned west to where we sweated behind B Co 116 Engrs bulldozing our new road.

From L Co's Biak narrative, we can appreciate the shortage of water which our M Co and other 3/Bn outfits also had to endure. Supposedly starting out from the coast with 2 canteens full on 2 June, "L" had no water at all issued next day, on 3 June. On 4 June, "L" actually received a whole canteen full for each man! On 5 June, we had no water issue. Col Newman expected to have to stop the whole waterless Regt dead in our tracks. But about 1200, a heavy rain pooled our open ponches and was funnelled into our empty canteens while we drank and rejoiced. Then on 6 June, water arrived up that lengthening road from Bosnek, and L Co had 2 full canteens to fight on again.

On 5 June, after the rain had filled our canteens, K Co's 1/Pln about 1400 found an approach up over the southern ridge above Mokmer Strip. Our 3/Bn — of course with M Co — immediately positioned on the ridge-top where through thick jungle we could glimpse Mokmer Strip, 2500 yards SW.

Well resupplied by 6 June, especially with water, our 3/Bn with 1/Bn on our left was now ready to seize Mokmer Strip. And on 7 June, after some bombing by 5 Air Force and 30 minutes' preparation by 121 FA, who had followed on our overland trek, we marched downhill. We seized Mokmer Strip without fighting. By 0850, our lead Pln was on Sboeria Beach. By 0915, attached 2/Bn 162 Inf had closed in behind us, and the rest of 186 Inf was following us into Mokmer Strip.

Mokmer Strip now seemed like an easy conquest. But about 0945 from Mokmer Ridge where we had bypassed them, the Japs impacted us with all the FA and MG fire that they could bring to bear. It was a 4-hour blasting. Especially vicious were heavy mortar and 20 mm fire from the direction of East Caves where our FA could not range in. And from NW along the low ridge behind West Caves, 75 mm cannon or dual purpose AA fire whistled down, but our observers could not locate them. By calling fire on positions which they could pinpoint on the ridge that we had just crossed, our FA and 81 mm mortar observers did diminish that fire by 40 per cent. By late afternoon, at least 6 Jap positions were silenced, and mortar fire had become lighter.

On that 7 July, M Co had more casualties in that 1 day than on any other single day in our whole war — 2 killed, 7 reported seriously wounded. Killed were Ogburn, Hanes Larsen. Reported seriously wounded were 1/Lt Malo, T/Sgt Hathaway, and Sgt Decker — along with Payne, Cortez, Garcia, and Jensen. (Nearby L Co lost 5 dead, 6 wounded. Of the 14 killed in all 186 Inf that day, "L" plus "M" had 2.)

Even as early as 1040 while Jap FA bombarded us, 186's CO Col Newman tried to run in supplies and tanks from the sea. Besides tanks, we needed medical supplies, especially blood plasma. Our 3/Bn reported having only enough plasma for 50 men. But not until 1236 could 1/Bn men locate a beach at Sboeria Village where barges and LSTs could land.

In the face of remarkably accurate fire from the ridges, it was hard to beach the tanks and supplies. And in a 12-foot coral seaside cliff, Japs held caves with MGs, backed by mortar bunkers near the coast road. When they first tried to land, 3 tank-loaded LCMs and some LCVs had to sheer off because of direct fire from the cliff caves. Although 2 of the LCMs with tanks were damaged, 3 tanks landed by 1340.

The tanks crunched a few shore bunkers that they could sight near the road with their guns, but they then turned inland to fight Nippo positions on the ridges. And 186 Inf still had to clear out the caves in the 12-foot cliff where tanks could not bring their guns to bear.

While I and K Cos fought the Japs in this cliff, at least one M Co man volunteered to help them. Although a supply Sgt in M Co, S/Sgt Ten Eyck with an unnamed assistant went into action. Killing a number of Japs, Ten Eyck cleared numerous caves, even put a 20 mm machine cannon out of action. Once, he even stood up on a ledge in full view of a Nippo gun pit and slew the crew. No doubt other "M" men fought that cliff also.

That night, Jap patrols harassed I Co's 3 Pln from the beach. About 2230, their MG fired over us. They showered grenades within 25 yards of our holes. Firing for effect 100 yards before our perimeter, M's 81 mm mortars weakened their harassment so that I and L Cos could stop the assault. The Japs seemed to attack for 2 purposes. Mainly, they wanted to keep our supply parties from landing in the protecting dark. But they also may have been on recon to locate our lines for the great night assault of 8-9 June.

We did not then know that Lt-Gen Takazo Numata had assumed personal command of the Japs' western area. He had issued orders for a final attack by all available men to retake Mokmer Strip.

The full moon was up by 2100 that night of 8-9 June. About 2130, K Co opened fire on 12 advancing Nips whom the full moon outlined against the white coral Strip. "K" shot rifle grenades and 60 mm shells at them, with unknown results. Presumably some of those same Nips went to ground and struck back at "K" with knee mortars.

After the mortar fire, the Japs seem to have sent trained dogs to help them accurately locate our holes. Several dogs did trot up to within 100 yards of 3/Bn's position at the west end of 186's perimeter. Two of them halted and barked. Other dogs trotted up soundlessly, then returned to the west. Japs then moved up past where the line of dogs had stopped.

A Jap whistle blew. The Japs attacked under cover of the mortars, which now began lifting and moving east. Our .50 caliber HMGs of 3/Bn Hq searched for the mortars, but heavy Jap fire flailed at them with each burst. We ordered our .50s to cease fire. But M Co's .81 mortars blasted out the Jap mortars. Then M's mortars detonated so dangerously close to our lines that we had to cease fire also.

L Co's 3/Pln with at least 1 "M" HMG was positioned on an inland road that turned north off the main beach road. In that position, the road became an obvious corridor of Jap attack. Despite close in fire of our .60 mortars, grenades, and rifles, Nippo bayonet men got through to kill. Bayonets and other weapons killed 7 "L" men and wounded 3 more.

In a hole near gunner Lapham, a Nip reared up and bayoneted an "L" rifleman in the back. Another Yank in the same hole shot the Nip dead. While the dead or dying Nip fell on an "L" man, he knifed the Nip again because he thought the enemy still endangered him.

Lapham rose to his knees and called for a Medic nearby. A probably wounded Yank fired a tommie at Lapham. A .45 slug caromed off his helmet just above the right ear but failed even to draw blood. A Jap or Yank rifle bullet would have killed him.

About 0500 at dawn, 3 blasts of a Jap whistle ordered their withdrawal. Still in our holes, we had killed 42 known Nips and lost 13 killed and 38 wounded in all 186 Inf. (Of these, our 3/Bn had 8 dead and 20 wounded.) On 9 June, "M" reported Sykora and Gitelson as both lightly wounded.

Despite failing to destroy 186 Inf, the Japs' story was different. They credited 222 Inf with advancing halfway down the Strip (where we were not even dug in) before we halted them. A Co of 19 Naval Garrison ("Marines") had infiltrated across the Strip into our rear but were too few to hold the ground.

Next morning, M's Lapham witnesses the desperation of our night fight. We saw a dead "L" rifleman with a bullet in his throat. While he fired his M-1, the bolt had caught his jacket lapel and held him while the Jap bullet killed him. A mortar had blown 2 "L" men from their hole; they found half a body 50-60 yards away. And in one of their shell-craters of 7 June, he found 8-10 dead Nips.

Such is the main tale of M 186 on Biak, but we had more combat still. On 10-24 June, we had 7 more losses. Quirk was lightly wounded on 10 June, and Wilson lightly injured, 15 June. On 19 June, the day that 3/Bn cut the West Caves supply lines, Short and 2/Lt Gallagher were lightly wounded. On 20 June, the day that K Co tried to take Hill 320, Verdugo was lightly wounded. On 21 June, the night of the West Caves Banzai, Levi was seriously injured. Martinez was seriously wounded, 24 June, the day that 3/Bn attacked Jap gun positions in the hills. Nothing more can be found about these last "M" casualties.

On Biak, M Co 186 Inf had just 3 killed, from a total of only 25 casualties. Despite the hardships and risk that "M" endured, we served the 41st well, with but few losses in action.

HEADQUARTERS CO., 1/BATTALION 163 INFANTRY:
(MEMORIAL ALSO TO SERVICE COMPANY'S 1/LT FRANK NUGENT)

Wire and Water on Wakde

by DR. HARGIS WESTERFIELD, Division Historian,
and NATHAN J. (SONNY) SONNENFELD

CREDIT: Most important sources are 2 undated cassettes sent by Sonnenfeld with the sound-track from him, John Drum, and Clifton James. Sonnenfeld backed those cassettes with some 21 Pp handwritten letters dated 28 Feb, 26 July, 12 Aug, and 21 Aug — all 1982. Ray Heinitz sent an undated letter in 1982 also. I used data also from Award Stories of Sonnenfeld, T/5 John Drum of 163 Inf — and Capt John Panek (C Btry 218 FA) and 1/Lt Frank Nugent (SV 163). I used also Gen Eichelberger's comment on our "fine" 163 Infantry in **Dear Miss Em**, and a comment from Col Moroney at our North Aurora (Ill.) Reunion of Mid-America several years ago. Background is from 163 Inf's Casualty List of 18 May 1944, and RR Smith's **Approach to the Philippines.**

About 0735, May 1944, 1/Bn 163 Inf's Hq Co safely landed on Arare Beach across from Wakde Island which we expected to occupy safely tomorrow. Beaching was easy because light cruisers *Phoenix, Nashville,* and *Boise* had salvoed 6-inch shells into Wakde on our left flank for 50 minutes. Two LCIs rocketed the rear of our beach, and 3/Bn 163 Inf landed before us, with A Co 116 Engrs and 27 Engr Combat Bn after them. After settling down in 163's perimeter, T/5 Drum's wiremen (with Sonnenfeld) had little to do but go swimming from that fine long sandy beach.

Next morning, 18 May, was beautiful to 1/Bn wiremen — "clear, sunny, picture perfect," Sonnenfeld called it. Enhancing that beauty were 30 A-20s of Fifth Air Force which swooped to blast silent Wakde. Thirty minutes before our embarkment for Wakde, destroyers *Wilkes* and *Rode* fired 2350 rounds of 5-inch and 6-inch shells, and then little 20 mm and 40 mm machine cannon. Ten minutes before our barges left Arare, rocket LCIs began barraging the 60-yard beach with its little jetty. Wakde took a total of 850 rockets that day.

Meanwhile, wiremen and other 1/Bn Hq men laughed and joked cramming into barges to take over pathetic, battered little Wakde. We enjoyed the impact of bombs and shells and rockets on Wakde. We stood while barges circled in the water and waited for the exact moment to charge the beach.

Now our LCVP coxswain called, "O.K., fellows, it's time to take your kneeling positions. The rules say you got to get down on your knees." We wanted to keep on standing up, but we would be happy that we obeyed that order.

Then our barges straightened out to hit the beach abreast; Jap MG bullets struck us. They punched holes in wooden gunwales. T/5 Drum thought that he heard Jap mortars impact. As Drum tried to shrink into himself on the boat bottom, he saw that AT Pln's Mackowsky seemed to lie where he seemed to shield Drum from the bullets. Every time Mackowsky moved, Drum moved to keep Mackowsky between himself and the bullets. Drum was not selfish about hiding behind him. Something else had put Mackowsky there, and Drum was going to make use of him.

Driving for Wakde Beach even in the third or fourth waves, Hq Co lost Herwig from a shot in the right forearm. On the same LCVP with Heinitz, Cpl Zwieczkowski was wounded in the hand. Zwieczkoski had been firing a heavy .50 HMG into the beach. The barge grated the sand. As the ramp clanged down and we piled out of the craft, McIlvanie died from a bullet in the throat.

Now all Hq Co flattened on a bare beach with a low 30-40 rise ahead of us. We risked our eyes to look up over the sand to coconut palms, brush, and coral outcrops. We waited on our chests and faces for what seemed forever, although it could have been only 10 minutes. We were under fire from both flanks and before us. Finally, 1/Bn's CO Maj Wing stood up and yelled, "Let's get the Hell out of here," and strode forward. The fire had died down. And all 1/Bn reinforced charged off the beach, happy to be alive.

We wiremen set up our switchboard in our new Bn CP near a cross-roads centrally located on a slight rise. T/5 Drum our leader had already searched the beach-head for "wire-heads" and connected them with all our Cos. While Jap MG and rifle fire streamed overhead, he discovered 2 damaged lines and repaired them. After our switchboard was in operation, we discovered an unexploded bomb next to the crater where we had sheltered that switchboard. We let that bomb stay there for our whole time on Wakde.

Fire fights seemed to go on all around us. Wireman James took an unusual wound. Sent down to the beach for water, James came under Jap fire, and crawled under the dock for safety. Bullets blew up a nearby truck tire. Fragments hit him in the mouth, knocked out teeth, broke his jaw in 2 places. James did not rejoin 1/Bn until we had landed on Biak.

Late that afternoon, 1/Bn's wiremen had a risky assignment for an important link-up north into Wakde. By now, A Co held a fine tactical position north of the Strip in NE Wakde, but the Jap garrison still fought hard. When night came, "A" would be isolated and exposed to Jap attacks north of that Strip and would need all the mortar and FA protection they could get. But "A" had travelled so far and fast west of the Strip and then around the cape eastward that they had no wire connection with Hq.

To connect with A Co, a 6-man team of T/5 Drum, Sonnenfeld, and 4 others left Bn Hq with 2 phones, and wire coils. Except for Sonnenfeld with his tommie, we had only our M-1s for protection, but our route was through an area where "B," "C," and the tanks had supposedly cleared out the Nips.

We hooked a roll of light combat wire to the switchboard and snubbed it around a tree to keep from disconnecting it. Moving out and unrolling the wire on the ground, we hiked much like a rifle Co patrol. Treading at 20-30 foot intervals with Sonnenfeld as point, we had our sixth, get-away man trailing slightly to the rear.

Somewhere on the way, we briefly endured sniper fire. We took some near misses, but no fire heavy enough to pin us down.

But crossing open Wakde Strip was harder. At the south side of the narrower middle of the Strip, we could look across open surface to what seemed a long distance to the trees on the other side. Actually, it was only some 150 yards across, but C Co had lost some men when they crossed. But we would have a long hike to round the west end of the Strip as A Co had done earlier, and perhaps meet some bypassed Nippo riflemen who would see us before we saw them. We had to cross the Strip under threat of fire from the jungle.

Pointing out a spot where we could regroup on the other side, we took off with our extra wire coils and ran like Hell. We panted across in a weaving straight line. As Sonnenfeld wryly remarked, "A weaving straight line is the shortest distance between two points — when you are in combat!"

No Japs fired as we dashed across and fell exhausted but safe in the brush on the north side of the Strip. It was a sweaty, heat-struck dash in a temperature of 110+ degrees. Hearing heavy fire to our right, we warily brought our line over the ground that A Co had cleared when they pushed eastward.

A Co welcomed our phones with great relief. We gave tired A Co most of our food and ammo and water and turned back for "home" in Hq Co. It was late in the day, and we became a little foolhardy. We accepted a tank commander's offer to ferry us all back on top of his vehicle across the open Strip. Yet we crossed without drawing fire.

Back in 1/Bn Hq, Sonnenfeld and Drum and the other wiremen still had to try to dig in for the night. But at that late hour, we could only dig in about 3 inches into solid coral below an earthen surface. We tried to sleep between turns on guard, but Jap harassment broke up our sleep.

The worst attack was about 0200 next morning from perhaps a whole Jap Pln. D Co's HMGs ably defended our 1/Bn's CP. Eder, Reid, Retterath, and S/Sgt Henry, among others, fought off a desperate attack. Henry was hit in left shoulder; Pender lost the toes of his right foot. Nordmark took both bullets and grenade fragments in his legs. They killed at least 12 Japs and knocked out their MG by pointblank fire from Eder's own MG. Our 163 Journal reported that 10 of the Japs were Marines — probably from 91 Naval Garrison unit. They were wellfed and physically fit, with new weapons and ammo.

By our second day on Wakde, one of 163's main problems was to get water from the beach-head to the front. Wakde was too small an island to have a permanent stream, and combat fire had damaged the cisterns that normally supplied it. Drinking water for us must be ferried over from the mainland, then stockpiled on the beach until forwarded to the companies inland. But evidently because only a little resistance was expected on Wakde, not enough plans had been made for supplying the front-line Cos, even after the water was deposited on our beach.

Men up front drank from coconuts between intervals in combat, but in some areas, the coconut supply was exhausted. We would have to expose ourselves to Jap bullets for more coconuts. A number of men not in the line units because especially concerned about this front-line thirst — like Service Co's 1/Lt Nugent, C Btry 218 FA's Capt Panek, and 1/Bn 163 Hq Co's Sonnenfeld. These men made memorable efforts to bring up that crucial water.

SV Co's 1/Lt Nugent made a heroic but tragic attempt to forward water. On 163's second day on Wakde, on the morning of 19 May, Nugent heard that an earlier water-party had failed, through no fault of theirs. Jap bullets had bled the cans of a forward Co. Calling together his assigned carriers, Nugent took them down to the beach for water from Toem.

About 250 yards from their start, Jap rifle fire wounded 2 men whose names are unknown. Jap fighters had slipped between F and C Cos and shot them down. Nugent called for 5 volunteers and tried another route down to the beach for water.

This time, Nugent's water-party made only a short distance. A burst of HMG fire fatally wounded Nugent, but he still had strength to order his assistants to carry on. Reported wounded about 0920, by 1440 Nugent was dead from those bullets in right arm and chest.

The leader of a 218 FA observer party had better luck, however. When he heard of 163's suffering up front, Capt Panek offered his party's services to carry water in the alligator which had ferried them from the mainland. Borrowing an MG and crew lent by Col Wing, Panek took 218 FA's Swails and Sgt John Hanson with him. Boldly they lumbered their water-laden alligator through the dangerous scrub jungle and across the east end of the Strip to thirsty B Co. On the way, they slew 3 Nip riflemen, but did not have to fight off a heavy attack. They returned to the beach with B Co wounded. Later, Panek decided that the Nips had failed to fight his alligator because they thought that it was a tank.

About the time when Nugent got his death-wound, 1/Bn Hq Co was short of water also. Even if Japs lurked somewhere between us and the beach, Sonnenfeld decided to act on his own.

Taking only one young man with a tommie gun to guard him — a man whose name he did not remember, Sonnenfeld slipped through coconut aisles and brush down to the beach. Here he found 163's CO — tall, thin Col Moroney, who seemed to Sonnenfeld 6 feet, 4 inches above ground. Looking around him, Sonnenfeld watched a group of Air Force Ground men who had prematurely landed on Wakde. While 163's men were thirsty in battle at the front, "Air Force" was writing letters, reading magazines, or making coffee. (Others were caught stealing wallets or watches from our casualties, and the order had come out for us to shoot to kill.)

Emotionally, Sonnenfeld grasped 163's CO by the shirt and drew him close. Emphatically, he informed Col Moroney about our lack of water. Moroney could have arrested Sonnenfeld for confinement and court-martial, but this old Regular Army and West Pointer asked simply, "What should we do?" Pointing to a 6x6 truck with the driver under it deep into a comic book, Sonnenfeld replied, "Colonel, just hook that truck to that water-trailer and give me that driver."

Col Moroney said to the driver, "Do what this man tells you to." (This was an example of Col Moroney's way with the men of 163 Inf. Later, he was heard to say, "The 163 Inf was already a going concern when I took command." Moroney had clearly seen that the best way to deal with the average 163 man was to give him head as you do with a good horse and let him run.)

After the hook-up with the trailer, Sonnenfeld gave the orders that may have saved them from dying like Nugent. He and the young man with the tommie gun lay down in the bed of the truck — one man on each side of it alert and ready to fight for his life. He told the driver to run the motor in low gear.

And the truck growled up the road where Nugent had been shot, all the way in low gear. Sonnenfeld thought that the growl of the motor scared off lurking Japs — that they may have believed that the truck was a tank that would machine-gun them or run them down and crush them. The water arrived safely at 1/Bn Hq Co where men drank happily. Sonnenfeld thought that big James downed 3 quarts himself, and for all of Hq Co, no water could ever taste better.

These were some of the adventures of 1/Bn 163 Inf's wiremen on Wakde. They will never forget their landing under the Jap MG ambush, laying the wire to A Co across the open Strip, and their thirst on waterless Wakde.

B CO 116 MEDICAL BATTALION, and
G COMPANY 162 INFANTRY MEDIC:

Medics at Toem and Parai Defile

by DR. KE VAN BUSKIRK and
G 162's MEDIC LEWIS WEIS

CREDIT: Dr (then Capt) Van Buskirk's 2-page single-spaced typescript dated 16 July 1982 is personal source of the Toem story. I used also my own "War of Nerves at Toem," (**Jungleer**, June 1979), **Reports of General MacArthur, Japanese Operations in the Southwest Pacific,** and RR Smith's **Approach to the Philippines.** Parai Defile story is from 4-page typescript of G 162's Medic Lewis Weis dated 20 Mar 1983 with 162 Inf's Biak Casualty List, and RR Smith's **Approach to the Phillippines.** Weis was inspired by Charles Brockman's **Jungleer** history, **"First Two Days In Parai Defile,"** (K 162) in **Jungleer** for April 1983.

I. MEDICS AT TOEM

Just before dark 27 May 1944, B Co 116 Medics blissfully relaxed for a good night's sleep, even in the jungle of Toem Foreshore across from conquered Wakda Island. For the first time since Arare Beach 10 days ago, we had dined under our newly erected canvas mess-fly. We had had our first mail-call since our landing. Luxuriously, some of us opened up cots with musquito bars and flotation bladder pillows — on the ground outside our hole. Now we gathered in little groups for small-talk and the cigarettes before lying down. For we rejoiced because 163's "Wakde War" was over.

At our officers' meeting in Tornado Task Force Hq, Brigadier-General Doe had congratulated our 163 Regtl Combat Team for our victory and told us to get out of our holes. There were no Japs within 20 miles, said Gen Doe. We were to set up above ground and live like men.

But as we started to bed down, we heard a Jap bomber — "Washing Machine Charlie" — swooping in from the east. No doubt he was targeting plane-packed Wakde Strip, but each explosion came closer and closer. After each bomb, we tensed because we felt that the next bomb was labelled for us. Then came our long wait until it exploded somewhere else.

Sitting on the edge of his foxhole while the bombs fell, CO Capt Van Buskirk observed far eastward on his right front above the jungle, a series of exploding flares. Thoughts of Japs' attack were farthest from his mind. He assumed that while he met at Task Force Hq, another AA unit had moved into what had been vacant jungle.

CO "Van" paid no more attention to the flares. Dark had fallen. He left the edge of his hole, crawled under the musquito bar into his cot, and took off his fatigues for the first time since Aitape. He donned red-white-and-blue pajamas that had come in the mail that day. Now he lay comfortable on his back on clean canvas, gazing up into the dark above his musquito bar. Although relaxed on his cot, he was still a little skittish at sleeping above ground.

(And if Van had known what that series of flares meant back there in the jungle, he would have already been back in his hole and reaching for a grenade. He might have had his finger already in the locking ring of the grenade. For those flares were not from a new AA battery position, but surely summons for Col Soemon Matsuyama's striking force from 224 Inf to assemble before an attack.)

And B Co 116 Medics was in an exposed position between the road and the sea. North across the Tementoe Creek-to-Tor-River Road was our Medics' lightly guarded ambulance park. (We did have a line of holes along the road.) We lay outside the larger perimeter of 1/Bn 163 Inf to our left — which extended from the sea deep inland. And that 1/Bn 163 perimeter was defended with only a few scattered front-line holes. On our right flank close to the sea, there really was an AA detachment, but it could not defend our front from an attack. (And to the right of the AA detachment alongshore was Dr Garlick's totally exposed 3 Portable Hospital.)

About 15-20 minutes after Van had blissfully stretched out for a whole night's sleep on his cot, Jap rifle fire struck B 116's bivouac from our front and deep right flank.

We Medics hit our holes — some men hit so fast that they took their mosquito bars with them. Dinky new carbines and heavier M-1s of old-timers leaped out from the crotches underneath our cots and into our arms. Hands on trigger-guards, we held fire and waited tensely.

Jap mortar shells arced into B 116 — mostly into the mess area in a roadside corner towards our far left. Some Jap grenades armed against trees and landed in our holes, but we threw them back before they exploded. The AA gunners on our right flank threw down on the Japs' charge. They levelled their 20 mm guns and battered the area where Van had seen the series of flares.

T/5 Zelasnakar lay in hole in mid-front of our defensive area near the road. He had with him a new man — from a group of 12 replacements. The Nippo rush surrounded Zelasnakar and the new man and isolated them. He tried to restrain the rookie, but the man leaped out of his hole and ran for the rear. Zelasnakar leaped out of his hole to tackle him and save his life. In that black confusion, one of our Medics fired on this supposed Jap, and slew Zelasnakar. Two other Medics were lightly wounded that night — their names forgotten and unrecorded on 163's casualty lists. It now seems as if the Japs fought merely a holding action on their left flank against us. Their main attack was against 163's infantry.

Luckily, B 116 had no patients in our area. We merely brought in sick men or casualties from the front, and forwarded them to Hollandia hospitals. To our right on the coast on the other side of the AA men, Dr Garlick's 3rd Portable Hospital was not so lucky. With their patients, they lay exposed and undefendend. Garlick's Medics made an orderly and safe evacuation of their patients, however.

Although 224 Inf did not drive home their attack on us, the fight lasted until nearly morning. Van estimated that 70 dead Japs were found in the whole 163 combat team's area. But including B 116 Medics, our probable losses of dead were 4 men of 163 Inf, 5 Engrs of A Co 116, and another unknown Medic from another outfit besides our T/5 Zelasnakar.

Although we repulsed the Nips' attack, their reports admitted no repulse. Next day, Tokyo Rose radioed that our few survivors of the night action had escaped by water from Toem. Final Jap report of their attack was more restrained. The report said that Col Matsuyama's 224 Inf had quietly assembled under cover about 2 miles north of Toem and had made a surprise attack with limited success. Part of his detachment had penetrated as far as the beach. It had forced a number of us to flee in landing craft. But in that newly made salient, our Naval and FA guns had caused heavy Jap casulaties. (This is the first recorded report of any Navy or FA action in the 163 area!) Fearing that his narrow salient would be pinched off, Matsuyama had withdrawn his advance elements and had given his exhausted troops a breathing spell.

Enough of this face-saving Japanese account! But what can we say about Gen Doe's permission for us to sleep out of our holes because no Japs were within 20 miles? In the first place, even in jungle terrain, 20 miles was not great distance for the march of a die-hard Jap regiment. And during 23-27 May, Gen Doe had plenty of data to suggest that Jap infantry was in force close to 163 Inf. On 24 May, an outpost of 1/Bn 163 had killed a Jap Lt with sketches of our positions on his corpse. On 23-27 May, Japs had strongly held a log bridge across Tementoe Creek in 2/Bn's area and had pulled back fighting the very day before the night when Matsuyama struck. It is hard to understand Doe's permission to let 163 Inf relax while the Japs were anywhere near by.

But as for B 116 Medics, we were twice lucky that we lost only 1 man killed, and 2 apparently lightly wounded. First, we were lucky that the Japs' main attack was not meant for us, but only to kill our infantry. Second, we were lucky that the attack had only slanted across our front and left us in relative safety. We had hit our holes fast and stayed there until the charge was ended and the last Japs had fallen back. But it had been a night that B 116 never forgot.

II. MEDICS AT PARAI

About 1000 hours on G Co 162 Inf's second day on Biak, Medic Weis' real Battle of Biak began. At 1000, Weis was hiking in a column of twos with G Co 162 behind 3/Bn towards Jap Mokmer Strip. Just as Weis saw Parai Road leave the coast and start the climb up Parai Ridge, Jap fire crashed down to cut off 3/Bn.

A Jap mortar shell exploded on Weis' near right. He took a little steel fragment in his hand, but it was a minor wound easily dressed. A G Co cook to Weis' right had a left arm wound, but Weis cannot remember who gave first aid to the cook.

While G Co flattened under fire behind palm logs or coral outcrops, Weis heard the call of "Medic!" down on the beach. Weis ran towards the sound of the call as he was trained — indirect lines in short bursts of speed to avoid shell fire, and found the prone wounded man. While both men tried to hide behind a coconut log, Weis cut away his pants with scissors to bind the wounded man's buttocks. It was hard to wrap a gauze bandage around legs and a 40-inch waist. Weis rejoiced with the wounded man that he had an ideal excuse for rest out of combat. This wounded man — probably from G Co — seemed happy.

Then a 3/Bn rifle Co Medic called Weis for help in the area where G Co and 3/Bn were in contact when the Jap bombardment started. Past where 3/Bn was grounded, Weis saw the 2 casualties. A mortar shell had shattered between them. A young Lt lay there gashed head to foot by fragments, and Weis — himself a veteran from Roosevelt Ridge — pronounced the Lt dead. (The Lt may have been L Co's 1/Lt Minner, although K Co's 2/Lt Barnes was the other 162 officer killed that day.) The other man, a Sgt with unremembered name, had a broken leg from that same mortar shell. Passing where men still hugged the ground on both sides of Parai Road, Weis wondered why he was running, for by then the noise of battle had died down.

Soon Weis saw a flatbed truck with Medics and litters on it, probably from 116 Medical Bn. How they came so close to the front, Weis wonders, but they were more than welcome.

The NCO in charge lent Weis 2 litters, and a litter squad offered to bring out the 2 casualties. Although a detail carried back the Lt's body, Weis decided not to take the live Sgt to the rear, with his leg now splinted to a rifle. (Probably this casualty was L Co's S/Sgt Koelfgen.)

Orders had come that while 2/Bn was withdrawing, all 3/Bn rifle Cos would have to go forward to consolidate the forward positions of 162 Inf in Parai Defile. Weis feared that Japs would infiltrate through the gap that these moves would open up. With 2 riflemen's help, we Medics carried the wounded Sgt west towards 3/Bn Hq. Beach was so narrow and congested here that we had to carry the Sgt through the sea — waist-deep and sometimes up to our arm pits. At 3/Bn Hq we found too many men jammed on a strip of sand at low tide.

About this time, some 4-5 DUKWs of 542 Amphib Engrs were maneuvering offshore with ammo and medical supplies. From a Jap gun high on Parai Ridge, exploding shells splashed geisers high around the boats, but all were near misses. The first brave pilot drove his craft straight into the beach and climbed it up on its tracks safely below the Jap gunner's trajectory. And in turn, the other DUKWs would also gun their motors inshore while the Jap gun continued to miss. (As at Zamboanga in 1945, a floating amphibian craft looked easy to hit from the land, but actually while in the water, it became a small, elusive target.)

After the first DUKW's supplies unloaded, Weis boarded it with the wounded Sgt and the volunteer litter men and other 162 wounded.

For the first 50-100 feet, the DUKW pained our Sgt horribly as its tracks lurched over the coral hunks on the beach. Then in deep water, it was like riding on a cushion. We never knew why the Nippo gun did not harass us again from Parai Ridge.

Such were Weis' memories of that first day of 162's defeat in Parai Defile. And never did he forget a poignant casualty of 29 May, 162's second day of frustration in that first attempt to force Parai Defile through to Mokmer Strip.

About noon on 29 May while talking to our 2/Bn medical officer, Weis idly watched a destroyer moving alongshore. Suddenly a smoke ring showed that it had fired. Then he heard the shell explode — either on the cliff wall or in a large tree topping the cliff. Weis and the 2/Bn medical officer were almost deafened.

After momentary silence, Weis heard the call for the Medic. Here lay a young man dead on the ground, with no mark on him — K Co's Newman whose name was on the current list to go home. Weis thinks that he himself made out the tag with "KIA" on it. Our own Navy actually slew 4 "K" men there: Copp, T/Sgt Higgenbotham, S/Sgt Portel, and Newman, who should never have been up front on a home roster.

Such are the lasting memories of T/5 Weis in Parai Defile.

C CO 162 INF:

Sgt. Camp's Patrol Against Oba's Raiders

by C 162's SERGEANT RICHARD C. CAMP, with DR. HARGIS WESTERDIELD, Division Historian

> CREDIT. Prime source is Camp's 5-page typescript, "A Soldier's Experience." Australian David Dexter's **The New Guinea Offensives** supplied helpful data. Camp's story about what Aussie Hoffman told him, confirms my beliefs about why Hoffman's patrol was overrun. Neither David Dexter (I wrote to him years ago) nor Canberra's Australian War Memorial has given me primary information on Hoffman's patrol. It was an Australian disaster. I have omitted mention of another scout and his native who became separated from Camp.

During the last week of 1/Bn 162 Inf's siege of Mt Tambu, C Co's Capt Newman called Sgt Camp into CP and gave him important orders. Camp was to accompany a small patrol of 3 natives and penetrate the mountain jungle down to the coast and warn our FA that some 200 Japs were raiding to destroy our guns that had turned Mt Tambu and Roosevelt Ridge into death-traps for Jap garrisons. C Co's wire was cut.

This was 14 Aug, third day of Lt Messec's B 162 patrol's pursuit of Maj Oba's raiders who were mainly Capt Arai's Co of Jap 102 Inf. Messec had sent back information about purpose and direction of the raid.

After memorizing details from Newman's map — only map available in C Co — Camp headed into the jungle at 0800 with 3 natives — Tomanda, Myra, and one other. At the start, with experienced native scouts, we did double time when that rough jungle terrain permitted it.

About mid-afternoon, we met a native family that had fled from Jap invaders. We gave them what rations we could, and told them that our Army was setting up a refugee camp for them.

We continued our careful patrol down to the coast. Entering into a swamp, we came upon a river unnamed upon the old maps. Late that afternoon, we heard firing in the distance off to our right and headed toward it, still beside the river. It ran into Lake Salus, which was SE of our FA.

By now, darkfall was nearing. We sensed Jap movement all around us. Finding some low bushes, we settled down for the night. We could hear Jap talking far too close.

We waited out a miserable night with Japs all around us. The Guinea rain began falling. Camp had a shelter half to cover himself, and could take out some of the chill with his breath under the cover. But the natives had only one small piece of canvas. It was not large enough for all 3 natives, and Tomanda squatted shivering. Camp said, "Tomanda, get under here with me." At first, Tomanda refused. Naturally, the rain increased.

"Get in here!" Camp insisted. Tomanda crawled gratefully under the half with him. Tomanda said, "You sleep, I watch."

It was a bad night there in that rain among Japs in their temporary bivouac area, but no Japs discovered Camp's outnumbered patrol.

At daybreak, Tomanda said, "Jap him come." We heard more talking. Some Japs moved out — who had bedded down a few yards away. We trailed them, with Myra bringing up our rear.

After about 30 minutes tailing the Japs, we came to an inlet maybe 30 feet wide. The Japs turned left inland. Camp suggested that we cross and get ahead of them.

We waded through water fairly deep, for 2 of our natives had to swim across.

On the other side, we faced a mangrove swamp some 50 yards wide, which we had to cross by stretching our legs from root to root. Again on solid ground, we looked for tracks but found none. Nobody seemed to be ahead of us or anywhere near.

After half a mile, we saw a trail up a mountain. About halfway up, we halted for a break. Then we heard somebody coming along the side of the ridge almost level with us.

It was an Aussie with a rifle. We watched until he was a short distance off, then called to him.

He hit the dirt at once. Camp had a hard time to convince him that we were no Japs. Finally, Camp said that he would stand up, and the Aussie could shoot if he wanted to. But if he shot, Camp said, "Four men will be looking down on you."

When Camp stood up, the Aussie came forward, after still holding back a little.

This Aussie was Lt WN Hoffman, whose approximately 30-man Pln had been shot up and driven into the jungle. Their fight had caused the firing which Camp (and also nearby B 162's Messec) had heard last night.

Hoffman stated that when his patrol had bivouacked beside Lake Salus, the Japs had struck them. Most of his men were in swimming, without many guards. Hoffman's Pln was scattered.

The morning after the Jap victory, Hoffman himself was trailing 8 Japs — who must have come up the same trail which Camp's men had used. Hoffman had taken to the mountain in hope of getting ahead of these 8 Japs.

Then Hoffman valiantly left Camp's men and went up the mountain to search for his men for whose ambush he had been responsible. Just as Camp started to move, fire broke out. Hoffman called for help. He shouted that he was hit in the arm.

Camp shouted to Hoffman to join us for protection. As soon as he spotted Hoffman coming back, a grenade was thrown over his head to where the Jap fire came from. The fire stopped while Hoffman came to us.

It was an ugly wound. The bullet had struck Hoffman's right forearm 4 inches above the hand. It had broken both bones in his forearm.

While bandaging Hoffman, Camp had someone hold his carbine clear of the damp ground. One native said that the Japs were following Hoffman. All 3 natives started to run.

Camp yelled, "Merchinee, you bloody Mary!" (Come back here, you woman!) Tomanda and Myra returned; the other unnamed third native ran off with Camp's carbine.

Camp had Myra and Tomanda each throw a grenade at the Jap noise in the jungle while he finished binding up Hoffman. The 2 grenades may have caused the Japs to think that a large force opposed them; they held back while Camp, Hoffman, and the 2 natives escaped. After 100 yards, Myra saw Camp's carbine 15 feet off the trail and retrieved it. Camp at that time had to stop and make a tourniquet to halt the flow of Hoffman's life-blood.

Farther along in our flight, we were in a little depression. Firing broke out back up the mountain to our left. We thought the Japs were shooting at us and hit the ground. Then from another ridge to the right, we heard more fire. Japs yelled, and the shooting stopped. We thought that they had fired on their own men. We ran as low to the earth as we could and got out of there.

Hoffman would later report that he had encountered 50 Japs that morning of 15 Aug when he was wounded, on a spur NW of Lake Salus. Perhaps some armed remnant of Hoffman's patrol was putting up a fight. Maybe this fight kept the Japs too busy to pursue us.

We were down in the low country near the sea now. Hoffman was becoming weak and exhausted from loss of blood and our hurry. At a native village, Camp loosened and retied the tourniquet. While Myra stayed with Hoffman, Camp and Tomanda checked out the native village. It was vacant, and we went on.

Soon we arrived at a clearing with another ridge across it. Tomanda spotted a fox-hole ahead. Watching it awhile, we saw a Yank helmet and head.

Camp called across the clearing to identify us and say that we were coming to the hole. Crossing that clearing was hard work, for he still did not know that the guard believed him. They were a ragged group, and Camp with his Aussie hat and shirt.

After explaining his patrol to the Yank in the foxhole, Camp phoned the battery commander with his warning about the Jap raiders. (Camp does not remember the name of the FA formation, whether 205 FA or 218 FA). He took wounded Hoffman to the hospital, then returned to the FA kitchen. It was 2 days since he had last eaten.

"C" ration cans were boiling in a kettle. Camp gave each native a can and opened one for himself. He was looking into a box of cigarettes. Someone walked behind him and profanely quiried what he was doing. "Just what it looks like," said Camp. The other man said, "That's the way with you blasted Aussies. We give you an inch and you take a mile."

Turning around, Camp realized that he was talking to the battery captain. The captain saw the US dog-tags hanging out of the unbuttoned shirt and asked Camp's name and why he had on the Aussie uniform. Camp explained, that our US uniforms were worn out.

This was the same officer whom Camp had talked to on the phone. When Camp told him that they had not eaten for 2 days while coming down to warn the FA — or had had no cigarettes on Tambu for 3 weeks — Camp, Myra, and Tomanda could have had the whole kitchen.

Now the first Jap raider fired on the outpost. Camp, Myra, and Tomanda stayed to help the FA garrison all that day and night. But the fire was evidently only to harass this battery; no Japs drove home an attack.

Leaving the FA next morning after breakfast, Camp went first to visit Hoffman at the hospital. On the way, they saw an Aussie outfit, and maybe 30 natives with this outfit. While Myra and Tomanda talked with natives whom they knew, Camp went on to the hospital.

The Dr told Camp that Hoffman was still weak, but plasma transfusions were making him convalescent. (Camp would still like to know the condition of Hoffman's forearm today, after the bullet had broken both bones. Hoffman surely lived, for the detailed Australian War Memorial history does not list him as killed.)

Returning to Myra and Tomanda, Camp ran into trouble. He arrived just in time to see an Aussie officer glaring at Tomanda. The officer put his hand to his pistol and said, "You will do as I say, or I will shoot you right here."

Camp saw red at the treatment of his native cobber. He jabbed his carbine into the officer's flank and said, "Hold it — unless you can get your gun out and shoot before I can." Camp told Myra and Tomanda to leave.

The Aussie said that he was a captain and had trained these men as scouts. He had a claim on them to go fight the Japs with him. (Perhaps this officer was Capt EP Hitchcock, head of the Papuan Infantry Bn).

Camp replied to the captain that these men were assigend to his outfit and that they were leaving with nobody but Camp. Camp refused to identify himself and left. He warned the officer to remain where he was until Camp was gone.

Farther up the beach that 16 Aug, Camp and the natives found an AA outfit in time for dinner — mashed potatoes, meat, brown gravy, and corn. Camp had been without this kind of food for so long that it made him briefly sick. His natives also felt queasy.

Camp helped the AA men to set up a better defense against the raiders. He put out booby traps on an inland trail into the swamp. As night fell, he posted the natives nearby for observation — with himself just a few yards behind them.

The night was quiet, but a Jap did come. He took one of Camp's booby traps apart, looked around, then headed back into the swamp, without giving any more trouble.

Then Camp and his men reported to 3/Bn Hq farther up the coast and asked what was the best trail he could take back home to C Co. Col Roosevelt asked Camp to escort some officers to inspect C Co.

Next morning, Camp's party started out with the officers to go to C Co — a 12-mile hike. About halfway up to Mt Tambu, the natives heard a noise near the top of a high ridge. Camp and a native scouted forward.

They smelled coffee! Here was a tent pitched and 2 Aussie Salvation Army men with a fire going under a coffee-pot for travellers — 5 or 6 miles from anywhere safe. Camp never forgot that coffee-break.

Back with C Co, Camp was sure that he would be called in for getting the drop on that Aussie captain. But he heard nothing. Back in Australia with 162 Inf, 1/Bn Hq called Camp over to get full details of his patrol. They wanted to give him a medal!

But when they learned of the run-in with the Aussie, they perceived that there was the danger of trouble from this officious captain. Camp got no medal for his hard work.

Such was the great patrol of Sgt Camp and New Guinea men Myra and Tomanda. At dire risk to themselves, they saved the life of crippled Aussie Lt WN Hoffman, and helped warn the coastal gunners of the swoop of Oba's raiders. This patrol is one of Camp's finest memories of World War II and 162 Inf.

186 INF'S 2/BN HEADQUARTERS CO:

Into The Slot At West Caves

by DR. HARGIS WESTERFIELD, Division Historian,
with MACHINE-GUNNER CASIMER HEBDA

---

*CREDIT: Casimer Hebda's 3.5 page typescript sparked this history. He typed it about 14 Feb, and sent additional data to me about 7 Apr 1984. Most useful also were 186's **Narrative of Operations** on Biak, RR Smith's **Approach to the Philippines**, Fred Larey's letter of 3 Sept 1964, and I 186's Roger Jensen's letter of 10 July 1969. Useful also were 2/Bn 186's Award Stories of Theodore Howe, Chester Klovas, Howard Lang, T/Sgt William Hall, Casimer Hebda, and Gillis Labbee. Other sources were Arthur Vesey's story, "Dear Hirohito, Better Tell Your Boys About Chicago" (**Chicago Tribune** — 22 June 1944), and 186's Biak **Journal**. Most of this history that you are now reading, supersedes my earlier story, "Battling Kuzume's Big Banzai," which appeared in the Dec 1970 **Jungleer** and was reprinted in **The Fighting Jungleers.***

When Hq Co of 2/Bn 186 Inf landed on Biak, we hit the wrong beach. An unexpected 6-mile an hour current pushed our tracked landing crafts too far west. Smoke and dust of the bombardment obscured landmarks. We grounded in a mangrove swamp at Mandom in water and muck. Hq Co's machine-gunner Hebda slipped into water up to his head.

Col Newman landed here with his CP group and all of our 2/Bn — along with a D Co MG Pln and an .81 mm mortar section. Although isolated in Jap country, they quickly moved inland to Bosnek Road and by 0745 were hiking east to our original beach.

Despite confusion of unscrambling units which had landed in the wrong places, 2/Bn was ready for action at Bosnek by 1200. Rifle Cos of 2/Bn began probing the low coastal ridges. Soon we discovered the dangers of the caves and Jap holes. One Sgt looked down into a hole and was shot in the head. We dropped a grenade into the hole and disposed of the Jap.

From 27 May to 31 May while 162 was repelled from Parai Defile far west of us, 2/Bn 186 Inf patrolled to help secure the Bosnek area. On 28 May, men found a large cavern near 2/Bn Hq Co with some 15 Japs hiding in it. On that day, several Japs died trying to escape, but the day when the cavern was finally cleared has gone unreported.

Scouting about 4 miles east of Bosnek alongshore on 29 May, men of 2/Bn found a rough motor road curving back west from Opairef Village. This road led to land surveyed for a Jap Strip directly north of Bosnek — the start of the long road that 116 Engrs would build for 186 to seize Mokmer Strip.

On 31 May, 163 Inf's 1/Bn and 3/Bn came from Toem to relieve 186 Inf Regt from Bosnek Beach. First, however, 2/Bn had to march east to Opairef and slay the few Japs holding out nearby. With B Co, our own F Co had trouble with them. But by 1500 that 31 May, we had overrun those Opairef Japs.

Next morning, 2/Bn turned inland from Opairef to follow the road west to the Survey Strip. Forty-five minutes after 3/Bn climbed up from Bosnek and perimetered at the west end of the strip, our 2/Bn dug in near the east end. When Nips of 1/Bn 222 Inf attacked that night of 1-2 June, 3/Bn slew 86 Japs. Our 2/Bn had only slight action. At dawn of 2 June, a Jap officer did perish under an E Co LMG.

By 0900 2 June, 186 Inf began our hard trek west towards Mokmer Strip. While 1/Bn and 3/Bn with 5 tanks advanced abreast down the road, 2/Bn with AT Co patrolled north of the road. We protected 186's right flank and line of communications. By 3 June, however, 2/Bn also had to assist Regtl Supply Officer to carry food to the forward battalions.

On that agonized 5-day march to seize Mokmer Strip from inland, thirst was our greatest problem. On one day near the end of the march, 2/Bn's Hq Co had halted because we lacked water. Then arrived a truck with 5-gallon cans.

Laying down his pack, Hebda took Howe's and Miller's canteens and his own to fill them at the truck. A Medic and 2 other Yanks were also filling canteens. Suddenly from the dark scrub jungle, 4 Japs leaped out and began firing. Hebda dived into a ditch. Labbee had his .50 HMG set up already and shot them down.

All 2/Bn was rushed from watering to prepare new defense positions. Hebda had to leave the empty canteens which he had tried to fill. Miller and Howe left Hebda's pack which he had dropped near them. That night, he had to borrow others' rations, and a shovel to dig in.

(Perhaps this action occurred on 5 June north of Mokmer Ridge near the Strip. Some 15 Japs hit 2/Bn's flank and rear with grenades, knee mortars and rifles. A G Co patrol was credited with clearing that area. Twelve Japs died.)

That night, Japs walked around shouting, "Hey Joe, where are you?" We kept quiet. One Jap did step into a hole with a Lt from another outfit who had a carefully sharpened machete. He chopped the Jap to death. The Lt laid the machete back on the edge of his hole, but it fell and cut his own leg.

Next day, some men returned for their canteens. All were shot full of holes. Hebda's pack was gone — with his gold pocket watch inside.

By 6 June, 186 Inf had positioned on or north of Mokmer Ridge above Mokmer Strip. On the morn of 7 June, after 30 minutes' fire mainly from 121 FA's 75s, 186 Inf's 1/Bn and 3/Bn marched down and occupied undefended Mokmer Strip by 0850. ("F" was attached to 1/Bn.) The other 2/Bn outfits hand-carried supplies over the ridge-crest and onto the Strip — as did CN Co and a SV Co detachment. Reported booby-traps caused us to follow the trail carefully.

Suddenly at 0945 when we had hardly dug in, Jap shell fire impacted 186 Inf. From the ridges where we had bypassed them unawares, Jap FA, AA, mortar, and automatic weapon fire rained down.

Leaping into their hole on the NW flank, Hebda and Howe watched a mortar shell impact 50 yards away. Another exploded within 25 yards. "It looks like we're next," said Hebda. But Shell No. 3 struck another outfit's hole, where an officer lost a leg.

But Hq Co 2/Bn survived the heavy bombardment throughout 7 June with just 3 wounded. Seriously wounded was T/4 Cline with T/5 Dunlap and Cpl Hall lightly wounded. Our whole Regt had 14 killed, 68 wounded. On 8 June, Blankenship and McClain were lightly wounded.

After 186 Inf loosened Jap pressure on Mokmer Strip, 16 June was the day when our 2/Bn closed the Great Gap on Mokmer Ridge between 162's 2/Bn and 3/Bn. This Great Gap had existed since 12 June, when 162 Inf first topped Mokmer Ridge. By 15 June, those 2 Bns had narrowed the Gap to 500 yards. On 16 June, 186's 2/Bn finally closed the Gap and turned the ground back to 162 Inf again.

For Hebda in 2/Bn Hq Co, that 16 June was a day of long, fearful waiting. Hq Co had climbed the ridge after the rifle Cos of 186 Inf until they felt surrounded in the dark jungle heights. Then they halted and dug in to back "E," "G," and "H" fighting ahead of them.

In his hole under a bush to the left, Hebda heard a big Jap gun fire across the trail. Force of the trajectory was so great that he thought that its wind would lift off his pants. He could even hear the Jap officers' firing orders ahead of him.

Here Hebda waited for 12 long hours. After the Gap was closed in the morning, smoke bombs had to be fired to cover the Cos' retreat from their advance too far. When he left his hole, he saw 5-6 Yank dead around him. Seeing 3 men carry a wounded man, he went to help them. The man's leg was swollen huge as a balloon. He was screaming with pain.

Besides closing the Great Gap, our 2/Bn had found the western Jap lines defending West Caves. Although 2/Bn lost 15 killed and 35 wounded — an outstanding loss for a day in the 41st Div — 65 Japs were dead. In 2/Bn Hq Co, our Phipps was shot in the ankle. Lightly wounded was 1/Lt Blanton, other circumstances unknown.

On 19 June, 186 Inf dug in north of West Caves and severed Jap supply lines into the Biak hinterland. On 20 June, 162 Inf from the south began to flame gasoline drums into the caves. The die-hard Japs must come out fighting, or burn.

And on that night of 20 June, 2/Bn 186 Inf held the slot that the Japs had to charge through. Facing south towards West Caves, T/Sgt Hall's AT Pln of 2/Bn Hq held the actual roadblock with two .50 HMGs, one on either side of the road. A steep ridge protected Hall's left flank. To his right, G and F Cos held the lines with their .30 LMGs and .60 mortars to brace up their rifles. Two Sherman tanks backed their lines, maybe 100 yards to the rear. M Co's .81 mortars were also dug in to support us.

On that night of 20 June, Japs with knee mortar coverfire tried to penetrate 2/Bn's lines. Some of these Japs may have scouted us to feel out our positions for the next night's great attack. But 12-15 Japs came through Hq Co's perimeter, and we held fire in that deceptive dark. Hebda said that they carried gun barrels that seemed to be 7-8 feet long. Whatever the aims of this little night offensive, 11 Japs died that night.

This night fight of 20 June may well have been the prelims for the coming great night battle of the night of 21-22 June. For this battle, the Jap officers had selected a striking force from mainly 2/Bn 221 Inf, some of the most effective Japs still alive on Biak. They were not originally in the Biak garrison; they had slipped ashore from barges into Korim Bay after a night run of over 75 miles from Noemfor Island to the west. (They were not members of the 36 Div already on Biak, but of the 35 Div at Manokwari on the New Guinea mainland.) For most of them, the daylight hours of 21 June would be their last hours on earth.

After the attack of 20 June, 2/Bn Hq's machine-gunners had stretched a trip-wire across the road and attached it to a great heap of empty 5-gallon drums. Our 2 HMGs were sighted to hit that trip-wire, even in the dark.

Attack No. 1 came in the dark night of 21 June. At 2100, Japs charged up the road. They tripped the wire; falling cans clanked. Gunner Howe with second gunner Lang and gunner Labbee with his second gunner Klovas loosed their heavy .50s at the unseen wire. Wounded Japs moaned. Other Japs impacted knee-mortars around us, machine-gunned our lines. Sheets of flame made the jungle bright as day.

As we silenced the screaming charge, G 186's Sgt Jensen fired .60 mm mortar shells as close as 50 feet from our holes to drive crawling Japs into our fire-lanes. Col Maison sensed that the Japs' deployment area was a small clearing around a great tree 100 yards back. They did not know that the great tree was zeroed in for our mortars. M Co's heavy .81s blasted around that tree and scattered the Jap support troops.

Attack No. 2 came at midnight. They first lobbed in knee-mortars, futile in the dark. Our mortars and MGs repulsed their attack. Remarkable was the action of 2/Bn Hq's .50 HMGs. They were not exactly right for anti-personnel fire. They would be best against tanks or strafing planes. But even without the firing speed of .30 MGs, they could do plenty of damage. They were so conspicuous, however, that they became a main objective of Jap Attack No. 3.

Attack No. 3 came at 0400 in the late dark of before dawn 22 June. It was a forlorn hope — stealthy and desparate — mainly grenades and bayonets. And our MG ammo was running low. From his hole, Hebda called back to Sgt Dailey to gather ammo to carry.

It was 30 feet back to Sgt Dailey — but the longest 30 feet that Hebda ever traveled in his life. But he got back safely with the ammo. So dark was the night that he never knew whether any Japs ever fired at him. T/Sgt Hall also carried ammo up to the holes.

But the die-hard Japs closed in. All along 186's line of holes, hand to hand combat began. When a Jap landed even in the hole of Capt Pendexter, Bn Medic, he slew him with a machete.

Howe's MG jammed. An already wounded Jap rushed the gun, and bayoneted Cpl Miller in the shoulder. Howe gripped the Jap by the throat. Frenziedly the Jap pulled out a grenade. It exploded between them; both fell dead.

Meanwhile, second-gunner Lang wrestled a Jap rifle from him and killed him with the bayonet. Lang leaped from his hole and slew 4 more Jap grenadiers.

Second-gunner Klovas rushed back 50 yards from Labbee's gun and called forward a Sherman tank. Sgt Synakiewicz' tank rolled up and blasted the Japs' charge at us. I Co 186's .60 mortars angled fire in from the west across our front and finished Jap Attack No. 3.

Howe was only 186 man killed that night. Cpl Miller's bayonet wound was light. In all 186, only 4 more wounded were reported, on 21 and 22 June. In 2/Bn 186 Hq, Irish was seriously wounded, but we cannot find out whether any man but Miller was wounded actually in that night fight.

Jap report is that 150 men attacked that night. As Attack No. 3 ended, 109 were dead. At 0815 next morning, G 186 slew 9 more behind a tree, and 10 others playing dead by the road. Total Jap dead, therefore, was probably 128.

When Gen Eichelberger came up to investigate last night's firing, a Jap knee mortar shell dropped harmlessly 2 feet before Klovas, T/Sgt Hall, Hebda, an unknown Lt, and Eichelberger himself. Probably this was the final Jap shot in 2/Bn 186 Inf Hq's night fight of 21-22 June 1944. Now we needed only to load the dead Japs into trucks to be hauled away for a mass burial, and continue the siege of West Caves.

HEADQUARTERS CO. 2/BN 162 INF:

From C Ridge Into Salamaua — First!

by PFC JOE BRADSHAW
with DR. HARGIS WESTERFIELD, Division Historian

CREDIT: In a 37-page single-spaced typescript written in 1980 with 2 undated 1980 letters, Joe Bradshaw has supplied our only detailed story of 2/Bn 162's fight for Scout Ridge after Roosevelt Ridge was stormed. Background is from Aussie David Dexter's **The New Guinea Offensives** *(mainly the Australian story), and Col AR MacKechnie's "Report of Operations of 162 Inf 29 June - Sept 1943." Col MacKechnie's Chapter VII summarizes his 2/Bn's actions. (Journal of 162 on the operation was almost useless. Casualty List of 162 cannot be located in Federal Archives, nor personnel lists.) Dexter claims that Capt AG Ganter's patrol led Aussie 42 Bn into Salamaua the day before Bradshaw's entry. But Bradshaw's group found no Aussies in Salamaua, as his manuscript points out. (I cannot verify the spelling of Lt "Glauscen;" there was a "Glockzin" in the 41st, but he was a Lt. in 186 Inf.)*

After storming Roosevelt Ridge on 15 Aug 1943, 2/Bn 162 Inf had to capture the Japs' Scout Ridge, which lay north of "Roosevelt" and at right angles to it and extended half-way to Salamaua Town. While the other 2 Bns pressed on our left flank, 2/Bn had to fight uphill on 3 parallel ridges that climbed from Dot Inlet to Scout Ridge — ridges named only "B," "C," and "D."

But first, our scouts had to locate the Jap positions above us in that overhanging hill jungle. On 16 Aug, 2/Bn Hq Co's PFC Bradshaw and Sgt Daniel found B Ridge clear of Japs three-fourths of the way up. Marking the limit of our patrol by branches across the trail, we then scouted all the way up C Ridge.

From the highest point of C Ridge — a tree that we named "King Dick," we saw no Japs clearly. But looking NE across a draw to a rounded hill later named Berger Hill, we seemed to discern bent forms struggling up it.

To be sure that they were Japs, we patrolled through the draw of giant ferns towards Berger Hill. Suddenly, we heard Jap voices — saw maybe 10 armed Japs coming from Berger Hill towards B Ridge, next to Roosevelt. They laughed and sang like a bus-load of US school-children picknicking.

When hidden Daniel rose to see better, his rifle-butt scraped a stone. They silenced; we heard steps of a grim patrol encircling our fern thicket.

Back to back, fingers on triggers, we looked up to netted Jap helmets in sunset. Suddenly, frightened wings whirred up from the ferns before us. The Japs decided that we were birds, and marched on.

A 6-man section of the same patrol with Bradshaw and Daniel had seen Japs bivouacking near Lokanu Village, northwards before D Ridge. They had watched Japs cook or hang laundry.

Thus, our patrol of 16 Aug learned that Japs held D Ridge, but that C Ridge was clear. (Later, a patrol of other 2/Bn Hq men contacted Japs far up on the B Ridge summit.) Using the tree King Dick on Jap-free C Ridge, FA observers began calling fire on B and D Ridge. Then on 26 Aug, F Co seized the C Ridge summit after a needless FA preparation.

Then Capt Munkres ordered Bradshaw and Daniel to take 13 men (among them, Reser) with a recently attached Capt to locate Jap positions on D Ridge. Munkres cautioned us to watch out for a 1/Bn patrol coming over from the SW.

Starting on the west slope of F Co's new perimeter where D Ridge Japs could not see us, we patrolled up an almost waterless creek-bed of pot-holes, then up a faint track that put us near a tunnel of interlocked foliage. Bradshaw tried to crawl up the tunnel to observe D Ridge, but the patrol's riflefire recalled him.

Daniel said that he had shot 2 Japs, but was uncertain whether they were Japs or men of our 1/Bn patrol. Our men sporadically fired, although unsure of whom they fired at. Bradshaw leaped into a sunny opening and cursed them. Their answering wild volley replied that they were Japs. Our firepower repelled them, and we were recalled without casualties. We do not know how many Japs we killed. Later, we learned that 1/Bn had called off their patrol.

With 2/Lt Polimac commanding, Bradshaw and Daniel led another patrol past F CO's position to search for Japs past the inland point of C Ridge.

About 250 yards deep in waist-high kunai, we found a Nip corpse beside his bullet-holed helmet. He had certainly died rushing into battle with our previous patrol. Then 3 Nips climbed up the slippery bank of Pot-Hole Creek and died under Bradshaw's tommie and Daniel's Springfield.

Deeper into kunai, 1,000 yards from F's perimeter, we struck a north-south trail pitted by Japs' hob-nailed shoes. Outposted Bradshaw and Daniel looked down a trail-curve around the hill — just in time to see and hear a noisy Nip Pln bouncing towards us.

Before BARmen could come up, Daniel fired prematurely and forced Bradshaw's tommie to fire also. The Japs hit our Pln on 3 sides — front, downhill, and up from Pot-Hole Creek. Over 50 Jap rifles fired; we were mortared, machine-gunned, grenaded.

But Polimac had our Pln already deployed; we blew them back on all 3 sides, had no losses. They threatened our rear; Polimac ordered our withdrawal, while Bradshaw's tommie discouraged any Jap pursuit.

Happy were Maj Berger and Capt Munkres. C Ridge had been safely captured. We had 2 fights in 3 hours without casualties. We had discovered a Jap supply trail. FA harassed the ridges 24 hours a day.

Three days later, Munkres tried to entrap those Japs who had forced Polimac's Pln from the Scout Ridge Trail. With 4 men picked by himself, Bradshaw was to lie in ambush where the trail came from a "wigwam" of interwoven jungle, crossed Pot-Hole Creek, and climbed a 10-foot bank. An unnamed 1/Lt was to drive the Japs into an ambush with his Pln. (Bradshaw's 4 picked men were an unnamed BARman with his assistant Cashley, Broome, and 41 MP's Moyer, a boyhood friend of Bradshaw.)

Forty-five minutes after Bradshaw posted ambush, heavy mortars briefly blasted the Japs. After 30 minutes' silence, the unnamed 1/Lt with his Sgt came to tell us that an attack was useless. Irritated Bradshaw now thought that he had persuaded the Lt to make a flank attack this time against the Japs. Bradshaw crawled back into ambush to await the attack.

From a distance, the Sgt fired his carbine. Then the Lt's Pln withdrew. Concealed Japs fired; Bradshaw's men returned fire. Feeling deserted, Bradshaw's men left the ambush. Cashly was wounded, Broome left dead. To cover their retreat, Bradshaw's tommie silenced the Japs below us.

Later, the Sgt said that his carbine had killed a Jap creeping up on Bradshaw. Broome exposed himself to look. Bullets struck Broome in several places for an instant kill.

Next morning, Polimac led a squad with Bradshaw and 41 MP's Moyer to recover Broome's body. Far ahead and alone, Bradshaw inspected ground in the Wigwam on all-fours, tommie slung on his shoulder.

Suddenly he looked up: 2 Nips slightly to his right at 10-15 feet aiming rifles at him. "Japs!" he howled, and flipped over. Their bullets missed. Again he rolled over as more bullets whizzed past. He came up on his knees, tommie exploding viciously. The squad found 3 — not 2 — dead Nips.

Before Polimac could place his squad for defense, Japs swarmed up firing. Our fire halted them, but we had to leave, after a probable number of Jap casualties. We do not know when Broome's body was recovered.

We thought that Japs held ground between B Ridge and Old Baldy, a hill slightly north of F Co on C Ridge. Bradshaw and Daniel guided 30 G and H Co men on this recon, with G's Lt Glauscen and Lt McHenry of "H" who resembled movie hero Clark Gable. (It was now hard to find 30 able men from any 162 Co.) Most of these men wore jungle caps — not helmets.

In a low meadow where a defile mouth between B and C Ridges touched the creek-bed, Bradshaw noted a suspicious-looking low mound. A Jap shot echoed up the defile. As he flattened, Japs volleyed bullets, grenades, mortar-shells.

Glauscen rushed up bent low and dropped beside Bradshaw. Lt. McHenry skillfully deployed his 30 riflemen firing prone in a wide, deep semi-circle. From a ridge-shoulder above the Nips where 3 trees were close together, Daniel's Springfield carefully picked off Japs who could be seen only from high up.

Bradshaw, Glauscen crawled to shelter behind a 4-foot bank just 2 arm-lengths from the low mound of the Jap MG. Bradshaw's tommie and Glauscen's carbine zipped bullets through the pillbox slot.

Jap fragments glanced from Bradshaw's helmet through Glauscen's cap; he crawled pack in pain. More Japs fired. Fragments lightly wounded Bradshaw in right side, abdomen. He looked back to see Lt "Clark Gable" bandaging wounded H Co's Fitzgerald's knee, only 200 feet behind him. From farther up B Ridge, another Jap MG fired down on us which Bradshaw duelled with his tommie.

The "G" Pln withdrew. Bradshaw took Fitzgerald's arm over his shoulder and bellied with him over the rough ground. Fitzgerald screamed when his toe caught on root or vine or rock. After 25 yards, Daniel came down to help drag him out. Another fragment wounded Bradshaw more seriously at the base of his neck. Ghastly Fitzgerald now begged us to leave him, but we dragged him back to perimeter and saved his life.

Like Fitzgerald, Bradshaw was hospitalized. With only 3 wounded, including Glauscen, we had blasted the Jap strongpoint. Daniel himself claimed 20 hits; the whole Pln must have wounded 20 more Japs.

Released from hospital a few days later, Bradshaw about 1030 1 Sept hit a slit trench when Nips mortared 2/Bn Hq. They wounded 2-3 men, but missed Bradshaw.

Returning to G's CP on C Ridge, he learned that Lt McHenry's Pln was again besieging the Jap strongpoint which had wounded him a few days before. The Pln had stalked the position for 2 hours, but still did not know whether any Nips were in it. Capt Ratliffe asked Bradshaw to look at that position.

When he probed past the inactive Pln of riflemen, that same pillbox fired as before. While he fell prone, a grenade bounded past, then exploded and seemed to paralyze him in the side. Then the Pln's rifles, grenades, MGs, and .60 mortars got fire superiority, but Ratliff wisely withdrew from a suicidal charge.

This time in hospital, Dr Maffeo told Bradshaw that he might have a homer. Another Capt-Medic said that a chunk of "oval shrap" was imbedded in his shoulder, too deep to be removed in that field hospital. Bradshaw was offered a homer again, but declined. After carrying that "scrap iron" in his shoulder through 2 more campaigns, Bradshaw still retains it.

After 9 hospital days — and a bombardment about the fourth day — Bradshaw was released. Returning to depleted 2/Bn Hq, he heard that Jap resistance on Scout Ridge was broken — that most of his outfit was already moving on Salamaua Town. If he hiked up D Ridge, he might catch his cobbers on the trail.

Panting up D Ridge, which the Aussie 15 Bn of militia had captured, Bradshaw arrived at the Scout Ridge trail crossing before 2/Bn Hq Co appeared. He joined Sgt Daniel to scout before 2/Bn moving on Salamaua Town. The combat-worn Japs had retreated. We hiked north up the wide Jap supply trail past empty Jap blockhouses with 3 coconut log tiers, guarded by trenches and pillboxes.

Before 0800 10 Sept, Maj Berger and Capt Munkres sent for Bradshaw and Daniel to cut cross-jungle to find a safe ford for 2/Bn across the Francisco River. We did not then perceive that we would find ourselves racing to be first in Salamaua.

With Sgt Robertson — a boyhood friend from Portland whose help Bradshaw had requested — we 3 plunged off Scout Ridge, down cliffs above the swirling, yellow Francisco River. Some times we climbed down sheer cliffs where a wrong step meant death. Down past soaring waterfalls, we clung desperately to vines. Or we took turns hacking through brush. We probed a silent village past abandoned Nippo gear.

Beside swirling Francisco River, an Aussie Signal detail welcomed us with hot billy-can tea. Although Aussies had crossed, they said that a whole Bn would be in danger. We asked them to connect us with 2/Bn for consultation. They said that they were trying hard to contact Maj Berger, but their failure all day made us suspicious. Were they trying to hold us back?

So at gray dawn 12 Sept 1943, we 3 helped each other into the sudden, treacherous currents. We probably crossed before that small detachment of 162's 3/Bn crossed on that same 12 Sept.

Scouting into Salamaua Strip with its wrecked Nip planes about sunrise, we were only 1500 yards south of the town.

341

HQ COMPANY 116 ENGINEERS:

Priefert's Battle of Biak

**by VIRGINIA and BURDETTE PRIEFERT,
with DR. HARGIS WESTERFIELD, Division Historian**

> CREDIT: Personal story comes from three letters (total 18 pages) of 18 and 24 July and 6 Aug 1981. While "Stub" Priefert told the story, Virginia wrote it up and typed it with journalistic expertise, and deserves a by-line. She is the first feminine 41st Division member to get a by-line. Some background comes from RR Smith's **Return to the Philippines**. The Prieferts give credit to B Co 116 Engrs' Capt. Argyle Armstrong for his poem which brought back the memories of his order to grade the great road on Biak. This poem appeared in the July, 1981 **Jungleer**, after Hargis found it in the archives at Dwight Eisenhower Library.

On Biak D-Day, 27 May 1944, when Hq Co 116 Engrs landed at Bosnek Beach, Engr Priefert watched a bulldozer fronting the uplifted ramp of our LST. With his engine hot and running, the driver sat alert at his controls, ready to hit the beach. Our LST drove for the land, grated coral under the surf, and dropped its ramp.

As the ramp levelled, the bulldozer plunged forward. It plunged into deep water; the LST had not really closed into the beach because the water was shallow. We Engrs thought that cat was lost, but the salt water could not kill the motor. The dripping driver made it ashore. He turned around, dropped the blade, and pushed down sand to make a causeway for our 10-12 supply trucks to land with their heavy loads.

After the trucks, Hq Co 116 Engrs hiked ashore. Jammed together among trucks and marching outfits below Bosnek's cliffs while other landing vessels poured in to unload, we were lucky that no Jap FA opened up. We know now that our Air Force had spent many bomb runs to make the Bosnek area safe for our landing.

First order for Hq Co was to secure our own unit. Every 2 men must dig a fox-hole together. Priefert and another Engr agreed to make an L-shaped trench for watching in all directions. Grabbing burlap bags from a truck, we filled them with sand and lined the holes to keep the loose earth from caving in. Then in confusion because other outfits worked through our area, we unloaded the trucks and sand-bagged our supply dump and a nearby field hospital.

About 1600 came the first Jap air-raid. Planes darted low from over Bosnek cliffs to escape radar detection. They struck at 4 LSTs side by side at one of the jetties. Because of the needed hurry to unload and a small beach area, Admiral Fechteler had let 4 LSTs moor too close together. But no bombs exploded. The strafing runs killed only 1 man, wounded 2 others. Priefert saw one plane land in the ocean from AA fire from Navy or beach AA. Another strafed the ships offshore but splashed down. Another dived too low on our ships and caught its wing-tip on a sub-chaser. It killed 2 sailors and wounded 9. That plane burst into flames and cart-wheeled into the ocean. The sub-chaser had to be towed off to Hollandia for repairs.

It amazed us when one Jap plane flew the entire length of the beach without harm from a ceiling of flak. We could almost see clouds of steel in the air. The pilot often zoomed so close to the ground that Priefert looked into his goggles. But the pilot maneuvered so adroitly and so fast that he escaped.

Another day when 2 planes came over, AA fire knocked one upside down. The capsized pilot fell into the sea. He was unhurt; 2 Yanks waded out and walked him ashore. And once, when a plane seemed to swoop for Priefert himself flat in his trench, a big "silver bar" Lt landed on top of him for safety. Priefert feared that the Jap plane would kill the Lt first. (Priefert still deeply regrets that he had no time to change places with that Lt to save his life.)

One of Priefert's first Biak details was to work on an airstrip for a Piper Cub FA observer plane. With 25-30 more Engrs, he helped to level the strip with entrenching tools from our packs. Our bulldozers were badly needed elsewhere.

When the Strip seemed ready, they radioed in a little Piper that landed all right. When it departed, it backed close to the cliffs as possible and then took off. It cleared the ocean by just a few inches and became air-borne again.

Then Engrs Priefert and Barum worked on a No. 12 grader to hack out a larger Strip on a coral base behind the cliffs. (While a bulldozer is a vehicle mounted on a track and pushes a great blade before it, a grader is a longish vehicle mounted on wheels. After a bulldozer does the harder work, it drops its blade from the chassis to smooth off the bumps on the ground.) Coral on this strip was so sharp that it tore up tires, but plenty more were handy to replace them as quickly as they blew out.

Out of somewhere came an officer to tell us to push the loose coral into the runway center. Even if this order seemed foolish, we had to obey the officer. The first plane that tried to take off, bogged down in loose coral. Then the officer ordered a jeep to pull a board over the strip to flatten the coral.

Another plane did get off the ground, but the coral retarded it. Pilot and plane ended up on the stumps of little trees at the end of the strip. Pilot was unhurt, and plane patched up to fly again.

Finally, we did what we should have done in the first place. We pushed all coral and loose sand to the sides of the strip. Engrs dynamited off some of the hard coral high spots, and it became a fair air-strip.

Jap planes still bombed our beach. During early morning twilight, a plane paralleled the beach and dropped a probable 500-lb bomb — seemingly aimed for Hq 116 Engrs. It luckily landed off-target into the sea. Two hundred feet away, our

342

hole rocked with the explosion. Sand and water flew all over us. Our teeth rattled. The crater was large enough to bury a jeep.

When B 116 Engrs' Capt Armstrong needed another grader, Priefert and red-headed Texan Barum got the crew assignment. They found Jap skulls everywhere when they graded a waterpoint road. Because they were unburyable in the coral, we had to push them aside with the grader. When Priefert put a Jap skull on the grader front, a Major politely objected, and Priefert took it down.

After finishing the new Strip behind Bosnek Cliffs, Priefert and Barum had orders to grade newly won Mokmer Strip. (Capturing it was the main strategic move of the whole Biak Operation.) Assurances were that the Japs no longer menaced us; they were all holed up in West Caves.

While we busily graded, the ground burst with an explosion right before us. We feared that a Jap mortar shell had impacted. We huddled under our grader. Then another "shell" blasted to our right. We shrank into the earth and expected to hear fragments hit the grader above us.

We trembled a long time under the grader, but there were no more explosions. We observed that those blasts were from the ground — and not from mortars above us at all. Later, we learned that the blasts were due to fumes from gasoline that other 116 Engrs had poured into West Caves during 20-22 June. The fumes had gathered in little coral pockets under Mokmer Strip and had ignited from the fires in West Caves to make the blast. After an hour, we returned to grading the Strip.

Then, some time around 9 July 1944, Priefert with Barum got the most memorable order that he ever had in the whole war. B 116's CO Armstrong told him and Barum to grade a new-made road into the scrub wilderness of upland Biak. He ordered us not to return under any circumstances until we had finished. From Armstrong, we feared court-martial if we disobeyed.

Priefert and Barum never knew where this road led, but it was surely 186 Inf's former overland route through the coral scrubland to Mokmer Strip, which road was now disused.

We believed that this road was for infantry supplies, but we never knew that infantry ever used that road. (After 186 seized Mokmer Strip and the Sboeria Foreshore, it was quicker and safer to move supplies by water. We heard also that FA used that supply road, but we saw no FA men.

For the first 2-3 days, we graded through the scrub with a small guard from an infantry squad's outpost. Two men walked ahead of us with M-1s. At night, we holed up with maybe 6-8 other men in little "pigpens" of coral that the Japs had piled up.

Nearby was a big Jap "pigpen" with a dead crew still manning a dead MG. The dead gunner still crouched behind the gun with his finger on the trigger. His 2 crewmen still slumped over the belt that they had fed into the gun. Moving closer to them, we saw that they were only skeletons.

All those 2-3 days, we worked 8 hours in the Biak upland silence, and returned nightly to the outpost. One night while trying to keep dry from the heavy Guinea rain, we stretched a canvas sheet over our ponchos on the ground. We tied one corner to our grader, one corner to our truck, and the other 2 corners to trees. With a guard posted, we others enjoyed a dry, smiling sleep while rain battered the canvas.

But the rain bulged our canvas with 50 gallons of water. The ties broke and dropped 50 gallons of water on us sleepers. One man awoke and screamed, "We're drowning! We're drowning!"

One night when tired Priefert and Barum returned to the outpost dog tired and fell asleep beside the others, Blankenship was on guard. Blankenship was a quiet, deliberate fellow of course not well know to Priefert and Barum.

Suddenly we sleepers awoke to the crackle of M-1 shots and sat up with our M-1s leaping into our hands. After the shots, we heard an empty M-1 clip ring in the coral. In the silence after the shots, we admired the dead whom Blankenship had made with his M-1.

Five Japs had sneaked up on the outpost to kill us. With 8 shots from 1 clip, Blankenship had slain all 5 Nips. From then on, Blankenship had our greatest respect.

After the first 2-3 days, the infantry guard left us. We worked on the road alone — just Priefert, Barum, and the No. 12 grader. We were in a remote and lonely place where the noise of our motor and scraper could carry for some distance. We were in blind low scrub where Japs could be anywhere.

Priefert and Barum took turns driving the grader. While one man sat high up under the canvas shelter and drove, the other man stood on the housing by the motor and with his M-1 tried to see a Nippo sniper before he fired on us. We were scared stiff most of the time, at brush that seemed to move with Nips when a man stared too long into it.

As the work went on, Priefert labored in a high fever all day, from the time when he awoke in the morning. Yet he remembered Capt Armstrong's order: he did not want a court martial. Besides, Priefert was a true Nebraskan of the finest breed, conscientious and hard-working.

Because of his illness, this fought-over scrub jungle became more horrible than ever. The jungle stink was stronger all the time. Rats ran over us and our bedding at night.

Finally, sick Priefert could endure no longer — Armstrong's orders or no orders. Court-martial or not, he could not go on. He left the grader, struggled back towards B Co. Late at night, he arrived at a field hospital.

He saw light at a tent: a doctor writing on make-shift desk beside a lantern. The doctor helped yellowed Priefert into the tent, tapped his back, and said, "Man, you're nearly dead. Why didn't you come in days ago?

The good doctor helped him into a cot. From then on, Priefert was so sick that he could not rise up to leave his cot even for necessities. He would roll from the cot onto the ground, then pull himself up to walk by using the cot to support himself.

Next day, he became sicker still. Three B Co Engrs working with an unfamiliar new detonator had a premature explosion. DuMarce was killed, and Clark and Carmichael blinded by the blast in their faces. An on-the-spot medical diagnosis was they could never see again, but Priefert would never know whether they would attain even partial sight. Priefert's morale was near its nadir.

Along with jaundice came another agony that the jaundice may have caused. Perhaps because bile had accumulated in his body from the jaundice, his legs were swollen up to look like gallon pails — to over 5 inches in diameter. Actual cause of this leg infection was never determined, but the legs had to be slashed open and drained.

The Medics carried Priefert to the beach for an airplane evacuation. When the plane failed to come, they took him by beach-craft to the hospital ship *Comfort* en route to Milne Bay. His illness was finally diagnosed as jaundice, and he hoped that he would die soon.

Priefert is today uncertain how long he lay in hospital at Milne Bay — but anywhere from 30 to 60 days. When finally cured, he had lost at least 90 pounds. Returned to Biak, he was put on water-point detail and had no more of that horrible road. (Later, he learned that his No. 12 grader was ill fortune for another man. In March, 1945 at Zamboanga, B Co's Libera died from a mortar blast while he was grading a road with that No. 12). But for Priefert, that outback scrub-land road on Biak is still a nightmare where he runs a grader while deep in a fever and in fear of a Nippo shot.

F CO 163 INF ON BIAK, I:

Probing Ibdi Pocket

by S/SGT RALPH MARLOW,
with DR. HARGIS WESTERFIELD, Division Historian

> CREDIT: Essential part of this history is S/Sgt Ralph Marlow's detailed handwritten manuscript of 10 pages from a total of 83 pages about F 163 on Biak, backed by 163 Inf's Biak Casualty List and Journal. Other sources are Volume VIII, "New Guinea and the Marianas," in Samuel Eliot Morison's great **History of US Naval Operations in World War II,** and Lt-Gen Robert Eichelberger's report of trouble-shooting on Biak. This report is in Ch VI, "The Ridge Pockets," from I Corps **History of the Biak Operation, 15-27 June 1944.** The second history of F 163 on Biak will appear later.

After F Co 163 Inf helped storm Wakde Island and hold the Toem Foreshore for 3 weeks, we boarded an LST on 9 June 1944 to reinforce our 41st Div on Biak. So heavily loaded was our LST that we waited for high tide to lift us off the sand. While we were still in sight of Wakde across the darkening sea, an air raid alert sounded. We blacked out the ship, but "All Clear!" soon let us light up again.

All day on 10-11 June, "F" sailed west towards Biak with our other 2/Bn 163 Cos and attached outfits. Convoy consisted of 10 LSTs slowly pushing the waves at 8 knots per hour. On our crowded LST, men slept under trucks. The chow-line circled the entire deck. Our food was tasteless, concentrated, dehydrated.

S/Sgt Marlow, F's Communications Sgt, never forgot the wondrous tray of food that a sailor brought to him. The sailor refused any pay and apologized for the left-overs, but Marlow rejoiced in fresh bread, fresh mashed potatoes and vegetables, spiced ham, and fruit salad. It tasted marvelous!

Towards dusk 11 June, F Co sighted Biak, but our ship's officers would not land. Because of Jap air threats, they never docked over 8 hours at a time. All night we cruised in circles and waited for daylight.

When F Co landed on 12 June, 1/Lt Overby and Comm/Sgt Marlow were the advance party to find our assembly ground. Biak was a rocky shore of brush and coral chunks rising to a high stony ridge heavily jungled with here and there columns of tall white trees. Just to our left on the shore, long AA Guns pointed at that ridge, with Nippo flags stencilled in red on them for the planes that they had shot down. Marlow heard the blasts of heavy guns where a destroyer shelled the high ridge close inshore to the west.

Soon after "F" grouped and dropped packs, the air alert sounded. Running for cover, we saw destroyers shoot red AA tracers far out at sea where 3 Jap bombers were diving on ships. Twice we heard loud explosions. Geysers rose from the water from near misses on our destroyers. A Jap bomber fell from the sky in a ball of flame. As we cheered, a second bomber burned in the sky. But huge columns of smoke lifted from a hit on Destroyer *Kalk*. Then a third Nippo plane flamed, bounced over the waves, and sank. But that one bomb on Destroyer *Kalk* had exploded torpedoes on the deck, which exploded torpedoes in turn damaged forward engines and boilers. Fires were put out, but 30 sailors were killed, 40 wounded. Crippled *Kalk* had to be towed to Hollandia for repairs.

About 0900, trucks carried F Co about 5 miles west and unloaded us by several FA batteries. The gunners were delighted, for they had no infantry protection. At noon, FA cooks gladly fed us.

In a little coconut grove, "F" spent hours digging in and putting up shelters against rain, but we had to move again. After trucking about 4 miles west, we had to get out and hike because the rocks would wreck the trucks.

At the base of a 300-foot cliff covered with dense brush, we came to a cool clear stream flowing from the solid rock of the cliff. Here were the ruins of a bridge that the Japs had destroyed — but no Japs. We were now in that Parai Defile that had long held up 162 Inf. But that very 12 June, 162's AT Co and C Co had pinched out the remaining Japs. The last 162 men had already marched through to join their Regiment, which was already fighting to secure Mokmer Strip.

F's 1/Lt Rottman (our CO) outposted 2/Lt Houser's 2/Pln 400 yards west across the stream from the cliff, and placed our main perimeter 100 yards east of the stream. Crossing to lay wire to Houser's Pln, S/Sgt Marlow and Cpl Mueller saw men of 116 Engrs building a temporary bridge. Marlow and Mueller saw 3 American corpses of men who had died probably when Parai Defile was opened that day.

At night, "F" tried to sleep on the rocky ground. Directly overhead was 300-foot Parai Cliff that Japs might fire down from. With darkness came the roar of FA and 4.2 mortars arcing above us and shaking Parai Ridge.

About 2300 in the dark, an M-1 fired. Something was stumbling toward F's main perimeter. After a little silence, another M-1 fired and grenades boomed. A groan died away at the cliff base. Then in the quiet, we heard 3 rifle shots to signal an air alert. Nippo planes coursed overhead but ignored us to drop their bombs close to Bosnek Jetties where we had landed. The Guinea rain soaked us wet and shivering before dawn. At daylight, was found 2 dead Japs. At a few feet, Russo had slain the stumbler, and Romer had killed the other Jap.

By 14 June, the Parai Bridge was fully repaired. Bulldozers were widening the road from Bosnek Jetties to Mokmer Strip, and a steady stream of traffic was passing in both directions. Our offensive to secure the Strip was well supplied.

And F's assignment in Parai Defile was completed, except for Lt Houser's outpost west of the stream a few days more. We moved 300 yards eastward on the inland side of the road and positioned against the dark ridges concealing Ibdi Pocket, about whose Japs and their locations we knew almost nothing.

We knew only the positions of our 2/Bn's rifle Cos. The day that 2/Bn landed, E Co pushed west through Parai Defile to guard the road from the Japs' East Caves garrison. East of us at Ibdi, G Co had found Old Man's trail to penetrate the ridges and turn west to find the Jap lines. And our F Co lay between "E" and "G" at the cliff base to fight the Japs who might slip down defiles from the ridges to block the road.

On 14 June, F Co began to reconnoiter the coral cliffs above us. Sgt Reeves' recon patrol climbed a short way overhead, but soon Marlow back at Hq heard the Sgt's low voice on the phone. They had found 2 Japs guarding the cliff path. Reeves' patrol was ordered to withdraw.

At dusk came the vicious blasts of 2 Jap .75s down from the ridges — although other reports said 3 guns fired. They shelled E Co and 2/Bn Hq but did not strike at us.

Next morning, Sgt Reeves led an 8-man patrol into the ridges behind 2/Bn Hq to find the Nippo guns. Penetrating a no-man's-land high in the sky below dark shadows from tall trees or steep ridges, they were suddenly cut off from the phone. Dreading an ambush, they slipped back to safety. When flown over the dark ridges later, Reeves could not even see his route through that dense jungle. We never found the guns.

On 18 June, 2 "F" patrols went out. T/Sgt Brent took the same route which Reeves had used yesterday to find the Jap gun. And Reeves had his third patrol in 3 days.

Reeves sought for another route up the cliffs behind our perimeter. A few minutes later, he phoned down that they had found a possible upward route, about 200 yards east of "F."

After an hour and a half of silence from the phone, rapid rifle fire and grenade blasts sounded above us from the ridges. Reeves phoned, "We shot 2 Japs and will continue on." Just a few minutes later, came more rapid rifle fire and more roars of grenades.

On the first ridge, Reeves' men had discovered a good east-west trail. Two Japs came down from the east. Although both were unarmed, we had to kill them — then a third coming from the west. We feared that they would run and bring down the other Jap on us. Then 4 more armed Japs came from the north, and we killed them. We were so close to the Nips that we smelled their food cooking.

A few minutes later, Japs attacked us up a cliff from the north. We could even hear their superiors giving orders. They threw in plenty of grenades and shells from mortars. Reeves' patrol had to withdraw.

Meanwhile, 1/Lt Rottman ordered Marlow to take a message and follow the wire to Reeves. With Hernandez, Marlow went as far as the cliff base and started to connect his phone to the wire. Marlow knew better than to climb into an attack of grenade-slinging Japs.

Seconds later, loose rocks crashed down near Marlow and Hernandez. Bleeding, grim-faced men of Reeves' patrol warned Marlow and Hernandez to get out. Reeves' men said that Japs on the sides of the ravine had tossed grenades down on them; they could only retreat without firing.

Marlow saw Ellwood's BAR open up while the riflemen crawled off under Jap fire. Then they rose up with M-1s to cover Ellwood's retreat. Ellwood's helmet toppled off. When he picked it up, Nippo bullets shot it from his hands.

F lost 3 wounded to hospital in this skirmish. Fragments seriously wounded Taapken in left hand, Schutt in right hand and knee, and Campbell in left leg. Reeves' men claimed 14-15 dead Japs, and 6 probables.

In the ridge-jungle behind 2/Bn Hq, T/Sgt Brant's patrol had followed the wire past where Reeves had halted yesterday — and deeper still into the brush. Heavy MG and rifle fire stopped them, but with no casualties. They claimed 8 dead Japs, and 2 probables — but could never find that Jap .75 cannon.

Only a week after our Biak landing, "F" was down to 110 men. When 2/Bn CO Maj Irving phoned to ask why 19 of us were on sick-call that morning, Lt Rottman replied that we had dysentery and strained backs and legs. When Irving ordered Torrman to inspect each of our 19 men personally, Rottman tactfully replied that he was no member of the medical profession.

Later that 19 June, F Co had orders to find a better approach to getting at the Japs. We were to bypass them west of us and cross over the 10 coral ridges north of the beach. Then we could patrol down from the NE and try to find an easier entry into their positions.

On 20 June, we straggled under heavy equipment to the north side of the coral ridges. Trees were much smaller here, and the brush less dense. Soil was still so rocky that we could not dig in. We heaped up little pigpens of coral around the ponchos we slept on, with flotation bladders for pillows.

On 21 June, "F" hiked along a narrow footpath towards the high cliffs of the NE corner of Jap country. After 600 yards, we turned left through high brush. Suddenly we came to a ghastly white area of solid rock darkened by branches of great trees growing from that rock. Over this rock were scattered large, jagged boulders, among craters 20-30 feet deep. Visibility was 75-100 yards. Cliffs stood up about 100 yards ahead.

Rottman advanced 3/Pln to climb the cliff before us. At wide intervals, 3/Pln began the laborious ascent until thick foliage hid them from the rest of "F" waiting below.

Suddenly volleys of Jap MG fire cracked down from the cliff-tops all around us. From that fire, 3/Pln's men rolled back down the cliff. Pursuing Jap riflemen fired down on us. A stampede of F Co almost began.

Lt Rootman shouted to "F" to stand fast. Giant trees on the coral flat concealed us from aimed Jap rifles, but bullets whined into trees and coral around us. Walter was missing in action up there, to be found dead later. Sgt Grilley bled from a wound in back or right thigh, but refused to be carried.

Now withdrawn about 100 yards to where we could hold, F Co learned exactly what happened when 3/Pln topped the cliff. From the next cliff and high ground came the Nips' fire-blast. Walter fell forward dead, and 3/Pln jumped down the cliff to save themselves. Jap fire was coming from 3 sides.

Now Lt-Col Rankin phoned F Co to shoot a flare to orient his mortar batteries down on the Japs. But Rankins' mortars fell short; his first 2 mortar rounds bracketed us. When "F" fled our own mortars 200 yards east, Rankin requested another flare. This time, our own flare brought down the Jap mortars on us. One Jap shell struck a tree almost overhead, but hit the ground among us without exploding. In confusion, "F" raced east again. Returned to last night's perimeter, we heard our FA fire battering the Japs. It was the most intense FA we had ever heard, but it failed to dislodge the Japs from Ibdi Pocket. They were the entire 3/Bn 222 Inf reinforced, about 1,000 men.

On 21 June, F Co failed to storm Ibdi Pocket, and we did not then realize that our recon in force was important in the final destruction of the Japs. While we fought, a HMG from D or H Co fired for us from high ground over our heads. Evidently the Japs thought that an all-out storm-force was attacking. They opened up all along their positions on the high ground to the south of us. From the volume of fire, 163's Exec officer decided that we were facing an entire Bn. It would take more than F Co to clean them out. The real Battle of Ibdi Pocket had begun.

Such were F 163's first 9 days on Biak — 12-21 June 1944. Landing when 3 Jap bombers dived on Destroyer *Kalk* and seriously damaged her, we endured a war of nerves while we guarded Parai Defile. In 2 bitter skirmishes, we felt out the Japs with 1 of ours killed, 4 wounded to hospital — and some 23 dead Japs. Such was our start of the Battle of Biak.

CANNON COMPANY 162 INF:

Assault Guns at Zamboanga
(Dedicated To CN's Al Morrow)

by GUNNER HAROLD ARKOFF
with DR. HARGIS WESTERFIELD, Division Historian

> CREDIT: Most important author is Gunner Harold Arkoff who wrote a complete history of CN 162 for all World War II—a single-spaced typescript of 9 pages. For this history alone, he wrote one typescript entitled "Description of Cannon Company's 105mm Howitzers and Their Operation," 3 pages long, and another typescript, "Cannon Company, 162nd Infantry Regiment Zamboanga, March-April, 1945," 5 pages long. Important also was detailed Award Story of Joseph Cappola. Useful archives were 162's "Report of Operation, Zamboanga Area..." and 162's Journal throughout March, 1945. Two previous CN stories are in my Fighting Jungleers. Story of CN 162 for entire World War was also in the Dec. 1960 Jungleer, and Al Morrow's story of CN in Parai Devile was in July 1973 Jungleer. Death of Al Morrow directly caused this new CN-162 story when a letter from Edna and Susan Morrow gave me Harold Arkoff's address.

The 105mm assault guns of Cannon Co 162 Inf played an important part in defeating the Japanese in the Battle of Zamboanga. These were front-line cannon designed for close support of riflemen against pillboxes and bunkers.

But even if CN 162 began training with our guns at Toorbul Point in Queensland in February, 1944, we still had to fight as riflemen throughout the New Guinea Campaign. In fact, **we even landed as a rifle Co at Zambo, on 10 Mar 1945.**

Beaching from our LCI at 0934 19 minutes after 162's first wave, we pushed inland through the ridge of rubble that had held up 162's first landing barges. Warily with ready rifles, we scouted behind 162's line Cos towards Wolfe Field, 600 yards inland. Already, however, by 0930, I and K Cos ahead of us, had crossed the Strip without fighting.

Quickly, we carried out CN's first Zambo assignment. We found that the 600 yards from Wolfe Field back to the beach was clear of bypassed Japs. Then we dug in opposite the Strip to secure Zambo Road, 162 Rgtl Hq, and the supply dumps. We also helped unload an LST on the beach. That afternoon, Jap guns fired down from the hills at us. Biel took a fragment in the stomach--although marked lightly wounded. Crabtree had a fragment in the leg.

Next morn at 1040 11 Mar, Jap FA and mortars flamed a gas dump and ammo dump 200 yards east of 162's CP--and just 50 yards from CN. our nearest men had to leave their holes because of the heat of the fire and the danger of more explosions. The rest of 11 Mar, our CN observers helped to spot Jap 75s in the hills and call down 205 FA shells on them. When F Co in Ratliff Force pushed west towards Caldera Point, 162 Hq believed that 2 of our cannon would go forward to help 162's small flank offensive. But we were never called there.

At about midnight 12-13 Mar, 8 Japs raided the dumps to burn those gasoline drums which their FA had failed to burn. These 8 Japs crossed the Strip and Zambo Road and touched off those drums. They mined the road also.

Spotting a CN Co position, they pinned down its men with a light .25 caliber "Woodpecker" MG. They fired this LMG pointblank on us. We fired back with rifles and carbines until we drove them off. Jap MG slugs riddled the whole area. Next morn, a Jap lay dead only 5 feet from our holes. And next day, we found 3 dead just 30 yards up the road. We believe that CN killed those 3 from the 8 raiders in last night's fight.

But not until 16 Mar 1945, did CN 162 become a true assault gun cannon Co. Then, our 6 big 105s became our principal weapons. We were no longer just another rifle Co!

By 16 Mar, assault guns seemed to be necessary against the fixed positions of the tenacious Japs above in the jungle ridges that were close together. Regular long-barreled 105mm guns of our FA would not be accurate or safe to fire because of their flatter trajectory. Distances between our riflemen and the Japs on the next ridge would be only 200-300 yards.

And the Japs were holding out well against 162's 1/Bn and 2/Bn in the ridges above the bitterly contested San Roque area. Fighting in rain forest 1500 yards NW of Masilay, 1/Bn was halted before Jap mortars and FA. To the right on high ground north of San Roque, the Japs also held back 2/Bn. These Bns could not close the gap between them. Now CN Co's 4 guns of our 2/Pln and 3/Pln had to close that gap.

On the morn of 16 Mar, Sgt. Padnuk's 3/Pln's 2 guns went to gith for 1/Bn north of Masilay. It was a formidable small procession. A jeep of 2/Bn 162 Inf guided us into the hills. Our CN Co jeep followed with Sgt Padnuk, Lt. O'Hare and his driver. Next followed our 6-wheel trucks, each with a 105mm Howitzer trailed behind it. On each truck was a 6-man gun-crew. Both trucks were piled high with hundreds of partly loaded rounds. Each partial round was a brass cartridge case 20 inches long with a fused projectile in its head. Also piled in the trucks for propellants were posder bags still stowed separately in wooden racks. As needed, we would insert 2-4 bags into each cartridge before we fired.

From San Roque Perimeter a mile-and-a-half behind the lines, our convoy of 3 trucks and 2 command jeeps made a scary trip to the front. Going was slow up wet slopes and over muddy trails. Our loaded truck with No.1 gun slopped into tracks that a carabao could not have waddled through. Finally, our 6-man crew had to manhandle it into place. Our No.2 gun ahd the guns of 2/Pln were set up nearby. With Cpl Strickland in charge of No.1 Gun, Computer Fire Director Arkoff and crewmen Di Stifano, Stallings, Naebar, and Gadaloun, we grunted and groaned the cannon forward. Finally, we had this 4977-lb. 20-foot gun into firing position.

Our gun now stood atop a ridge above a draw 400 yards from the next ridge where an estimated Co of Japs were holed up. (This war probably the beginning of the of the attach of I and K Cos of 16 Inf against a height which "K" men would call Cram Hill. Probably we were about to fire for I Co's attack. We separated the gun trails and dug them in and were ready to fire.

But the Japs saw our gun. A Jap LMG rattled and shattered 2 trees overhead. Several 25-caliber bullets zinged from our guns and made little chips on the olive drab muzzle. But our own riflemen silenced the LMG.

In 5 minutes, No.1 Gun was ready to fire—aimed straight across the valley into the Jap ridge a few hundred yards off. We swabbed the muzzle, leveled the gun-sight bubbles. We jammed in the shell. Cpl Strickland pulled the lanyard for our first shell fired in action.

First round was white phosphorus to verify the range. The white puff on the crest of the targeted ridge told us that our range was correct. Now we fired for effect along with the other 3 guns—30 minutes' rapid cannon fire—5-6 rounds a minute—300 rounds. We pumped shells through the gun as fast as we could load and fire. As fast as we threw out the hot spent cartridges behind us, we jammed new shells into the breech. We feared that new shells would prematurely explode in the barrel, but they never did.

Suddenly 2 Filipino scouts burst out of the rain forest beside us. They said that a few of our shells had gone wrong, into a detachment of their own guerilla 106 Div. They were across the ridge from near Moroc Village and pressing the Japs towards us.

After we corrected range and continued firing, I Co overran the blasted Jap position ahead. Regtl Hq reported a count of 40 dead Japs, with surely as many more sealed inside caves blasted shut by our fire. CN Co lost nobody; I Co had 1 dead, and 10 wounded.

As our first shoot-out on 16 Mar demonstrated, CN Co's Assault Gun was effective for the shorter ranges of the Zambo ridges. The regular 105mm "field piece" of our FA had too flat a trajectory to impact the close-in Jap valleys. Our Model M-3 was not a field piece but a Howitzer. It had a shorter muzzle for the size of the projectile, which enabled it to fire over our advancing troops and hit targets close to them. Despite its range of 12,000 yards, we shot it mostly at 200-300 yards. We could turn it 23 degrees left or right without shifting it. We could depress it 65 degrees to fire downhill. Our M-3 was a fine battle-field cannon.

Thus, beginning 16 Mar, we were finally a real infantry cannon Co. From 16 Mar through 17 Apr, our 105mm shells aided riflemen to dig out die-hard Japs from their ridges. We hauled guns over mountain roads that were almost impassable. Instead of trucking in ammo, we used jeeps. Or we hand-carried it. Instead of our maximum range of 12,000 yards, most of our fire was *point-blank* shots from the top of one ridge to the top of the next ridge—200 to 300 yards. Often we sighted a gun through the bore. Our 3 Plns fired independently, often 20 miles apart, for 162, 186, or 163 Inf.

On 16 Mar, 2/Lt Swanson's 1/Pln supported F Co's unopposed invasion of Basilan Island. On 18 Mar, other CN guns moved up to fire from I 162's ridge position. On 19 Mar, we sent 2 guns to Kawit far west of Zambo City to fight for K Co 163 Inf against a Jap gun at Caldera Point. On 22 Mar and again on 27 Mar, we assigned a Pln of our guns to 1/Bn 186 Inf after they took over from 162 Inf on West Ridge.

When 2/Lt Swanson's 1/Pln's 2 guns returned from Basilan Island, they almost met disaster on the Zambo mainland. On 21 Mar, they had orders for direct fire support to 2/Bn near Masilay, where they were trying to advance up East Ridge to capture Mt. Capisan. On 21 Mar, 2/Bn was to advance 1,000 yards up East Ridge.

Swanson's guns were positioned dangerously close to the Japs. They set up a gun in a valley 300 yards from the Japs—and the other in a palm grove only 150 yards from the lines.

Suddenly the guns took fire from both flanks. Rifles, MGs, and mortars flailed us. Sierra, near his truck, took a FA fragment in his right shoulder.

Jap phosphorus shells flamed the brush less than 5 feet from an ammo pile near one of the guns. An explosion might have wrecked Swanson's Pln. Cappola rushed in to stamp out the fire. Although exposed to heavy Jap mortar shelling, Cappola kept on fighting the flames. Other men ran forward and helped put them out. Then they withdrew the gun to a position where the Japs could not strike it.

But 2/Bn's attack on that 21 Mar was a failure. Spearhead E Co pushed just 500 yards safely up narrow East Ridge. Here they took fire from an estimated 50 Japs in a strongpoint of numerous pillboxes and trenches. E Co's position was untenable. Bn Co Caulfield ordered E Co back to their position of early morning.

Next day, however, with CN support, our 2/Bn attached again over the same ground where E Co was halted yesterday. Fighting up parallel ridges behind a successful air strike and heavy FA fire, both Cos seized yesterday's objective 1,000 yards ahead. Dead Japs totalled 74. And on 23 Mar, with CN's support again, E and F Cos contacted at the ridge junction closer still to Mt. Capisan.

Thus, on 24 Mar, stage was set for 162's 2/Bn and 3/Bn to storm Mt. Capisan. Rain made Wolfe Strip useless and kept the Air Force grounded, but the Bns climbed grimly uphill. When 2/Bn met heavy resistance about 0900 before Bald Hill guarding Capisan, CN guns fought gallently. Our salvos silenced numerous Jap MGs as soon as they opened up. G Co captured Bald Hill and forwarded to overrun Mt. Capisan itself. Forty Japs died on Bald Hill and Mt. Capisan. For 162 Inf, the main battle of Zamboanga was ended.

On the morning of 28 Mar, however, CN men became riflemen again. Guided by Graves Registration officer, Sgt Padnuk led a 12-man patrol from CN's Hq perimeter near San Roque to bring back a dead man. After some 400 yards cross-country trek through a clearing and over several ridges, we found the body, started him back on a 4-man stretcher.

As we crossed a clearing, a Jap LMG and rifles fired down at range 400 yards. They seemed to be in a large hole. Their grazing fire pinned down most of our 12 men, but some of us managed to return fire. From up the valley also, a Jap mortar tried to zero in on us with 2 rounds.

But the clearing chanced to be covered by CN's own 3/Pln overlooking the Japs. Our 3/Pln shot a .30 and a .50 HMG into the probable Jap position. Padnuk's patrol leaped up and got out of there just as the third Jap round impacted where they were pinned down. Near casualties were T/4 Howard and Jenkins. Howard had 3 holes in his fatigue jacket, and Jenkins had a bullet hole through his pants at the knee.

Last action of CN Co's 105mm assault guns in World War II was the 5-day struggle for Sibago Island. Lying 28 miles SE of Zambo City at the eastern end of Basilan Strait, this little lighthouse jungle island of 2 hills had a die-hard Nipps garrison of probably Jap Marines of 32 Naval Guard. When I & R was repelled on 267 Apr, an L Co Pln with probably 2 M Co 81mm mortars reinforced I & R.

For close support, CN sent 2 assault guns to fire from Lanhil Island, 1,000 yards across the channel. CN's guns got 3 direct hits on the lighthouse tower, but it still stood. By later afternoon, our guns had cleared the brush around the lighthouse and exposed a Nippo cave-mouth. Yet not until 0930 on 30 Apr did I & R count 58 Japs dead and report that the island was Filipino ground again. We had lost 1 L Co man killed, and 2 wounded.

At a cost of just 3 wounded, CN Co had fought for our Division in the Battle of Zamboanga. We had won our battle with an uncounted number of Japs wounded or dead.

★★★★★★★ IN MEMORIAM: ★★★★★★★★★★
FRANK VIVORITO (G-163)

Night in the park: great elms,
A far away football band:
The drums beat: Star spangled banner.
I am back in New Guinea forth years ago—
The American flag over dull jungle,
The narrow sand. We had sniper fire.
The surf was bad. We walked in under water.
Vivorito drowned. We never found his body.
The band beats out the picture: the boy
We never saw again—the blue water, the flag
In New Guinea, peace in this city.
                    HARGIS WESTERFIELD

★★★★★★★★★★★★★★★★★★★★★★★★★★★★★★

C COMPANY, 163 INF:

Bob Burns' Story of Toem-Wakde

by DR. HARGIS WESTERFIELD, DIVISION HISTORIAN
and COMPANY 163's BOB BURNS

Credit: Justification for C 163's second Wakde story comes from discovery of Bob Burns' Diary with important personal information—and Ltrs of 27 and 28 Aug 1977. Other new data are from Casualty Lists unavailable to me in 1969. I used also RR Smith's Approach to the Philippines and my earlier story with Lt Walt Larson, "C Co 163's Coconut Hell on Wakde" (Story No. 46 in June, 1969 Jungleer). Burns' Diary also gave me C Co's story on Toem Foreshore. These new sources have caused me to correct some statements printed in earlier story. Earlier story also named some men as wounded but not hospitalized. My practice is to omit names of men wounded but not hospitalized. (Burns owns and operates Evergreen Farm at Worthington, Minn.)
C 163 Wakde II

Leaving Korako Beach at Aitape about 1600, 15 May 1944, C Co 163 Inf rode an LCI in the convoy to capture Wakde Island. Enjoying a cool offshore breeze, we watched the sinister jungle move past in its endless green. Although our convoy hugged the shore, our flat-bottomed little LCI began pitching and caused some seasickness. C Co's Burns feared destruction; waves heaved C's LCI almost clear of the sea, then let it drop with a bang. He expected the LCI to split in tow, but it was stouter built than he thought.

Arriving at Hollandia at 0600 16 May, we anchored until dark, then slipped out in convoy to sight the Toem Foreshore by Wakde at 0530, 17 May 1944. From Sarmi Village far west and along the shore to Wakde on our left flank, Navy and planes blasted every possible target. Burns saw 6-8 shells at a time strike into Wakde tarkets. Great fires flamed on Wakde Island, silent under the coconut palms.

Landing on Toem Foreshore some time after 0715 from LCIs, "C" waded in waist-deep. Climbing an 8-foot bank, we staggered through shell-torn ground and sent out patrols that found no Japs. Col Moroney turned us left down a little truck trail. On both sides of us, blind jungle threatened ambush, but our sweaty hike under full pack for 3 miles made us forget our worries.

C Co dug in close to the shore, with FA batteries just 50 yards behind us zeroing in on Wakde. Almost 40 guns hit Wakde—105s from CN 163 and 167 FA, and 155s of 218 FA. Destroyers pounded Wakde; PT boats ran in close and broadsided Wakde.

But after "C" dug in during early afternoon, Burns likened it to a family reunion rather than a beachhead. Kitchens sat up; we went swimming. Mail bags were opened. Burns read his 6-7 letters while guns roared behind him.

Burns could not sleep that night in his hole because the big guns impacted Wakde from behind him. But he lay happy—sure that no Japs could be alive there tomorrow.

And when "C" crammed into LCMs at 0845, 18 May, with cannon firing even more heavily, Burns was still happy. As we shoved off, great waves threw his LCM up and slapped it down into the troughs. We looked across the waves to quiet Wakde Beach.

But when we got between Wakde and our MGs firing from little Insoemanai Island behind us, Jap bullets flailed us from Wakde. While our first waves from A and F Cos were already ashore, we were still out in the water under heavy fire.

Bullets flew overhead—or holed the gunwales around us. We hugged a light metal sheet near the boat's floor—as close as we ever hugged anything before in our lives. T.J. Smith was hit in the windpipe. Leonard was gunshot in right temple in our LCM at 0920.

About 0924, our coxswain drove us far up on land. We piled out and hit the beach prone, where Smith was slowly dying. Under Jap MG fire which missed us by inches, we spread flat on the beach and worked our way forward. While moving inland, our cook, T/4 Sunderman, was probably killed, reported dead at 0930. Hayes may have got his death-wound then; a falling tree broke his back.

Burns had hit the beach, prone behind a big coconut log. Here he waited until the Cos began fanning out inland. Then he was up and dodging, tree to tree. Having lost contact with his squad, he joined C's 1/Pln and moved forward with it. Ahead, he saw our 2 tanks shatter a few pillboxes. Probably in this advance, Cpl Suits died, and Leonard was shot in left temple—both reported casualties at 0945. Kraus was gunshot in the head—time and place not recorded.

Returned to his squad by noon, Burns ate K rations with them on a little rise of ground where they could still see the beach. Occasionally, stretcher-bearers passed with wounded, but Burns thought that the fight was practically over.

But Burns' Wakde war was far from over. Main part of C Co regathered and moved to the south edge of Wakde Strip where unharmed palms still stood upright among supply dumps and intact buildings.

Then Burns had the greatest fright of his life. "C" had orders to cross the Strip and contact A Co pushing Japs east along the north shore. Tanks were to guard us across the open Strip.

But when S/Sgt Seeger's recon squad crossed the Strip and returned safely in about 30 minutes, Capt Kent of Wing's 1/Bn's Staff decided to send us all over minus tank protection—although with a mortar barrage as preparation.

About 1400, Lt Moore's 1/Pln started, followed by 2/Lt Larson's 2/Pln with 2 squads. Suddenly 2 Jap MGs opened up. Burns ran faster than he had ever run before in his life, or would ever run again. Dust spurted up all around his feet. He saw only 1 small shell hole in the Strip; his only salvation was to get across. His 200-yard run seemed to take hours. He misjudged the distance to the ditch, dived in too soon and cruelly skinned head and knee.

Two of Burns' squad were hit—on each side of him. Yates made the ditch but died a few minutes later, a wound in the abdomen. Zerr was wounded in right leg and left thigh. In Moore's 1/Pln, Kleeman died from a shot in the chest. Wounded also in Plns unspecified, were Henry Johnson with a bullet in the thigh, and Hurley, shot in right leg. Burns wondered how MGs could fire over 200 bullets at our crowd, yet kill only 2 and wounding 3.

Weapons Pln with 167 FA and 218 FA now silenced the Japs, and at 1545, the other "C" men safely crossed the Strip. When a tank with A Co in from the west joined us north of the Strip, we went with them to clean up NE Biak—which was "Coffin Corners." Once a sniper fired on "C" from a coconut tree, but our heavy fire smashed his tree and probably slew him. We passed many wrecked Jap planes and unexploded bombs on the Strip. At the east end was wreckage of maybe 2 Yank planes and shoes and charred clothing of what 2/Bn Hq reported as 4 dead fliers—and notebook of airman 2/Lt Vanderbeck.

C's first battle-day on Wakde was closing. Leaving "A" still connecting the Japs, we spread out and recrossed the Strip. South of the Strip, Japs sniped at us along the trails—especially from a small knoll eastward among warehouses. LMGs fired every few rods and drove us into ditches. Reported wounded at 1800 going into bivouac were S/Sgt Perkins in left leg, and Schwartz in left hand. Japs sniped heavily at us now, but we dug in by pitch dark to help B Co on our left cordon off the Japs eastward. C's right flank was on the sea south of Wakde.

On 19 May, "C" again fought the Japs penned in Coffin Corners. While "B" and "F" pushed on our left, we teamed with all 3 tanks of 603 Tank Co to fight along the shore slanting NE to the rounded rump of Biak. Tanks' names were "Wake Island," "Hellzapoppin", and "Shangri-La." 1/Lt Stanfield's 1/Pln had 2 of the tanks; Larson's 2/Pln with Burns had the other.

Topping a slight rise east, we found the Japs. Bullets rang on armor as our tanks shattered pillboxes and riflemen shot at Japs fleeing from pillboxes. Sgt Siemkiewicz was probably wounded during one of these actions, at 1045 in right shoulder while he directed an attack on a Jap position. Rifle bullet penetrated his back to the spine. He never walked again. Gullo had a fractured right patella. Time and circumstances of Gullo's wound are unreported.

While Lt Larson directed fire by radio from behind a tank, a Jap leaped from a trench and on top of the tank, in nothing flat. He tried to shove a grenade into a gunport.

At first, excited Larson merely stared and said, "There's a Jap getting on the tank". Then S/Sgt Seeger fired; Laron fired; others fired. It took 8-10 bullets to kill that Jap. After that, the tank stayed bolted up, all the time.

This Jap had charged from a T-shaped shallow trench just 3-4 yards before the tank. Only 4 feet deep, the trench lay hidden under dried palm branches. Now we saw 14 live Japs in it. Big Martinez lifted his heavy BAR. "Let 'em have it!" we yelled, but he seemed scared to fire. Then a Jap officer jumped out screaming, with lifted saber. "Marty" cracked 20 rounds from his BAR and killed 7 of the Japs. Later, he said that he had held fire because he feared a jam.

When the Jap officer screamed, all Larson's "C" men reared up and went in firing. The brush was alive with Japs. We advanced firing into some 28 Japs. Our quick M-1s killed half, drove off the others. Some 14 Japs lay dead—big "Tiger Marines." They were probably members of a 150-man Co of 91 Naval Garrison Unit—rumored advance party of 1200 men unable to land.

Soon "C" had no return fire, but Lt Stanfield was sure that hidden Japs still faced us on our left. He did not want to risk hitting "F." Two tanks went elsewhere. Tank No. 3 and Larson's 2/Pln fought slowly east in line of skirmishers, then turned NE at the beach. We combed the brush for Japs.

At 1647, Col Moroney reported that Wakde Strip was now all 163's. Surviving Japs crouched in an oval pocket 500 yards long on the curved cape of NE Wakde. Our Lt Foster's 3/Pln had counted 200 Jap corpses where "C", "B", and "F" had fought. Leaving "A" and "F" men to contain the Jap pocket, we withdrew with "B" and some other men to the beach for a hot meal and a good night's rest.

About 0530 at daylight 20 May, we watched from our holes while 6-8 Japs of a bypassed 37-man group ran around with flaming torches among trucks of probably 836 Engr Aviation Bn. Prematurely parked on Wakde, the trucks had been poorly guarded. Fearing to hit other troops, we could not fire. Avenging Engrs slew 36 Japs and caught a prisoner, at cost of 3 dead Engrs.

On 20 May, some "C" patrols checked for Japs in rear areas, and others moved toward the pocket where "F" would help on the left. Crossing the south end of the Strip, we met some resistance. Pussich was probably shot in the face here. Then working on the pocket, we contacted 5-7 Japs in a cave about 1115. Storming the cave with probably a flame-thrower, we pushed against the Japs under a coral beach shelf, and finally contacted "F" down from the north at 1539. C's war on Wakde was finished, and at 1910 after supper, we left Wakde forever.

Returned to Toem Foreshore, C Co, like almost all 163 outfits, cut jungle poles and framed our tents for a garrison camp. On the narrow shore between dark jungle and surf, lights shone long after dark. Our security was only a squad on guard in holes behind the tents.

Yet our Jap war was still going on. A graveyard was growing on the shore behind "C". After 163's Insoemanai and Wakde burials, corpses of 158 Inf were arriving—in truckloads. From 158 Inf's fights west of Tor River 10-12 miles west of Toem, 42 corpses were buried on 23-25 May, with more to come.

This growing graveyard behind us should have alerted 163 Inf to the continued danger of Jap armies striking us to cut off 158 Inf's supply ships on the shore behind us. On the night of 25-26 May, a Jap officer died on a recon patrol before our lines. Rumor had it that he was mapping our defences.

But when the night attack of 27 May struck, "C" was unready. Tents were alight "like a church," with card-players. An estimated 50 Japs burst through our tents and charged right through C's security squad behind the tents—12 surprised men in 4 holes, 3 to a hole. We blazed away, but they ignored us and galloped on to their defeat on the beach.

Yet "C" had 9 casualties that night. A shot in the head killed Buck; a shot in the abdomen killed Gilkison. Spear was hit in both legs but did not die until 30 May. Schneekloth took a bullet wound in right shoulder, Limpert in left knee, Schoening in the chin. T/5 Lindway was shot in right arm, Prerost in left arm and right foot, Bystrek in the ear. We have no more details of the fighting where "C" lost these 3 killed and 6 wounded.

For next night, 28 May, 163 sternly dug in to fight a human sea of Jap bayonet men. Nerves were taut. Early in the night, most of 163's MGs fired most of their bullets—from 3/Bn on our left flank to H Co on Tementoe Creek. Under a moon coming in and out of clouds, our front flamed like sunrise. No Japs charged. Thousands of rounds of ammo were wasted because tense guners probably misunderstood an order. But from his hole, canny Burns saw no Japs and restrained his 2 rooky riflemen from crazy blasting away.

"C" was glad to leave spooky Toem. On 30 May, we embarked with 1/Bn and 3/Bn to fight on Biak. At Toem-Wakde, we lost 7 killed (3 of them at Toem) and 16 wounded (6 of them at Toem). Aided by tanks on Wakde, we had fought well.

Eight boys in a jeep on Emu Park-Yeppoon Road. Back row: Stewart, Kim, Aldape and Cranston. Front row: Weingartner, Francis, Carvalho and Patrick. (Courtesy of O. Patrick)

B CO 163 INFANTRY:
BAYONET CHARGES AT SANANANDA
by 1/LT (THEN 2/LT) WALTER L. MCKENZIE
with DR HARGIS WESTERFIELD,
DIVISION HISTORIAN

Understandably homesick, this Jungleer surveys what had been a dry area when he selected it the previous night before several inches of rain fell during the night. Sanananda Area. (Courtesy of Rohlffs)

At Sanananda, B Co 163 Inf began with defective ammunition—armor-piercing (AP) shells jamming our semi-automatic M-1s. First round would misfire; we had just one ramrod for every 9 riflemen to eject bullet. Ingenious Sgt Fiscus found that working the M-1 trigger guard would recock the rifle. The cartridge usually fired the second time. But each squad's BAR and the 1903 bolt-action rifle would fire AP. The squad tommie gun shot .45 cartridges all right, but we had only one spare clip per gun. One man had to reload that clip while the other fired.

Yet B Co had to fight with defective AP ammo in our first fight when we relieved Aussie 2/7 Cavalry Regt in Musket Perimeter. At once, the Japs struck to defeat our untried men. Despite AP, we repelled them, but in 45 mintues, we were short of ammo. Then Sgt Russ forwarded the right ammo instead of AP. Russ and 2/Lt McKenzie ran from hole to hole and laid out clips. We stopped 2 Jap attacks, 2 hours apart.

Knoepfle's shoulder was hit, Del Castillo's left elbow, Miller's left hip. Guider and Sgt McKinster were shot in lower parts of body. Robdjek's left arm was broken.

By day, Japs harassed us with unlimited MG ammo. They lacked grenades, however. When our automatic weapons drew fire, we hid them where they were safe. Then we turned accurate rifle fire on the Jap MGs and often silenced them.

Thus for almost 2 weeks, "B" held Musket Perimeter—like a frontier outpost against Indians. Japs held P Perimeters 300 yards south, and Perimeters Q-R 25-50 yards north. Only access to Musket was through and around Jap Perimeters P.

Only a few feet above swamps, Musket Perimeter was an oval space 75 by 50 yards. It was a grassy, brushy flat overlooked by tall snipers' trees above dense undergrowth—a deadly perimeter hard to defend.

At once, "B" began trying to break out. BARmen fired up our last AP bullets to destroy snipers each morning. Then we moved around fairly safe until the Japs' mid-day attacks—7 attacks on 7 consecutive days. The Japs then failed their daily attacks; then they tried 5 night attacks. Our grenades stopped those 5 consecutive night attacks.

B's first attempt to break out of Musket was a Weapons Pln attack, 5 Jan., 3 days after we occupied Musket. Fiery Capt "Red" Hamilton planned it—Col Doe's nephew, trained as a Field Artillery officer. His battlefield tactic was simple—a bayonet charge. Weapons Pln specialists held no line positions for Musket, and so Hamilton used them-perhaps more 60 mm mortarmen than any other Weapons men.

About 1235, 5 Jan, 1/Lt Ellers' Weapons men assaulted. We lined up 25 men, fixed bayonets, and charged when a police whistle blew. Hidden Jap MGs stopped us dead, number of casualties in that first charge unknown.

"It should have worked," said Hamilton. Another charge of 25 with police whistle and fixed bayonets failed also. Perhaps all of 4 hidden Jap MGs shot men dead.

In one of these charges, Limbocker died. McMeel and Potter tried to save him, but Jap tracers stopped them. Both men were killed also. We never found McMeel's body—only mementos his own mess-gear left in Jap Hqs. Mendoza was wounded and had to be left to die under Jap guns that night. Killed also was S/Sgt Sullender. Pickenstein was shot in the neck, and 1/Lt Ken Ellers in right arm.

As sole remaining front-line officer besides Capt Hamilton, 2/Lt McKenzie must be part of every important patrol or attack. His weapons were limited. Only once could he ever get a LMG; they were protecting B Co Hq. HMGs were protecting 1/Bn Hq.

Sgt Gaskell was killed that day, precise circumstances unknown. Maybe he threw himself on a grenade to save others. Maybe he saved a supply party by grenading pillbox slots until the supply party passed and he was killed. That night, Conner's grenade rebounded from a tree to kill both Koustrop and him in the same hole.

On 7 Jan, a sniper bullet struck across S/Sgt Lockman's back and killed him. Gorishek was slain also, on 7 Jan.

On 8 Jan, "B" charged bayonets again. Aussie Gen GA Vasey permitted Doe to attack. While "C" hit Perimeter Q, Doe would strike where we had lost out on 5 Jan—against Perimeter R.

Aussie Hanson Troop's 25-pounder cannon first wasted 15 minutes' fire on Perimeters Q-R. Their only shells had delayed fuzes which penetrated the ground and often even failed to explode. Our charge was a walk with bayonets and no whistle.

Our charge stopped instantly in thick jungle brush only 25 yards from Jap MGs. Marly in 2/Pln heard heavy fire before his squad even left their holes. S/Sgt Eder of Weapons said that the Japs let us get only 5-10 feet from our holes before they blasted us. Backing 2/Pln's rush, Sgt Rubens found the men grounded, dead or wounded. Old-style long bayonets caught in vines when we raised them to fire. After first rush, McKenzie ordered our bayonets left behind.

With Pln/Sgt Henry "Boak" Wilson, McKenzie's 3/Pln started through E Co holed on our left flank. When Jap MGs opened up, we hit the ground. Moving on, we veered left to where McKenzie thought that we ought to pierce the Nippo lines. When Wilson sensibly objected, McKenzie withdrew 3/Pln to Musket.

"B" had 9 killed, 8 wounded, perhaps our highest total of any World War II fight. Dead were Russell, Genther, Foltz, Carroll, Sgt Holmes, and Cpls Irmen and Rogers. Nore died of wounds. We never found Berg's body—like McMeel's on 5 Jan. Besides Sgt Rubens reported shot in the right hand, wounded included Castillo, hit in shoulder and left hip; Laabs shot in left shoulder; Cpl Petrovich in left shoulder and arm. Shot in the hips was McFarland, Kjemhus in left hand, Martin right foot. Cawiezell's right ear drum was traumatically ruptured. After futile bayonet attacks, morale was low in Musket.

The Japs seemed to have an empenetrable cordon northwards. But why didn't Col Doe prepare our attacks with 37 mm guns or 81 mm heavy mortars? Sighting 37 mm guns into pillbox slits would have smashed the Jap crews. Instead, their shells blasted off tree-crowns concealing snipers above Musket Perimeter. In our final assuaults, the 81s almost unaided blasted out surviving Jap perimeters. McKenzie felt that Doe and Hamilton reserved 37s and 91s to secure their Hqs.

Departing Aussie garrison had left us a 3-man outpost just 15 yards from the Nippos. McKenzie called it dangerous and worthless; Hamilton insisted on keeping it. We had to replace those 3 men every 24 hours to remain sane after long silence close to death. Every day, McKenzie had to point the way for one man at a time to and from these holes, but on 10 Jan, Hamilton sent him elsewhere. Relieving men that day, Sgt Fiscus died with a shot in the brain. Outpost was then abandoned.

"B" suffered horribly in water in our holes. McKenzie never remembered sleeping at all. For warmth, he sat back to back with his runner in a clammy pool—once bailed 200 consecutive helmets of water but failed to lower the level.

In 2 weeks, most of "B" had malaria, but a man had to have 103 degrees of temperature before hospital. Malaria or not, we had to hold Musket Perimeter.

McKenzie suggested that Hamilton should relieve a few men at a time into higher, dryer, parts of Musket for a few hours. They could dry out awhile and keep water-wrinkled hands able to handle a rifle. Hamilton replied, "Those men can stay out there 30 to 60 days if necessary. There is no limit to human endurance." But to save Hamilton himself from the danger of a Jap breakthrough, McKenzie finally prevailed on him to rotate men back to a few hours of heavenly dryness and warmth.

On 12 Jan, Australians' 3 tanks and 2 Bns failed to raise our Musket siege by storming Perimeters P south of us. Lt-Col, Hatsuo Tsukamoto's 3-inch shells smashed all 3 tanks. Aussie infantry casualties were 151—34 dead, 51 missing in action—with minor ground gains. Gen Eichelberger and the Aussie generals feared to attack again. They agreed the "P" would fall only after intense mortaring and constant harassing—slow work indeed through poisonous swamps.

But B Co triggered downfall of Perimeters P. About dawn 14 Jan, a "B" patrol found a sick Jap lying in bushes south of Musket. Some men wanted to kill him. In the nights, we had heard screaming that sounded like McMeel or Berg under Jap torture. McKenzie saved the Jap because Div Hq wanted to question him. When he fainted, we gave him a "C" ration. He actually broke off twigs for chopsticks to eat it! Sgt Wilson had to carry him part way down the Supply Trail. The prisoner told Div Hq that all able-bodied men had left "P" 2 days ago. Aussies and our 2/Bn at once liquidated "P" and slew 252. Sanananda Road was opened; Musket Perimeter siege was raised.

On 15 Jan, Hamilton told McKenzie's 3/Pln to strike Perimeter R again. But Col Doe ordered us to join other Cos east of Musket. No one told them that we were coming. "K" men believed that we were Japs—shot Sgt Wilson across upper lip and holed Sgt Pickett's pack before ceasing fire.

We learned that battered B Co was in reserve for A plus C's attack on Jap Perimeter S across Sanananda Road. Next day, on 16 Jan, A Co lost heavily in a deadly attack that failed across almost open terrain. But McKenzie and B Co did not know of A's failure. He was wrongly told that A and C Cos together had won Perimeter S already; we had only to mop up. He was to lead 3/Pln in single file into "S".

But McKenzie had learned to doubt every order. Halting 3/Pln and all B Co, he probed forward with Bermudez and Sgt Lee. Jap fire cracked at them, they never knew how they managed to escape alive.

Angrily Hamilton rushed up to lead "B" forward instead of McKenzie. McKenzie gripped Capt Hamilton by the shoulders, turn him back—and surely saved his life.

Now the truth came out about 163's attack that morning. A Co's CO told Lt-Col Lindstrom of 1/Bn that this attack would fail. Lindstrom relieved him. C Co's Capt Van Duyn also refused to attack but was not relieved. A Co pushed alone and failed—with 9 killed and 37 other losses.

McKenzie then volunteered to lead 3/Pln beside the Jap lines and contact A Co still facing the Japs. Jamilton attached S/Sgt Johnson's 2/Pln to fight under McKenzie's command. But just a minute or two before the jump-off, Hamilton suddenly withdrew 2/Pln from the fight—without informing McKenzie. Johnson rose up to call to ascertain that his last man was out—and died form a bullet in his head.

Still unaware of 2/Pln's withdrawal, McKenzie's 3/Pln was now in place before the Jap perimeter. Heavy fire lashed us. Set up on left flank, S/Sgt Eder's LMG could not draw fire enough from the Japs to help us. Like Johnson, 3/Pln's Cpl Lingle died with a bullet in the head. BARman Cpl Morin got his death-wound—a bullet through nose and left eyebrow. Marly and Blumenthal tried to save Morin. A Jap slug in the spine paralyzed Blumenthal who died 10 days later. Trying to tell McKenzie that dead Johnson's Pln had gone, Runner Hapke died a few feet from the Lt. With 2/Pln's help, we might have surprised and routed the Japs. After 2/Pln left, we were lucky that the Japs did not wipe us out. Only in semi-darkness could our 3/Pln escape the Japs.

Next day, 17 Jan, McKenzie and Sgt Lee guided officer observers to where they watched the Jap lines just 20 yards off. By their perimeter size, McKenzie estimated that it held 150 Japs on the side where we had attacked the day before. An Aussie veteran observer advised mortars and an attack at once.

So on 18 Jan, we were promised a barrage—81 mm mortars for the first time. Although 90 rounds were promised, just 30 fired—total misses near unburied Johnson. Attack failed.

On 19 Jan, "B" kept fighting—with a Pln-sized Co. On 20 Jan, Plotts was hit in right leg, and Goricks by "shrapnel" in right leg also. Medic Abbott would die of wounds 2 days later.

On 21 Jan, came finally the 81 mm barrage McKenzie had long wanted—2,000 rounds preparing a 4-Co attack on Perimeter S. B's Burnham took fragments in right arm, left side of face; Henninger was shot in left leg. Compa was killed; Beck died of wounds. But we slew the Japs in droves and seized Perimeter S. Still, on 23 Jan, Estes was shot in right arm, other circumstances unknown.

In B Co's Sanananda Battle, we began wtih 187 men, but ended with 21 on duty. We lost at least 27 killed, 27 wounded, and 112 out with malaria. All 163 Inf had just 96 dead, but over 25 per cent of those dead from "B". In all of our attacks, we had just one mortar blast of 30 wasted rounds. So much for bayonet charges that never touched a Jap! For Good Soldier McKenzie and others, these are proud but bitter memories.

Surely Lt. McKenzie's excellent history explains why B Co lost 27 out of 96 men killed in action in 163 Inf's Battle of Sanananda. Prime credit is due to McKenzie's letters dated 8 Aug, 14 Sept, 3 Oct, and 23 Oct all in 1984, plus additional notes in 1984. I used also official Casualty Lists, and Dr. Samuel Milner's Victory in Papua (where Milner does not contradict McKenzie). We owe a great debt to B 163's Cpl Bernard Marley who contacted McKenzie by phone and letter and helped to break his 41 years of silence.

Photo below: Papua. Sanananda Area. A native boy saw a Japanese run into a dugout from where he immediately opened fire at Australians carrying ammunition towards the front line at Buna. The Australians were some distance away and could not decide exactly the position of the Japanese. Keeping the dugout under observation the native boy told three Americans who crept up to the dugout and ordered the Japanese to come out. When he did not do so they killed him with machine gun and rifle fire. This picture shows the Americans after they had entered the dugout. One keeps his Tommygun ready to fire in case the Japanese was pretending to be dead. (Courtesy of Rohlffs)

146 FA AND 2/BN 163 INF:

Bongao and Sanga Sanga Islands

by DR. HARGIS WESTERFIELD, DIVISION HISTORIAN
and 146 FA'S CAPT ROBERT ALLEN

A Prime source was 6-page typescript entitled only "D-Day," attributed to Capt Robert Allen. Used also but often vague and sketchy were 2/Bn 163's "Narrative Report," with "Casualty List," and 5-page "Journal." I also cited 163 Regt's April, 1945, Morning Report. Important data also were from Sulu White Task Force Field Order No. 1, Lt-Col Alfred Hintz' "V-4 Sulu White/Sanga Island," and Award Stories of Ernest Cortez and Herman Stier. Background came from RR Smith's **Triumph in the Philippines, Reports of General MacArthur/Japanese Operations in the South-West Pacific,** *and* **Terrain Study No.102/Sulu Archipelago** *(from Allied Geographical Section, SW Pacific, Area 1). G 163's great CO Buck Braman first suggested this story to me by his gifts of F.O. No. 1, a map of Bongao Island, and an Air Command Sketch of Bongao. We have only one more FA story left to publish: 218 FA's second history of the Wakde Operation. We want more FA stories!*

At 0800 31 Mar 1945, Btry B 146 FA and 2/Bn 163 Inf with attachments sailed from Zamboanga City to seize Sanga Sanga Island Strip and Bongao Island that guarded the Strip. Some 200 miles SW of Zambo City at the west end of the Sulu Archipelago, these islands held an estimated 500-man Jap garrison who might reinforce Jolo, where 163 would soon attack. Capturing these islands would cut off a night escape route by small craft from Jolo into Borneo. To assist the coming Aussie invasion of oil-rich Borneo, Sanga's all-weather coral strip was needed by our 13 Air Force.

Our Sulu White Task Force made an imposing small convoy. Destroyers *Phillip* and *Waller* and at least 4 LCIs protected us from suicidal attacks by small launches. Overhead was cover from Marine Detachment A, 419 Night-Fighter Squadron; we might expect frequent sneak-plane attacks. We also carried a Pln of Btry C 202 AckAck, a 116 Combat Engr Pln, B Co 658 Amphib Tractor Bn, some 116 Bn Medics, and 12 Portable Station Hospital. We took A Co 873 Aviation Engr Bn to work on the Strip.

At 0600 2 Apr, we sighted our beach, in Sanga Sanga Bay. Less than a year ago, in June 1944, an enormous Nippo Combined Fleet had assembled at the great deepwater anchorage south of nearby Tawi Tawi with plans to wipe out our Division on Biak. Nakajima sea-planes had based near Bongao. Sanga Strip had teemed with planes. But the Jap fleet and Air Force had broken themselves in battle for Leyte and Luzon. Now the sea was bare of any ships but ours. For 10 days before our landing, Marine and Army planes had pounded the beaches with 500-lb bombs and strafing. PT boats had shot up coastal targets.

Thus we drew no Jap fire on 1 Apr. Destroyers' guns were silent. Our 4 support LCIs—2 mortar craft, 2 rocket craft—held fire. We feared to endanger Filipino guerillas already holding Sanga Sanga. In 3 years' valiant struggle, they had laired in the wilderness of large Tawi Tawi Island just across channel from Sanga Sanga where our submarines had supplied them. Their observers had radioed submarines in to sink ships of the Japs' Combined Fleet. From Tawi Tawi had fared guerilla supplies and men to build up the harassed freedom fighters of Jolo.

Rough seas and the reef delayed our Amtracks' landing for 40 minutes. About 0930, F Co beached with a section each of H Co's mortars and HMGs. Forming a line 1,000 yards inland north of the Strip, "F" tied in with E Co and another "H" HMG section protecting our right flank.

Guerillas happily guided our 2/Bn staff from the beach to Filipino-Spanish Col Suarez' HQ near the Strip. The son of a Spanish father and a Tiruray mother, this fine Moro Col was somewhat taller and lighter in color than other Filipinos. He said that a Jap force of 100-175 had fled from Sanga Sanga cross the narrow channel to Bongao Island, that rocky little chunk of low mountains. instead of 500 Jap Marines, the garrison was probably 300. Already our striking force of G and E Cos with an "H" HMG section was forming to take Bongao.

Btry B 146 FA's guns were being landed. For freedom to maneuver offshore, they were lashed onto landing barges, one gun to a barge, with two FA men in charge. LSMs had towed them through the Sulu Sea. These barges now cast off from their LSMs and hit the reef before the beach.

Tractors easily dragged the guns across calm water 3-4 feet deep between reef and land. Then a mud-hole bogged them down. A DC-4 bulldozer had to heave tractor-teams up the slope. Not until 0930 were 146's guns ready to fire.

Bongao Island is small and roughly oblong, some 4,500 miles east-west by 3,000 yards north-south—some 4 square miles. A narrow spit some 800 yards long curves from its NE corner. North coast was then rice paddies and some fields. Southern two-thirds is cliffs and dense jungle rising to Bongao Peak (1030 ft) on the SW, and Kabogan Peak (706 ft) on the SE. Connected by a low saddle, these jungled peaks made a formidable wilderness. Six years ago, island population had been only 975.

A March Air Force recon had noted 3 AA positions on high ground near the spit beside Bongao Town and 3 more AAs and 3 37 mms in the southern mountains. We never accounted for all of those guns.

About 1300, understrength G, E, and H Co men deployed on Sanga Sanga for the 500-yard Amphtrack dash across channel to Bongao Island. We chose to hit a probably undefended area 1,000 yards east of Bongao Channel's western exit. Across the channel, we saw rugged Bongao Peak and dark jungle below.

After Marine air strikes at suspected AA positions above Bongao town and on Bongao Peak, the Navy barraged our landing site. While our Amphtracks' guns raked the foreshore, G Co was borne across Bongao Channel at 1330, with no casualties.

Then "G" guarded E's and H's crossings. G Co cut the east-west trail to the south and patrolled the overgrown trail to Pahut Village on Sibutu Passage, but found no Japs. Scouting 100 yards south, "E" saw 5 Japs, killed 1. All outfits dug night perimeters at a 4-trail crossing. At 1630, a few Jap mortar shells impacted harmlessly.

Back on Sanga Sanga meanwhile, ineffective Jap 20 mm fire struck from the Bongao spit at 146 FA's pilot Lt Parks with driver and mechanic assembling a Piper Cub. Some 20 mm fire hit our unloading ships but without casualties. By 1500, Parks was flying above Bongao to guard our infantry until night.

About 2130 that night, "G" men in holes saw 7 Japs come at us down the trail from Bongao Town, probably trying to escape into the mountains. We killed all 7. We found new rifles with them, plenty of ammo, and a radio in good condition.

Next morning, "G" and "E" patrolled from their cross-trails perimeter. East towards Bongao Point, "G" found Jap food and medicines scattered all along the trail. We checked deserted trucks, empty mess-halls and barracks, undefended cement pillboxes. At the edge of Bongao Town, a silent 40 mm gun was in position.

Scouting southwards, "E" drew fire from Kabogan Peak but worked around it and probably penetrated through the low pass between Kabogan and Mt Bongao, to the south shore. "E" then rounded the coast NE to contact G's Bongao town patrol.

The Japs struck as hard as they could, ambushed a FA wire-party coming from Sanga Sanga with its FA guides and infantry guards. Hidden Jap rifles caught us in an open flat, wounded Btry B's Dillard, Cpl Lisuzzo. Other casualties probably were H Co's: Zoumandakis, Sgt Fralin—and Legleiter, who died of wounds. While others hugged the earth, H's Cpl Cortez rose to give aid to one of these wounded and carry him to safety.

Some die-hard Japs were still on Bongao Point. About 1530, a twin Jap 20 mm gun made light hits on 2 LCMs unloading supplies back on Sanga Sanga. Capt Wilkins, Lt Parks emplaned, caught the gun still firing, killed it with a direct 105 mm hit. With HE and time fuze, we silenced 2 more guns nearby. About 2100 that night, Lt Simpson's gunners saw lights in the same position, put them out with time-fire.

We first had to find and kill 2 Jap 20 mm guns on Hill 101 north of the peak. To pinpoint the guns, FA men had to climb to the top of Hill 101 itself to sight the guns below. Lt Simpson, Lt Swanson, S/Sgt Remme, Cpl Westerman, a Marine observer scouted to the unguarded top of the hill.L

After setting up defenses, we marked the guns with our shells, then killed them with a 27-plane Marine air-strike. Then G Co with the observers overran the hill and 706-foot Kabogan Peak, but found only a wounded Jap, who escaped. G's 2 Plns wisely did not follow any one of the many trails leading into deep ravines where the Japs were surely in ambush. On 5 Apr, a Formosan prisoner led an E Co patrol and FA observers back up Mt Kabogan. He said that he knew where 300 Japs hid in a cave. Climbing the SE slope first, we then crossed to the SW slope. This Formosan—a civillian laborer—showed us a mountain rift with sheer cliffs on both sides. Japs guarded it at both ends. Fearing that the prisoner had led us into a trap, "G" withdrew and did not fight. Before 11340, E Co had caught 7 Japs in the cliffs and killed 4. E's Smard was wounded some time this 5 Apr.

On 6 Apr, 163's Maj Munkres and 146's pilot Park flew over Kabogan's NW slope to adjust fire. At 0920, 100 H Co's 81 mm mortar shells and 142 shells of 146 FA impacted the area. Then 163's men moved up to the base of the NW slope, but got no farther. Jap riflemen slipped back into the impact area and fired down on us. Our men were too valuable to waste.

The Japs were now certainly at bay in the mountains, and all their 20 mm or 40 mm machine cannon out of action. We never found any of their alleged 37 mm guns. The Japs seemed to have sufficient ammo and food, but they lacked enough water on little Bongao where there was just one small stream on the south shore. Guerillas could readily replace our ground troops, outpost the water-points and harass the Japs to extinction. By 1700 on 6 Apr, all our troops were gone to Sanga Sanga.

But next day, 7 Apr, there were again small actions on Bongao. A 7-man souvenir-hunting party of Engrs met an ambush. Perhaps 2 were wounded; but 3-4 others died. We do not know what outfit they belonged to—but probably not A 116.

On 7 Apr also, a small "F" patrol from Sanga Sanga covered Pahut Village and Tampat Point on SW Bongao. Three-fourths of the way up Mt Pajar (660 ft), we drew rifle-fire, and returned to Sanga Sanga. B 146 marked the area; Marine bombers hit Pajar with 3 out of 8 Napalm bombs that they dropped in that area. "F" had killed 2 Japs somewhere on that patrol.

Then most of the Sulu White Force embarked on 10 Apr to help our 163 in the Battle of Jolo. F Co remained to protect Marine Engrs expanding the Strip. Remained also 12 Portable Hospital, and a detachment of Amphib Engrs for water transport.

Bongao still had a tragic finale—found only in a terse entry dimly read on a microfilm Morning Report in Federal Archives. On Bongao on 15 Apr, an "F" patrol met an ambush under mortar, MG, and small arms fire. Killed were Ash, Girardo, Bloomquist, Conner. F Co had to send a reinforced Pln to recover Conner's body at 1430. Seriously wounded were Garner, Stites, Brady, Quattrocki.

And what became of Bongao's Jap garrison, Marines of 33 Naval Guards, overestimated as 500 strong when Sulu White Force landed? Originally 4,400 had occupied Tawi Tawi on 1 May 1944 to secure this great Jap fleet base and war viciously with the guerillas of Col Suarez. After the Jap Combined Fleet departed, 3,700 went to Zambo to fight well against us, until we annihilated them. Some 300 died in their tenacious defense of Mt Daho on Jolo. The remainder held the Bongao area beside the larger 25 Independent Mixed Regiment, part of the Jap 37 Army of eastern Borneo. When 25 Regt withdrew to Borneo, the Guards were left to die alone.

Instead of 500, they were then only 250 strong—3 groups, Infantry, Engrs, and Air Ground troops. Under harassment of guerillas and our planes, they were down to 200 by 26 Apr, with diminishing rations and critically short of water. Next day, they tried to escape in various hidden craft across 40 miles of Sibutu Passage into Borneo. Our planes and surface craft—presumably PT boats—killed all but 24 whom our naval-air personnel rescued. Only 16-17 arrived in Sandakan to continue military service.

By 2 May, Marine Engrs had lengthened the 2,800-foot coral Strip on Sanga Sanga to 5,000 feet. Fighter planes of 13 Air Force based there for close support of Aussie landings in Borneo. By mid-May, Royal Aussie planes had replaced our American planes to continue supporting raids on Borneo.

About 20 May, an LST brought back soldiers of 93 Inf Div to relieve homesick F Co to rejoin 163 Inf at Zambo. Most of us gladly said farewell to the sheer red cliff of Bongao above the harbor.

And surely by the end of 1946, little Bongao Town was rebuilt and carrying on business as usual. The third port in the Sulus after Jolo and then Siasi ports, it had exported dried fish and railroad ties. It was another Moro town much like Taluksangay of Zambo City. From the little pier, a broad path led into the single street on piles above the water. Chinese shops lined both sides of the street. We are happy that we liberated Bongao Town.

Such is the story of B 146 FA's and 2/Bn 163 Inf's Sulu White Operation. It was a necessary task, to subdue still potentially dangerous men of 33 Naval Guards. A veteran combat team had carefully planned this action in order to conserve every available soldier for the infighting which we expected in attacking the Japanese Home Islands.

162 INFORMATION & RECON PLN ON BIAK:

Last Days of 1/Lt Myron Folson

**by DR. HARGIS WESTERFIELD, DIVISION HISTORIAN
with John Justin Smith, Arnold Nierman, and Al Grauerholz**

> CREDIT: Personal stories are from Smith's letter of 5 Jan and 21 Nov 1977, and 9 Jan 1978; Grauerholz' letters of 24 Apr 1963, and 10 and 18 Jan 1978—with Ray Russell's letter of 10 Jan 1961. In a voice thick and pained with throat cancer, Nierman phoned 1 May 1978. Nierman died shortly after this phone call. For background, I used 162 Inf's Biak Casualty List and Narrative and Journal with 41st Div Training Note 9 of 14 Oct 1944. Where Nierman contradicted this Training Note, I took Nierman's word as authoritative. History of Folsom's I & R in the Salamaua Operation appeared in **Jungleer** for Mar 1963, and also in **The Fighting Jungleers**.

When 162 Inf landed on Biak 27 May 1944 and started to penetrate Parai Defile, 1/Lt Folsom's I & R vets led the recon and fighting. While some of us scouted the high flanking cliffs, 162's "point of the point" was Folsom', Nierman, and John Justin Smith scanning beach and brush and Mokmer Road for the first Jap fighters.

Folsom said, "We must keep the Regiment advancing." This was the way the athletic and saintly Folsom talked to his devoted men. "Must" was the strongest word that he ever used.

And keep the Regiment advancing we did. About 1115, we sighted perhaps a squad of Japs in the Defile just east of a steep limestone cliff. When our Navy blasted, these Japs retreated westward. We had begun that obscure first day's battle for Parai Defile. It was a battle that even frontline men have a hard time remembering—because of the disastrous next 2 days.

In that first day's fight down Parai Defile, I&R contacted Japs 13 times, but we do not remember in what order the contacts came.

Slipping along the coast road to a rise in the ground, Scout Smith confronted a Jap scout with rifle at port. Luckily, the Jap's rifle was on safety; Smith killed him before the safety came off. (Later, Smith learned that the Jap never had a chance. Japs orders were to carry the rifle loaded but locked at all times. The safety rod of his .25 rifle was knurled and behind the bolt. To unlock that rifle, a man's sweaty, nervous hand had to push in knurled rod, turn it, then let it spring out. God pity a Jap with this safety!)

Another time, a rifleman in a tree shot at Smith. Firing downward requires special technique of leading a target. The Jap missed; Smith killed him in the tree.

Once an I&R man glimpsed 2 Japs in the brush at a road-bend in the Defile. Not knowing how many more Japs were with them, we called up riflemen from our following Co—probably "L." With their help, we fusilladed and slew 2 men hiding by their MG.

Our most spectacular shoot-out occurred where the coast-road disappeared and we had to walk the sand because the ridges came down to the water's edge. The slopes had eroded into little caves—great places for unwary men to get killed.

Our lead scout looked into a cave and saw a Jap foot with a boot on it. One volunteer I&R man lobbed in a grenade. Then we ran back to where the other two men waited in the sand, with their fingers on triggers.

An officer charged out and swung up his saber with the ight light flashing on his blade. We shot him down. Next arged an enlisted man in meticulous uniform. We shot m down. Another charged behind him and was shot down, and another and another. All charged in single file—men larger than usual—perhaps Jap Marines. We slew all 15 who came out.

Still unsure of how many other Japs lurked in those caves, we called for help from the sea. Nearby floated an LCI with racks of rockets. Using an improvised kind of elementary arm-semaphore, Smith signalled to the LCI to open fire. Dozens of rockets blasted the cave. The hillside collapsed and buried the dead Japs and possibly some live one—even the officer's saber that Smith had coveted.

These 5 were the most remembered of I&R's 13 contacts when 162 Inf penetrated Parai Defile that first day on Biak. All 13 times, I&R succeeded in encountering these Japs without losing a single wounded man. We lost no men partly because of our experiences under Folsom with New Guinea scouts like Tapioli at Salamaua. There were other reasons for our safety: the alert quickness of our scouting, and the ferocity of our support from Navy, Air Force, FA, and tanks. In all 162 Inf that day, we had only 1 killed and 6 wounded—against a total of 16 known dead Japs. These men were from 3/Bn 222 Inf and 14 Division Shipping Unit—these last perhaps the "Marines" slain the cave. In those encounters, Smith had fired an entire bandolier of .30 shells—in a front-line "Hogan's Alley."

Regimental records say that 162 Inf with heavy fire support battled the Japs just 4 times—at 1115, 1235, 1400, and 1450. But our 13 encounters tell more accurately the deadly tale of 162's first day in Parai Defile.

That night, I&R still had a holiday attitude on Biak. A disliked officer wanted to hole up with I&R for greater protection, but we kept him out of our diggings. He did hole up nearby, and we spent the night alarming him against creeping Japs who never attacked.

But with daybreak 29 May, our mission began to look grim. Worried because most of 162's front was constricted back in the Defile, Col Haney ordered us to move faster. To save time, he withdrew I&R's right flank scout because he had to slow us down when he checked out the rough land edging Parai cliffs. Short, slender, dynamic Haney rebuked Smith for protesting. Haney had lain sleepless last night.

On this 2B May, Smith evidently scouted with 2/Bn's G Co which moved westward along a terrace behind L and M Cos. We were to the right rear above 3/Bn's main attempt to capture Mokmer Strip from the Beach Road. Above us were jungle- covered cliffs which had never been secured.

Within 30 minutes after Haney rebuked him, Smith was down on his face with the forward elements of probably G Co, under a heavy barrage of MGs and mortars. Fire came from where that right flank guard should have been.

At first we were safe below the MGs' trajectory. Beside probably S/Sgt Cassidy of G Co, Smith tried to crawl up with others to kill the MGs. Mortars impacted nearby. A fragment struck a "G" man in his cartridge belt and exploded the shells in it, clip by clip. This man and others died.

Shortly, someone came up behind Smith and crashed his leg with a sledge-hammer—so Smith thought when the mortar- fragment whammed him. Frightened Smith slit open his pants-leg; blood squirted out 6 inches at a squirt from his thigh. In seconds seeming minutes, he got the bandage from his first-aid packet and pressed it hard into his leg. It took 3 minutes to stop the intense bleeding.

By now, Smith was alone in the quiet with the dead under Parai Cliffs. Others had pushed ahead, or retreated. He crawled more than a mile to 2/Bn Hq Medic Sparrage who tied up his thigh and said, "I told you you were going to get in trouble with that I&R Pln."

Jeeped back to a Portable Hospital on the beach, Smith had a visit from Folsom that evening. "What some guys will do to get out of combat!" he joked and shook hands and wished well to Smith. Smith long remembered that simple goodbye, for 2 days later, Folsom lay dead under Jap MGs above Mandom.

To CO 1/Lt Grauerholz of SV Co, Folsom seemed to foreshadow his coming death. He said, "All I know to do is just go out and look and see everything I can and come back and tell Regiment what I saw. And I'll keep going until they get me." Next day, Grauerholz saw an I&R Sgt bring the bad news to 162's Exec, Lt-Col Bailey.

Folsom's death-patrol occurred because 2 previous patrols could not locate Japs' positions in the dark ridges above Mandom Water-Hole. Jap rifle-fire or small raiding parties from the ridges constantly harassed our men at 162's water-point there. When our patrols moved into the ridges 700 yards north of Mandom, mortar and automatic fire had halted them.

On 31 May, Folsom sought those positions with a 9-man carrying carbines and tommies. A captured Javanese (or possibly Korean) guided us. Nierman and the Javanese went first; Peel and Folsom followed. Other patrol members included Gene Sullivan, Svagdis, Thodoropoulos, Ray Russell, Sczpanski, John D. Williams. Nierman, the Javanese, Peel, and Folsom moved far ahead of the others.

Past CN 162's outguards at Mandom Water-Hole, we climbed the first of 6 ridges between us and the Jap heights. We filed over 4 low, sharp ridges through dense rain-forest. Only a little thin soil covered the coral bedrock in places, but trees grew close and slender and tall—8 to 20 inches thick and 100-150 feet high.

On these first ridges, we found no Japs—only Biak jungle silence and heat as we slipped ahead silently—carbines and tommies ported, finger near trigger. We sweated in the shady brush cutting off the light breezes. Outcrops and rolls of slippery loose rocks underfoot tried to trip us. Loose stones might roll under us. We scouted up dangerous crests, wound down into 50 feet deep. Laboriously we climbed 4 crests, still thinking ourselves unobserved.

About Ridge 4, we began hearing Jap talk around us, but saw nobody. Our Javanese guide now led, with Folsom, then Nierman and Peel close behind. Five men patrolled after us, for visual contact with Folsom's group and for flank security. Back on Ridge 4, 2 men stopped to guard our rear and give cover if Japs attacked.

Topping Ridge 5, the Javanese said that he saw 2 Japs sitting at a tree-base. Still hearing Jap voices nearby, Folsom, Nierman, Peel, and the Javanese stood a little off the trail to map what we had observed.

Nierman thought that we were far enough into deadly Jap country. He said that we ought to turn back, but Folsom ordered us to move farther up the trail.

Now Folsom was first in line, the Javanese in a jungle suit second, and Nierman third. Folsom followed the guide. Both bent low in the foliage to tread the trail which was the only concealed route of approach.

From 2 emplacements a short distance left of the trail, Jap MGs lashed out. A burst in the chest killed Folsom instantly. We returned some fire, and threw a few grenades to blast the brush nearby. But heroic Folsom of Salamaua lay dead: Black-eyed Folsom the handsome all-American boy—a Roman Catholic whose friends described him as "saintly." We could not bring out his body then, but we could map the terrain for revenge.

Cover and concealment were meager on these heights. Jap movements in the brush revealed the 2 positions where Folsom was shot from. One MG was emplaced on a knob left of the trail. Another gun flanked it on the left, a bit lower downslope.

But these positions were only part of a large Jap semi-perimeter. Left of these guns, Gun No. 3 guarded a ridge gap. Left again, Gun No. 4 was on the shoulder of the gap. Gun No. 5 was on the left flank of these 4 guns, north across the second ridge from them. On the right of the trail, Nos. 6, 7, and 8 guarded it and secured the right flank of the semi-perimeter—3 guns on 3 different ridges. No guns protected the rear of this semi-circle of positions, but they were unnecessary in this phase of the Battle of Biak.

While we sadly reported the death of great Folsom to 162 Hq, the Javanese guide reappeared. He was smiling all over his face. We thought that the Jap gunners had spared him because he was in collusion with them. We still believe that he decoyed Folsom forward to his death under Jap fire. We threatened to kill him. Nierman took the man by the throat an roughly led him to the prisoners' stockade. We heard that the Javanese died trying to escape.

But we could not bring out Folsom for days. Heavy and accurate fire must be laid on the positions which we occupied later without casualties.

Mjr Caulfield led the party who recovered Folsom. In Folsom's fatigue jacket, we found the silver bars of a captain, which Caulfield had presented him because Folsom would soon have been promoted to that rank.

Many of 162's officers and men attended Folsom's funeral. Borne on a hospital stretcher, and wrapped in a wrinkled poncho, the body seemed unbelievably small to SV Co's CO, 1/Lt Grauerholz, his close friend. We stood in a hollow square while the bugle played "Taps." We buried him at the base of the coral reef near Mandom. Such were the final ceremonies for Great Scout Myron Folsom, hero of the Salamaua Operation, who died at the head of his patrol on Biak, 31 May 1944.

An Australian climbing to a Japanese observation post built by the Japanese to direct the fire of two 3-inch naval guns against Allied troops advancing on Buna. Australians captured the guns and observation post, then used the observation post to direct the fire of the 25-pounders. (Courtesy of Rohlffs)

1/Bn 163 INF AT ZAMBOANGA:
PASANANCA AND THE RESERVOIR PERIMETER
BY DR. HARGIS WESTERFIELD, DIVISION HISTORIAN

> **CREDIT:** Basic for this history are letters of 1/Bn Hq Co's Clifton James (8 Nov 1978), A's Clifton James—different from the other James—(3 Oct 1968, Robert "Ace" Helman (30 Oct 1968), B's Art Merrick (5 April, 9 July, 7 Sept, 23 Nov—all 1979), and C's George Irish (9 Oct 1976). Only Hq Co's James gave almost full coverage of his Co's action. Other writers gave scattered but important details of their Cos. I used these Federal Archives: March 1945 Morning Reports, 163 Inf Journal, First Bn S-1 Journal, 146 FA's Capt Robert Allen's "Zamboanga Recaptured", and "Atrition in Pasananca"—with 716 Tank Bn's "A Co on Zamboanga-Jolo." Also I examined Award stories of Byron Cline, Nicholas De Serio, Gordon Foster, Raymond Heinitz, George Irish, James Kent, Francis Madden, Joseph Seiler, Clarence Stout, and Harvey Stuart. Now won't one of your readers give me story of A, B, C, or D Cos—or other stories of 162, 163, 186 or any FA outfits at Zambo? (James' story of Hq Co 1 Bn was No 115 in Dec 1979 Jungleer.)

This is the saga of 1/Bn 163 Inf's Zamboanga Battle in the overgrown Tumaga River coconut groves, against the Jap Marines of 33 Naval Guard and 54 Independent Mixed Brigade's FA. Beaching after air-strikes and 162's first waves, 1/Bn landed at San Mateo, under light Jap FA and mortar fire. As his LCI grounded, Hq runner James thought that all the Jap 20 mm guns in Zambo were firing around us.

Despite more FA and mortar fire after we landed, 1/Bn's casualties were light, because we were at first in Division Reserve. By 1535, we had perimetered at the east end of Wolfe Strip. In C Co., fragments wounded Eyre in right thigh, Mahl in right hand.

On 11 Mar., next day, our real war began. At 1050, a Jap shell near Hq CP wounded 1/Bn's CO, Maj Alfred, killed Reichenberger. Later, 2/Lt. Seiler died. He had risked himself the day before to deploy vitally needed vehicles of supplies. That shell also wounded Leach, S/Sgt. Duvall, T/4s Barnes, Barnard; and T/5 Kisser.

With Maj Kent CO now, 1/Bn crossed Baliwasan River, east towards combat. NE of us, near Santa Maria, F Co took heavy fire: mortars, 20 mm machine-cannon. At 1430, 1/Bn relieved 'F.' With 146 FA help, we smashed the Japs' first Line. Hq Co's 1/Lt Foster killed a Jap 20 mm gun too close to us.

The Japs fell back to their already fortified line 200 yards to the area, and we made perimeter against a possible night counter-attack. That day, A Co lost Boguslav seriously wounded, and Stricland and S/Sgt Joe Smith lightly wounded. Lightly injured in action were McRae and Cavanaugh. D Co's Cunat was lightly wounded.

That night in C Co, nervous green men threw grenades at carabao who blew booby-traps. One grenade blew the leg off an unnamed man. Our grenades panicked another soldier; he dashed from his hole across the perimeter. A guard killed him because he seemed like a Jap in the dark. Killed also were Boyle, Rothchild—and Haught seriously wounded.

On 12 Mar, 1/Bn faced our strongest defenses since Idbi Picket. Some 2,000 men of 33 Naval Guard (Marines) were entrenched behind barbed wire, with 20 mm cannon, 75s, mortars, MGs—invisible in 4 miles of coconut jungle from Santa Maria to Pasanaca. We must draw their fire to find them.

At 1010 A Co advanced with our right flank on Tumaga River, and B Co left of 'A.' (And 2/Bn advanced on our left flank west of Route 8-A.) At once, small arms and moderate FA fire hit us. Passing through Santa Maria, 'A' and 'B' took a heavy FA barrage about 1200. B Co viciously slew a Jap observer team directing cannon fire on us. By 1230, 'B' met HMG fire. Perhaps then, 2/Lt De Serio had a scout seriously wounded. Directing fire to pinpoint 2 Jap positions, De Serio crawled over open ground and rescued the scout.

B Co had to call for 3 tanks; they evidently sashed pill-boxes before us. Meanwhile on B's right, 'A' evidently quelled their Japs with mortars and bazookas and would have advanced at 1510. But a pillbox held up B's right flank, with a Jap crossfire from the left where 2/Bn was held up.

That night, A Co on B's right hand had to set up in an isolated perimeter. On that 12 Mar, 1/Bn had made only 400 yards through coconut groves from the south to north of Santa Maria. 'B' lost most men. When 1/Lt Starr led his Pln up a draw, a HMG or 20 mm shell struck him. We luckily saved him. Killed that day were Frazier, Sgt Immerman, with Flaig to die of wounds 14 Mar. Besides Starr, Sgt Coop was seriously wounded; Czarnick, Humphreys, Fishman, and Zapp slightly wounded. T/Sgt Davis of Hq Co was seriously wounded; T/5 Stern slightly wounded. 'A' lost Collins, lightly wounded.

Fighting for both Bns, 716 Bn's tanks had killed 6 20 mm guns, several MGs. And 146 FA had 2 direct hits on Jap 75s. After all-night harassment, 146 FA reported a great decrease in Jap FA fire.

But on 13 Mar, the day of Blow-Out Hill, 1/Bn had hard fighting. Our first action that day was easy. A 'B' patrol found a Jap position vacated 400 yards ahead; a Pln seized it. Without waiting for tanks, all 1/Bn advanced those 400 yards—on the way saw a dead 20 mm gun that had fired last night—a live clip still in the breach.

C Co mistakenly fired on 'B' ahead of them. When T/Sgt Yates of 'C' stopped his Co from more shooting, a Jap rifle killed him. Replacing 'B' on the front at 1048, 'B' lobbed mortars before 'A' and helped that Co to come up beside it.

C Co made 200 yards more. 2/Lts Worthly and Moore killed a 5-man pillbox crew. When we found a mined bridge over a little stream, AT Co deloused it for 2 tanks to cross.

Farther across the stream, both Bns fought for the hilly jungle just south of Pasanaca. Straddling Route 8-A to 2/Bn's right, C Co met heavy fire in a small farm area at a hill-base.

Supino was perhaps killed here, another man wounded. Crouched in a farm building, a scout pointed for 1/Lt Irish the Jap MG and supporting riflemen holding up 'C.' Irish called a bazooka team to come up, but a Jap rifle shot him through the groin. Capt. Houston bandaged him. The pillbox was later gutted.

About 1440, the Japs blew up a hill close to C's left flank among forward elements of E Co. Fragments flew 1500 feet high. For minutes, 'C' cringed under whole falling trees, stones, and clods. C's Burns embraced a tree for safety. Uhler was evacuated to die later of a broken neck. 'C' had to casualties that 13 Mar—but not all from Blow-Out Hill. Other 1/Bn men also suffered.

But no Jap offensive followed the explosion—perhaps because the heaviest destruction was on their side of Blow-Up Hill. On C's front, Burns and others heard loud, confused Jap voices. Burns turned a LMG on the sounds and heard anguished moans; but no attack followed.

Both Bns kept advancing. While 2/Bn got a foothold on the west ridge over Pasanaca, 1/Bn drove to the clearing just before the village. Taking fire from 3 sides, we recoiled to the woods and dug in. Our helping tanks that day had killed a 20 mm gun and a 40 mm gun for us.

In 1/Bn, 'C' was hurt worst on Blow-Up Hill day. Beside dying Uhler, these men were marked 'lightly injured:' Tyree, Ross, Tomaso, Favara, Siefert, Martinez, Mahl, Popp. Injured also were T/Sgts McKeller, Wronkiewicz, and S/Sgts Sarnowski, Pesavento. Kosola, Tegeler, Stewart were 'lightly wounded.' On C's right, A Co's Long and Sgt Hyde were killed, Phipps and Gilvin seriously wounded. Other wounded were Baker, Aikin, Buckner, Boc. In 'D,' Nyberg was lightly wounded and 4 lightly injured: Riggs, Olsen, Bradford, S/Sgt Neilson. Except for C's Uhler, we do not know which of these 3 dead and 26 other casualties were mine victims. ('A' did report that 4 of their 9 losses were from the mine, but did not name them.)

We had now located the Japs' main line. On 14 Mar, after 32 minutes' air bombs and FA, both Bns advanced at 0954. But in an hour, heavy fire stopped us from a Jap pillbox concentration. And 146 FA's Piper Cub spotted a high-velocity .75 cannon commanding Route 8-A into Pasanaca.

When 'C' called for tanks, one came, but could not find the Jap gun. Gould of 'C' offered to lead the tank in, but the tank returned with a report that Gould was killed. With his squad down under Jap fire, Sgt Stuart tried to guide the tank into its target. Stuart leaped before he could shelter at its side, 20 mm shells ricocheted from the steel and killed him. S/Sgt Madden then led the tank to silence the 20 mm gun and route a rumored 100 Japs in that area.

On that 14 Mar, B Co's Capt Merrick saw S/Sgt Leisnig die from a bullet in the head when he walked near the Co CP. B's seriously wounded were Franklin, and Anthony; Falcone and S/Sgt Lindl were lightly wounded. In 'C,' Lamphere was hit, to die on 15 Mar. Sgt Kocyon was seriously wounded; Lopez, Wheeler, and Tom lightly wounded; and Stanko lightly injured.

On that 14 Mar, 'B' claimed 1 700-yard advance. Coordinated with FA, planes, tanks, our pressure was getting results. By 1500, we heard explosions in Pasanaca!

The Japs were indeed leaving Pasanaca. On 15 Mar, first 1/Bn recon patrols reported no activity ahead. By 1350, word came that a small patrol, probably of C Co, had passed through the village on the right of Route 8-A. Probably this patrol found a badly burned 20 mm gun on the road, and the abandoned high-velocity .75 that had fired on us yesterday.

And before 1350, 1/Bn had already pushed on to our next objective after Pasanaca: to sieze Zamboanga City Reservoir and Power Station, 2 miles north. Still, we must overwhelm Japs on surrounding ridges—Japs with FA, mortars, 20 mm guns, MGs, and small arms. Our 146 FA fired 600 rounds that day.

An A Co patrol pressed for the Reservoir on our left, and a 'B' patrol on our right. B's patrol crossed Tumaga River—about 1.5 feet deep—and slew 3 Japs in a cave. By 1435, the 'A' and 'B' patrols contacted at the disused oval Reservoir. While 'B' secured the Reservoir, 'A' hunted farther and found a deserted emplacement with 3 silent .75s. Forty-five minutes later, all 1/Bn had followed the 2 patrols and had dug an oval perimeter around the Reservoir.

HQ men told A's Sgt James that a nearby tunnel was clear of Japs, but he checked it out with a flashlight. From the depths, 5 Japs rushed him. James hurled his light at them, fled for the tunnel mouth. But he tripped; they ran over him. An officer shot his pistol at James' stomach, but missed at 10 feet. The Japs disappeared into the brush.

Two silent Jap AA guns pointed skyward some distance from our perimeter, but a 'B' patrol returned uncertain whether Japs could still fire them. B's CO Merrick led a second patrol to enquire and found them harmless. From nowhere, a Jap bullet smashed the left lens of his glasses, deflected on the nose-piece, and splintered the right lens. Merrick escaped with a slightly bloody nose, glass fragments in his upper cheek. Besides Merreick, only casualties listed in 1/Bn on 15 Mar were Delrial of Hq slightly wounded, and C's Clarence Smith and Eramo also slightly wounded.

Reservoir Perimeter was an easy target, constricted under total observation from ridges on 3 sides up to 1,000 feet. At 0710 16 Mar, a vicious Jap 20 mm gun forced Maj Kent to dive for a hole, shells exploding at his heels. Two 'D' gunner failed to kill it with a HMG. AT Co's .57 recoilless cannon silenced the 20 mm with 4 rounds.

Assisted by a 20 mm gun and mortars, Japs reoccupied positions before an A Co Pln. Wounded to die later, 1/Lt Stout adjusted mortar fire on the Japs and destroyed them.

All day Jap fire continued. At 1425, a mortar shell blasted 1/Bn officers in council. A chest fragment killed Lt Call of 116 Engrs; C's Capt Houston was hit in the side to die later. B's Capt Merrick took a head wound; his runner Garcia survived in shock after he was blown off the ground.

In 1/Bn Hq, Maj Kent was wounded in both knees; runner Jones thrice in the head. Hurley was badly torn up, Exec Capt Skaugit wounded also. The Japs holed a rescue ambulance, but the 2 volunteer drivers loaded most casualties and escaped at 80 miles per hour.

Wounded Maj Kent remained to direct fire for an hour; S/Sgt Cline especially helped him. S/Sgt Heinitz laid new wire under mortar fire to assist Kent until shock forced Kent to give up command.

Besides Lt Stout killed 16 Mar, 'A' lost Curtis, Capell, and T/Sgt Dore lightly wounded. Besides Garcia and Capt Merrick wounded, 'B' had Blount seriously wounded. S/Sgt Snyder died in 'D.' Graychee was lightly injured, and 6 men lightly wounded: Huguley, Hunt, Parker, Richards, Serek. Total losses of 1/Bn were 4 dead, 15 wounded, 1 injured.

But the heavy shelling of 18 Mar was the Japs' last. FA, planes and 1/Bn's patrols were killing their most lethal weapons. On 17 Mar, 'B' killed 3 Japs, lost Higbon, S/Sgt Klingsporn seriously wounded. On 18 Mar, with 2/Bn on our left, we sortied from the Reservoir to drive the Japs off the ridges. Losing Brill killed before a Jap position, 'C' overran it with 2 tanks. On 20 Mar, 'B' used .81 mortars and tanks to help sieze Jap positions. At 2330 that night, knee mortars or small arms killed Born—with a fragment in his heart. Rasberry was killed, Andrew, Junior Brown, S/Sgt Michi lightly wounded. On 23 Mar, C's Hetterman was lightly wounded. By 23 Mar, 1/Bn's battered Cos were being relieved from action.

In 1/Bn 163's Zambo Battle of 1023 Mar, we had maybe 19 killed, 70 wounded against Jap 33 Naval Guards. their losses were far greater, but they made a tenacious defense—with our planes and tanks—and against heavier FA. Our 1/Bn 163 Inf had won probably our hardest battle.

New Guinea. Milne Bay. This monument has been erected in memory of officers and men who died defending Turnbull Field. The sign on the monument reads: "This marks the western-most point of the Jap. advance Aug.-Sep. 42. 85 unknown Jap. Marines Lie buried here." (Courtesy of Rohlffs)

186 INF and 532 ENGINEER BOAT & SHORE REGT: THE HOLLANDIA FIRE AND LAKE SENTANI
by DR. HARGIS WESTERFIELD, DIVISION HISTORIAN

Outstanding source is Amphibian Engineer Operations, which is Vol IV of "Engineer Operations in the Southwest Pacific/1941-1945." (I discovered this out-of-print volume while on a Division History Grant at Duke University's General Eichelberger Collection) Help comes also from RR Smith's Approach to the Philippines, which in turn relies heavily on "Reckless Task Force Report" of Hollandia Operation. Useful also was Terrain Handbook No 25 (New Guinea), of Allied Geographical Section, SW Pacific Area. I also used Karl Dod's The Corp of Engineers: the War Against Japan.

Surely the most important Jap victory against out 41st Div was the blast of just one aerial bomb on White Beach 1 at Hollandia. Ironically, jungle terrain forced us to lay out a perfect target for a lone plane to fire off our congested ammo and gas dumps on White Beach 1.

For Hollandia beaches were impossibly narrow for wartime landings. Best of those beaches, White Beach 1, was 800 yards long, but just 70 yards wide. Behind most of this Beach, a wide, water-logged mangrove swamp could never be a dump site—or even an exit road without heavy labor. Air photos had failed to reveal the swamp because the jungle hid it. And abandoned Nippo dumps were scattered too close on the dryer 70 yards of beaches. Our FA and AA batteries also took up space among the old Jap and new US supply dumps. A perfect target for a Nippo bomber was Hollandia's White Beach 1.

But we Amphibs—532 Engr Boat & Shore Regt—had to land cargoes of at least 7 LSTs before dark. Shortage of ships in New Guinea was too crucial to idle the LSTs for even a day. It was not sensible to risk cargoes in ships for a Nippo bomber. So the Shore Party of our Amphibs, the Naval Beach Party, and Cannon Cos. of 162 and 186 Inf unloaded all 7 LSTs before dark on D-Day, 22 Apr 1944. They drove off trucks, jeeps, and bulldozers, and off-landed 2625 tons of bulk cargo. Smaller craft lightered ashore the cargo form Australian Attack Transport Westralia.

Then White Beach 1 exploded and roared up in flame in our faces. In mellow tropical twilight just before dark, we heard a Jap bomber overhead. Flying through mountains, then too low above the beach for radar detection, it evaded out Act which never fired. Evidently guided by the light of a flaming Nippo dump, the plane loosed just 1 stick of 5 bombs on the north part of White Beach 1. Three bombs merely geysered up sand and water, but No 4 hit the edge of a Nippo ammo dump.

Instantly the dump exploded. Thundering blasts went on all around us. A Jap gas tank blew up. And an alleged "signal control mishap" let the plane escape without AckAck fire.

E co's Amphibs and other beach outfits desperately went to work. We tried to cut a fire-break—rolled gas drums away and carried off other supplies to make that break 30 yards wide down to the sea. Roller conveyors trundled other supplies to safety. Human chains passed other equipment out of immediate reach of flames.

At first, we seemed to confine the fire by this fire-lane. Then flames hit another ammo dump. When it exploded, bullets and metal fragments sprayed the beach. Some Amphibs were hurt; survivors fell back under the rain of death.

The fire leaped our 30-yard break and flamed new heaps of supplies. Flames raced from dump to dump. Again and again, explosions showered the beach with murderous missiles.

Although repelled by this flame-wall, we Amphibs worked frantically to save what we could. By now, all personal gear was lost. Vehicles burned up; roller conveyors were destroyed.

Facing exploding shells and searing flames, our little landing crafts beached in the heat and evacuated men who were burned or wounded. There were many heroic rescues.

One herioc action was by 4 enlisted men on a B Co 532 LCVP. When explosions started, the LCVP was offshore near Hamadi Island. Blinker signals said that wounded men were cut off from rescue by shore—and the LCVP drove for the beach. As we closed in, a heavier explosion rained fragments into the sea around us, but we charged on in.

We grounded, helped men aboard, and shoved off. Explosions shook the beach and wounded 2 of the men we were saving. We carried out casualties down-shore south across Jautefa Bay Channel to White Beach 3—and returned to save more men. (The author omits names of these B 532 men.)

A B 532 Amphib officer—probably 1/Lt Heath—remembered that a wounded soldier had been borne in from danger and placed in a dugout among the dumps. This Lt organized a rescue party for the wounded men. Amid fires and explosions, they carried him to safety from the flames.

2/Lt Dalton of 532 Shore Bn's Hq Co aided 6 wounded men caught in the middle of the fire-break that was overrun. gasoline flamed within 25 feet. After ascertaining that the 6 were safe, Dalton rescued a seventh man from a fox-hole threatened by flames.

Collecting Pln. of B Co. 162 Medics had set up their aid station centering the dumps. They seemed to be in the path of the flames. Despite falling metal fragments, letter men moved thorugh the blazing, smoking dumps on rescue missions. Aid men worked under the same menace to save wounded whom the bearers brought in. Several times, they had to move the station itself away from the flames. Named for outstanding heroism were these 3 doctors: Maj. Makart, Capt. Cunningham and Capt. Swisher.

All through that night of 23-24 Apr and all next day, great fires still blazed on White Beach 1. Ammo still exploded; more men were wounded or burned. Desperately, we still tried to drag supplies and equipment from the flames' path. Many Amphib officers and men worked 36 hours—or until they fell exhausted.

Well into 24 Apr, the great fires raged. Over 60 per cent of the rations and ammo that had landed by twilight 23 Apr was destroyed—an estimated value of $8,000,000 in 1944 dollars. Dead were 24 men, 100 burned or wounded. Our devoted Amphibs had saved many more from the casualty list. Last reported losses occurred in late afternoon, 24 Apr while the dumps still burned. Heat set off a 90 mm shell into our Regt area. Killed was another Amphib, and another wounded.

But this holocaust of rations and ammo could have caused temporary failure of the Hollandia Operation, at least, with many more casualties. While advancing inland, 186 Inf had to halve rations and conserve ammo. Although 162 Inf did seize Hollandia Town, orders were to limit operations to patrolling and making defenses, until further notice. Lucky was it that the Japs lacked even a small air force and even one reinforced Inf Bn to attack our crippled beachhead.

While Beach 1 fires still burned, 12 heavily laden LSTs arrived offshore from eastern New Guinea. Seven were originally destined for our 41st Div on Humboldt Bay, but 5 were turned from 24 Div at Tanamerah Bay because its narrow beaches and muddy tracks were impractical for staging supplies. The 24th Div must use the same supply beaches as the 41st.

Because Hollandia Harbor with Challenger Cover was studed with coral reefs, the Amphibs had to continue using the same outer beaches. White Beach 3—which was south cross-channel from Cape Tjeweri—would be hard to land on. The off-shore gradient was unsuitable to beach large LSTs.

Then an experimental LST hurled itself full speed at White Beach 3. It grounded 40 yards offshore, but unloading was possible when the tide fell 4 feet. Shore parties waded out waist-deep to unload. Vehicles drowned out as soon as they drove off the LST ramp, but tractors heaved them ashore.

Then LST CO Capt Cutler ordered his commanders to run all their vessels at high speed to ground as close to the foreshore as possible. They rammed the beach so hard that after they were unloaded, extricating them was hard work.

With White Beach 3 as a temporary dump area, the Amphibs in small craft then transferred LST cargoes 2500 yards over water to White Beach 4. Here within Jautefa Bay was a dump area wide enougth to store supplies to help our 41st to capture the Hollandia strips. Men of 24 Div's 34 Inf assisted our Amphibs. (These 34 Inf men had been unneeded in combat.)

While our Amphibs were fighting the great fire and their problems, 186 was already advancing up the inferior Jap road 18 miles from Pim Village on the coast, to Lake Sentani, south of the Hollandia strips. FA and supply trucks followed this fragile road so close that it turned to muck. Under heavy rains, 186 Inf labored forward, mudhole to mudhole. Where the road crossed sago swamps, some culverts and 2 bridges caved in, to make land traffic almost impossible.

Then our LVTs of 2nd Special Brig Support Btry forwarded to assist in moving supplies. They helped greatly, but by dusk, 7 LVTs and 2 DUKWs were bogged down. Next day, we yanked them from the mud and dragged FA and supply trucks onward again. But on 26 Apr, Nippo destructors blew up bridges along the narrow road. Well before noon, 186's spearhead 1/Bn was stalled indeed.

By now, 1/Bn 186 Inf was just about 6.5 miles from Cyclops Strip, most eastern of the 3 Hollandia airfields that were Task Force objectives. But over 3 miles of this road led among the steep slopes and cliffs of the north shore of Lake Sentani. If the Japs blasted down the lakeside road cuts, 186 Inf would have an almost impossible task to bypass damaged portions.

Col Newman of 186 perceived that tactful usefulness of our Amphibs. While 3/Bn pushed on the north shore road, he would embark 1/Bn on LVTs and outflank the Jap positions.

(Probably largest lake in New Guinea is winding Lake Sentani, which fills the great gorge between coastal Cyclops Mtn and lower mountains southward. Lying west of Hollandia, it is about 8 miles wide at its widest, and 14 miles long at its longest. For 186 Inf, it became an east-west water-borne approach to the 3 Hollandia Strips.)

At Koejaboe Jetty, we unloaded supplies from LVTs, and reloaded them with 2 Cos of 186's 1/Bn. (We know that C Co was one of them.) With 2 combat LVTs and 2 DUKWs in the van, this convoy moved west along the lake. Surprised Nips manning lake-shore mortar batteries and inshore AA guns tried to fight, but our rockets quickly silenced them. The Japs' bursts damaged 2 of our LVTs but without casualties. At 1150, we landed both Cos at Nefáar Village, the rest of 1/Bn later. By 1530, 3/Bn also arrived unopposed over the lakeside road to meet us in Nefaar.

Next day, 26 Apr, while 186's main body maneuvered towards Cyclops Strip, our Amphibs were water-borne again. We loaded 2/Bn 186 at Koejaboe Jetty, and again started out with our Amphibs' 2 combat LVTs and 2 rocket DUKWs leading. We voyaged some 2.5 miles west of Nefaar Village to the jetty south of Ifaar Village.

Nearing the jetty, we took Jap fire from an island and a peninsula to the west. Their fire sank 1 LVT, but we silenced the Japs. Leaving Sentani Lake with 186's men still "on deck," our LVTs clanked up Ifaar Road to rejoin 2/Bn to their 186 Inf at the Strips. By 1645, 186 Inf held all 3 strips, and had contacted 24 Div men pushing east from Tanamerah Bay. Since 186 Inf held Hollandia Town already, Hollandia Operation was completed.

But our Amphibs continued inland labor for 186 Inf and 24 Div. Combat LVTs carried on extensive recons into every island and inlet of Lake Sentani, but met only token resistance. We also laid wire under water form Koejaboe to near Sentani Strip. Because the north shore lake road was still nearly impassible, for some 7 days, we carried ammo and supplies over the water highway of Lake Sentani.

Back down at the beaches, our Amphib unloading continued—the major reason why we were there. Now based mainly on difficult sloping White Beach 3 beside Lake Tjeweri, we emptied LSTs into our LCMs. By mid-afternoon 25 Apr, we had our barges lined up in groups of 5 where they awaited orders to cross 2-3 miles of Jautefa Bay to unload at Pim Village to be trucked inland. Since only 3 of each of these 5 LCMs at a time could unload at Pim Jetty, often 25 LCMs had to idle offshore for their turn at the dock.

Overworked men and machines broke down; for we were now supplying both 41st and 24 Divs over that swampy road up to Lake Sentani. For example, on 25 Apr, Maintenance Co had 5 LCMs and 6 LVPs deadlined for repairs. (In one day, 9 LVTs were seen out of action on Sentani Road. One LVT sank in Sentani; a rocket DUKW fell apart beyond repair.)

This is a small part of the saga of 532 EB&S Regt's crucial fight in the Hollandia Operation. We beached the front-line riflemen. We battled the Great Fire, the mud on Sentani Road, and the hold-out Japs on the Lake. Our labor, our firemanship, and our skirmishes on Lake Sentani—all of these were a major contribution of our Hollandia victory for the United States.

New Guinea: Komiatum Ridge. Cpl. Charles Letters, of Sydney, and Cpl. Frank Young, of Port Moresby, display a Japanese flag found on Komiatum Ridge after the enemy had been forced from it. Cpl. Joe Bartlett, of Newcastle, is holding a Japanese computator or adding machine. It is comprised of a lot of beads arranged in a framework. Bartlett is sitting in a captured Japanese chair. (Courtesy of Rohlffs)

Papua. Australian-manned General Stuart tanks attack Buna. After the first wave of tank attack at Buna had passed, one of its Japanese defenders lies dead in the forground. (Courtesy of Rohlffs)

Papua. Sanananda Area. A forward Section Post less than 30 yards from Japanese positions. These Australians live and fight in mud and water. The photographer who took this picture could hear Japanese speaking, but could not see them. (Courtesy of Rohlffs)

★★★★★

205 Field Artillery on Biak

by Dr. Hargis Westerfield, Division Historian

CREDIT: Documentary sources found at Washington National Records Center from the fourth Visitation Grant of our 41st Division Association were 3. I used 205 FA "Narrative Report," "Log of Observations," and "Casualty List." I still had to use R.R. Smith's *Approach to the Philippines* to get the full picture of 205 FA's place in the operation. Award stories were just 2 available: of 1/lts Steven King and Klemens Nelson. Although I had promises of help from 205 FA men as early as 1968, no one would give me his personal story, which would have made this history much more interesting.

On 28 May 1944, second day of the Biak Operation, 205 FA's 105 mm guns landed at Bosnek. We came on Z+2 because our first mission was only general support of an expected easy capture of Mokmer Strip. Capt Wise, 1/Lt Jendrzewski, and 3 men of our advance party led us down the coast to positions below the low, dark-green Ibdi ridges.

Landing on Biak at 0825, all batteries by 1130 were emplaced below Ibdi and waiting for firing orders, 100 yards behind 146 FA Bn closest to Parai Defile. Suddenly our mission changed from general support to combat for 162 Inf.

For in Parai Defile 90 minutes before we were ready to fire, 3/Bn 162 Inf was already in trouble. The Japs had pocketed them; they needed every gun that could bear on the Japs surrounding them.

Ten minutes after our guns began firing, 2 Jap mortar shells impacted among our guns — and 20 minutes later, 2 more shells. Although reported "slightly wounded," 2 FA men were evacuated. From 1140 to 1500, mortar fire blasted into us.

At 1200, these first 2 men were wounded, in B Btry. Bodine was hit in right shin bone; Montana in head and right arm. Also in "B" 30 minutes later, Georgepoulos was wounded in right leg.

By 1300, 3 men of 205 FA suffered also when on detached duty in 146 FA's command post. Stout of our HQ Btry was lacerated in right shoulder, and SV Btry's 1/Lt McClendon was reported as "seriously wounded" in an unnamed part of his body. But Hill of Hq Btry died of wounds.

And by 1330, B Btry again had casualties — 5 wounded, and 1 dead. Hayes was killed from fragments that penetrated the right side of his head. Medic Bonior was wounded in right shoulder blade, and Augustini in right thigh and left upper arm. Landis was wounded in left shoulder blade, and Jackson lost his little finger. Fagundes was wounded in the left arm.

All told, 205 FA had 2 dead, 11 wounded and hospitalized — and 3 more men hit who remained on duty.

Meanwhile, we were unable to relieve 162's 3/Bn from the overwhelming fire of Japs concealed in the Parai Ridges. Effect of any FA shells was limited because the Japs were in deep fissures crosswise to our fire, or in caves and crevices ending towards the sea.

Offshore destroyers and rocket craft were best positioned to fire on the Parai Japs, but that fire became impossible. About 1200, Ensign Travis, Naval Fire Support Officer, was killed forward with C 162. Naval Fire Support became impossible, for no replacement for this liaison officer was at once available, and direct communication to destroyers and LCIs became erratic for 2 whole days. It was impossible to concentrate enough shells to neutralize Jap fire. So 162 Inf would have to retreat from Parai Defile, but could not complete that retreat until the next day, 29 May.

By 1220, while 205 FA endured mortar fire, 41 DivArty changed our mission from general support to direct support of 162 Inf. Knobbs and Wilson, both 1/Lts, forwarded 2 observers' parties to call down fire for 3/Bn and 2/Bn about 1500 yards west of Parai Village. By 1845, also, an observer for attached 121 FA's 75s was also delivering fire. All night, we harassed the Japs with our shells.

About 2000 that night, a Jap plane lobbed 3 antipersonnel bombs on A Btry. Bombs did little damage; a man was lightly wounded but stayed on duty. Fragments did dent the carriage of No 2 gun. An ammo pit flamed up, but we quickly put out the fire.

On 29 May, we battled for 162 Inf who had to fight Jap tanks in early morning before our men had to leave Parai Defile. At 0847 for a time, we neutralized Jap mortars on the ridge above 162 Inf. At 0916, our observers brought down fire to drive off one of the 7 Jap tanks that attacked 162 Inf. A minute later, 60 rounds from Jap mortars impacted our firing area, but harmlessly.

Thirteen minutes later, a mountain gun and mortars shot down on us from the reverse slope of a high ridge to the north. We requested an air-strike, but we have no report of any Air Force assistance. Forty minutes later, perhaps because of our own shelling, we took no more mortar or cannon fire from that ridge.

On that 29 May, however, we mainly lobbed shells behind or on the north flank of retreating 162 Inf. We believe that we saved many lives for our infantrymen who reformed with us that night in perimeter 500 yards west of Ibdi. Although the Japs could have wiped out 162's 2/Bn and 3/Bn, losses were comparatively small. Efforts of 205 FA, 146 FA, and other support units had kept 162's losses of 28 - 29 May down to 32 killed, 94 wounded, and 3 missing in action.

Our 205 FA casualties included a man wounded and marked "Duty," and Toronto struck by falling flak in B Btry. He was slashed in right thigh and evacuated.

On 30 May, we were largely inactive while 162's patrols sought new routes to attack the victorious Japs north and west of us. At 0740, our destroyers shelled the Parai coast. At 1300, probable knee-mortars impacted near B Btry.

That night, 205 FA was secure in a thousand-yard long perimeter some 500 yards west of Ibdi. With us were some tanks, C Co 186 Inf, D Co 542 Amphib Engrs, and 162's Regtl Hqs, 1/Bn, and CN and AT Cos.

Early on 31 May at 0740, our own B-25s strafed our Bn area. Our Narrative reports that 4 men were wounded, but Casualty List has just one name. Cpl Menghelli suffered a total fracture of his left thigh from a .50 HMG bullet. At 1300, some 15 - 20 rounds of a Jap MG struck 200 - 300 yards from our Command Post, but did not wound any 205 FA men.

On the morn of 31 May, our front lines towards the Parai Japs were only about 300 yards of our 2 forward A and C Btrys. We could not fire close support without endandering our Inf protecting us. We dug new positions and laid new wire, then despatched "C" to the rear a half mile, and "A" one mile back. While the forward B Btry remained on call to fire, "A" and "C" were out of action just a minimum time because they dropped at once into previously prepared stations. By 1800 Hours, "A" was registered on a new base point, and "C" also was registered by 1900 Hours.

By 1 June, Gen Fuller had begun his new offensive for Mokmer Strip — a two-pronged offensive. While 162 Inf continued fighting to liquidate the Parai Defile Japs, 186 Inf would advance overland to capture Mokmer Strip from the rear. With offshore destroyers' aid, 205 FA would support both Regts.

By 2015 that night of 1 June, 205 FA caught hell from those 75 mm mountain guns on Ibdi Ridges overlooking our perimeter. At 2015 Hours, 4 guns zeroed on our area and threw down screaming ("Whistling Charlie") shells on us.

That cause of this shellfire was the arrival of tanks of 603 Tank Co at 2015. The tanks buttoned up and ran away, but the Jap guns seemed to plunge down shells with such accuracy that we wondered how they failed to destroy our Btrys. At midnight, they fired 100 rounds that exploded a gas and ammo dump on the left flank of long-suffering B Btry. To save them from the flames and explosions, we had to move 3 howitzers and 2 of our defending MGs.

Lt Rector observed the .75s gun-flashes 5,000 yards off, and began counter-battery against them.

But not until 0230 on 2 June were the valiante Jap gunners shelled into silence. For the rest of the night, we turned to deliver harassing fire against Parai Defile. At dawn, we opened up against the same mountain gun battery to be sure that we got no more fire from that area. Before dark again, we fired a normal barrage to secure us against their 75s.

Our Journal reports that 4 men were wounded that night — 2 from Hq Btry and 2 from SV Btry. The Casualty List has only 2 of these names. At 2330 that night of 1 - 2 June, a .75 wounded Bushaw in Hq Btry — struck him in left side. At 0330 just as we finally silenced the guns, Lewis was hit in upper right side.

Already, 162 Inf had begun probing again to expel the Japs from Parai Defile. From an ambush position at a stream crossing halfway through the Defile, 3/Bn pushed on 3 June. L Co pushed with 7 tanks. An observer party under 1/Lt Oakes and a liaison party with 1/Lt Ross accompanied "L" with the tanks.

But in that narrow foreshore below tall cliffs, the Japs held a nearly impregnable roadblock. A Jap charge briefly cut off L's lead Pln. Then a lone warrior disabled a tank which had to be towed out. Our guns blasted probable Jap positions, but we had to retreat.

On that same 3 June, we marked with smoke 3 different targets for air-strikes. The Air Force credited us for accurate marking of those positions which resulted in precision bombing. At 1000 that morning, B Btry's Crouch was wounded by a .50 HMG — a simple fracture of his left forearm.

On 6 June, 1/Lt Knobbs scanned the Mokmer coast from his floating observation post — an LCV — "Landing Craft Vehicle" — of 542 Amphib Engrs. He called down effective fire on troops, tanks, trucks, and guns. Two large fires started in Japanese dumps. Japs fired back, but Knobbs was only grazed in left ear — other men in the craft unhurt.

Meanwhile, 2/lt Shea boarded a destroyer better to call down fire against the Jap roadblock and other positions in Parai Defile from which 3/Bn was forced back on 3 June. All afternoon and night, our Bn harassed that area.

But the Japs still held Parai Defile. On 7 June after 186 had seized Mokmer Strip from inland, our troops needed the fastest way to supply that isolated Regt. Supply by landing craft from Bosnek was far too slow. To get a truck route, Gen Fuller had to liquidate the Parai Defile Japs. He had to land troops west of the roadblock to press against L 162 on the other side.

On that 7 June, 21 LVTs — "Landing Vehicles Tracked" — loaded reinforced I and K Cos to land at Parai Village, west of the Defile. Before they landed, 205 FA and the destroyers fired a heavy preparation so aimed as to clear the area but not damage Parai Jetty. Capts Wise and McDougall also rode those LVTs with an observer party to call down fire on the Japs overhead in the ridges. (Despite the successful landing, it was not until 1335 12 June that Parai Defile was cleared of Japs.)

On 8 June, 205 FA continued the offensive for 186 and 162 Inf now in fighting to drive the Japs from positions above Mokmer Strip. To range the Japs at a farther distance than before, we had to displace A Btry to a new position west of Ibdi before B and C Btrys. Our 205 FA pilot, 2/Lt King, began using our new little air-strip for his Piper Cub observation plane (By the close of the Biak Operation, King would have flown over 175 missions for 205 FA, from the Salamaua Operation onward.)

Radio communication with our forward observers at Mokmer Drome were difficult through Parai Defile. We had to relay all messages from Hqs through our floating OP out in the sea. Despite danger from Jap shore parties, we had to man that position 24 hours a day.

All that 8 June, we fired heavily on the Japs holding that low ridge above Mokmer Strip. On 9 June, our 105s shelled to prepare the landing for supply craft at Mokmer Beach. On 10 June, we shelled Mokmer Ridge against the Japs firing down on 186 Inf on Sboeria Beach. At 1800, Lt Wilson shot up pillboxes and 2 AA guns. From the air, 1/Lt King called down fire that put a Jap dual purpose AA gun out of action. (In the Papuan and New Guinea Campaigns, King would fly over 175 combat missions, with over 400 hours' flying time.)

On 13 June, B and C Btrys moved forward by landing craft past the Parai Defile Japs, then marched to new positions by Mokmer Drome. Despite some Jap fire that wounded 3 unnamed men, we were ready to fight by 1930. "A" Btry rejoined us next day.

When 1/Bn 186 Inf attacked West Caves approaches, 1/Lt Klemens Nelson led an observer party to assist. When Japs attacked 186 Inf with tank support, our FA men fought them off in the front lines. Nelson himself killed 2 Japs. Under small arms and FA fire, they brought down 105 FA shells to help defeat the Japs.

On 10 June, our last big shoot-out of our Btrys as a whole was to help 186 Inf cut off the Japs escape route behind West Caves. Much later, on 30 June, C Btry had perhaps the last memorable firing mission of 205 FA, against the few die-hard Japs still in East Caves. From near Mokmer Village, we arced 800 rounds of smoke and high explosives into the caves. Little Jap resistance was left after our bombardment.

In our Battle of Biak, 205 FA Bn lost only 2 killed and 16 actually reported hospitalized from wounds. Under continuous Jap menace, we helped win victory on Biak.

F Co 163 Inf II: Fighting the Ibdi Pocket Cliffs
By S/Sgt Ralph Marlow and Dr. Hargis Westerfield, Divsion Historian

> CREDIT: This is our second story of G 163 on Biak; the first story described F Co in Parai Defile security guard, and in probing the Ibdi Cliffs. Essential part of this history before you is another 11 pages of a total of 83 pages from S/Sgt Ralph Marlow's detailed handwritten manuscript about Biak. Backing comes from 163 inf's Biak Casualty List and Journal. Other sources are Volume VIII, "New Guinea and the Marianas," in Samuel Eliot Morison's great *History of US Naval Operations in World War II*, and Lt-Gen Robert Eichelberger's report of trouble-shooting on Biak. The Eichelberger report is in Ch VI, "The Ridge Pockets," from *I Corps' History of the Biak Operation, 15 - 27 June 1944*.
> We now have four stories of F 163 at Sanananda and on Biak; but we still need F's Zamboanga story.

After F Co 163 Inf had made 2 reconnoisances in force against the Japs' 3/Bn 222 Inf entrenched in Ibdi Pocket, we regrouped south of the Pocket on Bosnek Road. We probed again for a ravine to climb to fight those 1,000 Japs in their low deadly dark-green jungle ridges.

At 0800 24 June, Sgt Reeves' patrol nosed along the cliff base and began to climb the first ridge. After an hour's wait at Hq below, rifles cracked and grenades blasted. Reeves phoned that they had slain 2 Nips. But grenades were showering the patrol. Later, we heard that they killed another Jap, while one escaped. CO 1/Lt Rottman at once ordered Reeves' return. BARman Ellwood covered retreat. We had no casualties.

After 11 days on Biak, "F" had only 100 men remaining. We had 1 killed, 3 wounded, but mainly dysentery had depleted us. Morale was low; we faced ridges like stone walls.

On Sund 25 June, Maj Irving ordered us to find another trail into the ridges. Sgt Myslinski's patrol found a ravine seeming to lead to the top of the first ridge.

So on 26 June, "F" planned to push up the ravine in Pln columns and storm Ibdi Pocket. On that 26 June, A and B Cos would attack from the west, with "C" supporting. G Co would strike on the east, and F Co would drive up from the south.

Early 26 June, F's 1/Pln began climbing up the jagged coral cliff. Progress was slow, sweaty. We had to hang on to trees to keep from backsliding. With ready guns, our scouts advanced warily a few yards at a time.

A beautiful white Biak cockatoo perched peacefully on a branch overhead. We wished that we too had wings and could fly away.

After 2 hours, Comm Sgt Marlow in Hq Pln could see the flats far below. He knew that our 1/Pln had neared the top. When 1/Pln topped the summit, all F Co would follow and turn left to strike where reports were that the Jap lines blocked the way.

About 1010, a single rifle shot, then several more cracked from near the ridge-top. Our 1/Pln was down under Jap bullets that rang on the splintering coral sides of the ravine. Twenty yards above them, Rottman and Marlow in Hq glimpsed 1/pln's riflemen prone in coral. Maj Irving phoned to Rottman to reach that summit — at all costs.

A Jap grenade thudded dully above. In the small seconds before the explosion, all men flattened against the ravine sides. From smoke and dust, S/Sgt Krull stumbled down bloody on back and arms. He had rolled away from the grenade, but multiple steel fragments had penetrated back, face, left arm, and right hand.

Although 1/Pln could not move without drawing fire, Maj Irving again phoned to advance F Co. Rottman ordered 2/Lt Houser's 2/Pln to advance east of the ravine, if at all possible.

At 1/Pln's rear, Houser's men climbed a series of boulders like stairs. Inch by inch on smoother rock and flat on their stomachs, they disappeared from view into the silent brush on the summit.

After 30 minutes' silence, rapid Jap rifle fire crackled into Houser's Pln. They sounded like caps detonating in July fireworks back home. Our M-1's return fire sounded duller.

Lt Houser phoned down that Chyboski and Cowan were badly wounded. Unable to get to Chyboski, they asked for immediate aid to bring down Cowan.

Lt Rottman phoned to Maj Irving that "F" could not advance farther without great losses. Rottman said that Houser's 2/Pln was flat on the ground and could not even see where the Nips were firing from. Irving ordered Rottman to send in our last Pln.

Although Rottman seemed calm and cool leaning against a tree by the phone, Marlow thought that he saw pain on Rottman's face. After a few minutes, Rottman ordered a runner to forward 3/Pln into combat.

When 3/Pln moved up, a Jap volley halted them. From near Rottman, T/Sgt Floyd Smith phoned down to our 60 mm mortars to range in on the Japs. But we could observe by sound only, and had to cease.

Dr. Holcombe arrived, and crawled up over a 15-foot ledge to try to save Chyboski and Cowan, while 2 litter squads waited below. An hour and a half later, Holcombe slid back down over the ledge, and told the bearers to carry out our 2 casualties. Chyboski was already dead, but plasma kept Cowan alive.

Crawling flat, our Medics brought Chyboski down, dead from a bullet in the forehead. Marlow wired Chyboski to the stretcher to keep him from rolling out when they carried him down the steep ridge.

Cowan was still alive, after grenade fragments in chest and stomach. It took 8 men just to lift him down the ledge, for we could not wire him to the stretcher without pressing the steel deeper into his wounds. Cowan would die tomorrow.

The Japs fired occasional bursts to keep our Plns down. S/Sgt Oliphint crawled back and reported the death of Regular Army S/Sgt Edmund Williams — shot square through the heart when he exposed himself to locate a Jap sniper. Texan Compton crawled up and took Williams' watch but said that the body could not be moved without endangering others. (Compton would be killed later.)

Maj Irving wanted "F" to set up defenses where we were, but Regtl Hq ordered immediate withdrawal. Marlow saw Rottman beam with relief.

While T/Sgt Mills' 1/Pln covered the others with rifle fire, they slipped back down. Our 2/Pln was down under Nippo threats from higher ground, but they had only a few yards to slide down to safety.

While 3/Pln withdrew, we heard a nearby rifle-shot — then a body rolling down the steep slope towards us — then an exchange of more shots above. A small tree stopped the body; Marlow rushed out to find 3/Pln's Staley, still alive, with just a few cuts and bruises.

As Staley had risen to retreat, a Jap only a few feet away fired and struck Staley's canteen. The bullet spun Staley around to roll 40 feet. Sgt Hutchison killed that Jap. But Staley's name never appeared on the casualty list.

With better cover, 1/Pln now slowly left the ravine. Back in F's perimeter, the cooks had coffee and hot cereal, for we had not eaten since early morning.

Then "F" got bad news. On 28 June, we were to attack Ibdi Pocket again, in a different direction. Back on the inland side of the Pocket, we were to contact G Co already facing the death-ridges. With "G" on left flank, we were to try to flank and overrun pillboxes that had stopped "G" on 26 June. Bad news also was that Cowan had died of yesterday's wounds.

Yet F Co got one good laugh. That night of 26 June in semi-dark, a lone Jap ran down the road past our holes. First guard who saw him could not fire because a parked jeep blocked off the Jap. When Jap ran past other holes, it was too late to fire. It made us somehow happy that a Jap had escaped alive.

Leaving our mortars back at Ibdi with G's mortars, we entrucked to 2/Bn Hq on 27 June, then hiked over the ridges again. Now we were close to where Walters died on 21 June. About 200 yards from the Jap ridges, we perimetered atop the rocks behind little walls of coral. All night, FA shells splintered among rocks; fragments ripped tree-tops overhead. Trying to crawl up under our helmets for protection, we chilled in a heavy soaking rain before daylight.

At 0800 28 June, FA ceased fire. With T/Sgt Mills' 1/Pln leading, "F" scouted slowly towards the Jap pillboxes to the SE. On a knoll, Mills' scouts halted for 1/Pln to come up.

As 1/pln topped the knoll, many Jap MGs crackled like rattlesnakes. F Co flattened in brief confusion. Crawling up over a 5-foot ledge in the rear, 1/Lt Rottman learned from T/Sgt Mills that 1/Pln's right flank was under cover, but that our left flank was unprotected. Rottman called for 2/lt Houser to come up to discuss committing his 2/Pln.

A Jap grenade thudded too close. Jumping into a big hole, Sgt Marlow heard the explosion. Houser jumped in beside Marlow and said that Rottman was hurt badly — and asked for Exec 1/Lt Overby to come up. With bloody face and shoulder, Rottman ran back, his jaw so impacted that he could only mumble.

Maj Irving directed our new CO Overby to have a 1/Pln man up front to mark the Japs' positions with a smoke grenade. Our mortars registered on the smoke, and F got retreat orders.

Our smoke grenade gave away our position. Before, we took just a stray Jap shot or so, but now lead from countless Jap MGs arced over our whole Co area.

Sgt Reeves of advanced 1/Pln ran unhurt past Compton, but a slug pierced Compton's left hip — to finally kill him. One bullet shattered Tucci's left arm; another bullet tore his thumb completely from his right hand.

An "F" superior ordered Marlow to phone for 2 stretchers, but Maj Irving reprimanded Marlow. Despite Marlow's description of the wounds, Irving said that only Medics could call for stretchers. These wounded men would have to walk. Volunteers carried Tucci in shock back to our perimeter, with Compton complaining of stomach pains. Then Medics' litters bore them back to the aid station.

Returned to our stony perimeter, we remaining "F" men had wonderful food. We 42 men each had 5 doughnuts from an unknown unit south of the ridges.

"F" had shrunk to 42 men, mainly because of dysentery. We could not dig latrines in our rock, but had to use crevices in the coral. But on 30 June, a bulldozer made us a road and heaped off the rocks so that we could dig for field sanitation. Our kitchen crew trucked in to set up for hot meals. Morale also went up when we had a mail call.

Luckily, the Japs did not attack — shelled us just once, but totally missed our perimeter. Lt-Col Rankin told us that the diary of a dead Nippo Sgt-Maj said that our FA was causing many casualties, and that the Japs were running out of ammo. Maybe our FA and their lack of ammo saved us from Jap raids.

Heavy shellfire still sliced the air overhead against Ibdi Pocket to keep us from sleeping. Our muscles twitched as we waited for shells to impact and feared that they would hit us. On 2 July, Medics brought G Co's dead Schmidt to wait near us for a truck to the graveyard.

On that same 2 July, S/Sgt Dunlap's patrol crept to within bazooka range of a Jap pillbox without being seen. Next morning, Sgt Reeves took a bazooka team that hit the box 4 times. We saw no Japs in that shattered emplacement.

And that night of 3 July, F Co had orders to take 18 men to try to penetrate Ibdi Pocket near that demolished pillbox. While 1/Lt Overby planned the patrol that night, the phone rang again. Orders were that F Co with all 2/Bn were to raise the siege of Ibdi Pocket. On 4 July, we left forever that filthy little perimeter of stones.

Our Compton, however, was slowly dying in hospital. The bullet in his left hip had shattered the bone, but deflected upwards. Stomach was holed 18 times, and bladder twice. Although sent home, Compton died a few days later.

Unforgettable was F Co's night of 4 July when free of Ibdi Pocket. Instead of lying on guard in coral pigpens we 40-odd men slept above ground again as God meant us to. At 163 Hq, we blissfully sprawled in hammocks lent by AT Co men who were out on listening posts. Instead of being awakened to clutch a grenade in the blackness in a soaking rain, we looked out in the moonlight and talked in natural tones.

F Co never fought in Ibdi Pocket again, nor any other 1/Bn and 2 Bn Cos. On 10 July, 3/Bn took up the Pocket siege and pressed the Japs until 22 July when B-24 500-lb bombs silenced the Pocket forever.

Later, "F" learned how incredibly lucky we were not to attack Ibdi Pocket again. Centering the Pocket at a high point of 180 feet were 4 large caves. One could have held several hundred men. Ringing the 4 large caves were 17 smaller connected caves. Circling the 17 caves were 75 4-man pillboxes of logs and coral. Outside this central core of pillboxes were some 200 hastily constructed pillboxes.

Originally, 800 men of 3/Bn 222 Inf with 200 attached men had garrisoned this rectangle of 400 by 600 yards. Minimum heavy armament was 3 75 guns, 8 90 mm mortars, 2 37 mm guns, 2 20 mm guns, 3 HMGs, numerous LMGs, and at least 100 rifles. Our FA and Air Force had shattered many more weapons, or our Engrs had sealed them into caves. And the 1,000-man garrison was gone, dead or in flight before the bombing.

Without the Air Force, 163 Inf would have been shattered attacking Ibdi Pocket. As for F Co, we were lucky that we had to attack where the cliffs made it impossible to go farther. On easier terrain, A Co lost 12 killed, and G Co lost 10. "F" was lucky indeed to have just 5 too many men to lament for: Will, Chyboski, Williams, Cowan, and Compton.

Papua. Nearing the end of the Papuan Campaign against Japan. Native boys and Americans examine a captured 75mm. anti-aircraft gun, near Sanananda. An Australian takes advantage of the opportunity to make a cup of tea. The Japs in their retreat, took with them the breech block of the gun so that it could not be used against them. (Courtesy of Rohlffs)

Headquarters Co. 2/BN 186 INF: THIRST ON BIAK
By Capt. Luis (Lew) Turner
with Dr. Hargis Westerfield, Division Historian

> CREDIT: Most important part of this history is Capt. Turner's pages 796 - 882 of his 220,000 word manuscript which he sent to me in Nov. 1985, shortly before he died, 3 Dec. 1985. Highly useful also were 186 Inf's 35 page single-spaced typescript "Narrative" of Biak, and RR Smith's *Approach to the Philippines*. ("Journal" of 186 Inf on Biak was of little use.) Important also were casualty lists. Already published in Jungleer were two stories of this 2/Bn Hq Co on Biak: "Battling Col. Kuzume's Big Banzai," Jungleer Dec. 1970, and "Into the Slot at West Caves," Jungleer, July 1985. "Battling Col. Kuzume's Big Banzai" is also in *The Fighting Jungleers*, first edition.

Tense, heavily armed Hq Co of 2/Bn 186 Inf peered from our charging landing crafts into black smoke slashed with sudden orange flashes of rocket fire. Smoke and orange flashes were all that we could see at dawn 27 May 1944 as we led 186 Inf to strike on Biak.

To our confusion as the smoke lifted, we faced a swamp of mangroves. An unexpected 6-mile an hour current had carried smoke-blinded coxswains 3,000 yards west of Bosnek Beach into the only mangrove swamp on Biak's south shore.

About 0743, our amphibian trucks pushed halfway into the swamp before the mangroves sprung us back. With all 2/Bn and Col Newman's command group, we slipped into waist-deep brine and pushed heavy weapons and rifles through snarled branches. Past 162 Inf marching against Parai Defile, we slogged 3,000 yards to our Bosnek Beach objective. If Col Kuzume had used reports from his scouts, his 11,000 men could have driven the 41st into the sea.

Digging in near Bosnek, 116 Engrs and we mopped up a token Jap resistance force 1/Bn 222 Inf. About 150 yards east of CP, we found a cave at the end of a sunken ramp with some Jap supplies. The cave held a die-hard Jap shooting at us. A Nisei US Jap pleaded with him to surrender; the Jap enemy kept on firing from behind heaped up packing cases.

Our Sgt Hand crawled into the cave mouth. To shoot the Jap, he had to move a crate out of his way. There was a loud "Crack!" Hand turned his back just as a booby trap exploded — staggered with a back bleeding from small fragments. We called for a bulldozer which sealed the Jap up alive.

When Jap bombers dived on us, they did little damage. Many Jap planes died from a new computerized sighting control which was tied in with several trailers carrying twin .50 HMGs.

After 162 Inf retreat from the Parai Defile trap, 163 Inf's 1/Bn and 3/Bn from Toem relieved us from Bosnek Beach. We were now to march overland behind Bosnek to bypass Parai Defile and sieze Mokmer Strip from the rear. Our 2/Bn was first to turn east alongshore to Opiaref and then turn inland up a rough, twisted road. After ending minor Jap resistance near Opiaref, we were to turn west to the flat behind Bosnek which was surveyed for a Jap air strip. There we were to join 3/Bn to march on Mokmer Strip.

Hiking behind Opiaref, we had to round a 20-foot coast artillery gun barrel mounted on 2 wooden sleds. It weighed 7-8 tons. The Japs had dragged it to mount in a concrete revetment. Bore was about 14 inches in diameter. If set up in time, it could have played hell with us at Bosnek.

Turning west on the upland road, we heard the end of a skirmish between Japs and K and AT Cos. By 1500, we were digging in on the flat east of the surveyed Jap strip.

As night fell 2/Bn Hq's CO Turner was without a sleeping hole. Nobody had replaced his saki-filled orderly now under arrest by the MPs. His men set up for Turner a parapet of abandoned white bags of Jap rice. Tiredly behind his parapet, Turner ate a K-ration, smoked a cigarette under poncho, and slept. He expected no fight that night.

About 0330, Turner awoke to the thump of a Jap knee-mortar, 2 rifle-shots, and a Jap scream. Japs and Yanks shouted. M-1s, carbines, and Jap Arisaka rifles volleyed.

Alone behind his raised and visible white bag shelter, Turner helmeted himself. A grenade exploded close; he put his helmet over his lower abdomen. Then fearfully, he replaced it on his head. Should he have his head blown off, or be emasculated? Turner finally left his head uncovered.

After 4 hours, the firing ceased. From Cannon Co., a Yank shouted, "Help!" A blade was thudding into another man. A Jap officer had slashed CN's Gee deeply across his shoulder. Our mild Lt Moore went berserk. With rusty machete, Moore hacked the officer to pieces, had to be pulled off him. Slight blond Moore with weak light blue eyes in thin gold glasses, was nickname "Grandma." After that duel, Moore lost that nickname.

On that night of 1-2 June, our 3/Bn with help killed 86 Japs. We lost 3 killed and 8 wounded — but no one in 2/Bn. And at 0900 2 June, all 186 Inf marched west.

Our 1/Bn and 3/Bn pushed abreast along the faint trail towards Mokmer Strip. With Turner's 2/Bn Hq Co, 2/Bn had to patrol north of the road or to hand-carry supplies and water. Six tanks were in support, beside 121 FA's 75s on call.

From 1/Bn 222 Inf, small Jap patrols fired rifles and MGs at us from north of the road. Our tanks or FA 75s slew or scattered them. By dusk, 96 were dead, with 6 Yanks killed and 10 wounded. Recovered Japanese soldiers said that a Jap Hqs was north of us. Our 121 FA 75s destroyed it.

By next day, 3 June, water had become the most important problem of our westward advance. For all 186 Inf plus newcome 2/Bn 162, we had only one 900-gallon water trailer with a few 50 gallon drums extra which had to truck up from the coast.

And we patrolled and fought down under blazing sun between thick walls of 12-foot scrub that cut off even the slightest cool from a breeze. Mere marching nad patrolling without fighting made us sweat. We lacked enough water to replace our lost moisture. When Jap patrols struck us, we had to run low and crouch and fire and run over and over. We had more sweat and more thirst.

Our danger was in fainting from sunstroke, dehydration, or waterless shock. Lucky were we not to have to face any large Jap attack; we would have lost many men.

Although every man must have started out with 2 full canteens on 2 June, we had no issue of water at all next day. On 4 June, Col Newman retarded our start until water arrived from Bosnek. Then about one canteen full per man was issued. At 1000 just as we were moving out, Gen Fuller halted us. We had to wait for new orders because the Jap Navy was about to hit Biak. Their Navy turned back. Our few patrols found no Japs.

Water failed to come on 5 June, but despite advice of Bn COs and his Staff, Col Newman ordered an advance about 0800. By 1200, 186 was east of the rugged ridgecrest above Mokmer Strip — east of that ridge which curved north of the sea. Newman sent out 2 patrols from every Bn to seek a route over that ridge.

But our waterless men trekked too slowly. Newman thought that by mid-afternoon, thirst would stop us dead in our tracks.

But a miracle happened! Before 1200, a gigantic dark cloud gathered overhead. About 1430 hours began a sprinkle. In 10 minutes, a heavy tropical rain slapped down hard.

Without orders, we stopped dead. In groups of 4-6, we help up a poncho. As rain cascaded through the neck holes, we took turns to fill our helmets from them. We drank deep again and again and filled our 2 canteens. Some men swallowed an entire canteen! Lightning struck the earth around us while thunder crashed. Turner thought that God was relenting in his disapproval of our senseless war, by this rain.

Col. Newman had nagged his officers to speed up our march. But now he stood soaked like all of us with his helmet full of water. He laughed hard and shouted, "Game called on account of rain!"

While the rain stopped, K Co's 1/Pln found a jungle path to the top of the 300-foot ridge above Mokmer Strip, which crest all 3/Bn then occupied. Our 2/Bn now had to guard 3/Bn's rear and provide carrying parties. At that time, 2/Bn was at the end of the new supply road. Two trucks were parked nearby, some distance apart.

Rifles, grenades, and knee-mortars from some 15 Nips blasted out of the scrub against 2/Bn's flank. One small Jap leaped onto the road before Hq Co with his long bayoneted rifle. Turner with his carbine drew a bead on him — shot him twice — but without pushing his safety. Other 2/Bn men fired — even with MGs. The Jap hid in a truck; their bullets wrecked it. He escaped unhurt into the brush.

Although creased twice already that day, G Co's 1/Lt Minor had orders to smash that 15-man attack. Losing 2 dead Yanks, 17 wounded, Minor killed 13 Nips. A grazing shot rimmed his jawbone — looking as if a hot iron had burned it.

On that 6 June, 3/Bn patrols from the ridge-crest searched for a passable route down to Mokmer Strip. Newman resupplied all units for an expected all-out assault on the Strip. After hand-carrying supplies up to 3/Bn all day, Turner's men and others dug in near the crest. Water finally came. Ration was just one canteen full plus a canteen cup. We did not know when we could get water again.

In that heat, men would drink too much that night. Turner wisely issued only a canteen full — reserved the cupfuls in a lister bag for tomorrow.

That day, patrol from probably K Co had found a fair route to descent to the Strip. But a heavy Jap attack badly wounded Julius Jones. They tourniqueted his leg and cut saplins for litter poles with a poncho between them. In darkness, they carried Jones back up the rough trail among jagged coral, brambles, and tripping rocks. They feared to smoke, they ran out of water.

They topped our ridge and collapsed. Col. Newman woke Capt. Turner and demanded the water he had saved for his own Co. The patrol was down on hands and knees — one man on his back with a parched tongue protruding. Most of Turner's lister bag passed down their thirsty throats.

Newman now wanted time to thoroughly search for Japs on the heights, but Gen Fuller ordered immediate siezure on Mokmer Strip. On 7 June after 121 FA's shellfire for 30 minutes, all 186 Inf jumped off, with attached 2/Bn 162 Inf. At 0730 from a line of departure below the 100-foot contour, 1/Bn and 3/Bn abreast pushed on the Strip, with 2/Bn 162 securing their rear. Our 186's 2/Bn hand-carried supplies, helped by CN, SV, and Regtl. Hq Cos.

By 0945, 2/Bn entered the dispersal runway of Mokmer Strip. In column of twoes, we scouted the surrounding trees for snipers. Jap rifle fire began — then mortar and FA shellfire. One burst blasted gear from 2/Bn's Maj Bradbury and stunned him. For 4 hours, 186 was pinned down in old shell craters by FA, mortars, and MGs. In 2/Bn Hq Co, T/4 Cline, Cpl. Hall, and T/5 Dunlap were wounded — Cline marked "seriously." (All 186 Inf lost 14 killed, 68 wounded that day.)

On 8 June still being shelled, 1/Bn Hq Co had Blankenship, McClain reported lightly wounded. When Jap fire cut wire on the Strip to our recon patrols, Turner told 2/Lt Pouser to send a repair crew. Refusing to expose his men, Pouser sat cross-legged on the open Strip and spliced the wire. In cover, our riflemen duelled Japs trying to kill Pouser, but he was unhurt.

By 10 June, all of 162 Inf had joined 186 to fight for Mokmer Ridge. While 162 fought on the Ridge, 186 secured the coastal flat below. Sgt Rockeman of 2/Bn Hq was lightly wounded. On 16 June, 2/Bn closed the Great Gap on Mokmer Ridge between 2 162 Bns. In 2/Bn. Hq Phipps, 1/Lt Blanton had light wounds.

By 20 June, Mokmer Ridge was cleared. Siege of West Caves was begun — Japs' last important stronghold on Biak. Some 162 Cos fought to take the Caves, and 186 men blocked the Japs from escaping up the road to the north.

About dark 20 June, 2/Bn Hq men found an explosive dump in a trench before our perimeter. About 1.5 tons of bright yellow picric acid cases lay in a trench pointed at us. A stray bullet could detonate them and destroy Hq Co. That night, we emptied the trench and scattered the cases before our holes. Trucks hauled it to a safe place next morning.

In early dark 21 June, 20-30 men passed through our lines laughing and speaking English. We held fire — but later learned that they were Japs escaping from West Caves.

That night of 21-22 June, West Caves Japs made 3 desperate attacks — the final at 0400. Irish of 2/Bn Hq was seriously wounded. Cpl. Miller took a light bayonet wound. Gunner Howe died by his .50 HMG from a Jap suicide grenade.

At dawn, Gens. Eichelberger and Doe rode up in tanks to complain that our bullets had shot up their kitchen.

On the road, a .50 HMG lay on its side with a dented breach and a Jap corpse hugging it. Past the gun was a scene of red devastation. Bloody mangled corpses stretched into the distance. Some Yanks stalked with rifles and grenades to make mercy killings.

Thus ended 2/Bn 186's main actions on Biak. Luckily, Bn Hq Co lost only 11 wounded, and 1 killed. In great danger, we had landed on the wrong place, marched in a waterless hell, closed the Great Gap, fought off the Big Banzai before West Caves. Our history was a marvel of endurance.

AT Company 162 Infantry: MINE PLATOON ON BIAK
By Dr. Hargis Westerfield, Division Historian & AT Co's Sgt Counts & Lt Schatzman

> CREDIT: AT Co's Fred Kielsgard contacted Stephen Counts to help me. (Counts later became T/Sgt of Mine Pln at Zamboanga.) Core of this second story of AT 162 on Biak are Counts' letters of 21 Mar and 26 Dec 1979, and 27 Jan 1980. Important on AT's ridge fight of 3 June and the later death of Jimmie Shields is Pln leader Lt Ed Schatzman's undated letter written about Sept. 1980. Other sources are AT 162's Morning Report (June, 1944), 162 Inf's Biak Casualty List, and RR Smith's *Approach to the Philippines*. A previous story of AT 162 on Biak appeared in *Jungleer* (Sept-Dec 1974), reprinted in *The Fighting Jungleers*.

On Biak D-Day, 27 June 1944, AT 162's Mine Pln marched with 162's 3/Pln into Parai Defile to try to capture Mokmer Strip. We carried old World War I minedetectors, heavy backpacks and sweep discs with 12-inch diameters and 5-foot handles and ear-phones. But 3/Bn never called us up to use them.

Our lead Cos easily forced the lightly held Defile. By dawn 28 May, Mine Pln thought that Biak was another easy Hollandia victory. Then, in the flat brushland west of Parai, the real Battle of Biak started. With perfect observation from the ridge, the Japs plunged HMG and mortar fire on 3/Bn. S/Sgt Counts recalls our despair under 2 hours' heavy Jap blasting. We couldn't even group for reliable orders from the COs. Rumor was that a Bn officer said, "Every man for himself."

When 162's Col Haney ordered retreat, 603 Tank Co's Shermans tried to silence Jap fire from the cliffs. They broke through with guns blazing, but Jap MGs continued firing. AT's Mine Pln desperately ran through Jap fire-lanes — a few men at a time.

Waiting his turn, Counts was in a sniper's sights. The first bullet zipped by; he dived behind a log. More bullets struck smoke and steam from the log near his face. They seemed like dum-dums. They cracked so hard that he could hear the muzzle-blast and detect that Japs' positions. He crawled over a coral ledge and ran through MG fire-lanes. AT's Foley was down with a bullet through his thigh. Counts helped 2 Yanks to move him to safer ground for Medics' care.

On 29 May after a quiet night, Jap tanks and infantry attacked 2/Bn entrenched above and to the right of where AT's Mine Pln had dug in on the beach. From our positions, Counts saw an occasional Jap advance on the sky-line, while we tensely looked back for a Jap charge. After the 4 tanks died above us, he heard Jap officers' orders, and a fire-fight. Two Jap Inf attacks failed; 3 more Jap tanks were killed.

On that 29 May, Mine Pln lost Sgt Lynn Miller and Claude Johnson, both marked "lightly wounded." A destroyer's 6-inch shell went wrong and put a fragment in Johnson's left shoulder. A Jap MG hit Fuller also. In Parai Defile, Mine Pln abandoned our mine-detectors. We fought as infantry thereafter.

We rejoined AT Co to fight Ibdi Pocket ridges — the Japs' eastern bastion for Parai Defile. When on 2-4 June, 2/Bn 162 Inf fought north on Young Man's Trail through the Pocket to join 186 marching westward, "AT" had a new mission. "AT" was to help CN Co keep open 2/Bn's supply line from the coast.

On 2 June, Mine Pln got orders to make perimeter on Ridge 4 in a tangle of rain-forest on knife-edged coral ridges. Ridge 4 was so far inland from AT Hq that we laid wire to keep in touch. Climbing to the Ridge 4 crest, we passed a new Jap corpse, surely left after 2/Bn's push.

Ridge 4 was all solid coral — a poor perimeter position. We huddled in natural depressions and heaped coral chunks around us. With our LMG, we had M-1s and 2-3 grenades a piece. Counts' squad held the trail back to AT Co. Kielsgard's squad lay in the depression below Ridge 4 to act as a listening post.

Counts feared that Jap killers would trail us on that wire down to AT Hq. It went dead about dusk.

Night fell. Heavy fire broke out on AT's other ridges, to continue all night. Mine Pln spent a quiet time, however. The Nips evidently had failed to locate our positions. Then just at first light, 2/Lt Schatzman heard Jap trucks being started, and Jap voices.

Just at daylight also, down the steep slope on Mine Pln's rear, Counts' men heard Japs chattering, yawning, and laughing — like men just awakening from sleep at a country club. We were more scared now; they felt safe and did not need to be quiet. Had they already planned to attack us?

Now 2 Nips came down the trail behind us where our wire was laid. One "AT" man first waved and called to them, but he stopped when he realized that they were Japs. In a position or two past Counts, a rifleman fired twice too quickly at them and missed. They dropped into a draw, then disappeared, certainly to alert the Jap outfit below us.

About an hour later, a Jap sniper fired — maybe from a tree with a full view of our whole perimeter. His first shot wrecked our LMG. Then the Japs moved on us — a whole Co, as Schatzman estimated.

On the perimeter side behind Counts, at least 100 Japs climbed up the steep slopes and attacked. Schatzman let them get close before we opened fire. He hoped to pile them on the trail, but they crouched in the brush or climbed trees and fired down on us.

Their push failed. Fighting kitchen man Shields was one reason for their failure. He seemed careless of his life — fired standing up exposed, like sighting on targets in a shooting gallery. Shields claimed a kill of 28. Perhaps his marksmanship saved Mine Pln from any casualties.

No charges hit Counts' side of the perimeter, but he had unbelted all his M-1 clips and lined them on the rock before him, with his 3 grenades. Expecting the Japs to break our perimeter, he prepared to stuff clips into his M-1 as a butcher stuffs a meat-grinder. Expecting death from a sustained attack, he hoped, like every man, to slay many Japs before he died.

After the attack, heavy shells burst haphazardly between us and AT Co below. Later we learned that Cannon Co thought that we were overrun and fired their mortars to help us escape.

Probably deciding that Jap mortars or own FA might soon knock us off Ridge 4, Lt. Schatzman ordered retreat. Leaving our shattered MG, Mine Pln started back down-trail to safety. Counts happily saw Kielsgard and his squad below them, who fell in as rear guard.

After AT's fights of 2-3 June, Gen Fuller closed 2/Bn 162's supply trail across Ibdi Pocket and attached that 2/Bn to 186 Inf on the plateau. Fuller also decided that he could not force Parai Defile until Ibdi Pocket was cleared. He ordered 1/Bn 162 to attack east from Young Man's Trail, and "AT" to push west with attached A Co 186 Inf on our right. Our western attack hit a stone wall in the heavily fortified depths of Ibdi Pocket.

On 7 June when "AT" patrolled west from Young Man's Trail Shields and Schatzman scouted ahead of Counts' point squad. Lt Schatzman had chosen Shields as first scout because he appreciated this fighter's alertness and aggression.

All went quietly until they hit a bald spot 25-35 yards long on the ridge. After a brief wait, Shields crossed, with Schatzman 15 yards behind him.

Shields fired suddenly; Schatzman saw that he had hit a Nip. Then Schatzman thought that Shields moved up to prepare to throw a grenade. Heavy Jap fire broke out; Shields was down. Schatzman fired at the Jap sound of fire but himself drew MG fire. He called to Shields but had no answer.

Crawling back to Mine Pln, Schatzman contacted Lt. Harbaugh. We brought up a MG to fire on the Japs and also tried to use a bazooka to try to fell some of the big trees. The bazooka did not smash the trees — merely drew more MG fire. We could not bring out Shields' body.

(A week or so later, G Co 163 men attacked past Shields' post of honor, on a water-rutted ridge. Somebody had covered him with an Aussie blue blanket. Nearby, a little dead Nip in swollen puttees hung head down in vines over the cliff. Beyond them, the narrow ridged lifted over a heap of brush and rocks into a grassy glade. A cross-cliff about 15 feet high walled the glade, with 2 pillboxes on top. Below that cliff on the other side, were 3 Jap emplacements to fire over that cross-cliff. We might knock out the 2 pillboxes. But after silencing the pillboxes, we would have to crawl over the cliff in a slot between 2 big trees — a man at a time. A touch of a Jap MG trigger would topple his corpse back over the cliff. Such was Shields' bed of honor.)

On that 6 June, Jap fire forced us to retreat to a safer night position. We perimetered on a narrow ridge with a bald knob in the direction where Shields had died. We had to hold that knob to keep Japs from seizing it and raking AT Co from our narrow ridge behind it.

Now 2/Pln with their LMG and Counts' Mine Pln squad got orders to hold Bald Knob. McCormick and Gardner placed their LMG at the end to fire west. Counts' men held the north side; 2/Pln men guarded the south side.

Bald Knob's white coral gleamed under the nearly full moon. We dared not sky-line ourselves; we were already taking some rifle-fire. We heaped coral chucks around us and hugged the ground. McCormick took a leg wound, Kielsgard replaced him on the LMG. The ridge than quietened for awhile.

As night deepened, Counts heard, far down the ridge, iron tires on a rock — a Jap mountain gun repositioning. Yet he slept — after midnight and but little sleep since D-Day while Kees and Kessler guarded him in their turn.

Counts did not sleep long. Jap howls and our MG's crackling awoke him. Main Jap thrust seeemed against Kielsgard's MG, but our grenades burst all around Bald Knob — against Japs in the brush below.

All night, Bald Knob rocked with explosions — our own grenades, and some knee-mortar blasts. Kielsgard kept his MG bursts short, but fired too frequently. We had just 3 grenades apiece. Worried Counts sent a man crawling bach to Hq for more.

Just below us, Japs were again dragging that heavy metal object over coral. Counts feared that they were trying to place a mountain gun fire into the depression between Bald Knob and the rest of "AT." Counts threw a grenade. The scraping halted, then started again. The grenade has arced too far below. He sparked another grenade in his hand, held it briefly before throwing it. It also exploded too far downhill. Now he laid an M-1 clip on the rock to help point his M-1 in the sound's direction. He stabbed the next sound with a full 8-round clip, reloaded, and waited. He never heard the supposed wheels on the rock again.

Bald Knob vibrated all night with knee-mortar and grenade blasts. Kielsgard's LMG was running out of ammo. Too few grenades came up from AT Co behind us on the ridge.

Daylight was coming. On this bare hump, we would be clear targets for Jap snipers. Since the Japs had failed, Counts ordered withdrawal. Later, he found 2-3 helmets of grenades that "AT" had collected for us, but somehow, they had never come up to help us.

On that 7 June, AT Co pushed on the Japs' positions — this time from the west. Hidden pillboxes of blazing MGs stopped us. Grenades bounded down on us. When 1/Lt Harbaugh called for reinforcements, a Pln of A Co 186 Inf arrived under Sgt Platko, with satchel charges.

"AT" and A 186 crawled up to a waist-high coral cliff, with Japs on the other side on higher ground. Flattened at the cliff-foot, we seemed safe from riflemen. The Japs threw a few ineffective grenades down on us.

An A 186 man — probably Roy — rose up and looked for a place to throw his satchel charge. A Jap blasted him at close range. Clutching his chest, Roy lay back sighing and died.

Probably at that time, 2 more A 186 men were wounded — Stukel, and Banks. "AT" lost Mine Pln's Entzminger, S/Sgt Palmer, and 1/Lt Harbaugh marked lightly wounded. Mine Pln's Gunia escaped from a bullet all the way through his helmet. (At Zamboanga, Gunia would escape miraculously also. At Zambo, he disarmed a Bouncing Betty, it blew up and wounded only the tip of a little finger.)

After our failure, AT 162 and A 186 could not gain more ground along the ridges west of Young Man's trail On 10 June, Gen Fuller relieved both Cos to bypass Parai Defile and help the fight for Horseshoe Ridge above Mokmer Strip. Some days later, AT 162 was occupying a ridge half a mile east of West Caves, after dragging some Jap corpses down into a draw. When Counts took a detail to evacuate some wounded from near West Caves, Strawser was seriously wounded. The last time Mine Pln saw Strawser, he was laughing and joking and smoking a cigarette. But he died of that wound — a small, evil blue hole in the abdomen. This is the last time that Counts remembers that Mine Pln was under fire on Biak.

Such was the war of AT 162's Mine Pln on Biak. After having to lose our mine-detectors at Parai Defile, we ably defended Ridge 4 and Bald Knob against fierce Nippo attacks. We had 7 wounded. We were lucky to have just 2 dead, but men never forgotten, Shields and Strawser.

HQ. CO. 2/BATTALION, 162 INF.: PATROL WITH GUERILLAS IN MINDANAO

by Joe Bradshaw
with Dr. Hargis Westerfield, Division Historian

> CREDIT: Most of this history comes from last 16 pages of Joe Bradshaw's 27-page, double-spaced typescript, "Battalion Two and the Philippine Liberation." (Pages 1-11 are Bradshaw's story of Zamboanga Battle and Basilan Island.) Typescript is on pages 15 inches long and 12 inches wide. Useful as background were "Addendum/Activities of 2nd Battalion (162 Inf) from 3 May 1945 through 7 July 1945...V 4 Operation," R. R. Smith's *Triumph in the Philippines*, and Reports of General MacArthur/*Japanese Operations in the Southwest Pacific Area*, Vol. II. Also useful were 162 Inf's *Report of Operation*... 4 May to 30 June 1945, and "Journal — 162nd Infantry Regiment," beginning 3 May 1945.

On 4 May 1945, Scout Joe Bradshaw landed in 162 Inf near Cotabato City about 100 miles overseas east of Zamboanga — but still on Mindanao Island. We beached peacefully, for 24 Div ahead of us already fought Japanese 100 Div 100 miles eastward above Davao City. After 162's 3/Bn at once reembarked for Davao around the coast to help 24 Div, we other 162 men had to secure Cotabato Province which 24 Div had already passed through.

Guerillas said that bypassed Jap outfits holed up south of us on Mt. Blit and Dalican Village in a partly explored swamp and mountain jungle. We had to find out how dangerous those Japs were.

About 12 May, 2/Bn's C.O., Lt.-Col. Wayne Bailey, briefed Joe to lead a guerilla patrol to reconnoiter the Japs to the south. Although Joe was only a PFC, Maj. Ratliffe made Joe his personal representative — knowing Joe's cleverness.

To keep the patrol as secret as possible, Maj. Ratliffe himself drove Joe to the guerilla camp. Ratliffe introduced Joe to the guerilla Lt.-Col. as his recon officer. Joe saw a few tents and double-manned sentry posts with wide fields of fire. The guards said that we were already behind Jap lines!

Joe dined beside the Lt.-Col. with 16 other officers. The Col. asked for Joe's rank. Joe discreetly replied, "Sir, this mission is strictly hush-hush. Col. Bailey advised me to say that I am his personal representative." The Col. answered, "No one less than a major could hold this important duty." Joe gave the Col. 12 cigars, and 12 packs of cigarettes.

Next morn, Joe led his recon patrol forward — 2 Sgts with tommies, 2 Cpls with carbines, and a turbaned Moro carrier whose conscience was against killing.

We hiked 9 miles to a hidden path to the advance post. It was too late to explore a Jap canyon between the guerilla outpost and US lines. (Mt. Blit is an elliptical-shaped 4051-foot height about 25 miles south of Cotabato City.)

We scanned a Jap detachment on a flat below us. Sentries seemed to spend more time in horse-play than in watching. Men lolled among the scattered grass huts. We spotted munition and supply dumps.

On the third morning, we explored the Jap-held canyon, looking from heavy jungle down into the chasm. Often, the Lt. asked, "Don't you see them? There they are." But Joe could not see any Nips under the jungle canopy below us. Three Filipino peasants came up from the canyon and also affirmed that they had seen the Japs. But Joe remembered too well the false reports that 162 Inf had from timorous men on Roosevelt Ridge.

Entering the canyon, we found that the Japs had left hastily, probably 4 hours before. Ashes were still warm, equipment strewn everywhere. The peasants had perhaps lied, to keep the guerillas from what the peasants considered to be their rightful loot.

On the fourth day of their patrol, Joe and his 2 Sgts and 2 Cpls sought for heavier Jap concentrations. The Lt. with his Pln lurked back 30 yards to secure us.

At a Jap outpost, only 2 men guarded; others lay asleep in a grass shack. A LMG sat on its bipod. Two knee mortars lay on the ground, and 3 baskets of grenades. Farther back were camps totalling about 100 men, with ammo dumps and supply dumps. A small hospital stood on the edge of a garden, with a handful of patients. We saw horses and carts, but no motor vehicles. We wondered why there were many sacks of rice.

Before noon, we had patrolled along a path on the side of a gorge above a turbulent stream. Now the clay sides of the gorge were over 100 feet high. Through jungle breaks, we saw tents, but mostly grass shacks where Japs were washing clothes in a big old drum, polishing sabers, or just lying around.

Also through that jungle, we saw a large, squat, thatched building. The Lt. said that this was Col. Yamashita's Hqs. He was the son of Gen. Tomoyuki Yamashita fighting in Luzon.

We wanted to fire on them. We knew we could slay some 10 and escape in the confusion. But our patrol was incomplete. The Japs would horribly punish Filipino civilians, long before we could move Yanks from Cotabato to save them.

Joe planned to kidnap Col. Yamashita that night. While the guerillas waited outside, he would slip into the Col.'s room, knock him out, gag with an extra sock, tie his arms, and drag him into the jungle. Yamashita would be imprisoned in Cotabato Town before his officers would know that he was gone.

The Filipino Lt. seemed to like the idea. He located Yamashita's sleeping area, and said that we could enter the building from the rear. If Joe failed and was entrapped, his tommie would fire. We would scatter to the jungle, and hopefully, rendezvous tomorrow. The scared Lt. looked at Joe with an expression that still haunts Joe.

In dull twilight, we moved out, single file. In 15 minutes it was darker, but Joe still saw the Lt.'s back ahead, and the Lt. saw back of second of the two best trackers leading us. Thirty minutes later in blackness, Joe held to the Lt.'s pack-strap, and the man behind held onto Joe's pack. Every few minutes then, Joe whispered, "How much longer?" Always came the answer, "Only a few minutes."

Morning light came after long hours. We were back in the corn-field where we had started — tired and hungry. Holding down his fury, Joe slowly smoked. Finally, he controlled his voice to ask, "What happened?" "Loco guides lose way," replied the Lt. in pretend scorn. Every night, Joe had slept lightly because he feared treachery, but now he stayed awake until noon when he awoke the guerillas.

But Joe still had another mission. We were to spy on Japs at Dalican, a port some 3-5 miles west of the Filipino outpost, on Talayan River, which flows into Mindanao River near Cotabato Town. The Lt. said that we lacked the men to examine this allegedly well-fortified Nippo town, but Joe said, "As a soldier, I must carry out my orders!"

Using jungle cover beside the dusty road for the first 1.5 miles, we saw an opening 200 yards long, with 50-75 yards of bare ground on each side of the road. As point, Joe planned to run through the opening, while the guerillas doubled after him, man by man. As each man halted, he would cover the rear for Japs. But nobody followed Joe. He had to slip back and order them ahead of him with his tommie.

In another 1.5 miles from Dalican, we found a rice plantation of many thatch-roofed buildings with Moro workers. Women wore ornamented vests and baggy pantaloons, tucked in at the knees. Two bearded older men told us of a little known nearby way into Dalican. All day, they said, Japs had patrolled every inch of Dalican, both sides of the river, and both sides of the road. The Moros did not know how we had missed that dragnet.

Patrolling deep into green jungle, we found the overgrown trail. It ended behind an abandoned old grass shack. Nobody noticed us in Dalican until we came to some impressive riverside docks.

We talked to a few citizens. In fair English, one said that US troops had docked in an LCM a few minutes, then dropped back downstream. These had drawn the Nippo patrol from Mt. Blit. The Pln had left just 30 minutes before.

Many natives were not trustworthy. We told the truth where it was common knowledge, but exaggerated the size of US forces in Cotabato. We spoke of thousands of troops and tanks. While taking compass bearings, we visited the marketplace. We left by a hillside exit, which was closest to Cotabato — to throw off any Jap informants from our trail.

Although returning to Cotabato was safer, Joe had promised to banquet at the Moro plantation that night. Refusing Moro hospitality might alienate them. Our guerillas wanted to be where women were.

Welcomed by the Moros, we chose a bivouac house. Knowing that they would turn out any household to let us rest unmolested, Joe chose a sagging old grass shack on the outskirts near the jungle. Its odor was unpleasant but endurable. Later, we found that it was a disused hogpen.

We dined of course with our arms by our feet. Hosts were all male — the top men of the plantation. Women sat outside on the steps to enjoy the show — and warn against the Japs.

Joe was served first. Each waiter marched with a round wicker tray raised on 5 fingers high overhead — a dish to a tray. First came a bowl of chicken soup; then boiled rice; then chopped pork with rice, bean sprouts, and spring onions; then coarse brown sugar in coconut shells. Dessert was rice biscuits with coffee and milk — milk which Joe prized indeed.

Outside the hall, we merely allowed ourselves handshakes. But middle-aged women hugged us, and their hugs prompted the girls to embrace us with passion unexpected from Moros. The men looked on indulgently. With songs and a mandolin, we were escorted to bivouac in our ruined hut.

About 0300, our guard on duty awoke us. Loud Jap voices demanded and threatened. An estimated 50-man Jap patrol was ransacking every building to find and kill us. Moro voices wept and wailed and pleaded hysterically.

Back to back in the death-dark of our smelly old hut, we crouched, hands on trigger-guards. If the Japs got within 20 yards, we'd blast them and while they were still in disorder, dive back into the jungle, and hopefully meet tomorrow. But now, Moros were laughing, and a Jap voice was saying in English, "So solly, please!" We heard the measured tread of their retreating patrol.

Searching, ready to shoot, the Japs had turned out all the men, women, and children from all the Moro homes. The Moros loudly screamed that we had left last night. The Japs failed to examine our shack; they could not believe that Americans would sleep in a hogpen.

In early dawn, we made a total reconnaissance back in Dalican. We mapped every street, road, by-path, house, or wayside thicket. In the market-place, we told the arriving morning crowd the names of islands already freed from the Japs. Then we retreated towards Cotabato Town and safety.

By twilight, we had arrived at either E or F Co 162 Inf. Here, a heavy-set 1/Lt. seemed to find fault with us when he said, "Figured you'd turn up a couple of days ago." Joe replied, "We could have been here four days ago, if we'd have shirked our responsibility." Then Joe said that we were famished.

The 1/Lt. said that Joe could eat — but not his comrade guerillas. Joe said, "We all eat or nobody does." He unslung his tommie. "Lt., I do not intend to argue. I am Col. Bailey's representative until this patrol is over." The Lt. gave in. We ate fresh potatoes with jungle rations, toast, plum pudding.

At 1430 the next day in 2/Bn Hq, Col. Bailey examined the guerilla Lt.'s map with Joe's entries of Japs' positions. Bailey said that air photos confirmed Joe's maps, and Joe's data.

As Bailey had requested, Joe offered his plan for a 3-pronged attack to secure Dalican from the Mt. Blit Japs. But Bailey replied that by now, those Japs were no real threat. (For 2/Bn was needed — 100 miles east to drive Lt. Gen. Gyusaku Morizumi's men into the Mindanao Mountains.)

Then Col. Bailey had the grandest surprise of all for Joe Bradshaw long after midnight. Joe was going home! Joe had come back from patrol just in time to board a truck leaving Cotabato Town that morning to begin the trip.

At 1100, Joe embarked with some 20 more men to truck 100 miles east across Mindanao to embark from Davao. We were unarmed and in sun-tans. As we drove through a battle area near Davao, Jap FA and automatic fire fell near us. We saw a dead man lying beside an overturned jeep and two men of a Service Bn trembling in fear. SV 162's 1/Sgt. Bob Fleming and a motor pool man righted the jeep and with the dead man in it, followed us into Davao City. The rest of Joe's return Stateside via Leyte and Norfolk, Va., was routine. About June, 1945, Joe was discharged — but with a

30-day furlough to decide whether he desired to remain in the Army.

Epilogue on Joe's patrol. From Jap reports, we believe that Joe had patrolled against a detachment from 1/Bn 74 Jap Infantry. Assigned to gather rice for Morozumi's 30 Div, they were cut off by the US invasion. (This could explain why Joe had seen many piles of rice bags on his patrol.) From 2/Bn 162 Hq, we have notes on a 4-5 man patrol of 11-15 May, which seems to be Joe's patrol. Earlier Filipino civilians' reports were that some 300 Japs were in the Mt. Blit area, but this report — probably Joe's — was that an estimated 100 Japs were in the Mt. Blit garrison.

OUR NAVY AND AMPHIBIOUS ENGINEERS: FIRST WAVE FIGHTERS FOR WAKDE

by Dr. Hargis Westerfield, Division Historian

CREDIT: Most important sources are Capt. Bern Anderson's "Report of Operations; Capture of the TOEM-WAKDE Island Area..." of 7 June 1944; and *Amphibian Engineer Operations*, which is Vol IV of "Engineer Operations in the Southwest Pacific 1941-1945." Other sources are Capt. A.G. Noble's "Report of the Toem-Wakde Operation," of 22 Sept. 1944; "It's a Crazy War Up on Wakde," probably by Cpl. George Bick from *Yank Down Under* (21 July 1944); *Sarmi*, which is Terrain Handbook No. 26 of Allied Geographical Section; 163 Inf.'s Casualty Report; Samuel Eliot Morison's *New Guinea and the Marianas*, which is Vol VIII of his *History of United States Naval Operations in World War II;* and R.R. Smith's *Approach to the Philippines*. Our 163 Inf. historians were unaware of the full contribution of Navy and Amphibs in averting disaster on the beach. I regret that more data cannot be had on the casualties of the Amphibian Engineers in the charge for Wakde Beach. (Most important facts of this history came from visits to U. S. Navy Yards Archives at Washington, D. C., and Gen. Eichelberger Collection at Duke University, Durham, North Carolina. Our 41st Div. Assn. financed these visits.)

Most 41st Div. veterans are unaware of the front-line fighting and casualties of our Navy and Army Amphibian Engineers when 163 Inf. stormed Wakde Island Beach. Yet without firing of Navy Destroyers and LCIs ("landing craft, infantry"), and without the dogged Amphibian Engineers, 163's charge for Wakde Beach would have been a disaster. It would have been a pile-up of wrecked barges and scarlet 163 corpses idly rolling in the surf. This is how the Navy and "Amphibs" helped us. (Right name of "Amphibs" is "Engineer Boat & Shore Cos," EBSR.)

On D-Day morn, 18 May 1944, our leaders were still uncertain of how many Japs held Wakde, but they expected heavy resistance. So at 0750, the Wakde assault began by 36 medium bombers (A-20s) of Fifth Air Force. At 0830 while 163's 1/Bn plus E Co loaded into barges of A Co 542 Amphibs, the Navy opened fire.

At 0830, Destroyers *Wilkes* and *Roe* began bombarding Wakde from opposite ends of the invasion corridor between Insoemanai Island and Wakde. In 15 minutes, they blasted Wakde with 240 5-inch shells, an average of 16 per minute. At 0830 also, SC 703 stationed itself 600 yards south of Wakde in the invasion corridor, and 1200 yards west of the actual landing beach. SC 703, a submarine chaser, was the "control boat" for our beachhead.

In 6 waves, a total of 27 landing barges were to leave Toem Foreshore at 5-minute intervals. Each wave would drive due north from Toem past the west end of Insoemanai Island on their right. When each wave reached SC 703, it was to turn right between Wakde and Insoemanai and charge for the 150-yard stretch of sand north of Wakde Jetty.

About 0850, 2 LCIs led 163's first wave around the "corner" between Insoemanai and Wakde — the "corner" which SC 703 was marking. The LCIs exploded 850 4.5 rockets on the landing beach and the jetty. On past the LCIs drove the barges — with just 1,200 yards of water to cross before the beach.

But the Japs were now tensed in ambush at their MGs and mortars on the beach to the left of the barges. The 6 waves of barges chugging hard abreast had to expose their longest sides to the Wakde mainland just a few hundred yards north of them. There the Japs had emplaced MGs in dugouts, or in the gun turrets from wrecked planes. The MGs were cleverly camouflaged and covered. A reef protected that coast from a direct landing.

The Navy had suspected this Jap MG attack from Wakde on the left flank of the barges charging for Wakde Jetty. An air photo of Wakde in a Terrain Handbook had revealed that reef-protected coastal strip about 300 yards long, suspiciously clear of tropical growth. A third LCI, No 31, impacted it.

End of LCI 31's rocket fire seemed to be the Japs' signal to open up. A MG barrage impacted from that coast at our barges. LCIs Nos 73, 34, and 31 stood 150 yards offshore and struck back at the Jap MGs with every machine-cannon they could bring to bear. Farther back, SC 703, the control boat, fired also from her 3-inch cannon and 20mm guns whenever she had an interval between the waves of barges passing by.

Despite Naval superiority in fire-power, it was a hard fight against those hidden Jap MGs. Their positions were hard to find. Spotters on SC 703 found 6 MG positions in fairly close limits. But to do this, they had to backtrack the line of bursts that fell close to the vessel. Spotters also located the MGs' dugouts by wisps of bluish smoke apparently from defective ammo.

They were expert, well-trained veteran Nippo gunners. Among them were surely men of 224 Inf Regt of the Jap 36th "Tiger" Division after warfare in China — or the 91 Naval Guards ("Jap Marines"). All of their carefully controlled MG bursts ranged from 12 to 20 shots and then ceased awhile to keep our spotters from locating the dugouts. Our own LCIs' fire and that of SC 703 flailed the beach and helped the Jap gunners to remain concealed. Jap fire came also from mortars and rifles whose positions we never could discover.

The gallant LCI crews paid in death and wounds for their courage in close combat. LCI 173 had 1 dead, 3 slightly wounded, including their CO. A Jap 20mm shell started a fire in their 40mm shells near the bulwarks before it was put out. Another 20mm shell alighted in her 40mm ready box but failed to explode. LCI 34 had 6 casualties — 3 of them severely wounded, of whom 2 died. By later figures, losses of those 2 LCIs totalled 14, 20 per cent of the total number of about 70 in their crews. (LCI 31, which was farthest west from the Jap gunners' concentration on the barges, luckily had no losses.)

Those 3 little LCIs deserve more honor from the 163 Inf than they have ever received. They were only light little 100-foot craft with guns fore and aft and amidships, and fine Jap targets high in the water.

Yet the 3 LCIs kept up constant fire while our 1/Bn had to run a possible 1200-yard gauntlet of Jap MGs. Our barges had to run broadside to the MG fire and in ranks that they had to keep — 3 to 6 craft abreast. Without the LCIs, we would have beached with many dead and wounded already in the barges. Or more likely, we never could have grounded on the beach at all. (We can find names of just 2 killed and 5 wounded in all 163 Inf before we actually touched down on the beach.)

Despite the Navy's rockets and gunnery, A Co 542 Amphibs (with a B Co detachment) suffered 3 deaths and many wounds before they landed on Wakde. When the 6 barges of Wave No 1 was some 300 yards from beaching, light Jap MG and rifle fire began. Some fire came from the southern, right flank; but most of it was from the beach to the north and left where those LCIs were fighting the MGs. Against Wave No 1 with 6 barges, the fire was irregular and weak — and against Wave No 4 with 4 barges, which followed close after.

Then against the last 4 waves of 163 Inf, the Japs threw in all the MG and mortar fire that they could bring to bear — against 17 barges broadside.

Although 163's men could at least flatten behind the steel gunwales of the barges, the Amphib Engrs had to expose themselves to guide and steer. Coxswains must especially be exposed while they steered on the small platform aft of the troop space. They had to see over the ramp. Bow lookouts had to lift their heads from the gunwales to watch for submerged coral reefs that could rip open the bottoms and drown men or let them be picked off while they tried to swim.

In one barge, a correspondent for *Yank Magazine* saw a coxswain die from a bullet in the head. In A Co barges 2 coxswains died. (One of these may have been the man mentioned by the *Yank* correspondent.) One coxswain had saved himself by crouching low behind the gunwale, except for quick glimpses ahead. When the barge was 10 feet from the shore, he put out his hand for a signal for a soldier to loosen the left side of the ramp. A rifle bullet wounded his left hand.

When an Amphib crewman was hit, another took his place — until sometimes no Amphib was left to steer. A Jap 20mm shell struck one ramp and killed or wounded several men. Later, they found 68 flattened bullets in the barrage, beside the 20mm fragments. At least 3 times, the final steersman was a man who had never before had his hands on the controls of a barge.

In a barge of B Co 163 men, all Amphibs were wounded — the coxswain and other crewmen. B Co's Sgt. Bilbao seized the controls unfamiliar to him, and lurched the barge over to ground on Insoemanai Island. Another man returned it to land on Wakde. A war correspondent guided in one barge. Still another amateur coxswain was a Red Cross photographer. After its coxswain was killed, the Red Cross man kept the barge in formation until the engine-man took over the helm.

After the barge hit Wakde, he exposed himself to Jap bullets to turn the winch to lower the ramp.

One handicap to succoring casualties was the lack of available Medics. One Medic was assigned to ride in just one of 4 barrages. Often he was in the wrong barge when a casualty needed him in another barge. Several barges lost time in running their wounded back to the destroyers.

Total number of A 542 Amphibs' losses was 2 officers and 3 enlisted men killed, and 2 officers and 28 men wounded. Attached B 542 had 7 wounded. A Co lost 33 per cent of their men; over a fifth of all Wakde casualties were Amphibs. In 3 days' fight on Wakde, 163 Inf, however, had just 23 dead and 80 wounded. Like the Navy, the Amphibs were important to help 163 Inf.

After A 542 beached 163's fighters, Amphibs still had combat and hard labor ahead to land supplies. E Co 593 Amphibs took over port battalion work on Wakde. With their Shore Bn's Weapons Pln from Bn Hqs, they were rushed to Wakde prematurely. Because 163 was fighting Japs just 200 yards inland, E 593 had to dig in under heavy MG and rifle fire.

After the Japs died or fell back, "E" begain unloading fuel and other bulk cargo from barges brought from Toem by A Co. Beach was sandy with a slope right for dry landings, but there were other difficulties. Jap fuel drums and debris must be moved. Sporadic sniper fire caused several casualties, but we worked hard to unload 4 LSTs.

Guarding E's flanks that afternoon, Amphib Weapons Pln slew several more Jap riflemen and killed a beach pillbox that 163's men had missed. As soon as the surviving Japs fell back, we extended the dump area farther inland. By day's end, we had a dispersal ground 200 yards long and 100 yards into Wakde. For the Amphibs, the remainder of the Wakde operation was without fighting — only hard labor.

Of the 800-odd Japs on Wakde, largest company was 280 men mostly from 3/Bn 224 Inf, with a few weapons Co men also from 224 Inf. Besides fragments of other commands, there were 150 "Jap Marines" of 91 Naval Guards. Lt.-Gen. Hachiro Tagami had planned to move 2 more Marine Cos to Wakde, but waited a day too late before 163 Inf landed.

After the Wakde battle, Amphibs helped the Inf Regts on the New Guinea mainland. To serve the Regts attempting to capture Sarmi Strip, A Co 542 Amphibs ran a ferry of 3 barges for crossing the wide Tor River towards Sarmi. All went well as long as 163 Inf secured Toem Beachhead. But when 163 Inf had to reinforce their 41st Div on Biak, 158 Inf had to fall back towards Toem.

Two strong Jap forces were preparing a counter-attack on the Toem-Arare Beach, but Brig.-Gen. Edwin Patrick did not discern the danger, even after the first attack. On 27 May, shortly before 163's first 2 Bns departed for Biak, Col. Soemon Matsuyama's men of 224 Inf had attacked. They broke through 163's carelessly defended front at Toem and were finally halted only at the beach.

Yet Patrick was unaware of the coming attack of Col. Naoyasu Yoshino's 223 Inf from the southwest. Patrick's few jungle patrols had found no Jap menace from the southern jungle. Patrick had no defenses in depth now that 163 Inf was gone.

On the night before Yoshino's attack, he had 21 different little fortified positions alongshore for 12 miles. Five of them were little gun positions of 202 Antiaircraft Arty Regt between Arare and Unnamed River.

On 30 May at 1830 about dusk, some 100 Japs of Yoshino's 223 Inf struck AA's No 6 Gun Position on the beach. They caught AA men in swimming, and 593 Amphibs relaxing after a hard day's work on shore party.

The Japs drove No 6 gun crew from their position and captured at least a .50 HMG. This gun they turned on the swimmers and on 593 Amphibs' Shore Bn. The Amphibs manned their .30 MGs and with rifles and grenades repelled the Japs. Fight continued for hours after dark. The Japs overran 2 out of 4 gun positions that they attacked.

About 2200, the Japs struck again at the south end of the Amphib area. Trying to burn Task Force supply dumps, they had a suicidal fight with B Co 158 Inf. They left 52 known dead for a US loss of 12 killed, 10 wounded. Amphibs had 2 slightly wounded.

On 24 June, Amphibs landed I and K Cos of 1st Inf Regt with tanks into a hot fight near Rocky Point to cut off Japs holding Lone Tree Hill. A Jap 75 cannon sunk one barge-load of wounded men, but a .37 gun on another barge silenced the 75 and saved all the wounded.

Until June's end, 593 Amphibs' Shore Bn helped defend Toem Beach against Jap infiltrants. They cleared 2 miles of fire lane 150 feet wide belted with barbed wire and studded with pillboxes. For 10 consecutive days, They helped guard that lane against four furious attacks, with only light losses.

Such were main actions of US Navy and Amphibs at Toem-Wakde-Maffin Bay. Without Navy-Amphib expertise, Wakde Beach would have been a disaster. After Wakde, Amphibs fought and labored for 163 Inf, 158 Inf, and 6 Div. They fought and labored hard and well.

"C" CO. 163 INFANTRY: BATTLING PERIMETERS R AND S

by STAN "BLACK BART" DAVISON
with DR. HARGIS WESTERFIELD, DIVISION HISTORIAN

> CREDIT: Thanks to A 163's Howard McKinney's help, Stan Davison has sent to me his fine 23-page Diary (now a single-spaced typescript), and a 2-page handwritten letter of 5 Mar 1985. Other assistance has come from 163's Sanananda Casualty List, Dr. Samuel Milner's *Victory in Papua*, and the original handwritten "War Diary/163rd Combat Team" provided by R. L. Arnett. In some ways, this is probably more accurate than the earlier published story of C 163 at Sanananda (*Jungleer*, Oct 1978), which was republished in *The Fighting Jungleers*.

On 1 Jan 1943, 3/Pln's Sgt. Davison squelched into muddy Sanananda Battle. In C Co 163 Inf's advance party, all squad-leaders and some officers slogged up the Supply Trail knee-deep in mud to little Moore's Post across Sanananda Road from Huggins (later Musket) Perimeter. Here we donned Aussie helmets to keep Jap watchers from knowing that we were fresh troops.

Farther up-trail, we passed unaware a Jap MG 30 yards leftwards, and arrived at our deadly Perimeter Kano (later Fisk Perimeter). The Aussies said that the Jap Army totally encircled us but were on the defensive. With Japs cooking fires 50 yards off, "C" men did not sleep well. Next day in an Aussie patrol, 1/Lt. Fisk killed C Co's first Jap.

On 3 Jan, all "C" replaced the Aussies in Kano Perimeter. In 3-man holes, we shared 24-hour guard duty — an hour on, 2 hours off around the clock. Two men per squad had to lie on outguard all daylight hours — hard indeed to lie motionless all day. Nights were restless because we had to grenade Japs prowling outside our perimeter.

On 6 Jan, a 3-man patrol unmasked a Jap MG nest. Holmes died from a MG burst in his chest, another shot between the eyes. We never found his body. S/Sgt. Don Dixon was hit in his big toe. Kassing was treated for shock.

On 7 Jan, Jap raiders struck our perimeter — killed Richter with a bullet in the brain. Kundert took a shot through the back into left abdomen. Carrying out Kundert, Malizzio was wounded in the head to die in Australia three weeks later.

On 8 Jan, Col. Doe had permission of Aussie Maj.-Gen. Vasey to attack perimeters Q-R. Q-R blocked Sanananda Road between C's perimeter and Musket Perimeter to the south. Behind an Aussie FA barrage, B Co would attack "Q" west of the Road, while our "C" would stike "R" east of the road.

But first, an Aussie "short" exploded in our mid-perimeter, killed Raley and Aubrey Jones. Sherman would die in hospital on 11 Jan. T/5 Callantine was pierced in left abdomen and 1/Lt. Ferris in right flank. McJames and Harrison were struck also in unrecorded parts of body.

FA rolling barrage and our advance were uncoordinated. Aussie shellfire among our forward men killed McLemore and Meek. Gillaspy lost his left arm. A tourniquet around his right thigh saved Steen.

Actual attack failed. The Aussies had only shells with delayed fuzes that exploded mostly in deep muck. Despite cover of 15 minutes' FA shelling with C's mortars and MGs to help, "C" failed to storm Perimeter R. (B Co failed also — in bayonet charges against Perimeter Q.)

"C" had to fight across a waist-deep swamp that had filled up the night before. Killed was 1/Lt. Fisk when he stood up to hurl grenades. Sgt. Nelson was shot in left arm, Roy Smith in left hand and left shoulder, Cornish in right thigh. Records do not state parts of body wherein Strand, Cpl. Martin, and Sgt. Wheat were wounded.

In this attack, Sgt. Mohl and 4 men narrowly missed being mowed down by a Jap MG. In escaping through blind jungle, they faced a 2/Bn 163 perimeter which they thought to be Jap. They fired into it; a grenade blew a mosquito net sky-high. They shouted apologies; no one was hurt.

C Co fell back to Moore's post which part of 2/Pln held, opposite Musket Perimeter. Col. Lindstrom ordered a second attack again — across the swamp. CO Capt. Van Duyn refused to make such an attack in face of sure death.

While part of "C" fought, Sgt. Davison was on the Supply Trail with a 60-man carrying party. There probably Murphy was shot in left knee and borne back to Bn Medics.

C Co's morale was down to sub-zero with five killed and 14 wounded. Sherman would die of wounds. Back in Kano Perimeter, renamed Fisk, we cowered under almost steady rain. With just a few bits of ground above water, we had to lie in clammy slit trenches. Dry cigarettes and matches were few. Then came our first mail. We sat in water up to armpits to read it. Davison had seven letters; morale went up; one man even smiled.

On 10 Jan, Davison began the most nightmarish patrol in his life. At 0400, he headed a 3-man patrol to scout Jap Perimeter S across Sanananda Road. With him were C's Nowlin and a man from another Allied outfit whom we'll call "Tommie."

Through thick jungle, we crossed the road and hiked about 200 yards before we turned right. Davison had decided that it would be a better plan to circle behind the Jap perimeter than to follow the Road. We tracked four different azimuths, first 340 degrees, then 355, then 10, and finally 140 degrees to put us in a half circle behind Perimeter S.

Daylight had come. Just as we settled down to observe, a lone Jap with a knife wandered out towards us. Without time for good cover, we dropped to earth just where we were.

The Jap was digging around in the tree roots for food. Hacking around all the time, he circled before Nowlin, then before Tommie. Finally, he circled in front of Davison, who lay covering him with his Thompson gun.

The Jap stopped and peered into the brush. Davison looked him right in the eye — a Jap with a long black beard, glasses ¼ inch thick, filthy clothes, and a rank odor.

With his tommie covering the Jap, Davison leaped up. The dazed Jap put up his hands and dropped back. With left hand, Davison motioned him to come closer. Davison now decided to knock him out with a left hook, drag him back into the brush and kill him.

Suddenly Tommie from another outfit panicked. He jumped up, pointed his M-1 at the Jap. Tommie's M-1 shook like a leaf — his face pasty gray, his eyes popping out. The Jap bounded back screaming what sounded like "No! No!" He fell flat on his back, rose, rushed back to his perimeter, falling several times.

Tommie crashed throuogh the brush opposite from the Jap. Davison and Nowlin caught him, hastily decided what to do.

We could hurry northwest towards Gona Battle, west to 2/Bn who might shoot us for Japs — or try to find our way back through Jap country. We were totally lost. When Tommie bolted, we had lost our azimuth.

We failed to retrace our path. We blundered into a knee-deep swamp. Vines and undergrowth hampered us. One kind of vine would hook to our clothes and rip them off if we did not stop to pull the barbs out just as they went in. Clouds of mosquitoes whirred down and bit our faces.

From 0900 to about 1230, we wandered in the swamp and dodged huts and dugouts on rising ground. We skirted a partial clearing with several Jap tents and Japs sitting outside. Snipers pecked at us, but we kept mostly out of sight. We crossed Jap parallel tracks with wire on them — north to Sanananda Point. Japs talked behind us; we hid.

Cover was excellent; a 30-man Jap patrol passed within five feet. From 1300 hours to 2030 near dark, we flattened without movements — except for relieving our dysentery — Tommie's uncontrollable. His continual moving about did not reveal us. Yet all afternoon, Japs walked and laughed and talked all around us. Even our own FA harassed us; a fragment missed Nowlin's back by some three inches.

Always, we sought the direction of C's perimeter. Then we heard a wondrous sound — the sharp crack of Mohl's Aussie grenade launcher which an Aussie had passed on to him. It went off several times. Azimuth was 180 degrees south.

About dusk, a Jap sniper came from a tree just ten yards ahead. Maybe he missed seeing us because he had looked to the front with the thick foliage below and behind him.

At 2030 in moderate dark, we headed south along a stream bank, as quietly as we could. Tommie crashed along, however. We heard Nips right and left, but they may have thought that we were raiders headed for the front.

Finally, we entered Fisk Perimeter clearing, marked by a bent tree. After Davison called "Black Bart!" Mohl ordered C Co to hold fire until we rushed in. Nowlin and Davison gratefully bolted a can of herring and smoked their first cigarettes in 26 hours. They were as happy to see us as we were to see them.

After resting all 14 Jan and shooting through the back a Jap who came down the Road too close and then decided not to surrender, Davison had another patrol order. With 15 men, he was to check out the jungle to the rear and left of Jap Perimeter S.

At 0400 15 Jan, this patrol marched to a point some 200 yards past the Road. While Seeger, Rummel, and Davison observed, four 3-man patrols cleared the jungle for 250 yards but found nothing. Returning, we saw dead Japs and faced two of them alive near an outpost. Nobody fired. To dodge them, we crawled 150 yards the full length of a clearing and homed to Fisk Perimeter by 1100. At 1200, "C" made a small attack.

Although the Japs had deserted the smaller Perimeter R east of the Road, larger Perimeter Q to the west still held out — a labyrinth of trenches and bunkers 150 by 300 yards. On 15 Jan, A Co sneaked inside this Perimeter. With B Co men, our C Co's 2/Pln cordoned the tenacious Japs and fought them.

Killed were C's Tague and Staub. Baskin was shot in left ankle, and Urnikis in left shoulderblade. Cos A, B, and C's 2/Pln were relieved from fighting Q Perimeter, for they would fight with the rest of C Co for Col. Nordstrom against Perimeter S.

Thus at 0600 16 Jan, "C" had battle orders. With "A" on our right, we were to attack Perimeter S from near Sanananda Road. At the first Jap resistance, "C" would form a skirmish line to the left.

After the heaviest barrage Davison had ever known — FA, mortars, MGs — C Co moved down Sanananda Road, in column of Plns. We saw shell craters six feet deep. Barrage had blasted Japs from a first line into a second line.

Because this was the area of his patrols, Davison's squad led, with scouts Rummel and Seeger. When they found a "dead" Jap on the ground, Rummel said that he had never seen one dead with his eyes closed. Mohl fired his tommie into the live Jap; Van Duyn shot him in the head to make sure.

Co A lost heavily on the right, but "C" fanned out to the left without fighting. Near the swamp where Davison and Nowlin had hidden the day before, Col. Nordstrom decided to set up Perimeters A-D in the rear of the Japs' route to the sea.

Now "C" had orders to make a perimeter protecting 1/Bn's north flank. But Van Duyn's patrol of Davison, Seeger, Rummel, Robles, and Swiec could find no good site for a perimeter. We did find a strange trail with US wire on it and cut that wire because we thought the Japs were using it. Later, Swiec learned that it was 2/Bn's wire. We had to re-splice it. We routed a bunch of Japs on the Road and killed two. C's only casualty that day was Dye, shot in the knee.

On 19 Jan, "C" became part of 163's all-out push against remaining Jap perimeters S-T-U-V in the Road-bend area east of Musket. A barrage began about 1700 hours, and we attacked just before dusk amid rain and mud. This 19 Jan was the day that S/Sgt. Mohl and Cpl. Rummel crossed a creek and broke into a line of Jap pillboxes with grenades, because their rifles would not work. They killed six pillboxes.

But "C" lost two killed, ten wounded. Dead were Don Smith, Cpl. Freitas. Most wounded had to lie in the mud all night, with Smith and Freitas. S/Sgt. Don Dixon took a bullet in the back above the right hip. Bullet shattered his ammo belt; six to eight pieces had to be extracted from his body. Gunter was shot in right leg, Toelaer in right thigh and head, Tylick in thigh and biceps. Perry was hit in left shoulder-blade, Praznowski in the middle of his back. Busse was shot in right chest and arm, and Robles in right cheek and arm. A bullet perforated Nowlin's right cheek; Mall was hit in left index finger.

On 20 Jan, supported by our 60mm mortars, we shot our way into the Jap lines. Report was that Levy slew 22 Japs but was wounded four times — most serious in left knee. We had two killed and two more wounded besides Levy. Nance and Whitney both died of wounds. Nielsen was hit in head, Slosar in right leg. Davison's detail counted 200 dead Japs.

On 21 Jan came "C"'s final big attack. Although main thrust was by A and K Cos under strong FA and 81mm mortar barrage, "C" fought into the Jap positions without this barrage. After "A" overran their objectives, they helped "C" finish their fight. "C" lost only newly promoted Cpl. Hanenkrat, a bullet in left leg. All 163 Inf counted 500-525 dead Japs that day.

Thus ended C 163's Sananada Battle except for more mopping up. Battle and disease had cut Co strength from an original 185 to 115 by 17 Jan. By 20 Jan, Davison's 3/Pln alone had shrunk from 40 down to 15. Fifteen men had died, out of 96 deaths in all 163 Inf. Such was the price of victory.

Maj. Gen. Horace Taylor gives Edwin Rashkind the Silver Star earned in Salamaua Campaign. Edwin Rashkind was a medic in 3rd Bn., 162 Inf. (Courtesy of Clark)

Allied capture of Mubo. With their fingers on the trigger of a rifle and light automatic, Corporal Max Hamilton of Melbourne and Sergeant Jim Garrick of Newburg, Oregon, examine a hut in a native village abandoned a few minutes earlier by the Japs as they retreated towards Mubo. Later the Japs were forced out of Mubo. The Nassan Bay-Mubo Campaign cost the Japs 950 casualties. Allied casualties were light. (Courtesy of Rohlffs)

Papua. Giropi Point. This is what Japanese Chevrolet trucks look like after Australian manned tanks had finished with them during the Giropi Point battle. Private R. Francis of Adelaide has a rest on this battered farm truck. (Courtesy of Rohlffs)

New Guinea: Goodview Junction. Typical jungle country and typical Japanese defences from which the enemy were driven by the Australians between Komiatum and Salamaua. Fox holes were connected by trenches and extremely well camouflaged. (Courtesy of Rohlffs)

1/BATTALION 186 INF HQ CO.: WOUNDED NEAR DEATH ON BIAK
by AL H. HOFFMEISTER
with DR. HARGIS WESTERFIELD, Division Historian

On bloody Biak, 1/Bn 186 Inf Hq Co's Al Hoffmeister was wounded horribly and a long time close to death. Up until 7 June 1944 when 186 Inf captured Mokmer Strip, Al had it about as good as any enlisted man could have it in a combat outfit. Al was in S-3 (Operations), a S/Sgt and a topographical draftsman. Al's duty was to keep all locations of Japs and Yanks plotted on a map at all times.

Although 1/Bn 186 landed in the wrong place on Biak — about 2½ miles west of where we were ordered to land — we hiked east to Mandom and bivouacked for six days until 2 June. When Hq Co climbed the coastal cliffs to join in 186's overland march to Mokmer Strip, Al did not suffer as much from thirst as riflemen did. He had an extra Jap canteen, and in 1/Bn was closer to sources of supply from the water convoys. But still, he never forgot that wonderful rain of 5 June when a long, heavy downpour kept 186 Inf from being halted dead in their tracks.

Once in that march, Al saw a Jap jump from brush a few feet off and arm a grenade. He put that grenade under his helmet and blew off his head. On the afternoon of 6 June, a mortar shell blasted near 1/Bn Hq. A fragment almost entirely amputated the left arm of a Rifle Co runner.

Before daylight 7 June, Al's Co was awakened on Mokmer Ridge to get C rations before the push down to the Strip. Al then heard of the landing on Omaha Beach in Normandy. He saw that of his three ration cans, he had two supper cans and no dinner can. He had a cold premonition that he would not be there for supper.

Then with 3/Bn on our right flank, Al's 1/Bn marched down the brushy slope to Mokmer Strip and crossed the opening without Jap opposition. Al's 1/Bn formed a line of Cos to defend the east end of the Strip, all the way from the ridge down to the beach.

Near a crushed coral road, Hq Co men looked for the best site for 1/Bn CP. Among the several dead Japs along the road, Al searched for maps, letters, orders, or other information to identify units, positions, and numbers.

And then Al's disaster premonition came true. With S/Sgt Pharr of S-2 (Intelligence) and recruit Nelson also of S-2, they scouted along the coral road. On the ridge above them, the heavily armed Japs whom they had bypassed were still hidden and silent beside their guns and mortars and stacked ammo.

On their right, Pharr and Al saw a crevice — or perhaps a cave entrance. Despite its silence, Al took no chances. He threw his last two grenades as far as he could into the black mouth. He heard the blasts but never knew whether they had hit any Japs.

A few yards farther on the road, there crashed before them and around them the thunderous openings of the Japs' four-hour bombardment of 186 on the Strip — on 7 June 1944.

Pharr had been scouting ahead of the other two men. He was on the right side of the road — Nelson the left — and Al on the right a number of yards behind. All three men flattened into the roadside ditches to hope for the end of the shelling.

But the shells never stopped falling. Tops of the palms between the road and beach were being "blown the hell off." If the Jap guns depressed a little more or the mortars angled a little higher, all three might be killed.

Al decided to slide back down the ditch and crawl into the opening where he had thrown the grenades. He could shelter there 30 inches below the surface and recall Pharr and Nelson to hole up with him. (Perhaps Al feared that a Jap Inf attack was coming.)

Prone in the entrance, Al covered Pharr and Nelson with his carbine. Deep in the dark behind him, he heard a sound like somebody stumbling over broken wooden boxes. Al thought that his earlier two grenades had left some wounded Japs alive. He ought to get out of the entrance where he was outlined against the daylight. He might get a grenade lobbed at him.

Just as he straightened up, while the shellfire still blasted from the ridges, several red-hot battering rams hit Al in the abdomen. They blew him out of the hole, blew his carbine out of his hands, even blew off his ammo belt. A hole about 6 by 1 inches was torn into his lower left abdomen. Al feared that it was deep enough for his death.

Still cool as a cucumber, Al tried to save himself, as shell fragments and MG bullets impacted nearby. He dared not take sulfa because his stomach or intestines might be pierced. For a long time, he did not know that he was holed through right thigh and ankle, for the shock from this abdominal wound hurt him too much to realize these other two wounds.

While Al was still in shock, four young, sparsely bearded Japs boiled up from the cave with long rifles and long bayonets. Al faced them almost eye to eye — four scared but determined men. And before them lay unarmed Al almost mortally wounded.

Why did they fail to shoot Al dead from a distance? Had daylight after the cave dark dazzled them? Or was it the shellfire? Or did they just want bayonet practice?

They jabbed at Al with their bayonets, but somehow missed. Al shouted to Pharr and Nelson for help.

Under the bombardment, Pharr could not hear Al. But he did chance to look back, and shot at once. His carbine hit the first two in the belly; they folded up like rabbits and died close to Al.

In frenzy, Al pressed his belly wound with his right hand. He rolled over, crawled and half ran several yards down the ditch, and huddled behind a large coconut log. By now, Pharr had slain the last two of the four Japs.

But three more bayonet men leaped from the cave into the daylight. Nelson slew one; Al never knew what became of numbers 6 and 7. As for the cave, Al heard, months later, that the cave ran all the way down to the beach. It would take riflemen and flame throwers to wipe out 50 Japs left in the cave.

Other 1/Bn Hq men were moaning in pain nearby. Almost at once, Al got first aid — from an older Bn Medic whose name he forgot. This Medic put a compress on Al's belly wound, but never knew about the two leg wounds. A morphine shot relieved the pain but let Al's mind think clearly.

Half an hour later, littermen packed Al about 100 yards to the sheltered side of rock outcrops parallel to the beach, among many wounded on stretchers and some walking wounded. Al guessed that of some 85 casualties from the bombardment, 70 still lived. He saw Cpl Hopkins from Hq Co with a phosphorous fragment in his back. Craig lay unconscious near Al — with a right arm wound and a hole in his skull just over the ear. (But Craig lived to beget 11 children down in Louisiana; Al still gets letters from him.)

About 1400, landing craft drove in under fire for Sboeria Beach where Al lay wounded. He saw water spurts leaping around them from Jap fire. One craft lurched under a hit; smoke and flames flared high into the sky. (Actually, three tanks were landed, but two craft were damaged, and most craft never beached. A previous landing attempt was a total failure.)

Twice as the day grew later, the wounded were again moved; the second time into a huge bomb crater on the open cliff-top above the beach. Al saw more than a dozen litters around him.

About dark, a Hq man said that Col Fields and other 1/Bn officers at CP talked of moving from the Japs' overhead field of fire. They did not know what they would do with their wounded. Lying helplessly wounded, Al was never more scared in his whole life than at that moment. Next time that he saw a man from his outfit, he asked for a weapon to protect himself from Nippo killers. A recent transfer to 1/Bn Hq Co but an old-timer overseas, Minnesotan Amdahl kindly brought a loaded carbine to Al.

Lovingly, Al laid the carbine butt on his chest and pointed it between his toes at the crater rim. He could silhouette Japs on the rim in the dark and maybe shoot a few. He could fire his last two bullets into his brain. For the only time in his whole life, Al thought of suicide.

But 1/Bn 186 Hq Co did not leave their position. Al believed that he might have dozed off until dawn. Every time that he moved, he felt warm and wet under his rear. The fragment that had passed through his right leg had pierced a vein. The Medic had missed that wound, and another that had grazed his right thigh farther up. He was of course in dire danger of infection.

About daylight 8 June, Amphib Engrs beached with supplies and ammo and began to evacuate the wounded. But when carried down to the beach, Al heard a Mjr and Cpl agree that they lacked room enough for Al. They would have to leave without him.

Al swore at them, "I can't hack it another day; I got it yesterday morning. I can't hold out much longer." The Mjr flashed a light on Al's wound tag and said, "He's right. We have to take him!" They lashed Al's litter on the hood of the buffalo out before the windshield and headed into the open sea. Salt spray drenched Al; the wounds burned like fire as they drove east towards Bosnek — about mile offshore.

Lying on his back, Al was first to see three Jap planes zoom towards them from the direction of Bosnek Beach. Al alerted the Mjr, who ordered the Cpl driver to zig-zag to save them. One plane left formation and charged down with MGs blazing. To protect Al, the Mjr placed his own helmet over Al's head. The strafing missed them, and the plane flew on west. (Probably the Jap airman was short of gas after a raid on Bosnek shipping, and he had a long flight back to his field on Vogelkop Peninsula at the head of western New Guinea.)

In mid-morning, about 24 hours after his wound, Al and litter were borne to Bosnek for major treatment. Here, sandbags surrounded the wounded in their litters around the operating pit. Operating pit was bulldozed out of the hard coral 5-6 feet deep and the spoil stacked in bags around the pit. Medics carried Al and litter down into a large dug-out roofed with tarps and electrically lighted. Other doctors were working on other patients all around him.

Operating lights burned Al like red-hot iron. Silently, doctors ran probes through both leg-wounds that were treated for the first time. They cleaned the wounds and packed them. From his belly they picked out fragments of ammo clips and chunks of dirt. Having only novocaine as a local anesthetic, Al passed out for the first time since his wounds.

When Al came to, he and his litter were carried up a long, narrow gang-plank into a Navy LCI — "Landing Ship Infantry." (This was a small ship about 100 feet long with several decks and usually 3-4 machine cannon mounted topside.)

Al rolled from his litter into a clean, white-sheeted cot — the first sheets Al had seen since a Sydney furlough a year ago. Sheets were surprise enough, but then a Navy Lt asked Al whether he would like an unbelievable lunch — green peas, mashed potatoes, and steak with gravy.

This menu was an indirect medical verdict that was the most glorious news of Al's life. This menu indicated that Al had no holes in stomach or intestines. This American food was delicious with his hope to live!

That afternoon of 8 June, the LCI left Bosnek and about mid-morn on 9 June, it hove to beside a giant hospital ship with dazzling red crosses. It seemed about ten storeys high — probably a converted luxury liner. We were out of sight of land in the middle of the sunny blue Bismarck Sea.

A boom swung down from tall ship's after deck and flattened on the LCI deck. With Al's and maybe six others' litters on a pallet, the boom lifted out over the open sea and even spun around. Al was as scared as he had been when he feared that he would be deserted while lying wounded back on Biak.

But Al landed safe on the after deck and was carried into a large room the size of an auditorium. Here were real beds with clean white sheets and many nurses and doctors for the 60 patients. The hospital ship waited out in the sea for several days until it was full of the casualties who kept arriving.

Landing at Finschafen, Al entered 364 Station Hospital, a first-class outfit. In 10 days, his leg wounds healed so that he could stand. After three weeks, he was on the operating table to finish off his abdominal wound. Doctors went to work again on the 6-inch jagged cleft across where his belt would be. Cutting all around the perimeter below the skin layer, they pulled the outer skin together and stitched it. It looked like a large baseball cover. But after the stitches were cut, the skin pulled apart to leave a scar over inches wide. Al could never wear an ammo belt again. Al was transferred from 1/Bn 186 Hq to wait about six months in casual outfits until his discharge 17 May 1945.

Al really had his death-wound on Biak. But S/Sgt Pharr's carbine, Amphib Engrs and Medics saved him for a ripe old age.

> CREDIT. In many ways, this is the history of many men's front-line wounds. Over 95 per cent of this history comes from Al's two marvellous single-spaced handwritten letters on sheets 8½ by 11 inches in size. First letter is eight pages long, dated 1 Mar; second letter is twelve pages long, dated 11 Apr — both in 1986. Other documentation comes from S/Sgt Pharr's Silver Star Award, and RR Smith's *Approach to the Philippines*.

Taking a bath at the old swimming hole. McIntire, McEvoy, Rasmussen, Stiteler, Kourbelas, Timothy and Byrum. (Courtesy of Kourbelas)

205 FA BN (and K Co 162 INF): FORWARD OBSERVER SCHROEDER ON ROOSEVELT RIDGE

by LT. DON SCHROEDER
with DR. HARGIS WESTERFIELD, Division Historian

On 23 July 1943, 205 FA's forward observer Don Schroeder first fought the Japs. Still a rookie from overseas officer candidate school, Don volunteered to help K Co 162 Inf. In their first major assault on Roosevelt Ridge, on 21 July, they were repelled by Maj Kimura's 66 Regt's 3/Bn. "K" was almost pinned down in black jungle on the south slope of the Ridge.

But even finding K's front lines nearly killed Don. He was sent alone to follow wire into the jungle up the Ridge.

Past 3/Bn Hqs' outguards near Boisi, he felt suddenly alone in heavy jungle with his borrowed carbine. He could see just 20 feet at best. He could hear no firing, not even birds, only his own heartbeat. But he wrongly believed that he was safe in US territory. Actually, he might bang into Jap killer patrols anywhere north of Boisi.

Now Don faced the Ridge itself. Rapidly it steepened, and the jungle grew thicker than before. Soon he had to climb by grasping roots and vines.

About three-fourths of the way up, he passed some K Co men who would have been lying down — if the ground had been level. Passing more "K" men, he expected to find the Forward Observer he was to relieve — or at least someone to brief him.

As he climbed, he heard shots, but no bullets hissing above or impacting nearby. Suddenly the jungle thinned out, and Don was on the rounded top of Roosevelt Ridge and looking down the reverse side into Dot Inlet. He saw barges on the beach, and Japs moving far down there.

But why were no "K" men around him firing on the Japs? An Army bugle sounded. Instantly a Jap HMG — a "Woodpecker" — thudded bullets at him from the left. Don himself was the whole front line.

Instantly, he threw his body backwards over the Ridge — fell 12 feet and landed on his back. But he was unhurt. The gunner surely believed that he had killed Don, and ceased fire. Shocked Don realized why "K" could not storm Roosevelt Ridge. From the left or west, hidden Jap MGs enfiladed the bare crest to topple dead anyone who stood on it.

Still shaking, Don found Capt Gehring and the other observer whom he had missed seeing just 20 feet below the crest. After briefing from this departing Forward Observer and Gehring, Don spoke to his new Communications man, Cpl Simpson, who would handle his phone wire to 205 FA on the beach.

Gehring feared that the Japs would seize the unoccupied ridge-line above us, and fire down on "K." Don had Gehring drop "K" down the slope to be safer from our own shell-fire.

Then Don registered 105mm cannon of B Btry 205 FA on the seemingly lower crest of the Ridge to the west. Then he tried to move the registration of his shells east along the ridge-line. It sounded simple, but it wasn't. The summit was narrow; he could not be sure just how far over some shells went. Shorts falling on our side could be disastrous.

After careful and accurate adjusting, Don impacted the top of the Ridge before K Co. "K" then started to move up, but heavy rifle and automatic fire and a few mortar shells blasted "K." We had some casualties, and at that late time of day, Gehring got permission to withdraw.

K Co bivouacked that night back in 3/Bn's perimeter. This was contrary to Australian advice not to give up the ground which "K" had gained that day.

On his second day of combat, 24 July, Don started out with K Co just before noon. To be sure not to get lost again, he followed close with Cpl Simpson behind Gehring. Don wanted to be quickly at hand for Gehring when he would be needed.

We moved farther east, then turned up towards the Ridge. The climb seemed steeper than the day before. Simpson was laying wire, but needed help. It took plenty of dogged sweaty labor to roll up that wire coil and carry other gear.

On the Ridge top, "K" men were already partly dug in under light fire from front and that vicious left flank. Don could not see Dot Inlet on the other side, for this time he dared not raise his head high enough to be shot at. He did see some Japs on a high knoll or pimple to the east.

Desperately, Don tried to identify some of his registration points of yesterday. Although not over 200 yards from yesterday's location, he failed to identify any point.

Jap fire increased; "K" took some light casualties. Don had to call for a round of white phosphorous to orient himself. Since he feared to burn "K" men, he ranged it too far away. He heard the shell whistle overhead, but he could not hear it thud in the jungle, as he could have heard the impact of high explosive shells. For safety, he had to keep his head down but observe at the same time. He decreased the range, prayed, and fired a second white phosphorous shell. This time, he saw the smoke plume after a few seconds, and had an aiming point.

Don changed fire to high explosive, with a delayed fuze. He hit the knoll where the Japs were digging in. He exploded some rounds just north of the crest, and also on it.

Frontal fire ceased, and far to his east or right. But fire persisted from his west or left. Even with several carefully adjusted barrages, he could not pinpoint the source of that fire.

A Jap bugle blew, and a few mortar shells struck among us. Gehring pulled back K Co, while Don covered it by a withdrawal barrage. K Co retreated again with their wounded, and Don spent the night with "K" a little north of Boisi. (By this time, Gen Coane had orders from his Aussie CO not to leave the ground which we had won to huddle into a compact 3/Bn 162 perimeter on the beach.)

On his third day of battle, 25 July 1943, Don fought Roosevelt Ridge with a new team. Battered "K" rested and hoped for replacements. Simpson rested also. Instead, Don climbed with giant Australian Sgt Fred Makin of Papuan Inf Bn and 3 Papuan native soldiers. (Australian historian Dexter says that Makin was a 34-year-old laborer from Canberra who was born in West Midland England.)

his most vivid memory of the war. Makin and he both lived to perpetuate their comradeship.

CREDIT. Basis for this gallant history is a 13-page letter-size single-spaced typescript which Don Schroeder wrote before his return from overseas. Important supplementary documentation comes from 162 Inf's 1943 Journal — and from Australian David Dexter's excellent *The New Guinea Offensives*. I have also a photoprint of Capt Frederick Gehring of K Co urging him to come down from Roosevelt Ridge on 24 July — and also Schroeder's medal award. This story corrects or amplifies two of 205 FA's earlier histories: "Cannoneers of Salamaua," and "Cannoneers of Salamaua II," republished in my first *Fighting Jungleers*, and originally in *Jungleer Magazine* on March 1965 and on October 1972.

---

1. I CO 163 INF ON JOLO: TOMMY GUNNER GONZALES ON MOUNT MABUSING

by JOHN ZANIER AND DOMINIC GONZALES

2. AT CO 163 INF AT ZAMBOANGA: DEATH OF KEENAN AND SULLIVAN

by RAMON GALVIN
(both histories with DR. HARGIS WESTERFIELD, Division Historian)

1. I CO 163 ON JOLO. This is the story of I Co 163 Inf's main fight on Jolo Island against Mount Mabusing — and of S/Sgt Dominic Gonzales, champion tommy-gunner. After A and C Cos secured 163's beachhead on 9 Apr 1945, "I" had to storm 823-foot Mount Patikul above the road south to Jolo City. Despite 12 500-lb Marine Air Force bombs on Patikul, "I" still had a small fight.

Two Moro guerillas guided our combat patrol. When 5 Japs lashed out automatic fire, we fixed them with a Pln in their rear, then mortared them with 60s. We slew nine Japs, had Grate slightly wounded, and took Mount Patikul.

That night, I Co had to slog through dark to regroup with 3/Bn near Mount Mabusing, about 4 miles south of Patikul Beach. The night was black. We had to hold to one another to keep from losing contact. Zanier held onto Barnard with a bag of mortar ammo on his back.

Suddenly Zanier heard a snap like a twig crackling underfoot. Then a grenade exploded. Barnard cried, "Help me!"

Barnard had carried grenades in the same pouch with his mortar shells. The pin had worked out of a grenade and detonated it. Yet the .60 mortar shells did not explode! The blast almost split open Barnard's side, yet Zanier holding onto the pouch was unhurt. S/Sgt Gonzales and some men remained behind with Barnard until dawn, and the rest of "I" slogged on in the dark to rejoin our 3/Bn.

Barnard probably recovered; his name is not on 163's death list.

Later, I Co had to bed down in the dark. We formed a protective circle. Our 1/Lt Amans lay shivering like a poplar leaf in a wind because of chills from malaria. Zanier lent Amans his poncho for covering, but the chills kept on. Next morning, however, Amans refused to turn in to the Medics. Perhaps this was when Amans signed his own death warrant, for a Jap MG would slay him two days later.

Probably on the night of 11 Apr, I Co had a Jap shoot-out. Shortly before daylight, Sgt Cunningham heard a great amount of human noise outside I's circle of sleeping men. Believing that the noise was from a crowd of Moro refugees, Cunningham still crawled up on them to be sure. To his surprise, early light revealed a group of Japs preparing for breakfast. Somehow or other, no one had strayed off to see I Co's men.

Cunningham crept back to range in our mortars and a MG, the last probably manned by Petersburg. Shortly afterwards, we had 17 more dead Japs.

I Co's biggest fight against the Japs was against Mount Mabusing, altitude 874 feet. About four miles south of Jolo City, Japs of 54 Infantry Mixed Brigade held a line of low Mounts — Mabusing, Pula, Agao, and Dato (also spelled "Datu"), according to guerilla reports. Our 3/Bn had to storm Mabusing, easternmost of those mounts. While I Co on 11 Apr had rested from Mount Patikul and the night march, "L" had assaulted Mabusing and was thrown back — with an officer and 11 men wounded.

Although "L" had easily fought their way to the summit of round-topped Mabusing, heavy fire repelled them from an unnamed low ridge behind Mabusing and connected with it by a saddle. An estimated 40 Japs with at least three HMGs and two mortars struck back at "L." The Japs knocked out two LMGs and repulsed "L"'s 2/Pln — even cut off a whole squad for three hours. Because the Japs had cannily dug in on a reverse slope, 146 FA's 105mm guns could not arc in on the Japs; the guns would overshoot the target.

On 12 Apr, the second day of 3/Bn's attack, it became I Co's turn to try to conquer Mount Mabusing. This time, we had help from an air-strike, guns of 146 FA and 716 Tank Bn, and our own 60mm mortars with 3/Bn's 81s.

Neither air-strike nor guns nor mortars expelled or even weakened the Nips to leave Mabusing, however. We tried to move on them with tanks and two I Co Plns, to one of which S/Sgt Gonzales belonged. But the tanks could not climb the steep slopes of Mabusing. One I Co Pln had to attack alone, with Gonzales' squad in the lead. Ahead of him, Gonzales now saw Jap trenches connected by foxholes.

Suddenly, Gonzales observed a Jap MG positioned forward with its two-man crew. For some reason, it did not fire on him. When he moved towards the Japs, they put down their heads as if they were praying. Gonzales slew each of them with a burst of 5-10 shots from his tommy. They slumped down in their same positions, dead.

When 2/Lt Thompson came up to find out what had happened, Gonzales warned him to stay back in a safer position. Gonzales said that every time he killed, he would lift one, two, or three fingers to signal the number.

Main mission of Don against Roosevelt Ridge now was to keep the Japs uncertain and insecure against a storming party. Don tried to top the Ridge again and knock out those automatic weapons that had expelled "K" from the Ridge. He also searched for Jap mountain guns that had harassed 3/Bn at other times.

In a hot, humid climb, we reached a spur maybe 20-25 feet below the Ridge crest. After 30 minutes, a five-man Jap patrol passed east of us on that crest. They halted and started digging in before our eyes. A Papuan spotted to the west what looked like an observation post. Through glasses, Don saw much movement there, surmised that it might be a Jap FA emplacement.

Don had a real problem to adjust 105mm fire on these targets. We were without wire, which enemy patrols could find and track to kill us. We had only Papuan runners to contact our Btrys far below the Ridge. Don's old map was inaccurate. Rain-forest and rugged terrain made it hard to get a clear view. Jap patrols could be on any Ridge shoulder.

But with such tempting targets waiting for the cannon before him, Don wanted to fire "so bad that I could almost taste it." He decided to fire by the FA observer's "2 BGs method" — "by guess and by God." His message form requested several rounds of high explosive, with a 50-yard decrease in range towards us.

Don gave the message to a Papuan, and started timing his delivery to the waiting gunners in the flats. Uncaught by any Jap patrol, the Papuan did a marvellous job of fast slinking down through the mountain jungle to the gunners waiting below.

In just 35 minutes, the first shell arced over. It crossed the Ridge to where we could not see or hear where it landed. A few seconds later, the next two rounds geysered the Ridge summit, but were short of the suspected emplacement.

Suddenly the whole Roosevelt Ridge popped out with Japs. Like ants, they leaped up where the rounds had impacted, and up before us, and eastwards. They were shouting; they seemed to Don to expect another attack from Tambu Bay.

Don wrote a second message for a Papuan runner. Besides necessary corrections to shell that emplacement, Don asked for just two rounds each on two other targets, with another 50-yard decrease in range. First, the gunners were to fire for effect on the suspected gun emplacement, then space out fire on the other two targets.

These were tricky adjustments, for once Don had sent the message by runner, he had no way to stop the fire, even if he brought down shells on our own observer party.

It took 48 minutes for Don's second runner's message to get results. The volleys for effect looked fine. Shells impacted all around the emplacement areas. Some shells seemed like direct hits.

One round for the other targets dived too close to us. Fragments flew close overhead. Another round to the farthest east struck a tree on our south slope and blew debris everywhere.

Don now feared that the Japs knew that we were observing close to them, and that they were searching to kill us.

Our second Papuan runner returned with a worried message from Capt Ghering, signed at 1305 Hours. Gehring strongly urged Don to come back in that night. Worse still, the runner himself said that Japs in force were behind us down the slope.

We moved west beside the Ridge until we found another spur with a small indentation concealed among some brush. We dug in.

Don sent our first runner down again with a new fire order. Agonizing over our unreliable map, he wrote: "One-fifty left. Repeat range. Repeat Btn 3 rounds. Am digging in." Don signed off, "LOVE AND KISSES." He never knew why he closed thus. As the runner took off, we tried to deepen our indentation in the scrub, even with our hands. Japs were all around us.

After 50 minutes, new shells flew over — shells to our right and left, overs and shorts. Fragments sheared the scrub too close; concussions shook the earth and almost deafened us. The Papuans especially seemed to be dazed. Then Btry B seemed to increase the range; they fired another five rounds or more — even across the Ridge.

It seemed the right moment to escape! We hoped that the shell blasts had cleared off some of the Japs in our rear. Breathlessly we stumbled behind our Papuans to the Ridge base and scouted along the trail to 3/Bn's perimeter. It looked to Don as if we had made it safely.

Suddenly a Papuan waved us off the trail. Makin dropped back and said that a Papuan had smelled Japs. Dark was falling. We crouched and observed for several minutes. It was silent and hard to see in the jungle shadows, about 1700 Hours.

Don watched a shadow slip across the trail, from one tree to another. Yet because we were so close to 3/Bn's perimeter, Don was sure that the shadow was a Yank. He called out to the shadowy figure.

Jap bullets flew at us. Although behind a tree, Don heard other bullets impact trees behind him. He knew that he would soon be hit.

He dived left and came up behind a prone little log about two feet above ground. He was safe from concealed fire from the rear, but a slug from in front hit the log above his head.

Desperately in the dim light, Don tried to see the Jap who had fired. Too late, Don saw him; the Jap shot smashed into his chest. Not yet in pain because shock had numbed him, Don was full of adrenalin. His carbine killed the Jap. Makin's tommy and the Papuan's Enfields drove off the Japs, with four dead and one wounded whom they carried off.

Makin tapped the wire to 3/Bn; a patrol came with a stretcher. At 15 Portable Hosp, Don said that he was hit in his lung. Yet the X-ray showed no lung damage. When he took a deep breath, Don and the doctor heard blood rush in and out of the wound into the cavity between ribs and lung. The bullet had pierced Don's back at a flat angle, rebounded from his ribs, and bounced out again. Luckily, the bullet was a Jap .25 instead of a Yank .30, which would have killed him.

Don had 52 days' hospital. Almost hooked on morphine, he had to stop the shots. He contracted a fever like malaria until the remaining blood was siphoned from his chest cavity. Then came recovery.

Back at Tambu Bay, Don was shocked to discover that Roosevelt Ridge was blasted and burned bare of its lordly rain-forest — even its gigantic jungle trees. This mountain was just a chunk of pockmarked red earth. Don rejoined 205 FA Bn still as a Forward Observer until tranferred to 6 Div, but observing on the Ridge was

Now Gonzales led his squad with the rest of his Pln inside the Japs' perimeter — long connecting trenches in the brush, with many foxholes. Following a trench and crouched low, he saw two Japs crawling towards him on hands and knees. When they noticed him, they started to back up — a look of total surprise on their faces. Gonzales shot them dead.

Meanwhile, the Pln was attacking with fire right and left of Gonzales. But he was so close to the Japs that he began to fear that men behind him might take him for a Jap and slay him.

Crawling low with his Thompson ready, Gonzales could see a long Jap rifle with bayonet slanted above a head in a hole to his right. Taking cover behind a tree, Gonzales watched that brave Jap in his last fight. The Jap lifted his head and picked out a Yank target. Then he stood up, fired a few shots, and dropped back down to the safety of his hole. Again the Jap stood up.

With perfect timing, Gonzales emptied a full 20-round clip into his body.

All the while, the Japs were firing rifles and MGs at the I Co men firing back at them. They threw grenades also. One grenade exploded near Gonzales; the blast knocked him down. But he was up unhurt and throwing grenades himself. As Gonzales' own grenades ran out, men of his squad passed more up to him.

Handling his tommy gun like a part of himself, Gonzales had a field day of killing through the brush among those Nippo foxholes and trenches. Mostly he fired from the hip and at short distances; he triggered short bursts of 2-5 rounds and hurled back dead men. When he made a kill, he raised a finger on his right hand for a signal.

Still unhurt but for the grenade concussion that had knocked him down, Gonzales kept on fighting. Carried away by the magic of combat, he wondered why he was not killed or wounded.

While he was firing his last of six 20-round clips, his Thompson jammed. He fled from the fighting front. One of the observers from the tank Co donated another tommy and five more clips, and Gonzales hurried back to battle. By now, the battleground was quiet; dead Japs were contorted everywhere for the souvenir hunters.

Forty-five Japs were killed by I Co that day. Of these forty-five, Gonzales was sure that he had killed eleven, but he had stopped counting with that number. Shooting from the hip with his tommy, he had needed instant coordination to aim and fire and stay alive. Watching Zanier, however, credited Gonzales with fully 22 of the 45 whom "I" killed that day.

By 1300 on that 22 May, mainly by Gonzales' fire, I Co had overrun Mount Mabusing. Besides 2/Lt Thompson slain, I Co lost at least Marek and Newton wounded by rifle-fire.

About 1542 that same 12 Apr, 1/Lt Amans also died. Although he was due to be rotated home, Amans and L Co's Joe Walters went to examine Jap corpses. They now believed that the area was safe for them. Walters was also a souvenir hunter.

Amans already had a beautiful Jap saber, among his many Jap souvenirs. L Co's Walters was something of a loner — known throughout 3/Bn as a man who went by himself into the jungle on souvenir searches. Often he would be gone for hours — a thin, shortish man, a little stoop-shouldered. He always carried a tommy gun slung over his shoulder.

But we doubt that Walters this time had a chance to fire his tommy. A Jap MG waited in an ambush — one that we had bypassed earlier — which the Japs had set up after we had stormed Mabusing. Walters lost an eye when the MG flamed out — a wound unreported in 163's Jolo casualty list. (Zanier would later see Walters stateside, at O'Reilly General Hospital in Springfield, Missouri, in the last months of 1945.)

Allied capture of Mubo. American troops near Nassau Bay carrying captured Jap equipment ot Headquarters for examination by Intelligence officers. From L to R: Lieutenant Verne Jubenville, Private William Childers, Private Gerald Schulte and 1st. Sergeant Richard Vanosdel. (Courtesy of Rohlffs)

When Amans was mortally wounded, the Medic tried desperately to save him. He used his own T-shirt to staunch the burst of blood, but Amans died.

Such is the story of I Co 163 Inf during our first four days on Jolo Island — from the beach to Mount Patikul to Mount Mabusing, highlighted by S/Sgt Gonzales' gallantry.

2. AT CO 163 AT ZAMBOANGA.

On 15 Mar 1945 during Zambo' Battle, S/Sgt Galvan's squad of 163 Inf's AT Co had orders to make a road-block west of newly won Santa Maria Village. Purpose of this road-block was to secure left flank and communications line of 2/Bn 163 Inf whom Jap fire had halted from the ridge NW. On the day before, Galvan's squad had obeyed orders to go through that same jungle with an AT Co 37mm gun, but we had drawn Jap fire and halted.

After Galvan's squad set up our road-block, a reinforcement squad from AT Co passed through our position and tried to contact 162 Inf pressing for Mt Capisan on our left.

About 0915 that 15 Mar, Galvan heard firing from that reinforcement squad ahead of us. They radioed back that they were pinned down, and needed help. Pln/Sgt McGiffen ordered Galvan's squad to save this endangered squad.

Galvan's squad pressed forward into a heavily jungled area with too much underbrush for us to see any Japs prone with rifles to kill us. First contact with our squad were radioman Galle and a "Lt Tex" of AT Co.

Two wounded men, Sgt Brackett with PFC Marx, crawled back from the pinned down squad, and then First

Scout Sullivan. Sullivan was most concerned about his buddy and fellow-scout Keenan. Sullivan knew only that Keenan was wounded. He did not know whether Keenan was dead or still alive.

Sullivan led out. Galvan followed with his squad and Medic Galle. Bent low and working forward to where Sullivan knew that Keenan was down in that brushy jungle, we dared not raise our heads. Japs fired on us twice, but hit nobody.

Medic Galle slipped up to examine Keenan. Anxiously, Sullivan lifted his head to find out whether Keenan still lived.

All this time, we were shot at and FA was impacting too close. As Sullivan raised up his body, a Jap bullet in his left side killed him. In dying, Sullivan turned over on his left side, and his feet were close to prone Galvan behind him.

Medic Galle rushed back from dead Keenan and cried, "Oh my God, what happened?" All this time, we were shot at, and our own FA was striking too close.

To get out Sullivan's corpse, Galvan called back for a man in his squad to detach a rifle sling and pass it up to us.

Still prone, Galvan and McGiffen slipped a loop of that sling around Sullivan's feet and pulled him back to us. Medic Galle now made sure that Sullivan was dead.

There was nothing else that we could do now for dead Sullivan and Keenan. We had to save ourselves. We crawled sweating out of that deadly place and left their bodies behind. Not until 18 Mar, three days later, were they recovered for burial. Galvan believes that a tank crew brought them back.

After the area was secured, Sgts Galvan and McGiffen returned to examine that place of death. To their surprise, main source of Jap fire was a pillbox just 50 feet away, but hidden in the brush. They believe that just one Jap had manned it.

As in other operations of 163 Inf, main assignments of AT 163 Inf was to probe for mines, guard our Regt's flanks with road-blocks, and go on nerve-wracking patrols where anything could happen. Later in Zamboanga Battle, we had two fire missions into Japanese areas. Only notable casualties, however, were S/Sgt Church killed in action back on 12 March about 1900, and Sgt Scott reported lightly wounded but hospitallized. Perhaps the worst of AT 162's fights, however, was during the probing patrol where Keenan and Sullivan died.

Co A 116th Engineers waiting to go to Nassau Bay. (Courtesy of Rohlffs)

> CREDITS. I 163's John Zanier is responsible for History No. 1 with two letters totalling 29 pages written 9 Oct and 10 Nov, both in 1981. After San Jose Reunion, Gonzales sent me a four-page letter on his shoot-out on Mount Mabusing. For background, I used two earlier *Jungleer* stories: 146 FA's "Fighting the Jolo Mountains" (Jungleer, Jan 1979), and 163 Inf's "Winning Mounts Mabusing, Datu"(*Jungleer*, July 1980). "Fighting the Jolo Mountains" was published early enough to be reprinted in my first *Fighting Jungleers*.
>
> AT 163's Ramon Galvan's was a single-spaced 1½ page typescript which was undated. Help came also from 163 Inf's Morning Report of March 1945, and 163 Inf's Zamboanga Journal.

Eugene E. Tepoorten 1st Sgt., 148th FA HQS. Btry. Ft. Lewis, Oct. 1941. (Courtesy of Tepoorten)

B Co 162 Inf:
OUR "SOEPIORI CAMPAIGN"
by Dr. Hargis Westerfield, Division Historian
with Major James Gray,
General Kenneth Sweeny

This is B Co 162 Inf's story of the "Soepiori Campaign" of Sept-Oct 1944. After the Battle of Biak ended when Ibdi Pocket fell, an estimated 1,500-4,000 Japs still were capable of final suicide attacks. (Division G-3 estimated that only 1,500 Japs were surviving; but from other reports, we judge that 4,000 was the more accurate number.) Although 186's landing at Wardo on 17 Aug broke up the final Jap attempt to regroup for a suicide attack, we still had to hunt down those refusing to surrender. We had to hunt them into their logical place of retreat from Wardo on Biak, into wilder and more mountainous Soepiori Island, NW of Biak.

Separated from Biak only by narrow Sorendidori tidal rift, rugged Soepiori was the natural retreat for Japs driven from Korim Bay and Wardo. Although with less than 300 square miles, Soepiori was a third the area of Biak, it had cliffed wilderness hide-outs and food supplies from native gardens. Two mountain ranges run generally SE to NW across Soepiori. The central mountain rises to 3,300 feet. Southwards, the lower coast range is as high as 1,500 feet in places. Between the two ranges was the narrow garden area stretching NW from Korido Bay. Population was then about 15,000. To reach this narrow garden area, the Japs would have to trek 16 miles along an exposed coastal corridor.

On 7 Sept 1944 at 0900, Col Benson's 1/Bn 162 Inf and E Co landed unopposed at three different places on the south Soepiori coast. Farthest west, A Co reinforced, landed at Napido. Main Benson Force landed at Korido Anchorage centering the south coast — with most of B Co in it. A detached "B" Pln landed farthest east of all, at Amirweri (also spelled Aminosweri) to set up a route-block. This B Pln's position turned out to be the most interesting position of the whole "Soepiori Campaign."

Back at Korido, 1/Lt Gray's main body of B Co beached and passed through "C" already ashore at the hill-base north of the village. Up the trail about 50 yards, we found three skeletons, and a few cases of mortar and rifle ammo. And 100 yards north, we had to kill two Japs, one of whom died as he reached into a box after we challenged him. Both were in poor physical condition. Next day, a patrol hunted up a stream-bed until a 40-foot cliff with a waterfall blocked further hiking.

Although A and C Cos had to kill a few Japs, and "A" at Napido took a prisoner, most action was with 2/Lt Grimm's Pln back at Amirweri. This village was located well around the nearly 90-degree bend in the shore which twisted NE back up towards Biak and the saltwater creek between Soepiori and Biak.

On 10 Sept at 0630, a native warned us that a number of Japs were coming down the beach from the NE. About 400 yards from Amirweri, we saw 20-25 Japs, about half bearing rifles. Because they offered no resistance, we signalled them to surrender. But some dashed into mangroves, and we fired, killed two officers, two men. Others tried to hide in the brush or fled back up the coast.

Reinforced by a second squad, we pursued about 1,000 yards. At different points along the way, we captured 12 prisoners, singly or in pairs.

Then on that 10 Sept, it happened just as on Biak: B Co found death again. After the 1,000-yard chase, 2/Lt Cate with two men turned inland a short distance to check out a small opening in the mangrove thicket. A hidden Jap MG threw down and slew all three. The MG had withdrawn by the time the other "B" men could deploy.

We sent a patrol around the mangrove thicket to strike the Japs from the inland side. To make that move, we had to climb hills that were close to the coast. When the lead scout crossed an exposed ledge, a Jap rifle shot rang out and killed him. We could not then recover his body.

Since the main Jap force had escaped, we withdrew to night perimeter. Besides Lt Cate, Ellis, Pearce, and DeLoof were dead. Exact place where the enlisted men died was not recorded. Two men's bodies were not recovered until much later — one not until 15 Sept, and the last not until 24 Sept.

Back at 1/Bn's Korido Base, the radio informed us of the fight. An LCM of "B" men left their patrol off Pimonsbari Point and brought Lt Cate and one enlisted man back to Korido. At once, Col Benson ordered the other B Co men and a section of D Co's 81mm mortars to Amirweri to destroy the Jap fighters.

Although a veteran of Salamaua and Biak, Lt Gray felt his first real hatred of Japs. He was angry because Cate had survived the battle of Biak with two wounds, yet now was dead from Japs we had tried to save. He carefully planned his next action against them.

But next morning at 0830 before Gray could effect his plans, our beach outpost sighted maybe 15 Japs hiking SW along the beach at 1,000 yards' range. Gray posted a rifle Pln and a LMG in ambush at the mouth of Amirweri Creek. At 30 yards, we challenged them, but they tried to run. We killed ten, and two probables at 1020. Fifteen minutes later, we polished off another Jap in a palm tree 30 yards NW of our perimeter. We found two rusted Jap rifles. All the corpses were in poor condition.

An angry Gray set up D's 81s for an immediate fire mission against the Japs who had killed Cate. This was one for old John Cate, God rest his soul — a good Irishman and a good soldier. Gray carefully checked targets with Lt Grimm and others who had been on the deadly patrol of 10 Sept.

D Co's projectiles impacted the jungle where Cate had attacked the Japs. The blasts covered an area 100 yards long by 100 yards wide.

The Japs were there all right. A captured diary said that they were sitting up in the trees and singing war songs when the first surprise rounds impacted. Tree bursts struck several Japs. Most of the others died on the ground. Thus ended the Jap resistance, after a great combat salute for Cate and our other dead. Not until 15 Sept, four days later, was the third man's body recovered from a point 1,000 yards NE of Amirweri. We found his dog-tags and M-1.

From 14 Sept through at least 15 Oct, B Co held Amirweri coastal block and ran patrols. We patrolled mainly on foot and occasionally by LCM on the 7.5 miles of Soepiori coast slanting SW from Biak to Pimonsbari Cape. We soon discerned the Japs' escape routes — even if no native trail ran down the coast, and hills rose to mountains immediately from the mangrove swamps.

Crossing over from Biak, the Japs might take a rough inland route. For food, they could hop from garden to garden on their way SW. Or they could stock up on yams on Biak and take a coast route. They could move in the open on coral just outside the fringe of heavy mangrove thickets.

Among those fugitives was Rear-Admiral Sadatoshi Senda, CO of 28 Special Base Force. With Commander Mayeda and an organized group, Senda was trying to rendezvous with a submarine probably to return across Geelvink Bay to his Manokwari Hq. We never knowingly contacted Senda or Mayeda, but we did contact the group. The diary disclosing this information came from the body of a Jap accompanying the Admiral. Senda did escape to Japan.

Some time after we avenged Cate, DeLoof, Ellis, and Pearce, natives said that a sizable body of Japs was coming down shore toward us. They moved slowly because they waited for low tide each day to be safe from ambush out on the bare, drying beach away from the opaque mangrove thickets.

Since killing them could be certain, CO Gray decided to give them a chance for life — but only if they surrendered without fighting. The inland terrain was so rough there that they could hardly deviate from their route unless they reversed and ran back up the beach. Gray made detailed plans to receive them.

Near Amirweri Village, Sgt Gilbert set up an ambush so planned that on a signal his men would rise up and capture the Nips whom they would have already encircled. For security, Gray also placed placed BAR teams where they could fire at once. Realizing that suddenly startled Nips might run, Gray stationed himself before them on a point across the village lagoon. He would call to them when they entered the ambush. His phone could reach his ambush group to order them to fire or not to fire.

As their point appeared, Gray stood up before them. In Japanese, he called for their surrender. The leading men halted and seemed confused. Other Japs seemed not to know what went on. He called "Surrender!" a second and third time, then phoned to Gilbert's men to stand up.

Then everything happened at once. The Japs yelled and started to run back up the beach. Gray thought, "None of this chasing them back into the mangroves and getting the John Cate treatment!" He ordered B Co to fire; it was all over in 10 minutes. Some died; some escaped; and four did surrrender about a week later to the connecting patrol up from 1/Bn at Korido.

Natives also helped capture Jap prisoners from Soepiori. Once our Division Chief of Staff, Col Sweeny himself, saw the natives help us. Embarking on a Coast Guard frigate with a Navy Lt speaking Japanese and a Dutch officer speaking "native," Sweeny visited the Soepiori coast.

Natives in dugouts with outriggers hailed the frigate. Two really handsome semi-nude bronze people paddled up to the frigate. The husband in front had a wicked-looked spear. The wife in back had long hair, shoulder length, tied behind her back with a string. Lifting matting from the dugout floor, they uncovered and delivered two skinny, bewildered Japs.

A second dugout brought a Jap sitting a third of the way back from the bow and facing forward. A 10-year-old sat confronting him with a club like a policeman's night-stick. Behind the Jap, a man and a woman had paddles to use on him if necessary.

Dugouts kept coming with 2-3 Japs in them. Usually, they lay in the bottom under rattan nets. Crowning the day was the arrival of a chief in a giant double-outrigger dugout manned by 7-8 men or boys paddling on both sides. Six more stood in the center. As they drew up, the chief wearing coat and pants distinctly counted up to "three" in his language. Then all saluted. From under the mat, they brought out five dazed Japs to surrender to us.

All told, Sweeny's frigate caught 26 that day. After the sailors placed all 26 on the fore-deck together, the ship's doctor inspected and treated them where needed. We fed them and took them to the Biak stockade for interrogation.

Back with "B" at Amirweri, eight starved Japs on 13 Sept gave up to the beach outpost. On 19 Sept occurred another memorable Jap execution. In gardens 2,000 yards east, we sighted 30 Japs at 1125. With bazookas and rifles, we deployed on the ridge above them — slew 25, with three probables. Our bazookas were notably effective. The Japs had six rifles and 60 cartridges, all in good condition.

On 19 Sept also, excited natives ran into B's area. On daily trips into their gardens, they had normally taken a few young men as guards. But with us nearby, they had sent the women and children with only an old spearman. But this time, two Japs seized his spear and murdered him. Our patrol was too late to catch the Japs.

These coastal natives had stopped headhunting long ago, but they reverted to the old days now. On 23 Sept, a war party brought back a Jap head on a spear, reported killing another Jap. That night, B Co was invited to the celebration of chanting and dancing around the head, down by the water's edge.

This was a solemn affair, no doubt for the natives' feeling that justice was done and the old man's spirit appeased. On CO Gray's suggestion, an American participated. Our Sgt Kekipi stood up in the full light of the fire on the beach which shone on the Jap's head. Kekipi obliged with an old Hawaiian war-chant. To us "B" men with our rifles across our knees, it became a victory-chant for our Battle of Biak.

After 15 Oct, B 162 left Soepiori Island for the comparative luxury of the new Biak Base. For our four dead, we had slain 85 Japs, with five probables, and one suicide near our perimeter. We had taken 16 prisoners. The natives had killed 25, brought in a prisoner. (We are of course unsure just how many of the 17 surrendering were actually Japs, or Koreans or Formosans unwilling to die for Nippon.) Our "Soepiori Campaign" had been a hard but necessary mop-up. Yet we do not forget that lonely desert jungle wasteland beyond Biak.

CREDIT. Sources are Maj Gray's 4-page, single spaced typescript, "Soepiori Campaign," written about Sept 1962, "Unit Journal of Co B 162 Inf Soepiori Campaign," Col (now Brig Gen Retired) Sweeny's "Incident of Naval Support During the Biak Operation." Important facts also appeared in "Operation Report" of Hq 1/Bn 162 Inf (9 Sept 1944), 162's Sept 1944 "Morning Report," 41 Div's G-3 Addendum to "Hurricane Task Force Narrative of Biak Opn," *Terrain Handbook 27/New Guinea/Schouten Islands,* and RR Smith's *Approach to the Philippines.* (Brief and less accurate version of this story appeared in B 162's Biak story of Apr 1972.)

33rd NAVAL GUARD (JAPANESE): SAGA OF A JAPANESE "CIVILIAN" MARINE
by Makoto Ikeda
with Dr. Hargis Westerfield, Division Historian

This is how Makoto Ikeda of Tokyo finally became a Japanese "civilian" Marine of 2nd Co, 33rd Naval Guard in Zamboanga Battle. (He was called "civilian" because he was not originally trained as a Marine.) He was trained to speak Malayan at the "Raising Asia Special School" in Tokyo. With 22 classmates, he boarded *Manko-Maru* from Kure Naval Base on 7 July 1944 — for rich Amboina Island in Indonesia about 300 miles west of New Guinea. They were to influence Amboina farmers to win independence from the Dutch — and to build up the Japanese "Greater East Asia Cooperative Sphere."

Ikeda never saw Amboina. On 31 July, a US sub sank *Manko-Maru* in Bashi Channel between Taiwan and Luzon. After 12 hours drifting, he was luckily saved by a rescue ship, but 16 of his 22 classmates had died. From Manila, he embarked on *Kokuzan-Maru* to voyage south and west by Zamboanga and Biak — safest way to reach Amboina. But a carrier-bomber of Admiral Halsey's force killed *Kokuza-Maru* in Malso Bay of Basilan Island.

Because the US 41st Div had already secured Biak, Ikeda was forever severed from his Amboina language mission. At Zambo, the seven remaining young language specialists of 18-19 years' age were no more useful than Formosan laborers and were treated like them. Attached to 103rd Naval Stores Dept of 33rd Naval Guard, they protected a salt warehouse from Filipino thieves. They also labored to transfer enormous loads of munitions, salt, and other supplies to cave warehouses near the base of Mt Pulungbata north of Pasananca.

As D-Day neared, US air raids increased. On 8 Mar, a lookout discovered a long line of US fighting ships in Basilan Strait. From where they were guarding a salt warehouse at Talontalon east of Zambo City that day, they hurried back to their Branch Office in Pasananca. A Marine Corsair machine-gunned them, but wounded nobody.

Zambo Battle had begun. The Japanese Marines of 33rd Naval Guard defended the central sector from Zambo City west to San Mateo Beach. Inland, they also held the terrain from Pasananca and Mt Pulungbata westward through San Roque Strip and Mt Capisan. The Marines' sector was strategically the most important for guarding the Zambo area. The Army's 54th IMB (Independent Mixed Brigade) secured both flanks of the Marines.

As battle began, Ikeda and five other language specialists became members of the Marines' Signal Unit. Slender Ikeda and his classmate Yokota were now part of a four-man group of runners. They were two teams of two men each. If one runner was killed, the second runner must still strive to deliver the message. Runners were crucial to the Marines because heavy shellfire often cut phone wires, and radios were scarce.

Naturally, Zambo Battle went against the Japanese.

They lacked planes and tanks and long-range FA. Still, they fought like Japanese. The Marines still honor two outstanding heroic acts.

Marines still remember Lt (jg) Rensho Masho of 129th Air Defense Co. On 13 Mar when a US tank attacked, Masho followed the Imperial Navy code of honor. He said, "A commander must lead in battle." With a heavy explosive charge in his arms, he charged the tank headlong. After his death, his 20 men also charged the tank to die there.

On 13 Mar also, Blow-Out Hill before Pasananca was a scene of Marine heroism. They could not halt the US advance by detonating the mine at a distance by electricity. At the cost of their lives, two Marine petty officers blew the mine by hand and caused E Co 163 Inf 83 casualties.

These heroes were Eizo Sakanishi, "Naval Higher Fitter Petty Officer," and Akiyo Yamauchi, "Naval Fitter Petty Officer 2nd Class," both of the 27th Torpedo Adjusting Squadron. For their valor, the Admiral of the Combined Fleet posthumously promoted each of them two ranks. (The promotion of two ranks was normally given to a *Kamikaze* pilot!) Sakanishi became a Naval Sub-Lt, and Yamauchi a Warrant Officer.

Zambo Battle was proceeding to a Japanese defeat. Ikeda never forgot the message that he and runner-partner Yokota had to carry from Lt-Commander Masaji Fujimoto at Cabatagan to Lt-Commander Sasaki of 103 Naval Stores Dept of Pasananca. Nor did he ever forget the dangers of that run.

Under heavy shellfire, they arrived at Marine Hqs in one of the tunnels near Cabatangan in the San Roque area. On the hill overhead, 3rd and 5th Marine Cos still desperately held positions despite FA, tank, and Inf attacks.

In the tunnel was Lt-Cmdr Sasaki, 33rd Naval Guards Exec. Sasaki courteously thanked them for their services. In a bombardment shaking heaven and earth, he was steady as a rock. (He would die during the great retreat after battle.)

Back into the hell of shelling went Ikeda and Yokuta to relay a message from Hqs of the SE Fleet to Lt-Cmdr Fujimoto at Pasananca. Shells were falling outside the tunnel, like a rain-torrent. They ran but repeatedly flattened when shells impacted too close. Once Yokota covered Ikeda with his body when a shell burst threatened him.

Finally arrived in the Pasananca cockpit under intermittent FA fire, the runners saw that supplies were being destroyed before evacuating. White smoke emitted from cave mouths. A black stream of sugar was afire. As they reported to Fujimoto, a bloody Army Pvt fell from nearby cliff ledge. He shouted, "The shells kill even before we see the enemy."

Without even glancing at the wounded soldier, Fujimoto listened intently to the runners. They had to shout; Fujimoto was half-deaf from destroyer guns when he had fought at Guadalcanal. The message from the Naval Guards Co was from Hqs, SE Asia fleet: "Choose a way to survive at all costs. Expect the day of restoration of the Empire to come." The message forbade acts of suicide.

Now the two runners got orders to rejoin their Defense Unit of 103rd Naval Stores Dept in the Moroc area about five miles north of Zambo City. Here were ridges 1200-1500 feet high where the Marines fought guerillas and 186 Inf. This Moroc Pocket was the final strongpoint of Zambo Battle.

After their report, Ikeda and Yokuta began running and dodging shell bursts up the narrow Moroc Trail. They passed a file of Formosan laborers with shoulder loads of rice or salt bales. Some were taking a trailside break without permission. Ikeda and Yokuta warned them to hurry — shouted "American tanks are coming!"

The runners found their 2-squad Depense Unit entrenched on a ridge for cover against the guerillas before them. An unwieldy 13mm MG helped secure the ridge. Eastward was an open slope of a former open field. About 150 yards ahead, the rain forest stood up — ideal cover for the guerillas.

Next day, guerillas opened up with rifle fire and grenade launcher blasts. Although they blasted the Japanese from their holes and captured the MG, the ground was retaken in about an hour. Guerilla arms were superior, but morale was poor. Guerillas were undisciplined troops never trained to stand in battle. The MG was safe where the guerillas had abandoned it in their hurry to withdraw.

Squad-leader Okamoto had fought bravely here, but a bullet pierced his arm. Ikeda's classmate Tanioka was wounded also. Lacking hospital facilities in the coming retreat into the mountains, both would perish from wounds from which they normally would have recovered. Tanioka would die on 22 May, and Okamoto on 27 May.

After more confused fighting in the Moroc area, the Defense Pln fell back under heavy shellfire. They gave up their cumbrous, almost unused MG. It was impractical for combat in the muddy jungle. Never intended for land use, it was formerly mounted on a motor launch sunk in Zambo Harbor. Not an Inf weapon, this salvaged MG was a clumsy carry. It broke down into only two heavy assemblies — the barrel, and the complicated base. They could not emplace it for effective use in jungle mud.

But back in the safer rear echelon, Engr Warrant Officer Onue grew wildly angry at the abandonment. Although he was no longer with the Defense Pln, he still retained command of it. He ordered his men to recover the MG. And no matter how unreasonable he was, they must obey his order. For among Japanese armed forces, a superior officer's order was considered to be an order of the Emperor Himself. They had to obey this murderous order.

Higher Petty Officer Oda picked Ikeda among only ten men to retake this gun. As darkness fell, they started forth with Oda himself leading. They were just lightly armed, for two men would have to carry the heavy barrel on their shoulders.

The MG lay hidden under bushes in the bottom of a valley, and they did safely infiltrate close to it. But carrying it off was more dangerous than finding it. The guerilas had silently let them enter the valley while they held fire all around. Now they fired from all directions. The Japanese were pinned down on a brushy slope with a clump of trees. They flattened fearfully prone in despair of their lives.

Soon the fire ceased. They hoped that the guerillas believed that they were dead, or had escaped. In a low voice, Oda told his men not to move. Later, he slowly removed his helmet and carefully lifted it up on the end of a stick. Instantly, a bullet whizzed by his helmet.

Their last hope left was for the night to come soon. A heavy attack before dark would wipe out all eleven men.

In time, night did fall — a long black tropical night. In the first light of dawn, they were safe to leave their valley of death. Nobody was hurt. They still took an entire day to rejoin the Naval Guard up front.

Of course they could not recover the useless MG. Oda reported to W/O Onue that the guerillas had destroyed it. Oda brought back some smaller parts of the MG to prove that the detachment had tried hard to recover it. The report did not ruffle Onue. Nonchalantly he said, "I had already struck your names from my roster." The villain had ordered them to retake a useless MG — not expecting them to return alive!

At Moroc, they heard that the Army had let down 33rd Naval guards. On their east at Zambo City, the 360th Bn had failed to attack on the Marines' flank. Another time, an Army Btry had pulled out from support without even informing the Marines.

Worst of all, the Army had diverted rice — that vital necessity — from the Marines. The Army had often robbed rice from Naval laborers' carrying parties. Supposing that both Army and Marines had enough rice, the 103rd Naval Stores group followed orders to burn the remaining supplies of rice in the caves. For the months when they would keep on fighting the US, the Marines were left with rice for only 2-3 weeks.

On 31 Mar, the Marine 33rd Naval Guard began their long hunger-and-death march into the starved Zambo mountains. (Ikeda and his classmate Akira Makita became assigned to 2nd Co 33rd Naval Guards.) Their march was over 300 twisting miles long, over a period of five months. It was continual foot-slogging in muddy mountain jungle and fighting guerillas and US troops — mostly while near starvation. Places of many deaths on the west coast were Sibuco, Panganuran, and Annungan. Lt-Cmdr Masaji Fujimoto was killed by a US mortar shell at Sibuko on 8 May. On different days there died also Naval Guards' CO Capt Keinosuke Ikeda, his Exec Lt-Cmdr Heiji Sasaki, and other officers like Higher Petty Officer Tetsuo Okada, and Squad-Leader Tetsuo Oda. (The Supreme CO of the Zambo trooops, Lt-Gen Tokichi Hojo, himself committed suicide — not by slitting his abdomen, but by a bullet in the brain.)

Dead also were the last five of Ikeda's classmates who had started out from Kure on 7 July to be interpreters in Indonesia: Tetushi Kishini, Eichi Kato, Yoshito Tamioka, Terue Yokoa, and Akira Makita, who had been closest to Ikeda in battle. After Makita dropped behind the ranks between Panganuran and Annungan, Ikeda kept supporting him and encouraging him. Finally, he must leave him to die.

The Marines' 2-week rice ration was soon gone. They ate *camotes* — Filipino sweet potatoes, from a few fields. They ate wild things when they could catch them. Ikeda ate a big snake, a small frog, slugs — anything to keep alive. As military formations broke up, Ikeda teamed with men of Naval Stores. Protected by his rifle, they gathered food for all three of them.

After hiking to the west coast of Zambo Peninsula, the Marines crossed the mountains to the east coast and hiked north again. Finally came peace, and Emperor Hirohito's order to surrender. Five months after Moroc fighting, they laid down their last arms — and went home to rebuild battered Japan. Out of 4365 men of 33rd Naval Guards (Marines) plus attachments, only 560 survived. But Ikeda was one of them!

> **CREDIT:** Most credit for this history is due to Japanese "Civilian" Marine Makoto Ikeda's manuscript, "Experience of a Certain Japanese Naval Civilian Employee at Zamboanga." This is an 8-page 7 × 10-inch document in English — in small, clear handwriting, prepared in 1986. More assistance came from four letters of 8 Mar, 8 Apr, 28 Aug, and an undated letter — all written in 1986 — and then Ikeda's corrections to my final MS. RR Smith's *Triumph in the Philippines* was also somewhat useful.
>
> When Ikeda wanted our US history to help him in his own history of the Japanese Battle of Zamboanga, he contacted the Washington (D.C.) Center of Military History, and the Center contacted our Division Assn, which contacted me. I have called my friend Ikeda a "Civilian" Marine because that was his precise Japanese status. (But to me, he ended up his war a true Japanese Marine because he seems to have acted as one.)

Papua, New Guinea, January 1943, near Sanananda. Moving into forward area to relieve the Australians. (Courtesy of Merrick)

B CO 163 INFANTRY: BERNARD MARLY'S BATTLE OF SANANANDA
by Cpl Bernard Marly
with Dr. Hargis Westerfield, Division Historian

B Co 163 Inf began our Sanananda Battle about two miles up the muddy Supply Trail to Musket Perimeter. From nearby Jap Perimeters P, a .50 HMG fired overhead, but we dropped unhurt into trackside grass. The fire stopped. In 15 minutes, we sloshed up the muddy trail again. Each rifleman carried two extra bandoliers and six grenades. Within 30 minutes, we passed a line of Yanks we were relieving — under 100 32 Div men, survivors of a whole Bn. We crossed a small stream on a slippery log. The guard warned us to hurry because of sniper danger. In a jungle gap, we filed into grassy little Musket Perimeter with tall trees looking down on us.

On the south side of Musket, Rifleman Marly and "Red" Shell cleared up a trench which departing Yanks had already dug. It was sandy and V-shaped for two men with a pool for drinking water in one end. We sat on the ground at the other end when no snipers fired down. On that first day in Musket Perimeter, B Co fought off two hour-long Jap attacks — had six wounded that first day of battle, 3 Jan 1943.

For Marly, night was worse than day. Millions of mosquitos descended on him. With right arm, he wiped off forehead, right side of face, neck, and left arm. Then his left arm wiped mosquitos from the opposite places he had missed before. Aussie repellent burned his face; he had to put out the "fire" by rubbing with wet sand.

About 0220 that night, crawling Japs fired a small-caliber automatic weapon at us. Marly saw the flash of its fire. In turn, Shell and Marly threw four grenades before it ceased fire. (Grenades were those fine Aussie pineapples that did not spark and reveal our positions.) The Jap gun shifted to the north side of Musket and again drew grenade throws. Broken twigs and our own grenade fragments fell before our holes and made men think that they were Jap grenades. But the Japs had no grenades! Soon all scared "B" heaved grenades at Japs who were not there. About 0400, Jap automatic fire harassed us again. And, of course, the Guinea rain soaked our sleepless bodies.

B Co did have hot Aussie tea for breakfast — indeed had it at first three times daily. Australian was our "C" ration — a square grand can pale golden with corned mutton, tea sack, and 3-4 hard, round "biscuits" to crack our teeth. Soon cans came up dented — sometimes with minute holes. "A bite near that hole would gag a maggot," said Marly.

Early on 5 Jan, Marly and Limbocker patrolled north of Musket. About 50 yards out, two hidden snipers opened fire from trees 40 yards apart. One Jap tried to kill Limbocker; the other tried to kill Marly. Both Yanks knelt and fired back at the rifle reports. They would fire twice apiece, one shot of each two at each Jap.

Marly heard a bullet "sput" too near him — just before he heard the Jap rifle crack. While squeezing a new clip into his M-1, Marly glanced slightly to his left rear. In terror, he saw where the Jap bullets were striking — on a barkless stump close to his heel. Sun had found a place to pierce the jungle; sun had lighted up his heel for a Jap target.

Marly jerked his heel from that deadly sunlight. You could have covered the bullet holes in that stump with a quarter; they had missed his heel by a fraction of an inch. What saved Marly from crippling or death was that the Jap sights were set a little too high for firing down at an angle.

Seconds later, two small Jap automatic weapons fired on Marly and Limbocker from the ground. They went from kneeling to prone, wormed silently back to Musket. In a few more automatic bursts, a ricochet from trees would have struck them, if not a direct hit.

On this 5 Jan, Limbocker died — probably in the bayonet charges that Capt Hamilton ordered against hidden Jap MGs. McMeel and Potts tried to save Limbocker, but Jap stopped them. They died also, and S/Sgt Sullender — and Mendoza who had to be left to die under Jap guns that night. McMeel's body we never found. Pickenstein was shot in the neck, and 1/Lt Ellers of Weapons Pln in right arm. A .50 HMG bullet had pierced a log that he lay behind and wounded him. No bayonet even touched any Nip!

And "B" was back in our wet holes for another sleepless and fearful night. It did help morale that Col Doe himself inspected our outer holes. Always he wore a fatigue cap with the silver eagle plain to see, but he inspected on his belly. A stocky, middle-aged man of 42, he crawled close enough for every rifleman to see him. After Doe, when it was almost too dark to see, ammo and grenades were thrown close to us — and cans of corned mutton or beef.

On 7 Jan S/Sgt Lockman died, whom Capt Hamilton called his best soldier. Probably from a tree inside our lines, a sniper holed Lockman's helmet in front into his brain. On 7 Jan also, Gorshek was slain.

On 8 Jan, B Co charged bayonets again in our biggest attack, and with our greatest losses in all Sanananda Battle. While C Co struck Perimeter R east of the road, "B" would hit nearby Perimeter Q west of the road.

This time, we had 15 minutes' preparation from the 25-pounder cannon of Australian Hanson Troop. But they had exhausted all their shells except those with delayed fuzes. The shells impacted like coconuts falling from trees, but the fuzes delayed them to explode harmlessly underground - if they exploded at all. (B Co's 81mm mortar shells would have smashed the Jap, but they were protecting Regt 1 and 1/Bn Hqs. At Musket Hqs also were .37mm AT guns whose frequent, accurate fire could have pierced Jap bunkers, but B Co never had the use of them.)

After the harmless 25-pounder shells, B Co charged bayonets again. Only this time, we blew no whistle, and our charge was a walk in a ragged line. We got nowhere.

Heavy Jap fire started against our first line even before Marly's 2/Pln left Musket. The Japs seemed to have an automatic weapon every 10 feet of their line, said Weapons Pln Sgt Eder. We could do nothing against interlocking fire from at least four MGs.

Lockman's former Pln suffered grievously. Eight men died: Berg, Russell, Genther, Foltz, Carroll, Sgt Holmes, Cpls Irmen and Rogers. Berg's body disappeared. Eight were wounded: Castillo in shoulder, left hip; Laabs in left shoulder; Cpl Petrovich in left shoulder and arm. McFarland was shot in his hips; Kjemhus in left hand; and Martin in right foot. Cawiezell's left ear-drum was traumatically fractured. Sgt Rubens was hit in left hand and right temple; he never fought again. (While B's attack failed, "C" failed also, with six killed, and 13 wounded.)

After about mid-Jan, Marly and Shell were moved into a hole on the north side of Musket. Here, Jap attacks seemed more determined than before. They seemed to ignore our grenades, or maybe our arms were giving out.

Next day to counter this new Jap fury, a direct line was connected to a 60mm mortar of S/Sgt Eder's Weapons Pln. In zeroing in, the mortarmen found that they must slant their tube at the minimum range — dangerously close to the holes. Base-plate had to ground in the sodden sand, which made their accuracy theoretically unreliable. But the piece would not fire except in dire emergency, we were told.

Next night when the Japs attacked furiously again, somebody called for the mortar's help. Marly heard the "sloop" of the shell leaving the barrel, and cowered flat in our hole. Seconds later, the shell impacted, and two to three more before us. Jap automatic fire ceased. When they struck again that night after three or four of our futile grenades, the 60s again silenced the Japs, with three rounds. Weapons Pln men aimed the mortar so accurately that they could have lobbed a shell into a canteen cup on the parapet of our hole.

One night after we saw our first sunset from Musket Perimeter, 15 inches of rain waterfalled us. By dawn, just our heads were above water — our rifles and ammo belts and grenades on grass outside our holes. When we tried to bail, the water flowed right back.

Water had wrinkled hands and feet. Marly's feet hurt as if they were in boiling water. When he slipped off a sock with his feet submerged, they burned even worse. Their wrinkles even had wrinkles — sidewise and lengthwise.

After 84 hours of their septic tank, Shell and Marly crawled forward to dig a new hole, despite Jap danger. Shell said he preferred a shoulder wound to lying in water. Quietly, they dug into an infantryman's luxury — a new hole only damp, but not deep in water. When orders came for all "B" men to dig drier holes, Jap fire drove them back into their holes like turtles. Only Marly and Shell luxuriated in drier holes.

By 14 Jan, Sanananda Battle began its final and victorious phase. Continual Aussie-US pressure and semi-starvation were beating the Japs. South of us, Perimeters P were overrun; the Road was opened. Northwards, our 2/Bn had cut off Jap retreat. The Japs had deserted Perimeter R, and A and K Cos were fighting inside Perimeter Q which had killed too many good "B" men already.

On 15 Jan, B Co moved east to join our 1/Bn in the final actions against Perimeters S-T-U east of Sanananda Road. Already deployed against Perimeter Q, K Co was not told that "B" was hiking east. An M-1 scorched Sgt Johnson's upper lip but drew no blood. A second "K" M-1 bullet holed Sgt Picketts' pack, but deflected on a metal mirror and merely felled him. K's fire was halted before anyone was actually wounded.

On 16 Jan, A Co's push on Perimeter S was failing with 49 losses. Capt Hamilton ordered McKenzie's 3/Pln up from reserve to attack against an unbroken Nippo MG line.

Now down to 20 men, we moved out in small groups over kunai grass among low, sparse brush. Farthest left, Marly's three-man group was hit hard. Before we ever fronted the Jap line, a sniper mortally wounded BARman Cpl Morin — a shot into nose and left eye. When the other two men tried to help Morin into a shallow ditch, the sniper shot Blumenthal in the spine and paralyzed his lower body. Marly brought up littermen to evacuate them, but both Morin and Blumenthal died later. At every chance, Marly's M-1 duelled the nearby Jap sniper, but another, unknown "B" man made the kill. On that 16 Jan, more "B" men died — Cpl Lingle and Runner Hapke from 3/Pln, and 2/Pln's Sgt Johnson when Capt Hamilton suddenly withdrew 2/Pln before 3/Pln attacked.

Marly returned to Musket Perimeter. When Jap fire struck near his new hole on the west side, Marly expected an attack. His M-1 fired so fast that linseed oil ran from the overheated stack. Later, he went with 2 Graves Registration men to search for Johnny Lorr, missing in action after separation from a buddy on patrol. (Lorr did return later.)

Finally, on 21 Jan, B Co became part of 163's last fighting at Sanananda. After some 40 minutes' Aussie fire and US MGs and mortars, all 1/Bn rifle Cos plus "K" advanced. B Co entered terrain where brush was blasted out into long open vistas. We passed a corpse heap of an estimated 300 large Korean Marines — men averaging 180 pounds in weight and in height 5 feet, 8 inches — close to average US height. We passed three immense unfired dual purpose cannon with a huge ammo supply stacked like cordwood. Ammo was in clips of 6, each big cartridge 24 inches long and 3 inches in diameter. Marly never has learned why these guns had not fired on us.

Suddenly Marly saw his first live Jap — a man running away. Coop and he fired and knocked him into a hole, where they dropped in a live grenade and left him. They shot a second running Jap and dropped a second live grenade into the hole that he fell into. They grenaded two thatched huts, but found only four dead attendants around a corpse on the table in each hut. Perhaps one was a surgeon. Officers' swords hung on the walls. In 30 minutes, 163's successful storming party was over, and we counted 165 Jap corpses in B's area alone. "B" had no casualties.

Thus ended Marly's Battle of Sanananda. He found himself suddenly a Cpl and leading an honor-guard for Aussie Lt-Gen Herring and other "brass" three miles up the road to the sea and the Aussies who had overrun the coast. Then came for Marly a hospital session with malaria and a cyst. He was placed on limited service and transferred to Medics. Like the other surviving "B" men, Marly had lived through a swamp in Hell. Out of 96 deaths in 163 Inf at Sanananda, 27 of them were in B Co alone.

CREDIT. Bernard Marly's original typescript is 26 pages long, single-spaced — a thorough coverage of almost everything a historian would want to know, down to the last detail of his equipment. I wrote this also with the "framework" provided by B Co's 1/Lt Walter McKenzie's history entitled "Bayonet Charges at Sanananda," published in the 1985 *Jungleer*. Other "framework" is 163 Inf's Sanananda Casualty Lists, where I have mainly used dates of deaths. Much of this history may contradict the official history, Dr Samuel Milner's *Victory in Papua*, and my earlier *Jungleer* publications on B 163 in July 1974 and October 1978. I believe that Marly's and McKenzie's stories are much more correct, however.

218 FIELD ARTILLERY BN: PANEK'S CAREER WITH 218 FA
by Dr. Hargis Westerfield, Division Historian with Major John Panek

On 18 Mar 1944, Capt Panek's forward observation party from C Btry 218 FA was first assigned to charge into Wakde Beach in an LCVP of A Co 163 Inf. Probably we would have been in the same LCVP where a coxswain was killed and A's CO Lt Rhodes was wounded and put out of action. But suddenly, we OP men discovered that we had our own private amphibious craft — an alligator with chauffeur for our war on Wakde.

Since 218 FA already had difficulty receiving from our "610" radio, Panek conferred with Wire/Sgt Hewitt about whether we could lay our own underwater cable from Arare Beach to Wakde. Hewitt said that the cable might be practical. We hurried to load a portable switchboard, "130" wire, and wire-laying gear from 218 FA. Also on board besides Panek were Swails, Bates, Cpl Hale, Sgts Hanson and Lauzon, and Lt Leigholt. (Although Panek was CO of C Btry, he had a special assignment as observer for Col Green, 218 FA Bn's CO.)

By the time our alligator was loaded and seaborne, 163's 1/Bn plus F Co was already ranked and charging for Wakde Beach. Running much slower than the LCVPs, we cruised some distance behind them. We still got the attention of Jap MG fire but were not hit.

When we set up our switchboard on Wakde Beach, Panek found that his project of an underwater cable was successful. For three days, this wire was 191 FA Group's main communication with our fire-base at Toem. (This 191 FA Group consisted of 218 FA with 155mm guns, and 167 FA and Cannon Co 163 with 105s.) And Wakde Force's CO Maj Wing was happy because he too might use our cable.

But when Panek told Major Wing that we were ready to call fire from our 155s, Wing was extremely cautious. For the night before, our own FA had shelled E Co guarding our Provisional Groupment on Insoemani Island across from Wakde. Seven men were seriously wounded: two of them would soon die. Luckily, Wing believed, however, that 167 FA had shelled E Co the night before — not our 218 FA — and finally consented to use our cannon. (The CO of 191 FA Group accused inexperienced CN 163 of the disastrous shellfire, but a CN spokesman denies this accusation.) Panek thus fronted for 167 FA's Col Beach until Wing consented to let 218 FA fire. Of course, both Bns then fired! Later that 18 May, when Jap MGs cut C Co in two when trying to cross Wakde Strip, both 218 FA and 167 FA silenced the Jap MGs. All of C Co then crossed the Strip.

Now it was late in the afternoon of 1/Bn 163's first bloody day on Wakde. Panek heard Wing conferring with another officer about the difficulty of forwarding water and ammo — probably to B Co. (Evidently our expectation of an easy victory on Wakde had caused laxity in planning to supply our men against those stubborn Japs.) And the Japs were slipping around B Co's right flank and menacing our beachhead.

Panek then volunteered the services of our alligator to carry ammo or water to the front. He asked only that Wing lend him a MG with its crew.

When soldierly Wing granted Panek the MG with gunner and loader, Panek put Lt Leigholt as exec with the alligator. With Leigholt were 218 FA's Swails and Sgt Gene Hanson.

We feared that the Japs would gut our open alligator with grenades when we rumbled towards B Co through the brush. Seeing several Nippo riflemen, we were badly scared, but we slew three of them. We were also scared when we crossed the open Strip, but nobody shot at us there. B Co welcomed us with our water cans and ammo. Loading some of B's wounded, we returned safely through that dangerous overgrown coconut plantation.

During the next day or so on Wakde, while the battle still went on, our alligator made more successful supply trips to the front and did not lose even a man wounded. Why did the Japs fail to attack this obvious and easy target? We concluded later that the Japs must have thought our alligator was a heavily armored tank which might readily blow them to pieces, or run over any Japs who tried to escape.

Throughout most of 18 May, 218 FA's fire on Wakde was continual. Sometimes against those formidable and deep bunkers and pillboxes, all 12 of our 155s would fire a concentration. Sometimes we directed 10 rounds from every gun on a target — a salvo of 120 rounds at a time. And we might keep on firing for effect after all of those 10 rounds of 12 of our guns. Our batteries called for so many more shells that even the cooks were drafted to truck them to our gunners.

That night, Maj Wing called for 20 rounds per hour on the Japs' final positions in the corner of NE Wakde. When knee mortarmen harassed B Co's holes early that night, Wing had us range our guns as close to B's front as we could. Then 30 rounds silenced the Jap mortarmen — whether rounds from 167 FA, 218 FA, or CN 163 is not known.

At daylight 19 May, Panek awoke from his hole before the alligator. The morning was quiet as he looked out over the terrain. Out front lay a number of dead Nips, and rifles shattered by grenades. As Panek dropped back into his hole for more rest before the hard day ahead, he heard a little "zing" over his head. A bullet hole appeared in the line of fire which would have passed through his brain.

For two days more, Panek's observers were assigned to Wakde. On the morning of 20 May while we stood in the alligator, we saw 6-8 Japs setting fire to poorly guarded Engr aviation trucks. (Aviation ground forces had landed prematurely on Wakde even during our first fighting on D-Day.)

We FA men opened up on the incendiary Japs with our carbines, but could not save the trucks. Despite the long range for our short-barreled little carbines, Panek was sure that he killed an apparent Jap Marine of 91 Naval Garrison Unit. He was probably a S/Sgt — 6 feet tall and weighing about 190 pounds. Panek still has his picture. A Sioux Sgt, formerly a 163 Inf member, hastily organized his Air Force counter-attack and slew all 54 Jap raiders.

Returning from conquered Wakde on 20 May, Panek was complimented by Bn CO Col Green for his good job. Green also said, "John, would you mind going out tomorrow with a forward observation group? I need someone of your caliber." Panek was to take his alligator and crew west across Tor River to cover 158 Inf's attempt to capture Sarmi Strip. For the Jap 70s of 36 Div were giving 158 plenty of trouble. They would fire 25-30 rounds, then cease. Although our guns' counter-fire would seem to silence the Japs' guns, after 1-2 hours, they would open up again.

Panek decided to scout up the beach in his alligator for closer ovservation of the Jap guns. Perhaps he would observe from out in Maffin Bay. And so we drove about a mile west across Tor River.

But our alligator became a prime target for the Jap 70s. A first round hit below us — and a second round in front. Round number 3 split the bracket; it exploded under our vehicle.

Packs and supplies around us padded us from serious wounds but for a few trivial cuts in Panek's chest.

We piled out of the alligator and took cover from shellfire among the arching aerial roots of tropical trees above us. As we withdrew under jungle protection, Panek glimpsed on his right a Jap bayonet attached to a rifle. And a Jap was also attached to that rifle. Panek seized the rifle from the Jap and killed him.

About a mile back down the beach, safe from the shells, we discussed what to do. We were an OP without communications. Radio, telephone wire were all back with the alligator — perhaps destroyed, along with our rations and water cans.

Cpl Hale, our MG-gunner, said, "I know how to drive. I'll get it back." He planned to work up under jungle cover until abreast of the alligator, then make a dash for its controls, if any were operable.

About an hour later, Hale chugged back in the alligator. Only damage was a 6-inch hole between the tracks. It was now useless on water and obviously a slow target on land. In the rest of the Maffin Bay Operation, we used a jeep to carry our FA observers as close as possible to our target.

Panek and his observers spent about three weeks with 158 Inf. Every 3-4 days, he rotated some men up from his own Btry C. He wanted to help their morale — to have them see the effect of their hard work and gunfire upon the Japs.

Panek never forgot that especially fearsome night of about 26 May. When 158 men dug a night perimeter, our OP had to be out in front of them to range in our 155s for protection against a Jap night attack. We notified the 158 outfit's CO that we would be before their perimeter, and that we would phone him to alert the men in their holes when we were ready to pass through in the dark. We did not want 158's MG to fire a final protective lie through our flesh and bone.

Adjusting fire was difficult on this evening. Darkness fell before we had registered our 155s. We tried to phone that 158 CO to ask him to pass through the lines, but we got no reply. Rather than risk trying to pass through those alert pickets with their hands on their grenades in their holes, we dug in on the beach. We spent that weary night between our venomous infantry and the Japs who might crawl in on us with knives in the dark.

Ours was an interesting method of adjusting fire to protect our infantry perimeters. We began by shooting one gun into the sea. From observing the splashes, we could bring in fire parallel to our lines as close as it was safe. Of course we fired just one gun at this time to conserve our store of heavy 155 shells. Then we could turn the guns inland before our perimeter, and then fire a Btry volley to be sure that all guns were adjusted right.

Thus we fired on defense. Our offensive fire — especially in counter-battery fire — was much more difficult. For often the Japs sheltered their guns in caves and rolled them out to fire. When we ranged in on them, they wheeled their guns back into the safety of the caves. Finally after our observers located them, a Navy cruiser had to silence them by direct frontal fire from the sea. For final security, 158 Inf flamed out the caves.

After 218 FA withdrew west of Tor River, we forwarded one gun every day to range and destroy an important Jap footbridge across a river towards Sarmi. (Name of that river is not remembered.) After demolishing that bridge, the gun was retreated back across the Tor River into our Bn's main emplacements.

In these shoot-outs, Sgt Rutherford and Cpl Hicks of C Btry were often gunners with that advanced gun. They needed only 2-3 rounds to smash that bridge. But every night, persistent Japs rebuilt that bridge. This action of blowing apart and rebuilding the bridge went on for 30 days!

For working our guns, T/4 Lloyd "Skip" Willis gained special recognition. He invented a new kind of gas pad to fit in the 155mm gun breach and keep the guns firing more accurately, and at longer ranges. When a gun fired, explosion of gases in the breach would impact the shell to fire harder and farther.

These pads were made of fiber, but with sustained usage, the fibers dried out and let the gases escape harmlessly into the air behind the gun. Then ingenious T/4 Willis got tape from the Medics. He wrapped several layers securely around the used-up pad. He discovered that his "medical" pad worked better than a new pad. For this achievement, Willis was called all the way up to the Battle of Biak to demonstrate this effective new pad. (We believe that "Skip" Willis should have had a bronze star for his originality.)

PANEK AT ZAMBOANGA. Such were high points of Capt Panek's war on Wakde Island and at Maffin Bay. At Zamboanga Battle in our Southern Philippine Campaign of 1945, Panek daily made two recon flights over the Jap lines to pinpoint targets for our 155s. Pilots were either Lt Case or Lt Janssen. On our third day at Zambo, about 1745 on 12 Mar, his pilot had to swoop at dangerously low heights to see into the jungle foliage. A Jap 20mm machine-cannon struck one of the plane's main struts, but Panek continued observing, and calling down fire.

Seeing small fires on the ground and Japs milling around a large hut and many tents — surely a headquarters area — he saturated the area with all of the available 12 guns of 218 FA. After firing this mission, he attacked a gun position. Fifty Japs ran from it into a nearby rain-forest grove. He dropped eight volleys into that grove; they surely caused numerous casualties.

On Wakde and at Maffin Bay and Zamboanga, Panek was a front-line artilleryman. On deadly Wakde, he led a daring alligator crew of FA men and infantry to carry water for thirsty infantry. His ground or air observation at Maffin Bay or Zamboanga were risky — and accurate. Panek richly deserved his promotion to the rank of Major by the war's end.

CREDIT. Basic personal history comes from Maj. Panek's 9-page handwritten letter of 19 Apr 1982, backed by his two Award Stories — for his actions on Wakde and at Zamboanga. I used also Cpl. Maurice Hale's Award Story for action at Maffin Village 1. Documentary sources include 24-page typescript history entitled "218 Field Artillery Battalion in World War II," and 36-page legal-size typescript "218 Field Artillery Battalion/Annual Historical Report (1944)," and R. R. Smith's *Approach to the Philippines*. Other documentary sources include my own Division History published in *Jungleer*, "Toem, Wakde, and Maffin Bay" (*Jungleer*, Oct. 1981), "218 FA BN Unit Journal" (Zamboanga), and "Zamboanga Campaign Historical Report of 218 FA Bn (10 Mar 1945 - 20 June 1945)."

C COMPANY 162 INFANTRY: BATTLE BEFORE DAWN AT ZAMBOANGA
by C 162's BOLT, QUAIVER, AND GRIGAR
with Dr. Hargis Westerfield, Division Historian

In Zamboanga Battle, veteran C Co 162 Inf did a disciplined job against our Japanese enemy. Most poignant experience, however, was our night of agony before dawn on 16 June 1945, when desperate Japanese charges might have destroyed "C."

On 10 Mar 1945 at 0750, we jammed into landing craft off San Mateo west of Zambo City and watched planes and Navy bomb the beach. We landed dry and orderly on Yellow Beach II.

Our 1/Bn's objective was to seize unused Wolfe Air Strip 500-600 yards inland. While A and B Cos moved forward, "C" secured National Highway with a roadblock — until F Co passes us west to Caldera Point and so closed off 1/Bn's left flank.

By 1530, "C" was digging in 500 yards from the coast before deserted Wolfe Strip. While enemy FA shelled this coastal ground, a lucky hit fell on C's 3/Bn. It wounded Cunningham in the arm, and Kuznierz in the leg. Sam Allen was slashed in the stomach.

About 2230, Japanese barraged us on the left with small arms. They seemed to want to draw fire to spot our holes; we stayed quiet. They ceased after an hour of intermittent volleys. Next morning, we merely contacted "A" and "B" with 1/Pln's patrol, and dug in 200 yards ahead of yesterday's position.

On the third day, 12 Mar, 2/Pln led "C" about a mile ahead to dig in near Masilay. This Pln caught six Japanese sleeping in an outpost and slew them.

As we dug in on a hill, enemy mortar shells made four "C" casualties and 1 "D" casualty. 2/Lt Larsen was hit in the shoulder, T/Sgt Gardea in head and hand — all light wounds. S/Sgt Noah was seriously wounded in several places and badly shaken up. Combat fatigue hospitalized Patterson. D's Dooley was seriously wounded while with C Co.

On 13 Mar in the same position near Masilay, "C" had our first death. This was when two squads of 2/Pln moved up at 1200 to the outpost where they had slain six Japanese the day before. The two squads then separated and tried to hit the enemy's two flanks in a surprise attack. But MG fire gave Burgos his death. Rusch was wounded in right arm, and Hultgren "lightly injured in action," other circumstances unreported.

On this 13 Mar, 1/Bn's recon had found the main approaches to Japanese Hqs on Mt Capisan. About halfway inland between Masilay Village and Mt Capisan, one ridge separated into two. The Japanese held both East Ridge and West Ridge with pillboxes and trenches.

Orders were for 1/Bn to move west to Sinonog River, then north on West Ridge. On this march, "C" secured Bn rear. "B" in the lead took rifle and MG fire from higher ground and had five wounded to hospital. On recon with B Co, Col Benson was shot in the stomach and came back wildly cursing. B Co had met 1/Bn's first determined resistance which we had yet encountered at Zambo.

On 15 Mar, an armored bulldozer of 116 Engrs cut a jeep supply road to C Co. While cleaning his rifle, Gonzales shot himself in the foot and was marked "lightly injured in action." But 2/Lt Larsen reported back for duty after three days' hospital for his shoulder wound. (But C Co knew nothing about our most important event of 15 Mar. Japanese scouts had precisely located our holes to help plan one of the bloodiest night attacks which the 41st ever had in World War II.)

Probable main reason for the big night attack of the Japanese before dawn 16 Mar was that they planned to demolish the armored road-builder that the Engrs had parked in C's perimeter before dark. (The heavy frontal attack of 50 Japanese on B Co seems to have been a diversion to take attention from the unrestrained charge on our C Co. B's 60mm mortars and D's 81s readily beat off their attack, with 25 enemy dead counted.)

The carefully planned attack on C Co from the rear (south) seems to have been in three commands, with three different missions. No. 1 mission was to wipe out automatic weapons positions. No. 2 was to destroy Hq Pln where Capt Krist, 1/Sgt Hackos, Orderly Bocko, 2 FA observers, and maybe some others were sleeping above ground instead of in holes. And No. 3 mission was to demolish the armored bulldozer with a mine and boxes of TNT.

Came then at the dead hour of 0300 this die-hard Japanese attack — apparently in one 50-man charge. Even in darkness, they seemed fairly sure of where our holes were, from daytime scouting.

For "C," it was luckily timed just as the man on guard in each hole awoke the next man who was to relieve him. But even so, mortarman Sgt Bowman was unable to fire. He had told us that if the Nipponese struck, he would fire flares to highlight the charging bayonet-men. Bowman never got a round off from his 60mm — died with a bullet in the forehead.

Other men fought heroically. When firing and grenading broke out, Weekley piled up half a dozen enemies. He may have hit the demolition man running with his mine to blast the bulldozer. This Japanese blew himself up — was found at daylight with his body split apart in two different areas.

Suddenly aroused at the barren, black hour of 0300, T/Sgt Grigar heard footsteps nearing his hole and "came to attention like a house on fire," and waited his chance to shoot.

A body thudded into Grigar's hole. Grigar raised his rifle to club the supposed Nipponese. "No, no Tom! It's Gus!" It was S/Sgt Gus Falgout. From the rim of his hole, Grigar, Falgout, and Lt Petersen slanted rifles in three different directions. They waited for a Japanese body to skyline itself.

One enemy squatted before the rifle of Grigar. Easing his M-1 towards the man, Grigar fired. The dying man gurgled so horribly that Grigar silenced him forever with a bullet through the head.

Canadian-born Brownhill was "the bravest of the brave." If he fired his BAR in the dark, it would mean death. His BAR lacked a flashhider. Just as Japanese bayonet-men ran wild over our holes, Brownhill's BAR spouted fire like a blowtorch. His automatic clips may well have shattered the great rush, but a rain of grenades blasted his hole. Fragments blinded Brownhill for life, blew off the right foot of Layne his helper and killed him. S/Sgt Azevedo was also wounded in that hole, part of body unknown.

And one grenade meant for Brownhill exploded in the hole with T/Sgt Grigar, 2/Lt Petersen and S/Sgt Falgout. They jumped out in different directions — Petersen with fragments in his rear.

Grigar was tangled up in phone wire. He just rolled over the parapet and stayed prone in the dark. Then he realized that all he had with him were his helmet and six M-1 rounds left in his rifle after he had slain the other Nipponese. His other gear was still down in the hole.

Then a Japanese leaped into Grigar's hole. Grigar heard the man chipping the grenade on his helmet to arm it. But the Japanese blew himself up instead.

Just as before, another enemy squatted before prone Grigar. As he eased up his M-1 to fire, three more Japaense stumbled over Grigar's outstretched legs.

Grigar remembered his disciplined training. If he shot the man in front, the three men behind would certainly slay him. He lay hardly breathing — could almost feel the bullet-shock into his body. But the three believed that he was dead. They moved off and stumbled into Kelly and two more Yanks who killed them. Grigar never knew what became of the man squatting before him whom he had feared to shoot.

Firing and grenading died down. The whole attack had lasted only half an hour, but the longest half-hour in the lives of most men. Grigar heard one young Yank cry for help, but nobody dared aid him. Came the long wait until day while Grigar listened to other Americans with Japanese moaning all over the black perimeter. He was horribly thirsty, but his canteen was down in the hole with the shattered remains of the enemy suicide. Rain fell. He cupped his hands and drank from his palms gratefully.

In that painful daybreak of 16 Mar, Medics and unhurt C Co men gave what aid they could to the wounded and helped bear them away. They examined the many dead in the little heaps of corpses.

As early as possible, seriously wounded Capt Krist was rushed back to the surgery that would save his life. Krist had taken a bayonet lunge into the chest, but for hours, devoted orderly Bocko had held him down and clamped the wound with his fingers. Prime credit for saving the life of his Capt goes to Bocko.

Another memorable wound was that of an iron man, signaller Glen Hansen. A saber — a weapon usually carried by an officer — had lopped off Hansen's left hand at the wrist. Instead of dying from bloodletting and shock, tough Hansen reportedly shot dead with his carbine the man who had severed his wrist. After making his tourniquet, he was said to have fired a total of three clips and killed two Japanese attackers. From his dead hand, he retrieved a ring that his mother had given him for Christmas. He wanted to have the Medics pickle in alcohol for his mantel at home.

Besides Brownhill, Azevedo, Capt Krist, 2/Lt Petersen, and Hansen, a sixth man was wounded — Falgout who had narrowly missed a clubbing from Grigar in the dark. Details are unknown.

Besides Bowman and Layne, our dead were Pat Sullivan, S/Sgt Myers, Colucci, and Sumpter, who died of wounds.

And so "C" lost six killed and six wounded — all but Petersen marked "seriously wounded," although Petersen was also hospitalized. For these 12 casualties, the Japanese left 26 dead. (They usually carried off any casualty who could not walk.) Despite their gallant attack, they failed to destroy the Engrs' bulldozer.

But "C" never fought again on West Ridge. For when F Co had orders to occupy big Basilan Island south of Zambo City, our whole Bn with tanks and AT Co were ordered to take over the San Roque fight from 2/Bn elements.

Although by 16 Mar, 162 Inf had secured San Roque Strip and Village, a strong pocket of Japs laired in the stream valley still in the San Roque area north of Zambo City. By the time our 1/Bn took over the front, the Japs had retreated from a system of trenches and pillboxes. But they had mined the little roads up the valley, and still retained their fighting organizations. On 17 Mar, 1/Bn patrols to the NW drew LMG and rifle fire.

And so on 18 Mar at 1400, C's Lt Larsen with 2 Plns and a LMG section went to knock out a pillbox blocking 1/Bn. One tank supported us. A Japanese road mine exploded under the tank. Killed were C's Joe Sullivan, and five men wounded. 2/Lt Larsen got his second wound, more serious than the wound of 12 Mar. Seriously wounded also were Karnbad, S/Sgt Crucitt — and Knouff and Briesky lightly wounded.

The Japanese covered the mined ground with intense MG fire, and our force retreated to Bn CP. During that 18 Mar, our C Co. CP was taking sporadic 20mm fire. But the main body of "C" still pushed 900 yards NW of our former position against the enemy.

On 19 Mar, 1/Bn's advances steadily continued. By 1100 hours, our A Co had contacted K Co, and encirclement of the new Nipponese positions in the valley was completed. Several times during the day, however, a 20mm machine-cannon and a LMG fired on 1/Bn. At 1700, a LMG wounded Witbeck and Peyton. And on 20 Mar, in a search for the 20mm gun, Koehn of 1/Pln was wounded — all circumstances unknown.

Koehn was C's last Zambo casualty. With other 1/Bn men, "C" had to mop up — with help of FA and Marine air-strikes. Patrols found the nuisance 20mm gun, but we have no reports on its destruction. On 29 Mar, 1/Bn moved to Pitogo and Maasin Valleys about six miles west of Zambo City on the south shore.

Our Bn easily cut the main Japanese escape route up the west coast — the Mt Capisan-Batal Trail. When we found a dug-in position, they briefly held it and then withdrew. On the night of 31 Mar, "C" took slight knee-mortar fire. On 4 Apr, "C" spotted a small group of Nipponese 200 yards north and had them shelled out. Everywhere, fleeing Japanese took to the rain forest.

And on 27 Apr, 162 Inf alerted to move to the Mindanao Mainland. We had fought well at Zamboanga, with just eight dead and 19 wounds that hospitallized men. We had bravely done all that was asked of us — even on that deadly night battle of 16 March, at 0300 hours in the dead of night.

CREDIT. Tom Bolt is most responsible for his preparation of this history which Westerfield has sought for over 17 years. Tom Quaiver contributed his 6-page typescript of his diary of 9-20 Mar 1945. Quaiver also sent Tom Grigar's 3-page story of his night fight. Bolt's letters are dated 10 and 25 Mar; 1 and 15 Apr; 12 and 18 May; 1 June; and 20 July — all in 1985. Bolt forwarded a copy of Robert Ripley's "Believe It Or Not" from San Diego's *Union Tribune* of 13 Nov 1946 about Glen Hansen's severed hand in the 15 Mar night fight. Useful data came from 162 Inf's Casualty List of 10 Mar-27 Apr 1945, 162's First Battalion/Zamboanga Operation 162nd Infantry, 162's Regimental Report of Zamboanga Battle entitled "Report of Operation/Zamboanga Area," and "Journal, 162nd Infantry Regiment beginning 27 Jan 1945."

1/BATTALION 186 INFANTRY: BLUNTING COL KUZUME'S LAST OFFENSIVE
by Dr. Hargis Westerfield, Division Historian

On 13-19 June 1944, 1/Bn 186 Inf took part with 162 Inf's 1/Bn in probably the most important maneuver of any 186 Bn in World War II. This maneuver on Biak was to drive west in the rear of the Japs battling 162 Inf on Mokmer Ridge. We were to cut behind those tenacious Japs on Mokmer Ridge and strike other Japs guarding what natives had told us was the last remaining Jap "waterhole" on Biak.

As of 13 June, we thought that we were to attack a waterhole garrison. We did not realize that this "waterhole" was Col Kuzume's West Caves. We did not expect that Kuzume's last tanks would team with massed Jap infantry to crush us dead in that hilly jungle.

For this great maneuver, Gen Doe attached 186's 1/Bn to 162's 1/Bn. Once we had crossed Mokmer Ridge going north in a safe place while the 162 men crossed on our left, we were to team with them and drive west at Kuzume. D Co's .81 mortars would stay behind in Regimental Battery. We got a kind of reinforcement. This was our own A Co — less a Pln — which had been detached at T-Jetty for special duty with 162 Inf. Covering fire would come from 641 TD's 4.2 mortars and the 75mm cannon of 121 FA — a Bn especially attached to the 41st for Biak.

By this time in the New Guinea Campaign, 1/Bn 186 were seasoned jungle troops, perhaps the most experienced on our Regiment. At Hollandia, we fought on Borgonjie River and in the final showdown at Cyclops Drome. On Biak, we were first to attack Mokmer Ridge on 9-10 June. We were already tempered for our greatest test on Biak.

On 14 June at 1800, Lt Col Field's 1/Bn moved out to battle. We marched in column of companies. C Co was advance guard, followed by A's 2 Plns. After "A" hiked Field's command group, then 2/Bn Medics with attached Meds from 116 Clearing Co. Next came D's HMGs and 1/Bn Hq's AT Pln. B Co secured our rear.

While 1/Bn 162 men moved north over a trail through 3/Bn fighting on Mokmer Ridge, our 186 Bn had to trek on a wide arc farther east. First we followed a trail leading north of the east end of Mokmer Strip. We crossed Mokmer Ridge about 500 yards east of 162. Now we moved NE along a rough trail leading toward the ridge crossing which 186 Inf had used to occupy Mokmer Strip on 7 June.

C's advance now prowled in blind jungle and rough country. It was a dark land of dense second growth with some large trees — rolling terrain broken abruptly by low commanding heights. At 0930, shots rang out on the trail, about 800 yards north of Mokmer Ridge. C Co men took fire from a small Jap group and killed three.

Our Bn's march became even slower and more careful. Turning a "corner," we scouted west in almost a straight line to where the yet unknown strongpoint of West Caves awaited us.

About 1035, T/Sgt Ackley's first squad of C Co surprised Japs in hasty positions astride the trail. Severson killed four Nips in one long BAR burst. To the right of the trail, Sgt Wilkinson detected a Jap ambush before it was sprung. His squad wiped out a whole Nip squad, killed 15. Schlabach was wounded.

While protecting Ackley's Pln, Horn, T/5 Viscioni, T/Sgt Snell fired on two Japs to the right of the trail. The Japs took cover among giant ferns, shot back. Fifteeen more Japs opened fire on a long line beside the two. Horn got a leg wound, Edwards a wound high in the head. The Nips howled and rushed; our BARs and grenades repelled them. We counted twelve dead.

Evidently 20 Jap riflemen originally held a ridge 100 yards long to the right of the trail and parallel to the trail. To finish off the survivors, we loosed Lt Peterson's A Co Pln. His men shot their way down the ridge, slew four men, two officers.

About 1200, "C" moved out again and killed two more Japs. With 2/Pln and 3/Pln abreast on either side of the trail, "C" advanced in line of skirmishers, scouts out ahead. At 300 yards, a Jap LMG, rifles, and a grenade launcher shot from a knoll at 2/Pln left of the trail. Heavy growth blocked us frontally. Placing BARs to cover side trails, Ackley called Lt Strong for company mortars. Five rounds of C's 60s smashed dug-in Japs; our advance killed another Jap and took the gun. Boggs was wounded from the fragment of a Jap suicide grenade. In the next 800 yards, "C" lost four men from heat exhaustion.

By 1430, C Co was in line with B 162 300 yards south of us, and both Bns moved forward abreast. Since 162's men had also met Jap opposition that 14 June, we could not make physical contact until 735. Both Bns were 400 yards short of assigned objectives, but we dug perimeters, tiredly, tensely.

For that day's action, 1/Bn claimed 20 known dead, 10-12 possibles. Four "C" men were wounded. C's lead scouts evidenced thorough training; they saw the Japs' camouflage in time, slipped up and fired first. Not one scout was wounded. Then our lead squads opened fire at once. "A" men also fought well.

But on 14 June, we had hit only die-hard Jap outposts, mostly riflemen, in hastily prepared positions. And 121 FA's 75s had helped us greatly. From 0800 to 1640, they had fired 1608 shells of interdictory and preparatory fire at the northwest ridge above the location of the suspected Jap waterpoint. Yet both Bns were still some 400 yards short of our objectives.

Our real fighting was only begining. For before dark, patrols discovered that 1/Bn 162 south of us was on the periphery of West Caves. We now realized that it was the major Jap strong point on Biak — Jap HQs with a 1,000-man garrison.

Col Kuzume struck at us with tanks and infantry in the early darkness. At 1930, his tank-infantry fighters expelled B 162 from a semi-isolated position NW of their main Bn perimeter. B 162 men sheltered awhile in B 186 holes. A B 162 squad leader said that Japs had captured two HMGs, presumably from D 162.

Then from the darkness near the road into our perimeter from West Caves, perhaps an entire company of Japs attacked us in small commands. They struck between B and C Cos astride the road. They struck between two flaming "D" HMGs and our M-1s and grenades. They harassed all night. In early morn, 50 men charged C's left flank near the road, and against "B" men farther to the left. At dawn, we counted 30 Jap dead, including an officer on a "B" parapet with his saber ready to slash.

Next morning, on 15 June, 1/Bn expected storming parties of tanks and infantry. At 0700, 121 FA's observer adjusted fire on possible tank approach routes northward. In tight perimeters, our 186 Bn waited in holes. C Co held our NW perimeter; "A" shouldered against "C" at a 45-degree angle for the NE perimeter. B Co with D's HMGs closed the gap between A and C's perimeters on the south, with 1/Bn AT's 50s to fire final protective lines. Our whole Bn was on a slight rise of ground.

Then with daylight, "B" had orders to dig in left of the road from West Caves, where D's HMGs and 1/Bn Hq were positioned already. From brush high above "B," heavy Jap rifle and MG fire flailed out. B's M-1s and BARs lashed back at suspected Jap snipers in tall trees. When four Japs moved out at us from a cave opening, we killed them or drove them back. "D" men machine-gunned the cave entrance; now and then, a few Japs ran out and fell.

At about 0715, two Jap tanks, each with an infantry Pln, hit us from the West Caves road. Men from B 162 ran from them to shelter in our holes. At 250-300 yards, each tank opened with its .37mm cannon and its .25 LMG and charged our holes. Our rifles and mortars killed or scattered the tank-infantry while D's HMGs flailed the tanks. Just as the tanks turned to flee, the .50 HMGs of Bn AT Pln were brought forward into action from the east. The AT gunner on the north emptied his whole bag of cartridges into the broadside of the last tank. That tank smoked, turned off the road out of sight. A column of smoke rose from that dead tank a long time.

Thus ended the first attack of 15 June. (On our left, B 162 had fought a third tank-infantry team of Japs. When some "B" men's fire scattered the infantry, the tank ran away.)

It was probably during the first attack on our 1/Bn that A Co's 1/Lt Lester Hansen reconnoitered behind our holes to set up flame-throwers as a final protective line. But a .37 shell fragment hit him in the spine, kept him from ever walking again.

At 1400, two tanks attacked our holes again. This time, 121 FA's .75s impacted 600 rounds on the Japs. The .75s hit no tanks, but they neutralized MG and rifle fire against us. They kept Jap Inf from forming for the attacks.

Tank No. 1 hit C Co and D's HMGs head on, while Bn AT Pln's 50s blasted it. C's bazookamen Schultz with loader Jewell fired three ineffective rounds — two of them not exploding. At a "D" HMG, a Jap slug almost tore the helmet from gunner Click's head, but he continued firing. At 200 yards, T/Sgt Cottingham's bazooka shell hit the tank just above the turret. As the tank turned, Wilkinson with Hyde his loader got a rocket into its rear. Les DeWitt arced the AT shell from his grenade launcher into the tank. It disappeared into the brush, halted, and burned.

Blazing with automatic fire, Tank No. 2 closed in on "C." Its .37 gun struck at emplacements. But the .50s crippled the rotor mechanism in its turret. The Schultz-Jewell team fought Tank No. 2 with three more rockets, hit it three times. Last shot destroyed the tool rack, probably damaged the tracks. Trying to bring the .37 to bear on us from the damaged turret, it stripped its tracks on the coral. Despite heavy rifle fire, the crew escaped from the dead tank.

Thus ended our tank-battle of 15 June with three dead tanks, at least 20 dead Japs. Besides A's 1/Lt Hansen, we counted 13 more wounded. "B" lost Englund, Grassmeyer, Sgts Greigg and Guy More. "D" lost McKenzie. C's wounded were not recorded. Others of 1/Bn's wounded were perhaps light wounds of men never hospitallized.

Even during battle, patrols went to find Jap concentrations and prepare for the next push at West Caves. A's patrol found no Japs, but C's found them. A Jap patrol chased S/Sgt Neeno Schena's three-man patrol. Our men fired MGs on him, in error. Yet on the right flank of our next day's offensive, he found a 50-man Jap entrenchment on a hill NW. Our FA neutralized this position before the next day.

That night at 2130, we called in FA on a column of Japs marching with flashlights on the high ground above us, and put out their lights. While D Co's HMGs on the road guarded five tanks which had joined us that afternoon, knee mortars barraged "D." A Jap suicide squad with satchel charges crept up under our HMGs to kill the tanks. Our guns slew seven Japs and saved the tanks.

On 16 June, 2/Bn 186 closed the Great Gap on Horseshoe Ridge for 186 Inf. For 2/Bn, our 1/Bn secured a road down which Jap reinforcements might come. Jap small arms fire killed B Co's 2/Lt Redding. "C" killed 7 Japs.

On 17 June, we marched again with 1/Bn 162 on West Caves. While AT Pln's .50s secured our roadhead, A Co led out with five tanks. (A's detached Pln had returned to us on 15 June.)

Although 162 with tanks had to clear two MGs and a .75 cannon from the heights, we found that the Japs had evacuated our side of those heights. "A" killed two Japs in a pillbox. In "D," Maisey was wounded; and Hoagland wounded in "B." C's Bernheisel died of wounds. "A" killed ten Japs that night.

On 18 June, we held our holes with almost hourly exchanges of Jap and D Co mortar blasts. Stress of command responsibilities caused relief of our fine CO, Lt-Col Field, with stomach ulcers.

And on 19 June, 1/Bn 186 Inf reverted from attachment with 162 Inf, back to 186 Inf command. At 1230, we marched to link up with other 186 Bns to cut off West Caves from reinforcements from the north.

And so concluded 1/Bn 186 Inf's most important maneuver of World War II. Coordinating well with 4.2 mortars and FA, we blunted Kuzume's final tank-infantry attacks. We had minimum casualties, for so important a maneuver. We attained a position where we could end the Biak war. Our 186 Inf reached a level of efficiency that would continue into the Battle of Zamboanga, and on into the Japanese invasion — if that invasion had ever come to pass.

CREDIT. Prime data are from "History of First Bn 186 Inf (while detached from Regimental Control...13-18 June 1944)," R R Smith's *Approach to the Philippines*, "Narrative Historical Report of Biak Operation" (121 Field Artillery), and Award Story of 1/Lt Lester Hansen. I also found a few meager notes called "History of A Co 186 Inf, 2-15 June 1944." Histories of B, C, and D Cos were republished in *The Fighting Jungleers*. B's Biak story appeared in *Jungleer* for Nov 1966; C's in June 1969; and D's in Mar 1976 and Jan 1977. A letter from 186's Ibsen Nielsen (10 Mar 1980) says that unfortunate Lester Hansen — despite becoming a paraplegic — graduated from law school and became a practicing lawyer.

THE JAPANESE NAVY: "KON" OPERATIONS TO RELIEVE BIAK
by Dr. Hargis Westerfield, Division Historian from Naval and Air Historians

During 2-13 June 1944, our 41st Division came as near destruction in World War II as it ever would. The Japs mounted three "KON" or "sea army" operations against us. Without the aid of the U.S. Air Force and especially our weaker Yank and Aussie fleet, Jap guns would have sunk our LSTs and destroyer guards offshore. Jap guns would have pulverized our beachhead into bloody froth. A Jap Special Landing Force would then have driven us against the reinforced Jap defenders of Biak. God surely took a hand in our salvation for the failure of KON Operations was ultimately due to forces beyond our Army and Navy and Air Force control.

Main reason why Jap admirals wanted to crush our 41st on Biak arose from fear of a new Biak air-base. Their supreme battle-fleet hoped to demolish our Navy in the Philippine Sea north of New Guinea. Our new air-base on Biak would put their fleet in mortal danger.

On 2 June 1944, KON I assembled in Filipino Davao Gulf. Called the KON or "sea army" fleet, it was formidable against our weaker Navy in Biak waters. Besides an old battle-ship *(Fuso)*, it consisted of three heavy cruisers *(Aoba, Myoko, Haguro)*, one light cruiser *(Kinu)*, eight destroyers, two mine-layers, and smaller craft. It carried a new special landing force, two Amphibious Brigade of 2500 — perhaps three infantry Bns, 12 75mm cannon. This fleet expected air cover from the reinforced Jap 23 Air Flotilla which would strike from Sorong and other New Guinea fields west of Biak.

When this deadly KON I fleet left Davao Gulf about 2400 2 June, it had a horrible opportunity to kill our 41st. Despite submarine and plane reports of Jap Navy movements, Gen MacArthur's G-2 wrongly believed that fleet elements were merely convoying supplies and troops for Davao or the Palau Islands.

Except for perhaps six destroyers covering the beachhead, our Navy was far from Biak. Only on 3 June — the day before KON's expected arrival — did Allied Naval Forces order a weak fleet to head for Biak. To oppose the Japs' Battleship *Fuso,* three heavy cruisers, one light cruiser, eight destroyers, we had only one heavy cruiser, three light cruisers, ten destroyers. Their battleship and heavy cruiser could sink Rear Admiral V.A.C. Crutchley's squadron while still out of range. This Aussie CO would have fought at night when our Hollandia and Biak air cover would have been useless.

But the Jap invasion plan had a fundamental weakness. The plan did not provide an effective air-force. Although Jap Headquarters had reinforced their decimated 23 Air Flotilla at Sorong with 166 planes, most of those planes never fought over Biak. On arrival in New Guinea, most of the pilots took malaria. Some pilots fought, of course. On 2-3 June, raid of only some 50 Jap planes swooped on Biak. We had no air cover, but a sheet of flame struck from our Ack-Ack around Bosnek — downed 23 planes, with small damage only to Destroyer *Reid, LTS 467.*

The blunder of a Jap recon plane was the main reason KON I failed. About 2025 3 June, the recon pilot saw a strong U.S. carrier force approaching Biak. Maybe the pilot was malarious. Maybe he mistook destroyers for battleships, LSTs for carriers. Maybe he merely saw Crutchley's weak fleet from Hollandia.

KON I's CO had already reported a periscope of ours that watched his fleet in the Philippine sea. Two Navy bombers had traced his moves. Now Rear-Admiral Naomasa Sakonju got orders from Jap Combined Fleet Headquarters to withdraw. For the moment, our division was saved. Only important U.S. loss was light cruiser *Nashville,* holed in an air-raid.

KON I failed — except for a minor success. While U.S. attention was on KON, some Japs slipped through from Mankowari to reinforce Col Kuzume. On that tense night of 3-4 June, Capt Ozawa's 6 Co 221 Inf and two light guns landed at Korim Bay, and perhaps 5 Co 222 Inf. This landing was small success for the Japs' lost chance to wipe out Bosnek and our shipping with Battleship *Fuso's* twelve 14" guns.

KON II followed immediately. Probably air recon, early on 4 June, informed the Japs that we had no carriers in Biak seas. Now, instead of larger, slower cruisers, the Japs tried to slip in six destroyers. Of these six destroyers, three were to carry 200 infantry apiece; and three (or maybe six) were to tow a landing barge apiece, with 30-50 men to a barge.

Leaving Sorong on the far western end of New Guinea about midnight 7 June, the six destroyers coasted the farthest northern point of New Guinea, the Cape of Good Hope. At dawn, they expected air cover from six planes of their 23rd Air Flotilla. On 8 June, KON II's success appeared certain. Without carrier plane opposition, they were safe because most of our heavy bombers had massed for Palau Islands far north. Jap raids of 5-6 June on Wakde Strip had caught over 100 of our planes parked wing to wing, and made the Strip useless.

Yet KON II found trouble in broad daylight in the seas north of Cape Good Hope. About 1330, P-38 fighters from Hollandia Strip attacked the covering six Jap planes. The P-38s shot down at least three Japs, drove off the others. With eight fighters protecting them, ten B-25 bombers swooped on the destroyers. (Other sources alleged that we had 50 planes.) Attacking in pairs, they shot in mast-high. Before Squadron Leader Major Tennille got his plane into bombing position, two destroyers' concentrated fire tore his plane apart, slew him and 2/Lt Wood. But their sacrifice enabled other bombers to crosscross the six destroyers with low-level strafing and bombing.

An underwater bomb exploding holed *Harusame;* she sank in five minutes. A fragment penetrated *Shiratsuyu,* but she did not slow down. Strafing damaged topsides of *Samidare* and Adm Sakonju's *Shikanami*. We lost three bomber crews.

But when our planes left, the Japs rescued *Harusame's* castaways and steamed on for Biak. Then about 1800, a flyer reported that a fleet was speeding at the little convoy from east of Biak: one battleship, four cruisers, eight destroyers. No doubt Sakonju remembered that erring plane report of 3 June that aborted KON I. Valiantly, he drove on into tropical night. The moon rose at 2023, two days past full. Passing showers often hid that moon.

This time, however, a battle-fleet was coming, far heavier than Sakonju's. Adm Crutchley came for a kill — with

Aussie heavy cruiser *Australia,* Yank light cruisers *Phoenix, Boise,* fourteen destroyers, two of them Aussie.

Crutchley's first contact occurred when a recon plane spotted five Jap planes 60 miles WNY of Korim Bay. Crutchley sent U.S. destroyer *Mullany* to check the dark little fjord. The Japs had not arrived. About 2320, a Jap plane marked *Mullany* with a flare, but the bomb missed by 100 yards.

After *Mullany* rejoined us, cruiser *Boise,* Yank forward destroyer *Fletcher,* and Sakonju made radar contact at 2320 — at 23,400 yards. Outgunned Sakonju turned to escape. Destroyers cast off their towed barges of Jap infantry and turned north.

Although Adm Crutchley had ordered Yank Cmdr Jarrell to fall back to the fleet's port quarter, Jarrell probably disobeyed. Three miles ahead of Crutchley, he was working speed up to 30 knots. Nine minutes later, Jarrell opined that the Japs had loosed torpedoes. Eleven minutes later, cruiser *Boise* saw a torpedo in her wake. All our cruisers turned north; the torpedoes missed.

The Japs ran NW at 32 knots — in two lines, three ships on the left, two on the right. Three minutes later, we passed the castoff barges of Jap Inf, and fired on them, results unreported.

We settled into a long stern chase — our destroyers at 35 knots, slower cruisers at 29 knots. Commander Jarrell's four-destroyer division was closest to the fleeing Jap. Racing parallel to Jarrell on the north was Cmdr McManes' division with four destroyers — but 7,000 yards behind Jarrell.

By 0018, Cmdr Jarrell had closed down his flagship *Fletcher's* range from 23,400 yards to 17,000 yards. He now ordered *Fletcher* to open fire. At this distance, Jarrell hardly expected a hit, but he hoped that the Japs would zigzag to avoid shells, and lose distance. But Sakonju trusted in speed and kept on in two straight lines.

By 0045, Crutchley was sure that no Jap cruisers supported the destroyers. With eight of his destroyers closing in on just five Japs, he had no reason to burden his slower cruisers any longer at full speed ahead. He ordered destroyers to continue pursuit until 0230, when they would have good reason to break off. At 0100, before Jarrell's first shots, he turned the cruisers back at 15 knots, with a four-destroyer screen, and sent Aussie destroyers *Arunta* and *Warramunga* to find the cast-off Jap barges, but with no reported results.

Our pursuing destoyers were closing range on the Japs, but orders were to cut off pursuit in 65 minutes. At 0125, Jarrell tried to trick the Japs into destruction. At 13,000 yards, he directed all of his four destroyers to turn to port and shoot broadsides. During those seven minutes, we saw the bright flare of Jap gunfire through heavy smoke columns.

Jarrell had rightly assumed that the Japs did not know that McManes' division was closing in on them from the right. Replying to Jarrell's broadsides, the two Jap destroyers on his right also turned rightwards. First, they shot torpedoes; at 0144, a torpedo track passed Jarrell's *Fletcher.*

While the Japs' two destroyers turned and lost speed and distance, Cmdr McManes' 4 destroyers had cut their range to 15,000 yards; at 0205 they opened fire. In six minutes, we saw an explosion on destroyer *Shiratsuyu*. She lost 1,000 yards at first, then picked up speed. At 0227, our range was down to 10,000 racing yards, but we could get no nearer.

In the entire two hours of the chase, we had exchanged 1,300 rounds with the Japs. Besides "straddling" *Shiratsuyu,* we had slightly damaged *Samidare* and Flagship *Shikananami.* But even our most endangered Jarrell's *Fletcher* was untouched.

For good reasons, we broke off the chase. The seas west of Mapia Island were restricted for Yank planes; they might bomb us by mistake. During daylight, destroyers needed safety under fighter cover, close inshore.

KON II did not wholly fail; some Japs in the barges reinforced Kuzume on Biak. Perhaps 2-3 barges landed — men of either 2/Bn or 3/Bn 219 Inf — maybe 5th Co, 222 Inf.

KON III was the final plan of the frustrated Jap Navy against Biak. Core of this invincible fleet was battleships *Musashi, Yamato,* superior in power world-wide, with a total of 18 18" guns. (Battleship *Fuso* of KON I had just 12 guns of only 14" caliber.) Supports were heavy cruisers *Myoko, Haguro, Aoba,* light cruisers *Noshiro, Kinu;* and seven destroyers. Without turning back, they were to pulp Bosnek and Owi, and land troops.

Although positioned at Batjan Island SW of Morotai on 12 June, this fleet never struck Biak. On 13 June, it sailed east to help defend the Marianna Islands from our 5th Fleet.

We never suffered Naval bombardment in all three KON Operations; but we fought a sizable Jap infantry reinforcement infiltrating during this time. As mentioned already, in KON I and II, probably two Cos, two guns, and 2-3 other barge-loads landed on Biak. Otherwise, Jap records are vague. Conclusions are that, during 3-25 June — ending 12 days after KON III aborted — these numbers arrived: 225 men of Kuzume's own 222 Inf, 400 of 221 Inf, and 500 of 219 Inf. (Not a man of the Navy's 2nd Amphibious Brigade ever landed.) Total was about 1125 infantry, a fair-sized assistance to Kuzume's 4,000 infantry already on Biak, and 7,400 other troops.

These 1125 men surely delayed our capture of Mokmer Drome. They prompted Gen Fuller to request reinforcements on 13 June, and so helped effect his request to be relieved from 41st Division command.

But besides losing Destroyer *Harusame,* the Japs took more significant losses from KON — almost all trained pilots who reinforced 23rd Air Flotilla against Biak. They lost maybe half from Malaria or combat over Biak. Most of the others died from bad weather or our Air Force when trying to return to the Mariannas.

At the time of the KON Operation, we seemingly had no idea of the menace to our Division. In KON I, only an erring Nippo pilot's report saved us from *Fuso's* twelve 14" guns. In KON III, our 5th Fleet's Mariannas attack saved us from *Musashi's* and *Yamato's* eighteen 18" guns. We can well say that the hand of God saved our 41st Infantry Division.

CREDIT. Books already published were my sources here, for their authors have researched this area of our history further than I need to go. Books included *Japanese Operations in the Southwest Pacific Area,* from "Reports of General MacArthur;" Samuel Eliot Morison's *History of U.S. Naval Operations in World War II* — Vols II, V, and VIII; and Walter Karig's *Battle Report/The End of an Empire.* Also useful were Frank Craven and James Cate's *Army Air Forces in World War II,* Vol IV; George C. Kenney's *General Kenney Reports;* and R. R. Smith's *Approach to the Philippines.* Smith is finely detailed on possible Japs' troop landings, but he omits much of interest about our Navy and Air war, which I gathered mainly from Morison and Karig. Kenney is best on the saga of Major Tennille.

1/Bn 163 INFANTRY: CONQUERING MOUNT DAHO ON JOLO
by Dr. Hargis Westerfield, Division Historian

On 15 Apr 1945, Cannon Co of 163 Inf began 163 Inf's battle for the Jap Marine fortress of Mt Daho. CN joined 146 FA, Marine bombers, Moro infantry to destroy the great outwork of Daho. This outwork was a tenaciously held strongpoint of three mutually supporting 20mm guns at Kilometer 7½ on Route 10 SE of Jolo City.

On 15 Apr, CN and 146 FA fired 300 rounds in 30 minutes. After an air-strike, the Moros overran the outwork. Then on 16 Apr, 163's 1/Bn took over the operation to fight Daho to a finish.

Looming on the southern sky, 2247-foot Mt Daho was an enormous flat-topped ridge with the crest slanting down slightly from right to left. At least seven dark ravines led up through the jungle to its summit. Daho was actually a dead volcano with the top blown off, the fourth highest mountain on Jolo.

Main Jap positions were on the crest of two partly bare ridges climbing south to Daho's summit. Emplaced here were 90 20mm twin-gunned machine cannon. Supports were HMGs, LMGs, mortars well dug in. Between the ridges were deep, forested ravines connecting with another deep ravine between the two ridges and Daho's north slope. The ravines well concealed communication lines, dumps, and cover for reinforcements.

Except after heavy losses, Daho was impregnable to infantry. We needed all the guns and planes we could get. Daho was potentially as deadly as Sanananda — only Sanananda tilted.

On 16 Apr, we dug in A and C Cos on each side of Route 10. 'B' now had orders to fight SE from Kilo 7 — a recon in force. About 1300 'B' met 20mm fire near 4 Kilo 8. By 1315, 20mm fire had wounded two B men, one D man, one guerilla. At 1330, we had plunging fire from the base of Daho on the north slope. We called for an air-strike that probably never happened because of fear of hitting 1/Bn's recon patrols.

On 15 Apr, 163 reported 19 Japs killed, but not specifically killed by B Co. We lost D's Don Marshall wounded, with Caldwell and Drake probably from "B."

By 17 Apr, we had located Jap positions. This morning Daho endured our heaviest air-strike so far. Then at 0755, three combat patrols got orders to strike straight west to Daho, if unopposed.

Transferring grenades from a tight pocket to his pack for ready throwing, B Co's S/Sgt Coppege pulled a pin accidentally. We scattered at this warning, but not enough to save ourselves. Coppege fell on the grenade and died for us.

As "B" in the middle patrol started up the ridge, MGs lashed us and a 20mm gun halfway up the ridge — perhaps the gun that shot yesterday. FA air observers neutralized the gun with several battery volleys, then called for precision fire, saw two direct hits, destroyed the gun.

But Jap rifles still fired. From a position on East Ridge, a hail of MG fire and mortar shells fell on "B" men. Another 20mm gun fired; Jap Marines counter-attacked. Perhaps at this moment, B's lead scout Edgerton was heroic. Japs fired from three sides; his platoon was prone. Edgerton charged the Jap 20mm gun, killed it, and died there.

Although "B" slew some 15 Japs in this counter-attack and called down 36 FA rounds on the others, "B" was repelled, in a two-hour fight. FA reported that "B" had one killed, three wounded, four missing — later three who finally returned safely.

Three more 20mm guns opened up from another position on the slope of Daho, south of East Ridge. To save "B," 146 shelled and screened with smoke. From the ground, FA's Lt Allen caught gun flashes in an aiming circle. At 7,000 yards through BC scope, he called down fire and silenced the guns. Before Allen could fire, A Co also lost three wounded. Besides Coppege, "B" lost killed: Frank Shaw, Howard Moore, Edgerton, Courtney. B's wounded were Coward, Denevan; 1/Lt DeSerio was injured. "A" lost Conley, Gorby, Bellet wounded; Hendrix, Fox, Wes Bailey, John Compton were injured. Killed from an unidentified outfit was T/3 Madden, and Gamble wounded.

On 18 Apr, 45 planes hit Daho twice; FA fired some 500 rounds. FA's Lt Allen placed a bomb salvo where a 20mm had shot yesterday. The salvo tore off foliage, revealed a half-closed cave. CN Co dragged a 105 to B's forward position, under cover of bombardment. A 37mm AT gun came up also.

Jap MGs, rifles, and this last 20mm gun smothered our fire. CN men and FA observers crouched in a bomb crater; 20mm projectiles bracketed that crater. Jap fire halted; we surfaced and fired back; the 20mm drove us under again. After several more firings, we withdrew under FA smoke at 1600. CN's Conant was wounded; B's S/Sgt James A. Smith was injured, perhaps in this same action. With air observation, FA later silenced that last 20mm gun with two direct hits.

On 19 Apr 1/Bn positioned to storm Daho. After two 18-plane strikes by 0730, we moved to Kilo 9, Route 10 to set up observation post and base of fire. On the hill 2,000 yards NE of Daho, we emplaced a 105 cannon and a two 57mm AT recoilless cannon, with light and heavy mortars. Our rifle Cos made perimeter near Kilo 8 beside our line of departure.

Hub of Mt Daho's defence was the crest of West Ridge climbing south to Mt Daho, with another defence on East Ridge. Mjr Armstrong planned to overrun weaker East Ridge first. A Co would lead the attack; "B" would fire in support. Once we took East Ridge, C Co from reserve would storm West Ridge under support fire of both other companies.

Greatest day of battle for Mt Daho was 20 Apr. Beginning 0800, planes dropped 45 1,000-pound bombs. (At Ibdi Pocket, 163 had used 64 1,000-pound bombs from planes.) Then .50 caliber MGs ricocheted quick patterns of red on the ridges. After this 45-plane strike, 146 FA hammered reeling ridges with "fuze delay" and "fuze quick." CN's 105 and two 57s fired; mortars drummed steadily into the smoke-pall; debris flew everywhere.

Suddenly firing ended; silence was startling. A small smoke-plume from burning grass lapped up toward Jap lines. About 1910, A and B Cos. advanced covered by trees. Dense brush and slippery rises made us advance too slowly.

In 40 minutes, we were half-way up the slope. Jap machine-gunners were firing but not hitting close — perhaps because gunners were unadjusted to downhill fire. At 1015, "B" on the right took MG fire. FA's Lt Hornefius ordered return fire on that pillbox, splintered it with delayed fuze. At 1100, "B" took 25 mortar shells,

fire from one HMG, three LMGs, had four men wounded. FA smashed back for "B."

At 1140, "A" tried to drive our attack home. Breaking into the open centering East Ridge two-thirds up the slope, we fell prone under intense fire from two pillboxes, rifles, mortars, and MGs. Our 57s and CN's 105 with 146 FA scored direct hits on both pillboxes; a delayed fuze FA shell killed one pillbox.

But Jap fire halted A's next try to advance. Probable reason was B Co's failure to support "A" with fire. For "B" took the wrong direction on Daho's twisting trails among brushy ridges, came out high on West Ridge, 200 yards below the Japs' strongest position.

B's CO — probably 1/Lt Lunney, bravely tried to right the mistake. Dispatching a platoon back to East Ridge for "A," he threw all other "B" men into a desperate attack on the supreme Jap position above him.

Although using only two die-hard platoons instead of two companies as originally planned, "B" almost took West Ridge. After two BARmen — Earl Harris and an unnamed man — killed two Jap MGs, intense rifle and MG fire stopped us. Lead platoon could not move without heavy losses. 2/Lt Saratowicz crawled up and smashed a MG nest with a grenade, was wounded to die.

We silenced the Jap rifles but had no flank security. We retreated firing on more Nip riflemen. Only BARman Harris still in action, Harris helped break three counter-attacks. Harris, McFaull, Sgt Estes, and others secured our retreat under smoke. B Co records say that intense automatic fire had pinned our attack for four hours. At 1500, we attacked again around right flank but after an hour's fight withdrew because of ammo shortage.

On East Ridge to B's right, spearhead A Co fought well minus expected support of "B," but withdrew after heavy combat. On the ridge, S/Sgt Fritz spotted a trench system with a MG holding back A Co. Deploying his squad skillfully to cover him, Fritz charged the MG. Firing as he ran, he silenced the gun but was seriously wounded.

The platoon leader — probably 1/Lt Dupont — was wounded, but T/Sgt Carpenter drove home our attack. We held the ridge briefly. When an overwhelming Jap force countered, Carpenter slew six Japs. We had to withdraw, but Ewing, Shultz, Jin secured our retreat and died.

The Japs pursued "A" too far down the slope. Before they could disengage, an accurate, intense FA barrage slew many. Spotting many Japs scrambling down the rear of East Ridge, our Piper Cub had called fire on them.

For Jolo fighting, losses were heavy — five dead, 29 wounded. A's Jin, Shultz, Ewing were dead. Wounded were Allen, Broadhead, Ellsworth, Frye, Jarouse, Jocoy, Kohut, Konradt, Cpl Cummings; S/Sgts Fritz, Helman, Willard Wilson; T/Sgt Ingram. B's 2/Lt Saratowicz was dead. Wounded were James E. Brown, Burdick, Cross, Ferguson, Gamble, Richard Hansen, Krowiorz, T/Sgt Delsi. D Co had two MGs knocked out, Claude Bailey dead, and four wounded: Gritter, Hayslett, Cpl Satterthwaite, Sgt Frankowski. "A" did not number Japs killed; "B" claimed 32 dead, 20 probables. All units killed an estimated 100.

Reasons for failure to storm Daho 20 Apr go far deeper than failure of all "B" men to support "A." Ammo was running short before our retreat. Despite four days' FA and 36 dive-bombing missions, much fire was useless. Because of ravines cutting sharply in all directions, projectiles had to hit vertically to impact inside them. Worst of all, bombardments had failed to cover high, open ground of the strongest emplacements.

We planned to assail Daho tomorrow, 20 Apr, but bad weather grounded planes at Zamboanga. We kept the Japs on edge and prepared for battle tomorrow. At 1425, all our cannon, mortars, MGs fired on Daho to pretend an attack. About 1530, 27 planes bombed, with some 25 per cent of the bombs actually on target. Nine planes at a time strafed twice. Our supports made it a point to blast that high, open ground neglected yesterday.

Patrols found that the crests of our bitterest fights were deserted, but Japs held caves on reverse slopes, and on the side of Daho above those crests. One patrol discovered a covered approach for tomorrow's attack. That night while FA shelled Daho, we heard explosions above us.

At 0850 23 Apr after 37 planes struck — four with rockets — we grimly attacked — into the silence of a dead mountain. For after dropping their bombs, our Marine planes returned over their targets three more times, but without bomb-loads. The simulated bomb-runs were to keep remaining Japs under cover until 1/Bn reached their holes. By 1035, however, all three Cos had reached initial objectives with no Jap fire. By 1700, we had found 147 Jap bodies and killed two more Japs — presumably those whom C Co reported having seen before 1005 that morning. We had no casualties in 1/Bn. Daho was ours, a week after 1/Bn's first attack. By Gen Suzuki's order, the Japs had begun withdrawing the night of 20 Apr after our great assault.

Original Daho garrison was 500 Imperial Marines of 33rd Naval Guards, and 100-150 men of 363 Inf Brigade falling back from Mt Datu. We counted 288 recognizable Jap bodies, but believed that all arms had killed 350 of the 500 Guards. (We lack figures on 363 Inf Bn.) Many were blown to fragments, or sealed in caves we feared to penetrate. Our battle losses — mainly in 1/Bn — were 11 dead, 39 wounded to hospital, five injured.

In the attack of 20 Apr alone, FA had fired 600 rounds of 105s. (Total rounds for 146 FA's entire Battle of Jolo is unknown.) Marine planes had some 35 strikes, 300 sorties, and dropped 1400 tons of bombs — half of their action on Jolo, in fact. They had also fired 32 rockets. In an area some ⅓ miles long and 200 yards deep, not a whole tree was standing. In those deep, narrow ravines, concussion must have been terrific. One prisoner said that after each strike nearby, his senses left him for 6-7 hours.

Such was 1/Bn 163 Inf's great siege of Mt Daho. Ibdi Pocket, Wakde, Pasananca — all of these are formidable positions that we think of when we remember storming Mt Daho.

CREDIT. Main sources are 146 FA's Capt Robert Allen's "Reduction of Mt Daho," and 163 Inf's Journal 13-25 Apr 1945. I used also medal stories: Edgerton, Coppege, Harris, Saratowicz, McFaull, Estes, Fritz, Ewing, Shultz, Jin, Sheeran. Other sources were "Operational Monograph No. 10," 163's May, 1945, Morning Report, Casualty List called "Sulu V-4 Operation/Jolo Island," A and B Cos' payroll lists, Robert Sherrod's *History of Marine Aviation in World War II,* and report of Lt Col Alfred E. Hintz. (Morning Reports are incomplete and casualties' outfits hard to identify.) With no personal narratives to help me, I had to piece together some actions from medal stories — a difficult and unreliable process. (146 FA's story of Mt Daho appeared in June, 1963, *Jungleer,* reprinted in my *Fighting Jungleers.* Title is "146 FA Blasts Mt Daho.")

167 FIELD ARTILLERY ON BIAK: FIRING FOR 186 INF AND 24 DIV
by Dr. Hargis Westerfield, Division Historian and 1/LT Willaim B. Morse, 167 FA

On 18 June 1944, 167 Field Artillery Battalion landed our 105 mm guns on Biak. From 17 May through 15 June, we had fired for 163 Inf and other units afterwards in the Toem-Wakde-Maffin Bay Operation. On LST 181 which took us to Biak, we had manned the craft's .50 caliber HMGs against Jap air attacks — which never came.

As was his way for all landings, Col. Beach had wisely waterproofed all gear, although told that he would not need to waterproof for Biak. (He was fooled on other occasions.) He was short of tractors; he needed 18, but had just 13. Yet by 1435, our guns were emplaced near Mokmer Drome. Before dark, Btrys B and C registered on a base point and fired all night.

Only named casualties of 167's Biak Operation were 4 on that 18 June. About 1/LT O'Laughlin and T/5 Lieblong, we know only that they were wounded. T/5 Siegfried had a hand wound about which we know nothing more. 1/LT Kobliska had an unusual "wound." Assigned to sweep about half a mile of the second ridge ahead with light fire, he tried to climb a tree on the first ridge to observe. For his first time, he used lineman's irons. He moved his knees too close to the trunk, fell 20 feet, and sprained an ankle. Kobliska tried to refuse a purple heart, but could not avoid the medal.

That evening, a sniper zeroed in on the forward observer team of 1/LT Morse, Four Jap rounds whistled too close to Morse's ear. The team dug in prone. Then the sniper moved his fire 100 yards to Bn aide station and made some stomach hits on men not named. (A Journal page is missing.) When we spotted him on a high coral ridge, several thousand rounds of MG fire silenced him.

Next morning, we had orders for direct support of 186 Inf, that strategic day of 19 June. This was when 186 Inf was to cut off the Jap's West Caves from the rear. Our 186 Inf was to seize the first long, narrow, steep rise of the 100-foot ridge NW of West Caves. Holding that ridge, 186 Inf would cut off the Jap's main supply route and reinforcements from north Biak. The newly arrived 34 Inf (24 Div) would secure 186 Inf's left flank for the attack.

Probably the night before 186 attacked, 34 Inf's CO called on 1/LT Morse. This CO had learned that 167 FA had excellent overlapping air photos of the terrain. This CO began questioning Morse — not his own 34 Inf officers. And Morse found that he was actually himself planning next day's Regtl attack. Morse was scared that something would go wrong and the 41st DivArty would fault him.

But the plan worked. With observers attached to 186's E and F Cos, 167 FA fired 10 minutes' preparation up to 1030. Then we shot 7 concentrations. With just a few casualties, 186 Inf had taken the ridge and cut off West Caves, the Jap's last Biak strongpoint.

Now 34 Inf had orders to capture Boroko and Sorido Strips. These two Strips lay about 2.5 miles west of already captured Mokmer Strip. The Japs had used Boroko Strip only slightly. Probably main Jap opposition would come from 500 men of 219 Inf, 35 Div. Called "Nishihara Force," these men had recently landed during the Jap Navy's abortive plans to reinforce Biak.

About 0830 on 20 June, 167 FA observers with 34 Inf pushed from the beach to a low coral ridge about 2,000 yards inland. Resistance was only a little sniper fire.

By 1600, 167 FA had forwarded our guns to new positions. We set up a Fire Directions Center, and Btry C adjusted fire on Korim Track to the north. We shelled 500 yard intervals down 3/Bn 34 Inf's front. Beginning that night at 1900, A and C Btrys fired harassing shells on Korim Track all night.

After battling Jap raiders back at Toem, 167 FA took no chances! Besides keeping normal FA perimeter defense with machine-gunners and riflemen, we kept an observation line 150 yards into the jungle on front and flanks. And in the first 3 days, recon patrols searched ground before our observaton line. We found no Japs.

On 21 June while 34 Inf patrolled and consolidated, all 167's Btrys fired concentrations on Japs on Korim Track. Btry B fired 2 concentrations on a Jap strongpoint and a small warehouse. Liaison parties now were at all Bn HQs of 34 Inf, and forward observer parties with A, F, G, and I Cos.

On the morn of 22 June our Cub Pilot 1/LT Van Dyke with observer Capt. Ramstead sighted a Jap Btry of undiscerned caliber. One long barrel pointed towards Mokmer Strip, and a second barrel towards Sorido Strip. Other 2 guns pointed south to the beach. Eight Japs were in the gun-pit to fire on Mokmer Strip.

By 1220, Btry A began firing for effect on the Nippo Btry, then Btrys B and C — with another unnamed FA Bn also concentrating. Van Dyke reported all our Btrys 75 per cent effective.

At 1815, Btry A fired a precision adjustment against No. 3 piece. A's direct hit on the gun exploded nearby ammo. "A" dropped a shell into No. 1 pit and damaged the gun there. Then a direct smashed No. 2 gun. (But when Van Dyke landed, his plane cracked up against a phone wire accidently strung across the field. Van Dyke and Ramstead were unhurt, and the plane repairable.)

After West Caves resistance ended, 186 Inf with other 41sters still had to fight Japs holding ridges above West Caves. Our decimated 41st Div badly needed 167 FA. With fresher 34 Inf. First Bn of 34 Inf led 2/Bn eastward into the ridges, with 167 FA observers.

Penetrating into the tangled coral ridge jungle, 1/Bn 34 Inf (less C Co) occupied old Jap positions on the "Finger — a long, narrow ridge running NW from the "Teardrop." (The "Teardrop" was a box canyon from which 200 well-armed Japs had previously slipped off between 186 Inf and 3/Bn 163.)

Most 1/Bn men easily occupied the Finger, but "C" had trouble. Ordered to take a different route north of the Finger, C hit a Jap ambush of unknown strength and was repelled south. "C" could not rejoin 1/Bn until the next day.

On 27 June, 167 FA fired for 1/Bn scouting north and east into the ridges to feel out Jap lines. At 1100, a Jap position was spotted. Btry B covered it with bracket fire. At 1245, 2 Jap MGs were observed about 3,000 yards from our FA basepoint eat of Korim Track. A Bn concentration of shells hit there, but they were well dug in. We had to shoot more concentrations that day, and harassing fire that night.

Meanwhile, 1/Bn's patrols north of the Teardrop area brought information that caused officers to fear that more Jap trouble was coming. From their coral cliff strongholds north of 1/Bn, they might be preparing for a die-hard stand — or a suicidal counter-attack.

So Gen. Doe ordered 34 Inf's 2 Bns to attack on both flanks of this cliff area and clear it. While 2/Bn pushed from SW and west, 1/Bn would push from the SE.

At 0700 28 June, F and G Cos patrolled east along a ridge to try to contact A and B Cos expected from the SE. They found 11 dead Japs in a probable hospital area, then brushed aside a little Jap patrol and wounded some of them. A 0930, Japs attacked with mortars, A MG, and small arms.

The Japs slew 1 Yank, wounded 2 more, and caused 4 to be temporarily missing in action. Fearing to strike our own Inf, 167's gunners dared not shell. Although continuing to advance, both F and G encountered repeated sniper fire. They finally dropped back to a ridge to dig in.

During that day fight of 28 June, 2/Bn's E Co was useless. In those confusing twisted jungle ridges, they had been guided into the wrong positions — could not fight that day.

On that 28 June also, 1/Bn pushed — but had almost no resistance, except late in the day in A Co. Advancing between 1/Bn and their 2/Bn, A Co saw no Japs during most of the day. About 1600, they unwisely chose to set up on a bare coral knoll about 50 by 85 feet in area.

When A was trying to dig in, an unknown number of Japs lashed out at them. Knee mortars impacted on the bare knoll; MGs rowelled it. Came then riflemen with long bayonets. Green A Co pulled out too fast; in fact, then turned and ran!

Our 167 FA observer party had to leave also. Lt. Flory and his men hid a No. 610 radio in the brush at the foot of the knob. They held together and helped save A Co from the useless casualties that happen when men turn their backs and run. (Flory was not a regular 167 FA officer. He was one of several officers attached from probably 6 Div for combat experience. Like some other attached officers, he liked 167 FA enough to want to transfer into us, but this was not allowed.)

With 167's Cpl. Wieland, he helped save a wounded A man. With some stubborn A Co men, they organized a rear guard — carried off rifles and protected the wounded men. They rejoined A Co safe in last night's perimeter. Losses were 4 killed, 3 wounded, and 2 missing.

After a night of our harassing shellfire and a heavier morning preparation, C Co on 29 June probed into the ground A had fled from. "C" had only a little resistance.

Main fight of 29 June, however, was on the 2/Bn fronts. Today, our guns were prevented from firing until 1130. It was hard to adjust accurate shellfire into that vague, scrubby jungle of low ridges. We had to avoid hitting nearby Inf. But F and G did manage to advance 100 yards farther than yesterday.

F Co kept probing for the end of the Jap's left flank until about 1500 hours, when a Pln worked itself around the end of that flank. A bloody fight began. The 34th Inf's 2/Bn had 9 killed, 15-20 wounded, and some 4 missing — although 2 of those missing evidently turned up that night. Since 2/Bn had to halt in a poor defensive position, they withdrew 150 yards — 50 behind yesterday's position, and dug in. Our 105s covered their withdrawal. (Not until 6 days later did 186 Inf recover the radio that Lt. Flory's observer party had to leave on 28 June. It had lain hidden in the brush all the time.)

On 30 June, 2/Bn's patrols found 2 of the "G" men missing in action since yesterday. For half the night, they had secreted themselves in caves inside the Jap area. They credited 167's night shellfire for keeping the Japs under cover until their escape back into our lines.

The rest of 34 Inf's last day of combat on Biak was limited to recon patrols, evacuation of wounded, and recovery of corpses. For 34 Inf had orders to assemble on the beach on call to embark for the Noemfor Island Operation farther west off the head of New Guinea.

While 34 Inf withdrew to the beach, 167 FA fired concentrations to secure from Nippo pursuit. By 2330, all outfits had retreated without further casualties. Report of 2/Bn was that F Co had killed 100 Japs, G had killed 33. And 167 FA had credit for slaying 66 more that day.

On the morn of 1 July, a DivArty concentration was hurled down on the Japs to keep them from realizing the departure of 34 Inf. Later, 167 FA learned that we had slain 34 more Japs. And later, 167 FA was reassigned to directly support 186 Inf again. We now fired to help mop up, but our real Battle of Biak was over.

We have one nauseous memory of green 34 Inf on Biak. Over a period of several days after they left, flies began buzzing over 167's positions. They became a serious health hazard — a frightful pest. (while you were eating from a messgear with one hand and fighting them off with the other, did you ever have a New Guinea fly dive down your throat and into your stomach and STAY there?) Searching the vacated 34 Inf area, our surgeon and Medics found open garbage pits and a dead pig covered with flies. It took a long time to get rid of those flies. We complained through channels, and an unverified rumor says that the 34 Inf CO was relieved.

Actually, the 34 Inf were good guys, but a typical green *unblooded* Inf Regt. After Biak, they fought well in the Philippines; we FA men surely helped train them. As for 167 FA, our harder battle down at Toem had already turned us into a Bn of seasoned veterans.

CREDIT. First, I thank Bill Morse for his personal memories of 167 FA, in a 2.5 page single-spaced typescript of 18 Feb 1986. Most useful was and 8-page single-spaced typescript entitled "Unit History of 167 FA Bn/Biak Island Campaign," with an "Introduction" about leaving Toem, and a list of 4 purple hearts. Useful also was Lt-Col. Dwight Beach's "Apendix I/Lessons Learned in Combat" — a well written 3-page typscript. RR Smith's Approach to the Philippines has a large map of 34 Inf's Biak days, and a 2-page commentary of that Regt. I consulted also Journals of both 167 FA and 34 Inf. My other story of 167 FA is "167th FA Fights a Toem," in Dec. 1960 *Jungleer* (No. 13), reprinted in my *Fighting Jungleers*.

A CO 116 ENGINEERS: NIGHT FIGHT AT TOEM
by A Co 116 Engrs' G. D. "TONY" ROHLFFS, GEORGE D. MOORE, and GEORGE KRAEMER
with Dr. Hargis Westerfield, Division Historian

On 17 May 1944, A Co 116 (Combat) Engineers beached in the second wave following 3/Bn 163 Inf on the Toem Foreshore opposite Wakde Island. The other 2 Bns of 163 Inf landed after us. Attached to 27 Engr Bn, we began clearing bivouac and dump areas, and helping Amphib Engrs offload ammo and other supplies from ships. With 27 Engrs, we began building a 2-lane truck road alongshore from Toem to Arare.

Our Toem-Wakde Operation was to be the usual beacheading Engrs' hard work; but it would also be where we had our one bad night of Jap attack.

On the morning of 18 May when 163 Inf's 1/Bn plus E Co stormed Wakde, George Moore was among the Engrs sent to help B Co 116 Medics set up inshore from A 116. Casualties were flooding the Medics from a total of 40 killed and 107 wounded. It seemed to Moore that there were many trucks of US dead. In the afternoon, Moore was on a detail to dig graves inland south of A 116's camp. Only known Wakde casualty of A 116 was Ren-teria, marked "seriously wounded" with a gunshot through his right arm. He was shot on 22 May on Wakde; we have no report on what he was doing on Wakde.

But by 27 May, the Japs seemed no longer to menace our men at Toem. Battle was going on about 20 miles east of us, where 158 Inf was assailing Lone Tree Hill towards Sarmi Strip.

On that peaceful early night of 27 May, A 116 Engrs' camp had almost a holiday atmosphere. Men were swimming from the beach north of the new 2-lane road. Electric lights shone from kitchen and showers. In kerosene-lighted tents, cots were spread for card games or sleeping. (So luxurious was Toem that nearby B 116 Medics had 2 gasoline-powered washing machines.)

We Engrs looked forward to another great night of unbroken sleep—but for the guards in a listening post and in a pillbox with 3 men and a heavy .30 caliber MG. Yet dense jungle to hide Jap charges, began just 100 yards in from the beach and ran back 6 miles to mountain foothills. But A 116 Engrs did not worry that a surprise rush of Jap bayonets from the dark could readily overrun our HMG post. Our 163 Hqs gave us no warning of any Jap danger.

On our 2 inland jungle trails were sets of booby traps for night security. But here also, security precautions were lax. The man in charge of those booby traps, A Co's Artificer Rohlffs had to go alone to set those traps just before dark, and just after morning lightfall. A 116's operating procedure was that every man assigned a job was on his own to get that job done. Despite his pleas for a trigger-man to crouch on guard over him, PFC Rohlffs could get no security while his nervous hands adjusted delicate explosive mechanisms.

And so that night once more, Rohllfs leaned his tommy-gun against a tree and worked with sweaty, trembling hands among grenades, land-mines, and bouncing betties. Often he started at dark jungle noises, but he could not risk an explosion in his face if he seized his tommy-gun to defend himself. But no lurking men of Col Soemon Matsuyama's force bayoneted him kneeling over his booby traps.

After setting the traps, Rohlffs looked forward to a quiet talk with his tent-mates, then sleep in the peaceful jungle dark. On the way back, he talked a little with T/5 Mossman at his listening post ahead of the .30 HMG which was our only security to warn against a Jap onslaught. Mossman was a nice, quiet boy whom other Engrs guess to have enlisted when still only 16 years old. Mossman too had set booby traps before his listening post which he shared with just one man, a Canadian born Indian, Vic Paul. This was the last time he would ever talk to Mossman, who did not have long to live.

Then Rohlffs homed to his tent—a little 3 man officers' tent in the western section of the camp where Hqs personnel slept. Beside the tent was a large 8 man air-raid hole covered by metal airfield ground nets and earth. Here slept men of Hqs personnel unassigned to squads—command car drivers, cat-men, mechanics, and Co clerks. East across a wide lane down to the sea were the ordnance tent where Rohlffs worked, the supply tent, the kitchen, and random squad tents. The showers were just south of them, closest to the jungle.

With tent-mates Roberts and Lucy, Rohlffs quietly chatted before turning in. Surely they talked about going home, for the rotation points system had begun for the 41st. On 23 May, Bell, Beaver, Franklin, "Scotty," and "E.V." had already emplaned for the States. Since most "A" men had twice the needed 85 points for home, names were drawn from a hat. Rohlffs' name had come up. Since he had been overseas even in the surf landing on Nassau Bay that began the Salamaua Operation, he would be happy to rotate home in June. Nothing could be more on his mind than "home" and the fear that he would not live to make it.

That quiet talk over the cigarettes was reassuring to Rohlffs. At the same time in a larger squad tent, Moore watched other men tranquilly playing cards by the light of a kerosene lantern.

Suddenly Rohlffs, Lucy, and Roberts heard a loud "Pop!" "Sounds like a field kitchen blew up," one man said. (A Jap had tripped a wire that exploded a grenade.)

Tommy-gun fire rattled from the listening post of Mossman and the Canadian Indian Paul. Then we all heard the opening bursts from the 3 man crew at the MG. With that fire came "all kinds of hell"—grenade blasts, rifle and automatic fire, screaming Japs, bugle calls, and whistles that sounded foreign.

Before they heard the echoes from the first shots, Rohlffs, Lucy, and Roberts seemed to feel their guns leap into their hands. They slipped under the tent-sides into the great 8 man hole and readied to repel the Jap charge that seemed certain to come.

The screaming and firing came in waves, then suddenly quieted and started over. Crouching Rohlffs saw a body darken his loophole. The body said nothing, but it lay right against the muzzle of Rohlffs' tommy.

"Let him have it!" whispered one man. "Hold it!" said the other man in a low voice. We expected all kinds of horror to break out: Nips ringing us to strike with long bayonets, a grenade about to be rapped outside to arm for blasting us, and death in many more ways.

After at least 10 long minutes, the alleged Jap blacking out the hole spoke in good old American English. He only wanted to share the hole with us. The noise of the attack was dying down.

But the men in Moore's squad-tent were not near any 8 man hole. After that first booby trap popped, somebody turned out the kerosene lantern. Moore dived for the tent floor, with Morris prone before him. Other card players dived into small holes outside.

Moore heard rifle-fire from his right near the CP area, from T/4 Kraemer, and Cpls Robin and Richardson. Our .30 HMG kept on firing. Moore heard Japs in the tents of 2/Pln on his left. He heard a final whistle, and thought that this was the signal for the Japs' withdrawal. But he still did not dare to leave his tent in the dark. Japs might be lurking behind to kill him, or some Engrs might slay him by mistake. All the remaining night, Moore crouched by his gun in tent shadows.

T/4 Kraemer had to lie flat on ground behind a palm tree about 20 feet left of his 2/Pln tent. A Jap grenade exploded too close to his right leg but did not wound him. He fired a clip and a half and thought that he surely wounded one Jap.

In ugly daybreak, we looked tiredly and bleary-eyed on our camp that was peaceful last night—and now a corpse-littered battlefield. Moore could not talk at first; his voice may have left because of his fear. Moore seemed to see many corpses, mostly Japs', but even a few Engrs. (God knows, even one dead Yank was one too many.)

We thought that we could reconstruct the time sequences of the attack. First, the Japs struck the listening post of Mossman and Paul. It was a small round hole, maybe 3 feet around, and 4 feet deep, with no overhead protection.

Mossman had died on his tommy-gun but alerted our camp to fight back in seconds. He had piled up 6 twisted corpses with his tommy—although Paul may have killed more than one of these. Mossman died with a hole in his head. Paul said that he had hidden all night under Mossman's body to save his own life.

Secondly, the Japs had flailed the 3 man pillbox armed with the .30 caliber water-cooled HMG with its flash-hider. This pillbox was formidable. It was shaped something like a horseshoe behind a curved sandbagged barricade, and roofed to repel grenades and plunging baynet men. Entrance was from the rear down a ramp.

Regular Army Sgt Wisnieswki commanded, with gunner Nichols and assistant Murray. From the dark, the Japs had used preparatory automatic fire. They had set up a shoulder-operated little automatic weapon on a bipod. Moore believed that Mossman had slain the gun crew before they had struck the pill box slot. But the bayonet charge came anyhow. Japs rushed with bayoneted rifles. Some ran with boyonets lashed to long poles.

They charged the pillbox in ranks, shoulder to shoulder. Moore saw bodies piled on tops of bodies. As the MG mowed down the first rank, the second rank charged and was shot, then another. Moore could see just how many waves had charged. Nichols' continuous fire had slashed the corpses over and over. He could not risk grenades from men still alive.

When Moore saw them, the corpses lay where Nichols' MG had piled them. They were not yet stacked to truck off for burial. Moore wishes that he had counted them, today, but he was far more concerned with the number of Engr casualties.

One lone Jap did start a bayonet attack towards the pillbox entrance behind the gun, but Murray shot him down. It was a silhouette shot into a dark blur in the night.

Probably at the same time of the pillbox charge, other Japs had charged to the left of our listening post and pillbox—on the side closest to the sea. They seemed to fan out to catch our men in showers and squad tents.

Four or five Japs were sprawled dead in the showers. Two more lay silent in the opening behind the showers and before the squad tents nearer to the coast. Six lay before Mossman and Paul's listening post, and an uncounted number before the .30 HMG. Rohlffs estimated a total kill of 35.

A Co 116 Engrs had 5 dead, and 2 seriously wounded. Besides T/5 Mossman shot through the head, T/5 Wilde was found dead near the HMG with a bullet in his pelvis. Larsen's body lay between Rohlff's tent and the jungle near a dismounted truck hood used as a tent. Bullets had pierced Larsen's head and chin. Eichenlaub was dead across the road near the beachside palms—arm shot off and a fragment in his left side. A shot in the chest had killed Renkel. Where he was found is unknown, but Moore saw him carried off for burial. B 116 Medics' Zelesniker also lay dead in our area; he may have come to aid our Engr casualties.

Two men were reported seriously wounded. Thomas took a bullet in the groin; Robets was shot in the jaw. And there were mental casualties, one of them Rohlffs' close friend. While visiting him at B 116's hospital, Rohlffs watched 3 Engrs crawling around on the earth and making queer noises. The sound of a distant shot would jerk them into spasmodic moves.

Near Toem, A 116 Engrs had listed only a few casualties after that 27 June fight. On 29 June, Sgt McNulty was accidentally killed when he came too close to our HMG in the dark. On 29 June also, John D. Brown was reported missing in action. A "John D. Brown" appears in an overall roster of our Division's dead—perhaps the same man. On 30 May, Grizzle was shot in his left hand, and recorded "seriously wounded."

Not until they read these words will many A 116 men realize that the night attack of 27 June was merely a "diversion"—an attack to draw attention from the main attack. Main attack struck 163's lightly held 1/Bn perimeter farther inland. By hitting us Engrs, the Japs hoped to panick 163 Inf, or to weaken them by sending forces to help us. But this attack from Col Soemon Matsuyama's 224 Inf (36 "Tiger" Division) had merely lost good men whom he could have used elsewhere. As for hard fighting A 116 Engrs, we are lucky that Col Matsuyama did not throw all of his men at us and drive us into the ocean.

CREDIT. George Moore's letters of 21 Feb and 24 Mar 1987—10 pages handwritten—helped to complete what Tony Rohlffs began—a full length story of A 116 Engrs at Toem. (George Kraemer also helped from a 2 page letter of 9 July 1987.) Rohlffs began it all with 18 pages handwritten—an undated letter and a second letter of 12 Apr—both in 1982. Important also for this story were 2 Federal Archives studies entitled "Japanese Raiding Parties in the Wakde-Sarmi Campaign," from a typescript called "Enemy Tactics, Materiel and Terrain." Background comes from RR Smith's *Approach to the Philippines*. (Smith never mentions this study of Jap raiding parties.) I used also 163 Inf's Wakde-Toem "Casualty Lists," which includes A 116 Engrs' casualties. (Calling all Engineers: We still have no Engrs' stories about Zamboanga and other Southern Philippines actions.)

H COMPANY 162 INFANTRY: PARAI DEFILE & MOKMER RIDGES
by LT. CHARLIE JACHIM
and Dr. Hargis Westerfield, Division Historian

On the second day of Biak Battle, 28 May 1944, H Co 162 Inf heard that 162's 3/Bn was in trouble and needed us. In pushing down the south Biak shore to take Mokmer Strip, 162's forward Cos were being repulsed.

Suddenly H Co began a forced march to hold a defense line in Parai Defile. We marched a long, hot distance at a fast pace with breaks that were few. 2/Lt Jachim of our HMGs estimated that we slogged 12 - 15 miles per hour at 3.5 miles in 3 - 4 hours. (Jachim was Pln leader of H's 1/Pln of 4 HMGs.)

Jap mortar rounds menaced us as we neared our assigned positions to cover the Parai Defile withdrawal. The mortar blasts increased when Jachim and some gunners crouched in a beach depression. A Jap mortar fragment somehow missed others of us but hit Jachim's runner Caro in his wrist. Although the wound was judged light, it caused such damage to Caro's nervous system that he was evacuated Stateside.

Jachim's HMG Pln got orders to entrench across the road from Mokmer Strip. Pln/Sgt White took our second section a little way inland and anchored G Co's right flank on the first rise up from the sea. This second section straddled the road, with a gun on the inland side and a gun on the seaward side. Cpl Carter had one squad, and Cpl Hermanson the other squad.

Jachim and his new runner Shoemaker dug a hole behind the second HMG inland from the sea across the road. The sand here made easy digging — unlike the coral over most of Biak. Visibility was fair in that neglected coconut grove, but undergrowth limited the forward view.

Units of 3/Bn started to retreat through H's position until late afternoon. Jap mortar fire seemed heavier as the day grew later.

During one Jap mortar concentration, riflemen protecting a withdrawing tank suffered several casualties. Going bravely into the mortar impact area, Medic T/5 McNiel gave first aid and directed evacuations. Under intense fire, McNiel administered first aid and morphine to a seriously wounded man and helped carry him to a safer place. For performing similar duties days later, McNiel was seriously wounded, on an unknown date.

A company retreating through shallow water along the beach took withering mortar fire and was disorganized. T/Sgt Lynch took command and directed most of them into a safe retreat. When they told him that they had to leave one man under fire, Lynch rescued him.

Besides Caro first reported lightly wounded, "H" lost 4 men seriously wounded that 28 May: Hatton, Naserowski, Stringer, and Poremski — who had just a finger wound.

Later that afternoon, Jap mortar fire slowed down. "H" readjusted or consolidated positions. Lt Uppinghouse of the flanking G Co Pln agreed with Jachim that H's HMGs should be pulled back 50 yards to a new position for better fields of fire and cover for the beach on our left.

H's mortar Co, 1/Lt Ivey, came up to register in our 81s to guard Jachim's new HMG position. Outstanding mortarman Ivey pulled his 81s in close before our HMGs — within 50 yards or less. Next day in combat, Jachim wished that the big tubes were closer still.

By dawn of our third Biak day, 29 May 1944, Jap tanks and Inf massed to wipe out 162's men still holding Parai Defile.

In gray dawn, Lt Jachim awoke from his hole to volleys of his HMGs. About 0700, a Jap column rout — marched down the road towards "H." Seeming a company-sized unit, they marched in disciplined order — upright and on their feet even in a battle area — they rounded a downhill road curve and headed towards us on a long straight road section.

It was a machine-gunner's dream come true. They were unaware that we were sighting them, low in holes over our guns.

An officer led. They still hiked in route-march formation, rifles slung on their shoulders, in columns of twos. By now, the officer seemed almost on top of our holes.

Suddenly the officer seemed to spot our holes. He halted to give an order. Our 2 closest MGs opened fire.

The officer fell about 50 feet from our guns. We mowed down his column of riflemen following him. Japs piled up already dead or writhing and screaming on the road.

Surviving Japs fanned out towards our inland right flank and fought G Co's riflemen in their holes. They stood up and attacked frontally against G Co and were shot down from foxholes. H's 1/Lt Ivey's mortars also blasted H and G Co's front. While they died, "H" did not lose a man killed or wounded.

Our front somewhat quieted down but for sporadic Jap mortar shells. We busied ourselves to bring up more ammo and to reorganize. For we had shot about 1300 rounds already.

Now we heard engine mortars humming from the Jap rear, out of sight up the hill and around the curve. Remembering his intelligence briefing, Jachim was certain he heard tanks. He still believes that if they had charged when he first heard them, they would have panicked and overrun our lines. He still does not understand why they did not strike at once.

Jachim headed back for nearby 2/Bn 162 Hqs to call for our tanks. Shortly a mortar shell exploded about 15 feet to his left. Concussion grounded him; he was not even scratched. But about 75 feet ahead of Jachim, 2 "H" men running for ammo were hit — Hill and Terry both lightly wounded for hospital.

Jachim safely arrived at 2/Bn CP and asked for tank assistance. Back at his front-line HMGs, he still heard Jap motors, but the tanks had not moved. After what seemed forever, we heard our own tanks rumbling forward to defend us. Now the Jap tanks were moving out of sight also.

We saw a beautiful sight behind us — 2 Gen Sherman tanks, each with a 75 mm cannon mounted on it. Tensely, we watched them halt near us. We looked for the Jap tanks up the road.

The first little Jap tank tottered into sight around the downhill road curve and fired. Our tanks knocked it out. Another Jap tank rounded the flank of the first tank and was also knocked out. Our shells pierced their armor, but being only light tanks with 37 mm cannon, they could not penetrate our heavier tank armor. Our 75s with AP shells easily struck dead 4 tank crews.

After the first wave of 4 tanks, a second wave of 3 tanks made a charge. One Jap 37mm shell actually hit the armor near a 75mm gun barrel and locked the gun so that it could not be accurately sighted. But the tank CO backed partly into a shell hole to elevate his cannon and managed to destroy one tank. After all 3 tanks of the second wave were dead, their accompanying Jap tank-Inf retreated.

Jachim's "H" men took no fire at all from the Jap tanks. In gratitude, Jachim and his gunners presented the tankmen the Jap officer's saber. Jachim himself gave them the big silver chain and pocket watch from the officer's corpse. He sent back the maps and papers to Bn Hqs. We felt truly safe with those big Sherman "iron horses" near us.

But 162 Inf could not knock out the Jap mortars and MGs on Parai cliffs. Our position was untenable. Our whole attack force had to escape from the Defile. While all 2/Bn but G Co and some "H" men and 3/Bn riflemen left by water, most of 3/Bn retreated up the shore.

Pln/Sgt White volunteered to command some men of "H" who withdrew on land. Lt Jachim left by water. Too well, Jachim remembers the fears he had waterborne with Parai cliffs overlooking us, and knowing that the Japs were behind those cliffs. Jammed tight with others in the little DUKW, he moved by its one slow speed from under threat of those cliffs from which Japs might throw down shells at any minute.

H Co's detachment's land retreat was fairly safe, but we still lost a man killed, exact name uncertain. The planes covering our retreat made strafing runs. One plane mistook us for Japs and slew that "H" man.

On that 29 May, H Co's casualties were 2 killed and 4 wounded. Of the 2 dead, either Brooks or Cpl Soroken died by fire from our own plane. Besides Hill and Terry already mentioned, whom a Jap mortar wounded when they ran back for HMG ammo, we had 2 more men listed as lightly wounded. They were Katz and Morell, details unknown. (Morell would be killed 10 days later.)

After 162 Inf's retreat from Parai Defile, 186 Inf began their dry overland march from behind Bosnek to capture Mokmer Strip from the rear. Our 2/Bn 162 was attached to 186 Inf for this move. Although the 3 rifle Cos of our 2/Bn joined 186 Inf by climbing across the ridges west of Ibdi Pocket over Young Man's Trial, H Co with heavy weapons marched a longer way. We followed 186 Inf on the inland road and rejoined our 2/Bn on or about 5 June.

On 7 June with 186 Inf, our 2/Bn easily occupied Mokmer Strip but came under heavy bombardment from the bypassed Japs still on the ridges. Killed was Siscavage. Seriously wounded were Hartoon and Rogers, and Weis lightly wounded.

On 8 June, the Jap bombardment continued. When our 2/Bn tried to move east over the flats to contact other 162 Cos which had arrived by sea, "H" had more casualties.

Sgt Bishop's squad had a position with some tree cover and concealment. Probably a Jap shell fragmented on a nearby tree. Sgt Bishop died there, and Rasmussen and Morell — Morell who had already been hospitalized for a light wound in Parai Defile 10 days before. Somewhere else in H Co, Noel was killed, Evans seriously wounded, and Davis and McGowan lightly wounded.

At the close of that 8 June, H Co perimetered close to the sea, on the flats above the usual first beach above the water. Cover was sparse and ground hard; we could not dig. We had to shelter in natural depressions. Occasional Jap mortar shells fell above us.

T/Sgt Tom Lynch's HMG section was on the right flank of 2/Bn near the beach. There the Japs attacked that night. Lynch first saw a few shadows and himself fired the HMG at them. Then he saw more shadows slipping to his right to flank the gun and kill him.

Lynch ordered Grizzle to replace him to fire the MG. Lynch moved over to cover Grizzle on the right flank with an M-1.

We repulsed the attack, but Grizzle died on the HMG. A grenade blasted Lynch's face and blinded him. He had to be led back to aid station, but he gratefully recovered his sight in the beauiful light next morning. Meanwhile Sgt White had reorganized this MG position and held 2/Bn's flank. Next morning there, we slew 2 Japs going for water with their empty canteens.

During the days from 8 June to 19 June, H Co rejoined 162 Inf coming west from Parai Defile and was in the final infighting for the Japs' West Caves. By about 13 June, "H" with our 2/Bn was fighting for the low Mokmer Ridge west of 162's 3/Bn. Harry Smith was lightly wounded on 11 June, and Cpl Burgen killed on 17 June.

On 18 June, the Casualty List says that 2/Lt Harris died of wounds. Rocheville and Cpl Lindley were seriously wounded, and McCormack lightly wounded.

We are unsure whether these casualties occurred during H's almost forgotten night fight of 18 - 19 June. About 0400 on 19 June, a heavy Jap attack with mortar preparation overran F 162's lightly held left flank with 3 holes widely separated. They threatened to roll up 2/Bn's line on Mokmer Ridge.

Here died 2/Lt Curtright, a lad of 19 beside an H Co HMG, no one knows precisely how. Curtright may have died while he stood up behind the MG to direct its fire. Or he may have been fireing the HMG himself. Or he may have stood up to fire his own M-1. The attack was stopped, and F Co men counted 28 dead Japs.

Last reported "H" casualties were Spence, lightly wounded on 19 June, and Kazmierczak, lightly injured on 23 June.

All told on Biak, H Co lost 11 killed in action. This number includes Grizzle and Lt Curtright, neither of whose names is listed in Westerfield's Fighting Jungleers, although men remember that they died. Twenty more were wounded and hospitalized, of whom Morell was later killed after return to duty. For a heavy weapons Co, our number of 11 dead was fairly high. On Biak, H Co had fought reliably, wherever we were needed.

CREDIT. Most credit for this history is due to H 162's Charlie Jachim's letters of 4 June, 25 June, 30 July, 17 Sept, 5 Nov (two letters), and 16 Dec — all in 1986. They would cover about 10 pages of single-spaced typescript, business letter size. For help in these letters, Charlie also contacted H Co's Tom Lynch and Al Cesliak. Charlie verified also 2 Award Stories — of Medic T/5 Don McNiel and T/Sgt Tom Lynch. Background data are from RR Smith's *Approach to the Philippines*.

E CO 163 INFANTRY:
BLOWOUT HILL AT ZAMBOANGA

by Dr. Hargis Westerfield, Division Historian
with E. 163's BARman Robert Sams

This is the story of Blowout Hill at Zamboanga Battle, on 13 Mar 1945. The mine under Blowout Hill played havoc with the Pln of E Co 163 Inf who were on the hill when the Japanese blew the mine by 2 suicidal Marines. But despite the agony of men of E Co and other outfits, this is basically a tale of Japs' failure to make full use of their deadly weapon. It is also the harrowing story of BARman Robert Sams and the grievous wound that he suffered on Blowout Hill.

On 12 Mar 1945—the day before Blowout Hill—E Co 163 had not suffered many casualties. On that 12 Mar, we had begun pushing in our 2/Bn towards the heavily fortified Jap Marines of 33 Naval Guard at Pasananca. Our 2/Bn push began in column of companies. G Co led out with "E" following, and "F" in the rear. By 1230, G Co had encountered heavy FA and MG fire, and had lost 2 killed and 2 seriously wounded. E Co had echeloned to the left to protect G's flank, but had less trouble. By nightfall, 146 FA's 105 guns with 5 tanks of 716 Tank Bn had made easier the way for farther advances next morning up the highway to Pasananca Village. Our 2/Bn had advanced some 400 yards against that fortress of overgrown bunkers and hidden 75 mm cannon.

On the morning of 13 Mar, the day of Blowout Hill, G Co went into 2/Bn reserve and hoped to rest, and our E Co led out with "F" behind us. At first, our advance was easy towards what would become Blowout Hill. Without vicious fire from the Jap 75s which had been silenced the day before, opposition seemed much lighter. With tanks and 105s to assist us, we had only rifle fire and mortars to fight. At 1000 when a Jap mortar fired, our own mortars knocked it out. E Co overran an abandoned Jap 20 mm dual purpose gun. By 1040, we had pushed 200 yards north of 2/Bn's forward CP and had contacted men of 1/Bn advancing in the jungle on the eastern side of Pasanaca Road.

E Co's main effort that day had been to march directly forward towards Pasananca Village. This frontal push meant that we had to drive the Japs from a low jungle hill. Heavy jungle crowned its top. It was almost flat on the top, with a gentle curve for a summit. This was deadly Blowout Hill.

E Co's BARman Sams remembered afterwards that "E" had that morning come to an open area of 300-400 feet before we started up the hill. On our first try across the open area, "E" took several casualties. S/Sgt Wieder must have died here, for his death was reported at 1020, but we have no way of finding the names of the wounded at that time. The Japs were dug in at the base of the hill, and their MG and rifle fire was heavy. We had to call for the tanks to blast out the Japs with our 75 mm cannon.

It was probably E Co's 2/Pln that started over the hill with the other rifle Plns on our flanks. After a rough climb to about the middle of the hill, 2/Pln began advancing too far ahead of our flanking Plns on rougher ground. A halt was called.

BARman Sams and his assistant were left a short way to the rear to guard a cross-trail. They endured much Jap rifle fire and were about to dig a hole and pull the hole in after them. As could be expected then, they had orders to go forward again.

Once more, E Co's officers called a halt. Sams and his unknown assistant took the usual infantrymen's positions in battle. They dropped down for rest and shelter close to an unknown Medic. (Sams was a new man in E Co. He had joined only at Mindoro, and had hardly begun to know the names of other "E" men.)

When the explosion lifted up Blowout Hill beneath them, neither Sams nor his BAR assistant knew when it happened. He thought that it killed his assistant outright. The nearby Medic was mangled and broken horribly, but Sams knew nothing about either man at that time. Sams recovered consciousness to find himself crawling downhill in unbearable pain.

About 1440 that 13 Mar 1945, Japanese Petty Officers Eizo Sakanishi and Akiyo Yamauchi blew the mine by hand. Thus they died gamely for the Emperor. They exploded many tons of TNT, naval depth charges, and torpedoes. The whole hilltop lifted skyward. Flying at 1500 feet, the cub pilot of our 146 FA Bn saw a column of smoke and debris far over his head. Below, trees and chunks of earth and stone fell back into a crater over 200 yards in diameter.

Before the explosion, the reserve G Co had moved to the hill base near the waiting tanks. About the time that we arrived, we could still see E Co's Pln on top of Blowout Hill. Then the entire hill seemed to fly high in the air. Hunks of rock and coral weighing tons flew skyward. While the earth shook, pieces of equipment and maybe men looking like old sacks were blown high overhead. A sheet of flame shot upward 100 feet.

For a few seconds, "G" stood dazed by the thunder. Then all G Co dived for cover. Rocks and dirt rained down on a nearby tank; a huge chunk of rock struck about 200 feet away from cowering "G" men. But no G Co man was hurt. Choking smoke and dust then rained on us, and we heard the agonized call for Medics.

When Sams of E Co came to himself after painful crawling, many Medics and rear echelon men were working on his body. They cut off all his clothes, gave him a shot, and lifted him into a litter.

Just as maimed Sams was placed on a cot in a tent of a beachside hospital whose number he does not remember, a lone Jap raider dived from the setting sun. Twice the plane bombed and strafed the hospital area. Sams later heard that Naval AA fire had downed the plane. This was the only reported air sortie at the Battle of Zamboanga of the depleted Jap Air Force in the Philippines.

Strangely enough, Sams' X-ray showed no internal damage. But that quaking ground above the explosion had beaten him into a pulp. He was black and blue all over. He had a knot in his spine. Even after a month's hospital and rest camp, he was hardly able to walk. He said that it was found that his spine was fractured, months later.

E Co men on top of the blast suffered most of the casualties, of course. For the whole day, "E" listed a total of 34 names in the Morning Report, but it did not state exactly which of these men were in the explosion. E Co had been in combat before the explosion. (As mentioned before, S/Sgt Wieder was killed long before, at 1020.)

Hanenkrat and Brandell were reported dead at 1500, about the time when the mine blew up. Besides these 2 killed, we have the names of 31 E Co men who were also reported as casualties on 13 Mar.

A strikingly large number of these "E" casualties were reported as "lightly injured in action," an unusually large number for a Morning Report. We therefore believe that these injured were almost all explosion casualties—and no doubt a large number of the wounded.

There were 14 wounded in action. Seriously wounded was Pios. Lightly wounded were 2/Lt MacMillan, S/Sgt Williamson, and Sgt Spinella. Other lightly wounded were Parker, Olsen, Marshall, Raykov, Meyer, Ashby, Deston, Neithercutt, Scott, and Moody.

There were 17 marked lightly injured in action. Strange as it seems, Sams himself was reported lightly injured in action! Also injured were S/Sgts Newton and Alfred Nelson, and Sgt Moran. Others were Beyer, Brand, Bernard Jones, Austin, Lowe, Loney, Pannick, Breckenridge, Norman, Falasca, and Pena.

Finally, the last two names on the casualty list seem to deserve special mention as casualties of the blast. Perhaps because of the confusion in the dust and smoke after the explosion, Brenton and Bridegam were first marked as missing in action. Later, their names appeared on the list as lightly injured in action.

Thus, of 33 possible casualties of the explosion, 2 were reported killed, 1 seriously wounded, 13 lightly wounded, and 15 lightly injured. Hanenkrat and Brandell were surely killed in the blast, and most of the other 31 were also blast casualties.

And in 1/Bn 163 Inf across Pasananca Road, a fair number of the casualties there were surely victims of the blast. Here, C Co men cringed under entire trees falling on their ground. Euler of C Co was carried away to die of a broken neck. Besides Euler, on 13 Mar, "C" reported 3 lightly wounded, and 8 lightly injured. On C's right in A Co, 2 were named as killed that day, 2 others seriously wounded, and 3 others lightly wounded. (Although "A" spoke of 4 mine casualties, their Morning Report failed to name them.) In "D" there were 1 lightly wounded, and 4 others lightly injured. As in E Co, however, we are fairly sure that most if not all of the lightly injured were mine casualties, perhaps because of the unusually high proportion of them in combat.

Despite the number of 163's casualties and the size of the blowout—all of 300 yards in diameter—why did the Japs fail to realize only meager results from the blast—in comparison to what they should have realized? Why did they fail to destroy almost all of E Co and most of the tanks? Why did they fail to follow through on the blast with an all-out Marine attack at a time when the forward Cos of both 163's Bns might have been demoralized?

The Japs may have failed to begin a die-hard offensive because the hill blew off in the wrong direction for them—on the Nippo side of Blowout Hill. Perhaps for concealment from our scouts and observation planes, they had been forced to dig in from the wrong side. And perhaps their misguided explosion demoralized them also from taking the offensive. On 1/Bn's front, they seemed to have prepared no attack. After the blast, C Co had heard only disorganized shouting and movement on their Jap front—and had silenced the noise with only one MG belt. In 2/Bn, a G Co patrol around the left of Blowout Hill found that the Japs had not even left their entrenchments around what G Co would call "Death Valley."

And after that momentary dazed halt from the blast, 163's offensive continued the rest of that bloody day of 13 Mar. Despite G's halt at Death Valley, other elements of 2/Bn moved up. Before dark, 2/Bn had a foothold on the west ridge that commanded Pasananca Village. And 1/Bn had advanced to the woodland edge just south of Pasananca, where heavy fire and the dying light finally repelled them. Both Bns still needed several more days to overrun Pasananca, but despite Blowout Hill, they were now positioned for final victory.

Of E Co's 33 alleged casualties of 13 Mar which were mostly from Blowout Hill, we have the later history of the suffering of just 1 man—Sams, whose first agonies we have mentioned already. His spine was fractured, and by Oct 1972, he had endured 2 spinal operations. A seriously diseased kidney showed signs of previous injury. It bled continuously and must be removed. Yet Veterans Administration gave Sams only a 40 per cent disability payment—and not for his kidney. Because Sams could not remember which Zambo beach hospital had treated him, he could find no evidence that the damaged kidney was a battle injury. Like probably some other Blowout Hill casualties, he would never get adequate compensation for this necessary kidney operation.

Such was the Blowout Hill disaster and its agony, as epitomized in maimed Robert Sams. The Morning Reports of 13 Mar name just 57 casualties, and not all from the mine. Another official report goes up to 83. Yet the blast did not get its fullest effect and did not halt 163's 13 Mar advance.

POSTCRIPT Best proof of 163's Inf's good luck on Blowout Hill comes from the story of Americal Division's blowout at Go Chan Hill, about 2 miles north of Cebu City in the middle Philippines. On 29 Mar 1945, 18 Inf prepared to withdraw from heavy fire on Go Chan Hill. It was a low, brushy rise with a shallow curve, much like our Blowout Hill.

When the Japs blew an ammo dump on Go Chan Hill's eastern spur, A Co 18 Inf lost 20 dead and 30 wounded. B Co. 716 Tank Bn lost a tank and crew and had 2 more tanks damaged. Already under strength from Leyte Battle, A Co's survivors went to other 1/Bn rifle Cos. Not until the close of 30 Mar did 18 Inf storm Go Chan. In contrast to this American holocaust, E Co's agony was far easier than most E Co men have ever realized.

CREDIT Indispensable core of this history is BARman Robert Sams' letters of 4 Sept and 30 Oct 1972, and 3 Jan 1973. The 30 Oct letter was over 2 pages, single-spaced. Backing these letters were 163 Inf's Zamboanga Journal and Casualty List, and Capt Robert Allen's 146 FA history, "Ring of Fire at Zamboanga," from Mar 1970 JUNGLEER. (For 163 Inf itself left no narrative report—only their Journal.) I used also these published histories: 1/Bn 163 Inf: "Pasananca and the Reservoir Perimeter" (*JUNGLEER*, Feb 1966), and the Japanese Marine's "Saga of a Japanese Civilian Marine" by Makoto Ikeda (*JUNGLEER*, May 1987). Story of the successful Japanese explosion under Go Chan Hill in Cebu comes from RR Smith's *Triumph in the Phillippines*.

162 INF and 532 ENGR BOAT & SHORE REGT: MIRACLE LANDING AT NASSAU BAY

by Dr. Hargis Westerfield, Division Historian

Few 41 Div men realize the importance of 162 Inf's Nassau Bay invasion in 1943. Until then, mountain jungles and Japs had halted a strong Allied offensive. Fighting from inland to capture Mubo Strip, the Aussies could not truck enough supplies and ammo over roadless mountains for their campaign. They could not build roads fast enough; air-drops were of limited use. Confined to a narrow jungle shore, our 162 Inf could make only slow advances. The Jap Army of over 6,000 securely held Salamaua on the coast with a strong line along the Bitoi South Fork inland to 15 miles SE of Mubo Strip. They secured Nassau Bay with an advance strongpoint on Cape Dinga.

Using 532 Amphib Engrs' barges, 162's Col MacKechnie planned to land 162 Inf 1/Bn at Nassau Bay and expel the Japs. We would then have a convenient supply base by sea close to the Aussies fighting for Mubo. After cutting off the Dinga Point Japs, we could team with the Aussies to envelop Mubo and fight for Salamaua Town.

But the Nassau Bay landing would be hazardous. Our only terrain information was from a hurried scout of 2 Aussies of 2/6 Inf who had found a long stretch of unguarded sand between Dinga Point Japs and other Japs some 2 miles west on the Bitoi River. For secrecy, our voyage to the beach must be at night—54 miles in open sea mostly by 36-foot landing barges. In always dangerous weather, we would land on an enemy shore in darkness. Yet orders were to land at midnight, storm or calm.

Number of Amphib barges was limited. The Amphibs would use 29 LCVPs—"Landing Crafts, Vehicle, Personnel," 36 feet long; 1 LCM—"Landing Craft, Mechanized," 50 feet long, and 2 Jap barges, length unspecified. With the help of 4 PT boats—80-foot craft—the flotilla would carry 1,090 men, crewed by 87 A Co men and 7 D Co men of 532 Amphib Engrs.

To guide and guard those helpless barges, we had 4 PT Boats. Actually ships, these little 77-80 foot plywood destroyers cruised at 25-40 knots. Designed for shallow water, they carried machine cannon, depth charges, and torpedoes.

PTs 143 and 120 loaded 70 soldiers each. PT 142 carried just 10—for reasons unknown. Without troops aboard, PT 168 patrolled against Jap barges and submarines. The 23 LCVPs took 36 men each, the LCMs each 60, and the 2 Jap barges at least 50.

Already, there were portents of a bad night passage over 54 miles' rough waters in open barges. Outside Morobe, high winds chopped the seas. Rain began falling in sheets. Maj Rising of 532 Amphibs advised Col MacKechnie to postpone the operation. But poor radio communications kept him from permission from 6th Army Hq.

Starting at 1830, at 20 minute intervals, the barges in V-formation in 3 waves left Morobe. A PT Boat was to lead each wave. Because of rain and high billows, trouble began at once. Waves 1 and 2 readily followed their PT guides, but Wave No 3 failed to find PT 120 in the blackness. An Amphib Engr had to herd the 11 LCVPs and the Jap barge. (They failed to land at Nassau Bay that night.)

Losing contact with PT 120 was just the first mishap. At 25 knots an hour, PTS 142 and 143 could not keep contact with barges laboring along at 7-8 knots. Blackness, driving rain, high waves made the barges hard to see.

Leading PT 168 without troops became totally separated and patrolled alone, although there was no threat from the Jap Navy that night. The three barge groups struggled on. Although 162's I&R men were stationed on 3 offshore islands to show flashing lights as guides, even the PTs could not see the lights through darkness and rain. Compass and watch and the dim loom of the land were their only navigational aids.

Meanwhile, Capt Burke's Aussie guides performed splendidly in trying to light us in to Nassau Bay. After a struggle through jungle and swamp behind the beach, they came upon the open sands just 5 minutes after the scheduled midnight hour. Burke's group set up 3 lights on the beach—2 red lights 600 yards apart and a white light halfway between. Lt Urquhart's group set up 2 lights farther south. The Aussies cut a Jap communication wire and posted 10 men on each flank, with 7 by the center white light between the 2 red lights.

This was the most heroic half-hour of those Aussies of 2/6 Inf Regt. They lacked a radio to say whether or not 162's convoy had turned back in the storm. If the Aussies waited too long, many Japs would certainly find them and slay them.

Meanwhile, 162's convoy had battered its way through or over 12-foot waves and heavy rain over 54 seasick miles. Even the phosphorescent wake of the barge ahead was hard to see to keep in contact.

Leading Wave No 1, PT 142 overshot Nassau Bay, ran far up the coast, and had to turn back from perhaps Lokanu Bay past Roosevelt Ridge deep into Jap country. In turning back, PT 142 blindly ran among the barges of Wave No 2, which crossed before it. PT 142 narrowly missed a collision and scattered the 12 barges like minnows. Meanwhile Wave No 3 with probably 2 FA Btrys and an AA Pln gave up the voyage and returned to Morobe.

Having regrouped Wave No 2's barges, the officers of Waves 1 and 2 could see no guide-lights—not even the shore itself. But they reckoned that they were opposite Nassau Bay, and turned in where they hoped that it might be. Wave No 1 led the way.

Suddenly in the dimness, they saw lights. The Amphibs' CO said that it was "perhaps the greatest of all coincidences" that they found the bay and the lights. At first they saw only the 2 lights of Urquhart's group, but they landed where they saw the 3 lights of Burke's group. In surfs 10-12 feet high, it was a confused, battered "shipwreck landing."

But Amphibs' orders were to land at any cost. Thus, about 0035 hours, Wave No 1 pointed their ramps straight for Lt Burke's 3 lights, and charged the shore with their throttles wide open. Waves tossed the barges around like matchsticks, but they impacted the sand and dropped ramps. All 12 of them unloaded their troops safely. Except for 2 LCVPs, the Jap barge and 9 other LCVPs hit so hard that they could not ret4ract from the shore. The 12-foot breakers 'broached' them—beat them sideways and flooded engines and interiors.

About 0035 hours also, Wave No 2 of 11 LCVPs and 1 LCM struck for the beach. Again, they unloaded safely—even the bulldozer from the LCM, whose motor may have scared off a lurking Jap patrol who thought it was a tank. Some barges collided with the barges of Wave No 1, or ran over their ramps which they had dropped already. Like most of Wave 1, all of Wave No 2 broached in the surfs.

The 2 LCVPs of Wave No 1 which were still afloat returned to one PT boat and took aboard 70 men, including Task Force CO Col MacKechnie himself. All

70 got ashore safely, but one of these LCVPs also broached and was wrecked. A total of 23 barges were battered into twisted masses of steel and wood by the pounding surfs.

It was lucky for 162's stranded men that Wave No 3 had never tried to land but had safely returned to Morobe. Our Amphibs' CO had wisely decided to hold 8 more barges in reserve, also. For some days, these remaining craft would be the only transportation for supplies, ammo, and reinforcements.

Marooned at dawn on an enemy coast were some 740 men—405 from 162 Inf, and others from various support units. No FA guns had landed. Men faced attack from unknown numbers of Japs, and without means to withdraw if defeated or out of ammo. Throughout the morn, sporadic Jap rifle fire harassed the beach. The wrecked Amphibs formed a provisional Inf detachment of 68 men with rifles and MGs salvaged from battered barges.

When A Co 162 Inf fought the Japs on that first morning of the beachhead on the north flank, the Amphibs took part. When the Aussie Pln ran out of ammo, we took over the front along with a detachment of A Co 116 Engrs. Although the Japs were defeated on the north, they overran a C Co Pln on the south flank of the beachhead late that afternoon. When the Japs formed for a night attack on the beachhead, the Amphib detachment were ready.

Shortly before dark, Amphibs formed a defense line on the right flank beside detachments of A 116 Combat Engrs, D 162's mortarmen, and Hq personnel. About darkfall, we had to move from the right flank to dig in the left or southern flank—in time for the strong Jap attack that went on all night.

They fired furiously with LMGs, mortars, rifles, and grenades. But their fire was wild and erratic, and we returned heavy fire with our rifles and LMGs. When they infiltrated, we met them with grenades, bayonets, and knives.

Towards the bleak morning, some Japs slithered through the brush close to us and called clearly in English, "All you Engrs fall in! Hey, Joe, your boats are coming in!" One even shouted, "532nd Engrs, we'll get you!" No doubt some of their scouts had crawled close enough to our lines to learn the number of our Regt. But when they closed in on us, we had to disembowel only a few of them to make the others run.

In the dark about dawn, a screaming band of Japs made a headlong charge. Some did manage to break through. Then we slew at least 12—in return lost 7 killed, 8 wounded. Afterwards, Col MacKechnie credited us Amphibs for saving his whole command. He had already committed his reserves on the north front except for us.

It was wise that the Amphibs' CO had reserved 8 barges from last night's stormy voyage. Lucky also was it that heavy seas had held back Wave No 3 from beaching. For now these were Col MacKechnie's only connection with Morobe supply base.

On the second morning while 162 Inf was still fighting, 10 LCVPs arrived with badly needed supplies and 190 men of Wave No 3 which had failed to land before. Despite 5-foot combers, we drove for the shore. First barge beached right into a nest of Nippos who had not yet retreated. With rifles and MGs, troops leaped ashore and expelled the Japs. On the right beach, an officer exposed himself to flag the other barges into the right area. Only 2 capsized in the 5-foot waves.

Regular supply missions of us Amphibs had begun. On the night of 2-3 July, PT CO Lt Atkins convoyed a convoy to land at Nassau Bay. While Lt-CO fired on remaining Japs still holding Cape Dinga, 11 barges beached on their own power. Little Aussie trawlers towed others. Perhaps this convoy brought in Btry B 218 FA whose 4 75s bombed possible areas of Jap concentration north and south of the beachhead.

The 54 miles of sea between Morobe and Nassau Bay was menaced by Jap air raids, but we Amphibs kept on voyaging, but mainly by night. Japs searched the seas from above, and attacked at every chance. Not until 10 July did our Air force gain superiority over Nippo planes.

In one encounter, 2/Lt Keele and a 4-man crew were strafed by a low-flying plane. MG bullets mortally wounded Keele, and damaged his barge. Although probably still close to Morobe, Keele refused to turn back with desperately needed supplies. Before his death, the crew landed their cargo at Nassau Bay.

On 9 July, an LCM crew evacuating wounded 162 men, saw 4 Jap Zeros shoot down a B-25. Changing course, we rescued the surviving flyers clinging to floating parts of the plane. Evading the bombs of the Zeros, we fought off the planes with our .50 HMG. Finally we beached back at Morobe with 5 wounded Amphibs and 59 jagged holes in the hull of our LCM.

By the 11th day after the Nassau Bay landing, our little Amphibian fleet had labored hard over the 54 miles from Morobe base to Nassau Bay. We had carried 2 Inf Bns, 2 FA Btrys, 1 AA Btry, and a Co of Combat Engrs. We had also carried an Engr Shore Co (less a Pln), 480 native carriers, 3 portable hospitals, and 450 tons of supplies. On return to Morobe, we bore with us the sick and wounded for extended treatment.

While 162 Inf was marching overland towards Roosevelt Ridge on 17-20 July, we landed FA and a medical group for them on Tambu Bay. The guns we landed included 12 105 mm and 12 75 mm guns and 8 Australian 25-pounders—important to win Salamaua. In our regular runs to Tambu Bay, we often endured shelling from Jap Roosevelt Ridge.

When on 20 July, Tambu Bay troops sorely needed phone wire, 7 Amphibs volunteered to run a barge to beach under Jap FA observers. Need was so great that we could not wait until darkfall. As we landed, large caliber shells exploded all around the barge but without hitting us. We unloaded the wire, quickly lifted ramp, and saved ourselves.

These are highlights of the Samamaua Operation for A and D Cos of 532 Engr Boat & Shore Regt, plus men of 562 Engr Boat Maintenance Bn, and 587 Signal Co. Our losses in battle were comparatively light: 8 killed, 3 missing in Action, and 9 wounded. But without our barges, the Allied victory at Salamaua might well have been impossible.

CREDIT Basic document for this history is *Amphibian Engineer Operations*, by Office of the Chief Engineer, General Headquarters, Army Forces, Pacific. With these, I considered Samuel Eliot Morison's *Breaking the Bismarcks Barrier*, which is Vol VI of his *History of United States Naval Operations in World War II*, Australian David Dexter's *The New Guinea Offensives*, and Col AR MacKechnie's *Report of Operations of 162 Inf, 41st Inf Div in Papua New Guinea*. All are contradictory, but I judged them from the positions taken by *Amphibian Engineer Operations*, a book discovered at Duke University's Eichelberger Collection in a visit financed by our 41st Div Assn. (McCartney's *JUNGLEERS* indicated that 218 FA's guns landed on D-Day at Nassau Bay, but I find no other statement of what I believe to be an inaccuracy.) Thrilling story of Aussie guides who lighted the landing appears in David Dexter's *The New Guinea Offensives*, published by Australian War Memorial in Canberra.

THE 41st INFANTRY DIVISION: BIAK: OUR BIGGEST BATTLE

BY Dr. Hargis Westerfield, Division Historian with R.R. Smith and other scholars

Our 41st Infantry Division fought a crucial battle on Biak. For Biak was the southern anchor of almost the last strategic defense line before Japan itself. And the Japs needed Biak for land-based planes in an expected all-out naval battle near Biak.

Combat started at once with our Biak landing. On Biak ridges above our supply base, 186 Inf and Amphib Engrs killed Japs in cave. Our 186 Inf destroyed a pillbox guarding the inland pass. It took 4 hours for 162 Inf with 6 tanks to slay Japs guarding Parai Defile and push on to Parai Village. That night back at Ibdi, Japs of 3/Bn 222 Inf shot or grenaded or bayoneted men of C Btry 146 FA — killed 4, wounded 8.

Our 3/Bn 162 Inf passed Parai Defile and dug in for the night. On our second Biak morning, we suffered 162 Inf's greatest disaster of World War II. Just past Parai Defile was an inland terrace about 500 yards wide under 15-foot scrub trees. Across K and I Co's front, Jap MGs hacked an impenetrable line. From East Caves and other ridges, Japs lobbed heavy mortar shells down on us like tropical raindrops. Brush was low enough for Japs to see our troop movements, but high enough to obscure our aim.

Heavy fire support was impossible. Our 146 FA up the shore could not hit defiladed Jap positions facing seaward. When main naval fire observer was killed, communications become erratic with offshore destroyers and Amphib craft gunners.

While 4 of 603 Tank Co's Shermans protected us, 3/Bn retreated in small groups under fire to shelter behind 162's 2/Bn in Parai Defile. So went 162's first battle day.

On 162's third Parai Defile day, Jap tanks with Inf tried to destroy us. In the first tank attack, H Co's HMGs struck down Jap Inf still marching in formation — Their Lt. leading. Then 2 of our Gen Sherman medium tanks holed 4 thinly armored Jap tanks — even blew off turrets. Jap's 37 mm guns could not pierce our thicker armor. Thirty minutes later, our tanks destroyed a wave of 3 tanks while our Inf slew their Inf.

Jap Inf attacks kept on, cut the coast road under Parai Defile cliffs. With close mortar support, B 162 and Cannon Co (acting as riflemen) dislodged them.

Col. Haney saw that mortars and MGs on Jap ridges had defeated his direct drive for Mokmer Dromes through Parai Defile. While D Co 542's Amphib Engrs with rifles and LMGs landed to guard the cliffs, 162's 2/Bn and 3/Bn retreated on foot. For close support, 641 TD impacted 400 rifled mortar shells on the ridges, then destroyed their mortars, and marched east. Our 1/Bn left on Amphibs' craft. In 2 days' combat, 162 Inf lost 32 dead, 186 other casualties — the Japs even more.

Next few days, "L" 162 outposted in Parai Defile and patrolled for Jap positions, On 3 June, L led 3/Bn and 7 tanks to force the Defilie. Japs cut off the forward Pln, which the tanks rescued. A Jap in Yank uniform leaped on the tank, dropped a grenade inside. He slew the driver, wounded another crewman. A "cat" dragged out the crippled tank. "L" luckily had only 3 dead, 1 wounded.

To bypass the Parai Defile Japs, Mj. Gen. Fuller ordered 186 Inf to move overland from Bosnek to capture Mokmer Dromes from the rear. On 1 June, 186 placed 2 Bns north of Bosnek ridges to start west. That night, 3/Bn stood off a heavy attack from 1/Bn 186 Inf. That night, 1/Bn 222 Inf attacked. We slew 186 Japs, while we lost 3 dead, 8 wounded.

On 2 June, with 2 Cos abreast and 5 tanks, 186 advanced west. Support fire came from 121 FA Bn's 75s (attached to the 41st only for Biak). Jap's small arms and LMGs killed 4 Yanks, wounded 10. We slew 96 Japs. By mid-afternoon, 2/Bn 162 Inf had fought up from the coast to aid us.

On 3 June, 186 Inf still marched thirstily west in scrub desert and heat. Reduced to a canteen of water daily we lugged heavy gear through 12-foot scrub blocking all breezes. Our greatest aid was the road built by B Co 116 Engrs. With our 2/Bn, they forwarded some supplies and water from Bosnek. The 1/Bn 222 Inf Japs had withdrawn ahead of us to Mokmer Ridge.

By 5 June, 186 had assembled behind Mokmer Ridge above Mokmer Dromes. This tangle of sharp coral ridge and jungle was 240 feet high and about 500 yards wide. We could find no route over it. And we had no water ration since 4 June morning.

Luckily, about 1200, heavy rains flooded our up-turned helmets and ponchos. K Co finally found a rough way up to the ridge-top, and all 3/Bn led the Regt to the summit.

Next day the 41st made an error as serious as trying to force the Parai Defile. Col. Newman of 186 had planned to clear the Japs from Mokmer Ridge before we dropped down to take Mokmer Dromes. But Gen. Fuller refused Newman's request. Fuller was under pressure from Sixth Army's Gen. Krueger to sieze at least one airfield. A poor recon found no Japs.

With heavy FA preparation, 186 plus 2/Bn 162 took Mokmer Dromes unopposed. Then the bypassed Japs on that same Mokmer Ridge hurled tons of steel down upon us — from cannon, dual-purpose AckAck, 20 mm guns — a 4 hour firestorm. Finally, counterfire from 121, 146, 205 and 947 FA silenced them. In the next few days, 186 tried but failed to storm Mokmer Ridge.

So Gen. Fuller made a fine strategic move to reinforce 186 Inf. He decided to bypass the Japs' Parai Defile stronghold by water and land 162 Inf west of it.

On 7 June while 186 Inf was still blasted at Mokmer Dromes, 162's I and K Cos beachheaded at Parai Jetty. At once fired on from the ridges, they had help when Cannon Co and 6 tanks landed. "CN" at once pushed east, but the Japs cut them in two to halt their offensive. L 162 had remained behind the Regt to push west against those Japs, but could do no better. (Not until 5 days later did 162 Inf use AT and C Cos to liqudate the Parai Defile block.)

By 8 June, most of 162 Inf was ashore at Parai Defile. Led by Cos C, I, and K, we advanced towards Mokmer Dromes. But East Caves' hidden mortars grounded us. We were stopped where 3/Bn had failed back on 28 May.

Next day, we pushed on, with concentrations of 81 mm mortars, 205 FA's 105s, and 641 TD's rifled mortars. We moved only in small groups and huddled for safety behind every slight rise of ground. Next day after that, 1/Bn and 3/Bn waded in often waist-deep surf to avoid shellfire. Each concussion in the water slammed us like a foul punch below the belt.

Finally, 162's 1/Bn and 3/Bn contacted 2/Bn which had trekked overland with 186 Inf. We grouped below Mokmer Ridge to battle 600-700 Japs above us on the ridge and the terrace behind it. Jap Col. Naoyuki Kuzume knew that so long as he held the crest, he could prevent Aviation Engrs from repairing Mokmer Dromes to make them operational.

The Ridge terrain was covered with dense rain forest or scrub. Inf defenders were the surviving 120 men of 1/Bn 222 Inf, with maybe 2 Cos of 2/Bn, fragments of Engr units, and some FA and AckAck guns and crews — about 600-700 men.

Attacking on 11 June, 3/Bn 162 hit a wall of Jap fire which grounded us almost when we started. Only by mid-afternoon did 947 FA's 155s help I Co get atop the 60-foot contour. On 12 June, all 3 Cos of 3/Bn did advance doggedly west along ridge-top and terrace behind it. Helped by M Co's 81 mm mortars, I Co fought through 2 Jap defense lines, found a third line 50 yards farther, and discerned a fourth strongpoint.

On that 12 June also, 2/Bn fought Mokmer Ridge farther west and placed F Co on top. A 900-yard gap was left between the two Bns, and hard to clear. Next day, we still failed to close it. So on 14 June, Jap fire from the Gap impacted near Aviation Engrs repairing Mokmer Dromes. Gen. MacArthur badly needed that field for planes to support Central Pacific battles.

Because Japs tenaciously held Mokmer Ridge, Gen. Doe decided to send 1/Bn 186 and 1/Bn 162 around the right side of the ridge. With these Bns in their rear, Doe expected that the Japs would fall back from Mokmer Ridge.

On 14 June, 1/Bn 186 crossed Mokmer Ridge east of 1/Bn 162 Inf where there were no Japs. Turning west about 800 yards north of the Ridge on the Jap's flanks, 1/Bn 186 overran Japs in 2 fire-fights, and advanced over 1200 yards west to line up with 1/Bn 162 Inf to the south. (1/Bn 162 had also fought Japs, but had a shorter distance to move.) Before dark, patrols discovered that we were on the rim of Col. Kuzume's great West Caves Hqs, estimated to have a garrison of 1,000.

In early dark, Jap tank-Inf teams struck from West Caves, expelled semi-isolated B 162 from their advanced position into an orderly retreat. That night, a probable Co of Japs harassed B and C 186. Fifty Japs charged the two Cos at dawn and left 50 corpses when their charge failed.

About 0715 that 15 June, 3 Jap tank-Inf teams charged both Bns. Rifles and mortars scattered their protecting Inf. Tanks turned back. The .50 HMGs of 186's bn AT Plan killed the hindmost fleeing tank. In the last attack, 121 FA's 75s disrupted their Inf formations. Our bazookas destroyed both tanks. So died the last tanks to fight us on Biak.

On 17 June, both Bns with tank aid stormed Horseshoe Ridge, final barrier before West Caves. But there were Japs still in strength behind us towards Mokmer Ridge.

While the 2 Bns were still fighting towards West Caves, Gen. Doe had ended the problem of closing the great Gap on Mokmer Ridge behind us. Thinking that 2/Bn and 3/Bn 162 needed a rest, he decided to use 2/Bn 186 Inf to close the Gap.

On 16 June after heavy shellfire, E Co of 2/Bn struck east from the Great Gap on both sides of Mokmer Ridge. Heroic Morales cleared out 2 silent gun positions held by riflemen, but died there. When Jap automatic weapons halted E 162's advance, G Co's 1/Pln advanced abreast of "E". In under 2 hours, E's 2/Pln contacted 3/Bn on the Ridge and closed the Great Gap. Later, "E" and "G" actually fought West Caves before being withdrawn. With a loss of 15 killed and 35 wounded, 2/Bn had closed the Great Gap and slain at least 65

Papua - Smashed Japanese landing barge and dead Japanese litter this beach at Buna. (Courtesy of Rohlffs)

Japs. It was one of the 186 Inf's finest exploits in World War II.

But the underground sump-hole complex called West Caves held out still. The strong garrison had access to reinforcements and supplies by the road from NW Biak. Gen Eichlberger decided to cut that road. (Eichlberger had replaced Fuller in command on Biak.)

Although Doe feared that we would be knee-mortared to death above West Caves, Eichlberger attacked. On 19 June, supported by heavy shellfire, 2/Bn moved up from the SW, with 3/Bn in support. F Co readily cut the Jap access road and with E Co secured a strategic jungle ridge just past the road. Only a few Jap 90 mm AckAck guns from an unknown location did cause a few wounds. Eichlberger assigned 162 Inf to undertake final reduction of West Caves, with their 3 large sumps.

Striking West Caves on 20 June with 2 tank's help, 1/Bn 162 Inf found that 186 Inf had cleared out most Japs north of the sump-holes. But rifle and automatic fire kept us from sending men into the sump-holes. Flaming gasoline into the sumps did not halt the shooting. Next night, the Japs sallied out in 3 waves to try to escape. Next day, 22 June, 186 Inf counted 115 Jap dead, against 186's loss of 1 dead, 5 wounded. Col. Kuzume had ceremonially burned 222 Regt's colors, but did not commit suicide. Jap reports are that he was killed on 2 July north of Boroko Drome. Despite 116 Engrs explosion of 2 500-lb TNT charges in a sump, West Caves was not cleared until 27 June.

Our Biak war seemed over. By 22 June, P-40 "War Hawk" fighters used Mokmer Drome. Excepting a few stragglers, formidable East Caves was deserted by the end of June.

But Ibdi Pocket held out. Here on 7 jagged ridges in thick jungle, 3/Bn 222 Inf's 800 plus 200 FA and weapons crews had fought 162 Inf beginning on 1 June. When 162 Inf took over on 12 June, we planned to storm Ibdi Pocket.

But the great attack of 1/Bn and 2/Bn (less E Co) only compressed the Japs into 600 square yards. Our restrained attacks lost 18 killed, 46 wounded. Thereafter, our patrols mainly found targets for ground and air Bombardment.

Taking over on 11 June, 3/Bn 163 Inf constricted the Japs into a smaller area. About 200 Japs escaped. We marked the ridges for the bombers. On 22 July, 8 B-24's in 3 waves dropped 64 1,000-lb bombs followed by mortar and FA shelling. Ibdi Pocket become a tangle of coral jungle and corpses.

Losing about 375 killed and 1,700 wounded, our 41st killed about 4,700 Japs and captured 220. Biak became an important air-base. The 41st well remembers the Parai Defile ambush, 186 Inf's jungle desert march, and fighting over Mokmer Ridge. Biak was a gallant operation for us Americans (and for the Japanese).

CREDIT. This is the brief but scrupulously accurate history of our 41st on Biak. Main source is R.R. Smith's *Approach to the Philippines* — 5 chapters, 117 thoroughly researched pages. Other contributing scholars are Samuel Eliot Morison in *New Guinea and the Marianas* from his History of US Naval Operations in World War II; Japanese scholars in General Douglas MacArthur's *Japanese Operations in the Southwest Pacific*; General Robert L. Eichlberger and Milton MacKaye in *Our Jungle Road to Tokyo*; and Hargis Westerfield in "Montana's Great Combat Regiment: 163rd Infantry Regiment in World War II." from editor Chester Shore's *Montana in the Wars*. I have also used my memories from at least 60 published or unpublished histories compiled by me and other Division Association members.

Papua. Allied troops on the move from Buna to Sanananda. (Courtesy of Rohlffs)

K CO 162 INFANTRY'S PAPUAN CAMPAIGN
by Dr. Hargis Westerfield with K-162's Jim Litke, John Feeley, Others

Early on 20 July 1943, K Co 162 Inf left bivouac south of Boisi Village and marched to seize Roosevelt Ridge. But that Jap fortress would not fall for over 3 weeks.

The night before, Scout Lipke heard that he was to lead "K" through Boisi Village just below Roosevelt Ridge. His 3/Pln said that he was lucky that the Japs never shot the first man—only the second or third. Lipke did not sleep much.

In the morning, our Papuan Pln slew Japs in an outpost and "K" destroyed their MG. Lipke led out K Co. He was indeed lucky to scout with Papuans. As he had a foot poised above a windfall tree trunk, a Papuan's whistle kept him from putting it down. The Papuan uncovered a land-mine from a heap of fallen leaves where Jim could have lost his foot.

About 1200 Hours, they entered Boisi Village. Capt Lovell and the Papuans saw Japs run out the other side. Colossal blue jungled Roosevelt Ridge towered just 1500 yards north. While the other Plns stopped behind them, Lipke's leading 3/Pln made a small perimeter and began to eat.

Then began K's real war! Shells from Jap .75 mm mountain guns and mortars smashed down from Roosevelt Ridge, and enfilade fire from taller Scout Track Ridge to the left. FA shells landed behind 2/Pln and before 3/Pln.

Lipke heard 12 shells hiss overhead, but just 9 exploded. For safety, he ran behind a tree 12 times. Mortar shells fragmented close to probably 1/Pln with Capt Lovell and 1/Lt Dorigan his Exec, just as they started forward.

First mortar shell burst wide of them; the second impacted close while Lovell and Dorigan hugged the swamp. Shell No 3 was almost on them; Shell No 4 on top of them.

Lovell had 2 rations of bully beef in his pack. They stopped some fragments and perhaps saved his spine and maybe his life. But another fragment put him out of action with a wounded left arm.

Lovell told Exec Dorigan, "Jim, I guess it's all yours now." Dorigan tried to stand up, but then realized that a fragment of the same mortar shell had slashed his foot. Lt Gehring was now K's new CO.

The sweetest sound that Lovell ever heard in his life was our guns down on the shore thumping at the Jap guns a few minutes after he was hit. They were probably 218 FA's 75s firing from Cochran Beach. They silenced the Jap guns or mortars on Roosevelt Ridge, and enfilade from the heights on our left.

Papuan litter bearers arrived quickly and took the 2 officers and enlisted man Henderson to the rear where Medics gave blood transfusions.

The Japs had caused a total of 12 "K" casualties. Names of the wonded besides Lovell, Dorigan, and enlisted men Henderson and Carney are unknown; but there were 10 wounded. Killed, however, were Hatton and S/Sgt Schirmer. (Carney and Capt Lovell were both returned to the USA.)

At 0700 22 July, 2 days later, "K" attacked Roosevelt Ridge, against an estimated 200-250 Japs in jungle cover. L Co attacked on our left. Our FA tried to make our fight easier by a concentration just before we jumped off. North of Boisi, M Co's 81s readied to support us.

Almost every advance up that Ridge had to be in small, narrow columns. Passable tracks were all so narrow and so constricted by heavy brush or large trees that we could not move freely on a broad front. K Co had to divide into 2 attack lines on 2 separate ridge shoulders.

But the mountain-side jungle helped "K" on our "first run up the hill." It hid us from the watching Japs. About 1200 Hours, a squad actually reached the top unopposed—made it between 2 manned Nippo positions.

From the uphill corner on the right of this squad, tough little New Jerseyite Kettner watched and ate his "C" ration. When a Jap came, Kettner killed him and kept on eating.

Later the Japs combined against our storming party and repelled that attack line that was first to top Roosevelt Ridge. In scrambling to escape, we had to dodge grenades rolling down on us. Swede Gullstrom of Tillamook was lucky. A grenade caught in his fatigues. Feverishly, he tore at clothing to pull it loose and save his life. The grenade did not explode; many Jap grenade fuzes were unreliable.

To escape from their death near the summit, Scout Lipke, another scout, and his Pln/Sgt had much trouble. They had been near the top in the right column, and the withdrawal order never reached those 3 men up front. Concussion grenades exploded above them, and they slid for safety.

Somebody told Lipke that all "K" men had withdrawn from above him on the slope. Then he saw a head covered with green cloth coming down the trail behind some bushes. Thinking he saw a Jap, Lipke lifted his tommie gun and fired 3 .45 slugs where he thought the target was. Then a Yank came leaping into his sights. He was another observer from another Regt in a green fatigue hat. Lipke's 3 shots had passed just 3 inches from the man's nose. Lipke learned not to be trigger-happy. (In a similar situtation at Zamboanga 2 years later, Lipke would have fire held and save 3 more men's lives.)

Lipke now rejoined his Pln and helped form a skirmish line to secure the slower withdrawal of men on his right. Men carried Levit—K's only casualty in that assault. A bullet had grazed Levit's left ear and had broken his ear-drum. Levit had never been heard to swear—or seen to smoke or drink. Now he swore like a mule-skinner.

Next day, 23 July, 205 FA's observer 2/Lt Schroeder helped give "K" more knowledge of why Roosevelt Ridge was formidable. Sent alone to contact CO Gehring, he failed to find Gehring, climbed up past him by grasping roots and vines. Unexpectedly, Schroeder found himself on the bare top of the Ridge—saw Japs below far down by Dot Inlet.

Suddenly a Jap bugle sounded. From the west of the Ridge, a Jap HMG thudded bullets on the summit. Instantly, he threw his body back downhill and saved his life. Schroeder called 205 FA fire on the Ridge, left and right. But he couldn't hit the source of the HMG fire to his left.

After a valorous 3-day action for "K," Observer Schroeder took a serious rifle wound in his chest and went to hospital. But "K" patrols and FA harassment continued.

"K" suffered also. On 28 July, K Co was mortared. Hanrahan was killed, and S/Sgt Stark wounded in neck and shoulder. Hickey had a bad arm wound. On 2 Aug, 6 days later, Jap mortars killed 2 more: Lekberg, Bn Supply Sgt; and Mail Clerk Pineo. Six more unidentified men were also wounded.

Then after 2/Bn breached Roosevelt Ridge with heavy FA fire and stormed and wiped out surviving Japs on the east end, "K" still fought. In pushing the stubborn Japs back towards Salamaua Town, we operated on 3/Bn's flank. On 17 Aug, a combined "K" and "L" patrol found that Jap positions were still in depth along Scout Ridge and to the NE.

Next morn, 18 Aug, with an "L" Pln supporting, K Co tried a direct frontal attack on Jap positions and suffered.

At 1815 that day, with the "L" Pln securing our rear, a "K" combat patrol confronted a high barricade of brush and logs before the Japs' concealed positions. Through holes blasted by our mortars, we crawled under the fence. We couldn't get much past that fence. Jap LMG and HMG fire grounded us. L's fire neutra-lized the Japs' MGs. We squirmed back to safety through those mortar holes under the fence.

On that 18 Aug, "K" had our greatest total of losses since that first day at Boisi—10 of us this time instead of 12. Three were killed: Frost, Barber, and Sgt Harwood. Seven were wounded: Belloni, Lega, Welch, Jenney, Jacobs, Medic Rashkind, and Lt Reed.

By 26 Aug, "K" and our 3/Bn fought against Japs closer to Salamua. They now held the intersection of Scout Ridge and B Ridge. At 0725, a 16-man combat patrol in two groups of 8 men scouted the highest parts of B Ridge. We also must fight to distract Japs from interfering with 2/Bn's move up C Ridge. At 1140, Jap fire menaced us higher on B Ridge, and the false ridge between "B" and Roosevelt Ridge. We withdrew 200 yards but kept on observing.

Next day, 27 Aug, "K" took the same route as yesterday, and slipped up to where we could observe the Japs. As Lipke remembers it, this was a 12-13 man patrol with a phone. When we faced the concealed Japs, orders were to shoot to draw their fire so that we could estimate their numbers.

BARman Arney we posted on our left. He was to open fire—but only at a good multiple target.

Arney was cautious at first. He finally opened up. Then he ducked, moved about 10 feet aside, and fired again. It was a clever move, but he ducked again, and returned to the same spot too many times.

So now a canny Jap LMG man waited for Arney to lift his head to fire the BAR. The Jap lanced a whole clip through Arney's head. As Arney's eyes dilated, Lipke bravely crawled up to him. Lipke pulled back Arney and his BAR back to safe ground.

(Official 162 Journal says of this fight that the patrol divided into 3 sections. Section No 1 moved right and located a pillbox with 3 Japs in it. We grenaded all 3 to death. Section No 2 moved left into rifle and LMG fire. We retaliated with BAR and rifles. We grenaded a pill-box. Section No 3 shot up a LMG position and a hut containing 8 Japs. Of an estimated 50 Japs, we slew 24- with only losing Arney.)

Hastily we buried Arney, and evacuated that ridge slope. We halted in thickets for safety. We crossed open spaces low and at the double—a man at a time.

Back in perimeter, they asked us separately to pinpoint where we had buried Arney. Days later, he was found for Graves Registration to bury him properly in a graveyard.

Instead of 50, total Jap strength in this position was estimated at 300.

Arney was last "K" man to die. K's last wounded man was McGoldrick. A sniper shot off his right thumb. A Portable Hospital did a fine job repairing his hand, but we never saw McGoldrick again—believe that he was sent home.

By 10 Sept, K Co with other Yanks and Aussies had fought free of those everlasting ridges and jungles. We were pursuing the retreating Japs towards Salamaua Town.

On 12 Sept morn, "K" started hiking from the western curve of Bayern Bay. But we hiked in the direction opposite Salamaua. We could readily have crossed Francisco River unopposed and turned right to enter Salamaua. We could have been first into Salamaua! At this point, the river ran slow and was just waist deep. But we had orders to let the Aussies enter before the Yanks.

Instead, we marched inland back from Salamaua along the south bank of the Francisco. Then we turned hard right and waded the river where it was deep and rapid. Then we circled Salamaua Aerodrome and returned almost across the river from where we had started out that morning.

Near the end of the hike, we caught a sick Jap lying in a hut—K's only prisoner. With blackwater fever, he was looking at us through mosquito netting. When we saw him, our Pln Lt could not draw his pistol fast enough. Then he found that he could not murder the poor sick man looking up at him with both empty hands in sight. The Jap was so maddened at being left by his outfit that he told us all that he knew about the other Japs. Later, Medics gave him blood transfusions and he was still alive when Lipke last heard of him. Next day, 13 Sept 1943, "K" entered Salamaua. Our Papuan Campaign was ended.

"K" had fought a deadly war into the ridges above Tambu Bay and Dot Inlet. Once, we were down to a total front-line strength of 39—although on 12 Sept before Salamaua, we had an officially reported strength of 64. This last number no doubt included men in hospital. Yet most of our decrease was due to illness, not battle casualties. From 29 June through 12 Sept, we had a reported only 6 killed, 14 seriously wounded (3 of those wounded, officers), and 23 lightly wounded. (No attempt is here made to harmonize these figures with the previous number of K 162 casualties in this campaign.) In return, we claimed 91 Japs killed out of our 3/Bn's total of 316, second after I Co with 119. But as with most infantrymen's wars, K Co 162 Inf's was mostly digging and climbing and taking sleepless turns on guard against a heroic Japanese Infantry. Such was our World War II.

CREDIT. With this K Co 162's history, we have printed one or more stories on every 162 Inf rifle Co in the Salamaua Operation. K 162's history was hard to get. Most K 162 leaders never bothered even to answer my letters. Capt Don Lovell did write on 25 Sept 1967, but he was too early wounded and evacuated before he got to know his outfit.

Three most useful sources are Jim Lipke's 5-page handprinted letter received in Nov 1987; John Feeley's Casualty List in a letter of 16 Nov 1984, and 162's detailed Journal of 9 July-13 Sept 1943. Excellent contributions are from Ed Wildfong's letter of 13 June 1984, and 146 FA's Don Schroeder's History No 175 in *Jungleer* for Feb 1987. Useful also were Hal O'Flaherty's report in *Chicago Daily News* (22 July 1943), and Lt Leonard Jermain's "Battle Saga of Northwestern's Own 41st" (undated, probably from *Portland Oregonian*). Other references are Col AR McKechnie's *Report of Operations of 162 Inf/8 July-13 Sept 1943*, and Australian David Dexter's *The New Guinea Offensives*. But official list of 162's casualties in the Papuan Campaign is lost, and McKechnie's report omits most of what 3/Bn 162 did before Salamaua. Getting K 162's Salamaua history is almost miraculous.

167 FIELD ARTILLERY ON PALAWAN: CONCENTRATION 476 to RESCUE E CO 186 MEN

by 167 FA's Bill Morse with Dr. Hargis Westerfield, Division Historian

On Filipino Palawan Island, C Btry 167 FA fired one of the most effectively coordinated missions of any FA Btry in World War II. This was Concentration 476 to rescue 1/Lt Robert Revees' 2/Pln, 186 Inf, on 2 Mar 1945.

Three days after 186's unopposed landing, Reeves' E 186 Pln hunted Japs in the tall hills west of Puerto Princesa Bay. With them were C Btry 167 FA's observation party: S/Sgt Richard Tyrell, T/4 Edwin Benckart, and Pfc Charles Petley.

As we rounded Hill 1125, we killed a Jap and heard chopping dying away. As we took a break on a knoll before turning back to the coast, we realized that we were under observation from a higher knoll across a ravine. When 2/Pln filed down the forward side of the hill, rifles and MGs shot from a bunkered position on the second knoll. Lt Reeves and a scout were wounded, another scout slain. Like these casualties, other "E" men were pinned down behind or under some logs.

The "E" Pln called for FA help to rescue the men, but we lacked a map of the area. From his Piper Cub, 167 FA's Lt/Col Dwight Beach flew to adjust our 105 mm shells on the target. For Tyrell had used the mirror on his FA compass to call Beach for assistance.

After a few rounds by Beach, Tyrell was able to locate the bursts and take over the rescue mission. To avoid hitting our own Inf, Tyrell did not use the faster method of firing "shorts" and "overs" and then splitting the difference. Our 41st Div procedure was called "creeping fire." It meant firing rounds over, then shortening range by small steps until we were on target. Even this slowly, Tyrell rapidly brought our 105s just over the heads of the patrol, and within 100 feet of the wounded. This fire was unavoidably close to the wounded, and done only in the most threatening situations.

Back at the gun positions, we fired faster and faster. For we got our fire commands quicker than Bn Fire Direction Center could give them. By the time "Fire Direction" told us, we at the guns knew them already. We had listened to the radio messages between Tyrell and Direction Center. We could foretell all orders—like a new one to change to fire half smoke-shells.

Morse helped gunners' morale by keeping them informed on the situation up front. He told Btry C what the target was—that it was a rescue mission—and that their own S/Sgt Tyrell was Forward Observer.

As soon as heavy fire began, we foresaw that we would have ammo supply problems. Our ammo Sgt asked Morse for help to carry ammo from Btry dump to the guns. Ammo supply lay 150-300 feet to left rear of our howitzers, and still stacked on the ground or on trailers. Ammo Sgt had only a small ammo section group and a 3/4-ton truck. But 1/Sgt Mel Davis ran up to say, "I just closed the kitchen, and sent all but one man to help carry ammo."

All drivers, mechanics, machine gunners, and communications men were now uncrating and carrying ammo to help out the 3/4-ton truck which took too long to load.

Exec Officer 1/Lt Ray Hahn then took command of our ammo detail. He left 2/Lt Morse at the phone from Fire Direction with T/5 Cecil Harrison to record fire commands and pass them to C Btry's 4 guns. All others frantically rushed to feed shells into C's guns.

Suddenly Tyrell ordered "Cease Fire" to Numbers 1 and 4 guns. They were the outside pieces. Tyrell had found that he was getting tree bursts from those outside pieces. Tall trees diverted their shells off the target. But Tyrell could keep Guns No 2 and 3 hitting target because the trees were low before their trajectory. Nos 2 and 3 were now shooting over Tyrell's head and about 60 feet before E's wounded to hold off the Japs.

S/Sgt Edling, Section Chief of No 1 gun, rushed to Morse in anguish to ask, "What did we do wrong?" Morse patiently explained why No 1 gun had to cease fire. Morse told Edling and his gunner to remain at their piece to wait for new fire orders. Except for Section Chief and gunner, both idled gun crews also began to carry shells to Guns No 2 and 3.

Fire order now was "Shell one-half smoke, one-half HEC (high explosive)—fuze delay."

We had a hitch about smoke. No 2 and 3 gunners reported, "Only 10 rounds smoke are left." Ammo Sgt reported, "No more smoke in C Btry dump."

Tyrell called E 186 men to halt rescue attempt until we could get more smoke. We kept up rapid fire with HE to keep Japs neutralized.

Fire Direction ordered B Btry half a mile off to despatch all their smoke shells at once. To Morse, it seemed like hours waiting, but in very few minutes, he saw a 3/4-ton truck overloaded with shells turn into C Btry at high speed.

But the load of shells was not from B Btry but from A Btry. For as soon as Morse reported the need for smoke, A Btry's Capt Howard Perry had ordered all his smoke shells heaped on the truck and forwarded. It was a record run for Palawan Island roads—7 miles in 9 minutes—and without orders.

With smoke on hand, our fire mission reached crescendo. We ordered the fastest fire possible. We were lucky that the ground under the Btry was heavy clay and very dry. There was no wheel-bounce. Trails were firmly set. There was no lateral or rear displacement of the pieces in firing. We were shooting "Charge 5"— maximum being "Charge 7"—at an elevation of 400-500 mils—about 30 degrees.

Both crews moved so fast that the breach opened and the empty cartridge case was ejected as the tube reached full recoil. Many times the new round was already loaded as the tube returned to Btry firing position. We fired as fast as the famous French 75s in World War I—but almost never that fast with 105s in World War II.

Roar of rapid fire was almost continuous, with chant of commands at the piece and the smell of burned powder. When the tube was back in firing position, Section Chief reached out to set the gunner's quadrant on marks at the top of the level. Number One Gunner quickly checked elevator bubble and called "Set!" Gunner instantly checked his sight for direction, called "Ready!" and Section Chief yelled "Fire!" Then the 2 guns blasted. "Set-ready-fire!" "Set-ready-fire!" "Set-ready-fire!" were all the words that Morse could hear.

But to fire that fast ammo must arrive on the run. All must be hand-carried. It took too long to load it on the truck and unload it on the run.

About this time, Capt OD Maxie, Bn Surgeon, stopped to watch Morse on the phone. Some ammo problem slowed rate of fire, and Morse had Maxie spell him on the phone, 4-5 minutes. So Maxie, for the only time in his career, had violated the Geneva Convention against participation of a Medic in combat.

During all this fire, observers Tyrell and Benckert alternated their duties. One man forwarded to observe impact; the other man talked on the radio. When the observer had to make a correction, he crawled back to the radio. Then in turn, the other man crawled forward to observe.

Third man of the observer party, Petley of Brooklyn, volunteered with the Inf rescue party to help save E's wounded. He crawled up with the "E" men covered by our smoke. Above him roared delayed action fuze shells that burst several feet underground. Petley helped carry wounded to Medics.

All of E Co's 2/Pln then fell back some 200 yards to better ground for defense, with Petley still in rear guard. While "E" disengaged, rapid FA shellfire continued at first, then rapidly slowed down as they found their new position. It was now 1600 Hours, 1 hour and 20 minutes since 167 FA had our first fire orders.

Not until 40 years later might Morse read of E 186's casualties, which 167 FA kept down. There were a few more than 1 killed and 2 wounded. Sansbury died of a neck wound. After his first wound, Maurer moved and drew more fire to finish him. Five men survived their wounds. Most serious were probably wounds of 1/Lt Reeves and Dwight Shonyo who dragged Reeves out of fire. Although merely grazed in one leg, Reeves lost 2/3 of a knee-cap from the other leg. A "pork chop" was sliced from Shonyo's back. A bullet hit Vezane on his wrist. Watkins' type of wound is unknown. (Reeves so well recovered from his knee-cap wound that he could walk only a little stiff.)

So strongly defended was Hill 1125 that it took 1/Bn 186—who had replaced E Co—with 167 FA to overrun that tough position. On the first day of fighting when 1/Bn 186 took over, "A" had 1 killed, and "D" 2 wounded. On the second day, B Co failed in 3 pushes. MGs grounded us on our first try. After C 167's 1/Lt Ehrlich adjusted shellfire, "B" was stopped dead again by MG fire from a pillbox. C Btry neutralized that pillbox, but "B" failed again—with a total of 1 killed, 4 wounded all day.

Only on the third day did "B" seize that pillbox, after FA, mortar, and MG fire—341 shells in 3 concentrations. C Btry made a direct hit on the pillbox, but "B" finally killed it with a flamethrower. Only 1 B Co man was wounded. The Japs withdrew, but abandoned 2 20 mm guns and 2 MGs, with a few corpses. (They usually carried off most of their dead.)

In 167 FA, Morse still well remembers that great first day of saving E's 2/Pln from annihilation. He remembers incidents and men of that day like clicks of a fast-moving slide projector. He remembers Mess/Sgt Herbst with a big grin as he trotted up with 2 40.1-pounds of shell, one under each arm. He remembers 1/Sgt Mel Davis when he closed the kitchen and all other Btry details to forward ammo. He never forgets the tottering overloaded truck of A Btry's Capt Perry who delivered smoke shells without order. Perry's initiative was crucial in saving E Co lives—a whole Pln of them.

Key observer Tyrell told Morse that he was surprised to find both canteens empty after the fight. Yet Tyrell had no memory of taking even one drink from them.

Along with fine gunnery and observation, under-strength 167 FA's was an outstanding achievement in supplying abundant shells. Although Btry tables of organization called for 95 men, we had just 52 men to pass ammo and fire. A single round weighed 42.1 pounds. Each unopened wooden case held 2 rounds—weight 84.2 pounds. Number of rounds we fired was 507. We had to lift each round 4 times before gun-crews jammed it into howitzer breaches. Besides normal exertion of lifting, we must add the work of lateral movement of 6 to 10 feet at the guns, with 150-300 rounds to move from the Btry dump.

Since 52 men carried and passed ammo, each man handled an average of 1,824 pounds. Shells were of an unwieldy shape and size. We loaded and fired all 507 in 1 hour and 20 minutes. (Actually, most of the passing occurred in 40 minutes in the middle of firing.) And remember that we had to police gunpits of empty brass and powder bags so that crews could move and load and fire unhampered. We had to bring up a new supply of shells—160 rounds, 40 per gun, although just 2 men did most of the firing.

We had good reasons why 167 FA was so skilled a "gun-crew"—observers, gunners, and supply men. After 3 years overseas, we were all proud of our outfit, and knew our job. Cross-training for all jobs was routine; Btrys operated more by suggestions than by orders. Years of training and job skills and loyalty converged to save Inf lives. No Btry ever fired a more worthy mission than C Btry 167 FA. Lt Morse well remembers every man in 167 FA Bn. And of all these men, S/Sgt Tyrell was the best technical FA man he had ever known in his whole life.

CREDIT. Finest source was Bill Morse's typescript of an estimated 3,158 words—13 pages. These were Morse's personal memories, or from 167 FA's untitled history of the Palawan Operation. Morse wisely backed his memories by letters from Dick Tyrell and Ed Benckert—and discussions with Mel Davis, Tom Pettifer, and Don Marsaw. Morse's son, Maj Dwight Morse (FA) checked on ammo weights of World War II 105 mm howitzers. I also consulted 186 Inf's "The Palawan Story," and E 186's "First Blood on Palawan," both from my *Fighting Jungleers*. "The Palawan Story" was first printed in *Jungleer* in Oct 1979, and E 186's "First Blood" still earlier, on Feb 1962. (This "First Blood" was submitted by Dwight Shonyo—the first 186 Inf story ever to appear in *Jungleer*.)

41st CAVALRY RECONNAISSANCE TROOP (MECH) AT ZAMBOANGA:

by Dr. Hargis Westerfield, Division Historian with 4 Recon Awards Winners

In Zamboanga Battle, 41 Cavalry Recon Troop (Mech) was truely a cavalry outfit. Instead of fighting on foot as on Biak, we maneuvered with 42 armed vehicles. Core of our cavalry was 13 M-8s — 6-wheeled armoured vehicles, each with an open turret forward mounting a .37mm cannon and a .30 HMG. Another .30 MG was in each bow. For hauling supplies and pulling other vehicles from the mud, we had 5 half-tracks mounting .50 HMGs. Most of our 22 jeeps had 60mm mortars or MGs.

We could scout ahead or flanking our 41st Div to find the Japs. Then, like old-time horse cavalry, we could strike in a weak place, then withdraw and bring up infantry.

On 12 March 1945, the mounted 2/Pln of 2/Lt. Mitchell scouted on right flank of 163 Inf fighting for Santa Maria Village. Div Intelligence said that Santa Maria was already secured. But we probed to find only a crossroad between us and the Japs. A FA tree-burst halted us.

Mitchell jeeped to Inf CP and got permission to continue seeking for Japs on 163 Inf's right flank. As we were about to move, another tree-burst hit us. Pln/Sgt. Froio was wounded on the side and Mitchell's gunner had right arm and nerves cruelly damaged. Sgt. Olson left his shell-hole under fire to bring a Medic for the 2 wounded. Froio would return to fight in a week, but the gunner rated a "homer."

Next village we hit had a supply dump with about 12 Japs trying to close the dump. We slew 2 probables; the rest escaped. Mitchell told 41st HQ that he found many saki cases; so HQ took all cases (next time he found saki, Mitchell brought it back for 41 Recon in the M-8 turrets).

Then we spotted a Jap HQ with a cave. Although Olson's jeep tried to draw fire, no Japs shot at him. Mitchell let 163 Inf deal with that cave.

Reaching 2/Pln's next objective for that day at Mercedes Village north of Pasananca, Mitchell heard that Div Intelligence had ordered 41 Recon and Air Force bombers to attack it at the same time. Mitchell had the bombers grounded and seized Mercedes without casualties, Yanks or Filipino civilians.

Next day, acting Lt. Rundle's Pln raced to rescue loyal Filipinos imprisoned in San Romon Penal Colony near the coast west of Zambo City. We feared that Japs or collaborators would murder them. A good blacktop road — Route 8 West — led to San Ramon.

Through binoculars at a distance, Sgt. Charlson spotted the entrance guard, a lone Filipino with a shotgun. While Sgt. Nason covered him with his M-8s guns, Charlson rushed the guard and grabed the shotgun. Not a shot was fired.

The Japs had fled; we scouted the area and found none of them. One prisoner was a schoolteacher named "Ray," (perhaps spelled "Rey" in Filipino Spanish) who spoke fine English. Ray was crammed into a cell just 5 by 5 feet, and condemed for execution tomorrow. Among the collaborators was Head Warden Moreno whom we turned over to our MPs as soon as we got orders. All Filipinos insisted that Moreno was guilty, but we do not know what became of him.

That same day, Rundle's Pln drove about 5-6 miles up the west coast to contact our guerillas near Labuan. When a Filipino stepped out into the road with an American flag, we had made our contact. Leader was a mestizo named Johnstone.

Thus, within 3 days, 41 Recon had scouted around and secured both flanks of our 41st Div in Zambo Battle. We had helped to force Jap withdrawal to the Pasananca cockpit and Mt. Capisan.

Our new CP now temporarily located at Mercedes which Mitchell's Pln had captured, north and east of Pasananca. On 16 march, we moved on the Japs at Malapugan. But they had fled last night. So 1/Pln tried to head them off at Lunsuran, about 6 miles north of Zambo City. Fires were observed in Lunsuran. But as 1/Pln entered that village, Japs fled disorganized into the mountain jungle behind it. They left documents, rations, ammo, and poorly laid mines. East of Tumaga River, no Jap organized units existed — all the way to our guerilla lines cutting them off at Moroc-Brea heights.

Led by US guerilla leader Capt. Donald LeCouvre, 41 Recon now hunted 23 miles north and east of Zambo to contact the hidden city of Filipino Curuan. On the way, we met many roadblocks and had a minor skirmish. Entering Curuan, we found 5,000 refugees from Zambo City. Doctors, lawyers, and businessmen had tilled the soil for food to stay alive. We began to bring them home — first the Zambo mayor with the police chief and other city officials.

After Jap withdrawal from Pasananca and Mt. Capisan, 41 Recon still had many patrols and some bloody fights. For by late March, the Japs had broken through the guerilla lines and held high ground near Moroc, about 7 miles north of Zambo City. We had to locate the new Jap lines and establish contact by radio with the guerillas.

And so, about daylight 29 March, 1/Lt. Cieslik's 7-man patrol entrucked from base camp at Ft. Pilar in Zambo City to contact some 30 Filipino guerillas near Moroc. Besides Cieslik, known US members of this patrol were S/Sgt. Tippett, and Sgts Bourlier and Alsup, who was the radioman. Near Moroc, the climb was steep and Alsup almost fainted before we found the guerilla camp at mid-day.

At once, Alsup made radio contact for the guerillas with 41st HQ. He gave the guerillas current frequencies, procedures, and codes to help them cooperate with the 41st. When Alsup saw that his comrades were going on an evidently hopeless mission, he volunteered to go with them — at least to draw fire.

Patrol's mission now was to determine strength and main Japanese positions. We were also to find a possible Yank supply line.

Our Pln Leader, 1/Lt. Cieslik, was a newcomer to 41 Recon from an outfit garrisoning Panama. Cieslik was desperately eager for combat. Like Alsup and Tippett, he carried a carbine. At least one patrol member had a tommy-gun. Bourlier and most other men had M-1s. For hand-to-hand combat, most of us had managed to "acquire" a pistol, one way or another.

Choosing what seemed to be safest terrain, Cieslik led his patrol into the rear of the Japs. Soon he probed into a small pocket and began to draw fire from 3 sides — from rifles and MGs. He spotted a Jap MG's field-of-fire and saved our patrol from being wiped out.

When Jap fire seriously wounded a guerilla scout, Cieslik ordered covering fire from his 6 men and went in under heavy Jap fire to rescue him. Cieslik's alertness, quick thinking helped him to complete our patrol's mission far ahead of the expected length of time.

Boulier's bravery was outstanding. When Jap fire hit 2 guerillas and cut them off, Bourlier went in to save them. Under much fire, he brought out one wounded man and gave him first aid. He tried to save a second guerilla, but Jap fire repelled him. As dark began to fall, he kept on creeping up for the second guerilla. Only after dark could he rescue that second wounded man. (Not until 7 days after Cieslik's patrol and a final counter-attack could Inf spring the Japs from their Moroc stronghold.)

Back at San Ramon Prison which Rundle's Pln had liberated, his 3/Pln fought off a night attack by about 30 Japs. We had no casualties, but they bayoneted many civilians outside the prison. We cleared the area and slew 6 more Japs. Meanwhile, AT Co 162 Inf took over security for the prison.

On 12 April, 41 Recon's 1/Pln began a recon patrol that led into battle with the Japs. Led by 2/Lt. Petre, we were to scout Jap movements on the east coast of Zambo Peninsula, probably near Curuan. Being inexperienced, Petre wisely had S/Sgt. McKinsey take the lead.

From a perimeter of armoured cars and jeeps, McKinsey took a 10-man patrol with a Filipino guide up an almost unused trail. Lt. Petre accompanied us. With Cpl. Thompson, McKinsey took the point of the recon patrol.

In over 4 hours scouting we found no Jap tracks. A Filipino came down the trail and said that he had seen no Japs. (McKinsey admits that he should have taken the Filipino back up the trail with him.)

The trail gave out suddenly. Just 30 feet ahead, we saw some 25 japs eating or resting. They could not see us in the darker jungle behind us. They lacked outguards also.

As McKinsey was placing his 10 men, a shot rang out, whether Yank or Jap, he never knew. Japs scattered in every direction. Our 11 men charged in cursing and snap-shooting with M-1s and carbines with tommies to back us.

Behind McKinsey, a Yank yelled, "Grenade!" McKinsey stopped. A hammer seemed to crash McKinsey in the hip. T/5 Lightcap and 2/Lt. Petre riddled the Jap officer-grenadier. Full of adrenalin, McKinsey charged ahead firing.

We overran the panicked Japs to where we could see 100 yards down a draw. Here Japs were setting up MGs or mortars. We toppled several mortar teams to the ground, but there were too many Japs. Light mortar shells chipped leaves on us. Ammo ran low, and McKinsey signalled "Retreat."

Of an estimated 20-22 dead Japs, McKinsey and Thompson claimed 3 apiece. Betts claimed 2; Petre, Lango, Cpl. Moody and T/5 Ortega one each. S/Sgt. Alipio Manahan our guerilla guide killed one also. Sgt. Schneider our radioman did not score, and was angry. We do not know who slew the other Japs.

Next day, Division ordered line Inf to clear that pocket of probably 150 Japs. Our Thompson and Nelson voluteered to take the point ahead of the Inf to find them. but the Japs cannily ambushed us a mile closer than where we expected them. They shot Thompson and Nelson both in the hips and forced the Inf to dig in.

Despite orders against it, a fine Inf Sgt. dragged both men from under fire down the trail, gave first aid, and bore them to Medics. Nelson survived; rumor says that Thompson died. Of course, the Japs were dispersed, those still alive.

With McKinsey's and Petre's fight of 12 April, our Zamboanga Battle seemed to be over. Lt. Downs' Pln returned from a month on Jolo Island with 163 Inf. We planned for 2-3 weeks labor on our overworked vehicles. But 4 days after Downs' return, "Division" ordered us to help out Inf pursuing the defeated Japs up the Zambo Peninsula. Our specialized radiomen, gunners, drivers and mechanics were set afoot in the hungry, wet mountains of disease and death. We left only 25 men behind to construct a camp and complete heavy maintenance on our 40-odd "cavalry" vehicles.

About half of 41 Recon was ordered up the Zambo Peninsula west coast to assist 1/Bn 186 Inf in the Siocon Bay area. We were to set up ambushes to intercept the Japs.

But the Inf CO failed to obey his orders to have ambushes set up. He merely sent out 41 Recon and 186 patrols to kill Japs. Mitchell's men's orders were to ride an Amphib craft down the coast, beach, and work back to 186 Inf.

We trailed a Jap squad to the jungle edge of a native garden. Bees stung some of us. We fled and scared the Nips to flee also. That night, it was hard to pull out stingers; 2 men must take morphine. We still heard the Japs — rose at crack of dawn and slew all 8-10 of them.

Main Jap body hid in the mountains. Rundle's 18 man patrol searched for the Japs — found them in a native garden. When their fire grounded us, Rundle had to get a Piper Cub to call down 12 FA rounds to expell the Japs. Pursuing again, we were ambushed from 2 sides. To save our scouts, we flanked the Japs from high ground and drove them out.

Despite just 2 days' rations, we had to continue the pursuit. we chased them for 4 days. Often a die-hard ambush of sick and wounded fought us until they died. On Day No. 4, an LCM brought food with Inf to relieve us — even while we looked down on some 30 surviving Japs.

Joyfully, we left the Japs for Inf combat, and boarded the LCM for our Zambo camp. By 2 June, a third of 41 Recon was confined with foot and body ailments — and bee stings.

Our 25-man rear echelon also suffered. Floods continually soaked our camp area. We had to remove vehicles and tents to a dryer area — start laborious overhauling, and cleaning all over.

In Zambo Battle, our 41 Recon Cavalry was a highly trained, hardworking and hard fighting outfit. Our recons saved many US and guerilla lives. We slew 133 Japs. (Killed or found dead in mountain patrols were 86 of them.) In return, we had just 9 wounded in action — none killed. Ours was a top-level performance of expertly trained mechanized recon cavalry.

CREDIT. Discovery of this 41 Recon history is miraculous! I had heard nothing from 41 Recon men since 1964. Then from a dark corner of Washington National Records Center, I found Awards citations of William Alsup, Larry Bourlier, Everett Charlson, Ted Cieslik, Ed "Curly" Mitchell, Ray McKinsey, Dawin Olson, Russ Thompson and William Rundle. Bourlier and Cluff Tippetts each had a sworn statement of Ciesliks' Award. Letters come from Alsup (9 and 25 Nov), Mitchell (15 and 17 Dec), McKinsey (undated), and Chester Cheney (undated), all in 1987. Rundle wrote, 12 Jan 1988. McKinsey sent 2 undated clippings, probably from a Laramie, WY newspaper. Total pages were 48. This history would still be impossible without an over 5 page letter-sized single-spaced portion of an official report merely labeled "Headquarters, 41st Cavalry . . ." 26 June 1945. For over 20 years, I had it in the bottom of 163 Inf's Col. Moroney's footlocker in my possession, useless until my discovery of the Awards Stories in June, 1987. (Story of 41 Recon on Biak was in *Jungleer*, Feb. 1964, and republished in my *Fighting Jungleers*.)

5th CO 33rd NAVAL GUARD (JAPANESE MARINES): AGAINST U.S. TANKS AND MOUNTAIN JUNGLE

by Shinji Suzuki, Naval Paymaster Lt. Senior Grade
with Translator Makoto Ikeda and Dr. Hargis Westerfield, Division Historian

During the first week of Zamboanga Battle, the Japanese Marine's veteran 5th Co, 33 Naval Guard, were entrenched in their strong point on a low rise of ground at Cabatangan. Cabatangan was about 25 miles inland, NE of San Roque's doggedly held valley. This strongpoint anchored the right flank of 128 Air Defense Co's position in the Pasananca cockpit were US 163 Inf Regt and 146 FA fought them. CO Suzuki named 5th Co's position "The Emperor's Shield." Against US air strikes, FA barrages and tanks, 5th Co's only weapons were rifles, LMG's, 20mm machine-cannon and sticky grenades.

On the day the tanks first attacked, heavy shellfire began in the morning and continued deep into the afternoon. Shelling never ceased. US planes precisely guided the shells.

Yet, deep in log-braced bunkers, Jap Marines actually slept in helmets, with rifles under their arms. Digging, carrying supplies, and turns on guard had tired them. Unbroken roar and explosions were soothing like waves on a beach. And while FA fired, US tanks dared not risk an attack.

When a shell hit close to CO Suzuki, earth and sand grated on him. A hot wind blasted through his dug-out. He awoke, found that he had no casualties, and slept again.

About 1400 hours, silence did awake Suzuki. The sentry shouted, "Commander! Tanks! Tanks come!"

"Be ready for action," Suzuki ordered. Grasping his saber, he peered over the parapet. At 200 meters (about 180 yards), he saw the heavy monsters moving from concealment behind a fold of the earth.

Soon they halted, half hidden in bamboo undergrowth. They did not fire; Suzuki's Marines had orders not to fire. In death-like silence, the tanks seemed to watch carefully the Marines. Then the tanks' cannon moved quietly from right to left to back again — for 3 minutes, 4 minutes, 5 minutes. Then with motors throbbing, the tanks heaved their whole bodies above the bamboo bushes and stopped short.

The lead tank's big gun turned its black muzzle toward 5th Co. Muzzle flashed red flame. Now all 3 tanks' guns roared; their MGs opened up. They shrouded 5th Co's right pillbox.

Suzuki had a harrowing muzzle view of the salvos aimed to kill him and 5th Co, but most of the fire missed them. Tracer tracks seemed to pass 4-5 feet over 5th Co's heads. Guns were not sighted to fire on the trench on the rising slope. Only a few Japs would be wounded that day.

To help morale, Suzuki and Orderly Tanabe crawled up to talk to the 20mm gunner at the most forward curve of their convex position. Suddenly Suzuki realized that the lead tank aimed directly at him. Muzzle flamed dark red; he lowered his face. The shell dashed sand and earth on him. His cheek was hot, perhaps from a graze.

Tanks slowly closed in, were now only 110 yard off. Casually, Suzuki crept to 1/Pln's position, 150 yards to left rear. First-Warrant Officer Akana exposed half his body above the trench to hear Suzuki. A shell exploded a black pall above Akana. Suzuki feared that his casual words had ordered Akana to raise his head to his death.

But Akana's helmet lifted up. He waved his left hand, but held right to his face, as if lightly wounded. Suzuki motioned him to hide again.

By now the tanks had closed in to about 40 yards, in a slanting line. US BARmen crouched on top behind the lead tank turret. Seeming to fear a charge from the trench, they still fired and halted and advanced, in fear of a Jap charge.

In this 40 yards, Suzuki was about to order "Fire!" But the tanks halted. Lead tank's turret opened slowly. For his first time in the war, Suzuki saw US faces — tank Inf gathered on the ground beside the lead tank. One tankman dropped from turret to the ground — talked loudly to the Inf.

For his first time, Suzuki heard the voices of the men he was fighting. He discerned sunburnt ruddy faces and disordered fair hair. A big tankman was throwing out empty shell casings, 4 or 5 at a time. Another tankman on his tank was drinking coffee.

Seeing coffee caused Suzuki to crave a cigarette. Still withholding firing orders, he crept back into a trench and smoked. His Marines gazed at him down the trench: riflemen, gunners of 3 20mm guns, a flame-thrower man, others with sticky grenades to burn into openings in tank armor.

The unwary tank-infantry teams were advancing again. But instead of guarding the tanks from the ground, the infantry were riding. The teams seemed to think that no fighting men still lived in the trenches. Now they were just 10 yards away — a golden opportunity for blasted Japanese.

"Fire!" shouted Suzuki. His 3 20mm cannon opened up — with LMG's, automatic rifles. All bullets hit tanks or men. Infantry scattered in disorder; tanks backed and turned and ran.

A Formosan "special volunteer," Okamoto laid down his sticky grenade to beg for a rifle. After a shot too high, in the next four rounds, he collapsed one American.

But Suzuki heard no fire from his right pillbox. He found a trench almost caved in, 2-3 men flat on their faces. A shell had buried their LMG into sand. He exhorted those men to fire. About 110 yards away, he shot an American prone on a fleeing tank. Warrant Officer Inamori and his pillbox crew also began to fire.

Red tracers of 20mm shells sparkled on the turrets of all 3 tanks. About 150 yards off, Tank No. 2 had halted evidently in mechanical trouble.

Suzuki wanted to destroy that tank. He ordered Tomito with his *nikko* to creep over the ground to strike that tank. (For 5th Co was tactically divided into 5-man fighting teams called *Nikko*.) They crawled to within 50 feet, and would have flamed the tank by a sticky grenade, but it suddenly fled.

Back in their trenches, 5th Co jubilated. Losses all day were just 7 seriously wounded. First-Warrant Officer Akana was burned in the face. For their 7, they claimed 30 US wounded, but no American dead. The Marines' heroic fight well deserves a place in Japanese history.

For 5 days, Suzuki's 5th Co held the right flank of 128 Air Defense Co's Pasananca cockpit. Well had he named this Cabatangan strongpoint *Mitate-Kochi*, "the Emperor's Shield."

But 5th Co was down to 20 men — 2 of the 3 20mm guns destroyed, Hakoneyama's pillbox pulverized, Petty Officer Tsurumi's party all slain. Americans were infiltrating from the direction of the almost neutralized Pasananca cockpit. US tank fire rumbled from 5th Co's right rear.

At darkfall, Suzuki went to HQs to discuss a suicide attack tomorrow. Over shell battered ground, he first visited the tunnel of 5th Co's wounded. There he thought of the beloved picture in his chest pocket — of parents and brother and sister last seen 3 years ago. He refused to let an enemy hand touch this picture on his corpse.

He lighted a corner of the picture. The flame slowly turned those beloved faces to ashes. With no more regrets, he went to Marines' Vice CO Sasaki to prepare for death in battle.

But Sasaki refused Suzuki's desire for a suicide charge. New orders were for all men to survive and hope to restore the Empire. All Marines began to retreat from near Zambo City into the northern rain-dripping jungle mountain wilderness. For over 3 months, they would slog and fight northward alongshore, then east across Zambo Peninsula, and drop their many dead from starvation, disease, or combat.

On 20-27 March, 5th Co fought rear guard actions north from the caved-in position at Cabatangan. Jap COs tried to build a new strongpoint near Moroc. Suzuki's men seized and held Moroc heights until 54 Indep Mixed Brigade relieved them.

Near Tumaga River headwaters, 5th Co changed from rearguard to vanguard. By now, this 2-man Co was reinforced to 300 Marines.

Fighting Suzuki was unequiped to lead the Guards into unknown mountains. Map was incomplete. "Compass" was a bar magnet suspended from a string to indicate north. Assets were hardworking, zealous scouts, and his own abiltiy at quick, accurate decisions. He was terribly responsible for all the Marines.

On 30 March, 5th Co hiked north, then over 2 weeks curved west over mountains about 25 miles to the coast. On 17 April, through a rift in seaside mist, they saw a planted field. They routed a band of 100 probable guerillas and dug *camotes* — Filipino sweet potatoes. Suzuki felt full of energy again. A nearby deserted village gave supplies for 2 weeks — both for 33 Naval Guards, and Indep Mixed Brigade.

Again marching north, they looked down to Sibuco Bay Strip. Morale was still high; they wanted to sabotage the Strip, but HQ refused permission. Instead, orders came for 5th Co to lead north for the rice-lands of Siocon Bay — impossibly far.

Disease was now rampant — notably malignant malaria that could kill with brain-fever. Tropical skin ulcers pained and crippled many. Horrible little leeches sucked their blood. Cripples had to fall by trailside and die.

At Anungan on 14-19 May, 5th Co fought their last great fight against Americans. They captured "delicious" US rations, enough to feed entire 33 Naval Guard for a month.

But the entire Naval Guard failed to come to 5th Co. US troops had closed in between 5th Co and the main body, and forced them to try a circuitous route through the starved mountains. Suzuki's men went in to rescue them — found them thinned down to half the strength of a few days back.

Moving still farther north on the coast to Siragauy, 5th Co fought off Americans landing from LCIs, and waited for their main body. Again, Suzuki's Marines had to rescue 2 of the remaining Co's from the jungle mountain maze. But Suzuki was deeply worried. The unit of his beloved Vice-CO Sasaki was still missing. (Sasaki would die apart from him on 1 September.)

Orders came to give up the march for Siocon and the rice fields and turned inland. Diseased, thinning 5th Co left the heavily guarded west coast of Zambo Peninsula and limped east. In 5 days, they made 20 more hard mountain miles to near the east coast. At Tapilisan, they dug abundant food from the fields and had an actual 5 days' rest.

By 25 July, 5th Co had slogged north again and had dug in on Gariguan Heights. By October, Suzuki now hoped to march east off Zambo Peninsula and join the Jap army near Davao on the southern Mindanao. He did not know that those Jap divisions were already broken fragments in the mountains. On Gariguan Heights, so sick were his own men that only 20 at a time were available for duty.

But suddenly, 5th Co's war was over. On 28 September under roadside rain, a Fleet liaison offcer told Suzuki that his Emperor had ordered a surrender of all Jap forces.

For 6 days, Suzuki agonized in the dilemma of any chivalrous Jap officer in World War II. His duty was to obey his Emperor and surrender. But an easier way for him would be to commit suicide and avoid the humiliation of surrender. He desired death without surrender, like Sasaki.

Finally, Suzuki had his solution. He would be a coward to die and leave his men by themselves to undergo that disgrace of laying down their arms.

Near Sanito, 60 miles NNW of Zambo City, Lt. Suzuki had a gallant finale to his war. After a tearful speech before decimated 5th Co erect in ranks, he drew his saber and ordered, "Mark time! Right shoulder arms! Forward, march!" With measured tread, 5th Co marched proudly and straight before the ranks of the surprised Americans.

He took their chivalrous salute and returned their salute in the spirit of Japanese *bushido* — the way of the warrior. He himself ordered 5th Co to disarm. They were the surviving 109 of the 300 whose retreat from Tumaga River headwaters had started 5 months ago. What Americans could call Suzuki's "Appomattox" occurred on 9 October 1945. It was Japanese honor to surrender thus, and American honor to receive their surrender thus.

(Final comparative statistics of Naval Guard's Mokoto Ikeda will demonstrate the hardships of those Marines. Beginning with 5,197 native Japanese, the Army's 54 Independant Mixed Brigade finished with 1,166 native Japanese to return home. Beginning with almost as many, 4,365, the Marines had just 560 survivors. Army survival rate was 22 percent of the 5,194; Marine survival rate was just 13 percent out of 4,365.)

CREDIT. Mr. Makoto Ikeda of Tokyo, a "Civilian Marine" also of 33rd Naval Guard, translated Mr. Suzuki's 3 manuscripts. titles of Suzuki's 3 MSS are *"The First Day of the Fighting Against Tanks"* (6 pages), *"Determined to Make a Suicide Attack"* (2 pages), and *"Dairy"* from 1 January 1945 through 10 March 1946 (17 pages). These MSS all came to me written in English, in Ikeda's small, clear, painstaking handwriting. Provenance of Suzuki's "Diary" is unusual. Suzuki's original "Diary" disappeared into hands of US troops after he surrendered. But about 9 months later, Suzuki rewrote it from memory; he needed it for his own post-war rehabilitation. Ikeda himself supplied an excellent large-scale map of the presumed Marines' retreat north from near Zamboanga City, then west to the Zambo Peninsula coast — then back and forth across the Peninsula to the place of his final surrender. After I rewrote Suzuki's original work, I returned in to Tokyo for Ikeda's final revision. (Shinji Suzuki is now president of Tokyo's Nitto Boseki Co;, Ltd., a conglomerate that manufactures fiberglass, textiles, building materials, and many other important products.)

Service Company, 186 Infantry: Hard Labor, Wounds and Death

by Dr. Hargis Westerfield, Division Historian

In January 1943, Service Co embarked with our 186 Infantry from Australia for our first time in New Guinea. We landed at Port Moresby on the way to relieve 32 Div on the north coast. By nightfall, we lay in luxurious jungle hammocks with zipper mosquito nets for tired sleep. We were near the airstrip.

But we did not know about Aussie AckAck emplacements nearby. When Jap bombers hit the strip that night, Aussie 90 mm guns blasted us awake. Some men slashed or dived right through the mosquito nets to the ground. Mail Clerk Scofield and others did total flip-flops in their hammocks and ended up in a tangle.

Several days later, we boarded the filthy Dutch freighter *Bontekoe* for our voyage around the end of eastern New Guinea to Oro Bay. Two destroyers and two minesweepers guarded our little convoy. Once, two Jap Zeroes made a single strafing run on us, then flew on past.

Bontekoe had a filthy Javanese crew using shower stalls for latrines. Creosote was used to cover the odors of this converted cattle boat. Odors were sickening, especially for men already afflicted with malaria or dysentery.

Landing at Oro Bay, we had to hike 18-20 miles up the shore towards Simemi. A Jap plane futilely strafed us; we futilely returned fire with M-1s. Natives came to carry our gear and assist our sick. When we forded streams thigh-deep to waist-deep, we posted outguards against crocodiles and Japs.

At Simemi, we even ran some patrols and found Japs more sickly with malaria than ourselves. But mostly, we carried on the complicated assignments of a Service Co which has to support the many needs of 18 other Regtl Cos.

SV Co had the payroll section, the mail section, the medical detachment, vehicle maintenance, and three ammo sections, one for each of 186's three rifle Bns. Above all, we "kept on trucking" ammo, food, water and medicines to 186's Cos.

Along with Regtl Hqs Co, Cannon Co, and Anti-Tank Co, we were in the Provisional Bn. All three companies could be "decentralized"; that is, assigned partly or wholly to other outfits. For example, SV Co was detached from 186 Inf's main body and held back six weeks from returning to Australia. We were assigned to detached 2/Bn 186 Inf to defend 6th Army Hqs at Milne Bay. (There was no fighting.)

About six months later after refitting and training in Australia, SV 186 embarked for Biak. On May 27, 1944, main body of SV landed dry and unopposed on Bosnek Jetty. With Regtl Hqs, we bivouacked at the base of Bosnek cliffs. Jap raiders flew over us to bomb and strafe our ships. First *kamikaze* of World War II happened here. The plane sideswiped a 110-foot sub chaser and started a fire quickly put out.

Since 162 Inf was halted in three days of combat at Parai Field, 186 Inf made their dry fighting overland march to take Mokmer Strip from the ridges behind it. After six days pushing west, 186 Inf was ready on June 7 to strike down on the strip from Mokmer Ridge east of it. While 186's 2/Bn and 3/Bn waited orders to advance abreast into the strip, SV Co men were to follow them with 2/Bn.

After early morning FA preparation that June 7, 186 Inf started down to Mokmer Strip at 0730. By 0850, the leading 2 Bns had seized the strip without fighting and was beginning to organize the beachhead bordering the strip. About 0915 most of SV Co was hand-carrying supplies down to the beach, along with 2/Bn and SV Co.

On the strip half an hour later, SV men were under heavy shellfire from Mokmer Ridge which we had bypassed because of misguided pressure from Gens Fuller and Krieger. SV Co had our first casualties on Biak. T/5 Lenaburg was seriously wounded and T/5 Crane lightly wounded — other details about the wound unreported.

A third SV man was wounded — although he was not with our company but on another part of the ground. T/4 Pasvogel was attached as a typist to Regtl Hqs Section. When shell fragments from a Jap .75 mm mountain gun — "Whistling Charlie" — caught Hqs men in the open, they dived into the handiest shell crater. In it, Pasvogel was safe — with Col. Newman, Majors Dillon and Anderson and other officers.

Or Pasvogel was safe, if he had stayed in the hole. But the radio operator with his bulky equipment still lay prone outside the crater. Pasvogel crawled out to drag him below ground to safety.

A fragment tore through Pasvogel's pack and lightly wounded him in his upper back. It just missed the bottle of beer he had treasured in his pack. After returning, patched up by the Medics that night, he reclined in his hole and drank that precious beer. It never tasted better!

During 186's first days on Mokmer Strip, two more men were lightly wounded. Capt. Marx was hit on June 8, and T/5 Pingelton on June 10. Other facts on these wounds are unknown.

But all of SV Co did not march with our Regt overland to take Mokmer Strip from the rear. Other SV men helped to make a seaside base between Mokmer Strip and Sboeria Village to stockpile supplies from Bosnek.

It was probably on the night of June 7 that Mail Sgt. Scofield with others boarded a landing craft for run to Sboeria. As our Amphib Engrs nosed their crafts through darkness to seek landing, Japs fired down on us from Mokmer Ridge. We heard their shells rip the air above and splash into the sea behind us.

Our leaders said that we had nothing to worry about, for the ridge-top Japs could not depress their guns low enough to hit us. But they still kept us on edge.

As we closed into shore, lights flashed to help us make contact with waiting 186 men. Jap radiomen kept trying to jam our signals. When our operator swore over it, "Shut up, you slant-eyed SOB!" the Jap operator replied, "Same you, ME-I-CAN bastud. Same you!"

The Amphib Engrs had to circle until daylight because they were unsure whether or not they might land among lurking Japs. Then we did land under shelling from Mokmer Ridge, and ran zig-zag from shell crater to shell crater. MGs firing down from the right raised the dust close to us.

Yet as our FA counter-fire killed their guns, we could set up a SV base. We went back to our routine of carrying mail for our Regt, maintaining vehicles, and hauling supplies.

First truckload of mail came sopping wet. Many packages had fallen apart. Address labels had dropped off. Water had blurred handwritten names and addresses. Wrist watches, pocket knives, rings, pipes, tobacco — even whiskey — lay loose outside mail containers.

Normally, most of this pile would have gone to the San Francisco dead letter office. But through company clerks, we asked men to tell us what gifts they had expected and to try to identify them. Judging by our compliments plus lack of complaints, we feel sure that most of the gifts went to their rightful owners.

Scofield never forgot his happy encounter with truly courteous Gen. Fuller. Returning to SV Co from hospital in his suntans, Scofield got orders to "ride shotgun" to guard Pappy Chastanier's 6 x 6 ammo and ration truck to the front. Still in suntans, Scofield carried not a shotgun but a tommy when he jumped into the truck.

On the way to the front, they drove into a one-way lane. Lined with coconut trees, it was too narrow for two vehicles to pass. A command jeep then came at them from the opposite direction.

Chastanier flashed warning lights, but the command jeep kept right on coming. Gen. Fuller was in it. His driver called, "Can't you see this is a command car?" Chastanier shouted, "We got rations and ammo for the front!" Fuller ordered his drive to back up until he could pull aside to let Chastanier pass.

They unloaded near the front lines at nightfall and had to try to sleep there until morning. Gunfire never ceased all night. At dawn, a lieutenant and 7-8 other men loaded into their 6 x 6.

That night, some Japs had felled a roadblock of trees to stop us to make easy targets. They shot at us. While Scofield fired his tommy at the sound of their rifles, Chastanier put his truck into high and jolted across the logs to the open road and safety.

After Biak Battle officially closed on Aug. 20, Nippo planes hit SV Co in a deadly little air raid about two weeks later, the night of Sept. 7-8. SV was then in garrison, camped in a line of pyramidal tents with other Provisional Bn Cos. On the low ridge above Mokmer Strip, we bivouacked in tents gleaming in bright moonlight. At 0230, most SV men slept deeply after hard labor. They had been tuning up 186's vehicles for the Philippine invasion.

Only T/4 Rudie of the gas detail and T/4 Linklater of the Parts Department were awake — just off guard. At 0230, Rudie was still awake enough to hear the air raid warning. With Linklater and T/4 Trif, he alarmed others in the tent, mostly mechanics. Of maybe 10 men, they roused out six — all but T/4 Distefano and T/5 "Zeke" Jones. Jones was delirious and could not be saved in those few moments.

Rudie heard a plane dive down the tent row. The first bomb whistled down and exploded. At 150 yards down the tent row, the second bomb also whistled and exploded. Rudie rightly expected the third bomb to explode in his tent.

Twenty feet behind the tent lay a deep sandbagged bomb shelter. Rudie almost flew into this hole. M/Sgt Lyon, T/4s Berriocha, Linklater, and Trif; Kowaluska and Barbee — all leaped in. Hull and Trif had dug the hole, but Hull was crowded out. T/5 Hull flattened under a 2-1/2 ton GMAC truck.

The leaping men cleared the top sandbag tier on ground level just as the third bomb blasted. They called it a daisy cutter, but it actually shredded the tent and smashed a hole a foot deep into the coral. The impact bounced Rudie around in their hole and creased his helmet. Rudie, Linklater, Berriocha took light flesh wounds. Hull's arm was blown off.

Hull lay still living outside the hole, his arm blown off, the bone exposed. Rudie started to doctor Hull, but about a mile away, the planes were circling back. But Mokmer Strip searchlight guided AckAck to explode shells ahead of them. They disappeared back into the moonlight.

Out of the hole again, Rudie deftly tourniqueted Hull to halt the massive bleeding, and sprinkled sulfa on raw flesh. Two tents away, they found the Medic and recovered morphine capsules from his shell-torn kit to somewhat ease the pain for Hull and Imus. Both men survived. (On June 28, 1944, Hull's parents wrote to thank Rudie. Alive and recovered stateside, Hull was just about to leave for the hospital for his artificial arm.)

A small detachment from AT 186 also suffered from the bombing. Waller died of wounds; four more were wounded to hospital: Nelson, Mayer, Baker and Berzelius. Nothing more is known at the time of this writing about AT 186 on Biak.

This Jap air raid of Sept. 7-8, 1944, was perhaps the only even lightly effective raid against our 41st Div on Biak. Only known results were a shredded tent, an oil dump briefly aflame, three deaths, at least two lifelong cripples, and some light wounds.

The raid was so quick that accurate facts on the Nippo planes are hard to find. We have statements that they were a fleet of 12-14 planes — and another that there were only 4-5 planes. We are sure that one was a medium bomber. They might have slipped in from a hidden airfield in western New Guinea, or north of us from Halmahera.

Such are almost all of the available facts of the history of Service Co 186 Inf on Biak and the New Guinea mainland. Except for that final air raid and earlier dangers in taking Mokmer Strip, SV Co's main achievement was hard, dependable labor for our Regt.

CREDIT: Basis for this history is Roger Scofield's 2-page single-spaced typescript (1984), a similar five pages from Ray Pasvogel (Apr. 26, 1983), and 5 pages handwritten from Don Culp (Sept. 24, 1988). Trif sent a note of corrections (Jan. 6, 1989). For the air raid, besides Trif's note, I have these undated sources (all from 1988): Gordon Trif and Edward Linklater's 3-page single-spaced typescript, another handwritten note also by Trif, with 2.5 pages by Frank Rudie, with his letter from Mr. and Mrs. Ben Hull (Jan. 28, 1944).

This SV 186 history was a "sticky" one to write. Too many men who could have helped did not answer my numerous letters. Nobody bothered to tell me about the air raid. Only because of my Division History Grants was I able to find that casualty list which no clerk in Washington National Records Center had mailed to me. (The raid came after the New Guinea Campaign of the 41st was officially closed.) I owe a final thanks, however, to William F. Johnson of SV Co who contacted men to tell me of that final air raid. (*Banzai!*)

---

162 Inf Regt in the Salamaua Operation: Results of a Divided Command

by Lt. Col. Carl Webber with Dr. Hargis Westerfield, Division Historian

As Exec Officer of Maj. Archibald Roosevelt's 3/Bn 162 Inf in the Salamaua Operation, Capt. Carl Webber experienced the farce of divided command. After Col. Archibald MacKechnie beach-headed his 1/Bn 162 Inf on Nassau Bay, our 41st Div's Maj. Gen. Horace Fuller detached MacKechnie's 2/Bn and 3/Bn.

Fuller assigned Col. Mack's detached 2 Bns to the command of his 41st Div's chief of artillery, Brig. Gen. Ralph Coane (pronounced "Co-ANE" to rhyme with "grain"). About 10 miles north of Mack's beach, Coane was to emplace guns on Tambu Bay to blast the Japs' Salamaua Strip northward across the ridges.

Those 2 162 Inf Bns taken from MacKechnie would have to secure Coane's FA base. To secure his guns, the Bns would have to seize the ridges above the guns. Japs already held those ridges — most important of which became named Roosevelt.

While Coane's guns shelled Salamaua, Col. Mack's 1/Bn was to climb the mountains above Nassau Bay, drive the Japs from Komiatum Track, and storm Mt. Tambu. Col. Mack's force would be commanded by Australian Lt. Gen. Sir Stanley Savige.

While Savige commanded MacKechnie, Coane was also to be commanded by the commander of the Aussie New Guinea Force. *Yet Coane was to be still under American Fuller's command!*

At once, Fuller's Chief of Staff. Col. Kenneth Sweany, objected to Fuller's formation of this divided command. Since MacKechnie's men would be part of New Guinea Force, Sweany said, Fuller would have no command over their fighting. Sweany also objected to placing artilleryman Coane in command of infantry while experienced MacKechnie himself was deprived of his Bns. (This historian also reasons that Mack should have commanded capable FA officers like Col. William Jackson of our 41st.)

Fuller would usually take Sweany's recommendations after some thought, but this time, Fuller refused. Sweany realized that Fuller still wanted to keep control of MacKechnie.

Misunderstandings quickly arose. Aussie Gen. Savige asked who commanded Roosevelt's 3/Bn — Savige, or

U.S. Gen. Coane. Isolated in jungle mountain Hqs, Savige had not yet been clearly informed about Coane's mission. (Probably also, he had not seen a copy of Fuller's complicated order which put Roosevelt under Coane and thus under Savige's orders.)

Puzzled, Savige then radioed to his own Aussie superior CO to ask who commanded whom. From far south across New Guinea at Port Moresby, Lt. Gen. Sir Edmund Herring replied, "... all units Mack Force are under control of your 3rd Australian Division." Savige naturally thought

As Exec Officer of Maj. Archibald Roosevelt's 3/Bn 162 Inf in the Salamaua Operation, Capt. Carl Webber experienced the farce of divided command. After Col. Archibald MacKechnie beach-headed his 1/Bn 162 Inf on Nassau Bay, our 41st Div's Maj. Gen. Horace Fuller detached MacKechnie's 2/Bn and 3/Bn.

that he commanded 3/Bn, and passed down orders to Roosevelt's 3/Bn. Herring's message should have settled everything, but it did not.

Roosevelt refused to obey Aussie orders, for he understood that Fuller commanded him. He said that he would take orders only from his own 41st Div. COs.

On July 12, Roosevelt's long letter to Gen. Coane complained that total confusion prevailed back at Nassau Bay where no one was in authority over Aussie forces, Coane Force, and U.S. forces. Roosevelt had confusing and contradictory orders; his own 3/Bn Hqs had too small a staff to handle problems of supply for the three different forces.

His letter also warned of danger from the Japs. If they attacked now, they might bring shame and disgrace to everybody. Roosevelt asked Coane to send a high ranking officer to command at Nassau Bay. We have no record that Coane even replied to his letter.

Yet Roosevelt followed Aussie orders — led his 3/Bn north to guard Coane's move to emplace guns at Nassau Bay. He well knew that the Aussie order was dangerous. He would have to leave Nassau Bay unprotected but for service troops, although it was the head of the Australian and U.S. mountain supply line.

Roosevelt lacked a supply train also — neither native carriers nor an Amphib craft detachment. To cross his Bn over deep, swift Bitoi River, he had just one Amphib assault Boat.

Yet Exec. Officer Webber had so well organized 3/Bn's movement that it was completely crossed by 0900 hours. Then I and L Cos attempted an inland hike to reach Boisi Village below the ridges above Tambu Bay. They followed a secret inshore trail which Papuan Infantry scouts had told them about. It was believed that the Japs had used it to escape from MacKechnie after he beached at Nassau Bay.

But the secret trail was impossible. They had to machete jungle all the way — over one series of razorback hills after another. During the next two days, rations were exhausted and many men's shoes became unserviceable. "I" and and "L" had to rejoin K Co waiting for us after only a day's march up the coast. So 3/Bn was unable to deploy on arrival at Tambu Bay and move on a wide front against the Japs on the ridges.

Thus, two days after leaving Nassau Bay, on July 20, K Co entered Boisi Village and came under fire from Jap guns on Roosevelt Ridge 1500 yards northwards. Capt. Lovell and Exec 1/Lt Dorigan were both wounded. Eight men were wounded, and two were killed. Probably 218 FA's 75s silenced the Jap cannon from their new positions on the coast.

On July 22, K and L Cos tried to storm the eastern part of Roosevelt Ridge. One "K" squad actually topped the ridge, between two concealed Nippo positions. After the repulse, the Cos fell back to their new Boisi positions.

But the problem of divided command continued. It would be some three weeks before 162 Inf could capture Roosevelt Ridge. Two probable reasons for this delay seem to be evident. One is that Coane understood that he had only to emplace guns by Tambu Bay to fire over Roosevelt Ridge at Salamaua. Another reason is that aggressive and experienced Col. MacKechnie was relieved from commanding 162 Inf — even from his 1/Bn remnant left to him after the rest of 162 Inf went under Coane's command. Gen. Fuller relieved Col. Mack during a squabble resulting from that same misunderstanding as to who commanded 3/Bn 162. Col. Mack was "kicked upstairs" to become liaison officer between 162 Inf and Gen. Savige's Aussie 3/Div.

After K and L Cos failed a frontal attack on Roosevelt Ridge, Aussie Savige clearly told Gen. Coane the best strategy to take it. Maps revealed that the ridge was higher on the western, inland edge than on the eastern edge. Papuan scouts had reported that the western edge was just lightly held. Savige told Coane to attack the Jap's positions from the west; we now had 5 FA Btrys to support such an attack.

Coane did send probably I Co to the west — even promised Gen. Savige to be on the way to success before dark on July 25. On that day, with FA support, 3/Bn did gain 50 yards up the ridge before a counter-attack forced them back. Coane's force remained safely and compactly perimetered in the Boisi area, although Papuan scouts begged to lead them back against the Ridge again.

The Roosevelt Ridge situation improved, however, by July 27-28. From newcomer 2/Bn, E and F Cos gained a firm hold on a small ridge slightly below the crest. By July 27 also, I Co of Roosevelt's 3/Bn had made a significant gain near the west end of Roosevelt Ridge.

I Co had fought up Scout Ridge at right angles to Roosevelt Ridge and captured Bald Knob. This was the highest "pimple" on that area which 162 Inf now held. Only 2.5 miles from Salamaua Town, it became a perfect observation point from which to bombard Salamaua Town and Strip.

On Bald Knob, I Co almost continuously battled the Japs. Now it was I's turn to repulse them by rolling down grenades.

Webber made a trip with signal men up from 3/Bn to inspect I's new position. Climbing the almost vertical ridges in tropical heat was indeed hot pain. Only guide was the wire leading up past a heap of I Co's Nippo corpses. They picked their way past a water hole which "I" and the Japs shared at different times by mutual agreement. They climbed past trip wires lined with K-ration cans where grenades could be attached for night protection.

At nightfall, Jap mountain gunfire opened from about 600 yards away. It seemed to be ranged in from a Jap perimeter just 200 yards off.

Occasional tree bursts made the shells extremely effective. When a shell slashed a tree directly above the perimeter, "I" had many wounded.

Webber had a foxhole in the CP with CO Lt. Colvert, but they had to leave it. Medics needed the hole for the wounded, to give them plasma transfusions.

Webber had to wander around under FA fire to seek an empty foxhole. When he found one, he bailed it out and dropped dead asleep in the mud. The shellfire had stopped.

By daylight, Webber started back to 3/Bn through L Co's position. He met no Japs, but going down was harder than going topside. He slipped in mud and tripped over roots and saplings. At the ridge-bottom near Boisi, he halted for a creek and waterhole he had used before. He was encased in reddish mud from the wet trench on Bald Knob. While washing off the dripping mud, he had a hot battle with "piss ants" that kept dropping from the shrubbery above him. About a half-inch long, they bit viciously. When crushed, they smelled sour, pungent.

Back at 3/BnCP, Webber learned that Jap mortars had slain four men, wounded several more, including Lt. Mikesell, Bn intelligence officer. CP had to move to a safer place.

Despite successes of I, E, and F Cos on July 27-28, Roosevelt Ridge was still untaken. There was no real progress deep into August. Because of that same old dispute about command of 3/Bn, Fuller had fired Col. MacKechnie from any control of 162 Inf — MacKechnie ablest U.S. field CO of all.

Perhaps about this time, Maj. Roosevelt decided to complain to Gen. MacArthur himself about lack of leadership in the siege of Roosevelt Ridge. To do this, Roosevelt would have to risk his military career and be subject to court martial.

After Gen. Fuller and most other 41sters had returned to Australia, Chief of Staff Sweany was left in charge of the continuing fight for the Ridge. About noon one day, haggard Maj. Roosevelt entered Sweany's office at Dobodura. He asked permission to see MacArthur about relations with the Aussies, and about the divided command.

Sweany forbade Roosevelt to visit MacArthur's Hqs — or write anything to him. Sweany also ordered him to remain at Dobodura until commanded to return to Roosevelt Ridge.

On July 12, Roosevelt's long letter to Gen. Coane complained that total confusion prevailed back at Nassau Bay where no one was in authority over Aussie forces, Coane Force, and U. S. forces.

It is still unknown whether Roosevelt really complied with Sweany's order not to talk to MacArthur. But the siege of Roosevelt Ridge was about to conclude successfully.

After Fuller relieved Col. MacKechnie on July 22, he assigned MacKechnie to Coane. Coane made him liaison officer to the Aussie 3/Div, "just to get rid of me," said Mack.

But on arrival at 3/Div Hqs, Col. Mack learned that the canny Australians were for him. They had gone over Fuller's head and persuaded MacArthur to restore MacKechnie back to command 162 Inf. His Regt would now be detached from Fuller to the command of Aussie New

Guinea Force generals.

With Col. Mack's return to command 162 Inf, Gen. Coane was needed no longer. He rejoined Gen. Fuller in Australia.

For the final assault on Roosevelt's Ridge (Aug. 14, 1943), Col. Mack now used Maj. Lowe's 2/Bn. For preparation, he did what artilleryman Coane should have done — ranged in all Aussie and U.S. guns he could bear on it. He also called down Bofors AA guns with 20 Air Force bombers. To keep Japs from reinforcing their Ridge garrison, H Co 162's Capt. Heiser hammered the rear slope with an 81 mm mortar barrage.

Triumphant MacKechnie watched the ridge top literally lift with the bombardment. As shellfire moved before them, the troops easily occupied the ridge without casualties. Thus ended this great barrier to capturing Salamaua.

Capt. Webber did not see the Ridge again until after 162's great assault. Just after his night with I Co on Scout Ridge, a long, vicious malaria attack had hospitalized him. While furloughed down to Sydney, he had recurrences of his malaria for a month in and out of a Sydney hospital.

When he did return to 162 Inf, his long absence had caused his replacement as Exec Officer. He was transferred from infantry and promoted. He became a major and an Air Force Inspector-General. He had a well-merited high type of public relations assignment. He finally became a Lt Col!

Thus resulted Gen. Fuller's divided command of 162 Inf before Salamaua. Fuller probably retarded U.S. victory

> **CREDIT:** Most responsible for this history is Lt. Col. Carl Webber's 13-page single-spaced typescript entitled "From Nassau Bay to Tambu Bay, Boisi, Roosevelt Ridge & Salamaua," with a postcard marked Nov. 12, 1989. Webber's typescript contains a copy of Maj. Archibald Roosevelt's letter to Gen. Ralph Coane (Aug. 13, 1943) and Coane's letter to appointment to command (Jul. 11, 1943). Almost equally important are citations from Australian David Dexter's *The New Guinea Offensives* (Canberra: Australian War Memorial, 1961), and Gen. Ken Sweany's letter of Dec. 30, 1988 (3.5 pages, single-spaced typescript). First-hand information about Col. Archibald MacKechnie's return to command of 162 Inf and the seizure of Roosevelt Ridge comes from the Colonel's two-page letter of May 1, 1959. (In answering two letters I wrote to him in 1969, retired Col. Roosevelt refused to help me twice.) I made an earlier study of the Salamaua command problem in *Jungleer* magazine's story No. 58, "162 Inf HQ: Good Soldier MacKechnie's Salamaua Operation," re-published in my *Fighting Jungleers*.

for a month. Luckily, the Japs were too defensive-minded for an offensive during this time. Luckily, the Australian generals were wise enough to get Col. MacKechnie returned to rightful command of all 162 Inf. This divided command was a bitter farce that never should have happened.

Papua. The beach at Buna with the remains of Japanese landing barges and dead Japanese soldier. (Courtesy of Rohlffs)

F 163's Most Accurate History of Sanananda
by Ralph Marlow with Dr. Hargis Westerfield, Division Historian

At 0400 in the dark, 5 Jan. 1943, F Co 163 Inf trucked without breakfast to a Port Moresby Strip to fly to Sanananda Battle. Past debris of a loaded bomber that had just blown up accidentally, we boarded Aussie Hudsons — 16 men to a plane. Airborne, we saw New Guinea jungle unroll ahead — a gigantic tufted carpet. Soon our pilot was dodging between pinnacles of the Owen Stanley Mtns. We lurched in currents from the north side.

Only 45 minutes after Moresby, F 163 hit Dobodora Strip. Groaning wounded with bloody bandages waited to load on a big transport plane for Moresby. We lurched ankle-deep in mud in six-foot kunai grass north towards combat. We drank well water near three 25-pounder Aussie cannon. Jap raiders had blown to ribbons the muzzle of the fourth gun. Other three guns were firing for men in battle eight miles away.

On 6 Jan, we perimetered near Soputa, still fairly safe. But that night, Dehort was accidentally killed, our first dead.

After an idyllic 7 Jan. of sun and riverside bathing, on 8 Jan., "F" plunged into sunless jungle-swamp east of Sanananda Road, to avoid Japs on that road. Stumbling over hidden roots and logs, we often sank waist-deep in mud. Rifle and MG fire sounded nearby; we slipped aside for natives carrying our wounded in litters. We perimetered on higher ground east of 1/Bn's Musket Perimeter. Stray rifle bullets cut the leaves overhead.

For 9 June, we got battle orders. Second in the 2/Bn line of Cos, we were to follow G Co through the south side of Musket Perimeter, then slog west 1400 yards to cut Killerton Track. The Track was the escape route of three Jap Perimeters "P" that had long blocked Sanananda Road.

After 500 yards, we filed through 1/Bn's Musket Perimeter. A 1/Bn man warned us to hurry across Sanananda Road; a Jap MG had fired down it that morning. While hurrying F Co across the road, Marlow heeded another man's warning to keep low. A Jap bullet wounded another man sitting on the edge of a hole. Medics carried him off with a stomach wound.

Our cruellest march of all was the 1400 yards down "Suicide Trail" to Killerton Track. We climbed over huge logs and jumped into deep, muddy holes. Some men dropped their rifles into thick mud which made them useless.

When G Co fired at Japs on the Track, F Co forwarded 2/Pln to help them. Soon our 2/Pln was prone in the kunai while fighting Jap MGs a few yards ahead. Medic Bays ran through Jap fire to bandage Green, shot in the back, and Herman, shot in the shoulder. Then 2/Pln crawled back to safety.

And so, on 9-14 Jan, "F" with our 2/Bn blocked Killerton Track with "Perimeter Rankin," and cut off the Jap escape route. Perimeter Rankin was actually a ring of Co perimeters. Each rifle Co detached a Pln to take its turn to the front closest to the Japs, for 24 hours.

Fronting the Japs, men sat neck-deep in water in the long night. Guns grew so muddy that we rinsed them in the water in our holes. When relieved wet and sleepless back to our Co perimeter, we let Hq men clean and dry our guns and ammo while we slept.

Rain every night and Aussie shells kept us awake. The ground shook sand on us in our holes. To avoid shellfire, Japs crept close to our holes and duelled us with grenades. After the night of 11 Jan, we found Toth killed five feet from his hole.

On 14 Jan, a Jap sniper twice drove "F" into our holes. Suspecting that he shot from a tall, vine-covered tree, Jacobsen, Marlow, and 2/Lt Rader twice tommie-gunned the tree, top to bottom. The Nippo sniper never bothered "F" again.

By the end of 14 Jan, Perimeter Rankin became useless. While the Aussie 18 Brigade struck from the south, our G and E Cos pushed from the north and crushed the Perimeter "P" Japs. Our Weapons Pln had the repulsive chore of burying some 300 Japs who had held "P." Victorious Aussie 18 Brigade passed north through Perimeter Rankin to battle the Japs on the coast. And "F" got marching orders and new fighting orders.

Orders were to follow the Aussies about 1.5 miles up Killerton Trail to the Coconut Grove. Then we were to turn east and then south again to strike the Japs' rear on Sanananda Road where we had come from on 9 Jan.

By 16 Jan, F 163 was back into battle. From perimeter in the kunai east of Coconut Grove, we were to push through a Nippo jungle to Sanananda Road. After a medium bombers' air strike of 30 minutes and FA shelling, we were to push abreast of G Co on our left flank.

Leaving our packs, we macheted through jungle and swamp to more open ground and marched in three parallel Pln columns. But we lost an hour and the effect of the preparatory shells and bombs. The jungle separated our Plns; we had to regroup near G Co.

Orders now were to cut Sanananda Road on the north or rear of Perimeter S — where A Co suffered heavy casualties in their attack of that 16 Jan. In single file, we followed a winding trail into ground which the Japs had cleared for a field of fire. Intense rifle fire grounded us.

Racing up with orders from Col. Rankin for "F" to retreat, Marlow found everybody down under Jap fire from everywhere. No matter which side of a tree a man covered behind, the fire came from that direction.

Counts was down with a large hole torn in his right thigh. Earlier in the fire-fight, Marlow heard, Sgt. Ellis Olson had orders to deploy his squad on our right flank. He died with a bullet in the brain.

After Marlow contacted CO Ellers, we were told to retreat, a man at a time. When Ordish dashed back, a whole Jap volley cut him down. With Marlow and Medic Malanca helping him, Ordish crawled into jungle cover and a waiting litter. He was wounded in the left elbow, buttocks, and back.

Regrouped safely again, we saw G Co file into jungle to our left and heard their rifles open up. F Co's CO had orders to push beside G Co at a 50-yard interval. Lead Pln would be 2/Lt Ogden's. It was mostly open ground ahead, among big trees on dry and level ground.

"F" had hardly advanced more than 50 yards before a MG burst drove us to ground. Even Hq Pln was down. Ellers twice ordered the advance to continue, but we did not move. Word came back that Lt. Ogden was dead. When Medic Marcus tried to aid Ogden, a MG burst slew him also.

Already, Prinz was dead, and Sgt. Raush dying from a head wound. Ellers ordered us back, but retreat was impossible under grazing fire. A main source of this fire came from two MGs in a narrow ravine before F Co, but we did not know that source.

Ellers then ordered 2/Pln from the rear of our column to hit the Japs on our left flank. But 2/Pln failed to maneuver far enough leftward to avoid Jap fire. Their fire stopped us; a bullet grooved the skull of Sgt. Willard Johnson. He was paralyzed below the hips.

After 2/Pln failed, Ellers tried once more to advance "F." He told Cpl. Tidrick's squad to run from our right flank and kill those MGs.

Tidrick's squad doubled 40 yards from our right flank, hit the ground, and emptied their guns at what they thought was the MG nest — a dangerous looking native hut. Concealed in the ravine, the two Jap MGs opened up — hit Tidrick three times: in shoulder, chest, left forearm. They shot Paul three times also: in shoulder, thigh, and left forearm.

Tidrick half carried, half dragged Paul to safety. We saw the two bloody men with Tidrick supporting Paul with his good right arm. Tidrick's left wrist hung shattered; he bled from a hole in his chest as large as a fist. Tidrick insisted that Paul be treated first, and refused treatment himself until he reported the Nips' positions. Both men lived. (That night, E Co's Capt. Buckland with Steiner and Sgt. Lund wiped out those Jap gunners who slew Ogden, Prinz, and Raush, and wounded Counts, Ordish, Johnson, and Paul.)

Now we had to leave our four dead on the field. We took the trail after G Co which had easily fought through the Hospital Lot to Sanananda Road. That night, we perimetered in water among Jap corpses on the west side of Sanananda Road. Here we remained on 17 Jan., except for 1/Pln guarding 2/Bn Hq.

On the night of 17-18 Jan, Japs blundered into isolated 1/Pln's perimeter and fought us. Cpl. Ray died of a wound that night; Horrocks was shot in the neck, but we repelled the Japs.

On 18 Jan, F Co filed down Sanananda Road to begin our bloodiest fight of all Sanananda Battle. While trying to bring Sgt. Hundahl's Pln closer to us, Cpl. Pulliams scouted too close to Nippo lines. His body was recovered four days later.

Patrolling down the east side of the road, we slew many Japs in small armed bands, without casualties to ourselves. In late afternoon, we took low traversing fire from several Jap MGs, and then some mortar shells — but again had no losses. We were now on the edge of our objective, Perimeter V, which was part of Perimeter U.

Scouting east, 1/Pln found a group of hospital huts. Able-bodied Japs ran to hide among the sick and wounded. We had no choice but to shoot anyone who moved.

Scouting farther east and south, 2/Lt Raber's Pln saw Japs carry laundry down to the stream across from them. Heisler's BAR was to begin the shoot-out; it jammed after two shots and stampeded most of the Japs. In the fire-fight then, Krull's rifle was shot from his hands. Lt. Raber was shot in left arm and neck. A third bullet pierced his helmet, grazed his head, and bloodied his face. Most of the Japs escaped.

On 18 Jan, "F" claimed 54 Japs killed, with only Lt. Raber wounded and Cpl. Pulliams killed. But next day, 19 Jan, was our deadliest day of battle at Sanananda.

On 19 Jan, main action began by Cpl. Cameron of Weapons. With rifleman's protection, Cameron crawled dangerously close to Nippo lines to call down fire on them. For 30 minutes, without shorts into our own Co, he called down Aussie FA and 163's 81 mm mortar battery into a perimeter 150 yards wide.

Now "F" got orders from an unremembered source to charge the Japs with fixed bayonets down into the draw and across the little stream. While we still deployed in line, Nippo fire began. Only waist-deep in a little Jap hole, Marlow himself incurred three near-misses by Jap bullets and dived for a coconut tree.

With 1/Pln and 2/Pln in line, we screamed and charged the Jap positions across the draw. But despite Cameron's great barrage, the Jap MGs blasted away. From behind a tree that MG fire was cutting, Marlow saw our shattered Plns retreating, while a Jap MG enfiladed us in the draw. Some men dangled shattered arms; some limped; some were carried. Some able men cried hysterically.

This charge cost "F" at least seven dead, 14 wounded, and one seriously injured. Cpl. Reynolds and Sgts. Dickey and Billsborough died within a few feet of a Jap p11box. Reynolds warned us not to risk our lives to save him. Other dead were Scott, Beighey, Kramarik, and Molitor. Although 163's Casualty list says that Helmer was wounded in the neck, Marlow says that Helmer died later. Casualty list does not report his death.

Despite agony of a rupture, Cpl. Ward Williams save BARman Fallstick from drowning from his wounds. Fallstick lost a lung from a bullet in his chest; he had a hand wound also. Zimmerle was shot in right leg; Al Brown in right leg and arm; and Sgt. McLean in right foot.

Other recorded wounds were mostly higher up — Lawrence and Arguello both with a bullet in left shoulder apiece. Denton was hit in right elbow, Brune in right hand, and Babicz in right wrist and left shoulder. De Risco was only man hit by grenade fragments — in left arm and mouth. Unreported was the nature of Hahn's, Caswell's, Mitchell's and Payne's wounds.

After Perimeters U-V were liquidated four days later, F Co learned that we had prematurely charged an almost impregnable position until much more FA fire and mortaring. We had charged 19 log bunkers heavily manned by MGs. Centering the perimeter were trucks buried in the ground with MGs bolted to their motor blocks. Storming the "Motor Pool Perimeter" on 19 Jan would have cost the lives of several understrength Cos.

E Co replaced F Co on that 19 Jan, but did not have to charge the Nips' lines. On I and L's successful assault of 23 Jan, E Co had only to provide fire support.

Marching back north up Sanananda Road, we spent the sunny morning of 20 Jan washing uniforms that were a mass of solid mud. We dried our billfolds and photos in that sun and cleaned three days' rust from our guns. Although our pathetic little Co still had much marching and patrolling in mud and rain still to do, our Battle of Sanananda was ended. We had probably 15 killed, 22 wounded, and one seriously injured. After marching to cut Killerton Track on 9 Jan, we had fought bloodily and well in our two great fights of 16 and 19 Jan 1943.

CREDIT: Core of this history is Pp. 31-79 of Ralph Marlow's 293-page handwritten manuscript which F 163 leaders unofficially commissioned him to write while it was happening. Background sources include 163's Sanananda Casualty List, *Yank Magazine's* Staff Correspondent Dave Richardson's "Sunset Division Eclipses the Rising Sun," Dr. Samuel Milner's *Victory in Papua.* Two earlier "F" stories of Sanananda already in the *Jungleer* are Jess Fallstick's *BARman at Sanananda* (*Jungleer,* June 1960), and "Two Days' Infighting at Sanananda" (*Jungleer,* Jan. 1977). Marlow's history corrects or adds to these narratives. Milner and they omit F's fight of 16 Jan. Sgt Olson did not throw away his life and five other men's in a charge of 19 Jan; he was killed on 16 Jan. Sgt. Billsborough did not waste these men's lives either. The deaths were the result of a bayonet charge ordered by officers superior to the men of F Co. This charge was not even mentioned in Training Note No. 2 — evidently because the officials did not like to admit their failure in judgment.

---

146 Field Artillery on Biak: Wet Landing, Night Combat

by Dr. Hargis Westerfield and Capt. Robert Allen, 146 FA

When 146 Field Artillery's 105 mm howitzers beachheaded on Biak on 27 May 1944, our landing was part of a calculated risk. So important to Gen. Fuller was the early beaching of guns, tanks, trucks, and bulldozers that they were loaded on eight special LCTs ("Landing Craft, Tanks"). These long barges were to be driven by Navy coxswains up the outer reef and over it as far as possible, then into the shallow water before the beach. So important was this cargo of guns, tanks, trucks, and bulldozers to assist our infantry that Fuller had to accept the risk of damage on the coral. Immediately after securing our landing, 146 FA must turn to support the westward rush of 162 Inf to capture Mokmer, Sorido, and Boroko Strips.

As our LCTs raced for the smoky shore, Btry A's LCT came under fire from a Jap MG already in A's proposed position. But pointblank fire from a watching destroyer knocked out that MG.

All of our three gun batteries had to make wet landings from the LCTs. Some of our guns and vehicles had to be dragged across 50 feet of water 3-4 feet deep, but we landed and got into position in good time. The LCTs were just slightly damaged. Only guns to land ahead of 146 FA were

Btry C 121 FA's pack 75s.

Btry B of 146 FA dropped gun-trails just inland of the new jetty at Bosnek, while "A" and "C" positioned on higher ground some 400 yards east. When our CO Lt-Col. Anderson found that 186 Inf did not need support near Bosnek, he had our Fire Direction Center mass the fires to support 162 Inf's march towards Mokmer Strip. Btry A was ready to fire at 1000 hours, and "B" and "C" by 1030. (The 155 mm guns of Btry C 947 FA were ready at 1230.) At 1500 hours we had our first Biak casualty. Sv Btry's Sgt. Stewart was killed when a falling limb impacted him from a shell-torn tree.

About 1300 hours, 162's 3/Bn in the lead halted before heavy rifle and MG fire from 1500 yards east of Parai Jetty where the road begins to enter the Defile between cliffs and sea. Fire seemed to come from the cliff caves and lower coral terraces.

From our new LCV observation post offshore, Capt. Bedke registered a 146 FA Btry on those Jap strong points. But we knew that our firing results would be limited. We would have to fire from an angle east up the shore, and many Jap weapons were in caves and crevices facing seaward to the south.

We decided to call for Naval assistance. Lt. Wolffer radioed a destroyer offshore which directed heavy fire on the caves and coral terraces. But for maximum effect, Wolffer exposed himself to wade out on the reef to contact a rocket LCI. With signal flags, he wigwagged to penetrate the cliff caves with rockets that would accurately explode inside. (Meanwhile, another man of Wolffer's observation party, Sgt. Donaldson, dared Jap fire to rescue a wounded 162 infantryman.)

When 3/Bn 162 dug in for the night near Parai Jetty, 146's Communications Section strung wire for shellfire to protect them. Jap sniper fire was continual against our Communications men. During exchanges of fire, Sgt. Burnette slew a Jap — 146 FA's first known kill.

Finding that 186 Inf's opposition at Bosnek was only light, Btrys B and C in late afternoon displaced forward down the coast to Ibdi with a skeleton Fire Control Center. By 1725, Btry C was registered. We prepared for defensive fires to support 162 Inf against night attacks at Parai, but they had no need to call us that night.

Our forward Btrys B and C had unknowingly placed themselves in danger of a desperate Jap night attack. Btry C was up ahead, closest to Mokmer Strip. No units but Japanese were in front of "C" but for 162 Inf, three miles away at Parai. Btry B was 200 yards to our rear.

It was bad enough to have this exposed forward position, but we were unable to entrench ourselves properly. Before we could set up a secure defensive perimeter, we had to organize fires to defend 162 Inf. Thus our registration fires helped to reveal our new positions to Japs of 3/Bn 222 Inf who were on the Ibdi heights above us.

They were well concealed in those vague dark-green jungle terraces overhead. (3/Bn 222 Inf would be the last formation on Biak, which 163 Inf and the bombers would not destroy until seven weeks later.)

Absolute security was also impossible to use because elements of 162 Inf were still streaming past on the way to Parai Village for the great assault on Mokmer Strip tomorrow. Btry C prepared our inadequate defenses with the belief that Inf troops would be strung along the beach road just a few feet from the left front of our gun positions.

We placed two MGs in a stronghold a few yards to the right of No. 1 Gun. Their fire lanes were to the right and the front of our gun positions. We sighted another MG a few yards to the rear of this stronghold. Its field of fire was to our right and our right rear. Not one MG guarded our left flank on the road.

Fifty yards to our rear, an Air Corps AA unit had positioned across Parai Road to the left. Btry C placed only one sentry as liaison between the Air Force and us.

Besides failing to protect our flank on the road, we also made another disastrous error. Because the early night hours were quiet, we allowed some men to sleep outside of their holes. Only about 30 yards off the road and 30 yards back of No. 4 Gun, our wiremen huddled down in a close-packed group, a ready target for bayonet-men. Behind them also on the road were men of our Maintenance Section.

We were a perfect set-up for a mass Jap attack. It could have wiped out a whole Btry of men and guns, and even caused 162 Inf to hold up their Mokmer offensive to secure their rear. Lucky were we that only a small raiding party with almost no demolition charges for our guns hit Btry C that night.

At midnight, Jap bayonet-men charged down the road toward the open side of Btry C's Perimeter near the road. From the brush, six to seven Japs with levelled bayonets drove off the lone sentinel contacting the Air Corps Engrs. With those levelled bayonets, they swarmed in among the close-packed sleeping communications men; they pinned some of them to the ground with bayonets. Their officer slashed half-awakened men with his saber.

Grunting bayoneting Japs drove the Maintenance men back into the brush. Our gun crews and machine-gunners were already cut off from the road by thickets that our bulldozers had not had time to level last night. Our other fighters could only feel sick while they listened to the helpless cries of men being butchered near the road.

Howerton and Cpl. Lashappel were slashed or stabbed to death, probably while still in their sleep. Thurlow took a thrust in his abdomen and was left for dead. All night, he lay agonizing alone, and died the next morning before the attack ended and Medics could come to him.

A few yards off, Sgt. Dutton was found dead. He had

put up a fight, but a saber cut him down before he could flee into the brush.

Thus died four men. Bayoneted and seriously wounded was Peeler, but he did slay the Jap who had thrust into him. Like Cpl. Postelthwait, also pierced and badly wounded, Peeler escaped into the inner perimeter. Both men took refuge at the CP behind the guns and underwent Medics's treatment while the fight still raged.

T/5 Hunt was less seriously wounded and escaped. He saved himself by rolling under a vehicle away from where he was struck and lying still. Also less seriously wounded, T/5 Craig also escaped in an unreported way during the confusion.

Meanwhile, our MGs could not fire down the road because our guns and other equipment lay in the line of fire. But Cpl. Young and crew rushed a MG to an exposed position behind No. 2 gun and slew two Japs. The main Jap force then moved back down the road in front of our guns and equipment and blocked off Young from firing again.

But Young's first burst had flamed a pile of powder bags. For several seconds, the position was lighted up like noonday. We heard Jap voices chatter along the road. They soon attacked again — with grenades, rifles, and LMGs. Some slipped around to the right flank also and hurled grenades into the perimeter. One placed a demolition charge near No. 4 gun, but it failed to damage the piece. This is the one time in the entire night attack that the Japs did what should have been their reason for the raid — to kill our guns.

One little Jap group subjected Btry B to a brief attack before a gun position. They grenaded our outpost there and fired into the perimeter. Our .50 HMG tired to enfilade them beside the perimeter, but it jammed after the first round. The Japs fired back with their LMG and continued throwing grenades.

Outpost guard Zeulner left his hole and shot at the Jap MG with his carbine. He got off four rounds, but the carbine jammed. He threw a grenade; it failed to explode. The Japs rained in grenades on the outpost, but they hurt nobody. Later, blood on the road showed that Zeulner's few rounds surely got results.

At daybreak, the Japs broke off their attack. While Medics tended our wounded from outlying positions, we counted casualties. We added to our roster Lish, wounded by a sub-machine gun. So far, we had four dead, five wounded. But we would have two more serious casualties.

After daylight, Antonovich and Murray were searching into the sinister brush on our right flank to see whether they could find signs that our MGs had hurt any Japs on that side. A moment later, we heard a terrific explosion. We rushed out to find Antonovich and Murray both badly burned and wounded by a Jap explosive trap. A wounded Jap had lain quietly all night where he and another Jap had fallen under our MG fire. The other Jap had died during the night, and his own blast killed the Jap who set it off. Neither Antonovich nor Murray died of wounds.

We found only certain proof that six Japs were killed — and one of those in the Air Force position nearby. Those Air Force Engrs had lost one killed, and one wounded. Bloody trails showed evidence of other casualties — whether dead or wounded, we did not know, since the Japs even carried off their own corpses.

In early morn, Btry A and the remainder of 146 FA's men moved up beside us. Lt. Setzer and his Btry CO's party took fire from a Jap MG between Btrys C and B. So the rest of 146 FA positioned on the other side of the Bosnek-Parai Road. We cut broad fire-lanes on the right flank across the road, and received no further attacks that morning.

On that morn of 28 May, 205 FA and 947 FA came down from Bosnek and set up near us. We were all now ready to give full support to 162 Inf's fight for Bosnek Strip.

Such is the saga of 146 FA's first day on Biak — our landing and emplacement at Ibdi and our vicious little night fight against the Jap raiders who were probably from 3/Bn 222 Inf. Considering the precarious position that 146 FA lay in below Japs on the Ibdi ridges, we were lucky to lose only four killed, and finally, seven wounded.

We lost no guns. Although we know of only six Jap casualties for sure in contrast to our five dead, and seven wounded, it was in the end only a minor skirmish. From here, it seems that a heavier attack would have wiped out at least Btry C and caused 162 Inf to fall back from their forward position at Parai Village. And so, their night attack remains only a bitter and proud memory of 146 FA on Biak.

CREDIT: Personal basis of this history is "Bosnek Beachhead," a 3-1/2 page single-spaced typescript by Cpt. Allen, which is a small part of his coverage of 146 FA throughout World War II. Useful also was R. R. Smith's *Approach to the Philippines*. I found Allen's narrative in Federal Archives, but I have found no trace of it in McCartney's *Jungleers*. Story of 146 FA in Bongao-Sanga Sanga was in *Jungleer* for June 1985. Hollandia story was in May 1968 *Jungleer;* Parai Defile (Biak) story in April 1972 number; Jolo Mountain Story in Jan. 1979 number; Mount Daho story (Jolo) in June 1963 number; and Zamboanga story in March 1970 number. Of these six stories, only the Bongao-Sanga Sanga story did not appear in my *Fighting Jungleers*. (Although I covered 146 FA's overall Parai Defile story in an earlier *Jungleer*, I could not then give them full credit for their landing and night battle. Such is my reason for this history. I have already stockpiled for publication the detailed history of 146 FA's escape from Parai Defile.)

The Division History, No. 199

I Co 186 Inf At Zamboanga, II: BARman Wins DSC at Anungan

by Dr. Charles Solley, Ph.D. with Dr. Hargis Westerfield, Division Historian

Before he slugged it out with his BAR to win his Distinguished Service Cross near Zamboanga, Charlie Solley had already fought well on Biak. Still under 20 years old, Solley was a dedicated combat soldier of high morale. Earlier, although he had thought of becoming a minister and hated to think of killing anyone, he fought governments that murdered German Jews or Americans at Pearl Harbor. Throughout the war, he bore a New Testament in his pack.

Charlie's Southern Philippine of 1945 actually began before the real campaign. It started up north on dusty Mindoro Island near Manila where the 41st staged for Zamboanga. I Co 186 Inf sent a Pln on security patrol for Japs. As we walked on an air strip, U.S. soldiers fired on us. A bullet wounded Gilbert in his left arm. We dropped and yelled to cease fire. Gilbert survived his wound, rejoined us at Zambo.

On Palawan, this Pln had another small action — during our pursuit of fugitive Japs on the rocky surf-swept coast of western Palawan. In some places, the only trail below the ridges had to be along slippery rocks dashed over by the waves. We hiked on GI shoes with rifles, extra heavy ammo, extra rations. Some men almost slid into the surf to drown, but we grabbed them and saved them from being carried out to sea and battered to death against the cliffs. (Thus died K Co's Campbell.)

One I Co Sgt and six men were still lost in the mountain wilderness. Solley, Sgt Shrimp, Wissel, and three others sought them for three nerve-wracking days. Japs had cut the phone line and hidden the wire under rocks. We never found them, but they escaped the Japs and returned to life.

Then "I" with our 3/Bn left Palawan to reinforce 186's 1/Bn who had already helped 162 Inf to storm Mt. Capisan, Jap stronghold of Zambo Province's western defenses.

First combat of Solley's 3/Pln came on 1 Apr 1945 when we relieved K 186 fighting for Sugarloaf Mtn north of Zamboanga City. Ten die-hard Nips held 3/Pln from crossing the low ridge before the mtn. Our FA and Marine bombers had bared the ridge of jungle. Every time we tried to crawl over the rocks, rifles and a MG stopped us. Knee-mortar fragments holed Solley's helmet.

Finally at 0710, FA shelled again, and 3/Pln dashed across the ridge. Other I Co men found the 10 Japs in three pillboxes on the reverse slope of the Mtn. Two Japs were persuaded to surrender; the other eight were dynamited to death.

Next sharp action of Solley's Pln was on 3 Apr when 186 attacked Moroc Pocket. This was a plateau some five miles north of Zambo City, held by mortars and MGs, on 3-5 April.

On 3 Apr, Sgt Shrimp's squad patrolled near Moroc Village. After crossing a wide trail with big trees to our right, we sensed Japs. Then two MGs and 20-30 rifles fired on us. We flattened to the ground, hid behind the trees.

Now we had to retreat across the opening back to our officers. While we took turns drawing fire, a man at a time would dart across the trail and drop behind an old dead tree. BARman Solley ran last. Nobody was wounded; Solley and three others got holes in their fatigues.

While we hugged the ground, 2/Lt Pierce, surely a rookie, stood up behind us in plain view. We heard the Japs talking. Pierce ordered us back across that deadly ground. He threatened to "bust" us and jail us when we refused.

A Jap bullet shot Pierce in the throat. We had to crawl to pull out the badly bleeding Lt. Pierce seems to have survived, but we never saw him again.

After stubborn resistance on 5 Apr and a Jap counter attack, 186 overran Moroc Pocket. Probably next day, 3/Pln patrolled down the narrow trail. Men in Shrimp's understrength squad were BARman Solley, assistant Wissel, Steward, Johnson, Wieczorek, and a man nicknamed "Swede." Like a mountain goat's footpath, our narrow little trail followed the edge of an 80-foot drop — so narrow that we had to hang onto any brush that would support us. The drop was almost straight down.

Stewart's helmet fell off his head, made alarming noises as it bounced down 80 feet. Lower down, the trail grew easier and wider. We found many Jap "houses," brushy lean-tos, small saplings and leaves. (Stewart recovered his helmet.)

The Japs had fled but for a sick man. Some men wanted to kill him then, but Solley prevented them. Solley talked to him in the few Japanese words that he knew, gave him food and water. The Jap said that there were nine Japs close by near the river. Solley thought that the prisoner said, "Nine Japanese," but he had actually said, "Ninety" — Solley's deadly mistake.

Slowly we patrolled down the riverbank trail. Johnson ran first scout, with Sgt Shrimp next in line, then BAR team Solley and Wissel, then "Swede," Wieczorek, and Stewart.

Suddenly Scout Johnson sensed death in the brush ahead, and dropped into a crouch. A Jap Nambu (LMG) fired. It seemed to fell Johnson, but he wasn't hit. Solley knelt and volleyed his BAR the Nambu sound, and retarded its fire. Johnson rose and ran back. Solley and Wissel fired

"... [Charlie] Solley was a dedicated combat soldier of high morale. Earlier, although he had thought of becoming a minister and hated to think of killing anyone, he fought governments that murdered German Jews or Americans at Pearl Harbor. Throughout the war, he bore a New Testament in his pack."

in a second Nambu — results unknown.

On the trail behind us, more Japs were closing in. We couldn't retreat or advance without annihilation.

Sgt Shrimp helped us to escape sideways — down across the Missaloy River. We sat safely and unseen behind boulders.

(Just before crossing, Solley looked straight back at his tall young Jap prisoner, who looked straight back at Solley. The Jap accepted his death, with a formal bow. Solley shot, yet he still feels guilty, even if he had to kill to secure himself and his buddies.)

Darkness fell. Jap mortars still impacted the trail we had come down. We heard voices of the Japs trying to find us. We huddled silently behind our boulders safe across the Missaloy.

After about two hours, Solley crawled to the other men of the squad and coaxed them to eat from their rations. About 0400 in that dark, we faced up to the fact that we had to do something desperate about our predicament. It was easier than we thought. On wet bellies, we crawled back across the river past the Japs in the dark, and tensely made it back up the mountain.

(Meanwhile, the 1/Lt with his other two squads had retreated back up the wider trail. Nobody with him was wounded. They were hopeful for us because they still heard the Japs firing, even if we were silent.

After we climbed the mountain trail, our own FA began to fire down into the area where we had fought the Japs and hidden. We had escaped our own shellfire. Back home with I Co, we were slapped on the back and hugged to be alive.

Next day, "I" returned to look for the Japs again. They had vanished and left behind two corpses. Solley looked for a bunch of ripening bananas which he had carried along for snacks for his squad. The Jap he had to kill had also shared them. They were all shot up!

This nightmarish Missaloy patrol ended the first phase of I Co 186 Infantry and Solley's Battle of Zamboanga. By 18 May, I Co was in rest-camp down by a coconut grove. We slept blissfully dry on cots under canvas near a cool stream where Filipina women laundered their clothes. We watched cock-fights and movies.

While in rest-camp, Solley and a young Filipina woman became very good friends. To take her to a GI movie, he would walk the 10 miles from her home to the show, with her grandma as chaperone. He wrote a fine poem which he gave this "tiny slant-eyed goddess, to love by sight and touch." Yet the poem says that he kissed her just once, and that was to say good-bye. Celia was the mother of a child by her guerilla husband whom the Japs had killed. Theirs was a brief, innocent friendship of the kind that some other 41sters still remember. But Solley was called back to battle; he would see her only once more for the rest of his life.

About a month after our rest-camp, we had our second Zambo Battle. This was against the retreating Zambo Jap garrison, probably members of 33rd Naval Guards (Jap Marines). Theirs was an orderly retreat up the west coast into a jungle rain forest wilderness like New Guinea's.

Landing from Amphib craft on 17 May we had hot, sweaty or rain-chilled patrols to kill a few elusive Japs. On 22 May Solley with Sgt Shrimp's little squad found battle somewhere up the dry bed of what was probably Montibug River, near coastal Anungan Village. We penetrated into a bivouac area of 100 Japs still heavily armed with rifles, MGs, mortars.

Sgt Shrimp told Solley and Bernie Wieczorek to check out a small cave the Japs fired from. We climbed on top of the cave. Below us, outside the cave, was a hidden Jap rifleman positioned to fire down on I Co.

Bernie held fire on that Jap until Solley with his BAR crouched near the cave-mouth and nodded to him. Then Bernie slew that Jap. Rifleman Bernie and BARman Solley then shot into the cave-mouth. Either he or Solley killed two Japs coming out to fight with an old U.S. BAR. Solley ran into the cave to seize the Japs' BAR.

More Japs blazed from inside the cave, but missed. Solley rolled from the mouth and hurled a grenade back into darkness. Thinking all were dead, he tried to get that BAR again.

Living Japs fired again from the dark. Solley threw a second grenade — this time, followed through. Crawling in with a knife, he felt bodies and stabbed them to be sure they

> "At a Zambo hospital, it took 30 minutes for doctors to extract the bullet from his intestines. He was still paralyzed. His girlfriend Celia walked 40 kilometers for his last visit from her, but his follow-up letter probably never reached her."

were dead. The cave was silent. Solley and Bernie had slain eight Japs at the cave.

Thus on 22 May began Solley's greatest and final day of battle which won him a DSC — "Distinguished Service Cross." After the cave victory, he advanced in I Co's forefront towards a high hill surrounded by wide trees and thick brush.

About 300 from that brush, unseen Japs flailed us, with at least two Nambu LMGs. Scout Bernie Wieczorck dropped with bullets in stomach and intestines. Medic Mascio ran to help him, but an arm wound halted Mascio. Our Lt was pinned behind a tree bole — the Japs still invisible.

Although safe behind a tree, BARman Solley and helper Wissel knew that Bernie must be saved. To locate the Japs' fire, Solley had to draw fire himself. He simply arose and fired his BAR on automatic. His first clip emptied; he slipped in a second clip and fired on.

Now he saw two Japs with a US BAR and three riflemen and slew all five. Wissel kicked one body, found it alive, and killed him for sure. But around Solley were still two Nambus firing from the blind brush. With another clip in his BAR, he stood up and strode forward until he saw two Nippos shooting their Nambu. He slew that gun-crew, while their guard of three Jap riflemen missed him. He killed that trio of riflemen, and fired at several other fleeing Japs.

Now Solley fired standing at the second Jap LMG high on the hill. Then from a tree top directly above, a Jap rifleman shot straight down into Solley's back. The bullet penetrated into his intestines. He fell, like being hit with a sledgehammer. Weissel killed the Jap who had shot Solley.

But the Jap had paralyzed Solley's legs. He still crawled as far as he could to fight that final LMG. He still doesn't know how he managed to empty his BAR into that Nambu with his left hand. With his right hand, he then lifted his body to roll it down the slope. Bernie Wieczorek still lived, and transfusions saved Bernie's and Solley's lives. The Japs broke off the fight and scattered in all directions.

(Official US report is that the fight of 2 I Co 186 Inf Plans was against over 100 Japs in a large bivouac area between high ridges. It lasted four hours, in three phases. In Phase 1 our fire superiority drove them back a few hundred yards. In Phase 2, they made a second fighting stand as soon as our Plns continued advancing. Only in Phase 3 did we finally break the back of their resistance and scatter them. In return for wounds of Mascio, Wieczorck, and Solley, we killed 41 Japs, even took a prisoner.)

But Solley's war was over. At a Zambo hospital, it took 30 minutes for doctors to extract the bullet from his intestines. He was still paralyzed. (His girlfriend Celia walked 40 kilometers for his last visit from her, but his follow-up letter probably never reached her.) Solley was finally able to walk, and was discharged from the Army in Temple, Texas, about seven months after his wound. Although never fully recovered, he managed to get a Ph.D. in psychology, and is now a college professor. He is still rightly proud of his great war in the SW Pacific.

CREDIT: Credit begins with publication of two Solley letters which Secretary Chester Clark of Great Lakes Chapter placed in August 1986 *Jungleer*. Core of this history is 28 pages of double-spaced typescript which Solley sent the Historian in the next two years. Also useful was his poem, "By the Shining Sulu Sea." Framework of this history is I 186's "Two Battles of Samboanga," rewritten and adapted for *Jungleer* (No. 122, April, 1980). I referred also to 3/Bn 186's "Casualty List" and I 186's report, both under heading of "Panganuran-Anungan-Sibuko Operation." Despite his serious wound, Solley recovered to get his Ph.D. from the University of Illinois, now is a college professor in Psychology at the University of Detroit.

K Company, 162 Infantry: Balut Island to Calinan

by Dr. Hargis Westerfield, Division Historian, with K 162's Charles Brockman & Bob Irick

This is the story of K Co-162 Inf's wars in southern Mindanao, when we fought for the 24 Div to defeat the Jap 100 Div north of Davao City. We had two main actions. First came the amphibious expedition far south of Davao City into Sarnagani Bay on the southernmost tip of Mindanao. Most memorable part of this expedition was the landing on Balut Island. Second action was the hard battle to capture Calinan north of Davao City. Calinan was the center of resistance for the Second Defense line of Gen. Jiro Harada's 100 Div.

Leaving newly won Zamboanga City at 1300 hours 3 May, "K" with our 162 Regt voyaged over 150-mile Moro Gulf and arrived at Parang on the main part of Mindanao Island at 0800, 4 May 1945. Leaving most of the 162 Inf to guard 24 Div's lines of communication across southern Mindanao to Davao Gulf, "K" started with the rest of 3/Bn on its detached mission.

With our 3/Bn and attached C Btry 205 FA, we got orders to join 24 Div in the Davao City area immediately. Traveling in LSTs, we voyaged an estimated 300 miles around the great southward projecting mass of mountains and swamps of southern Mindanao. Rounding Tinaca Point, which is the farthest southern land on Mindanao, we traveled north into Davao Gulf for about 100 miles. Landing at Talomo on the western side of Davao Gulf about 20 miles southeast of Davao City, we saw that battle was going on close by.

Marine Dauntless dive bombers were striking at Nippo positions so close that we saw white stars on the fuselages. Farther left, we viewed tall, snow-topped Mt. Apo (9,693 feet) and feared that we would have to storm it.

About 1200, "K" boarded 6x6 trucks and rode north down a narrow concrete two-lane highway through the jungle. We were still surprised to ride again on the right side of the road instead of the left side, as in Australia-New Guinea. We saw many 155 mm guns towed by heavy tractors. All bridges were blasted away and replaced by temporary structures.

That night in perimeter, Brockman heard eight M-1 shots and a grenade blast. Next morning, Ball exhibited a fine saber to reward him for last night's shooting. (We do not know how many Japs died that night.)

After 2-3 days' security patrols when some 90 mm Jap mortars landed too close to us, we trucked south again. We were riding down the shore to Malalag where PT boats had a base near their supply tender.

On the afternoon of 12 May, K's convoy halted while advance elements scouted the area. We heard a terrific explosion. A mine had blown up our command jeep. First/Sgt De Ryk died at once; Capt Watson died of wounds that same day. Lucky Driver Gribbons survived with only a face wound.

In this Malalag area on the west coast of Davao Gulf, K Co spent about two weeks in routine security patrols. With other 3/Bn 162 Cos, 162's I & R and 640 TD, 205 FA, and guerillas, we secured routes across southern Mindanao back to the west coast. We protected large Padada Strip, and the rear of 24 Div which was now fighting from Davao City northward. For to the south of us above Sarangani Bay were 2,000 organized Nips who potentially threatened the rear of 24 Div.

Then after two weeks, "K" embarked from Malalag on one of our Div's last amphib raids of the war against Sarangani Bay Japs. "K" was the core of a sea-borne force to clear the last Jap bases on the southernmost part of the Mindanao coast. Here Japs had set up motor torpedo boat bases to raid our Navy, but too late in the war to be effective.

It seemed a large force. Guarded by Destroyer Escort Leland E. Thomas, Destroyer Flusser, PT boats and LCIs with rockets or guns, we boarded some 10 LCMs. Including 12 men of Naval Fire Support, our force totalled 260.

K Co made three landings. First was on 1 June at Luayon, about 30 miles downshore from our Malalag base. After an hour's destroyer bombardment and air-strike, we landed and destroyed the radio station. We found three Japs dead already, killed two, and wounded one who escaped. (As of 30 May 60 Japs had garrisoned Luayon with several MGs and AA guns.)

Second landing on Balut Island 3 June, was most eventful. Located off Tinaca Point, most southern tip of all Mindanao, Balut Island is 23 square miles in area, with a volcano 29,895 feet in height.

But men like K Co's BARman Irick saw no volcano. To him and other "K" men, Balut was just another jungle terrain for tiresome, sweaty hiking in full pack. Balut was the hottest place that we had ever known in the Philippines. Almost everybody seemed to suffer from heat exhaustion.

Landing at 0800, "K" started out in open, flat country

and patrolled slowly and steadily inland. Covering several miles, we saw no Japs or Filipinos — of a post-war population of 1,377 Filipinos.

Next day, 4 June, Balut seemed still hotter, but we again found no Japs of the estimated garrison of 40-50 — largely naval personnel, with a mobile radio station. Relieved, we expected to leave our harmless objective and head "home" for Malalag without fighting.

Then suddenly, intense rifle fire struck at us. We thought that a whole company of Japs were firing — steeled ourselves for a charge.

Fearfully hiding behind a large rock, Irick did not take time to look around. Encumbered by his BAR and heavy equipment, he painfully slid down a stony gorge. At the end of the slide, he was in pain. Medics bandaged him and splinted his leg. Although carried on a litter back to the barges, he had nothing broken. (Irick spent just some 10 days at 52 Field Hospital before rejoining K Co.)

But Jap rifle fire ceased before us; nobody charged. Of those 40-50 estimated Jap "marines" on Balut as of 26 May, we slew just three. We demolished their radio station, and all other installations, and a three-inch gun. MGs had already been smashed before we landed.

K's third and final landing was on 5 June at Cape San Agustin, back eastward across 30-mile wide Davao Gulf. Cape San Agustin was another of the southern points of Mindanao. PT boats had already brought off two plantation owners with accurate data on the Japs. Earlier reports had credited this 100-man garrison with two 6-inch guns, two .50 HMG guns, but the bombardment chased the Japs deep into the jungle. With no reported Jap or U.S. casualties, we destroyed a radio, two large generators, two fuel dumps, a 20 mm gun, and small arms ammo.

For all three landings, we finally claimed a total kill of six Nips, one probable, besides another 10 whom the Filipinos reported as killed. (It would be many years before "K" men realized that 2,000 Japs, well-fed and in good condition, were alive in the Sarangani Bay hills.) With about 450 naval troops were some Cos of 167 and 168 Jap Inf, and some FA. Five weeks after "K" left Sarangani Bay, a special U.S.-Filipino task force concluded organized resistance on 25 July after killing 450 Japs. Ironically, Sarangani Bay was where Gen. MacArthur had planned his first invasion to reconquer the Philippines. It became the site of the last attack against unmolested Japs in the Philippines.

K's return from Cape San Agustin meant the finish of our first main action in southern Mindanao. In our second main action, "K" with our 3/Bn fought the entrenched Jap 100 Div. These Japs still held out bravely, only 17 miles northwest of Davao City, in the dark abaca hemp jungle of the Talomo River bottom. The 24 Div had broken Gen. Jiro Harada's First Defense Line in six weeks of battle, but now the worn 24 Div men moved to the flank while 162's 1/Bn and 3/Bn and our attached 3/Bn entered the Talomo cockpit. With 24 Div, our 41 Div units shared in probably the hardest fighting of the campaign to seize the Mindanao mainland from the Japs.

Relieving 3/Bn 34 Inf 4,000 yards north of Ula on 13 June, 3/Bn was to secure the road junction 3,000 yards east of Calinan, and from there strike Calinan itself.

When I and K Cos moved on 14 June, "K" was in reserve. At 1045, a Jap knee mortar harassed us. It fired a few rounds, then moved several hundred yards and fired again. Our 60s evidently silenced that mortar, which only damaged a LMG of ours. But ahead of us, I Co suffered heavily from a Jap mortar and a 75 mm cannon — had three killed, 12 wounded.

Next day, 15 June, K Co passed through I Co now in reserve — and pushed with two tanks of 716 Tank Bn. At 1800, "K" slew 17 Japs at a village road junction. Lightly wounded were Corolla, Lt. Baldwin. We dug in for the night just south of that road junction.

At dusk 16 June, "K" suffered the tragic instant death of four Sgts from one shell. The morning had gone well enough. Despite 90 mm mortars, knee mortars, and even Jap fire from M-1s that they had captured somewhere else, we had knocked out a pillbox and were within 75 yards of the next road junction. That morning, we had lost two wounded, and at 1340, a Jap MG wounded three more men. Only this is known about the five men.

When "K" gathered for close about dusk, a Jap 75 shell hit with such accuracy that we suspect observers were close. Probably because of this pin-pointing by nearby Japs, four Sgts were killed. Sgt Torre died, with S/Sgts Hartmann, Kmicinski and McShane. We believe that not one man of the four knew what hit him. Irick surmises that he too missed death with Torre and "Chink" Kmicinski only because he was then on outguard. Marked seriously wounded was Lopez. Arcangeletti, Gerlach, Earl Hall, Litke and McElroy were lightly wounded. That night, mortars harassed us from the northwest. Small Jap groups shot into our perimeter, but caused no casualties.

The Japs before us fought as bravely as ever. Lacking planes and tanks and with only outranged 75 mm cannon short of ammo, they still resisted doggedly. They did have the advantage of concealment among dark, tall acres of abandoned and overgrown abaca (Filipino hemp) fields. And Gen. Harada had thrown in his best troops (probably 167 and 168 Inf Regts) until the survivors had escaped into the mountains.

On 18 June, although all fronts still resisted heavily, 162 Hqs said that resistance was more scattered than before. The attached 3/Bn 163 Inf had not seized Calinan Village on 18 June, and thus relieved 162's 1/Bn to fight westward from Calinan. K Co's own 3/Bn fought strong Jap positions northwest of Calinan. It failed to crack the Jap strong point west of the first road junction 700 yards northwest of Calinan. Here I Co was forced to dig in. K Co

CREDIT: Charles Brockman supplied a three-page manuscript. Bob Irick wrote on 12 May, about 1 June, then 19 June, 21 June, 29 June, 20 July, 4 Sept., 9 Oct. — all in 1981. I used also 162's V-5 Operation "Report of Operations," and "Journal" beginning 4 May 1945, along with "Preliminary Joint Discussion on Clearing the Davao Gulf Shore" (26 May 1948), and 162's "Casualty List" — although the V-5 List wrongly omits any mention before 13 June 1945. Important was Samuel Eliot Morison's Vol XIII of his *History of U.S. Naval Operations in World War II,* on Luayon, Balut Island, and Cape San Agustin. Useful also were R. R. Smith's *Triumph in the Philippines* and Gen. Douglas MacArthur's *Japanese Operations in the SW Pacific Area.* This is the only full-length history that I have of any 162 Regt outfit in Central Mindanao.

lost Lyon, lightly wounded. But the Japs again withdrew, now that they had lost Calinan.

Now our 3/Bn had to clear Japs from north and far northeast of Calinan. We had cleared Villafuerte, Dacodao and Lascon Plantation.

On 19 June, "K" advanced up Villafuerte Road on ground that Japs had held shortly before. About 1600, we met heavy MG and rifle fire from a Jap pillbox and vicinity, 300 yards north of the road junction. Two more pillboxes then fired. Our patrol withdrew and called down FA on the pillboxes, but too late that day to appraise results. On that 19 June, Parrish was lightly wounded, Stambaugh lightly injured. At 2230 that night, "K" in perimeter slew three Japs. Next day, the pillboxes were deserted.

On 20 June, K Co again met heavy resistance northeast of Villafuerte road junction. Lightly wounded was Gibert — Turner lightly injured. Wilkins Sr. was killed, our final battle death of "K."

Next, 3/Bn had to fight in the Mt. Monoy ridge mass where some Japs still held out. On 21 June, while 1/Bn 162 cleared the southwest section, 3/Bn had to storm the northeast part. Despite Jap 75 FA and mortars, L Co with our FA preparation took Mt. Monoy. "K" joined "L" on the summit about 1830.

Finally, "K" was in probably the 41st Div's last fight of World War II. After an AT 162 patrol recoiled from the fire of four automatic weapons on the dirt road southeast of Lorenzo, "K" acted. On 27 June, we seized high ground near where "AT" had escaped. On 28 June, L Co passed through our position but met a small holocaust — five dead and 12 wounded. ("K" lost nobody.) Not until 30 June, after CN 162's preparation and with two tanks' help, did 3/Bn advance again. The Japs' 22 pillboxes were totally deserted. The whole 62 Inf sector was now totally cleared of Japs.

Thus ended K 162's war for the 24 Div in the Davao area. Losses were luckily few, but we still lament the death of four fine Sgts by one shell, and excellent Capt Watson with 1/Sgt DeRyk. We would be happy for the close of K Co's final action of World War II.

Wau-Mubo area, New Guinea. Australian Pvt. Keith McLeod of Malla Couta, Victoria advances through the thick jungle undergrowth. (Courtesy of Rohlffs)

E Company, 163 Infantry: Insoemani, Liki, and Toem Foreshore

by Dr. Hargis Westerfield, Division Historian

In the Toem-Wakde Operation, E Co 163 Inf endured our own shellfire on Insoemanai Island, then seized Liki Island, and finally skirmished with Matsuyama Force at Toem.

Landing safely on 17 May 1944 under furious air and navy bombardment, we had a brisk little engagement with the Japs. Patrolling from Toem, T/Sgt Larsen heard Jap talk ahead of him. When his patrol stepped up to shoot, 2 Jap scouts saw them too soon. We killed the first scout, but the second ran. One man, name unknown, chased the Jap, but fell wounded but still under fire. Larsen divided his patrol to flank the Japs, then took 3 men down-trail to draw fire.

When Jap fires drove Larsen and his 3 to earth, Larsen saw that the Japs had turned their rifles on the wounded man. Larsen leaped up and rushed to save him. His 3 front men and the flankers hit the Japs right then. They broke and ran and left behind weapons and packs — and 12 dead.

Meanwhile, E Co readied to seize Insoemanai Island to fire to secure for landing our Provisional Groupment of heavy weapons. They were to blast Wakde Island tomorrow before 1/Bn landed. Wakde lies half a mile north of Insoemanai. Tiny Insoemanai is between Wakde and the Toem mainland, and roughly parallel to Wakde. About 750 yards long and 200 yards across, it was covered with thick brush and a few coconut trees.

About 1045, with needless preparatory fire from 2 destroyers and 2 rocket LCIs, 2/Lt Ritzenhein's E Co's Pln's landing craft grounded on a coral reef off Insoemanai. Wading in 75 yards, we found no Japs. Then most of "E" with the Provisional Groupment of heavy weapons landed and positioned. E Co's and AT Co's .50 HMGs first arrived, and D and H Co's HMGs and .81s completed the Insoemanai garrison. The Groupment was ready for enfilade fire on Wakde to protect 163's waterborne attack tomorrow.

On Insoemanai we found no Japs — only 5 long deserted native huts. But on Insoemanai, "E" suffered 5 — or probably 6 — killed and 5 seriously wounded — our top number of daily casualties in the whole New Guinea Campaign.

We dug in our MGs on the open beach. Although we were about 500 yards from the long southern peninsula of silent Wakde Island, we believed by now that no Japs could menace us from there.

Suddenly a Jap sniper struck from Wakde. Our 1/Lt Hutton was shot in the right chest and fell in the sniper's sights. Lampe left a safe place and began to drag Hutton behind rocks and trees. That same sniper hit Lampe in the head, but he kept on dragging Hutton. Lampe died a few minutes later. (As for Hutton, the Casualty List calls Hutton "seriously wounded," but our final Division roster of the dead carries the name "William G. Hutton." First name, initials, last name are the same as our Lt's.

S/Sgt Nolan was seriously wounded, gunshot in right knee, and Ellingham lightly wounded, shot in his chest. (One of these 2 men may have been earlier wounded that 17 May in T/Sgt Larsen's patrol's fight near Toem.)

Mortars neutralized the sniper fire, which we now think to have come from near Wakde Jetty. But Insoemanai would still be a place of death or wounds for 6 more "E" men.

In the dark about 2200, our own misguided FA shells impacted on our Insoemania position. They deflected eastward and missed the long southern Wakde cape by 500 yards. Everyone not on guard was blasted awake. E Co's Capt Zimmerman reported 5 air bursts and 5 impacts. Killed was Sgt Thomas. Cpl Sarno was slashed in abdomen and Schmidt in right side; both would die tomorrow at Toem. Sgt Serino was gouged down his right side — right hand, right leg, and right hip. Seriously wounded also were Peterson — right side; Reeson — left ankle and right hip; and Richardson — lower hip. Because of the number of hip wounds, perhaps these 4 men were all caught asleep on their sides.

The first shell severed the phone line of our Insoemanai FA observer. He raced past H Co's HMGs to Group Hq to phone to halt the shelling while other men furiously dug at the coral stone to grovel from any more fire. But no more shells hit Insoemanai that night. We lay on that remote little island with only the wounded or dying while Medics worked on them — and the fear that another wild shell might blast us.

Which battalion of 191 FA Group at Toem fired those projectiles on us — 218 FA, 146 FA, or Cannon Co 163 Inf? The 191 FA Group Hq reported that CN Co fired on our own Regt because they were inexperienced in gunnery.

But next morning, we jaded, sleep-starved "E" men crouched at our HMGs. With AT and D and H Cos, we volleyed Jap Wakde, then took Jap fire in return while our landing barges drove for Wakde Beach. We easily won our morning duel — fired until the attack waves of 163 men came between us and the struggling Japs.

But E Co did not fight on bloody Wakde. At 1148 18 May, while 1/Bn and F Co battled for Wakde Strip, "E" had orders to capture another remote little islet for a 5th Air Force radar warning station. The islet was Liki, 20-25 miles west of Insoemanai, and 16 miles out at sea from Jap-held

After a small holocaust from our own shells on Insoemanai, we island-hopped to land safely on Liki. Then we had fought well on rear-guard at Toem. We had 5 or 6 dead, and 7 wounded. But our action in the Toem-Wakde Operation was only a prelude to harder fighting on Biak.

Sarmi Town on the New Guinea Mainland. Much larger than Insoemanai, Liki was 4 miles long, about 20 miles square. Against an alert, aggressive Jap garrison, E Co could encounter bitter jungle fighting.

On 19 May, E Co joined a sizable landing force to capture both main Koemamba Islands, the name of the group Liki belongs to. Convoy consisted of 2 attack transports, 2 LCTs, with 2 destroyers. Aboard with "E" was I Co 163 Inf, whose mission was to land on Niroemar, a smaller island a few miles east and secure the ground for another radar station.

While "E" waited for the destroyer bombardment to cease, we saw before us on the SW side of Liki, a sandy, flat beach — only beach in the whole steep-sided island. Covered with jungle, Liki rose before us to 3 wooded peaks, the center and highest peak 1039 feet.

Landing was unopposed. By 1140, Capt Zimmerman reported that "E" had entered Saoe Village, and by 1245 had scouted 600 yards east of Saoe, and found no Japs. By 1248, we were on the west coast, 200 yards past Isjuma Village. Isjuma had been evacuated by Japs several days ago. By 1430, an LST was unloading the Air Force radar; and by 1847, all of "E" but 2/Lt Ritzenhein's security Pln was returning to Toem.

By 20 May, Ritzenhein's Pln had picked up 5 natives with their chief, whom the pre-landing bombardment had slightly wounded. We found just 31 natives on Liki, although others may have easily hidden in the uplands. Only Jap signs were a few saki bottles, maybe 12 L-shaped trenches, a grave, and Jap clothing on some natives. The natives said that 30 days ago, the 38-man Jap detachment had forced them to gather all available food for the Japs to take to Sarmi. After sending an "E" squad to replace all I Co on Niroemar, Lt Ritzenhein would soon rejoin "E" at Toem.

When E Co returned to the Toem Foreshore, we dug in strongly in our 2/Bn on rear-guard of 163 beach-head, on Tementoe Creek. (Hollandia was about 143 miles east of the Tementoe.) Left of us, G Co anchored 2/Bn on the seashore, and battered D Co back from Wakde, lay holed up on our right. With other 2/Bn men, E's objective was to secure 163's rear from Col Soemon Matsuyama's 224 Inf. We were in the possible line of a drive from Matsuyama Force, which had earlier trekked east to recover Hollandia from the 41st. Maj-Gen Hachiro Tanoue, however, had recalled Matsuyama to help defend Sarmi. About 3,000 survivors of the Hollandia garrison had also made their way through 143 miles of jungle from Hollandia to join Gen Tanoue.

While 1/Bn 163 Inf set up tents west of us under protection of a few scattered MG positions, 2/Bn 163 Inf slept every night in holes on guard, and patrolled daily. Soon we found the Jap fighters.

On 23 May, an "E" patrol marched east across Tementoe Creek towards Kedir Village, about 2 miles away. Thick flat jungle was everywhere except on the narrow beach. We sighted 11 Japs in 3 groups — one of 5 men, another of 4, and a third of 2. In the fire-fight, Sgt Peters was seriously wounded — gunshot in right shoulder. After our fire-power repelled the 11, we were in turn halted by Jap rifles. Every move drew fire from what we thought to be a small defense position, which we could not see. We fell back in order, while our FA hit their hidden positions.

Next day, 25 May, 2/Lt Larsen's G Co patrol of 28 men with extra BARs went out to search for the 11 Japs. This time, when "G" tried to cross a stream on a log footbridge, an estimated 20 Japs with 2 automatic weapons crossfired on the bridge. "G" lost scout Freddie Marooch of the Netherlands Indies Civil Administration (NICA), and G's Vitosky with a head wound. G's patrol fell back without recovering Marooch. In mid-morning next day, a 6-man "G" patrol found 5 freshly dug foxholes on the coast track to Kedir Village, and saw 3 Japs crossing the track west of the holes. Japs had certainly occupied this area.

Next day, 26 May, E Co sent 6 men, including a Sgt and another NICA man to find NICA Marooch. At 1145, we saw his body, but no longer on that log bridge. It was removed to the far side of the stream, as if to tempt us into ambush. We saw no Japs, but just as we tried to cross, a LMG opened up from near the trail. We escaped unharmed.

On 27 May, E Co moved out in strength to force that log bridge crossing and recover Marooch. Attached to our 67 from "E" were an officer and 2 men of H Co's 81s, an officer and 3 Cannon Co men, 2 Intelligence men, and 5 Medics. This patrol turned out to be a recon in force that should have alerted the whole Regt to strengthen our perimeters.

This time, a probable preparatory bombardment seems to have helped "E" cross that stream on that log bridge. We advanced 500 yards before Jap contact. After a vicious fire-fight, the Japs pulled back down the trail.

Although we advanced 100 more yards, Jap firepower drove us to earth. We tried to flank the Japs with a squad, but their rifles stopped us. Moxey lay mortally wounded, his body exposed on the side of the log which Jap eyes watched over their rifles. Their close fire kept us from dragging Moxey's corpse over to the safe side of the log. Finally, S/Sgt Muchmore crawled to the log and pulled the body over to what would have been safety if Moxey still lived.

Our slightest move now drew Jap bullets that seemed to come from everywhere, but S/Sgt Newman noted direction of the main fire while Muchmore pulled Moxey back over the log. Although he drew some shots, Newman crawled towards the log. A few yards from the sniper, Newman stopped crawling, lay quiet as if dead. Suddenly he stood up to his full height and fired rapidly. He killed 2 Japs and neutralized the most dangerous position.

Now Muchmore and Newman redeployed and attacked. Our M-1s repelled the Japs. Instead of the expected bunkers, we found only deserted Jap foxholes.

Besides losing E's Moxey killed, we lost also H Co's Holbrook wounded some time during this fight. We brought back the corpses of Moxey and NICA Marooch. We had won our small battle, but the Jap outfit that we had fought, was still intact deep in that blind jungle.

On the night of that same 27 May, a command from Matsuyama Force charged into 163's tents at Toem. Wisely avoiding our 2/Bn's deadly perimeters on the Tementoe, they chose a vacant jungle near B 116 Medics for deployment. Some 200 Jap riflemen, mortarmen, and machine-gunners broke into 163's camp. Motor pool guards finally smashed them near the shore. Except for men well dug in like our 2/Bn, 163 Inf had a wild night until the last Japs were expelled.

Today it seems that the Japs fighting "E" and "G" on 23-27 May were a decoy force to conceal Matsuyama's plans to overrun 163 Inf. They had left that log bridge unbroken to draw us over it in their direction — and had moved Marooch's body across to be sure that we would follow. Their ruse succeeded.

But as for E 163, our Toem-Wakde action was finished, although we did not reinforce our 41st on Biak until 12 June. After a small holocaust from our own shells on Insoemanai, we had island-hopped to land safely on Liki. then we had fought well on rear-guard at Toem. We had 5 or 6 dead, and 7 wounded. But our action in the Toem-Wakde Operation was only a prelude to harder fighting on Biak.

CREDIT: This history I pieced together mainly from award stories of Leo Lampe, T/Sgt (later Lt) Don Larsen, and S/Sgts William Muchmore and John Newman, with help of 163's Toem-Wakde Journal. Much help came also from R. R. Smith's *Approach to the Philippines,* and *Terrain Handbook No. 26* (Sarmi) from Allied Geographical Section, Southwest Pacific Area (New Guinea). Help came also from my own "War of Nerves at Toem," (*Jungleer,* Jan 1979). E Co's Don Torgerson identified Larsen as being an E Co man also.

Our Amphibian Engineers (542 EB & SR, 2 ESB): Beachhead Battles for Biak

by Dr. Hargis Westerfield, Division Historian

Amphibian Engrs of 542 Engr Boat and Shore Regt with other Amphib attachments played crucial parts in the 41st's Biak victory. In combat, we helped make Bosnek Beachhead. We rescued many 162 Inf men from the Parai Defile disaster — especially the wounded. In combat also, we supplied 186 Inf to hold Mokmer Strip during their first crucial days after capturing it.

At daybreak 27 May 1944 after Navy and Air bombardment, we Amphibs launched our barges from LSTs and loaded infantry to hit Bosnek Beach. At 0657, Wave No 1 of 20 LVTs (tracked) formed and headed for Bosnek. Second and third waves, each of 20 LVTs, followed 5 minutes apart. Waves Nos 4 and 5 went next — 13, and then 12 DUKWs — amphibious trucks. After small support ships fired 684 rockets, our MGs quickly silenced light Jap mortar and MG fire.

But coxswains could not see the beach through bombardment smoke. An unknown 4-knot current deflected our prows west. Instead of coral beaches, Wave No 1 saw only a mangrove swamp. First 4 waves landed 2-3,000 yards west of Bosnek Beach.

Luckily, the Japs' 2/Bn 222 Inf did not attack, and 186 Inf's men landed safely. Only near Bosnek, the Japs would fight piecemeal from fixed positions. Most of Waves 1-4 and part of Wave 5 beached wrongly, and 186's men marched to their original objectives.

Meanwhile Amphibs of 542 Regt's Shore Bn tried to find a landing beach for 8 LCTs. For protection against possible Jap attacks, their tanks and guns must be quickly beached. But everywhere, the reef was a solid barrier to flat-bottomed craft. Finally, Amphibs found that opposite the shore farthest east, the reef curved inward to within 10 yards of the sand.

When an LCT struck for that reef, Jap fire began. The LCT pulled back to safety, and a destroyer and a rocket LCI impacted the Japs while 186 men flanked them on the beach. After the Japs' defeat, the LCT unloaded in 3-5 feet of water 10 yards out. The other 7 LCTs had to unload tanks, guns, bulldozers into small Amphib craft to ferry them ashore.

Landing was lightly opposed, yet dangerous. E 542's Gleespen fell off an LST and was drowned. While scouting close inshore for landing sites east of Bosnek, our barges had grenades thrown at them. Five planes struck at these barges, but our gunners claimed that they themselves downed all 5.

At 1000 while seeking a road inland, E 542's Capt De Ford had a call for help from probably 186 Inf. Japs in 2 caves 50 yards apart had halted them, wounded an officer still lying near one cave. Their own rifle fire could not reach the Japs inside the caves. Our men were out of grenades.

Capt De Ford, Lts Rial and Brim, Cpl Martin, and 5 other men fired and silenced Jap return fire from snipers' holes in the cliff and from the 2 caves. Smith and Lorix blasted the caves with grenade launchers. Closing in, they found that the Inf officer had died. As they were about to throw hand grenades into one cave, a Jap officer with saber and an enlisted man with bayoneted rifle charged them.

DeFord put a .45 bullet into the officer's brain, but Lts Rial and Brim finished him off. Lorix was wounded in arm and shoulder. An enlisted man slew the Jap rifleman.

An Amphib bazooka team arrived to fight the east cave. After 6 rockets with rifle and tommie gun fire, we rushed into the cave and found 60 dead Japs. Then we cleaned out the west cave — in 2 hours' battle had slain 100 Japs.

When seeking a place to tie up a floating dock, Lt Norris and an enlisted man drew grenade blasts from a cave. Return grenades killed the Japs. On recon, Goldberg and Laurie also killed 2. At 1500 hours, Inf asked us to launch rockets from an LCI into the cave. Instead, White and Brumhall brought a bazooka; its 3 rounds killed at least 2 Japs and silenced the cave.

A few planes raided us. About 1700 the first day, several Jap fighters and perhaps 4 bombers swept undetected on our LSTs from over the low cliff northward. Despite the surprise, AA crews and Amphibs of 542 Regt and 2 Engr Special Brigade Support Btry fought back. Three bombs hit an LST deck, but failed to arm because they fell at too low a height. They merely cracked open and were thrown overboard.

One of those bombs narrowly missed our Brigade CO Gen Heavey, but wounded his aide. AA fire destroyed one bomber that fell on the LSTs. A crippled bomber dived for destroyer Sampson, but missed and briefly flamed a subchaser when a wing brushed it. Other 2 bombers and the fighters were also knocked down. Our Engr Support Btry

For Amphibs of 542 EB & SR and 2 ESB, the Battle of Biak was a competent operation. After landing and fighting at Bosnek Beach, we helped save 162 Inf from destruction in Parai Defile.

claimed a kill of 2 bombers and one probable bomber.

By 1730 D-Day, when LSTs embarked for Hollandia, Amphibs with Inf assistance had unloaded 2 tanks, 28 guns, 500 vehicles. They had unloaded the whole assault force of 12,000, and 85 percent of their bulk supplies.

On the second Biak day, the Japs trapped 162 Inf's 2/Bn and 3/Bn in Parai Defile. At their cry for help, 11 LVTs and all available LCVPs were loaded with supplies and ammo and raced down to Parai Defile.

The LCVPs could not cross the reef before Parai Jetty, but the LVTs crossed on their tracks. When Jap guns and mortars on Parai Ridge tried to destroy the LVTs, we fought back with rockets and 37 mm guns, knocked out one Jap position.

From Support Btry barges, we lost 3 wounded. A FA man from the 41st was killed therein. Our LVTs evacuated many of 87 wounded and ferried ammo and medical supplies from the LCVPs. D 542's Amphib Engrs repaired Parai Jetty. They landed a 947 FA observer to crash down a 155 mm gun barrage.

On that first battle-day of 162 Inf in Parai Defile, it was a costly but orderly withdrawal. But they were still in the Defile. Next day, 14 LVTs of 2 ESB's Support Btry had to evacuate many of 162's 96 wounded. Jap fire stopped the LVTs' first try to reach Parai Jetty, but on the second try, they landed and carried those wounded back to Bosnek.

But on that second day, 29 May, 162 Inf had to escape from Parai Defile because they could not destroy the Japs' mortars and guns on the heights. Most of 2/Bn and part of 3/Bn retreated under fire from the cliffs into the tracked landing craft. Hundreds of men waded through surf to the reef to embark in LVTs and LCVPs. Two combat LVTs and a flak LCM fired from them and knocked out at least one Jap mortar position. From Parai Jetty, Lt Stewart's LVT loaded vehicles and other heavy equipment. But by now, the Japs had closed in to mortar the LVT and damage it. One Amphib lost his leg.

Evacuation continued well into the night. One DUKW remained ashore to save 2 fugitives and make a final search.

Earlier, however, during the daylight hours of 29 May, Amphibs formed a landing party for a rear guard of 162 Inf. With 6 other officers and some 100 men, D 542's Lt Steward climbed Parai Cliff to make a covering shell for retreating 162 Inf.

Fortunately, Nippo riflemen had been cleared from the cliff before we topped it. But our little command was in great danger; we had just one fire unit per rifle, and 200 rounds for each of our 5 MGs. Because we must fight only if attacked, we held fire on the number of Japs we saw or heard close to us. After several hours' tense picketing, we marched east paralleling the main body until we reached the new barrier to the Japs. A Jap mortar destroyed Spears' rifle and wounded his finger — our sole casualty. Meanwhile, Amphibs' Lt Portch of Hq Co 542 set up 5 37 mm guns at the barrier. They killed 2 Japs before they turned over the 37s to 162 Inf.

Meanwhile, Amphibs of 2 Eng Special Brigade's Shore Btry were scouting the small palm-fringed Padaido Islands SE of Biak for setting up a PT base and an air strip. Finding no Japs on Owi or Mios Woendi Islands, they still landed A 163 Inf for security, on 5 June. Capt Wells' barge convoy fought 2 strafing Nippo planes and hit both. Capt Buck claimed downing a plane with his rapid-fire 37 mm gun. An LCT captured a live Jap pilot from the sea.

These planes were part of a 15-plane raid. They bombed Bosnek beaches, but too late in the day to hit any LSTs, which had departed already. But a bomb blew off the shoulder of Shore Bn Hq Co's Bouquette at this MG and killed him. F 542's Reese took 15 slugs in hip and back, but lived.

Back in Parai Defile, the Japs still held a long, unbroken roadblock. So on 7 June, Amphibs led a major drive to end this block by striking its rear from the west — while part of 162 Inf pushed from the east. Amphibs loaded 162 Inf's I and K Cos on 18 LVTs of 2 ESB Support Btry and convoyed them to Parai Defile. Guards were 2 combat LVTs, a rocket LVT, and 4 rocket LCVPs. After a barrage of 264 rockets, "I" and "K" landed unopposed, and CN 162 later. In a few days, Parai Defile would be finally cleared of Japs.

On 7 June also, Amphibs embarked to assist 186 Inf. By now, 186 had bypassed the Japs' main army by a westward overland march. That morning, they had captured Mokmer Strip, but unbeaten Japs still surrounded them. Reports were that 186 Inf had 300 yards of beach open where it was safe to land to supply them.

Early on 7 June, a convoy of 10 LVTs and 3 LCMs left Bosnek to help 186 Inf. Each LCM carried a medium tank, of which 186 Inf could have brought none through the ridges. Escort was 4 rocket LVPs, 2 flak LCMs, and an LCS — all from our Amphib Support Btry.

Scouting the shore, we saw no 186 men, but Japs fired mortars and MGs at us. We feared to hit 186's men if we fired back. About 1300, 186 men marked a part of the beach with a ground flare, and we started to land the 3 tanks. As the 3 LCMs reached the reef before the beach, 30-40 Japs rushed from native huts. We slew most of them. The tanks landed and silenced Japs MGs and mortars, and then a 75 mm mountain gun and a 20 mm machine cannon on low Mokmer Ridge before us. Two of the 3 tank-carrying LCMs were so damaged that they could not retract ramps — had to retreat in reverse 9.5 miles back to Bosnek to keep from shipping the seas.

Until all Jap fire on the beach was silenced, we decided to run in supplies and evacuate 186's wounded only at night. But still as dusk fell, we had no clear idea of the location and extent of 186's beachhead.

Trying for a night landing on Mokmer Beach was a frustrating experience. Shortly after 2400, 2 LCVPs of a convoy of 14 followed an LCS to the reef. There they waited 25 minutes for 186's men to wade out and unload them. But they saw nobody. (CO Col Newman of 186 Inf thought that we failed to land because Div Hq had failed to relay his signals, and also because of Amphib over-caution.)

At 0400 with some moonlight, however, 7 LVTs with a covering flak boat lumbered across the reef. Brief and harmless Jap fire came from the shore. Unloading a third of 186's daily rations with heavy weapons ammo, our LVTs evacuated 92 casualties.

On our returning LVTs in sight of Bosnek, a Jap divebomber wounded 2 already wounded 186 men and a 4-year-old native child. (Off Parai in another command, a man of 2 ESB Support Btry was killed.

Next night, on 8 June, 18 LVTs again supplied 186 Inf at Mokmer Beach, despite Jap fire on our flanks. Our LVTs transferred 94 casualties across the reef to LCMs for Bosnek.

Final runs to Mokmer Beach were on 9 June. Our combat LVT intentionally drew fire from an isolated Jap pocket which threatened our landings. Tanks later fired from LCTs and destroyed those gun positions. That night, 13 LVTS resupplied 186 Inf and evacuated 44 more casualties. By next day, 162 Inf had ended Jap resistance in Parai Defile, and it became more efficient to supply 186 Inf by truck rather than by water.

With Parai Defile opened, our Amphibs' war on Biak was almost over. Final combat was at Wardo, on Biak's west coast. There the Jap army tried to regroup for a final attack. On 17 Aug at 0830, after Air-Navy preparation, 5 LVTs dashed for the shore, then 15 LCMs 2 minutes later. Opposition was light; small arms hit a support LCS. A shell wounded 2 Amphibs. After 75 Japs were found dead, Wardo Operation became a routine mop-up.

For Amphibs of 542 EB&SR and 2 ESB, the Battle of Biak was a competent operation. After landing and fighting at Bosnek Beach, we helped save 162 Inf from destruction in Parai Defile. We fought open a supply corridor to 186 Inf at Mokmer Beach. We lost 5 killed, 40 wounded, and 1 missing in action. Jap fire damaged some Amphibian craft, but none were sunk except a DUKW of attached 812 Amphib Truck Co at Parai Defile.

Emblems of our 41st Div were the low gray landing craft of the Amphib Engrs. Our 41st Div was actually an Amphib outfit!

> **CREDIT:** Outstanding source is *Amphibian Engineer Operations,* which is Vol IV of "Engineer Operations in the Southwest Pacific/1941-1945." (I discovered this out-of-print volume while on a Division History Grant to Duke University's Eichelberger Collection.) I have combined this source with an earlier history which I wrote from a 43-page typescript called "A/A Report/542 Engineer Boat and Shore Regt." R. R. Smith's *Return to the Philippines* was useful also. Below are some abbreviations which I have had to use to save space:
> EB&SR — Engineer Boat and Short Regt
> ESB — Engineer Special Brigade
> DUKW — Amphibian 2-1/2 ton truck
> LVT — Landing Vehicle, TRACKED
> LCM — Landing Craft, Mechanized
> LCPR — Landing Craft, Personnel
> LCS — Landing Craft, Support
> LCT — Landing Craft, Tank
> LCVP — Landing Craft, Vehicle & Personnel
> LCI — Landing Craft, Infantry
> LST — Landing Ship, Tank

Papua. Japanese prisoner captured by the Australian troops. (Courtesy of Rohlffs)

Papua. Buna. Captured Japanese pom pom on the Buna strip. (Courtesy of Rohlffs)

Papua. The fall of Gona. Japanese killed in the final assault on Gona (Courtesy of Rohlffs)

Planning Invasion of Japan (Kyushu Island)

by Dr. Hargis Westerfield, Division Historian

On 1 Nov. 1945, our 41st Div would be one of nine Divs assigned to start the first invasion of Japan. We were part of Gen. Innis Swift's I Corps. Teamed with other veteran 25th and 33rd Divs, we were to land on big Kyushu ("KOO-SHOO") Island. Based on south Kyushu 400 miles south of Tokyo, we were to defeat desperate large air-ground armies — then garrison that new staging area to overrun heartland Kanto Plain on Honshu Island and capture Tokyo.

For Yanks and Japs, this Kyushu invasion might be the most important operation of World War II. It might have quickly ended the war. On Kyushu, Japs would surely have expended most of their kamikaze planes — really their crucial defense line. If their Kyushu defense had failed — it would be limited to 10 days' battle — they might have sued for peace to avoid the occupation of Tokyo.

For we did not need to occupy all Kyushu's 16,000 square miles. We planned to hold only a strip averaging 100 miles wide east and west by 80 miles north and south on the lower end. There would be a roomy seaside base for attacks on the heartland Kanto Plain with Tokyo.

Our nine Divs would find this strip easy to hold. Kyushu was mostly a mountain massif 80 miles wide. The national highway around the southeast coast was mostly a single two-lane gravel road. Inland secondary roads were for light traffic, single-laned, from which ran narrow dirt tracks. Single-tracked coast railroad had many bridges and tunnels readily smashed by our planes. Kyushu Japs would not expect reinforcements from the defense of Tokyo.

We had two great naval forces with carrier planes and two land-based air forces to land our infantry on Kyushu with minimum casualties. These four forces were necessary against Jap suicide pilots.

Fleet Admiral W. F. "Bull" Halsey's 3rd Fleet would strike first. Including a British task force, Halsey had 17 fleet and escort carriers, eight battleships, 20 cruisers, 75 destroyers, and necessary support vessels. For 67 days, to 23 Oct., 3rd Fleet would damage Jap air forces, and disrupt passage between Honshu and Kyushu. Eight days before D-Day, 3rd Fleet's carrier groups would join with carrier groups of Admiral R. R. Spruance to soften up the Kyushu landing area.

Spruance's 5th Fleet had a Fast Carrier Force of seven fleet and three light carriers, with an Escort Carrier Force for closer support. It also had a Gunfire and Covering Force, a Mine Force, and three Amphibious Forces — these three under one commander.

Two land-based Army Air Forces would also strike. Beginning 23 Oct., Lt. Gen. G. C. Kenney's Far Eastern Air Force would cut communications from north Kyushu to the assault area. They would collapse strategic bridges, and cut rail lines to areas for reinforcements from seaport bases like Nagasaki and Sasebo. With B-29s and B-32s, Gen. C. A. Spaatz's Strategic Air Force would mine straits between Honshu and Kyushu.

Eight days before we landed, Spruance's 5th Fleet would charge the shores. While carrier planes controlled the air, 16 escort carriers would soften up the beach approaches. Surface fire support groups would bombard to cover our fleet of minesweepers who would drag the inshore waters over and over again. Five days before we landed, underwater demolition teams would clear the underwater defenses and Japanese frogmen crouched below the surface.

On 1 Nov. 1946, nine Inf. Divs, including our 41st and three Marine Divs would beachhead on southeast Kyushu. For security reasons, however, four Regts must first seize outlying islands, 4-5 days before the nine Divs would hit the Kyushu mainland. On 27 Oct., 40th Div's three Regts and 158 Inf would capture offshore islets south of Kyushu — for unsinkable bases for radar and fighter stations to protect our landings. At Okinawa, too many outposting destroyers had died under kamikaze swoops.

Five days later, on 1 Nov. 1946, three Corps of three Divs each would attack Kyushu on a shore front roughly in a half-circle 150 miles long from near Kagoshima on the west to Miyazaki on the east.

On the west, Marines of 2nd, 3rd, and 5th Divs would strike, and on the far east, Army I Corps would beach with our own 41st Div. Most of the 150 miles were narrow beaches under heavily fortified cliffs. Behind them were two wide bays, Kagoshima Wan and Ariake Wan. Past the cliffs were excellent airports — among them, Kagoshima, Chiran, and Miyakonojo — which last the 41st might have to take.

North of Ariake Bay were long white beaches with the widest plainland in all south Kyushu. Here our 41st would land.

On the far west, the three Marine Divs would have the strongest Jap force to battle — three Inf Divs, an Inf Brigade, a tank Brigade and a whole Artillery Command. The Marines had to capture the western Kagoshima Bay shores, consolidate and move north.

East of the Marines, XI Corps (43rd Div, America 1 Div and 1st Cavalry Div would secure the eastern shore of Kagoshima Bay and Ariake Bay.

Farthest east and north, our 41st Div would hit Miyazaki Beaches as part of Gen. Innis Swift's I Corps, with 25th and 33rd Divs. We would fight the Japs' 154 Div straddling Miyazaki City, and 212 Div on the north and 156 Div on the south. We had two missions. We had to turn south to overrun Miyakonojo Strip. We also had to turn north and come up on line with XI Corps and the Marines in the mountains to cordon off south Kyushu from north Kyushu attacks. (If not needed elsewhere, three days after these troops beached, IX Corps — 11th Airborne, 98th and 81st Divs would reinforce the Marines and XI Corps.)

Now this was the Miyazaki battlefield for our 41st Div. Foreshore were two different beaches, both 750-1000 yards long. Behind each beach was a mile-long lagoon. Oyodo River separated those beaches. Miyazaki City of over 100,000 people was near Oyodo Mouth.

Oyodo River was deep enough for LSTs a few miles up, but tracked vehicles were needed to cross the two beaches and the lagoons behind them. Behind North Beach were rice paddies impossible for tanks without help, and miles of guns emplaced above this beach. Mortars and automatic weapons pits guarded South Beach from the hills. Yet past the heavily defended beaches was a plain where our armor could fight the Japs.

The corridor south to Miyakonojo Air Field would be hard to fight through. There was only one road through mountains with many tunnels and bridges. Such was the 41st beachhead near Miyazaki in eastern Kyushu.

Japanese Defense Plans. Japanese defense plans certainly sounded formidable. Because of the kamikaze menace, air defenses were the most powerful, but we could also fear a Navy-Army surface fleet of small suicide craft, and big guns in caves. Finally, regular Inf Divs and Coastal Defense Divs would hold the beaches or fill them with their dead.

By dawn on D-Day, a four-fold air attack would swoop from the air. While our advancing fleet was still in the open seas, 2,000 Army/Navy fighters would battle for air superiority over Kyushu. A special force of 330 Navy pilots would strike our main body to hold it from using their guns and planes to protect their transports. With those two forces already in battle, a third force of 825 kamikazes would bomb our 180 personnel transports and 70 supporting ships. Near our night's transports' anchorages, we'd be struck by 2,000 more kamikazes in waves of 2-300, hour by hour.

How successful would these air attacks be? Based on Jap estimates of their results in the Okinawa Operation, they expected up to 50 percent losses on us. But these estimates erred. They thought that they had sunk 196 ships. Actual number was 35 sunk, with 31 more heavily damaged. Yet the kamikaze attacks at Okinawa did sink about five times as much as non-suicide attacks of trained flyers did sink.

The Japs also hoped to defeat our invasion because they had thousands of planes to fight over a short distance for a long time. They noted that our land-based planes would have to fly back 350 miles to Okinawa to rearm and refuel. Our Navy planes and AckAck guns would be left to fight without land-based help. Continuous fire would cause our Navy weapons to malfunction. Battle fatigue would exhaust their crews by darkness. And all night and nine more days afterwards, the remaining Jap planes would smother and sink our fleets.

(But surely our air force Generals Kenney and Spaatz had foreseen Japanese plans to wear us down by sustained attacks day and night. Kenney and Spaatz would surely have organized their flights of planes in stages from Okinawa to keep on target day and night.)

The nearly destroyed Japanese Navy could have almost no part in resisting invasion. But it did produce the suicidal "kaiten," a midget submarine which had potentials. It was a modified "long lance" torpedo manned by a pilot. Launched under water from submarines, kaitens had sunk a U.S. tanker and damaged two transports in early 1945. But only 450 kaitens were ever built.

Both Navy and Army had suicide motor boats. Essentially, they were light plywood craft 18 feet long with automobile motors, maximum speed 25 miles per hour. With a bomb of about 500 pounds in the bow, a sailor was to crash a vessel wherever he could hit it. With two depth charges on each side of the cockpit, the soldier was to target the vessel's engine. Both soldier and sailor would get quick deaths.

With jagged shores, the south Kyushu coast was made for fire on our ships — front, flank and rear. For example, Ariake Bay was guarded by 18 heavy or medium cannon in caves or behind embankments. There were four 280 mm howitzers, four of 240 mm, two 120 mm guns, and eight 100 mm guns with the lighter divisional pieces of 86th Div. Where our 41st Div would land near Miyazaki, seven 150 mm guns would strike us — along with reinforcements from more heavy FA units.

Even if U.S. forces did beach, close combat would redden the sands. First, massed "coastal combat divisions" would jam the beaches to fight to their death. Secondly, unleashed "line divisions" would charge in over the bodies of coastal defense divisions.

Evidences of Japanese desperation were these "coastal combat divisions." With fewer fighters than the regular line divisions, they had superior fire power. They would have many MGs, grenade launchers and knee-mortars. Yet they were almost immobile, with only a fourth of the horses and vehicles of the regular line divisions — and only to forward rations and ammo. Deployed in caves and bunkers, they would charge to strike our Inf as we hit the beaches. Greatest drawback was that their personnel were poorly trained civilians.

But Jap line combat Divs were the decisive reserves. They would charge into battle as soon as the coastal Divs were committed. Infantry, tanks and heavy FA would attack even over the screaming wounded and corpses of the coastal Divs. Jap line Divs and coastal Divs would be so tightly compacted in struggle that our Navy and planes would be unable to find Jap targets because they would fear to kill our Inf hitting the beach.

At all costs, the Japs planned to hold us at the water's edge. If we could dig in on the beaches, our FA and flame-throwing tanks would clear our way to the mountains bordering their coastal plains. Our thick-armored tanks with 75s or 105s would outrange and gut their tanks. If we reached the foothills to entrench, their Inf would lack the power to overrun our lines. Yet all of their largest air fields lay on or near the coast plains; they had to die holding them.

Such were the U.S. offensive and Jap defensive plans for "Operation Olympic," our name for the Kyushu invasion. The Japanese evinced their desperation by marshalling enormous air and ground forces. For some historians, it seems that the Kyushu battles would have been the only battles in the Japanese home islands. The slaughters on both sides would surely have caused negotiations for peace — if only to forestall a Russian invasion from the north.

We are absolutely certain of just two truths. First if our 41st had fought on Kyushu, there wouldn't have been much left of our Division. Second, we are happy that no Japanese or Americans were killed or wounded in Operation Olympic, that unfought Battle of Kyushu. No blood was spilled on Miyazaki Beaches!

CREDIT: Discoveries of new documents about our Jap invasion has led to my total revision of this history. Most important was the study of U.S. battlefields from Gen. E. J. Winslett's 17-page typescript, "Defense of Southern Kyushu (KOO-SHOO), dated 3 June 1946. Other documents now used were Richard O'Neill's book *Suicide Squads* (New York: Ballantine Books, 1984); and James Martin Davis' *Top Secret/ The Story of the Invasion of Japan* (Omaha, Nebraska: Ranger Publications, 1986). (AT-163's George Philip Morris supplied this last brochure.) Two more books were Prof. K. J. Bauerle's "Olympic," in *Marine Corps Gazette* (Aug. 1965); and Lee Enderlein's "Greatest of All Invasions," in *Military History* (Aug. 1985). (Irwin Soliday of 163 Inf. sent me this publication.)

In this new history, I have still included citations from my earlier unpublished history. Most important were two magnificent volumes: *Reports of Gen. MacArthur: Japanese Operations in the Southwest Pacific Area*, printed in 1950. Okinawa background of kamikazes I found in Samuel Eliot Morison's *Victory in the Pacific*, Vol. XIV of his *History of United States Naval Operations in World War II*. (O'Neill's *Suicide Squads* is a small, carefully documented encyclopedia of Italian, German, British, and Japanese plans, diagrams, and operations of kamikazes, land, sea, and air.)

G Co's Bongao Action (Philippines)

by Dr. Hargis Westerfield, Division Historian
with G Co 163 Inf's S/Sgt Kermit Dulian

On 1 Apr 1945, G Co 163 Inf awoke before daylight for our voyage southwest from Zamboanga to seize Bongao Island. We embarked with our 2/Bn, B Btry 146 FA, and attachments in a small convoy with Destroyers *Phillip* and *Waller*, four LCIs with rockets or mortars, and Marine planes overhead.

Briefed in our LCI, we learned that G's CO Capt. Braman, had scouted Bongao from a plane and drawn Jap fire. G Co was to land first on Sanga Sanga Island and then on Bongao at the far western end of the Sulu Islands. By defeating the Nippo garrison, we would cut off other Japs' escape routes from Jolo, last important stronghold between Zamboanga and Borneo. On mountainous little Bongao, the Japs had FA, and AA in concrete emplacements.

At daylight on 2 Apr from our LCI, we saw blue mountains of northeast Borneo in the distance. We steamed close to little Bongao with two large peaks — that looked too much like Biak.

We watched some 50 Liberators drop 500-lb. bombs on Bongao. The Marine Corsairs loosed lighter bombs and strafed. Destroyers *Phillip* and *Waller* silenced some Jap 20 MM AA fire.

Our convoy steamed close to Sanga Sanga Island just east of Bongao. Guerillas stood knee-deep in water for welcome; the U.S. flag flew on the beach. Landing in bouncing rubber boats, we heard guerillas say that all Japs had left for Bongao across the channel. G Co was to storm Bongao.

An hour later, "G" had hiked through heavy jungle to Sanga Sanga Strip. Its coral surface would need but little labor to ready it for heavy bombers. As we reached the Strip, Jap 20 mm fire hit the beach behind us. Our destroyers silenced them.

Leaving F Co to guard the Strip, G Co led H and E Cos to the southwest coast of Sanga Sanga Island. Across the channel lay the thick jungle of Bongao. While lunching on K rations, we heard some spatters of fire from Bongao that hit the beach where we had landed. Still, our war didn't look bad so far.

After G Co beached, we were to push in to the first high peak westward, to probably the lower slopes of Bongao Peak, height 1030 feet. With Kabogan Peak (706 feet) across a saddle eastward, the Japs had observed for the former battle-fleet anchorage of Tawi Tawi Island to the south. We heard that the Japs still garrisoned both of those peaks. And we already knew that they held Dila Point with 20 mm guns on the northeast end of the island where Port Bongao was located.

At 1200, our landing was prepared by a Marine air-strike and a barrage of B Btry's 105s and H Co's 81 mm mortars. Then G Co boarded Alligators armed with .50 HMGs. Because the bow HMG was mounted high on the Alligator, Dulian made Moyer — his tallest man — the gunner.

After the heavy barrage, G Co's Alligators' .50s sprayed the Bongao foreshore as we crossed the 200-yard channel. We had no opposition, but both of 2/Pln's Alligators stuck in mud about 50 feet out. We waded in with water to our armpits.

Still drawing no fire, "G" started inland through dense jungle. Jap 20 mm fire sounded somewhere east of us, but it again shot on the beach at unloading craft. So safe was our march that Kern found a pineapple and ate it on our first break. We hit an opening in the jungle about one-fourth mile inland and scouted to the base of the first hill southward. A "G" patrol west along an unused track to the coast found no Japs.

Most of the Japs were evidently laired on Kabogan and Bongao Peaks to the south and were waiting for us. We had come in behind the other Jap stronghold around Port Bongao to the northeast, and the Japs would have to leave fast to keep from being trapped there.

Meanwhile G Co came down a jungle track to a wider north-south trail that crossed the unused east-west trail. That north-south trail led between Kabogan and Bongao Peaks to the coast. We held an important strategic position in the approximate center of Bongao Island.

With E Co, we halted and outposted all four ways. Suddenly Jap sniper fire and mortar shells struck at us, but hit nobody. A Pln of H Co HMGs reinforced us. Tiredly, we dug perimeter, and relaxed in our holes. On this strange island, the night blacked us out — all quiet but for a few Jap mortar shots.

About 2100, the Japs counter-attacked from the nearer peaks, probably Kabogan Peak. We thought afterwards that they misjudged our location in the darkness. From the noise, we believed that there must have been a whole Co on each flank — an over-estimate of maybe 400-500 Japs.

Without warning in that black night, H Co HMGs opened up in short bursts. Hand-grenades blasted. Japs yelled or screamed. A Jap officer gave orders; then came more screaming. Jap rifles were firing over our heads. Then their attack ended suddenly but for more screaming — and moaning.

At daylight, we found seven dead Japs on the trail with five new rifles, much ammo and food, and a battery radio to send and receive codes. They wore new uniforms.

But all was quiet that morning of 3 Apr. No Jap snipers harassed the men clearing the area. After breakfast near the corpses, S/Sgt Dulian got orders for a four-man outpost down-trail towards the south coast. Scouting south with BARmen "Tony" and Moyer, Dulian and MacNamara found that they had to set up in the open. They kept low, for they could be seen from both peaks behind them. And 1/Pln had heard Japs digging in probably on Kabogan Peak before daylight.

After the outpost, Dulian's squad had to run a patrol with his six men, 2.5 miles to Pahut Village on the west end of Bongao. This trail skirted the foot of Bongao Peak past a Jap observation post with AA defenses. At the end of this trail 42 Japs had outposted with native police. Dulian complained that they might hit an ambush when returning, and have trouble bringing back any wounded. Capt. Braman gave him T/Sgt Reese and a medic who brought up the rear.

Dulian pushed his patrol west as fast as was reasonable. Much of the trail went through dense jungle, with plenty of Jap signs. At the island's end, Pahut Village had wooden huts unlike the usual native huts of nipa palm. Hogs and chickens pecked or rooted around the clearing. While MacNamara and the medic secured our rear, we checked out all the huts — a double tier 1/4 mile along the beach. We found no Japs.

Returning safe to G Co, we heard an occasional firecracker report of a Jap rifle. Sniping on G Co came from a peak at 600 yards. A bullet narrowly missed our Catholic Chaplain Father Lynn, who was usually up front with 2/Bn.

Meanwhile on that same 3 Apr, T/Sgt Kozing's Pln warily moved east towards Port Bongao, the most important Jap stronghold on the island. Medicines and foods were scattered all along the trail. We thrust our M-1s into empty barracks, mess halls and concrete pillboxes. A silent 40 mm gun was still mounted at the edge of Port Bongao. An E Co patrol contacted us here. The "E" patrol had followed a trail south between the two peaks, and turned to search the coast of southeast Bongao before it met us at Port Bongao. "E" had seen no Japs.

About 1600, most of our 2/Bn left the "Four Corners" between the two peaks and occupied Port Bongao. Only an "E" rifle Pln with the "E" Weapons Pln remained to garrison this strategic post against the Nips on the two peaks.

G Co could not understand why the Japs had left for the peaks. Everywhere were roads and trails covered by emplacements with fine fields of fire. Even with help from air power and FA, they would have been hard to overrun.

On the way into Port Bongao, Dulian's squad acquired a bottle of whiskey and two bottles of Jap beer. With 7-Up from Waskovich, we had our first whiskey since Biak. Dulian's and Waskovich's men dug in on a slight rise above Port Bongao. Our kitchen crew had hot food for us. Moyer and Kern brought up a collection of souvenirs, including a full case of Jap soft drinks, a bicycle, cans of Jap tomatoes, silk shirts, socks, another bottle of whiskey. After whiskey and a Jap soft drink as chaser, we holed up at dusk, near H Co's HMGs.

About 0200, Jap MGs fired — probably at some fires that guerillas had lighted near the port. Dulian wakened BARman "Tony" to take over guard. As "Tony" rolled over on his face, a stray Jap bullet drew blood from a fleshy part of his body. The Jap rifleman had aimed too high at H Co in the dark; they had heard the bullet hiss over them. Our positions were on ground a little higher, and so "Tony" had caught the bullet.

On 4 Apr, Reese's Pln — now just 24 men — got orders to knock out 20 mm guns on low Hill 101 above Port Bongao. On 27 Mar, Air Intelligence had reported three guns there, with 200 Japs. We were then to attack Kabogan Peak frontally.

Waskovich's squad led. We made a steep climb to top Hill 101. FA and planes had pounded it. A low plane radioed that the pillboxes seemed to be empty. We found four twin 20 mm guns set in concrete pillboxes, but all damaged from shells or bombs. Lamb slew a stray Nip. In Jap huts, we found three cases of beer for refreshment — a bottle for every two men.

Low Hill 101 was a fine observation post for our Marine observer to direct bombs on Kabogan Peak before our assault. But first wave of Corsairs bombed and strafed too high above it. Most bombs missed; two Corsairs almost collided. Next flight missed at first; we saw one bomb splash the bay a half mile off. Finally, the Corsairs smashed some bombs where we wanted them.

After 146 FA fired also, our Pln went up the road for our frontal attack on Kabogan while 3/Pln attacked from the west, at about 1140. First, we had to take only a small hill below the main peak. We worked our way slowly up the hillside into well-placed defenses through barbed wire tangles. They were fine, naturally well-protected positions with small fields of fire. The Japs were gone, however, except for torn up bodies and much equipment. The radio ordered us to push on, 400 feet up to the top of the 706-foot peak. Jungle was thick, with many caves and rough but much-used trails.

After setting up defenses at the base of the sheer slope, 2/Lt. Beale sent Dulian's squad to find a way to the top of the peak from our side. Jap signs were plentiful, but we could find no way to climb. As we withdrew, rifles opened up on us, but missed. It now made no sense to dig out a few die-hard Japs at the cost of good G Co soldiers who would be needed on Jolo or in Japan. Guerillas could take care of those Nips.

About 1500, Reese's Pln got orders to spend the night with E Co's 2/Pln down at the "Four Corners" where we had fought off Nips in the night attack of 2 Apr. We had 1500 yards to hike.

With just 300 yards left before E Co, Lt. Beale suddenly said, "Let's go!" Dulian's squad hurried after him, without scouts.

At a sharp trail-bend, Beale yelled suddenly, "Put 'em up!" He drew back behind Dulian. There were two Japs ahead, one lying down. The Jap on the ground said, "More Japs there."

Suddenly the prone Jap moved. Beale emptied his carbine into him. Later, we found that he was a one-legged Jap. The second Jap started to run; Dulian killed him. Bolts clicked across the trail. Dulian saw a third Jap there and killed him. Two Jap shots missed Dulian.

Now on Beale's orders, Dulian's squad started up the trail. Kern and MacNamara opened up on a Jap. At the trail-curve, hidden Japs fired back. Putting his other four men in line, Dulian told them to fire when ordered. Kern, MacNamara, and Dulian moved in close and threw grenades. Then the whole squad raked the trail-curve. After silence, we found five live Japs pinned in the ditch, and slew them.

Dug in beside E's men, we heard that they had sniper fire from the peak at 1200. About midnight, booby traps exploded, and several Japs bypassed our perimeter — probably seeking water. Dulian heard movement before us about 0100 and awoke MacNamara and Kern. An unseen Jap tried to pick us off in the moonlight. He knocked his grenade on wood to arm it. As we ducked, it exploded before our hole and hurt nobody. We had no more Jap trouble that night.

After a few more nerve-wracking patrols, G's Bongao Action was ended. Japs still hid on the peaks, but we turned Bongao over to 375-400 guerillas to outpost the water-points and thus draw out the Japs. And by 1545 6 Apr, "G" and other 2/Bn men were safe across the channel to Sanga Sanga Island.

As for the originally estimated 300 Japs on Bongao, the last 200 bravely held out until 26 Apr. On 27 Apr., they tried to escape to Borneo, but PT boats gunned them down, but for some 40 survivors. Already, however, on 10 Apr., G Co had left for Jolo and our last fighting in all World War II. Our Bongao Action had been brief and efficient.

CREDIT: Basic personal story comes from a 12-page, double-spaced typescript from G Co 163 Inf's S/Sgt. Kermit Dulian. I collated this history with another history published in the *Jungleer* in June, 1985. This story is "146 FA and 2/Bn 163 Inf: Bongao and Sanga Sanga Island." For both this history and that one, I used also "Sulu White Task Force Field Order No. 1," and 2/Bn 163's "Narrative Report," "Casualty List," and 5-page "Journal." My historical background comes from R. R. Smith's *Triumph in the Philippines, Reports of General MacArthur/Japanese Operations in the South-West Pacific,* and *Terrain Study No. 102/Sulu Archipelago* (from Allied Geographical Section, S. W. Pacific, Area 1). G Co 163 Inf's great CO, Capt. Arthur (Buck) Braman first suggested this story to me by his gifts of F.O. No 1, a map of Bongao Island, and an Air Command Sketch of Bongao. Since writing this history, I credit Mr. Makoto Ikeda of Tokyo for writing that our enemies were "Japanese Marines" of the 33rd Naval Guard to which Mr. Ikeda also belonged.

Horseshoe Hill and A Company Ridge (Biak)

by Dr. Hargis Westerfield, Division Historian with S/Sgts. Monford Kruger and Thomas Grigar and 2/Lt. Richard Leukhardt

These are the stories of three memorable fights of 1/Bn 162 Inf's A and C Cos against Col Kuzume's last great offensive from West Caves on Biak. After our other two Bns of 162 Inf still had hard fighting on Mokmer Ridge south of West Caves, 1/Bn 162 flanked Mokmer Ridge on the east side and then drove towards West Caves. With 1/Bn 186 Inf on our right, 1/Bn 162 advanced westward against heavy infantry and tank opposition on 14 June 1944. And on 15 June, Kuzume's infantry and tanks began their all-out attack against us.

I. A Co 162 Inf fights a tank. On Biak on that 15 June 1944, S/Sgt Krueger's LMG squad of A Co 162 valiantly helped to repulse a Jap tank hammering in 37 mm shells at close range.

When the tank attacked about 0930, Krueger's LMG squad awaited orders in our shallow holes built up with coral chunks around the sides. We were then attached to Lt. Des Champs' Pln on A Co's right flank. West from dug-in A Co was the strategic south-to-north supply road for West Caves.

At 0930, we heard the ominous throb of the Nip tank's motor from behind a small hill some 300-400 yards to our left in Jap territory.

Confidently waiting S/Sgt Krueger expected D Co's nearby .50 HMGs to open up and halt the advancing tank.

But as the tank's throbs came nearer, D Co's 50s opened up only for seconds. Then in fear, we heard no more HMG fire.

The tank was clanking down the road directly towards A Co and our LMG squad. The saplings went down as the tank left the road some 50 yards away and turned towards us.

S/Sgt Krueger's first impulse was to withdraw from the death in the tank's 37 mm cannon. But he quickly thought what retreat would mean: panicking with maddened Jap infantry shooting him and his men in their backs while we ran.

Krueger ordered his LMGs to fire. Bullets rattled off the tank. Our LMGs sprayed the ground on both sides of and behind the tank to drive off the Jap infantry whom we expected to follow through its attack with grenades and bayonets. The black little careening monster seemed to grow larger and larger as it closed in.

Its 37 mm cannon hit the position next to Krueger only two yards away, but caused no casualties in that little pigpen of coral. Then, suddenly, it ceased fire and turned and chugged off, and Krueger felt alive again.

Later, we learned why D 162's HMGs stopped firing on the tank after a few rounds. Krueger reasoned why the tank probably called off the attack.

D Co had ceased fire because their HMGs could be sighted on the tank only the short time when it came over the hill. Then the hill curve had masked the fire. The tank had withdrawn because A Co men from their holes had opened up with a BAR and thrown grenades. Our resistance had demoralized and repelled the tank crew and their supportive infantry. The tank's 37 mm gun was ineffective even against moderately good emplacements at short range.

On that 15 June, A Co had six wounded, although we do not know whether they were hit in the tank attack or some other time. Fenstormacher and Koskoff were seriously wounded. Reported lightly wounded were Price, Thomas, Heller, Sgt Wiecrek. It was a slight price to pay for our victory — when B 162 that same day had 15 casualties, eight of them serous wounds.

II. C Co storms Horseshoe Hill. On 17 June 1944, C Co 162 Inf stormed Horseshoe Hill in one of C's bloodiest fights on Biak since Parai Defile. Actually a long, curved ridge, Horseshoe Hill blocked the advance of 1/Bn 162 Inf 1/Bn 186 to the rim of West Caves. This hill extended from north to southwest in a curve directed towards our march like the front of a horseshoe, and thus got its name.

On that morning of 17 June, C Co was in reserve when 162's A and B Cos began 1/Bn's drive west. But by 1005, despite help from our FA and 603 Tank Co's 1/Pln, heavy automatic fire from Horseshoe Ridge halted A and B Cos.

That fire came from ground that was originally 1/Bn 186's objective. But 186 had been forced to delay their march because they had to take a roundabout route to avoid overlapping our 162's 1/Bn. The 186 men had to turn east from bivouac, then swing north to approach Horseshoe Hill from the northeast, and so could not come up in time to halt Jap fire on A and B 162.

So "C" had to attack Horseshoe Hill. Confidently we waited while FA and mortars pounded it for 90 minutes. This barrage was well placed, but not fully effective. We did not know that the Japs were waiting for us under cover of caves or crevices in the cliffs.

Yet the attack still looked easy. While our three Sherman tanks advanced and delivered direct fire from their 75s, C's 1/Pln and 2/Pln lined up about 150 yards from the hill, with

3/Pln in reserve. As our Plns advanced, D Co's two .30 HMGs delivered overhead fire on that ridge.

But to S/Sgt Grigar in that advance, all timing of the attack seemed to be lost. He thought that when the FA salvos ended, C Co should have been at the ridge-foot, not 150 yards away. Grigar also believed that we needed not two but four heavy .30s — or even heavy .50s to fire overhead for us.

At the immediate crest of the hill, "C" met the Japs. Our barrage had badly shaken them. We saw several wounded or dying who lay behind the crest. We saw where they had huddled from our shells in caves and crevices from a foot to 6-8 feet in depth. We had knocked out several pillboxes.

But two Jap MGs still fired on us from protected positions back in caves. We could not silence them. About 1140, we had to fall back down Horseshoe Hill while our tanks fired uselessly on the two MGs.

Before our C Co's second attack, the three tanks shot fro 45 minutes at the crest, with their .30 HMGs and .75 cannon. They destroyed a Jap .75 and the two MGs that had repelled us.

About 1230, we again assaulted the hill with two Plns forward, and the other in reserve, as before. This time, our tense men climbed the hill under perfect silence from the crest before us. No Japs fired. Their automatic weapons crews huddled in their holes and died from our rifle and BAR fire or grenades. A few unorganized Nippo riflemen still wandered in the brushland behind the crest and waited for death. Our security patrols or outguards picked them off.

Just as our C 162 ended resistance on our section of Horseshoe Hill, 1/Bn 186 men began approaching the high ground from the east. With far less resistance, A 186 contacted "C" about 1330.

Now A and B 162 resumed their drive westward, but scattered MG and rifle fire harassed them from positions southwest of our C Co, from Mokmer Ridge. On the day before, 16 June, G Co 186 Inf had cleared this area when 186's 2/Bn had closed the Great Gap between 162's 2/Bn and 3/Bn. Japs had reoccupied this part of Mokmer Ridge. C 162 had to clear this brush from scattered MG crews and riflemen before dark.

Although nobody was killed on that 17 June in C Co, we had our top number of casualties on Biak. (Back on 8 June at Parai Defile, we lost one killed, four seriously wounded, four lightly wounded, and one lightly injured — a total of 10 casualties.) But in this fight for Horseshoe Hill, or elsewhere that day, we had 12 casualties — with three seriously wounded, seven lightly wounded, and two men lightly injured. Seriously wounded were Orosco, Mascarella, and 2/Lt Landrum. Marked lightly wounded were Munroe, Hedell, Lumpkin, Svaboda, Steforsky, Sgt. Groff, S/Sgt Gardea, Stelmach and Liebson.

III. A Co 162 Inf defends a ridge. After A 162 had captured a small ridge 150 yards north of West Caves on 17 June, we prepared for battle that night. (This was the same day that C Co won Horseshoe Hill.) Our CO, 1/Lt Mitchell, knew that A Co was too short of men to hold that ridge unaided, for the whole West Caves garrison might come boiling out that night to slay us. Even with the fire of our attached section of D 162's 1/Pln's HMGs, we could not be safe.

Mitchell called forward A Co's own 60 mm mortarmen who had supported his day's fight from near 1/Bn Hq. Bn Hq also granted him 12 A & P men, and a section of .50 HMGs especially for possibly necessary AT defense. These reinforcements brought the total garrison of Mitchell's ridge up to 100. (Already a small outfit after 20 days' action on Biak, "A" had suffered 22 casualties on this 17 June — four dead, and 16 wounded into hospital.)

Carefully rechecking the entire area, Mitchell felt most secure in our rear, for reliable C 162 would help protect us. He reorganized A Co and detachments into two rifle Plns and a Weapons FLN. He emplaced 1/Pln on the west side of the ridge with the 12 A & P men and D's HMGs. He put 2/Pln with A's own 60s to guard the east side. Most of our firepower he concentrated to the south towards West Caves. He told us to dig 3-man holes.

Although undergoing constant harassment from snipers and knee-mortars while organizing our perimeter, the Pln leaders personally inspected every position to see whether our men had carried out instructions.

Our Pln leaders — T/Sgt Berry and 2/Lts Descamps and Leukhardt — checked all holes to see that we had linking and overlapping fields of fire — which were to be cleared as much as possible. We must have a complete barrier of booby traps. Perhaps most important was the order to limit our fire with small arms and MGs. We must always use grenades — unless Japs closed on us within five yards. These reminders were necessary; we were jaded and tired after 1/Bn's fourth day drive to the West Caves rim.

The expected Jap attacks began about 2100 in the dark. In the first phase, they tried the south nose of our ridge — which was the closest to West Caves. Jap scouts hoped to draw fire by peculiar noises. A Jap with a small pick continually struck it on the rocky ground before him. Despite noises, the Japs failed to draw fire to located our positions. Grenades rained down to keep them at a distance. (We found the pick beside a dead Jap the next day.)

One Jap officer with an NCO did infiltrate to within four feet of a MG position. Totally unseen until four feet away, they rose to lunge bayonets into our gunners. They toppled dead from MG bursts. Ont he west flank of our ridge also, two Japs rushed on a MG, and died from close-range fire.

In the second phase of A's night fight, Japs began to probe for a weak spot in our perimeter. They hit our mortarmen on the east side and failed. Then they circled our perimeter and tried other places, but still could not find a breach to penetrate with a knot of bayonet men.

In the third phase, towards morning, the Japs waited until they had coaxed a provoked Yank to throw a grenade. They would try to trace back the chain of sparks to the thrower. This tactic boomeranged on them. Their return fire revealed their positions above ground and identified targets for our more accurate grenade bursts.

By daylight, the Jap detachment — an estimated 60 — had left our front but for some of their dead whom they could not bring out. We estimate that they lost 12 killed, and an unknown number of wounded whom they had evacuated.

As for little A Co with 12 A & P men and D Co HMG crews, we had nil losses. Decimated A Co was happy indeed to have no more losses. On the day before, 17 June, we had 21 casualties, almost half of our 1/Bn's total of 46. We had four dead: Robinson, Thacker, Rinholt, and Yoka. Magg and Martinez were seriously wounded. Marked lightly wounded were 15: Schroeder, Shelton, Skatzes, Lough, Terracciano, Fischer, Carey, Karns, Ward, Norman Williams, Dave Williams, and Bragg. Also marked lightly wounded were T/Sgt Burkhartsmeyer, T/Sgt Yancy, and Sgts McHugh and Neely. On 17 June, A Co had our top score of casualties in the entire Biak campaign, but that night, the last men of A Co had survived with no more casualties.

Such were three memorable fights of A and C Cos in 1/Bn 162's flank thrust on Col. Kuzume's West Caves stronghold. Refusing to panic, A Co repulsed a tank threat. C Co painfully stormed Horseshoe Hill, and A Co held the ridge which they had captured against a night attack.

CREDIT: Reports of these 3 fights for the east rim of West Caves on Biak are from "Lessons Learned/41st Inf Div/162 Inf Regt" dated June - August 1944. Kruger reported on the tank fight, and Grigar on Horseshoe Hill. Leukhardt reported on defending "A" Ridge. Important help came from R. R. Smith's *Approach to the Philippines*, and 162 Inf's "Report of Casualties." In December 1981, I tentatively located Horseshoe Hill from maps in "I Corps History of Biak Operation 15-27 June 1944." Other sources include "Historical Record" of 603 Tank Co (28 June 1944), and 162 Inf's "Narrative" and Journal." Here are the first little histories of A Co. 162 Inf which I have ever been able to locate.

(Could some member of A Co 162 Inf help me with the story of "A" on Biak or at Zamboanga. Please!)

---

146 Field Artillery Battalion on Biak: Escaping the Parai Defile Death-Trap

by Dr. Hargis Westerfield, Division Historian
with 146 FA's Capt. Robert Allen

By daylight 28 May 1944 near Mokmer Village, we gun crews of 146 FA manned our 105 mm cannon while forward observer teams went to help 162 Inf. On the 41st Div's second day on Biak, 162 Inf had already passed easily through formidable Parai Defile last night. They expected to occupy Mokmer Strip before mid-morning. In the tangled brush ahead, scouts had spied only little scattered groups of Japs in the brush.

By 0930, 3/Bn 162 had gained 1500 yards beyond Mokmer Village. Then battle began!

Suddenly K Co met a storm of MG and rifle fire. We slew eight Japs, but too many held Mokmer Road, and struck our right flank. Forward 3/Bn units pulled back 600 yards to where the road leaves the shoreline on a 200-foot cliff. (Perhaps this is where 146 FA's Sivula and T/4 Roger Comstock became missing in action. Wounded by mortars and trapped in cave by rifle fire, they hid in coast cliffs for 16 days.)

1/Lt Schild's C Btry's forward observation party strung wires up to K's point. They had to spread out along both sides of narrow Mokmer Road, for here was the only open ground for any observation at all. As we arrived, heavy small arms fire came from ahead and the inshore flank. And we heard the clanking advance of Jap tanks up the road from the Strip. At 0942, Btry C opened up on the Jap tanks.

Meanwhile, Lt. Wolffer with the Naval Shore Fire Control Party came up. Wolffer's party called down destroyer gun-fire, and worked with his 146 FA's guns to block that tank attack. Four of our own M-4 tanks forward to fight the Jap tanks — but also drew fire down on Schild's observer party.

Although our tanks took two direct hits from the Japs, they continued firing. The Jap tanks dropped into defilade, but a heavy barrage of mortar and dual purpose cannon fire crashed into 162's point. Under intense fire, infantrymen fell everywhere.

During these barrages, Lts Wolffer and Schild exposed themselves continually to rise up and call shelling down on Mokmer Road to the Strip. This helped to lessen the furious fires of the Jap Inf attack and neutralize the fire from the high ground.

All that day, Sgt Donaldson was notable in his expert and brave work as a lineman. When Jap fires held up 162's advance, he kept the phone line operating between Lt Wolffer and the Naval Shore Party which called down destroyer fire. Jap mortars cut the line numerous times, but Donaldson continually repaired it. When the Jap riflemen surged forward, he assisted in evacuating the naval radio.

Lts Schild and Wolffer took advantage of a lull during the Jap attack. They back-tracked along the road 75 yards to where they had better observation of the heights on our right flank where the fire originated. At 1120 hours, Schild brought a 146 FA shell concentration into the midst of the Jap mortar and artillery positions.

Our tanks withdrew to a station near our observers and drew a vicious barrage. Our 105s duelled that ridge until about 1300 when we had to shift fire to another hard-pressed section. From 1300 until retreat at 1730, 3/Bn endured intermittent Jap mortar fire.

Schild's and Wolffer's teams did gallant work that day, exposed to heavy fire to keep the phone line open from the forward observers to the Bn radio. Besides Sgt. Donaldson, there were Gambecurte, Kocich, Jarvis — with Sgt Marvel, S/Sgt Haug, T/4 Bock, and T/5s Olson and Perry.

Meanwhile that morning while 146 FA fought for that part of I and K Cos near Mokmer Strip, we fought also for other 162 Cos, for Jap scouts had spotted a fine field of fire to cut off 3/Bn from 162's connecting 2/Bn on the coastal strip behind 3/Bn. This was near Mokmer Village where the road drops to the beach, then rises 50 feet to go on to Mokmer Strip.

From near Mokmer Village (maybe East Caves) the Japs threw down murderous fire. They struck L Co at the end of 3/Bn and G Co at the point of 2/Bn. Despite several casualties, "L" with an "M" weapons detachment found a safe way to rejoin 3/Bn. (One cut off "L" Pln had to fight east to 2/Bn's protection.) But 3/Bn was thus cut off from the Reg't.

Observing for Btry B, 146's Lt Thompson was with G Co's point in the defile. With his party and G's mortar observers, Thompson repeatedly tried to scale Parai Ridge to call fire on Jap emplacements. Shells and point-blank MG fire thwarted us.

Then the Japs retaliated against 146's Btrys in our advanced position near Mokmer Village. At 1330, Service Co's 2/Lt Silva saw Jap mortar fire adjusting from the sea 100 yards away. Silva warned our CP, but we could do nothing because we were firing a vital concentration for 3/Bn to halt a tremendous Jap attack.

As Jap observers adjusted their range, they walked their heavy mortar shells into us and increased fire. At 1400 hours, a shell burst on Mokmer Road near the Bn radio jeep. Hq Btry's Sgt Paulson got his death wound. Others in 146 FA and 205 FA 100 yards east drew wounds from Jap mortars.

Three 146 men showed outstanding bravery here. T/4 McClintock lay by a phone controlling 2 Btry's fire. Only protection was two supply boxes beside him. When he had to shift fire, he had to get up in the open to check his charts for firing data. After switchboard and operator were hit, 1/Lt Ridenoure supervised repairs of wire connections. Later, he continually exposed himself to load wounded into trucks.

Mortar shells landed close to the jeep where T/4 Woltersdorf's radio was mounted. Fragments hit the jeep. But Woltersdorf kept on relaying commands and sensings to our fire direction center.

Our Bn aid station was already crowded with 146 FA and 205 FA casualties. A shell exploded only a few feet from the tent where Capt Katz and medics treated our wounded. The wounded were in shallow cover, but the medics worked over them in open ground. Katz got his death-wound, yet would not leave his wounded men until he had written out their evacuation orders. Medics Houghton and Cpls Kelley and Siefferman were also wounded. S/Sgt Anderson and T/3 Benites replaced Katz and the others to supervise aid to more casualties.

Mortar blasts stalked up and down our gun positions. One shell made a direct hit on a Btry A slit trench. Killed was Schortgen, and T/4 Owsianka wounded. Even offshore rocket-fire could not silence the Jap automatic fire from the ridge-line above us.

Btry B's CO, 1/Lt Wilkinson, formed an attack patrol and mounted the ridge — but was recalled before they could fight.

After two hours of vicious Jap fire, "Division" ordered withdrawal from this untenable position east of Mokmer Village. We had 25 casualties: one officer and two men dead, and three officers and 19 men wounded. After orders at 1540, we quickly displaced back to our previous position near Ibdi. By 1730, we were ready to fire for 162 Inf again.

But we feared an ammo shortage. In our hurried retreat, we had left too many shells near Mokmer Village. Commandeering trucks along Mokmer Road, Sv Btry's W/O Dugan, M/Sgt Fowler, and S/Sgt Engert led back a supply party. By 1830, Sv Btry had brought back to our gunners over 1,000 rounds.

While Jap mortars and artillery forced 146's retreat to Ibdi, 162's Col Haney planned 3/Bn's retreat from the Mokmer-Parai death-trap. When 3/Bn left the Parai area, all FA and Navy guns would fire to cover the Inf's disengagement. Our 146 FA's 105s, with 947 FA's 155s, and 121 FA's 75s — all would impact west and north of 3/Bn. After 162 had passed the defile at Mokmer Village, most of our fire would shift onto the area of heaviest Jap gunnery — near the beach north of Mokmer Village — where were East Caves.

At 1700 that 29 May, 3/Bn's retreat began. The three observation parties of Lts. Schild, Wolffer, and Ducommun linked up with the Inf rear-guard and four tanks. Although the first retreating men of 3/Bn did not draw heavy fire, withering

MG, mortar, and rifle blasts hit most of 3/Bn streaming east through the defile.

Under almost point-blank rifle shots with mortar shells bursting all around, our FA parties moved in rushes. Yet T/4 Plourde leaped from a tank-protected jeep to destroy a naval radio which had been with the party of slain Ensign Travis.

Fire became so deadly that retreating rear-guard Inf and our FA observers had to drop down over the cliff, then one by one cross the bullet-swept beach to shelter in 2/Bn's perimeter.

As soon as 3/Bn had passed through 2/Bn, 146 FA placed defensive fire across the west and inland sides of 2/Bn. Especially heavy concentrations impacted the cliffs commanding the beach. We fired all night.

But at 0500 next morning, 29 May, shells from unknown guns impacted 3/Bn's perimeter. To clear 146 FA from accusations of firing on our own Inf, we had to risk observers' lives in the pre-dawn tropical dark. Sgt Marcel and Lts Ducommun and Wolffer had to expose themselves to being shot by our own men. To readjust fire accurately, we had to walk through 3 Inf perimeters in the dark.

We ceased fire at 0600; but at 0630, we had to fire again. A Jap tank-Inf attack started against 2/Bn. At 0645, we held fire to keep from striking our own Sherman tanks moving to kill the Jap tanks. After 603 Tank Co destroyed seven Jap tanks, they reported that our FA caused great losses to attacking Jap Inf.

Waves of mortar, MG, and rifle fire now fell on F Co holding the northwest lines of 2/Bn's perimeter closest to the Japs. An observers' duel began between Jap and 146 observers.

Lt Thompson, S/Sgt Meyer, and Cpl Mackey assisted F Co. They set up in a MG hold on the coral terrace. This MG position was on the seaward side, but where they could observe the high ground north of Mokmer Strip.

For still better observation, Thompson with Mackey extending the phone wire, inched forward from the MG position to a vantage position north of the coral ridge-crest. They brought telling fire on the Japs until rifle and MG fire drove them back into the MG hole — and then from the MG position.

Thompson realized that Jap observer teams were striking at them from the main ridge. Moving back under the shelter of the coral terrace, he again scaled the ridge from E Co's perimeter. From here, he safely adjusted fire on the cliffs. Soon all Jap fire ceased.

While Thompson's observer party fought the Japs, a destroyer of ours erred in target identification. It caused death and wounds in 3/Bn. Although wounded himself, T/4 Bock stuck to his radio and got through to the destroyer to stop the shelling.

Now began 162 Regt's great retreat through Parai Defile. For they could not dislodge the Japs from the ridges. In fact, except for water communications, 162 Inf was totally cut off from the Division. To extricate his Reg't, Col Haney planned for 1/Bn to hold west of Parai while his other Bns passed through.

Withdrawal began at 1400. Most of 2/Bn left by amphib craft from Parai Jetty. While 146 FA and 947 FA observers protected their rear, the other 2 Bns and tanks marched east. Our observers called down a prepared barrage from Parai Jetty north to the cliffs. Afterwards, we observed an accurate creeping fire behind 1/Bn's exposed rearguard.

Entire withdrawal was from 1400 to 1700. It was without casualties. Inf COs credited their safe withdrawal to our FA's continuous creeping fire.

When 163 Inf (less 2/Bn came from Toem on 30 May, 146 FA was reassigned from 162 Inf. We supported 163 Inf through the end of their Biak Operation at Ibdi Pocket. Meanwhile, we assisted 186 Inf in their overland march to capture Mokmer Strip from the rear. But our most crucial exploits on Biak were to save 162 Inf from disaster at Mokmer Village and Parai Defile.

In fighting for 162 Inf on 27-29 May, we lost no guns to the Japs, but our casualties were the highest of any 41st Dis FA Bn in World War II. We had eight killed and 44 wounded — as many as some Inf rifle Cos in the whole New Guinea Campaign. Such was the price we had to pay for the honor of our forward position to back 162 Inf's first assault for Mokmer Strip.

CREDIT: Core of this story is a 6-page legal-sized typescript on the Biak Operation attributed to 146 FA's Capt. Allen. Sub-titles are "Battle for Mokmer Drome" and "Withdrawal." (For background, I have used also R. R. Smith's *Approach to the Philippines;* but where his hours conflict with Allen's, I have used Allen's. Allen I know to be closer to the action than Smith.) Other sources are 146's Biak casualty list, and award stories of Capt. Seymour Katz; 1/Lts Otto Schild and Frank Ridenoure; S/Sgt Paul Anderson; Sgt John Donaldson; T/4s Vernon Woltersdorf and Roger McClintock; and Cpl Elbert Mackey. An earlier, less detailed report appeared in the April 1972 *Jungleer,* with the misleading title "Battle in Parai Defile," reprinted in my first edition of *The Fighting Jungleers.* Published in August 1989 was a third 146 FA story of Biak called "Wet Landing and Night Combat." Capt. Allen covered all of 146 FA's action with the 41st: Hollandia, Biak, Zamboanga, Jolo, Bongao-Sanga Sanga, and Central Mindanao.

E Co.162 Inf. (Salamaua, Hollandia, Biak): BARman Floyd West's War

by Sgt. Floyd West with Dr. Hargis Westerfield, Division Historian

E Co 162 Inf's BARman Floyd West never forgot that morning when a Jap Zero pilot flew close overhead and did not slay him. On that morning of 1943, West was in a convoy of LCVs (Landing Crafts, Vehicles) which was chugging up the Guinea Shore to seize Morobe before the Salamaua Operation.

On that sunny New Guinea morning, West's LCV was helplessly lashed to an immobilized LCV. That evening before in the other LCV, an unaware Yank had lighted his last cigarette and chucked the empty foil pack into the sea. The LCV sump pump had sucked up the foil and plugged itself. Because water leaked under the closed ramp, that pump was needed to draw water from the LCV floor.

The 30-man cargo had to bail the LCV with their helmets. The coxswain had to halt the LCV until the pump was unplugged. While the rest of the LCV convoy drove onto Morobe, the mobile LCV with West in it was lashed to the crippled LCV to help hold up the crippled craft.

We did not dare to beach the two barges on that unknown Guinea Shore under dark mountains. Any straggling Japs, whether or not they had a MG, could murder us all at once. We lashed our two anchors together and let them drag below until they hooked into the shallows at a safe distance offshore.

All night the barges banged and bumped together in the waves. Men like West became seasick from the endless bouncing. Even if the men in West's barge kept dry and tried to sleep, it was a hard night.

Men in the immobile barge took turns to bail with their helmets all night from the water seeping under the ramp. One man had a flashlight to help start the complicated repairs, but not until morning could they actually work the pump.

Early next morning, out of the west from the direction of Morobe, a Jap Zero flew low less than 100 yards above the helpless LCVs. That Jap Zero flew low less than 100 yards above us. West looked up to see two more Zeros flying at 10,000 feet.

The lowest Zero was low enough for us to see the sunglasses on the pilot's nose, and his white silk scarf with the red ball of the Jap insignia on his forehead. But the pilot did not strafe us dead in our barges. He flew by and waved his wings, like saying, "You're lucky, boys!"

In BARman West's belt was a clip of .30 shells with tracers — MG shells which he could fire in his BAR. But he had sense enough not to fire on the plane. But the Lt. in the other barge shot at the Zero with his .45. Luckily he must have missed, for the pilot seemed unaware of the shot.

West shouted, "Stop that shooting! Look up!" The Lt. looked up and quickly sheathed his pistol. West still rejoices at our luck. If the Lt. had brought down three Zeros on our barges, we 60 men and four crewmen would have been just a temporary bloody spot in the ocean. But maybe the Zeros ignored us because they saved gas and ammo to strike richer targets farther west.

Soon the sump pump was repaired. We chugged on to Morobe and arrived at noon. Five minutes after West landed, he was seasick no longer.

At Morobe, 162 Inf had another notable encounter with a Nippo plane. Every night, "Washing Machine Charley" flew over, awoke us, and drove us into slit trenches. But a Black Widow Spider — a radar night fighter — called on Charlie. One night we hard gunfire and saw a flaming red ball. Washing Machine Charlie was forever silent.

West bitterly remembers one death at Morobe. One day, some 163 Inf men were swimming in the darkened brackish water near the river mouth. We had a guard for sharks. Suddenly, soundlessly, a man disappeared under the dark water. He had stood just 10 feet from three buddies. A crocodile must have dragged him down to cold, black, agonized death.

By 4 Apr., 162 Inf was mostly based at Morobe, except for detachments back down the coast to Gona, to mop up Jap stragglers. A short way up Morobe River, PT crews had a base to refit their little boats to harass and sink Jap barges. Our 162 Inf's main task, however, was preparation for Salamaua.

But not until some nine months later did E Co 162 Inf go into battle for our Division. We were not in 162's beachhead at Nassua Bay, but we reinforced our 3/Bn whom strong Jap forces had held from capturing Roosevelt Ridge — 3,000 feet of jungle mountain running in from Tambu Bay. On 27 July, 3 162 positioned for our fight to storm Roosevelt Ridge, and on 28 July BARman West was in the attack force. Having outshot the whole 2/Bn, West was assigned the heavy BAR which he could never permanently exchange for an M-1.

His climb to combat on the ridge-crest was heartbreaking. He had to literally crawl up a 60-degree slope hand to hand to hand from one brush clump to another. His BAR weighed 22 pounds, and 22 steel clips weighed almost as much. He wore a 40-pound combat pack with at least four grenades in it.

In the area where "E" fought, the slope was less than 20

degrees, with visibility into the jungle less than 100 feet. As his BAR opened up, he worried about hitting F 162 men in the jungle who might have already taken the ground before him. Yet he had to spray the leafy tangle to cover E Co men, and hope not to hit any Yanks.

Here he expended all of his BAR clips against unseen Japs, and called for more. No BAR clips came, and he refilled his clips with MG cartridges. Every fourth was a tracer. These tracers may have caused him his painful wound.

West continued his fight for Roosevelt Ridge. Again he sprayed the jungle — his gun now so hot that he lightly burned his left hand on the barrel.

West went great now in the magic of combat when a man's own life seems not to matter. He could not hear any other fire over the blasts of his BAR, and his MG bullets seemed to have halted Jap fire completely. West never stopped to think that even if he couldn't see where his tracers were hitting — that the Japs could see where they were coming from.

Then two Jap bullets found West. One really played havoc. The BAR was shot out of his right hand. A bullet hit his partly loaded BAR clip and blew it up while it was only partly fired.

The explosion smashed the knuckle above his right first finger. It stripped 90 percent of the flesh from the other side of the middle finger. Only a couple of strips of the clip remained in the BAR breach. His hand was permanently blackened from powder burns. Small fragments of cartridge casings and clips — dozens of slivers — dug into his right hand and shoulder and chest still to be removed by doctors years later.

He also had a hole the size of a half-dollar in his right cheek. The Medic — West remembers his name as Williams — said, "You're sure lucky. It missed your jugular vein by less than an inch."

Most important first aid that Medic Williams gave West was for the middle finger with its 90 percent of the skin loose and dangling. Probably Williams wrapped the loose skin back with a bandage over a tongue depressant. "I can save that skin for you," he said. "Don't let anybody unwrap it." Despite the offensive odor, West kept the bandage on and saved 90 percent of the skin with but a little scar tissue. He still has a sharp pain when he touches hard surfaces, but the finger has served him well over 40 years.

Leaving Roosevelt Ridge forever on his first day there, West noticed one wounded man with a chunk quarter-size on his bare rear. A mortar fragment had hit that part of his body which a training Sgt had told West is hardest to keep down.

Wounded West found his descent down Roosevelt Ridge easier than the climb, even if he now had just one good hand to grasp the roots of the almost sheer slope. He descended mostly on the seat of his pants.

On that 28 July 1943, he left Tambu Bay by PT boat. He lay forward on the bouncing deck, which bounced like all PT boats even in calm water. After a week in Dobodura Hospital, he was flown over the Owen Stanley Mountains first to Port Moresby, and then to Townsville, Australia.

Again hospitalized at Townsville, West had his purple heart pinned on his pajamas by Mrs. Eleanor Roosevelt. Behind among the beds strode two generals, one wearing three stars. As a civilian years later, West still needed outpatient treatment from a doctor. Three times, he had to have sharp quarter-inch squares of brass from the exploded clip extracted from deep in his right hand.

Rejoining E 162 regrouped at Rockhampton after Salamaua, West got a six-day Melbourne leave — all the leave he ever had in four years of military service.

Landing on 22 Apr. 1944 with 162 Inf at Hollandia, West again saw action — this time with a bazooka. At 0750, E 162 led our 2/Bn from the west shore of Jautefa Bay to cut the track from Pim Village on the coast to Hollandia.

Across a narrow mangrove beach covered with Jap supplies, we entered a wide mangrove swamp, not shown on the sand table we had seen earlier. We had to walk on slippery mangrove roots above the mud — hardly 100 yards in an hour. West fell on his bazooka and bent it on a root. But with others' help, he managed to straighten it out between two trees.

Above us on the Pim-Hollandia Track, we saw a Jap HMG firing down the track from a shelf 10 feet above it. Cliffs behind and over the shelf protected the gun-crew. The crew never saw E 162, for they had never expected us to come in from the swamp upon their flank. We were well concealed on a slope 50 feet below.

West loaded a bazooka round and killed the HMG. This was the major act of his war at Hollandia.

When E 162 landed on Biak, West had regained his BAR to use it well. On 27 May 1944, shortly after 0900 hours, West with "E" landed dry at Boxnek Jetty and scouted towards Parai Defile. "E" was securing the inland flank of 3/Bn pushing westward down the beach towards Mokmer Strip.

After patrolling about 500 yards to his left along the ridge above the jetty, West still saw only white cliffs ahead. Then he was recalled. For so far, marching 3/Bn had seen no Japs and thought that they needed no protection.

While falling back, West suddenly heard a noise and rose up to look over a bush. A Jap was up also and preparing to shoot West with an automatic weapon. This Jap "BAR" had a long curved top cartridge clip, unlike West's BAR with the clip under the gun.

Instantly West fired first — squeezed his trigger to loose six shots a second. First bullet hit the Jap near the left shoulder. Other bullets then cut a strip across his body to the right ear. West felt hot blood on his own hands and face. He had beheaded the Jap, and the wind had blown the blood on West.

Slipping around the bush, West saw four Japs including the beheaded man lying with their backs up, like playing possum. The living three lay face down in a six-foot pocket in the brush. They had three automatic rifles, but they made no further attempt to use them. West saw that the headless Jap had a star on his shoulder.

Telling his Pln to hold fire, West executed the live three. Blood from an artery or lung squirted several feet up in the air. These four Japs had let our patrol bypass them on the way up the ridge. For an unknown reason, they failed to fire and slip away. Before we recovered from our surprise, they could have slain a number of us and then escaped.

West later wondered whether we should have tried to take the three live Japs for prisoners. But he could also think that they might have hidden grenades on their bodies to blow up "E" men who might try to capture them. West left the corpses for foolish souvenir hunters.

West soldiered on with E 162 in our great Parai Defile disaster until the third day. On 29 May, he was again wounded.

At that time, West's Pln was waiting for orders down in the Defile. A real sniper — not just any Jap rifleman whom we miscalled a sniper — seems to have fired down from Parai Cliff — less than 1,000 yards away.

When the bullet hit, West was near a large tree. It pierced his helmet and cut his cheekbone just before his right ear. Perhaps the bullet hit the large tree and spent much of its force before it rebounded and struck him. For by just a half-inch, it missed his eye, temple, or ear and did not bore in. After 10 hospital days, West rejoined E Co — with just a small patch on his cheekbone.

Such are outstanding memories of E 162's Floyd West. Home on furlough, he was transferred into Air Corps as a mechanic. But he still in heart belongs to 162 Inf and our 41st Infantry Division.

> **CREDIT:** Predominant sources are Floyd West's letters of 15 Feb, 6 Apr, 25 June, and 22 Nov — all written in 1985. These consist of 19 legal size pages and 16 letter size pages — single-spaced and handwritten. R.R. Smith's *Approach to the Philippines* was useful for reference on Hollandia and Biak — and on Salamaua, Col A.R. Mackechnie's *Operations of 162nd Infantry in Salamaua Campaign in New Guinea*, a typescript submitted to the Infantry School at Fort Benning, Georgia, in May 1944.

41st men on maneuvers. (Courtesy of Rohlffs)

Occupation revealed this Japanese factory for two-man suicide submarines. Kure, Japan. (Courtesy of Watson)

Japanese cannibalism was discovered by 41st man John Watson and as this Formosan laborer was eaten without the courtesy of being killed first. He was still alive when Sgt. Watson photographed him. (Courtesy of Watson)

148 Field Artillery Battalion from Darwin to Luzon

by Willard A. (Bill) Heath with Dr. Hargis Westerfield, Division Historian

Copyright: in usual places in *Jungleer*, in year of publication.

Credit (smallest type, boldface, box). Only official archive is *History of 148th Field Artillery Battalion*, June 1-December 31, 1945. Bill Heath wrote a softback 41-page book named *Unit History/1940-1946* with a list of 36 contributors. Important also are Cliff Causton's 72-page handwritten manuscript, and the *Horace Brown Story*, which Heath parlayed into half a dozen manuscripts averaging 35 pages. Part of 148th Field Artillery's saga appears in a number of books. Australian books are Douglas Lockwoods's *Australia's Pearl Harbor*, and Dudley McCarthy's *SW Pacific Area: The First Year*. American Books are John Miller's *Cartwell: The Reduction of Rabaul*, Samuel Eliot Morison's *Breaking the Bismarks Barrier* from his 14-volume *History of U.S. Naval Operations in World War II*, and Robert Ross Smith's *Triumph in the Philippines*. (Data on 148th Field Artillery in the Philippines are meager, despite above archive and Smith's volume.)

Some of most notable among contributors to Bill Heath's Unit History are Jack Allured, Horace Brown, Cliff Causton, Vernon Dubbert, Lloyd Henrichs, Louis Kohl, and Joseph Tomecek.

When the radio announced the disaster at Pearl Harbor, 148th Field Artillery was already in convoy west of Hawaii to join the Philippine Army. At once, our convoy began zig-zagging to dodge possible submarine torpedoes. Aboard stinking old liner *Holbrook* (copra and jute cargoes), we repainted it battleship gray. We donned life jackets with full canteens.

At Suva, the Fiji Island Capital, orders re-routed us to Australia. From Brisbane, we passed between Australia and New Guinea to land at Little Darwin for new orders.

After midnight six weeks later, we left Darwin in a fool-hardy convoy to reinforce Aussie fighters on Timor Island in Indonesia, 400 miles north across open sea without air cover. Only protection was heavy cruiser *Houston* with aged destroyer *Peary* and two Aussie sloops. We had five transports with Aussie engineers and AT guns and crews on three of them. Our 148th Field Artillery was on USS *Portmar* Aussie *Tulagi*.

On our second day out, a Jap recon plane dropped bomb sticks that missed B and C Batteries on *Portmar*. On the fourth day, 35 Mitsubishi heavy bombers and nine flying boats attacked in four flights from four directions. But to kill us, they had to kill veteran cruiser *Houston* first.

Under a transport's smoke screen, *Houston* fought off the 44 planes with 900 rounds in 45 minutes. Lying on his back with binoculars, Captain Rook turned *Houston* aside from the bombers. When Their flights criss-crossed with sticks of bombs, he backed *Houston* full speed astern. Near misses covered *Houston* with splashes several times, but she came up striking back. Total casualties from a near miss to one transport were three Aussies, one seriously wounded.

Back at Darwin, 148th Field Artillery's transports with 33 other vessels took a raid like that on Pearl Harbor. On February 19, 1944, CO Mitsu Fuchida's 242 planes blasted crowded Darwin Harbor. (Fuchida had also commanded at Pearl Harbor). While his powerful fleet circled offshore, the planes sank eight ships, drove one onto the beach, damaged 11 more. (Twenty-three went undamaged). They slew 243 including 52 civilians and wounded 52 more.

U.S. destroyer *Peary* was blown out of the water, her last .50 HMG still blazing. U.S. transports *Meigs* and *Mauna* Loa were sunk, also British tanker named *British Motorist*, and Aussie passenger ships *Neptuna* and *Zealandia*. Aussie hospital ship *Manunda* was savagely damaged. U.S. freighter *Admiral Halstead* was also blasted, but her captain floated ashore a cargo of high octane gas in 44-gallon drums. These were outstanding examples of Nippo victories.

When the attack began, 148th Field Artillery's *Tulagi* and *Port Mar* trapped in the back bay. Hoping to be unnoticed, *Tulagi's* soldiers were all below deck, except for MG crews and Lieutenant Kohl. (Nobody could find the custodian of the key to the real AA guns.)

Just as they were leaving, the planes tried to sink *Tulagi* and *Port Mar*. While firing .50 HMGs, C Battery's Skelton were killed, and A's Wofford and Meade, with Belknap seriously wounded. On Likkel's gun, assistant Wilbur died. Lieutenant Kohl credits Sam and Sergeant Hulse with saving *Tulagai* from sinking. While diving and machine gunning, a Jap bomber tried to drop his last bomb on *Tulagi's* deck. The under water explosion did cause the captain to try to beach the ship.

Much less is known about *Port Mar's* battle for survival. Evidently she took five hits from 50-pound bombs. Perhaps two did not explode. One fell harmless below on a mattress. A B Battery man carried it up and dropped it safely overside. The other three caused damage below the water-line. Ninety-eight holes penetrated *Port Mar's* sides. She headed for the dock but an ammo ship (name unknown) blew up there. *Port Mar* grounded on an Aussie lepers' island where the men were rescued.

Men climbed down ropes or jumped from sinking *Tulagi*, then swam to safety or caught little boats. Although a boat was coming alongside for him, Lieutenant Colonel Patterson wanted to be last off with *Tulagi's* captain. Bertol and Technical Sergeant Kemp had to throw him into the sea for the boat to pick him up. But Bertol and Kemp were carried out to sea in the tide. For three hours, they took turns gripping a 2x4 or swimming. Two Aussies in a motor boat finally bore them ashore.

Wofford, Meade, Skelton, and Wilbur in *Tulagi* were 148s only dead. (Wilbur had discharged himself from hospital to join the Timor convoy). In either transport, 148 had many wounded. Major Whitely was hit in his arm, and Second Lieutenant Henrichs in his calf. Other known wounded from either of the two ships were Belknap, Horace Brown, Lieutenant Les Brown, Blake, Brook, Brogan, Nickolauson, Tieman, and Walton. We had actually 35 Purple Hearts.

Only five Jap planes and five probables were reported. The Japs downed 24 U.S. planes and damaged two.

Why did the Japs hit Darwin almost instantly after our Timor convoy returned? Their spy was a wheelchair "cripple" who managed the Darwin curio shop. Since he was crippled while a prisoner, he was kindly released on parole. After the raid, a Darwin civilian saw him walking. In the back of his shop, officials discovered plenty of sophisticated radio equipment. He was executed.

After garrison duty at Darwin, 148th Field Artillery took our salvaged 75mm guns into southeast Australia to trade them for 105s. We had over three months training and rest in happy Ballarat city. (There were at least seven marriages to Aussie wives.) Nine months after the Darwin raid, we finally struck the Japs in combat.

We became part of Operation Cartwheel to defang Rabaul on New Britain north of New Guinea. With its deepwater harbor and four airfields, Rabaul was the main staging area for invading New Guinea. We teamed with horseless 112 Cavalry to land at Arawe (Cape Merkus) on the south shore of New Britain, 300 miles southwest of Rabaul.

At 0510 on December 15, 1943, our forward observer Lieutenant Schermer with a team of Battery A men was overside in a rubber boat with 14 more rubber boats of Company A 112 Cavalry to attempt the Arawe landing. Noon was four days past prime over the dark unknown shore. Destroyer *Shaw* stood by to fire support.

The Jap garrison of two companies of 53rd Infantry Regiment crouched to fire down our throats from the beach enfiladed by MGs. At 0522, about 100 yards from the beach, Jap MG and rifle fire broke out. Of 15 rubber boats, 12 were punctured and sank. Cavalry losses were 12 men killed, four missing, and 17 wounded. Destroyer *Shaw* could not see where the three boats did land and had to hold fire.

An AA Battery killed Lieutenant Schermer and sank our field artillery boat. His Battery A men were in the water three hours before a landing craft chanced to pick them up.

Other 112 Regiment men landed on other parts of the coast to help secure the beach for advances inland. We saw some Yanks borne past us for burial in blanket-covered stretchers. Our field artillery lost good men also, names unknown. About 150-200 Japs died.

Most effective Jap resistance was from planes—dive bombers daily for 30 days. They sank a small coastal transport, damaged two sub-chasers, and four LSTs. Nightly, "Washing Machine Charlie" disturbed our sleep, dropped a bomb or so. One moonlit night, all our HMGs gathered and scared hell out of him. He revved and jerked the throttle to save himself—surely needed two new wings and a change of underwear.

Two Jap battalions tried to expel us. Major Komori's 1/Battalion 181st Infantry crossed 15 streams from the north coast while Tobushi's 1/Battalion 181st Infantry landed from the sea. We got reinforcements. With two companies of 158th Infantry, a tank company, and medium bombers, we defeated their greatest onslaught of January 16, 1944. (By January 21, Komori Battalion alone had lost 116 killed, 117 wounded, 14 dead of disease, and 80 sick.)

Our best remembered shoot-out came when Puli River Canyon halted 112's advances. Across the river, Japs were formidable in pillboxes and caves. Our field artillery officer lacked confidence in Fire Direction Center to fire over advancing men and kept down losses.

Instrument specialist Corporal Nielsen asked the 112 Cavalry officer to assign our field artillery officer for temporary duty elsewhere. With the help of a spotter on the river-bank, he walked our 105's shells into the Jap pillboxes and caves and dislodged them. Our guns followed 112 Cavalry across Puli River to pursue the Japs.

In Arawe Battle, 148th Field Artillery fired 4,400 rounds—at times a continuous bombardment. Several gun barrels had to be relined. And at least once, we fought as infantry. Once, while on forward liaison duty, Headquarter Battery's Captain Cook with Sergeant Boyd blasted two grenades into the rear of a pillbox and thought they had killed the men in it. But they found a Jap still living and took him to Intelligence for questioning.

On March 17, 1944, 15 men were seriously burned; some died. In a class on thermite grenades, a new second lieutenant exploded a white phosphorous grenade. Harry Harris was among those taken out of action for some time.

After Arawe, 148th Field Artillery had three more wars to fight. In mid-1944, we helped 112 Cavalry hold the Drinumor River line in New Guinea. In the fall, we fired for 112 Cavalry on Leyte. And by February 1945, we had begun our final long action on Luzon Island. This was mountain fighting against the Jap Shimbu Group east of Manila.

With 112 Cavalry, we protected 6th Army's communications lines from their supply depots in the Luzon central plain. Sixth Army's mission was to destroy the 50,000 man Shimbu Group holding the mountains east of Manila. Thus on February 19-26, we fired for 112 Cavalry from Muzon Village, Bulacan Province. Near here, Corporal Durham endured heavy Jap shellfire to dash 100 yards and put out a fire near his battery ammo dump.

Through February 26, we had Corporal Barraclough killed, and six wounded: McKnight, Hamilton, Kirk, Brandt, Lieutenant Engle, and Sergeant Purnell. (No other information is available on these casualties.)

Next operation with 112 Cavalry was to help capture Wawa and Ipo Dams deep among mountain precipices. These dams impounded most of the water supplying wrecked Manilla city. Mainly, this was a war against tropical diseases, with few casualties.

In four months, 148th Field Artillery had just 10 more casualties, including two attached Filipinos. Killed were Crosby, Lethrop, and guerillas Martin and Second Lieutenant Mendoza. Wounded were Duling, Fox, Hilker, First Lieutenant Tabaka, Second Lieutenant Crissman, Sergeant Young, and Corporal Duling. We know only how Crosby and Lieutenant Mendoza died.

On Crosby's and Mendoza's death night, Battery B was for the second night on detached duty under a bright moon. A "Jap" demolition team (actually eight tall hairy Koreans).

Sentry Taylor's carbine wounded the first raider. Even in the abdomen, the carbine impact was too light. The man fled. Awakened Causton of service battery volleyed at six Koreans with his tommy but missed. The Koreans returned rifle fire, threw a harmless grenade.

Automatic rifle fire slashed at Causton and Cohalan, pinned them in shallow wash. From the Korean came a continuous shaft of flame, but it missed. Causton had fallen flat on his tommy gun and feared to rise up to use it.

Covered by automatic fire, two Koreans shoved a demolition charge under the rear of a 6x6 truck, and placed another under the maintenance truck. A third Korean poured gas from a bidon on that truck.

The exploding charge flamed the truck and lighted up the whole area. O'Donald and his gun crew of two cooks mounted a .30 MG on the hill by the kitchen. Three Koreans charged the gun uphill, one by one. Despite having to clear 20 MG stoppages, O'Donald slew all three.

Behind Causton in that tricky light, Bales mistook him for a Korean and fired twice at him. First bullet slashed Causton's left ear lobe and left side of his neck—a lucky wound despite much blood. Second shot was a near miss. Causton swore at Bales and rushed back down the wash and dropped beside him.

Guerilla Second Lieutenant Mendoza panicked from the kitchen and ran out yelling for us not to shoot. We accidentally killed him.

Meanwhile, the Korean Taylor had shot, was crawling slowly through a narrow rice paddy to the kitchen with a bandage around his abdomen. We fired on him but missed. In a kitchen slit trench, he found Crosby, an 18 year old replacement who had joined us yesterday, and cut his throat. After the Korean tried to escape, we counted 22 Yank bullet holes in him.

This was perhaps 148th Field Artillery's last notable fight—with two of us dead and two trucks destroyed. (Hilker was also reported wounded that day, but probably not in that fight.) Out of maybe nine to 10 who attacked, Causton estimated four to six dead Koreans.

By June 25 all gun batteries of 148th Field Artillery were back into rest camp. Massive rotation Stateside has already begun. Called by one reporter, "The Little Giant of the Pacific" (with 112th Cavalry Regiment), we had been overseas 44 months—had seen action in Australia, New Britain, New Guinea, Leyte, and Luzon. Such is 148th Field Artillery's epic of pride in combat.

ADDENDUM-Three Arawe wounded deserve to be remembered. Irving and Corporal Drake volunteered (probably) to go on patrol up the New Britain coast on a landing craft and hiding out by day. But one of our P-39s with .37 guns saw the amphib craft and thought that it was Japanese. Irving survived with a silver plate in his head, and Drake despite a torn left shoulder. Plumlee was wounded at another time and evacuated by LCM. Although ordered to loosen the bandage around his knee, the busy medics neglected him, and he had to have an amputation.

163rd Ind. Regimental Chapel, 1945. (Courtesy of Huck)

162 Inf Medical Detachment: From Zamboanga To Namnam

by Pharmacist Don Cortright with Dr. Hargis Westerfield, Division Historian

On Filipino Mindoro Island in 1945, Don Cortright's medical career began. (And Don is still a "Medic" today — a pharmacist in Monroe, Michigan.) Although coming to Mindoro as a rifleman, he was reassigned to 162's Medical Detachment. With five others — including friends Turner, Schenk, and Kornbluth — high IQ exam ratings had caused reassignments to Medics.

On-the-job training at first was attendance for sick call with an experienced Medic to supervise. Don painted sores and bandaged feet, learned names and uses of various medicines. He had medical lectures each morning. Next came classes on bandaging, injecting morphine, and giving plasma. He had also close-order drill, hikes, reveille, retreat.

There was litterbearer training for the coming campaign. Officially called noncombatants, they carried carbines "for personal protection only." Although unmarked as Medics on helmets or armbands, they would be identified by carrying medical kits and litters.

One windy, dusty day on Mindoro, Don saw 162's first campaign "casualty." A rifleman blew off his big toe with an M-1. He said that he had shot it off accidentally.

Don came in time to grasp a large severed tendon — kept it from retracting into the foot before the doctor came. Don never saw the man again.

On 8 Mar 1945, 162's Meds boarded small LCIs ("landing craft Inf") for Zamboanga. Beaching on 10 Mar, 18 minutes after H-Hour, Don landed safely.

Hardest work at first was carrying litter, carbine, and pack. The shouldered carbine would slip down his arm and try to fall off when he had to lift the litter to carry a casualty. He also had to carry a heavy medical kit. It held tourniquet, rolled bandage, triangle bandage, scissors, sulfa powder packets, and calamine lotion. He also had packets of 1.5 cc syrettes holding half-grains of morphine tartrate, and several large and small sizes of "field brown" dressings in sterile waxed paper for gunshot wounds.

On D-Day, he helped bear wounded to an aid station. He helped move that aid station several times. It was set up a few yards behind advancing Inf. That first night, Don lay in a hole and watched tracers overhead.

Medics' living conditions improved quickly — with hot food from a kitchen instead of "K" rations. The kitchen also had a few hundred Filipino refugees down from the hills everyday. Most of them wore big grins and were very polite.

In late light of 13 Mar., a plane roared by, not 400 yards away. A soldier yelled "Zero!" Everybody scrambled for the little cover. Half a mile past them, it bombed and strafed the beach, then veered off under harmless AA fire. Nobody had bothered with a slit trench, but two hours later, four were deeply dug into the hard ground.

Don found three abandoned ponchos. He connected them for a mosquito-proof sleeping shelter. On his second night in it, he heard the opening rustle, levelled his carbine at the sound. It was just Episcopal Chaplain Smith's assistant asking for shelter from the venomous mosquito stings. Don "smugly" let him sleep in safety.

Near one aid station were sweet corn fields and sweet potatoes, and nearby coconut trees. There were many vacant huts left standing by the Japs. With his buddy Turner, Don checked them for souvenirs. Because of possible stray Japs, they often approached a hut from opposite sides with fingers on carbine triggers.

Once they found eggs and sweet corn that they guessed that the Filipino owners had left. While they carried this food out, the owners caught them. Don and friend became red faced!

They offered to trade C-ration cans for their plunder. The Filipinos happily agreed. They said that Japs seized their food — never offered to pay. That night, two Medics enjoyed a fresh unrationed supper.

Don traded a pair of suntan pants for a Jap battle flag, found another in the helmet of a Nippo corpse. He acquired a cache of Jap blankets covered with designs, and Jap diaries which he gave to "Intelligence" to translate.

But all the while, Zambo Fight went on as 162 Inf and other Regts drove the Japs deep into jungle mountains. Like his other three litter bearer cobbers — Turner, Schenk, Kornbluth — he endured the labor of carrying 150-180 pound Yank casualties up and down the foothills.

Don had to cope with the menace of snipers trying to sight him through telescope attachments from tall trees. Like other Medics, he had to take his turn on the killing grounds. But no one was hit while he served there.

One troublesome sniper was indeed hard to kill; he must have fired 50 times without results. Automatic fire was useless against suspected trees. Finally, mortars silenced the sharp reports of his rifle.

Some days later, men bore a dead 2/Lt into the aid station. While leading his men up a hill, he took a sniper's bullet between his eyes — never knew what hit him.

After a fairly comfortable life in garrison beginning 2 Apr, Don was sent to a Pln up front. Heaviest combat was over, and F Co was mopping up surviving Japs. Don now had to sleep on the ground in his poncho and eat front-line rations that he had to carry himself. He could become a sniper's prime target because a Medic casualty would leave the "F" Pln without badly needed medical attention.

Yet Don was pleased that his "F" men called him "Doc," and placed him for security in the middle of the column on patrol. At night, he slept on inner perimeter.

Suddenly he got a real initiation into duties of a frontline Medic. Asleep in perimeter with only combat boots off, he woke to rifle shots, then the call "Medic!" Back into boots with aid kit, he slipped into a trench with a wounded Yank.

With diarrhea, this man had crawled outside perimeter without telling anyone. When he tried to crawl back, his own squad leader thought him a Jap and shot him three times.

Before treating the wounds, Don injected a 1.5 cc morphine syrette into the man. He powdered all wounds with sulfa, bandaged them under a flashlight. It was an ordeal to dress them. Every time he moved the man, he found another hole — three entrance and three exit wounds. One was in the chest, one in the side, and one in the elbow. Entrance M-1 hole was about the size of a little finger. Exit hole behind it was as large as a fist where a chunk of flesh was blasted out.

Trying to comfort him, Don stayed beside him until daylight. Then came other Medics with plasma. They splinted his broken arm to a carbine and carried him back in a litter.

(Like this man, Don himself was once almost shot accidentally. From sleep in a tent back in garrison, he went to the latrine in the dark. Returning to lift the entrance flap, he stared into an M-1 muzzle. But the man was not trigger-happy — merely warned Don never to leave the tent without informing somebody.

Although 186 and 163 men still hunted down retreating Nips in the Zambo mountains, Don's 162 Inf embarked to help 24 Inf Div regain Central Mindanao from the Japs. By 4 May after voyaging some 150 miles east from Zambo over Moro Gulf, Don debarked from an LST ("landing ship tank") at Cotabato. Here he spent two weeks on aid station duties — mostly treated Filipinos with nasty sores and ulcers.

Then Don became part of 2/Bn 162's final fighting in World War II. While 162's other Bns reinforced 24 Inf Div far southeast of Cotabato to fight north of Davao, Don's 2/Bn moved on the Japs northwest of Cotabato. In mountains east of Pulangi River, Jap survivors of 30 Div still held out.

Jammed into a tiny LCM ("landing craft mechanized") on 19 May, Don endured a torturing trip eastward up Mindanao River deep into the island. It was a dismal 10 hours in an open boat under hot sun as Mindanao River bored inland.

All along the banks, natives came out to stare at this liberating convoy. They yelled — clapped hands — danced jigs.

Most of their children were stark naked. Soldiers threw part of their K-rations to them, laughed as they scrambled for what we had rejected.

Our LCM voyage ended after about 50 miles east from Moro Gulf to near Kabakan Village where the river kept on east. For trekking 100 miles north to Valencia Airport, we boarded trucks of 1.5 tons — 6x6 trucks. Journey was hard labor — up twisted trails — through jungles and mountains, along cliffsides and down gorges.

Don's "six-by-six" dragged a 3-ton ammo trailer, so was stuck in mud or on grades more than other trucks. Like the others, Don's truck had a powerful winch on the front. Sometimes, they had to use the winch just to pull the truck a few yards at a time. Once they took seven hours to move 15 miles. Don still remembers their camp in a rubber plantation. A gash in a tree would produce "rubber juice," a thin, white milky sap.

It took over two days to reach Valencia Airport, about centering wide Mindanao Island. Don was now in Bukidnon Province, a land of grassy savannas and high mountains, much like West Texas, with its southwest continental climate. Days were hot; nights were cold. At night, he needed two wool blankets. But the chill did keep down the number of mosquitos.

At Valencia, men had "Jap scare." One night 200 men panicked before a movie screen. At the edge of the watchers, 10 men rose and crowded towards the center. Then men began to shove and scramble and crawl. They cowered — as if defenseless from a hail of grenades or a Jap bayonet-rush. Screen was knocked over; a major lost a tooth. The cause was that one man thought that he had seen a Jap — nothing else!

Expecting front-line Medic's action again, Don finally solved his problem of carrying a litter with the slung carbine sliding down his shoulder. A passing soldier peddled him a .45 automatic for $50, with two 7-shot clips.

On 13 June, Don's 2/Bn 162 was part of the Namnam move to help clear Japs from the Iglosad-Namnam area east of Valencia. Five columns advanced east across Pulangi River — elements of 31 Div with 180th Regtl Combat team and   2/Bn 162 Inf attached.

Through rain forests and mountains, they floundered in knee-deep mud and across hip-high streams. Starting down a big hill above a valley before more high mountains, they were in danger. They were halfway down the hill when Jap fire broke out. They hit the ground and started to crawl back up, hoping that the tall grass would help conceal them. It was tough to have to crawl under heavy packs. As the sweating men rested, a burst of bullets thudded the ground near Don.

One slug struck near the heel of the man before him. That scared man crawled uphill to escape past three men above him. Exhausted, angry Don wanted to snatch an M-1 to empty down the valley.

This fight lasted several days while mortars and planes even with napalm impacted the Japs until Inf expelled them. Meanwhile, Don was almost killed. On the hill crest, he scanned Jap positions with borrowed binoculars. Maybe they reflected the light. A Jap sniper's bullet clipped so close to him that it threw dirt into his mouth. Don rolled over to safety and thankfully returned the borrowed binoculars.

Yet only reported casualties for 162 Inf were Maj Ratliff and PFC Morris. Native bearers had to carry Ratliff by stretcher all the way back through mountain jungles to Valencia.

After 21 days, 2/Bn 162's "Namnam Mission" was over. There had been a victorious 3-day fight near Miligan, and five days more combat near Pulangi River. But FA and planes carried on most of the battles. Then the Yanks turned over the pursuit of the fleeing Japs to the Filipino Inf, and marched 20 miles back to Valencia in two days.

Don Cortright's real war was ended. But to go home again, he must return to Zamboanga and participate in 162 Inf in the Japanese occupation.

For Don, the war was great. Besides coming home alive and unwounded, he had gained an incentive through his Medic's experience to become a civilian professional. Today, Don has his own pharmacy in Monroe, Michigan.

CREDIT: I believe that all front-line Medics will smile in memory as they share Don Cortright's experience. Inspiration for this history is from his carefully written book based on his diary. Title is *A GI in World War II*. It's an attractive 89-page softback illustrated with Don's own photos. Other sources are Don's four letters dated 7, 10, 13 Feb, and 18 Apr — all written in 1989. "Report of Casualties of 162 Inf in Central Mindanao" names just two wounded near Namnam.

G Co 163 Inf (2/Pln): Combat in the Zamboanga Ridges

by S/Sgt Kermit Dulian with Dr. Hargis Westerfield, Division Historian

After G 163's 2/Pln's four-day fight against Japs in "Death Valley" at their Pasananca stronghold, we had to battle them again on the Zambo ridges. On 17 Mar 1945, 2/Pln advanced again into that deadly defile with a ridge holding pillboxes 10 feet apart and a 40 mm gun emplaced. This time, no tanks marched with us, but the valley and its gun were forever silenced. Past hundreds of shell-torn Japanese corpses, 2/Pln climbed our first ridge while laying wire back to CO Capt Braman.

With E Co on our right, "G" was to push against Japs still holding the ridge running from southeast to northwest above Pasananca. We were also to contact and support 162 Inf operating against Mt Capisan to our left. With two air-strikes and shells from 146 FA's 105s and 218 FA's a55s, we moved safely into the ridges. The night was quiet but for a 146 FA "short" that landed too near S/Sgt Dulian's hole.

On 18 Mar, E Co passed us climbing high, steep hills. In a park-like valley, we found a Jap Hqs with motor pool and switch board for detonating mined hills. We destroyed the board.

On a 4-man patrol up a steep trail to a hill-top, Scout Lamb saw four men with backs turned who sat eating coconuts. With "E" to our right, and 162 to our left, Lamb thought that the four were 162's Yanks. But Dulian knew that even the most careless Yanks would watch a little.

Tommie gun ready, Dulian slipped into the clearing and shouted, "Hi, fellows!" Four Japs leaped up to face us — and drop under Dulian's Tommie and Lamb's M-1. Later we found two helmets and blood. Probably a fair-sized Jap outpost had fled with the four bodies.

Capt Braman had "G" occupy that ridge. Now T/Sgt Reece saw movement at a cliff-base 60 feet below. Going down with Ford and McInerney to clear the brush near the cliff, Dulian saw leaves shake. He reached for a grenade. Suddenly he realized that he was a target for a concealed Jap 30 feet off who might have a bead on him that very instant.

As he whirled to run for cover, a Jap bullet went all the way through his left forearm, near where another bullet had wounded him last year on Biak. All three took cover; the Jap escaped. Dulian's arm burned and stung and bled freely, but the wound was too minor for him to earn a hospital rest.

While Braman and radioman Armstrong examined Dulian's wound in a seemingly safe spot — but in the open —

we heard a loud "Crack!" A Jap bullet in the shoulder felled Armstrong and did hospitalize him — and not Dulian.

About 1405, a 30-man "G" patrol from another Pln contacted 162's men on our left flank across a 500-yard gap. Although pressing Japs before us, "G" was again in a hot spot.

About midnight of 18-19 Mar, Japs struck 3/Pln below 2/Pln — killed Utigard, wounded Rudningen. G and H Cos slew probably 19 Japs. Firing continued until daylight.

On 19 Mar, G's 2/Pln had some bloody little fights. Early that morning, we heard Jap rifle fire below. Fields' squad was working through brush to scare out the Japs.

Meanwhile, 2/Pln's Bleck and S/Sgt Waskovich were neutralizing booby traps 30 feet apart. Wasko looked around just as Bleck crashed to the ground as a rifle cracked. Bleck saved himself by crawling back to a stretcher.

Now five shots rang out like a Jap HMG. Scared Ford ran from outguard back to Dulian trying to eat a "K" ration. As Ford reached for a cigarette, he had seen a Jap trying to kill him from the brush. Without aim, Ford fired five shots fast as a Jap MG, and ran. Dulian took Abramowitz back to support Ford on his guard, and returned to his "K" ration.

Then Sgt Reece and 2/Lt Beall asked for Dulian's help. Scout Fiorello of S/Sgt Fields' squad lay wounded in brush under hidden Jap riflemen. Fields himself had tried to save Fiorello and had died with two bullets in his head.

Dulian heard that Fiorello lay in jungle on the right of the trail, but we could not see him or hear him. The Japs were somewhere left of the trail — but probably only a few of them.

Dulian had his BARman Tony and Bates from Wako's squad take a 50-foot interval between them and spray the brush left of the trail. They fired several clips low in the brush. We waited 10 minutes to give the Japs time to leave.

With Tony and Whip covering, Lamb and Dulian went in for Fiorello. The Japs were gone, but Fiorello could not be heard. Lamb finally saw Fiorello; Dulian softly called to him. At first, Fiorello would not answer. But he was still alive!

Later, Fiorello said that every time he cried for help, the Japs shot him again. He had lost much blood, from a bullet in the right leg, and three in the chest. But after plasma and bandages, he survived in hospital. (Early in April, Westerfield spoke to him afoot in Zambo, about to head home for the States.)

Fields, McCorkle, and Bombardier were dead, and other sick or wounded — out of action. G's 2/Pln was down from 38 to 16 men — "the 16 fighting fools," as we called ourselves. Fields' disbanded squad joined with Dulian's and Waskovich's squad to bring both up to seven men apiece.

Pressing on into the hills on 20 Mar, 2/Pln narrowly escaped from a dark night trap. That morning, 2/Pln worked carefully down a steep slope into a village that the Nips had just left. Returning villagers gave us tomatoes and fresh eggs tasting wonderful when we boiled them. F Co sent a patrol up a ravine into the next hill and brought back their dead — a handsome blond young man, blood-covered. The "F" Lt said that Jap dugouts and pillboxes were everywhere. Filipino refugees also reported Japs in force a mile up the ravine.

About 1400, 2/Pln got orders to advance up that ravine. G Co's Sgt Kosing already held the hill shoulder on the left. "E" was trying to push up the shoulder on our right.

In 2/Pln, Dulian's squad moved out first. His two BARmen were in front for heavy fire instantly on any Jap who might open up. The BARmen were Dulian's Tony and Fields' Bowers.

After 100 yards past Kosing, a Jap LMG fired, with several rifles. Dulian's squad dropped under fire. Our glasses spied pillboxes on both sides, but not the Jap LMG, which Kosing's BARs could not kill because the gunners could not see it.

Around the ravine bend, Dulian dodged back to the main G Co, and brought back withdrawal orders. They left, a man at a time, while H Co covered with a HMG barrage.

Orders now were to entrench in the throat of the ravine for the night. We might as well have had our graves dug in advance. It was a downhill lie where Japs could roll grenades on us in the dark. We were drawing occasional sniper shots; the LMG was zeroing in on us. And to hold this ravine, we had only 1/Lt Brandon's detachment — Beall's 16 men of our Pln, part of 3/Pln, and a section of LMGs.

Japs cut our wire behind us. When Griffith and Goodman went to splice it, a shot missed them from a pillbox cleared earlier. Around a bend, Goodman with his tommie suddenly faced a Jap with a Yank BAR across a boulder. The surprised Nipp ducked. Goodman and Griffith raced back around our bend to tell our little detachment that we were cut off.

Brandon sent Wasko's nervous squad back to clear our rear and repair the line, if possible. They reconnected the wire without firing a shot. There Bates found a Jap pistol lying on the trail. We were sure that we were deep in a trap — high ground on both sides, Japs everywhere, and dark just an hour away.

Thank God that Capt Braman phoned with orders to leave as fast as we could. E Co on our right had retreated. In the falling light, F Co reported a Jap force in the ravine.

Back in last night's perimeter, we had no supper. Our kitchen party had drawn fire on the trail and had to turn back. About daylight, a Jap 75 shot at our hill, hurt nobody.

On 21 Mar, our Pln against cleared the water-hold down by the village. No Japs had reoccupied the nearby pillboxes. About 1200, our Pln had to clear out those same pillboxes in the ravine that we had cleared yesterday. While "E" moved uphill on our right, we climbed also while leaving Waskovich's squad to guard a demolition crew for those pillboxes.

Once while climbing in the open, we saw a Jap patrol some distance across the ravine. We were fine targets in the open, but they did not see us. When Wasko's squad forwarded from behind, they drew rifle fire the last 100 yards but arrived unhurt. Jap fire continued for an hour.

On the next ridge (probably "Brown Nose" Ridge) that 21 Mar, Kosing with 1/Pln and 3/Pln had to retreat under heavy Jap rifle fire, MGs, and mortars. Here 3/Pln's Hoffman took a little bullet hole in his forehead — the last man killed in G Co. Vanderwelt of the MGs was paralyzed for days with a bullet near his spine, but recovered for duty. Before dark, our H Co 81st seemed to make a direct hit on a pillbox. Bodies and a bundle of rags flew up. (By 1643, E Co did seize Brown Nose Ridge.)

On 22 Mar, G Co was almost destroyed. After a barrage on the hill next to where "G" was dug in, Marine Corsairs dived on it, bombing and strafing. Then a Corsair dived for the wrong hill — for G Co's hill!

G Co's warning flag was not up, but we were out in the clear to be seen plainly. A lone Corsair decided that "G" was Japanese. Its first 500-lb bomb missed and fell into a ravine below us. He had missed from a high altitude, but he carried a second bomb. He circled and dropped that bomb on us from a lower level.

This 500-pounder seemed to plummet directly into the middle of G Co. Then, at the very last second, it missed our summit completely. It fell over a sheer bank to strike far below. It just grazed the bankside.

The explosion knocked standing men into the ground. A few of us had minor cuts from fragments — could not hear for days. Two men were bomb-happy a day or so, but recovered. Luckily Dulian's BAR team had changed position just a little while ago. In the position they had just moved from, a fragment had torn a tree apart, just two feet above the ground.

Back on the flats at 2/Bn Hqs, Col Munkres howled, "There goes my G Co!" Men heard him call over the radio: "I don't care if you are a Colonel! Get your damn planes to hell out of there." While "G" was calming down after its near miss, Father Lynn came up with our supply party. He came to take Hoffman down for burial. (He did not have to dig in the ruins for our bodies.)

Munkres then humanely ordered G Co to defer our next attack until tomorrow. From our hilltop, Sgt McInerney saw a Jap with leaves on his helmet try to crawl across an open spot to Jap Hqs. McInerney picked him off at 600 yards. Occasional Jap return fire totally missed us.

On 23 Mar, 2/Pln pushed towards Coconut Hill where Hoffman had died. This was the second hill from where the bomb had missed us. Climbing the first hill in line of skirmishers, Dulian's squad saw no Japs. Then we waited for a barrage, and Kosing's Pln to reinforce us.

From this hill, Dulian's squad led out to take Coconut Hill, two miles off at the end of a saddle. Our first 500 yards was through open brush. Three mortar shells impacted close. Moving more carefully, we soon climbed at a 45-degree angle. We saw mouths of two huge caves and a deserted 20 mm gun just off the trail. Three more Jap mortar shells exploded nearby. A dud fell nearer still where a live shell could have hurt us. While Dulian's men watched the caves, Wasko's squad took over the advance. Barrages had cleared Wasko's move to the hill summit. They found only deserted shacks. Kosing's 1/Pln then dug in on Coconut Hill after we took it.

And except for picking off a few stray Nips back at those two large caves, our Zamboanga Battle was over. On 25 Mar when B Co replaced us, we trucked back to Santa Maria for a hot meal, a bath, and clean fatigues. That night, we bedded down above ground on cots under ponchos. After 16 battle days — eight of them in the Zambo Hills, we rejoiced in our brief rest.

But by 2 Apr, G Co was landing at Sanga Sanga Island 200 miles southeast of Zamboanga in the Sulu Archipelao. We were to cross Sanga Sanga to storm Bongao Island peaks if we had to. G Co's 2/Pln was lean, understrength, combat hardened. We were indeed seasoned veterans for what could lie ahead. But for Japan's surrender, we would have had to storm Miyazaki Beach on Kyushu Island.

CREDIT: Main source is a 15-page typescript by G 163's S/Sgt Kermit Dulian. Other sources are from 163 Inf's "Journal" of 18-25 Mar 1945, and from 146 FA's Robert Allen's "Battle for the Ridges," in Allen's sheaf of stories headed by the title "Zamboanga Recaptured." We have already published Dulian's fine histories of G 163 in Death Valley at Zamboanga and the invasion of Bongao Island. Another of his histories stockpiled for later publication details his deadly patrol of 19 June 1944 on Biak where Otis Belin was killed. In this forthcoming history at a later date, I have included my own narrative of the deadly wound of Arnold Johnson, also on 19 June 1944 on Biak. (I omitted Dulian's name on earlier histories because he asked me to, but I see nothing wrong with the details which I have selected. Like other 41sters, Dulian deserves all the honor that we can give him.)

E Co 163 Infantry on Biak: East Caves and Ibdi Pocket

by Dr. Hargis Westerfield, Division Historian

On 12 June 1944, hardened E Co 163 Inf landed from action at Toem (Wakde Operation) to fight on Biak. At once, anti-aircraft gunners shot down 3 Japanese planes trying to kill us. By 1205, "E" was trucking down the coast to our positions below the Japanese menace in the sinister dull green ridges above us. This pocket of Japs was guarding the formidable East Caves strongpoint which 162 Inf had bypassed to battle for Mokmer Strip.

On 13 June began E's combat patrols to seize high ground above the little stream that ran out of the cliffs into Geelvink Bay from Parai Defile. On that 13 June, 2/Lt Ritzenhein's Pln patrolled into high ground above the stream. Easily occupying a good ridge position, we probed on into Jap trouble.

S/Sgt Art Morris' squad advanced 100 yards until Jap fire briefly halted us. Overcoming heavy fire, we thrust into Jap positions. Selmer Olson was probably killed here by a shot in the head. Terrific Jap volleys grounded Morris' squad. A Jap flank movement threatened to cut off his squad from Ritzenhein's 2/Pln.

By quick, precise commands, Morris aimed his squad's fire and silenced the Nips. Morris killed 3 Nips; we slew the other 3. We held ground against a counter-attack, then acted as Pln rear guard to withdraw to the ridge-top already secured. Morris had a bullet wound on the left side of his chest, yet continued to guard our withdrawal.

On 14 June, Johanson took a flesh wound in his right leg — had to be helped down to a truck. After surgery probably on Owi Island, he went into hospital at Hollandia. About 6 weeks later, still limping, he was back with E Co for the Korim Bay landing.

So despite Japs' opposition, "E" held a high ridge above the Parai stream, about 500 yards east of Parai Jetty. Position was 20 feet wide and 250 yards long. On this solid coral, each reinforced rifle Pln spent 2 days in turn, then rotated down to bathe and rest by the stream.

On 15 June about dark, a Jap 75 mm mountain gun boomed from the ridges NE of E Co. "Whistling Charlie" seemed to aim at every man in E Co below the ridges. We flattened in terror. Fragments in head and leg killed Sgt Quam. Metzger was wounded in left arm, Ed Morris in his left hand. Appleton was also wounded in his left hand — and ankle. Railsback was hit in left lower side. All men were reported seriously wounded. Since almost all wounds were on the left parts of their bodies, all men seem to have lain on their right sides.

When the first shell landed, Torgerson and 4 others were playing poker in a tent. During next few seconds, Torgerson with 3 others dived for a shell hole in solid coral just outside the tent. But the hole was big enough for one man only.

Not being that one man, Torgerson looked up from lying flat on bare rock to see Marshall still out in the open. Marshall was counting the money left behind, heap by heap. He wanted every man to recover exactly his own money.

(We are sure today that the Nips had at least 3 guns back in those ridges. One they could pull back around the right angle of an L-shaped cave where our FA could not hit it. Firing from near 2/Bn 163 Inf's HDQs, Rebone and Lund knocked out one gun with a little 37 mm cannon.)

On 17 June, Sgt Persefull was seriously wounded — fragments in his back. On 19 June, Steptoe took a lighter wound from a fragment in the head. We know no more about these 2 casualties.

Back on 18 June near Parai Jetty, a Jap flank attack hit a patrol of ours. The second-in-command, Sgt Larsen, intentionally moved out into the open to draw fire and fight back. When the Japs fired, he slew 4 of them with his rifle. Then his patrol leader used automatic weapons to smash the Jap attack. (This patrol was not fully reported, however.)

On 20 June, E Co tried to penetrate deeper into the Parai Defile ridges to hold a trail which we believed to be close by. On this mission, we sent out 2 successive patrols. S/Sgt Walker led the advance patrol; 1/Lt Langston led the second patrol to finish this action.

S/Sgt Walker took his 13 men to seize a new perimeter area to hold the new trail. They soon met heavy resistance and slew several Japs. The other Japs held fire and drew back.

Through light sniper fire and then intensive fire, Walker's patrol continued forward. They still dug a new perimeter. Then his radio operator told Walker that they were cut off and facing a fight to the death.

In the following patrol, 1/Lt Langston began with a recon patrol of 4 men including Sgt Patch. A strong Nippo force cut them off — gave Langston his death-wound. Jap fire grounded Patch and his 2 men. The fourth got away through a Jap position to get help.

Patch meanwhile tried to drag dying Langston into a coral hole, but every time he tried, heavy fire concentrated on Patch. He still guarded Langston until he died. When Langston's men came up, Patch darted across open ground to help them disperse the Japs.

Seven days later, 27 June, S/Sgt Finnicum took 12 men to recover Langston's corpse. The Japs had left Langston out in the open while they watched from caves and prepared positions. Twice that morning, they repelled Finnicum's men.

Finnicum tried again that afternoon. After quick recon, he placed his men under cover to pin down the Japs with rifle fire. He dragged Langston into shelter, called litter men to drag the dead officer back to decent burial.

After 27 June, E Co had no more casualties reported while we held our ridge position above Parai Road. After receiving no more fire on 1-2 July, we believed that the Japs had left the area. On 3 July at 1030, our 10-man patrol checked out the cliffs westward to East Caves — saw just one Jap who escaped. Meanwhile an "E" Pln penetrated the caves and found ammo and rusty guns unfired for a long time.

In East Caves, we found 5 20mm guns, 5 90 mm mortars with 500 shells, and 2 HMGs. This formidable position had helped cut off 162's 3/Bn in the early Biak days. It kept our trucks from the coastal road on 7-13 June. East Caves was a 240-foot coral cliff honeycombed with tunnels and heavy weapons positions with a garrison of 1,000 Japs. They had plenty of food. Nobody knows why "E" found it undefended.

On 9 July, E Co left the Parai ridges with East Caves forever. With F and G Cos, we moved to patrol the jungle north of Ibdi Pocket where 3/Bn 163 now fought the Japs.

On 12 July behind Ibdi Pocket, we lost 2 men wounded from F Co's 2/Pln's patrol. A K-9 hunting dog and handler led the "F" patrol. Coming up a bull-dozed road in our rear, the dog smelled E Co men instead of Japs. It lacked training to discriminate between Yank and Jap body odors. Probably when the trainer drew back the dog, the "F" scouts forwarded and fired. Before the fire was halted, 2 "E" men had gunshot wounds. Moyer was slashed in the cheek, Merkel in the left side of the neck.

One night in this jungle north of Ibdi Pocket, "E" set up positions in bamboo thickets. For night security, Capt Zimmerman ordered Sgt Torgerson to place his 2 LMGs to crossfire over the trail. As they were sighting the guns, Torgerson saw a Jap coming down the trail. He saw Torgerson and ran off unharmed. Capt Zimmerman was unhappy that the Japs now knew that we were posted on the trail.

Torgerson then placed his 2 LMGs for crossfire 100 feet down the trail. He cannily laid fragments of bamboo trunks and branches on our side of the planned crossfire for the Japs to tread on and alarm us.

About 2000 in black dark, our gunners heard feet crackle on the bamboo in the trail. Their belts flamed the dark. With daylight, we found 15 dead Japs and discarded packs where the surviving Japs had dropped them and fled.

On 13 July came another brave patrol of E 163. In a mission to lead an E Co advance north of besieged Ibdi Pocket, S/Sgt Porter's squad received fire from Jap rifles and automatic weapons. The fire came from a grass hut and a coral fort. After a brief skirmish where 2 Yanks were knocked out of action, Porter pulled back his patrol to avoid more casualties. Then Porter alone shot tommie gun slugs into the hut and arced 2 grenades into the coral fort. He slew 4 Japs and cleared the way to a successful patrol. Probably here Nordstrom died from a shot in the back, but we have no idea at all of the other man's name.

After bombing planes wiped out the remaining Ibdi Pocket Japs on 22 July, E Co with our 2/Bn had a final Biak mission. This was to mop up Japs around Korim Bay on the north side of the island.

Johanson never forgets his fright on one of those patrols. (At this time he ranked as Cpl while also leading a squad. While checking out a shore village, he padded past an open vent hole high as his head, then up a stairs made of a notched coconut log to look into the hut. Three Nips were huddled on the floor. One had his rifle poked out the vent hole which Johanson had just passed. Johanson shot the 3 men so fast that he himself fled half scared to death. Twelve Nips were killed on that Korim Bay patrol.

E Co's New Guinea Campaign was ended. After casualties from our own FA wrongly ranged on Insoemanai Island in the Wakde-Toem Operation, we had fought well there on Tementoe Creek. Then on Biak in our war for East Caves — hard little jungle patrols, we had our final training to become a great jungle company. Yet we lost just 4 wounded to hospital, and 4 killed — Olson, Quam, Nordstrom, and 1/Lt Langston.

NOTE A. More About Fighting for East Caves

Along with West Caves and Ibdi Pocket, East Caves that E 163 battled, was 1 of the 3 formidable strongholds on Biak. At the end of Parai Ridge, it was really a little "mountain" 240 feet high which must be climbed hand over hand.

Centuries of New Guinea rain had eroded this mountain into a tangle of caverns made for stubborn resistance. Tactically the most important part of East Caves was a wide coral ledge about 180 feet up this 240-foot cliff on the seaward side. On this ledge were 2 wide sumps at least 50 feet wide. One was 75 x 200 feet. Both were honeycombed with tunnels.

In these sumps were 90 mm mortars, 20 mm "machine cannon," HMGs, and many light mortars. From 50 feet deep in the sumps, heavy weapons could safely fire over the protecting shoulders on U.S. troops. Jap observation parties could range in on Parai Defile and terrain all the way into Mokmer Strip. One HMG pillbox defended the steep seaward side. On the land side, 5 HMG pillboxes guarded the sheer slope.

East Caves' heavy plunging fire was the main cause for 162 Inf's defeat in Parai Defile on our first days on Biak. On

7 June, East Caves' weapons blasted 186 Inf and 2/Bn 162 Inf when they seized Mokmer Strip. On 9-11 June, they caused many more casualties when 162 Inf bypassed Parai Defile.

Garrison was 800 strong — 300 Marines of AA and service units mostly, 500 Engrs, a mortar unit of 2/Bn 222 Inf, and some riflemen. (There were also 200 civilian laborers.) CO was a Lt-Col Minami — also CO of 17 Airdrome Construction Unit.

Yet after 11 June, the Japs failed to use their heavy firepower and 800 men efficiently. They could have drawn back badly needed US Cos from infighting for West Caves. But E 163 and 3/Bn 163 outfits battled any sallies of the garrison. Backing our infantry were fires from 641 TD Bn's 4.2 mortars, 205 and 947 FA Bns, tanks, off-shore destroyers and Air Force bombers that pounded East Caves through 23 or 24 June.

On 28 June, the East Caves CO, Lt-Col Miname killed himself, and his garrison in small groups began escaping north towards Korim Bay. Not until 20 July, however, were the last 40 Japs killed off in East Caves.

But 11 days earlier, E Co 163 Inf had left East Caves ridges to patrol near Ibdi Pocket. To this day, historians do not know why the Japs failed to make full use of their third great stronghold on Biak Island.

CREDIT: Basic for this fine history are award stories of 6 E Co NCOs: Max Larsen, Arthur Morris, Charles Patch, Carl Walker, Thomas Finnicum, and Alfred Porter. Don Torgerson and Ernie Johanson sent letters, both in Feb. 1983. Scholarly background came from a 3.5 page typescript by 2/Bn 163's Maj Robert Irving and R.R. Smith's *Approach to the Philippines*. Other sources include 163's Biak Casualty List, Journal and Narrative plus Ralph Marlowe's history of F Co 163 Inf.

148 FA Battalion: From Timor Convoy to Luzon

by Willard (Bill Heath) and Others
with Dr. Hargis Westerfield, Division Historian

When the radio announced the Pearl Harbor holocaust, 148 FA Bn was already in convoy west of Hawaii to join Filipino defense forces. At once, convoy began zigzagging to dodge possible submarine torpedos. Aboard stinking old liner *Holbrook* (copra and jute cargoes), we repainted her battleship gray. we donned lifejackets with full canteens.

At Suva, Fiji Island capital, orders re-routed us to Australia. From Brisbane, we passed between Australia and New Guinea to dock at little Darwin for new orders.

After midnight 6 weeks later, we left Darwin in a foolhardy convoy to reinforce Australians on Timor Island in Indonesia — 411 miles north in open sea, without air cover. Only protection was heavy cruiser *Houston* with aged destroyer *Peary* and 2 Aussie sloops. We had 5 transports with Aussie Engrs — and AT guns on 3 of them. Our 148 FA was on US *Portmar* and Aussie *Tulagi*.

On our second day out, a Jap recon plane dropped a bomb that missed our B and C Btrys on *Portmar*. On our fourth day, 35 Mitsubishi heavy bombers and 9 flying boats attacked in 4 flights from 4 directions. But to kill us, they had to sink heavy cruiser *Houston* first.

Under a transport's smoke screen, *Houston* fought off the 44 planes with 900 rounds in 45 minutes. Lying on his back with binoculars, Capt Rooke turned *Houston* aside from the bombers. When their flights crisscrossed with sticks of bombs, he backed *Houston* full speed astern. Near misses splashed over *Houston* several times, but she came out striking back. Total casualties from a near miss on a transport were 3 Aussies, one seriously wounded.

Back at Darwin, 148 FA's transports with 33 other vessels took a raid like that on Pearl Harbor. On 19 Feb, CO Mitsu Fuchida's 242 planes blasted crowded Darwin Harbor. (Fuchida had also commanded at Pearl Harbor.) While his powerful fleet circled offshore, his planes sank 8 ships, drove 1 onto the beach, damaged 11 more. They slew 243 — 52 civilians, wounded 52 more civilians.

US destroyer *Peary* was blown out of the water, her last .50 HMG still blazing. US transports *Meigs* and *Mauna Loa* were sunk, also British tanker name *British Motorist*, and Aussie passenger ships *Neptuna* and *Zealandia*. Aussie hospital ship *Manunda* was savagely damaged. US freighter *Admiral Halstead* was bombed also, but her Capt floated ashore a cargo of high octane gas in 44-gallon drums.

When the attack began, 148 FA's *Tulagi* and *Portmar* were trapped in the back bay. Hoping to be unnoticed, *Tulagi*'s soldiers were all below deck, except for MG crews and Lt Kohl. (Nobody found the custodian of the keys to the real AA guns.)

The last bombers tried to sink *Tulagi* and *Portmar*. While firing .50 HMGs, C Btry's Skelton was killed, and A's Wofford and Meade, with Belknap seriously wounded. On Likel's gun assistant Wilbur died. Lt Kohl credits Sam and Sgt Hulse with saving *Tulagi* from sinking. They diverted a Jap bomber from dropping his last bomb on *Tulagi's* deck. But its underwater explosion caused the captain to try to beach the ship.

Much less is known about *Portmar's* battle to survive. Evidently she took 5 hits from 50-pound bombs. Perhaps 2 did not explode. One fell harmless below on a mattress. A B Btry man carried it up and dropped it safely overside. The other 3 caused damage below the water-line. Ninety-eight holes penetrated *Portmar's* sides. She headed for the dock, but an ammo ship blew up there. *Portmar* grounded on a lepers' island where the men were rescued.

From sinking *Tulagi*, men climbed down ropes, then swam or caught little boats to safety. Lt-Col Patterson wanted to be last off with *Tulagi's* Capt. T/Sgt Kemp and Bartol had to throw him into the water for a boat to pick him up. But the tide carried Kemp and Bartol out to sea. For 3 hours, they took turns gripping one 2x4 or swimming until 2 Aussies picked them up in a motor boat.

Wofford, Meade, Skelton and Wilbur in *Tulagi* were 148's only dead. (Wilbur had left hospital to join the Timor convoy.) In both transports, 148 FA had many wounded. Maj Whitely was hit in the arm, 2/Lt Henrichs in the calf. Other known wounded from both ships were Horace Brown, Belknap, Lt Les Brown, Blake, Brook, Brogan, Clauston, Tieman, and Walton. We totalled 35 purple hearts.

Only 5 Jap planes and 5 probables were reported. The Japs downed 24 US planes and damaged 2.

Why did the Japs hit Darwin almost instantly after our Timor convoy returned? Their spy was a wheel-chair "cripple" who managed the Darwin curio shop. Because he had become crippled while serving a sentence in prison, he was kindly paroled. After the raid, a civilian saw him walking. In the back of his shop, officials discovered concealed, sophisticated radio equipment. He was executed.

After garrison duty at Darwin, 148 FA took our salvaged guns into SE Australia to trade for 105s. We had over 3 months rest in happy Ballarat city. (We had at least 7 marriages to Aussie wives.) Nine months after the Darwin raid, we finally struck the Japanese in combat.

We became part of Operation Cartwheel to defang Rabaul on New Britain Island north of New Guinea. With a deepwater harbor and 4 airdromes, Fortress Rabaul was the main staging area to invade New Guinea. We teamed with the now forever horseless 112 Cavalry Regt to beachhead at Arawe (Cape Merkus) on the south coast of New Britain, 300 miles SW of Rabaul.

At 0510 15 Dec 1943, our forward observer Lt Schermer with a team of Btry A men was overside in a rubber inflated boat with 14 more similar boats of A Co 112 Cav to attempt Arawe Beachhead. Moon was 4 days past prime over that dark unknown shore. Destroyer *Shaw* stood by to fire blind support.

The Jap garrison, 2 Cos of 53rd Inf Regt, crouched to shoot down our throats from a beach enfiladed by MGs. At 0522, about 100 yards from the beach, Jap rifle and MG fire shattered the night. Of 15 rubber boats, 12 were punctured and sunk. Cavalry losses were 12 men killed, 4 missing, 11 wounded. Destroyer *Shaw* could not fire in the dark for fear of hitting the 3 boats that managed to land.

An AA Btry slew Lt Schermer and sank our FA boat. His Btry A men huddled in the brine for 3 hours before a landing craft chanced to drag us out chilled and dripping.

Other 112 Cav men landed on other parts of the coast to help secure the beach for inland advances. We saw some Yanks borne past us for burial from blanket-covered litters. Our 148 FA men lost good men also, names unknown. About 150-200 Japanese perished.

Effective Jap resistance was from dive-bombers daily for 30 days. They sank a small coast transport, damaged 2 subchasers, 4 LSTs. "Washing Machine Charlie" dropped a bomb or so. One moonlit night our assembled MGs almost blew him from the sky — surely wrecked both wings.

To expel us, Maj Komori's Bn from 181 Inf crossed 15 streams from the north while Tobushi's Bn of 141 Inf landed from the sea. With reinforcements — 2 158 Inf Cos, a tank Co, and medium bombers — we defeated their great attacks of 16 Jan 1944. (By 21 Jan, Komori Bn alone lost 116 killed, 117 wounded, 14 dead of disease, and 80 sick.)

Best remembered victory came when Puli River Canyon blocked 112 Cav's advances. Japs were formidable on opposite bank in pillboxes and caves. Our FA CO feared to fire over advancing men and keep down losses.

Instrument Specialist Cpl Nielsen persuaded the 112 Cav officer to put the FA officer on temporary duty elsewhere. Using an observer on the river-bank, he walked our shells into the Japs' caves and pillboxes and dislodged them. Our guns crossed with 112 Cav over the river to pursue the Japs.

In battle, 148 FA fired 4,400 rounds — at times a continuous bombardment. We had to reline some gun barrels. One on forward liaison duty, Hq Btry's Capt Cook with Sgt Boyd blasted 2 grenades into a pillbox and slew all but one Jap. They took him to Intelligence for interrogation.

Cpl Drake with Irving patrolled in a beachhead craft up the New Britain coast — hiding by day. But a P-39 mistakenly wounded them with a .37. Irving survived with a silver plate in his head, Drake with a torn left shoulder. At another time, Plumlee had a wounded knee under treatment. A busy medic failed to loosen the bandage; Plumlee lost his leg.

In mid-1944, 148 FA displaced to New Guinea to help 112 Cav hold the Drinumor River line. That fall, we fired for 112 Cav again, on Leyte. By Feb 1945, we had begun our final long operation on Luzon in the Philippines. This was in mountain fighting against the Japs' Shimbu Group east of Manila.

With 112 Cav, we protected 6th Army's supply line from their depots in the Luzon central plain. Sixth Army must destroy the 50,000-man Shimbu Group holding the mountains east of Manila. Thus on 19-26 Feb, we fired for 112 Cav from Muzon Village, Bulacan Province.

Through 26 Feb, we had Cpl Barraclough killed, 6 wounded: McKnight, Hamilton, Kirk, Brandt, Lt Engle and Sgt Purnell. (No other information is available on these casualties.)

Next operation with 112 Cav was to help capture Wawa and Ipo Dams deep among mountain precipices. These dams impounded most of the water supplying wrecked Manila City. Mainly, this was a war against tropical disease, with few casualties.

In 4 more months, 148 FA had just 10 more casualties, including 2 attached Filipinos. Killed were Crosby, Lathrop, and Filipinos 2/Lt Mendoza and Martin. Wounded were Fox, Hilker, 1/Lt Tabaka, 2/Lt Crissman, Sgt Young, and Cpl Duling. We know only how Lt Mendoza and young Crosby died.

On Crosby's and Mendoza's death night, Btry B was for a second night on detached duty under a bright moon. A "Jap" demolition team struck — actually 8 tall, hairy Koreans.

Sentry Taylor's carbine hit the first raider. Even in the abdomen, the carbine impact was too light. The man ran. Awakened Causton of Service Btry volleyed at 6 Koreans with his tommy, but missed. The Koreans returned rifle fire, and threw a harmless grenade.

Automatic rifle fire slashed at Causton and Cohalan, pinned them in a shallow wash. A continuous shaft of flame slashed from the Korean, but it missed. Causton cowered flat on his tommy gun and feared to lift up to use it.

Covered by automatic fire, 2 Koreans shoved a demolition charge under the rear of a 6x6 truck, and another under the maintenance truck. A third Korean poured gas from a bidon on that truck.

The exploded charge flamed the truck and lighted up the whole area. O'Donald and his gun crew of 2 cooks mounted a .30 MG on the hill by the kitchen. Three Koreans charged the gun uphill, one by one. Despite having to clear 2 MG stoppages, O'Donnell slew all 3.

Behind Causton in that tricky light, Bales took him for a Korean and fired twice at him. First bullet slashed Causton's left ear lobe and left side of his neck — a light wound with little blood. Second shot was a near miss. Causton swore and rushed down the wash and dropped beside Bales.

Guerilla Lt Mendoza panicked from the kitchen — ran out yelling for us not to shoot. We killed him accidentally.

Meanwhile the Korean Taylor had shot with a carbine was slowly crawling through a narrow rice paddy to the kitchen, with a bandage around his abdomen. We fired at him but missed. In a kitchen slit trench, he found Crosby — an 18-year-old replacement who had joined us yesterday — and cut his throat. The Korean failed to escape; we counted 22 bullet holes in him.

This was 148 FA's last notable fight — with 2 dead and 2 trucks destroyed. (Hilker was wounded that day also, whereabouts uncertain.) Out of 9-10 who raided, Causton estimated 4-6 dead Koreans.

By 28 June, all Btrys of 148 FA were enjoying rest camp. Stateside rotation was going on. Called by one reporter, "The Little Giant of the Pacific," 148 FA had been overseas 44 months — had fought at sea, in Australia, New Britain, New Guinea, Leyte, and Luzon — and would occupy Japan. Such is 148 FA's proud epic of combat.

CREDIT: Only official US archive is *"History of 148 FA Bn... 1 June - 31 Dec 1945."* Bill Heath wrote a 41-page manuscript named "Unit History/1940-1946," with a list of 36 contributors. Important also are Cliff Causton's 72-page handwritten manuscript, and the "Horace Brown Story," 35 pages of single-spaced typescript. Australian book sources are Douglas Lockwood's *Australia's Pearl Harbor,* and Dudley McCarthy's *SW Pacific Area: The First Year.* American book sources are John Miller's *Cartwheel: The Reduction of Rabaul,* Samuel Eliot Morison's *Breaking the Bismarcks Barrier,* from his great naval history of World War II, and R.R. Smith's *Triumph in the Philippines.* (Data on 148 FA on Luzon are meager.) Besides Bill Heath, some of the principal contributors are Jack Allured, Horace Brown, Cliff Causton, Vernon Dubbert, Lloyd Henrichs, Louis Kohl, and Joseph Tomecek.

162nd Inf. Rgt. Hq. staff, 1941. Ft. Lewis, WA. L to R. front row: Ralph Connell, Milton Kielsmeier, George Eisneros, Harrington. Back row: Don Allen, John Armstrong, Donald O. Nelson, Charles Chase, Richard Johansen, John Kutcher. (Courtesy of Ralph B. Connell)

41st Infantry Veterans

Publisher's Note: All members of the 41st Infantry Veterans Association were invited to write and submit biographies for inclusion in this publication. The following stories are from those who chose to participate. The biographies were printed as received, with only minor editing. The publisher regrets it cannot accept responsibility for omissions or inaccuracies within the following biographies.

All Second Lieutenants. Called into active service December 1941 and all assigned to the 41st Infantry Division, Ft. Lewis, WA. A class on the heavy .30 cal. MG. January 1942. (Courtesy of Arthur W. Merrick)

GUIDO, J. ABBRUZZESE, was born Jan. 13, 1925 in Brooklyn, NY and grew up in North Plainfield, NJ. Mr. Abbruzzese entered the Army on Sept. 17, 1943. Basic training was at Ft. McClellan, AL and then on to Ft. Ord, CA. He joined the 41st Div., G Co., 2nd Bn., 163rd Inf. in April 1944 at Finchhaffen, Dutch New Guinea. He landed on Aitape, Biak, Zamboanga, Jolo and all other areas that G Co., 163rd Inf. was involved.

He went on to land at Hiroshima, Japan on Oct. 6, 1945. He left Nagoya, Japan in December 1945 when the 41st Div. was disbanded.

He was honorably discharged on Jan. 25, 1946 with the rank of staff sergeant. He received the following decorations during his service in the military: Purple Heart, Bronze Star, Combat Infantry Badge, Asiatic-Pacific Medal with Bronze Arrowheads, three Bronze Service Stars, Philippine Liberation Ribbon, Victory Medal and Japanese Occupation Ribbon.

He married Mildred Sacco on March 7, 1943. They have eight children, 22 grandchildren and one great-grandchild.

Mr. Abbruzzese is now retired after having spent 40 years in the construction industry and currently resides in South Plainfield, NJ.

WILLIAM H. ADAMS (BUD), was born Aug. 5, 1919 in Elmore City, OK. He entered the service on Feb. 25, 1941 and was assigned to the 41st Div., 162nd Inf., AT Co.

He was stationed at Ft. Lewis, WA; Australia; and New Guinea. He will always remember the hospitality of the Aussies and the lasting friendships he made while in the service.

Was discharged June 6, 1945 with the rank of technical sergeant.

Married 45 years to Helen, a girl from Melbourne. They have two daughters, four grandsons (one in the Army). He was a hospital engineer and retired six years ago.

DOMINICK M. AIELLO, was born Dec. 8, 1913 in Chicago, IL. He graduated from grammar school in 1929 and worked at a candy factory until drafted into the service Sept. 18, 1941 at Chicago, IL. Was assigned to HQ Co., 1st Bn., 163rd Inf., 41st Div.

Was stationed at Camp Roberts, CA; Ft. Lewis, WA; and New Guinea.

He was discharged Oct. 1, 1945 with the rank of private first class.

Employed with the city of Chicago as a garbage man until his retirement on Feb. 1, 1978.

MARVIN W. ALBAUGH, was born Aug. 28, 1924 in Phillipsburg, KS. At the age of 12, his family moved to Portland, OR. He graduated from Lincoln High School in June 1942 and worked as electricians helper until inducted Feb. 23, 1943 into the Army at Ft. Lewis, WA.

Was assigned to 131st Inf. Regt. in Ft. Brady, MI for basic and trained as radio operator. The 131st was reassigned to Ft. Benning, GA, then sent to Ft. Ord, CA. He joined the Hqs. Btry., 41st Div. Arty. in Rockhampton, Australia, serving as operations clerk.

Participated in D-Day invasions on Hollandia, Biak Island, Zamboanga, and occupied Hiro, Japan.

Left from Nagoya on Dec. 21, 1945, arrived in Seattle, WA Dec. 29, 1945 and was discharged from Ft. Lewis on Jan. 8, 1946 with the rank of sergeant.

Married to Betty since Jan. 18, 1946. They have five children and 16 grandchildren. He has been a business man with service stations, heating oil distributors, investment company and currently is a real estate broker in Beaverton, OR.

CHARLIE ALBERTI, was born Aug. 15, 1918 at San Rafael, CA. Entered the service Feb. 25, 1941 and assigned to the 41st Div.

Stationed at Ft. Lewis, WA, Philippines, New Guinea, and Australia.

Discharged Sept. 10, 1945 with the rank of tech 5. His awards include the Philippine Liberation Ribbon, one Star, Asiatic-Pacific Campaign Medal, Good Conduct Medal, American Defense Ribbon and the Purple Heart.

Married 44 years to Gloria, and they have two sons (Bob and Richard), one daughter (Gloriann), and six grandchildren.

Alberti is semi-retired and lives on a farm raising pigs and cattle in Stevinson, CA.

JAMES L. ALBERTSON, was born Jan. 29, 1920 in Iroquois County, IL. He was raised in Kelso, WA and graduated from Kelso High School in 1939. Joined the National Guard Medical Detachment Hqs., 41st Div. on March 23, 1939. Was inducted into active service on Sept. 16, 1940.

Transferred to 41st MPs in the winter of 1940. Left for the Philippines on Dec. 5, 1941 on USS *A.T. Etolin*. Returned to the U.S. on Dec. 9, 1941 and returned to Ft. Lewis, WA. The division was streamlined and he was transferred to Co. B, 186th Inf.

Left for Melbourne, Australia on May 13, 1942. Next was sent to Rockhampton on July 19, 1942 Australia and to Buna, New Guinea in January 1943. He returned to Rockhampton in July 1943. Was then sent to Hollandia first part of 1944.

His memorable experience was going under the Golden Gate Bridge on Dec. 5, 1941.

Returned to the U.S. on July 29, 1944 and went to SCU, Ft. Missoula, MT in August 1944. From there he went to Ft. Lewis Separation Center and was discharged Aug. 26, 1945 with the rank of corporal. His medals include the American Defense Service Medal with clasp, Asiatic-Pacific Service Medal with two clasps, and a Good Conduct Medal.

Married to Margaret Smith since Jan. 29, 1948. They have four children: Gale, Linda, Diana, and Mark. They also have two grandchildren, Darin and Natalie, and one step-grandson Ryan.

He has worked as farm hand, truck driver, butcher, surveyor, carpenter, shingler, saw mill worker, and ended up working in a paper mill for 31 years as a paper maker before his retirement on Feb. 1, 1962. He now lives on his brother's Christmas tree farm, doing a little yard work, gardening, fishing, and does some traveling.

CLAUDE B. ALLEN, was born May 9, 1919 in Sallisaw, OK. Entered the service at Yakima, WA in March 1941 and was sent to Ft. Lewis, WA. The second day there he went to the hospital (appendicitis) for six weeks.

Assigned to the 41st Div., 163rd Inf. Medical Detachment, 1st Bn. Left for Seymour Australia on March 19, 1942 on the *Queen Elizabeth*, then to Rockhampton. Landed in New Guinea in December 1942. Flew on the Owen Stanley Range without a side door. Went into combat Jan. 1, 1943 at New Guinea. Memorable experience was when a wild boar bit a soldier on Biak.

He was discharged in August 1945 with the rank of sergeant. He received the Purple Heart, Combat Infantry Badge, Unit Citation, and Good Conduct Medal.

Married for 45 years and has four children, nine grandchildren and nine great-grandchildren. After 30 years with the post office, he retired in 1976 as postmaster. He makes his home in Gold Hill, OR.

LEEON F. ALLER JR., M.D., was born Sept. 27, 1920 in San Francisco, CA and educated in Seattle, WA. B.S. degree from the University of Washington and M.D. from University of Pennsylvania in 1951.

He joined the 146th Field Artillery, 41st Inf. Div. on Aug. 3, 1937; transferred to 116 Med as first sergeant in 1939; attended Carlisle MFSS, PA, then overseas with 41st Inf. Div. in New Guinea, NEI, Philippines, Japan in combat and occupation.

Came home as captain and attended Med School, then active duty, 101st Inf. Div., began med practice in 1953 remaining in ARNG. Became Washington State Surgeon then active duty in Central America until he retired as colonel MC in September 1984.

He received the Silver Star, Distinguished Service Medal, Meritorious Service Medal, Bronze Star, Combat Medical Badge, and others. Was given Prefix "A" by surgeon general, U.S. Army.

He now continues mission work in Third World, Professor at University of Washington and family practice.

475

Married Virginia Sorgenfrei in December 1945 and they raised 76 of their own, adopted, and foster children. He was in scouting for 58 years (last 30 as scoutmaster), 27 years M-2 job therapy prison ministry, composer and writer. Was U.S. Family Physician of the Year 1987-88 AAFP.

Also, see *Once There Was A City* ... a tale of Hiroshima; his music composition, *Song of the Medical Corps*, and a book of poetry written by his father, CWO Leeon F. Aller Sr. *North of the Coral Sea*. Leeon Sr. was with the 41st Inf. Div. from 1934 until 1943 when he was transferred to a higher headquarters in the SWPAC Theatre. They went overseas together on the USS *Argentina* in April 1942.

EVERETT BURTON ALLISON, was born Dec. 11, 1920 in Cleborne, TX. Entered the service in March 1942, trained at Ft. Leonard Wood, MO and in July was assigned to the 41st Inf. Div., Co. A, 116th Combat Engineers. Stationed at Rockhampton, Australia, New Guinea, Biak, Philippines, Zamboanga, and Jolo.

His memorable experience was throwing charges to slow down the Japanese resistance while the infantry rolled gasoline drums into the Biak Caves and set them afire.

Was discharged in August 1945 with the rank of sergeant. He was awarded the Bronze Star Medal, Good Conduct Medal, Asiatic-Pacific Campaign Medal with four Battle Stars, and the Philippine Liberation with one Battle Star.

Married to Rose Ann and they have four children, and four grandchildren. He is retired from the copper mines and resides in Superior, AZ.

DAN B. ALMOSLINO, was born June 26, 1919 in Seattle, WA. In 1939 he joined the 146th National Guard and was assigned to the 41st Inf. Div. from 1941-1943. From 1943-1945 he was at Puget Sound Navy Shipyard. Was with 105th Army Transportation Corp from 1945-1947.

Was stationed two years on Philippine Island, then spent short-time in Yokahama.

Discharged from Ft. Laughton, WA with the rank of T-corporal. He received awards for sharpshooting.

Married to Minnette in October 1948. They have three beautiful children: Michelle, Michael, and David, and granddaughter Suzy. Retired teamster; P/T driver at old-age home; and building chairman. He enjoys playing golf and poker.

WILLIAM A. ANDEL, was born June 15, 1920 in Bruno, NE. Entered the service on Nov. 3, 1941. Basic training at Ft. Leonardwood, MO. Was assigned to 41st Inf. Div., Regt. HQ, A Co., Co. B, 11th Engineers. Stationed at Australia, New Guinea and Biak.

His memorable experiences include landing at Sanananda, Biak, and Hollandia; when he crushed his hand at Buna; and when he had a 11 day furlough in Sydney, Australia.

Discharged Aug. 26, 1945 with the rank T/5. His awards include the Asiatic Theater of War Ribbon with two Gold Stars and the Presidential Unit Citation ribbon with Co. B Engineers.

Married Mary in 1950, has five boys (one in Navy for 17 years) and nine grandchildren. Was farming near David City, NE, now retired but still living on farm.

ARNOLD J. ANDERSON, was born Jan. 26, 1915 in Tonopah, NV. Entered the service in February 1941 and was assigned to the 41st Inf. Div., HQ2 163, in February 1941. Was stationed at Ft. Lewis, WA and Biak Island.

Discharged with the rank of sergeant. He received all the usual division awards.

He is a retired postmaster and makes his home in Tonopah, NV.

JACK M. ANDERSON, was born June 16, 1923 at Saco, MT. He enlisted in Co. G, 163rd Inf. on Dec. 8, 1938. He graduated from high school in 1940 and was inducted into the service with the 41st Div. on Sept. 16, 1940. Trained at Ft. Lewis, WA.

Departed for overseas aboard the *Queen Elizabeth* on March 19, 1942 and served with Co. G until he received a battlefield commission as second lieutenant and was transferred to Co. I, 186th Inf. on Biak, NEI. Went to Kaidaichi (Hiroshima) Japan with Co. K, 186th Inf. and returned to the U.S. on Nov. 11, 1945.

Jack served seven months with the 1st Bn., 38th Inf., 2nd Div. in Korea and was WIA, MIA, and POW during that time. During his military service, Jack received two Bronze Star Medals, Army Commendation Medal, two Purple Heart Medals, POW Medal (Korea) and the Good Conduct Medal.

He married Betty J. Hallock at Scappoose, Oregon on Dec. 16, 1945. They have three children.

After retiring from the Army in 1963, Jack was a firefighter for 15 years at Lakewood, WA. He relates that knowing the Lord Jesus Christ as his personal savior is his most memorable and most important experience.

NORMAN H. ANDERSON, was born at Chicago, IL on Oct. 23, 1919 where he lived and went to school until he was drafted into the service on Sept. 19, 1941. He was sent to Camp Roberts, CA for basic training and was there when war was declared. He was sent from there to Ft. Lewis, WA where he joined Co. D, 163rd Inf. Regt. of the 41st Div. He remained with Co. D for the duration of the war and was discharged on Oct. 13, 1945.

After the war he moved to southern California, where he now resides. He was attending the University of Southern California when he took part in the Korean War, serving in the U.S. Navy.

In 1953 he finished his education and taught science at Los Altos High School for the next 30 years. He never married and remains a bachelor to this day. He says he loves Chicago but after four years in the tropics has learned to love Southern California as well.

ROBERT E. ANDERSON, was born Aug. 4, 1914 in Aurora, IL. Was drafted in October 1941 and sent to Camp Roberts, CA for basic training.

War was declared and he was sent to Ft. Lewis, WA to the 41st Div. He served with the 41st, Co. G with the 163rd landing in Welbourne, Australia in February 1941.

He fought in New Guinea making numerous beachheads at Buna, Gona and Sanananda.

He attained the rank of sergeant and after many bouts with malaria and shrapnel wounds, he received the Purple Heart. He returned home on points in November 1944. Transferred to the Air Corps for the remainder of his service.

Married to Betty. They have four children and five grandchildren. Was employed as an engineer for the Southern California Gas Company, he retired in 1976 after 31 years of service. He is a member of the Visalia United Methodist Church and the 41st Division Association. He lives in Visalia, CA.

EDWARD A. ANKLAM, was born June 17, 1907 in Roulette, ND. He entered the service Sept. 16, 1940 and was assigned to 41st Inf. Div., Co. E, 163rd Inf. and Co. C, 186th Inf. at Ft. Lewis, WA.

He served about 60 days with the Australian Papuan Inf. Bn., a company of New Guinea natives. They were very loyal to them and very bitter to the Japs.

Discharged April 24, 1946 with the rank of major. He was awarded the Asiatic Medal with two Bronze Stars, Bronze Star Medal with one Arrowhead, Combat Infantry Badge, American Defense Medal, World War II Victory Medal, and American Theater Medal.

He has one son, and two daughters. His wife passed away in 1981. He worked 30 years for the post office before retiring. Now he enjoys museum work.

BRUNO ARCANGELETTI, was born July 17, 1926 in Scranton, PA. He was inducted into the U.S. Army on Oct. 3, 1944. Took basic training at Camp Wheeler, GA. Onto Ft. Ord, CA as his port of embarkation to Leyte, Philippine Islands.

Was assigned to the 41st Div., K Co., 162nd Inf. at Zamboanga on the island of Mindanao. Fought battles at Luayon, Balot Island, Cape San Augtin and was wounded at Calinan on June 16, 1945. Along with Francisco Lopez, Gerlach, Earl Hall, Jim Litke, and Hank McElroy.

After recovery at McGuire General Hospital, Richmond, VA, he was re-assigned to Aberdeen Proving Grounds, MD as a military policeman.

Honorably discharged from Ft. Meade, MD on Aug. 11, 1946. During his tour of duty, Bruno received the Combat Infantry Badge, Good Conduct Medal,

Purple Heart Medal, Bronze Star, and ribbons for the American Theater, Asiatic-Pacific Theater, Philippine Liberation, and World War II Victory.

Bruno is widowed with three grown children and three grandchildren. He is retired from the U.S. Post Office after 26 years as a letter carrier. He resides in Morton Grove, IL and enjoys walking, cycling, traveling, cooking and collecting baseball cards.

HAROLD ARKOFF, was born Aug. 20, 1925 at Ft. Dodge, IA. Enlisted in the Army in 1943 the day after high school graduation at the age of 17.

After infantry basic at Camp Fannin, TX, he joined Cannon Co., 162nd Inf. during the Biak, New Guinea Campaign. He fought in the Philippines including Zamboanga, Mindanao as gunner on 105mm Howitzer. He was awarded the Bronze Star Medal, Combat Infantryman's Badge and numerous campaign and battle ribbons.

Later he was stationed in Onomichi, Japan near Hiroshima where the first A Bomb was dropped.

Discharged in January 1946, he entered college and graduated with honors from the University of Iowa, School of Journalism.

He has spent his career as an executive for broadcasting and publishing firms, including KMA, Shenandoah, IA; KGIL, Los Angeles; and KKHI, San Francisco. From 1965 to present, he has been an owner of a California magazine publisher.

Harold and his wife Helen have two children and live in Calabasas Park, CA.

LELAND S. ARMSTRONG, was born June 10, 1922 in Hubbard, OR. He entered the service June 10, 1940 and was assigned to the 41st Inf. Div., stationed at Ft. Lewis, WA.

He was discharged Aug. 12, 1945 with the rank of private first class.

Married since July 6, 1947. He is retired from farming and lives in Gervais, OR.

VERNON A. ARNOLD, was born May 4, 1919 in Crockett, TX and was raised in Rusk, TX. He joined the Army on Oct. 7, 1941 and was sent to San Antonio, TX and Camp Roberts, CA for basic training. At Ft. Lewis, WA he was assigned to 163rd Inf. Regt., 41st Div., E Co.

Sent to Australia and transferred to 41st Military Police Det. Served in New Guinea and Biak. Discharged in San Antonio, TX on Aug. 9, 1945 after three years and 15 days of foreign service. His rank was private first class.

He became a carpenter and maintenance foreman, retiring in 1977. Married to Joyce since 1950 and reside in Pollok, TX. They have four children and three grandchildren.

WILLIAM ASHER, was born May 9, 1925 in Chicago, IL. He entered the service Oct. 4, 1943. Basic training at Camp Wolters, TX then assigned to the 41st Inf. Div., E Co., 163rd Regt. Stationed at New Guinea, southern Philippines, Japan.

He participated in the Korean Conflict from July 12, 1950 to July 10, 1953.

Was discharged with the rank of tech sergeant. His awards include the Combat Infantry Badge, World War II Victory Medal, Asiatic-Pacific Theater Ribbon with two Bronze Battle Stars and one Bronze Arrowhead, Philippine Liberation Ribbon with one Bronze Battle Star, and Bronze Star Medal.

Widowed after 40 years of marriage. He has two daughters and two grandchildren. He had quad heart bypass operation in 1981. He is now retired and lives in Morton Grove, IL.

FREDERICK A. ASHMAN JR., was born June 1, 1922 in Malden, MA and grew up in Malden until 15 when family moved to Melrose. Graduated from high school in June 1941 and joined the Army on Oct. 4, 1942.

Stationed at Camp Croft, Spartansburg, SC for 13 weeks at 31st Training Bn. Shipped out in May 1943 to Camp Stoneman, CA to Oakland, CA to Brisbane, Australia. Joined the 41st Div. in July 1943 at Rockhampton as a replacement in Co. B, 1st Platoon.

Served in Aitape, Wakde, Biak, and Philippines. Landed in Ft. Lewis, WA on Dec. 20, 1945. Received his discharge with the rank of private first class on Jan. 4, 1946.

Married to Martha "Marty," they have no children. Retired in August 1985 from the profession of bookbinding. He belongs to the VFW, American Legion, Masons (32% degree) and Aleppo Shriners (also belongs to the Minute Men of the Shrine).

LES AXLING, was born in October 1922 and graduated from high school in June 1940. He joined Seattle National Guard on Aug. 3, 1940 and was separated by point system from 41st Inf. Div. on July 25, 1945.

Seattle unit was Hqs. Btry., 1st Bn., 146th FA. Sent from Ft. Lewis to Melbourne, Australia in April and May 1942. Transferred to H&S Co., 116th Combat Engineers in October 1942 at Rockhampton. Was equipment operator and truck driver in Papua, Hollandia, Biak, Mindoro Island, Zamboanga, Jolo.

Hired by Bell Telephone as installer-repairman in August 1945 near Seattle. Transferred to AT&T in January 1984 and retired from there Sept. 30, 1986. He still does some telephone work.

Back to the Army in August 1950 and a U.S. sponsored trip to Fukuoka, Japan then to Korea January 1951 as wire chief then communications chief in experimental "battlefield illumination" company. Returned to the States the end of August 1951.

Married in June 1952, has three fine daughters and six grandchildren. He makes his home in Kent, WA.

KENNETH BAILEY, was born in Dec. 29, 1914 at Los Angeles, CA. He entered the service March 28, 1941 and was assigned to the 41st Inf. Div., F. Co.,

163rd Inf. Regt. Stationed at Tacoma, WA; training in Australia; combat at Sanananda, New Guinea and invasion of Philippines.

Discharged with the rank of staff sergeant. He received all the usuals medals and ribbons awarded the 41st Div.

Married to Betty and they have two sons Michael and Craig. He is retired and enjoys traveling and fishing. They make their home in El Monte, CA.

ALFRED W. BAKER JR., was born Feb. 8, 1922 at Pawtucket, RI. He entered the service July 17, 1944 at Ft. Devens, MA. Assigned to the 41st Inf. Div., Co. I, 186th Regt. as rifleman. Stationed at Palawan Island, Zamboanga, Mindanao, Philippine Islands, Kure Naval Base, Japan.

His memorable experience was the forced march into the interior of Zamboanga to the edge of the Rain Forest and the tragic loss of a medic buddy and his best friend.

Discharged March 6, 1946 from Ft. Devens, MA with the rank of private first class. His awards and decorations include the Good Conduct Victory Medal, Asiatic-Pacific Theater Ribbon, Philippine Liberation Ribbon, Meritorious Achievement Medal, C&B Badge, and Marksman.

Married 18 years to Thelma Rose Baker. No children. He retired August 1984 from Hughes Aircraft Company with 33 years of service. He is a member of Lodge #933, IAM for 39 years. His hobbies are traveling and photography.

GAIL J. BAKER, was born Jan. 7, 1919 in Bicknell, UT. Was drafted into Army on Feb. 27, 1941. He received basic training at Ft. Lewis, WA with the 41st Inf. Div. He served with H Co. and HQ Co., 2nd Bn., 162nd Inf.

He manned anti-aircraft gun on troop ship *Santa Paula* from New York to Melbourne, Australia. Next to Seymour, Rockhampton, and Kumusi River outpost in New Guinea.

Participated in landing at Nassau Bay encountering 10 foot surf, and in the Tambu Bay, Roosevelt Ridge, and Salamaua campaigns. Left 41st at Hollandia, New Guinea. Sent to San Francisco, CA and assigned to an MP unit with 9th Service Command.

Discharged Sept. 17, 1945 with the rank of staff sergeant.

Married Winona and has two children, Carol and Robert.

Owned a dry cleaners in Bicknell, UT; sold it and moved to Salt Lake City, UT in 1953 (also has residence in LaVerkin, UT). Retired building supervisor, Mountain Fuel Supply, 1980.

LINCOLN P. BAKKEN, was born Feb. 12, 1917 in Caledonia, ND. Was inducted into service Sept. 16, 1940 for one year training (took six and one-half years to get his one year in), Co. D, 163rd, 1st Bn., Officers Training School, Brisbaine, Australia, tactical instructor 18 months. Prior to that Sanananda, New Guinea, trained Melbourne and Rockhampton, Australia, Ft. Lewis before going overseas.

After three years and seven months overseas, 250 of them and one nurse came home on converted bomber. They sat on folding chairs, but it was better than on the boat. They made five stops for fuel from Brisbane to Sacramento.

Discharged in October 1945, he re-enlisted nine months later. Was discharged again six months later. Retired as first lieutenant. He received numerous awards.

He has two children, a son and a daughter.

KENNETH RUSSELL BALDWIN, was born Aug. 29, 1927 in Methuen, MA, grew up and was educated in Salem, MA. He entered the service Dec. 8, 1941 and was assigned to 1st Inf. Div., then to OCS. Went overseas in late 1942. Came to Division Hqs. from infantry in very early 1944 due to shortage of officers and recovery from wounds. Was attached and assigned to Division Ordnance Section as division ammunition officer. He was commended for the ammunition supply during the Biak, Hollandia, and other campaigns. Transferred to 6th U.S. Army Hdqs. and thence to Gen. MacArthur's general headquarters.

Left the Army in February of 1946, transferred to Reserves, was called back for Korea and served as battalion, brigade, and general staff officer with the 300th Service Command, 70th Division Hqs., and 91st divisions. Retired as a colonel (P) GS from the Reserves. His awards include the Silver Star, Bronze Star, several Purple Hearts, Bronze Arrowheads etc. with theater ribbons and Battle Stars.

Married with four sons and one daughter. His sons, Kenneth Jr., Robert and James served during the Vietnam War in the Army and Bob served in the Marines.

Kenneth served as assistant to the general manager and as National Business Manager for the Cadillac Mtr. Car Division of General Motors Corporation. Retired from there and formed his own company, Baldwin Associates.

He belongs to the Masonic Order, Sons of Confederate Veterans, Jeb Stuart Chapter, VFW Military Order of World Wars, and is president of the Ives Train Society (a toy train hobby group). He has served on many civic groups and freely volunteers for needy organizations. He founded the Cadillac-LaSalle Car Club, a club for antique car buffs in 1958.

ROY A. BANNER, was born May 9, 1913 in Alberta, Canada. He entered the service March 5, 1941 and went through basic training with 116 Medics Co. A. Transferred Jan. 21, 1942 to 29th Engrs. in Oceanside, CA. He spent eight months in Alaska with the 29th.

On April 21, 1944 he was shipped with 29th (now called 1641) to Hollandia, New Guinea on Biak where he met his old company, 116 Medics. His Engineer Company then moved on to Luzon and Manila where he was wounded. He spent about four months in a hospital and was returned to the U.S. in October 1945.

He was discharged from Fitzsimmons Hospital Jan. 5, 1945 with the rank of staff sergeant. He received the Purple Heart.

He attended the University of Washington and graduated in Fisheries in 1949. He worked for the state of Washington until he retired in 1976.

He is married with two sons.

HERBERT BANNERMAN, was born Oct. 8, 1921 in Seattle, WA. He entered the service Sept. 16, 1940 and was assigned to the 41st Inf. Div., 146 FA, F Btry., 167th FA, C and HQ Btry. Stationed at Ft. Lewis and South Pacific.

Discharged with the rank of tech 4 sergeant. He joined the reserves and was recalled for Korea, CO Petroleum Products Lab., northern New Guinea, south Philippines.

Married (wife deceased). He has four grandchildren. Herbert is retired from the Federal Bureau of Prisons.

EDWARD P. BARBEE JR., was born Oct. 7, 1923 at home on the banks of North Grosbek near Quanah, TX. At age of five, he moved with his family to a farm between Ropes and Levelland, TX. Graduated from Ropesville High School in May 1940. Moved to San Diego, CA and worked for National City Ship Constructors from 1941 to April 1943.

Was inducted into the U.S. Army at Ft. McArthur, CA. Took basic and advanced training at Ft. Hood, TX and Ft. Ord, CA. Boarded USS *President Grant* at Oakland, CA for Brisbane, Australia, Ascot Replacement Depot. (His father also boarded this same ship in 1917 in WWI.)

Assigned to Service Co., 186th Inf. Regt., 41st Inf. Div. in December 1943 at Rockhampton, Australia. In 1944, he boarded ship at Gladstone, Australia for Finchhaven, New Guinea staging area. Boarded LST for landing at Hollandia, New Guinea. After Jap bomb hit PIM Supply dump, he fished barrels of Jap aircraft gasoline from Lake Senteni in order to operate vehicles.

In 1944, he boarded an LST for landing on Biak Island, NEI. On the second night there were approximately 13 Jap bomber raids. No. 13 came across OWI Island and Bosnek and he shot it down with a 50 caliber machine gun from truck mount and received a Bronze Star. Earned another Bronze Star for taking truck loads of supplies through Jap roadblock at Parari Defile, to Mokmer Drome Beachhead. Those Jap tanks kind of give you a start when you don't know that they have been knocked out, and Jap mortar shells dropping.

In 1945 he boarded ship for staging area on Mindoro Island, Philippine Islands. Boarded ships for landing at Puerta Princesa, Palawan Island Philippine Islands. Saw caves where Japs had burned POWs. Saw Iwahig Penal Colony of Palawan. Boarded LCI for landing at Zamboanga, Mindinao, Philippine Islands, was assigned to Philippine guerillas most of time here. In September 1945 they boarded ships for landing at Kure, Japan on Oct. 7, 1945 and stationed at Kaidachi in Hiroshima area. Made several trips in and out of Hiroshima for various reasons. In December 1945 he boarded train for trip to Nagoya, Japan for return on USS *Admiral Eberle* to Seattle, WA, then to Ft. McArthur, CA.

Married Mary Means Jan. 25, 1946. They have two children, James Edward and Mary Jeanne. They also have three grandchildren, Amber, Kendall, and Mary Nell. They reside in Lubbock, TX. On Dec. 31, 1988, he retired from the U.S. Department of Agriculture as a warehouse examiner. Edward and Mary enjoy square dancing.

Received honorable discharge on Jan. 13, 1946. His awards include Bronze Stars, Bronze Arrowheads, Combat Infantry Badge, Philippine Liberation Ribbon and Good Conduct Medal.

ORVILLE BARKSDALE (SPARKY), was born May 16, 1923 in Oregon, MO and moved to Stafford, OR in September 1928.

He enlisted in the Newberg National Guard Sept. 13, 1940 and was sent to Camp Murray, a muddy suburb of Ft. Lewis, WA. His unit Bn. F, 218th FA Bn. was renamed Btry. B, 218th FA Bn. He was assigned to the 3rd Gun Section on a 155mm Howitzer where he spent the balance of his almost five years of his one year enlistment.

He held the ranks of private first class, corporal, buck sergeant and section chief. He served in Australia from Melbourne to Rockhampton. Twice to New Guinea at places like Oro Bay, Wadke Island, Hollandia and Biak Island where he was rotated back and discharged May 25, 1945.

He retired in 1978 and lives in Woodburn, OR where he and his wife Margaret enjoy their home. They have two children, two grandchildren, and two great-grandchildren. They also enjoy using their motorhome.

JAMES E. BARNARD, was born Jan. 23, 1922 at Lamar, CO. Joined Oregon National Guard Co. L, 162nd Inf., 41st Div. in January 1940. Was called to Federal Service in September 1940 and trained at Ft. Lewis, WA.

Shipped overseas to Australia in March 1942, he participated in Salamua Campaign in New Guinea in June 1943. Attended OCS in Australia, graduating with rank second lieutenant in September 1943. Served as infantry platoon leader with C Co., 127th Inf., 32nd Div. Participated in landing and ground action at Aitape, New Guinea. Patrolled interior of New Guinea for 50 days on reconnaissance with Recon Troop of 32nd Div.

Rotated to USA in September 1944 and separated from service as first lieutenant in November 1945. Served with Oregon National Guard until 1962 and retired as major. He received the Combat Infantry Badge and all the usual ribbons.

Married to Ramona Lenaburg. They have two daughters and two grandsons. He attended Oregon State University and graduated in 1949. Taught high school for three years, then started his own general construction business. Retired at Beverton, OR after 33 years and now looks after investments, plays golf and fishes.

CLARENCE W. BARTON, was born July 14, 1918 in Oelrichs, SD. Was drafted July 21, 1944. Basic training at Camp Roberts, CA, then assigned to Co. G, 162nd Inf. He served in New Guinea, Philippines and Japan. Joined 41st in February 1945 at Mindoro, Philippines.

Served in south Philippine liberation at Zamboanga, Mindanao, then sent to Kure, Japan. Went through Hiroshima, Japan two months after the Atomic Bomb (he would love to see Hiroshima now).

Discharged at Ft. Lewis, WA on Aug. 15, 1946 with the rank of tech fifth grade.

Married Grace in 1959, she passed away in 1982. No children. He is now married to Lucile. Worked 43 years in sawmills and retired in July 1980. Still runs a small farm at Colville, WA. He enjoys riding their Arabian horses at the farm and on organized trail rides.

They spend August salmon fishing off Vancouver Island in Canadian waters. He is a member of Eagles Lodge.

NICHOLAS S. BATANIDES, was born Aug. 3, 1919 in Tacoma, Washington. He entered the service Oct. 9, 1941 and was assigned to 41st Div., 162 Medics and 41st Div. MPs, 162 Bn. Stationed at Camp Roberts, Ft. Lewis, and Ft. Mason.

His memorable experiences include: playing the part of Uncle Sam in a Special Service stage presentation of "Meet the Soldier in Rockie" and taking 40 prisoners to Finchhaven.

Discharged Aug. 26, 1945 with the rank of private first class. He received the Medical Aid Badge. The litter carrier was sent to him after the war from Washington, DC.

Married 46 years to a wonderful wife. They have two sons, two daughters, and nine grandchildren. He is retired and lives in San Francisco, CA.

DWIGHT E. BEACH, was born in Chelsea, MI on July 20, 1908. He attended the University of Michigan for two years prior to entering the U.S. Military Academy from which he graduated in 1932, commissioned a second lieutenant in field artillery and detailed to the Army Air Corps. Prior to WWII, he served with various horsedrawn field artillery units.

Shortly after Pearl Harbor and the beginning of WWII, Gen. Beach was transferred to the Southwest Pacific where he organized and commanded the 167th FA Bn. using wild horses purchased in Australia. After converting to tractors, his unit in the 41st Inf. Div. participated in campaigns in the Southwest Pacific area from Australia through New Guinea to the Philippines and Japan. In the Philippines he became executive officer of the 24th Div. Arty. He participated in four amphibious assaults at Aitape, Maffin Bay, Wakde and Palawan and in the follow-up phase of amphibious operations in Biak and Zamboango. He also participated in overland operations at Davao.

Since WWII he has commanded the artillery of the 11th Airborne Div., the artillery of the 45th Div. in Korea, and served as artillery officer and deputy chief of staff for Plans and Combat Operations, 8th U.S. Army in Korea. In November 1954 he was appointed chief of staff of 8th U.S. Army.

Following Korea, Gen. Beach was assigned to the U.S. Continental Army Command as the director of the office, Special Weapons Development. He was then assigned to the Department of the Army in the Office of the Deputy Chief of Staff for Military Operations as the Director of Guided Missiles.

General Beach commanded the 82nd Airborne Div., Ft. Bragg, NC from June 1959 to April 1961. In May 1961 he returned to the Pentagon as the deputy chief of Research and Development.

On July 1, 1962 he was promoted to the rank of lieutenant general and assumed the duties of Chief of Research and Development. He was designated Commanding General, United States Army Combat Developments Command on Aug. 20, 1963, a position he held until May 24, 1965 when he was promoted to his current rank and transferred to Korea as Commander in Chief, United Nations Command; Commander, U.S. Forces, Korea; and Commanding General, 8th U.S. Army. On Sept. 1, 1966, he became commander in Chief, U.S. Army, Pacific with station at Ft. Shafter, HI.

During his service, Gen. Beach has been both a student and an instructor at the U.S. Military Academy, the Field Artillery School, the Command and General Staff College, and the Army War College. He has also attended the Amphibious Training School, the Armed forces Staff College, and the Infantry School Airborne Course.

His decorations and awards include: Distinguished Service Medal with Oak Leaf Cluster, Silver Star, Legion of Merit, Bronze Star Medal, Air Medal with Oak Leaf Cluster, American Defense Service Medal with Foreign Service Clasp, American Campaign Medal, Asiatic-Pacific Campaign Medal, World War II Victory Medal, Occupation of Japan Medal, National Defense Service Medal, Korean Service Medal, United Nations Service Medal, Philippine Presidential Unit Citation, Philippine Liberation Ribbon, and Senior Parachutist Badge.

General Beach is married to the former Florence Clem of San Antonio, TX. They have five children: Ann (Mrs. Donald E. Jaekle), Capt. Dwight E. Beach Jr., Cynthia (Mrs. Richard Guthrie), Lillian Beach, and Florence Beach.

WIN M. BEATY, was born Dec. 12, 1914 in Laurel, NE. In 1922 his family moved to eastern Oregon where Win attended school at Baker. In 1930 the family moved to Portland.

Win joined the Oregon National Guard in 1932 and was inducted into the Army on Sept. 16, 1940. His unit, the 218th FA, was camped at Swamp Murray where he trained as a gun sergeant. His unit went to Melbourne in 1941 and then to New Guinea. Later the outfit returned to Rockhampton and then back to New Guinea from where he returned to the U.S. in 1944. He served in a training cadre in California and Texas and was discharged July 29, 1945. Win received the Asiatic-Pacific Service Medal, the American Defense Service Medal and the Good Conduct Medal.

In 1949 he married Dorothy Denfeld in Wisconsin. Together they have five children and 10 grandchildren. He worked as a paint salesman and retired nine years ago.

His time is now spent doing the usual chores and yard work around the house. He enjoys walking, going to the beach, playing with the grandchildren and going on occasional trips and tours.

ALLEN K. BECK, was born Sept. 25, 1919 in Everett, WA. He graduated from Everett High School in 1938. Was employed by Boeing Aircraft 1940-1944. Drafted into service in 1944. Had basic at Camp Wolters, TX.

Departed from San Francisco for overseas in January 1945. Was assigned by replacement depot at Leyte, Philippine Islands to A-163. Joined the 41st on Mindoro. Made landings on Mindanao and Jolo. Occupation duty in Japan. Transferred to 24th Div. when 41st deactivated.

Was discharged with the rank of staff sergeant in May 1946. He received the Combat Infantry Badge and Purple Heart.

He retired from the Federal Civil Service as a full-time technician for the Washington Army National Guard in 1977.

Allen is single and lives in Seattle, WA.

ELDON E. BECK, was born July 27, 1919 in Lewistown, MT. He entered the service on Sept. 16, 1940 and was assigned to Co. K, 163rd Inf., 41st Div. Stationed at Ft. Lewis and the South Pacific.

His memorable experiences include the whole tour of duty and his first campaign flying over the Owen Stanleys into the Sanananda Campaign.

Discharged with the rank of sergeant, he received the Combat Infantry Badge, two Bronze Battle Stars (New Guinea), Asiatic-Pacific Campaign Medal, American Defense Service Medal, Good Conduct Medal, Unit Citation, and Bronze Star.

Married 45 years to Neta. He had one son, one daughter, three granddaughters, and one grandson.

He is retired and lives on a ranch in Lewistown, MT.

AUGUST BENITES, was born Feb. 5, 1919 in Hawaii and raised in San Leandro, CA. Graduated from high school in 1937 and was drafted in 1941. Entered the service June 2, 1941, assigned to 146th FA Med Detachment. Basic training in Camp Roberts, CA, joined the 41st in September and was shipped to Australia then New Guinea and the Philippine Islands.

Participated in five invasions, New Guinea, Hollandia and Biak; Philippine Islands, Zamboanga, Jolo, and Tarvi Tarvi.

Discharged in September 1945 with the rank of staff sergeant. His awards include the Bronze Star and Purple Heart.

Married Jean Stacy Young in 1948. They have two daughters, Marilyn and Marta, two grandchildren, Justin and Brianna. He was in the clothing business and had his own men's shop. Retired in 1984 to Twain Harte, CA.

ALBERT W. BENNETT, was born Sept. 20, 1915 at Ely, NE where he graduated from high school. He was inducted into the service March 28, 1941 at Ft. Douglas, UT and was sent to Ft. Lewis, WA. Assigned to Co. L 162.

Departed the U.S. on March 4, 1942, arrived in Melbourne, Australia on April 9, 1942, then to Rockhampton Queensland, then the full length of New Guinea to the Philippines. He was in the battles for Salamaua, Biak, Zamboanga, and Davao on Mindanao.

Returned to the States Sept. 26, 1945. Discharged with the rank of staff sergeant on Oct. 2, 1945. He has the Philippine Liberation Ribbon, Asiatic Pacific Campaign Medal, Good Conduct Medal and American Defense Service Medal with four Bronze Stars, one Bronze Arrowhead, and the Combat Infantry Badge.

Married to Flora Milne of Rockhampton Queensland. They have a son and a daughter. He is a retired electrician from Westinghouse Hanford Company. He makes his home in Kennewick, WA.

FORREST E. BENNETT, was born April 19, 1918, raised in Long Branch, NJ and graduated from high school. He was inducted into the Army on Dec. 12, 1940 and was assigned to and trained with Co. A, 114th Inf., 44th Div. at Ft. Dix, NJ; Camp Claiborne, LA; and Ft. Lewis, WA. In April 1942, he was transferred to Co. L, 186th Inf., 41st Div.

He went to Australia and made beachheads at Hollandia and Biak, New Guinea. He also made a beachhead at Palawan Island in the Philippines. From the Philippines he was sent to Ft. Dix, NJ and discharged in July 1945.

He attained the rank of staff sergeant and was awarded the Bronze Star along with the Combat Infantry Badge.

In 1946 he married Betty Caliendo and remained in Long Branch, NJ. After 32 years in the postal service, he retired in 1978 and now plays golf.

GORDON F. BERG, was born May 7, 1920 in Greenwood, IL. He entered the service Sept. 21, 1941 and was assigned to K Co., 163rd Inf., 41st Div. as a cook.

Discharged Oct. 2, 1945 with the rank T/4.

Married Beulah in October 1945. They have one son, two grandsons, and one great-grandson. He retired from the post office in 1972.

ALBERT C. BERGER, was born Sept. 19, 1921 in Leduc, Alberta, Canada. Entered the service Sept. 29, 1939 and was assigned to Co. F, 162nd Inf., 41st Div. Stationed at Portland, OR; Camp Murray and Ft. Lewis, WA.

Was discharged Feb. 7, 1942 for not being a citizen of the U.S. Ten months later was drafted on Dec. 7, 1942 and put in the 104th Inf. Div. at Camp Adair, OR. Trained in the U.S. for two years then transferred into the Canadian army and became an instructor at an advanced infantry training center in Camp Ipperwash, Ontario, Canada where he was until his discharge after the war in March 1946. Rank achieved was corporal.

His awards include the Good Conduct Medal, American Defense Medal, Infantry Badge, Expert in .45 auto, 38 colt, 30.06 rifle, 22 rifle.

Married to Elsie for 22 years and has two daughters, Kathy and Karen. He retired in 1978 and moved to Cascade, MT next to the Missouri River in the Big Belt Mountains.

ARTHUR L. BERGER, was born Dec. 8, 1914 at Hay Lakes, Alberta, Canada. Entered the service in 1935 at Portland, OR. Was assigned to 41st Div., Co. F and Co. C, 162nd Inf. Stationed at Portland, OR, Ft. Lewis, WA, and Australia.

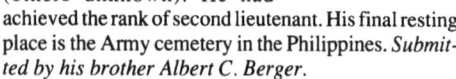

Arthur was killed in action on June 12, 1944 at Biak Island. His awards include the Purple Heart, Combat Infantry Badge (others unknown). He had achieved the rank of second lieutenant. His final resting place is the Army cemetery in the Philippines. *Submitted by his brother Albert C. Berger.*

EDGAR D. BERLIN, was born Dec. 2, 1917 in Denver, CO. Raised through high school in northwest Oregon, He attained officer rank in Army Infantry Reserve while completing college through the junior year in 1941 at Oregon State University.

Reported to 41st Inf. at Ft. Lewis on Dec. 26, 1941. He made the trip on the *Santa Paula* as platoon leader with 2nd Bn., 162nd Inf. from New York to Melbourne, Australia. He became Battalion S2 at Buna-Gona, then participated in amphibious landings at Nassau Bay, Finchhaven, Hollandia and Biak. Ed made the rotation list after Biak was secured and trained infantry recruits until war's end at Camp Fannin, TX. Two more years college resulted in a master's degree in mechanical engineering, then employment as an aerospace engineer with General Dynamics in San Diego until retirement.

HYMAN BERMAN, was born May 4, 1916 in Rochester, NY. Entered the service November 1941 and assigned to HQ Co., 1st Bn., 186th Inf., 41st Div. Stationed at Camp Wheeler, GA; Ft. Lewis, WA and Buna.

Participated in the action at Palawan, Hollandia, Biak, and Zamboango.

Discharged October 1945 with the rank private first class. He received four campaign medals and Battle Stars, six Overseas Bars and numerous ribbons.

Married to Revelle, had son Marshall, daughter Harriet, and granddaughter Davina. Was traffic manager, retired, and lives in Highland Park, IL. Hyman passed away from lung cancer on Oct. 4, 1992.

STANLEY W. BEVER, was born May 4, 1921 in Spokane, WA. Joined the National Guard in October 1938; assigned to 41st Div., HQ 2nd Bn., 146th FA HQ 167th FA.

Spent 41 months in the South Pacific. Driver and orderly for Dwight Beach who later became a four star general. He formed the 167th Pack Artillery preparing to go to the Owen Stanley Range. In 90 days they took range horses in Ingham, Australia and trained them to pack the 75 mountain guns. When the Owen Stanley Range was secured, they decided Pack Artillery was not needed so they returned to truck drawn 105th Artillery and proceeded to New Guinea, Wadke Island, Biak, Mindora, Mindanoa, Palawan, and Zamboanga.

Discharged with the rank T/5. He married Dec. 15, 1954 and has four children and 10 grandchildren. Was in the printing plate business two years, electrotyper four years, and real estate broker 40 years. Presently retired and enjoys golf, travel, fishing, and investing.

LYLE BISHOP, was born Dec. 31, 1917 in Mitchellville, IA. Drafted on Oct. 29, 1941. Was at Ft. Des Moines, IA for two weeks then went to Camp Wolters, TX for basic training. From there went to Ft. Lewis, WA and joined the 41st Inf. Was in I Co. 163 until they got to Seymour, Australia than put in 3rd Bn. Medics 163.

Moved to Rockhampton, Australia and on to Port Morsby. They flew over the Owen Stanley Range to Dobadurak, New Guinea, then walked up a log road to Buna. After they took Buna, they went through the jungles to Gona, to a peninsula, back to Dobadurak. Flew to Port Morsby and took a boat to Australia for additional training.

He had a furlough in Melbourne, Australia and had a good time. After leaving Rockhampton, they made two landings in New Guinea and on to Biak and the Philippines. Made a landing at Zamboanga and Holo.

Atomic bomb was dropped. Came back to the States Sept. 15, 1945 and after a 30 day leave was discharged Nov. 2, 1945 with the rank private T/4.

Married to Elma and they have two children and four grandchildren. Worked at VA Hospital, Des Moines as attendant then as janitor till March 15, 1973, then for A.A. Schneiduhahs, D.M. as janitor until Nov. 1, 1983.

DWIGHT D. BITNER, was born April 22, 1923, Butler, MO, Bates County. Graduated Amoret High in 1941. Drafted into Army 1944, took infantry basic training at Camp Fannin, TX. Went overseas December 1944 and was assigned to Co. E, 163rd Regt., 41st Inf. Div. Served in Liberation of Philippines and Occupation of Japan near Hiroshima. Returned to States in May 1946. Achieved the rank of staff sergeant.

He attended Agricultural School, farmed, owned car agency and was insurance sales manager.

Married Loraine in 1948 and has three children: Teresa De Ann (deceased); Lt. Col. Teddy D., Air Defense (participant of Desert Storm, his hobby is jumping with Golden Knights); and Annetta Bethene, RN with BSN and teaches college nursing.

Dwight served as president of local hospital board, optimist, and member of American Legion and DAV.

FRANCIS R. BLACK, was born Dec. 6, 1912 in Vancouver, WA. Entered the service in April 1930 and served with Btry. A and D, Service Btry., HQ Btry., Div. Arty., at Townsville, Melbourn, and Rockhampton, Australia; New Guinea; Salamaua; Hollandia; Mindoro; and Mindanao.

Discharged in 1946 with the rank CWO. He received all the usual awards of the 41st Div.

He was a heavy duty mechanic for a rock crushing and road building company in Coos Bay, then worked for the Alaska Pipeline seven years. After retirement from pipelines he spent five summers at a Jade mine near Nome, AK.

Divorced, he has two children and six grandchildren. He lives on five acres outside of Coos Bay, OR. His hobbies are Model A Fords (present project is installing an overdrive in his A Ford).

JOHN L. BLACK, was born Oct. 29, 1918 in Miles City, MT. Entered the service on Sept. 16, 1940. Served with Co. L, 163rd Regt., 41st Div.

Went to South Pacific Theater in early 1942. Participated in combat duty in New Guinea, Biak, and surrounding area.

Discharged Aug. 26, 1945 with the rank staff sergeant. His awards include the Combat Infantry Badge, Purple Heart, and Unit Citation.

Married and has two daughters. He is a member of the American Legion, VFW, DAV, and 163rd Infantry Association. He is a retired carpenter.

DUDLEY B. BLATCHLEY, was born Dec. 21, 1921 in Seattle, WA and grew up in Portland, OR. He entered Oregon National Guard in November 1939. Inducted into Army Sept. 16, 1940 at Ft. Lewis, WA. he served with HQ Co., 162nd Inf.

He was shipped overseas from Ft. Dix, NJ to Australia, arriving early 1942. He fought in fall of Salamaua, at that time the longest continuous combat for any troops in Southwest Pacific (76 days). He made landings at Nausau Bay, Hollandia, Finchhaven, Biak, and Zamboanga.

He was awarded the Combat Infantry Badge and Bronze Star. He returned to U.S. in Aug. 14, 1945 (V-J Day). Was discharged Aug. 18, 1945 at Ft. Lewis, WA.

He married Betty J. Stedman Sept. 6, 1945. They have three children and six grandchildren. He retired as captain with 28 years of service on Eugene City Fire Department.

He is a member of VFW, life member of Elks, 100F and Valley River Baptist Church. He is an ardent RV traveler, covering much of the U.S.

WALTER E. BLOOMER, was born July 26, 1924 in Kearny, NJ. Drafted on May 18, 1943. Went to Camp Wheeler, GA for 17 weeks basic training, then to Ft. Ord and Camp Stoneman, CA.

Was sent to Brisbane, Australia to Camp Ascot and then sent to H Co., 162nd Inf., 41st Div. Reassigned to A Co., 186th Inf. for the duration. Took part in battles at Hollandia, Biak, Palawan, and Zamboanga and then occupied Japan.

Discharged Jan. 13, 1946 with the rank technical sergeant. He received the Bronze Star, Bronze Arrowhead, Good Conduct Medal, Asiatic-Pacific Campaign Medal, World War II Victory Medal, Combat Infantryman's Badge, Sharpshooter Badge with Rifle Bar.

Married to Marie Rose Walberg in 1946 and they have six children. He was on the Kearny Fire Department for 36 years and retired in 1985. He now resides in Toms River, NJ with his wife.

BILL BOLSTER, was born April 30, 1919 in Plentywood, MT. Drafted February 1943 in Billings, MT, sent to Ft. Lewis, WA. Trained at Camp Roberts, CA for 13 weeks.

Arrived at Brisbane, Australia on July 26, 1943. Joined B Co., 163rd, 41st Div. at Rockhampton on Aug. 7, 1943. Had jungle training until March 18, 1944. Sailed on *Victory Cape Cleare* to Finchhaven, New Guinea. After three weeks sailed on LST 241 for invasion of Aitape, New Guinea at 0701 hours in April 1944. Was in hospital at Lae, New Guinea for two months then rejoined his company at Biak on July 27, 1944.

Was transferred to Division Quartermaster on Oct. 22, 1944. Left Biak on Feb. 2, 1945 on *Liberty John Lande*. Invaded Mindoro Island, Philippines on Feb. 9, 1945. Left in March on LST 579. Invaded Zamboanga on March 10, 1945. Left Sept. 17, 1945 on AK 31 and landed in Hiro, Japan on Oct. 7, 1945 as occupation forces.

Left Japan Dec. 12, 1945 on USS *Magoffin* and arrived in San Francisco on Dec. 25, 1945. Was discharged from Ft. Lewis on Jan. 3, 1946 with the rank T/5. His decorations include: Victory Medal, Asiatic-Pacific Service Medal, Philippine Liberation Medal with one Bronze Service Star, Bronze Service Arrowheads, and Good Conduct Medal.

He worked for John Deere Company, Portland, OR for 30 years before retiring on Jan. 6, 1979. Has resided in Twin Falls, ID for 26 years being a resident credit and insurance representative for Deere in this area.

Bill and wife Shirley Anne are enjoying their retirement and try to spend a lot of time with their four sons in California, Washington State, and Japan.

THOMAS L. BOLT, was born June 24, 1926 in Portsmouth, VA. Enlisted in Army April 7, 1944. Basic training at Camp Roberts, CA. Joined 41st Inf. Div. on Feb. 23, 1945, at Mindoro, Philippines, and participated in landing at Zamboanga, Mindanao on March 10, 1945, and served as rifleman in Co. C, 162nd Inf. and also in Davao Province. Army of Occupation in Japan stationed at Kure and Matsue until Dec. 24, 1945 when division demobilized.

Discharged Aug. 24, 1946 with rank of sergeant. Served in Enlisted Reserve Corps until Aug. 24, 1949. Attended U.C. Berkeley with B.A. degree in anthropology and MSW degree in social work.

Married to Joanne with two children, Katherine and Ronald. Remains as social worker on Fresno County, CA psychiatric ward.

JOSEPH F. BONDS, was born Dec. 5, 1923 in Bower Cave, CA. Entered the service Dec. 28, 1942. Served with Co. M, 186th Inf., 41st Div. Stationed at Zamboanga, Mindanao, Philippine Islands, Hiroshima, Japan.

California Mi-wok Indian, raised on Indian Reservation Intuolomne, CA (Yosemite Tribe). Military Police during WWII in southern California.

Discharged with the rank squad leader, corporal.

He is the father of five children and grandfather of seven.

TROYCE M. BOONE, was born Jan. 4, 1925 in Caddo, TX and raised near Ranger. Went to school in Ranger and Olden, TX. Entered the Army July 21, 1944 and took his basic training at Camp Wolters, TX.

Left the States Jan. 1, 1945. Got off the ship in Leyte about Feb. 10. Went to Mondoro where he was assigned to the 41st Inf. Div. Served with Co. I, 186th Inf. They made a beachhead at Palawan on Feb. 28, 1945. After about 30 days, they were sent to Zamboanga. When the war was over, he was sent to Japan for occupation for 10 months. After returning to the States, he got his discharge Aug. 20, 1946 in San Antonio, TX.

Married Effie M. Boone on May 1, 1944. They have five children and 10 grandchildren. He retired in March 1990 from the oil fields. Does a little ranching for past-time.

VIRGLE R. BOX, was born Oct. 29, 1921. He was drafted into the service Aug. 26, 1942, at Ft. Oglethorpe, GA. He took basic training at Ft. McCellan, AL. From there he went to Camp Butner, NC and joined the 41st Div. with Co. A, 116th Engineers Combat Bn. in 1942.

He was then sent overseas to serve in New Guinea GO 58, WD45, southern Philippines GO 67, WD45. They then made landings at Zamboanga and Holo. He was then sent to Japan after the big bomb was dropped.

He came back to the States and was discharged on Dec. 5, 1945 with the rank of sergeant.

He married Norene Moore on Jan. 9, 1946. They have two children, Michael and Bryant, and three grandchildren, Chad, Stephen, and Crystal. He was a member of the VFW Post of Decatur County, Lions Club, and served as Circuit Court Clerk for Decatur County for eight years. He owned and operated the Parsons Texaco Service Center from 1970 until his death on July 21, 1985.

RUSSELL O. BOYD, was born June 18, 1917 on a farm in South Dakota. Drafted March 27, 1941 and served with F-146 and C-167, stationed at Ft. Lewis, WA. Participated in Aitape action.

His memorable experiences include: going over on *Queen Elizabeth,* first landing, coming home under Golden Gate Bridge, and first family get together after several years.

Rotation after 34 months overseas, then Ft. Sill, OK. Was discharged from Camp Beale, CA in June 1945. He received the Asiatic-Pacific, Good Conduct and all the usual division medals and ribbons.

Married since 1947 and has a daughter, two grandchildren, and one great-grandchild. His wife passed away in 1988. Retired after 30 years with city of Los Angeles. He still likes to camp and fish.

FRED D. BOYER, was born July 4, 1919 in Roseburg, OR where he grew up and went to school. He joined the Oregon National Guard in 1936 in Roseburg and was called to active duty in September 1940 going to Camp Murray, Ft. Lewis, WA and overseas to Australia.

Combat duty in New Guinea and the Philippines. Went to Officer's Candidate School before going to the Philippines. After being commissioned, he joined the 24th Div.

Discharged the fall of 1945 and was retired as a major in the Oregon National Guard. He received two Silver Stars and was awarded the Purple Heart.

Married in 1946 and has a daughter Becky and granddaughter Tiffnay. He went into the meat business when he got out of the service, selling it in 1980 and retired.

He is a member of the Purple Heart Club, VFW, Moose Lodge, Elks Lodge, and Umpqua Valley Round-up Association, also served on the local fair board and Glide School Board. He was grand marshall of the annual rodeo parade in June 1990.

JAMES BRADLEY (DAVE), was born Dec. 21, 1919 in Vancouver, WA. Raised in Portland, OR and graduated from Jefferson High in 1938.

Inducted in Army Oct. 8, 1941. Took basic training at Camp Roberts, CA. When Pearl Harbor was attacked, he joined Co. L, 186 at Raymond, WA. Was assigned to S-1 Hqs., 186, transferred to AG Section, 41st Div. HQ. Served in Australia, New Guinea, and Philippines.

Discharged from Army Oct. 4, 1945 at Ft. Lewis, WA.

He married Gwen in 1946 at Oregon City, OR. They have two children, Lisa (surgical nurse in Omaha, NE) and Andy (employed by Carbomedics in Austin, TX).

James worked for Magnus Metal, a producer of brass bearings in Portland, OR, French Camp, CA and Fremont, NE for over 42 years. He retired in 1983 and travels half the time in their motor home. He is a member of Good Sam RV Club, AARP and Coast to Coast Resorts.

ARTHUR J. BRAMAN, was born Aug. 12, 1914 at St. Edwards, NE. Entered the service Jan. 29, 1942. Served with 163rd Inf., Co's F, I, G, 2nd Bn. Hqs. Stationed at Australia, New Guinea, and Philippines.

His memorable experiences include first day of combat at Buna, New Guinea Jan. 9, 1943 and commanding G Co. for two years.

Discharged Jan. 31, 1946 with the rank of captain. His awards include the Silver Star, Bronze Star, Combat Infantry, Asiatic-Pacific Ribbon with two Bronze Stars, Philippine Liberation Ribbon with one star, Congressional Distinguished Unit Badge, and Bronze Arrowhead.

Married to Helen and they have one son and two daughters. He is retired after 48 years with Union Pacific Railroad.

WILLIAM W. BRANDON, was born Jan. 24, 1917 in Ellwood City, PA. Entered the service October 1942. Served with G Co., 163rd. Stationed overseas.

His memorable experience was seeing the shoreline of Seattle, WA when he came home.

Discharged in March 1946 with the rank of captain. He received the Bronze Star and Presidential Unit Citation with cluster.

Married Dayna in 1946 and has two daughters, Dianna and Sandy, and five grandchildren. Has been retired since 1982.

LEWIS ROSS BRANDT, was born April 18, 1925 in Spencer, NC. He entered the service Aug. 6, 1943. Was assigned to 41st Div. on Dec. 15, 1943 at Rockhampton, Australia.

His most memorable experience was landing in Kure, Japan as a member of the Occupation Army. Friendships formed during battle have meant a great deal to him and he cherishes each one of these men and the memories of their life together in the jungles.

Discharged with the rank of staff sergeant. His awards and decorations include the Bronze Star, Good Conduct Medal, American Campaign Medal, Asiatic-Pacific Medal with two Bronze Stars and one Arrowhead, World War II Victory Medal, Army of Occupation Medal with Japan Clasp, Combat Infantry Badge, and Philippine Liberation Ribbon.

Married Mary Ruth Thompson in August 1949 and has three sons, Lamar, Phillip, and Gordon and two grandchildren.

He retired from the DuPont Company (Nylon Div.) in Martinsville, VA after 36 years on Jan. 31, 1984. He is enjoying retirement, woodworking, gardening, travel, and the grandchildren.

He is a member of the American Legion, Potomac Chapter of 41st Inf., National Chapter of 41st Inf. and the Methodist Church.

ALEXANDER BRASCHAYKO, was born Feb. 28, 1917 at Vanderbilt, PA. Served with Co. B, 162 Regt., 41st Div. Stationed at Ft. Lewis, WA; Australia; New Guinea; and Philippine Islands; Mindanao.

Memorable experiences include: Mt. Tambu, Battle of Salamau, Hollandia, Zamboanga, and West Caves in Biak Island.

Discharged with the rank of technical sergeant. He received the Bronze Star and Combat Infantry Badge.

Married since 1947 to Elizabeth, they have three children, Mary, Katheleen, and Steven. He worked for Detroit Police Department from 1946-1971 and as hospital security from 1971-1982. Now retired and lives in Utica, MI.

ARTHUR R. BREMER, was born Sept. 18, 1918 in Fairfield, MT. Entered the service Feb. 27, 1941. Assigned to 41st Div. as lineman-telephone 238. Stationed at Australia and New Guinea. He participated in action overseas.

Discharged with the rank of private first class. He received the Asiatic-Pacific Service Medal, American Defense Service Medal, and the Good Conduct Medal.

He is single and retired from farming early due to military disability.

CLYDE H. BREMERMAN, was born Jan. 17, 1915 in Flemington, MO. Drafted March 4, 1941 into 162nd Inf. Medics from Yakima, WA and served almost a year at Ft. Lewis before war was declared.

Rode troop train from Ft. Lewis to Ft. Dix, NJ, then to Brooklyn, NY. From there took ship through the Panama Canal to Bora Bora Society Islands, then to Auckland, New Zealand and Melbourne, Australia. From Australia to New Guinea, to Biak Island in Netherlands East Indies. Came home on rotation, separated as dental technician at Ft. Lewis on Aug. 31, 1945 with the rating T/5. He is lifetime member of DAV.

He worked for NP Railroad 10 years in the backshops in Tacoma, WA; 20 years at Yakima Valley College as carpenter and cabinet maker. He retired in 1983.

Married Maxine three weeks before entering service. He has one son and five grandchildren. Lost Maxine to cancer after 41 years of marriage. He married Alnora in 1985. They own four rentals which keeps them busy.

GILBERT BRIMEYER, was born June 3, 1922 in Sioux Falls, SD. He joined the Army July 29, 1942.

On Dec. 27, 1942, he went through Panama Canal to Brisbane, Australia. When replacements were sent to the 41st Inf. in New Guinea, he went into town, missed departure and was AWOL. On his own he traveled by train to Townsville, obtained a ride on an Australian airplane to Port Moresby.

In February 1943, he joined the 41st Signal Co. at Dobadura. He was at Hollandia, Biak, Palawan, and Mindanao. Although promoted to staff sergeant before going to Japan, the general cancelled all promotions so he remained a T/5. In Japan he toured Hiroshima.

He married Leone in 1949. They have two daughters. One is a teacher and the other an attorney. Gilbert retired as vice-president for a large health care center.

MELVIN B. BORKOFSKY, was born Aug. 10, 1919 in Avon, SD. He entered the service on July 8, 1941. Was assigned to 41st Div. on Oct. 12, 1941, Btry. D, 148th FA, Btry. B, 205th FA, Ft. Lewis, WA.

His memorable experiences include: the bombing of Pearl Harbor; the sea voyages; the field artillery training; and the five months in the hospital in Australia.

Discharged September 1943 with the rank of corporal. His awards include the Southwest Pacific Expedition, American Defense Service, Asiatic-Pacific Theater, and Good Conduct Medal.

Melvin owned and operated a garage after leaving the service for several years until his MS worsened. He has spent the last 20 years in a wheelchair. Melvin has done volunteer work at the local VA Hospital for over 19 years. He has studied computer and has been writing family histories.

Married to Pearl since 1944. He has two sons, Larry (Vietnam vet) now with the FBI and Rick, retired from AT&T and now with a communication firm at SAC HQ in Omaha.

Melvin is a life member of VFW, American Legion, DAV, and PVA. He lives in Grand Island, NE.

FRANCIS M. BROWN, was born May 16, 1920. Graduated from Mt. Vernon, WA High School in 1938. Joined the Army Sept. 16, 1940. Served with 116th QM. Later called 41st QM.

Trained at Ft. Lewis, then went overseas to Australia in March of 1942. From there to New Guinea, Port Morsbey, Dobadura, Buna, Hollandia, and Biak.

Returned to the U.S. from Biak and was assigned to the 4900 Military Police in the old armory in Seattle, WA. Was discharged Aug. 26, 1945.

Married to Dorothy Buchanan on Feb. 22, 1945, whom he met while stationed in Burlington, WA. They have two daughters, Nancy and Christine, and five grandchildren. He spent most of his working years as a salesman for Marie'e Dressing Incorporation. Now retired and lives in Seattle, WA.

He is an active member of 41st Infantry Division Association, Seattle Chapter. and past president of Ballard Eagles #172.

DOYLE E. BRUCE, was born April 24, 1916 in Appleby, TX. He entered the service on Oct. 6, 1941. Served with 163rd Inf., 2nd Bn., G Co., 41st Div.

Stationed at Camp Roberts, CA and Ft. Lewis, WA. Overseas at Sanananda, Australia, New Guinea, Wakde, Aitape, Biak, Zamboanga, Jolo, Sanga Sanga. Engaged in Kumusi River Patrol. He never missed a day in combat.

Discharged on June 15, 1945 at San Antonio, TX with the rank of staff sergeant. He never had a furlough.

Married in November 1945 to Helen Slack. They have two sons (each has a set of identical twins) and a daughter who has a son. Doyle retired after 31 years as masonry contractor in Lufkin, TX.

ROBERT F. BRUNSWICK (BOB), was born May 22, 1923 in Oregon. He entered the service September 1940, assigned to Co. E, 218. Saw combat in HQ 167 in South Pacific, Australia, New Guinea, and Philippines. Made several beach landings in New Guinea and Philippines. Was liaison team radio operator.

Discharged with the rank T/5. He received the Good Conduct Medal, Philippines Liberation Medal and others whose names he has forgotten over the years.

Married 39 years to Jeanne. He is retired and lives in Alpine, CA.

ALLSON F. BUCHANAN, was born Nov. 10, 1925 in Detroit, MI. Entered the service in July 1944. Assigned to Co. D, 186th Regt., 41st Div.

Made landings at Palawan, Zamboanga, and Japan. Discharged with the rank private first class. He received the Philippine Liberation with one Bronze Star, Asiatic-Pacific with two Bronze Stars, World War II Victory Medal, Combat Infantry Badge, Good Conduct Medal, Expert Medal (rifle and pistol), and the Purple Heart with one Bronze Star.

Married to Eleanor and has son John. He worked 39 years with Chrysler Inc. in Cuba, Columbia, Mexico, Palawan, London, and Switzerland. Retired since 1989 and lives in Port St. Lucie, FL.

WALTER E. BUCKLAND, was born Dec. 25, 1917 in Highwood, MT. Joined the service Sept. 16, 1940 and served with OLD D, A, and B Co., 116 Med, 41st Div. Attached to 1st Bn., 163rd Combat Team. Overseas duty at Dobadura, Huggins Perimeter, Sanananda, Papua, Biak, New Guinea, Zamboanga, Jolo, and Tawi-Tawi, Philippine Islands.

Discharged July 25, 1945 at Ft. Lewis, WA. Received the Distinguished Unit Badge.

Married to Iris (Australian) and has son Dana. He is retired at Seattle, WA and enjoys golf and skiing.

BOYD E. BUDGE, was born Jan. 26, 1914 in Ogden, UT. Called to one year active duty Aug. 11, 1941. Was assigned to 41st Inf., Ft. Lewis. Served in Co. A, C, HQ 163, and DHQ. His military specialty was assistant AC of S G-3. First combat: Huggins Perimeter, Sanananda, Killerton Point, Gona. Second Phase: Aitape, Toem, Wakde, Biak. Participated in battles at Papua, Dutch New Guinea, and south Philippines. Attended Ft. Leavenworth 22nd Class C&GS School. Then to Zamboanga, Subic Bay (planning Olympic OPN), Kure, and Hiroshima.

Returned December 1945, one of the 143 officers remaining of the 1,400 that left Ft. Lewis in February 1942. Was discharged March 22, 1946 at Ft. Douglas. His awards and decorations include: Air Medal, Bronze Star, Distinguished Unit Badge, Combat Infantry Badge, American Defense Service Medal, Asiatic-Campaign Medal with three Bronze Stars, one Bronze Arrowhead, Philippine Liberation Ribbon with one Bronze Star, World War II Victory Medal, American Campaign Medal and seven Overseas Service Bars. He retired from USAR in 1974 with the rank lieutenant colonel.

Married Jessie in 1939 at Boise, ID. They have three children, seven grandchildren, and one great-grandchild. Boyd retired from civilian life in 1982. He is a member of the Kiwanis International and Elks.

RALPH BULLOCK, was born Dec. 8, 1917 in Los Angeles, CA. Graduated from Los Angeles Polytechnic High School in 1935 and from Whittier College in 1940.

Enlisted in Army on Feb. 26, 1941. Stationed at Ft. Lewis, WA. Served in Co. K, 162nd Inf. Regt., 41st Inf. Div. in Australia and New Guinea. Assigned to HQ Co., 127th Inf. Regt., 32nd Div. and assigned to Div. HQs as assistant G-3. Served in New Guinea and Leyte Philippine Islands campaigns.

Discharged as sergeant on Sept. 27, 1943 at OCS in Australia and commissioned on Sept. 28, 1943. Retired as major AUS.

Married on Feb. 3, 1945 to Alice E. Andrews of Los Angeles. They have two daughters, Evelyn and Patrica, and four grandchildren. Ralph worked as branch manager, YMCA of Los Angeles, a teacher, principal, superintendent of a school district, and assistant to the county superintendent of School, county of San Bernardino, CA.

OSCAR DOUGLAS BUMPAS, was born Aug. 15, 1913 in Marshall County, MS. He was inducted in the U.S. Army on June 17, 1941 at Camp Shelby, MS. Occupational speciality was cook 060 and his qualification and date was CIB.

He received most of his training at Ft. Lewis, WA. He was in camp in northern California for a few weeks before departing on April 22, 1942. Stationed in Australia, he participated in the battles and campaigns of New Guinea, Papua and Southern Philippines.

Discharged at Separation Center, Camp Shelby, MS on Oct. 6, 1945 with the rank private first class. His decorations and citations were: Good Conduct Medal, American Defense Service Medal, APTO Medal, Philippine Liberation Ribbon with one Bronze Star.

Married June 2, 1946 to Wilma Blondine Renick. They have one daughter Carlie Rose who married Rudolph Wilson. Oscar was a Baptist, barber, farmer, and school bus driver. Oscar passed away Aug. 19, 1989 and was buried in Pine Grove Cemetery in Benton County, MS.

EDWARD W. BUNCH, was born Sept. 25, 1912 in Linn Creek, MO. Joined the service Feb. 26, 1941 and was assigned to 41st Div., Service Co., 186th Inf. Stationed at Ft. Lewis, WA.

His memorable experience was the last conflict on Biak Island, taking of airfield from Japs. He received the Bronze Star Medal. Discharged Aug. 22, 1945 with the rank staff sergeant.

Married to Catherine, they have one son and three granddaughters. He worked 30 years as over-road driver. Presently retired and lives in Kansas City, KS.

JOHN BUSHA, was born June 21, 1914 in Luzerne, PA. Inducted Oct. 2, 1941 at Detroit, MI. Assigned to Co. B, 163rd Inf., Ft. Lewis, WA. Trained at Camp Roberts, CA. Participated in battles at Sanananda Trail, New Guinea. Stationed at Rockhampton, Australia.

Was BARman and wounded at Sanananda. After hospital stay at Sydney (place called Merrylands) went back to Brisbane, then to Rockhampton to rejoin his outfit. Only there two weeks and his leg started swelling again. He was sent back to Sydney then to 4th General Hospital in Melbourne. Left for U.S. in middle of January on Italian Hospital Ship *LaPloma (Dove)* and landed at San Pedro. Sent to Hoff General Hospital, Santa Barbara, CA.

Discharged Oct. 27, 1945 at Ft. Story, VA with the rank of corporal T/5. His awards and decorations include the Purple Heart, Good Conduct Medal, Bronze Star, American Defense, Presidential Unit Citation, Asiatic-Pacific, and World War II Victory Medal.

Married to Anna since June 4, 1949.

WILLIAM P. BUTLER, was born May 25, 1916 in Murphysboro, IL. Drafted Aug. 7, 1941. Took basic

483

training at and helped build Ft. Leonard Wood, MO. He joined C Co., 116th Engrs. on Dec. 7, 1941. He later joined B Co., 116th Engrs., 41st Div., Ft. Lewis, WA.

He made several landings in New Guinea. While there he got typhus and was hospitalized at Australia for five months.

Discharged July 13, 1945 with the rank of corporal T/5. He received a Bronze Star for Biak Island.

Married Regina Qualls on Oct. 15, 1944. They have two children, Merle E. Butler (Vietnam veteran) and Linda R. Crafton. William worked for Luhr Brothers Inc., Columbia, IL for 40 years. Alois Luhr was his relief operator on a bulldozer with B Co. on Biak Island. He retired from Local 520 Operating Engineers in 1983.

TRUMAN K. CALDWELL, was born July 6, 1923 in Rauenden, AR. Inducted Feb. 2, 1943 and assigned to Co. B., 163rd Inf., 41st Div. Trained at Camp Roberts, CA. Stationed at Australia, New Guinea, Biak, Philippines, and Japan.

Made landings in Aitape, Wakde, Biak, Mindoro and Jolo. He was wounded on Jolo.

Discharged Dec. 22, 1945 with the rank private first class. He received the Asiatic-Pacific Theater Ribbon with two Bronze Battle Stars, Bronze Service Arrowhead, five Overseas Service Bars, Good Conduct Medal and the Purple Heart.

Married Hazel in 1943 and they have one son, one daughter and three grandsons. Truman is retired from Ford Motor Company.

WILLARD M. CALLAHAN, was born Dec. 1, 1917 at Redstone, MT where he grew up and graduated from high school in 1936. He then went to work at Ft. Peck, MT on the dam.

Went into the service Sept. 16, 1940 at Glasgow, MT. Training at Ft. Lewis, WA also training at American Lake, CA. Went overseas with the 41st Div. on March 19, 1942. Theirs was the first infantry outfit to reach the Southwest Pacific after Pearl Harbor. They landed in Australia and from there went to New Guinea where he fought at Buna-Sanananda Campaign at Salamaua, Aitape, Hollandia, Wakde, and Biak, in-brief up the entire length of New Guinea. Was with the 163rd Service Co.

Came back to the StateS Dec. 25, 1944 and was in the hospital at Texas until he went back to Ft. Lewis, WA to be discharged on June 2, 1945. His rank was T/4. He received the American Defense Medal, Combat Infantry Badge, Asiatic-Pacific with one Bronze Star, the Distinguished Unit Badge, and the Good Conduct Medal.

He got into construction work and worked in Idaho, then went to Oregon where he met his wife Ruth. They have one son Terry, who works for Northwest Bell, and two granddaughters Karen and Janet. From Oregon he went to San Diego, CA where he worked for Western Salt, Nelson and Sloan Sand and Gravel and National Steel Shipbuilding Company as a crane operator. He retired in 1980 and passed away March 27, 1986. He was very proud to have served with 41st Div.

RICHARD C. CAMP, was born March 2, 1920 in Ruggles, OH. Lived in various places in Ohio and moved to Reading, MI at the age of 16. Entered the Army in October 1941, and was stationed at Camp Wolters, TX and then at Ft. Dix, NJ. Was assigned to the 41st Inf. Div., C-162 when they left the States during WWII. He served in Australia and New Guinea and took part in numerous patrols.

Received honorable discharge as staff sergeant in 1945. He was awarded the Good Conduct Medal, three Battle Stars and Bronze Star.

Married Ellen Avery in 1946, become step-father to Ann, Wes, Dean, and Jim. Richard and Ellen had a daughter Dorothea who died at two days. Richard became a widower in 1974 and married Patricia G. Corser in December 1975.

Richard was a farmer most of his life and became a truck driver in Brooklyn, MI in 1951. He was forced into early retirement as a result of a stroke.

Richard is a member of DAVA, American Legion, VFW, and the Masons.

RICARDO CARDENAS (RICK), was born in El Paso, TX but was raised in the Mojave Desert of California. He joined Co. B, 163rd Regt. in July 1943. He was part of the first group of infantry replacements (who were 18-19 years old), to arrive in Australia and help fill the depleted ranks of the 41st Div. The regiment had just returned from the Buna-Gona fight in New Guinea. Assigned as a rifleman (scout), Rick remained with the regiment through New Guinea, Philippines and Japan.

He returned home as a staff sergeant, was later recalled for the Korean Conflict where he served two tours in a rifle company. He was battlefield commissioned on his first tour. He commanded the rifle company he had served as squad leader, platoon sergeant and later first sergeant.

Rick subsequently served two tours in Vietnam. His military assignments took him to a number of installations in the USA to include duty in Germany and North Africa. He is a graduate of infantry branch schools to include the command and general staff college at Ft. Leavensworth, KS.

He retired in 1972 as a lieutenant colonel. His highest command was a battalion. His decorations include: Distinguished Service Cross, Silver Star, Bronze Star with clusters, Purple Heart with clusters, and other awards and decorations to include personal decorations from the government of Korea and South Vietnam.

In 1953 he married Katherine Patton and raised two sons and a daughter. He finally became a grandfather in 1990.

EVERETT W. CARLSEN, was born Dec. 13, 1923 in Cannon Falls, MN. He entered the service May 22, 1943. Assigned to 41st Div., 167th HQ Btry. Stationed in Australia, New Guinea, Philippines and Japan.

Discharged with the rank T/5. He received the Asiatic-Pacific Service Ribbon, Good Conduct Medal, Philippine Liberation Ribbon with one Bronze Star, and Bronze Arrowhead.

Married Ione in 1949 and has three children, Susan, Pamela and Wayne, and three granddaughters. Everett retired from George A. Hormel Company on Aug. 31, 1984.

ELWOOD L. CARLSON, was born Oct. 20, 1924 in Duluth, MN. Entered the Army in June 1943 after high school graduation. Basic training at Camp Fannin, TX, then sent to Australia and joined E Co., 162nd Inf. at Rockhampton.

After landings at Hollandia and Biak, where he was wounded, he transferred to the S-2 Section, 2nd Bn., HQ 162 Inf. Made landing at Zamboanga, Philippine Islands, went to Cotabato and central Mindanao where he was assigned to a U.S. Command Group with the Philippine army for a move into eastern Mindanao.

Went to Japan with the occupation forces before returning to the States in January 1946. Highest rank held was sergeant. He received the Combat Infantry Badge, Purple Heart, and Bronze Star.

Married to Sarah Coker with two children. Retired in 1982 after 32 years with Dow Chemical as a chemical engineer. Now resides near Angleton, TX.

LARRY CARPENTER, was born Feb. 28, 1920 in Weesaw Township, Berrien County, MI. He graduated from New Troy High School in 1939.

Drafted into Army in October 1941. Infantry training at Camp Wolter, TX. He joined G Co., 162nd Inf. at Ft. Dix, NJ in March 1942. While in New Guinea on Roosevelt Ridge, he went on patrol behind Jap lines and was hit by machine gun fire on Aug. 13, 1943. He spent four and a half months in hospital.

Left Co. G, 162nd on restricted duty. Was assigned to 17th Replacement Depot at Camp Ascot, Brisbane; rotated back to States in October 1944 with 32 months overseas. He was assigned a clerk at Ft. Custer.

Discharged Aug. 19, 1945 as a T/5. He received the Purple Heart and Combat Infantry Badge.

Married Juanita in 1960. He has one daughter Maria (married to Tony Seal) and two granddaughters, Glory and Faye.

He retired from Whirlpool Corporation in 1979. He is past commander of American Legion Post 518 in New Troy, MI and DAV Chapter 126, Stevensville, MI.

BILL CHAINEY, was born June 26, 1918 in Boliver, TN. Assigned to 41st Div., 162 KC. Stationed at Ft. Jackson, SC.

Discharged in 1945 with the rank technical sergeant. He married in 1950 and has one daughter. He is owner/president of V-B Machine Company since 1962.

JOHN H. CHIPLEY, was born March 28, 1908 in Saskatoon Sask, Cananda. Graduated from Grants Pass High School, was president of senior class. Received only scholarship given Willamette University, then Pacific University, graduating from Southern Oregon College with teaching degree in 1936.

Inducted in 1924, Grants Pass, OR. Trained at Camp Clatsop, Camp Jackson, Camp Stevens, and Ft. Lewis. He assisted "Chappy" Blinkesop, Chaplain Div. He participated in many sports.

Discharged in 1956 with rank Warrant W/2. Spent two years in Reserves, served two and a half years in Oregon National Guard. Received Sharpshooter Award, Marksman and Expert.

Married Neva L. Chipley in 1936. They have a son John H.C. Chipley and daughter Karen Chipley Waide. He taught school for 40 years in Oregon. In 1968 was nominated to Who' Who-biography in Library of Congress. In 1990 Grants Pass nominated him to Hall of Fame. He is retired in Mesa, AZ since 1975.

Not bad for a young man who was left an orphan at age 16!

MEHRAN CHOOLJIAN, was born March. 27, 1917 in Delrey, CA. Entered the service July 10, 1941. Assigned to 41st Hqs. Stationed at Ft. Lewis, WA, Australia, and the Pacific. He spent 41 months overseas.

Discharged with the rank staff sergeant. He received the Philippine Liberation Medal and Good Conduct Medal.

Married to Madeline in 1948. They have three children and five grandchildren. He is engaged in farming and packing raisins.

JOHN M. CHRISTENSEN, was born April 13, 1920 in Hillsboro, OR. Enlisted in Oregon National Guard Sept. 25, 1939. Inducted National Service Sept. 16, 1940. Assigned to 41st Div., Btry. E, Co. A, 218th FA Bn., stationed at Ft. Lewis, Camp Murray, WA.

Overseas April 22, 1942 to Australia. Combat missions at New Guinea and Southern Philippines. Returned to Ft. Lewis and discharged Aug. 12, 1945 with the rank of sergeant. He was awarded the Bronze Star and Philippines 1945.

Enlisted in Reserves July 18, 1950. Served SGM, 413th Committee Group, 104th Div. Training USAR, Ft. Vancouver, WA. Awarded Department of the Army Commendation Medal for U.S. Army Reserve Service Oct. 20, 1970 to Sept. 20, 1976.

He has three children, Joan, Patricia, and Matthew. Retired from General Foods Corporation. He is a member of 41st Infantry Division Association.

CHAUNCEY A. CHRISTOFFERSON, was born Jan. 26, 1912 in Everett, WA. He grew up and graduated from high school in Marysville, WA. He volunteered and was inducted into the Army March 4, 1941. Being assigned to the 41st Div. Signal Co. as radio man he trained at Camp Murray, WA and participated in war games at Hunter Liggett in California.

On Dec. 8, 1941 following Pearl Harbor, his unit took up position on the Olympic Peninsula of Washington; but a little later, due to the death of his father, he was honorably discharged, account dependency. He left his unit March 16, 1942 with the rank of private and served as shipfitter helping to build floating drydocks, etc. and in maintaining other Navy vessels.

In 1949 he married Nellie Risa and after graduating from college they both became school teachers. In 1958 he graduated from seminary and pastored churches until retirement in 1977. Since then he has been beekeeper, choir singer, member of a Lions Club, historical society and beekeeper's association.

He has three sons, Charles, Mark, and Kenneth plus two grandchildren. Charles serves the U.S. Army with the 82nd Airborne, Mark with the Air Force as an F-16 fighter pilot, and Kenneth in the Air Force as a communications expert.

CHRIST J. CHRISTOPHERSON, was born Feb. 1, 1920 in Charleston, WI. Entered the service Nov. 26, 1941. Assigned to 41st Div., Co. I, 186th Inf. Stationed at Camp Wheeler, GA, Ft. Lewis, WA, and overseas.

His memorable experiences include Battle at Buna and when he was wounded in action at Humboldt Bay, Dutch New Guinea.

Discharged June 1, 1945 with the rank private first class. He received the Bronze Star, Purple Heart, Combat Infantry Badge, Asiatic-Pacific Campaign Medal, American Defense Medal, Good Conduct Medal, three Battle Stars, Victory Medal, and five Overseas Bars.

Married to Margie Ibe on Nov. 6, 1946. They have two sons, Gary and Daniel, and six grandchildren. He is retired after 41 years as orchard supervisor and now owns and operates a 80 acre farm.

R.C. CISCO, was born July 3, 1919 in Cisco, AR. Entered the service Sept. 16, 1940. Assigned to 41st Div., Co. K, 186th Inf. and Co. K, 163rd Inf. Stationed at Ft. Lewis, WA.

Participated in action at Sanananda Point, Gona, New Guinea, Wakde, Aitape, Biak, Mindora, and Zamboanga. Was wounded at Zamboanga.

Discharged in 1945 with rank technical sergeant. He retired in 1965 with rank first sergeant E-8.

Married Sue on Nov. 14, 1946. They have two children, Donna and Brad. Was with LP Gas Company and retired from there in 1980. Now enjoys traveling.

CHESTER F. CLARK, was born Feb. 3, 1918 on a farm near Howell, MI. Went to rural school, graduated Howell High High in 1935 and ROTC at Michigan State College. Drafted Oct. 9, 1941 and sent to Camp Roberts, CA.

Basic training was cut short at eight and a half weeks due to Pearl Harbor. Assigned in Ft. Lewis WA to Med. Det. 162, 41st Div. in December 1941.

Aid man with I-162, 1st Bn. Medical Clerk 162, Medical Clerk and Graves Registration, MacKechnie Task Force, Nassau Bay to Salamaua 1943 (Presidential Citation), Personnel Clerk Med-162 1944-1945 through to Zamboanga, two furloughs to Melbourne, returned to U.S. in September 1945 as a T/3 and discharged Oct. 6, 1945.

Married Yvonne in 1946. They have five children and eight grandchildren. Manager of farmers large Co-op, press operator at International Paper, in retail of furniture, petroleum, and hardware.

His diary was used in book *Yanks Down Under*. Toured Australia with Yvonne three times (1979-1984-1988) in 40 different Aussie homes. Had six Aussie couples as guests in Michigan 1979-1990.

Edits bi-weekly historical column in local newspaper. Numismatist and exonumist. Chairman, 41st Div. National Convention in Dearborn 1976. Registration chairman in Dearborn 1983.

EARL J. CLARK, was born April 16, 1918 in Acton, MT. Enlisted in the 163rd (Montana NG) in March 1935, received a Reserve commission in 1939. He traded his sergeant stripes for Gold Bars at induction in 1940.

He trained with the 41st at Ft. Lewis, Ft. Benning, Camp Nagambe, Seymour, Rockhampton, and New Guinea. Saw action in the Papua-New Guinea Campaign and in Leyte and Luzon in the Philippines.

Left the 41st in November 1943 for duty at the Fox Farm. He flunked out at this duty and ended up on limited service at Base 7 in Sydney. The war had never dealt him such a winning hand before!

Went home on 30 days TD over Xmas 1944. Returned to the SWP landing in Tacloban, Leyte, Philippine Islands. His last duty station was with the Motor Command, Base X, Manila, Philippine Islands.

Returned to the U.S. in August 1945 and went on inactive duty in December 1945. He later reactivated the 3rd Bn., HQ Co., 163rd Inf., Montana National Guard in 1947.

He attained the rank of captain and was awarded the Presidential Citation, Combat Infantry Badge, Bronze Star, American Theater, American Defense, South Pacific with three stars, Philippine Liberation with one star, and Victory Medal.

He is the father of three children, one pre-war and two post war. He has been retired for 10 years and is back in Billings, MT.

LEWIS E. CLARK, was born June 4, 1917 at Madera, CA in a tent with no doctor. Entered the service June 6, 1933 with I Co., 162nd Inf. located at Silverton, OR. Next to L Co., 162nd Inf located at Dallas, OR; then to A Btry., 218th FA. In 1940 was sent to Swamp Murray (Ft. Lewis) and then shipped overseas to Australia.

Transferred to the MP Platoon in 1942 and was with them throughout the SWPA. He had many memorable experiences. A few of these are: the entire division camping at Camp Rilea, the mules running away during parades at Camp Rilea, being honor guard at

Gen. White's funeral in Portland, the fires on Hollandia, sleeping through air raids, serving as training cadre sergeant at Ft. Lewis, being commander of the guerilla unit for three years while in the 249th AD at Camp Rilea, being given a Letter of Commendation by the commanding general of the 6th U.S. Army, and knowing Generals Marshall, MacArthur, and Eisenhower.

Was an expert with all infantry weapons and was asked to become a sniper with Merril's Marauders. Went to Alaska for cold weather training January-February 1977 at age 59 (the oldest ever permitted to go there and receive such training.

Arrived home after the war was over and was discharged Sept. 12, 1945 with the rank of sergeant at Ft. Lewis, WA. Re-enlisted in the HQs Btry. in 1955. Retired in 1964 with 20 years and rank of master sergeant. He went to Japan where he served as the educational advisor to the American International Schools in the Far East (1965-1968). He rejoined 2nd Bn., 162nd Inf. in 1973 when he was told that his prior 20 years was not 20 years and served in that unit until July 1977 when he retired for good as a MSG-E8 with 35 years in the 41st Div. and the 41st Brigade.

His awards include Letter of Commendation, Good Conduct, Shooting Medals, and the Combat Infantry Badge.

Married E. Jean Robertson on July 27, 1941. They have one daughter Laurinda Sue who was born shortly before their 24th wedding anniversary. He retired in 1977 after 35 years as teacher, administrator, and science consultant. His wife retired from teaching in 1982. They are both active in church, garden, and bridge playing. They live in Eugene, OR where they enjoy friends, traveling, beach-combing, photography, cooking, and reading.

JOHN FRANCIS CLARKE, was born March 13, 1918 in Portland, OR. Entered the service Sept. 14, 1940, National Guard. Assigned to 41st, Sept. 16, 1940, Federal Service. Stationed at Camp Murray, WA; Seymour; Rockhampton; New Guinea; Leyte and Panay.

On Dec. 7, 1941 at at 10 minutes to 11:00 a.m. on the Pacific Ocean, they got a SOS of a lumber schooner ahead torpedoed. He was sitting in the sunshine and the next thing he was in the shade heading back to the States. On their second trip they were allowed one canteen cup of water or coffee a day going from New York to Australia.

His awards include two Bronze Battle Stars, Pacific Campaign Medal, American Defense Service Medal with one star, Good Conduct Medal, Philippines Liberation Medal and six Overseas Service Stripes.

Married, had two children. Remarried in 1988 to Ida. Retired from over the road truck driving. He keeps busy on his one-half acre of land.

LUVERNE CLAUSEN, was born in Alden, MN and entered the Army on March 1, 1943 at Ft. Snelling, MN, then to Camp Roberts, CA. Joined the 41st at Rockhampton, Australia, and from there to New Guinea.

Was wounded at Biak on June 28, 1944. Next to the Philippines and from there to Jolo Island. Stationed at Kure, Japan and spent one day at Hiroshima.

Discharged Feb. 2, 1946 with rank of T/5. Was a radio man, mail clerk, and company clerk. Medals awarded were the Purple Heart, Combat Infantry Badge, Asiatic-Pacific Theater Ribbon with two Bronze Stars, Bronze Service Arrowhead, the Philippine Liberation Ribbon with one Bronze Star.

Married in Albert Lea, MN. He has two daughters and six grandchildren. Was a partner in a farm store for 17 years, then sold wholesale to elevators and farm stores. Presently retired and spends his time golfing, traveling, and his wood shop.

WILLIAM A. CLINE, was born Sept. 12, 1919 in Leavenworth, WA. Raised in Seattle, WA and graduated from Lincoln High School in 1937.

He joined Washington State National Guard in February 1938. Unit HQ Btry. 2nd Bn. 146th FA Regt. Inducted into federal service on Sept. 16, 1940. Trained at Ft. Lewis, WA. In 1941 the division was streamlined and the 146th Regt. was split into two separate battalions with the 2nd Bn. becoming the 167th FA Bn.

He served 32 months overseas in Australia, New Guinea and the Netherland East Indies. Participated in combat at Aitape, Wakde Island, Sarmi and Biak.

Returned to the U.S. on rotation in September 1944. After 30 days leave, he was assigned to the Artillery School at Ft. Sill, OK. Discharged on Dec. 15, 1944 at Ft. Lewis, WA. Achieved the rank of technical sergeant.

His most memorable experience was the year 1943 when their field artillery battalion was chosen to train as a horse pack artillery unit.

Married to Claire and has two sons, one daughter, and four grandchildren. He retired in 1980 from Pacific Northwest Bell Telephone Company. They reside in Edmonds, WA.

JOHN R. COFIELD, was born Feb. 8, 1918 in Newell, AL. Entered the service Sept. 14, 1941. Assigned to 41st Div., Co. E, Medics, 162nd Inf. Stationed at Camp Croft, SC; Ft. Dix, NJ; Ft. McClellan, AL; and overseas.

His memorable experience was the 42 day journey on *Santa Paula* from New York via Panama Canal to Aukland, New Zealand to Melbourne, Australia.

Married to Bernice Bailey on May 25, 1951. They have two children, David and Emily. John retired after 32 years in education, high school science and elementary principal. He is a member of American Legion, VFW, Historical Society.

ELBERT WALTER COLLINS, was born in June 11, 1922 in Wytheville, VA. He entered the service Jan. 1, 1943. Assigned to 41st Div., A Btry., 167th FA, BA Horse Pack outfit in Ingram, Australia, New Guinea, Philippines, and Occupation Forces in Japan. Caught typhus and malaria fever.

Memorable experience was seeing the destruction caused by Atom Bomb at Hiroshima.

Discharged with the rank of staff sergeant. He received the World War II Victory Medal, Asiatic-Pacific Campaign with two Bronze Stars, one Arrowhead, Good Conduct Medal, and Philippine Liberation Ribbon.

Married to Doris in 1946. They have three sons (oldest son was killed in Vietnam in 1969), seven grandchildren, and one great-grandchild. Elbert was shift supervisor in hosiery mill for 35 years, retired and now farms for fun.

JOSEPH S. COMLEY, was born May 15, 1926 in northeast rural Missouri near Gorin where he grew up and graduated from high school. While working and living in Ft. Madison, IA, he was drafted Aug. 10, 1944. Basic training was completed at Camp Fannin near Tyler, TX.

In February 1945, he joined G Co., 162 of the 41st Inf. Div. at Mindoro in the Philippines. From there he participated in the landing at Zamboanga on the island of Mindanao. After the Mindanao Campaign he went to Japan and served in the Occupation Forces in the Military Police. In August 1946 he was discharged having attained the rank of buck sergeant.

He received the Combat Infantry Badge, various unit and campaign citations.

After service he graduated from college and spent the greater part of his working career in the insurance business, retiring in June 1988.

He married and has two children, Mark an attorney and Kathy a commercial artist.

RALPH B. CONNELL, was born May 2, 1919 in Minneapolis, MN. Inducted Feb. 26, 1941 at Spokane, WA. Trained at Ft. Lewis, WA and was assigned to Service Co., 162nd Inf., 41st Div. Was regimental file clerk at 162 HQs.

He took part in maneuvers at Hunter Liggett Reservation, Olympic Peninsula, sailed from Brooklyn on SS *Santa Paula*, Seymour, Victoria, and Rockhampton, Queensland.

Was hospitalized: 33rd Surgical, 105th General, Letterman, McCloskey and Veterans at Wood, WI. Due to hearing loss, he was discharged June 8, 1943. His Awards include: American Defense, Asiatic-Pacific, Good Conduct, Victory Medals.

The GI Bill resulted in a B.A. degree from Stanford University and a 30 year career in insurance administration. Married Florence A. Noyes, a U.S. Cadet Nurse, and they raised six children. Ralph and Florence retired to the banks of the Stanislaus River in Oakland, CA where they are active in senior affairs—especially dance, which they teach.

LEE H. COOK, was born Dec. 30, 1921 in Spartanburg, SC. Entered the service Aug. 28, 1940 and was assigned to 41st Div., I Co., 162nd Inf. Stationed at Australia and New Guinea.

His memorable experience was the Biak Campaign.

Discharged with the rank of staff sergeant. He received the Good Conduct Medal, American Defense, Asiatic-Pacific Theater Ribbon with two Bronze Battle Stars, and Combat Infantry Badge.

Married to Ruby and has two sons, Phillip and Lyn, and four grandchildren. He is presently retired in Greenville, SC.

FRANCIS E. COON, was born Sept. 15, 1922 in Mt. Vernon, IN. Entered the service November 1942. Trained at Ft. Bragg, NC and Ft. Sill, OK. Assigned to the 218th FA of the 41st Div. in Australia, New Guinea, Biak, and Zamboanga Philippines.

Left Zamboanga in September 1945 en route to Tacoma, WA then to Camp Atterbury, IN for discharge in November 1945 with the rank of staff sergeant.

Married Sept. 5, 1942 to Mary Elizabeth Cleveland, has two children and four grandchildren. Retired product engineer for Chrysler Corp. in 1979. Sold real estate and owned his own company, retiring second time in 1987. He and his wife now reside Manchester, MO.

DON A. COOPER, was born May 24, 1917 in Sidney, MT. Entered the service Sept. 16, 1940. Assigned to Co. D and A, 116th Med. Regt., stationed at Camp Murray, WA.

Discharged with the rank of private first class. His awards include the American Defense Medal, Unit Citation, Asiatic-Pacific, and Good Conduct Medal.

Married to Lois since 1944. They have two sons and four grandsons. Don is retired and a life member of VFW 1087 and Elks 214.

DION W. CORBELL, was born Dec. 30, 1918 at Spanish Fork, UT. Graduated from high school and attended Brigham Young University for two years. Joined the CCCs in 1939 and inducted into the Army on Feb. 21, 1941 at Ft. Douglas, UT.

Sent to Cantonment, Ft. Lewis for basic training with 82nd Inf. Brigade, assigned to E Co., 162nd Inf. Regt., Dec. 7, 1941, guard duty at Puget Sound area, to Ft. Dix February 1942, sailed from Brooklyn on *Santa Paula* and arrived Melbourne, Australia on April 9, 1942. Field training at Seymour and R&R in Melbourne. Moved to Rockhampton, Australia July 1942.

Sent to New Guinea in February 1943, debarked at Oro Bay, walked to Gona (55 miles through jungle), rations were short and many did not make it. First combat on Roosevelt Ridge ending at Salamaua after 76 days of combat. Returned to Rockhampton September 1943, took leave to Melbourne then put in the Fox Farm. Rejoined unit on Biak, made landing at Zambo, war ended and was sent home. Only three were left from the original company that left the States. They were Ed Jarvis, Kenneth Baker and Dion.

Discharged Oct. 1, 1945 with the rank of technical sergeant. He finished school and went to work at the Hanford Project, Richland, WA. Retired in 1983.

Married to Florence and they have two sons, nine grandchildren, and one great-grandchild.

DONALD W. CORTRIGHT, was born Jan. 22, 1925 at Coldwater, MI. Graduated from high school in June 1944 and was drafted July 14, 1944. Basic training at Camp Wolters, TX. POE Ft. Ord, CA. Overseas duty at Leyte, Mindoro, and Mindanao, Philippines and occupation of Japan.

In February 1945 he was assigned to a medical unit attached to the Hqs. Co. of the 2nd Bn. of the 162nd Inf., 41st Div. Originally with an aid station then as an aidman with the 1st Platoon of F Co. Made initial invasion of Mindanao at Zamboanga and clearing Japs from throughout the island, including the Namnam mission.

Discharged on Aug. 21, 1946 with the rank T/4. His awards include the Good Conduct Medal, World War II Victory Medal, Asiatic-Pacific Medal, Bronze Star Medal, Combat Medical Badge, Philippine Liberation Ribbon with two Battle Stars and Bronze Arrowhead, and Army of Occupation Medal for Japan.

Graduated as a pharmacist in 1951. Married Wilma in July 1951. He is now retired and lives in Monroe, MI.

STEPHEN F. COUNTS, was born April 16, 1918 in Bishop, CA. Went through basic training at Camp Roberts. Was assigned to AT Company-162 in December 1941 right after the Japanese attacked Pearl Harbor.

Went to Australia with the 41st Div., took part in the Salamaua Campaign. Made the landing at Biak, and several others in the Philippines. The memorable experiences came so hot and heavy that none stands out above the others. He wouldn't take a million dollars for the experiences, but you couldn't pay him enough to ever want to do it again.

Returned to the USA after the Japanese surrender and was discharged in October 1945 with the rank of technical sergeant (or platoon sergeant).

Took up his former occupation as a beekeeper and diversified farmer in California and also in Oregon. Later worked as a surveyor with the Josephine County Road Department. He retired in 1982 after 20 years with the department.

In 1947 he sent for and married Lette, his Australian sweetheart. They just celebrated their 44th wedding anniversary. They have three daughters and four grandchildren.

He still farms and lives on the same land he bought in 1955 when they first came to Grants Pass.

BURL L. COX, was born Feb. 18, 1919 in Walton, OR. He moved to Salem, OR in 1930. He has lived in Salem since that time. Graduated from high school in 1936.

Enlisted in Co. B, 162nd Inf. Oregon National Guard in November 1934 at age 15. Was ordered to federal service on Sept. 16, 1940 at Ft. Lewis, WA.

Went overseas from Ft. Dix, NJ on March 4, 1942. Commissioned December 1942 and assigned to 186th Inf. where he remained until returning to the States on June 19, 1945 from the Philippines.

He participated in operations at Buna, Hollandia, Biak, Zamboanga and Palawan. Was awarded the Silver Star, the Bronze Star, and Purple Heart.

He enlisted in the Oregon National Guard in February 1947. He retired in 1972 with the rank of colonel.

Married to Cleo Bales in 1940. They have a daughter and son who each have two children. He was employed by a seed company from 1946 until his retirement in 1984.

CHARLES WM. CRARY, was born Oct. 1, 1923 in Los Angeles, CA. From June 1932 to Sept. 16, 1940, lived and attended school in Salem, OR. Joined B Co., 162nd Inf. in Nov. 22, 1939. He was mobilized with his unit on Sept. 16, 1940, which was sent to Camp Murray at Ft. Lewis.

He was in the landing at Nassau Bay, New Guinea in the Sanananda Campaign, and was wounded on Mt. Tambu Aug. 3, 1943. Charles was evacuated through Wau, New Guinea having been carried there by natives in a seven day trek.

Eventually, sent to the States. He was discharged with a certified disability discharge from De Witt General Hospital on July 28, 1945, after having spent two years in hospitals. Earned the Purple Heart, Good Conduct, American Defense, Asiatic-Pacific Campaign, World War II Victory, Unit Citation and the Combat Infantry Badge.

On Aug. 10, 1947, he married Hester Ann Akes of Yakima, WA. There are three grown daughters and six grandchildren. Charles trained as a teacher and taught in the Salem Schools (Oregon) for eight years, moving to Monterey, CA where he taught and was an assistant high school principal for nine years. For the next nine years, he was the principal of the Valley Adult School located at the Correctional Training Facility in Soledad, CA. He retired to Carlsborg, WA, where he built a house and then worked for several years for a local veterinarian before going into full retirement.

JOE H. CRAWFORD, was born Nov. 13, 1921 in Kansas City, MO. Enlisted Feb. 7, 1942. Basic training at Camp Wolters, TX. Assigned to 21st Inf., 24th Div., Oahu, HI. Graduated OCS, Brisbane, Australia in January 1944. Assigned Co. E, 186th Inf., 41st Div., February 1944.

Participated in Hollandia, Biak, Palawan, and Zamboanga campaigns. Was wounded at Biak. In charge of Hiroshima area to scrap out Japanese weapons.

Discharged as first lieutenant, Ft. Leavenworth Jan. 19, 1946. Received the Purple Heart, Bronze Star, Air Medal and campaign ribbons.

Graduated with B.S. in mechanical engineering from University of Michigan in 1950. Principal work was research in machine tools and jet engines.

Married to Betty for 45 years, has five children and nine grandchildren. Presently semi-retired and doing consulting.

MARION R. CRISWELL, was born May 8, 1920 in Ottumwa, IA. Inducted into the Army on Oct. 28, 1941 at Ft. Des Moines, IA. Infantry basic training was at Camp Wolters, TX. He served with D Co., 186th Inf. Regt. from March 1942 to August 1945 through all campaigns of the regiment.

Discharged Oct. 7, 1945 with the rank of staff sergeant. During the Korean War he was recalled to active duty on Sept. 27, 1950 to Aug. 16, 1951 and was stationed at Ft. Leonard Wood, MO

Married Dorothy in 1948. They have a son, daughter, and four grandchildren. He is retired from the U.S. Postal Services.

MERLE E. CROFT, was born Oct. 4, 1919 at Iona, ID, graduated from high school, and joined the military at Ft. Douglas, Salt Lake City, UT on July 10, 1941. He requested the Air Force but ended up in the Army Medical with training at Camp Grant, IL.

After 13 weeks of basic and medical training at Ft. Sill Army Hospital, Lawton, OK was his duty station until April of 1942 when he was relocated to Corpus Christi, TX as a member of the 175th Station Field Hospital unit being organized for service in the Southwest Pacific. It was deactivated at Charlieville, Australia without hardly any service because of substantial accomplishments of the forces to the north.

His reassignment was with 116th Med. Bn., Co. C attached to the 41st Inf. and assigned to the 186th Inf. Bn. They traveled up the long coast of New Guinea from Port Morsby, Buna, Sanananda, Senimi, Oro Bay, Douglas Harbor, Lae, Salamaua, Finchhaven, and Hollandia.

After a time of R&R at Hollandia, the 41st shipped out for the Japanese held fortress island of Biak where he was severely burned from his waist up. Following over 10 weeks in Lae Field Hospital and near death, added to about three months of R&R at the Oro Bay area, he rejoined his Co. C, 116th Med. unit in time to participate in the beachhead on Palawan Island.

With Palawan secured, the 41st Div. was sent to Zamboanga, Mindanao to assist in mopping up action. It was from Zamboanga his stateside orders were issued for 30 days then reassignment. It was August 1945 and the A bombs on Japan changed his leave to an honorable discharge at Ft. Lewis, WA on Sept. 10, 1945 with the rank staff sergeant. He received all the usual awards and medals.

He returned to Idaho Falls, ID, his wife Rhea and his old job at the auto dealership where he continued to work until Dec. 10, 1962. He left the dealership and went back to the government for work as a security officer for the Department of Energy at the INEL Site west of Idaho Falls. He retired from there in December 1980. Rhea and Merle have two daughters, two sons, and 12 fine grandkids.

L. DONALD CULP, was born July 29, 1915 in Lima, OH. Enlisted for three years on Sept. 25, 1939 in Co. E, 186th Inf., Oregon National Guard, at LaGrande, OR. Inducted Sept. 16, 1940 into Federal Service and stationed at Camp Murray and Ft. Lewis until sent to South Pacific in April 1942. He served with Service Co., 186th Inf. in Australia and New Guinea until May 1944 as personnel sergeant in regimental headquarters.

Returned to the States in May 1944 and was assigned to HQ Co. Army Ground Forces Replacement Depot #2, Ft. Ord, CA in charge of all enlisted pay of replacements and cadre. Supervised 40 clerks. Was discharged as master sergeant in September 1945.

Married to Betty with three children and six grandchildren. He retired in 1978 as vice-president from the First National Bank of Oregon. They reside in Beaverton, OR. He is currently secretary of Portland Chapter, 41st Infantry Division Association.

ROBERT J. CUMBEE, was born Sept. 19, 1918 in Maybrook, VA. Entered the service Oct. 4, 1941. Assigned to Co. F, 162nd Inf., 41st Div. Stationed at Camp Lee, VA.

Participated in battles at New Guinea, and southern Philippines and combat on Biak.

Discharged with the rank of staff sergeant. He was awarded the Asiatic-Pacific Theater Campaign Medal with two Bronze Stars, one Bronze Arrowhead, Good Conduct Medal, and Philippine Liberation Ribbon with one Bronze Star.

Married to Rachel in 1946 and they have two children, three grandchildren, and one great-grandson. He was a car salesman and owned a grocery store for about 15 years. He retired in 1981, developed cancer in 1986, and passed away May 1, 1987.

EDWIN WOODROW CUSICK, was born Jan. 16, 1917 in Fairfield, CA. He entered the service from Berkeley, CA in September 1941 at Camp Roberts, CA. Was assigned to 186th Regiment of the 41st Div. in December 1941 at Ft. Lewis, WA.

Went to Australia as a medic with the 186th in all of their operations until awarded a battlefield commission in Zamboanga and was transferred to the 162nd Regt. Served with the 162nd in the Philippines and in the occupation of Japan where he was one of the first American soldiers in Hiroshima. Served in the Pacific Theater for 44 months and was discharged as a first lieutenant.

Was recommended for the Silver Star for leading a rescue party through Japanese lines at night in order to locate a litter party which had been cut off by a Japanese counterattack. He found the party and brought them safely back through the lines. Did not receive the award because it was submitted 10 days to late for consideration.

Was awarded the Combat Medical Badge, Bronze Star, numerous Arrowheads and Campaign Stars and service medals.

Worked as trucking superintendent for Bigge Drayage of Oakland, CA and then formed his own company "Big Cargo," a consulting firm until his retirement for health reasons.

CLIFFORD A. CUTCHINS III, was born July 12, 1923 in Southampton County, VA. Entered the service April 6, 1943 and assigned to 162nd Inf., stationed at Zamboanga, Mindanao, Philippine Islands.

Discharged with the rank of captain. He received the Commendation Medal, Pacific Theater and American Theater.

Married to Ann W. Woods on June 21, 1947. They have three sons, Clifford A., IV, William W., and Cecil V. He was chairman of the board and chief executive officer, Sovran Financial Corporation from 1983 until retirement in 1989 after 42 years in banking. He resides in Virginia Beach, VA and is active in community and civic affairs, serving on numerous boards throughout the state, rector for VPI&SU.

HARVEY V. CUTTS, was born April 8, 1919 in Mitchell, SD. Entered the service Sept. 16, 1940, 41st National Guard, D Co., 116th Med Bn., stationed at Ft. Lewis, WA.

Overseas April 1942 to Australia. Spent war years in New Guinea and Philippines. Discharged Dec. 6, 1945 at Ft. Lewis, WA with the rank of first sergeant.

Married Audrey in 1946. They have two daughters, one son, and four grandchildren. He retired in Albany, OR in 1982. Now enjoys traveling, gardening, and fishing.

OTTO L. DAEMS, was born Aug. 11, 1918, in Butte, MT. Joined the National Guard in February 1936. Assigned to 41st Div., Co. C, 163rd Regt. on Sept. 16, 1940. Stationed at Ft. Lewis, WA and overseas.

Saw action at Sanananda, Gona, New Guinea, all combat with the 163rd through Biak.

Retired September 1970 with the rank of major. He received the Legion of Merit, Bronze Star with cluster, Commendation Medal with cluster, Purple Heart and numerous campaign medals and ribbons.

Otto is a widower with four children. Now fully retired in Colorado Springs, CO and enjoying every minute of it.

GARLAND N. DALEY, was born April 23, 1919 in Rushford, MN. Garland came to the Kalispell, MT area in 1925 where he grew up and graduated from high school in 1938.

He was drafted in the Army in Oct. 9, 1941 where he was sent to Camp Roberts and Ft. Lewis for basic training. Garland was sent overseas in 1942 with L Co. of 186 on the *Queen Elizabeth*. They landed in Sydney and were stationed in Seymour, Australia. Transferred to 818 and served in New Guinea and Biak, Philippines.

He left Manila for the USA in October of 1945. Was discharged from Ft. Lewis on Oct. 14, 1945 with the rank of technical sergeant.

Garland later returned to Sydney, Australia in April of 1946 and married June 8, 1946 to his Australian girl friend. They then moved back to Kalispell, MT where Garland was a building contractor for seven years. He then went into the logging and cattle ranching business. Retired from the logging business after 35 years but still raises a few cattle.

Garland and wife June have two daughters in the teaching profession and are living in Arizona. They had one son who passed away when he was 15. They went back to Australia in 1974 and 1983 and are currently planning another trip back.

JAMES G. DARR, was born April 2, 1922 at Sioux Rapids, IA. His father was a WWI Army veteran and a farmer. James joined the Army in March 1943. He trained at Camp Roberts, CA and at Rockhampton, Australia. He served as a field lineman with HQ and HQ Btry., Division Artillery, participating in campaigns at Hollandia, Biak, and Mindanao, followed by occupational duty in Hiroshima.

Discharged on Jan. 9, 1946. His awards included the Good Conduct Medal, Bronze Service Arrowhead, and the Philippine Liberation Ribbon. He achieved the rank of T/4.

Married to Arlene Utley on March 2, 1947. They have two sons (both Vietnam Army veterans), one daughter, and five grandchildren. He is a retired Iowa farmer, but still resides on the farm. Each Memorial Day he participates in the local service, wearing his 45 years old uniform.

HERMAN F. DAVENPORT, was born Dec. 3, 1917 at Hurst, GA. Raised in Fannin County, GA. Graduated from high school in 1936. Drafted Sept. 13, 1941 at Ft. McPhearson, GA then went to Ft. Dix, NJ. While at Ft. Dix he was assigned to the 41st Inf. Div. and served in Australia, New Guinea, Biak, and the Philippines (with the exception of time spent in a malaria rehabilitation camp). Made landing in New Guinea and the Philippines. Left Mindanao, Philippines for the U.S. in September 1945.

He received his discharge on Oct. 4, 1945. He achieved the rank of sergeant.

Married Myrtle Hunt in 1945. They have two children, Joan and David, and two grandchildren, Jeffrey and Drew. He is a retired county forest ranger from Georgia Forestry Commission.

WARD F. DAVIDSON, was born July 13, 1918 in Liberal, OR. He grew up in Molalla, OR, and graduated from high school in 1938.

Volunteered and was inducted at Portland, OR on March 28, 1941. Was sent to Ft. Lewis, WA. Assigned to I-163 and transferred to D-186 for basic training. He drove a truck until after maneuvers in California the summer of 1941. Upon return from California, he joined the Cooks Force D-186. Was sent to Cooks and Bakers School at Ft. Lewis for three months, returned to his company and was appointed mess sergeant at Buna, New Guinea in 1943, staff sergeant rating. He has recollections of making meals with limited supplies of poor quality.

Left D-186 at Biak Island in October 1944 for 30 day rotation furlough home, arriving just before Christmas. On return to duty, he came down with malaria so did not return overseas. Was sent south to Alexandria, LA (recruit training center) to be mess sergeant again.

Transferred to Camp Shelby, MS for discharge on July 20, 1945. His medals include the Purple Heart, Good Conduct Medal, American Deployment Medal, Combat Infantry Badge, Asiatic-Pacific Theater Operation Medal and two Combat Stars.

Married to Mona on July 27, 1945. They have four children, 10 grandchildren, and one great-grandson. Two sons joined the Navy. He managed an egg processing business about 35 years and retired as a mechanic (warehouse equipment) at age 70.

HERBERT B. DAVIS, was born April 24, 1921 in Portland, OR. Graduated from high school in Newberg, OR in 1939. Joined the Oregon National Guard and was inducted into federal service Sept. 16, 1940.

Stationed at Ft. Lewis (Swamp Murray), WA, Btry. F (later Btry. B), 218th FA Bn. Served in that unit as battery clerk until war's end in 1945. Served overseas in Australia, New Guinea and the Philippines.

Entered Willamette University September 1945 and graduated June 1949. Employed by Chevron Corp. in wholesale marketing until his retirement in 1979.

Married to Shirley, September 1945. Their daughter Sally Williams lives in Beaverton, OR with her husband Jeff. She is a senior forecaster with NIKE Corp.

JORDAN W. DAVIS, was born July 27, 1912 at Dunlap, IA (Harrison County). Enlisted in National Guard on Sept. 11, 1940 and called to active duty on Sept. 16, 1940. Assigned to G Co., 186th Inf., 41st Div. Trained at Ft. Lewis, WA.

Shipped to Australia in April 1942. Participated in battles at Buna, New Guinea, Hollandia, and Biak. Also spent time at Melbourne, Rockhampton, Townsville, Milne Bay and Palawan Island in the Philippines. Took part in landing at Hollandia, Biak, and Palawan. Was wounded June 3, 1945 at Palawan.

Discharged Aug. 22, 1945 with the rank of staff sergeant. He married December 1945 to Marie. They have two sons and four grandchildren. He worked as an insurance agent and adjuster for 26 years. Now semi-retired. He is a member of American Legion, life member of VFW and DAV. His awards and medals include the DSC, Purple Heart, Bronze Star, Good Conduct Medal, Combat Infantry Badge, American Defense Medal, Asiatic-Pacific Campaign with two Arrowheads and four stars, the Philippine Liberation Ribbon with one Bronze Star and the World War II Victory Medal.

LLOYD E. DAVIS, was born Dec. 6, 1924 in Dillon, MT. Joined 10th Light Mountain Inf. (Ski Troops) in March 1943. After training in Colorado, he volunteered for overseas service. Replacement Depot in Buna, New Guinea assigned him to 41st Div., joining K Co., 186th on Biak in 1944.

Staged on Mindoro, Philippine Islands, he made landings on Palawan and from Zamboanga up the coast of Mindanao. Landed in Japan October 1945 and was based in Kaitaichi. Our recon patrol through Hiroshima was said to be first after the bomb.

Left Japan in December 1945, discharged in Ft. Lewis, WA in January 1946 as first sergeant. Awarded Combat Infantry Badge, Silver Star, Bronze Star, Purple Heart and Bronze Arrowhead.

Returned to Dillon, married Millie, graduated from college and moved to California. Left position as national sales manager in automotive field to start own business as manufacturers representative where he is still active traveling northern California, Nevada and the northwest. He has two children and four grandchildren.

MELVIN R. DAVIS, was born Jan. 15, 1915 in Seattle, WA. Entered the service Sept. 16, 1940, Washington State National Guard, assigned to 41st Div., Btry. A, 146th FA and Btry. C, 167th FA. Stationed at Camp Murray, Ft. Lewis, WA and overseas at New Guinea, Zamboanga, Mindanao, and Philippines.

Discharged June 12, 1945 with the rank of first sergeant. He received the American Defense Service Medal, Asiatic-Pacific Service Medal, Good Conduct Medal, Philippine Liberation Service Medal with one Bronze Service Star.

Married to Helen and they have one daughter and one grandchild. Melvin is retired from Boeing Aircraft Company, working 23 years with Boeing Security.

WILLIAM R. DAVIS, was born April 11, 1925 in Gilmer County, Ellijay, GA. Was inducted July 20, 1943, assigned to Co. D, 162nd Inf., 41st Div. He trained at Ft. McPherson, GA; Camp Wheeler, GA; Ft. Ord, CA; and Camp Stoneman, CA. Asiatic-Pacific Theater of War, he participated in battles New Guinea, Southern Philippines Liberation.

Discharged at Ft. McPherson, GA on Jan. 19, 1946 with the rank of corporal. His awards and decorations include SS Rifle, Combat Infantry Badge, Asiatic-Pacific Service Medal with two Bronze Stars and one Bronze Service Arrowhead, Philippine Liberation Ribbon with one Bronze Star, one Bronze Star Medal, Good Conduct Medal, and the World War II Victory Medal.

William is a barber/hair stylist and in the business

of real estate. Married Estelle Southern Bearden on Nov. 28, 1948. They have one son Winston Davis and twin grandsons, William Thomas & Jacob Oliver Davis.

LESLIE V. DAWES, was born July 19, 1924. Entered the service May 25, 1943, the day after graduating from high school.

Basic training at Camp Wheeler, GA. Joined the 41st Inf. as a replacement in Rockhampton, Australia in January of 1943. Was one of the first to be put on guard duty in Hiroshima. Says the radiation ruined his health.

Retired with rank of staff sergeant. He received the Bronze Star, Combat Infantry Badge, Good Conduct Medal, World War II Victory Medal, Philippine Liberation Medal, and the Asiatic-Pacific Campaign Medal with three Bronze Stars and three arrowheads.

JOHN G. DAWSON, born Dec. 11, 1922 in Seattle, WA. Graduated high school in Ilwaco, WA in 1940. Enlisted A Btry., 146th FA on Sept. 18, 1940.

Discharged Sept. 28, 1941 with the rank of corporal. Re-enlisted A Btry., 146th FA Bn., on March 11, 1942. Served with A Btry. through WWII. Discharged June 11, 1945 with rank of staff sgt. at Ft. Lewis, WA.

Received B.A. degree from University of Washington in June 1949. Designated distinguished military graduate of ROTC and appointed by congress as RA second lieutenant infantry Aug. 7, 1949.

Subsequent military career included: Korea service with 9th Inf., 2nd Div.; Vietnam with HQ U.S. Army and MACV Advisory Team 68, Vinh Long, RVN. Was medically retired in October 1972 with rank lieutenant colonel at Madigan Army Medical Center.

Married Eileen in 1949 and they have two children, Charles and Janet. They live in Lakewood, WA near Ft. Lewis. He is a member of Seattle Chapter, 41st Division Association, The AF&AM (Masons), a member of Board of Directors of Washington National Guard State Historical Society, and a member of DAV.

JOHN P. DAY, was born Oct. 11, 1916 in Bossburg, WA. Entered the service on Feb. 21, 1941 at Spokane, WA. Military specialty was automotive mechanic.

Participated in action at New Guinea and Papuan. Discharged May 31, 1945. He received the Asiatic-Pacific Service Medal, Good Conduct Medal and American Defense Service Medal.

Married to Elsie Feb. 12, 1941. They have one daughter, four sons, six granddaughters, seven grandsons, three step-grandsons, and one great-grandson.

John retired in 1979.

ANGEL D. DAYOT, was born Aug. 7, 1920. Was inducted Dec. 8, 1941 at Basilan City, Philippines. Served with E Co., 106th Inf.; HQ Co., 2nd Bn., HQ 121st Inf.; E Co., 2nd Bn., 121st Inf. attached to 186th Inf., 41st Div. for combat-mopping operations.

Wounded in action during Japs landing at Zambo City and again at Sibuku. Saved Lt. William Whitley in Murok. Killed 17 Japs in Sibuku (See *Jungleer* May 1990 issue).

Discharged April 7, 1949. He received the Purple Heart, Bronze Star Medal, and Good Conduct Medal.

Graduated from Eastern University with BSE in biology, Spanish and science. Was high school teacher, high school principal, and college instructor. Graduated with master's (1968-1970); graduate professor (1970-1972). Called to active duty (1972-1978) and assigned southern command, Zambo City, retired lieutenant colonel; graduate professor (1978-1984); 1984 to present-elected Barangay chairman/captain, Baliwasan, Zambo City. Married since 1953 and has five sons and one daughter.

EDWARD DEBELAK, was born Aug. 21, 1922 in Avella, PA. Inducted into the Army January 1943. Completed infantry basic training at Ft. McClellan, AL. Accepted for OCS, graduating from the Infantry School at Ft. Benning in December 1944.

Was assigned to IRTC at Camp Croft, SC and shipped to Philippines. Was assigned to Co. I, 162nd Inf., 41st Div. in May 1945. Participated in the mopping up operation in central Mindanao. Transferred to the 524th QM Group in Kobe, Japan when the 41st was inactivated.

Returned to the States June 27, 1946. Was recalled to active duty on Sept. 11, 1950 with the 298th Transportation Truck Co. Trained at Ft. Bragg, NC. Later was transferred to the 513th Transportation Truck Co. in Korea.

Returned to the States and released from active duty on May 28, 1952. He is a life member in the Reserve Officers Association.

Married to Theresa and raised two sons and two daughters. He retired from Westinghouse Electric Corporation as a supervisor in a metal machining department.

RUSSELL R. DECKER SR., was born Dec. 3, 1919 in Waukegan, IL. Graduated Waukegan Township High School in 1938. Joined the Army June 24, 1941. Was sent to Ft. Sheridan, Camp Roberts, Ft. Lewis, 41st Div., D Btry., 146th (later A Btry., 167th FA). Spent all his time with the 41st to the end at

Zamboanga. Sent home on temporary duty in April 1945, was discharged on points.

His gun section, 1st Section, A Btry., 167th FA sunk the only two man submarine by accident at the mouth of the Thor River. "The Jezabel" was painted on his gun.

Married to Vi, his high school sweetheart. They have five children, two girls and three boys.

At the time of his discharge he was first sergeant of A Btry., 167th FA and say they were the greatest bunch of bastards in WWII, South Pacific. He is a member of the Lions, Eagles, and Elks.

LOUIS J. DECOTEAU, was born Dec. 19, 1919 in McLaughlin, SD. Entered the service Sept. 16, 1940. Assigned to 163rd Inf., 41st Div. Participated in New Guinea Campaign. Was a boxer and fought in Melbourne, Australia in 1942.

Discharged Sept. 25, 1944 with the rank of private first class. His awards include the Purple Heart, Unit Badge, Defense Service Ribbon, Asiatic-Pacific Campaign Ribbon, two Bronze Stars and four Foreign Service Bars.

Married Gladys in 1945. They have four children: Louis Jr., Joyce, JoAnn, and Robert.

Louis was a track inspector for BN Rail Road. He is a member of Elks, DAV and American Legion.

SAMUEL A. DeGASPERIS, was born Oct. 12, 1924 in Trenton, NJ. He was inducted in the Army in August 1943 and took his basic infantry training at Ft. McClellan, AL.

He shipped out for the South Pacific from San Francisco in March 1944 where he landed in a replacement center in Australia. He joined Co. A, 1st Bn., 163rd Inf. Regt. While at Finchhaven, New Guinea waiting for the Hollandia Invasion he was assigned to Division HQ, Finance.

Later served on Biak, New Guinea and Zamboanga, Philippines Campaigns. After the Atomic Bomb was dropped on Hiroshima, Japan, he served with the occupational forces for five months.

Left Japan for the U.S. in January 1946. Was discharged at Ft. Monmouth, NJ.

A graduate of Rider College, NJ and presently employed with the Division of Taxation, Treasury, state of New Jersey.

Married to Regina with one daughter Trish, who is a television reporter with NJN News. He is a 30 year member of the American Legion Post 414.

GAETHANO DeMAYO (TOM), was born Oct. 27, 1922 in Newark, NJ. Joined the service Jan. 9, 1941 and trained at Ft. Bragg, NC with 9th Div., 60th Inf., E Co. Was assigned to 41st Div. February 1942, Camp Dix, NJ.

Left for overseas from New York Port in March 1942 on the ship *Santa Rosa*. Assigned to G Co., 162nd Inf. Arrived in Melbourne, Australia and had further training, then shipped to New Guinea. Was seriously wounded in the battle for Salamaua, Roosevelt Ridge on Aug. 13, 1943. Shipped to an Australian hospital then eventually to USA.

Given sick leave, then assigned to 66th Inf. Div. Casual Co., Camp Joseph T. Robinson, AR. Re-entered hospital, then discharged because of the seriousness of his wounds on March 4, 1944. His awards and decorations include: Combat Infantry Badge, Bronze Star Medal, Purple Heart Medal, Good Conduct Medal, American Defense Medal, American Campaign Medal, Asiatic Pacific Medal, and Victory Medal.

Married, divorced, and has one child. Retired as license inspector attached to police department for city of Newark, NJ.

MARVIN H. DESLER, was born April 28, 1921 in Enterprise, OR. Raised in Pendleton, OR and graduated high school in 1939. He joined the National Guard that same year. Inducted into federal service Sept. 16, 1940 and served the entire war in Australia and New Guinea.

Discharged from the 41st at Ft. Lewis, WA in June 1945.

He married Jean in 1946. They have one son who is an electronic engineer. Went to work in a furniture factory and became head of design and development department. Retired from the furniture business in 1985.

JOSEPH DiDOMINICIS, was born April 4, 1918 in Chicago, IL. Entered the service Oct. 10, 1941. Assigned to 163rd Inf., 3rd Bn. Med., Aidman Co. K, 1st Platoon.

Overseas March 18, 1942. Made three landings. Returned Stateside March 11, 1945. Received all the awards for the New Guinea Campaign plus the Bronze Star. Discharged with the rank T/3.

Married and has four children and five (soon to be six) grandchildren. He retired in 1982.

ROBERT J. DILLMAN, was born Dec. 10, 1919 in Wabash County, IN. Inducted Sept. 22, 1941 at Ft. Benjamin Harrison. Basic training at Camp Wolters, TX. Sent to Ft. Dix, NJ to Co. M, 135th Inf.

On March 3, 1942 was transferred to Co. B, 162nd Inf., 41st Div. Sailed on the *Santa Paula* to Melbourne, Australia and camp at Seymour. Then on to Rockhampton for more training.

Landed at Nassau Bay, went inland to Mt. Tambu. Next landing at Hollandia, then Biak. Was on patrol to capture the first Jap prisoner. He was sent back to Hollandia because he caught typhis fever. Rejoined Co. B in time to move on to Philippines and was on first wave at Zamboanga.

He went home on rotation the next month April 1945 and was discharged at Camp Atterbury, IN on June 10, 1945.

RAYMOND F. DOERING, was born Feb. 23, 1920. Entered the service May 10, 1942. Assigned to HQ Co., 116th Engrs. Stationed at Australia, New Guinea and the Philippine Islands.

He will always remember the New Guinea natives and how the children could sing our folk songs.

Discharged with the rank T/4. He received all the usual awards and decorations of his division. He is presently retired and lives in Clear Lake, MN.

HAROLD D. DOTY, was born June 18, 1924 in Thurman, IA. Entered the service in 1942 and was assigned to Co. B, 218th Inf., 41st Div. Stationed overseas in the South Pacific.

Discharged with the rank corporal, T grade.

Married to Mary. They have two sons, Mike and Harold Jr., Mike lives in Nebraska and Harold Jr. in New Jersey. They also have five grandchildren. Harold and Mary enjoy traveling all over the U.S. He retired after 42 years as a truck driver.

CLARENCE WENDELL DOUGHERTY, was born April 1, 1918 in Castle Rock, WA. Graduated from high school in 1936. Attended Lower Columbia Junior College one year and two years at Pacific University at Forest Grove, OR. Was inducted into service in Kelso, WA on Sept. 16, 1940 as sergeant in Medical Detachment Special Troops, 41st Div.

When division was streamlined he was transferred to Medical Detachment, 186th Inf. Served in Australia, New Guinea, and Philippines. Had furlough to U.S. in December 1944. Returned to Zamboanga in February 1945.

Was discharged as first sergeant of 186th Medics with the rank of technical sergeant at Ft. Lewis, WA on Aug. 23, 1945.

Married Leatha in 1958 and has two step-children, four grandchildren and two great-grandchildren. He owned a grocery store for 25 years and lived in Kotezebue, AK for three and a half years. Was clerk/treasurer in Castle Rock for 11 years, then retired. He belongs to American Legion, VFW, Lions, Eagles, and Elks.

FRANCIS L. DOUGHERTY (LOWELL), was born May 11, 1917 in West Frankfort, IL. He entered the service Jan. 28, 1941 and was assigned to Co. D, 116th Med. Bn. Basic training at Ft. Sheridan, IL, then sent to Camp Grant and worked in hospital ward. More training at Fitzsimmons General Hospital in Denver, November-December 1941. Joined the 41st Div. in July 1942.

Discharged Oct. 27, 1945. Married Nov. 4, 1945 to Army nurse, 1st Lt. Dorothy Jacob. They have two daughters, two sons, and eight grandchildren. He was a letter carrier in Elgin, IL for 32 years. Now retired and lives in Tomball, TX.

REV. THEODORE E. DRAKE, was born April 8, 1924 and his wife Geneva O. (Wren) Drake, Cherokee Indians from Oklahoma. Can trace his white side back to 1776. His great-grandfathers fought in the Civil War (one North and one South).

Trained at Camp Roberts, CA for 13 weeks, shipped to Australia and joined Co. B., 163rd Inf. Fought in major battles on Tome, Wakde, Zamboanga, Jolo, and other places (he can't remember names).

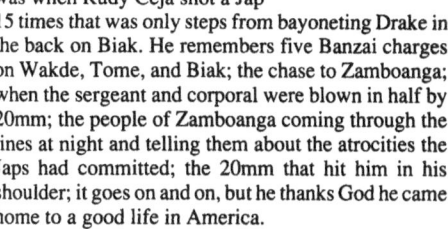

His memorable experience was when Rudy Ceja shot a Jap 15 times that was only steps from bayoneting Drake in the back on Biak. He remembers five Banzai charges on Wakde, Tome, and Biak; the chase to Zamboanga; when the sergeant and corporal were blown in half by 20mm; the people of Zamboanga coming through the lines at night and telling them about the atrocities the Japs had committed; the 20mm that hit him in his shoulder; it goes on and on, but he thanks God he came home to a good life in America.

Married Oct. 6, 1942. He has five children, David, Barbara, Ted Jr., Terrie, and Wayne. Also has 12 grandchildren and one great-granddaughter.

MILTON DREXLER, MD, was born April 3, 1914 in New York, NY. He graduated Bern Medical School in 1937. Volunteered for reserve duty in 1939. Assigned to active duty in June 1941. Trained at Camp Shelby, MS with 151st Inf. Regt. He joined 162nd Inf. Regt. as battalion surgeon at Ft. Dix. Served in Australia, New Guinea, and Biak as captain M.C.

He returned to the States on a stretcher in 1945 and was discharged from active duty in 1946. He received the Legion of Merit, Silver Star, Bronze Star, Combat Medical Badge, and Purple Heart.

Went into private practice West Chester County, NY. Is faculty member of city hospital in New York City; director Family Practice and president of medical staff, United Hospital; joined VAMC, Bronx; associate chief of staff and president of medical staff Diplomate Board of Family Practice, adjutant professor Clinical Medicine, Brooklyn College of Pharmacy; Faculty Cumberland Hospital of Long Island University. Retired 1986 to Greenwich, CT and Palm Beach, FL.

Married to Mollie in 1941. They have two children, Andrew (an endocrinologist) and Sharon Stem (a botanist). They have two grandchildren, Teddi and Samuel Stem.

ROBERT E. DROTZIGER, was born Dec. 11, 1918 in Chicago, IL. Inducted Oct. 11, 1941 and stationed at Camp Roberts, CA and Ft. Lewis, WA. Was assigned to F Co., 163rd Inf. 41st Inf. Div.

Departed March 19, 1942. Served in two battles in Papuan New Guinea, was light machine gunner and chaplin's assistant. Served in C Co., 186th and F Co., 163rd, HQ Det. OCS.

Was discharged June 16, 1945. He received the Distinguished Unit Badge, Good Conduct Ribbon, American Defense Service Ribbon, Asiatic-Pacific Theater Ribbon with two Bronze Stars, six Overseas Service Bars.

Married Verna on Feb. 17, 1942 in Washington.

Went home in May 1945 for 30 day leave and had delayed honeymoon in Florida. They have two children and four grandchildren.

Robert was a commercial artist and played the piano since he was five years old. While in the service he and Ralph Marlow entertained the boys with shows and music. He wrote a song *Till I Come Home Again*. He had a brain aneurysm surgery in June 1983. He is now in a nursing home with Alzheimer's.

EDMOND G. DUCOMMUN, was born Nov. 11, 1918 in Alhambra, CA. Entered the service July 12, 1941. Assigned to 41st FA Bn. at Ft. Lewis.

Made landings at Hollandia, Biak, Zamboanga, Jolo, Philippine Islands, occupied Hiroshima, Japan and finally after 42 months sailed for San Francisco.

Discharged with the rank of major. He received the Silver Star and Bronze Star.

Married to Sharon in September 1948. They have one son, who is a doctor, and three grandchildren (two girls, one boy). Edmond is retired from industry and from the Army Reserve with the rank of colonel.

ROY M. DUFF, was born October 1920 in Steptoe, WA. Moved to Whitefish, MT six weeks later. Joined Montana National Guard, 163rd Inf. Medical Detachment in September 1939. Inducted September 1940. Spent entire war with 163rd and 116th Medical Bn., 41st Div., Murray, Lewis, Australia, New Guinea, Philippines, and Japan.

SWA June 1944. Direct appointment of second lieutenant in April 1945. Returned to States and Whitefish in January 1946. Back to Montana National Guard and helped organize units Western Montana. Various assignments until military retirement October 1980 as member of State Headquarters Staff with a total 41 years of service.

Founded public transportation company in 1946, civilian retirement in 1988. Married Norma, Rockhampton, November 1944. They have two sons, one a school administrator and the other with CEO transportation company.

GLENN EUGENE DUGAS, was born in Bemidji, MN on April 17, 1918. Inducted into Army at Portland, OR on Oct. 9, 1941. He was in L Co., 186th Inf. for two months following outbreak of war. Was assigned to L Co., 163rd in February 1942. Transferred to Service Co., 163rd, January 1944. Basic training at Camp Roberts, CA; Ft. Lewis, WA; and Seymour and Rockhampton, Australia.

Participated in New Guinea Campaign at Sanananda, Huggins-perimeter, and patrol and mop-up operations around Gona and Kumusi River. Took part in landing at Zamboanga, Mindanao, Philippines, March 10, 1945.

Discharged from Army at Ft. Lewis, WA on June 14, 1945 as a private first class. He received the Asiatic-Pacific, Philippine Liberation, Good Conduct, and American Defense Medals and the Distinguished Unit Citation and Bronze Star.

Married Vivian Elizabeth Moore on March 5, 1946. They have three daughters and three grandchildren. Retired from Manville Corporation after 32 years. Moved to Vancouver, WA from Lakewood, CA in 1979. He is enjoying life in the great northwest.

DELMAR S. DUNHAM, was born March 5, 1919 in Paulding, OH. He moved to Michigan at the age of four. Graduated from Britton High School in 1937. Drafted into the Army Oct. 8, 1941. Trained at Camp Roberts, CA.

After Pearl Harbor he was sent to Ft. Lewis, WA and assigned to HQ Co., 1st Bn., 162nd Inf. In March of 1942 he boarded *Santa Paula* for trip to Australia. He was in the New Guinea Campaign and also Biak.

After a bout with yellow jaundice and malaria, he was sent home weighing 124 pounds, a loss of 40 pounds. After a 30 day leave he was assigned to Ft. Knox, KY. Discharged Oct. 27, 1945.

He married Wilma and has a daughter Linda and son Gary who also served in Okinawa and Vietnam. He retired in 1982 after 41 years working in refrigeration and air conditioning at Tecumseh Products Company, Tecumseh, MI. He now lives in Britton, MI.

HARRY V. DURBEN, was born on Sept. 8, 1918 and graduated from Plainfield High School, Plainfield, OH. On Nov. 17, 1941, he was sworn into the Army at Ft. Hayes in Columbus, OH.

After seven weeks training at Camp Wheeler, GA, he was assigned to the 41st Div. and sent to Ft. Lewis, WA on March 1, 1942. Set sail at San Francisco on April 22, 1942 and arrived at Melbourne, Australia on May 13, 1942. Went on to Rockhampton, Australia. Flew from Port Moresby, Australia to Buna Gona Airstrip in New Guinea. Freed New Guinea, the East Indies, Philippines and was preparing for departure to Japan when Japan surrendered.

On September 21, 1945, he received an honorable discharge from Camp Atterbury, IN. Received the rank of corporal with seven hash marks, Asiatic-Pacific Theater Ribbons, three Bronze Stars, American Defense Service Medal, Philippine Liberation Ribbon, and the Good Conduct Ribbon.

Was married to Phyllis T. Smithson on Oct. 5, 1955 until her demise on May 5, 1980. Retired from the U.S. Postal Service on Sept. 8, 1983 and now residing in Newcomerstown, OH.

DON E. DUVALL, was born Nov. 27, 1917 in Monticello, IL. He entered the service Sept. 23, 1941. Assigned to HQ Co., 1st Bn., 163rd Inf. at Ft. Lewis, WA and overseas.

His memorable experience was playing basketball with the guys, playing poker, and shooting craps with Clifton "Jesse" James.

Wounded outside of Zamboanga on March 11, 1945. Discharged Sept. 19, 1945 with the rank of staff sergeant. He received the Bronze Star for meritorious achievement in the Pacific Theater on Jan. 23, 1943, the Purple Heart, Good Conduct Ribbon, Asiatic-Pacific, Combat Infantry Badge, and three Bronze Campaign Stars.

Married Jeane on May 19, 1946, has one child and two grandchildren. Don was employed by Revere Copper and Brass Inc. at Clinton, IL for 30 years. The last 10 years of his employment he served as group traffic manager for the Clinton, IL plant, the Alussco, AL plant and the Rome, NY plant. He retired Jan. 31, 1982.

He is an enthusiastic golfer and a member of the Clinton Country Club for 45 years. He has won every annual club tournament, including club championship and senior championship.

EUGENE EDEN, was born on April 29, 1924 in Monett, MO. Joined the service Oct. 3, 1943. Assigned to Co. E, 163rd Inf. Stationed at Biak and Mindoro.

His memorable experience was moping up on Biak. Discharged with the rank private first class.

Married to Norma and has three children and nine grandchildren. He retired in 1986. Now enjoys gardening, fishing and traveling.

MERLE EDMUNDS JR., was born March 9, 1919 in Bloomington, IL. Graduated from high school in 1938 and attended Illinois State University from 1939 through 1941. Was drafted Sept. 26, 1941. Basic training at Camp Roberts, CA. Joined the 41st Inf. Div. at Ft. Lewis, WA on Dec. 12, 1941. Was assigned to Co. H, 186th Inf.

Went overseas March 17, 1942 to Australia and New Guinea. Was assigned to Division Hqs. in Special Service and made a sergeant in July 1942. While in Rockhampton, Australia, he wrote and directed the first Army musical there.

In April of 1943 he was assigned to Co. G, 163rd Inf. Fell out of a tree and broke his collar bone and shoulder. Was operated on in Townsville, and never returned to the 41st. Spent time in Special Service in Townsville and Brisbane.

Returned to the States on Thanksgiving of 1944. Was discharged from the Army on Sept. 26, 1945. Married twice and has two sons, Terry and Stan, both served in Vietnam. He is a member of VFW, American Legion, Elks Lodge, and a 32 degree Mason and Shriner.

LAWRENCE C. EDWARDS, was born Nov. 20, 1920 in rural Shobonier, IL. Graduated from high school in 1939. Enlisted in Army Signal Corp on Aug. 10, 1942. Reported to Ft. Sheridan, IL. Then went to Camp Crowder, MO for basic training. Joined the 41st Signal Company on Aug. 27, 1943 at Rockhampton, Australia.

He made D-Day landings at Hollandia, New Guinea and Palawan, Philippine Islands with 162nd and 186th Inf. Regts. Also participated in the Biak Campaign. He left Zamboanga, Philippine Islands on Sept. 19, 1945 for occupation of Japan.

Returned to States where he received his discharge Dec. 6, 1945 with the rank of master sergeant. Married Louise in 1948. Retired from Illinois Bell Telephone Company in 1981 after holding various management positions. They reside in Rural Rochester, IL.

LEONARD RALPH EDWARDS, was born Sept. 10, 1919 in Muskingum County. Entered the service Nov. 18, 1941. Participated in the action at southern Philippines, Papua, New Guinea, and Australia.

His memorable experiences include flying over the Owen Stanley Range; the time spent in Sidney, Melbourne, Rockhampton, and Brisbane, Australia.

Was wounded in 1943 and received the Purple Heart and Oak Leaf Cluster. Also received theater ribbons and nine Bronze Stars. Discharged with the rank of T/5.

Married Lucy Moutz Dec. 23, 1945. Has two sons, Robert and Keith, daughter Susan, and 10 grandchildren. He retired from Brockway Glass in 1980 after 36 years of service.

MORRIS EHRLICH, was born Dec. 30, 1918 in New York City. Inducted into Army Sept. 8, 1941. Went to Camp Croft for basic infantry training, followed by Combat Intelligence School. Transferred to Ft. Dix in February 1942 and shipped out March 4, 1942.

Recruited for Medics on board ship and served with Medics in all the campaigns of the 3rd Bn., 162nd Regt., 41st Div. throughout the war until discharge Sept. 30, 1945 as technical sergeant.

Married Frances in 1947. They have three children and four grandchildren. He became a retailer with real estate holdings in Queens and Nassau counties in New York and also New Jersey. Formerly resided in Queens, NY, retired in 1985 and now lives in Pompano Beach, FL.

JOHN P. EPPARD, was born Sept. 25, 1918, in Staples, MN. Entered the service on Feb. 21, 1941. Assigned to I Co., 186th Inf. 741 Ord. L.M. Co., stationed at Ft. Lewis, WA.

Discharged Sept. 12, 1945 with the rank of T/3. He received the American Defense Service Medal, Asiatic Pacific Campaign Medal, Philippine Liberation Ribbon, Good Conduct Medal with one clasp.

Married Sept. 24, 1949 to Rita. They have a daughter Robin and son Mark. He retired in June 1980. Is now attending college in California, majoring in horticulture.

ALDO ERAMO, was born March 6, 1926 in Ortona Dei Marsi, Italy. Raised and currently lives in Boston, MA. Entered the service on May 26, 1944. Was assigned to 41st Inf. Div., C Co., 163rd Inf. at Mindoro. Stationed in Southern Philippines with landings at Jolo and Zamboanga. Occupation at wars end in Nagoya.

Discharged May 7, 1946 at Ft. Devins, MA with the rank of technical sergeant. Decorated with the Purple Heart, Bronze Star, Good Conduct Medal, Asiatic-Pacific Theater Campaign Ribbon with a Bronze Service Arrowhead, Victory Medal, Philippine Liberation Ribbon with one Bronze Service Star, and Army Occupation Medal of Japan.

Has been active in VFW since return to U.S. on April 28, 1946. He is member of New England Chapter of 41st Division Association. Retired and enjoying life with his family.

PIUS ERCK, was born June 7, 1911 in Esmond, ND. Entered the service March 4, 1941. Assigned to Co. A, 116 Med., stationed at Ft. Lewis, WA.

Went to Australia, from Seymour to Rockhampton to New Guinea to the Philippines at Mindoro and Mindanao. There he got a rash and was sent home on hospital ship. Landed at San Francisco July 4, 1945.

His memorable experiences include his first combat on Mt. Tambu and when the shooting started, he went in numerous times and brought back the wounded; eating Australian rations with biscuits full of weevils; and the still on Biak. They made about 25 gallons a week and had a real happy company. They also supplied the infantry.

Discharged with the rank NCO 014. He received the Silver Star, Distinguished Unit Badge, Bronze Star, and Service Arrowhead.

Married for 30 years, he has stepchildren and grandchildren. Was in the paper making profession from 1937 to 1974, now retired and taking it easy.

CHARLES ERICKSON, was born April 20, 1920 at Badger, IA. He graduated from Eagle Grove High School in 1940. He was inducted Oct. 24, 1941 at Des Moines into the Army. He took basic and then overseas training at Camp Wolters, TX and Ft. Lewis, WA where he was assigned to Co. D, 186th Inf., 41st Inf. Div.

He sailed on a converted passenger ship the *Argentina* from San Francisco to Melbourne, Australia arriving on May 13, 1942. He campaigned and saw action in New Guinea. Left New Guinea on points July 13, 1944 aboard a liberty ship.

Memorable experience was drawing ticket back to U.S. out of a hat and seeing the Golden Gate Bridge.

After a brief furlough he was assigned to Co. B, 211 ITB at Camp Blanding, Fl where he was a heavy weapons crewmen instructor until time of his discharge Oct. 4, 1945.

Married to Pauline Lucius Oct. 29, 1945 at Ocala, FL. They returned to Ft. Dodge, IA to make their home. They have two sons, three daughters, and 15 grandchildren. He retired from the U.S. Gypsum Company in 1982.

JAMES A. ESBRANDT, was born July 18, 1926 in Balto, MD. Entered the service Oct. 3, 1944 and was assigned to F Co., 163rd Inf. Regt. Stationed at Zamboanga, Jolo, Sanga Sanga, Japan.

Discharged with the rank of staff sergeant. He received all the usual awards.

Married to Thelma in 1954, he has four sons and seven grandchildren. After two heart attacks, he retired on disability in 1978.

LESLIE N. ESKOLA, was born in Eveleth, MN on March 9, 1925. He entered the service at Ft. Snelling, MN on July 24, 1943. Was assigned to Co. E, 275th Inf., 70th Div., Camp Adair, OR; Ft. Ord; Camp Stoneman, CA; and overseas.

7th Replacement Depot, Oro Bay, New Guinea. Was assigned to 41st Div. in July 1944. Served with Co. B, 163rd Inf., Biak, Philippines (Zamboanga, Jolo), Hiroshima, Japan.

He remembers observing his 20th birthday on an LCI the day before the Zamboanga landing and visiting Hiroshima in November 1945.

Left Japan January 1946, discharged at Ft. McCoy, WI on Jan. 31, 1946 with the rank of technical sergeant. He received the Combat Infantry Badge, Bronze Service Arrowheads, and Good Conduct Medal.

Married to Betty and has four sons and a daughter. He retired in April 1987.

NEWTON L. ESPE, was born in Prairie Farm, WI on March 25, 1922. Was raised in Minnesota, Wisconsin, Bolivia, and Iowa. Resident of Portland, OR since 1938.

Participated in New Guinea campaigns at Salamaua, Hollandia, Wakde, Biak, and at Zamboanga in the Philippine Islands.

Served in the radio section of HQ Btry., 218th FA Bn. (formerly HQ Btry., 3rd Bn.) from 1939 until his honorable discharge in 1946 with the rank T/4.

Married with two children and two grandsons. He retired as graphics department manager at Tektronix, Inc. in 1983. For the last seven years has operated his own business as technical writer and graphic designer.

CLIFFORD WILEY EVANS, was born April 13, 1919 in Warren, OR. Entered the Army on Sept. 16, 1940. In the early part of 1942 was given yellow fever inoculations in preparation for deployment to the South Pacific with the 41st Inf. The serum was bad and he came down with yellow jaundice (hepatitis) along with many other young men. Upon his release from the hospital at Ft. Lewis, his records were not available because they had been sent to the South Pacific with the rest of the division.

When the records were received, he was sent to Ft. Sill, OK for training as an artillery mechanic, sometime after this he was transferred to Georgia to an airborne division and trained. Later he was sent to England and Wales for training for D-Day invasion.

Served in Europe until his discharge in October 1945 and received many commendations for his service to his country.

After his discharge he came back to Salem and worked for an aircraft company making and repairing carnival rides for a couple of years, then became a recreation pilot.

Married to Evelyn Killin on Dec. 10, 1949 and never had any children. He worked for International Paper Company in Salem for a number of years. Later he became a stone mason/brick mason and worked in the construction industry. Took a college course in commercial art, but found he was not cut out for the big city life, where the money was, so went back to construction, later was a service representative for a Chrysler/Plymouth dealer in Klamath Falls, OR.

In 1972 he became ill and was unable to work until his death in July of 1990 of cardio-vasculor complications.

C. GILBERT EVANS (CHARLIE), was born Jan. 29, 1923 in Osage City, KS. Inducted at Ft. Leavenworth, KS with basic training at Camp Roberts, CA. Joined 41st Div in Rockhampton, Australia in July 1943. Served with 163rd Inf. Regt., B Co., 1st Bn. HQ Co. and as regimental mail sergeant in Service Company.

Participated in the Aitape, Biak, Zamboanga, and Jolo landing and battles and the occupation at Hiro,, Japan. Player coach of the Service Company basketball team.

Discharged Jan. 7, 1946 at Ft. Logan, CO. He returned to college and played on the Kansas and Creighton Universities basketball teams. He received a BSBA from Denver University and MBA from San Diego State University.

He practiced as a public accountant and in corporate accounting management for Haskins & Sells, Foremost McKessan, General Dynamics Corp. and Beatrice Company. He married Dorothy Krische, a registered nurse, in Topeka, KS on Sept. 6, 1948. They have six sons, four daughters and 19 grandchildren. They have resided in Kansas, Colorado, New Mexico and for the past 30 years in Southern California.

JAMES G. EVESON, was born April 10, 1916 in Raymond, Alberta, Canada. He became a U.S. Citizen in Brisbane, Australia. Entered the service on April 10, 1941. Went to Ft. Lewis, WA for basic training with the 103rd Anti-tank unit. Joined the 41st Inf. Div. at Ft. Lewis, WA. Served with Service Company, 186th Inf. Left for overseas on April 10, 1942 to Australia. Transferred to 163rd Inf. at Biak as a warrant officer. Served in Australia, New Guinea, Biak, Hollandia, Zamboanga, Mindanao, and Japan.

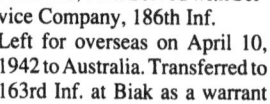

Discharged Dec. 31, 1945 at Ft. Lewis, WA. He received the Combat Infantryman Badge and Bronze Star.

Married to Colleen Martin and has three sons, Ross, Ray, and David. He is a member of the Lion's Club, Elks Club, American Legion, VFW, American Institute of CPAs and Oregon Society of CPAs.

MARCUS A. FALCONE, was born April 6, 1922 in Alliance, OH. He was inducted in the Army Dec. 16, 1942. Trained at Ft. McClellan, AL. Shipped overseas in May 1943 to Sidney, Australia. After two months of duty there he shipped north to Rockhampton and was assigned to Co. B, 163rd Regt. on July 20, 1943.

Was in the invasions of Aitape, Wadke Island, Toem, Biak, and Zamboanga. On March 14, 1945 was in the attack of Santa Maria Mission. On Zamboanga he was wounded by a sniper's bullet in the right shoulder. He was evacuated stateside and after surgery and a stay of six months in the hospital was discharged from Mayo General Hospital.

He retired as a certified welder in 1975. Married to Margaret for 49 years. He enjoys fishing and woodworking. He is the holder of the Purple Heart, Combat Infantry Badge, and other campaign battle ribbons. He was proud to be a part of the 41st Div. and regrets he didn't make it to Japan.

LAVERNE A. FALK, was born Dec. 9, 1917 near Courtland, KS where he grew up and graduated from high school and a three year business course. He entered the Army Oct. 3, 1941 at Ft. Cook, NE. He was in Unit HQ Co., 2nd Bn., 163rd Inf. Anti-tank Platoon.

Trained at Camp Roberts, CA; joined the 41st Inf. Div.; served on Coast Guard duty; and on March 19, 1942 was sent to Pacific Theater.

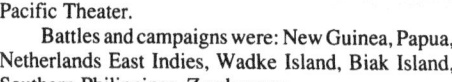

Battles and campaigns were: New Guinea, Papua, Netherlands East Indies, Wadke Island, Biak Island, Southern Philippines, Zamboanga.

Discharged as staff sergeant on Oct. 9, 1945 at Ft. Logan, CO. His awards and medals include the Combat Infantry Badge, Presidential Unit Citation, two Bronze Stars, four Campaign Stars, Discharge Pin, one Arrowhead, and numerous Campaign Battle Ribbons.

He is a retired carpenter contractor. Volunteers at veterans hospital and VFW Post 1650 Topeka Funeral Detail.

Married to Esther in 1946, he has one son Ronald; two granddaughters, Holly and Jamie; step-son Eugene; and two step-granddaughters Laura and Shannon. This marriage ended in divorce and he married Evelyn in 1965.

VICTOR E. FARON, was born Nov. 24, 1924 at Creve Coeur, MO. Was drafted Sept. 27, 1944 and went to Camp Robinson, AR for 15 weeks basic training. Was sent to Ft. Ord, CA to go overseas Feb. 15, 1945.

Joined 41st Inf. Div. at Zamboanga April 6, 1945 and two days later made landing at Holo Island as a rifleman with Co. B, 163rd. Was hit by mortar shrapnel. Another round fell at his feet but was a dud. After Holo they landed at Piacon to intercept the Japs moving across the island. Also made landing on Mindanao and was in occupation of Japan. After deactivating of 41st, he was sent to 534th Engr. Boat and Shore Regt. It was also deactivated and he was then sent to the 24th Div., stationed throughout Japan including Hiroshima and Nagasaki.

Came back to the States Sept. 7, 1946. After a 60 day furlough, he received his discharge on Nov. 25, 1946. Was a service station owner for 38 years. Married to Marge and has two sons. He is semi-retired and lives in Creve Coeur, MO.

JOHN FEATHERLY, was born Nov. 27, 1916 in Dillon, MT. Moved to Omak, WA in 1924 and graduated Omak High School in 1934. Joined the Army March 6, 1941, stationed at Ft. Lewis, Tacoma, WA. Assigned to Co. D and A, 116th Med. Bn., 41st Div., serving entire war with 116th Med. Bn. in Australia, New Guinea, and the Philippines. Trained at Ft. Lewis, Hunter and Liggett Military Reservation, CA.

Participated in battles/landings at Salamaua-Lea, Hollandia-Biak in New Guinea and Dutch East Indies, Mindoro Island and Zamboanga in the Philippines.

Discharged from the 41st Div. at Ft. Lewis on Aug. 27, 1945 with the rank of staff sergeant. He received the American Defense Service Medal, Good Conudct Medal, Purple Heart with one Bronze Oak Leaf Cluster, and the Philippine Liberation Medal with one Bronze Service Star.

Married Bernice on April 22, 1946. They have three children. He retired from heavy construction in 1979. Enjoys trap shooting, fishing, bowling, and gardening. He winters in Arizona in his 5th wheel trailer, following senior trap shooting circuit.

RICHARD T. FEDDERSEN, was born in Iowa. He graduated with honors from the State University of Iowa and advanced ROTC. He completed the officer's course at Ft. Benning in 1941. He joined the 162nd Inf. Regt. at Salamaua during the battle. Colonel MacKechnie directed him to do a combat questionnaire and action report. This involved interviewing leaders in the forward fighting units.

He also served as regimental personnel officer G Co. commander and regimental S-3. He commanded G Co. during the latter part of the Biak Campaign and its proud capture of Mt. Capisan at Zamboanga. He developed the training program and directed the Philippine Guerrilla Officers' School for Gen. Doe at Zamboanga.

His rank and awards are Colonel, Infantry, AUS, Bronze Star Medal with two Oak Leaf Clusters, Combat Infantry Badge, Philippine Presidential Citation, Combat Assault Landing Arrowhead, Presidential Unit Citation U.S., and was senior officer to accept the surrender of the admiral of the Imperial Japanese Naval Academy at Eta Jima, Japan.

He is now an Iowa farm owner and manager. He is married and has two children and one grandchild.

FREDERICK H. FELDSCHNEIDER, was born April 12, 1925 in Marshalltown, IA. He entered the service Aug. 29, 1944. Served with Co. G-162, Weapons Platoon; stationed at Zamboanga, Mindanao, Philippine Islands, and Japan Occupation.

Received honorable discharge in 1946 at Ft. Sheridan, IL. He achieved the rank of T/5.

Married Marilyn in 1948. They have three children, Janet, Barbara, and Luann. Also have five grandchildren, one girl and four boys. He is a retired farmer and lives in Marshalltown, IA.

FRED W. FELDT, was born July 14, 1924 in New York City. Entered the service on July 28, 1942. Was assigned to 41st Signal Co., G Co., 163rd Regt. Stationed overseas in Australia, New Guinea, Southern Philippines, and Japan.

Discharged Dec. 3, 1945. He received the Combat Infantry Badge, Battle Stars for New Guinea Campaign and South Philippine Liberation and Bronze Service Arrowhead.

Married to Dorothy in 1951. He retired in 1978 and moved from Croton-on-Hudson, NY to Stuart, FL. He is enjoying life.

EVERETT J. FERBRACHE, was born in Lewistown, MT on Aug. 11, 1919. He moved to Portland, OR in 1922 and graduated from high school in June 1938.

He joined the Oregon National Guard in 1935, was inducted into federal service September 1940, stationed at Ft. Lewis, WA with Service Company, 186th Inf., 41st Div. He served in Australia and New Guinea.

Received a medical discharge, service connected, on Nov. 3, 1944 with the rank of staff sergeant.

Married Betty in 1947 and raised three sons, attended college, majored in geology and was employed with the Corps of Engineers for 34 years. He retired in February 1981.

KEITH W. FERGUSON, was born Dec. 9, 1916 in Niagara, ND and raised in Tillamook, OR. He enlisted in K Co., 162nd Inf. in September 1933.

Inducted in 1940, trained at Ft. Lewis, WA. Went overseas with 41st on March 4, 1942. Was commissioned December 1942 and assigned to C Co., 163rd Inf. for Sanananda Operation. He commanded F Co., 163rd on Wakde and F Co. at Zamboanga and Sanga Sanga landings.

Rotated to the States May 1945 and released from active duty January 1946 at Camp Fannin, TX with the rank of captain. Activated Co. M, 186th Inf. at Tillamook, OR in May 1947. Was recalled to active duty November 1948. Graduated from the Army Language School (Russian) in June 1950. Served two tours in Germany and one in Korea.

Married Irene Bishop in November 1937. They have a son Roger. Retired in December 1963 at Ft. Lewis with the rank of major. He makes his home in Eugene, OR.

MICHAEL FERNANDEZ, was born 1918 in Ewa Mill, Honolulu, HI. Entered the service March 28, 1941. Assigned to Co. M, 162nd, stationed at Ft. Lewis, WA and overseas.

Memorable experiences: Roosevelt Ridge in New Guinea and Biak Island in New Guinea.

Discharged Oct. 1, 1945 with the rank staff sergeant. He received the Good Conduct Medal, American Defense Service Medal, Asiatic-Pacific Campaign Medal, and Philippine Liberation Ribbon with one Bronze Star.

He never married and is retired in San Francisco, CA.

WARREN E. FICHTNER (HAPPY), was born Jan. 23, 1918 in Medford, OR. Entered the service Sept. 16, 1940. Assigned to 41st Div., A Co., 186th Regt. Stationed at Ft. Lewis, Camp Murray, WA and overseas.

Arrived in Australia May 14, 1942 at Camp Seymour out of Melbourne. From there went to Rockhampton, Queensland. During this time his duty was assigned as the armour artivicer (ordinance mechanic, small arms). His most interesting experience was bootlegging beer, wine, whiskey, gin, etc. and selling it to the fellows and officers over the fence under Col. Murrary's nose. Another time while at Seymour and Rockhampton, he ironed clothes for the enlisted personnel instead of going out and digging foxholes. From here, they went to New Guinea, Port Moresby by boat and flew over the old Stanley and made camp at Buna.

Was wounded on island of Biak. Discharged with the rank T/5. His awards and decorations include: Purple Heart, one Bronze Service Arrow, Philippine Liberation, Asiatic-Pacific Service Medal, American Defense Service Medal, Good Conduct, and Combat Infantry Badge.

Married Helen Crichton in 1942, divorced in 1945. Married Gloria Pittock in June 1946, three sons were born to this union, divorced in October 1985. Married Carol Maas March 11, 1988 in Sidney, Australia and daughter Clara Mae Camille was born Dec. 12, 1989. She is the joy and light of his life. Also has stepson Jonathan Maas.

He is retired and has visited Australia three times since 1984. Lives on three acres, has 38 chickens, and three geese for watchdogs.

LAWRENCE H. FITCH, was born April 25, 1913 in Springfield, SD. Entered the service Feb. 29, 1941. Assigned to 41st Div., 163rd Regt., 3rd HQ Bn., stationed at Ft. Lewis, WA.

Overseas for 38 months of active duty in New Guinea, East Indies, Philippine Islands, Jolo and Sulu Islands. Spent a week's furlough in Sidney, Australia. Spent time in General Hospital in Sidney with typhus and malaria.

Discharged at Ft. Levenworth, KS on May 25, 1945 with the rank of sergeant. He received the Bronze Star, Good Conduct, Asiatic-Pacific Campaign, American Defense, American Campaign, World War II Victory Medal, and Combat Infantry Medal.

Married Adeline Borschelt on June 9, 1946. Has one daughter Laurie. His wife passed away in 1974. He married Betty Jane Kirsch on Nov. 1, 1975. Retired in Montana, spent three years in Mission Service Corps, retired and now lives in Mesa, AZ with Betty Jane.

MELVIN A. FORREST, was born March 20, 1918 in Morton, WA where he has spent all of his life, excepting when he served in the Army in WWII in Co.'s I, E, C, and B of the 116 Medics.

Was inducted March 4, 1941 and trained at Ft. Lewis, WA. He was sent overseas April 22, 1942. Was in the battles at Sanananda, Aitape, Toem, Wakde, Biak, and Zamboanga as an ambulance driver.

He arrived home May 13, 1945 and was discharged May 19, 1945. He achieved the rank of sergeant and received the Presidential Unit Citation.

He spent the next 36 years in logging and farming, before retiring in 1981. He married Ellen Coleman Allison in 1950. They have four children and seven grandchildren. They reside near Morton on 40 acres that keeps him busy. He is a member of the VFW and the Moose Lodge. He and his wife enjoy traveling.

DAVID H. FOSSELMAN, was born Dec. 24, 1917. As member of 185th and 162nd Inf., he treasures the honor of 12 years association with the dedicated men of the 41st Div. Their mission was defense of NW United States against the Russkies.

While serving at Army General Hospital, he protested bizarre psychiatric treatment of troops, thus incurring wrath of hospital commandant and was "boarded." Request for either civilian counsel or JAG assistance was refused; an active duty pharmacist was appointed as "counsel," but argued unsuccessfully. During appeal, assistance was requested from NG echelons and from Army Chief of Chaplains—both declined. Honorable discharge was "accepted."

Employment since discharge has consisted of student counseling and pastoral activity, San Jose State University; director, Youth Service Bureau of White County, IN; and clinical social work, Wabash Valley Hospital, Lafayette, IN. Current assignment as associate pastor of St. Joseph's Church, Reynolds, IN. Pastor is Rev. Robert Fosselman, CH (Lt. Col.) USAR, Retired.

His hobbies are golf, reading, writing for publication, and happily reflecting on memories of service with the 41st Div. God bless 'em all!

Motto: Illegitimi non carborundum.

HOMER W. FRANKLIN, was born Oct. 28, 1917 in Oakman, AL. Drafted Nov. 13, 1941, he went to Camp Wheeler for basic training with the 13th Bn. Assigned to 41st Div., Co. I, 186th Inf. Regt. in February 1942 at Ft. Lewis, WA.

Served in Melbourne, Australia and assigned to

HQ Co., Buna, New Guinea during the war achieving the rank of sergeant T/4. Involved in the battles of Hollandia, New Guinea and received the Infantry Combat Badge.

Returned to the States October 1944 and was reassigned to Ord. 4th Service Command at Ft. Jackson, SC. Discharged in September 1945 in Atlanta, GA.

He joined the National Park Service in June 1947. Assignments included Death Valley, CA; Hawaii National Park; Big Bend, TX; Lassen National Park, CA; Joshua Tree National Monument, CA and Roosevelt-Vanderbilt Estate, NY. He retired in August 1975 and currently resides in Tuscaloosa, AL.

He married Pauline Ralston on Nov. 8, 1941. They have two children, Sharon and Paula Karen, and two grandchildren, Eric and Ryan Gilnak.

WILLIAM A. FREDLUND, was born April 3, 1924 in Brooklyn, NY. Was raised in Freeport, Long Island, graduating from Freeport High in June 1942. Drafted Feb. 17, 1943 at Camp Upton, Long Island and took basic training at Ft. Brady, MI. Served at Camp Wolters, TX; Ft. Benning, GA; and Ft. Ord, CA.

Went overseas to Doomben, Brisbane, Australia in January 1944; Goodenough Island off New Guinea; Lae; and Finchhaven. Joined Service Co. 186 at Biak in June 1944. Served with L Co. 186 at Mindoro and landing at Puerto Princesa, Palawan, Philippines. Returned to Service Co. 186 and went to Mindanao, Philippine Islands and Hiroshima, Japan.

Returned to the States in January 1946 and was discharged with the rank of T/5 at Ft. Dix, NJ on Jan. 18, 1946. He received the Philippine Liberation with one Bronze Star, Asiatic-Pacific Service Medal, World War II Victory Medal, and the Good Conduct Medal.

Graduated from Auburn University in December 1950 in civil engineering. Worked for E.I. Dupont and municipal engineer before becoming village engineer of Herkimer, NY in 1963. Retired in June 1989, remaining in private practice as professional engineer.

Married Marjory on Nov. 1, 1952. They have two daughters (Nancy and Amy), two sons (Richard and Carl), and six grandchildren.

KENT S. FREEMAN, was born July 3, 1920 in Portland, OR. Joined the 41st Div. on July 29, 1937. Served with Medical Detachment, 162nd Inf. Regt.

Retired June 23, 1964 with the rank sergeant first class, senior drill instructor. He was awarded the Combat Medical Badge, Expert Infantry Badge, Bronze Star with V Device for Valor, Germany 1945, Medal of Rhine Danube, and Medal of French Liberation.

Married and divorced. He has one son and two daughters. He is now completely retired in Beaverton, OR and does volunteer work.

VERNON A. FREY, was born July 8, 1919 in Elizabethtown, PA. Enlisted in Air Corps, October 1941 with Flight School to follow basic training. Called to duty March 4, 1942; received infantry basic at Camp Wheeler, GA and assigned to 4th Inf. Div., Camp Gordon, GA.

Selected for Infantry Officers School at Ft. Benning in October 1942, graduating as a second lieutenant in January 1943. Was assigned to Camp Roberts, CA.

Following eight months with the 44th Inf. Div. at Ft. Lewis, WA, he left the States as replacement in 41st Div. for landings at Hollandia, Biak, Palawan, and Zamboanga with H, M, Cn. Co. 186 and Division HQ in Japan.

Returned to the States Feb. 6, 1946 for duty at Camp Robinson, AR and Ft. Benning Officers School prior to entering reserve status with the rank of major in June 1947.

His awards include the Bronze Star, Victory Medal, Army Commendation, American Theater, Philippine Liberation, Occupation and Pacific Theater Ribbons with three Battle Stars and Arrowhead, and the Combat Infantry Badge.

Became owner-manager in food brokerage, commercial real estate and leasing companies, retiring in 1981. Married to Naomi and has son, daughter, and four grandchildren.

ALEX FRIEDT, was born Sept. 28, 1919 in Center, ND. Was raised in Billings, MT. Served with Co. L, 163rd, 41st Div. then Co. C. In Seymour, Australia, he transferred to 41st QM. In Rockhampton he served in New Guinea Campaign and returned to Rockhampton in 1943.

Sent Stateside in rotation in 1944. Served with 49th MPs in San Francisco, CA. Sent to Ft. Lewis in 1945 for discharge on Aug. 25, 1945.

Married Elizabeth in 1944. They have five children (one deceased), and 12 grandchildren. He retired in 1983 and they reside in Sedro-Woolley, WA. He is a life member of DAV.

HARVEY P. FRIEND, was born July 14, 1924 in DeQueen, AR. Was raised in Los Angeles, CA. Graduated from high school in 1943. Was inducted Feb. 24, 1943. Completed basic training at Camp Strongs, MI. Stationed at Ft. Brady, MI. and Ft. Benning, GA with Cannon Co., 131st Inf. Regt.

On Jan. 16, 1944 he was assigned to D Co., 116th Med. Bn. of the 41st Div. in Rockhampton, Australia. He was in the landings at Hollandia, New Guinea, at Biak Island and in the Philippines at Santa Fe, Mindoro, Zamboanga, Mindanao, and Holo, Zulu.

He was in the peaceful invasion and occupation of the Kure-Hiroshima area of western Honchu Island, Japan.

Returned to the States on Jan. 13, 1946 and received his discharge at Ft. MacArthur, CA with the rank of Tech/5.

Retired from the Los Angeles Police Department and the Department of Airports after working 33 years as a peace officer.

He married Norma in 1946 and they have five children, Sanda, Cathy, Harvey Jr., Charles, and Cynthia, plus nine grandchildren and one great-grandchild.

BASIL C. FRISBEE, was born June 1, 1918 in Grand Junction, CO. Has twin brother Cecil. Entered the service Oct. 9, 1941 and served with K Co., 162nd, 41st Div., light machine gun. Training at Camp Roberts, CA. Participated in Battle of Soloman.

Discharged Jan. 26, 1944 with the rank of private first class. Received the Combat Infantry Badge and Bronze Star.

Married Grace Stricklen March 25, 1944. They have a son and daughter, Burton and Cathy. He retired in February 1980.

CECIL B. FRISBEE, was born June 1, 1918 in Grand Junction, CO. Has twin brother Basil. Joined the service on Oct. 9, 1941 and was assigned to 41st Div., K Co., 162nd Inf., light machine gun. Basic training at Camp Roberts, CA. Participated in the Battle of Soloman.

Discharged February 1944 with the rank of private first class. He received the Combat Infantry Badge.

Married Marjorie Thornton in February 1944. He retired in 1982.

HARVEY D. FUCHS, was born June 21, 1920 in Chicago, IL and raised in Cicero, IL. Graduated from Morton High School and Northwestern University.

Inducted in October 1941 and took basic infantry training at Camp Roberts, CA; was sent to 41st Div. as a replacement after the Pearl Harbor attack. Originally assigned as secretary to Gen. Thomas E. Rilea, assistant division commander. Spent the war with 41st Div. in Australia, New Guinea, and the Philippines, mainly in the G-3 Section of Division Headquarters. Participated in the Buna/Gona Campaign, landings at Hollandia, Biak, Zamboanga, and Palawan. Discharged on June 20, 1945 at Ft. Sheridan, IL with the rank of sergeant.

Married Laura in 1948. They have three children, Lorelei, Leslee, and Lawrence. Started his accounting career after the war as a CPA with Arthur Andersen and Company. Entered private accounting as a vice-president of the J.R. Short Milling Company in Mt. Vernon, IN. Retired from this company in 1987 to do volunteer work with the AARP as a tax consultant.

ARTHUR N. GAGNIER, was born May 12, 1916 in Butte, MT. Enrolled in service Feb. 26, 1941, Ft. Missoula, MO. Was sent to Ft. Lewis, WA and assigned to 186th HQ 41st Div. Served in New Guinea, Papuan, and Southern Philippines. Served in South Pacific from April 22, 1942 to June 26, 1945.

His group had the record of being pinned down in their fox holes for the longest period of time. Discharged Aug. 8, 1945 with the rank of staff sergeant. He received the American Defense Service Medal, Philippine Liberation, Bronze Star, Asiatic-Pacific, Good Conduct and many ribbons to numerous to mention.

Joined Army Reserve on Aug. 4, 1948 as sergeant first class and served 363rd QM Service Co. (ORC) until May 28, 1952.

He spent 34 years in government service, retiring as a administrative contracting officer in the Defense Department. Was an active member in the 41st Infantry Division Association and a long time member of the Eagles. He was also elected Father of the Year. Arthur passed away April 5, 1991.

Married Phylis G. on Oct. 18, 1947. They had four children, John, William, Jeri Lynn, and Phillip, and eight grandchildren. His widow lives in West Linn, OR.

RAMON GALVAN, was born July 6, 1919 in Ft. Worth, TX. Entered the service Feb. 14, 1941. Served with Anti-tank Co., 163rd Inf., 41st Div. Stationed at Ft. Lewis, WA.

Received honorable discharge with the rank of staff sergeant.

Married to Bella and has five children, Ramon Jr., Velma Lu, David, Gina, and Jimmy. Retired 10 years ago in Murray, UT and now is just enjoying life.

HERBERT QUINN GARTMAN, was born Oct. 14, 1924 in Green County, MS. Was inducted at Camp Shelby, MS in July 1943. Basic training at Aberdeen Proving Ground, MD. He left Stoneman, CA in January 1944 for Brisbane, Australia. He joined the 41st Inf., 162nd Regt., 2nd Bn., 3rd Platoon, Co. E.

Battles included Hollandia, Biak, and Zamboanga; relieved the 186th on Mindanao, back to Zamboanga; then to Kurie and Onamachee, Japan as occupation forces.

Left Nagoya, Japan on the *Explorer* in December 1945 to Camp Kilbourne, NJ. Was discharged at Camp Shelby, MS on Jan. 6, 1946. Medals earned were the Bronze Star, Good Conduct Medal, Asiatic-Pacific Campaign with three Bronze Service Stars and Arrowhead, World War II Victory, Army of Occupation with Japan Clasp, Philippine Liberation Ribbon with two Bronze Service Stars, Combat Infantry and Philippine Presidential Unit Citation.

He is a retired steel fabrication business owner and father of seven children. He now lives in Lake Butler, FL.

CHARLES GAZDIK, was born Dec. 30, 1923 in Sheridan, WY. Inducted Feb. 23, 1944 at Ft. Logan, CO. He served with Co. B, 163rd Inf. Regt. Trained at Camp Roberts, CA and served in the southern Philippine Liberation, Zamboanga and Jolo Islands. He was stationed at Mindanao and Tokyo, Japan. Was clerk/typist at Gen. MacArthur's Headquarters.

Discharged March 29, 1946 with the rank private first class. His awards include the American Theater of Operations Service Ribbon, Asiatic-Pacific Theater Service Ribbon, Philippine Liberation Service Ribbon with one Bronze Star, Good Conduct Ribbon, Purple Heart Ribbon, Combat Infantry Badge, and Bronze Star Medal.

Married and has a lovely wife, six grown children, and 14 grandchildren (soon to be 16). He is retired from the grocery store business.

J. RICHARD GERTTULA, was born March 2, 1918 in Astoria, OR. He joined Btry. A, 218th FA at Camp Murray, WA as a second lieutenant U.S. Army Reserve on Feb. 1, 1941 and was assigned as reconnaissance officer. Transferred to Btry. D, 218th FA, which later became Co. C, 641st Tank Destroyer Bn.

Was sent to San Francisco, loaded on USAT *Etolin* and departed for parts unknown on Dec. 5, 1941. After Pearl Harbor returned to San Francisco for several weeks of guard duty and gun emplacements. Back to Ft. Lewis and to coastal watch at North Cove for several weeks. Then entrained to Ft. Dix, NJ and the USS *Uruguay* for the 40-day trip to Australia.

Served at Camp Seymour, Victoria, Australia then moved to Rockhampton. There he went to Chemical Warfare School, then sent to New Castle, NSW, Australia to joint overseas Operational Training School. Learned combat loading of troop transport. Upon completion Co. C, 641 was detailed to Gladstone to combat load ships to New Guinea for the 41st Div.

Next was assigned to Base B at Oro Bay, maintaining roads and building the dock and water supply for hospitals. After several weeks of intensive training, Recon Co. was attached to 186th for the Hollandia Operation.

During preparation for the Biak landing, 641st was redesignated 98th Chemical Mortar Bn., motorized Recon Co. attached to 162nd Inf. From May 27 to July 12, 1944, they fired 7,986 rounds in support of 41st Div. After Biak Operation, battalion was assigned to 6th Army Special Troops.

Rotated home from Lupao. In the States he was assigned as assistant S/3 of the Tank Destroyer School, Ft. Hood, TX. Was discharged as disabled for recurring malaria on Feb. 2, 1946. He attained the rank of captain.

Became cattle rancher, breeder of Charolais cattle and Arabian horses and operator of artificial insemination organization for livestock with active partner and mate, Doris. They have a son Russell and daughter Ardith Barton. He is now retired.

PETE GIANOPULOS, was born Aug. 22, 1924 in Taft (Kern County) CA. Was raised and educated in Taft, having graduated from high school in 1942, Taft Junior College in 1947, and Fresno State College in 1950.

Joined the Army Reserve Corps on Dec. 14, 1942. Basic training at Camp Roberts, CA. Left States July 7 and landed in Brisbane, Australia. Assigned to M Co., 163rd Regt. and two weeks later to Regt. HQ Co., I&R Platoon, as a truck driver.

Participated in amphibious landings at Aitape, Toem, Wakde Island, Biak Island, Zamboanga and Jolo Island.

Became part of the Army of Occupation of Japan in the Hero, Kure, Hiroshima area. Most memorable experience included the I&R Platoon patrol across Biak Island, which resulted in being ambushed and visiting Hiroshima.

Returned to the States after 30 months in December 1945 and received honorable discharge at Ft. MacArthur, CA on Feb. 9, 1946. Awards and decorations include Combat Infantry Badge, Bronze Star Medal, Republic of Philippines Medal with one Bronze Star, the Presidential Unit Citation Badge, Asiatic-Pacific Campaign Medal with three Bronze Stars and one Arrowhead, the World War II Victory Medal and the Army Good Conduct Medal.

He retired in June 1986 after 36 years in education as a teacher, counselor, and director of Pupil Personnel Services at Taft Union High School. He was a member of the Taft City Council, Mayor of Taft, and first director on the Kern County Water Agency, member of the California Teachers Association, the National Education Association, Taft Midway Masonic Lodge, Bakersfield Scottish Rite of Free Masonry, and the Al Malaika Shrine of Los Angeles.

PATRICK V. GIBSON, was born Dec. 10, 1920 in Canby, OR. When he was two, the family moved to Bend, OR where he attended school. He joined the Oregon National Guard in June 1936 and was activated to duty Sept. 16, 1940, stationed at Ft. Lewis, WA. He was assigned to Co. I, 162nd Inf., 41st Div.

He achieved the rank of staff sergeant, serving in New Guinea, Biak, and the Philippines. He was discharged Sept. 7, 1945 in San Francisco, CA.

Married Marjorie Wade in 1946. They have four children. He was owner and manager of Gibson Air Service in Bend, OR from 1951 to 1974 and was also past commander of the VFW and the Civil Air Patrol. He loved to hunt, fish and fly. He also loved music and played in a band as a drummer. He passed away April 4, 1990.

WALDO A. GILBERT, was born Jan. 12, 1920 in Rushsylvania, OH. Entered the service Nov. 17, 1941. Served with Co. F., 186th Inf., 41st Div. at Camp Wheeler, GA for basic training. Further training at Ft. Lewis, WA. Joined Co. F, 186th Inf., 41st Div., March 1942.

Left San Francisco April 25, 1942 and landed at Melbourne, Australia May 13, 1942. Training at Rockhampton and Seymour for nine months. Went to New Guinea February 1943 for Papuan-New Guinea campaigns. Got typhus fever from ticks and lice.

Back to the States October 1944 and home to Ohio for two weeks furlough. Then sent to Miami, FL for R&R. Had physical, then sent to Camp Atterbury, IN for discharge Jan. 1, 1945 with the rank private first class. Received Marksman, Good Conduct, Asiatic-Pacific Ribbon, and the American Defense Ribbon.

Retired after farming and working for Ohio Department of Natural Resources. Married Dorothy M. Ward on Nov. 22, 1945, no children.

DONALD D. GILSTRAP, was born Dec. 18, 1924. Entered the service in early 1943. Served with 186 HQ Co. INR. Stationed at Australia, New Guinea, and Biak Island. Was wounded June 7, 1944 on Biak Island.

Discharged with the rank of corporal. He received the Combat Infantry Badge, Good Conduct Medal, Purple Heart, and Bronze Star.

Married to Billie and they have a son Doug and daughter Donna Potts. He is a real estate developer, builds and owns apartments, shopping center, office buildings, and condominiums.

BERNARD A. GINGERICH, was born Sept. 12, 1923. Entered the service on March 1, 1943. Served with A Co. and Service Company, 163rd Inf. Regt., 41st Div.

Saw action at Biak, Jolo, and Zamboanga. Discharged with the rank T/4. He received the Combat Infantry Badge Rifle, Bronze Arrowhead, Victory Medal, American Theater Ribbon, Asiatic-Pacific Ribbon, Good Conduct Medal, and Philippine Liberation Ribbon with Bronze Star.

Married to LaVonne and has four children and one grandchild. Was with Mack Trucks Inc. for 24 years, supervisor service engineering.

ALPHONSE F. GIRDWAIN, was born Sept. 24, 1922 in Chicago, IL. Entered the Army Jan. 11, 1943 at Camp Custer, MI. Was assigned to Ft. Brady, 131st Inf., 33rd Div. Co. A for training and guarding the 500 locks.

Went to Ft. Ord, CA and on Feb. 6, 1944 sailed on the *Sea Corporal* for Australia to join the 41st Div., Co. B, 162. Participated in the Hollandia, Biak, and Soepiori Island Campaigns. Reassigned as a truck driver for AFWESPAC, in the Philippines. Left for the USA in March 1946.

Discharged as T/5 on April 4, 1946 at Camp McCoy, WI. His awards include the Combat Infantry Badge, World War II Medal, Good Conduct Medal, American Campaign, Asiatic-Pacific Campaign, Army of Occupation, and Philippine Campaign Ribbon.

Married Bernice Okunis in Chicago in 1950. They have son Robert, daughter Theresa, and two granddaughters. He worked five years for the CTA, owned a tavern for 18 years, and worked 16 years for the state of Illinois. Retired to Beverly Hills, FL in 1988. He belongs to the American Legion, Midwest Chapter 41st Division, and the Loyal Order of Moose.

JO E. GLENN, was born Feb. 24, 1925. Was inducted July 14, 1943 and trained at Camp Adair, OR. Was in Co. K, 276th Inf., 70th Div., Co. G, 362nd Inf., 91st Div.

Left for overseas in May 1944. Was assigned to Co. K, 163rd Inf. in July 1944. Transferred to 3rd Bn. Medics 163 in September 1944. Was in the battle for Biak Island, made the landing at Zamboanga and Jolo Island and the battle at Davo. Was wounded at Zamboanga.

Left for home from Nagoya, Japan on Dec. 24, 1945. Was awarded the Bronze Star, Purple Heart, and Combat Medics Badge. Discharged at Ft. Logan, CO on Jan. 16, 1946 with the rank T/4.

Married to Jean and has five children and 11 grandchildren. He is retired and presently post commander of Post 76 American Legion, Concordia, KS.

DONALD D. GOODWIN, was born June 12, 1919 near Blanchester, OH where he grew up on a farm. Graduated from high school in 1937 and inducted into Army on Oct. 20, 1941 at Ft. Thomas, KY. He received basic training at Camp Wolters, TX.

Joined the 41st at Ft. Dix, NJ on March 1, 1942. Was assigned to Co. H, 162nd Inf. Arrived in Melbourne, Australia on April 10, 1942. He saw combat in New Guinea in the Salamaua Campaign in 1943, Hollandia and Biak in 1944. Was hospitalized after Biak Campaign and never rejoined unit.

Arrived back in States April 1945 and discharged as a staff sergeant on July 14, 1945. He received the Combat Infantry Badge, Asiatic-Pacific Theater Ribbon with one Bronze Star, American Defense Service Medal, and Good Conduct Ribbon.

Married Mary Alice Bailey on Nov. 7, 1947. They have two sons and six grandchildren. He retired as vice-president of First National Bank, Blanchester, OH in 1981. He is a life member of the American Legion and VFW and member of the Rotary Club, Jr. OUAM Lodge, and the Second Creek United Methodist Church.

LYNN J. GORDON (FLASH), was born Aug. 11, 1918 in Marysville, CA. Graduated from high school in June 1936. Inducted into Army on June 17, 1941. Trained at Camp Roberts, CA. Was sent to Ft. Lewis, WA in September 1941 where he was assigned to Co. G, 162nd Inf. as a bugler and mortar gunner. Served remainder of tour of duty with G Co.

Made landings at Nassau Bay, Hollandia, and Biak in New Guinea and Zamboanga in the Philippines, where he was wounded and sent home. Was discharged from Ft. Lewis, WA on June 18, 1945 with the rank private first class.

Spent 30 years with the U.S. Post Office and retired as supervisor in August 1980. He is happily married and lives in Placerville, CA.

He is past national president of 41st Infantry Division Association and member of DAV Association and the American Legion.

ROBERT T. GORES SR., was born Nov. 10, 1919 in Brooksville, FL. Entered the service Oct. 14, 1943. Served with 162nd Regt., Co. B., 8th Bn., 41st Div. Stationed at Ft. McClellan, AL and Maryland. He served in the South Pacific as rifleman.

Went overseas June 15, 1944; landed on Guam July 20, 1944; and was 1500 miles from Hiroshima when the atomic bomb was dropped.

Discharged with the rank of corporal. He received the World War II Victory Medal, Overseas Medal, and Good Conduct Medal.

Married to Lillian on June 29, 1959 and they had four children. Robert was general painter and decorator until he passed away on April 2, 1990. He belonged to the American Legion and DAV.

GENE GRAVES, was born May 15, 1925 in DeWitt, AR. Entered the service Dec. 11, 1944 and served with L Co., 163rd Regt., 41st Div. Stationed overseas at Zamboanga. Was discharged with the rank of corporal.

Married to Elnora Bullock on Aug. 30, 1952 and has five children (Kenneth, Suellen, Nancy, Patricia and Debbie) and four grandchildren. He is a retired farmer, a widower, and lives in DeWitt, AR.

PERCY T. GRAY, was born Dec. 30, 1918 in Plains, MT. Entered the service Oct. 9, 1941. Sent to Ft. Lewis, WA; then Camp Roberts, CA for seven weeks basic training; back to Ft. Lewis; then off to Australia; New Guinea; Netherlands; East Indies; and the Philippines. Participated in operations on Palawan and Philippine Islands. Served with 186th Inf., HQ Co., 3rd Bn., 41st Div.

Discharged Aug. 18, 1945 with the rank sergeant. He received the Bronze Star Medal.

Married Margie (a buddy's sister) in 1948. They have two sons, one daughter, and four grandchildren. He is a retired builder and enjoying life in Independence, KY.

CHARLES F. GREEN, was born July 7, 1913 in Portland, OR. Was a Field Artillery Reservist and called to active duty in July 1942.

Was sent overseas to Australia in December 1942. He joined the 167th FA Bn., C Btry. in May 1942 at Crystal Creek near Townsville, Queensland, where the 167th was training as a Horse Park Artillery Battalion.

He spent his remaining active service with the 41st Div. He served with the 167th, which had been motorized, at Aitape, Wakde, and Biak, the 218th and Divarty at Zamboanga and completed his active duty with Divarty on occupational duty at Hiro.

Was discharged with the rank of captain in June 1946. He and his wife Reba have two children, Charles Jr. and Ann. He is still active as a petroleum geologist and lives in Santa Barbara, CA.

RAY E. GREEN, was born Jan. 17, 1917 in Hot Springs, AR. Entered the service Oct. 6, 1941. Assigned to Co. F, 163rd Inf., 41st Div. Stationed at Ft. Lewis, WA and overseas.

Fought from Australia to the Philippines. Made Biak Beachhead. Discharged with the rank staff sergeant and received the Combat Infantry Badge with two Oak Leaf Clusters.

Married Doris Blackmon in 1946. They have two daughters, Marla and Sandra, and two granddaughters, Aimee and Jaime. He is a retired chef.

BRASHER K. GREGG, was born Oct. 31, 1916. Entered the service Nov. 13, 1941. Assigned to F Co., 186th Inf., 41st Div. Basic training at Camp Wheeler, GA; Ft. Lewis, WA; then overseas to Australia and New Guinea.

Discharged Dec. 27, 1944 with the rank private first class.

Married Ruth Kennedy and has two daughters, Brenda and Jennifer, two grandsons, and one granddaughter. He worked 41 years with Textile and retired in 1981.

BERNARD G. GREINER, was born Nov. 29, 1917 in Stillwater, OK and raised in Vinita, OK. Joined the Army on June 10, 1942. Stationed at Ft. Sill, OK; Camp Clairborne, LA; Ft. Belvoir, VA; Camp Edwards, MA; and Ft. Devins, MA.

Joined 41st Div., 162nd Regt. in New Guinea, then back to Australia and reassigned to 163rd Inf., 1st Bn. In March 1944 made two landings and joined division at Biak Island, to Mindoro, Philippine Island and made landing at Zamboanga and Sulu Jolo Island.

Visited at Hiroshima on Oct. 6, 1945. Landed in Ft. Lewis, WA Dec. 19, 1945 and was discharged April 10, 1946. He received the Bronze Star with Oak Leaf Cluster, Purple Heart, and Combat Infantry Badge.

Joined the 45th Inf. Div. in May 1949. Called to active duty for Korea in August 1950. Back to the States and discharged in 1952. Retired from Oklahoma National Guard in 1962. Retired from U.S. Post Office in 1977. He is a member of 41st Division Infantry Association and American Legion.

WILFRED E. GUNDERSON, was born Jan. 6, 1914 in Portland, OR. Was raised in NW Washington. Inducted April 23, 1941 at Ft. Lewis, WA. Served in 116th Medics, 41st Inf. Div. 1941-1944 in States, Australia (Camp Seymour and Rockhampton) in Papua New Guinea, and Biak Island.

Formed valued lifelong friendships with several who came to know the Lord while in military service and with fellow-Christians in Australia.

Returned to the States in October 1944. Discharged from Ft. Lewis with the rank of technical sergeant.

He remained single and lives with his sister Vivian and shared in the care of their parents until their deaths in 1962 and 1972. Graduated from college in Bellingham, WA and from the University of Washington in Seattle with M.L.S. and Ed.D. Was a public school teacher, librarian, and administrator for 33 years; is a volunteer pastor of community church for 12 years; authored elementary science textbook, periodical articles, and assisted his sister Vivian in several writing projects.

His travels include Australia, New Zealand, Europe, and Israel.

ROBERT J. GWALTNEY, was born Oct. 27, 1922 in Harlem, MT. Joined the Montana National Guard May 6, 1940. Served with Co. M, 163rd Regt., 41st Div. Stationed at Camp Murray, Ft. Lewis, WA; New Guinea and Australia.

Discharged Oct. 8, 1945 with the rank of sergeant. He received the Bronze Star, Combat Infantry Badge, and Presidential Unit Citation.

Married to Betty in 1944 and has two children, Nicki and Bob III. Retired in 1974 after career with DOD (Navy). He is enjoying retirement in Bremerton, WA.

KENNETH E. GWIN, was born March 20, 1920 in Cokeville, WY. Enlisted Sept. 9, 1940 with A Co., 116th Combat Engrs., Camp Murray, Ft. Lewis, WA. Joined D Co., 116th Engrs. and sent to Washington State, they became A Co., 116th. Took part in the Hunter Ligget Maneuver. Departed for the South Pacific March 19, 1942. Combat experience began at Port Moresby on June 23, 1943. Did various kinds of construction on bridges and road, lots of time under combat conditions. He disarmed booby traps, land mines, sea mines etc. Was also assigned to a tank unit at Zamboanga and Jolo. They restored water supplies at Zamboanga and Jolo that was bombed out by the Air Force.

Shipped home from Jolo for discharge on June 17, 1945 at Ft. Douglas, UT.

Lost his wife Helen after 40 years of marriage in 1982. Also lost a son Jimmy when he was 16 years old due to a heart condition. He has another son Ken Jr. and a daughter Susan. He retired eight years ago and has made several trips to Australia in that time. He is enjoying life.

OLIVER CLAYTON HAGEN, was born Dec. 7, 1923 in Richland County, ND where he grew up on a farm and graduated from Colfax High School. He entered the Army in June 1943 at Ft. Snelling, MN.

He trained and was assigned at several locations, Camp Tacoa, GA; Camp Haan; Camp Irwin; Ft. Ord; Camp Stoneman, CA; Camp Howze, Camp Fannin, TX; and Ft. Meade, MD. He joined the 41st Div., 146th FA Service on Mindoro, Philippine Islands in February 1945.

He participated in initial landings at Zamboanga and Jolo. Left the 41st in January 1946 after it was disbanded at Kure, Japan and joined the 32nd Div. on the Island of Kyushu. Was discharged as a technical sergeant at Ft. Lewis, WA in July 1946.

Married Dawna (Roy) on Feb. 14, 1948. They have two daughters, Vikki in Woodbridge, VA and Stacey in Los Angeles, CA. He spent 32 years in the Federal Civil Service, 24 and a half years with the Bureau of Indian Affairs and 7 and a half years with the National Park Service. He retired Dec. 31, 1978 from the Washington, DC office as chief, Division of Contracting and Property Management. He is a member of the Elks, VFW, American Legion, NPS-E&AA, AARP, and NARFE.

BILLY S. HALE, was born in Hunt County, TX on Feb. 21, 1919. Entered the service Nov. 5, 1941. Assigned to 41st in February 1942. Member of Co. K, 186th Regt., stationed in Australia and New Guinea.

His memorable experience was the battle on Biak when Sgt. McGill was hit by shrapnel and died later that night. The same shell got Billy but his wounds were superficial.

Discharged with the rank of private first class on June 29, 1945 from Ft. Sam Houston, TX. His awards and decorations include: American Defense Service Medal, Purple Heart, Asiatic Pacific Campaign Medal with two bronze stars, and the Combat Infantry Badge.

Married to Dorothy Guillory in 1949. He has three sons, two daughters, and 12 grandchildren. He retired in 1979 after 30 years with E Systems, Garland, TX.

CHESTER J. HALKA SR., entered the service May 20, 1943 inspite of a farm deferment. Trained at Camp Wheeler, GA. Assigned to Co. B of the 186th Inf. Regt. at Rockhamptom, Australia. From Australia he was sent to New Guinea attached to the 542nd Amphibious Engineers. Operating LVT-Buffalo.

His memorable experience was while delivering blood plasma etc. to field hospitals in Biak, he learned of wounded GIs from the 162nd Inf. He and another person, under fire, picked and loaded wounded GIs and took them to the field hospital. They refused a citation at the time but now, if possible would like to receive it.

Participated in battles in Hollandia, Biak, New Guinea, Palawan, and Mindanao, Philippines. After combat was stationed at Honshu, Japan.

Discharged Jan. 13, 1946 with the rank of sergeant. He received the Asiatic-Pacific Theater Ribbon, Philippine Liberation Ribbon, Good Conduct Medal, Bronze Arrowhead, and the Victory Medal.

Married to Elsie with two children and five grandchildren. He presently operates a 2,000 acre tree nursery with his son Chester Jr.

WAYNE S. HALSTEAD, was born Nov. 1, 1918 in Kansas City, MO. Entered the service July 10, 1944, took infantry training at Camp Wolters, TX. Served with Co. G, 186th Regt. Joined the 41st on Mindoro, Feb. 25, 1945. Made the invasion of Palawan and was also at Balbzc, Pandanan, Zamboanga, then Japan.

He still has nightmares about watching his best friend, Bob Garoutte, trying to stuff his intestines back in his stomach after his belly was ripped open by .50 caliber machine gun bullets. He will never forget the look of horror on Bob's face.

Discharged Jan. 30, 1945 at Ft. Levenworth, KS with the rank of private first class. He received the Combat Infantry Badge, Bronze Star, Purple Heart, World War II Victory Medal, Soldiers Medal with Star and Arrowhead, Army of Occupation Medal with Japan Clasp, Asiatic-Pacific Campaign Medal with Bronze Arrowhead and Bronze Star, Philippine Liberation Ribbon with star and the Good Conduct Medal.

He is now a semi-retired painter foreman after having run paint crews for various contractors in Kansas City and in the county for 42 years.

Married to Helen whom he met in 1938. They have four kids, five grandkids and two (soon to be three) great-grandkids. He belongs to the VFW Post 8615 and American Legion Post #496. He is a life-time member of International Brotherhood of Painters and Allied Trades (Painters Union) and the National Rifle Association.

FRED HAMMERLE, was born Sept. 2, 1916 in Brooklyn, NY. Served with 116th Medical Bn., stationed at Ft. Lewis, WA and overseas.

Made landings in New Guinea, Hollandia, Biak, Mindanao, Zamboanga, and Jolo. Returned to the States September 1945 and was discharged a week later at Ft. MacArthur.

He has four children and 10 grandchildren. He is retired and lives in Sun City, AZ.

JAMES G. HAMMOND, was born Jan. 13, 1918. Raised on a farm in St. Clair County, MO. Graduated from Weaubleau High School in 1937. Inducted into the Army on Sept. 25, 1941. Took basic training at Camp Roberts, CA.

Joined I Co., 163rd, 41st Div. at Ft. Lewis, WA in December 1941. Served the entire war with I Co., 163rd in Australia, New Guinea, Biak, and in the Philippines at Zamboanga, Holo, and Davao.

Was discharged at Jefferson Barracks, St. Louis, MO on Oct. 5, 1945. He achieved the rank of sergeant.

He retired from General Motors Assembly Division in November 1978 after 32 1/2 years. He is a life member of VFW. He is enjoying life one day at a time in Independence, MO.

CARL W. HANKS, was born Aug. 21, 1926 in Hillsdale, IN. Drafted Sept. 28, 1944. Training at Camp Wolters, TX with the 53rd Inf. Training Bn.

Went to Zamboanga, Philippines in March 1945. Combat Team, H Co., 162nd Regt., 41st Inf. Div. Was in Victor 4 & 5 Operation on Mindanao Island.

Discharged from Deshon General Hospital, Butler, PA on April 6, 1946 with the rank of private first class. He received the Combat Infantry Badge and Bronze Star Medal.

Married Mary Craig on Nov. 26, 1946. They have two children, Craig and Carole, and three grandsons. Carl is a retired mail carrier.

CHRISTIAN A. HANSEN, was born Dec. 25, 1920 near Sidney, MT. Graduated from high school in 1938. Joined the Montana National Guard 163rd Inf. Regt. in March 1939. Called to active duty Sept. 16, 1940. Trained at Ft. Lewis, WA with Co. A of the 163rd Inf. Served in Australia, New Guinea, and the Philippines. Received a battlefield commission on Biak, Was transferred to Co. B, 162nd Inf., later transferred to Co. F, 162nd Inf. Wounded at Sanananda, New Guinea. Received white phosphorus burns on Basilan Island near Zamboanga, Philippines.

Returned to the States in September 1945. Remained in the Organized Reserve Corp. Assumed command of Co. A, 163rd Inf. Montana National Guard in December 1947. Remained with the Montana Army National Guard both in military and civilian capacity until retirement in 1980 as a lieutenant colonel. He received the Purple Heart Medal, Bronze Star with Oak Cluster, and the Combat Infantry Badge.

Married Marjorie in January 1946. Has four children, Karen (a teacher in Houston, TX), Carl (former combat photographer in Vietnam), Allen (a graduate of the U.S. Naval Academy, now a commander in the U.S. Naval Reserve and the Registrar of the Massachusetts Maritime Academy), Elizabeth (home health aide in Vermont), and four grandchildren.

EUGENE G. HANSEN (GENE), was born June 9, 1920 in Upland, NE. Joined Btry. B, 218th FA, Oregon National Guard in September 1940 at Ft. Lewis, WA. Played on the 1941 41st Div. football team; transferred to Btry. C, 218th FA; to Melbourne, Australia in April 1942.

Fought with Aussies in cutting Komiatum track in New Guinea, forcing Japs to give up Mt. Tambu. Was involved in landings at Hollandia, Wakde Island, and Zamboanga, Philippine Island.

Discharged as first sergeant on July 10, 1945. Attended Oregon State University, graduated in 1949 in business; has lived in Corvallis, OR since Aug. 15, 1945. Married Helen Epley on Dec. 18, 1945. They have three sons: Bob in Salem, OR; Eric in Washougal, WA; Gary, Seattle; and daughter Karen Oldfield, Tigard, OR.

A career life insurance agent for 43 years, his hobby is managing the American Legion Baseball team. He chaired the 1990 American Legion World Series, hosted by Corvallis, OR.

CLIFFORD L. HANSON, was born June 17, 1920 in St. Anthony, ID. Joined the service Sept. 9, 1940. Served with 116 Med. Co. D, stationed at Ft. Lewis, WA and the South Pacific.

Discharged August 1945 with the rank of sergeant, back in the National Guard to the rank of first sergeant. He received the Silver Star.

Married and has four children and six grandchildren. He retired in 1985 and lives in Idaho Falls, ID

RAYMOND RODNEY HASBROOK, was born May 19, 1914 in Dickinson County, IA. He graduated from Superior High School in 1932. His occupation was farming until the draft board called him from Jackson, MN. He was inducted at Ft. Snelling, MN on July 10, 1941. He had basic training at Camp Roberts, CA, then to Ft. Lewis, WA with the 41st Div., 167th FA for six months.

He boarded the *Queen Elizabeth* in Spring of 1942. Landed in Sidney, Australia where he went by train to Melbourne, Australia. He served in Australia, New Guinea, and the Philippines. While in the service he was involved in the training of pack horses to carry supplies. He was discharged at Jefferson Barracks, St. Louis, MO on June 10, 1945 with the rank of T/5 corporal and with many honors. After being discharged he had a session with malaria.

On June 14, 1947 he married Irma McMullen and they lived in Estherville, IA. He took more training in mechanics and worked at Thomas Motors Garage, then at Mobile Oil Company where he delivered LP gas in rural areas. Before retiring he worked as maintenance custodian for Esterville Public schools. He retired in 1976.

He is a typical senior citizen, having done his duties in various organizations. At present he is trying to maintain his health and learn the mysteries of Medicare.

CHARLES W. HASH, was born May 26, 1910 in Billings, MT. He attended school in Billings where he met and subsequently married Alma Heisler on July 4, 1931. He joined H Co., 163rd Inf. Regt. on March 13, 1930. Was inducted into federal service on Sept. 16, 1940, and his unit moved to Ft. Lewis, WA for training.

During WWII he served with the 41st Inf. Div. in Australia at Sanananda and Hollandia, New Guinea and at Biak, Schouten Islands.

He is a graduate of military schools that include: The Battalion Officer's Course and Glider School at Ft. Benning, GA; The Command and Staff College, Ft. Leavenworth, KS; The U.S. Army War College, Carlisle Barracks, PA; and the Surface to Air Missile School, Ft. Bliss, TX.

Post WWII duty assignments include: 6th Inf. Div., Ft. Ord, CA; HQ I Corps, U.S. Army, Korea; MAAG Indo-China, Saigon, Vietnam; HQ 6th U.S. Army, San Francisco, CA; 32nd Missile Brigade, Germany; and U.S. Army School, Europe, Oberammergau, Germany.

He retired at Ft. Bliss, TX on Jan. 31, 1965 with the rank of colonel. His awards include: the Silver Star, Bronze Star with Oak Leaf Cluster, Purple Heart, U.S. Presidential Unit Citation, Vietnamese Presidential Citation, Combat Infantry Badge, and the Glider Badge.

He and wife Alma reside in McMinnville, OR. They have one son Richard, three grandchildren (Jerold, Judy, and Sue Ann), and two great-grandchildren (Aaron and Joseph).

JAMES A. HAUFF, was born July 5, 1915 in Chicago, IL. Entered the service in September 1941; served with K Co., 186th and C Co. 163rd; stationed at Ft. Lewis, WA and overseas.

Was commissioned a second lieutenant May 3, 1945 at Zamboanga, Philippine Islands. Released from active duty Dec. 18, 1945. He received the Bronze Star Medal, four Bronze Battle Stars, and one Bronze Arrowhead.

Married since Jan. 19, 1946, he has three children and five grandchildren. He is retired and lives in Chicago, IL.

DON W. HAWES, was born Feb. 24, 1915 in Donnybrook, ND, but lived near Berthoff until he was

13 and family moved to Washington, then to Oregon. He entered the Army on March 5, 1941 at Ft. Lewis, WA. Assigned to Co. C, 116th Medical Regt. of the 41st Div.

On April 22, 1942 he was shipped to Melbourne, Australia. After a short training period went to New Guinea, Lae, Salamaua, Finchhaven, Hollandia, Biak, Mindoro and the Philippines.

One day at Mindoro, one of the junior officer said to him, "Hawes, how would you like to take a furlough back to the States?" At first he didn't believe it, but he was selected to go. While waiting for transportation, they assigned him to a LST supply ship and made two landings, Palawan and Zamboanga. They received word that their boat was over at Leyte and they were going to fly them there. On the way to Leyte the most frightful thing happened. When they were over the mountains, the airplane's engines began to sputter and they had to make a forced landing and no airstrip. The engine didn't quit but they were losing altitude. The crew saw a boat off the coast, so they landed in the ocean and were picked up by the PT boat. All survived, but what an experience!

He was given a 45 day furlough and during that time the war ended in Europe so he didn't have to go back overseas. He was discharged Aug. 26, 1945. He received the American Defense Medal, Asiatic-Pacific Service Medal, Philippine Liberation Medal with one Bronze Star and the Good Conduct Medal.

He married on Aug. 8, 1953 to a ready made family. Marjorie had a son George and a daughter Karen by a former marriage. George now has three sons and Karen is still at home.

Worked as a mechanic for nearly 28 years in a heavy equipment shop and retired in 1978. He now repairs lawn mowers and garden tillers in a little shop at his home. His hobby is old cars and he has a 1930 Ford Model A tudor sedan and a 1935 Ford V-8 touring sedan. He is a member of the Model A Ford Club, Early Ford V-8 Club, VFW, and the Masonic Lodge.

STEPHEN A. HAYWOOD, was born April 23, 1916 in Idaho. Lived on a ranch until drafted into the Army. Inducted at Salt Lake City, UT and sent to Ft. Lewis, WA for basic training. Placed with the 218th FA Bn. H, 41st Div.

Went overseas on March 4, 1941 on the USS *Uraguay* with stops at Bora Bora, Aukland, and New Zealand. Arrived at Melbourne, Australia after surviving a typhoon in the Tasmain Sea. Traveled by train to Seymour and set up camp in the sheep paddocks of Australia. Later journeyed to Rockhampton where a permanent camp was established.

Battery B was given job of guarding airport in that city. Later, he boarded Dutch freighter *Bontiki* at Gladstone, Australia and headed for New Guinea. Ship was attacked by 105 Japanese planes. There was loss of ships, personnel, and several injured. Arrived in New Guinea on a rainy, stormy night. The stench of death and decay was everywhere. Established a camp on a hill overlooking Oro Bay and was intermittently bombed by Japanese planes. He tried to sleep in the mud and rain.

Co. H changed to 641st TD Bn. Saw action at Aitape, Sarmi Dutch New Guinea, Tnsomonen Island, Biak, Nooemfor, then to Tannomera Bay area to prepare for the Philippines in November.

T/4 Haywood was injured when accidently shot at Sarmi. Sent to 27 General Hospital at Hollandia, then hospital ship *Monteray*, then sent back to the States to Letterman General Hospital, then Baxter General Hospital in Spokane, WA.

After a short furlough, he was sent to Santa Barbara, CA where on May 7, 1945 he was discharged from the Army with a 50% disability.

Married to Gwendolyn and has one daughter and two grandchildren. He became active in construction for several years and finally worked in education for 15 years until his retirement in 1981. He is a happy warrior and spends much of his retirement researching for old Army buddies with much success.

WILLARD A. HEATH (BILL), was born Feb. 15, 1919 in Portland, OR. Raised and educated there and attended the University of Oregon. Was inducted June 7, 1941 and assigned to the 148th FA at Ft. Lewis, WA.

Shipped overseas Nov. 22, 1941 as part of *Pensacola* convoy with the destination of Philippine Islands. Arrived Brisbane, Australia on Dec. 22, 1941 and continued to Darwin where troops disembarked and encamped.

Transferred to Far East Air Force, and Bill proceeded to Java missing ill-fated Timor mission and bombings suffered by 148th FA in Darwin Harbor on Feb. 19, 1942. Escaped during Battle of Java Sea and continued to serve Air Corps. Graduated OCS and was assigned to the 403rd Bomb Sq. in New Guinea. Returning to States in November 1944, he served out the war at Mitchel Field, NY. Was released Dec. 4, 1945.

Worked for United Airlines for 34 years and retired to Boise in 1980 where he lives with his wife Barbara. They have three children and two grandchildren.

CARL J. HEFFELFINGER, was born in Rochester, NY on Aug. 9, 1924. Primary and secondary schooling was accomplished in Buffalo, NY. Inducted into service early 1943. Basic medical training at Camp Robinson, AR, followed by immediate transfer to a pacific voyage on the Klipfontein (Dutch) to Brisbane, Australia. From Ascot, off to Ingham, Queensland and the 167th FABN (pack artillery), where a city boy and horses worked together with mutual distrust. Then a decision that horses and New Guinea might be incompatible caused Carl to become one of the "cowboys" chosen to herd the horses the many miles from Crystal Creek to Townsville.

Participated in combat/occupation of Aitape, Wakde Islands, Biak, Palawan, Zamboanga, and Japan for additional experience, memories, and a love for the ocean.

Departed from Nagoya in December 1945 and was discharged Jan. 12, 1946 with the rank of staff sergeant.

Carl earned a Ph.D in physical chemistry. Married to Lois Arnold in 1950, he has three children, Ann, Sue, and Paul. Carl retired as a research fellow from DuPont in 1985 and still consults for them. During his career he has revisited Australia and Japan. Carl lives by the ocean in Pine Knoll Shores, NC.

RICHARD N. HEIDRICK, was born Aug. 14, 1919 in Edinberg, Scotland. Entered the service June 20, 1941. Basic training at Camp Roberts, CA, Ft. Lewis, WA was assigned to 186th Regt., 3rd Bn., Co. I, 41st Div.

He had many memorable experiences. He will always remember how the guys backed each other all the way.

Discharged with the rank of staff sergeant. He received the Purple Heart, Good Conduct Medal, Combat Infantry Badge, three Bronze Stars, and three Campaign Ribbons.

Married May 12, 1945 to Angie Heidrick at Witchita Falls, TX. Has no children. His hobby is making wood items, fishing, pets, garden and flowers. He is retired and lives in Springfield, MO.

KARL L. HEIMAN, was born May 1, 1924 in Oberdorf, Germany. In 1933 when Hitler came to power, Karl was eight years old. Within a few short years, very methodically, his family was relegated from well-to-do Germans to subhuman outcasts. They lost their homes, businesses, belongings and their human dignity. His father survived Dachau concentration camp and received among his many decorations the Iron Cross. His extended family lost 22 men, women and children during the Holocaust.

Karl fought WWII in the American Army, joining July 22, 1943 and served with Co. C, 163rd Inf., 41st Div. Stationed at Rockhampton, Australia. He participated in battles at Aitape, Toem, Wakde, Biak, Southern Philippines, Zamboanaga, Mindanao, and Jolo. He was among the first of occupation troops in Japan, stationed near Hiroshima.

Discharged with the rank of sergeant, he returned a much decorated combat veteran. Among his awards are the Purple Heart, Bronze Star, Presidential Unit Citation, Combat Infantry Badge, Bronze Arrowheads and numerous campaign and battle ribbons.

He is a retired Sears Roebuck executive. He frequently speaks to audiences, young and old, students and parents, Christian and Jewish congregations, about his experiences and life before, during, and after the Nazi tyranny.

His son Howard, a neonatalogist, is a doctor and major in the U.S. Army and stationed with his family at Ft. Sam Houston, TX. His daughter Elisabeth is a successful business executive and lives with her family in Connecticut. Carl lives in East Meadow, NY.

HENRY N. HEINE, was born Dec. 15, 1919 in Scholls, OR. He enlisted in the 41st Div. in 1940. Trained at "Swamp" Murray near Ft. Lewis, WA. Shortly after Pearl Harbor, they shipped out of San Francisco for Sidney, Australia on the *Queen Elizabeth* (its maiden voyage).

Before the war's end, he had sailed on at least 21 different craft. From Melbourne, they went up the coast to Rockhampton, over the Owen Stanley Range by air, ending up at Buna. After contacting malaria and yellow jaundice, he was flown back to Townsville, Australia to a hospital for several months in a rest camp recovering as a casual.

Next he went to Hollandia, Biak Island, Philippines, and Zamboanga. Rotated back to the States (there were only six people with as many rotation points as he had in the entire 41st Div.) and was near Seattle when the bomb was dropped on Japan.

Separated from the Army in 1945 as a T/3. He received the Bronze Star Medal, American Defense Service Medal, Asiatic-Pacific Service Medal, Good Conduct Medal, and the Philippine Liberation Medal with one Bronze Service Star.

Married for 42 years to Jeanette. He has four grown boys, Gary, Bradley, David, and Kevin. Henry is a retired high school art teacher.

EDGAR S. HEINEMAN, was born Dec. 2, 1917 in Merril, WI. Entered the service Aug. 14, 1942. Assigned to G Co., 163rd Regt., 41st Div.

Participated in action at Biak, Philippine Islands, Mindoro, Zamboanga, Mindanao, Jolo, Tawi Tawi, Bongao, Honshu Island, Japan.

Discharged with the rank of staff sergeant. He received all the usual awards.

Married to Mary. He is retired and lives in Dailey, WV.

DEAN DENNIS HENRY, was born Feb. 13, 1917 in Sheyenne, ND. His memorable experience was serving in the 41st Div. with his buddies.

Discharged with the rank of staff sergeant, he received the Silver Star and two Bronze Stars.

Married Mary Cavan and had four children and two grandchildren. Mary passed away in 1981. In 1983 he married Gladys Williams in Harlowton, MT, where he lived until his death on Feb. 14, 1990. He enjoyed attending the reunions and visiting with his army buddies.

Dean worked as a carpenter and became a building project engineer. He worked on such jobs as the launch system at Kennedy Space Center and the Minute Man Missles installed in Montana.

CLYDE D. HENSLEY, was born July 1, 1918 in Henry County, VA. Drafted Oct. 7, 1941; basic training at Camp Croft, SC; assigned to 34th Div., 135th Inf., Ft. Dix, NJ, then assigned to 41st Div., HQ Co., 2nd Bn. 162nd Inf.

Left Brooklyn, NY on March 3, 1942 for Melbourne, Australia. Participated in the campaigns of Buna Gona, Salamaua, Finchhaven, Hollandia, Biak (where he was wounded), Philippine invasion, Zamboango, then war ended.

Returned to the States and was discharged Oct. 5, 1945 with the rank of staff sergeant. His awards/medals include the Combat Infantry Badge, Purple Heart, Bronze Star, Philippine Liberation Ribbon with one Bronze Star, Philippine Presidential Unit Citation Badge, Asiatic-Pacific with three Bronze Stars, one Arrowhead, American Defense, Good Conduct and Victory Medal.

Retired from National Homes in October 1982. His hobbies are woodworking and gardening. Married to Geneva since March 1946 and has three children and four grandchildren.

RUDOLPH HEPPNER (RUDY), was born April 24, 1918 in Plentywood, MT. Entered the service Sept. 16, 1940, Montana National Guard, M Co., 163rd Inf. Stationed at Ft. Lewis, WA and South Pacific.

His memorable experience was returning home after three and a half years overseas. Discharged June 6, 1945 with the rank of master sergeant. His awards include the Bronze Star, American Defense Service Medal, Asiatic-Pacific Service Medal, Bronze Service Arrowhead, Philippine Liberation Medal and star, and the Combat Infantry Badge.

Married to Arlene in 1942. They have four daughters, one son, seven grandsons, and two granddaughters. Rudy is totally disabled from a stroke in 1981.

SID HERMANSON, was born Oct. 4, 1917 in Oakland, CA. Graduated from high school in 1936. Was selected for the Army Feb. 24, 1941. Stationed at Ft. Lewis, WA, assigned to AT Co. 162.

In Rockhampton, he transferred to Can. Co. 162, as supply sergeant. Saw action in New Guinea, Hollandia, and Biak. Discharged from the Army September 1945 with the rank of staff sergeant. He received the Combat Infantry Badge, Good Conduct Medal, Asiatic-Pacific Campaign and American Defense Service Medal.

Married Elsie in 1947 and has four sons, three daughter-in-laws, and 10 grandchildren. He worked as a carpenter and retired in 1982. Has been able to travel and enjoyed many 41st reunions. He belongs to two mens' clubs and plays two games of cribbage everyday with Elsie.

STANLEY E. HERTENSTEIN, was born March 4, 1926 in St. Marys, OH. Drafted into the Army on Jan. 15, 1945. Received basic training at Camp Robinson, AR, and Ft. Ord, CA. Assigned to Co. G, 162nd Regt.,

41st Inf. Div. at Zamboanga, island of Mindanao, Philippine Islands. Went to Kure-Hiroshima area of Japan with 41st Div. as part of the Occupation Forces.

When 41st Div. was deactivated, he was assigned to a Medium Automotive Maintenance Company in Kobe-Osaka area.

Discharged from Army with the rank of T/5 at Ft. Sheridan, IL in November 1946.

Married Dorothy Nuesmeyer on June 4, 1949. Has three children and eight grandchildren. Retired in 1985, after 40 years service with the Ohio Department of Natural Resources. Lives in New Bremen, OH. He is a charter member of the 41st Infantry Division Association.

ROY M. HESSENFLOW, was born May 18, 1925 in Lawson, MO. Drafted into the Army Aug. 18, 1943. Took basic training at Camp Roberts, CA. Was sent overseas March 7, 1944 to the 41st Inf. Div.

Was assigned to Co. E, 163rd Regt. Made landings at Aitape, Wakde, Hollandia, and Biak Island, New Guinea. Had foot surgery and was sent back to the States Feb. 7, 1945.

Discharged Feb. 24, 1946. He was awarded the Combat Infantry Badge.

Married to Evelyn and has three grown children and five grandchildren. He retired from Remington Arms Ammunition Plant in Independence, MO in 1984 after 33 years of service. He resides in Henrietta, MO.

LAWRENCE A. HILLIG, was born May 29, 1919 in Boyd, MN. Graduated from high school in Dayton, OR. Was member of 41st when it was activated Sept. 16, 1940. Was gun mechanic for Btry. B, 218th FA at Camp Murray, Ft. Lewis, Australia, New Guinea, and Philippines.

Discharged Aug. 15, 1945 and was awarded the Bronze Star.

Larry was painter, building contractor, and retired as paint foreman for Portland General Electric.

He and wife Marge had three children, Sue, Hank, and Nan, and six grandchildren, one deceased. His hobbies were restoring classic cars, bow hunting, fishing, and gardening. He was a member of Auburn Cord Duesenberg Club, and won trophies for distance driving with his '36 Cord Westchester.

Larry survived spinal cancer in 1982, but died of lung cancer Dec. 11, 1989. He asked that memorials be sent to the Oregon Military Museum at Camp Withycomb, the 41st's own museum. Other B-218th families have followed suit when buddies have died.

ARNOLD W. HOEHN, was born Sept. 21, 1919 in Lyndon Station, WI. Graduated from Mauston, WI High School in 1937. Was drafted into the service Nov. 4, 1941; stationed at Macon, GA and Ft. Lewis, WA; assigned to HQ Co., 2nd Bn., 186th Inf. with 41st Inf. Div. and served with infantry division in Australia, New Guinea, Philippines, Zamboanga, and Palawan.

Was discharged Oct. 4, 1945 at Camp McCoy, WI as a technical sergeant.

He married Tess on Nov. 11, 1945. They have one son, daughter-in-law, and two grandchildren. In 1945 with his father, he started Hoehn Lumber and Construction Company in Lyndon Station, WI. He is still active in his business with his wife and son.

He is a charter member of the Maurice C. Havey VFW Post 5970 and member of Harold B. Larkin American Legion 187.

ERNEST P. HOFF, was born May 25, 1921 in San Francisco. Raised in Vancouver, WA. Graduated Vancouver High School in 1940. Many of the VHS football team were in the Oregon National Guard, assigned to G Co., 162nd Inf. and they answered the federal call on Sept. 16, 1940.

The next year was spent at Camp Murray, WA and the 2nd Bn., 162nd Inf., performed the original guard duty around Boeing Aircraft plant and related manufacturers in Seattle. He shipped out to Melbourne, Australia in 1942, and thence to Rockhampton.

Injury caused him to leave the 41st Div. prior to New Guinea, and he was subsequently assigned to OCS in Brisbane, teaching unarmed combat. Returned to Vancouver, WA for assignment to Barnes General Hospital in March 1945 and was separated Sept. 2, 1945. Highest rank was sergeant.

He spent the next five years at the University of Washington, including ROTC. Graduated in 1950 with second lieutenant's bars and returned to Army for Korea. Retired from Army in 1966 as a captain.

He taught school until retirement in 1984. Married Dorothy in 1946 and produced two boys and one girl. He is involved with Boy Scouts, Special Olympics, Masonry, American Legion, and currently coaches the Edmonds High School divers.

AL HOFFMEISTER, was born Armistice Day, 1921 in Oregon City, OR. Entered the service Dec. 1, 1939. Served with HQ 1st Bn., 186th Inf., Ft. Lewis, Australia, New Guinea, and Biak.

His memorable experiences include: Pearl Harbor Day; patrol of NW U.S. Coast; pet python snake at Rockhampton; Mokmer Strip, Biak Island in June 1944; and the two weeks spent in Mt. Morgan, Queensland.

Wounded in action, he received the Purple Heart, Bronze Star, Good Conduct, and American Defense Medal. Discharged at Ft. Lewis, WA in July 1945 with the rank of staff sergeant.

Married to Ethel since 1948. They have a son, daughter, and two grandchildren. Al is a retired wildlife biologist. He is back on the farm in Gresham, OR and raises a few sheep.

MARK D. HOLCOMB, was born June 18, 1907 in Centerview, MO. Entered the service Sept. 16, 1940. Served CO 163rd Med. Det., CO Co. B, 116th Med. Regt.

His citation reads in part, "for meritorious achievement in connection with military operations against the enemy on Mindanao, Philippine Islands, from March 10 to 27, 1945. Major Holcomb's medical section achieved outstanding results in the quick recovery of wounded soldiers. The superior treatment of the wounded under most difficult circumstances saved many men's lives. The superior organizing of his men and their technical skill due to previous training he had given them, gave the troops great confidence in their medical personnel and was a define boost to morale. Major Holcomb's work is a great credit to himself and the Medical Corps."

He received the Legion of Merit for conspicuous service during the Sanananda, New Guinea operations. He also received a Presidential Unit Citation, Letter of Commendation from Gen. Douglas MacArthur, and a combat Medical Badge. Dr. Holcomb graduated from the University of Louisville School of Medicine in 1936.

Married to Kara in 1932. She has passed away. They had four children and six grandchildren. After 50 years he retired from medical practice. He resides in Enid, OK and does gardening, and aqua aerobics (three times weekly).

C.A. HOLMGREN (BUD), was born June 5, 1923 in Portland, OR. He entered the service in February 1943. Took basic training at Camp Roberts, CA then shipped to 41st Div. in Rockhampton as replacement in July 1943. Was put in I Co., 163rd Regt.

Made five beach landings: Aitape, Wakde, Niroemoar, Biak, and Zamboanga. He made sergeant on Biak.

About 20 minutes on the beach on March 10, 1945 at Zamboanga, Bud heard Japs talking. He stopped his squad and went forward a few steps. He was charged by 10 screaming Japs. As the first Jap lunged at him, Bud put his M1 in the chest of the Nip and fired. Another took his place and Bud kept firing. As he fired his eighth round, Bud was run through by a Jap bayonet. With the help of the men behind him, this was the only Jap to reach him. That Jap was beat to death by his men.

After 14 months in the hospital, Bud was discharged in November 1945 with the rank of sergeant. He received the Purple Heart, Infantry Badge, Bronze Star, and all the usual medals/awards.

Married to Ruby, he has one son, three daughters, and eight grandchildren. They live on the beach in Oregon.

WILLIAM L. HOLT, was born Jan. 19, 1917 at Mt. Judea, AR where he grew up and graduated from high school. He was drafted in the Army on June 27, 1941 at Camp Robinson, Little Rock, AR. Sent to Camp Roberts, CA for basic training.

He joined HQ Btry., 41st Div. Artillery, at that time 55th FA Brigade HQ, on Oct. 12, 1941. Served with this unit through the Zamboanga Campaign. He was sitting at Leyte waiting on a ship home when the "bomb" was dropped on Nagasaka and the Japanese surrendered.

Returned to the States where he was released from active duty on Sept. 13, 1945. Married to Shirley on Thanksgiving Day 1945. They have one son William Charles. Graduated from college in 1950. He was called to active duty during the Korean War and served nine months before being released from active duty.

He joined Phillips Petroleum Company as a chemical engineer. Retired in 1982 and now spends his time playing golf, swimming, and keeping up the homestead. He is a member of the DAV, American Legion and other engineering societies.

JOHN F. HOOD, was born July 21, 1919 in Breckenridge, TX. Took basic in Camp Robinson, AR and went to the Pacific in 1944 to New Guinea. Was assigned to Co. I, 162nd Regt., 41st Div on Mindoro, Philippine Island. Was appointed rocket launcher (Bazooka) shooter until end of war. Made the initial landing at Zamboanga, Mindanao, Philippines.

Was discharged at Ft. Sam Huston, TX in April 1946 as a staff sergeant. He received the Combat Infantry Badge.

Married Bernice on Feb. 15, 1941. Daughter Brenda was born in 1944 and John Jr. was born in 1949.

EARL S. HOOKER, was born Jan. 6, 1912 in Great Falls, MT. Sworn into Co. I, 163rd Inf., Montana National Guard in June 1930. Inducted into federal service September 1940 as first sergeant. Commissioned second lieutenant October 1940 at Camp Murray, WA.

Promoted first lieutenant October 1941 and transferred to Anti-Tank Co. Completed Rifle and Heavy Weapons Course at Ft. Benning in February 1942. Was shipped with unit from Ft. Lewis to Seymour, Australia on *Queen Elizabeth* in April 1942. Reached Port Moresby by December 1942. As ranking infantry officer, was in command of 900 troops aboard *Van Houtz* around to Oro Bay. Promoted to captain in February 1943 and back to Australia to take command of Cannon Company. Transferred to L Co. on return to New Guinea. Participated in beach landings at Toem, Wakde-Sarmi and Biak.

Was awarded the Combat Infantry Badge, Bronze Star, Distinguished Unit Citation with three Battle Stars. Discharged at Ft. Douglas on Oct. 21, 1945.

He raised eight children. Presently is retired and weekend prospector. He is member of VFW, SAR, and GPA.

EARL M. HOOSLINE, was born April 18, 1915 in Schaefer, ND. Joined the service in November 1941. Served with HQ and HQ, 186th Inf. Regt., 41st Div. Was in the Wire Section the complete times except for a couple of trips to the hospital with malaria.

He remembers the great times in Australia (where he played on the 186th baseball team) and the not so great times in New Guinea, Biak, and the Philippines.

Discharged with the rank T/5, he received all the usual awards/medals.

Married to Mabel Pladson on June 1, 1968. She had five children. Her husband passed away in 1966 and was also in WWII. Earl is a retired B.N. Railroad conductor and lives in Bloomington, MN.

PAUL WALLER HOYE, was born March 3, 1912 in McHenry, MD. Inducted July 24, 1942. Served with 116th Combat Engrs., 41st Div. Trained at Ft. Belvoir, VA. Served entire war with 116 at Biak, Dutch New Guinea, Philippines and Zamboanaga.

Discharged at Ft. Meade, MD on Aug. 13, 1945, with a rank of technical sergeant. He received the Bronze Star and the Legion of Merit.

Until his retirement in 1968, he managed the American Legion Post 71, Proctor Kildow, the Oakland Country Club and is now a distributor of paper and glass products to restaurants and clubs where he lives in Oakland, MD.

He is married to Kay and has two children and two grandchildren. He is a member of the American Legion Post 71 for 46 years, VFW, Moose, and Elks.

JACK HOYLE, was born April 17, 1921 in Washington, DC. Entered the service May 1, 1942 and served with Signal Company, stationed at Rockhampton, Dobadura, and Hollandia.

His memorable experiences include the Samboga River flood at Dobadura and landing at Hollandia. Left the 41st and served from February 1944 with 83rd Signal Bn. and landed at Leyte with the 24th Div.

Discharged Sept. 15, 1945 with the rank of staff sergeant. He received all the usual medals/awards.

Married to Elenore and they have two sons and one daughter. He retired in 1989 after 40 years in the Aerospace industry.

CURTIS M. HUCK, was born July 8, 1923 in Iron Mountain, MI. He graduated from high school in 1942. Was inducted into the Army Feb. 8, 1943 and trained at Camp Roberts, CA. He left for Australia (without a furlough) and joined the 41st Inf. Div. in Rockhampton. Was assigned to HQ Co., 3rd Bn., 163rd Inf. in July 1943.

He participated in assault landings at Aitape, Toem-Wakde, and moved on to Biak. Made landings at Zamboanga and Jolo and went to Hiroshima.

Discharged Jan. 12, 1946 at Camp McCoy, WI. He achieved the rank of corporal and was awarded the Bronze Star.

Married Dorothy in 1946. They have two children, Gary (Vietnam veteran) and Lynda, and three grandchildren. Grandson Marty is in the Air Force and stationed in Spain.

Curtis is retired from Scott Paper Company and resides near Foster City, MI. He is a life member of VFW.

FRED O. HUGGINS, was born June 24, 1924 in Canada near the Montana border. Moved to the U.S. in 1942. Worked for Illinois Central Railroad until drafted in March 1943. He took basic at Camp Roberts, CA. He joined the 41st Div. in Rockhampton, Australia in July 1943

Made landings along North Guinea coast then Biak and on to Philippines. He was wounded March 1945 at Zamboanga and a month later was wounded on Jolo Island. Due to lack of medical supplies and slow evacuation, he lost his leg due to gangrene. He returned to U.S. and was hospitalized in Texas until discharge in February 1946 with the rank private first class. He received four Campaign Stars, Purple Heart with cluster and Bronze Star.

Married Ann in November 1942. They have two sons and a daughter. He and his father operated a grocery store until 1960. He then moved to Boulder, CO. He worked in construction and was superintendent for 24 years, retiring in October 1984. Ann died during surgery July 1982. He married Helen Kaiser in October of 1986 and resides in Boulder, CO.

RICHARD F. HUGHES, was born March 30, 1917 in San Francisco, CA. Was inducted from Oroville,

CA in February 1941. He trained at Ft. Lewis, was assigned to 218th FA, Training Btry., HQ Btry. 218th FA, 205th FA HQ Btry., then to HQ Btry. Div. Arty., 41st Div.

Before war broke out, he went with 218th FA and headed for the Philippines. Troop ship turned back to Frisco just a day or two before Pearl Harbor was bombed.

Was in the battles of Nassau Bay, Salamaua, Hollandia, Biak, and Zamboanga. After Zamboanga invasion, he was sent home on points and discharged at Camp Beale, CA in July 1945.

He says his best experience was getting the hell out alive. His worst experience was Biak.

His family includes, Wife Melba, son Richard, daughter Vicki and three grandsons. He went to work for the California Division of Highways in late 1945 and retired in 1977.

EDWARD J. HULA, was born Dec. 3, 1920 in Columbia Falls, MT. After school, he entered the Civilian Conservation Corps at Glacier National Park, MT (1938-39). On Sept. 9, 1940, he joined the Montana National Guard in Kalispell, MT which was F Co., 163 Inf. Regt. of the 41st Div. He was inducted with the division and served with the same outfit at Camp Murray/Ft. Lewis in Washington state before WWII as a machine gunner. He married Lula Ness while on furlough in July 1941.

He left with the unit for Australia in March 1942, and served with the same unit in the Weapons Platoon until leaving them from Zamboanga, Mindanao, Philippines.

Was discharged under the point system at Ft. Douglas, UT in June 1945. He re-entered the service again in 1955 with B Battery of the 190th FA as gunner and section chief. Left the unit in 1964 and worked as a construction surveyor and later was employed in the aluminum industry until retirement in 1977. There are four children, nine grandchildren and one great-grandchild from this marriage.

His memberships include CCC Alumni, DAV, VFW, 41st/163 Association, RSVP, AARP, MSCA, and NVSC.

CHARLES HUNTLEY, was born Nov. 29, 1917 in Ashland, WI. Inducted into the service Sept. 16, 1940, 41st Signal Co., Ft. Lewis, WA; New Guinea; Australia; and the Philippines.

His memorable experiences include: being strafed in the Philippines and the hospitality of the Australian people.

Discharged with the rank of sergeant. He received the Good Conduct Medal, American Defense Service Medal, American Campaign Medal, Asiatic-Pacific Campaign Medal with one Arrowhead, World War II Victory Medal, and the Philippine Liberation Ribbon with three Bronze Stars.

Married Shirley on Oct. 16, 1948. They have three children. Charles is retired and lives in Portland, OR.

ORA H. HURD, was born July 22, 1917. He entered the service on July 5, 1941. Served with HQ and Service Btry., 167th FA Bn.

Discharged with the rank private first class. Was married to Mildred. Ora passed away on Dec. 19, 1983

FRED JAMES HUTCHENS, was born in the Labelle area, the seventh child of a family nine children. Attended school at Labelle and Rigby. On completion of school, he worked at a CCC camp as a heavy equipment operator for two years.

He was a member of the National Guard, 116th Engrs and was one of the first to be called to active duty at the beginning of WWII.

He spent over five years in the South Pacific and received the Asiatic-Pacific Service Medal and American Defense Medal.

After returning from the war, Fred worked for Roger Brothers Seed Company until their business was moved from Rigby. He then became employed by the city of Rigby (10 months as truck driver, 38 years as public works director). He was a volunteer fireman for 33 years, served as cub master and district commissioner for 25 years and hold the coveted Silver Beaver Award in the Scouting program. He has served as Elders QM president, in Stake Young Mens Organization, chairman of Stake Service and activity comm., 14 years as bishop's counselor under two bishops, five years on the high council.

In 1983 he was honored in the Who's *Who of the West* book. Most recently was sustained as Bishop of the Rigby 5th Ward.

Fred passed away Nov. 30, 1988.

HAROLD F. INGLE, was born April 5, 1920. Raised in Toledo, OH and drafted November 1941. After basic training, they were sent to Ft. Lewis to fill out 41st Div. He served as machine gunner, 2nd Platoon, H Co. 163rd Regt.

In spring of 1942, he sailed to Australia for training near Seymour and later at Rockhampton. Shipped to Port Moresby in December 1942 and flown into combat at Sanananda. Served in combat at Aitape, Toem, Wakde, Serra and Biak.

Was wounded at Zamboanga, returned to serve with H Co. on Jolo. In July 1945, he left for home on points. Liberty ship took 41 days to get to San Francisco. After Labor Day, war ended so was discharged Sept. 10, 1945 from Camp Atterbury, IN with the rank of staff sergeant.

Married to Mildred since September 1945. They have three children. Harold retired in 1986 from the Toledo Post Office.

ROBERT A. IRICK, was born Jan. 6, 1925 at Logan, OH. Inducted July 22, 1944 at Ft. Hayes, Columbus, OH, then to Ft. Benjamin Harrison, IN. Trained at Camp Fannin, TX with Co. K, 162nd Div., 41st Div. 544th Engr., Boat and Shore Regt., 4th Engr. Special Brigade in Japan.

Participated in battles at Leyte, Zamboanga, Mindanao, Philippines and Occupation of Japan.

Discharged June 20, 1946 at Camp Atterbury, IN with the rank of private first class. His awards include:

retired as lieutenant colonel in 1958. His awards include the Bronze Star, Purple Heart with Oak Leaf Cluster, Combat Infantry Badge, Asiatic-Pacific Ribbon with three landings and other pertinent awards.

Married Betty Richardson in February 1948. They have four daughters, one son, and 10 grandchildren. He is retired from insurance and real estate business. He is living on the beach at Manzanita, OR.

ERNEST LAVOIE, was inducted into the Army Sept. 16, 1940. Trained at Camp Murray, WA. Served entire tour of duty with Co. I, 186th Inf. as company clerk, supply sergeant, and squad leader.

He led the 1st Squad to land on Hollandia, New Guinea. Company mission was to capture anti-aircraft guns guarding entrance to bay while remainder of division was to capture airstrip. Next battle was on Biak Island where they spent 60 plus days in fox holes on front line. Also made landings on Palawan, Mindoro, and Zamboanga in the Philippines.

Sergeant Lavoie was discharged June 1945 after three years overseas duty. There was only one original member of company left. He was given seven ribbons and the Bronze Star.

Married in 1945 and had six children and nine grandchildren. He worked for Sherwin-Williams Paint for 27 years and retired in 1981 as branch manager. He enjoys horseshoes, boxing, genealogy and writing. He lives in McMinnville, OR.

JAMES VERNON LEACH, was born May 27, 1917 in Tillamook, OR. Joined the Oregon National Guard March 10, 1936, K-162, 41st Div. Stationed at Camp Murray, Ft. Lewis, WA and overseas at Australia, New Guinea, and the Philippines.

Discharged with the rank of staff sergeant. He received the Purple Heart, Bronze Star, Good Conduct Medal, and all the usual medals/ribbons. Married a Navy nurse, has one daughter, one son, and one grandchild. He retired from the Power Company as a lineman. He is active in the American Legion.

ALVIN E. LENABURG, was born Jan. 7, 1915 in Bessie OK. He graduated from there in 1931. Was drafted Sept. 30, 1941 and went to Camp Wolters, TX for basic training. He joined the 41st Inf. Div. at Ft. Lewis, WA. Served with 186th Inf. in Australia, New Guinea, and Biak where he was wounded and received a Purple Heart on VE-Day June 7, 1944.

He returned to the States in September 1944 and was discharged in May 1945. Married Holly in October 1944. They have three children and six grandchildren. He worked for Union Equity Cooperative Exchange, a large wheat cooperative for 35 years. He retired Feb. 1, 1977. Alvin passed away April 13, 1989.

ROBERT L. LENTZ, was born March 4, 1919 in Hutchinson, KS, where he grew up and attended the Hutchinson schools. He entered the Army July 8, 1941 at Ft. Leavenworth, KS. He went to Camp Roberts, CA for basic training and then to Ft. Lewis, WA for overseas training with Btry. D, 218th FA, and then the 41st Div. Anit-tank. Was on the way to the Philippines when Pearl Harbor was attacked and had to turn around and come back to the States.

Sailed from New York March 4, 1942 and landed in Australia April 10, 1942. Served in New Guinea, northern Solomons and Bismark Archipelago.

Discharged May 30, 1945 with the rank of T/5, with the 98th Chemical Bn. Motorized. His awards were the American Defense Service Ribbon with two Bronze Stars, pre-Pearl Harbor with star, Asiatic-Pacific Ribbon, and the Good Conduct.

Married to Marjorie in 1944 at Rockhampton, Queensland, Australia. They have five children and nine grandchildren. He was employed by the Hutchinson School System for 26 years before retiring. He is a member of the American Legion Post.

RAYMOND G. LEUZE, was born in the western New York State. Inducted into the service on Aug. 13, 1943 in Buffalo, NY and sent to Camp Upton, Long Island for indoctrination. He took his basic training at Camp Wheeler, GA. Upon completion of training, he was sent to Ft. Ord, CA and then to Camp Stoneman.

He departed the USA on Jan. 27, 1944 and landed in Brisbane, Australia. He joined Co. I, 162nd Inf. at Rockhampton. He took part in the Hollandia, Biak and Philippine landings and earned the Purple Heart, Bronze Star, Combat Infantry Badge, two Arrowheads and three Campaign Stars. He took part in the Occupation Force, landing at Kure, Japan on Oct. 20, 1945 and left the company on Dec. 7, 1945 on rotation.

He achieved the rank of T-5. He was discharged at Ft. Dix, NJ on Jan. 14, 1946. He worked for the DuPont Company for 35 years and retired in 1985. He is also very active with the Boy Scouts of America and has achieved many honors in scouting. Has been married 34 years to Janice A. Graw and has a son and a daughter.

ALBERT J. LEVENDUSKY JR., was born July 13, 1925 in Passaic, NJ. Inducted Sept. 16, 1943. Infantry basic training at Ft. McClellan, AL then to Ft. Ord, CA. Was sent to SW Pacific in March 1944 and assigned to H Co., 163rd from April 1944 to June 5, 1944.

Wounded at Toem, Dutch New Guinea on June 5, 1944. From then until September 1945 he was a patient in 10 different Army hospitals overseas and the States.

Discharged with the rank of private. He received the Bronze Star, Purple Heart, Good Conduct Medal, Asiatic-Pacific Medal with two Battle Stars, Combat Infantry Badge, and World War II Victory Medal.

Graduated Fordham University College of Pharmacy in 1949; owned and worked in community pharmacies. Last 17 years employed at VA Hospital, East Orange, NJ retiring as supervisory pharmacist.

Married to Lorraine on Sept. 12, 1954, no children. They reside in Clifton, NJ. He is past national president (1984-1985) of the 41st Infantry Division Association.

JOSEPH S. LIBRIZZI, was born Nov. 13, 1919 in Chicago, IL. Inducted on Oct. 13, 1941, 41st Div., Co. G, 186th Inf. Trained at Camp Roberts, CA. Participated in battles in Central Pacific, New Guinea, Port Moresby, Buna, Lae, Salamaua, Finchhaven, Hollandia, Biak, Zamboanga, Leyte Manila. Stationed at Central Pacific Australia New Guinea.

Discharged on Sept. 11, 1945 with the rank of private first class. His awards include the World War II Medal, Good Conduct, American Defense Medal, Asiatic-Pacific Campaign with four Battle Stars, Bronze Star Medal and Combat Infantry Badge.

Married with three children and five grandchildren. He was overseas 42 months with no R&R and no furlough in four years. Never received furlough money or bonus that was promised for overseas duty. Retired and lives in Oaklawn, IL. He had major heart surgery six years ago.

ALBERT D. LINDEN, was born June 22, 1923 in Seattle, WA. Joined A Co., 116th Med. Bn., 41st Div. at the Old Armory in September 1940. Started out in the platoon of Sgt. Robert B. Logan. Stayed with A Co. until his discharge on June 13, 1945.

He remembers the first days in old Swamp Murray; California maneuvers; the train trip he took from Sidney to Seymour, Australia after he got off the 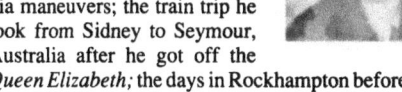 *Queen Elizabeth;* the days in Rockhampton before and after combat in New Guinea.

Married Ingegerd in Sweden in 1956, has one son Eric who works out of Los Angeles and New York as the U.S. Representative for a European manufacturer of clothing. Albert was in his own business from 1962 to 1983 as an independent importer of new European cars. He introduced many of the new models before the dealers got them, at least in the Northwest. Retired, he keeps busy with community work in Seattle.

JEROLD O. LINDENMUTH, was inducted into the service on Feb. 17, 1942 at New Cumberland, PA. After clothing and shots, he was put on a train and taken to Camp Roberts, CA. He trained there for 13 weeks and then was shipped to Australia where he joined the 41st Div. They made stops at Suva, Fiji Island and Auckland, New Zealand on the way.

Was in the 162nd Cannon Co. and took jungle training in Rockhampton, Queensland, Australia. Next to New Guinea and southern Philippines. They spent three Christmas's in Australia. The Nips called them the 41st "Butchers." They had 105 Howe and also served as infantrymen. Discharged at Ft. Dix, NJ with the rank of staff sergeant. Married over 45 years and worked as truck driver for 40 years. He is commander of VFW Post 129 in Pottsville, PA.

CALVIN LOCHER, was born Sept. 30, 1915 in Auburn, CA. He graduated from college in 1939. Drafted Feb. 24, 1941 and was assigned to Co. K,

511

162nd Inf. at Ft. Lewis, WA. Transferred to Service Company, 162nd in 1943.

Left U.S. on March 4, 1942 from New York for Melbourne, Australia via Panama Canal. Served with 41st in Australia, New Guinea, Netherlands East Indies and Philippines. Left Davao, Philippine Islands June 30, 1945 for one year rotation to U.S. Was on a ship that broke down five times between Leyte and Oahu. Finished trip on a liberty ship. Arrived in States three days after Hiroshima was bombed. Good timing! Highest grade achieved was T/4.

Married to Roberta two days before he was drafted, they celebrated their 50th wedding anniversary on Feb. 22, 1991. They have four children and six grandchildren. He worked for the state of California 32 years in six different agencies and a variety of management positions. He retired Dec. 1, 1977.

DONALD F. LOCKE, was born Sept. 25, 1916 in Jordan, MT. His childhood was spent in Missouri and California. Drafted February 1941 and went to basic training at Ft. Lewis, WA.

Shipped out to Australis in 1942 and later to New Guinea. Made three major landings at Salanavas, Hollandia, and Biak. They also made many small landings. He served with the 41st Inf. Div., 205th FA Btry. C as a staff sergeant.

Married to Lela who was a teacher. They have no children. He worked in the automobile, mobile home and RV business in Milton-Freewater, OR and Wallowa Valley, OR. Retired in 1979, he lives in Enterprise, OR and enjoys fishing and traveling.

ARNOLD S. LOMAX, was born in 1916 in Bushnell, IL. Was inducted into the Army Oct. 21, 1941. Went to Camp Roberts, CA for basic training. A week after the Pearl Harbor attack, he was sent to Ft. Lewis, WA and assigned to Co. D, 162nd Inf. Regt.

Left the U.S. on March 4, 1942 and arrived in Melbourne, Australia on April 9, 1942. Was stationed in Rockhampton, Queensland before service in New Guinea where he participated in landings at Douglas Harbor, Hollandia and Biak. In the Philippines he was in assault beachhead operations at Zamboanga, Cotabato, and Davao. Was assigned to HQ Co., 1st Bn. 162.

After the Japanese surrender, he was returned to the U.S. where he was discharged from Ft. Sheridan on Oct. 12, 1945. He received the Combat Infantry Badge, Bronze Star as well as Battle Stars and Arrowheads for the Service Ribbons.

He married Maxine in 1952 and they have two children, Tracey and Stuart. He received his bachelor's and master's degrees from Western Illinois University. He worked for the U.S. Postal Service for 38 years, retiring in 1979. He lives in Bushnell, IL.

ROBERT R. LONZWAY, was born March 14, 1922 in Baker, OR. He graduated from Baker High School in 1940. Entered the National Guard in November 1938, mobilized Sept. 16, 1940 into 41st Inf. Div. with F-186 and E-163 at Ft. Lewis, WA. First overseas assignment was at Camp Seymour, Australia. He also served in Buna, Gona, and Ora Bay in New Guinea.

Received the Purple Heart, Combat Infantry Badge, and Bronze Star. Upon returning to the States in March 1945, he was assigned to Port Command at New Orleans, LA. Was released from active duty February 1946 with the rank of first lieutenant.

Married to Arnetta Turner of North Powder. They have two children and one granddaughter. He graduated from Oregon State University in 1949 and worked for the U.S. Soil Conservation Service for 35 years. Retired in 1977 at Oregon City. He plays golf, bowls, and travels.

JESUS E. LOPEZ, was born Jan. 30, 1922 in El Paso, TX. Entered the service June 24, 1944, assigned to Co. C, 163rd Inf. Regt., 41st Div. At Mindanao and made landings in Zamboanga and Jolo Island. Was in Hiro, Japan in 1946 in Army of Occupation near Hiroshima.

Discharged March 10, 1946 with the rank of private first class. He received the Asiatic-Pacific Campaign Medal, World War II Victory Medal, Good Conduct Medal, Philippine Liberation Ribbon with two Bronze Stars, and Bronze Service Arrowhead.

Married to Mary Lou for 49 years. They have two children and two grandchildren. He retired in 1987. They reside in Coachella, CA and enjoy gardening and taking it easy.

KELLY A. LOUVIER, was born Dec. 22, 1917 in Jeanerette, LA. Joined the service Nov. 13, 1941 and was assigned to K Co., 186th Inf., 41st Div., stationed at Ft. Lewis, WA. Was a rifleman.

Overseas, he participated in Papua New Guinea Battle and a couple of others. Discharged July 28, 1945 with the rank of private first class. He received the Asiatic-Pacific Campaign Medal with two Bronze Stars, American Defense Service Medal, Rifleman 745, and Combat Infantryman Badge 5.

Married Lerlene Johnson on June 21, 1946. They have three children, Jimmy, Joe, and Laura, and five grandchildren, Jaci, Jesse, Jonathan, Joseph, and Daniel. Kelly retired from Lone Star Steel Company after 30 years. Wife Lerlene retired after 37 years of teaching school. Both he and his wife enjoy seeing the "Ole Cobbers" and their wives at the annual Mid-South Chapter meetings.

ALAN LOWELL ZURFLUEH, (for business reasons, surname was dropped after college and he has since been known as Alan Lowell), was born June 24, 1920 in Tillamook, OR. Inducted Sept. 16, 1940 with National Guard Unit K Co., 162nd Inf. Regt. Departed U.S. for Australia on March 4, 1942.

Went into combat in New Guinea as 60mm mortar section leader and fought in all major battles with K Co. including Buna, Salamaua, Hollandia, and Biak. His battalion commander in New Guinea was Maj. Archibald Roosevelt, son of President Teddy Roosevelt. He was a feisty and fearless leader like his father. Alan remembers once when they were under rather heavy Japanese mountain gun fire, Maj. Roosevelt walked among them as they were frantically digging their fox holes deeper, and jokingly remarked that after the war the men of Co. K shouldn't have any trouble finding jobs as ditch diggers.

Rotated to U.S. Dec. 7, 1944 and was assigned to an infantry training detachment at Ft. Sill, OK. Separated from the service July 3, 1945 as staff sergeant.

Earned a bachelor's degree from University of Oregon where he met his wife Betty. He became a widower in 1987. After a career as administrative hearing officer with the California State Department of Motor Vehicles, he retired in 1980. Serves on the Board of Directors of Widowed Persons Association of California, Elderhostel Advisory Board at California State University, Sacramento and as a volunteer guide at Sacramento Zoological Gardens.

RICHARD LUND, was born Dec. 15, 1923 in Seattle, WA. Entered the service Feb. 22, 1943, assigned to 163rd, 2nd Bn., HQ Co. Anti-tank, stationed in Australia, New Guinea, Biak, Philippines and Japan.

Discharged with the rank of platoon sergeant and went to Alaska. He married Katherine and they have a daughter, a son, and four grandchildren. He retired in July 1981 and lives in Camano Island, WA.

HAROLD J. LYON, was born Nov. 13, 1918 in Madison, NE. Graduated from high school with class of 1936. At the age of 17 he traveled to NW Montana to work for four years as farmer and logger. The next four years he was engaged in the manufacture of combat aircraft in Southern California. Was called to service July 1944 and trained at Camp Wolter, TX.

Overseas duty found him at Zamboanga, Mindanao, where he joined K Co., 162nd, 41st Inf. Div., actively engaged in combat May 3 to June 18, 1945. A shell fragment wound sent him to a hospital on the island of Leyte. Those six weeks included the operation known as "Balut Island to Calinan" with K Co. 162 attached to the 24th Div.

Returned to active duty at Zamboanga with K Co. a few days before they set sail for Japan aboard the USS *Darke* (APA-159) on Sept. 19, 1945. After nine months with the Army of Occupation in Japan and 13 days of fog, the harbor at Seattle was a pleasant sight.

He received honorable discharge with the rank of sergeant on Aug. 17, 1946. He received the Combat Infantry Badge and Purple Heart.

Married to Betty and they have four children and seven grandchildren. He is a member of the VFW and American Legion.

JAMES B. LYONS, was born April 23, 1924 at Stoneburg, TX. He attended school and grew up on a farm in the same ares. Entered the service May 25, 1943 at Camp Wolters, TX. Received basic training at Camp Campbell, KY and advanced infantry training at Ft. Sill, OK. Joined the 41st Div., A Co., 162nd Inf. Regt. at Rockhampton, Australia in January 1944 and remained with A Co. 162 through Finchhaven, Hollandia, New Guinea, Biak, Zamboanga, and Davao, Philippines to Kure, Japan.

Left Nagoya, Japan Dec. 18, 1945 for the USA. He received the Asiatic-Pacific Campaign Medal with two Bronze Stars and one Bronze Arrowhead, Philip-

Grammer School (8 years) Ascension of our Lord School.

Drafted into Army On Oct. 13, 1941. Entered the service Oct. 13, 1941 in Chicago, IL. Transported to Camp McCoy, WI for immunization shots, left by train to enter Co. A, 77th Inf. Training Bn. in Camp Roberts, CA. Left Camp Roberts shortly after attack on Pearl Harbor and joined the 41st Inf. Div., F Co., 163rd Div.

Briefly hospitalized after Aitape New Guinea Campaign. Rejoined F Co. on Biak Island, went to the Philippines for landings on Zamboanga, and Tawi Tawi Islands. The war ended after President Truman dropped the "Nice One."

Returned to the States, went to work for the Cook County Highway Sheriff's Police for eight years, then worked as an automobile investigator (12 years) for the state of Illinois. Now holds a Chief's Star as a private detective for American Detective Enterprises, Inc.

Was married (divorced) has three daughters, Sheryn (married to Tony), Judy (married to Jon), Laurie (has boyfriend Rob), and lost a son Ronie in motorcycle accident. He has four grandchildren, Micheal, Jason, Erika, and Stefanie. He has a sister Genevieve and lost a brother to cancer.

Married the second time over 20 years ago to Hazel and is living happily ever after. Retired and lives in Evanston, IL.

CLAIRE F. KONO, was born March 17, 1917 in Rockham, SD. Assigned to 41st MP Detachment, Ft. Lewis, WA and overseas Rockhampton, Australia.

Was wounded on Hollandia landing and received the Purple Heart. Discharged with the rank of private first class.

Married to Vivian, they celebrated their 45th anniversary in May 1991. They have two daughters, two sons, seven grandsons and one granddaughter. He farms 600 acres near Faulkton, SD.

JOHN F. KORIENEK, was born April 9, 1925 in Chicago, IL. Entered the service May 18, 1943, truck driver with Service Battery, 218th FA, Rockhampton, Australia.

His memorable experience was visiting Hiroshima, Japan after the Atomic Bomb was dropped.

Discharged Jan. 10, 1946 with the rank of private. He received the Asiatic-Pacific with two Bronze Battle Stars, Philippine Liberation with one Bronze Star, World War II Victory Medal, Good Conduct Medal, and four Overseas Bars.

Married June 21, 1947 and has two children and three (soon to be four) grandchildren. He is still working for city of Chicago Water Department as a machinist. He plans to retired in July 1993.

NICK S. KOURBELAS, was born Jan. 6, 1919 in Green River, WY. Enlisted September 1940 as private in 41st Div. MP Co. Stationed at Camp Murray, WA for training. Departed Dec. 5, 1941 on USS *Etolin* from San Francisco, returned Dec. 9, 1941. Departed San Franciso on *Queen Elizabeth* in March 1942 for Australia.

Transferred to 41st Div. Hqs. on July 13, 1942, was sent to Rockhampton and reached rank of T/3. Next to Port Moresby Feb. 4, 1943 by Aussie flying boat and on to Division Headquarters near Dobodura, New Guinea. Was evacuated April 1943 by air to Port Moresby Field Hospital for a two weeks bout with jaundice and malaria.

Received appointment to OCS, Brisbane June 1943, graduated Sept. 28, 1943 as second lieutenant and assigned to Oro Bay, New Guinea. There until Dec. 12, 1944 when rotated back to U.S. on small Dutch freighter. After seeing Chili, Peru, went through Panama Canal to New York arriving Jan. 27, 1945. After R&R at Santa Barbara was assigned to San Francisco Port of Embarkation as trans officer. Discharged as first lieutenant on October 1945 at Ft. Beale, CA.

Following the service, he attended University of Southern California and Utah. Received B.S. degree in aero engineer and private pilot's license. Worked as engineer for Consolidated Vultee Aircraft (now General Dynamics) until retirement in 1983. Resides with his wife Mary in El Cajon, CA. They have two children and two grandchildren. He is a member of the American Legion Post 282 and does a lot of traveling. His hobby is helping neighbor rebuild old airplanes.

GEORGE L. KRAEMER, was born March 3, 1917 in Bellevue, KY. He entered the service Sept. 8, 1941, 41st Div., Ft. Lewis, WA. Discharged Sept. 12, 1945 with the rank of T/4.

Married and has two sons Dave and Dan, and four grandchildren. His wife Edna passed away. George retired in April 1979 and still lives in Bellevue, KY.

ROSS C. KREAGER, was born March 11, 1916 in Newton, IA. Lived on farm until drafted on Oct. 28, 1941. From Ft. Des Moines went to Camp Wolters, TX for basic training. After war began was sent to the West Coast to join the 41st Div. On Feb. 24, 1942, he was assigned to Co. D-186 and served the entire war with this unit in Australia, New Guinea, Biak, and the Philippines.

On July 29, 1945 he left the Philippines on the point system and arrived back in the States on August 14, and was discharged on August 22 with the rank of sergeant.

He will never forget the living conditions in New Guinea or the combat experiences in the Philippines where he was awarded the Purple Heart.

Married to Virginia in 1946. They have three children, Charles, Gwen, Kenton, and seven grandchildren. They owned and operated a farm near Adel, IA where they now reside.

GORDON F. KRIEG, was born May 13, 1917 in Halder, WI. He entered the service Nov. 26, 1941. Stationed at Ft. Sheridan, IL, New Guinea and Australia.

He served with the 186th Inf., 41st Div. as a rifleman. Gordon spent 32 months overseas and participated in the campaigns of Papua and New Guinea.

Discharged at Pine Camp, NY on Oct. 2, 1945 with the rank private first class. His medals include the Asiatic-Pacific Theater Ribbon, American Defense Ribbon, one Bronze Star, and the Combat Infantry Badge.

Gordon married to Mary Barton on Aug. 22, 1964. Worked for Krieg Bros. Terazzo in Lafayette, LA and later for Iowa Terazzo in Cedar Rapids, IA. He retired in 1983 and passed away Oct. 16, 1989. His widow lives in Cedar Rapids, IA.

ERNEST J. KRIEGER, was born May 4, 1917 in Forest Grove, OR. He grew up in a farming community of Verboort, worked on a farm, then at logging, then became a mechanic. Inducted Sept 16, 1940. Assigned to I Co., 186th Inf., 41st Div. He trained in Forest Grove National Guard and Camp Murray, Ft. Lewis, WA.

Was among the first ones to go overseas on April 22, 1942, remaining there for 39 months. He participated in battles at Papuan, New Guinea, and southern Philippines.

Discharged July 20, 1945 at Ft. Lewis, WA with the rank technical sergeant IV. His medals include the American Defense Service Medal, Purple Heart, Good Conduct Medal, Asiatic-Pacific Service Medal, Philippine Liberation Medal with one Bronze Silver Star.

Married Phyllis Hulsman on Sept. 18, 1945. They have four children and five grandchildren. They owned and operated Ernie's Tavern for almost 25 years and he was employed with General Tire and Rubber Company in Portland, OR. He is now retired.

HENRY KROPP, was born Nov. 17, 1919 in Great Falls, MT. Entered the service Oct. 10, 1941. Assigned to I Co., 186th Inf., 41st Div. Stationed in the South Pacific, Australia, and New Guinea. Was wounded at Humboldt Bay.

Discharged with the rank of staff sergeant. He received the Purple Heart, two Bronze Stars, and the Asiatic-Pacific Campaign.

Married in 1945 to Ann Schloser. They have two sons and five grandchildren. His wife passed away in 1982. He is retired from farming but still runs the Barrel Cafe and Lounge in Great Falls, MT.

FRANK R. KUNZE, was born Oct. 29, 1919 in Twin Falls, ID. Was raised in Boardman, OR. Drafted in the Army from Portland, OR on Oct. 10, 1941. He was taking basic infantry training in Camp Roberts, CA when the war broke out.

His battalion was shipped to Ft. Lewis, WA on December 7 to the 41st Div. He was put in E Co. 186th for about six weeks, then transferred to C Co., 116th

509

Engrs. Stayed with them until the war ended. Went to Australia, New Guinea and the Philippine Islands. Participated in the campaigns at Buna, Gona, Sanananda and the invasions of Hollandia and Biak Island. Was in the U.S. on furlough when the invasion of the Philippines was started; however, he participated in the mop up operations around Zamboanga and was there when the war ended.

Discharged with the rank of staff sergeant, was leader of the 3rd Platoon. After discharge, he worked in construction and eventually became a general engineering contractor. Married to Eleanor in 1947. They live in Temecula, CA.

EUGENE C. LADOWSKI, was born in Sobieski, WI on Sept. 21, 1919. Drafted into the Army Oct. 11, 1941 at Ft. Sheridan, IL. Stationed briefly at Camp Roberts in California and Ft. Lewis in Washington.

Left the U.S. on March 19, 1942 for Camp Seymour, Sydney, Australia. He served in Rockhampton and Gladstone until Dec. 21, 1942. Arrived Christmas Day at Port Moresby, New Guinea. Moved to the front lines on Jan. 1, 1943 at Sanananda. Was wounded in action at Biak Island, Dutch New Guinea on June 29, 1944.

Discharged with the rank of sergeant on June 20, 1945. He received the Purple Heart and the Bronze Star.

Married Eleanor Piechota on June 22, 1946. They have four daughters, Sandra, Catherine, Patricia, and Ellen. Worked at Northwest Engineering as a welder until his retirement in September 1984. Currently living in Green Bay, WI. He is the proud grandfather of Angela and Benjamin Lindbo and Michael Dobkoski.

WILLIAM G. LAMBERT, was born Feb. 2, 1920 in Langford, SD. Called into federal service with the Oregon National Guard on Sept. 16, 1940. Was a member of Co. D, 186th Inf., 41st Div. Served at Ft. Lewis, WA until his unit was sent overseas in early 1942.

Served in Australia and New Guinea to the rank of staff sergeant. Was assigned to Officer Candidate's School in Brisbane in 1943. Commissioned that year and assigned to the 32nd Div. Served there with Co. M, 126th Inf. in New Guinea, Morotai and Leyte. Participated in Saidor and Leyte Campaigns.

Rotated back to the States in 1945. Served in the Army Reserve until his retirement in 1962 as a major. His awards include the Combat Infantry Badge and Bronze Star Medal.

A well-known journalist and consultant, he has worked for Newspapers, TV, and for *Time* magazine and *Life* magazine, to name a few. Was recipient of numerous awards including the Pulitzer and George Polk Awards.

Married to Jean Kenway Mead on July 7, 1945. They have two daughters, Kathryn Woolen and Heather Oxberry. He lives in Villanova, PA.

LOUIS LANDESMAN, was born April 26, 1917 in New York. Raised in Spotswood, NJ and attended high school in South River.

Moved to San Francisco in 1937 and drafted into the Army on Feb. 27, 1941. Was assigned to the 146th FA and then to the 167th FA Bn. in the 41st Inf. Div. at Ft. Lewis, WA.

Arrived in Australia in March of 1942 and trained in areas from Seymour to Townsville.

Participated in landings and campaigns, Aitape, Hollandia, Sarmi Wakde, and Biak Island in and near New Guinea. He achieved the rank of corporal.

Rotated to the States and transferred to the Air Force, stationed in Sarasota, FL when the war ended. Was discharged Sept. 4, 1945.

He was employed at I. Magnin in San Francisco for 30 years and retired at age 70. Married to Eleanor for 32 happy years and has a wonderful family. He is proud to have served in the famed 41st Div.

ANTON J. LANGE, was born June 18, 1917 on a farm near Westphalia, TX. He attended school at the Westphalia School. Inducted into the Army on Nov. 13, 1941, at Ft. Sill, OK. Assigned to Co. A-137, IRTC. Basic training at Camp Wolters, Mineral Wells, TX. As he completed basic, Japan bombed Pearl Harbor. As a result he was sent to Ft. Lewis, WA, where he was assigned to the 41st Div., Co. D-186.

After several stops in Australia for overseas and landing training, he went to Port Moresby, New Guinea. After flying over the Owen Stanley Range, he eventually landed on Biak Island. He helped secure Biak and several other islands. Was put on rotation to return to the States. Upon arriving in the States he became ill with malaria just as he received orders to go to Italy.

Was sent to Camp J.T. Robinson in Arkansas to recuperate and was discharged on Sept. 24, 1945 as a private first class. Duty as NCO, a rifleman, and #3 gunner on the 81mm mortar in the New Guinea Campaign.

Anton received the Combat Infantryman Badge, four Service Bars, American Defense Medal, Asiatic-Pacific Medal with two Bronze Stars and numerous campaign and battle ribbons.

He married Amanda Wilde of Ballinger, TX on Jan. 22, 1946. They have five children and five grandchildren. Since their marriage they have farmed and ranched at Norton, TX. Now retired, they continue to attend St. Mary's Star of Sea Catholic Church in Ballinger. He is a member of the Norton Lions Club and is involved in community affairs.

EDGAR LANGSTON, was born Sept. 2, 1921 on Fish Creek, Harlowton, MT. Attended Langston grade school and Harlowton High School.

Joined the National Guard D Co., 163rd Inf. in 1936. He was inducted Sept. 16, 1940 at Harlowton, MT. Received basic training at Ft. Lewis, WA.

In March 1942 sailed from San Francisco on the *Queen Elizabeth* and headed for Australia and jungle training. Next to New Guinea where he spent most of the remaining time, winding up in Biak.

Was attached to the Air Force at Ft. Lawton, WA. After several months, he was discharged at Ft. Douglas, UT on Sept. 16, 1945 with the rank of sergeant.

He and his wife Shirley have three children. He served two terms as state representative (1957-1959) and 20 years as county commissioner. He is a member of Masons, Shriners, American Legion, VFW, and the hospital board. He also farmed/ranched and is now retired.

WALTER E. LARSON, was born July 15, 1909 in Billings, MT. He entered the service March 2, 1942. Assigned to C Co., 2nd Bn., HQ 163rd Inf., 41st Div.

After two years service in U.S., was sent overseas in February 1944 to New Guinea, Philippines, and Japan. His memorable experience was joining the very fine fellows of the 163rd Inf. as a replacement and getting ambushed on a patrol. Made landings at Aitape, Toem, Wakde, Biak, Zamboanga, Tawi Tawi, Jolo and occupied Hiro, Japan. Was at Hiroshima.

Discharged with the rank of first lieutenant. He received the Combat Infantry Badge, American Theater, Asiatic-Pacific with two Bronze Stars and Arrowhead, Philippine Liberation with one Bronze Star, and the World War II Victory Medal.

He has a wife Margaret, sons, Walter Jr. and Ben. Walter was a farmer and had a business, Overhead Door Company. He is now retired.

ROBERT C. LASALLE, was born Feb. 18, 1920 at Battle Creek, MI. Raised in Portland, OR and attended Benson High. Joined Oregon National Guard, Co. K, 162nd Inf., Tillakook, OR on Sept. 12, 1940. Inducted into federal service with 41st Div. on Sept. 15, 1940.

Served entire war with 41st Div., Co. K, 162nd Inf. Commissioned second lieutenant Jan. 24, 1944, Co. B, 186th Inf. Participated in campaigns of New Guinea, Biak, Philippines, and Army Occupation Kaidachie, Honshu, Japan, and Hiroshima.

Was discharged Jan. 25, 1946 at Ft. Lewis, WA, U.S. Army Reserve captain until he joined Oregon National Guard as CO, Co. E, 162nd Inf., on Sept. 23, 1949. Retired April 30, 1963 as lieutenant colonel.

Married Janet on July 15, 1941. They have three sons, five grandchildren, and four great-grandchildren. He retired from Union Oil Company in 1982 and now resides in Tigard, OR.

THOMAS W. LATTANZI, was born in Manila, Philippine Islands on March 17, 1920. His father was with the 31st Inf. Regt. in Vladivostok where he married his mother in 1919 during the Russian Revolution during WWI.

He enlisted in the 186th Inf. Regt. in August 1937 and was inducted in September 1940. He served in Service Company, Regt. HQ Co., HQ Co. 3rd Bn., L Co. and the regimental band.

Wounded twice on Biak Island, first on June 6, 1944 while serving as 3rd Bn. company commander. After two months of hospitalization, he was again wounded on Aug. 10, 1944 while serving as battalion communication officer.

Transferred to the active reserve in January 1946. After 31 years of active Army and Reserve duty, he

Zamboanga, Philippines. Landed at Parang and went to Ft. Picket and ended up at Davao. Later was in the occupation of Japan at Kure Naval Base.

Discharged Nov. 22, 1946 with the rank of staff sergeant. He received the Asiatic-Pacific Theater Campaign Ribbon with one Bronze Star, Good Conduct Medal, Occupation Ribbon, three Overseas Service Bars, the Japan Victory Ribbon, and the Philippine Liberation Ribbon with one Bronze Star.

Married to Marjorie in 1944. They have two children, Marie and Brent. He was in the retail business and a investor. Retired in 1972, he resides in Austin, TX.

EDWARD H. KAPELLE, was born April 8, 1925 in Baldwin, KS. Entered the service July 1943. Assigned to A Co., 163rd and Service Co., 163rd at Camp Roberts.

Went overseas to Australia, Biak, Wakde to Hiroshima, Japan. Discharged with the rank of sergeant T/4. He received the Good Conduct Medal.

Married to Ann in February 1947. He has four children and seven grandchildren. He sold his wholesale auto parts store and now is enjoying retirement in Topeka, KS.

MITCHELL B. KASPEREK, was born June 5, 1917 in Buffalo, NY. Entered the service Aug. 29, 1941. Assigned to Co. C, 163rd at Ft. Lewis, WA, Sanananda, Wakde, Toem, and Biak Island.

Discharged with the rank of technical sergeant Sept. 8, 1945. He received the American Defense Service Ribbon, Asiatic-Pacific Theater Ribbon with three Bronze Battle Stars, five Overseas Service Bars, one Service Stripe, Good Conduct Medal, Purple Heart Medal, Combat Infantry Badge, and first Bronze Oak Leaf Cluster.

Married to Irene since May 29, 1947. He is retired and lives in Deerfield, MI.

PHILIP S. KEARNEY, was born May 9, 1920 in Truckee, CA. Before enlisting in the Army just after Pearl Harbor, he had completed teacher training in California. Entered the service Dec. 31, 1941, served with 41st Signal Co., stationed at Ft. Lewis.

His memorable experience happened on Aitape when Kearney and two of his buddies set off to examine some of the abandoned Japanese encampments

Discharged with the rank private first class. He received the Purple Heart.

After his discharge in 1945, he took a job teaching science in high school in Orland, CA. He found out that he was not cut out for teaching. He returned to college and took up electrical engineering at the University of California at Berkely.

In 1948, he got a job as an assistant electrical engineer for a firm in San Francisco, where he met and married Eileen Ormsby, a woman from Mason City, IA. They bought a home in Marin County just north of San Francisco, where their four children were born. In 1961, he was hired as an associate electrical engineer by the state of California, Department of Water Resources, in Sacramento, CA where they now reside. He retired in 1983 as a senior electrical engineer in the electrical design section. His major engineering accomplishment was the design of the remote control system and automation of the California Aqueduct which delivers northern California water to the southern part of the state.

ELDON A. KEEBAUGH, was born Aug. 19, 1914 in Milwaukee, OR. Was in the National Guard, 162nd Inf. Medics. Inducted into 41st Div. on Sept. 16, 1940, stationed at Ft. Lewis, WA.

Was sent to South Pacific on March 4, 1942, served in northern Australia training with Aussie troops, then to Papuan, New Guinea. He had charge of Medics during battle of Roosevelt Ridge. He contracted malaria, later typhus and spent nine months in Port Moresby, Townsville and Melbourne Hospitals.

Sent to U.S. on Feb. 8, 1944 to hospital in Santa Barbara, then to Ft. Lewis, WA hospital. Demobilized Dec. 15, 1944 with the rank T/4.

Married Genneth Meese Garrick on July 9, 1948. He has two step-children, Daniel Garrick and Sharron Shattuck, six grandchildren, and four great-grandchildren.

He worked for National Hospital in charge of First Aide Station covering Lumber Mills in Molalla area. Later had charge of drug room for Multnomah County Edgefield Manor. Was custodian foreman for Beaverton, OR School District at the same time he managed Park West Apartments in Portland, OR.

He retired in 1973. Has travelled to Old Mexico, Catalina Island, Canada, San Juan Islands, Denmark, Germany, Austria, Egypt, Israel, and Hawaii.

ARTHUR B. KELLER, was born in Buckeystown, MD on Jan. 25, 1923. He enlisted July 1, 1941 at Buffalo, NY and was sent to Ft. Monmouth Signal Training Center for cryptography training and was assigned to the 41st Signal Co., Ft. Lewis, WA where he was known as "the Kid."

He remembers landings at Morobe, Finchhaven, Hollandia, and Biak. In November 1944, the little Dutch freighter pulled under the San Francisco bridge, a pilot came aboard and then left, the ship was unable to dock because of a strike at San Francisco Harbor. It took three more days to Seattle where a band played as the soldiers boarded GT trucks for Ft. Lawton which provided a great welcome with hot showers, necessary after three weeks on the crowded freighter; a new uniform with all stripes etc. sewn on by German POWs; good food and a cot, the only one except for a hospital bed in Australia. He was discharged Sept. 27, 1945.

Married Margaret Page on April 7, 1945. They have three children and four grandchildren.

He retired as Alaska manager of an industrial insulation firm and lives with his wife near Rochester, WA.

WARREN S. KENT (BILL), was born Oct. 28, 1919 in Portland, OR. Entered the service Sept. 16, 1940. Joined Btry. E, 218th FA. Served with 218th A Btry. in Australia and New Guinea. He was in 4th General Hospital, Melbourne for five months in 1943. Than assigned to HQ Base Section, Australia, Engine Depot, Townsville, Australia. Participated in battle at Roosevelt Ridge and Salamaua Campaign. Discharged Nov. 10, 1945 with the rank of sergeant.

Home on furlough for the month of December in 1944. Was married to Inez on Dec. 31, 1944. They have one daughter and one grandson. He was a sand and gravel manager and retired in October 1984. He is very active in Eagles Lodge (past president five times). He lives in Bend, OR.

ARTHUR J. KESSENICH, was born Feb. 15, 1918 in Waunakee, WI. He joined the Wisconsin Army National Guard in October 1939. Mobilized for active duty in October 1940 with Co. G, 128th Inf., 32nd Inf. Div., Stationed at Camp Beauregard, Livingston, LA; Ft. Devens, MA; Ft. Ord, CA; Camp Woodside and Cable, Australia.

Participated in the Buna Campaign, then was sent to Officer Candidate School at Camp Columbia, Brisbane. Assigned as second lieutenant to HQ Co., 3rd Bn., 162nd Inf., 41st Inf. Div. in October 1943. Later transferred to Hqs. Co., 162nd Inf. and assigned as personnel officer and adjutant. Participated in New Guinea and Philippine campaigns.

Was awarded the Legion of Merit, Bronze Star with two clusters, Meritorious Service Medal, Good Conduct Medal, American Defense and Campaign World War II, South Pacific with three Battle Stars and Beachhead, World War II Victory, Reserve Force Medal with two 10 year devices, Reserve Components, Achievement Medal, Combat Infantryman Badge, U.S. and Philippine Presidential Citations.

Following WWII he rejoined the Wisconsin National Guard 32nd Inf. Div. Served with the division and the adjuant general's office as a full time federal employee until retirement from the military in February 1978 as colonel, infantry.

Married Dora Kuehn and has nine children.

FREDERIC T. KIELSGARD, was born Oct 15, 1915 in Fairfax, VA. He graduated Oakton High School in 1932 and was drafted May 7, 1941. Basic training with the 28th Div., 116th Inf., Ft. Meade, MD. Was among first contingent to leave division for overseas duty March 3, 1942. Joined the 41st Div., 162nd Inf. at Ft. Dix, NJ as a casual.

Sailed through Panama Canal to West Coast then to Brisbane, Austraila. Continued to Melbourne and Camp Seymour. After four months of training, they moved to Rockhampton for further training. Sailed to Oro Bay, North Guinea, marched up coast to Buna/Gona and set up defensive positions, then began the drive for Salamau, then back to Rockhampton to re-equip. Next was D-Day at Hollandia. Next landing was at Biak, NEI. Several months later they sailed for Mindora, PI to prepare for D-Day at Zamboanga, PI. Left Zambo August 1945.

Was discharged Sept. 11, 1945 from Ft. Bragg, NC, after 42 months overseas duty, with the rank of staff sergeant. Received the Bronze Star (Biak).

Married Alice in 1951 and has one daughter Sandra Lee and one grandson. Frederic has been a real estate broker since 1954 and is now semi-retired. His most memorable experience was as a machine gunner on Biak while under constant attack—all night strafing by Jap planes. He is a member of Lions Club, VFW, 41st Divisions Association, Potomac Chapter.

CLAUDE C. KILE, was born July 7, 1917 in Dalton, GA. Entered the service Aug. 18, 1943. Assigned to Co. M. 162nd Inf., 41st Div.

Stationed overseas in Southwest Pacific area. Participated in the battle of Biak and others islands.

507

Discharged with the rank of corporal. He received the Combat Infantry Badge, Pacific Service Medal, three Bronze Stars, the Purple Heart with one Bronze Star.

Married to Ollie Kile and has three sons, one daughter, and eight grandchildren. He is retired in Dalton, GA and enjoys sports and traveling.

FREDERIC L. KING, was born Nov. 6, 1918 in Clinton, MA. Entered the service Jan. 16, 1941. Assigned to 186th Inf. A, B, and E Co.'s

Discharged in 1945 with rank of first lieutenant, 26th Div., retired 1971 with rank lieutenant colonel, 26th Div. He received the Combat Infantry Badge.

Married to Janice Howe in 1941, he has two sons, Richard and Jonathan. He is retired from the U.S. Postal Service, lives in Clinton, MA, and enjoys playing golf etc. He is a member of the Shriners and Elks.

RAYMOND E. KING, was born Oct. 5, 1918 in Vandalia, IL. Entered the service June 27, 1942. Assigned to 41st Signal Co. Stationed at Camp Crowder, MO. Left the States June 27, 1942 on troop ship USS *Hermitage*. Landed in Brisbane, Australia in February 1943 and stationed in Dobodura, New Guinea.

Memorable experience was the two landings in New Guinea, one in Biak, Zamboanga, Mindanao, Philippine Islands, and being division message carrier.

Discharged November 1945 with the rank of corporal. He received two Bronze Stars, one Arrowhead, Asiatic-Pacific Medal, World War II Victory Medal, Philippine Liberation Ribbon, and Good Conduct Medal.

Married to Wanda in 1946. They have three children, Esther, Alan and John, five grandchildren, and one great-grandchild. He was a store owner for over 25 years. Presently retired in Assumption, IL and does a lot of fishing and traveling.

CHARLES H. KISTER, was born March 3, 1925 in York County, PA. He entered the service May 3, 1943. Assigned to 186th Inf. Med. Det.

Participated in action at New Guinea, Hollandia, Biak, Philippines, Palawan, Mindoro, Zamboanga, occupied Japan, Hiroshima.

Discharged Jan. 11, 1946 with the rank of T/5. He received the Good Conduct Medal, Philippine Liberation Ribbon with one Bronze Star, Asiatic-Pacific Campaign Medal with two Bronze Stars and one Bronze Arrowhead, World War II Victory Medal, Bronze Star Medal.

He corresponded with Jean Reeser the entire time of service and met her for the first time Jan. 11, 1946 the day he was discharged. They married Sept. 8, 1946 and have four children, Brenda, Douglas, Rebecca, and Pamela. Also eight grandchildren, Jeffrey, Bradley, Todd, Chad, Matthew, Kristina, Tacey and Grant.

Retired after a lifetime employment in the heating and air conditioning profession. His hobbies are traveling, woodworking, and counted cross stitch.

JOHN F. KLABOE, was born Aug. 30, 1918 in Wolf Point, MT. Raised in Great Falls, MT and graduated from high school and completed Montana State College (Engineering). Drafted Feb. 24, 1941 in Ft. Missoula. Basic training in Ft. Lewis, WA, 81st Brigade Hqs., 41st Recon, staff sergeant supply.

Left from San Francisco to SW Pacific on April 22, 1942, arriving in Seymour, Australia May 14, 1942. Served entire war with 41st Recon. in Austrlia, New Guinea, Philippines, Biak Island. Made number of landings. Returned from Philippines to Finchhaven on Dec. 29, 1944. Arrived in San Francisco Jan. 20, 1945. After a short furlough, he returned to Santa Barbara, CA and had a rest period at the Biltmore Hotel.

Assigned to SCU 4902, MP, Portland AFB, April 10, 1945, provist sergeant, Portland, OR Police Station. Discharged with the rank staff sergeant on Sept. 3, 1945 at Ft. Lewis, WA.

Married Mary Feb. 28, 1945 at the Biltmore Hotel. They have three children and eight grandchildren. They reside in Butte, MT. He was owner of heating, ventilating, engineering firm. He is a life member of DAV, VFW, Elks, American Legion, and Society of Engineers.

WILBUR A. KLEMZ, was born April 7, 1924 in Maple Lake, MN. Entered the service June 7, 1943. Assigned to Btry. C, 146th FA. Stationed at Ft. Snelling, MN; Ft. Leonard Wood, MO; Ft. Ord, CA; Camp Stoneman, CA; Camp Lawton, WA; Camp McCoy, WI and Camp Roberts, CA.

Overseas at Milne Bay, Biak, Philippines, Biak, Zambo, Jollo, Davo, Kure, Japan.

Discharged with the rank T/5. Married to Margaret. They have six sons and 14 grandchildren. He is retired and lives in Brook Park, MN.

ELDON W. KLIEVER, was born Jan. 31, 1920 in Dallas, OR. Entered the service September 1938, National Guard. Called to active duty Sept. 15, 1940. With 3rd Bn., 162nd Anti-tank Section, Co. L, 162nd, USASOS HQ Small Ships. Stationed at Ft. Lewis, WA and overseas at Buna, New Guinea.

His memorable experience was being caught in typhoon off New Guinea on a flat bottom ferry boat. They had a good skipper, no lives lost.

Discharged with the rank master sergeant. He received the Bronze Star, New Guinea Campaign Defense Medal, and the Good Conduct Medal.

Married to Millie since May 1941. They had daughter Diane and son Richard (served in Desert Storm). Millie passed away in 1979 and he remarried to 1980 to Marianne. He is a retired printer and lives in Salem, OR. Presently enjoying his hobbies with camera and woodwork.

ARTHUR C. KLINE, was born Aug. 25, 1918 in Sebring, OH. He graduated from high school in Paintsville, OH. Inducted into the Army Jan. 6, 1942. After basic training at Ft. Leonard Wood, MO, he was assigned to Co. B, 116th Combat Engrs. Bn. at Ft. Lewis, WA then overseas two weeks later.

Rotated back home in February 1945 and reassigned to the Manhattan Engineers project in Los Alamos, NM until is discharge in October 1945 attaining the rank of sergeant.

He became a tool room foreman after serving five years as apprentice tool and die maker. His whole work life changed when he went to work for a pressure sensitive adhesive company where he became a production and inventory control supervisor. He retired in 1980 and now spends more time with wife Margaret, son Jon and his wife and four children.

ALBERT L. KLINGSPORN, was born in Minnesota in March 1919, one of eight children. He grew up on a dairy farm remaining there until drafted Sept. 19, 1942. Albert was in basic training in Camp Roberts, CA when Japan attacked Pearl Harbor. He was transferred to the 41st Div., remaining in Co. B, 163rd Inf. until wounded on Mindanao, Philippine Islands.

He fought WWII in the Asiatic-Pacific Theater, returning as a much decorated combat veteran. Among his awards are the Purple Heart, Presidential Unit Citation, Combat Infantry Badge, and numerous campaign and battle ribbons.

Albert married Helen S. Panas on Oct. 6, 1946. They have three children and six grandchildren. His wife is deceased. Following the service Albert attended the University of Minnesota, obtaining a B.S. degree in 1953, and a Doctor of Veterinary Medicine degree in 1954. Albert is a retired executive of the U.S. Department of Agriculture.

EMERSON P. KOENIG, was born Dec. 31, 1919 in Botkins, OH. Inducted Nov. 19, 1941, stationed at Camp Wheeler, GA. He joined the 41st Inf. at Ft. Lewis, WA and served with I Co., 186th Inf. in Australia and New Guinea. He was wounded at Biak on June 8, 1944 and hospitalized in USA for one year. He was medically discharged on May 19, 1945 on disability pension. He had achieved the rank of staff sergeant. He received the Purple Heart.

While stationed at Rockhampton, Queensland, Australia, he married Janet McDermott of Gladstone, Queensland and they parented 11 children and 25 grandchildren.

He joined a family business in 1945 and retired as chairman of the board of directors of Koening Equipment, Inc., Botkins, OH. He was active in many civic organizations and a devoted member of the Great Lakes Chapter of the 41st Infantry Division Association. He passed away March 28, 1991.

STANLEY KONESKI, was born and raised in Evanston, IL. Graduated from Catholic, Polish,

Combat Infantry Badge, Purple Heart, Good Conduct, Asiatic-Pacific Theater, Bronze Star, Philippine Liberation, and World War II Victory Medal.

Married to Phyllis and they had five children and seven grandchildren. He farmed after Army discharge and worked for Lima Engine Plant, Ford Motor Company until medical retirement in 1985. Robert passed away July 3, 1989.

ROBERT L. IRVING, was born Oct. 8, 1900 at Salem, OR and graduated from high school at Wilbur in 1919. Graduated from OAC (now OSU) with ROTC commission in 1925.

Enlisted in Co. D, 162nd Inf. in Roseburg, OR on Dec. 16, 1929 and was promoted on basis of ROTC commission to first sergeant in April 1930. He received a National Guard commission in March 1932. Was appointed as commanding officer of Co. D and promoted to captain in 1937.

Was activated with 41st Div. in September 1940 as CO, Co. DD, 162nd Inf. and promoted to major in August 1941. He served as XO and then CO of first Bn., 162nd Inf.

Reassigned to 186th Inf. in early 1942, he arrived in Australia May 13 and served alternately as XO of 2nd Bn. and CO of 3rd Bn. through training in Australia and operations in Buna-Gona area in New Guinea, returning to Australia in mid-1943.

He was reassigned to 163rd Inf. in August 1943 as XO, 2nd Bn. From March through May 1944, the 163rd was involved in landings at Aitape and Wakde-Toem during the Hollandia operations. On June 12, 2nd Bn., 163rd Inf. (Maj. Irving is now CO) arrived at Bosnek on Biak Island and was assigned to the reduction of Ibdi Pocket through end of July. In mid-August, the battalion landed at Korim Bay and moved south to link up with 162nd units moving north from Mokmer.

Upon completion of Biak Campaign, Major Irving returned to U.S. serving as CO of training battalions at Camp Roberts, CA until September 1945 when he was promoted to lieutenant colonel and assigned to recruiting duties in Oregon. On March 30, 1946, he was released to the inactive reserve.

By April 1947, he was sought to help reorganize National Guard units in Oregon and was appointed CO, 1st Bn., 186th Inf. with HQ at Medford. In 1952 he was promoted to colonel and assumed command of the 186th Inf. Regt. with headquarters at Portland and with battalions located in southern, northwestern, and far eastern Oregon. He retired from the National Guard in 1958 with 31 years of service.

In civilian life he was employed by various county and state agencies, retiring from the State Highway Department in 1967. He died at Salem, OR in 1972. He is survived by his wife Elsie of Salem and sons Robert of Pendleton and David of Salem.

CHARLES G. JACHIM, was born Jan. 3, 1921 in Rice Lake, WI. Graduated from Rice Lake High School in 1938. Joined the Wisconsin National Guard in February 1938. Called to active duty with the Guard in 1940. Served with 1st Bn., 138th Inf. through the Buna

Campaign. Joined H Co., 2nd Bn., 162nd Inf. in September 1943 at Rockhampton, Australia.

Landed with the unit at Hollandia, Biak, and Zamboanga. Participated and witnessed the first tank battle of the South West Pacific. Left the unit at Cotabato, Mindanao for rotation home in May 1945.

His medals and awards include: Bronze Star, Purple Heart, Combat Infantry Badge, American Defense Medal, Asiatic-Pacific with three Arrowheads and four Oak Leaf Clusters, Presidential Unit Citation with Oak Leaf Cluster, Philippine Presidential Unit Citation, Philippine Liberation Medal, Victory Medal, AFRM, National Defense and Army Commendation Medals.

Married to Kitty in 1945. They have three daughters, one son, nine grandchildren, and five great-grandchildren. Retired from U.S. Postal service in 1980. Lives in Rice Lake, WI.

GEORGE L. JACKSON (MA), was born in Seattle, WA on May 5, 1922, graduated from high school into the 116th Medics in September 1940. He became CQ (charge of quarters) of the barracks of Co. C selectees, dubbed "Ma" for taking care of them.

Sent to New Guinea with 2nd Bn., 163rd Inf. at Sanananda; with 3rd Bn. 162 at Hollandia; and to Biak in 1944 as medical aidman with Edwin Haraseth, Ed Harnack, Leigh DeVaney, Whitey Pluid and Dan Sullivan. Later wardmaster at Madigan General Hospital, Ft. Lewis.

Discharged Aug. 31, 1945 after five memorable years as private first class plus $3.00 for combat medical badge. With GI Bill he graduated University of Washington 1949-1950. Taught Middle School for 27 years, started Medic Chapter 41st Division Association 1966, and edited *Pillroller* newsletter for 23 years.

Married Doris in 1949, has three children and four grandsons. Younger daughter duplicated dad's Army career. Carole Jackson was promoted to major Jan. 1, 1991. George in Muklteo is busy with VFW, avid reader, writer, and stamp collector.

JAMES E. JACKSON, was enlisted in Co. H., 186th Inf. Oregon National Guard in April 1939. Was inducted into federal service Sept. 16, 1940. Was a member of Co. H., 186th Inf. until his discharge Aug. 11, 1945.

He served in the Southwest Pacific from April 22 until Aug. 2, 1945. Principal place of training was Ft. Lewis, WA.

Participated in battles of Papua Campaign, landings at Tana-Maria Bay, Biak, and liberation of the Philippines. Served throughout all overseas duty as machine gun section leader with the rank of staff sergeant.

He is now retired from the Burlington Northern Railroad after 40 years of service. He enjoys fishing, traveling, and rock hunting with good friends and former members of Co. H.

He has one daughter and two sons. Still has the same wife after 46 years.

CLIFTON JAMES (JESSE), was born in 1921 at Spokane, WA. Entered the service Sept. 16, 1940. Served with Co. D, 186th then Co. A, 163rd.

Memorable experience was bullet going through helmet; Sanananda and being blown up at Jolo.

Discharged with the rank of technical sergeant, he received the Silver Star, Purple Heart, and Bronze Star.

He has five grown children and is an actor living in Dix Hills, NY.

WILLIAM J. JANSKY, was born May 6, 1920 in Cicero, IL. Entered the service Oct. 10, 1941. Stationed at Ft. Lewis, WA, 41st Cantonment. Trained at Camp Roberts, CA. When Pearl Harbor was attacked, he was sent to Ft. Lewis and assigned to M Co., 186th Regt.

Sailed for Australia, Seymour, Rockhampton, Yepoon. Left the 41st at Biak Island and sent to Ft. Benning, GA. Was in School Troops training cadre of officer candidates.

His memorable experiences include: sailing into Sydney Harbor; viewing the thousands of military gear at Port Moresby; and the GIs ingenuity at Senemi encampment.

Discharged at Camp Shelby, MS with the rank of spec. T/5 (corporal). He received the SWP Campaign Ribbon with stars, Combat Medal, Good Conduct Medal, and Victory Medal.

Married to Dorothy since July 12, 1947. They have three children, Judy, Kathy, and Jon and seven grandchildren.

Was owner of food marts and officer in local bank until his retirement. He is commander of Riverside Post #488 American Legion, president of Lions Club and past president of the Chamber of Commerce.

JOSEPH S. JELI, was born July 24, 1923 in Mt. Angel, OR to a family of 10 children. He was inducted into the Army on March 4, 1943 in Portland, OR. Went to Camp Roberts, CA for basic training for 13 weeks.

Joined the 41st Div. in July of 1943 in Rockhampton, Australia. Served with HQ 1st 163 in initial landings at Aitape, Wakde, and Biak. Transferred to the Maritime Personnel Section HQ Det. AF Wespac to serve in Luzon.

Discharged Jan. 3, 1946 at Ft. Lewis, WA with the rank T/4. Married Vera Gilmore on July 10, 1948. They have 10 children and 10 grandchildren. He has been employed by Willamette Egg Farms for the past 38 years. Over 10 years ago he and four other men purchased the business.

He is a member of the VFW and American Legion. Presently he is working to keep busy. He likes to spend his free time fishing and hunting.

CLIFFORD A. JENNINGS, was born on Nov. 28, 1924 in Oak Harbor, OH. He entered the service Feb. 27, 1943. He had basic training at Camp Roberts, CA and was transferred to A Btry., 146th, FA Bn. and joined the 41st Div. in August 1943.

He was sent to Brisbane, Rockhampton, and Finchhaven. He fought battles in Hollandia, Biak,

Zamboanga, and Jolo, then on to Kobe, Japan for occupation. His rank was staff sergeant and he was one of the first Americans in Hiroshima after the Atomic bomb was dropped.

Discharged Jan. 9, 1946. He received two Asiatic-Pacific Theater with four Bronze Stars, the Philippines Liberation Ribbon with one Bronze Star, a Bronze Arrowhead, World War II Victory Medal, and a Good Conduct Medal.

Married Helen Louise Heisner on April 26, 1947. They have two children. Patricia is now an accountant in Akron, OH and James is operations director for a corporation in Denver, CO. They have four grandchildren.

He retired from Ford Motor Company after 30 and a half years of service. He is now serving as a township trustee. He is past commander of NCYC and is a member of Blue Gavel, the American Legion, the IOOF Lodge and the Moose Lodge.

SYDNEY M. JENNINGS, was born June 4, 1920 at Brookneal, VA. Graduated from high school in 1938. Drafted Feb. 14, 1942 and sent to Camp Roberts, CA for 13 weeks of basic training. Joined Cannon Co., 162nd Inf. at Rockhampton, Australia in July 1942.

Participated in the New Guinea Campaign. Landed at Hollindia and Biak Island in Dutch New Guinea, Zamboanga, Philippine Islands.

Sent back to the States in September 1945. Was discharged November 1945 as technical sergeant E-6. Re-enlisted February 1946 and served three tours in Korea. Also served at Ft. McClellan, AL; Ft. Knox, KY; Ft. Jackson, SC; and Ft. Gordon, GA.

Retired from Army in 1968 as SGM E-9 at Ft. Gordon, GA.

Married Kathleen Lominick in 1950. They have two children, Celia and John. Worked at University of South Carolina until 1980 when he retired. He now spends his time beekeeping, fishing, and gardening. He resides in Columbia, SC.

ROGER J. JENSEN, was born Feb. 15, 1920 in Council Bluffs, IA. He spent his youth in Pendleton, OR where he graduated from high school and joined the National Guard, Co. G, 186th Inf. on Sept. 28, 1939.

Inducted into Army Sept. 16, 1940 and went to Camp Murray, WA. Went overseas to Melbourne, Australia on April 22, 1942. Was wounded on Biak Island in June 1944. Sent home in April 1945. Was discharged Aug. 31, 1945 at Ft. MacArthur, CA.

Went to work at the Long Beach Naval shipyard, Long Beach, CA in October 1945 and enrolled in Engineering Night School. He retired as a marine engineer and administrative contract officer in February 1975. Went into the travel business and retired for good in February 1980.

Married Jessie K. McCarthy on Oct. 2, 1941 in Renton, WA. He has one son and two grandsons. Has spent much time traveling the world the last 25 years and now enjoys playing golf and genealogy. He is a member of the Elks, Amvets, and DAV.

EDWIN F. JEWELL, was born Feb. 13, 1915 in Kentucky. Entered the service Nov. 15, 1941. Assigned to 163rd Regt at Ft. Lewis, WA.

Returned to the States on rotation Aug. 23, 1944. Was discharged at Ft. Lewis with the rank of private first class.

Edwin is retired from the life of aviation and lives in Alton, IL.

CHARLES E. JOHNSON (CHUCK), was born Oct. 29, 1924 at Woodruff, SC. He grew up on a small farm and graduated from Reidville High School in the class of 1941. He was drafted into the Army in May 1943 and completed his basic training at Camp Wheeler, GA and advanced infantry training at Ft. Ord. CA.

Joined the 41st Inf. Div. at Rockhampton, Australia in January 1944. He was first assigned to Co. D, 186th Inf. and about six weeks later was transferred to the Intelligence and Reconnaissance Platoon, HQ and HQ Co., 186th Inf.

He participated in the landing and fighting at Hollandia, Biak in Dutch New Guinea and Palawan and Zamboango in the Philippines and the occupation of Japan.

He was awarded the Combat Infantry Badge and the Bronze Arrowhead (assault wave) at Hollandia. Johnson was among the first Americans to enter Hiroshima. He was separated from the Army at Camp Gordon, GA as a technical sergeant (platoon sergeant) in January 1946. He re-enlisted in the Army in May 1966, joining the Counter Intelligence Corps and served for over 20 years, retiring as a CWO W-3 in November 1963.

Johnson subsequently worked for the post office for over 20 years and retired to his yard and garden in 1986. He married Frances Cothran in 1952 and they have a son, a daughter, a granddaughter and a grandson.

DONALD L. JOHNSON, was born April 30, 1920 in Lewistown, MT. Entered the service September 1940. Assigned to K-163 and Division Headquarters, stationed at Ft. Lewis, WA.

His memorable experiences include: watching a B-25 being shot down in front of him; furlough in Sydney, Australia; watching naval bombardment of Hollandia and Biak to their amphibious landing.

Discharged in June 1945 with the rank of private. He received the American Defense Service Medal, Good Conduct Medal, Republic of Philippines Presidential Unit Citation Badge, World War II Victory Medal, Asiatic-Pacific Campaign, American Campaign, Combat Infantry Badge, and Bronze Star.

Married to Stephanie in 1963, no children. He retired from postal service in 1984. Enjoys playing golf and traveling.

NICK KALEMBER, was born Aug. 4, 1912 in Duluth, MN. Came to Los Angeles in 1930 and was drafted March 1941 into the 161st. After maneuvers in Washington and California, he was transferred to the 186th and was sent to Australia in June of 1942, then to New Guinea for six months of jungle patrolling. He served as Col. Newman's guard in the Hollandia landing, and then on to the landing on Biak. This is where he discovered the Jap beer dump. In combat at Mokmer Airdrome where they fought off three days of Banzai attacks with fixed bayonets.

Discharged September 1945 after bouts with malaria and jungle rot.

Married Marie in 1942 and has three sons. He retired from the Los Angeles City Schools in 1975 and now travels in the West and Southwest.

FRANK A. KAMP, was born Lewiston, MT on Oct. 19, 1919. His life centering around ranching, he often trailed cattle to lower ranch in Missouri River Breaks in spring and back in early winter.

He entered the service March 16, 1940, training at Camp Murray, Ft. Lewis, WA as a member of Co. K, 163rd Inf., 41st Div. He fought in New Guinea, and served in Australia, arriving in U.S. December 1944, mustered out of infantry into Air Force, Lowery Field Air Force Base, Denver.

Honorable discharge at Ft. Douglas, UT on March 24, 1945 with the rank of staff sergeant. He received the Bronze Battle Star for Papuan Campaign, American Defense Service Medal, Asiatic-Pacific Campaign Medal, Distinguished Unit Citation, and the Good Conduct Medal.

He returned to home ranch as manager, later a commissioned agent for Standard Oil, then ownership. Presently a school bus driver and city council.

Has wife Dodie and four children: Larry, Vicki, Greg, and Dana. His grandchildren are: Melissa, Lindy, Jenny, Nicholas, Derrick, Tyler, and Daniel.

ROBERT L. KANEWSKE, was born Aug. 18, 1924 in Sealy, TX. He graduated from high school in 1943. Inducted in the Army Sept. 27, 1944 at Ft. Sam Houston, TX. Went to Camp Wolters, TX for basic training.

Overseas with brief stops at Finchhaven, Hollandia, New Guinea and Leyte before joining 41st Inf. Div. at

pine Liberation Medal with one Bronze Star, Good Conduct Medal, Purple Heart Medal, and Combat Infantry Badge. Discharged at Ft. Sam Houston, TX on Jan. 14, 1946 with the rank of sergeant.

Married to Patsy in January 1947, he has two children, five grandchildren and one great-grandchild. Spent 38 years in the aircraft industry retiring in 1984 from Bell Helicopter Company. He is an active member of the Baptist Church, Masonic Lodge, Scottish Rite, Shrine and VFW.

LEON HANS MADISON, was born March 18, 1914 in Sidney, IA, reared in Nebraska, and graduated from Clark High School in 1932. He was a student at Nebraska Wesleyan University, Lincoln for three years leaving to reside in Oregon.

In 1939 he joined Oregon National Guard, Co. M., 162nd Inf. at Corvallis, OR. Inducted in federal service with 41st Div. in September 1940. Trained at Camp Murray, WA.

Departed U.S. from New York on March 4, 1942. After serving in Australia and New Guinea, he was returned home on first rotation. In January 1945 he was sent to Europe with 12th Inf. Regt., serving in France, Germany, and Austria.

Discharged Sept. 28, 1945 at Ft. Lewis, WA with the rank of staff sergeant. He received the Rhineland, Central Europe, and New Guinea Service Medals and Combat Infantry Badge.

He retired after 30 years from the Social Security Administration. Married Claudene in 1946. They had four children, one of whom was killed in an auto accident. He is the grandfather of two. Presently married to Lillie. He is a member of Sons in Retirement Branch 46, NARFE and Immanuel Lutheran Church, Stockton, CA.

LAUREN L. MAIN, was born at Monroe, WA on Jan. 10, 1922. He joined HQ Btry., 146th FA on Sept. 16, 1940 and remained with the unit until rotated home in April 1945. His station and training were at Ft. Lewis, WA.

He went overseas with the division landing at Melbourne, Australia. With the division he went to Port Moresby, New Guinea; and with the artillery survey section, he was flown to Buna Airstrip to complete survey for allied artillery fighting in the area. With the division he landed at Hollandia. In the battle for Biak Island, he was with Capt. Bedke on the LCV Observation Post offshore.

He made the landing at Zamboanga then rotated back to Leyte. From there he flew to Hollandia and caught a merchant ship for the States, arriving April 30, 1945. His position was survey and instrument NCO with a rank of staff sergeant. He was discharged at Ft. Lewis, WA on June 11, 1945.

After the war he continued his education earning a B.S. degree from Washington State University. He married and fathered two daughters and a son. He is retired and living with his wife of 45 years in Chehalis, WA.

FREDERICK W. MALL, was born in Feb. 11, 1916 in Green, KS to German-Swiss parents. He was the fifth of six children. He entered the Army in October 1941 at Ft. Leavenworth, KS. He went to Camp Roberts and Ft. Ord, CA for basic and overseas training, serving with Btry. C, 163rd.

Served overseas in Australia and in New Guinea. He served on Biak and some others. Discharged in October 1945 with the rank of private first class. He received the Purple Heart.

Married Jul Dulohery in 1948. They had two children Durwin and Nola and six grandchildren, Dustin, Jennifer, LaVerne, Derrick, Lauren, and Lance. He farmed for 30 years and retired in 1978. They moved to Clay Center, KS. He enjoyed city life very much; but in 1983, he became ill with cancer and passed away on May 21, 1988. He was a member of VFW, Eagles, Elks lodge, and the St. Peter and Paul Catholic Church in Clay Center, KS.

RICHARD A. MALOTKE, was born July 30, 1924. Drafted May 18, 1943. He had basic training at Camp Roberts, CA and joined the 41st Inf. Div. in Australia in January 1944. Assigned to M Co., 186th Inf. for a short time, he was reassigned to Btry. B, 218th FA.

He took part in three battles, Hollandia, Wakde Island in New Guinea and Zamboanga, Philippines. Also took part in the Occupation of Japan.

Discharged Jan. 10, 1946 with the rank of sergeant. He married Annabelle on Aug. 2, 1947. They have two children, Sandy and Cindy, and five grandchildren, Marc, Aaron, Arianne and Sarah (twins) and Natalie. Richard retired July 1988. He is a life member in the DAV.

DURAND V. MANDOLINE, was born Jan. 21, 1914 at Chicago, IL. He was inducted Nov. 18, 1941 at Ft. Sheridan, IL with basic training at Camp Wheeler, GA. Was assigned to Co. B, 186th Inf., 41st Div. at Ft. Lewis, WA in February 1942.

Went to Australia in April 1942, training in Seymour and Rockhampton. Then to New Guinea in January 1943. Back to Rocky in July 1943. Made landings at Hollandia, New Guinea April 1944 and beach landing May 1944 at Biak Island. Also made landings at Palawan, Mindanao in the Philippines, February to August 1945. Most memorable experience was when Japs tried a night attack on Biak of 186th Inf. perimeter. Over 100 Japs were killed with very few American casualties.

Headed for home from Leyte in September 1945. Was sergeant at the time of discharge. He received stars for four beach landings and the Combat Infantry Badge.

Has wife Bonnie, son Jim plus two grandchildren and five great-grandchildren. He retired from employment with state of California in December 1977 and moved to Farmer City, IL where he now lives.

JAMES C. MANDY, was born Nov. 19, 1918 in Lewistown, MT, the son of Scottish and Irish immigrants. As a young man he worked on the city and county roads and cattle ranches then moved to Idaho to work in the silver mines until he was drafted into the service April 3, 1941 in Spokane, WA. The next day he was sent to Ft. Lewis, WA. to train as a member of Co. A, 163rd Regt., 41st Div. He was nick-named "chaplain" for his assistance to a Catholic Chaplain with the dying during combat and later was called "Jungle Jim" for his keen ability to spot Japanese movement in the undergrowth due to his 40% color-blindness.

Discharged with the rank of platoon sergeant. He received about 14 awards including the Bronze Star Medal, Good Conduct, American Defense Service Medal, Asiatic-Pacific Campaign Medal, World War II Victory Medal, Philippine Liberation Ribbon, one Arrowhead, and five Bronze Stars.

He is retired from the U.S. Postal Service and lives in Wallace, ID

ROCCO MANGINO, was born Jan. 14, 1920 in New York. He entered the service March 19, 1942. Was assigned to AT Co., 162nd Inf., 41st Div., stationed at Leyte.

Discharged Feb. 1, 1946 with the rank of staff sergeant. He received the American Service Medal, World War II Victory Medal, Asiatic-Pacific Service Ribbon, Good Conduct Medal, Philippines Liberation, and Philippines Presidential Citation.

Married Aug. 24, 1946 and has three children, JoAnn, Roxanne, and Rosemary. He works in auto parts sales.

HAROLD E. MANN, was born Jan. 26, 1917 in Portland, OR. Entered the service Sept. 16, 1940, Army Infantry, Co. I, 186th Regt, Camp Murray, WA; Camp Seymour, Rockhampton, Austraila. Transferred to Air Corps and Chanute Field, Scott Field, IL.

Memorable experiences include: New Guinea; arrival Oro Bay for Buna-Gona Operation; support detached service, Camp Winstains, Brisbane, dock detail; landing Biak; Air Corps in Illinois, Teletype Division, Maintenance Division, Instructor, super. Chanutet and Scott Field.

Discharged Sept. 13, 1945 with the rank of sergeant. He received the Good Conduct Medal, American Defense Medal, Papuan Campaign, Dutch New Guinea-Hollandia-Biak Operation, and the Combat Infantry Badge.

Married to Lilian Webb in 1950, no children. Retired from RMS and P.O. after 40 years of service. He lives in Portland, OR.

HOLLEY A. MANWARING, joined Hqs. Co., 41st Inf. Div., on April 16, 1936 until discharge in

1945. Hqs. Co. was inducted into federal service on Sept. 16, 1940 and left for duty at Camp Murray, WA. He became a staff sergeant and served in that position until December 1941.

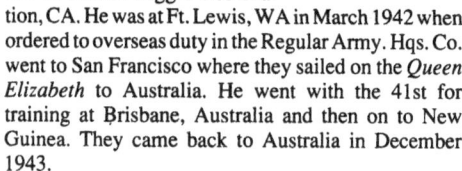

They trained in Blackfoot, had summer camps at Boise, ID and at Hunter Ligget Reservation, CA. He was at Ft. Lewis, WA in March 1942 when ordered to overseas duty in the Regular Army. Hqs. Co. went to San Francisco where they sailed on the *Queen Elizabeth* to Australia. He went with the 41st for training at Brisbane, Australia and then on to New Guinea. They came back to Australia in December 1943.

Was transferred to the 5603rd Engrs. Bn. leaving the 41st and went back to New Guinea. He served in refrigeration work and in the V-Mail program. He also installed refrigeration units for engineer units that had built and tinned their own walk-in coolers. He was made a technical sergeant in the engineers.

He entered the rotation program in the fall of 1944, leaving Milne Bay in January 1945 for the United States. He was stationed in Portland, OR in a MP outfit for six months. Then he left for Ft. Lewis, WA where he was discharged on Aug. 16, 1945.

Returning home, he became a letter carrier for the U.S. Postal Service retiring in 1974. Holley and his wife celebrated their 50th wedding anniversary in Nov. 24, 1987. They have seven children, 52 grandchildren, and five great-grandchildren.

SAM MARINKOVICH, was born Nov. 17, 1917 in Anaconda, MT. He attended elementary and graduated from Anaconda High School in 1937, then attended Butte Business College in Butte, MT.

He volunteered for the first draft and was assigned to the 41st Inf. Div. in Camp Murray, WA. His first experience was an overnighter without any warm clothing. The 41st later moved to Ft. Lewis, WA.

Departed for overseas duty April 1942. Destined for the Philippines, they were re-routed to Australia because of the Coral Sea Naval Battle. Landed in Seymour and later moved to Rockhampton which was to be their base camp.

His three and a half years in New Guinea brought much friendship and experience. Participated in beachhead landings in Hollandia, New Guinea, and Biak Island in Dutch New Guinea where he was awarded the Bronze star.

During his stay at the Presidio of Monterey, he enjoyed the people, golf, and the beautiful weather, which had a lot to do with his settling in Monterey. Started in the administration field in banks, savings and loans and 23 years with Coast Counties Land Title Company as a public relations officer and an escrow officer, retiring on Dec. 31, 1980.

Married to a wonderful woman named Lynn, for whom he is most thankful. They combined two families, making seven kids in all, and have 13 (soon to be 16) grandchildren. Sam and wife live in Murphys, CA in the Mother Lode.

He enjoyed his stay in Rockhampton where he was treated royally. He shall never forget them. He knows they were proud of the 41st Inf. Div. because they built a church in their honor.

DON H. MARKHAM, was born April 15, 1925 at Ontario, OR. Was at Camp Hood, TX for 16 weeks of basic training. Sent to Leyte, overseas, on Feb. 15, 1945. A couple of days later was in beachhead landing on Jolo Island as a rifleman, Co. B, 163rd in 41st Inf. Div. Was hit by debris or something from mortar fire but didn't try to get a Purple Heart.

Was also in landing at Mindanao. He went on numerous combat patrols. Was in Occupation of Japan, after the 41st was deactivated, in Hiro, Nagoya, and Honshu area. Was also in 534th Engr. and Shore Regt. and the 24th Div.

Came back to the States on Sept. 7, 1946. He is now a retired research scientist. He presently lives in Simi Valley, CA.

DONALD S. MARTENSON, was born July 26, 1923 in Boulder, CO. He entered the service Feb. 25, 1943, 205th FA, Rockhampton, Australia. Made landings in Hollandia and Biak, D-Day, Zamboanga and Mindanao D-Day-2 hours.

Discharged with the rank of staff sergeant. He received two stars and one arrowhead.

Married to Marian J. Bluhm on March 2, 1951. They have four sons and one daughter. He is retired.

WARREN C. MARTINSON, was born in Minneapolis, MN on April 2, 1920 to Lillian and August Martinson. He attended elementary and high school there and went to work for Arrowhead Steel Products Company. He married Mabel P. Scramsted on June 21, 1941 and accepted a job with McQuay-Norris in St. Louis, MO.

Was inducted into the Army at Ft. Snelling, MN on July 10, 1944, 741st Ordnance L M Co. He trained in Camp Roberts, CA and sailed from Ft. Ord on Dec. 30, 1944. He served in the Asiatic-Pacific Theater and the Occupation Army in Japan.

He was honorably discharged at Camp McCoy, WI on Aug. 9, 1946 with the rank of first sergeant. He received the Philippine Liberation Ribbon with a Bronze Star, Good Conduct Medal, Asiatic-Pacific Theater Service Medal, and the Army of Occupation Medal—Japan.

He retired from General Motors in September 1981 after 35 years of service. He has a son Lee and a daughter Laurie.

RAYMOND L. MARX, was born Aug. 31, 1917 in Phlox, WI. He graduated from high school in 1935 and was drafted in the Army Nov. 11, 1941. Basic training at Camp Wheeler, GA. From there he was transferred to Ft. Lewis, WA. Was assigned to B Co., Weapons Platoon, 186th Inf., 41st Div.

The division moved to Australia where he had amphibious training in preparation for landings at New Guinea, Biak Island and the Philippine Islands.

Discharged November 1945 with the rank of sergeant. Married Sept. 3, 1949 and has five children and five grandchildren. He owned and operated a grocery and hardware store and post office for 19 years. Now retired in Phlox, WI and enjoying life.

NORMAN F. MATHEWS, was born Feb. 13, 1924 at Prescott, AZ. Was inducted Feb. 18, 1943 and trained at Camp Roberts, CA. Assigned to HQ Co., 2nd Bn., 163rd Inf. Regt., 41st Div.

Overseas duty from July 7, 1943 to Dec. 23, 1945. Participated in campaigns/battles in Aitape, Wakde, Papua, New Guinea, Biak Island, Netherlands East Indies, Mindoro Island, Philippines, Zamboanga, Philippines, Jolo Island, Sulu Archipelago, Hiroshima, Kure, Japan.

Was discharged Jan. 10, 1946 at Ft. MacArthur, CA with the rank of technical sergeant. His awards include the Presidential Unit Citation Ribbons (U.S. and Philippine Republic), Bronze Star Medal with cluster, Asiatic-Pacific Campaign Medal with four Battle Stars, Philippine Liberation Medal, Good Conduct Medal, World War II Victory Medal, Occupation Japan Medal, and Combat Infantry Badge.

Entered Colorado Agricultural and Mechanics College in Fall 1946 and majored in forestry. Was a district forest ranger and later state forester for U.S. Bureau of Land Management, Santa Fe, NM.

He is an ardent hunter and fisherman and since retirement has been active in a number of wildlife conservation organizations. He has published in many state and national publications and is author of book on *Trophy Game Hunting*. Military Publications: 41st Div. History No. 143, 2nd Bn.; HQ Co., 163rd Inf. (Ammunition and Pioneer Platoon); Dr. Hargis Westerfield and Tech/Sgt. Norman F. Mathews.

Has been married to Ida for 44 years and has two grown children and one grandson.

JAMES J. MAYES, was born in 1913 in Missouri. He joined the Missouri National Guard in 1937. Was inducted into Federal Service with 35th Inf. Div. in 1940. Joined the 41st Div as a replacement officer in March 1944 and was assigned to Co. A, 163rd, Inf. as HQ Co. commander and 1st Bn. adjutant. Remained in that position until shipped back to the States from Hiro, Japan.

Was in the following engagements and landings, Aitape, Toem, Wakde Island, Biak, Zamboanga, and Jolo. Discharged with the rank of captain in 1946. He received the Bronze Star and Purple Heart.

In 1955 he was ordered to active duty as a lieutenant colonel and assigned as U.S. Property and Fiscal Officer for Missouri with the station in Jefferson City, MO. He remained in that position until his retirement in 1973 with the rank of colonel.

Married to Fern Miller on Nov. 20, 1941. They have two children and five grandchildren.

MICHAEL MAZIARCZYK, was born July 28, 1922 in Wilkes-Barre, PA and was raised in Cambra, PA. He served December 1942 to December 1945 without leave or furlough.

Basic training in Ft. McClellan, AL. Joined the 41st in Rockhampton in July 1943. Served his entire combat time with HQ Co., 1st Bn., 186th. He participated in every landing and operation the 186th was assigned.

While on detached service to 41st Signal Co., he

became friendly with a B-25 Sqdn. and flew on six bombing missions. He landed in Japan at Kure Naval Base, "borrowed" a jeep, and spent most of a day in Hiroshima. Flew out of Tokyo for the States November 1945 with the rank of staff sergeant.

Married Joan and has four sons, two daughters, and one grandson, He is still in real estate sales when not busy traveling.

JAMES I. McCLAIN, was born April 3, 1919 in Bend, OR. He entered the service Oct. 4, 1941 and was assigned to Co. I, 186th, 41st Div.

Discharged with the rank of staff sergeant and received the Bronze Star Medal.

Married to Eloise, has six children and 12 grandchildren. He is retired and lives in Bend, OR.

WESTON A. McCORMAC, was born March 5, 1911 in Tacoma, WA. He joined Btry. C, 146th FA Regt., Seattle in 1929. Active duty in September 1940 as plans and training officer of the 146th FA Regt.

He accompanied division overseas as assistant G-3, 41st Inf. Div. Served with Division Hqs. through Buna-Sanananda, Hollandia, and Biak.

Returned to the States in November 1944. Joined Regular Army in June 1946 and served two tours in Germany as FA Battalion Commander and assistant chief of staff G 1, 7th Army and FA Group Commander and deputy chief of staff of V Corps, retired as colonel in May 1966.

He was a professor at California Polytechnic State University (1968 to 1987) at San Luis Obispo, CA. Weston and wife Jeanne reside in San Luis Obispo.

BRAD McDONALD, was born Aug. 30, 1921 in Portland, OR. He joined K Co., 186th Inf., 41st Div., National Guards in 1940 at St. Helens, OR. Inducted into active service Sept. 16, 1940 at Ft. Lewis, WA.

Transferred to K Co., 163rd Inf. after Pearl Harbor. Left San Francisco on March 19, 1942 aboard the *Queen Elizabeth*. Arrived at Sidney, Australia on April 5, 1942. Transferred to Dutch freighter *Kramer* on April 6, 1942. Arrived in Melbourne on April 10, 1942. Trained out at Seymour. Left for Rockhampton by rail July 18, 1942, arrived July 25, 1942, trained at Yeppon Road.

Left Gladstone Dec. 18, 1942 aboard *Sloartzhount* (Black Dog) and arrived Port Moresby Jan. 4, 1943. Flew the Hump Jan. 8, 1943, landed at Dobodura, New Guinea. Combat at Sanananda Point, Buna, Gona. Landings at Aitape, Wadke, Tor River, Biak, Zamboanga, Jolo, Davao.

Left Leyte Philippines on July 23, 1945 aboard *Henry T. Allen* and arrived in Seattle, WA on Aug. 14, 1945.

Was discharged at Ft. Lewis, WA on Aug. 31, 1945 with the rank of staff sergeant. His medals include the Bronze Star, two Purple Hearts, Combat Infantry Badge, two Presidential Citations, American Defense Service, Asiatic-Pacific Service, Philippine Defense, World War II Victory, and the Good Conduct.

He married Aug. 25, 1946 to Donna and they have three children and four grandchildren. He retired Aug. 29, 1986 and lives in Portland, OR.

DAVID J. McELLIGOTT, was born Aug. 7, 1916 in Chicago, IL. Was drafted in November of 1941. Went to Camp Wheeler, GA for basic training.

Sent to Ft. Lewis, WA and from there went overseas in April of 1942 with HQ Co., 2nd Bn., 186th Inf.

Returned to the States in September of 1945. Was discharged in October of 1945 with the rank of sergeant. His decorations include the Combat Infantry Badge, American Defense Ribbon, Asiatic-Pacific Ribbon with four Battle Stars, and the Philippine Liberation Ribbon with two Battle Stars.

Married with one daughter Ellen (recently deceased) and one son David J. (a pulmonary specialist). David Sr. is retired after 35 years in the machinery business.

FRANCIS McGILVRA, was born in St. Helen's, OR. He joined the service in Sept. 16, 1940. Assigned to K Co., 186th Regt., 41st Div. Was discharged with the rank of sergeant.

Married to Laure and has three children and six grandchildren. He is a tree farmer in St. Helen's.

CHARLES E. McGRAW, was born Sept. 8, 1921 in Banks, OR. Inducted into federal service, 41st Inf. Div., Sept 16, 1942 from Oregon National Guard Unit, Forest Grove, OR.

He served with Co. I, 186th, and Co. I, 163rd, from Australia to Japan. Discharged from Ft. Lewis, WA in 1945.

Married Bulene Rolston at Forest Grove, OR in 1946. They have two children Charlene and Gordon. He joined Oregon National Guard Reserve, retiring in 1981 with the rank of colonel. Colonel McGraw passed away June 20, 1989.

HORACE A. McKELLER, was born Nov. 7, 1919. Drafted Feb. 11, 1942; basic training at Camp Roberts, CA; assigned to Regt. Hqs. Co., 162nd Inf.; August 1942, F Co., 162nd Inf.; December 1943, E Co., 186th Inf.; September 1944, Training Regt. at Ft. Ord, CA until February 1945.

Made amphibious landings to completion of campaign at Salamaua, 1943; Hollandia, 1944; and Biak (where he was awarded a battlefield commission), 1944.

Discharged in November 1945 with the rank of second lieutenant. He was awarded the Bronze Star at Hollandia and Oak Leaf Cluster at Biak.

He remembers the beautiful Aussie people; brave combat buddies; rigors of malaria; the fear and stench of death; and the mosquitoes that moved his hammock with him aboard.

Married Catheryne on Feb. 3, 1945. They have one beautiful daughter Martha and a handsome grandson William (Will) Buchanan. Horace retired as a hospital controller in January 1985.

LAWRENCE W. McKNIGHT, was born March 28, 1918 in Littlefield, AZ. Entered the service Feb. 24, 1941. Assigned to D Co., 1st Bn., 163rd Inf., Anti-tank. Stationed at Ft. Lewis and Asiatic-Pacific.

Discharged July 31, 1945 with the rank of technical sergeant. He received the Silver Star, Bronze Star, Distinguished Unit Citation and all the usual awards.

Married Louise Effinger on Nov. 24, 1945 in Las Vegas, NE. They have two sons, Michael and Jerry. Lawrence is a retired telephone installation supervisor.

GEORGE F. McMAHON JR., was born in October in New Haven, CT. Drafted Sept. 14, 1941 from Washington, DC. Went to Camp Croft, SC for basic training in heavy weapons and specialist training in Combat Intelligence. He joined the 41st Div at Ft. Dix, NJ.

Assigned to Hqs., 1st Bn., 162nd Inf. and served entire war with this unit in Australia, New Guinea, Biak and the Philippines. Returned home on rotation in July of 1945 and was discharged in October of 1945 with the rank of staff sergeant.

Married to Irene Coady. They have one son and two grandsons. He retired from the postal service with 30 years of service. He is an honorary life member of the K of C, council San Salvador #1 and John Barry Assembly #97.

ORUM J. McMASTERS (MAC), was born May 1, 1920 in Alliance, NE. Inducted into the Army Aug. 27, 1941 at Ft. Crook, NE. Was sent to Ft. Leonard Wood, MO for basic training. Joined the 116th Combat Engrs., 41st Div. in September 1941 at Ft. Lewis, WA. Served with the combat engineers in Papua, New Guinea building bridges, roads, and air strips.

Mustered out at Ft. Leonard Wood, MO. He was assigned the same barracks and the same bunk he had when he took basic training there. The best thing about serving was meeting all the wonderful guys and then being able to maintain these friendships through the years. Discharged Aug. 31, 1945 with the rank of T/4. He received the American Defense Service Ribbon, and the Distinguished Unit Badge.

Married Marcine and has two children, a son in New York City and a daughter and grandson in Omaha. He continues to run his own painting and contracting business in Alliance, NE.

DONALD R. McNEIC, was born July 5, 1923 in Spokane, WA. He entered the service Sept. 16, 1940, Med. Det., 162nd Inf., 41st Div. Stationed at Camp Murray, Ft. Lewis, Australia, New Guinea and Walla Walla, WA with Hospital Medics until his discharged.

Was wounded on Biak Island in June 1945. Received the Silver Star, Bronze Star, and Purple Heart. Discharged August 1945 with the rank of technical sergeant.

Donald is a widower with three sons and lives in Bethesda, MD. He administers an Archives at University of Maryland and consults with colleges and universities.

ROBERT A. MELINE, was born July 12, 1919 in Lake Bluff, IL. Graduated from high school in 1937.

Was drafted October 1941, Camp Grant, IL; basic training at Camp Roberts, CA; transferred to Co. G, 163rd Inf. immediately after Pearl Harbor.

Overseas from May 1942 to May 1945. Was discharged at Percy Jones Hospital Center, Ft. Custer, MI.

He retired from the VA Home Loan Div. in 1979. He makes his home in Decatur, GA.

WILLIAM G. MELTON JR., was born Jan. 1, 1923 in Oakland, CA. Raised in Square Butte and Lewistown, MT. He joined the National Guard, 163rd Inf. Div., Co. K on Nov. 16, 1938. Graduated from high school in 1940. Stationed at Camp Murray and Ft. Lewis, WA in new barracks.

Entered war and went to Bellingham, WA, then on to Australia on the *Queen Elizabeth*. They landed at Sydney, got on Dutch freighter *Cramer* and went to Melbourne, Rockhampton, New Guinea, Buna-Gona (where he became 1st Platoon leader), Jumbura (500 native carriers), Finchhaven, Aitape landing, Sarmi landing across the Tor River and 20 miles up coast to Biak, Philippines Islands, Zamboanga, Jolo, and Davao.

Was wounded in action at Mintal, Mindanao, on June 14, 1945. Discharged at Lewistown, MT by medical escort on April 17, 1946 as staff sergeant. His decorations include Bronze Star Medal, Purple Heart, Good Conduct Medal, Presidential Unit Citation, American Campaign Medal, Asiatic-Pacific, Ribbon with four stars and three arrowheads, World War II Victory Medal, Philippine Liberation Ribbon with three arrowheads and one Bronze Star, and seven Overseas Bars.

Married Veronica Ann Silverstrand on Aug. 18, 1956. Has five children: Tom, Doug, Becky, Mary, and Phillip and one grandchild Adam. Now retired as associate professor and curator emeritus, University of Montana, Missoula, MT.

ARTHUR W. MERRICK, was born in Great Falls, MT. Commissioned infantry 1940. Active service with 41st Inf. Div., 163rd Regt., Co.'s A, B, L, and S-3 (3rd Bn.). Huggins Perimeter and Sanananda, Aitape, Toem and Wakde, Biak, Zamboanga, Mindanao 1941-1945. IRTC, Camp Maxey and Camp Wolters, TX 1945; ROTC Dept., University of Washington and University of California (Berkeley) 1946-1948.

Inactive service with Montana National Guard 1948-1949; Army Reserve 1941, 1955-1972. Retired in 1972 with the rank of lieutenant colonel. He received the Silver Star, Bronze Star with cluster, Purple Heart with two clusters, Combat Infantry Badge, and Presidential Unit Citation with cluster.

Education: AB, BS, 1950, University of Montana; AM (Pharmacology) 1952; Ph.D. (Physiology) 1954, University of Missouri. Professional: was instructor, assistant/associate professor, professor and retired in 1985 as health scientist administrator, Heart, Lung, and Blood Institute, National Institutes of Health, Washington, DC.

Married since 1945. He has five children.

FRED MERRILL, was born Oct. 27, 1917 in Billings, MT. Entered the service in October 1941, assigned to Co. I, 186th Inf. at Camp Roberts, CA; Ft. Lewis, WA; Mangalove, Rockhampton, Australia; New Guinea; and Philippines. Discharged September 1945 with the rank of sergeant.

Married Grace Wheeler of Montana on Nov. 11, 1945. They have one son Grant, daughter Deborah, and one granddaughter.

Retired professor, University of Hawaii, social work. His entire family has lived in Honolulu since 1955.

GEORGE MILLER, was born June 10, 1919 in Portland, OR. Lived in Boise, ID since age one. Was inducted into the Army Sept. 11, 1941 and completed basic training at Camp Roberts.

Assigned to Btry. B of the 218th FA. He went overseas on April 22, 1942 and served in Australia, New Guinea, and the Philippines over a period of three years, four months, and 14 days. A most memorable experience was the 76 consecutive days he spent on Roosevelt Ridge in the battle of Salamaua.

Discharged Sept. 9, 1945 at Ft. Lewis with the rank of T/5. He was awarded the Asiatic-Pacific Service Medal, the American Defense Service Medal, the Philippine Liberation Medal, the World War II Victory Medal, and the Good Conduct Medal.

He worked for many years with the Internal Revenue Service and has been happily retired since June 30, 1974.

RUSSELL J. MILLER, was born June 19, 1919, in Detroit, MI. Graduated from high school in 1937. Drafted Oct. 6, 1941 and was assigned to Camp Roberts, CA in October 1941. Assigned to G Co., 162nd Inf., 41st Div. in December 1941. Served entire time with G-162 and on detached service with Service Company, Personnel Section, 162nd Inf.

Left Mindanao, Philippines in September 1945 and was discharged at Ft. Sheridan, IL on Oct. 12, 1945.

Married to Marilou with three sons and three grandchildren. Retired from Uniroyal, Inc. June 1980 and resides in Novi, MI.

PAUL R. MILLS, was born May 13, 1925 in Kenmore, OH. Entered the service Aug. 24, 1943. Assigned to Co. I, 163rd Inf., Biak, Zamboanga, Davao, Jolo, Japan.

Memorable experiences include: sitting under a palm tree at Zamboanga drinking beer when their newsreel crew came in and set up (they didn't get to see the movie); waiting alongside a road in Zamboanga and a tank company came up to help them. In their conservation one crew member asked, "When was the last time you have seen Fig Newtons." Most of us couldn't remember. He went back into the tank and began passing out packages of them. They were delicious; and seeing the total devastation of Hiroshima. It was hard to imagine that one bomb could do that much damage.

Discharged with the rank T/5, mail clerk. He received the Unit Citation, Philippine Liberation Medal and three Arrowheads.

Married twice, he has a son, daughter, seven grandchildren and nine step-grandchildren. He retired to Ft. Myers, FL after 30 years with General Telephone of Indiana and 13 years as contractor engineer.

EDWIN MILLSON, was born in June 1922 in Seattle, WA where he graduated from high school in 1940. He entered the National Guard in March 1939. In September 1940, he was inducted into federal service with Btry. F, 146th FA Bn. He was a gun section sergeant until March 1942 when he entered Aviation Cadets.

As a bombardier, he flew 48 missions over Germany. After WWII, he held assignments in training, research, and development and Strategic Air Commands. He retired in 1966 as permanent colonel from the position, executive secretary of the Joint Chiefs of Staff.

His decorations include: two Legion of Merits, four Distinguished Flying Crosses, Nine Air Medals, Bronze Star, French Croix de Guerre, and three Presidential Unit Citations.

After service he was vice president, Applied Technology, an aerospace company and executive director of the Sunnyvale, CA Chamber of Commerce.

Retired, he is married with three children, six grandchildren, and resides in Los Altos, CA.

WILLIAM A. MINNER (BILL), was born Jan. 12, 1920 in Masten's Corner, Felton, DE. Entered the service at Ft. Dix, NJ on May 14, 1943. Assigned to 41st Div. in January 1944 at Rockhampton, Australia after basic training at Camp Wheeler, GA.

Took part in the many landings of E Co., 186th and followed the actions and campaigns with time in Japan after the war was over. Memorable experiences include the landings on the many Jap held islands; a long bout with typhus; and minor injury from shrapnel in legs; and receiving the Purple Heart.

Returned to the States January 1946 with the rank technical sergeant. On the way home from California, he was taken from the train in Chicago with malaria. Was finally released at Ft. Dix on Jan. 18, 1946.

Married for 43 years to Anne. He has two daughter (school teacher and nurse), four granddaughters and one grandson. He is retired now from state of Delaware and has two harness race horses which keeps him busy. He served as mayor of Harrington in 1970s.

CASIMIR M. MISIEWICZ, was born Nov. 18, 1924 in Detroit, MI. Entered the service in August 1943, F Co., 162nd Inf., Ft. Riley, KS, Finchhaven, Hollandia, Biak, and Zamboanga.

Left 41st Div. from Zamboanga. approximately a month after landing to go to hospital. Did not return to 162nd. He became a member of Base M HQ on Luzon. Left PTO about December 1945.

Discharged with the rank of sergeant. He received a Bronze Star for bravery at Zamboanga and the Combat Infantry Badge.

Married with two children. Casimir is retired from Ford Motor Company.

EDWIN A. MOERI, was born April 27, 1919 in Madison Lake, MN. Enlisted in the National Guard in

1939 and was sent to Camp Murray when they were mobilized on Sept. 16, 1940. Shipped out on the *Matsonia* and landed in Melbourne, Australia in April 1942.

Was in the 41st Inf. Div. at first under Gen. White and in H Co. Fought in four major battles, Buna, Hollandia, Biak, and Puerto Princesa. Made three beachhead landings (including Hollandia and Biak) always going in on the third wave.

Was mainly gunner on an 81mm mortar team and took part in a lot of jungle warfare. Remembers once hot-wiring a Japanese truck and driving it alone at night to bring it up to where his unit was camped. He was wounded and received the Purple Heart.

After suffering several severe tropical diseases, he was sent back to the States arriving at Hamilton Air Base and was discharged Sept. 16, 1945.

Was married on Dec. 15, 1946 to Louise. They have three children and six grandchildren and live in Manteca, CA. Since the beginning of 1987, he has been in poor health and fights cancer just as hard as he used to fight the enemy.

GEORGE P. MORRIS, was born July 27, 1925 in Washington, IA. Was raised in Keota, IA and graduated from high school in May 1943. Drafted into the Army Sept. 9, 1943. Had infantry basic training at Camp Fannin, TX.

Left the States in March 1944 for New Guinea via Sidney, Australia with 10,000 other troops. Was assigned to 41st Div. on May 31, 1944 at Milne Bay, New Guinea. Joined Anti-tank Co., 163rd Inf., Biak, Dutch New Guinea. Served as company clerk at Regimental Hqs., 163rd Inf. In charge of regimental payroll section in Japan when the division was deactivated.

Discharged Jan. 31, 1946 at Ft. Leavenworth, KS with the rank T/4. Served in the Korean Conflict as an enlisted Reserve in the Japan Logistics Command at Camp Mower, Sasebo, Japan. Received the Combat Infantry Badge, Asiatic-Pacific with two stars and Arrowhead.

Married Darlene Weber on April 10, 1949. They have two children Dr. Michael A. Morris in Florida and Douglas Steven Morris in Minnesota. Spent his entire career in banking, retiring as president of First National Bank, Marion, IA in May 1983.

He is a member of El Kahir Shrine, Scottish Rite Bodies, ROJ, Lions Club, Elmcrest Country Club, Cedar Rapids, IA and Alta Mesa Country Club, Mesa, AZ.

JAMES R. MORRIS, was born Sept. 10, 1919 in Collingswood, NJ. Enlisted in Pennsylvania National Guard, 103rd Engrs., (C) Bn. Enlisted in Regular Army December 1941. Basic training at Ft. Lee, VA, Medical Training Center for six weeks. Assigned to Co. C, 135th Med. Regt. Served in New Guinea March-December, 1942 in support of 32nd Inf. Div. Assigned H&S, C Co., 116th Engrs. (C) Bn., Special Assignment, Alamo Scouts, 6th Army in 1944.

Overseas 32 months at Australia, Port Moresby, Buna, Gona, Sanananda, Oro Bay, Morobe, Hollandia, and Biak. Transferred to U.S. Ft. Belvoir, VA in October 1944, assistant provost marshall. Transferred to Army Reserve December 1945, captain of Corps of Engineers. Joined Pennsylvania National Guard, 103rd Engrs. (C) Bn., June 1947.

Participated in campaigns in East Indies, Papuan, New Guinea, Bismarck Archipelago, and Occupation of Germany.

Active duty during Korean War, 1950-1954, with 28th Inf. Div., 103rd Engineers, assigned S-4, S-3, assisted division engineers (28th and 9th), transferred to Army Reserve October 1954. retired from Army September 1979 with the rank of colonel, Corps of Engineers.

He received the Distinguished Unit Badge; Service with Papuan Forces; Bronze Star Medal with V; Army Commendation Medal; Special Forces TAB; Service with Alamo Scouts; 6th Army, 1944; Good Conduct Medal; Arrowhead Service Award; four Battle Star on Asiatic-Pacific Medal; American Defense; American Theater; National Defense; Army of Occupation (Germany); Army Reserve and World War II Victory Medal.

LESLIE M. MORRIS, was born Jan. 3, 1914 in Joppa, IL. Graduated grammar school at Salem, IL and high school at Tempe, AZ. Joined Arizona National Guard, HQ Co., 158th Inf., moved to California to work.

Drafted March 29, 1941, inducted at Ft. MacArthur, San Pedro, CA. Sent direct to 41st Inf. Div., Ft. Lewis, WA (National Guard Div.) Overseas to Seymore, Rockhampton, Gladstone, Townsville, Brisbane, Toorbul Point, Port Moresby, Soputa, Dobodura, Killerton, Huggins, Gono, Buna, Milne Bay, Oro Bay, Aitape, Toem, Wakde, Finchhaven, and Biak. Had malaria, jungle rot, sand flea bit infection, hearing loss, ear infection, dehydration, and surgery at Port Moresby, New Guinea for severe hemorrhoids. After CADRY was assigned to M Co., 163rd Inf. until his discharge June 20, 1945 at Camp Beale, CA with the rank communications sergeant.

He received the Good Conduct Medal, American Defense, Asiatic-Pacific with three stars, one Arrowhead, Bronze Star Medal, Distinguished Unit Citation, Combat Infantry Badge, five Overseas Bars, and one Hash Mark.

PETER J. MORRIS, was born Nov. 25, 1917 in Blacklick, PA. Entered the service Nov. 13, 1942. Assigned to Co. A, 116th Engrs. Stationed in Philippines, Japan, Australia, Biak, Hollandia, Holo, and New Guinea.

Discharged Dec. 5, 1945 with the rank of staff sergeant. He received the Asiatic-Pacific Theater Ribbon with two Bronze Stars, Philippine Liberation with one Bronze Star, Good Conduct, Legion of Merit, and the World War II Victory Medal.

Worked 36 years for Federal Dept. Agric. Retired 11 years ago and lives in Pittsburgh, PA. Married, his wife was in WACS two years. They have six children.

HAL S. MOTHERAL, was born Dec. 19, 1914 in San Marcos, TX. Entered the service Oct. 8, 1941. Assigned to H Co., 163rd Regt., 41st Div. Overseas to Australia, New Guinea, and Toem.

Was hit by artillery shell and lost left foot. Discharged with the rank staff sergeant. He received the Purple Heart.

Married to LaVerne and has son Hal Jr. and daughter Lynn. He retired Dec. 31, 1980.

BERNARD J. MOTL, was born March 30, 1915 in the town of Medina, WI. Was drafted Aug. 28, 1941 and was sent to Ft. Leonard Wood for basic training. Joined the 41st Inf. Div. at Ft. Lewis, Co. A, 116th Engrs.

Left for overseas March 19, 1942. Then made amphibious landings in New Guinea, then to Biak Island. During the landings in New Guinea, he was made line corporal. Received enough points at Biak Island to be sent back to the U.S.

Discharged from Ft. Sheridan on July 28, 1945 with the rank of corporal. He received the Good Conduct Ribbon, American Defense Service Medal, Asiatic-Pacific Theater Ribbon with two Bronze Battle Stars, and five Overseas Service Bars and one Service Stripe.

Married to Joan and has three children and three grandchildren. Retired in 1979 as a master plumber. Made a trip to Australia for two and a half months in 1983. He makes his home in Johnson Creek, WI.

ROBERT W. MOYER, was born Dec. 30, 1919 in New Madison, OH. Entered the service Nov. 17, 1941. Assigned to M Co., 163rd Inf. Regt. Stationed at Ft. Lewis, trained at Camp Wheeler, GA.

His best experience was when he was on furlough and stayed with an Aussie family on a ranch. They insisted he help brand calves and chase wallabies on horseback. They entered him in a rodeo riding a steer—he didn't win. His worst experience was Toem Village. He spent three and a half years overseas.

Discharged with the rank technical platoon sergeant, M Co., 3rd Platoon. He received the Asiatic-Pacific Theater Ribbon with four Bronze Stars and Oak Leaf Cluster, Philippine Liberation Ribbon with Bronze Star, Bronze Star, Combat Infantry Badge, Unit Citation Badge, Good Conduct Ribbon, American Defense Medal, and Philippine Defense Medal.

After service he went to work for Champion Paper Company, Hamilton, OH. He worked as a trouble shooter, construction, and maintenance electrician. Retired in 1977 after 32 years. Married to Mary and has three daughters, Miriam, Ellen, and Monica. He moved to Largo, FL in 1978.

WESLEY L. MULLENNEIX, was born July 28, 1919 in Moxee, WA. They lived in various places in Washington and Oregon, but mostly in Yakima, WA. He went into the Army on March 4, 1941 and was assigned to Co. F, 116th QM, 41st Inf. Div. He was with the 41st until Aug. 17, 1944 when he left on troop rotation from the Island of Biak.

At one time he was asked to drive Gen. H.H. Fuller to Rockhampton, Queensland, Australia. The general asked Mullenneix his name and after he was told, the general replied his name was really Molyneux as he had a Capt. Molyneux with him when he was the American Attache to France. From then on Mullenneix took an interest in his family and has published one family history, as well as edited the Grounds family newsletter for five years. He founded the International Molyneux Family Association and has edited their letter more than five years.

JAMES J. MUNZENMAIER, was born Jan. 8, 1919 in Des Moines, IA. Entered the Army Oct. 29, 1941 at Ft. Des Moines, IA. Basic training at Camp Wolters, TX in 1942. Assigned to D Co., 186th Inf., 41st Div. at Ft. Lewis, WA.

Departed from USA to Australia. Trained in Seymour and Rockhampton. He had one leave to Melbourne and Sidney, Australia. Was transferred to C Co., 186th Inf., 41st Div. on ship to Port Moresby. From there he flew to Buna, New Guinea. Other landings were Biak, Hollandia, Palawan, and Zamboanga, Philippine Islands.

Discharged with the rank of private first class. He received three Bronze Stars for the above campaigns. Departed from Leyte, Philippine Islands for the USA. Arrived in San Francisco on Sept. 24, 1945. Was discharged Oct. 4, 1945 at Jefferson Barracks, MO.

Married for 44 years to Cecelia. They reside in Des Moines, IA. They have one son Joseph and daughter-in-law Janet who are foster parents. He enjoys gardening since his retirement in October 1981 from a career in printing.

JOHN ROGER MURRAY, was born in Friend, OR. He entered the service in 1942. Was stationed at Ft. Lewis and overseas in Australia and New Guinea.

Discharged with the rank of sergeant. He received all the usual medals/awards.

Married to Eula. They had four sons, Charlie, Larry, Neal, and Pat and six grandchildren. John passed away.

WILLIAM R. MURRAY (BILL), was born June 21, 1919 in Roanoke, VA. He joined the Virginia National Guard in 1938. He served with HQ Co., 1st Bn., 116th Inf., 29th Div. He was discharged Aug. 1, 1941. He missed the landing at Utah Beach.

Was drafted Aug. 1, 1943. He trained at Camp Fannin near Tyler, TX. Then he joined the 41st Div. at Rockhampton, Australia in 1944. More training with Co. B, 162, then moved with them to Finchhaven, New Guinea.

His first combat was the invasion of Hollandia. After Hollandia was secured, his next action was Biak.

He was hospitalized on Biak and spent the remainder of his service time being cured of malaria and jungle rot.

He landed Stateside Dec. 13, 1944. After several months, he was sent to Ft. Story, VA for discharge with the rank of private first class.

He is now serving as a civilian following his retirement July 1, 1985. He has wife Phyllis, four children, and four grandchildren to keep him going and happy. He is an avid amateur radio operator and would like to establish a short-wave radio net with the 41st Div.

WOBLE T. MURRAY, was born May 4, 1919 in Suffolk, MT. He entered the service October 1936. Assigned to 163rd Regt., K Co., 1st Bn., HQ and Regimental HQ. Overseas in Australia, Papuan, Dutch New Guinea.

Discharged with the rank of sergeant. He received the Presidential Citation, Bronze Star, Combat Infantry Medal and all the theater ribbons.

He is a full time independent real estate appraiser.

GEORGE NALEZNY, was born June 9, 1917 in Brownsville, MN. He entered the service Sept. 19, 1941. Assigned to Co. C, 186th, joined the 41st at Ft. Lewis.

His memorable experience was landing at Biak Island. Discharged with the rank of sergeant. He received the Combat Infantry Badge, three Bronze Stars, Good Conduct Medal, and the Asiatic-Pacific Ribbon.

Married to Eva and they have five children, Joe, Jerry, Teresa, Krysteen, and Jane. He is retired and plays golf, fishes, hunts, gardens and wood works.

LESTER C. NEARGARDNER, was born April 26, 1925 one mile outside of Russia, OH. He entered the Army July 14, 1943 at Ft. Thomas, KY. He went to Camp Fannin, TX for basic training. He left for San Francisco, CA on Feb. 6, 1944.

He joined the 41st Div. in Australia. He was put in Hqs. Co., 2nd Bn., 186th. He went to New Guinea, Finchhaven, Hollandia, Biak, then to the Philippines, Mindoro, Palawan, Mindanao, next to Japan, Kure Harbor, Hiroshima. He left Nagoya on Jan. 2, 1946.

Was discharged January 23 from Camp Atterbury, IN with the rank of private first class. He received three Bronze Stars and the Bronze Arrowhead.

He is now retired and a member of the VFW.

TORAO NEISHI (PAT), was born March 12, 1917 in Oakland, CA. Entered the service Jan. 5, 1942. Basic training at Camp Robinson in Little Rock, AR. Went to Military Intelligence School at Camp Savage, MN via a few months of duty at Ft. Riley, KS. Learned Japanese military terms, translation of documents and POW interrogation techniques.

In September 1942, 14 graduates were ordered to join I Corps at Camp Stoneman, CA (point of debarkation). Arrived in Australia on Oct. 12, 1942. All were assigned to Gen. MacArthur's Hqs. in Brisbane where they translated the captured documents and interrogated several prisoners.

When 41st replaced 32nd Div in Buna, Harold Tanabe, Albert Tamura and Pat were assigned and stayed until Biak Island Campaign via Rockhampton, Finchhaven, and Hollandia. From Biak was sent to Buna to join the 38th Div. who landed Subic Bay to cut across Bataan Peninsula to San Fernando. Was stationed 15 miles east of Manila with the war ended.

Received field commission and Oak Leaf Cluster to the Bronze Star. Discharged December 1945 with the rank T/3 at Camp Grant, IL. He spent more than a year and a half with the 41st Div. and has many fond memories associated with comrades and his personal body guard, Ed Dombraski.

He is a widower with six children and four grandchildren. He is semi-retired and helps his sons operate a plant nursery.

CARL NELSON, was born Sept. 29, 1917 in Stambaugh, MI. Drafted Oct. 8, 1941 in Chicago, IL. Assigned to Camp Grant, IL for three weeks and then on to Camp Roberts, CA.

Immediately after Pearl Harbor, he was assigned to the 41st Div. and pulled three months of guard duty at Boeing Field in Seattle before going overseas to the Southwest Pacific until July 17, 1945 when he was discharged on the point system.

Spent one and a half years with G Co., 162nd Inf. and while in New Guinea the first time, he was fortunate to get a transfer to Division Headquarters Finance Section for the duration of his service before discharge.

Married 44 years and resides in Glen Ellyn, IL. He has three sons, seven grandsons, and one granddaughter. He retired 10 years ago.

EMIL L. NELSON, was born Aug. 1, 1921 at Brockway, MT. He joined Co. C, 163rd Inf. Regt. while at college in Bozeman, MT, was activated on Sept. 16, 1940.

While in Australia he attended Barney Rankin's Intelligence School and was the intelligence sergeant of Co. C in action in New Guinea. Wounded at Sanananda in 1943, he was awarded the Purple Heart. After hospitalization in Australia, he returned to Co. C in New Guinea.

In 1944 he was selected for OCS in Brisbane, Australia and upon graduation was assigned to MacArthur's Hqs. He served in GHQ SWPA in Hollandia, Leyte Island and Manila. He was sent back to the U.S. in 1945 and was released on Sept. 20, 1945.

He graduated from the University of Washington in 1948 and did graduate work at the University of California (Berkeley). He married his college sweetheart, Nina Vasilieff in 1950. They have two daughters, Natasha and Sandra, and three grandchildren.

He has worked in various federal government departments mainly in Washington, DC. He now does economic consultant work with long-time friend Dr. Andrew Brimmer at his firm, Brimmer and Company, Inc.

CHARLES F. NEMEC, was born in Roundup, MT on Aug. 9, 1921. He joined the 163rd Inf. National Guard in 1939. Inducted into federal service September 1940, 163rd Inf. Regt. and 41st Div. Was sent to Ft. Lewis, WA, Camp Murray.

The 41st Div. boarded *Queen Elizabeth* in San Francisco in March 1942, bound for Australia. He entered the Harbor of Sydney in April, boarded a Dutch transport, and sailed to Melbourne. By train to Camp Seymour for training then to Rockhampton for training. By boat in December to Port Moresby.

Flown to Buna, Sanananda, he took part in Papuan Battle until wounded in January. Returned Stateside as a medical casualty to Presidio, Ft. Walla Walla, WA.

Medically discharged on April 3, 1944 with the rank achieved of sergeant. He received the Purple Heart. Went to college 1945-1948. Received B.A. in economics and sociology and M.A. in history and political science. Was a high school teacher for 32 years before retiring.

Married and has three sons and one grandson. He is a member of the DAV and VFW.

HENRY W. NEW (BILL), was born April 8, 1925 in Charleroi, PA. He entered the service Sept. 17, 1943. Went to Ft. McClellen, AL for basic training. Then to Ft. Ord, CA and on to Angle Island.

He went overseas landing at Milne Bay. Joined the 41st Div in March 1944 at Finchhaven, Dutch New Guinea. Left two days later for the mainland near Weko Island, then to Aitape, both were D-Day landings. Went to Mindanao, Zamboanga, Jolo, and to Davao to Hero, Japan. They went to Magoya, Japan where they left in January 1946 for Ft. Lewis, WA.

Was discharged Jan. 24, 1946 at Camp Atterbury, IN with the rank T/5. He received the Combat Infantry Badge, Distinguished Unit Badge, Asiatic-Pacific Theater with two Bronze Stars, Philippine Liberation with one Bronze Star, World War II Victory Medal, and the Bronze Arrowhead.

Married to Rita on Jan. 10, 1948. They reside in Albuquerque, NM. They have two sons, James and William, one daughter Rita, and four grandchildren. He spent 25 years as a machinist with ACF and 15 years as a tool maker with GE in Albuquerque where he retired in 1988. He enjoys traveling.

DOUGLAS H. NEWTON, was born Dec. 27, 1918 in Hoquiam, WA, and raised in Aberdeen, WA. Drafted Feb. 17, 1941 and assigned to 82nd Brigade Hqs, 41st Div., Ft. Lewis, WA. Stayed with unit upon reorganization of division and outfit became 41st Recon. Troop Mecz., a cavalry unit.

Went overseas in May 1942 and served in Australia, New Guinea, Biak, Philippines (Zamboanga and Jolo). Was rotated from Jolo Island April 1945.

Discharged at Ft. Lewis on June 16, 1945 with the rank of sergeant T/4. He became advertising artist at the Olympian in Washington State capital city of Olympia.

Married to Virla in 1953. Happily retired in 1981 to RV traveling, fishing, oil painting etc. They have three sons, two grandsons, and one granddaughter.

WALTER R. NIEMASZYK, was born Dec. 16, 1919 in Chicago, IL. Inducted Nov. 13, 1941 at Camp Custer, MI, then sent for basic training to Camp Wheeler, GA. In March of 1942 was sent to Ft. Lewis, WA. Assigned to the Anti-tank Company, 186th Regt., 41st Div. Completed entire war service with the same unit, at various places such as Australia, New Guinea and Philippines.

At the end of WWII he was discharged from the 41st Div. in August 1945 while at Zamboanga, Mindanao, Philippine Islands. Later was separated from Army service on Sept. 24, 1945 at Ft. Sheridan, IL. He received the Bronze Star, Good Conduct Medal, American Defense Medal, Asiatic-Pacific Medal with three Bronze Stars and one Bronze Arrowhead, World War II Victory Medal, Combat Infantry Badge, and the Philippine Liberation Medal with one Bronze Star. Returned to civilian occupation as a machinist and other related fields. The last half of the working years were as LIC stationary engineer, until disabled with a cardiac problem.

BERNARD L. NOLAN (PAT), was born Jan. 29, 1924 in Detroit, MI. Entered the service in March 1943. Assigned to Co. E, 163rd Regt., 41st Div. Stationed at New Guinea, Biak Island, Zamboanga, Philippines.

Wounded at Zamboanga by a mortar shell which landed a few feet from his fox hole, shattering his left arm at the elbow. Was hospitalized for a year at Mayo General Hospital in Galesburg.

Discharged with the rank of sergeant. He received the Purple Heart with two clusters, Bronze Star Medal, and the Combat Infantry Badge.

Married Mary in 1946. They have five children and four grandchildren. He retired from United Airlines after 30 years of service.

EARL NORGARD, was born Dec. 2, 1920 in Portland OR. Enlisted in Co. H, 162nd Inf. on Sept. 16, 1940. Trained at Camp Murray and was company G-2, intelligence agent. Shipped to SWPA March 4, 1942 on the *Santa Paula*. Was the only survivor in a forward fire control OP when a heavy mortar shell landed at his feet. After the fighting from Port Moresby to Hollandia, Sgt. Norgard's detachment moved up to an advance island outpost making preparations for island landings that followed.

Returned stateside Dec. 13, 1944, he was confined to an Army hospital until discharged March 1, 1945 with 80% disabilities. Returned to college, he married Frances and raised three children.

Acquiring extensive construction knowledge, he became Portland's chief building inspector, retiring in 1982 after 22 years service. He has an enviable collection of war booty, mostly obtained by midnight requisition, including the last effects of Japanese Gen. Yamishito who was hanged.

LESTER R. NORMAN, was born Oct. 4, 1917 in Chicago, IL. Lived with his parents, Fred and Minnie Norman, until he was drafted into the Army on Oct. 11, 1941 at Camp Grant, IL. Army duty at Camp Roberts, CA; Ft. Lewis, WA, 163rd Sunset Inf. Regt., 41st Div., member of 186th E Co., 163rd E Co., Regimental Hqs.- T-4.

Was sent overseas March 1942 on the *Queen Elizabeth* to Seymour, Australia; Rockhampton, Australia; Finchhaven, Aitape, Biak. Rotated December 1944 to USA. Delay en route to Miami, FL. Assigned to Special Engineering Detachment in Los Alamos, NM.

Discharged Aug. 23, 1944 from Ft. Sheridan, IL. His awards include the Combat Infantry Badge, American Defense Medal, World War II Medal, Good Conduct Medal, Presidential Unit Citation, Bronze Star Medal, Victory with the Oak Leaf Cluster, Campaign and Service Medal, Asiatic-Pacific Campaign, Papuan, New Guinea, two Bronze Stars, and one Bronze Service Arrowhead.

Married to Phyllis B. Line on Sept. 8, 1945 in Evanston, IL and they celebrated their 45th anniversary in 1990. They returned to Los Alamos Feb. 28, 1946. They have three children, Dr. Elizabeth DeNiro, Lester R. Norman Jr. and Mrs. Mary Carlson, and 10 grandchildren.

Lester was the president of Society for Nondestructive Testing and president of Los Alamos chapter of AARP and is presently on the administrative board of the Methodist Church. He retired from Los Alamos Scientific Laboratory January 1980. Moved to Albuquerque, NM in 1985.

CHARLES E. NORTON (CHUCK), was born Feb. 14, 1910 in Sutherlin, OR. Worked in the family fruit canneries. Enlisted Co. D, 162nd Inf., ONG, 1930. Graduated OSU 1934, 2 LT FA, ORC, 1936-41 Continental Can Company Customer Services, Pac. Div. August 1941 assigned as 1 LT 146th FA, 41st Div., Service & C.

March 1943 transferred to Proc. Div. USASOS, SWPA. January 1943, 46 chief, subsistence proc. & inspection for Queensland.

Discharged as major and received the Bronze Star. Establishing technical services for CONTINCAN, Australian associate. Chicago, 1951-71, director tech. services CONTINCAN Overseas Div. 1951 assigned U.S. Army Engineering Labs. 1963 retired as lieutenant colonel, AUS.

He married Joanne Ganong in 1938. In 1971

retired to Monterey, CA. Activities: volunteer golf tournaments, Kiwanis Ecology/Conservation, Meals-on-Wheels. Belongs to ACS, IFT, AUSA and is a life member of ROA, TROA, MOWW.

RUSSELL E. NOYES, was born Nov. 10, 1921 in Beach, ND. Inducted into federal service with the 41st Inf. Div. National Guard on Sept. 16, 1940 at Ft. Lewis, WA.

Stationed South Pacific in March 1942 to December 1945. His units were Division Surgeons Office, and Co. D, 116th Med. Bn. Participated in battles in Dobadura, New Guinea, Finchhaven, New Guinea, Hollandia, Dutch New Guinea, Biak Island, Netherlands East Indies, San Jose, Mindoro, Philippines, Zamboanga, Mindanao, Philippines, Occupation Force Kure, Honshu, Japan.

Discharged in December 1945 with the rank first lieutenant. Awards received: five Bronze Campaign Stars, one Bronze Star Medal, Good Conduct Medal, American Defense Service Medal, Asiatic Pacific Campaign Medal, World War II Victory Medal, Army of Occupation Medal with Japan Clasp, Armed Forces Reserve Medal, Philippine Liberation Ribbon, and Philippine Presidential Unit Citation Badge.

His family includes wife, son, daughter (deceased) and three grandsons. He retired January 1984 in Santa Barbara, CA.

JOHN P. NUCHERENO, was born Nov. 7, 1923 in Buffalo, NY. Now residing in Tonawanda, NY. Graduated from high school in June 1941. Completed sophomore year Canisius College, Buffalo, NY prior to induction on Aug. 5, 1943.

Infantry basic training at Camp Fannin, TX. Joined L Co. 162nd\Inf., approximately March 1, 1944. Days later (he doesn't know if he volunteered or was drafted) joined Medics, 1st Bn. 162nd.

Wounded on Biak Island June 12, 1944; wounded at Zamboanga, Philippine Islands March 10, 1945; was evacuated to the States. Spent six months hospitalized at Ft. Devens, MA. Discharged Sept. 10, 1945.

Received his degree from Canisius College in 1949. Married to Peg in 1952. They have three children, Susan, John Jr. and Joseph. All have received college degrees. He has four grandchildren.

He worked for the U.S. Department of Labor mainly investigating union election and union finances. Transferred to and eventually retired from the U.S. Federal Labor Relations Authority in 1980. He enjoys golf, gardening, camping, and wood working.

FRANK L. NUENTHAL, was born Dec. 9, 1916 in Butte, MT. Entered the service June 17, 1941. Assigned to 41st QM and 741st Ord., stationed at Ft. Lewis, WA and overseas.

Spent four and a half years in Australia, New Guinea, Biak, and Philippines with 41st men who were great guys and good friends. Discharged with the rank of staff sergeant.

Married a Rockhampton girl, Nellie (Barry), in October 1943 and still happily married. They have a beautiful daughter Gail and a beautiful granddaughter Melissa.

ROBERT A. NYBERG, was born Jan. 6, 1924 in Chicago, IL. Entered the service March 4, 1943, assigned to Co. D, 163rd Inf., 41st Div. Basic training at Camp Roberts, CA.

Overseas to Australia, New Guinea, Philippine Islands, and Japan. Memorable experience was March 13, 1945, Blow Up Hill, Zamboanga, Mindanao, an observer team attached to A Co., 163rd Inf., his Buck Rogers imatation was authentic!

Discharged with the rank of private first class. He received the Purple Heart, Bronze Star, and Combat Infantry Badge.

Married Charmaine in 1948 and has two children, Nancy and Richard. He retired and now enjoys playing golf and traveling to see parts of the world he didn't see in WWII.

NOEL R. O'BRIEN, was Dec. 29, 1917 in San Francisco, CA. Educated at St. Ignatius High School and the University of San Francisco. He joined the Army on July 11, 1941. Took basic training at Ft. Monmouth, NJ from July to October 1941.

Transferred to Ft. Lewis, WA where he joined the 41st Inf. Div., serving with the Signal Corps for the duration of his enlistment. He shipped out to the South Pacific on May 19, 1942, and served in Australia, New Guinea, and the Philippines, achieving the rank of technical sergeant.

Noel was discharged from the 41st at Camp Beale, CA on July 11, 1945. He was awarded the Philippine Liberation Ribbon with one Bronze Star, the Asiatic-Pacific Campaign Medal, the American Defense Service Medal, and the Good Conduct Medal.

Noel married Patricia McCarthy on Sept. 25, 1948. They had four children and two grandchildren. He worked for 35 years for ASARCO/Federated Metals in San Francisco and Los Angeles. Noel was national president of the 41st Infantry Division Association from 1975 to 1976. Noel passed away on July 23, 1990.

VERNON O'BRYAN, was born Sept. 3, 1919. Entered the service in July 1942, assigned to C Co., 116th Combat Engrs. and Med. Stationed at Camp Wheeler, GA, Camp Butner, NC and overseas in Australia, Japan, New Guinea, Philippines, Zamboanga and Biak.

Discharged with the rank of staff sergeant on Dec. 7, 1945. He received the Philippines Liberation Medal, Good Conduct Medal, two Bronze Service Stars and Arrowhead, and World War II Victory Medal.

His family consists of wife Josephine; sons, Vernon Jr. and James; daughter-in-law Donna; and two grandsons, Jacob and John. Vernon worked as boat captain for 31 years. He retired in 1984 and lives in Pompano Beach, FL.

ROBERT PATRICK O'CONNOR, was born in Braddock, PA. Attended Catholic University of America, class of 1950. Joined the Hqs. 41st Div. Arty. in 1943 and with them till his discharge.

Was producer/director of Lenawee Players, Henrietta Loft, Rochester Arena Theater; agent for MCA; salesman; president of O'Connor Productions; secretary to editor in chief of *Silver Screen* and *Screenland* magazines; dance/theater critic; ghosted many books including a million copy seller called *The Monkees Go Mod*; started O'Connor Dance Library in Israel.

Currently a full-time ski instructor at Killington, VT and a part-time editor for *Warner Books* where he edits the work of Rev. Andrew M. Greeley among others. Also lectures regularly on writing and publishing at universities.

WAYNE E. OGLESBY, was born June 8, 1923 in Meadowbrook, OR. Entered the service Feb. 25, 1942. Assigned to 205th Regt., C Btry., FA at Camp Roberts, CA; Ft. Lewis, WA; and overseas to Australia, New Guinea, Philippines, and Japan.

Most memorable experience was entering Hiroshima after the bomb was dropped and inventorying the supply depot in the interior of Japan.

Discharged Jan. 2, 1946 with the rank of staff sergeant. He received the Bronze Service Arrowhead, World War II Victory Medal, Bronze Service Star, Asiatic-Pacific Service Medal and the Good Conduct Medal.

Married to Beverly on June 8, 1946. They live in Molalla, OR. He has two children, Tamara and Connie. Has been in TV and radio sales and service for 39 years. Also manager of bowling alley.

ADOLPH OLLEK, was born Jan. 4, 1914 at Hillsboro, KS. Entered the service July 1943. Was joined to the 70th Inf. Div. received his basic and overseas training at Camp Adair, OR, Ft. Ord and Camp Stoneman, CA.

Left for the Pacific Theater in May 1944. Landed at Milne Bay in June, where he joined the 41st Div., 116th Engrs. Combat Bn. He served at Hollandia, Aitape, Wadke Islands, Biak, Mindora, made initial invasion of Zamboanga, and the first landing at Hiroshima, Japan.

Arrived back in the States and was discharged January 1946 with the rank of T/4. He was awarded the Asiatic-Pacific Service Medal, Philippine Liberation Ribbon, Bronze Star, and WWII Victory Medal.

Married Laura Haas, has one daughter, son-in-law, and two grandsons, Jason and Ryan. He retired from Kansas Department of Transportation in 1979.

MANUEL LUCIANO ORDONEZ, was born May 5, 1926 in San Leandro, CA. Joined the 41st Recon., Hqs. Co. Trained at Camp Roberts, CA. His memorable experience was his first patrol, they didn't see any Japs, but they were all scared until they returned to camp.

Discharged Sept. 28, 1946. He received the Asiatic-Pacific Medal, Philippine Liberation Ribbon with Bronze Star, Army of Occupation Medal, and the Good Conduct Medal.

Married 36 years to Rose M. Ordonez. They have three children, Elizabeth, Gregor, and Manuel. Retired and lives in Auburn, CA. He is a member of the Northern California Chapter #31130.

HARRY E. OVERBY, was born July 1, 1918 in St. Louis, MO. graduated from Maplewood High School and attended St. Louis University. Drafted on June 14, 1941 and joined the 6th Inf. Div. at Ft. Leonard Wood, MO.

Graduated from Ft. Benning as second lieutenant in July 1942. Joined the 102nd Div. at Camp Maxey, TX. Left as replacement in October 1943. Arrived at Ft. Ord and left San Francisco in January 1944 for Brisbane, Australia.

Joined the 163rd Regt. at Rockhampton on February 20. Went to Finchhaven, New Guinea, Aitape, Toem, Wadke Island and Biak in F Co. Joined H Co. on Biak and went to Mindoro, Zamboanga, Sangi-Sangi, Bongo, and Jolo. Occupied Hiro, Japan October 1945 as company CO.

Left for the States via Panama Canal. Landed in Brooklyn on Jan. 3, 1946. Was discharged with rank lieutenant colonel at Jefferson Barracks in April.

Rejoined Wohl Shoe Company, retired after 41 years. He is a member of MONG and Reserve Officers Associations. Married 50 years to Virginia.

RAY OVERMAN, was born Dec. 8, 1918 at Iola, KS. Entered the service Feb. 28, 1941. Stationed at Ft. Lewis, WA.

Discharged with the rank of staff sergeant. He received two Bronze Stars, for Papuan and New Guinea Campaign, the Distinguished Unit Badge, and American Defense Service Medal.

Married to Betty Brookman on May 11, 1945. They lived on a ranch in Coleville, CA and moved to Southern California where he worked as an automobile salesman. He has one son Ray Jr. and two grandsons. He retired in 1984 and moved to Palm Desert, CA. At the time of his retirement, he was vice president and general manager of the Lincoln/Mercury dealership in San Gabriel and general manager of Deluxe Leasing Company.

He is a member of the American Legion Post 135, Alhambra, CA and a member of the Masonic Lodge 635, in San Marino, CA.

MINNEKUS PALTZER, was born Oct. 5, 1917 near Pella, IA. Entered the service Oct. 28, 1941 at Ft. Des Moines, IA, Co. D, 186th Inf. Stationed at Camp Wolters, TX, Ft. Lewis, WA, and overseas. Was in charge of an 81mm mortar in Buna, New Guinea, Biak and Southern Philippines.

His memorable experience was interviewing two sumatrans who spoke only Dutch. Discharged with the rank of staff sergeant.

Married to Florence in 1948. They have two sons,

Daniel and Seth. One is a child abuse investigator and the other a MD. Went to watch-making school in Kansas City, MO. Quit watch repair and started to work at Pella Post Office in 1965.

Retired in 1987 and has been making furniture for the family since then. He enjoys camping, hunting, and fishing.

GEORGE P. PAPADOPLOS, was born Sept. 12, 1923 in Wilkes-Barre, PA. Graduated from high school in 1941. Inducted July 29, 1943 and sent to Camp Adair, OR for basic training with the 70th Inf. Div.

Joined the 116th Combat Engrs., 41st Inf. Div. at Biak Island. Went on to the Philippines and Japan and helped close down the 116th Engrs. as their last sergeant-major when the 41st Inf. Div. was deactivated officially Dec. 31, 1945 in Japan.

Was discharged Feb. 13, 1946. Returned to college to complete his studies and on completion married Helen in 1950. They have two children, Peter and Anastasius, and five grandchildren. He became an active owner and corporation officer of a dry-cleaning firm and retired in 1989.

He is a member of the American Legion, VFW, Order of Ahepa, Masons, Consistory, and Shrine bodies. They reside in Kingston, PA.

FRANK J. PAPROCKI JR., was born June 14, 1919 in Laport, IN. Entered the service April 11, 1941, assigned to 162nd Inf., Hqs. & Hqs, 2nd Bn. at New Guinea, Zamboanga, Philippine Islands.

Discharged with the rank of private first class E/3. He received the Bronze Star and Purple Heart.

Frank passed away in 1959. He had two sons.

CALVIN C. PARENTEAU, was born July 2, 1917 in Scanlon, MN. Graduated from high school in Cloquet, MN in 1935. Moved to Los Angeles, CA in 1936. Was drafted Feb. 20, 1941 and went to Ft. Lewis for basic training. Was assigned to Hqs. Co., 163rd Inf.

Was in all New Guinea campaigns from Sanananda to Biak. Memorable experience was furlough in Melbourne, Australia. Came back to the U.S. on rotation plan Dec. 4, 1944. Was put in the 441st Army Air Forces Base Unit.

Received discharge in September 1945 with the rank T/5. He received the Good Conduct Medal and the Distinguished Unit Badge.

Worked 13 years on the Huges Flying Boat and 20 years at McDonald Douglas, Long Beach, CA. Presently retired and having a "ball." He is a member of the American Legion and the Elks.

He has two daughters, Nanette and Tina, one son, John, and four grandchildren.

HARRY R. PARKER, was born March 21, 1926 in Veronia, OR. He entered the service Sept. 30, 1944, assigned to I Co. 163rd. Stationed in the South Pacific.

Discharged with the rank of technical sergeant. He is married to Dorothy and has two daughters, Connie and Lorrie, and four grandchildren. He retired in 1988.

ROBERT LEE PARKER, was born Feb. 7, 1926 in Warren County, IA where he grew up and attended school until 1944. Was inducted in the Army June 14, 1944 at Camp Dodge, IA. Trained at Camp Hood, TX and joined A Co., 163rd in March 1945 at Mindoro.

Was with A Co. in beach landings at Zamboanga and Jolo Islands. Was transferred to Service Company and went to Kure, Japan with the 41st for occupation. When 41st was deactivated in December 1945, he was transferred to 4th Engr. Service Bn. and later to 864th EAB Engrs.

Left Tokyo, Japan on May 1, 1946 and was discharged at Ft. Leavenworth, KS on May 18, 1946.

Married Anne Roby on Sept. 10, 1946. They have sons, Bob Jr., John, and Dennis, and daughters Melinda and Julie. Also has five grandsons and five granddaughters.

He lives on a small farm in Warren County, IA. Retired after 40 years in building trade as a building contractor. He is a member of the VFW and the American Legion.

RAYMOND F. PASVOGEL, was born Sept. 10, 1918 in Rochester Twp. Entered the service Oct. 29, 1941. Trained at Camp Wolters, TX and Ft. Lewis, WA, I Co., Regt. Hqs, 186th Service Co.

He served 36 months overseas in Australia, New Guinea, Dutch East Indies and the Philippines with the 41st Inf. Div.

Discharged June 3, 1945 with the rank of sergeant T/4. He received the Combat Infantry Badge, Bronze Star, Purple Heart, Good Conduct Medal, American Defense Ribbon, Asiatic-Pacific Ribbon with three Battle Stars, and the Philippine Liberation Ribbon with one star.

He is a widower with one daughter and one

granddaughter. Retired in 1980 in Davenport, IA. He enjoys bowling and traveling.

OLIVER J. PATRICK, was born May 7, 1915 in Portland, OR. Entered the service March 28, 1941, 3rd Bn., 162nd Inf., 41st Div. Stationed at Ft. Lewis, WA, Camp Maxey, Paris, TX, and overseas.

Had 76 days of combat at Nassau Bay, Salamaua, Paval, Defile Ambush, bloody Biak, Buna, and Hollandia.

Discharged with the rank of staff sergeant. He received the Purple Heart, Silver Star, Bronze Star, and Combat Infantry Badge.

Married to Beatrice, has one son and one daughter, Brian and Darlene Fleming. Grandchildren: Robbie, Julia, Brian Bryn. He is semi-retired.

STEPHEN PARISH, was born March 1, 1914. Joined the service August 1943. Assigned to 162nd Regt., 1st Bn., Co. D. Stationed overseas in the South Pacific. Memorable experiences: Battle of Biak and Occupation of Japan.

Discharged with the rank of staff sergeant. He received the Bronze Star, three Battle Stars, Good Conduct Medal, Rifle Badge, and others.

Married and has sons, Steve and David. David served in Vietnam and died of cancer at age 38. Stephen is retired, lives in Lyons, IL, and enjoys gardening.

CHARLES P. PAUL, was born Dec. 26, 1909 in Max, ND. Entered the service in February 1941, Service Btry., 218th FA, Ft. Lewis, WA, Australia, New Guinea, and the Philippines.

Discharged with the rank of private first class. He made many friendships that last until today.

Married to Christine in 1949, daughter born in 1951, and widowed in 1975. He married Betty in 1984. They live in Portland, OR. He retired from Portland Parks Dept.

WESLEY EUGENE PAYNE, was born Oct. 26, 1924 in Maylene, AL. Entered the Army on July 16, 1943. Stationed at McPherson, GA, assigned to Co. A, 162nd Inf., 41st Div. Served as private at Camp Fannin, TX from August 1943 to December 1943.

Left California on Feb. 7, 1944 and arrived at Brisbain, Australia on Feb. 25, 1944. Engaged in battles at Hollandia, Biak Islands, Zamboanga Philippines on March 10, 1945.

Returned to the States as staff sergeant on Jan. 26, 1946. Discharged at Camp Shelby, MS on Feb. 1, 1946. His decorations include the Asiatic-Pacific Theater, Philippines Liberation Ribbon with one Bronze Star, Combat Infantry Badge, Good Conduct Medal, Bronze Arrowhead, and World War II Victory Medal.

Married to Kathryn Wallace in 1946. They have five sons, three daughters, 19 grandchildren, and one great-granddaughter. Retired from Southern Railway after 35 years as assistant track supervisor.

RALPH PAYTON, was born June 30, 1924 in Wallingford, IA. Drafted Feb. 22, 1943 and trained at Camp Roberts, CA. Shipped to Australia in July 1943 and joined 41st in August 1943. Served entire war with 205th FA, 162nd Regt. Combat Team.

Made landings at Hollandia, New Guinea, Biak Island, and Zamboanga in the Philippines and was attached to X Corps to liberate eastern Mindanao Island. Served in occupation in Kure, Japan. Was discharged with the rank of staff sergeant on Dec. 4, 1945.

Married Mary Francis Halstead in 1942. They have four children: Jim, Dick, Bob, and Mary Jean. He and Mary Francis reside in Emmetsburg, IA where they operate an antique store as their hobby.

DEAN P. PERKINS, was born Dec. 5, 1922 in Portland, OR. Enlisted summer of 1940. Assigned to Btry. C, 218th Service, 146th FA, C-205th FA, Ft. Lewis, WA and 40 months overseas.

Memorable experience was the time spent on Biak Island. Discharged with the rank of corporal, he received all the usual Pacific area medals.

Married to Myrna in January 1946. He has two daughters, Roberta and DeAnn. He retired as a Greyhound Bus driver.

ROBERT CLAY PERKINS, was born Sept. 15, 1923 in Seattle, WA. Enlisted Btry. F, 146th FA, 41st Div. June 25, 1940 at age 16. Active Army duty at Camp Murray, Ft. Lewis, WA from Sept. 16, 1940 to Aug. 9, 1941. Discharged as a private first class, specialist 6th class, for minority reasons to finish high school.

Joined the U.S. Marines Nov. 12, 1943. Boot camp and Anti-tank School followed in San Diego. Overseas from April 1944 to January 1946. Saw combat with Weapons Company, 5th Marines Regt., 1st Marine Div. against the Japanese on Peleliu, Okinawa and in the occupation of China. His unit was awarded two Presidential Unit Citations.

Robert credits his Army training as helpful for survival. After WWII, he returned to Seattle, graduated from the University of Seattle in 1949.

Married Dagny Myrwang on Dec. 31, 1947. They have seven children and six grandchildren. He retired as a transportation sales and traffic manager after 35 years of service.

He is a member of the 41st Infantry Division Association, life member of 1st Marine Division Association, American Legion, the China Marine Association, and the University of Washington Alumni Association.

QUINTEN E. PETERS, was born March 20, 1924 in Worthington, MN. He joined the Army February 1943. Basic training at Camp Roberts, CA, assigned to Co. E 163, 41st Div. July 1943, at Rockhampton, Australia.

Was wounded on patrol at Toem, New Guinea. Sergeant Peters returned to Co. E at Biak. While on Biak he was transferred to Army Forces Western Pacific Headquarters.

Returned to the USA from the Philippines in July 1945. Discharged October 1945, served later as a second lieutenant in Minnesota Guard until moving to California in 1957.

Married Phyllis in August 1945. They have two children, Susan and Todd. Quinten worked for the state of California DMV for 25 years. He was office manager at Turlock, Santa Barbara, Napa, and Sacramento. The last six years he was manager in charge of vehicle and vessel registration at headquarters. He retired in 1984. Quinten and Phyllis live in the Sierra foothills near Placerville, CA.

REINHOLDT PETERSEN, was born June 6, 1916 in Denmark. Arrived in USA at age 4 1/2. Graduated from Hayward Union High School in 1934. Drafted June 18, 1941. Went to Camp Roberts for 13 weeks training. Joined 41st Inf. Div. at Ft. Lewis, WA and served with Hqs. Co. 163.

Went to New Guinea at the end of December 1941. Was in the Battle of Sanananda. After about nine months in New Guinea, he got all kinds of jungle diseases and spent 14 months in Army hospitals.

Came back to the States on hospital ship *Maraposa*. Spent rest of time at Camp Maxey, TX training troops etc. Was discharged Sept. 24, 1945 with the rank private first class. His awards include the Combat Infantry Badge, Good Conduct Ribbon, Asiatic-Pacific Theater Ribbon, two Bronze Stars, American Defense Ribbon, and the Presidential Citation.

Married to Ebba and had three daughters and four grandchildren. He retired as a construction superintendent in 1980. He resides in San Carlos, CA.

CHARLES O. PETERSON, was born Nov. 26, 1918 in Logan, UT. Was inducted Feb. 20, 1941, trained at Camp Murray, WA and served in 148th FA for about six months. Transferred to Finance Office, 41st DHQ for remainder of service.

Went overseas on March 19, 1942 on the *Queen Elizabeth*. Stationed at Seymour, Australia; Rockhampton, Australia; Dobodura, New Guinea; Finchhaven, New Guinea; Biak, NEI; Mindoro, PI; Zamboanga, PI. Left for the U.S. on July 23, 1945 and was discharged Aug. 20, 1945 with the rank T/4. He enjoyed the time spent in Australia and cherishes the many good buddies while in the service.

Married in 1955 and has two daughters and one son. Retired after working for IRS for 35 years as

Internal Revenue agent, and chief, Review Staff for the district of Idaho. Passed CPA exam in 1955. His hobbies are playing at casual dance jobs, golfing, fishing, and upland bird hunting.

GEORGE W. PETERSON, was born June 8, 1917 in Chicago, IL. Joined the service Oct. 13, 1941. Assigned to 41st Div., 162nd Regt., 1st Bn., Co. C and served entire war with them. Stationed at Ft. Lewis, Australia, New Guinea, and the Philippines.

Discharged with the rank T/5. He received the Good Conduct, Asiatic-Pacific Service Medal, American Defense Service Medal, Presidential Unit Citation, Philippine Liberation Service Medal with one Bronze Star, and Infantry Combat Badge.

Married Marie Oct. 7, 1941 and has four children, Marie, Vicki, George Jr., and Ronald. He is retired from the Los Angeles Police Department.

WILLIAM L. PETERSON, was drafted into the Army June 26, 1941. He was one of five from his family in WWII. He took basic training at Camp Roberts, CA and was sent to Ft. Lewis, WA where he was shipped out Dec. 5, 1941 on the *Etalon* with the 218th FA Bn., Btry. A to the Philippines. They were 680 miles out when Pearl Harbor was bombed and the *Etalon* was sent back to San Francisco, CA on Dec. 10, 1941 where he spent a month on guard duty at the Presidio.

He later heard that the Japanese bombed a lumber ship of ours thinking it was the *Etalon*. He was sent to Satsop, WA as there was no room for them at Ft. Lewis. Without a leave home he was transferred to Btry. A, 146th FA. Was a gun crewman, light artillery #844, First Class Gunner. On April 22, 1942 was sent to Melbourne Australia and then to Rockhampton, New Guinea, Biak Island, Mindoro, and Jolo Islands.

Was sent back to Ft. Lewis to be discharged 41 months later on Sept. 9, 1945 with the rank of corporal. His decorations include the Asiatic-Pacific Theater Medal, Good Conduct Medal, American Defense Medal with clasp, and the Philippine Liberation Medal with one Bronze Star.

He and Florence Hawley were married Sept. 21, 1945 and have two boys, two girls, 13 grandchildren, and two great-grandchildren. He retired from the U.S. Forest Service June 1985 after 25 years of service.

ALAN B. PHILLIPS, was born Aug. 9, 1919 in Seattle, WA. Enlisted March 19, 1936 in Washington National Guard. Served with E Btry., 146th FA. Inducted into federal service Sept. 16, 1940.

Went to SWPA (Australia and New Guinea) March 19, 1942. Memorable experience was training as pack artillery for 10 months at Crystal Creek. Served with B Btry., 167th FA Bn. until October 1944 when rotated stateside.

After R&R in Santa Barbara, was re-assigned to the 536th FA Bn. at Camp Gruber, OK. VE-Day started the point system for discharge and he was discharged June 12, 1945. He received all the usual awards.

Married Ilmi on July 17, 1941. He has two daughters and three grandsons. Now enjoying retirement.

CARL E. PHILLIPS, was born Jan. 28, 1925 in Weiner, AR. Graduated from Weiner High School in 1942. Inducted into Army in October 1943. Stationed in Tyler, TX then served in New Guinea, Netherland East Indies, Philippines, and Japan.

Some battles were Biak, Jolo, Mindanao, and then went to Hiroshima after the bomb was dropped.

Discharged January 1946 with the rank of technical sergeant, he received the Asiatic-Pacific Theater Ribbon with two Bronze Stars and one Bronze Arrowhead, the Philippine Liberation Ribbon and one Bronze Star, and the Purple Heart.

Married Betty in 1947, they have three daughters, one son, and two grandchildren. He is president of C. Phillips Farms Inc., a family owned corporation, where he is still actively engaged in farming. All three daughters have degrees from Arkansas State University with two having master degrees. His son is currently majoring in agriculture, business, and economics at ASU.

He is past president of Lawrence County Farm Bureau, member of First Baptist Church, Walnut Ridge Country Club, and Elks Club.

KENNETH E. PHILLIPS, was born June 20, 1918. Assigned to K, Hqs. 3rd Bn., E, F, Hqs., 2nd Bn., Division Headquarters. Stationed at Ft. Lewis, WA, New Guinea, Philippines, Salamaua, Hollandia, Biak, Zamboanga, and Basilam.

Discharged with the rank of captain. He received the Combat Infantry Badge, Purple Heart (wounded twice), Bronze Star, and various campaign and service ribbons.

Married and has two children. He is a purchasing director.

ARTHUR J. PIERCE, was born Aug. 2, 1915 in Mason City, NE. Was drafted October 1941, Ft. Sheridan, IL. After basic at Camp Roberts, CA, was assigned to B Co., 186th Inf., 41st, Inf. Div., Ft. Lewis, WA.

Went to Australia in April 1942, transferred to division headquarters. In January 1943 went to New Guinea as Gen. Fuller's orderly. There contracted malaria and yellow jaundice. Hospitalized in Port Moresby and Townsville. Upon recovery was sent back to Dobodura, New Guinea, Rockhampton, Biak, and the Philippines. Worked in Div. A G Section.

Discharged at Ft. Logan, CO in October 1945 with the rank T/3.

Art returned to work at Chicago law-publishing company. Married Hazel (an ex-WAVE), has three children and four grandchildren.

Returning to Nebraska, Art operated his own sign business, retiring in 1980. Now he practices his avocation, calligraphy, as personal business and in Artists-in-Schools Program. He resides in Kearney, NE.

RAYMOND AUTHUR PLATTS, was born June 18, 1912 in Hubbard, OR. He graduated in 1930 from Jefferson High in Portland and in 1936 from University of Oregon in business administration.

During college he joined the National Guard serving as a staff sergeant, Hqs. Btry., 1st Bn. of the 218th FA. In September 1940, Ray was promoted to second lieutenant and in July 1941 to first lieutenant.

In 1942 the 218th shipped out to the Philippines. Ray was again promoted to captain between January 1943 and June 1944. Was at Wakde Island, Biak, Zamboanga and took R&R at Rockhampton. Before leaving the service in 1945 at the end of his rotation, he was up for promotion to major.

During his service in the South Pacific he received the American Defense and Asiatic-Pacific Theatre Ribbons along with the World War II Victory Medal, Air Medal, and Purple Heart. He was wounded during a reconnaissance flight.

He continued to be active in the Coast Guard Auxiliary, Depoe Bay Volunteer Fire District and Shriners. He was in the Masonic Lodge and a past patron of the Eastern Star at the Taft Lodge.

Married to Patricia Ruth Clark on Oct. 11, 1948. They had one daughter Marietta Lee. He owned and operated Coast Marine Service at Depoe Bay during their 10 year residence, moving to Portland in 1958.

During a business trip near Lewiston, ID in May 1960, Ray's car crashed. Complications from the accident resulted in his death June 10, 1960. He is survived by Patricia, Marietta and two granddaughters, Emily and Wendy Seymore, who live in Portland.

JOHN N. POAGE, was born Nov. 3, 1926 in Portland, OR. He entered the service Feb. 3, 1945, assigned to the 41st Div. Band, stationed at Zamboanga, Philippine Islands and Hiro, Japan. He also served with the 24th Div. Band and the 21st Army Band (Korean).

Memorable experience was the trip to Hiroshima aboard the U.S. *Cecil* and riding out a typhoon off Okinawa while moving to Japan for occupation service.

Discharged with the rank T/5. He received the Army of Occupation (Japan), Good Conduct Medal, Asiatic-Pacific, and the World War II Victory Medal.

Married with seven grown children and five grandchildren. He is a member of the VFW, American Legion, Elks, and Eagles. He is a retired public school music teacher and presently working as a shift supervisor for a security firm. He enjoys golfing and fishing.

LEONARD B. POHLMEIER, was born March 29, 1912 in Lawrence, NE. Graduated 8th grade from St. Stephen Parochial School. Raised on a farm and when the drought hit in the 1920s and 1930s, moved to Montana. He entered the service March 3, 1941 and was assigned to 116th QM at Ft. Lewis, WA. When the 41st was reorganized he was put in Ord. 741st.

Left San Francisco on April 20, 1942 for the South Pacific and landed at Melbourne May 14, 1942. Sent to

Sidney, Brisbane, Rockhampton, New Guinea, Biak, Leyte, Mindoro, etc.

Overseas 39 months. Arrived back in the States July 10, 1945. Discharged at Salt Lake City, UT. Returned to Helena, MT. and worked for the city until his retirement in 1976. Married in 1941, he lost his wife in 1977. He is living in a retirement home in Helena, MT.

DONALD L. POIRIER, was born April 1, 1916 in Cascade, MT. Entered the service on Feb. 24, 1941. Assigned to Co. F, 162nd, 41st Div. Stationed at Ft. Lewis, WA. Served as squad leader in infantry rifle company with campaigns in New Guinea and Philippines. Was injured in Dutch New Guinea on June 7, 1944.

Discharged June 8, 1945 with the rank of private first class. He received the Purple Heart, American Defense Service Medal, Asiatic-Pacific Theater Medal, and the Philippine Liberation Medal with one Bronze Star.

Married to Phyllis in August 1946, no children. He worked as auto partsman and retired in April 1978. Hobbies were camping, hunting, fishing, and square dancing. Donald passed away Nov. 16, 1981.

WAYNE W. POOL, was born Nov. 5, 1923 at Blunt, SD. Lived on a farm and graduated from Blunt High School in 1941. Enlisted in the Army in February 1943 and took basic training at Camp Roberts, CA.

Went to Australia in July 1943 and was assigned to Co. E, 163rd Regt. Served in New Guinea, Philippines, and Japan. Discharged in January 1945.

Married Patsy Mercer in 1950. They have two children, Randy and Tamara, and three grandchildren. He worked for a rural electric coop for 34 years and retired in 1984. Sparetime is spent hunting and fishing. He is a member of the Blunt City Council for 17 years and served as mayor of Blunt for 14 years. He is a member of the American Legion, Masonic Lodge, Shrine, Blunt Senior Citizens, Selective Service Board, 41st Division Association and life member of VFW.

PAT P. POTESTE, was born April 7, 1921 in Greenburg, PA. Entered the service July 16, 1942,

assigned to 116th Engrs., Co. B. Memorable experience was when two torpedoes went past troop ship. When torpedo boat sighted sub, sank same.

Discharged with the rank of sergeant, he received the Legion of Merit, three Bronze Stars, and Bronze Arrowhead.

Married in 1946 to grade school sweetheart. They have three children and six grandchildren. Was a merchant for 22 years and is now retired.

HYLE L. POTTS, was born Dec. 9, 1920 in Sioux City, IA. Entered the service Sept. 16, 1940 and assigned to Co. I, 162nd, stationed at Ft. Lewis, WA and the South Pacific.

Memorable experience was the day he left I Co. in 1944 to rotate home to his wife and daughter.

Discharged with the rank of staff sergeant. He received the Combat Infantry Badge, Bronze Medal, Good Conduct, South Pacific, American Defense, and the World War II Victory Medal.

Married in July 1941 and has two daughters, seven grandchildren, and eight great-grandchildren. He is retired from the civil service and just enjoying life.

CECIL C. POWELL, was born May 13, 1918 in Billings, MT. Migrated to the state of Washington as a baby and then to Torrance, CA in 1925. He graduated from high school in 1936. Entered the Army Feb. 16, 1941 and was sent directly to Ft. Lewis, WA. Assigned to D Co., 162nd Inf., 41st Div. on Feb. 28, 1941.

After Pearl Harbor, they were shipped to Australia and overseas training in Seymour, Victoria, and Rockhampton, Queensland, prior to going to New Guinea. He saw combat duty in Morobe, Nassau Bay, Salamaua, Hollandia, Biak, and Soepiori. He returned to the States on Jan. 1, 1945 for 30 days leave and was supposed to return to D Co., 162nd Inf. in the Philippine Islands but with the malaria bug going wild in his body, he couldn't stay out of hospitals long enough to rejoin the company.

He was discharged Aug. 28, 1945 after VJ-Day. His awards and decorations include the Bronze Star, Combat Infantry Badge, Presidential Distinguished Unit Badge, Good Conduct Medal, American Defense Service Medal, Asiatic-Pacific Campaign Medal, Victory World War II Medal, and American Campaign Medal.

Married his pre-war sweetheart Jan. 6, 1945. He has one daughter, two granddaughters, one stepdaughter, two stepsons with a total of four step-grandchildren.

He retired Nov. 15, 1976 after 40 years with the Torrance Municipal Water Department. With his wife he travels the USA, Canada, and other parts of the world. He has been back to Australia three times. They travel by ship, air, and motorhome.

WALTER W. POWERS, was born June 26, 1916 in Roseburg, OR. Entered the service in August 1935. Assigned to Co. E, 162nd Regt., 41st Div. Stationed at Ft. Lewis, WA. Was aboard ship 52 days going to Australia. He served in New Guinea.

Discharged with the rank of first lieutenant. He received the Asiatic-Pacific Theater Medal with one Bronze Star, American Theater Service Ribbon, and the World War II Victory Medal.

Married July 2, 1941 he has one son. He is retired in Reno, NE and recovering from a stroke.

KENNETH E. PRATT, was born 1921 in Colorado. He joined the Hqs. Btry. of the 218th FA on Sept. 1, 1940 in Portland, OR, the day the National Guard was inducted into the Army of the U.S.

At Camp Murray and Ft. Lewis until November 1941 when part of the unit was sent to the Philippines. Their unarmed ship left San Francisco and was entering Hawaii when Pearl Harbor was bombed. The ship returned to San Francisco, and they returned to Ft. Lewis and rejoined the division in January 1942.

With the troops that left San Francisco for Melbourne, Australia in May 1942. Served with the unit in Australia, New Guinea, up through the islands into the Philippines and in August 1945 was on a ship to Seattle when the nuclear bombs were dropped on Japan, bringing the war to an end.

After the war, he returned to Colorado and graduated from the University of Denver in 1949 with a degree in electrical engineering. After graduation was employed by Mountain Bell in Boise, ID, later transferring to Denver, CO then to New Jersey and back to Denver. Retired in 1983 after a career in engineering and personnel.

He married Jewel Jones in 1946 and has a daughter Lorraine, a CPA, and a son Ronald, an engineer. He and his wife now reside in Denver, CO. They have returned to the Pacific Northwest, their favorite vacation area, on many trips.

WILLIAM BURDETTE PREIFERT, was born on a farm southeast of Belvidere in Thayer County, NE on Feb. 27, 1921. Uncle Sam called him to Ft. Crook, NE where he was drafted and inducted on July 25, 1942. Boot training was at Camp Roberts, CA and after a train ride across the U.S. to Camp Butner, NC, he was trained to sleep in fox holes full of water, dry shave, bathe in his helmet and run two miles every morning before breakfast.

After another train ride across the U.S. he rode the *Delta Queen* three times out to the USS *O'Hare* for her maiden voyage out of San Franciso. Thirty days at sea found them unable to leave the ship even after they had landed in the Sidney, Australia harbor.

Volunteers were appointed to become the Provisional Engineers. This was a medical unit established to test atabrine. About 120 men were loaded onto a dilapidated New Guinea freighter and taken into the jungle where they were deliberately exposed to malaria. Although he was given atabrine he acquired P. Vivax malaria.

After spending time in the hospital in Toowomba, Australia for malaria he was assigned to the 116th Combat Engrs. of the 41st Div.

The initial invasion of Hollandia went like a text book invasion, but Biak was something else. He acquired yellow jaundice and hepatitis there and was put on the USS *Hope* Hospital Ship and taken to a field hospital in Milne Bay. After recuperating he was sent to the Basilian Island and Zamboanga where he was put into water supply.

The big bomb brought things to an end and he went in to Kure, Japan. He was one of three sent into Hiroshima to find water there 30 days after the bomb. They tapped into the underground iron pipe and pumped water into a canvas tank in the heart of Hiroshima.

T/Sgt. Preifert was happy to spend New Year's

Day in 1946 as a civilian again. Overseas he often thought if he ever got back to his Nebraska farm, he would never again leave it. He married Virginia Griffin and has two children, Jack and Leah. He intends to live his last day on his farm near Belvidere, NE.

NORMAN PROCESS, was born July 16, 1918 in Robinsville, WI. He joined the Service Sept. 7, 1941. Basic training at Camp Grant, IL; Camp Roberts, CA; and Ft. Lewis, WA. Served with Co. G, 163rd, 41st Div.

Overseas to Rockhampton, Australia, then to New Guinea. He fought in two major battles.

Discharged Oct. 5, 1945 with the rank of private first class. He received the Papuan Campaign Medal, New Guinea Campaign, Asiatic-Pacific Theater Medal with two Bronze Stars, American Defense Service Medal, Distinguished Unit Badge, Good Conduct Medal, and the Combat Infantry Badge.

Married to Irene 50 years ago. They have a son and daughter, Gaylord and Mary Jane, and four grandchildren, Shannon, Eric, Matthew, and Lori. He is a life member of VFW Post 9677 in Wisconsin.

DARREL WILLIAM PYLE, was born Oct. 15, 1920 in Burchard, NE. He joined the Oregon National Guard in 1939. Stationed at Ft. Lewis, WA; Australia; and Leyte.

He attended Cooks and Bakers School at Ft. Lewis. Was litter bearer and surgeons assistant on front lines. Returned to the States in December 1944 and given medical discharge March 24, 1945.

Married to Idella Buell on Nov. 27, 1945. They have two children, Charlie (Vietnam veteran) and Lorraine (married to James McCormick a Navy retiree), and four granddaughters, one grandson, and four great-grandchildren. He is retired from city employment after four bypass surgeries in May 1981. He lives in Everett, WA.

DANIEL RACHEFSKY, was born May 1, 1925 in Washington, DC. Drafted last year out of high school Sept. 16, 1943. Basic training IRTC Ft. McClellan, AL. Joined 2nd Platoon, L Co., 3rd Bn., 41st Div. at Finchhaven, New Guinea three days prior to beach landing at Aitape, New Guinea.

Served 96 days of continuous combat including Toem/Wakde area and Biak Island. He emerged from last battle, Ibdi Pocket, as one of 12 men of original 41 men. Was in combat 114 days in Philippines at Mindoro, Zamboanga, Davao, and Jolo. Was one eight men left out of 41 at end. Occupied Hiroshima at war's end.

Discharged January 1945 with the rank of staff sergeant. His citations included three Arrowheads, Presidential Unit Citation with Oak Leaf Cluster.

Married in 1980, has a daughter and lives in Beltsville, MD. His business includes grocery, dry cleaning and window coverings.

GRANT A. RAMEY, was born Oct. 30, 1920 in Bend, OR. He joined the National Guard on Sept. 15, 1940, G Co., HQ, 2nd Bn., 162nd Inf. He served at Ft. Lewis, WA, Australia, New Guinea and the Philippines.

Married Kate in 1956 and has three children, six grandchildren and six great-grandchildren. He spent most of his working years in the lumber industry. He owned a redwood re-manufacturing plant for 23 years, retiring in 1977.

He was elected to the Board of Directors of the McKinleyville Community Services District in 1970 and has served for the last 21 years. He also served on the Parks and Recreations Commission in a community of 10,000 persons.

He now enjoys fishing and traveling. He has been active with Cub Scouts, Grange, Commerce, Seventh Step Program within the prison system, Half-way House, and VFW and several political campaigns. He lives in McKinleyville, CA.

CHARLES RAVIOTTA, was born Nov. 23, 1918 in New Orleans, LA. Entered the service March 29, 1941, A Co., 186th Regt, at Ft. Lewis, WA for basic training.

He went to New Guinea, Buna, Hollandia, Biak, Palawan, and Zamboanga, Philippine Islands.

Discharged Aug. 20, 1945 with the rank technical sergeant. He received the Bronze Star, Good Conduct, American Defense Service, Asiatic-Pacific Campaign, World War II Victory Medals, Combat Infantry Badge, and Philippine Liberation Ribbon.

Married Garnet in 1947 and has one daughter and one grandson. He retired in 1980.

JOSEPH P. REBONE, was born Aug. 12, 1917 in Detroit, MI. Graduated from the University of Detroit in 1939. Drafted Aug. 27, 1941. Went to Camp Roberts, CA for basic training. Went overseas to Australia in July 1942. Assigned to HQ Co., 2nd Bn., 163rd Inf.

Saw action in the Papuan, New Guinea and Southern Philippines campaigns including five landings. Cited for the Bronze Star at Biak during the siege of Ibdi Pocket for knocking out a Jap 75mm cliff gun at night with a 37mm while under enemy fire.

Came back to the States and was discharged on Oct. 13, 1945 with the rank of technical sergeant.

Married Claire Whitman (now deceased) in 1947 and has two children, Joseph and Susan, and nine grandchildren. He retired from managing an asphalt refinery in Laketon, IN in 1985 and resides in New Carlisle, IN.

CARN R. REID, was born Nov. 4, 1911 in Philadelphia, PA. Enlisted April 1, 1942, 6th Armd. Engrs., Ft. Chaffee then OCS at Ft. Belvoir. Second lieutenant Dec. 8, 1942. Engineer Amphibious Command, Camp Edwards, MA. On May 10 left for Australia and joined S-3, 2nd Bn., 162 Inf., New Guinea as engineer amphibious officer; planned Hollandia landing and made first wave; next landing was Biak; then to field hospital with typhus in Lae.

Participated in Philippines Campaign, Mindoro and Zamboanga; injured and evacuated to General Hospital Luzon, hospital ship, then to General Hospital, Stanton, VA.

In August 1946 was ordered to Engineer Command, Ft. Belvoir to Ft. Monroe as landscape architect and assistant post engineer, Army Field Force Headquarters. Followed by Tokyo, Japan; Paris, France; Joint Construction Agency NATO; then to Ft. Dix, NJ until his retirement in October 1942.

His awards include the Combat Infantry Badge, Asiatic-Pacific Theater with three stars, Bronze Star, American Campaign, Army of Occupation, United Nations, Armed Forces Reserve, Victory Medal, and the Commendation Medal.

Married Nina Sawada in Tokyo in 1953. They have two sons. Presently working as a landscape architect.

DELMA L. REINECKER, was born Oct. 27, 1916 in Bellville, TX. entered the service Nov. 14, 1941. Assigned to Co. D, 186th Inf. Stationed at Australia, New Guinea and the Philippines. He spent 105 days chasing Japs.

Discharged with the rank of corporal. He received the Good Conduct Medal, three Bronze Medal Stars, one Bronze Battle Star.

Married to Minnie on Sept. 26, 1946. They live in Wallis, TX. He is retired.

LOUIS W. REUTER, was born Sept. 23, 1918, Mantowoc, WI. Graduated from high school in 1936. Entered the Army June 16, 1941 and served with C Btry., 218th FA Bn., Ft. Lewis, WA; Camp Cooke, CA; and overseas at New Guinea, Wakde, Finchhaven, Zamboanga, and the Philippines.

Discharged September 1945 with the rank sergeant first class. Re-enlisted immediately after the war in 1945 and was assigned to the 2nd Div. serving at Ft. Missoula, MT and Camp Cooke, CA. Re-enlisted again at Ft. Benning, GA. Transferred to Germany and was assigned to the 1st Div. with assignment as senior instructor in the Food Service School. Discharged from the Army in 1952 to enter civilian life.

Was a restaurant and motel owner/manager in Van Wert, OH; club manager of Columbus Mannerchor, OH; and club manager of Buckeye Lake Yacht Club, OH. Was PTA president, American Legion commander, member of the VFW, Lions Club, Eagles, Moose, and Elks.

He joined the 41st Infantry Division Association in the early 1950s. Elected to the Board of Governors at the Baltimore Convention in 1973 representing the Great Lakes Chapter, He became a member of the Portland Chapter in 1980. Served as co-chairman of the Portland Reunion in 1984. Now serving as president of the chapter.

Married in Germany to Willie in 1952. They have

two children, Cindy and Louis. Cindy is on the administrative staff at the University of Munich, Germany and Louis is a staff sergeant in the USAF stationed at Gila Bend, AZ.

HUGH Z. REYNOLDS, was born Dec. 21, 1919 in Harlowton, MT. Entered the service Sept. 16, 1940, assigned to Co. D, 163rd Inf. and trained at Camp Murray, WA until 41st Div. sailed to Australia on March 19, 1942.

Was an 81mm mortar observer, he served in Seymour and Rockhampton, Australia, Papua, New Guinea and again in Australia and Dutch New Guinea, making landings at Aitape, Toem, and Wakde. Was wounded at Ibdi Pocket on Biak and returned home December 1944. Transferred to Army Air Corps and became an airplane mechanic at Keesler Field, MS.

Discharged Sept. 18, 1945 with the rank of staff sergeant. He received the Combat Infantry Badge, Presidential Unit Citation, and the Purple Heart.

Married June in 1947 and they raised three sons. He re-entered the National Guard in 1949 and retired as a major in 1966. Was in the bar business for 28 years, then construction until retiring in 1982. He continues to hunt, fish and travel.

ANDREW (ZUANICH) RICHELLI, was born Feb. 29, 1924 in Bellingham, WA. He entered the service Feb. 20, 1943 and was assigned to the 41st on July 26, 1943. Stationed at Camp Roberts, Southwest Pacific. Most memorable experience was PT boat ride to get medical supplies from Sanga Sanga to Zamboanga, Philippine Islands and sleeping in the skipper's cabin.

Discharged Jan. 10, 1946. He received the Asiatic-Pacific Campaign Medal, Philippine Liberation Ribbon with one Bronze Star, Good Conduct Medal, Bronze Service Arrowhead, and the World War II Victory Medal.

Married to Mary on Aug. 17, 1947 in San Pedro, CA. They have three children, Larry, Martin, and Debra, and five grandchildren. He is semi-retired and still selling insurance.

BERT W. RIEBE, was born March 1, 1920 in Portland, OR. Entered the service April 7, 1937, D 218th FA, I-162nd Inf., A 186th Inf. Stationed at Ft. Lewis, WA; Australia and New Guinea, USC&GS, Kansas. Memorable experience was Melbourne furlough and Papua Campaign.

Discharged June 1977 with the rank of major. He received the Bronze Star, Purple Heart, Combat Infantry Badge, and theater ribbons.

Married Sept. 15, 1946 to Patricia. They have a daughter Judith, two grandchildren, and two great-grandchildren. He retired from an accounting practice in 1980. Now enjoys golfing, fishing, and traveling.

THOMAS E. RILEA (MAJ. GEN.), was born May 5, 1895 in Chicago, IL and raised in Agness, OR. Was a state forestry service ranger, studied engineering, then began his military career by enlisting as a private in Co. B, 3rd Oregon Inf. on Dec. 8, 1914.

Was a bugler in 1916 during the Mexican Border Campaign; was a regimental sergeant major until June 1918 when he was transferred to Gen. Pershing's staff reaching the rank of captain. Returned to the U.S. in September 1919 and became assistant to the adjutant general. In 1927 was promoted to lieutenant colonel, in 1931 commissioned brigadier general and was the youngest general officer in the U.S.

Entered active duty in WWII and named assistant division commander of the 41st Inf. Div. on Feb. 18, 1942. Participated in Papuan and Sanananda-Buna campaigns and was named commander of the Army service of supply base in Sydney, Australia in March 1943.

Gen. Rilea returned to the U.S. in 1945 and became commanding general of the infantry replacement center at Ft. McClellan, AL. He left active duty in December 1946 and resumed his position as Oregon adjutant general. Promoted to major general in the Oregon National Guard in 1948 and served as state director of selective service.

His decorations include the Distinguished Service Medal, Legion of Merit, Bronze Star, Purple Heart, Commendation Ribbon with metal pendant, and the National Guard Association Distinguished Service Medal.

Major Gen. Rilea passed away Feb. 3, 1959. He was a representative of the 6th Army area to executive committee of the National Guard Association; 32nd degree Mason; a Shriner; and member of American Legion and the Military Order of the World Wars.

He is survived by his wife, the former Mrs. Helen Coe Webster, whom he married in 1946; a son and daughter by a previous marriage, Thomas E. Rilea Jr of Salem, OR and Janet Farnam of Springfield, OR; step-daughter Betty Coe; sisters Myrtle Gadeholt and Mrs. Clara R. Allen; three grandsons, and three granddaughters.

ROLAND ROBETSON, was born Sept. 29, 1921 in Gurdon, AR. Entered the service Aug. 15, 1942 and assigned to Co. A, 116th Engrs., stationed at New Guinea.

Memorable experiences: when wounded May 27, 1944 at Toem; building roads over mountains from Ora Bay to Dobodura and Buna-Gona.

Discharged with the rank of private. He received the Purple Heart, Victory Medal, and all of the Asiatic-Pacific area awards.

He is retired from the railroad and receives 90% service connected disability.

LEO A. ROG, was born April 25, 1919 in Chicago, IL. He was inducted into the Army Oct. 8, 1941. He was in Co. G, 186th Inf. and trained at Camp Roberts, CA. Was stationed in Oregon and overseas. He fought in Papuan, New Guinea and Southern Philippines campaigns.

Discharged at Ft. Sheridan, IL on June 1, 1945 with the rank private first class. He received the Combat Infantry Badge, Overseas Service Bars, Good Conduct Ribbon, American Defense Service Ribbon, Philippines Liberation Ribbon with one Battle Star, Distinguished Unit Badge Go 21 (43) Asiatic-Pacific Ribbon and three Battle Stars.

Memorable experience was coming home and marrying his sweetheart, Norma. He also looked forward to the yearly conventions and seeing all is buddies again! He was a steamfitter and retired in 1983. He has six daughters, one son, and 10 grandchildren. After a long illness, he passed away Feb. 26, 1990.

JACK B. ROGERS, was born Nov. 22, 1920 at Choteav, MT. Graduated from high school in 1939. Joined Montana National Guard, Co. I, 163rd Inf., Sept. 12, 1940. Stationed at Camp Murray, WA. Served entire war with the 163rd in Australia, New Guinea, and the Philippines.

Discharged September 1945 as first sergeant. Married Ellen in 1945. They have four children: Tom, Jack Jr., and twins, Don and Dan. He owned and operated a floral and greenhouse business and then clothing business in Choteau, MT.

He is a member of VFW, American Legion, Lions Club, Chamber of Commerce, Country Club, and served as 41st Division Association national president, 1980-1981. He retired in 1982 and has traveled extensively. In 1970 he visited Australia with 41st Div. Group.

GENE D. ROHLFFS (TONY), was born Dec. 30, 1919 in Salem, SD. Entered the service on Sept. 16, 1940, HQ Bn., 218th FA, Co. A, 116th Engrs., Ft. Lewis, WA.

Made five landings after being picked to go home on rotation. Discharged with the rank private first class.

Married in 1942 to Dorothy. They have two sons, Tom and Dan. He coached American Legion baseball many years. Went to Hawaii two years with legion teams and to Australia in 1983 with basketball team. He retired from the printing profession in 1982. He enjoys painting with oils and greenhousing.

CHESTER EUGENE ROMIG, was born Oct. 11, 1918. Joined Oregon National Guard 186th Inf. Band in 1937. Inducted into Federal Service Sept. 16, 1940, supply sergeant. Band duty in Australia, Melbourne, Seymour, Rockhampton, New Guinea, Dutch East Indies, and the Philippines. Band duty consisted of supplying the band men with musical instruments, clothing, pack and ship supplies, doing parades, concerts, backing shows ie Joe E. Brown, Bob Hope, Jack Benny etc.

Went from infantry band to the U.S. Post Office as a letter carrier. Performed musically with Letter Carriers Band, Legion Band, Shrine Band and others. Now, still doing own Combo playing at circuses, concerts with community orchestras, dances, parties, weddings and funerals. He teaches clarinet, saxophone, flute with and for Northwest Music Teaching Schools.

Was appointed music librarian for Pacific Northwest Shrine Oriental Bands and later to the music librarian for the North America Shrine Oriental Bands.

Married Charline in 1947, they have one son, Chester Charles. They reside in Portland, OR. He is a member of Al Kader Shrine, Elks, Musicians Post, American Legion and Amvets Post 1.

JOE ROSCOE, was born Aug. 31, 1924 in Detroit, MI. Drafted September 1943 and entered service through Ft. Custer, MI before being shipped overseas to join Co. K, 186th Inf. in Australia.

He served in the occupation of Kadaichi Station, Hiroshima, Japan. Returned to the States and was discharged at Ft. Sheridan, IL on Jan. 10, 1946 with the rank of T/4 sergeant.

He received the Victory Medal, Asiatic-Pacific Theater Ribbon with two Bronze Battle Stars, Bronze Service Arrowhead, Philippine Liberation Ribbon with one Bronze Battle Star, four Overseas Service Bars, Combat Infantry Badge, and the Good Conduct Medal.

Joe married Jean on June 18, 1946 and they had two sons. He passed away March 20, 1991 at Wyandotte, MI after a long illness. He will be greatly missed by the Great Lakes Chapter in which he was very active even during his illness.

HAROLD W. ROSSOW, was born Sept. 2, 1919 in Redford, MI. Graduated from Plymouth High School in 1936 and drafted into the Army Dec. 3, 1941. He left Ft. Custer and arrived at Camp Roberts, CA just prior to Christmas.

After basic training he joined Co. B, 186th Inf. in Ft. Lewis in April 1942. He left the USA landing in Melbourne in May 1942. After the battle of Rockhampton and Brisbane, he made a stop in New Guinea, Biak, Hollandia, Palawan, Zamboanga, leaving Leyte in August 1945.

Discharged from Ft. Sheridan on Oct. 9, 1945 with the rank of staff sergeant. He received the Purple Heart for Biak.

Joined Michigan Bell Telephone in January 1946 and retired in March 1982 after 36 years. Married Cecelia in 1947 and fathered six daughters and two sons. Cecelia passed away in 1973. He remarried in 1978 to Marion and has three stepsons and 17 grandchildren. They moved to Sun City, AZ after retiring and became active in the Telephone Pioneers and Sun City Elks. He was co-chairman of the Michigan Chapter first two national conventions.

ROBERT L. RUFF, was born, Sept. 13, 1923 in East St. Louis, IL. Entered the service in March 1943, 218th FA Bn., Btry B, Rockhampton, Australia, New Guinea, Japan, and the Philippines.

Attended Navy Gun Control School, Goodenough Island off East Coast of south tip of New Guinea. He spent 17 days on ship from Frisco to Brisbane, Australia.

Discharged Jan. 6, 1946 at Jefferson Barracks, St. Louis, MO with the rank sergeant/technician. He received the Good Conduct, South West Pacific and Occupation of Japan Ribbon, and scored Sharpshooter with Enfield Rifle at Camp Roberts, CA.

Married to Nellie Jane Kerr (Heuy) Ruff. They have one daughter and one grandson. He is a retired sales representative with Johns/Manville Corp., Bldg. Products Div.

JOHN W. RUSSELL, was born Feb. 4, 1919 at Apollo, PA. Entered the service Dec. 7, 1944, Co. L, 186th, Co. M, 186th, 41st Div., IRTC Camp Blanding, FL; Ft. Meade, MD; Philippine Islands, and Japan.

Memorable experiences include: mopping up around Zamboanga, Mindanao, Philippine Islands; disposing of arms, ammo, poison gas and mines in and around Hiroshima Japan; and spending Christmas 1945 freezing in an airplane hangar.

Discharged Jan. 20, 1946 with the rank private first class. He received the Good Conduct Medal, Asiatic-Pacific with one Bronze Star, Philippine Liberation with one Bronze Star, American Service Ribbon and Combat Infantry Badge.

Married in 1937 and has four sons, one daughter, 19 grandchildren, and eight great-grandchildren. He is retired and enjoys his family, traveling, and hobbies.

WILLIAM R. RUTTER, was a good man, husband, and father. Rutter was a fish in the water. He also liked rock hunting and arrowhead hunting. He had five brothers and a sister. One brother, Pete, was William's twin. A car accident in 1962 took the lives of Pete and his dad instantly and his mom a few days later in the hospital.

He met Alma (from the borough of Manhattan in New York City) and they married in Medford. After the war they kept in touch with buddy Bill Badgley and his wife.

Medford, retired on February 1. He began his PP&L career as a groundman in special construction in 1945. He later joined the lineman ranks and became a working foreman in Medford in 1961. He retired as a district line foreman in Medford, a position he had held since 1979.

William passed away April 23, 1983 after a tough fight with cancer.

LLOYD P. SABBY, was born March 8, 1918 in Rolette, ND where he graduated from high school. He entered the Army at Ft. Snelling, MN on Oct. 23, 1941. From there he left for Camp Wolters, TX for basic training.

In April 1942 he left Ft. Lewis, WA for Australia. From there he went to New Guinea and the Philippine Islands. He served as a heavy machine gunner with Co. D of the 186th Inf. Also worked as a baker for a short time baking bread for Army personnel.

Was discharged at Ft. Lewis, WA on Oct. 4, 1945.

Married Naomi Peterson at Jewell, IA in June 1947. They have two sons, Ronald and Dennis, one daughter, Karen, four grandsons, Ryan, Nicholas, Evan, and Jeremy, and two granddaughters, Elizabeth and Briana.

He worked for John Morrell and Company in Estherville until retiring in 1980. He enjoys gardening, fishing, travelling, and helping the children.

HARRY SADO (SADOWSKI), had his name changed from Sadowski to Sado in 1947. He was born June 10, 1914 in Detroit, MI. Entered the service Dec. 3, 1941, 186th Inf., 1st Bn., 41st Div. Served entire war with B Co. 186th in Australia, New Guinea, and the Philippines. Participated in all their landings and actions.

Discharged with the rank of staff sergeant. He received all the usual awards/decorations of the 41st.

Married Oct. 27, 1945 and has one daughter and two grandchildren. They live in Troy, MI. He retired from Chrysler Corp. in 1974. He has traveled through 15 countries, Europe, Far East, China, Japan, Egypt, Greece, and North Africa.

EDWARD SAMS, was born April 26, 1923 in Marshall, NC. Entered the service September 1943. Trained at Camp Blanding, FL and went to Ft. Ord, CA, leaving there in March 1944.

Arrived at Goodenough Island, went to Finchhaven, New Guinea, and was attached to Co. B, 186th Regt., 41st Div. to Biak Island, Mindoro Island, Palawan, Zamboanga, Mindanao (went into Service Company 186th), Philippines, Kure Naval Base, Kaidaichi.

Left Japan in 1946. Was discharged from Ft. Bragg, NC on Feb. 6, 1946 with the rank T/5.

He is still working as radio technician at Radio Communications in Virginia. Married Betty Patrick from Kentucky and they have three daughters, Deane, Vicky, and Lisa, and one son David (with 82nd Airborne at Ft. Bragg, NC). His hobby is amateur radio. He is a member of the American Legion, AF&A Masons, and Scottish Rite.

ROBERT W. SANDERS, was born Feb. 8, 1924 in Crystal Falls, MI. Entered the service in March 1943. Received infantry basic at Camp Roberts, CA. Joined H Co., 163rd Inf. at Rockhampton in July 1943.

Participated in Aitape, Toem-Wakde, Biak Island, Zamboanga, Sanga-Sanga, Bongao and Jolo Operations and in the Occupation of Japan.

Discharged January 1946 at Ft. Lewis, WA as staff sergeant. He attended the University of Michigan and graduated with a master's degree. He spent 29 years in consulting civil engineering.

Married to Wilma and has a daughter Suzanne. Now retired and living in Ann Arbor, MI. He enjoys traveling, especially the modern accommodations which are so very superior to those on the LSTs, LCIs, AKAs and APAs of 1943-1945.

JOHN A SANTORO, L Co., 186th Inf. participated in all land and amphibious assaults engaged in by his unit during the New Guinea, Hollandia, Biak Island, Papua, Zamboanga, and the Philippines. Total foreign service was three and a half years including several months in Australia.

Apart from the usual combat experience, the most vivid memory he has is of the night his unit captured a Jap food dump. He opened and ate a can of preserved clams. That night during a fierce Jap attack on his platoon, he developed the most excruciating abdominal pain due to the dysentery caused by the clams. He crawled 20 yards back to the inner perimeter looking for First Aideman Baker. He found Baker in a slit trench with a carbine pointed at Santoro's head. Baker was trembling and about to squeeze the trigger when he luckily recognized Santoro's voice above the din. Baker hissed, "Sandy, you crazy SOB, I could have killed you!" Santoro replied, "Doc, I'm in so much pain either you pull the trigger or give me some codine, I don't care!" Ever since then Santoro considers every day his birthday.

John served during the Korean War (1950-1952) and was discharged in August 1985 as a master sergeant. His awards include the Combat Infantry Medal, Bronze Star Medal, Philippine Liberation Medal, and numerous campaign and battle ribbons.

He joined USPS in 1947 as a letter carrier and retired in 1981 as director of Customer Services, Brooklyn Post Office.

Married to Mary Pacitto in 1947. They have one daughter and two sons, Dolores, John and Richard, and six grandchildren.

DANIEL V. SATTERTHWAITE, was born in Crawford County, IL on July 24, 1917 and inducted into the service Aug. 29, 1941. He was sent to Chicago and then on to Camp Roberts, CA for training, put in 86th Anti-tank, then entered 41st Div. in December of 1941. Battles involved in were Papuan, New Guinea, Southern Philippine Campaigns.

Discharged Aug. 22, 1945 with the rank of corporal. He was awarded three Bronze Stars, Purple Heart, Good Conduct Medal, and the Combat Infantry Badge.

Married Ruby Christy in 1946 and raised two sons, Lewis V. and Danny L. Lewis is an aviation maintenance inspector and Danny works for AT&T and has three sons.

Daniel retired after 23 years of school bussing and 10 years as mechanic on farm machinery. His health is not so good as he has to be on kidney dialysis.

WILLIAM H. SCARBOROUGH, was born Nov. 26, 1919 in Crockett County, TN. Graduated from Alamo Tennessee High School. Drafted December 1942. Went to Camp Howze, TX for basic training. Joined 41st Div. at Finchhaven and served with Co. B, 1st Bn. 163rd Inf. Reg.

Transferred to Medical Corps while on Biak Island and had first aid training. Was assigned to Co. B as a medic and saw action on Zamboanga. He went with the division to Japan, rotating back to the States Dec. 15, 1945.

Discharged from the service Dec. 20, 1945 at Ft. Chaffee, AR. He was awarded the Purple Heart and Silver Star.

He married Jewell in 1949. They have two children and one grandchild. He retired in 1978 from the Veterans Administration with 32 years of service. He resides in Memphis, TN.

TED W. SCHENK, was born June 14, 1916 in Chicago, IL. He entered the service Dec. 11, 1941, 186th Inf. Regt., 641 TD Bn., 98th Chem. Bn. Camp Roberts (basic training), Ft. Lewis, WA and overseas.

Arrived Melbourne, Australia on May 12, 1942. From Seymour to Rockhampton, to New Guinea. Discharged from Wakeman General Hospital, Camp Atterbury, IN on April 20, 1945 with the rank private first class.

He is retired and lives in Sacramento, CA.

ARTHUR R. SCHERRER, was born April 13, 1923 in Dubuque, IA. Entered the service March 1943, 205th FA Bn., HQ Btry. Served entire war with 205th in Australia, New Guinea, and the Philippines. Was wounded at Zamboanga. He visited Hiroshima, Japan when quarantine was lifted, just before returning to the States.

Discharged at Ft. Sheridan, IL in December 1945 with the rank of sergeant. He received the Victory Medal, Asiatic-Pacific Theatre Ribbon with two Bronze Stars, Bronze Service Arrowhead, four Overseas Service Bars, and the Purple Heart Medal.

Married Joyce Lewis in 1947 and they have three children, Arthur, Robert, and Joann. He is a retired convenience store owner and likes to travel.

ANDREW A. SCHLEIFSTEIN, was born Nov. 16, 1918 in St. Louis, MO. Was drafted March 5, 1943. Went to Camp Roberts, CA for basic training. Left California July 6, 1943 for Brisbane, Australia, arriving there July 26.

Joined F Co. 163 at Rockhampton. First landing was at Aitape, New Guinea. Transferred to 1st Bn., HQ Co. 163. Other landings were Wakde, Biak, Zamboanga, Jolo, and Kure, Japan.

Arrived in Ft. Lewis, WA Dec. 10, 1945. Was discharged December 20 from Jefferson Barracks, St. Louis, MO with the rank of staff sergeant. He was awarded the Combat Infantry Badge with Bronze Star and Purple Heart.

Married to Virginia and has a married son and two grandchildren. Has been retired for 15 years after 25 years service with the St. Louis Fire Department. He is a life member of the VFW.

WILLIAM A. SCHMIDT, was born Aug. 5, 1922 in Marion, OR. Bill joined Co. B, Inf. 41st Div. in July of 1940. Co. B mobilized Sept. 16, 1940, trained at Camp Murray, WA, left New York on March 3, 1942, going through the Panama Canal, and landed in Melbourne, Australia on April 9, 1942.

Bill was stationed in Seymour, Australia for three months, then went to Rockhampton, Australia until the first part of 1943, then on to Port Moresby, New Guinea. From there his Co. B flew over the Stanley Owens Range landing in a cow pasture at Dobodura. New Guinea and started fighting the Japanese within 100 yards of the plane. His Co. B made a couple landings going up the coast of New Guinea and continued fighting up to Salamaua, New Guinea. From there he went back to Rockhampton, Australia.

After training more replacements, he left and landed at Hollandia Dutch New Guinea fighting the Japanese. From there he went to Biak Schouten Islands. His brother Alex Schmidt was with him in Co. B and was killed at the West Caves on Biak Island. After securing Biak, Co. B went to Mindoro in the Philippines and from there he went to Zamboanga, Mindanao and landed on the first wave. He fought there until he received orders to go home July 28, 1945. He landed at Seattle, WA the morning of Aug. 14, 1945. That afternoon was VJ-Day with Japan and being back home in the States was his most memorable day.

He was discharged Aug. 17, 1945. His awards and decorations include the Distinguished Unit Citation, Bronze Star, Good Conduct, American Defense Service, Asiatic-Pacific Campaign Medal, Combat Infantry Badge, Philippine Liberation Ribbon, and Honorable Service Lapel Button.

Bill married Theresa Wruble on Nov. 19, 1947 and has one daughter and three grandchildren. He retired in 1980 and lives on a small Christmas tree farm in Estacada, OR. He is a member of the 41st Infantry Division of Portland, VFW, and the American Legion.

FRED SCHUMACHER, was born June 17, 1917 in Portland, OR and lived there most of his life. He graduated from high school in 1935 and Oregon State College in 1939.

Was commissioned second lieutenant, field artillery as reserve officer in May 1939. Was called to active duty with 41st Div. in March 1941, assigned to HQ, 1st Bn. of 218th FA Regt. Transferred to HQ Btry., served as Anti-tank Platoon CO and member of 41st Div. FA Anti-tank Bn.

Was shipped to Plum, later to Ft. Lewis. In February 1942, he was transferred to 167th FA Bn., Hqs. Btry. In March 1945 he was assigned to the Field Artillery Training Center at Ft. Sill, OK, as CO of one of two pack training batteries. His most interesting experience was training in the only horse pack 75 pack howitzer battalion in history of U.S. Army.

He was in banking, machinery and finance business most of his career and retired as vice-president of a large industrial credit corporation. Married to Jacqueline and has two daughters and five grandchildren.

GEORGE A. SCHWENDNER, was born Dec. 23, 1919 in Chicago, IL. He graduated from Farragut High School. Entered the Army Dec. 12, 1941. Trained at Camp Roberts, CA. Was sent to Ft. Lewis, WA to join the 41st Inf. Div., 186th Regt.

Went overseas April 1942 to Australia, trained in Australia, and then was sent to Buna, New Guinea. Fought there and then made assault landings at Hollandia, New Guinea, Biak Island where he was wounded. Also made assault landings at Palawan, Mindoro Island, Philippines, Zamboanga, Mindanao. He was then sent to Leyte, Philippines.

Was sent home September 1945. He received the Asiatic-Pacific Theater Ribbon with three Bronze Battle Stars, Bronze Service Arrowhead, Philippine Liberation Ribbon with one Bronze Battle Star, seven Overseas Service Bars, one Service Stripe, Good Conduct Medal, Purple Heart, and the Medical Badge.

He married Gloria in 1948. They have two children, Lynne and Lee, and two grandchildren, Scott Harris and Eric Schwendner.

PAUL C. SCHWERTMANN, was born Oct. 11, 1923 in Kirwin, KS and moved to Portland, OR with his family at the age of nine. He joined the National Guard, Service Battery 218 FA, at the age of 17 and later was honorably discharged by giving his right age.

He was drafted on Feb. 25, 1943, trained at Camp Roberts and joined C Btry., 146th FA in Australia in September of 1943. He was in the initial landings at Hollandia, Biak, Zamboanga, Mindanao, and Jolo. He also fought at San Rose, Mindoro, and Davao, Mindanao.

He was among the first ground troops in Hiroshima and left the 41st in Japan on Dec. 12, 1945. Was discharged as a T/5 on Jan. 2, 1946. He was awarded the Philippine Liberation Medal with a Bronze Service Star, the Asiatic-Pacific Service Medal, the Bronze Arrowhead Medal and the Victory Medal.

He spent 34 years as a barber in Portland, owning and operating his own shop for 28 years, before retiring June 1, 1987. He has two daughters, Christy and Lori, and six grandchildren, Heather, Matthew, Jennifer, Jessica, Justin, and Courtney. He is enjoying his grandchildren and church activities.

R.W. SCONCE (LT. COL.), was born May 12, 1915 at Portland, OR. He graduated from Sacred Heart Grade School, Oregon State University with a B.S. in mechanical engineering and was commissioned a second lieutenant.

Military Service and Promotions: October 1933-June 1936, Btry. D, 218th FA, ONG; September 1935-May 1939, ROTC Oregon State University; May 1939-March 1941, ORC inactive; March 1941-February 1942, active duty with Btry. C, 218th FA, 41st Div., promoted to first lieutenant; February 1942-August 1942, Btry. A, 205th FA Bn., 41st Div.; August 1942-November 1943, Asst. S-2, 205th FA Bn.; November 1943-February 1944, S-2, 205th FA Bn.; February 1944-March 1944, Asst. S-3, 205th FA Bn.; March 1944-April 1945, CO, Btry. C, 205th FA Bn., promoted captain AUS; April 1945-August 1945, Ln. Off., 205th FA Bn.; August 1945-October 1945, Asst. C-2, Hqs. 4th Army, Ft. Sam Houston, TX; October 1945-February 1946, attached unassigned, Hqs. 4th Army; February 1946-March 1948, ORC inactive, appointed Captain ORNG; March 1948-January 1949, CO Hq. Btry., 41st Div. Arty.; January 1949, Ln. Off., HQ&HQ Btry., 218th FA Bn.; February 1949-March 1949, S-2 Ln. Off., HQ&HQ Btry., 218th FA Bn.; March 1949-May 1950, S-2, HQ 965th FA Bn.; May 1950-July 1951, S-3, HQ 965th FA Bn., promoted major ORNG; August 1951-February 1952, executive office, HQ 965th FA Bn.; March 1952-June 1958, S-3, HQ 965th FA Bn.; June 1958-March 1959, executive office 965th FA Bn.; April 1959-March 1959, S-3, HQ 41st Div. Arty.; July 1959, promoted to lieutenant colonel.

He served in the South Pacific three years and 26 days in New Guinea and South Philippines. He flew home on a 45 day leave from Zamboanga, but was reassigned to Ft. Sam Houston, TX.

Among his awards were the Bronze Star Medal (Biak, Hollandia and Dutch New Guinea); Asiatic-Pacific Campaign Medal with two Bronze Service Stars; American Defense Service Medal with one Bronze Service Star; and the Philippine Liberation Ribbon with one Bronze Service Star. He retired after 34 years of service with the rank of lieutenant colonel.

In civilian life, he was a mechanical engineer in the contract managing section of Bonneville Power where he worked for 30 years. Married to Ruth for 48 years. They had three sons, Ralph II, Richard, and Robert. Lt. Col. Sconce passed away in July 1988.

ALBERT C. SECREST, was born May 27, 1920 in Tacoma, WA. Entered the Washington National Guard in June 1938, 41st Div., 167 FA, Btry. B, Camp Murray, WA. He changed from Field Artillery to Pack Artillery and trained horses in Australia.

Discharged at Ft. Lewis, WA with the rank of staff sergeant. He received the American Service Medal and all the usual awards of the Pacific Theater.

Married to Lorraine and has two sons, Kendrick and James. He retired in 1986 and resides in Bremerton, WA. He says it's a strange feeling being one Army retiree amongst Navy retirees.

RUSSEL SERBY, was born 1920 in Marseilles, IL. Joined the service in August 1943, F Co., 163rd Regt. as rifleman. Stationed at Australia, New Guinea, Philippine Islands, and Japan. Memorable experience was being strafed by American Navy planes after landing at Aitape.

Discharged Dec. 23, 1945 with the rank of private first class. He received the Purple Heart at Wakde Island and the Bronze Star.

He married Anne Rutledge and has two children and three grandchildren. He retired from farming and lives in Ottawa, IL.

MARTIN J. SETTLE, was born May 20, 1919 at Chico, MT. He joined D Co., 163rd Inf. in 1937. Inducted into federal service in 1940. After Camp Murray he left for Australia in 1942. Went to 1st Bn. HQ 163 at Seymour, Australia. Was at Sanananda and Aitape.

Came home on troop rotation in July 1944. At Santa Barbara, CA he went through redistribution center then to Camp Wolters and Camp Maxey, TX. Discharged March 1945 at Ft. Douglas, UT with the rank of staff sergeant.

Married Adeline Mattila in July 1948. They had three children (two survived). He attended Montana State University and ranched all his life (sheep and cattle). He moved from Martinsdale to Canyon Creek, MT in 1961 and is semi-retired. His son, Scott, is taking over the ranch. He is a Mason, Shriner, Episcopalian, Republican, and life member of Sigma Chi Fraternity, VFW, and American Legion.

CAMILLO GEORGE SEVERINI, was born Feb. 25, 1922 in Newark, NJ. Entered the service March 18, 1943. Assigned to 41st, Pioneer and Ammunition Platoon, Hqs. Co., 3rd Bn., 162 Inf. Regt. Basic training at Camp Croft, SC. Assigned to Hqs. Co., 2nd Bn., 166th Inf. Regt. at Camp Shelby, MS, moved to Camp Hood, TX, then to 41st in Rockhampton, Australia.

Was trained as ranger commando prior to assignment to 41st. Made all landings in Hollandia, Biak, Zamboanga, Digos, Davao, Tocoma and many other skirmishes before Kure, Japan. Then to Fukuyama, Okazaki, Nagoya, then to Seattle and home. During the Korean War he served in Alaska Ground Defense Forces.

Re-enlisted in Army Air Force in Japan and changed to U.S. Air Force in 1947. Returned to infantry in 1948. Retired from Army Signal Corps in July 1963. His awards/decorations include: Combat Infantry Badge, Bronze Star, Good Conduct, American Theater Campaign, Asiatic-Pacific, Philippine Liberation, Philippine Presidential Unit Citation, World War II Victory, Japan Occupation, National Service, Reserve Officers Medal (11 years) and others.

Married to Felicia, he has two sons, one daughter, and six grandchildren. He is a member of the Elks, Masons, York Rite, Scottish Rite, VFW and DAV. Retired with rank of chief warrant officer after 20 plus years and from the Federal Civil Service with 22 plus years. Main profession was publications engineer in all types of military equipments.

DON K. SHAFFNER, was born Nov. 18, 1919 in Dillon, MT. He graduated from high school in 1938m and W.S.U., Pullman, WA with D.V.M. degree in 1949. He joined the 163rd National Guard Band while attending Montana State College in 1939 to get $1.00 per drill pay which he needed for college.

Called into federal service Sept. 14, 1941. Sent to Camp Murray, WA, transferred to Service Company in 1941. Shipped to Australia with 41st Inf. Div., 163rd Inf. in March 1942. Went to New Guinea, then back to Australia for training. Sent to Camp Shelby, MS in Spring 1944 for pilot training. About then the U.S. decided they needed ground troops not fly-boys so was sent to Camp Fannin, TX to train recruits. Discharged in June 1945 as a technical sergeant.

Married Helen Lloyd in 1946 and has two children, Sydney Gabel and Gail Kuntz, and two grandchildren.

He returned to Dillon, MT in 1949 to practice veterinary medicine for 30 years. He sold his practice in 1979 and is presently ranching.

DALE E. SHAVER, was born Sept. 2, 1920 in Liberal, KS. Entered the service Feb. 24, 1941, at 163rd,

Inf. Regt., Ft. Lewis, WA and overseas in Australia, Papuan, New Guinea, and southern Philippines.

Discharged June 8, 1945 with the rank T/5. He received three Bronze Battle Stars, American Defense Service Medal, Good Conduct Medal, Asiatic-Pacific Theater Medal, Distinguished Unit Badge, and the Philippine Liberation Medal. He was overseas four years and three months.

Married Freda on July 2, 1945. They had a daughter born Feb. 6, 1947 (died Feb. 8, 1947) and a son Robert born in 1948. They also had five grandchildren and one great-grandchild. They lived in Hughson, CA and moved to Ponderay, ID in 1951.

Dale passed away July 9, 1989 with cancer. They were married 44 years and Freda wouldn't have met him if it hadn't been for WWII. He threw his address out the window as he went thru Modesto, CA. She wrote to him and they met in San Francisco, CA before he left for overseas. They wrote for three years before marrying.

WARREN S. SHAW, was born Oct. 27, 1915 in Aneta, ND. Raised in Casper, WY and inducted in the Army Feb. 25, 1941 at Cheyenne, WY. After a brief stay in Ft. Snelling, MN, he was sent to Ft. Lewis, WA and joined the 41st MP Co.

He left San Francisco, CA March 19, 1942 on the *Queen Elizabeth* for Australia and arrived April 10, 1942. He served two tours of duty in New Guinea and was rotated back to the States from Biak, New Guinea Jan. 1, 1945. After a short furlough, he was assigned to the 2nd FA in Ft. Benning, GA. He was discharged Aug. 26, 1945 at Ft. Logan, CO.

Married Marie and has two daughters, Kathy and Wendy. He retired from the Postal Service in 1981. They reside in Panorama City, CA.

ALBERT R. SHOUP (BERT), was born Sept. 11, 1919 in Emporium, PA. Drafted in August 1943, trained at Camp Blanding, FL, and joined 163rd Inf. Regt. at Finchhaven in April 1944. Went to Biak, 1st Squad, 1st Section, 1st Platoon, H Co. 163. Made landing at Korim Bay.

Went to Philippines, attached to E Co. Made landing at Zamboanga. Was on Blow Up Hill and forward observation, chased off by enemy mortar company. Made landings at Sangi-Sangi and Bongao Village. Joined battalion at Jolo.

In July 1945 was transferred to E Co., GHQ Gen. MacArthur's Honor Guard. In August 1945 went to Yokohama and Tokyo. Discharged January 1946. He received the Combat Infantry Badge, Bronze Star, Good Conduct, Victory and Expert Rifle.

Got married in April 1946 and has five daughters and eight grandchildren. He retired as a carpenter construction superintendent. Left Reserves in 1954 with the rank technical sergeant.

OTHO VERNON SHUMAKER, was born Sept. 29, 1920 at Schuyler, VA. Drafted May 15, 1943. Went to Camp Wheeler, GA for basic training. Joined 41st Inf. Div. at Rockhampton, Australia. Served in Co. C, 186th Regt., made landings at Hollandia, Biak, Palawan, Mindanao.

Discharged Dec. 15, 1945 with the rank of staff sergeant. He received the Purple Heart, Bronze Star, and all the usual campaign ribbons.

Married Hazel on Oct. 4, 1941. They have four children, seven grandchildren, and two great-grandchildren. He retired from Dupont on March 31, 1979 after 36 years of service.

MELVIN Q. SIMMONS, was born Aug. 8, 1918. Entered the service in 1940, served with Co. I, 186th Inf. Discharged with the rank of sergeant. He received the American Defense Medal, Bronze Star, and Asiatic-Pacific Service Medal.

Married Rachel in 1945. He has two children, five grandchildren, and six great-grandchildren. He is retired.

HARRY G. SIMPSON, was born Jan. 17, 1920 in Salt Lake City. Entered the service Oct. 16, 1941, Co. C, 186th Inf. Regt., Ft. Lewis, WA. Served in Australia, Hollandia, Biak, New Guinea, Palawan, Zamboanga, and the Philippines.

Left Philippines on furlough May 1945. Discharged June 8, 1945 with the rank of staff sergeant.

Married wife Verna and has two girls, one boy, 12 grandchildren, and one great-grandson. He is a semi-retired school supply salesman.

JOHN D. SIMPSON, was born Oct. 22, 1914 in Mohler, WA. Entered the service April 22, 1941 at Tacoma, WA. Assigned same day to H. Co., 186th Inf. at Ft. Lewis, WA; Australia, New Guinea (Buna and Milne Bay), Papua (Hollandia) and Biak. Served as platoon sergeant and mess sergeant.

Memorable experience was being with a small detachment guarding a river crossing on the Mambana River and living by a native village, then going to mouth of river to observe a group of Japanese. Was detached from company for 49 days.

Back to the States Dec. 1, 1944 and Discharged July 11, 1945. He received the American Defense Service Medal, Asiatic-Pacific Service Medal with three stars, Good Conduct Medal, Bronze Service Star Medal, Sharpshooter Badges for carbine and pistol, and Combat Infantryman Badge.

Married Myrtle in 1945. They have three children, John Jr., Beth, and Catherine, and seven grandchildren.

He lives in Harrington, WA and is still raising cattle.

GORDON R. SITTON, was born May 2, 1916 in Carlton, OR. Graduated from Oregon State University and commissioned second lieutenant, FA, U.S. Army by ROTC June 1940. Ordered to active duty on June 24, 1941, 10th FA, 3rd Inf. Div., Ft. Lewis, WA. November transferred to 148th FA, which became 205th FA Bn., 41st Inf. Div. In April 1942 the division was stationed in Australia, Seymour, VIC, and Rockhampton, QLD until ordered to New Guinea for defense and recapture of Buna and Salamaua. Was executive officer of Btry. C, 205 FA.

Returned to Rockhampton for rest and preparation for the liberation of Hollandia and Biak, followed by Mindoro and Zamboanga invasions in the Philippines. Then to Hiro, Japan for occupation duty.

Returned to the U.S. and was released from active duty on May 16, 1946 with the rank of major. He was awarded the Bronze Star medal, Asiatic-Pacific Medal with two Bronze Stars and one Arrowhead, Philippine Liberation Service Medal with one Bronze Star, American Defense Service Medal, Army of Occupation Medal, World War II Medal, American Theater, and Honorable Service Lapel Buttons.

Married Veronica O'Brien in Australia in 1944. They have two children, Ruth and Patrick, and three grandchildren. Has Ph.D. in economics, Stanford University. Taught at University of California and Oregon State University where he was also director of International Education for 10 years. He retired in 1982 and lives in Corvallis, OR.

BILL SLAGA, was born Nov. 25, 1917 in Perronville, MI. Entered the service Sept. 11, 1941, G Co., 163rd Inf., 41st Div., Ft. Lewis, Seymour, and Rockhampton, Australia.

Discharged June 6, 1945 with the rank of staff sergeant. He received the American Defense Service Ribbon, Asiatic-Pacific Theater ribbon with three Battle Stars, six Overseas Service Bars, Good Conduct Ribbon, Philippine Liberation Ribbon, with one Battle Star, and the Distinguished Unit Badge.

He is a widower with two daughters, one son, and 10 grandchildren. He is retired

DARWIN FRANCIS SMITH, was born Jan. 28, 1919 at Cleghorn, IA. Inducted Nov. 8, 1941 at Ft. Des Moines in G Co., 186th Inf., 41st Div. and sent to Camp Wolters, TX for basic training. He was sent to Ft. Lewis, WA and left on the *Matsonia* for Australia (Melbourne, Brisbane, Rockhampton).

Participated in campaigns of New Guinea, Papuan, Biak Island, and the South Philippines. Discharged Oct. 7, 1945 from Jefferson Barracks, MO with the rank of staff sergeant. He received three Bronze Stars with V device and Oak Leaf Clusters, Philippine Presidential Unit Citation Badge, Philippine Liberation Ribbon, Combat Infantry Badge, World War II Victory Medal, Asiatic-Pacific Campaign Medal, American Defense Service Medal, and the Good Conduct Medal.

Married May 20, 1950 to Phyllis. They are the parents of three children: Jerry, Jane Ann, and Nancy. There are five grandchildren, Kyra, Jeremy, Tyler, Jay, and Kristin.

He was appointed postmaster of Cleghorn, IA in October 1957 and retired from that position Dec. 30, 1987.

FREDERICK H. SMITH, was born Nov. 2, 1923, Mystic, CT. Inducted Feb. 4, 1943 at Ft. Devens, to Texas for basic training, 86th Div. Went to Ft. Meade then Camp Patrick Henry, VA, POE. Went through Panama Canal to Pearl Harbor, Guadalcanal, New Caledonia, Milne Bay. Joined 41st Div., 186th Regt. at Finchhaven on Nov. 11, 1943.

Participated in invasions of Hollandia, Biak, Mindoro, Palawan, and Zamboanga. Was sent to Kaidaichi, Japan and stayed in Japanese camp on eastern outskirts of Hiroshima. (Still have tests to see about low-level radiation.) In 12th portable and 116th medical hospitals with malaria and jungle rot. Was hit three times but never received Purple Heart.

Discharged Jan. 17, 1946 and served four years in 26th Division Guard from 1949 to 1953, attaining the rank of staff sergeant. Among medals received were the Bronze Star, Presidential Unit Citation, Combat Infantry Badge, Bronze Arrowheads, and numerous campaign and battle ribbons.

Married Virginia in 1954 and they live in Massachusetts. He has one son, two daughters, and six grandchildren. He is a crane operator at Warren Pumps and plans to retire in Spring 1992. He enjoys backpacking, hunting in New Hampshire Vermont, and traveling with his wife. They have been to England seven times and have visited several other countries.

HAROLD S. SMITH, was born Oct. 22, 1921 in Lynnville, IA. Entered the service March 1943, Btry. B, 218th FA Bn., basic training at Camp Roberts, CA; overseas to Australia, New Guinea, Philippines, and Japan.

Made landings at Hollandia Beach, Biak, Finchhaven, Nassau Bay etc. Left Japan Dec. 13, 1945.

Discharged Jan. 9, 1946 at Ft. Leavenworth, KS with the rank of staff sergeant. Received the Philippine Liberation Ribbon w/1 star, the Good Conduct Medal.

Married Erma Jan. 23, 1946 and they raised five children, Roger, Pamela, Connie, Randy, and Jacqueline. They have 13 grandchildren and three great-grandchildren. He farmed for several years and was in the vending business from for 32 years in Grinnell, IA and Denver, CO. He retired from Martin-Marietta Aerospace in Denver in June 1985. He now resides at Holiday Lake, Brooklyn, IA. He travels some and enjoys just taking it easy.

MERLE O. SMITH, was born Nov. 22, 1919 at Dundee, IA. Inducted into the Army in Nov. 11, 1941. Received basic training at Camp Wolters, TX. Assigned to Co. D, 186th Inf., 41st Div., heavy weapons company at Ft. Lewis, WA. Served entire 38 months in this same company overseas in Australia, New Guinea, and Biak. Fought in the Battle of Buna, Battle of Hollandia, and Battle of Biak. He was sent home on rotation and given a month's furlough before being sent to Camp Lee, VA until discharge at Jefferson Barracks, MO on Aug. 13, 1945. Married Jean on Aug. 2, 1941 and has two sons and five grandchildren. He is president of the Iowa Chapter 41st Division and active in the VFW and American Legion. Owned and operated successfully an independent garage for 23 years and collects antique automobiles. He is semi-retired and winters in the Rio Grande Valley.

OSCAR H. SMITH, was born March 28, 1919 in Chicago, IL. Entered the service Oct. 6, 1941, HQ Co., 186th Inf., 3rd Bn., stationed at Camp Roberts, CA and Ft. Lewis, WA. Overseas in Australia, New Guinea, Philippines and Zamboanga.

Went home on rotation from Zamboanga and discharged with the rank of staff sergeant. He received the Philippine Liberation Ribbon with four Bronze Battle Stars, six overseas bars, Bronze Star Medal, Asiatic-Pacific Ribbon with four Bronze Battle Stars, American Defense Ribbon, etc.

Married in 1957 and has three children and eight grandchildren. He worked for Sears Roebuck for 37 years, retiring in 1982.

REX K. SMITH, was born Dec. 11, 1913 in Brownsville, OR. Entered Oregon National Guard, Co. K, 162nd Inf., 41st Div., Camp Murray, Ft. Lewis, WA.

His memorable experience was the 40 day trip on *Uruguay* to Australia and three years later the 20 day trip on *H. Lykes* to San Francisco. Discharged with the rank of technical sergeant (platoon sergeant). He received the Combat Infantry Badge and Bronze Star.

Married Emma Vantress in 1945. They have a son Ken and a daughter Barbara. Rex is retired and lives in Tillamook, OR.

JOHN SOBOTKA, was born March 23, 1918 in Omaha, NE. Entered the service June 23, 1941, HQ-167, Ft. Lewis, WA, as light truck driver and mechanic.

Discharged with the rank T/4. He received the Asiatic-Pacific Theatre Medal, American Defense Service Medal, and Good Conduct Medal.

Married Sept. 11, 1954 to Donna Ausdemore of Meola, IA. They have no children. John retired in June 1983 and passed away Aug. 1, 1989.

EDWARD F. SOKOLOWSKI, was born Sept. 18, 1918 in Detroit, MI. Moved to Hamtramck, MI about 1921. He graduated from high school in 1937 and was drafted in August 1941.

Basic training in Camp Roberts, CA. Then on to Ft. Lewis, WA. Was assigned to Co. D, 163rd Inf. Shipped overseas to Port Moresby. Flew over the Owen Stanley Range to Sanananda New Guinea. Their outfit made a number of beach landings and occupied many islands throughout the Pacific, ending up in Jolo, Philippine Islands. From Jolo he returned to the States with the rank of staff sergeant on the point system.

He retired from Wayne County DPW in 1983. He is a member of VFW and Knights of Columbus. Married to Jean for 40 years. They have one daughter Judy and live in Lincoln Park, MI.

IRWIN S. SOLIDAY, was born Feb. 24, 1918 in Chicago, IL. Inducted Oct. 13, 1941. Joined Co. E, 163rd Inf. Regt. on December 13 at Ft. Lewis, WA. He sailed on *Queen Elizabeth* March 19, 1942 and arrived in Sydney, Australia on April 6.

Trained at Seymour and Rockhampton. Arrived

Port Moresby, New Guinea on Dec. 27, 1942. Fought in division's first engagement, Battle of Buna, at Sanananda and was then on patrols and defense until May 8, 1943. To hospital in Australia and U.S. Was reassigned German PW Camp, Ft. Dix, NJ. Was discharged May 2, 1945 with the rank of T/5.

Married Roena on Feb. 21, 1948. They have two daughters, Debbie and Diana. Retired in 1980 as senior vice-president of Leo Burnett Advertising, after a 38 year career. He is a Mason and Shriner, Charter member of Midwest Chapter 41st Infantry Division Association, life member of DAV, VFW, and American Legion and lives in Oak Lawn, IL.

NATHAN SONNENFELD (SONNY), was born Sept. 29, 1919 in New York City. Drafted Oct. 13, 1941. Basic training at Camp Roberts, CA. On December 9, two days after the Japs attacked Pearl Harbor, he was sent to 186th Hqs. Co. on coast defense in Washington.

When 163rd was ready to ship out to Australia he was sent to 163rd to help bring it up to full strength. Was assigned to Hqs. Co. 1st Bn., 163rd Inf. Wire Section, the best wire section in the U.S. Army. Did it all at Buna, Sanananda, Wakde, Sarmi, Biak, Zamboanga, etc.

Came back to the States from Zamboanga in April 1945 on rotation. While on R&R in Atlantic City, he received his honorable discharge as a staff sergeant based on the point system in July 1945. He received a Silver Star for action of Wakde.

Married to Kelly in September 1945. Has one son Barry, a famous Hollywood cinematographer and director. Sonny is still selling theatrical and television lighting and dimming equipment.

ED SPANIER, was born March 30, 1921 in Helena, MT. Graduated Helena High in 1938. Joined Hqs. Co., 163rd Inf. National Guards to get three weeks vacation at Ft. Lewis at Uncle Sam's expense in August 1940.

He served in Australia and New Guinea with Hqs. Service 163, mostly in administrative capacity. Assigned to Fox Farm on return to Rockhampton, then rotated home September 1944. Assigned as cadre to Redistribution Station, Santa Barbara, and discharged at Ft. Douglas, Sept. 5, 1945, as staff sergeant.

Most of civilian life spent in sales, covered 11 western States for 18 years, living in Portland and San Francisco. Consultant to industry, San Francisco area for 10 years. Established and managed employee assistance programs for troubled employees. Retired from building management after seven years in August 1989.

One son, Barry, three grandchildren. Married high school sweetheart, Marnie, Christmas Eve 1989. Living happily in Boise, ID. He is past president of 41st Infantry Division Association, 1968-1969.

EARL A. SPEES, was born Oct. 13, 1919 in Corvallis, OR. Drafted April 21, 1941 and assigned to Hqs. Co. 81st Inf. Brig. Later the 41st Cavalry Recon. Tr. and served in Australia and New Guinea.

Highlights of service time was the month spent in Australia, New Zealand and the great barrier reef off Yepoon, Australia. Rockhampton is a modern city with two big bridges across the Fitzroy River (the old swinging bridge).

Left the 41st after Hollandia Invasion for the States on rotation. Assigned P.W. Section, Camp White, OR. Discharged Aug. 25, 1945 at Ft. Lewis, WA with the rank of corporal T/5.

Married Wilma in 1947. They have two daughters, Cheryl and Linda, and two grandchildren, Kim and Todd. He was a logger, did timber cutting and hauling and retired in 1984.

IRVINE H. SPRAGUE, was born July 4, 1921 in San Francisco. Drafted as a private in 1942, was rifle platoon leader in southern Philippines. Served with G Co., 2nd Bn., 163rd Regt., 41st Div.

Discharged with the rank of first lieutenant. He received the Combat Infantryman Badge, Purple Heart, two Bronze Stars, and the California Medal of Merit.

He graduated from Stockton College (English), College of the Pacific (economics), Harvard Advanced Management Program (business). Also attended George Washington University (law) and Indiana University (engineering).

Married to Margaret, they celebrated their 50th wedding anniversary on Nov. 3, 1990. They have three children, Michael, Kristine, and Terry.

He held a variety of positions of power and responsibility: chairman/director of FDIC (was principal architect of the bailout policy that saved Unity, Commonwealth, First Pennsylvania and Continental banks); member of Gen. MacArthur's Hqs. staff in Tokyo; director house whip office for congressman John McFall; executive director of House Policy committee for Tip O'Neill; California deputy director of Finance for Gov. Pat Brown; White House special assistant to President Lyndon Johnson. He is the author of *Bailout, An Insiders Account of Bank Failures and Rescues.*

He is retired with the rank of lieutenant colonel.

ARTHUR P. SQUIRE, was born Sept. 13, 1918 in Pentwater, MI. Drafted Jan. 2, 1943. Following basic was assigned to the 76th Inf. Div. then at Ft. Meade, MD. Spent 23 months in the weapons platoon, finally as mortar squad leader, all in Co. A, 385th.

Later from Camp McCoy, WI, two stints were spent in Michigan's upper peninsula learning winter warfare and testing that equipment. When everyone under sergeant and others were shipped to Europe, he was accepted for OCS.

Arrived in Leyte, Philippine Islands in February of 1945 and assigned to the 41st then staging on Mindoro. Given the 3rd Platoon in I Co., 163 and made two assault landings on Zamboanga and Jolo, collecting a Purple Heart in each operation. A bad knee finally gave out and he was reassigned to HQ AFWESPAC in Manilla as troop transport officer.

The knee and malaria put him on a hospital ship for home December 1945 with discharge in May as first lieutenant. He received the Combat Infantry Badge, Purple Heart with one Oak Leaf Cluster, and Bronze Star.

Finished college in 1951 and taught school in Flint, MI for 30 years. Married in 1948 to Eleanor, they adopted daughter Susan in 1962. Retired to hometown of Pentwater, MI in 1980. He renovated the family home and is living happily with his memories of the 41st Div.

EMMETT A. STALLCOP, was born Dec. 10, 1920 in Havre, MT. Entered the service Sept. 16, 1940, Co. M, 163rd Inf., Ft. Lewis, WA.

Discharged with the rank of technical sergeant. He received the Purple Heart with Oak Leaf Cluster, Combat Infantry Badge, and the Presidential Unit Citation.

He is a widower with one daughter. Retired after serving 30 years as city court judge in Havre, MT.

ERNEST STANGL, was born June 11, 1920 in Chicago, IL. Entered the service Oct. 13, 1941, Co. E, 163rd Inf., 41st Div., Ft. Lewis, WA. Stationed in Australia, New Guinea, and the Philippines.

Memorable experiences include: riding the barges in the China Sea and landing at Biak Island and Zamboanga.

Discharged with the rank of staff sergeant from Ft. Sheridan. He received Bronze Battle Star, Overseas Service Bars, Pacific Theater Ribbon and Philippine Liberation Ribbon.

Married Hazel from Rockhampton, Australia in 1947. He is a retired truck driver and lives in Orland Park, IL. He spends a lot of time traveling, mostly in Australia, and relaxing.

FRANK E. STEBLAY, was born Oct. 27, 1915 in McKinley, MN. He graduated from Biwabik High School. Drafted Sept. 19, 1941. Ft. Snelling to Camp Roberts to Co. G, 163rd Inf after Pearl Harbor. Then on March 19 boarded the *Queen Elizabeth* to Australia, later to New Guinea.

Left for the U.S. after almost 42 months overseas on July 23, 1945 and discharged from Camp McCoy on Aug. 23, 1945 with the rank of platoon sergeant. Was wounded Jan. 17, 1943 at Sanananda and received the Purple Heart and all the usual awards/decorations.

Married Margaret in 1946. They had a son Edward and daughter Donna Garland. Edward lives nearby and has two children Sara and Lee. Donna lives in Kent, WA and has two daughters Margie and Nicole. Margaret passed away in 1962. Frank retired in 1975 after almost 40 years in business counting almost four years in service. He does some gardening and goes fishing with his grandson Lee.

JAY K. STEHOUWER, was born Feb. 23, 1924 in Grand Rapids, MI. Drafted Feb. 25, 1943. Went to Camp Roberts, CA for basic training. Joined the 41st Inf. Div. on Aug. 8, 1943 at Rockhampton, Australia. He served with Co. F, 163rd Inf.

Participated in action in New Guinea, Hollandia, Biak, and the Philippines. Served with occupation forces in Japan.

Returned to the States on Nov. 3, 1945. After 30 day leave, received his discharge on Dec. 14, 1945 with the rank of staff sergeant.

He retired from the food business at 52 years of age and for the past 15 has served as pastor of a local Baptist Church.

MARVIN L. STEVENS, was born Nov. 27, 1921 in Billings, MT. Graduated from high school in 1940. Enlisted Feb. 5, 1942, was stationed at Ft. Lewis, WA, assigned to the 41st Signal Co., 41st Inf. Div.

Departed with the 41st Div. on March 19, 1942 for Australia and received his training there. While in New Guinea, he was sent from the Buna, Gona area around Oro Bay to Nassau Bay of the Salamaua, Lae Campaign. A few of them spent some time with the Aussies during that campaign. Made landing at Hollandia and Biak.

Came back to the States from Biak on points. Was discharged Dec. 15, 1944 with the rank private first class. Married his childhood sweetheart, Lillian. They have one daughter and two grandsons, Alan and Mike. He and Lillian live in Billings, MT. He retired in 1986. Marvin is a proud member of the 41st.

WILLIAM R. STEWART, was born June 13, 1924 in San Francisco. Entered the service March 1943, 163, I Co., 3rd Bn., HQ, Rockhampton. Made first landing at Aitape; furlough in Sydney; then landings at Wakde, Zamboanga, and Jolo; and rejoined the division at Biak for conclusion of that campaign.

Discharged with the rank of private first class. Married Jean on June 15, 1946. They have two children and one grandchild. He is a retired insurance agency owner.

FERDINAND F. STIEFFERMANN, was born Aug. 26, 1917 at Linn, MO, where he grew up and graduated from high school. He entered the Army in October 1941 at Ft. Leavenworth, KS. Went to Ft. Sill, OK for basic and overseas training. Joined the 41st Div. in June 1942 at Rockhampton, Australia. Served with HQ Btry., 146th FA Bn. in initial landings at Hollandia, Biak, Zamboanga, and Jolo.

Among his awards are the Bronze Star Medal, Bronze Arrowheads and numerous campaign ribbons. Discharged in September 1945 with the rank of technical sergeant.

Married to Mary Helen Wegman in 1946. They have one daughter Cheryl. He retired in 1981 after working 41 years for Southwestern Bell Telephone Company. He is a member of the American Legion, DAV, Elks, and the Midwest Chapter of the 41st Infantry Division Association.

CARROL STIRNWEIS, was with the 218th FA in the Oregon National Guard. Inducted into the Army on Sept. 1, 1940, he served with the unit through Camp Murray, Ft. Lewis, Australia, New Guinea, and up through the islands to the Philippines.

In August of 1945 he was on his way to Seattle to be discharged when the Atom bombs were dropped on Japan, bringing the war to an end.

He remained in Portland after being discharged and passed away in the 1950s. *Submitted by Kenneth E. Pratt.*

BEN B. STORY, was born April 22, 1920 in Paxton, IL. Entered the service Oct. 10, 1941, K Co., 186, 41st Inf., Ft. Lewis, WA, Australia, New Guinea, Biak, and Philippines. He made many good friends while in the service.

Discharged with the rank of T/4. He received one Bronze Battle Star, Philippine Liberation Ribbon, Pacific Theater Ribbon with three Battle Stars, Bronze Service Arrowhead, Combat Infantry Badge, one Service Stripe, Good Conduct Medal, and six Overseas Service Bars.

Married to Aileen May 7, 1947 and has three sons, Wayne and twins John and Jim. Jim is a major in the Air Force, John was a Marine for four years and now works for Merrill Lynch and Wayne is an insurance adjuster. They have two granddaughters, Sara and Samantha, and one grandson Sean.

FRANCIS ALBERT STOTT, was born at home in Athens, IL on July 2, 1924. Inducted April 27, 1943 while a junior at ACHS in Peoria, IL. Special gun mechanic training at Ft. Sill, OK; then Ft. Ord, CA; Camp Stoneman, CA; Brisbane, Australia; Rockhampton (167th FA, 186th Inf., 205th FA) finally Btry. B, 218th FA gun crew. Finchhaven, New Guinea, April 23, 1944; Hollandia; Wakde (telephone, radio, cook/baker school); Biak; Mindoro PI; Zamboanga; Japan occupation duty 1945.

Discharged Jan. 7, 1946 from Jefferson Barracks, MO. Enlisted in Army Reserves for three years 1946-1949. His awards and medals include: Good Conduct Medal, Asiatic-Pacific Campaign Medal, three Bronze Stars, one Arrowhead, World War II Victory Medal; Army of Occupation Medal Japan Clasp; Philippine Liberation Ribbon with one Bronze Star; and the Philippine Unit Citation Badge.

Memorable experiences: beach landing at Hollandia; feeding 80 year old American schoolteacher from the hills of Zamboanga; Gen. Douglas MacArthur's 40-miles per hour kitchen inspection; viewing Atomic Bomb destruction at Hiroshima.

Was home in January 1946, battled malaria for two years; obtained high school diploma following GED test and graduated in Army uniform May 1946 with younger brother. Went to four years Carpentry and Cabinetmaking School under GI Bill. Master cabinetmaker in Springfield, IL, retiring in 1985 due to ill health.

Currently active in the American Legion, Department of Illinois, served as 20th District Commander 1976-77; various chairmanships; and continuing volunteer with Illinois State Special Olympic Summer Games.

Married Phyllis Lorraine Simons on March 14, 1947 in Springfield, IL. They have one son Gary and two grandchildren, Elise Rose and Michael Francis.

CALVIN V. STOWELL, was born April 4, 1925 at Flasher, ND. He grew up in Independence, MO and graduated from high school there in June 1943. Was inducted into the Army on July 22, 1943. He took basic training with the 70th Inf. Div. at Camp Adair, OR. He left for overseas in May 1944 and joined the 41st Div. in July 1944 on Biak.

After Wardo Operation, he was assigned to 116th Med., 3rd Bn., 186th Inf. After Palawan Island Operation, he joined K Co., 2nd Platoon as aidman for Zamboanga Operation. He served with K Co. until the division was disorganized in Japan in 1946.

He obtained the rank of T/4 and was discharged Jan. 23, 1946 at Ft. Leavenworth, KS.

Cal married Joyce Holden in 1946. They have been married 44 years and have three children, Doug, Gwen, and Mark. He attended the International Fabricare Institute and worked 41 years in the drycleaning business. For 28 years he owned his own drycleaning shop in Independence. He retired Jan. 1, 1987.

JOHN R. STRETCHER, was born May 28, 1917 in Portland, OR. Attended local schools and the University of Oregon. He enlisted in 1936, assigned to 186th Inf., Oregon National Guard in Co. K and Co. M.

Re-enlisted in 1940 with Co. K, 186th Inf., 41st Div. and commissioned second lieutenant on mobilization Sept. 16, 1940. Overseas duty with Co. K then Cannon Co., Hqs. Co., Co. G, HQ-1, Co. B. Was also with 162nd Inf. at Nassau Bay, S-2 and S-3 for Brig. Gen. John T. Murray in Trobriand Islands Task Force.

Wounded at Hollandia Dutch New Guinea in April 1944. Spent time in numerous hospitals; then duty at Ft. Benning, GA; and Infantry School, 2nd Div., Ft. Lewis, WA. He retired in 1947 (due to physical) with the rank of major.

Married Lois in Montgomery, AL in 1946 and entered agricultural seed business in Oregon and California while raising two daughters. Retired in 1979 and now resides in Sarasota, FL.

REX J. STRINGER, was born July 29, 1925. Entered the service Sept. 15, 1943, Med. Det., 3rd Bn., 186th Inf. Regt., New Guinea, Biak, Philippines, and Japan.

Memorable experiences: Palawan landing; Zamboanga Operation; the friendships made, the day received orders to start back to good ole USA; and the pride felt in being a member of such a great division.

Discharged with the rank of technical sergeant third class. He received the Asiatic-Pacific Theater, Philippine Liberation, Bronze Arrowhead, Victory Medal, and the Combat Medical Badge.

Married in Ina and has three children, Lyn, Kenny, and Steve, and six grandchildren. He is semi-retired, dealing in investments.

ROGER F. STUCKER, was born June 7, 1914 in Logansport, IN. Entered the service Feb. 28, 1941, 41st Signal Company.

Discharged with the rank of sergeant. He received the Good Conduct Medal, American Defense Service, Asiatic-Pacific Campaign, Philippine Liberation Medal, and Unit Citation, one Bronze Star.

He has a wife, stepson, and stepdaughter. He is retired and enjoying life.

RAY L. SUMMERS, was born Oct. 24, 1918 in Murphysboro, IL. Entered the service Oct. 7, 1941, 186th Regt., 2nd Bn., E Co., Ft. Lewis, WA.

Discharged with the rank of platoon technical sergeant on Aug. 14, 1945. He received the Purple Heart and the Combat Infantry Badge.

Married Sonny Sorbits in 1946, they have no children. Presently retired after 35 years of service with B&O Railroad.

MARTIN T. SUNDSTROM, was born Nov. 23, 1917 in French River, MN. Entered the service Nov. 7, 1941. Basic training at Camp Wheeler, GA. Assigned to L Co., 186th Inf. at Ft. Lewis in February 1942.

Sailed for Melbourne, Australia in April 1942, then to Rockhampton by rail and to Port Moresby in December 1942 or thereabouts. Went by plane over the mountains to Dobodura Air Strip.

Shortly after he volunteered for duty operating small ships and transporting supplies and aviation gas from the ocean up the Embogo River to Dobodura, he was asked by the Australian officers of the Papuan Inf. Bn. to operate their reconnaissance ship. He accepted the assignment and in the next few months they operated in the area near Nassau Bay, losing one boat in heavy seas at Nassau shortly after the 162nd made their landing there.

An order came down that he was to work as an Australian Naval Warrant Officer. This indeed was a very memorable tour of duty. He has nothing but praise for the Australians and also the native Papuans.

Back to Australia in September or October 1943, then Hollandia and Biak Island. Went home on furlough to the States for Thanksgiving and Christmas in 1944. Returned to the Philippines in 1945 to join L Co., 186th on Zamboanga, then back to the States after VJ-Day.

Was discharged at Ft. McCoy, WI on Oct. 4, 1945 with the rank private first class. He received the Combat Infantry Badge, Bronze Star, Good Conduct Medal, American Defense Medal, Asiatic-Pacific with three Bronze Stars and Arrowhead and the Philippine Liberation with one Bronze Star.

He is married to Anna and is a retired locomotive engineer.

PAUL SWANSON, was born May 15, 1914 at Rock Falls, IL. In 1942 he became employed at the Green River Ordnance Munitions Plant at Amboy, IL.

Within the Fire and Rescue Department, he was promoted to lieutenant in charge of Station 2. Then in October 1943 he volunteered for active military service in the Army. Training in Anti-tank at Camp Blanding, FL. He was promoted to T/4 sergeant and shipped first to a casual camp at Leyte and then joined Co. K, 186, 41st Div. at Zamboanga.

He was in the occupational forces in the Hiroshima, Japan area. Departed Japan in late December of 1945 and discharged in Illinois on Jan. 9, 1946. Paul and wife Ethel now reside in Shingle Springs, CA. They have three sons, six grandchildren, and 12 great-grandchildren. He is a retired sign painter.

KENNETH S. SWEANY, was born July 13, 1902 in Maryland. Graduated U.S. Military Academy in

1923. Commissioned second lieutenant field artillery. Prior to WWII, troop duty, branch school, graduate of Command and General Staff School. Assigned to the 41st Inf. Div. in December 1941. Chief of staff for Gen. Fuller and Gen. Doe until July 1945. Transferred to 33rd Inf. Div., promoted to brigadier general commanding division artillery. In charge of Hyoga, Precture, Japan until deactivation of division. Reverted to colonel. PMS&T Arkansas State College; staff and faculty of C&GS, qualified parachutist, promoted to brigadier general, commander, 11th Airborne Div. Arty., commanded X Corps Artillery 14 months, 1951-1952 Korea. Commanding General U.S. Army Forces, Antilles.

Retired November 1955 as planner and deputy director, Maryland Civil Defense Agency for 14 years. His personal decorations include two Silver Stars, three Legion of Merits, two Bronze Stars, two Air Medals Commendation Ribbon, Korean Ulichi Medal with Silver Star, and Hatian Grand Cross.

Married Laura Lyon Ward in 1924. They have two children, seven grandchildren, and six great-grandchildren.

NOLAN F. SWEENEY, was born Aug. 7, 1915 near Dayton, OH. He rejoined his former National Guard Btry. F, 218 FA in time for February induction and trained at Ft. Lewis, WA. He served as artificer with F Btry.; a sergeant with H Btry.; a training cadre and when the 641st TD Bn. was formed he became the battalion motor sergeant.

In Australia he went to Service Company, 163rd Inf. Regt. as a WOJG in motor transport. In New Guinea, while on detached service, he helped salvage Japanese landing craft which 41st Ord. Team welded the bullet holes and repaired or replaced the engines. These boats were used in the landing at Nassau Bay.

Transferred to DHQ G-4 office as division motor transport officer. Went with the division to Japan. There he had the opportunity to both fly over and drive through Hiroshima and Kure Naval Base to see the devastation from the Atomic Bomb.

He left Okazaki, Japan and arrived in Seattle and Ft. Lewis the day before Thanksgiving 1945 and was discharged the day after. Among the many medals he received was the Combat Infantry Badge, Bronze Star, Oak Leaf Cluster, and Presidential Unit Citation.

He married Juanita Ross in May 1947 and has two sons, two daughters, and six grandchildren. His son Michael served three tours in Vietnam and Gary served in the Korean War. He retired after 10 years with L.A. Courtemanch Company and 20 years with Albers Milling Company, a division of Carnation. He enjoys hunting, fishing, and the ham radio. He is a life member of the Elks and the NRA.

RALPH G. SZEWCZYKOWSKI, was born Feb. 20, 1924. He entered the service March 22, 1943, 1st Bn. Med. Det., 186th Inf., Rockhampton, Australia.

Memorable experience was when sniper missed him and killed Lt. Redding next to him.

Discharged with the rank T/4 Med. He received the Medical Badge, Expert Rifleman, three Bronze Stars, and the Good Conduct Medal.

Married to Florence in 1947. They have five children, Ralph Jr., Edith, Douglas, David, and Paul. He is a bar owner.

FLOYD D. TAYLOR, was born June 26, 1919 in Carson, WA. Entered the service Sept. 16, 1940, HQ Btry., 218th FA Bn., Ft. Lewis, WA, New Guinea, Oro Bay, Dobodura, Moro Bay, Salamaua, Hollandia, Biak, and Wakde.

Discharged with the rank of staff sergeant, he received the Good Conduct Medal and all the usual Pacific Theater decoration.

Married Irene and has one daughter, one son, and four grandchildren. He is retired and lives in Auburn, WA.

RALPH L. TAYLOR, was born Nov. 9, 1919 at Gilford, MT. Inducted into the Army Sept. 16, 1940. A member of the Med. Det. 163rd Inf. Regt. Basic training at Ft. Lewis, WA. Member of the 2nd Bn. Aid Station and joined the Sanananda Campaign on Dec. 26, 1942. Joined the 3rd Bn. Aid Station and was involved in the battles of Tor River Crossing, Beach landing at Hollandia, Kamti Village Advance Aid Stations, and the Ibdi Pocket at Biak. Discharged September 1945 with the rank of T/3 sergeant.

Ralph retired from Bremerton Ship Yards after 30 years of service. Married for 42 years. He is a member of Washington State University, Team Master Gardener, and continues to speak at groups on horticulture subjects. He is a consulting rosarian, rose judge, and master gardener. He grew over 700 roses on two and a half acres in Gig Harbor.

ROBERT D. TEELA, was born April 30, 1922 in Havre, MT. Entered the service Sept. 16, 1940, Co. M, 163rd Inf., 3rd Bn. HQ, 163rd Inf., Ft. Lewis through Biak.

Discharged with the rank of private first class. He received all the usual awards/decorations plus the Silver Star, and Purple Heart (both at Aitape, New Guinea).

Married 46 years to Ruth and has two sons, three daughters, and five grandchildren. He retired after 33 years with U.S. Customs Service.

EUGENE E. TEPOORTEN, was born Jan. 7, 1917 in Vancouver, British Columbia, Canada. He moved to Detroit, MI in 1926. Enlisted in Civilian Conservation Corps 1933-1934; enlisted in the Navy in 1935, served in South China Patrol and Destroyer Squadron. Enlisted September 1940, E Btry., 146th FA, reassigned as first sergeant to Hqs. Btry., 148th FA.

Discharged November 1941 to work on B-17 armament for Boeing. When war was declared he went home to Detroit, enlisted, and went to Camp Custer, MI. He was reassigned to OCS Ord. School, commissioned June 1942 and served in ETO during WWII. He returned to Europe for occupation and Berlin airlift. He served in Korea and retired as lieutenant colonel USAF. He was awarded the Bronze Star in Korea.

He joined Boeing 1957 through February 1979. He and Evelyn were married in February 1943 and they reside in a cedar log cabin nestled among Douglas Firs overlooking Lake Washington. They stay busy going to CCC, Navy, Army, and Air Force reunions.

LEROY FRANK THIEL, was born Oct. 24, 1919 in Englewood, CO. He entered the service Sept. 16, 1940, 146th FA, 41st Recon, 41st MPs, Swamp Murray, New Guinea, Biak, and Philippines.

Discharged with the rank of private first class. He received the Soldiers Medal, Bronze Star, Purple Heart, and Philippine Occupation.

Married to Ina and has two daughters, Vicki and Randi. He lives is Dorris, CA and is the mayor.

CHARLES M. THOMAS, was born Sept. 19, 1912 in Maquoketa, IA. He entered the service as a private first class in 1940 with the 186th Inf., 41st Div., B, S, C, HQ 2, HQ 186, DHQ; Ft. Lewis, WA; Seymour, Australia; Rockhampton, Australia; Osaka, Japan; Buna; Sanananda; Hollandia; Biak; Zamboanga; Leyte; and Mindora.

Discharged with the rank of lieutenant colonel. He received two Bronze Stars and the Legion of Merit.

Married to Verda and has son Charles III. He is a retired superior court judge from the state of California.

JAMES C. THOMSON, was born Jan. 17, 1908 in Seattle, WA. He joined the Washington Guard A Btry., 146th FA in June 1926. Transferred to Regimental Hqs. Btry. June 14, 1927. Also served in 167th FA.

Commanding HQ Btry. when shipped to Australia in March of 1942. He was in Pack Artillery on Mt. Speck in Australia. Served as Liaison officer and commander in combat in New Guinea. Spent 32 months overseas and came home on rotation Oct. 30, 1944. After a short stay at Ft. Sill, OK, he was assigned to general hospitals as AGF liaison officer for two years.

Retired from the Army Dec. 3, 1946 with the rank of captain. His awards and citations include the American Defense Medal, Bronze Star, Asiatic-Pacific Theater Service with two Bronze Stars and one Arrowhead, American Theater Service Medal, and World War II Victory Medal.

Married in Seattle on Jan. 15, 1937. He has one son James L. and two grandchildren. He was very patriotic and could have gotten a deferment at Boeing but preferred to go with his men. Jim passed away Nov. 24, 1990.

WILLIAM D. TIDWELL JR., was born June 4, 1925 in Nashville, TN. Drafted into the Army immediately after graduation from Goodlettsville High School in 1943. He took basic training at Ft. McClellan, AL and was retained for a period of time as cadre personnel.

Transferred to the South Pacific, assigned to F Co., 163rd Inf., 41st Div. on Zamboanga, Mindanao as a platoon leader during the Sulu Campaign. He served with the 41st Div. until it was deactivated in Japan, and then served with the 25th Div. Occupational Force until 1946. He returned to the U.S. and served in various positions in the Army Reserve until 1951.

Recalled to active duty and again stationed at Ft. McClellan, AL. Later was transferred to the 28th Div. in Augsburg, Germany. He returned to the U.S. the latter part of 1952 and served with the 81st Reserve Div., 303rd Transportation Group, 401st MP PW Camp, 290th MP PW Bde. all located in Nashville, TN. He was then assigned to the 412th Engr. Command, Vicksburgh, MS and during this tour was promoted to major general.

He retired after 40 years of service in 1983. He holds the following awards and decorations: the Distinguished Service Medal, Bronze Star, the Army Commendation Medal, American Campaign Medal, Asiatic-Pacific Campaign Medal with Bronze Star, World War II Victory Medal, Army Occupation Medal, National Defense Service Medal, Armed Forces Reserve Medal with two 10 year Devices, Army Reserve Components Achievement Medal, Philippine Liberation Ribbon with Bronze Star, and the Combat Infantryman Badge.

Married to Elizabeth Ann Russell. They have two children, Bill and Teresa, and seven grandchildren. He is presently in the super market business. He is a member of Rivergate Church of Christ and is a member of the board of Goodpasture Christian School.

JAMES R. TILBURY, came from a family that had been in the U.S. over 150 years. Born in February 1918 and raised in northern Minnesota, he moved to Wisconsin during his high school years but came back to Minneapolis and graduated from Dunwoody Institute as an electrician.

After working four years he volunteered for his year and entered the service in the 6th Div. in February 1941. He entered Signal Corps OCS in October and graduated as second lieutenant in January 1942. Assigned to the 93rd Signal Co., he went overseas in 1943.

Re-assigned to 41st Signal Co. in November 1944 and received his captain bars as company commander. He came home Dec. 19, 1945 and rejoined his wife Elaine whom he had married when he graduated from OCS.

He has taught electrical skills at Dunwoody in Minneapolis and was head of the Electric Department for 10 years as well as in New Guinea for three and a half years; moved to Oklahoma as a customer engineer for IBM for four years; was the manager of electrical engineering at a plant that manufactured rooftop air conditioners until he retired in 1985.

His son, an electrician, is now owner and manager of machine shop. His three daughters, a speech therapist, a X-ray technician, and a real estates sales person, have presented him with nine wonderful grandchildren.

EVERETT E. TOLLE, was born May 16, 1925 near Mt. Sterling, IL. Was inducted into the U.S. Army in September 1943, Camp Grant, IL. Trained at Camp Wolters, TX, joined C Co., 163rd, Finchhaven, Papua, New Guinea, March 1944.

Participated in eight amphibious landings at Aitape, Tome, Wakde Island, and Biak in New Guinea; Zamboanga and Jolo in the Philippines. Went with the first occupation forces into Hiroshima, Japan.

Left the 41st in Japan in December 1945 and returned to the U.S. for discharge Jan. 6, 1946. He received the Combat Infantry Badge with star, Bronze Star, Purple Heart with two Oak Leaf Clusters, Victory Medal, Southwest Pacific Service Medal with two stars and arrowhead, and the Philippine Liberation Medal.

Was called back as a Reservist in 1950, went to Korea and joined 1st Cav. Was wounded near Seoul and returned to the U.S. in 1951.

Married Agnes Ambrosh in 1948 in Chicago, IL. They have one daughter Roseanne and one grandson Jonathan. He retired from Prudential Insurance Company and moved from Urbana, IL to Gilbert, MN in 1986 for fishing and hunting and to Florida in winter.

LESLIE TOTTEN, was born April 11, 1909 in Ansley, NE. Entered the service March 1935, 218th FA, Btry. D (later changed to C), Ft. Lewis, WA.

Memorable experience was spending 32 months during WWII in Australia, jungle of New Guinea, and Dutch New Guinea.

Discharged with the rank sergeant 4/c in September 1945.

Married Ruth on Dec. 8, 1941. They have six children, 21 grandchildren, and 10 great-grandchildren. He is a retired letter carrier and now does volunteer work.

ORVEL TREANGEN, was born Dec. 2, 1916 at Spring Grove, MN. On Sept. 9, 1941, he was inducted into the Army at Ft. Snelling, St. Paul, MN, and was in Anti-tank Company. His basic training took place at Camp Roberts, CA. On March 19, 1942, he was sent to the Southwest Pacific Theater and took part in New Guinea and Papua battles and campaigns as an automatic rifleman. He was wounded in fight at Sanananda and recuperated at a hospital in Australia and returned to battle.

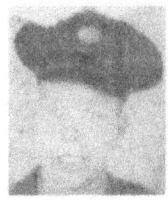

He was discharged in June 1945. He received the Purple Heart, five overseas bars, Combat Infantry Badge, Good Conduct Medal, Distinguished Unit Badge, Presidential Citation Badge, Asiatic-Pacific Theater Service Medal, and the American Defense Service Medal.

He is a retired farmer and now drives a school bus for the Spring Grove Public School, Spring Grove, MN. He is married and has two daughters, one son, and five grandchildren.

JOSEPH A. TRILLER, was born Aug. 3, 1921 in White Swan, WA. He entered the service Sept. 16, 1940, Oregon National Guard, Grants Pass, OR. Assigned to 41st Div., Regt. Hqs. Co., 186th Inf. Stationed at Camp Murray (later named 41st Contonemest), Tacoma, WA.

He saw action in the Southwest Pacific, New Guinea, Zamboanga, Biak, and southern Philippines.

Discharged with the rank of sergeant. He received the American Defense Service Medal, Asiatic-Pacific Service Medal, Good Conduct Medal, Philippine Liberation Medal with one Bronze Star, Combat Infantry Badge and Bronze Star.

Married Jean Pelkey on Oct. 25, 1941 at Seattle, WA. They had two children, Bonnie and Mike, and four grandchildren.

He worked at Hanford Atomic Energy plant 1945-1968. Ran an American burger shop in Brisbane, Australia for one and a half years. Then in 1970 took over a Texaco station in Pendleton, OR until 1987 when he retired. Moved to Albany, OR in 1989. Joe passed away Feb. 8, 1991 of cancer and was laid to rest Feb. 12, 1991 at Eagle Point National Cemetery, Eagle Point, OR.

ROB D. TRIMBLE JR., was born Dec. 21, 1917 in Lone Oak, TX. Graduated from Greenville, TX High School in 1934. Graduated from Texas A&M in 1940 with a B.S. in petroleum engineering. Commissioned second lieutenant from Texas A&M ROTC.

Called to active duty March 12, 1942. Spent three months at Ft. Benning, GA. Married Elayne Sanford on June 21, 1942. Assigned to overseas duty in July 1942. Joined 41st Inf. Div. at Rockhampton, Queensland, Australia in August 1942. Assigned to 2nd Bn., 163rd Inf. Regt. and airlifted into combat from Port Moresby to Dobodura, New Guinea. After battle for Sanananda Point, he returned to hospital in Rockhampton.

Appointed aide to Gen. Jens A. Doe and returned to New Guinea for three landing operations. Returned to USA on points from Biak after receiving the Silver Star. Released from active duty in September 1945. Practiced petroleum engineering and retired from the American Petroleum Institute in 1983. Moved from Dallas to new home at Holly Lake Ranch, TX to play golf. He is blessed with a daughter Toni, son Rob III, and five fine grandchildren.

FRANK A. TUROSIK, was born Sept. 13, 1917 in Concord, NY. Entered the service March 31, 1942, A Co., 116th Bn., C Engrs., Rockhampton, Australia, New Guinea, Biak, and trained at Ft. Leonard Wood, MO.

His memorable experience was meeting his older brother Paul in Rockhampton, Australia. They were stationed two miles apart but didn't know it until Frank received a letter from Paul. Paul had a hitch in the Army, was discharged at Ft. Lewis and was living in Tacoma, WA when called back to active duty with 99th Anti-tank, 41st Div. They hadn't seen each other in over eight years.

535

Discharged with the rank of corporal on Sept. 18, 1945 at Camp Perry. He received the Asiatic-Pacific Theater Ribbon with two Bronze Stars, Good Conduct Ribbon, Papuan and New Guinea Campaign, Purple Heart at Biak, and the World War II Victory Medal.

Back to Merrit, Chapman and Scott Corporation, Dunbar-Sullivan Marine Construction and Dredging Company, retired as superintendent in 1982 after 42 years. He enjoys gardening, cutting fireplace wood and the wildlife on his 83 acres.

PAUL FRANCIS TUROSIK, was born Aug. 25, 1912 in Great Valley, NY. Raised in Westline, PA and Cleveland, OH. He was a member of the "active federal service" in the Army of the U.S. from Feb. 26, 1941 to Oct. 15, 1941. Transferred to "Enlisted Reserve Corps: at Ft. Lewis, WA on Oct. 15, 1941 as private in Co. A, 99th Inf., Anti-tank Bn.

Recalled to active duty Feb. 3, 1942 as truck driver, Light 345. Departed for Asiatic-Pacific on March 4, 1942 and arrived April 10, 1942. Joined the 41st Inf. Div. stationed at Rockhampton, Australia, and New Guinea. Duties included driving command car and light truck. While stationed there, he met up with his brother Frank Turoski whom he hadn't seen in eight years. Paul participated in Aitape, New Guinea, Papuan, and Wakde Island campaigns.

On Oct. 8, 1944, Paul departed for the U.S. arriving on Oct. 25, 1944. His decorations and citations include the American Defense Service Medal, Asiatic-Pacific Theater Ribbon, five overseas bars, Good Conduct Medal, Victory Medal, Papuan and New Guinea Battle Stars.

He married Leona Baskett on Nov. 6, 1944. While waiting for Paul (her fiancee) to return from overseas, Leona did her part for the war as a logger in a logging camp and a logging truck driver day shift; and as a riveter on the B-27 and B-29 bombers at Boeing Aircraft Company swing shift. Paul was stationed in Missoula, MT for several months before being discharged Sept. 26, 1945 to Oakland ASF Regional Station Hospital Separation Point Detachment Veterans Administration Facility. Paul and Leona chose Tacoma, WA (where Leona was born and raised) as their home.

He was a member of DAV, VFW (Wild West Post #91), Catholic War Veterans, St. Peter and Paul's Post 1024, Knights of Columbus and Fraternal order of Eagles, Tacoma #3.

Paul worked for Baskett Lumber Company in Tacoma, WA for 33 years. He and Leona have three children, two daughters, George A. (Turosik) Malloy and Barbara E. Turosik, and one son Paul A. Turoski all of Tacoma, WA. Daughter George gave them two granddaughters, Sgt. Denise (Malloy) Palmer and Janelle Malloy. Denise and her husband Leon are both security specialists in the Air Force. Son Paul A. and his wife Andrea (Wolfe) Turosik gave them their first granddaughter Alissa Turosik and one grandson Jared Turosik. Paul Francis Turosik passed away Oct. 17, 1979 at the age of 67.

JOHN TURZA, was born May 6, 1920 in Detroit, MI. He lived in the Detroit area all of his life. He was inducted into the Army on July 12, 1944. He was stationed at Camp Wolters, TX for basic training.

On Dec. 30, 1944, he left for the Pacific area. He arrived on Feb. 8, 1945 and assigned to the 41st Inf., 162nd Cannon Co. He was involved with the first assault troops on Zamboanga, Mindanao. When peace was declared, his outfit made a landing at Kobe, Japan. He was with the occupational troops in Japan.

Discharged on Feb. 21, 1946 at Ft. Sheridan with the rank of sergeant T/4.

Married to Sylvia and has two sons and two grandchildren. He retired as tool and die maker in 1977.

EDWIN H. TYLER, was born Aug. 30, 1913 in Stockton, CA. Entered the service June 17, 1941, 162nd Regt. Service Co., Ft. Lewis, Australia, New Guinea, Biak, and the Philippine Islands.

He trained at Camp Roberts, CA after being inducted at Sacramento, CA. Discharged with the rank of T/4. He received the Philippines Liberation Ribbon with Bronze Star, American Defense Service Medal, Asiatic-Pacific Campaign Medal, and the Combat Infantry Badge.

Married Mary Frances Oliveira May 6, 1945. They have three sons, Kenneth, James and Roger. Kenneth manages the family business building custom farm equipment and repairs; James is employed at electric power plant in Craig, CO; and Roger is a lieutenant colonel in the Air Force (assistant air attache at American Embassy in London, England. Kenneth has daughter Bridget, James has son Phillip and daughter Treva, and Roger has daughters Melissa and Alexis.

Edwin is a member of the Crows Landing Lions Club (charter member since 1949), served 23 years on the board of education, chairman for 13 years, and served 42 years in the West Stanisluas County Fire Protection District, serving as fire chief in the Crows Landing Fire Department for 26 years. He is retired but acts in an advisory position at Tylers Welding Shop, Ind.

OWEN TYREE, was born Feb. 6, 1916 in Hayden, AZ. Entered the service Feb. 28, 1941, 218-C to 205-C, Special Services. Stationed at Ft. Lewis; Australia; New Guinea; Medford, OR; Santa Barbara.

Memorable experience was ship bombed in Milne Bay. Discharged with the rank of corporal. He is married, retired, and lives in Hemet, CA.

MICHAEL E. VAGENOS, was born Sept. 9, 1921 in Clarksburg, WV. He joined the National Guards, C Co., 175th Inf., 29th Div. in 1939. Was activated Feb. 3, 1941. Volunteered for foreign service in January 1942. He joined the 41st Div. at Ft. Dix, NJ and was assigned to E Co., 162nd Inf.

He trained with 29th Div. at Ft. Meade, MD. Amphibious training in Seymour and Rockhampton, Australia. Participated in battles in Hollandia, Biak, New Guinea, and southern Philippines. He contacted typhoid fever, dengue fever, and malaria.

Memorable experiences include: saving a comrade from drowning during amphibious training and was honored with regimental parade; meeting his cousin Tasso Lambrow in Finchhaven; and meeting a boyhood friend Steve Takos in Hollandia.

Returned to the U.S. April 1945 and was discharged at Ft. Dix, NJ on June 16, 1945.

He retired from the Department of Defense in June 1984. He married Theresa Wesolowski on Nov. 10, 1951 and they have two daughters, eight grandchildren, and six great-grandchildren.

ROBERT G. VAN CAMPEN (BOB), was born Nov. 27, 1914 in St. Paul, MN. Was drafted October 1940 and sent to Ft. Lewis, WA. Assigned to 3rd Inf. Div., 15th Inf. Regt., then assigned to 39th FA, then 60th Signal Bn. 1X Corps, all in 1941. Late in 1941 he was assigned to 41st Inf. Div. Sig. Co.

First week in December 1941 he shipped overseas to Philippines because of Pearl Harbor. Returned to the States and rejoined the 41st Div. and left for the Pacific Theater with Signal Company. Served in the Pacific Theater from March 1942 until August 1945.

Memorable experience was seeing the troop ship to the Philippines turn back to San Francisco.

Discharged from Camp Beal, CA in August 1945 with rank of sergeant. He received the Good Conduct Medal, American Defense Service Medal, Asiatic Pacific Campaign Medal, Philippine Liberation Medal with Bronze Star, and the Bronze Star Medal.

Married to Laina, he has one son by first marriage and one granddaughter Camille.

VIRGIL R. VANCIL, was born Oct. 20, 1924 in Vancil Bend, IL. Entered the service March 5, 1943, Co. F, 163rd Inf., Camp Roberts, CA. Served overseas in Australia, New Guinea, and south Philippines.

Discharged Jan. 8, 1946 with the rank T/5. He received two Bronze Stars and four campaign ribbons.

Married to Berneice Jan. 26, 1946 and has five children (son deceased 1965). He worked in the coal mines and was deputy sheriff of Williamson County, IL for eight and a half years. Virgil suffered a heart attack and passed away Dec. 31, 1989.

LOGAN E. VERMILLION, was born March 13, 1922 in Silver City, NM. Entered the service Sept. 16, 1940 into the 41st Div. Btry. A, 146th FA at Ft. Lewis,

WA. Overseas to Australia, New Guinea, Hollandia, and Biak Island.

Discharged on July 12, 1945 with the rank T/5 after 25 months of stateside duty, 32 months overseas duty. The day of his discharge he was told he was lucky to be alive, and when he asked why, he was told that a forward observers life expectancy was two and a half minutes. He thanked Cloyce G. Meneff, took his discharge papers, and headed for home.

His awards and decorations included the American Defense Service Medal, Good Conduct Medal, Asiatic-Pacific Service Medal, Sharpshooter, and Snipers Medal.

He married Delna J. Derickson on March 13, 1942. They have a son James Logan, daughter Michelle Carole, four granddaughters, and two grandsons. He retired from the Boeing Company on May 1, 1985 after 28 years of continuous service. His after retirement activities are golf, bowling, traveling, and owning a real estate office (Towne or Country Kenmore Inc.). His wife Delna is the designated broker manager and he is president of the company. He is looking forward to his second retirement in June of 1992. They recently made a trip around the world. They have visited Australia three times, New Zealand twice and New Guinea once since WWII. They play golf in the summer and go bowling in the winter.

GEORGE W. WADE, was born June 27, 1920 in Eagle Grove, IA. Entered the service Oct. 28, 1941, Co. I, 186th Inf. Stationed in Australia.

Discharged with the rank of private first class. He received one Bronze Star and the Purple Heart.

Married to Earlene and has two sons, two daughters, and 10 grandchildren. He is resident/manager of a 72 unit complex in Newton, IA.

JOE WAGNER, was born Dec. 24, 1919 in St. Paul, MN. Graduated from high school in 1937 and drafted on Sept. 17, 1941. Inducted at Ft. Snelling, MN. Reported to Camp Roberts for basic training on Sept. 20, 1941. Joined 41st Div. at Ft. Lewis, WA in December of 1941 and was assigned to D Co, 163rd Inf. Regt.

He left the USA on March 19, 1942. Arrived in Australia April 10, 1942 and took part in the Papua, New Guinea, and Philippines campaigns.

Discharged on Aug. 24, 1945 from Camp McCoy, WI with the rank of technical sergeant. He received the Presidential Unit Citation Badge, American Defense Medal, Philippine Liberation Medal and Bronze Star.

Married Ethel in September of 1946. He has three children and 10 grandchildren. He retired from 3M Company after 40 years of service.

EINARD R. WALITALO, was born Aug. 20, 1914 in Hancock, MI. Drafted in Detroit on Sept. 26, 1941. Basic at Camp Roberts, CA then joined 41st Inf. Div. right after Pearl Harbor. Assigned to C 162 Regt., guard duties. Sailed for 40 days on *Santa Paula* from New York through Panama Canal to Bora Bora, Auckland (Easter Sunday), Melbourne. Received training at Seymour as scout.

Transferred to division headquarters, moved to Rockhampton for amphibious training, then to Port Moresby and over Owen-Stanley's to campaigns at Buna, Gona, Lae, Salamaua, and Finchhaven. Returned to Rockhampton. Division brought up to strength, had one week of furlough to Sydney, Woulongong. Back to Lae to prepare for assault on Hollandia. Next to landing on Biak, Wakde. Was hospitalized for two weeks with jungle rot. Sailed to Philippines to prepare for assault on Zamboanga. Departed from Leyte on rotation plan for USA.

Discharged at Camp McCoy, WI on Aug. 23, 1945 with the rank of master sergeant. He was awarded the Bronze Star Medal. He had much malaria afterwards.

Married and has a son, daughter, and four grandchildren. He retired from General Motors in August 1973. They reside at Laurium, MI.

ALEXANDER B. WARNOCK (BEN), was born June 6, 1922 in Timber, OR. Inducted with the 41st from Salem, OR on Sept. 16, 1940. Graduate of Swamp Murray, Ft. Lewis. Served in B Hqs. Service 162 extended patrols up Kokoda Trail, Sanananda after the battle, went through Massau (Japanese landing barge) Salamaua, Hollandia, Biak, and Luzon.

Discharged July 30, 1945 with the rank of sergeant. Married 1948-1983 and lived in Portland. Now single, has two sons (one deceased) the other a captain in reserves, five daughters, and 12 grandchildren. He worked on Columbia River for five years, then ashore as truck diesel mechanic and foreman. Took an early retirement to hunt, fish, loaf, wood sculpture and carve.

CHARLES WARRICK (RAY), was born March 10, 1919 in Bloomfield, NE. Entered the service July 15, 1941, Ft. MacArthur, CA, Reg HQ 146 (later HQ 167). Basic training at Camp Roberts then went to Ft. Lewis, WA and overseas to Australia and New Guinea.

Memorable experience was being rotated home from Aitape New Guinea in May 1944. Reported to Camp Robinson, AR and was discharged September 1945 at Camp Bowie, TX. He received the Asiatic-Pacific with one star and one arrowhead.

Married Burnetta Saour in September 1946. They have two daughters, three grandsons, one granddaughter, one great-grandson, and one great-granddaughter. Was a plumber with the Los Angeles City Schools and retired after 25 years. Enjoys traveling and fishing.

WILLIAM H. WATKINS, was born April 19, 1921 in Wynona, OK. Inducted into the Army August 1943 and sent to Corvallis, OR to join the 70th Div. Anti-tank Co. for basic training.

On May 25, 1944, he boarded the U.S. *General John J. Pope* and arrived at Milne Bay, New Guinea on June 11, 1943, then on to Oro Bay, Finchhaven, then Biak where he joined the 41st Div. Cannon Co., 162nd Inf. Div.

Leaving Biak he began island hopping. Calinan, Davao Province, Philippine Islands, Okinawa, Kure, Japan, Izumo, Imaichi, Hiroshima and other cities. He

left Nagoya, Japan Dec. 24, 1945.

Discharged Jan. 16, 1946 with the rank of technical sergeant. He received the Purple Heart. He is now retired and lives in Odessa, TX with his wife Sue. They have one son who is now serving in Saudi Arabia.

JOHN WATSON, was born May 26, 1912 in Geneva, IN. Entered the service in October 1943 at Ft. MacArthur, Los Angeles, CA. Was sent to Camp Roberts, CA for basic training and two weeks after finishing, was given a company of his own to train. Assigned to a group going overseas as replacements and shipped out from Ft. Ord, CA. Even though there were 1,860 GIs and some outranked him, he was put in charge of the troop shipment.

In January 1945 he went into the G-2, 41st Inf. Div. He could take shorthand at 150 wpm and type at 80 wpm. He was promoted from buck sergeant to master sergeant and made head of G-2. For this accomplishment he received a Bronze Star.

Made several landings and ended on Mindanao at Zamboanga and made headquarters in an old fort, staying there until the war ended. While there was sent to Davao to check on cannibalism. On August 6, bomb was dropped on Hiroshima. They left for Japan, picked up an Atomic Bomb Survey Team at Okinawa, and pulled into Kure Harbor on September 16. One of the scariest times of his life was leaving Okinawa and trying to avoid the eye of a hurricane. Another of his assignments was to interview Hirihito.

In mid-December he was released and sent home with 1600 GIs. Again he was put in charge of the movement. They lost an engine and had to proceed on one engine at about half speed. They pulled into Seattle and were kept onboard ship for four days because there was no transportation available. Finally reached Ft. MacArthur and was discharged on Jan. 10, 1946.

ELDON G. WEAVER, was born Feb. 22, 1922 in Bremen, IN. Inducted July 12, 1944. Went to Camp Wolters, TX after basic training. Sailed from San Francisco on Dec. 31, 1944 and arrived at Leyte Philippines on Jan. 31, 1945. He joined the 41st at Mindoro Island.

Served with Co. L 163, made beach landing at Zamboanga, Mindanao as scout on March 10, 1945. Made beach landing at Jolo on April 9, 1945. Landed at Davao on May 10, 1945. Returned to Zambo on July 8, 1945.

Served with the 41st MP in Hiroshima area until division deactivated in January 1946. Was assigned to 530th MP Kobe, Japan until July 29, 1946.

Came back to the States Aug. 10, 1946. Discharged August 17 at Ft. Sheridan, IL with the rank T/5. His awards/medals: Victory Medal, Asiatic-Pacific Theater Ribbon with one Bronze Battle Star, Bronze Service Arrowhead, Philippine Liberation Ribbon with one Bronze Battle Star, three overseas service bars, Army of Occupation Medal (Japan), Good Conduct Medal, Meritorious Unit Award with Gold Star

Married Glenna in 1947. They have two children, son and daughter. He retired in July 1987 from Breman

Public School where he was transportation director. They live in Breman.

CARL E. WEBBER, was born Sept. 9, 1908 in Salem, MA. Graduated from Boston University and ROTC as second lieutenant in 1930. Served as lieutenant with 13th Inf. at Ft. Adams, Devens, McKinley and as CCC Company CO. Moved to Seattle in 1934 and served with 7th Inf. and CCC.

Called to active duty at Ft. Lewis in August 1940 serving at post headquarters. Reassigned to 162nd Inf. at time 41st Div. was ordered to Australia. As captain variously served as CO A Co., L Co., HQ Co. 3rd Bn. and Regt. Adj. During the Salamaua Operation served as 3rd Bn. executive under Maj. Archie Roosevelt. Hospitalized briefly during the campaign then returned to Salamaua as CO Regt. HQ Co. Subsequently transferred as in IG to 5th Air Force with promotion to Maj. (During Korean fracas served as Lt. Col. Aviation Engr. Force).

Upon return to civilian status headed Northwest News Bureau at Seattle and published a trade paper. With Supreme Court approval of the Social Security Act he joined the Federal Social Security Administration as a Field Representative. Some 25 years later he retired as area director of social security offices in northern California and Hawaii.

Widower in 1983 with three children, 12 grandchildren, and so far six great-grandchildren. He has remarried and lives at Vacaville, CA where he is currently serving a two-year stint on the Grand Jury of Solano County. Along the way he has been a Reserve Officer's Association chapter president, state officer, post commander American Legion and president of the Leisure Town Home Association, an adult community, where he now resides.

HANS C. WEDDUM, was born Jan. 21, 1913 in Elk Horn, IA, a Danish community, where he attended school and church. He entered the Army March 9, 1942, at Ft. Crook, NE, and was assigned to Camp Roberts, CA for basic training. Went overseas on troop ship *Matsonia* on June 22, arriving in Melbourne, Australia on July 16, 1942. Joined the 41st Div. at Rockhampton, Queensland, Australia. Discharged with the rank of staff sergeant.

Married to Elsie Nov. 23, 1947. They have two children, Dennis and Diane, and three grandchildren.

He was employed as secretary/manager of the Danish Mutual Insurance Association from 1955 to 1983, retiring at age 70. He is a member of the VFW, American Legion, and over 50 years of the Masonic Order.

CASPAR W. WEINBERGER, was born Aug. 18, 1917 in San Francisco, CA. Entered the service September 1941 and was assigned to Co. F, 186th Inf., Rockhampton, Queensland, Australia, Milne Bay, Dobodura, and New Guinea.

Transferred to Gen. MacArthur's Intelligence Staff

on Jan. 20, 1944. Served in that post in Brisbane, Hollandia, and Tacloban and Tolosa on Leyte Island.

Received honorable discharge in September 1945 with the rank of captain. He received the Bronze Star and Medal of Freedom.

Married with one daughter, one son, and two grandchildren. Civilian occupation: Of Counsel, Rogers and Wells; Publisher, *Forbes Magazine*, past Secretary of Defense.

RALPH O. WELLBAUM, was born May 9, 1911 in a pioneer family in north Pasadena, CA. Graduated high school, attended USC. Inducted Feb. 19, 1941 and assigned to Co. B, 162nd Inf. Trained Hunter-Liggett, Ft. Lewis and overseas at Camp Seymour, Rockhampton and Bribey Island, Australia.

Went to Papua from re-won Sanananda to Nassau Bay and Empire's rich Bulolo region. Reinforced Aussies, lonesome, clubby, generous, and perky in turn at Lababia, Green Hill Kitchen Ridge, Mubo, Buigap, Komiatum, but grave at formidable Mt. Tambu. B Co. directed barrages and contained Japs who fled it and once grand Salamaua, too.

Dutch Hollandia was easy; not Biak! Was wounded after three weeks fighting over ridges and cliffs on second day at East Caves by "friendly fire" from rear. Later check of enemy dead was 40 on flank and up from cave in initial day's fight.

Returned home and saw 1st Sgt. Larkins and cousin, also rotating. PFC Wellbaum was told Silver Star awaited him back at CO.

Discharged Jan. 31, 1945. Worked again as movie projectionist nearly 30 years at Stanley-Warner's Flagship Theater, Beverly Hills.

With Mary Eastman had two sons, daughter, and three grandsons, all doing nicely. Early life as one of 13 pioneers recalled as lucky!

HERMAN JOSEPH WELLE, was born July 20, 1917 in Lastrup, MN. Entered the service Oct. 24, 1941, 186th, Co. K, Inf. Ft. Lewis, WA and overseas.

Memorable experience was Papua, New Guinea, and South Philippines.

Discharged with the rank T/4. He received the Philippine Liberation Ribbon with one Bronze Star Medal, Good Conduct Medal, American Defense Service Medal, and the Asiatic-Pacific Theater Service Medal.

Married to Agnes April 30, 1946. They had two children Mary and Mike, and two grandchildren. Agnes passed away in 1983. Herman farmed for 39 years then sold it and moved to Little Falls, MN. Married Clarice July 30, 1988. He is a member of VFW, KC, Moose Lodge, and Little Falls Senior Center.

DONALD O. WELLS, was born Oct. 14, 1921 in Portland, OR and raised on a farm in Independence, OR. Entered the service Sept. 16, 1940, L Co., 162nd Inf., 41st MP Co.

Stationed at Camp Murray, Ft. Lewis, WA; Percidio Monterey, CA; Seymour and Rockhampton, Australia; Dobodura, Morobe, Nassau Bay, Finchhaven, and Hollandia, New Guinea; Biak, Schouten Islands;

Mindora, Zamboanga, and Leyte, Philippines.

Memorable experience was Dec. 7, 1941 when at sea, headed for the Philippines when bomb was dropped. Then ordered to return to San Francisco to rejoin the 41st Div.

Married to Marie, has son Steve in Bakersfield, CA and son Larry in Turlock, CA. Donald is retired from Modesto, CA Sheriff's Department. He enjoys traveling and woodworking.

ALFRED R. WENKE, was born April 6, 1919. Inducted into military service Oct. 8, 1941 in Chicago. Basic training at Camp Roberts, transferred to Co. F, 162 Regt., also Division Headquarters (AG) 41st Inf. Div., also Air Corps. Stationed in Australia and New Guinea. Discharged Sept. 17, 1945 with the rank of staff sergeant.

A memorable experience that Al recalls vividly was his emotional build-up and bursting anticipation to see and embrace his wife-to-be, Myrtle, in December 1944. Equally as thrilling was driving to Quebec to adopt their son in 1955. Over the years this has become a priceless memory. Al cherishes the memory of three close Army buddies, now departed, what a wonderful privilege and kindly destiny to have known them.

Al and Myrtle live in Scottsdale, AZ. They have mixed feelings about the expression "Golden Years" and cannot see a need for carrying around an assortment of aches and pains.

FLOYD W. WEST, was born Oct. 27, 1918 in Fostoria, MI. Graduated from high school in 1936. Entered the service Oct. 7, 1941, E Co., 162nd Inf, Camp Roberts and Ft. Lewis.

A few of his many memorable experiences include: when shot through helmet and hospitalized for a week. While there he gave three badly shot up fellows direct blood transfusions; when Eleanor Roosevelt, on one of her jaunts for FDR, pinned a Purple Heart on his PJs; and when in hospital at Port Moresby in September 1943, they talked about cutting off his shot up right hand, but then decided not to.

Discharged Aug. 31, 1945 with the rank of sergeant. He received the Combat Infantry Badge, two Purple Hearts, and Bronze Star.

Went back to school on GI Bill. Started teaching shop and vocational education in 1950. Received his master's in Vocational Education in 1953 and another in guidance and counseling in 1958.

Married Ann Hillman in 1950. They had a son Wayne and daughter Ellen. Ann died of cancer in 1960. Married Eleanor Kaller in 1972 and live on her family farm in Imlay City, MI. He suffered a stroke on June 8, 1975.

DR. HARGIS WESTERFIELD, was born Nov. 1, 1909 in Richmond, KY. Inducted Feb. 17, 1943. Trained in Army Finance School, Ft. Harrison, IN; earlier private with 107th Cav. (Horse), Ohio National Guard.

He participated in operations at Aitape, Toem-Wakde, Biak (New Guinea Campaign), and Jolo (Southern Philippine Campaign).

Discharged Feb. 16, 1946 with the rank of private first class. His awards include the Purple Heart, Combat Infantry Badge, Asiatic-Pacific Ribbon with two Campaign Stars (Spearhead Landing), Philippine Liberation Ribbon, and the Bronze Star (by Act of Congress).

Married to Nancy. He retired as professor of English, University of Nebraska at Kearney. (Ph.D. Indiana University). Presently licensed lay reader, St. Luke's Episcopal Church, Kearney, NE. He is still 41st Division Historian at age 81.

RALPH WESTERMAN, was born Nov. 28, 1915 in Ellsworth, KS. Entered the service Oct. 1, 1941, stationed at Camp Roberts, CA and Ft. Lewis, WA. Crossed the Pacific on the *Queen Elizabeth* to Australia, New Guinea, and Biak. Flew over the Owen Stanley Mountains to combat on Sanananda trail and went on patrols with fuzzy wuzzy natives.

Discharged May 30, 1945 with the rank of sergeant. He received the Good Conduct Medal, Sharpshooter, and all the usual awards of 41st Div.

Married Neva Phelps on June 10, 1945. They have four children: John, an attorney in New Mexico; Paul, farming family farm; Marilyn, an SRS worker; and Jeanette, a legal secretary. He also has seven grandchildren. Ralph has been on kidney dialysis for over four years. He is retired and still living on the farm he owned for 46 years in Ellsworth, KS.

E.F. WILDFONG, was born Nov. 21, 1921 in Bay City, OR. Graduated from Wheeler, Oregon High School in 1939. Enlisted in Co. K, 162nd Inf. (ONG) at Tillamook, OR in January 1940. Federal service at Camp Murray in September 1940.

Overseas to Australia in March 1942. Participated in Salamaua, Hollandia and Biak campaigns as a sergeant. Received field commission to second lieutenant in August 1944 and transferred to F Co., 186th Inf. Participated in Palawan Campaign in the Philippines. Returned to the States in May 1945 and finished WWII in School Troops at the Infantry School at Ft. Benning, GA. Released from active duty in October 1945 as a first lieutenant. He received the Silver Star with Oak Leaf Cluster.

Entered Oregon State University in January 1946 and graduated with a B.A. and B.S. in electrical engineering. He joined Portland General Electric Company and retired in 1983 as vice-president, division operations.

He has a wife and three daughters. They make their home in Portland, OR.

VERNON W. WILLEFORD (FOGARTY), was born Nov. 20, 1919 in East St. Louis, IL. Inducted November 1941. Received basic infantry training at Camp Wheeler, GA. Joined Anti-tank Company, 186th Inf. Regt., 41st Inf. Div. at Ft. Lewis, WA about February 1942.

Shipped overseas on the Matsonia April 25, 1942 arriving in Australia May 13, 1942. Moved to Buna, Papua in January 1943. Returned to Rockhampton, Australia in July 1943 for R&R. Had furlough in Melbourne.

Back to "island hopping," Port Moresby, Oro Bay, Buna, Hollandia, Biak Island, Mindoro, Philippine Islands, Palawan, and Zamboanga. Rotated from Zamboanga to the U.S. in September 1945. Discharged at Jefferson Barracks, MO on Oct. 4, 1945.

Memorable experience was the night on Biak Island when he felt he alone was fighting the entire war, only he could see the infiltrating enemy.

Married Irene in 1948. They have three children and five grandchildren. He was owner of an electronics company for 30 years; after heart bypass surgery, he retired in May 1985. Now he has "time to smell the roses." He is a member of the Moose and active in the VFW.

HUGH E. WILLIAMS, was born Oct. 1, 1917 in Dayton, TN. Graduated from Renton, WA High School in 1935. Enlisted Aug. 15, 1940 in Co. E, 116th Medical Regt., stationed at Ft. Lewis. In 1941 division was triangularized, he transferred to division headquarters as chief clerk, Special Service Section.

Overseas to Seymour, Rockhampton, Australia, Dobodura, New Guinea. In 1943 transferred to Quartermaster, Base Section, Service of Supply, Brisbane, where in 1944 he met WAC Cpl. Viola E. Bailey.

Returned Stateside August 1944 and was stationed at Camp Beale, CA. Discharged Aug. 10, 1945 as staff sergeant.

Married Viola in December 1945 after her tour to Hollandia and Philippines. He graduated in 1949 from the University of Washington in economics and business. They have one daughter and one granddaughter. He retired from his own electrical manufacturer's agency and now lives in Olympia, WA.

LEWIS E. WILLIAMS, was born Aug. 7, 1923 and raised in Alderwood Manor, WA. Graduated from Edmonds, WA High School in 1940.

Joined Washington National Guard in Seattle and was mobilized Sept. 16, 1940 with Co. F, 116 QM Bn., Hqs. Co., 41st Div., and Co. E, 162nd Inf.

In division headquarters he was the driver for Lt. Col. Downing G-2 in 1942 and 1943. In early 1944 he joined the 2nd Platoon of E Co. 162 and made the landings at Hollandia and Biak. Rotated home in August 1944 and was assigned to the IRTC at Camp Maxey, TX and in 1945 to OCS at Ft. Benning, GA. He then joined the Reserve and retired in 1970 with the rank of major.

Married to Lorna with one son. He retired in 1985, and they reside in San Diego, CA. He is a member of the American Legion, VFW, Elks, ROA.

HERBERT P. WILSON, was born April 26, 1918 in Tacoma, WA. Inducted into the service April 3, 1941. Assigned to A Co., 163rd Inf., 41st Div. on April 5, 1941 and given KP duty on April 8, 1941. Served entire enlistment with A Co., 163 except for hospital time.

Participated in the Buna, Gona, Aitape, Wakde, and Biak campaigns. Rotated back to the States in October 1944 and was discharged from the service in December 1944 on a medical discharge.

Married Margaret in February 1945 and has two children and two grandchildren.

Went back to the shipyard in Bremerton, WA and finished apprenticeship as a Marine electrician. Retired in 1973 as an electrical Marine surveyor in ship repair for the Navy. They reside in Tacoma, WA.

PAUL C. WILSON, M.D., was born April 28, 1925 in Bloomington, IN. Inducted into the Army in August of 1943 at Camp Custer, MI. He left Camp Custer and went to Ft. Riley, KS for basic training. Upon completing basic training, he went to Ft. Meade, MD for a short time and then was sent to Jackson Barracks, New Orleans and then to Camp Stoneman, CA.

The next move was on a ship SS *Lurline* to Milne Bay, New Guinea and then to Finchhaven, New Guinea where he joined the 41st Div, I Co. just before landing at Hollandia. From Hollandia he then participated in a beach landing at Biak. While in Biak he became a CW radio operator and was transferred to 3rd Bn. Hqs. Co.

The next beach landing was at Zamboanga. While in Zamboanga his regiment was sent to Davao to relieve the 24th Div.

Shortly thereafter the war ended and he was sent to occupy Kure, Japan. January 1945 he returned to Ft. Lewis, WA and then to Camp Grant, IL where he was separated from the service.

After leaving the Army he went back to college and then to medical school obtaining a MD degree. After graduating from a medical residency he married and had four children. He established a very successful practice in Crystal Lake, IL and remained there to the present.

LOREN H. WINDERS, was born June 22, 1920 in Wichita, KS. He was attending Wichita State University when drafted Sept. 25, 1941 at Ft. Leavenworth, KS. He took basic training at Camp Roberts, CA. After

Pearl Harbor he was assigned to Co. L, 186 and remained with this unit until his discharge Oct. 9, 1945 at Ft. Logan, CO. He attained the rank of staff sergeant and was squad leader. He was in foreign service over 41 months in Australia, New Guinea, and the Philippines.

Married to Becky in November 1948 and has two daughters, Jane and Ann, both are teachers. He worked 40 years in the lithographic trade as a pressman before retiring in 1985.

GROVER O. WINE, was born Aug. 18, 1919 in Wamic, OR. Entered the service Aug. 2, 1940, Co. H, 186th Inf., Camp Murray, Ft. Lewis, WA and overseas.

Helped raise, repair, and operate Jap assault boat; moved patrols in and out of New Guinea Rivers; January through April 1943, helped build sawmill between Dobodura and Oro Bay in 1943. Returned to the States July 22, 1944. Was discharged Dec. 8, 1944.

Married Imogene in 1945 and raised five children. Was airport operator, a pilot instructor, and aircraft and engine inspector for 35 years. Now retired and lives in Oroville, CA.

BENJAMIN H. WINKLER, was born July 26, 1919 at Wheeler, WA. Grew up in Eastern, WA and was section foreman on the NPRR, starting work on March 29, 1937. Was drafted into the Army March 6, 1941 and assigned to the 41st Div., Med. Det., 116th QM Regt. Took their training at the 41st Div. new barracks at Ft. Lewis. Washed a lot of windows there and joined the Med. Det. after training. At Rocky the 116th QM was made the 41st QM Co. which did away with the Med. Det. so the 41st QM Co. took us in.

Memorable experiences: Biak and Zamboanga landings; the 40 day boat trip from Leyte to San Francisco; and on Hollandia D-1 early in the morning before daylight and the ammo was blowing up on the beach. What a show! Discharged Sept. 8, 1945 with the rank T/5.

Married to Anna June 6, 1952 and they have a daughter Mary, two granddaughters, Shannon and Stacey, and three great-granddaughters, Emily, Jennifer, and Sarah—all are beautiful. Also has one son that is also a cousin. They got him when he was one and a half years old.

He retired from the railroad as a conductor on July 1, 1979 after 42 and a half years, including service time. He is a life member of VFW Post 1651, Pasco, WA. He loves to garden and gives most of it to the mission. Also loves to fish.

D.F. WINTERS, was born June 24, 1918 in Lewistown, MT. Entered the service Oct. 13, 1939; inducted for active service Sept. 16, 1940; Service Company, 163rd Inf.; Service Company, 162nd; Division Hqs. Co.; Division Artillery Company; stationed in the South Pacific.

Discharged Dec. 25, 1945 with the rank of warrant officer. He received the Asiatic-Pacific Theater Ribbon with two Bronze Service Stars, Philippine Liberation Ribbon with one Bronze Service Star and Bronze Arrowhead.

Married 1948 and has one son and two daughters. He retired as manager of Process Control Section, Nuclear Engineering in 1980. He lives at Lake James, Nebo, NC. Likes to fish and boat for amusement.

CHARLES J. WIRTH, was born April 17, 1920 in Wolf Creek, MT. Entered the service Sept. 16, 1940, Hqs. Co., 163rd Inf., stationed at Ft. Lewis.

Married Kay Peele (retired Army nurse) after discharge September 1945. Has two daughters, Barb and Anna, plus five grandchildren.

Retired after 36 years with Mountain Bell. He lives in Helena, MT.

JAMES W. WIRTH, was born March 15, 1921 in Harlowton, MT. Entered the service March 18, 1937, 163rd Inf., D Co. and called to active duty Sept. 16, 1940 at Ft. Lewis, WA. Transferred to Hqs. 2nd Bn, 153rd Inf. Arkansas National Guard. Sailed Feb. 22, 1942 from Seattle, WA on USS *Grant*.

Education and training completed: Bombardier (1035) AFBS, 1943; D R navigator course 1943; officer command training school, 1945; B-29 flex cnry, 1945; bomb refresher course, 1951; primary observation training course, 1954; aircraft observer Nav. bombardier, 1954; MB-Jet (1521B) advanced fly school, 1954; B-52 Trans. Training, 1957; academic instr. course (ECI), 1960; Air Force Instr. (ECI 7511), 1964; National Security Management, 1969; aircraft maintenance officer course accel., 1972; Sq. Officer School, 1960; Command and Staff College, 1962.

Memorable experience was destroying a German FW-190 and when he crash landed in a combat weary B-17 with over 200 bullet holes and flak holes.

He suffered a heart attack in October 1970 and retired with the rank lieutenant colonel USAF in July 1972 for medical disability.

Awards/decorations: Bronze Star, Purple Heart, Meritorious Service Medal, Air Medal with three Oak Leaf Clusters, Air Force Commendation Medal with two Oak Leaf Clusters, Vietnam Service Medal with three Bronze Service Stars, National Defense Service Medal with one Oak Leaf Cluster, Europe-Africa-Middle East Campaign Medal with one Bronze Service Star, World War II Victory Medal, Air Force Outstanding Unit Award with one Oak Leaf Cluster, Republic Vietnam Campaign Medal, Vietnam Service Award with one Bronze Service Star, SAEMR, Air Force Service Award with Oak Leaf Cluster, Good Conduct Medal (Army), Air Force Reserve Medal, National Defense Service Medal, American Campaign Medal, Asiatic-Pacific Campaign Medal with one Bronze Service Star, and the Distinguished Unit Citation with one Oak Leaf Cluster.

Married Margaret Allen in 1949. They met at the University of Montana in 1946. They had a son (deceased), daughter, and one grandson. Lt. Col. Wirth worked 10 years as a credit manager for a carpet company in Riverside, and retired as a vice-president in 1982. Since then he has traveled, played golf and volunteered at the museum.

ORVILLE K. WOIWOD, was born April 4, 1917 in Garner, IA. He entered the service Nov. 7, 1941, 186th Anti-tank, stationed in the South Pacific.

Discharged with the rank of private first class. He is retired and living in Dewey, AZ.

GEORGE WALTER WOLF, was born Feb. 14, 1920 in Covington, KY. He was inducted into service Nov. 14, 1941 at Ft. Thomas, KY. He trained at Camp Wheeler, GA. Went to Ft. Lewis, WA in February until April 1942, HQ 3rd Bn., 186th Inf.

Overseas to Melbourne, Australia on May 14 to a little place called Seymour. Moved to Rockhampton, New Guinea, where he became a cook, then back to Rockhampton and on to Biak.

Went home for 21 days in January 1945; then to Miami, FL for R&R. From there to Ft. Sill, OK until Sept. 22, 1945 when discharged with the rank T/5 corporal. His awards include the Asiatic-Pacific Campaign Stars and Good Conduct Medal.

Married Helen in July 1945, no children. He was a building contractor until 1965. Went to work in maintenance at the VA Hospital in Cincinnati, OH. He retired in January 1984 and now is enjoying life to the fullest. He has traveled over most of the U.S. and Hawaii. Also enjoys fishing.

LAWRENCE J. WOLLNEY, was born Aug. 10, 1922 in Brooklyn, NY. He entered the service Feb. 15, 1943, Co. D, 186th Regt., 41st Div. Basic training at Camp Hood, TX, radio operator then Camp Polk, LA, 45th Cav. Recon. Sqdn. Mechanized Troop B, supply assistant.

From there was shipped to Ft. Ord, CA, then to the Philippines in 1945 and assigned to 41st Div., Co. C, 2nd Platoon at Mindoro. Next to Palawan, Zamboanga, Shikopu, Japan as occupation until inactivated December 1945, Hiroshima.

Discharged with the rank of staff sergeant September 1945. He received the Republic of the Philippines Presidential Unit Citation Badge, World War II Victory Medal, Philippine Liberation Ribbon, Combat Infantry Badge, Good Conduct, and the Asiatic-Pacific Service Medal.

Married May 8, 1955 to Frances. He is a retired teamster of Local 707, having worked for 33 years. He is member of Knights of Columbus, and VFW Post General Francis V. Breene #71 as a life member.

VERNON C. WOLTERSDORF, was born July 22, 1918 in Bassets, WI. Lived in Salem, WI until 14, then moved to Somers, WI. Drafted June 14, 1941 and sent to Camp Grant, IL then to Camp Roberts, CA for basic.

Shipped to Ft. Lewis about October 1941. Served entire war in HQ Btry., 146th FA Bn., radio section. Overseas service at Camp Magalore, Rockhampton, Port Moresby, Milne Bay, Finchhaven, Hollandia, Biak (Bronze Star), Zamboanga, and Jolo.

Rotated home from Zamboanga, deloused at Angle Island, Frisco Bay, for two weeks. Discharged at Ft. Sheridan, IL on June 24, 1945.

Married his high school sweetheart Aug. 18, 1945. They have two sons and two daughters. Youngest daughter is an OTR in Adalade, Australia. Vernon retired as an electrician in 1982. He is a life member of American Legion and VFW.

ROGER S. WOODWARD, was born July 11, 1922 in Scrabble, VA where he grew up and graduated from Sperryville High School. Went to work for Safeway Grocery stores until inducted in U.S. Army April 15, 1943. Basic training at Ft. Riley, KS; advance training at Ft. Sill, OK; shipped overseas Jan. 19, 1944; joined 41st Div. in Brisbane, Australia in Spring of 1944 and assigned to K-162.

Participated in battles at Hollandia, Biak, and Mindanao, Australia. Went to Japan as occupation troops. Went to Hiroshima and saw where the A-bomb was dropped.

Discharged Jan. 15, 1946 with the rank of buck sergeant. He received the Good Conduct Medal, Rifleman Badge, South Pacific Ribbon, three Bronze Battle Stars, and the Japan Occupation Ribbon.

Went back to work at Safeway Grocery and retired July 11, 1982 after 40 years. Married Wilda E. Wright Dec. 24, 1948. They have two sons, Gary and Michael, and two granddaughters. He enjoys church work, gardening, family and Masonic Lodge.

GUS R. WRAGE, was born Sept. 5, 1924 at Ellis Island, NY and reared in Iowa. Was drafted Jan. 6, 1945 and trained at Camp Hood, TX. Went to Philippines and joined the 41st Div. at Zamboanga. Went on to Hiroshima, Japan.

Was discharged at Chicago on Nov. 18, 1946 with the rank of sergeant. Received the Asiatic-Pacific Theater Ribbon with one Bronze Battle Star, Philippine Liberation Ribbon with one Bronze Star, Victory Medal, Good Conduct Medal, and Army of Occupational Medal, Japan.

Married to Florence and now retired after farming 39 years in central Iowa. They celebrated their 40th wedding anniversary April 10, 1991. A tornado destroyed their home and most of their farm buildings in 1979. He is a member of Farm Bureau, United Church of Christ, and American Legion. They live in Gladbrook, IA.

VICTOR D. WRIGHT, was born May 17, 1919 in Fordyce, AR. Was reared in Little Rock, AR. Graduated from Little Rock High School in 1937.

Drafted into the Army at Camp Robinson, Oct. 3, 1941. Was transferred to Camp Wolters, TX for basic training. Shipped out to Ft. Lewis, WA in February 1942. Joined the 41st Div. at that time. Most of his unit was a National Guard Unit from Eugene, OR.

Left Ft. Lewis in March 1942 and landed in Melbourne, Australia in April 1942. Served with Co. M, 186th Inf. Served with this group from February 1942 until September 1945 when rotated home.

Made landings at New Guinea, Biak, Leyte, Luzon, Hollandia, Palawan, and numerous landings up and down the coast of Mindanao. Landed back in the U.S. in October 1945, and received his discharge at Camp Chaffee, AR with the rank of platoon sergeant/technical sergeant.

Married to Emma Birch Sept. 27, 1941. They have three children, Victor Jr., Ruth Ann, and Julie. Victor is retired, and lives in Little Rock, AR. He suffered a stroke in 1984.

DALE E. WYMAN, was born Dec. 10, 1923 in Anacortes, WA. Entered the service July 8, 1940, B 146th FA, B 116th Engrs., HQ 205th FA, Camp Murray, Seymour, Rockhampton, Australia

Saw action at Sanananda with 163rd, Hollandia, Biak, Soepiori, Zamboanga, Parang, and Davao.

Discharged Aug. 5, 1945 with the rank of corporal. He received the Distinguished Unit Badge, American Defense, Asiatic-Pacific, and the Philippine Liberation. Participated in Papuan, New Guinea, and Southern Philippines campaigns.

Married Mary Lou Moore on Sept. 24, 1946. They have two daughters and three granddaughters. Mary Lou passed away and he married Nora Fernandez on Aug. 8, 1990. They make their home in Las Vegas, NV. He is a retired merchant shipmaster and has traveled extensively to the Far East.

GEORGE A. YARBOUGH, was born Aug. 13, 1918, in Kerby, OR. He entered the service June 14, 1940, Co. C, 186th Inf., Ft. Lewis, WA and SW Pacific. Was wounded April 25, 1944 at Hollandia, New Guinea.

Discharged Oct. 14, 1944 with the rank of staff sergeant. He received the Bronze Star, Purple Heart, and Combat Infantry Badge.

Married to Jane and has sons, Craig, Jack, and Jim, daughter Jennifer, and seven grandchildren. He is a retired barber, now a campground host. They live in Cave Junction, OR.

CLAIR E. YORK, was born July 7, 1925 in Muscatine, IA where he grew up and graduated from high school in 1943. Entered the Army September 1943 at Camp Dodge, IA. Went to Camp Roberts and Ft. Ord, CA for basic and overseas training.

Joined the 41st Div. on June 28, 1944, at Finchhaven, Dutch New Guinea. Served with Btry. C, 146 FA Bn. in initial landings at Zamboanga and Jolo. Went to Davao to assist the 24th Division before returning to Zamboanga to rejoin the 41st on July 9, 1945.

Memorable experience was when separated with 16 infantrymen and four artillerymen by a Japanese wedge between our outpost and main unit for three days on Jolo Island without water in April of 1945.

Left the 41st when it disbanded in December 1945. Left Nagoya Japan on Jan. 14, 1946, for the USA. Was discharged Jan. 30, 1946 with the rank of sergeant. He received the Good Conduct Medal, Bronze Arrowhead, and the Philippine Liberation Ribbon with star.

Married to May in 1946, has two sons, Lanny and Randy, and three grandsons, Travis, Tyler, and Todd. First Lt. Lanny York USAF, gave his life for his country on Sept. 16, 1972 while flying reconnaissance during the Vietnam War. Randy is a practicing veterinarian in Wisconsin. Clair spent 34 years in the postal service in Muscatine and retired as Muscatine's Postmaster. He is a member of the VFW, American Legion, Elks, and Masonic Order. He has served 10 years on the City Council of Muscatine, serving as 3rd Ward Alderman, mayor, and presently serving as Alderman-at-large.

WALTER S. ZEUTENHORST, was born March 24, 1917 at Yakima, WA. He graduated from Central Washington State College and entered the service June 23, 1941. He served in the South Pacific with the 205th FA.

He was discharged Sept. 9, 1945. He taught school for 19 years, sold insurance, and operated an orchard. Married Elonora on Feb. 17, 1942. They have a son Terry and daughter Shirley. Both are married, but no grandchildren.

JOSEPH M. ZIMEL, was born June 8, 1917 in Paterson, NJ. Entered the service August 1943, 163rd Inf. Regt., stationed at Zamboanga, Hiro, Japan. Was platoon leader F Co. 163 and motor officer in Japan.

Memorable experiences: H-hour invasion of Zamboanga and landing in Hiro for occupation.

Discharged with the rank of captain. He received the Soldiers Medal, Army Commendation Medal, Bronze Star, Combat Infantry Badge, Presidential Unit Citation, and Bronze Arrowhead.

Married since 1943 he had two daughters and one grandchild. He is a real estate appraiser, consultant, and has been in practice over 30 years.

PAUL M. ZUSKY, was born Feb. 3, 1924 in Akron, OH. He graduated from North High School in 1942 and from Kent State University in 1950. Was inducted in March 1943 with basic training at Ft. Riley, KS.

Joined the 41st Div. in April 1944 at Finchhaven, New Guinea and was assigned to the 163rd Inf., 2nd Bn., G Co.

He participated in two beachheads in New Guinea. Then went to Biak where he was wounded. Participated in a beachhead at Zamboanga, Philippines. He also saw action in Jolo and Tawi, Tawi, Sulo Archepelago. He went to Hiro, Japan in October 1945.

He came back to the U.S. on Dec. 31, 1945. He was discharged on Jan. 11, 1946 as a staff sergeant.

Married to Henrietta (deceased) in 1948. They had two sons, Paul Jr. and Todd (deceased). He became an Internal Revenue agent in 1950 and retired from there in 1979.

Hq. Co. 3rd Bn., 163rd Inf. Cpl. Curtis Huck by Japanese Coastal Defense near Hiroshima, Japan - Nov. 1945. (Courtesy of Curtis M. Huck)

Basil C. Frisbee, New Guinea, 1943. (Courtesy of Basil Frisbee)

Hq. Co., 3rd Bn., 163rd Inf. kitchen and mess hall, Biak 1944. (Courtesy of Curtis M. Huck)

Reinholdt Petersen. (Courtesy of R. Petersen)

Constructed by the G.I.s, Chapel of the 1st Bn., 163rd, Biak 1944. (Courtesy of Arthur Merrick)

Pvt. Robert C. Perkins, Battery F, 146th FA, Camp Murray, WA. (Courtesy of R. Perkins)

Lester Jones, Japan 1945. (Courtesy of Karl Heiman)

Co. C., 163rd Rgt., Sept. 1945 - Zamboanga, Philippines. Siefert, Tamburelli, Burns, Johnson, Bouchard, Tobin, Heiman. (Courtesy of Karl Heiman)

Karl Heiman, Biak - 1944. (Courtesy of Heiman)

163rd Inf. Theater, Biak - 1944. (Courtesy of Curtis M. Huck)

Forward Observing Party. Winn, Parks, Ford, Bannerman, Tyrell, Lt. Green, 1944. (Courtesy of Dale E. Winn)

On the road to Buna, Australian troops cross a stream on an improvised bridge. (Courtesy of Rohlffs)

Jerome Patton, Edwin Pitt, George Meinicke, Bill Cline. Rockhampton, Australia. (Courtesy of W. A. Cline)

LuVerne Clausen by the mess hall at Biak. (Courtesy of L. Clausen)

L to R: Lieutenants Art Merrick, Cecil Rhodes, Butch Leibach and Dick Slade, 163rd Inf. Rgt, Rockhampton, Australia - 1942. (Courtesy of A. W. Merrick)

S/Sgts. Richard W. Kemp and William A. Cline. (Courtesy of W.A. Cline)

Lau and Siefert with 60 mm mortar. Zamboanga, P.I., Sept. 1945. (Courtesy of Karl Heiman)

Maj. Donald M. Cunningham at fire direction center, Aitape, New Guinea. (Courtesy of W.A. Cline)

www.ingramcontent.com/pod-product-compliance
Lightning Source LLC
Chambersburg PA
CBHW081142230426
43664CB00018B/2777